Historical, monumental and genealogical collections, relative to the County of Gloucester: printed from the original papers of the late Ralph Bigland, ... Volume 1 of 2

Ralph Bigland

ECCO

PRINT EDITIONS

Eighteenth Century
Collections Online
Print Editions

Gale ECCO Print Editions

Relive history with *Eighteenth Century Collections Online*, now available in print for the independent historian and collector. This series includes the most significant English-language and foreign-language works printed in Great Britain during the eighteenth century, and is organized in seven different subject areas including literature and language; medicine, science, and technology; and religion and philosophy. The collection also includes thousands of important works from the Americas.

The eighteenth century has been called "The Age of Enlightenment." It was a period of rapid advance in print culture and publishing, in world exploration, and in the rapid growth of science and technology – all of which had a profound impact on the political and cultural landscape. At the end of the century the American Revolution, French Revolution and Industrial Revolution, perhaps three of the most significant events in modern history, set in motion developments that eventually dominated world political, economic, and social life.

In a groundbreaking effort, Gale initiated a revolution of its own: digitization of epic proportions to preserve these invaluable works in the largest online archive of its kind. Contributions from major world libraries constitute over 175,000 original printed works. Scanned images of the actual pages, rather than transcriptions, recreate the works *as they first appeared.*

Now for the first time, these high-quality digital scans of original works are available via print-on-demand, making them readily accessible to libraries, students, independent scholars, and readers of all ages.

For our initial release we have created seven robust collections to form one the world's most comprehensive catalogs of 18th century works.

Initial Gale ECCO Print Editions collections include:

History and Geography
Rich in titles on English life and social history, this collection spans the world as it was known to eighteenth-century historians and explorers. Titles include a wealth of travel accounts and diaries, histories of nations from throughout the world, and maps and charts of a world that was still being discovered. Students of the War of American Independence will find fascinating accounts from the British side of conflict.

Social Science

Delve into what it was like to live during the eighteenth century by reading the first-hand accounts of everyday people, including city dwellers and farmers, businessmen and bankers, artisans and merchants, artists and their patrons, politicians and their constituents. Original texts make the American, French, and Industrial revolutions vividly contemporary.

Medicine, Science and Technology

Medical theory and practice of the 1700s developed rapidly, as is evidenced by the extensive collection, which includes descriptions of diseases, their conditions, and treatments. Books on science and technology, agriculture, military technology, natural philosophy, even cookbooks, are all contained here.

Literature and Language

Western literary study flows out of eighteenth-century works by Alexander Pope, Daniel Defoe, Henry Fielding, Frances Burney, Denis Diderot, Johann Gottfried Herder, Johann Wolfgang von Goethe, and others. Experience the birth of the modern novel, or compare the development of language using dictionaries and grammar discourses.

Religion and Philosophy

The Age of Enlightenment profoundly enriched religious and philosophical understanding and continues to influence present-day thinking. Works collected here include masterpieces by David Hume, Immanuel Kant, and Jean-Jacques Rousseau, as well as religious sermons and moral debates on the issues of the day, such as the slave trade. The Age of Reason saw conflict between Protestantism and Catholicism transformed into one between faith and logic -- a debate that continues in the twenty-first century.

Law and Reference

This collection reveals the history of English common law and Empire law in a vastly changing world of British expansion. Dominating the legal field is the *Commentaries of the Law of England* by Sir William Blackstone, which first appeared in 1765. Reference works such as almanacs and catalogues continue to educate us by revealing the day-to-day workings of society.

Fine Arts

The eighteenth-century fascination with Greek and Roman antiquity followed the systematic excavation of the ruins at Pompeii and Herculaneum in southern Italy; and after 1750 a neoclassical style dominated all artistic fields. The titles here trace developments in mostly English-language works on painting, sculpture, architecture, music, theater, and other disciplines. Instructional works on musical instruments, catalogs of art objects, comic operas, and more are also included.

The BiblioLife Network

This project was made possible in part by the BiblioLife Network (BLN), a project aimed at addressing some of the huge challenges facing book preservationists around the world. The BLN includes libraries, library networks, archives, subject matter experts, online communities and library service providers. We believe every book ever published should be available as a high-quality print reproduction; printed on-demand anywhere in the world. This insures the ongoing accessibility of the content and helps generate sustainable revenue for the libraries and organizations that work to preserve these important materials.

The following book is in the "public domain" and represents an authentic reproduction of the text as printed by the original publisher. While we have attempted to accurately maintain the integrity of the original work, there are sometimes problems with the original work or the micro-film from which the books were digitized. This can result in minor errors in reproduction. Possible imperfections include missing and blurred pages, poor pictures, markings and other reproduction issues beyond our control. Because this work is culturally important, we have made it available as part of our commitment to protecting, preserving, and promoting the world's literature.

GUIDE TO FOLD-OUTS MAPS and OVERSIZED IMAGES

The book you are reading was digitized from microfilm captured over the past thirty to forty years. Years after the creation of the original microfilm, the book was converted to digital files and made available in an online database.

In an online database, page images do not need to conform to the size restrictions found in a printed book. When converting these images back into a printed bound book, the page sizes are standardized in ways that maintain the detail of the original. For large images, such as fold-out maps, the original page image is split into two or more pages

Guidelines used to determine how to split the page image follows:

- Some images are split vertically; large images require vertical and horizontal splits.
- For horizontal splits, the content is split left to right.
- For vertical splits, the content is split from top to bottom.
- For both vertical and horizontal splits, the image is processed from top left to bottom right.

HISTORICAL,

MONUMENTAL

AND

GENEALOGICAL

COLLECTIONS,

RELATIVE TO THE COUNTY OF

GLOUCESTER;

PRINTED FROM THE ORIGINAL PAPERS

OF THE LATE

RALPH BIGLAND, Esq.

GARTER PRINCIPAL KING OF ARMS.

VOLUME THE FIRST.

LONDON

Printed by JOHN NICHOLS,

For RICHARD BIGLAND, of Frocester, in the County of Gloucester, Esq.

Son and Heir of RALPH BIGLAND, Esq.

"It is the prevailing Opinion of the World, that these Performances are solely
"fabricated by the petty Diligence of the obscuring Antiquaries who employ
"their Time in collecting Coats of Arms, poring over Parish Registers, and
"transcribing Tombstones.—But Histories of COUNTIES, if properly written,
"become Works of Entertainment, of Importance, and Universality.

"They may be made the Vehicles of much general Information, and such
"as is interesting to every Reader of a liberal Curiosity.

"What is local is often national."   WARTON.

SOLA VIRTUS INVICTA

TO THE MOST HIGH MIGHTY

AND MOST NOBLE PRINCE

CHARLES DUKE OF NORFOLK,

EARL MARSHAL,

AND

HEREDITARY MARSHAL

OF ENGLAND.

MAY IT PLEASE YOUR GRACE,

THE ILLUSTRIOUS HOUSE of HOWARD, and your GRACE
in particular, having for many Years patronifed my late
Father and his Family, I fhould juftly condemn myfelf if I
omitted

omitted this Occaſion of Publicly teſtifying my Gratitude And indeed, ſetting aſide the above Reaſon, to whom could the following Sheets be with greater Propriety addreſſed than to your GRACE, THE EARL MARSHAL OF ENGLAND?

Had it pleaſed GOD to have ſpared my Father ſome Time longer, there is no doubt that this Work would have been more compleat. It has been my Endeavour, ſo far as I was able, to prepare it for the Inſpection of the Publick; and though conſcious to myſelf, that it is by no means ſo Perfect as might be wiſhed, I yet take the Liberty to dedicate it to your GRACE; which I am the more emboldened to do, becauſe your GRACE, with your Wonted Affability and Condeſcenſion, has granted me that Liberty.

I have the Honour to be,

With the Greateſt Reſpect,

Your GRACE's

Moſt Grateful

and Obliged

Humble Servant,

Proceſter, *Glouceſterſhire,*
Novembır, 1786

RICHARD BIGLAND.

PREFACE,

By the late RALPH BIGLAND, Esq. Garter Principal King of Arms.

To the READER.

ABOUT thirty years ago, I began to make the Collection of Monumental Inscriptions which are to be found in the following Work. I entered on this laborious task principally to obtain from them that information relative to the Pedigrees of Families they are well known to afford. Though I term it a laborious task, yet it was not an unpleasant one to me, as it tended to encrease my knowledge in that branch of science which was become my Profession, and had been always my delight, and likewise furnished me with an agreeable amusement during the leisure hours I passed in the country.

Thus confined was my view when I first entered upon the employment; and I pursued it with as much assiduity as the duties of my office and other necessary avocations would permit; nor was it until I found the Collection become so very considerable, and myself repeatedly solicited by several of the Nobility and Gentry of the County, that I entertained any idea of offering them to the Public. Having however at length submitted to their solicitations, I formed the following Plan— I intended to have republished *Sir Robert Atkyns's* "Ancient and present State of Glocestershire," (which book was become extremely scarce) with such additions, and (as I hoped) improvements, as the intervening years gave me an opportunity of inserting, and at the same time to have introduced the Collection of Epitaphs I had made, together with a *Genealogical Account* of all the *Principal Families* in the County. Accordingly I purposed to have speedily carried it into execution, but the business of the College of Arms beginning about that time to encrease, and having continued ever since so to do, my design was unavoidably delayed, till the "New History of Gloucestershire" by Mr. Rudder, and the Republication of Sir Robert Atkyns, rendered it necessary for me to deviate from my Original plan— Instead therefore of giving a General History of Gloucestershire, as it first intended, I propose now to confine myself chiefly to the Monumental Inscriptions already collected, which amount to a much greater number than are to be found in any other work of this kind, and to the Genealogical Tables, I made and Collected, with proper references respecting many Families, who were formerly of property in the County, and are extinct as to Males, or are removed elsewhere, also of those Families still remaining in the County, and of Families of property lately removed into it from other Counties.

The Younger branches of Families often settle in places far remote from their native County. In process of time the Original stock or place of residence of the Family is either wholly forgotten, or becomes very difficult to be traced, and this has been productive of many considerable evils. The same may be observed of those branches of Families who have settled in foreign parts.

Monumental

Monumental edifices have been respected in all ages, and even among the most barbarous nations. Arrian writes, in his Second Book, that Alexander the Great, having found the tomb of Cyrus open and dirt thrown into it, was so enraged, that he offered a reward for discovering the offender, and when taken, punished him with an ignominious death.

It is likewise universally acknowledged, that Sepulchral Inscriptions have been always held to be of the most important consequences respecting the Rights of Inheritance. Burn * says, *that a copy of an inscription on a grave stone hath been allowed to be given in evidence.* They are undoubtedly some of the best evidences to prove the Connection of Families, and therefore, in that view, Collections of this kind may be considered as proper supplements to Histories of Counties, since they contain the History of the Inhabitants. And such Collections become still more interesting in a Commercial Country, where property frequently changes its owner, who thereby acquires a settlement far distant from his native one.

As to that part of the Work which contains the Genealogical History, from the post I have the honour to hold, I am furnished with materials, of which few other Writers could be so fully and authentically possessed.

I shall not pretend to set myself up for an Original author, but desire only that this Work may be considered (which I hinted before) as an Appendix to former Publications of the History of this County, not that I shall preclude myself from giving some account of the several Parishes within it: And I flatter myself, that the Reader will find in the course of this Work some few things deserving of Notice, which have hitherto passed unobserved. I would not have the Reader expect that All the Parishes should be equally Important or Amusing. This, from the Nature of things, cannot be. Some must be Short and Barren as to Matter, whilst others, it is hoped, will make Amends.

In order however to render the whole, so far as my Design goes, as complete and entertaining as possible, I have caused many Draughts of Churches to be taken on the spot, and engraved by able Artists, besides a great number of Armorial Ensigns of Honour, as they have occurred, and appear to have been Officially established. Remarkable Figures carved on brass or stone, and many other particulars with which several Churches abound, will be occasionally introduced.

In short, in the Histories of Gloucestershire, which precede mine, and indeed in almost all other works of the same nature, it has been usual to confine the accounts of the Families given therein, and their Pedigrees, to the possessors of Manors, or to a few others who are rendered eminent by their Births, Employments, or Estates; but in the following Work I have greatly extended this matter, and have taken due notice of many of the Inhabitants who are become what is commonly called Gentry, and are respectable in the County, making my Work in general rather an History of the Inhabitants of Gloucestershire, than of the Shire itself.

RALPH BIGLAND, Garter
Principal King of Arms

N. B. *The following Collections were brought down by the late Mr Bigland to the year 1781. But as several Monuments may have since been erected, and many Tombs, flat and head Stones, added, and more generally will be, before the publication of this Work, such as can be collected in due time will be inserted in their proper places, the others in an Appendix. The same method will be observed as to many recent articles, such as Canals, new Roads, &c. The Pedigrees or Genealogical Table will form a Work of itself.*

Plans of the Armorial Ensigns of those Families in the County whose Right to Arms is established, will be neatly engraved, in sheets as in Sir Robert Atkyns, and published towards the conclusion of the Work.

I. ABBENHALL.

THIS parish lies in the hundred of *Saint Briavels*, and *Forest* Deanery, adjoining to *Mitcheldean* on the fouth east, and twelve miles weft from the city of *Gloucefter*. It is a fmall parish, bordering upon the north fide of the *Foreft of Dean*, full of dingles and bottoms, and confifts rather of more arable land than pafturage, with feveral commons covered with fern and bufhes. The foil is chiefly light, fome of it fandy, and a fmall part rocky.

A fine fpring of water, which rifes out of a rock in the *Foreft*, at a fmall diftance from the parish, runs through a confiderable part of it, and, after fupplying feveral mills and three iron-forges, empties itfelf into the river *Severn* at *Hadbury*. This fpring near its fource, having paffed through a fmall grove, runs into a fquare bafon (made to receive it) about five feet deep, and large enough for a perfon to bathe in with fteps on one fide. The bafon is called *Saint Anthony's Well*, and the water, which is extremely cold, is much celebrated in all the adjacent country, as a certain remedy for cutaneous diforders of every kind: it has been known to cure an inveterate leprofy even by a few times bathing. Nearly the fame quantity of water iffues from the fpring during every feafon of the year, and there is fcarcely any vifible decreafe in the drieft fummers.

There was formerly an iron-furnace upon this ftream, which is now converted into a paper mill, and known by the name of *Guns Mill*. Mr Lloyd, to whom it belongs, has a good houfe adjoining thereto.

Confiderable quarries of a reddifh foft ftone, which ferves for paving and building, are found in this and the neighbouring parishes.

The Abbot of *Flaxley* had anciently a houfe here; and Sir Robert Akyns fuppofes, from the fimilarity of the found of *when* to *Abbot*, or *Abbey*, that it owes its name of *Abbenhall* to that circumftance.

Mr —— and Colchefter, Efq; poffeffes a confiderable eftate in the parish, and his a handfome feat here, called *The Wilderneft*, at which he now refides. It is fituated on the brow of a hill, and commands a profpect fo extenfive that thirteen counties may be difcerned from it.

Jofeph Pyrke of *Little Dean*, in this county, Efq; has a confiderable property in this parish; and Mr Chefton, an eminent furgeon at *Gloucefter*, has likewife an eftate here.

The living is a rectory, and the church, which is dedicated to *Saint Michael*, has an ifle on the fouth fide, and a good tower built of ftone, at the weft end, containing three bells.

INCUMBENTS	PATRONS	INCUMBENTS	PATRONS
1668 William Davis,	William Scudmore	1712 Thomas Mantle, M A	Charles Hyett, Efq
1685 Richard Hall, M A	Catharine Pawlings	171— Chriſt. Hoſkins, B A	John Howell, Efq
The above names and dates from Sir Rob. Atkyns		1785 John Probyn, Cler	John Probyn, Efq

PRESENT LORD OF THE MANOR,

EDMUND PROBYN, Efq.

B

At a Visitation of the county of GLOUCESTER, in the year 1682, by *Thomas May*, Esq Chester Herald, and *Gregory King*, Rougedragon, and in the year 1683, by *Henry Detbeck*, Esq Richmond Herald, and the aforesaid *Gregory King*, Rougedragon, Officers of Arms, Deputies and Marshals to S.r *Henry St George*, Knight, Clarenceux King of Arms, for the purpose of registering the descents and arms of all the gentry, by virtue of a commission from his Majesty *King Charles the Second*, under the great seal of England, the following persons, supposed to be resident in this parish, were summoned to appear personally, and bring with them such arms and crests as they used and bore, with their pedigrees and descents, that entrance thereof might be made and registered in the College of Arms, viz

Sir Duncomb Colchester, Knight,
Mr Davis, Clerk

The following is a Copy of the Summons issued upon this Occasion :

" Com GLOUCESTER

To the Bailiff of the Hundred of ———.

" I HESE are to require you, and in his Majesties name to charge and command you, that forthwith upon sight hereof you warn those baronets, knights, esquires, and gentlemen, whose names are within written, personally to appear before us, *Thomas May*, Esq Chester Herald, and *Gregory king*, Rougedragon, Officers of Arms, Deputies and Marshals to *Clarenceux* King of Arms, for the county of Gloucester, at the inn, in , on the day of August next, by nine o clock in the morning, where we intend to fit for registering the descents and arms of all the gentry within the said hundred, and that they bring with them such arms and crests as they use and bear, with their pedigrees and descents, and such other evidence and matter of record and credit, as (if need require) may justify the same, that we knowing how they use and challenge their titles, and by what right and authority they bear or pretend to bear arms, we may accordingly make entrance thereof, and register the same in the college of arms, or else to proceed as his Majesties commission under the great seal of England enjoyneth in that behalf. And those persons who may not conveniently bring such their antient evidences and writings as will serve to prove the antiquity of their race and family, but shall be desirous to have us come to their houses, upon signification of such their desires, for the furtherance of his Majesties service, we or one of us, will repair unto them so soon as conveniently we may. And if there shall be any of the degrees and qualities abovementioned omitted within your liberties in these our directions, that you likewise intent their names, and warn them also to appear on the day, and at the place abovementioned Accordingly hereof charge them not to fail, as they will avoid the peril that may ensue. Of these particulars you are to make a true and perfect return, together with this your warrant, and what you have done therein, at the time and place above appointed

Given under our hands and seals this day, of July, in the thirty fourth year of the reign of our most gracious Sovereign Lord Charles the Second, by the grace of God, of England, France, and Ireland, King, Defender of the Faith, &c annoque Domini 1682

THOMAS MAY, Chester
GREGORY KING, Rougedragon."

It appears from the poll-book of the High Sheriff, that at the contested election of a Knight of the shire for the county, in the year 1776, seven freeholders polled from this parish

ANNUAL ACCOUNT OF MARRIAGES, BIRTHS, AND BURIALS, IN THIS PARISH

A D	Mar	Bir	Bur.	A D	Mar	Bir	Bur	A D	Mar	Bir	Bur	A D	Mar	Bir	Bur.
1781	3	3	5	1791				1801				1811			
1782	—	3	3	1792				1802				1812			
1783	—	7	4	1793				1803				1813			
1784	1	6	4	1794				1804				1814			
1785				1795				1805				1815			
1786				1796				1806				1816			
1787				1797				1807				1817			
1788				1798				1808				1818			
1789				1799				1809				1819			
1790				1800				1810				1820			

MONUMENTAL INSCRIPTIONS.

IN THE CHURCH

ON THE NORTH SIDE OF THE CHANCEL IS A WHITE MARBLE MONUMENT, WITH THE FOLLOWING ARMS AND INSCRIPTIONS

Argent on a Fess Sable, 3 Mullets of the first, a Canton Ermine for Pyrke impaling Gules, a Cheveron between three Estoiles, Or for Colchester,

Near hereunto
lies interred the body of Nath
Pyrke, of Michel Dean, Esq who was descended
of an ancient Family, who had their chief seat
of Residence in this Neighbourhood ever since the
Conquest He married Mary, the Daughter of Sir Duncomb
Colchester, Knt and by her had issue three Sons and
two Daughters. Thomas the eldest married Dorothy
the Daughter of Richard Yate, of Arlngham, Esq
Duncomb the second married Elizabeth the Daughter
of Will Gwilliam, of Lingstone in the County of
Hereford, Esq and Jane married Rooke Walter, Son
and Heir of Thomas Walter of Stapleton, in the
County of Gloucester, Esq Nath and Deborah died
Infants, and lie interred near this place He was
a faithful Subject to his Prince, a good Father
to his Children, charitable to the Poor, and just
in his dealings He left behind him an inconsolable
Widow, who erected this Monument in
remembrance of so tender and loving a Husband
He died the 28 of October, 1715, in the sixtyeth
year of his age

Also in Memory of Deborah, the Mother of the said
Nath Pyrke, and Wife of Thomas Pyrke, Esq She was
a pious good Christian and lies interred near this
Place She died the ninth of February, 1602 But
Thomas Pyrke her Husband, and Father of the
said Nath lies buried in the Parish Church of
Little Deane

Also here lieth Dorothy, the Daughter of Thomas
Pyrke, Esq grand daughter of the said Nath
She was buried June 21, 1715

Also in Memory of Mary Pyrke,
the Widow and Relict of the abovenamed
Nathaniel Pyrke, who departed this Life
the 22d of December, Anno Dom 1738, Ætatis 70
And of Nathaniel, Son of Duncomb and
Elizabeth Pyrke who died January the
10th, 1735 aged XXXI year

ON A BLUE FLAT STONE, WITH THE EFFIGIES OF A MAN AND HIS WIFE AND TWO CHILDREN, IN THE HABIT OF THE TIMES, ENGRAVED ON BRASS

Chriſtus Mihi Vita,
Mors Mihi Lucrum

Here lyeth the Body of Richard Pyrke, of Michel Deane,
in the County of Glouc & Iohan his Wife, the Daughter
of John Ayleway, Gent which Richard died the 23 daye
of October, Anno Dni 1609   Aged LX Yeares

Here lyeth the Bodies of Thomas Pyrke, &
Robt Pyrke, Sonnes of the ſaid Richard &
Iohan, which Thomas died the   day of
Anno Dni   aged   Robt died the
day of   Anno Dni   aged

Here lyeth the Body of
Duncombe Pyrke, 2d Son of
Nathaniel Pyrke, Eſq who
departed this life October the
9th, Anno Dni, 1725, Ætatis ſuæ 34

ON MONUMENTS AT THE WEST END OF THE CHURCH.

JONATHAN VAUGHAN
of this Pariſh, Gent
died Oct the 24, 1742,
aged 46
ANNE his wife (Daughter
of THOMAS KING, Gent)
died Jan 14, 1758,
aged 54

In memory of
Richard Vaughan ſen
who departed this Life
April 24, 1728, aged 69 years
Alſo Mary his wife, who
deceaſed July the 10, 1718, aged 54 years.
Likewiſe Richard their Son
died May 11, 1723.
And John their Son
deceaſed May the 5, 1728

Near this place lies interred
the Remains of
Edward Hearne, Gent late of
Mitchel Dean in this County,
Died the 3d Sept 1776, aged 74

Near this Place lie the Remains
of Sarah his Wife, died the 27th
of July 1768, Aged 80

Near this Place lie Interred
the Remains of
Mr Tho Palmore late of
Scaldwell near Northampton,
and Nephew to the above
Edward Hearne, Gent died
the 16th May 1778, Aged 42

ON FLAT STONES

In Memory of George
Martin, of Huxley, Son of
Richard Martin, of this Pariſh,
who died Nov 23, 1728,
aged 48 Years

Alſo in Memory of George,
Son of Henry Martin, by
Elenor his Wife,
who died Jan the 4th 1723

In Memory of Henry
Martin of this Pariſh who
died Dec 20, 17__ , Aged 83

Alſo here lyeth the Body of
Eleanor the Wife of Henry
Martin, who departed this life
May 6, 1711 Aged 49 Years

Mrs Mary Hall, the wife of
Edward Hall of this Pariſh, the
Daughter of William Adee, Eſq
of Collon, in the County of
Middleſex, was here interred the
20th day of May, Anno Domini 1726,
Aged 74 Years

On the ſouth ſide hereof lieth
Edward, the Huſband of the ſaid
Mary, who was buried October
the 8, 1731, Aged 75 Years

In Memory of John Wood,
who was here buried November
the 5th, 1720, Aged 46 years

William his Son
was buried Aug 5th, 1723

James his Son
was buried April the 5th 17__

In Memory of
Thomas Wood who died
March 7, 1720, aged 60 Years

Also Mary, his Wife,
who died Dec 14, 1732, Aged 80 Years

Here lyeth the body of
Margaret, the Daughter of
James Sentom, by Mary
his Wife, who died March 15, 1723,
Aged 27 Years

Here resteth in Expectation
of a joyful Resurrection
the body of John Sloman,
who departed this Life one
day of October A D 1714,
Aged 76 Years

Also here lyeth the Body of
James Sloman who died the
the 31 day of March 17—

IN THE CHURCH YARD

ON TOMBS

Joseph Lloyd,
late of Guns Mills in this Parish,
died Nov 17, 1761, Aged 53

John Lloyd
died Aug 2, 1765, Aged 72

Sarah, the Daughter of
William and Mary Baynham,
died Dec 11, 177 , Aged 10 Years 5 Months

William Baynham,
Father of the above,
died 24 March 1780, Aged 59 Years.

Godwin Skidmore
died 12 March 1778, aged 93.

Elizabeth his Wife
died 12 April 1774, aged 73

Richard Cropp,
of Flaxley, died Aug 4,
1783, Aged 6?

Margaret, the Wife of
Richard Cropp died
October 4, 1766, Aged 82

Mary, Wife of
William Hardwick, and
Daughter of Joseph and Hannah
Lloyd, of Guns Mills in this Parish,
died May 17, 1769, Aged 29

Mary the Wife of
Joseph Lloyd Jun of Guns
Mills, Gent and Daughter of
John and Jane Robinson of Little Dean,
died Feb 24, 1784, Aged 37 Years

Robert Butcher
died May 2, 1765, aged 81

Elizabeth his Wife
died May 10, 1767, Aged 78

ON HEAD STONES

	Died	Aged
Mary the Wife of Richard Webb, Daughter of Richard Vaughan of Ruardean,	0 May, 1759	—
Thomas Webb	5 Jun 1757	76
Geo Widder	3 Oct 1751	41
William Vaughan	25 O 1733	70
Judith Butcher	2 Apr 1723	60
Joseph Butcher	23 Apr 1748	67
Robert Butcher	26 Apr 1759	—
Anne the Wife of Richard Halliday,	3 Nov 1686	—
Thomas Nelme	26 Jun 173	64
Alice Wife of Richard Nelme (deceased)	18 Nov 17 8	90
Thomas Meeke	1 Apr 17 9	59
Ann his Wife	6 Jan 1721	41
Abigail his second Wife Daughter of George Wright, of Leonard Stanley, and formerly Wife of John Cooke of Stalbridge in the County of Dorset, lie buried at Mitchel Dean She and the others of Nelme		
	2 Dec 1754	78
Richard Nelme	1 May 1759	80
Hester, Daughter of John and Mary Nelme,	1 Apr 176	13
Thomas, Son of Thomas and Elizabeth Jones,	17 M 1766	16
Peregrine Martin	27 Apr 177	15
Mary, Wife of John Nelme	20 M 1777	75

ABSTON and WICK.

THIS parish lies in the hundred of *Pucklechurch*, and Deanery of *Hawkesbury*, about seven miles east from *Bristol*, and thirty-four miles south from *Gloucester*. It consists chiefly of pasture and meadow land, with some arable. The soil is principally loam, and in several parts rather sandy.

Adjoining to the river *Boyd*, (which takes its rise at *Codrington*, a hamlet in the parish of *Waplet*, and runs through this parish to *Bitton*,) are several clifts rising perpendicularly to a great height, from the quarries of which is dug a stone that produces excellent lime. Coal is likewise found here, and two pits belonging to Richard Haynes, Esq; are now in work at *Wick*. Belemnites, Astroites, Serpent ne stones, and a flinty substance resembling Bristol stones, are frequently met with. A considerable iron work, the property also of Mr Haynes, is carried on in the clifts, for rolling and splitting iron to make hoops with, near which there is a paper-mill.

In a field called the *Chesties*, or *Castles*, there were formerly three large stones placed near together in a triangular form, and probably designed as monuments to some British chiefs, but only one of them now remains. Not far from this stone, several Roman coins, &c. have been dug up, and, in an adjacent field, a great number of bricks, undoubtedly Roman, have been discovered, and from the urns, bricks, &c. which remain, this place appears to have been a Roman pottery.

A feast or revel is held here on the Sunday before *Saint James's* day.

There are five hamlets in this parish, viz. 1 *Berdwic*, now written *Wick*. 2 *Holy Brook* so called from a spring which was dedicated to the *Holy Virgin*. 3 *Churchic*, or *Church-Asht*, which obtained its name from an ancient chapel dedicated to *Saint Bartholomew*, but the chapel is now in ruins, and the hamlet itself scarcely remembered. 4 *Bridge-Yate*, called in some MSS *Breach Yeat*. And 5 *Toghill*, not far from which are the remains of an old fortification and intrenchments, supposed to be Saxon.

Near the last mentioned place, happened one of the most memorable engagements in these parts during the civil war in the reign of King Charles. On the 5th of July, 1643, the King's forces were drawn up by Sir Ralph Hopton, and Prince Maurice, upon *Toghill*. The Parliament's forces, under the command of Sir William Waller, planted themselves upon *Laydown*, where they had a battery, and from whence Sir William detached a strong party of the horse and dragoons, with a regiment of Cuirassiers, to attack the King's horse who had never before turned from an enemy, but the attack was so vigorous, particularly by the Cuirassiers, that they were broke, and put to the rout, when a fresh party of troops belonging to the King, winged with some Cornish musqueteers, came up, and made an attack in their turn, drove back the Parliament's forces, and after a very bloody engagement, (in which Sir Beville Grenville at the third charge, his horse failing, after other wounds, received a mortal blow from a pole axe) gained the summit of the hill, and took possession of the battery. Upon this Sir William Waller retired behind some stone walls, where both parties continued in sight of each other during the remainder of the day, and at midnight the Parliament's forces retired to Bath, leaving lighted matches in the wall to deceive the King's forces who found themselves in the morning entire masters of the field of battle. The loss of Sir Beville Grenville in this engagement occasioned King Charles the Second, after his restoration, to confer the title of earl of Bath, and Viscount Lansdown upon Sir Beville's son, and in some mention of the same that some monument was erected upon *Laydown*, near the ... what I cannot discover.

The monument is a tall column with the following inscription.

On the several heights ... on the east the King's and those of Granville, and on the opposite Court ... the Grenville Croft.

THE FOLLOWING IS ON THE SOUTH TABLET

' In this battle, on the King's part, were more officers and gentlemen of quality slain in particular men ... [which] would have clouded any victory, and made the loss of others less look'd on, was the death of Sir Bevill Granvile. He was indeed an excellent person, whose ... in credit in reputation, ... on account of what had been done in Cornwall, and his temper ... so just ... that no accident which happened could make any impression in him, ... his soul, ere to be ... ing ... guilt, or at least seeming to do so. In a word, a bright ... court ... and gentleness ... on were never match'd together, to make the most chearful and innocent conversation. —*Clarendon's Hist.* vol. 1

Richard Haynes, Esq. has a handsome house at Wick, with a considerable estate.

The church, which is dedicated to *Saint James*, consists of one isle, with a neat pillars at the west end; and has a handsome tower, adorned with pinnacles, containing five bells. The situation of it is remarkably pleasant, as here are agreeable prospects towards *Dyrham*, and *Dunton*. The living is annexed to the vicarage of *Pucklechurch*.

BENEFACTIONS

Christopher Capel in the year 1662, devised one hundred and forty pounds, to purchase land, and erect a house for four poor people. A ground and house at *Holbrook* were settled for this purpose according to the will of the ...

Mr John Fanaway gave a yearly rent charge of ten shillings to the use of poor housekeepers.

Brown Willis, who died in the year 1727, left a part of his house at Wick for the habitation of two clergymens widows, to be chosen by the ministers of *Pucklechurch*, *Dyrham*, and *Dunton*, with ten pounds a year, and half a load of coal, to each. With the overplus of this estate, ... is to be chosen out of the fore mentioned parishes, is to be maintained at the University till he takes the degree of Batchelor of Arts. He also gave nineteen shillings a year, to be spent at the annual meeting of the trustees and ...

Mr William Hart, Clerk, has given twenty shillings yearly for two sermons.

Incumbents	Patrons	Incumbents	Patrons
1657 Walter Mountford, M A	Dean and Chapter of Wells	1724 Henry Gandy, B A	Dean and Chapter of Wells
1684 Henry Dutton, M A	The same	1768 George Swine M A	The same
16.. John Davis, M A	The same	1772 George Swayne, Jun M A	The same
17.. Henry Perow, B A	The same		
The above from Sir Rob Atkyn			

PRESENT LORD OF THE MANOR,

RICHARD HAYNES, ESQ.

At the before mentioned visitations by the Heralds in 1682 and 1683, the following persons were then more from this place.

Mr Raymond
Mr Seal, Cler
Mr Hart

At the Election in 1770 seventeen freeholders polled for this parish.

AN ANNUAL ACCOUNT OF MARRIAGES, BIRTHS, AND BURIALS, IN THIS PARISH

A D	Mar	Bir	Bur	A D	Mar	Bur	Bur	A D	Mar	Bir	Bur	A D	Mar	Bur	Bur
	—	1..	6	1791				1800				1811			
		1..	1												
		1..	1									1813			
												1814			
												1815			
									1796			1816			
												1817			
												1818			
												1819			
									1800						

MONUMENTAL INSCRIPTIONS

IN THE CHURCH.

IN THE BODY

ON FLAT STONES

Exuviæ Mariæ Hickes filiæ
Jacobi Hickes de hâc parochia, fub
hoc lapide jacent, quæ mortem obiit
per variolas, 8 die Novembris, Anno 32ª
ætatis fuæ, & A° Dom 1708

Infra item jacent exuviæ fupradicti
Jacobi Hickes, qui e vita hâc migra-
vit 25 die Augufti, An° 70 ætatis ejus,
& An° Dni 1709.

Cum fumus incerti quando moriemur, oportet
Hac de perpetuo causa nos effe paratos

Here lyeth the Body of Elizabeth
the Wife of David Milfum, Daughter of
James and Elizabeth Hickes of this
parifh, who departed this life the 1ft day of June,
1738, Aged 66 years

ARMS IMPALED IN A LOZENGE

On a fefs three roundles, between as many demi-
hinds, for Haynes—the impalement obliterated

Here lyeth the body
of Mrs Mary Haines,
the Widdow and Relict
of Mr Thoˢ Haynes,
of the City of Briftol,
Lord of this Mannor,
who deceafed the xviii day
of May, A Dni MDCCIX
Aged lxxx years

This Burial Place
of the family of Thomas
Haynes, Efq and
Sarah his Wife, was thus
difpofed, 1717

Remembering
that in the midft of
Life we are in Death

Here refteth the Body of
Richard Iveyleade of this Parifh,
Gent who departed this Life
the 24 day of January,
Anno Domini 1715,
Aged 55 Years

Also here Lyeth
Damaris Iveyleade Widdow
and Relict of the above
named Richard Iveyleade,
who died the 1 of December,
Aged 71
Years

In
Memory of
Richard Rufs, Gent
who died 12th June,
1767 Aged 54
Years

Here Lyeth the Body of Gabriel
Ivey, the Son of Richard Ivey,
of this Parifh, who departed this
Life the 22d day of March,
Anno Domini, 1727,
Aged 20 Years

ANTE OBITUM NEMO BEATUS.

Here lyeth the Body
of John, the Son of
Lewis Bryan, who
departed this Life
the 19th day of April,
and is buried
the 24th,
1684

Here
Lyeth the
Body of Charles
Bryan, of this Parifh, Son
of Lewis Bryan Senr who
departed this Life the
9th day of May 175 ,
Aged 51 Years

Here lyeth the Body of
Lewis Bryan Son of this
parifh who died the 11th
day of February 169

Under

Underneath Lyeth the Remaines of Mary Bryan, Relict of Lewis Bryan, of this Parish, who deceafed the 31st Day of August, 1704

Here Lyeth the Body of Lewis Bryan of this Parish, Jun who dep.ted this Life the 5th day of August, 1751, Aged 84 Years

In Memory of Guy, the Son of Lewis and Ann Bryan, who died the 11 day of June, 1708, Aged 12 Years and 10 Months

Alfo here Lyeth the Body of Ann, the Wife of Lewis Bryan, Sen of this Parish, who departed this Life March the 12th, 1741, Aged 73 Years and 10 Months

In Memory of Lewis, the Son of Lewis Bryan, Yeoman, by Mary his Wife, who died 12 April, 1767, Aged 13 Years and 6 Months

Underneath Lie the Remains of Lewis Bryan, of this Parish, Yeoman, who departed this Life, 12th January, 1744, in the 73rd year of his Age

IN THE CHANCEL

Here Lyeth the Body of Samuel Woodward, Gent who departed this Life the 2nd Day of July, 1648

ON A SHIELD BETWEEN THESE INSCRIPTIONS, ARE THREE CHEVERONELLS, FOR THE ARMS

Here Lyeth alfo the Body of Mrs Mary Seede, Widow, formerly Wife of the aforefaid Mr Woodward, who departed this life the 14th Day of Septem 1695

ON THE VERGE OF A FLAT STONE

CORPUS   IZA
BELLÆ PLAYER RELICTÆ ARTURI PLAYER
O QUÆ - - - - - - -

ON ANOTHER VERGE

HIC   - - CORPUS
ARTV - - - -
25 OCTOBRIS ANNO DOMINI 1591.

IN THE CHURCH YARD

ON TOMBS

Anon Spence died April 29, 1762, Aged no 18

Mary, Daughter of Stephen and Susannah Toghill died April 5, 1769, in the 2d Year of her age

George, Son of Stephen and Susannah Toghill died 28th April 1775, Aged 35

Stephen Toghill late of Kellston, Yeoman, died 10 Sept 1765, in 66th year of his age

Elizabeth, Daughter of Thomas and Sarah Toghill of Pucklechurch, and Wife of Henry Adey of Chipping Sodbury in this County, died the 16 June 1646, aged 9

Thomas Toghill of Pucklechurch, died 3 Aug 1720, Aged 5.
Sarah his Widow died Jun 6, 1763, Aged 86

George Toghill of Pucklechurch, Yeo died Jun 6, 1783, in 63d Year of his Age

Chri Booker, Son of
Christopher and Martha Williams,
died 19 April 1737, aged 20

Christopher Williams Son
died May 3d, 1743, in 77 Year of his Age

Martha, Wife of
Christopher Williams, and
2nd Wife of Charles Hill,
died July 4, 1745, Aged 68

Thomas Ashley,
died June 29, 1770, Aged 54

Martha, Wife of Thos Ashley,
died Aug 11, 1765, Aged 32

Richard their Son,
died May 4, 1774, Aged 15

Mary, Wife of John Sherborne
of Westerleigh, and Daughter
of Richard and Deborah Collins,
died the 8th of Dec 1748, Aged 67

Deborah, the Wife of James Palmer,
and Daughter of Richard and Deborah
Collins, died Dec 24, 1755, Aged 8

James Palmer
died 31st Dec 1758, Aged 85

Robert Collins,
Mathematician,
died 21 Jan 1733, in the
62nd Year of his Age

Richard Collins, Sen
died in the Year 1706, Aged 66

Deborah his Wife,
died in 1712, aged 52

Thomas, Son of
Thomas and Mary Lewis,
died Jan 20, 1740, in the
63 Year of his Age

Thomas Davis Son
died J 18, 1753, Aged 70

Mary his Wife,
died 31 Dec 1766, Aged 70

Ann, Daughter of
Thomas and Mary Lewis,
and Wife of Richard Spence,
of Newton Park in the
County of Summerset,
died March 31, 1752, Aged 52

Richard Spence,
late of Newton in said
County of Bristol, died
29 Sep 1752, Aged 44

William Ford, Gen
died 2nd Aug st, 0

ON HEADSTONES

	Died	Aged
Elizabeth, Wife of Thomas Bryant,	30 June, 1768	43
Mary, Widow of Samuel Bryan,	19 July, 1755	
Lucey Wife of Samuel Jerkins,	3 M 1756	56
Samuel Bryan	9 Nov 1754	49
Anna, Wife of Richard Bryan, of Mangetfield,	28 Nov 1770	60
Samuel, Son of Samuel and Mary Bryan,	20 Feb 1755	19
John Bryan	1 Dec 1755	60
Henry Doo	27 May 1753	74
Elizabeth, his Wife,	16 May, 1760	
Henry Door, Jun	Apr 1760	55
George, Son of Henry and Elizabeth Doo,	30 Oct 1755	52
Michael, Son of John and Mary Veniton, of Winchrington in the County of Dorset,	15 M 1755	27
Mary, Wife of John Ashley,	9 Feb 1753	40
Elizabeth, their Daughter,	1 July, 1760	3
Margaret Strange	Oct 1770	70
Sarah Strange	9 July, 1771	46
John Gay	June, 1757	7
Mary, Wife of John Gay, Daughter of Thomas and Sarah Tockhill,	Apr 1755	48
Robert, Son of John and Mary Smith	Jan 1745	
John Smith	Feb 1766	7
Thomas Sandum	Sept 17	6
Dorothy his Wife	Apr 17	
Mary, Wife of William Hooper, Daughter of and Deborah Sandum	15 June, 1741	
William Ashley	Mar	6
William Pearce	Feb 1756	
Henry Pearce, of Yate	1 Dec 1755	83
Mary his Wife	Feb 17	79
Jane, Wife of John Bryan	July 1755	63
Mary, Wife of William Luffell,	Aug 17	
William Luffell	Dec 1755	64

ON HEAD STONES.

	Died	Aged
Samuel Fussell - - - - - - -	23 Jan 1772	62
Mary Wife of James Bryan - -	14 Oct 1762	51
Ann Wife of Joseph England, of Waterleigh, Daughter of James and Mary Bryan, - - - - -	9 July, 1756	24
James Bryan - - - - -	12 June 1776	72
Joseph England - - - - -	24 June, 1776	47
Elizabeth Wife of William Bryan -	13 Aug 1775	6
William Bryan - - -	22 Dec 1756	82
Elliott Main - - - -	16 June, 1771	71
Edw Strange of Downton, - - -	4 Jan 1760	77
Thomas Fothill, Yeom - - -	15 Oct 1766	74
Sarah his Wife - - -	17 Apr 1780	84
Thomas Trubody - - -	11 Jan 1760	18
Martha his Daughter - - -	5 Aug 1765	12
Matthew Weeks - -	9 Feb 1782	8

III ACTON, or IRON ACTON.

THIS parish lies chiefly in the hundred of *Thornbury*, and deanery of *Hawkesbury*, about nine miles north-east from BRISTOL and twenty six miles south from GLOUCESTER. It consists of one third good pasturage, and two thirds arable. The soil is light, brash, and rich, and generally produces good crops, unless the season prove too dry, as it lies on a hard bed of stone the colour of which is between a red and a grey. In the year 1779, an Act of Parliament was obtained for inclosing a common in this parish, which was carried into execution; but when compleated it was not found to be advantageous.

This parish probably received the name of *Acton* from the Saxon word *Ac*, an oak, as it is said to have been much over-run with that tree, and it was named IRON *Acton*, to distinguish it from *Acton* TURVILLE, on account of the iron-works that were anciently here.

The adjacent country towards the forest of *Kingswood* being one vast bed of coal, the vein or strata extended themselves here also, but not so thick as in the adjoining parish of *Westerleigh*, which lies to the south. About twenty years ago, a coal-pit was worked at a place near this parish called *Nibly*, by the late Charles Bragge, Esq. but the stratum was too thin to answer the expence.

Two fairs are annually held here, one on the 25th of April, the other on the 9th of September.

There are two hamlets in this parish, viz. 1. *Lateridg*, or *Ladomite*, lying about a mile north-west from the church, and so denominated from its being situated on a rising piece of ground near the brook *Frome*, which, joining another brook that takes its rise at *Dodington* forms here the river *Froom*, and passes through *Frampton Cotterel*, *Stapleton*, &c. to Bristol. And 2. *Algar*, which lies in the hundred of *Grumbald's Ash*, and takes its name from *Algar*, or *Algor*, who held the manor in the reign of William the Conqueror.

In the last mentioned hamlet, Mr. Edward Huford has a neat house and estate. At *Acton* the same Thomas Nelmes Esq. has an estate and manor of a considerable extent, called *Cossewood* formerly belonging to the family of Crowther.

Acton belonged to Samuel Kent Esq. nephew of the late Thomas Kent, Esq. a worthy justice of the peace for this county, who served the office of high sheriff in the year 176-.

The house is a rectory and the church which is dedicated to *Saint James* was built by one of the *Poyntz* family in the late — century. It has a fine handsome tower, with a vane at the top, and pinnacles, in which are two bells and a clock. On the south side of the chancel there is a vault belonging to the manor house, near which, in the church-yard are two ancient crosses one of a most —

armour, the other of a woman in an antique drefs   In the church yard, on the north fide, is a very old
Gothic crofs, that appears to be coeval with, if not prior to the church   It has four fides   on each fide
two fhields, one or two of which are plain, two or three feem to have mechanical inftruments, fuch as
hatchets, &c carved on them, but thofe which had arms, are obliterated

----

BENEFACTIONS.

Mr HUMPHRY BROWN, a merchant of *Briftol*, gave, by will, Jan 27, 1629, 10 fhillings a year, for a
fermon to be preached on *St John's* day   He alfo gave to the church a pulpit cloth, cufhion, filver
flaggon, and chalice, and 40 fhillings yearly to the poor

Mr JOHN BRINKWORTH gave 20 pounds to the poor, by will, Jun 14, 1699   the intereft thereof to
be laid out in bread

Mr EDWARD BRINKWORTH gave 20 pounds to the poor, by deed, 25 Jun 1700, of the intereft, 10
fhillings for bread, the reft to be diftributed at the difcretion of the churchwardens and overfeers

Mr JOHN MORTIMER, rector of this parifh, who died in the year 702, gave 20 pounds to the poor,
the intereft thereof for bread

Mr SIMON SLOPER gave the intereft of 10 pounds for the benefit of the poor

Mr WILLIAM PAYNE gave the intereft of 5 pounds to be diftributed among the poor at the difcretion
of the churchwardens and overfeers

THOMAS LISTON, Efq by deed, July 4, 721, gave 10 pounds a year for ever for the benefit of the
poor

INCUMBENTS	PATRONS	INCUMBENTS	PATRONS
1574 Richard Talbot,	Nicholas Poyntz, Efq	1729 Ifaac Terry, Cler	Hugh Fuks, Efq
1577 Nicholas Ghudal,	Bifhop of Gloucefter	1736 Oliver Bately, B D	Chrift church, Oxford.
1581 Thomas Price,	George Hayworth	1763 Jofeph Jane, B D	Ditto
1580 John Loyde,	John Poyntz		
1593 John Wadlocke,	Sir John Poyntz		
1641 John Harvey,	Sir John Poyntz		
1694 John Mortimer, B A	Simon Sloper, Ger		
1703 Thomas Shure, M A	Ditto		

The above from Sir ROB ATKYNS

PRESENT LORD OF THE MANOR

WALTER LONG, Efq

At the Vifitation by the Heralds in 1682 and 168,, the following perfons were fummoned from this
place

The Heirs of Sir John Poyntz,
Mr Harvey, Cler
John Fuel, Gent

At the Election in 1776, forty Freeholders polled from this parifh

ANNUAL ACCOUNT OF MARRIAGES, BIRTHS, AND BURIALS, IN THIS PARISH

AD	Mu	Bir	Bur	AD	Mu	Bur	Bur	AD	Mu	Bir	Bur	AD	Mu	Bir	Bur

MONUMENTAL INSCRIPTIONS.

IN THE CHURCH.

IN THE CHANCEL,

AGAINST THE SOUTH WALL IS AN ANCIENT TOMB, AND ON A FLAT STONE NEAR IT ARE THE FOLLOW-
ING ARMS AND INSCRIPTION

Arms, Barry of 8 Or and Gules, a Mullett for difference

HIC JACET CORPUS HUGONIS POYNTZ, ARMIGERI,
UNIUS FILIOR' NICIOLAI POYNTZ, EQUITIS AURATI,
QUI IN IPSO JUVENTUTIS FLORE AB OMNIBUS
UNICE DESIDERATUS DIEM CLAUSIT EXTREMUM
UNDECIMO DIE MARTIJ, ANNO DOMINI JUXTA
USITATAM ECCLESIÆ ANGLICANÆ COMPUTATIONEM
1604, ÆTATIS SUÆ 26
CUJUS ANIMA IN ÆTERNA PACE REQUIESCAT

HIC JACET CORPUS ELIZABETHÆ,
UXORIS ROBERTI POYNTZ ARMI-
GERI, QUÆ OBIIT 12° DIE JAN
ANNO DNI 1631

ON THE VERGE OF A FLAT STONE IN OLD TEXT IS
INSCRIBED

Here lye the Remains of Robard Poyntz E

ON ANOTHER IN OLD TEXT

Ann the futte wife of Robard Poyntz

FLAT STONE ON THE NORTH SIDE

In Memory of
Mrs Alice Richmond,
Relict of Toby Richmond
of Chadlington, in the parish
of Lydiard Tregooze in Com.
Wilts, Gent. and Mother in Law
of the Revd Mr Thomas Shute,
A. M. Rector of this parish,
who departed this life
Nov the 3d A D 1726,
Luis sua 101

Her also lyeth the
Body of Mrs Alice Shut-
Widow, and Daughter of
the above Mrs Alice Richmond,
who died Oct 8 175
Luis fit 61

WITHIN A [...]

In Memory of Thomas Shute,
only Son of Mr Jonath Shute
of the City of Bristol, deceased
and Alice his Wife, who departed
this Life Sep the 1st, A D 1722, Æ 17

Here lyeth the Body of
Frances, Wife of John
Harvey, Rector of this Church,
who departed this Life
March the first 1689
Mors mihi lucrum

Here lyeth the Body of
Mr John Harvey,
Rector of this Parish,
who departed this Life
the one and twentieth day
of January, 169,
Rector 4 years

Here lyeth the Body of
Anne, the Daughter of
John Harvey, Clerk, who
departed this Life the
9 day of Jul 1693
Mortis, [...]

ON A MONUMENT AGAINST THE NORTH WA

The Arms a Chevron between 3 Crescents

Near this Monument lieth the Body
of William Wither, Servant to [...]
and Hester Wither of [...]
this Parish and Grandson of William
Webb of this Parish Father of the
said Hester Wither who departed
this Life Feb [...] A D 1, [...]
and 71 [...]

[...] memory
Ann P [...] Thomas Shute,
hujus [...] Rectoris,
qui obiit [...] Martij,
Anno Dom [...]
[...]

Præterea memoriæ
[...] Uxor Thomæ Shute,
qui obiit [...] Maij [...]
[...]

ON A SMALL MONUMENT NEAR THE FORMER.

To the Memory of
Mr John Trewman,
who departed this Life,
the 11 Day of August, 1686,
Ætatis suæ 82

ON A MONUMENT AGAINST THE NORTH WALL

The Arms and Crest, an Eagle displayed with 2
Heads

Dedicated to the Memory of William
Machin, Gent of this Parish, who
died May the 24, in 1717,
Aged 43 years

Also to the Memory of his wife
Elizabeth the Daughter of Thomas
Rickv of this Parish, and by her
3 children She died Sept the 4th,
1702, Ætatis suæ 32

Also 4 children by his later wife,
Elizabeth the Daughter of John
Bampton of this Parish, Yeoman

ON A FLAT STONE ON THE NORTH SIDE

In Memory of
Thomas Machin, of this Parish, Gent
who departed this Life
June 11, 1734, in the year of his age
Also of Ann, relict
of the aforesaid Thomas Machin,
who died Oct, 1744, in the 44 year of her age
Also in Memory of
ELIZABETH the wife of JOHN HARDWICK,
of this Parish Gent Daughter of the
aforesaid Thomas and Ann Machin,
who died May 1, 78, aged 46 years

Here lyeth the Body of Mr John
Mortimer, rector of this Parish,
who departed this life January
16, 1702, Ætatis suæ 56

ON A SMALL MONUMENT OVER ONE OF THE PIL-
LARS

On the Faith of a Resurrection
to eternal Life, is interred near
this pillar, Mary, wife of John Petty,
of the City of Bristol, Daughter of
Thomas Machin, Gent who while
living was deservedly beloved and
died much lamented Oct 12 sweet,
in the XXVI of her age

WITHIN THE PEWS ON THE NORTH SIDE OF THE
CHANCEL

The following inscriptions on flat stones

Here lyeth the Body of Richard
Lamb, of Chadesley Corbett, in the County
of Worcester, who departed this Life
in the City of Bristol, 25 May, 17-9,
aged 60 years

Also his Daughter Caroline Lamb, who
departed this life 2 day of June, 17-9, aged
4 months

Also of Penelope, Widow of the said
Richard Lamb, who was buried
Nov 15, 173, aged 45

IN THE BODY OF THE CHURCH

ON A FLAT STONE.

Hic sepultus est
Catherina,
Filia Guliimi Veele, Generosi,
de Chillwood,
February 25,
155

Here lyeth the Body of Hannah Roberts,
of Frampton Cotterell, Daughter of
William Roberts and Hannah his
Wife, who departed this Life the 27 day
of February 174

Here lyeth the Body
of George Coole of the Parish
of Frampton Cotterell Yeoman who
departed this life the 17 year 1755

In Memory
the aforesaid August
A D

Here lyeth the Body of
Mrs Elizabeth Mason,
Daughter of George Mason of Bristol, Merchant
and Dorothy his Wife Daughter and Heir
of William Lewis, Esq She was a Person
of most exemplary Character, which is
more amply set forth on her
Monument
She died Dec 8, 17 aged 45 years

In the South Isle on a flat stone
Here lyeth the Body
of John Godwin Gent
of Wetterleigh, who departed
this Life April the 5 17
aged 49
Also here lyeth the
Body of Mary his Wife,
who departed this Life
Mar 14 1727, aged

In Memory
of Sarah, wife of Robert Fitzherbert
of Bristol who departed this Life
17 April, 176, aged 56 years

Also of Robert Fitzherbert, who
died November 20, 1784, aged 51 years

Epitaphium

Epitaphium Johañis Crowtneri,
Generoſi, qui obiit May
5, A D 1624
Si nne fraude fides, pietas nõ ficta, modeftum
Os, prudens genius, mens proba, larga manus,
Cura dei patriæ reddant (poft funera) famæ
Vitam Crowtheri nefcia fama mori

Epitaphium Margaretæ, Uxoris
Johannis Crowtheri,
Quæ deceffit Oct 21, A D 1630
Conjux cara fuo jacet hic conjuncta marito,
Eft Cœlis unus ftratus utriq torus
Tali digna viro prudens, pia, cafta, pudica,
Viva fuit Chrifto, mortua nupta fuo.

Here lyeth the Body of John
Crowtler, fen of Chillwood, Gent, who
departed this Life 25 April, 1717, in the 77
year of his age

Alfo here lie the Bodies of three
Children of William Jones and
Anne his wife, of Chillwood

Samuel Crowther Jones departed
this Life 29 Oct 1719, aged 4 years
and 5 weeks.

Anne Jones died 12 Nov 1713, aged
One year, 7 months, and 3 days

Here lyeth the Body of Hannah,
Wife of Thoſ Ruffell, of the Parish of
Littleton upon Severn, Yeoman, and
late widow of John Lorringe, late of
the fame place, Yeoman, deceafed, and
Daughter of William Cotterell, late
of this Parish, Yeoman, deceafed, who
departed this life the 15 Nov Anno Dom
1751, in the 46 year of her age

In Memory of
Mr Giles Lorringe of this Parish,
who died the 29 Sept. 1731, aged
72 years

Alfo in Memory of
Mary Webb, widow, of the Parish
of Wefterleigh, who departed this life
June 5, 1762, in the 56 year of her age.

IN THE CHURCH YARD.

ON TOMBS.

Elizabeth, wife of Richard Hall,
died 24 April, 1710, aged 98

George Hall
died Sept 12, 1736, aged 77

John, Son of John
and Elizabeth Partridge,
died May 15, 1737, an Infant

John, fecond Son of that
name, died April 27, 1754,
aged 9

Elizabeth, relict of John Foord,
and late widow of John Partridge,
died Feb 4, 1765, aged 66

Giles Thomas,
died July 6, 1691, aged 43

John Smith,
buried Sept 9, 1728, aged 58

Sarah, his Wife,
died 24 Nov 1732, aged 80

Mary, Wife of John Smith,
died May 3, 1756, aged 56

Mary, wife of Samuel Webb,
died 10 Sept 1752, aged 51

Mary, wife of Edward Webb
died May 15, 1765, aged 19

Edward Webb
died Nov 18, 1772, aged 65

Thomas Andrews
late of Wefterleigh Yeo
died June 18, 1726, aged 29

Robert Andrews, of Kington,
in the Parish of Thornbury, Yeo
died Jan 13, 1754, aged 88

Sufanna, Wife of William Cotterell,
died Apr 19, 1696, aged 52
William Cotterell, Yeo
died Dec 11, 1704, aged 67
Elizabeth, wife of Edward Tire,
Yeo and Daughter of the faid
William and Sufanna Cotterell,
died Jun 3, 1721, aged 48
Sufanna, wife of Nathaniel Badie,
died 22 April 1732, aged 61
Mary Wife of Abraham Efford
died March 13 1762, aged 52

William Cotterell, Yeo
died 28 Sept 1756, aged 57

Elizabeth, Wife of John Smith,
of St Philip and Jacob, Briftol,
died March 17, 1765, aged 59

Robert Keeper
died Feb 14, 1757, aged 61

Mary his Wife
died Jun 10, 1750, aged 61

John Keepin
died April 1, 1779, aged 65

Nehemiah, the Son of
Hezekiah and Elizabeth Webb,
died Jan 7. 1722 aged 39.

Elizabeth, Wife of
Nehemiah Webb, died
Jan. 14, 1758, aged 80

William their Son died young

Hezekiah Webb, Yeoman,
died June 17, 1725, aged 79

Hezekiah his Son died young.

John Thorner, Yeoman,
who, after living many years in
this Parish, died in the Parish of Yate,
Nov 30, 1715, in the 67 year of his age

Anna his Wife
died 20 Oct 1720, aged 34
John their Son died an infant.

Michael Neale
died 18 March 1771, aged 33

Elizabeth, widow of Bluett Jones,
died 13 March 1773, aged 57

Bluett Jones, Gent
died Jan 25, 1767, aged 55

Susanna Jones
died Dec 5, 1772, aged 90

John Barrington
died July 11, 1747, aged 71

John his Son died young

William Payne
died Aug 20, 1702, aged 68
Anne his Wife
died Aug 2, 1720, aged 86
William Payne
died 1 March, 1707, aged 50
Mary his Daughter was
buried 2 Dec 1756, aged 2

Elizabeth, Wife of
John Median, of Cripping Sodbury
[?] entered Mr. Thomas Taylor at
[?] Five [?] 1737, died
[?] his Son
died [?] 1715, aged 1

Daniel Gregory
died Feb 22, 1735, aged 29.

Anne, his Widow,
died in August 1763, aged 66.

Daniel Gregory			Oct 2, 1747			17
Eliza Gregory	died		May 2, 1756	aged		19
Samuel Gregory			May 5, 1756			21

John, Son of Hezekiah Webb,
died Sept 25, 1712, aged 36

Arms, a Cross, and in the 1st Quarter an Eagle
displayed with 2 Heads

Robert Webb,
of Frampton Cotterell, Yeoman,
died April 16, 1711, aged 66

Mary, his Wife,
died July 18, 1728 aged 79

Nehemiah, their Son,
died May 24, 1686, aged 10 and half

Arms, a Dove standing on 2 Serpents for Sloper,
impaling on a Cheveron 3 Pheons

Simon Sloper, Gent
died May 6, 1706, aged 46.

Sarah, his Wife,
died May 3, 1689, aged 29

Hannah, Wife of Thomas Coules,
of Frampton Cotterell,
died Dec 7, 1697, aged 70

Thomas Coules, of Frampton Cotterell,
died Aug 15, 1707, aged 89

Thomas Sheppard
died 28 Feb 1770, aged 51

Susan, his Wife,
died 28 Feb 1769, aged 53

Mary, Relict of
Richard Sheppard,
and late widow of Charles Cox of Alveston,
died Dec 30, 1763, aged 77

Hannah, Wife of Thomas Cam,
died June 1762, aged 46

Thomas Cam
died 2 March, 1751, aged 2

ON FLAT STONES

Memoriæ
Willelmi Filij
Johañs Webb, Gen et
Annæ Uxoris ejus, qui
obiit xiiii° die Feb 1728,
Ætat sua septimo
Mense

Memoriæ etiam
Annæ Uxoris prædicti Johañis,
Qui obiit die Aprilis
1737, Ætat suæ 35

John Webb
died 5 day May 1741, aged 39

Giles, and Giles Loringe,
Sons of the above John Webb,
by Mary his 2d Wife,
both died very young

Gertrude, Daughter of
John and Catharine Godfrey,
died Nov 9, 1737, aged 9

Catharine, Wife of John Godfrey
of Bristol, died July 16, 1753,
aged 62

Martha, Wife of Thomas Woodward,
of Pucklechurch, died 28 July,
1742

Mary, Wife of Saml Webb,
died 30 Sept 1752, aged 31

ON HEAD STONES

	Died		Aged
Christian, Wife of Giles Jones, of Chepstow in Monmouthshire,	15 Aug	1728	84
Robert Holdbrook	4 Nov	1720	39
Mary, Wife of Jacob Highnam,	24 Apr	1713	56
Arthur Holdbrook buried	29 Sept	1750	68
Mary, Wife of William Still	22 May	1742	27
Ann his second Wife	12 May	1750	22
Benjamin Walker of Winterborne	23 Feb	1770	80
Mary his Daughter			34
Charity, Wife of Willm Knapp, of Oldbury in the Parish of Thornbury, Daughter of Robert Andrews of Kington, in the said Parish	13 Aug	1732	27
Edward Gifford	5 Mar	1746	45
Mary, Relict of Robt Drew of Rangeworthy	8 Nov	1770	62
Dan Stinchcomb	11 Mar	1730	44
Mary, Wife of Charles Stinchcomb,	2 Mar	1730	39
Hester, Daughter of Charles and Mary Stinchcomb	25 Feb	1730	6
Sarah Daughter of Charles and Mary Stinchcomb	25 Feb	1730	16
Charles Stinchcomb	20 Mar	1750	68
Thomas Button, of Cromhall,	3 Sept	1756	57
Thomas Smith	11 June	1743	58
George Rogers	26 Sept	1772	65
Mark his Son	15 Mar	1776	7
Robert his Son, by Ann his Wife,	4 May	1779	3
George Iles buried	1 Jun	1768	29
John Prigg	11 Jun	1750	30
Thomas Prigg buried	10 June	1750	
Ann, Wife of William Prigg	2 May	1750	65
William Prigg Sen	2 May	1755	74
Ann Wife of William Prigg	27 Aug	1747	78
James, Son of Thomas Cinn	30 Jan	1765	24

IV ACTON TURVILLE.

THIS parish lies in the hundred of *Grumbald's afh*, and deanery of *Hawkfbury*, adjoining to *Badminton* on the fouth, and five miles eaft from *Sodbury*. It is fituated on the verge of Wiltfhire, and confifts of more arable than pafture land in the proportion of about two parts in three. The foil is various, the chief part ftony, and in fome places clay, in general it is good.

In the middle of the village ftands a fmall antique ftone building, which was formerly a fanctuary dedicated to *Saint Margaret*. It is now converted into a dwelling houfe.

This place was poffeffed by the family of the Turbevilles foon after the Conqueft, and from them it probably received the addition of *Turbevill*, or *Turvile*, in order to diftinguifh it from *Iron Afton*.

A fair is held here annually on the firft Friday in Auguft, and a revel on the Sunday following.

The church, which is dedicated to *Saint Mary*, is fmall, confifting of one aile, and has a fpire in the middle. The living is a vicarage united to *Tormarton*, the rector of which parifh formerly had the prefentation of it. The impropriation belongs to Mrs Adey, of Old Sodbury. Service is performed here once a month, and being an extra parochial place, the parifhioners are married at *Tormarton*.

There are no Benefactions at prefent known of

INCUMBENTS	PATRONS	INCUMBENTS	PATRONS
1584 Edward Cox,	Edward Weike	1686 James Bernard, M A	Sir John Toppe
1588 Thomas Cadle,	Edward Weike	1719 Lewis Bridley, M A	Sir John Toppe
—— Stephen Banning		1735 Philip Blifs, M A	Thomas Peach Gent
From Sir Robert Atkyns		1775 Edward Griffin, B A	John Peach Hungerford, Efq
		1777 Newdigate Pointz, LL B	Nath Caftleton, Efq

PRESENT LORD OF THE MANOR,

JOHN PEACH HUNGERFORD, ESQ

The only perfon fummoned from this place by the Heralds in 1682 and 1683, was

Lady Toppe

At the Election in 1776, fix Freeholders polled from this Parifh

ANNUAL ACCOUNT OF MARRIAGES, BIRTHS, AND BURIALS, IN THIS PARISH

A D	Mar	Bir	Bu	A D	Mar	Bir	Bu	A D	Mar	Bir	Bu	A D	Mar	Bir	Bu
				1701				1801				1811			
	5			1702				1802					5		
		4		1703				1803				1813			
				1704				1804				1814			
	10			1705				1805				1815			
								1806							
								1807				1817			
				1708				1808				1818			
								1809				1819			
				1800				1810				1820			

MONUMENTAL INSCRIPTIONS.

IN THE CHURCH

IN THE CHANCEL

Here refteth the Body of
Richard Viner, Gent.
who departed this Life
the 21 of November, 1693,
Ætatis 57
Alfo here lyeth the Body of
Mrs Grace Wells, the
Wife of Mr George Wells,
of London, Vintner, and
Daughter of Richard Viner,
who deceafed
Auguft the 8, A D 1718,
Aged 33

Here lyeth the Body
of Mrs Mary, the Wife of
Robert Viner, Gent who
died Feb 11, A D 1719.
Aged 45

Here lyeth the Body of
Mrs Sarah, Wife of Robert
Viner, Gent. who died
April the 2d, A D 1721,
Aged 80 Years

IN THE BODY OF THE CHURCH

Here refts the Body of
Mr Jacob Latimer,
Vicar of this Parish, who
departed this Life, the   day
of November, 1696

IN THE CHURCH YARD

ON HEAD STONES

	Died		Aged
Sarah, Wife of William Eaftman,	9 Sept	17..	40
Sarah his 2d Wife	2 Nov	1772	36
Jeremiah Ifaac, Yeo	24 Sept	1744	100
Grace his Wife	7 Sept	1738	97
John Ifaac	17 Feb	176.	70
Jeremiah Ifaac, Yeo of Cottles Farm in the County of Wilts	18 Feb	1772	70
Charle Viner	13 Dec	172.	5
Charles, Son of Charles and Mary Viner,	2 Feb	174.	1
Nathaniel Evans	9 Oct	17..	80
Daniel Shellard	19 Nov	17..	
Jane his Wife	2 Nov	17..	
Thomas Hitt, Yeo	7 Jan	1...	
Rachel his Wife	4 Feb	1..	4
Betty, Wife of William Cambridge,	10 Dec	1..	
William Cambridge	1 ...	1..	
Thomas, Son of George and Elizabeth Hitt,		Jan	

V. ADLESTROP, or ÆDLESTHORP.

THIS parish lies in the hundred of *Slaughter*, and deanery of *St —*, about three miles north east from the town of *Stow*, and twenty-nine miles, in the same direction, from GLOUCESTER. It consists of nearly an equal proportion of meadow, pasture, and arable land, the soil being various, in some parts clay, in others loam, and in a few places sand.

The river *Evenlode* runs near the western side of it, and from thence makes its way to the *Isis*. The village is pleasantly situated on the slope of a hill fronting the south east.

In ancient writings this place is called *Eadelstrop*, and sometimes *Castlethorp*, the former name it probably received from the Saxon *Ædel*, noble, and *þorp*, a village, or habitation, and the latter from its being near *Castle barrow*, a round fortification, supposed to be Danish, on *Castleton Hill*, which lies not far from the verge of the parish. In the charter granted to Egwin Bishop of Worcester, who founded the Abbey of *Evesham*, about the year 700, the same is written *Tadlesthrop*.

James Henry Leigh, Esq. the lord of the manor, which lies in the old family seat, which is built in the Gothic style, and has been greatly enlarged and repaired.

The living is a rectory, and the church, which is dedicated to *Saint Mary Magdalen*, is annexed to *Broadwell*. The body and chancel were rebuilt in the year 1764, chiefly at the expence of the late James Leigh, Esq. but the old tower, with battlements, situated at the west end, still remains. There are two cross ailes in the church, and in the tower are five bells.

The inhabitants formerly interred their dead at *Broadwell*, but, about the year 1590, one of the ancestors of the Leigh family gave them land for a church yard, and procured it to be consecrated. In the year 1670, Doctor Johnson, the rector, built, at his own expence, a very large and handsome parsonage house, which has been much improved by the present rector Thomas Leigh, LL.B.

BENEFACTIONS.

Mr THOMAS BARKER, formerly an inhabitant of this place, gave 20 shillings a year, to the use of the poor.

LADY TURNER, by her will, gave in the year 1770, 50 pounds to the poor.

——— FLETCHER gave 5 pounds, the interest of which is laid out every year, at Easter, in bread for the poor.

INCUMBENTS	PATRONS	INCUMBENTS	PATRONS
1697 Edw. Wake, M.A.	Theoph. Leigh, Esq	1717 Theoph. Leigh M.A.	Theoph. Leigh, Esq
1699 Henry Bridges, M.A.	Theoph. Leigh, Esq	1763 Thomas Leigh, LL.B	James Leigh, Esq

PRESENT LORD OF THE MANOR,

JAMES HENRY LEIGH, ESQ.

The persons summoned by the Heralds, in 1682 and 1683, from this place, were,

William Leigh, Arm. Just.
Theophil. Leigh, Arm.
Madam Pentloe.

At the Election in 1776, only one Freeholder polled from this parish.

ANNUAL ACCOUNT OF MARRIAGES, BIRTHS, AND BURIALS, IN THIS PARISH

A D	Mar	Bir	Bur	A D	Mar	Bir	Bur	A D	Mar	Bir	Bur	A D	Mar	Bir	Bur.
1781	1	6	5	1791				1801				1811			
1782	—	6	6	1792				1802				1812			
1783	3	7	3	1793				1803				1813			
1784	2	3	1	1794				1804				1814			
1785	1	8	3	1795				1805				1815			
1786				1796				1806				1816			
1787				1797				1807				1817			
1788				1798				1808				1818			
1789				1799				1809				1819			
1790				1800				1810				1820			

MONUMENTAL INSCRIPTIONS

IN THE CHANCEL

H   I
THEOPHILUS LEIGH, Armiger,
Vir
Præstanti memoria fœlix,
Ingenii acumine valens,
A mendacio alienus,
Proposito tenax,
Cujus eximias animi dotes,
Collegium Reginæ Oxonii,
Et Templum Medium Londini,
Rite excoluerunt
Inter Gentes Europæ moratiores
Non sine Laude peregrinatus,
Virtutibus quæ probum decent ornatus,
Ad suos rediit,
Amore in Patriam, Fide in Regem, conspicuus,
In postremis vitæ annis
Privatum vivendi morem publico anteposuit,
cultui divino assidue interfuit in Ecclesia,
In statutis Regii non mediocriter versatus,
Legis divinæ indagator diligentissimus
E - - - - - - - - - adsertor fuit strenuus,
- - - - - - - - - mo duxit
Elizabetham Gulielmi Craven militis Filiam,
Postea accepit nobilem Mariam Brydges
Quæ hic juxta sepulta est,
Quatuor filii & quinque filiæ
mortuum plorarunt,
Obiit 10 Februarii, Anno Dom 1724,
Ætatis suæ 76

Monumentum hoc Gulielmus Filius
Patri Optimo
P C

William Leigh, Esq deceased June
the 17th, 1690, Aged 86 Years and 2 Months

Joanna Leigh, Wife of William Leigh,
Esq deceased June the 7th, 1689,
Aged 65 Years and 4 Months

Here

Heic juxta Conditus
Jacobus filius natu 2^{dus} Theophili Leigh, Arm.
Qui ad quindecim Annos Vexillarius,
inde Tribunus Militis gradatim evasit
Aufpicante ANNA REGINA,
apud LUSITANOS, IBEROS, ac BELGAS, feliciter
militavit
Hic tandem redux
ubi natus & renatus (Tibe correptis)
etiam denatus,
16 Janu: Anno Salutis, 171$\frac{5}{6}$, Ætatis
ultra 21um, 4 mentibus ægre perfectis

H S E
Thomas Leigh
Gulielmi Leigh Armig: ex Joanna Coniuge filius,
E plurimis eo quidem minimus,
Vir Ingenio,
Animi probitate, morum Candore in emeritis
Erga Principem fide, erga Ecclesiam observantia,
Spectabilis,
Dum bonis Literis feliciter incumbit
Heu libetactato Pulmone correptus
occubuit infoeliciter
7ma Calend: Martii Anno Salutis MDCLXXXVIII
Ætatem habens annos 24 Mens: 2um
H M Dilectissimo fratri pofuit T L

Here lyeth the Body of Mrs Rachel
Leigh, Widow, a Gentlewoman of exemplary Goodnefs and Piety who
died September the 19th, 172,, aged 66

H I
MARIA, Filia natu-maxima prenobilis JACOBI
Dni CHANDOS, *Baronis de Sudely,*
Cui Deus fummas dederat corporis animæque dotes,
Lumine fui Nobilitati pares,
Formam, Ingenii & Virtutis Indicem,
Foelicem Indolem, omnium capacem,
Religionis Studiis præcipue natam,
Pietatem affiduam, Prudentiam, amabili facilitate conditam,
Humilem mitemque animum, Sibi maxime decorum,
nec Genere indignum
Uxor erat THEOPHILI LEIGH Armigeri
Quem, quatuordecim fere annos Fide, Amore,
Suavissima Confuetudine, et multa prole, beavit
Sex primum Filiis, GULIELMO, JACOBO,
THEOPHILO, THOMA HENRICO, et CAROLO
Totidemq: Filiabus EMMA, ELIZABETHA
CASSANDRA, MARIA, CATHERINA, et ANNA
non fine matri interitui
Quarum CATHERINA morte matrem præiit,
ELIZABETHA paulo poft fecuta eft
Laetes ceteri, humanissimæ Parenti
Inftitutui et exemplo diu fruerentur,
Puerperio deceffit
(Fato fibi foli nec lugendo, nec improvifo)
Quam femper vitae ac mortem quotidie expectaffet
13° Junii Anno D: MDCCIII
Ætatis fuæ 3°

IN THE BODY OF THE CHURCH

Near this place in a Vault lie the Remains
of Theophilus Leigh, Efq who died on the 10th of
February, in the Year of our Lord 172⅘,
Aged 78 Years

Likewife in the fame place lie the Remains
of the Hon Mary Leigh, wife of Theophilus
Leigh, Efq and Daughter to James Lord Chandos,
Baron of Sudely   She died the 13 of June, in
the Year of our Lord, 1703, aged 38 Years

There alfo lie the early Remains of
James Leigh, Efq 2d Son of Theophilus
and Mary Leigh, who having honorably acquitted
Himfelf in the Command of a Regiment during
the latter part of the Wars which fell out in the
Reign of Queen Anne, died Jan 16th, in
the Year of our Lord, 171½, aged 21 Years only

Also in the fame Vault lie the Remains
of Mrs Rachel Lord, Widow, who departed
this Life Sept the 19th, in the Year of
our Lord, 1725, Aged 66 Years

In the fame Vault are placed the Remains
of William Leigh, Efq who departed this Life
on the 9th of Decem in the Year of our Lord,
1757, aged 66 Years   And alfo Mary,
the wife of William Leigh, Efq
who died July the 10th, in the Year of
our Lord, 1756, Aged 61 Years

In the fame Vault alfo is depofited
the Body of the Rev William Leigh,
2d Son of William Leigh, Efq
and Rector of Little Ilford
in the County of Effex,
whofe pious difpofition and
exemplary conduct rendered him
a real Ornament to his Profeffion,
and who by the moft innate
Goodnefs, & almoft unexceptionable
Innocence of Life, procured the Efteem
& Approbation of every true Friend
to Virtue & the Chriftian Religion
He departed this Life on the _ day
of April, in the Year of our Lord,
1764, Aged 3? Years

M S
Caroli Hanflap, Gen
Cujus anteceftores fub nomine Maldun five Mider,
cum Gulielmo Normanno in Angliam migrantes,
poftea Barones de Hanflip, in Agro Bucks devenere,
Nomen gentilitium inde mutatum,
Ad pofteros, longe diutius quam Baronia derivatum eft
Hic,
(Reous fimul a, Pietus Patriifque erga Principem indelitate,
tandem collapfis)
fortunam mediocrem æquo ferens animo,
vitam degit tranquillam & probam
Ex Margareta conjuge (Johannis James huius Parochiæ)
Binis cum amnibabus, Elizabetha & Anna relictis
Antiquiffimi Domicilii pariter ac Vitæ exitum potuit
poftridie calend Jan", Anno Saluris 175⁶, Ætatis 63,
opum omnium
conjux maeftiffimæ
H M P

On a handsome marble monument on the south side of the chancel are the following arms and inscription

Gules, a cross ingrailed, and in the first quarter a lozenge, Argent, for Leigh, impaling on a bend three fleurs de lis for Bee, and for crest an unicorns head couped, Or

Enclosed within iron rails on the outside of
this wall, rest the remains of Theophilus Leigh,
D.D (third son of Theophilus Leigh, Esq. and the
Hon. Mary Bridges) 56 Years the revered Master
of Baliol College, Oxford, and many years the
beloved Pastor of this Parish, he died Jan. 3,
1785, aged 91. And also of Anne his Wife, only
Daughter of Edw. Bee, Esq. of Beckley in Oxfordshire,
She died Oct. 5, 1765, Aged 65

In remembrance of the distinctive virtues
of these excellent persons,
and with all possible love & respect
to their honoured memories,
This tablet is erected by their daughters
Mary Leigh and Cassandra Cooke

In the same enclosure lie the Bodies of Cas-
sandra Wight (grand daughter of Theophilus
and Mary Leigh), of Mary & Emma Waldo their
Grandchildren and also of Anne Cooke, the beloved
Child of the Rev. Samuel and Cassandra Cooke
She died April 18, 1782, aged 12 years

Circles though small are complete

There are also interred in this chancel, Mary
Bee (Wife of Edw. Bee, Esq.) & four infant
Children of Theophilus and Anne Leigh

On a handsome marble monument between the church and chancel,
with a female figure resting upon an urn, and at the bottom of the inscription the arms and crest of
Leigh as mentioned in the preceding monument, impaling Argent, a cross Sable, charged in the
center with a leopards face Or for Bridges

In Memory of James Leigh, Esq. who died
Mar the 31st, 1774, Aged 49,
whose remains are deposited in a Family Vault near this place
Inheriting the Virtues of his Ancestors He shone in every
endearing character of private Life the best Husband, Father,
Brother, Friend In Public he was an excellent Magistrate, eve
studious to support justice and relieve distress Independant of,
Yet well affected to Government, a Friend to Liberty, an Enemy
to the Licentiousness of the Times, and zealous for Religion, this Church,
which he chiefly rebuilt, and its Worship, which he constantly
attended, declare Prepared as he was by his actions of Virtue,
A sudden Death received his reward
He married Mar 10, 1755, the Right Hon. Lady Caroline Brydges,
eldest Daughter of Henry Duke of Chandos by his first wife, Mary,
Daughter of Charles Earl of Ailesbury, by whom he has left an
only Son She erected this Monument in Testimony of his Virtues
and her affection

IN THE CHURCH YARD.

AGAINST THE NORTH WALL

Before this Place lyeth Buried
the Bodies of Anthony Greenhill,
late of Addleftrop, Yeoman,
and Anne his Wife, the which
Anthony departed out of this tranfa-
torie Life the 3 Jan 1596,
and the faid Anne departed
the 11 day of June, An° 1594,
in the Year of her age 63,
for whofe fakes Thom Dudlee
their Son in Law hath caufed
this Remembrance to be made

O N   H E A D   S T O N E S

		Died	Aged
Thomas Brandis		3 Sept 1758	66
Thomas Carter		13 Mar 1770	74
Deborah his Wife		31 Mar 1767	76
Samuel Tidmarth, of Cornwell, near this place, Oxfordfhire,		29 Nov 1771	81
John James		2 May, 1780	65

VI. ALDERTON.

THIS parish lies in the upper part of the hundred of Tewkesbury, and deanery of Campden, about four miles north west from Winchcombe, and fifteen miles north east from Gloucester. It consists chiefly of arable land, but there is some pasture, and in the hamlet of Dixton a good deal of wood land. The soil in general is a stiff clay, in a few parts sandy.

The name of this place seems to be derived from the Saxon Eldop, or Aldop, older, and Ton town. Dickleston, or Dixton, is a hamlet in this parish, seated upon a hill, about a mile westward from the church, which was formerly called Castle-Hill, from some ancient intrenchments there, that appear to be Saxon.

Sir Robert Atkyns relates, that about forty-five years before he published his work, a great quantity of wood and trees parted from the top of a hill, near the west end of a wood belonging to Mr Higford, and slipped away out of this county into Worcestershire, to which it lay adjacent. Some of the present inhabitants remember to have heard this circumstance related by their predecessors, and it still retains the name of The Slip.

The family of the Higfords have long been in possession of the greatest part of this parish, and it is at present held by the Reverend Mr Henry Higford, who has a large handsome house at Dixton, built of stone. John Higford, Esq one of this family, was knighted by Queen Elizabeth, in her progress to Sudley Castle, 1592. And William Higford, Esq who was a Justice of the Peace, and a very ingenious poet, was much honoured throughout the county.

The living is a rectory, and the church, which is dedicated to Saint Peter, is a small antique building, with an aile on the south side, and at the west end, a low strong embatled tower, containing six bells.

The family of the Higfords lie buried in the chancel, without any monuments or inscriptions, there are only the remains of the figures of old persons and flags. A sword and coat armour are to be seen for John Higford, Esq who was buried 30 March 1607, and whose body remained unconsumed for an unusual length of time, as was observed, upon its being taken up, fifty years after its interment, in order that another of the family should be laid in the same vault.

There is a small neat chapel at Dixton, in which divine service is performed for the convenience of Mr Higford's family.

BENEFACTIONS.

WILLIAM HIGFORD, Esq 28 Hen VIII gave to the church at Alderton, for the reparation and maintenance of its utensils and ornaments, 48 lands and lays (as they are described in the charitable gifts exhibited in the register of Gloucester, 1683), the yearly rent of which was of 3s 1d. These lands are situated in the fields of Alderton.

JOHN PAGE, Yeoman, in the year 1610, give 12 pounds for the use of the poor of this parish, for ever.

HENRY TOVEY, by his will, gave 40 shillings to the poor, for ever.

INCUMBENTS	PATRONS	INCUMBENTS	PATRONS
1577 Lawrence Hurlock,	John Higford, Esq	1715 Richard Smith, M A	Wm Higford, Esq
——— John Kinnin		1717 Prideaux Sutton, M A	Hen Higford, Esq
1695 Henry Higford, M A	John Higford, Esq	1724 Henry Meale, M A	Wm Higford, Esq
From Sir Rob Atkyns		1737 Henry Higford, M A	{ Wm Higford, Gent / Wm Jones, Gent }

PRESENT LORD OF THE MANOR

HENRY HIGFORD, M A

The following persons were summoned from this place, by the Heralds in 1682, and 1683,

John Higford, Gent
Lady Tracy,
James Creese, Gent

At the Election in 1776, six Freeholders polled from this parish.

ANNUAL ACCOUNT OF MARRIAGES, BIRTHS AND BURIALS, IN THIS PARISH

A D	Mar	Bir	Bur	A D	Mar	Bir	Bur	A D	Mar	Bir	Bur	A D	Mar	Bir	Bur.
1781	1	2	5	1791				1801				18 1			
1782	—	7	5	1792				1802				1812			
1783	—	5	6	1793				1803				1813			
1784	—	5	3	1794				1804				1814			
1785	5	5	8	1795				1805				1815			
1786				1796				1806				1816			
1787				1797				18 7				1817			
1788				1798				1808				1818			
1789				1799				1809				1819			
1790				1800				1810				1820			

MONUMENTAL INSCRIPTIONS.

IN THE CHURCH

James Cruse,
buried 7 Feb 1690,
Aged 86

Here resteth in hopes
of a Joyful Resurrection, the
Body of John Higens, of this
Town, who departed this Life

the 27 day of April, 1770,
Aged 43 Years

Here also resteth the Body
of Sarah, Wife of John Higens,
who departed this Life, the
14 day of March, A D 1782,
Aged 48 Years

IN THE CHURCH YARD.

Richard Greening, Sen
buried Oct 4, 1708,
Aged 69

Ann his Wife,
buried Nov 28, 1714,
Aged 62

Elizabeth their Daughter,
buried July 2nd, 1721,
Aged 34

Richard Greening Alcock,
died 15 April, 1707,
Aged 47

Richard Greening, Jun
buried July 25, 1713,
Aged 25

Thomas Hambourne,
Nephew of Mr Kinsman,
buried Jan 14, 1685,
Aged 25

John Ritter, Yeoman,
buried October 8, 1727,
Aged 73

Ann his Wife,
buried Aug 1, 1718,
Aged 66

Richard, their Son,
buried 9 day Nov 1728,
Aged 44

ON HEAD STONES

					Died		Aged
John Cox	-		-	-	16 Oct	1783	68
Anne his Wife					2 Nov	1772	70
John Town of Alstone,		-		•	16 Apr	1759	58
Christian, the Wife of John Town				•	3 Feb	1757	64
Elizabeth Wife of Richard Dobbins of Dumbleton,					1 Nov	1759	28
Mary Wife of John Horton,					15 Jun	1751	25
James Carpenter				buried	28 Mar	1758	65
Ann his Wife		-			5 Oct	1758	40
John Carpenter, Son					19 Oct	1756	67
Philip Howell	-			•	21 Mar	1778	83
Elizabeth his Wife					4 Mar	1779	71
Elizabeth Wife of John Howell				•	Dec 1653		80
John Horton					13 Sep	1771	74
Eleanor Cruse		•			18 July, 1779		79

VII ALDERLEY.

VII. ALDERLEY.

THIS parish lies in the hundred of **Grumbald's Ash**, and deanery of *Hawkesbury*, about two miles south-east from *Wotton-Under-Edge*, and twenty-one miles south from Gloucester. It consists of nearly an equal proportion of good arable and pasture land, with some woodland. The upper parts are appropriated to tillage, the lower to pasturage, and chiefly in the dairy way. The soil is principally a firm reddish sand, and towards the uplands upon a freestone.

The name of this place is probably derived from the Saxon *Eleop*, *Ealdon* or *Aldon*, Alder, and *Ley*, word which in that language signifies *untilled land* i. e. the older upland pasture.

Alderley is a small neat village, consisting chiefly of good houses, situated on an eminence which commands a most pleasing prospect towards the west and south-west. It is bounded on the north and south sides by two brooks, which after uniting their streams continue their course through *Kingswood* to *Berkeley*, where they fall into the *Severn*. Upon them are several corn and fulling mills. This parish was anciently considered as the uttermost of this side, or the *Forest of Kingswood*.

Behind this "Stones clearly fashioned by cockles and my party, such of great oysters, turned into "Stones, are found in parts of the hills the south-east of *Hele-ley*. These they mentioned by a early stratum which likewise contains various kinds of fossils are frequently met with upon this hill, but they are much more abundant in the adjoining parish of *Hatton-Under-Edge*.

The same writer informs us, in his "Account of the memorable matters that happened at Bristow" that "in the year ... a man of *Alderly* (which seem to be this place, ..., a man, ... did nearly pronounced in this manner by the common people) feigned himself Christ, who he was carried to Oxford and there ...

The family of Hele has been an ancient standing in this county, and have esteemed for their property and charity. *Alderley* is famous for being the birth place of Sir Matthew Hale, Knight, Lord Chief Justice of the court of King's Bench, whose extensive knowledge of the law especially in the administration ... to do ... and there ever met ... and rendered him at once an ornament to his country, and with ever to the county of Gloucester. This great and good man died in the year 1676 and lies buried in the church ... a tomb of blue marble.

Matthew Hale Esq ... descended from Sir Matthew, was the representative ... family estate, and a few years since ... who died ... in 1784 ... dismal, a ... spacious and elegant plan, one of the small manors ... which, being situated ... erected ... built the ... order that

where A

wherein the Chief Justice refided, has a moft extenfive profpect towards the weft into Wales. The eftate is now in the poffeffion of John Blagden Hale, Efq who having married the niece and heir of the late Matthew Hale, Efq was directed by his will to take the furname and arms of Hale, the king's fign manual for which is dated 11 Dec 1784.

The clothing manufacture is carried on in this parifh by two gentlemen of eminence in that bufnefs, viz Mathew A'Deane, Efq who married the heirefs of William Springer, Efq and has a handfome houfe here and William Larton, Efq who has likewife a genteel new-built houfe, pleafantly fituated on the fide of a hill fronting the fouth.

The living is a rectory and the church, which is dedicated to ——————, is a fmall, neat building, with an ile on the north fide, and a leffer one on the fame fide of the chancel, and at the weft end a tower with pinnacles, in which is one bell. On the outfide ftone work of the fouth window, is a fmall unique head of a King, and on the oppofite fide of the fame window another of a Bifhop, with the emblems of their dignity, a crown and mitre, on their heads. They are both in good prefervation, and are fuppofed to reprefent the founders of the church and as the face of the King fomewhat refembles that of Henry the Third, and neither pinnacles, nor images on the outfide, were in ufe till the beginning of that Prince's reign, it is probable that this church was founded about the middle of the thirteenth century. Over the outfide of the chancel door is likewife a fmall half length ftatue of a man, much defaced. In his hand is a fcroll written in the old Englifh characters, but too much obliterated to be made out. Adjoining to the image, on the wall, is the date, Anno 1456.

B E N E F A C T I O N S

Matthew Pontz, Efq 42 Ibz erected an almshoufe, confifting of two bays of building for the relief of two of the pooreft and moft impotent people of this parifh, who have lived here three years rent, for want of fuch the houfe to be let out for the ufe of the poor.

2) Above houfe being gone to decay, the late Mr Hale appropriated one of his to the fame purpofe. No record remaining of any fum being left by the abovementioned Mr Pontz for the fupport of the building, and this being the only charitable donation to the parifh known of, crecund has been made of

No benefaction.

INCUMBENTS	PATRONS	INCUMBENTS	PATRONS
1597 John Cooper,	Queen Elizabeth	1735 Potter Cole, M A	Matthew Hale, Esq and
1606 William Hern,	Eliz Pointz		Mary his wife
—— Thomas Shrewsbury	——		
1642 Thomas Dickenson,	Mary Barker		
—— Giles Workman,	Sir Matth Hale		
1663 Ev n Griffith,	Ditto		
1681 Jonath Moore, Cler	Matthew Hale, Esq		
1700 Will Atkinson, M A	Matthew Hale, Esq		
The above from Sir Rob Atkyns			

PRESENT LORD OF THE MANOR,

JOHN BLAGDEN HALE, Esq.

The following persons were summoned from this place by the Heralds in 1682 and 1683

Edward Stephens, Arm
Charles Mountenc, Arm
The Heirs of Mr Hale, or their guardian,
Mr William Crew,
Richard Workman

At the Election in 1776, only two Freeholders polled from this parish

ANNUAL ACCOUNT OF MARRIAGES, BIRTHS, AND BURIALS, IN THIS PARISH

A D	Mar	Bir	Bur	A D	Mar	Bir	Bur	A D	Mar	Bir	Bur	A D	Mar	Bir	Bur
1781	—	5	10	1791				1801				1811			
1782	3	9	3	1792				1802				1812			
1783	2	6	7	1793				1803				1813			
1784	-	7	12	1794				1804				1814			
1785	—	4	5	1795				1805				1815			
1786				1796				1806				1816			
1787				1797				1807				1817			
1788				1798				1808				1818			
1789				1799				1809				1819			
1790				1800				1810				1820			

It may be proper here to observe that in the list of burials, thirteen persons are included who were brought from other parishes

---

MONUMENTAL INSCRIPTIONS

IN THE CHURCH

ON MONUMENTS IN THE CHANCEL

ANNA,

Ilon Pettis in agro Oxon Generosi Filia,
Ægidii WORKMAN hujus Rectoris Uxor
Charissima, Septena Prolis Mater Sua
vissima, Cœlo æternum Fruitura,
Precenans Domum in Deo Male, &c,
A D 1655, Æ at 42, Conjecturae

Sancta, Pia, Pudica, Modesta,
Fidelis, Prudens, Mater dicta,
Conjugis Amor seu Ornamentum,
Conjux Religiosa semper flenda,
Qui pietatis posuit in Sempiterna
Pietas Amoris

Jesu Griffith huju Ecclef a Rec͠o , son m..s loci me cum exemplo venerabilis, P dhui pr cept men.i͡i ii. nem in fe rere, convers ione, d ferione tit, cift ate typ.. fui re . . & cont is preflinc ais doctrin.. Gnofticis rii & Pontieci um Ros e crontit pugna.. aui qua f fuum era. t t h fi.. t i n o.. rib.. comia vere..tu red...t deter ior & n.. o.. nitor, aui t ele.i , te tei i his ex aliquid de que t o io t n is d cere me ite tempere.. t d cnque perdin n m a io i i boni egi , pr abat tandem at..c.. mor bifq confe.tus.. on.. s in pre..b is, p.. t.. sui.. e i.. di..i..t cuam dit oli s & etc. cum Chrifto, vor que co apost fe es primo die Jun..s D MDCCLXXXVI
att ie iui LXXIII

<table>
<tr><td>

In
Memory of Frances
Hte wife of the Reverend
Mr Po tter Col,
Rector of th s Par.ih,
who die l May the 2 ft, 173?,
Aged 24 years

Alfo of Frances Paske,
Mother of h full
Frances Coll,
who die t the 10 Janu ry, 1759,
Aged 55 Years

This Monument
perpetuates the Memory
of
Mrs Mary Hale, of this Place,
Widow of Matthew Hale, Efq
She died the 11 day of July, 1775,
Aged 73

Alfo of Gabriel Hale, Efq
Son of the abovenamed
Matthew and Mary Hale
He died the fecond day
of October, 1774
Aged 4,

</td><td>

ON FLAT STONES IN THE CHANCEL

HERE LYETH INTERRED UNDER THIS STONE
THE BODY OF ELINOR THYNNE, THE
WIFE OF FRANCIS THYNNE, GENT AND
SISTER TO MATTHEW ROTES OF ALDERLEY
I THE COUNTY OF GLOUCESTER, GENT
DECEASED SHE DEPARTED THIS LIFE THE
ELEVENTH DAY OF NOVEMBER,
ANNO DOMINI 1693

HERE LIETH THE BODY
OF THE REVEREND
MR WILLIAM ATKINSON,
LATE RECTOR OF THIS PARISH,
WHO DEPARTED THIS LIFE THE
15 DAY OF NOV, 1734, ÆTAT 58

Here lieth the Body
of Mr George Atkinson,
who died the 24 of July, 1717

Here also lieth the Body
of M s Rachel Cosley,
Mother of the faid George
and William Atkinson
who died the 2d of July, 1720,
Ætat 60

</td></tr>
</table>

ON A FLAT STONE, THE FOLLOWING INSCRIPTION, THE FIRST FOUR LINES OF WHICH ARE ROUND THE VERGE

HERE RESTETH THE BODY OF WINEFED
ONE OF THE DOUGHTERS AND HEIRS OF HENRY WILDE OF CAMBERWEL
IN THE COUNTY OF SUREY
AND WIFE TO MATHEW JOYNTS LORD OF THIS MANOR
TO WHOM BEING
MARIED 24 YEARS
SHE BEAR 15 CHLDRN
IN WHERE OF 12
ARE YET LIVING
VZ NICOLAS JOHN
THOMAS MATHEW
EDWARD SLVESTER
RACHEL MARI AND
ELIZABETH ALCE &
IONE & DID IN YE CO
FESSID OF YE TRVE
CHRISTIA FAITH
IVNE 29
ANO 1578.
RRI
IO

Charles Seymour, of Callecombe in Com Wilts, Efq
born 2 April 1665, married 11 Nov 1699 to Agne ,
Daughter of Robert Codrington, of Codrington Efq
died February 6, 17.. and was buried here

IN THE BODY OF THE CHURCH

ON FLAT STONES

Under this Stone
lieth the Body of SARAH
the Wife of
WILLIAM LARION, Gent
of New Mills in this Parish
She died 30 March, 1760,
Aged 63 Years

Under this
Stone lieth the Body of
Mr ROGER JACOB, Clothier
He died 6 Aug 1752, æt 57

Also MARTHA, his Wife
She died 11 Sept 1757, æt 66

Martha their Daughter died
12 Aug 1758, Aged 38 Years

Thomas Phillips
died June 6, 17 8,
Aged 56 Years

ON A MONUMENT IN THE NORTH AISLE

Arms, three spread eagles, and ano r cross
between four eagles displayed

Near this Place lyeth the
Body of Christopher Devonshire,
late of the City of Bristol,
Merchant, who died July
1, 31, 1761, 7 Years

IN THE CHURCH YARD.

ON TOMBS

Hic inhumatur Corpus
MATTHEI HALE, Militis,
(ROBERTI HALE, et
JOANNÆ Uxoris ejus,
Filii unici) nati in hac
Parochia de Alderley,
primo die Novemb Anno
Domini 1609
Denati vero ibidem
vicesimo quinto die
Decemb Anno Domini
1676,
Ætatis suæ 67

ANNA Hi uxor MATT HALE, Militis,
ob 25 Sept 1664

MATT Hale, Vidui Testamentum fui Defideratissimi
interior be extruxit A D 1707

Under this Stone lyeth the Body of FRANCES
Daughter of ROBERT HALE, Esq by MARY his Wife
She was buried August 5, 1760, aged 63 Years

Also of Mrs RACHEL HALE, Daughter of
the faid ROBERT HALE, by ANN his Wife
She was buried Sept 8, 1760, aged 45 Years

Here lieth the Body of
MATTHEW HALE He
He died the 11 day of June,
in the Year of our Lord 1675

Here lieth the Body of MATTHEW
HALE Esq Son of MATTHEW HALE,
who departed this life the 9 day of Novemb
1725 aged 6

ON A HANDSOME TOMB OF WHITE MARBLE, ARE
THE FOLLOWING ARMS AND INSCRIPTION VIZ

Argent, a fess, and in chief three cinquefoils, Sable, for Hale, impaling, three greyhounds current
in pale, for Harding

H S E
MATTHÆUS HALE, Armiger,
MATT HALE, Militis,
Nepos et Hæres,
Quem avitis studiis sedulo incumbentem
Mors immatura corripuit
Jan XX A D MDCCVI
æt XXXVII

MARIA HALE, Uxor ejus mœstissima
Monumentum hoc honoris sui
Ob ne Memoriæ ponendum
Proprius Impensis
Extruxit

Here lyeth the Body of
MARY HALE, the
Daughter of ROBERT HALE,
late of Alderley, Esq
who was buried the 25
day of June 1762

Here lyeth the Body of
EDWARD ADERLEY, Esq
He was buried on the 9th day
of August in the Year
of our Lord 1675

Here lyeth the Body of EDWARD
ADERLEY, Grandson of Sir MATTHEW
HALE Knt who died the 10th
day of March 1

Under this Tomb
Lye depofited the Remains
of ELIZABETH HALE,
Relict of the late
EDWARD BISSE HALE, Efq
who died the 4th of June,
1762, Aged 59

As Alfo
of MATTHEW HALE,
eldeft Son of the faid
EDWARD BISSE HALE,
and ELIZABETH, who
died the 2ᵗ of Sept 1728,
Aged 3 Years and 6 Months

Here lyeth the Body of JOHN
STEPHENS, Gent Son of EDWARD
STEPHENS, of Alderley, Efq &
MARY his Wife, Daughter of Sir
MATTHEW HALE, Knt who died
the 27 day of April Anᵒ 1703,
in the 20 Year of his age

Here alfo lieth the Body of
HESTER, the Wife of JOHN
SOMERS, and Daughter
of EDWARD STEPHENS, Efq
and MARY his Wife, who
died the 13 of Nov A D 1708,
in the 27 Year of her Age

ANNA HALE, uxor MAT HALE,
Ann ob xvii Jan A D MDCLVIIII

MARIA HALE, Vidua, juftu Mariti
fui defideratiffimi marmor hoc
extruxit, A D MDCCVII

Here lyeth the Body of
Mrs ELIZABETH HALE, Daughter
of GABRIEL HALE, Efq by AMY
his Wife, who was buried June 24, 1753,
Aged 16 Years

Here lyeth the Body of
ROBERT HALE, Efq
who died 30 July in the
Year of our Lord 1690

Here alfo lyeth the Body of
MATTHEW HALE, fecond Son
of GABRIEL HALE and AMY
his Wife, both deceafed,
who departed this Life
March 30, 1733, Aged 34 Years

Hic etiam inhumatum Corpus
MARIÆ STEPHENS,
filii EDWARDI STEPHENS de Cherington, Armig
Uxoris Filiæque
Matthæi Hale, Militis,
patri maximi
matrem obut 7ᵗ die Septembris
Anno Dom 1733
Atque e is fuit

Here lyeth the Body of ANNA HALE,
Daughter of ROBERT HALE, late of Alderley,
Efq who died the 21 Nov 1694

Here lyeth the Body of GABRIEL
HALE, Son of EDWARD HALE, Efq and
ELIZABETH his Wife, who departed this Life
the 20 day of Septem 1756, in the 29th
Year of his age

Here alfo lieth the Body of EDWARD
HALE, Efq eldeft Son of
GABRIEL HALE & AMY his Wife,
both deceafed, who departed
this Life 10 March, 1735,
Aged 39 Years

Here lyeth the Body
of GABRIEL HALE, Efq fecond
Son of ROBERT HALE, Efq eldeft Son
of MATTHEW HALE, Knight, fometime
Late Lord Chief Juftice of the King's Bench
who departed this Life the 16 day of
June Anno Dom 1718,
aged 48 Years

RICHARD WORKMAN,
of this Parifh, Clothier,
was buried the 6 day of
September, 1695

MARGARET his Wife
was buried 18 day of January,
1668

RICHARD SHERMAN, Gent
was buried the 7th day of June,
1717, Aged 37

ANN WORKMAN, Relict of
RICHARD WORKMAN, of this
Parifh, Clothier, was interred
the 31ft of March, 1698

Here lyeth the Body of ALICE,
late Wife of THOMAS SHERMAN
of this Parifh, who was interred
Novem 10, 1688 Alfo the faid
THOMAS SHERMAN was interred
the February, 1725, ag 188

Under this Tomb are interred
the Body of ROBERT SHERMAN, and
ANNA his Wife, who was Daughter
of Sir GABRIEL LOW, Knt He died
26 Nov, fhe 21 Jun A D 1707

EDWARDUS CHEWE
I Eva Reane Rane

Avolat hinc quoriam facti eft domus incola
Rudis,
De iret citi intus erit clari forit pie niten
Materiam fuperibat opus, fed utunique Epelles,
Præ qui fordefcit quicquid hic orbis habet
At ius ut forget occidit perd mat Rumis,
Crefcet per montis vulneri majore at
Inget ex evenienus feum, pe Redneer
Incoli cum rede at non Rude Rudus eit

Here lyeth the Body of WILLIAM CREWE,
who was buried 7 Febr A D 1683

REBEKAH, Wife of WILLIAM CREWE, died
the 10th, and was buried the 13th of May 16_3

Mrs BRIDGET CREWE died June 14,
1746, aged 78

MATTHEW CREWE, Son of WILLIAM CREWE,
died the 30 of August, 1686

Here lyeth the Body of MATTHEW CREWE,
late of this Parish, who died the 29th of
Febrary, 1667, ætatis suæ 61

BRIDGET his Wife
died 23, and was buried 25 Dec 1658

By this Tomb lyeth the Body
of JOHN STANTON, Minister, who after
his Exile for Religion, began to preach
the Gospel of Christ in this Parish
Anno Do 15_8, and so continued
until his Death, which was Ano D 1579

MARY, Wife of
RICHARD KILMISTER,
died April 25, 1748, aged 63

RICHARD KILMISTER
died 4 Octo 1763, aged 75

MARY, Wife of THOMAS KILMISTER,
died 28 Decem 1754, aged 29

JOHN KILMISTER
died 14 June, 1765, aged 42

MARGARET his Wife died
4 May, 1766, aged 40

REBECCA HATHAWAY
died April , 1775, aged 7

To the Memory of
Mrs ELIZABETH FORTUNE,
who exchanged this Life
in full hopes of a happy
Eternity, Octo 26, 1767 aged 60

SAMUEL WATHEN
died May 6, 1757, aged 78
And SARAH his Daughter was buried here

MARY his Wife died
Decem 2_, 174_, aged 84

SAMUEL WATHEN
died July 8, 1756, aged 70

ANN WATHEN
died March 9 175_, aged 60

MARY HILL
departed this Life 27 Feb
176_, aged 80

JAMES GARDINER, Sen
died 29 April, 175_, aged 64

MARY his Wife
died 25 April, 176_, aged 83

JOHN COLLETT Yeoman,
died the 7th June, 1744, aged _

SARAH his Wife
died 18d Jan 175_, aged 70

SARAH their Daughter,
the Wife of JOHN A_ _son
died 2, Jun 1757, aged _, Years

JOHN COLLETT, Yeoman,
died June 2nd, 1732, aged 61

WILLIAM CANNOR
died May 2_, 1770, aged 74

ISRAEL his Wife
died Oct 29, 1777, aged 73

Here lyeth the Body of
WENTWORTH WOODROW, Gen
who was buried _ Jan 195_

MATTHEW GARDINER,
died Nov 23, 1780, aged 58

MARY his Wife
died March 4, 1781, aged 41

JOSEPH WALKER
died 24 May, 1780, aged 54

Elizabeth his Sister
died Feb 15, 1771, aged 47

JANE, Wife of THOMAS FREY,
died Aug 3, 17_, aged 54

Also Thomas and Sarah their
Son and Daughter,
Thomas died April 5, 1771, aged 19
Sarah died March 31, 1771, aged 12

MARY the Wife of
JOSEPH WALKER
died Aug 27, 1762, aged 33

JAMES ATWOOD
buried April 30, 1712, aged 35

James his Son
buried Mar 5, 1732, aged 33

RICHD LAITY
died 4th Dec 17_8, aged 75

Mary his Daughter,
Wife of William Winter,
of Hillsley, Yeoman,
died March 30 1770, aged 82

William Winter
her Husband died Oct 9,
1784, aged _, Years

Sub hoc _____ Cm __
Johnus Comper, de Holy ___ Enochus
de Huckelbury, Gentol _____
_____ non __ de July
Anno Dom 173_,
Ao ætatis 2_

DANL.

DANIEL LONG,	JAMES their Son
of Tresham, Yeoman,	died Sept 27, 1757, aged 23
died March 25, 1771, aged 61	Joseph their Son
MARY his Wife	died Dec 30, 1773, aged 38
died March 23d, 1782, aged 70	

ON HEAD STONES

						Died	Aged
Charles Long	-	-	-	-	-	18 Dec 17..	70
John Long	-	-	-	-	-	2 Sept 1700	55
John Seaborn, of Wortley, Sen	-	-	-	-	5 Jun 172..	85
Margaret his Wife	-	-	-	-	buried	1 Mar 1690	29
Elizabeth Hopkins, of Wortley,	-	-	-	-	1 Mar 176.	9.
William Eastmead, Son of Arthur Eastmead,	-	-	-	4 July, 1701	36
Arthur Eastmead	-	-	-	-	2 Jan 1759	6.
Elizabeth, Daughter of Arthur Eastmead, Sen	-	-	28 Feb 1712	3.
William, Son of Arthur Eastmead, Jun	-	-	-	2 Mar 1772	.
Sarah, Wife of Richard Harding,	-	-	-	-	26 Jun, 1771	80

N B *As we find that the* BENEFACTIONS *mentioned in the Parishes of* ABSTON *and* WICK, *and* ADLE STROP, *do not agree with the Returns lately made to the Clerk of the Peace, we insert them here, and advise the Reader to observe that the* BENEFACTIONS *given to the subsequent Parishes, in the following Numbers, are faithfully taken from those Returns*

BENEFACTIONS

ABSTON and WICK

Mr CHRISTOPHER CADLE, in the year 1662, gave by will one hundred and forty pounds to purchase house and land for four poor persons This sum is vested in the churchwardens and overseers, and the annual produce is 5l 10s

Mr JOHN HATHAWAY, in 1701, gave by will a yearly rent charge of ten shillings to the poor, issuing out of a ground called Ho estone, to be distributed among them by the churchwardens and overseers, in whom it is vested

RICHARD HAYNES, Esq date not known, gave to the schoolmaster of Abston and Wick a house and garden, the annual produce of which is 2l 2s It is vested in the schoolmaster for the time being

The Rev HENRY BERROW gave by will Dec 14, 1724, one hundred pounds, to be laid out in the purchase of land for the benefit of a charity school in the parish of Abston and Wick This sum, together with four hundred pounds given by the same person for the benefit of the charity school at Pucklechurch has been laid out in the purchase of an estate at Rangeworthy in the county of Gloucester, now let at 26l per annum out of which rent the tenant is bound the expence of repairs, rates, and taxes The proportion of the rent allotted to the school in Abston and Wick is 4l, or 5l It is vested in the rector of Doynton, Pulnt, the vicar of Soxbury, Yat, and the vicar of Hapler

Mr BERNARD WICKS gave by will, Sept 13, 1722, the rents and profits of an estate in the parish of Aylesford and Wick ten pounds per annum, part hereof to each of two widows of clergymen of the church of England to be appointed by the trustees six pounds per annum to the curate for improvements on the estate one pound per annum to each of the trustees and fifteen shillings per annum to each the surplus to be received till the sum shall be accumulated sufficient for the interest thereof to maintain one scholar of the school and at Oxford chosen out of either of the parishes of Abston and Wick, Pucklechurch, Doynton or Dyrham for the purpose of maintaining one scholar of the church of England The estate and is vested in the rector of Pucklechurch and the rectors of Doynton and Dyrham is now let at 5l per annum and with the savings has been purchased seven hundred pounds in the 3 per cent consols the annual produce 21l

ADLESTROP

Thomas BARKER, by will dated July 7, 1705 gave for the use of the poor the difference ... payable to him an annual rent charge of twenty shillings issuing out of a certain ... lands in the parish of Iceborough in the county now in the possession of Andrew Collins

... to be sold for the use of the poor five pounds which is now in the hands of ... who pay the five shillings per ann

... the current year by all to place poor children to school one hundred ...

VIII. ALDSWORTH.

THIS parish lies in the hundred of *Brightwell's Barrow*, and deanery of *Cirencester*, about four miles south-east from *Northleach*, and twenty four miles east from GLOUCESTER. It is situated near the road leading from *Cirencester* to *Oxford*, and the soil being light and stony, it consists chiefly of arable land, with a small proportion of pasturage. Adjoining to it are some fine extensive downs.

The name of *Aldsworth* is evidently derived from the Saxon word Ealb, Old, and Popð, an Habitation, or Farm.

The brook *Leach*, which rises above *Northleach*, runs through a considerable part of this parish in its course to *Leachlade*.

There is a feast held here the Sunday after *Saint Bartholomew's* day.

The church, which is dedicated to *Saint Bartholomew*, consists of one aile, and has a handsome spire at the west end, with three bells. It is an old stone-building, ornamented with pinnacles and grotesque images well executed, and as such decorations were not used till after the introduction of the pointed arch during the reign of Henry the Third, as observed in the preceding parish, it was probably founded in the 13th century. Being situated on an eminence, it is seen to advantage, and at a considerable distance.

The living is a perpetual curacy, in the peculiar of *Bibury*, and belongs to Christ church, *Oxford*, having been granted to the Dean and Chapter of that Collegiate church by King Henry VIII, soon after the dissolution of the monastery of *Osney*, by which it was then held. The vicarage of *Turkdean* and curacy of *Aldsworth* are given to the eldest unprovided-for Batchelor of Arts belonging to Christ-church.

No Benefactions to the poor.

Three cottages were given, by whom unknown, for the reparation of the church.

INCUMBENTS	PATRONS
1682 John Rawlins, B A	Christ-church, Oxford.
1707 George Isles, B A	Ditto
1731 Henry Massey, B A	Ditto
1757 John Saunders, M A	Ditto
1757 Thomas Bowen, B A	Ditto

PRESENT LORD OF THE MANOR,

LORD SHERBORNE.

The only person summoned from this place by the Heralds, in 1682 and 1683, was Sir Ralph Dutton, but by mistake, as they found from the bailiff's return that he resided in the neighbouring parish of *Sherborne*, still the residence of that family.

At the Election in 776, two Freeholders polled from this parish.

ANNUAL ACCOUNT OF MARRIAGES, BIRTHS, AND BURIALS, IN THIS PARISH.

A D	Mar	Bir	Bur	A D	Mar	Bir	Bur	A D	Mar	Bir	Bur	A D	Mar	Bir	Bur.
1781	1	5	6	1791				1801				1811			
1782	3	8	9	1792				1802				1812			
1783	3	7	2	1793				1803				1813			
1784	2	1	-	1794				1804				1814			
1785	1	7	7	1795				1805				1815			
1786				1796				1806				1816			
1787				1797				1807				1817			
1788				1798				1808				1818			
1789				1799				1809				1819			
1790				1800				1810				1820			

INSCRIPTIONS.

IN THE CHURCH.

Hannah, wife of
James Haines,
died May 1, 1711.

Thomas Broad
died March 2, 1703,
Aged 63 Years

Elianor, his Daughter,
died 23 January, 1682

Near this Place lyeth the
Body of Robert Palmer,
who died May 19, 1729,
Aged 76 Years

Mary, Daughter of
Robert and Martha Palmer,
buried May 5, 1685, Aged 6 Years.

Jane the Wife of
Richard Taylor
buried 7 March, 1691.

Mary, Daughter of
Richard and Isabella Taylor,
died July 3, 1726,
Aged 27 Years.

Edmund Hall
buried Oct. 16, 1707.

IN THE CHURCH YARD.

	Died	Aged
Anne Waine, Relict of John Waine the Elder,	30 July, 1743,	78
John Palmer	25 Mar 1728	68
William Palmer	1 Sept 1728	62
Mary, wife of William Palmer,	21 Jan 1750	47
Mary, wife of John Palmer,	6 Feb 1750	75
Richard, Son of Richard and Mary Palmer,	8 June, 1728	21
Richard Pacey	9 Mar 1759	56
Mary his Wife	17 Jan. 1766	67
James Pratt, Sen	14 Feb 1757	78
Anne the Wife of Giles Waine	18 July, 1759	50
Margaret the Wife of Thomas Broad	5 Mar 1761	63
Mary, Daughter of Thomas and Margaret Broad, and Wife of Joshua Arnill,	26 Aug 1758	31
Thomas Broad	10 Feb 1781	85
Giles Waine	12 May, 1771	70
John, Son of Giles and Ann Waine,	11 Feb 1779	28
John Waine	4 Sept 1776	37
Thomas Waine	13 July, 1763	69
Catharine his Wife	19 Sept 1771	67
Ann their Daughter	22 June, 1763	26
Richard Palmer	7 Apr 1779	67
Joan Palmer	9 June, 1773	66
Betty Palmer	9 May, 1777	66
Ann Palmer	9 May, 1778	73
John Evens	3 Mar 1777	66
Richard Taylor	8 Aug 1764	56
Robert Pencutt	24 Feb 1780	78
Elizabeth his Wife	13 Oct 1748	45
Edward Midwinter	1 Aug 1739	62
Edith his Wife	11 Oct 1771	87
Edward Midwinter	4 Dec 1779	46
John Midwinter	9 May 1781	44

IX. ALMONDSBURY.

THIS parish lies in several hundreds, but the principal tything, that of *Almondsbury*, where the church is situated, lies in the lower division of the hundred of *Berkeley*, about seven miles north from BRISTOL, five miles south-west from *Thornbury*, and twenty-eight miles south west from GLOUCESTER, and in the diocese of BRISTOL. The parish is very extensive, and consequently exhibits a great variety of soil, and, as in the lower parts it nearly adjoins to the river *Severn*, there is a great deal of marsh land in it, and the pasture considerably exceeds the arable. The occupiers of land are much obliged to the Commissioners of the Sewers for their great care in keeping the sea walls in good repair, as also the reens and ditches. But as all human efforts are exerted in vain against the fury of winds and tides, damage is sometimes sustained, and very considerable mischief was done, in the latter part of the present year 1766, on both sides the river, especially below *Chepstow* in the county of Monmouth. There is some cyder made in this parish.

The prospect from a place called *Almondsbury Hill*, on the main road leading from BRISTOL to GLOUCESTER, is so extensive, noble, and elegant, that it never fails to strike the eye of even an ordinary spectator. This hill seems to be one huge mass of rocky stone. Some copper and lead ore have been found here, but the quantity so small hitherto as not to answer the labour of digging.

The manor of *Almondsbury* belonged to Robert Fitz Harding, ancestor of the Berkeley family, who upon his founding the abbey of *Saint Augustine* in BRISTOL in the year 1148, granted it, with several other manors, to that monastery, and by Edw. I. a charter was obtained for holding a fair here on Whit Monday, to continue six days, and a weekly market on Wednesdays at *Over*, called anciently the town this of *Over*.

There are the under tythings in this parish, viz.

1. *Hempton* and *Let ho to this Patchway*, a bad common. this tything lies in the lower division of the hundred of *Langley* and *Swineshead*, about one mile from the church. The land here is generally poor, being a stiff clay, consequently with a blueish loam. *Woodland*, a hamlet in this tything, and consists of the land described.

2. *Over*, in the same division and hundred, about a mile and a half from the church. Here is a good pasture land with some good building stone. In this tything, Mr William Lacy of the manor of *Over*, has a good house, commanding a fine view of the Severn, and adjoins to it. George Lacy of *Over* the present occupier.

3. *Easter*, or *Eastward-Compton*, adjoining to *Over*, about three miles from the church. Here is some good pasture land.

4 *Gaunts-Urcott*, alias *Earthcott*, lying in the lower division of the hundred of *Thornbury*, about two miles distant from the church. poor land

Almordsbury is supposed to derive its name from being the burial place of *Almond*, a Saxon prince, father of King Egbert, or perhaps from an ancient encampment raised by him, near to the present windmill, on the top of the hill, some traces of which yet remain visible. At *Knole-House*, belonging to the Chester family, there are some old fortifications supposed to be Saxon. The house stands on a hill, in the middle of a well wooded park, surrounded by these fortifications, about three miles from the *Severn*, over which it commands an extensive and delightful prospect. But the ancient mansion stood in the bottom, near the church. what remains of it is converted into a farm-house, the barn, however, still remains, which, from its size, strength, and mode of building, well deserves notice

Within the manor of *Gaunts Urcott* is a farm called *Saint Swithin*. This is now in the possession of Alexander Edgar, Esq. a Justice of peace for this county. In the house there is a room still called the chapel. This farm is held under lease of the Mayor, Burgesses, and Commonalty of *Bristol*. Other farms are held under the same corporation by divers persons in this part of the parish, which, with *Urcott* aforesaid, is a separate manor called *Gaunts Urcott* and *The Lee* division. The hamlet received the first part of its name from the family of *Gaunt*, to whom it formerly belonged, and by whom the charitable hospital, within the liberties of the city of *Bristol*, was founded. It was intended by the founder as a dwelling for an hundred poor persons, but it was afterwards refounded by Queen Elizabeth, and is now applied to the use of the blue-coat boys

In the same year in which the abbey of *Saint Augustine* was founded at *Bristol*, there was a chantry erected in this hamlet, which was supported from lands in the manor of *Brokenbrow* in the hamlet of *Hempton* and *Patchway*. Part of the manor-house is standing in the memory of persons now living, and had the greatest appearance of being surrounded by a moat. The house was called *Standfhall Court*, and the grounds are now known by the name of *Standfhall*. Sir Robert Atkyns says that this chantry was under the patronage of the above mentioned abbey, and that the last incumbent was Mr. John Harrold

The living is a vicarage in the deanry of *Bristol*. the advowson and the rectory formerly, belonged to the abbey of Saint Augustine. At the dissolution they were granted to the Bishops of *Bristol* for the time being,

The church which is dedicated to the *bleffed Mary*, is large and handsomely pewed with Dutch oak. It has two iles of the same length and breadth with the nave, a loft organ loft in the middle, with a coat of efcutcheon on it, and the whole covered with lead. The chancel is in the improved stile of Norman architecture poised on four small pillars supported by heads resembling Monks well executed. the tower is plain with pinnacles. A very ornamental altar-piece with a neat pavement leading to it therein. In the tower are a clock and five bells, and several curious pillars of Dutch oak have lately been erected in the vestry and at the body of the church over the door at the top.

Since the drawing up of the foregoing deſcription, a very curious MS has been diſcovered among the archives at Berkeley caſtle, written by *John Smyth*, the elder, of *Niblcy*, in this county, Eſq dated Dec 1639, Anno 15 Regis Caroli, from which the Right Hon the Earl of Berkeley has, with great politeneſs, permitted the editor to copy ſuch paſſages as may ſerve to elucidate this work The following extract from that MS relates to the preſent pariſh of *Almondſbury*

" Almondſbury In Domeſday booke written Almondeſberie, id eſt, Almodes court, or the place of aſſembly, a manor whereof Thomas Cheſter, Eſq is lord, holden by knight ſervice in capite, viz the fortieth part of a knight's fee the demeſnes whereof, as that booke ſheweh, conſiſted in the time of William the Conqueror of two hides of land

" This townſhip, or manor, was, among divers others, given by kinge Henry the Second in the firſt yeare of his raigne, to Robert the ſonne of Hardinge and his heires, under the grant of *Berkeia et totam Berkelai herneſſe manerium cum omnibus appendicys ſuis* Howbeit, that Robert had the ſame by a former grant from the ſaid kinge Henry, in the time of kinge Stephen, when the ſaid Henry was but Duke of Normandy

" Upon Eaſter-day, then the xith of Aprill in the xiiith yeare of the raigne of kinge Stephen, in the yeare of our Lord 1148, the fower Biſhops of Worceſter, Exeter Landaff, and St Aſiph, conſecrated the church and buildinges, which the ſaid Robert had built neere to the towne of Briſtoll, dedicatinge them to God, and to St Auguſtine the Engliſh apoſtle, then newly by the ſaid Robert built upon his manor of Bileſwike, at the place ſince called St Auguſtine's Greene, and then inducinge the Abbot and Canons and (amongſt other poſſeſſions) then endowed that church and meruit in, by his deed, which he laid down upon the Altar there, with the manor of Almondſbury the manor of Horfield the manor of Aſhelworth, the manor of Cromall (ſince called Cromall Abbots), and with divers lands and tenements in Arlingham, with halfe of his fiſhings there, &c &c to hold in Frankelnouge, and wills in his ſaid deed that the ſame upon his bleſſinge ſhould quietly bee enjoyed

" The firſt Abbott, now ſtalled upon the foundation, was Richard, who died 4 September, 1186

" Morgin Gwillm was the 24th and laſt abbott, in whoſe time, after he had ruled three yeares, the monaſtery in 31 H VIII was diſſolved

" John Newland, the 21ſt abbott, made that remarkeable collection and pedigree of his founders, drawing downe the ſame from William the Conqueror to the 5th yeare of King Henry the VII, where hee ended, more than 20 times by mee vouched in all the three volumes of my Berkeleian history

" This manor, as it were by an equall poize reſteth with Hill and dale, upon which, hilly part, hath lead byn digged To which the faire caſtle of Berkeley, for part of her coveinage, doth acknowledge herſelfe belonginge

" The whole pariſh is within the dioceſſe of the Biſhop of Briſtoll and not of Gloſ'r As alſo of that deanery The church whereof I take to bee a mother church, honored with her two chappels of Filton and Elberton

" King Edward the Firſt, the ſecond of January, in the 13th yeare of his raigne, then at Briſtoll, granted to John de Marina, then abbot of the monaſtery of St Auguſtines by Briſtoll, and to the covent there, to have free warren in all their demeſne lands within the manor of Almondeſbury, &c And on the 8th of May followinge, in the ſame yeare of his raigne, granted to the ſaid abbott and covent to have a market each Wedneſday, and a faire each Whitſon munday, to endure ſix daies in his their manor of Almondeſbury

" In this pariſh was an ancient and remarkeable chantry, obvious in many records in the King's court, called *Brokenbury* chantry, dedicated to the ſervice of the bleſſed Virgin Mary, variouſly tumbled and roſted, in diverſe ages, which bleſſed Virgin by the charter roll in the Tower of London in 5 Hen V, ſeemes to be the tutelary ſaint and protectrix of this pariſh church of Almondſbury alſo, wherein this charity was founded "

B E N E F A C T I O N S

Houſes and lands, to the value of ſixty pounds per ann and upwards belong to the church, for the beautifying and repairing of the ſame The feoffees have a conſiderable ſum of money in their hands

Mr Edward Terril gave by will, 25 Sept 1683, the intereſt for ever of fifty pounds to be annually diſtributed among the poor

Mr Thomas Jefferis gave by will, 29 Sept 1737, an houſe, orchard and paddock, the reſidue of the rent, after keeping the premiſe in repair, to be given in bread to the poor

Mr John Sircocks gave by will, 29 July, 1741, the intereſt or produce of two hundred pounds to ſuch ſchoolmaſters and ſchoolmiſtreſſes that be choſen from time to time by Chriſtopher Griffith the elder, and Chriſtopher Griffith the younger, their executors, &c and the miniſters and church wardens of this pariſh of *Almondſbury*, and of the adjoyning pariſhes of *Filton Stoke Gifford*, and *Winterbourn*, for the time being, or the majority of them, for teaching poor children of the ſaid ſeveral pariſhes to read, whoſe parents receive no alms, and conſtantly reſort to the ſaid ſeveral pariſh churches and that an equall number of children of each pariſh ſhould be taught and inſtructed to read as aforeſaid —fifty pounds of the above charity belong to *Almondſbury*

Incumbents	Patrons	Incumbents	Patrons
1652 John Summers,	Bishop of Bristol	1775 William James, M A	Bishop of Bristol
1700 William Moseley, M A	Ditto	1778 John Davie, D D	Ditto
1733 William Taswell, M A	Ditto	1780 Thomas Blackburne, B A	Ditto

LORDS OF THE MANORS

Of the tything of *Almondsbury*

Mrs ELIZABETH LUCY, BROMLEY CHESTER, *Widow*

Of *Over*, and the manor of *Brokenbrow*

Mrs DOROTHY WILMOT, *Widow*

Of *Hempton* and *Patchway* (which includes part of *Almondsbury Hill* and *Woodland*)

The Rev JOHN SEDGEWICK WHALLEY,

in right of his wife, the daughter and heir of Edward Jones, of *Langford Court*, in the parish of *Banning ton*, in the county of Somerset, Esq

Of *Gaunt's Urcott* and *The Lee*

The MAYOR, BURGESSES, and COMMONALTY of the city of BRISTOL for the time being

The following persons were summoned from this parish and its hamlets by the Heralds in 1682, and 1683

From *Almondsbury* — { Thomas Chester, Arm and Just
                   { John Summers, Vicar

From *Hempton* and *Patchway* —Robert Brown, Gent

From *Over* —John Dowell, Arm

From *Gaunts-Urcott* —Edward Brown, Gent

At the Election in 1776, sixteen Freeholders polled for on this parish and its tythings

ANNUAL ACCOUNT OF MARRIAGES, BIRTHS, AND BURIALS, IN THIS PARISH

A D	Mar	Bir	Bur	A D	Mar	Bir	Bur	A D	Mar	Bir	Bur	A D	Mar	Bir	Bur
1781	5	25	26	1791				1801				1811			
1782	4	26	19	1792				1802				1812			
1783	6	23	20	1793				1803				1813			
1784	3	28	13	1794				1804				1814			
1785	9	22	17	1795				1805				1815			
1786				1796				1806				1816			
1787				1797				1807				1817			
1788				1798				1808				1818			
1789				1799				1809				1819			
1790				1800				1810				1820			

MONUMENTAL INSCRIPTIONS

IN THE CHURCH.

ON A CURIOUS ANTIQUE TOMB, SUPPORTED BY EIGHT COLUMNS OF THE CORINTHIAN ORDER, IN THE SOUTH CROSS AILE, ARE THE FIGURES OF A MAN AND HIS WIFE, IN THE HABITS OF THE TIME, AT FULL LENGTH, WITH THE FOLLOWING ARMS AND INSCRIPTION VIZ

Quarterly, 1st on a bend 3 calves passant — a chief Ermine 3 a chevron between 7 crosses patty 4 and — 4 Quarterly, in the first quarter a lion passant gudant 5 5 lozenges conjoined in fe 6 a lion rampant 7 a lion ram, ant ducally crowned 8 a fess ermine between 3 annulets 9 two bars in chief a lion passant —Impaling, Quarterly, 1st and 4th 2 chevrons, for KETTLEBACK 2d and 3d a 3 conjoelots, between 3 crossets fitchy

HERE LYETH THE BODIES OF
EDWARD VEELL, ESQUIER, WHO
WAS BVRIED THE 9 OF SEP 1577
AND OF KATHERINE HYS WYFE
WHO DEPARTED THYS LYFE
THE 10 OF NOVEM 1575
KARNE OF GENERAL AND 14
QVIS VIR TTA VIVAT ET NON
VIDEAT MORTEM PSAL 89
ALL FLESH AS GRASS ISA 40

In the NORTH CROSS AILE, ON A MOST NOBLE AND ELEGANT PYRAMIDICAL MONUMENT O VA-
RIEGATED MARBLE, WITH A FEMALE FIGURE, REPRESENTING GRIEF, RESTING ON A SARCOPHAG S ARE
THE FOLLOWING ARMS AND INSCRIPTION viz. Gules, a lion paſſant Ermine between 3 hawks lewers Ar-
gent, for CHESTER Efcocheon of pretence, on a feſs between 3 boars heads couped, a lion paſſant, for
GOUGH—Creſt, a lion's jamb erazed holding a dagger

To the Memory
of Thomas Cheſter, Eſq and in Record of his Anceſtry

Arthur Cheſter, Gent was buried June 17, 1603	
William Cheſter, Eſq	Oct 1 , 1607
William Cheſter, Gent	Oct 18, 1638
Thomas Cheſter, Eſq	Nov 24, 1653
Dominick Cheſter, Gent	Mar 19, 1669
William Cheſter, Gent	Oct 6, 16 3
George Cheſter, Gent	Sept 22, 1683
Thomas Cheſter, Eſq	Feb 26 1686
Thomas Cheſter, Eſq	Feb 26 1703

The Succeſſion of this Lineage was cloſed in the Death of Thomas Cheſter Eſq late of Kno' Some the
laſt record d of his Name He was by the unanimous Suffrage of his Country called upon to be Knight of
the Shire in five ſucceſſive Parliaments, and on his own part did the Honour that become him of their
Choice by the moſt inflexible Attachment to what He thought the true Intereſts of his Country and for their
He could never be prevailed upon to ſerve, nor during ſo long a Service by one Vote or Conniving at any
to deſe t, or diſappoint the Expectations of his Conſtituents

His Community at large felt long alſo in Him, the Loſs of an oft upright and uſeful Magiſtrate Juſtice was
his conſtant object improved by their compaſſion, as Occaſions called it forth which his benevolent Heart
would never ſuffer Him to eſtrange Himſelf from but never was he to be biaſed by any ſiniſter View or
private Intereſt from the Exertions of his proper Duty

Nor was he leſs amiable in his private Character, than reſpectable in his Publick under every Connection
in which He ſtood, anſwering with his beſt Powers to its reſpective Duties and ſuſtaining in Character, in
the different Scenes of Life they aroſe upon Him, the Neighbour, the Friend, the Brother, and the
Huſband, with no leſs Eſteem, Honour, and Virtue, than the Magiſtrate, and Senator, a Truth which
cannot be better evinced, than by the great and heart impreſſed Grief that not only attended his Loſs, but
has faithfully adhered to his Memory, and which, as long as any Trace of it ſhall remain with Thoſe who had
the Happineſs to know him, will in ore than anſwer This or any other Record that can be given of Him

His firſt wife was the Right Hon SARAH-HENRIETTA, the only Daughter of HENRY Earl of
SUFFOLK and BINDON, by Penelope Daughter of the Earl of THOMOND, who was buried April 6, 1722
In 1735 he married Mary the Widow of GEORGE GWINNETT, Eſq of Shurdington in this County, and
Daughter and Heireſs of JEREMY GOUGH, Eſq of London

He died on the 1ſt of Octo 1763 and having no Iſſue left his Eſtate to his Niece, ELIZABETH LUCY CHESTER,
wife of WILLIAM BROMLEY CHESTER, Eſq and only Child of his Brother RICHARD CHESTER, Eſq who
died on the 1 of July, 1760, and lies alſo buried near him

MARY CHESTER his ſurviving Widow, deeply afflicted for his Loſs, and venerating his Memory and Virtues,
took upon herſelf the Care and Direction of this MONUMENT

ON FLAT STONES IN THE SAME AILE

MARY CHESTER,
Reliq of THOMAS CHESTER, Eſq
[died] Nov ..., Æt 86

The 2 lady the Right Hon Dame
Henrietta ...ſter, Wife of Thomas Cheſter,
... th ...and Daughter of
Henry ... Earl of Suffolk and
... or ... in the Country of Life,
... departed this Life ... Anno Dom 17..,
... Pounds ... Years

... ... of ... William Cann,
of ... in the County of Somerſet
... ... died the ... of April,
... ...

ALſo

the ... of Peter Philldes Cann,
... of ... William Cann junior,
... ... of them
Cheſter ... and ... ſhe died
the ... ... A D ... ...

William Cheſter, of New Inn
Attorney at Law, ob primo July
Anno Dom 1728, Ætat 30

Charle Cheſter, 4th Son of Thomas Cheſter,
late of Knole in this Pariſh, Eſq who died
22 March Anno Dom 173 , aged 9

Richard How Cheſter, Eſq 3d Son of
Thomas Cheſter, Eſq late of this Pariſh,
who died July 16, 1760, aged 60

Bridget Hollworthy, Relict of Thomas Hollworthy
late of Korthborough in the County of Somerſet Eſq
and Daughter of Thomas Cheſter, Eſq
who departed this Life ... Oct ... , aged ...

The Body of ... Cheſter,
Relict of Richard How Cheſter, Eſq
and Daughter of ... Cheſter Eſq
in the County of Wilts Eſq
ob ... July 17.., aged 6

IN THE SOUTH CROSS AILE, ON A NOBLE MARBLE MONUMENT OF A PYRAMIDICAL FORM, ARE THE FOL-
LOWING ARMS AND INSCRIPTIONS

On the north side, Arms, Quarterly, 1st and 4th a lion rampant within a bordure engrailed, for
DOWELL 2d and 3d, Azure on a fess, between 3 swans necks erased Or, each gorged with a ducal
coronet Or, three cinquefoils of the last, for BAKER —Efcocheon of pretence 3 bars wavy, creft, a de
mi lion rampant

To the Memory of JOHN BAKER DOWELL, Efq and Elizabeth
his Wife, whose Bodys are deposited in a new Vault
made for them under the middle Isle of this Church, together
with three of their Children that dyed Infants

The said JOHN BAKER DOWELL, Esq was the son of John
Dowell, Efq Lord of the MANNOUR of 𝖔𝖇𝖊𝖗 in this Parish,
By MARY his Wife, one of the four Daughters and Coheiresses
of Sir JOHN BAKER, BARONET, the last of his Family,
Lord of the Mannours of 𝕾𝖎𝖘𝖘𝖎𝖓𝖌𝖍𝖊𝖗𝖘𝖙𝖊, 𝕮𝖔𝖕𝖙𝖔𝖓, 𝕮𝖔𝖒𝖉𝖊𝖓, 𝕾𝖙𝖔𝖓𝖊,
𝕾𝖙𝖆𝖕𝖑𝖊𝖍𝖊𝖗𝖘𝖙𝖊 and 𝕭𝖑𝖎𝖙𝖍𝖈𝖔𝖚𝖗𝖙, all in the County of 𝕶𝖊𝖓𝖙,
and departed this Life the twentieth day of 𝕺𝖈𝖙𝖔𝖇𝖊𝖗, MDCCXXXVIII

The said ELIZABETH DOWELL was the Daughter and sole Heiress
of JOHN BROWNING of 𝕮𝖔𝖆𝖑𝖊𝖞, Efq by ELIZABETH his wife,
Sister and Coheiress of ROBERT BRIDGES of 𝖂𝖔𝖔𝖉𝖈𝖍𝖊𝖘𝖙𝖊𝖗, Efq
both in the County of 𝕲𝖑𝖔𝖚𝖈𝖊𝖘𝖙𝖊𝖗,
and departed this Life the thirty first day of 𝕯𝖊𝖈𝖊𝖒 MDCCXXV

To his well deserving PARENTS,
JOHN BRIDGES BAKER DOWELL, Efq caused this Monument
to be erected

On the east side the arms and creft of DOWELL, as above described

The Family of the DOWELLS,
AUNCESTORS by the Father's side of the said JOHN BAKER DOWELL, Efq
are deposited in their Vault underneath this Monument

The Body of
JOHN BRIDGES BAKER DOWELL, Efq who erected this
Monument, and departed this Life March the XXXI,
MDCCXXXXIIII,
is also deposited in the same Vault with his Parents

On the west side the arms of BAKER as above described, with the Creft a naked arm, embowed, Vert,
in the hand a swan's neck, as in the arms

The FAMILY of the BAKERS,
Auncestors by the Mothers Side of the said JOHN BAKER DOWELL, Efq
are deposited in their Vault in the Parish Church of 𝕮𝖗𝖆𝖓𝖇𝖗𝖔𝖔𝖐 in the County of 𝕶𝖊𝖓𝖙

To whose Memory
(himself and his Son JOHN BRIDGES BAKER DOWELL,
Efq being their only remaining Issue)
He caused a Monument to be erected in the said
Parish Church of 𝕮𝖗𝖆𝖓𝖇𝖗𝖔𝖔𝖐

ON A FLAT STONE IN THE SAME AILE

Robert Nixon, the only Son of Jane Nixon, Widow, died
in Over House, 18 June, 1678, aged about 5 Years

ON A SMALL MONUMENT AGAINST A PILLAR UNDER THE TOWER ARE THE FOLLOWING ARMS AND IN-
SCRIPTION viz. Quarterly, 1st, Argent, a lion rampant Gules, for IVY 2 Ermine, on a chief Gules,
lions rampant Or, for QUINTINE 3, Azure, 3 scollops Or, for MAULE 4 Argent, a fef engrailed
Gules, between 3 annulets Sable, for VILE, impaling IVY

The above arms appear to be marshalled in the said deceased QUINTINE, wife of the deceased, the
said MAULE, his mother, who was no heirefs Whence they tho' they have been marshalled Quarterly,
1st and 4th, Argent, a lion rampant Gules, for I 2d and 3d, Azure a fef engrailed Gules, between 3
annulets Sable, for VILE impaling, Ermine, on a chief, lion rampant Or, to QUINTINE

HERE RIGHT AGAINST THIS PILLAR LYETH THE BODY OF
RICHARD IVY, SONN OF THOMAS IVY LATE OF WEST KI-
TON IN THE COUNTIE OF WILTES, ESQUIER WHO MA-
RIED ANN, DAUGHTER OF MICHAEL QUINTINE, LATE OF BUT-
TON IN THE COUNTIE OF WILTES, ESQUIER, WHO DE-
PED THIS LIFE THE 6 DAY OF DECEMBER ANNO DNI 16..
HIS RACE WAS AUNCHANT, HIS RICH SEAVENT NAYE
DEATH HEE HATH PAID, AND THOW MUST PAY IT TO

ON A MONUMENT IN THE NORTH AILE IS THE FOLLOWING SINGULAR INSCRIPTION

Of all the Creatures which God made under the fun here is none to miferable as man. For all dumb creatures have no misfortunes do befall them but what come by nature, but man, through his own folly, and against his own knowledge, brings himself into a thousand griefs both of foul and body

As for Example

Our father had two children, and against his knowledge he committed the fin of idolatry upon us. For had our father done his duty towards God but one part in a thousand as he did towards us when he prayed to God to fare our lives, God might have heard his prayers, but God is a jealous God and punifheth the faults of the parents upon their children. Though the fins of our father have deprived us of the light of the fun, thanks be to God we enjoy more great, more fweet, more bleffed light, which is the prefence of God the maker of all lights, to whom be all honour and glory

Beneath this Place lye the Bodies of John and Elizabeth Maronne, in the Memory of whom, her Father caufed this Monument to be put up. Elizabeth died in 1708, aged 6 — John died in 1711, aged 5

Their father was a poor man born in the province of Dophine in the kingdom of France, he believes that his fin ver. the caufe that God took the life of his children

Pecheur n'avanfe pas un pas fans panfer a la mort

This motto is in the Patois, or Provincial language of France, in English thus

A finner doth not advance a single ftep without an approach towards death

---

ON FLAT STONES, IN THE CHANCEL.

Intra
Conduntur Exuvia Johannis Smith,
Hujus Ecclefia non ita olim
paftoris   Dgri, qui obiit
Junii --, 1661
plenetfh e uxoris ejus
Sufannæ Smith, quæ obiit
Julii 12, 1660

Arms, 3 lions rampant ducally crowned
Here lyeth the Body of
John Lavford, of Stapleton, Efq
who departed this Life the 4 day
of January Anno Dom 1679,
Aged 35 Years

IN THE SOUTH AILE

John Day, of this Parifh, Yeoman,
died the 23d September 1708,
in the 73d Year of his Age

Mary the wife of William Tayler, Jun
and Daughter of the aforefaid John Day,
died 20 July, 1774, Aged 2,

IN THE MIDDLE AILE

William Mofeley, Minifter of Mangotsfield
Son of William Mofeley, Vicar of this Place,
who died 24 November, 1701, aged 41

Ifabella, Daughter of the Rev
William Mofeley, Vicar of this Parifh,
who departed this Life 5 April, 1708

Elizabeth, the Sifter of the Rev
William Mofeley, Vicar of this Place,
who died Aug 14, 1742, in the 71 year of her age

Thomas Mofeley S Johm of Merton College,
Son of William Mofeley, Vicar of this Parifh,
died the 12 of July 1720, in the 17 Year of his age

Anne the Daughter of the Rev
William Mofeley, Vicar of this Parifh,
departed this Life the 18 Augaft, 17 3

The Rev William Mofeley, Vicar of this Parifh,
departed this Life the May 1 1750, aged 77 Years

Anne Mofeley Relict of the Rev
William Mofeley, the Vicar of this Place,
died March 14 1757, in the 8th Year of her age

Edward Coules, of this Parifh, Yeoman,
died 16 of April, 1711, aged 41 Years and 11 Months
Alfo Edith, the Wife of Edward Coules,
died 16 Auguft, 1720, aged 49 Years and 3 Months

IN THE NORTH AILE

John, the Son of William and Sarah Taylor,
of this Parifh, died 28 Oct 1751, aged 16 Years
Elizabeth Daughter of William and Sarah Taylor,
died 1 Dec 1756, aged 3 Years and 5 Months
Sarah, Daughter of William and Sarah Taylor,
died Dec 21, 1762, Aged 19 Years
Ann, Daughter of William and Sarah Taylor,
died 6 May 1772, Aged 7, Year
William Taylor of this Parifh, Ser
died 18 Oct 1778, Aged 66

John Champneys, of the Parifh, Sen
died December the 24th, 1673
Alfo Elizabeth the wife of John Champneys

John Champneys, Efe of Lockington, Gent
Son of John and Elizabeth Champneys,
of this Parifh, and Grandfon of
the above John and Elizabeth,
died Feb Anno Domini 1720, aged 44

John Maronne of this Parifh, Gent
died May 24 1750, aged near 55 Years
Grace Wife of the faid John Maronne
died April 10 1744, aged near 70 Years

IN THE CHURCH YARD

ON A NEAT MONUMENT AGAINST THE WALL OF THE SOUTH CROSS AILE

Near this Place is interred the Body
of CATHERINA, wife of EDWARD PARROTT,
of *Over* in this Parish, who departed his Life,
16 June, 1781, aged 46 Years

ON TOMBS

John Rolph, of this Parish,
died 26 Jan 1737, Aged 86 Years

Elizabeth his Wife
died June 15, 1746, Aged 61

John, Eldest Son of George and
Susanna Rolph, of Thornbury,
died 13 Sept 1760, in the 9th Year of his age

Susanna, wife of the said George
Rolph, and one of the Daughters
of Thos and Eliz Cox, of this Parish,
died 28 Sept 1765, aged 41 Years

Henry Boulton, of this Parish, Yeoman,
died 24 Feb 1771, Aged 66

John Robbins, of Stoke Gifford,
died 20 November, 168,

Mary his Wife died
6 Nov 1709

Sarah and Mary their Daughters,
Sarah died in 1708
Mary in 1721

John, Son of Richard Dowell,
of Hempton in this Parish,
Gent died 28 of Jan 1724, Aged 63

William Hollester, Son of this Parish,
Gent died Sept 14, 1720, aged 77

Mary his wife died March
23, 1728, aged 65 Years

Also William Hollester, Gent
died August 27, 1726, aged 30

Muk Hollester, Gent died
Jun 15, 1735, aged 44

Grace Hollester, died Sept 25,
1740, Aged 46 Years

They were the Sons and Daughter of
the aforesaid William and Mary Hollester

Muk Grace, Anna, and Grace
Son and Daughters of Luke Hollester,
Gent all died Infants

Luke Hollester died 14 Jan 1756, Aged 56

Hester his Widow died 18 Jan 1771, Aged 69

William Hollester, Gent their Son
died June 20, 1774, Aged 4

Elizabeth Marth, wife of John Marth,
of Thornbury Gent and one of the
Daughters of Luke Hollester late
of this Parish, Gent by Hester his
wife died 1 July 1775, Aged 39

William Cotterell, of this Parish,
died Sept 10, 1727, aged 58

Susanna his Wife died
Jan 24, 1694, aged 21

Thomas Cotterell, of this Parish, Senr
died Sept 9, 1709, aged 81

Elizabeth his wife died
Jan 5, 1706, aged near 80

Thomas, Son of William and Mary
Cotterell, died April 27, 1729,
Aged 27 Years

Mary, wife of William Johnson,
and Daughter of William and Mary
Cotterell, of this Parish, died
June 23, 1723, aged 19 Years

William their Son was buried
April 5, 1724, aged 2 Years

Mary, the Relict of William
Cotterell, of this Parish, died
the 12th of Jan. 1764, aged 90.

Stephen Cotterell, son of William
and Mary Cotterell, died
May 4, 1747, in the 40th Year of his age.

Samuel Hollister, of Compton
in this Parish, died March 24,
1741, aged 62

Anne his Wife died Sept 4,
1743, aged 60

Edward and Mary their Children
died young

Anne, the wife of John Knight,
Daughter of Samuel Hollister, of
this Parish, Yeoman, died 21 Dec
1772, aged 64

Edw Bartlett, of this Parish, Yeoman,
died Jun 1669, aged 70

Elizabeth his wife died 14 Aug 1694

John Bartlett, of this Parish, Yeoman,
died Sept 28, 1718 aged 52 Years

Hannah his wife died 10 April,
1714, aged near 76 Years

Edw Bartlett, of this Parish, Yeoman,
died 12 Jan 1716, aged 71

Edward Champneys, of this
Parish Yeoman, died 14 March, 1728,
in the 73d Year of his age

Mary, Daughter of John Champneys,
of this Parish Yeoman, died 16 Apr
1711, in the 20 Year of her age

Hannah

Hannah, wife of Dan Turner,
of the Parish of Stoke Gifford, and
Daughter of Morris and Sarah Cook,
died June 1st, 1741, in the 38th Year of her age

John, Son of Morris and Sarah Cook,
died June 6, 1741, aged 30 Years

Daniel Turner, of the Parish of
Stoke Gifford, died May 16, 1743, aged 48

George Thornton, a native
of Virginia, the beloved Son of
William Thornton, of Rhapahanock River
in the County of King George,
was born the 19th Dec. 1724.

He came to this place November last,
and died the 19 day Dec. 1740,
having that Day fully completed
the 6th Year of his age

ON HEAD STONES

	Died		Aged
Benjamin Dobbins, Gent	2 Feb	1760	42
Three of his Children died Infants			
Anne, Daughter of Edward Stephens	8 Apr	1737	30
Edward Stephens, Yeoman,	15 Mar	1722	53
Mrs. Sarah Stephens born 11 1672,		1757	85
Philip Stephens	12 Nov	1712	54
William Stephens	19 Feb	1724	82
Mary his Wife	27 Oct		81
Stephen Stephens, Son of Edward Stephens,	29 Jan	1736	21
John, Son of Edward Stephens	19 Jan	1738	34
William, Son of Edward Stephens, Yeoman,	26 Mar	1729	27
Ann, Wife of Stephen Stephens,	17 Sept	1721	54
John Jayne, of Ellinghurst in this Parish, Yeoman,	27 Sept	1745	45
John Cox, Yeoman,	2 June,	1695	58
Elizabeth his Wife	1 Oct	1713	56
Susannah his Daughter	22 Aug	1694	—
John, Son of Thomas and Elizabeth Cox,	4 May,	1750	21
John, Son of John Cox,	10 Dec	1698	10
Thomas Cox, Yeoman,	15 June,	1754	58
Elizabeth his Wife	28 July,	1750	55
Thomas Bracey, Yeoman	5 May,	1739	66
Hester his Wife	3 Mar	1746	61
Stephen Bracey, their Son	19 Apr	1761	39
Sarah, wife of Philip Baker, and Relict of Stephen Bracey	19 Nov	1770	48
Hester, Daughter of Thomas Bracey	11 Feb	1710	
Mary, Wife of Thomas Bracey	4 Apr	1770	33
William, Son of Thomas and Hester Bracey	19 June,	1729	17
Hezekiah, Son of Thomas and Hester Bracey	21 Oct	1743	28
Christian, Widow of Hezekiah Bracey	9 Feb.	1766	52
Hester, Daughter of Hezekiah and Christian Bracey	12 Sept	1764	22
William Bracey	2 Dec	1723	37
Richard Bracey	27 Apr	1701	56
Mary his Wife	20 Dec	1706	59
Timothy Matthews	2 Mar	1764	76
Thomas Kemp	15 May,	1729	38
Anne his Wife	15 Jan	1729	34
Hester, wife of Thomas Kemp	4 Nov	1763	33
Edward Wade	9 Apr	1717	50
Jane, formerly Relict of Edward Wade, and late Wife of Timothy Matthews	5 May,	1738	70
Edward Wade, Son of the above	31 May,	1771	66
John Champneys, Yeoman,	24 Nov	1725	92
Elizabeth his Wife	15 Nov	1722	67
Robert Champneys, Yeoman,	12 Aug	1720	71
Elizabeth, wife of Stephen Bagg, of the Parish of St. Mary Redcliff, in the City of Bristol, and Daughter of Thomas Cox, of this Parish, Yeoman,	31 Dec	1743	26
Hester, wife of Henry Bagg	20 Dec	1775	55
Betty, wife of Simon Griffith	27 Sept	1760	34
Simon Griffith her Husband	5 Apr	1756	56
John Griffith	16 June,	1768	79
Ann his Wife	9 Dec	1754	73
Hester, wife of Richard Griffith	15 Jan	1776	47
Thomas, Son of Matthew Worgan	5 Aug	1775	19
Thomas Gunter	1 Feb	1761	83
Ann, Wife of Thomas Gunter, of Stoke Gifford	2 Nov	1775	31
Mary, Wife of Thomas Gunter, of Winterbourn	2 June,	1717	84
John Hollester	6 Mar	1716	11
Hezekiah, Son of John Hollester	1 Jun	1717	0
Isabell, Wife of Stephen Hollester	20 Mar	1760	70

Morris

O N   H E A D   S T O N E S

	Died	Aged
Morris Hill	22 Jan 1721	—
Robert, Son of Jonathan and Henrietta Houfe	3 Oct 1756	23
Mary their Daughter	2 June, 1762	22
Jonathan Houfe, of Frampton Cotterell, Jun	14 Apr 1769	39
Henrietta, Wife of Jonathan Houfe, of this Parish	16 Nov 1771	72
Jofeph Peafley	10 June, 1736	65
Hefter, Relict of Jofeph Peafley, late Wife of George Fry, of Stoke Gifford	29 Feb 1780	84
Edward Bowman, Yeoman,	10 Feb. 1758	63
Mary his Wife,	5 Mar 1757	72
George, Son of George and Elizabeth Croffman	6 July, 1762	26
Joyce, Wife of Mark Croffman, Yeoman	8 Oct 1763	46
John 2d Son of John and Ann Croffman	6 Jan 1741	31
John Croffman, Yeoman	25 Mar 1725	56
Ann, Wife of John Croffman	27 Sept 1760	87
Mary, Relict of Job Tovey	17 May, 1768	67
William Hoggard	26 Sept 1766	70
Ann, Wife of William Hoggard	4 Apr 1775	65
Sarah, Wife of William Johnfon	1 Nov 1768	53
Elizabeth, Wife of William Pugh	10 Feb 1769	55
Joyce, Wife of Jofeph Brown, of Stoke Gifford, and Daughter of George and Hefter Fry	21 Apr 1767	30
Jofeph Brown	15 June, 1770	47
Rachel, Daughter of Jofeph and Joyce Brown	10 Jan 1782	21
Sarah, Relict of Morris Cook, of Stoke Gifford	29 Jan 1743	64
Morris Cook, of Stoke Gifford	28 Apr 1735	39
Nathan Thatcher	8 Apr 1773	77
Hannah his Wife	27 Dec 1773	78
Peter, their Son	5 May, 1778	52
Thomas Bartholomew	16 May, 1744	53
Mary his Wife	24 July, 1747	—
Ann, Wife of Thomas Davis	4 Aug 1768	42
May, Wife of Richard Lee Strange, Yeoman	1 May, 1759	57
Richard Lee Strange	3 Aug 1754	87
Thomas Webb, of the City of Briftol	— 1779	—
Five Children of Thomas and Elizabeth Webb	— 1778	—
John, Son of Abraham and Grace Hughes	24 Dec 1759	33
Thomas Bailey, Yeoman	19 Oct 1728	58
William Cox, of Alvefton, Yeoman	12 Dec 1720	82
Elizabeth Crouder, firft, Wife of Thomas Dyer, of Henbury, and afterwards Wife of John Crouder, Gent	8 Dec 1718	65
Simon Rawlings	10 Aug 1750	53
Elizabeth his Wife	9 May, 1778	83
Thomas Webb	1 Nov 1769	36
Mary, Wife of William Britton, of Filton	7 Sept 1743	49
William Shepherd, of Northwick in the Parifh of Henbury	19 Jan 1753	36
Eleanor his Wife, and Wife of William Symes, of the fame place	21 Nov 1764	61
John Shepherd, of this Parifh	1 June, 1761	49
William Lewis	19 May, 1770	48
John Warren	23 Sept 1779	73
Ann his fecond Wife	16 Feb 1776	64
Elizabeth Spencer, Sifter of Ann Warren	25 May, 1772	58
John Warren	30 July, 1741	39
Richard Ponting	11 Nov 1743	49
Elizabeth fecond Wife of Richard Ponting	5 Feb 1756	70
Richard Ponting,	22 May, 1733	36
Thomas Powell	17 May, 1763	61
Henry Grace	20 Jan 1734	55
John Stallard	29 June, 1753	43
Sarah his Wife	29 May, 1768	48
John Stallard, Sen		
Elizabeth his Wife	20 May, 1768	82
Ann, their Daughter	15 Apr 1768	49
John Morris	10 Feb 1720	31
William Ambrofe, of Chipping Sodbury	22 June, 1733	33
Thomas Lewes, of Over	— 1710	—
Richard Seager, of Over, Yeoman	8 Nov 1731	82
John his Son	13 Nov 1714	25

ON HEAD STONES

	Died		Aged
James Long	19 Mar 1773		—
And allo Charles Morson	16 Feb 1770		—
They were natives of Africa, and fervants to Sir James Laroche at Over, who caufed this ftone to be erected			
Charles Brown	7 Jan 1777		44
William Moreton	22 Mar 1752		52
Elizabeth his Wife	21 Apr 1762		61
Ann, Wife of Giles Clarke, Daughter of John Hancock, of Woodland	5 Dec 1701		40
Mary, Relict of Samuel Tyfon,			
John Hancock	16 Apr 1726		52
Giles Hancock, of Shirehampton	16 Aug 1770		82
Elizabeth his Wife	31 Jan 1743		65
Grace, their Daughter	1 Sept 1731		18
John Hancock, of Henbury	21 May, 1750		90
Mary his Wife	28 Feb 1745		71
Mary Andrews, their Daughter	27 Mar 1762		60
Jofeph New	28 Nov 1760		71
Anna his Wife	30 Mar 1767		72
Jofeph Wathen	22 Nov 1725		63
Mary his Wife	11 Nov 1713		58
George Fawfett	23 Jan 1766		65
Elizabeth his Wife	15 Mar 1768		69
John, Son of Roger and Elizabeth Edwards	29 July, 1760		20
William Clements, Son of Arthur and Joan Clements	12 Mar 1758		45
Abraham Read	24 Mar 1772		45
Richard Dowell	23 Jun 1730		84
Thomas Dowell	6 Sept 1748		80
John Hughes	4 Nov 1763		70
Charles his Son			16
Hefter his Daughter			21
Mary, Wife of Ifaac Webb, and Daughter of John and Mary Tyler	27 May, 1771		29
Martha, Wife of John Birt, and Daughter of John and Anna Hollefter	14 Dec 1777		45
Betty Long, Widow of John Long of Tockington, and formerly Relict of James Webb, of this Parifh	18 Jun 1776		76
Sarah, late Widow of Thomas Bailey	9 Oct 1738		67
John Long, of Tockington	2 Jan 1771		70
Abraham Hughes	15 Feb 1767		70
Grace his Wife	14 Jan 1775		74

x. ALVESTON.

THIS parish lies in the diocese and deanery of BRISTOL, and in the hundred of *Langley and Swine-*
shead, two miles south west of *Thornbury*, six miles north-west from *Sodbury*, twenty-six miles
south-west from GLOUCESTER, and nine miles north-east from BRISTOL

The derivation of the name of this place is uncertain. Sir Robert Atkyns derives it from the Saxon
Ald, old, and from its being situated east of *Olveston*, but as *veston*, the termination of each parish, cannot be supposed to point out an *easterly* situation in the one instance, and a *westerly* one in the other, it
seems more probable that it owes its denomination to some Saxon chief of the name of *Alves*, who might
anciently have been the possessor, and therefore from him was called *Alves Town*. However that may be, it
must be observed that there are several places in this kingdom named *Alveston*, as may be seen in the Index
Villaris. It is now pronounced *Alston*

The parish lies high, and the soil is mostly clay, which, however, in a good season, yields very good
crops. A part of the soil is a coppery land on a lime-stone, which produces a great deal of what is
called Carnation-Grass. The western part forms a rock of limestone descending towards the *Severn*

The great road from BRISTOL and the West to GLOUCESTER and the North, passes through this place,
at which an inn, known by the sign of *The Ship*, has lately been fitted up in a commodious manner for
the convenience of travellers. A turnpike road is also making through it, leading to *Sodbury* through
Iron Acton, and which, when compleated from *Aust*, or the *Old Passage*, through *Olveston*, will be of singular advantage to travellers coming from the other side the *Severn*, being the nearest road to LONDON
from South Wales

There are three hamlets in this parish

1 *Alveston* village

2 *Rock Urcote*, or *Earthcote*, or *Herdcot*, situate about one mile from the church, it is written *Her-*
dicot in Domesday, and is, perhaps, derived from HERD, BIT handsome, beautiful, and COED a wood

3 *Grovening*, or *Crovesend*, this lies not far two miles from the church. Near to this place,
upon the brow of a hill (from whence there is an extensive view of the *Severn*, the town of *Thornbury*,
and the adjacent country) are the remains of a large round ancient encampment, which is called the
Old Abbey, as some say, from an abbey which stood near to it, but it does not appear from the monasticon, or any other record, that there was ever any abbey on or near this spot. Upon opening a large
barrow near to this camp, about the year 1670, several stone coffins, containing human bones, were
found. Each coffin seemed to consist of one solid stone, as Sir Robert Atkyns observes, no appearance of
any cement being visible. Perhaps they contained the remains of some british or Saxon chiefs, slain in
battle near the spot, as many engagements may be supposed to have happened in these parts, before the
former were forced to retire beyond the *Severn*

The manor belonged to the crown in the reign of King Henry III as that King made a reservation
of his park of *Alveston*, at the time when the *forest of Kingswood* was disforested. At the beginning of
the present century, it was held by the family of the Hills, and is now the property of Lewis Hoskins,
of *Stinchcomb* in this county, Esq a descendant, by the female line of the Hills, who has two
estates here, one in the occupation of Edward Dowd, of which the Ship inn makes a part, the other
of John Williams

At *Crovening* is a very old mansion house belonging to Henry Stephens, of *Cromhall*, in this county,
Esq now in the occupation of Mr Nathaniel Crewther

Adjoining to the church still remains the ruins of a large mansion house the rooms lofty and spacious,
commanding an extensive prospect. It belonged some time since, with a good estate to Edward Hill, Esq
and is now the property of Mrs Walmot. A farmer inhabits the house. This estate anciently belonged
to the family of Sitwell

About a mile and a quarter from the church, Henry King, Esq has a very good house and estate,
with a fine plantation of pear trees, of which is made excellent perry

Opposite Mr King, Mr Whittington of *Henfield near Tansloes*, has a good estate in the occupation
of John Pusto

Not far from this, Mrs Smith, relict of the late Captain Smith, has also a very good house and estate

A considerable estate, formerly belonging to Richard Hawksworth, Esq is now possessed by Christopher
Willoughby, Esq and occupied by John Church

The church, which is dedicated to Saint Helen, is a small building newly paved and fitted up within,
and has a low decent tower, that has lately been repaired with battlements containing three bells.
This living being annexed to *Olveston* for the incumbents thereof and pensions, see that parish

No Benefactions to the poor

PRESENT

The following persons were summoned from this place by the Heralds in 1682 and 1683

Nicholas Veele, Arm.	John Clark, Gent
Thomas Smith, Gent.	Thomas Heanes, Gent.
Guy Lawrence, Cler	Richard Hawkesworth, Arm

At the Election in 1776, ten Freeholders poled from this parish

ANNUAL ACCOUNT OF MARRIAGES, BIRTHS, AND BURIALS, IN THIS PARISH

A D	Mar	Bir	Bur	A D	Mar	Bir	Bur	A D	Mar	Bi	Bur	A D	Mu	Bu	Bur
1781	4	10	4	1791				1801				1811			
1782	4	7	3	1792				1802				1812			
1783	1	10	3	1793				1803				1813			
1784	1	5	4	1794				1804				1814			
1785	7	9	6	1795				1805				1815			
1786				1796				1806				1816			
1787				1797				1807				1817			
1788				1798				1808				1818			
1789				1799				1809				1819			
1790				1800				1810				1820			

INSCRIPTIONS IN THE CHURCH

Here lyeth the Body of
Colonel Thomas Veel,
who died 11 day of January
Anno Dom 1663

Here lieth the Body of
Nicholas Veel, Esq who
died tne 17th day of January,
1703

Here lieth the Body of
Dorothy, the Daughter of
Colonel Thomas Veel,
the second Wife of William
Holland, of the City of
Bristol, Gent who was
buried the 10 of January,
Anno Dom 1683

Here lyeth the Body of
Susan, the Daughter of
Thomas Clayton, Doctor,
and the King's Professor
of Phyfick, in the University
of Oxford, descended from
a ancient Family of
Clayton Hall in Yorkshire,
She was the 2d Wife of
John Milborn, Esq descended from a Family anciently
seated at Milborn Port
in Somersetshire, She died
the 19th day of July, 1654
Also the Body of Thomas
Milborn, second sonne of the
said John and Susan,
He died the 1st Day of October, 1676

Here lyeth the Body of
Alice, the Wife of Thomas
Clayton, Doctor of Physicke
in the University of Oxford,
She died Anno Dom 1657

Here lyeth the Body of
——— Hawksworth
who departed this Life the
24th day of October, Anno
Dom 1696, Ætatis suæ 42

1 John
Sarah } Children of Richard Hawksworth,
2 John } Gent and Sarah his Wife

John 1 was buried in May 1686
Sarah was buried in January 1687
John 2 was buried in Decem 1688

Here lyeth the Body of Thomas
Smith, Yeoman who died
May 2d, Anno Dom 1683

Also the Body of
Thomas Smith, of this Parish,
who died Aug 29, 1719,
Aged 63

Here lyeth the Body of Mary,
the Wife of Thomas Smith,
of this Parish, who died
March 23, 172, aged 60

ON THE VERGE OF THE SAME STONE

Here lyeth the Body of Thomas
Smith, Yeoman who departed this
Life the 9th day of September 1639

Here lyeth the Body of
Robert Smith, Son of Thomas Smith,
of this Parish, who died A D 1670

Here lyeth the Body of Margaret,
the Wife of Thomas Smith,
of this Parish, She died the
9th day of August, Anno Dom 1641

IN THE CHURCH YARD   ON TOMBS

Thomas Davis, Yeoman,
died March 31, 1744, aged 80

Elizabeth his Wife
died 16 September, 1736, aged 74.

Elizabeth, Wife of Thomas
Davis, of this Parish, Yeoman,
died Oct 31, 1757, aged 59

Thomas Davis,
died July 9, 1779, aged 79

Mary his Wife
died Jan 1776, aged 58

Sarah, the Wife of
Charles Hall, and the
only Daughter of John
Smith, of Wanswell, in the
Parish of Berkeley, Gent
died March 11, 1705, aged 26

Thomas Thomas
died 9 April, 1707, aged 36

Richard Cottell
died 21 May, 1717, aged 63

Edith his Wife
died 30 day Dec 1715, aged 62

William Watkins,
died the 29 Sept 1752, aged 60

Mary, late Widow
of William Watkins,
died the 8th day of May, 1755,
Aged 80 Years

Robert Shepard,
of Tockington in the Parish
of Olveston, died Nov 19,
1778, aged 66.

William Shepard,
Son of Robert and Hannah
Shepard, died April 13,
1747, aged 2 Years and 3 Months

ON FLAT AND HEAD STONES

	Died	Aged
Elizabeth, Wife of Thomas White,	6 Oct 1775	61
Samuel, Son of Thomas and Betty Smith,	25 Mar 1773	17
John, their Son,	28 Mar 1773	21
Thomas Raworth,	13 July, 1776	61
Anne Meredith, late of Tockington, Spinster, Daughter of Richard and Deborah Meredith, late of the same place, and Sister by the Mother to Mary, wife of Thomas Davis,	25 July, 1781	69
Samuel Wheeler	26 Apr 1756	37
Mary his Wife She lies buried at St Thomas in Bristol	2 July, 1757	39
William Webb Wheeler, infant Son of Samuel and Mary Wheeler,		
Mary, Wife of Benjamin Blanch, of Iron Acton, and Daughter of Samuel and Joyce Walker, of Tytherington,	26 May, 1776	25
Mary, Wife of Nicholas Webb,	23 Oct 1744	
Nicholas Webb	2 Feb. 1728	63
Elizabeth, Wife of Thomas Grove, of Elberton,	14 Feb 1735	82
Martha, Wife of Thomas Davis,	23 Aug ----	36
Elizabeth, Wife of James White, of Olveston,	11 Apr 1731	37
Mary, Wife of Thomas Davis, of Iron Acton,	--- Jun 1776	56
Mary, Daughter of Edward and Ursula Gardner, of Pamswick in this County, Cordr,	--- Jun , 1713	29
Mary Baker of Fortworth,	--- Aug 1720	25
John Nicholas	28 Apr 1737	1-
Richard Nicholas	1 Nov 1735	14
Ralph Nicholas	27 Feb 1741	3
Elizabeth, Wife of Ralph Nicholas,	1 May 1743	74
Hannah Nicholas	27 Mar 1755	6
William, Son of Ralph and Elizabeth Nicholas,	30 May 1733	27
Joan Webb	27 Nov 1748	26
Hester, Daughter of Charles and Hester Walker,		---
James and Nathaniel, Sons of James and Mary Whitcombe, of Tytherington,		
James	11 Mar 1768	16
Nathaniel	8 Sept 1752	
Ruth, Wife of Arthur Boulton,		46
William, Son of Richard Shepard,	May, 1740	51
Samuel, their Son an Infant,		
William Watkins	29 Sept 1752	60
Mary Thornford	26 June 1750	74
Edith Day	28 Jan 1717	51

N.B. In the church yard of Thornbay there is a tomb erected to the name of Purnell of Gre.. no clother of this family, viz the late John Purnell, D. D. Warden of New College, Oxford, and Vice-Chancellor of that University, A. D. 1714, 1718, and 1719

XI A L V I N G T O N

THIS parish lies in the hundred of *Blackstoe*, and *Forest* deanery, about seven miles to the east from *Colford*, and twenty two miles south west from GLOUCESTER. It consists of nearly an equal proportion of arable and pasture land. The soil is principally sand; in some places there is a little clay.

The *Severn* bounds on the east, and a small rivulet called *Caon Brook*, which takes its rise in the parish of *St. Briavel's*, after supplying a corn mill and iron forge in this parish, empties itself into that river.

In ancient times *Alvington* was a place of greater account than it is at present; the manor with its *markets* and *fairs* being held 49 Hen. III by the priory of *Lantwony*; but since their removal of the ferry to *Beachley*, it has been decreasing till it is now become only a village.

This place is supposed to have been the Roman station *Abone*, situated, according to Antoninus, on the journey from *Isca*, now *Caerleon*, to *Cara*, now *Wallingford*, and at which they passed over the *Severn* to *Trajectus*, now *Oldbury*. It was called *Abone*, or *Avone*, by the Romans upon account of its vicinity to the river *Severn*, *Afon*, or *Avon*, in the British language signifying a river. Camden derives its present name *Avington* from the same word, but it seems rather to be formed from the Saxon *Col*, all, *win*, a victor, and *ton*, a town, i.e. the town of some great warrior.

The manor continued in the possession of the priory of *Lantbony* till the dissolution of that monastery. The present proprietor of it is the Reverend Mr. Higford, of *Dixton* in this county, who has a pleasant seat here, together with a good estate. The ancient manor-house is now a farm, *Avington Court*, an antique building, belongs to Mr. Eaton.

The living is annexed to the rectory of *Woollaston*, and the church, which is dedicated to *Saint Andrew*, is called *Tre Chapel of Alvington*. It is small, with an aile on the south side belonging to the Lord of the Manor, and a tower at the west end, in which are five bells and a clock. The tower is partly stone and partly wood, covered with tile, and the whole building has the appearance of great antiquity.

No Benefactions to the poor.

INCUMBENTS	PATRONS	INCUMBENTS	PATRONS
1692 Thomas Davis, Cler	King William and Queen Mary	174 Somerset Jones, M A	Archbishop of Canterbury
1697 Richard Bell, B A	Duke of Beaufort	1769 Robert Penny, M A	Duke of Beaufort
1711 Robert Griffith, P A	Dito	1782 John Price, B D	Dito
1737 James Meredith, M A	Ditto		

PRESENT LORD OF THE MANOR,

Reverend HENRY HIGFORD, M A

The only person summoned from this place by the Heralds in 1682 and 1683, was

Mr. John Knight

At the Election in 1776, only two freeholders polled for this parish.

ANNUAL ACCOUNT OF MARRIAGES, BIRTHS, AND BURIALS, IN THIS PARISH.

AD	Mar	Bir	Bur	AD	Mar	Bir	Bur	AD	Mar	Bir	Bur	AD	Mar	Bir	Bur
1781	1	6	3	1791				1801				1811			
1782	3	7	4	1792				1802				1812			
1783	1	3	10	1793				1803				1813			
1784	1	4		1794				1804				1814			
1785	2	7	3	1795				1805				1815			
1786				1796				1806				1816			
1787				1797				1807				1817			
1788				1798				1808				1818			
1789				1799				1809				1819			
1790				1800				1810				18			

I

INSCRIPTIONS IN THE CHURCH.

ON A RAISLD STONE IN THE CHANCEL.

HERE LIES SIR ROBERT WOODROF KNIGHTE
AND MARYE HIS DEARE WIFE
WHOSE LIVES WERE VERIVOVS IVST
VPRIGHTE
BVT ATROPOS CRVEL KNIFE
SOONE CVT THEIR THREED THE FATE
IN THIS BEING KINDE
HIM HASTEING HENCE TO HEAVENS BLISSE
LEFT HER NOT LONGE BEHINDE
BOTH SPRVNG FROM OF-SPRING GENEROVS
AND LYVEING HERE AS ONE
THIS SEPVLCHER DOTH WELL BE FIT
THVS COVERD WITH ONE STONE

BVT READER VNDERSTAND
THAT HERE THOV READST NOT THIS
AT HEIRES OR EXECVTORS CHARGE
BVT AT A DWARIES OI HIS
WHOSE CHARITIE HIR HIRE MAINTAIND
AND NOWE THEY BEING DEADE
IN GRATEFVLL MEMORIE SHE CAVSD
THIS STONE ON THEM BE LAIDE
HE DIED THE XVII DAY OF MAY ----
AND SHE THE XIIII OF MARCH
1609

ON FLAT STONES

In Memory of JAMES PROCTOR,
who departed this Life,
3ᵈ day Feb 1757, Aged 78

Here lyeth the Body of
MARY, the Wife of JAMES PROCTOR,
who died 6 April, 1764,
Aged 56 Years

JOHN their Son died an Infant

Here lieth the Body of
MARY, Daughter of
JOHN and MARY HARRIS,
of Hutlebury in the County
of Worcester, who was buried
the 5th of July, 1743, aged 18

Here lyeth the Body of
DOROTHY HIGFORD, who
departed this Life the
14 day of March 1675,
being Lady of the Manor
of Alvington Spencer

H I
MARGARETA, JACOBI HIGFORD,
Armigeri, uxor, generosi Stirpe
Keyte, Baronetti Wat Keynfis, ort,
Obiit Februarii vigesimo primo
A D MDCCXVII Anno ætatis XXIX

M S
JACOBI HIGFORD Armigeri,
qui obiit 3 Septembri,
A D 1742, Anno ætat 18

Arms, On a chevron, between three bucks
heads caboshed, three mullets

HERE LIETH THE BODIE,
IN ASEVRED HOPE OF
EVERLASTING LIFE,
OF THOMAS HIGFORDE,
GENTL DESENDED
FROM THE FAMILII OF
THE HIGFORDS OF DIX-
TON IN THIS COVNTII,
SOMETIME LORD OF
THIS MANNAR, WHO
AFTER A VIRTVOVS LIFE
AND LONGE AND
WEARISOME SICKN
ESS, DECEASED THE
14 DECEMBER, 1651

Here lieth the Body of
DENNIS COMPTON
and JANE his Wife,
buried 28 day of March, 1640

Arms of HIGFORD, as before detailed

Here lieth also interred
JOHN HIGFORD Esq
Lord of this Manor,
who departed his Life
April 9, A D 1706

Here

Here lieth the Body of
THOMAS MEDCALFE,
who departed this Life,
the 20 Day of January 1729,
Aged 58 Years

Here lieth the Body of
THOMAS MEDCALFE,
who departed this Life
Oct 7 1776, aged 76 Years

Here lieth the Body of
MARY, the Wife of THOMAS
MEDCALFE, Jun who departed
this Life March 25, 1749,
Aged 42

Here lieth the Body of
WILLIAM the Son of
LEONARD and ELIZABETH MONK,
who departed this Life the
1st day of February, 1724

Also here lieth the Body
of LEONARD MONK,
late Coroner for this County
who departed this Life 9 Dec
1737

Also ELIZABETH his Wife
died June 5, 1739,
Aged 81

In Memory of
THOMAS BAKER, of
this Parish, who died
27 May, 1779, aged 65 Years

Here lieth the Body of
SAM LAWRENCE, Son of
EDWARD and SARAH LAWRENCE,
of Rodmore, who died the
13 of April 1782, aged 57

Here lies interred the Body of
SARAH, the Wife of EDWARD
LAWRENCE, of this Parish, Gent
She died the 15 Feb 1771, aged 4

Also here lieth the Body of the
abovementioned EDWARD LAWRENCE,
who died March 25, 1771 aged 69

Here lieth the Body of
SARAH, the Body of JOHN
IRELAND of this Parish,
who departed this Life July 6,
1750, aged 55

THE FOLLOWING INSCRIPTIONS
ARE ON TWO MONUMENTS

NEAR THIS PLACE
lieth the Body of MARY, the Wife of
GEORGE MEDCALFE
who died the 23d May 1763,
Aged 31 Years

Also GEO MEDCALFE,
departed this Life 2 Day of
Jun 1780 aged 45

NEAR THIS PLACE
lieth the Body of MARY
Wife of ROBERT HAWKINS,
AGENT TO
Alvington Forges, who departed
this Life
20 May 1767
Aged 23½ Years

IN THE CHURCH YARD; ON TOMBS

Mary, Wife of Thomas Ireland,
or Noverend, and last of all,
Wife of William Williams,
died Dec 5, 1724, aged 65

James, Son of Richard and
Elizabeth Hewett, died
April 18, 1770, aged 21

Thomas Son of Thomas and
Ann Cox, died 23 April, 1750
Aged 18

Anthony Cox, died 5 March,
1747, aged 20

William Lewis
died 11 Dec 1765 aged 55

Anne his Wife
died 15 April, 1766, aged 54

William their Son
died 15 July, 1766, aged 24

Mary Wife of
John Baker,
died 9 April 1772

Mary Wife of
John Williams,
died 19 ... 1754, aged 7

Sarah the Wife of
Robert Hickes, died Feb 1
1734 aged 76

Robert Hicks
died 9 Oct 1745, aged 77

ON FLAT AND HEAD STONES

	Died	Aged
Thomas George	11 Aug 1724	48
Anne his Wife	12 Mar 1750	67
Elizabeth, Wife of Thomas Cox,	11 Dec 172?	
Thomas Cox	11 Dec 1726	71
Edward Butcher, of Brockwear, in the Parish of Woolastone,	23 Dec 1743	26
John Butcher, of Woolastone,	13 Feb 1713	—
Ann, Wife of Warren Hopkins, of Brockwear,	3 Feb 1744	—
John, the Son of Warren and Ann Hopkins,	8 Jun 1744	—
John Butcher,	16 Dec 1724	—
John his Wife, late Wife of Richard Thorn, of Brockwear,	16 Sept 1754	71
Joyce, Wife of Christopher Miller,	16 Oct 1711	
Ann, Wife of Richard Hewlett, of Aylberton, buried	1 Jun 1750	39
William Weapin	27 Nov 17	38
Hannah Wife of John George,	3 May, 1776	61
Ann their Daughter,	1 Aug 177	30
Anne George, of Alberton,	1	6
John Hewett	May 1	8
Esther Willetts	11 Feb 1741	
Mary Wife of Joseph Willetts	7 Oct 1	
Thomas, Son of Joseph and Mary Willetts	Oct	13
John George	Nov 1776	60
Mary, Wife of John George,	Dec 17	76
John, Son of John George,	Sept 1	
Sarah the Daughter of John George	11 Feb 1	20
Elizabeth Wife of Josiah Thorn, of Alberton, in the Parish of Lidney	July 1	12
Josiah Thorn, of Alberton	Nov 17	
Kate Thorn	Dec 17	4
John Okley	Jan 17	

XII. AMPNEY CRUCIS.

THIS parish lies in the hundred of *Crowthorne and Minety*, and deanery of *Fanford*, about two miles east from *Cirencester*, and twenty miles south-east from GLOUCESTER. It consists of nearly an equal proportion of arable, pasture, and meadow land, and the common fields have been inclosed, agreeable to the Act of Parliament obtained for that purpose about the year 1770. The soil is principally a strong deep clay, and produces good crops of all kinds of grain.

Some of the houses belonging to this parish lie in that of *Ampney St Mary*, at least a mile from the church of *Ampney Crucis*. Indeed, the three parishes of this name are so intermixed with each other, that there is room to conclude they were anciently comprised in one. The road from *Cirencester* to LONDON passes through this place.

It probably received the name of *Ampney* from *Amnis*, the Latin word for a river, a clear stream of considerable breadth running through it, which, after passing *Down Amney*, falls into the *Thames*. The addition of *Crucis* was made to it, as some term was necessary to distinguish it from the other *Ampneys*, either upon account of the form of the church, which is built in the shape of a cross, or from a large cross that anciently stood in the parish, or which there are still the remains. The distinction might have been given to it, from the large possessions the church once held in the parish. In *Domesday* Book the name is written *Omenie*, and in some old grants it is named *Amney Holy Rood*, from the Saxon Hulᵹ, the cross.

An earthen urn, containing burnt bones and ashes, and also some Roman coins of the lower empire, were found, not many years ago, by some workmen, who were digging stone by the side of the London road.

The manor-house, formerly the seat of the Pleydell family, and lately belonging to Samuel Blackwell, Esq, is a good old building, and the only one worthy of notice in the place.

The living is a vicarage, and the church, which is dedicated to *Holy Rood*, is built (as already observed) in the form of a cross, with a tower at the west end, in which are five bells. Both the church and the tower are adorned with battlements, and have the appearance of great antiquity. The patronage of the church, and the impropriation, formerly belonged, with the manor, to the abbey of *Tewkesbury*, and part of the tithe and glebe were held by the abbey of GLOUCESTER. The impropriation now belongs to the heir of the late Samuel Blackwell, Esq.

BENEFACTIONS

The following is an abstract of the schedule delivered in to his Majesty's Justices of the Peace, September, 1786, from this parish.

" In this parish is founded a free school, supported by an annual rent charge of 8l. payable out of a farm in *Ampney Peter*, given in 1719 by Robert Pleydell, Esq. Part of this money is said to have been bequeathed for cloathing and apprenticing a number of children from the several parishes of *Ampney Crucis*, *Harnill*, *Ampney Peter*, and *Ampney Mary*, but in what proportion we know not, nor do we know that any directions were given, respecting the number of children from any one of these parishes. Thomas Tyndal late of *North Cerney*, Esq, has been considered as a trustee to superintend this charity, in whom the trust is now vested we cannot say, but suppose it to be in his representative. — See the inscription on Mr Pleydell's monument.

INCUMBENTS	PATRONS	INCUMBENTS	PATRONS
160, Henry Bishop,	King James	1710 John Sutton M A	King George I
1671 John Prevost,	King Charles II	1724 William Koger M A	Ditto
1674 Charles Serjeant M A	Ditto	1725 Samuel Rogers M A	Ditto
1658 William Hervey, M A	Ditto	1729 Thomas Lovell M A	King George II
—— Ilric Dilton	——	1765 Henry Davies M A	Lord Chancellor
The above from Sir Rob. Atkyns		1767 William Sandford D D	Ditto
		1783 Robert Stephen H B	King George III
		1786 Thomas Boy M A	Ditto

PRESENT LORD OF THE MANOR

The Heir of the late SAMUEL BLACKWELL, Esq.

The

The only perfon fummoned from this place by the Heralds in 1682 and 1683, was
Robert Pleydell, Arm

At the Election in 1776, ten Freeholders polled from this parifh

ANNUAL ACCOUNT OF MARRIAGES, BIRTHS, AND BURIALS, IN THIS PARISH.

AD	Mar	Bir	Bur	AD	Mar	Bir	Bur	AD	Mar	Bir	Bur	AD	Mar.	Bir	Bur.
1781	2	12	17	1791				1801				1811			
1782	3	14	8	1792				1802				1812			
1783	2	17	9	1793				1803				1813			
1784	4	16	12	1794				1804				1814			
1785	2	11	17	1795				1805				1815			
1786				1796				1806				1816			
1787				1797				1807				1817			
1788				1798				1808				1818			
1789				1799				1809				1819			
1790				1800				1810				1820			

MONUMENTAL INSCRIPTIONS.

IN THE CHANCEL

ON A HANDSOME WHITE MARBLE MONUMENT, ARE THE FOLLOWING ARMS AND INSCRIPTION VIZ.
Argent, a bend Gules, guttée d'eau, between two Cornifh choughs, Sable, a chief chequy Or and Sable, for PLEYDELL, impaling, Ermine, on a chief Sable, 3 battle axes Argent, for SHEPPARD

ROBERTUS PLEYDELL,
ROBERTI juxta fitum filius Unicus,
Natus 23 Julii, 1687,
Mortuus eft Maii 22, 1719
Fn' virum Sereniffimæ Frontis, Mitiffimi Ingenii,
Optimarum Artium Studiis libe iliter eruditum,
Prudentem, Pium, Juftum, Abftinentem,
Qui Filii, Fratris, Amici,
Officii omnii diligenter fancteq ie explevit
Si cictium quæ Maritum, quæ Patrem decerent,
Experiri per fata licuiffet,
Quam Beata fuiffet Uxor ! Progenies quam Proba !
Quan auem Curam in Suâ Prole inftituendâ
impendi vetuit Deus,
Iam omnem in Alienâ educandâ
(Largo ad id negoiii annuo fumptu in on ne Ævum dato)
Adhibuir, fic fera Pofteritatis fietus Pater
O Quot ex illo Pauperieris fuventut s Seminario,
Bcneola hujus Viri Munificentiâ extructo,
in Lctiori fola quotannis transferuntur,
Hinc Nomini Profperitatem fuam acceptum relaturi
et veluti illi Arbores quas, animi recreandi gratia,
Ipfe fua manu ferere folebat,
Præfenti et Futuris Seculis prodeffe poffit !
&c &c

He hath endowed a Charity School in this Parifh,
with a Rent Charge of Eighty Pounds per ann for ever,
for the yearly Apprenticing of two poor Boys or Girls
and for the Cloathing and Inftructing in Writing,
Reading and in Chriftian Knowledge, as many more
as the Refidue of that Sum will be fufficient for

Arms,

Arms of PLEYDELL as before described

Juxta jacet
SUSANNA, ROBERTI
PLEYDEL, Arm. Uxor, quæ
deceſſit IX Cal. July inter
horas XII & primam
noćturnas, innoque
Domini
MDCXLII

Non procul hinc
dormit JOHANNES PLEY-
DELL, Arm. qui vixit XXXII
Annos diebus XXX minus,
et exceſſit tertio non.
Auguſt, hora matutini
tertia, anno Dom.
MDCXLV

M S
ROBERTI PLEYDEL, Armig. Robti fili,
natu 2dᵘ mortuo fratre majori,
paternam hereditatem accepit, et auxit
Vir ſine fuco pius, ad conſilia
prudentiſſimus modeſtiæ ac temperantiæ
forma, beneficentiæ ſimul e bene
dictionis divina, in beneficos ingens
exemplar, φιλοξένος, Subditus,
Dominus, maritus, pater, amicus,
optimus,
ob IIII Kal. Jan. inter horas IIᵃᵐ & IIIᵃᵐ
matutinas an æt LVIII pene exacto,
Dñi MDCLXXV

In Memoriam
ROBERTI PLEYDELL, Arm.
qui vixit LXIII annos
VI menſes, & XVIII dies,
et exceſſit IX Cal.
Martii, hora diei XI,
Anno Dom.
MDCXLII

M S
Virginis Innocentiſſimæ SUSANNÆ PLEYDALL,
Filiæ natu tertiæ ROBERTI PLEYDAL, Arm.
et ELIZABETHÆ Uxoris, Quæ Hactenam Eon
ductam juxta parentibus natu, ut Moribus
Ætati, & ſexui conſentaneis informatur,
ea ad poſt octodecim menſes ibidem con
ſcripto commodum ex tempeſtate Et
domicum (Ventris torminis) incidiſſet et
multos dolores variosque cruciatus a Dys
ſenteria paſſa eſſet, per illum, ſupra
nituram ſpeciminæ per ſil quot dies ed to
[illegible], pur mente omnis Deo reddidit
Septemb. Vicesimo Sexto
{ Suoris MDCLXXVI
Anno { Ætatis ſui Anno

Prudete SUSANNA citeres ad hunc Locum
deferri, caribur pietatina ejus mater
ELIZABETH PLEYDALL ut et cum Exuviae
reliquis obdormient atque ad gloriosam
Omnium Reſurrectionem

ON A WHITE MARBLE MONUMENT

This Stone is erected
to the Memory of
SIR HENRY PLEYDELL DAWNEY, Baronet,
Lord Viſcount DOWNE,
whoſe Remains lie buried at MEERS, near WEZELL,
on the Banks of the LOWER RHYNE
He was Lord of the Bedchamber to GEORGE
the Third, both when KING, and PRINCE of WALES,
was twice elected Knight of the ſhire
for the County of YORK,
Colonel by Brevet,
Colonel of the Southern Battalion of Militia
of the Weſt Riding of the County of YORK,
and Lieutenant Colonel of the twenty-fifth
Regiment of Foot, which he commanded at the
Battle of MINDEN, Auguſt 1, 1759
And again at the Battle of CAMEN,
Octob. 16, 1760, where, being mortally wounded,
he died the ninth of December following,
in the thirty-third year of his age.

UNDER A HELMET AND SWORD, WHICH HANG
AGAINST THE WALL, ARE THE FOLLOWING ARMS
UPON AN OVAL SHIELD viz Quarterly, 1ſt and 4th,
PLEYDELL, as before deſcribed, 2d and 3d, Sa-
ble, a cheveron Ermine, between 3 bulls heads em-
boſſed, Argent

Arms, Per cheveron 3 elephants heads eraſed,
impaling a cheveron between 3 leopards faces

Obdormit prope Dorotheam,
JOHANNIS SAUNDERS, in Medicina
Doćtoris, Vidua, vixit ſeptua
ginta ſeptem Annos paucis
diebus minus, Viduitatis ornamentum, Pietatis Exemplum,
et Charitatis pene Miraculum,
deceſſit appropinquanti cre-
pusculo feſti diei meatis
 Octobris Anno Domini
MDCLXXIV

Hic legeſh poteris ſacris obduratis Oculis

IN THE SOUTH CROSS AILE

Arms, three arrows points downwards, one in
Pale, and two in Salter, encircled with a coronet,
impaling,—or a bend 2 pieces

I S I
MARIA, Uxor SWITHINI ADEE,
Plurimis ornata Virtutibus
Paucis conſpurcata maculis
Omnibus illi bonis
Honorabilis vixit
Et licut flebilis occidit
Vitam, quam elegante ornavit,
Contempſit fortiter,
Fato imminent placide ſuccubuit
Et vivere nos docuit e mori
Hydrops vitam moleſtum ſibi pene,
Sed Finem reliquit imiretum,
Die 10ᵐ Jul An Dom 1729

Juxta
Hoc Monumentum
S F
Swithinus Adee, Gen
Qui occubuit Nonis Martij
Anno Domini
MDCCXLVII
Ætatis Suæ
LXXII

Near this place
resteth the Body of
Mr Henry Ward,
Steward to the late Right Hon
Lord Viscount Downe
In which Capacity he served the
Family near 30 Years
He died July 2, 1760, respected
by his Lord, and regretted by his Tenants

On a marble monument in the North Cross Aile

In Memory of Thomas Powell, M A
Vicar of this parish for upwards of 35 Years.
His natural Chearfulness and Benevolence of Heart,
enlivened with a true Spirit of Piety
rendered him deservedly dear to his Friends,
Beloved and esteemed by his Family,
and respected by all his Parishioners
He departed his Life Dec 29, 1764,
in the 62d Year of his Age

Also of Margaretta Maria Powell, his Wife,
who departed this Life Nov 6, 1781,
in the 67th Year of her Age

Edward White died September 10,
1768, aged 79

Barbara his Wife died March 24,
1769, aged 8

In the North Cross Aile

Arms, three lozenges in fefs,—impaling,—a che
veron between three funs

To the Memory of
Anne (late Wife of
Robert Birkeley Freeman, Gent)
a Woman whose amiable Character
Added Lustre to her Family
She was pious without Pretence,
And charitable without Oftentation
She died much lamented June 29, 1763,
Aged 52

In the north aile is a fair free stone monument
on which are the figures of a man and his wife with
17 children. The man in armour, &c it length
There is no inscription but, from the Arms, it
probably was erected for one of the family of the
Floyds, or Lloyds, anciently Lords of this Manor
Upon the side of the monument, in relief, are his
five sons and seven daughters, represented as pray
ing

In Memory of John Radway,
Yeoman, and Frances his Wife
He died - - - 1735,
She - - 9, 1725
In Memory of
William Radway the Elder,
Yeoman, of this Parish, who
departed this Life the
4th Day of September, 1726,
in the 50th Year of his Age

Also Mary his Wife departed
this Life 30 December, 1730,
in the 65th Year of her Age

IN THE CHURCH YARD; ON TOMBS

John Wicks, Sen
died Nov 29, 167,

Henry Wicks
died July 20, 1728,
Aged 81

John Ash, Sen
died Feb 25, 1774,
Aged 5,

John Ash, Jun
died 19 April 1772
Aged 15

John Mayson
died 9 March, 1 , aged 7

Ann his Wife
died Jun 1, 1733, aged 71

John Leech, Sen
died in April 1774, aged 58

John Leech, Jun
died in Aug 1771, aged 49

Hester his Wife
died in April, 1 , aged 19

Mary their Daughter
died in May, 1781, aged 18

Rowland Newied
died May 3, 1776, aged 87

Richard Herbert
died July 2, 1774, aged 6

Deborah his Wife
died March 13, 1776, aged 66

Hester, wife of William Jordan,
died Jan 1, 1779, aged 12

Ann, the Wife of
Henry Radway,
died March 30, 1781,
Aged 33

Martha, the Wife of
John Radway,
died April 10, 1774,
Aged 74

Thomas King
died May 27, 1782,
Aged 65.

John May
died 10 June, 1780, aged 76

To the Memory of
Mr George Thomas, late of this
Parish, and in Testimony of his
honest and faithful Services, this Stone
was placed here by SAM BLACKWELL, Esq
he departed this Life 1st Day of April,
1774, aged 62

O N   H E A D   S T O N E S

	Died	Aged
John White, of North Cerney	1 May, 1768	77
John White	15 Apr 1760	58
Joan, the Wife of John White	13 Dec 1726	—
Edward Archer	2 Aug 1763	89
John Frampton, Sen	4 June, 1737	78
Anne his Wife	26 Dec 1752	85
Mary, the Wife of Jacob Frampton	16 Nov 1762	—
Hannah, the Wife of Ely Frampton, and Second Wife of Robert Humphreys	6 June, 1761	—
Roger Bullock	22 Feb 1729	62
Grace his Wife	18 Mar 1728	57
William Flburrough	3 June, 1747	77
Jane his Wife	2 Mar 1730	56
John Taylor	13 July, 1763	80
Suah his Wife	4 Nov 1761	78
Jonah, Son of Jonah and Mary Gorton	4 Aug 1731	18
Margare. his Wife	24 Dec 1779	84

XIII. AMPNEY ST. MARY,

OR

EASTBROOK.

THIS parish lies in the hundred of *Crowthorne and Minety* and deanry of *Cirencester*, about three miles east from *Cirencester*, and twenty-one miles so th-east from GLOUCESTER. It consists of rather more arable than of pasture and meadow land, and the soil is chiefly a strong clay. The common fields were inclosed at the same time with those of *Ampney Crucis*.

Ashbrook or *Eastbrook*, is the name by which it is usually known, and which it owes to a considerable part of the parish lying on the east side of the brook mentioned in the preceding parish, which runs likewise through it, and falls into the *Thames* about two miles to the east end of the river *Churn*. The road from *Cirencester* to LONDON passes also through this parish, and a portion of *Wiltshire*, which lies detached from the county, bounds it on the east.

The Church, which is dedicated to the *Virgin Mary*, is a small building, consisting only of one aile, without any tower. Some rude sculpture over the north door, and the round arches of the windows, seem to show that it was built in the time of the Saxons. It is situated near a mile to the southward of the village. The living is a perpetual curacy. The impropriation formerly belonged to the abbey of *Cirencester*, and is now held by the Heir of the late Samuel Blackwell, Esq. Thomas Boys, A. M. is the present curate, who was appointed in the year 1786 by Mrs Blackwell.

BENEFACTIONS.

For the Donation of ROBERT PLEYDELL, Esq. see *Ampney Crucis*.

There was given by the will of ———— the sum of twenty-eight pounds (seven pounds of which is now lost), and the annual interest of it directed to be distributed among the poor of this parish.

PRESENT LORD OF THE MANOR,

The Heir of the late SAMUEL BLACKWELL, Esq.

The following persons were summoned from this place by the Heralds in 1682 and 1683,

Robert Pleydall, Arm
Lewis Parker, Cler

At the Election in 1776, it does not appear that any Freeholder polled from this parish.

ANNUAL ACCOUNT OF MARRIAGES, BIRTHS, AND BURIALS, IN THIS PARISH

A D	Mar	Bir	Bur	A D	Mar	Bir	Bur	A D	Mar	Bir	Bur	A D	Mar	B	Pu
1781	·	5	3	1791				1801				1811			
1782	—	3		1792				1802				1812			
1783	—	5	1	1793				1803				1813			
1784	—	5	7	1794				1804				1814			
1785	2		6	1795				1805				1815			
1786				1796				1806				1816			
1787				1797				1807				1817			
1788				1798				1808				1818			
1789				1799				1809				1819			
1790				1800				1810				1820			

INSCRIPTIONS IN THE CHURCH.

JOHN HOWSE
died at the Still House,
July 22d, 1701, aged 94 years

WILLIAM CUIL,
of this Parish, Yeoman
died Nov 30th, 1735, aged 51

CATHARINE, Wife of WILLIAM
CUIL, she died Jan 27, 1768,
Aged 82 years

MARGERY, the Wife of
WILLIAM HINTON,
buried 2 June, 1690

JOHN WISE
died Sept, 8, 1720,
Aged 74

JOANNA, his Wife,
died January 1st, 1730,
Aged 75

JOHN HOWSE
died 18 March, 168_,

ELIZABETH, his Wife,
died 29 January, 1707

EDITH, the Wife of RICHARD HOWSE,
died Dec 17, 1716

ROBERT, Son of
WILLIAM and CATHARINE CUIL,
died Mi 30, 174), aged 29 years

JANE WISE, 1693

JANE WISE, 169_

JANE HOWSE,
died Dec 20, 16_

IN THE CHURCH YARD, ON TOMBS.

RICHARD, Son of JOHN and SARAH
HOWSE, died Jan 22, 1755, aged 47

EDITH, their Daughter,
died Feb 2, 1763, aged 65

RICHARD, the Son of JOHN and
ANN HOWSE, died Apr 2), 1766, aged 33

ANN, their Daughter,
died Feb 27, 1766, aged 31

THOMAS, their Son,
died Nov 11, 1775, aged 59

JOHN HOWSE, of the Chapel,
died 29th Sept 1731, Aged 7_

SARAH HOWSE, of the Chapel,
died 14 Mar 1721, Aged 5_

JANE, the Daughter of JOHN
and SARAH HOWSE, died
April 16, 1738, Aged 48

JOHN HOWSE
died Sept 10, 1765,
Aged 70

ANNE, Wife of JOHN HOWSE,
died July 7, 1774, Aged 64

ON HEAD STONES

	Died	Aged
R___ the Wife of Jonathan May,	_ May, 1761	7_
William Dr___,	6 ___ 1_8	)_

XIV. AMPNEY ST. PETER,

OR

EASTINGTON.

THIS parish lies in the hundred of *Crowthorne and Minety*, and deanery of *Cirencester*, about six miles east of that town, and twenty one miles southeast from Gloucester. It consists chiefly of meadow and pasture land, upon a light gravelly soil. The common fields have not been inclosed, as the parish is but small, and there is but little common age.

The name of *Eastington* was given to it, as it lies mostly to the eastward of the other two *Ampneys*.

An annual feast is held here the Sunday after *Saint Peter's Day*.

The church, which is dedicated to *Saint Peter*, is a small old building consisting only of one aisle, with a very low tower. The living is a perpetual curacy, the impropriation of which formerly belonged to the Abbey of Gloucester, and at present to the Bishop of that see, by whom the curates are appointed. Jeremiah Davies, M. A. is the present curate.

BENEFACTIONS

The return of donations to the poor made by the minister and church wardens is the same as for *Ampney Crucis*.

Two acres in the east field, and two in the west field of *Ashbrook*, and one in the ground near the church, called Mr Trinder's, in all five acres, were given towards the repairs of the church. And there is a small public common, called *the Moor*, open for the use of the poor all the year, the pasturage of which is remarkably rich.

It is not known with any certainty to whom the Manor now belongs or has belonged for many years. It is supposed by some to belong to the Heirs of Trinder, who formerly had property in the parish but is long since extinct. According to Sir Robert Atkyns, Robert Pleydell, Esq was the Lord of this Manor, at the beginning of the present century.

The only person summoned from this place by the Heralds in 1682, and 1683, was

The Heir of Mr Trinder

At the Election in 1776, five Freeholders polled from this Parish

ANNUAL ACCOUNT OF MARRIAGES, BIRTHS, AND BURIALS, IN THIS PARISH

A D	Mar	Bir	Bur	A D	Mar	Bir	Bur	A D	Mar	Bir	Bur	A D	Mar	Bir	Bur
1781	—	7	6	1791				1801				1811			
1782	1		4	1792				1802				1812			
1783	1			1793				1803				1813			
1784			11	1794				1804				1814			
1785				1795				1805				1815			
1786		9		1796				1806				1816			
1787				1797				1807				1817			
1788				1798				1808				1818			
1789				1799				1809				1819			
1790				1800				1810				1820			

INSCRIPTIONS

INSCRIPTIONS IN THE CHURCH.

Here lyeth the Body of
JOYCE TRINDER, the
late Wife of HENRY TRINDER,
who departed this Life
The first of Feb 1685

Here lyeth the Body of
EDMUND MILLES, who
departed this Life Oct 30
1683

In Memory of FRANCES,
Daughter of THOMAS and
CATHARINE LAWRENCE, who
died November 23, 1759,
Aged 30 years

ROBERT LAWRENCE
departed this Life
September 16, 1720,
Aged 73 years

IN THE CHURCH YARD, ON TOMBS

Guy Cull
died Sept 7, 1741,
in the 63d year of his age

Mary, his Wife,
died December 18, 1721,
Aged 47 years.

Guy, their Son,
died May 17, 1729,
Aged 20 years

Mary, the Wife of
John Allen,
died May 18, 1746,
Aged 34 years

John Howse
died September 23d, 1735,
Aged 42 years

John Howse sen
died Jan 10th 1746,
Aged 85 years

William Davies,
of Ampney Crucis,
died June 28, 1731,
Aged 82 years

Sabina, his Wife,
died Oct 28, 1731.
Aged 75 years

Betty, Daughter of
John and Margaret Howse,
died Mar 17, 1741, Aged 42

ON HEADSTONES.

	Died		Aged
Robert Taylor	5 Feb	1760	48
William Taylor	5 May,	1780	77
Betty, the Daughter of John and Margaret Howse,	17 Mar	1741	22
William Howse	4 Feb	1731	57
Edith, his Wife,	26 Jun	1747	63
Peter Emmett, alias Taylor,	29 July,	1748	66
Betty, his Wife,	30 Aug	1746	69
Daniel Tipper	13 Apr	1744	76
Anne, the Wife of Edward Bedford,	25 Mar	1745	—
Jane, the Wife of John Bedford,	15 Oct	1760	48
William then Son died at London	18 Aug	1767	48
Henry Creed sen	12 Dec	1764	—
Ann his Wife	1 June,	1765	-
Thomas Bishop	23 Mar	1781	36
John Bishop	19 Feb	1773	59
William Radway	15 Feb	1782	39
William Radway	14 Mar	1760	72

xv. ARLINGHAM.

THIS parish lies in the hundred of *Berkeley*, and deanery of GLOUCESTER, about ten miles nearly west from *Stroud*, and thirteen miles southwest from GLOUCESTER. It consists of good pasture and arable land, a deep rich soil and in general produces great crops of wheat and beans, some barley. There are likewise many orchards, the fruit of which make very good cider and perry, and walnuts grow here in great perfection, and are as plenty, if not more so, than in any other part of the county.

The situation of this parish being on the banks of the *Severn*, by which it is peninsulated in the shape of an horseshoe, some parts of it were formerly subject to inundations from that river, but, having been for several years under the care and inspection of the Commissioners of the Sewers, the banks are now kept in good repair.

There is a ferry here across the *Severn* to *Newnham*, the passage house belonging to which is on the opposite side. The river, in dry seasons, is fordable at low water, and loaded waggons pass through it without much danger. From an eminence, called *Barrow Hill*, there is a delightful and extensive prospect, it is said that thirty-six parish-churches are to be discerned from it in a clear day.

The name of *Arlingham* seems to be compounded from the British words Ar, Upon, Ing, a Meadow, or watery place, and Ham, a Village, i. e. a Village in a watery place.

In the parish register the following singular death is taken notice of among the burials of the year 1763, " Stephen Aldridge, who was suffocated by a flat-fish, which he unadvisedly put betwixt his " teeth when taken out of the net, but by a sudden spring it made its way into his throat, and killed " him in two minutes. It is here recorded as a warning to others, to prevent the like accident."

A feast is held here the Sunday after the Assumption of the *Blessed Virgin*.

In this parish are two places called *Overton* and *Milton Ende*, the former about one mile and half from the church, the latter about a mile, but they are not considered as hamlets.

There appears to have been anciently more than one manor in this parish. The Abbot of *St Augustine* in BRISTOL was seised of the manor of *Arlingham* 15 Ed I. A manor in *Arlingham* likewise belonged to the Abbey of *Flaxley*, which, after the dissolution of that monastery, was granted, 36 Hen VIII, to Sir ANTHONY KINGSTON. It, however, at this time, consists of but one manor, which has for seven Centuries been in the possession of the YATE family, who came into England with William the Conqueror, and it is now the joint property of LADY MILL, relict of the late RICHARD MILL, Baronet, and POWELL SNELL, Esq (niece and nephew of the late CHARLES YATE, Esq) to whom the estates and extensive fisheries in this parish, belonging to that ancient family, descended upon the death of the late JOHN YATE, Esq who died unmarried. LADY MILL resides in the old family mansion, called *The Court*, which is said to have been built near five hundred years. Around a side door, that leads into the court before the house, there is a good deal of sculpture in stone, executed in a style which proclaims its great antiquity.

A handsome old house, called *Slowwe*, which has long been in the possession of the HODGES family, being purchased by them of —— BRIDGMAN, 18 Elizabeth, is the residence of Mrs HODGES, relict of the Reverend Mr HODGES, the late Vicar. From some old writings belonging to the family, *Slowwe* is supposed to have been anciently a manor.

Mr GILES CARTER possesses a good estate in this parish, called *Puckpool*, which has long been in the family.

The church, which is dedicated to the *Virgin Mary*, is a long building, without any aisle, and has a good tower, with battlements, at the west end, containing six bells. It appears to have been founded in some of the early reigns subsequent to the introduction of the Norman architecture. A part of the ground whereon it stands was given by one of the YATE family. The inside is very neat, being remarkably well pewed, a good gallery at the west end, and two handsome brass chandeliers. The pulpit cloth and cushion, which are of purple velvet richly fringed, were given by LADY MILL, and a handsome service of Communion plate, by the late JOHN YATE, Esq. In the windows are some good painted glass, exhibiting the portraits of Saints.

The living is a vicarage. It was anciently held by the priory of *Leonard's Stanley*, to which it was given by Roger Lord Berkeley. In 1500, the abbey of St Peter GLOUCESTER presented to it. The advowson and impropriation were sold, a few years ago, by Henry Fox BRIDGMAN, Esq to Mr ELIZABETH ROGERS, who possesses a good estate here, which formerly belonged to the family of BYCK, at which she resides. The Vicarage House, which has been lately repaired, occupied by Mr Hodges, the relict of the late Vicar.

The following account of this place is taken from the before mentioned ancient MS in the possession of the EARL of BERKELEY.

" *Arlingham*, alias *Erlingham*, in Domesday Book written *ErlingeLane*, is one of those five interior manors or hamlets (parcell of the great manor of *Berkeley*), that adjoyne to the river of *Severne*, and on that part or side extendeth to the middle of the channell, wheresoever for the time the channell is, which often changeth its course.

" It is a parish of rich ground, and faire extent, wherein till of late years have byn several manors, the inheritance of several lords, the principall whereof is now the freehold of *Richard Yate*, Esq. All of

them

them within the lee or laweday of the hundred of *Berkeley*, holden at *Berkeley towre*, twice every yeare, whereat all the male inhabitants of this parish, above twelve yeares old, make their appearance

" In this parish the abbot of *St Augustines* by *Briftoll* had a manor raised in length of time out of divers lands and tenements given unto them at several times by the lord Berkeleys, which after the diffolution of that monaftery, was given to the dean and chapter of *Briftoll*

" In this parish the abbott of the monaftery of *Flaxley* had a little manor, raised like the former, by the gifts at several times of the lord Berkeleys, and other freeholders, which at the diffolution was granted to Sir Anthony Kingfton

" Alfo another little manor called *Wike*, alias *Arlinghams Wike*, now belongs to the *Yate* family

" A reputed manor called *le Berewe*, alias *the Berowes*

" In this parish the pryor of *Stanley*, thus *Leonard's Stanley*, a cell to the great monaftery of St Peter's, *Gloucefter*, held divers lands

" The moft remarkeable han bletts or names of places within this parish, whiche in the fcituation is a recke of land, iftmos or peninfula, are *Wike*, alias *Arlingham*, the *Berue*, the *Slo*, alias *Sloo*, *Overton*, i e the over towne, *Middleton*, alias *Milton*, alias *Millon end*, i e the middle of the towne, or the end of the middle town, and *Southend*

" In this parish alfo were divers lands and tenements dedicated to the fervice of the bleffed *Virgin Mary*, to whom alfo I thinke the parish church was dedicated, which lands in the time of kinge Henry the fourth were under the difpofinge and lettinge of *Procuratores frutiæ beatæ Mariæ Virginis de Arlingham*, the houfe the preift then before dwelt in, and after, was, and yet is, called our ladies preifts houfe

" In *Berkeley* caftle, is a deed made in 46 E 3 between John de Yate and 17 others, the chief inhabitants of *Arlingham*, on the one part, and Nicholas Wifhonger, Cementarian de Glou'r, of the other part, which perticularly fhews their compofition made with him for the buildinge of the tower or belfree wherein the bells do hange, and, of the moft part, if not all, the church of *Arlingham*

" Of able men for the warre, between 20 and 60 yeares of age, were in 6° Jacobi, which appeared at a general mufter before HENRY LORD BERKELEY, the Lieutenant of the county —98 And are now of trayned foldiers, under WILLIAM THORNE, Efq their captain, 4 corflets, and 12 muskets "

B E N E F A C T I O N S

JOHN YATE, Efq gave by will, 1751, an annuity of forty pounds, arifing from eftates in *Arlingham*, to fuch poor perfons, and in fuch proportions, as he poffeffor or poffeffors of the eftates, from whence the annuity arifeth, fhall in writing direct, or, in default of fuch direction, by the minifter and churchwardens, not intended for the eafe of the parifh rates, but as an additional fupport of the poor, vefted in Dame Dorothy Mill, and Powell Snell, Efq

N B Mrs MARY YATE, mother of John Yate, Efq carried into execution the will of her fon, refpecting this and the following charity, by proper deeds and conveyances

JOHN YATE, Efq alfo gave by will, 1754, an annuity of forty pounds, for the maintenance and fupport of a fchool mafter, to teach poor children of the parifh to read and write, and to inftruct them in the church catechifm, vefted in the fame hands as the former

Capt THOMAS LISTON, 1684, uncertain how given, gave to four poor perfons, not receiving relief from the parifh rates, a rent charge of ten fhillings, payable annually out of a field in the parifh, called *Woolcraft* at the difcretion of the minifter and churchwardens

ROBERT EARL OF LEICESTER, by an Act of Parliament in the 14th of Queen Elizabeth, founded an hofpital at *Warwick*, for the maintaining of 12 poor perfons of *Warwick*, *Kenelworth*, and *Stratford*, in the county of *Warwick*, and *Wotton under Edge* and *Arlingham* in this county The vacancies to be fupplied by equal turns, and the recommendation to be figned by the minifter and churchwardens of each parifh

The foregoing BENEFACTIONS from the Returns

Mrs YATE, in the year 1760, erected a houfe, at her own expence, for the benefit of the fchool which had been endowed by her fon, John Yate, Efq She likewife gave in her life-time, forty pounds annually for clothing the poor, which donation is continued by Lady Mill

Mrs YATE further left by will, 1777, ten fhillings for a fermon to be preached yearly on Good Friday, and the fame fum for one on Afcenfion day, and forty fhillings to be diftributed in bread to the poor on each of thofe days

INCUMBENTS	PATRONS	INCUMBENTS	PATRONS
1570 Robert Downs,	Queen Elizabeth	1732 John Webb, M A	Edward Toye, Efq
1573 William Downs,	Ditto	1750 William Toye, B A	Henry Toye, Efq
1598 Henry Child,	Ditto	1770 William Davies, M A	Henry Toye Bridgeman, Efq Abraham Turner Efq and Thomas Jacob White, Gent
1653 John Giles,	Bifhop of Glofter		
1681 W Churchuck, M A	Jos Brideman, Efq		
1689 Richard Butler, M A	John and James Bridgeman, Efqs		
The above from Sir ROBERT ATKINS		1756 Thomas Wells, B A	Elizabeth Rogers
		1760 Elifha Selwyn, Cler	Ditto
		1763 Thomas Hodges, M A	Ditto
		1764 Thomas Hickes, M A	Ditto

PRESENT

PRESENT PROPRIETORS OF THE MANOR,

Dame DOROTHY MILL, and POWELL SNELL, Esq.

The only perfon fummoned from this place by the Heralds in 1682 and 1683, was

Richard Yate, Gent

At the Election in 1776, thirty two Freeholders polled from this parifh

ANNUAL ACCOUNT OF MARRIAGES, BIRTHS, AND BURIALS, IN THIS PARISH.

A.D	Mar	Bir	Bur	A.D	Mar	Bir	Bur	A.D	Mar	Bir	Bur	A.D	Mar	Bir	Bur
1781	4	13	5	1791				1801				1811			
1782	7	14	7	1792				1802				1812			
1783	4	18	8	1793				1803				1813			
1784	7	13	24	1794				1804				1814			
1785	3	15	14	1795				1805				1815			
1786				1796				1806				1816			
1787				1797				1807				1817			
1788				1798				1808				1818			
1789				1799				1809				1819			
1790				1800				1810				1820			

INSCRIPTIONS IN THE CHURCH.

ON A VERY HANDSOME MARBLE MONUMENT IS THE FIGURE OF HOPE, KNEELING, HOLDING A HEART; AND UPON A LABEL IS WRITTEN,

" An Offering of a free Heart I give thee O my God "

Over which, on an oval fhield, are the Arms of YATE, viz Azure, a Fefs, in chief 2 Mullets Or

Motto,—*" Quo virtus vocat "*

Here lyeth the Body of JOHN YATE, Efq Lord of this Manour
The laft male Heir of his Family, and only Son of CHARLES YATE, Efq
He was in the Commiffion of the Peace, one of the Deputy Lieutenants of
this County, and Deputy Conftable of St Braivel's Caftle Defcended
from a long Race of worthy Anceftors He improved his native Virtues
with every amiable Qualification, that gains the Love and Veneration
of Mankind A lively fenfe and uniform Practice of Religion,
accompanied with Candour, Affability, and Sweetnefs of Temper, filled him
with Joy and inward Satisfaction Charity, Compaffion, and Univerfal
Benevolence, chiefly directed the Difpofal of his ample Fortune
Of pureft Morals, of an irreproachable Life, of filial Affection,
of Sincerity in Friendfhip, of true Honour, of Integrity of Heart,
He was an uncommon Example, with this admirable Affemblage
of Virtues, joyned to a polite Tafte of Literature,
The Scholar in Him accomplifhed the Gentleman,
As the Chriftian perfected the Man
In the Flower of Youth,
expecting, but not fearing, Death,
He willingly refigned his Soul to God on the 24th May, 1758, aged 27
To whofe ever dear and honoured Memory,
this Monument is erected
by his moft truly affectionate,
and much afflicted
Mother,
M Y

ON A HANDSOME MARBLE MONUMENT, ARE THE FOLLOWING ARMS AND INSCRIPTION VIZ

Quarterly, 1ft, Azure, a Fefs, in chief 2 Mullets Or, for YATE, 2d, Gules, a Cheveron between 3 Croffes patty Argent, for BERKELEY, 3d, Gules, a Buck's head caboffhed Or, for Box, 4th, a Lion rampant, for PRICE —impaling 3 lions heads erafed in chief, and a cinquefoil in bafe, on which impalement is an Efcocheon of Pretence, of quarterly 4 martlets —Motto, " *Qua virtus vera*

Bleffed are the Merciful, for they fhall obtain Mercy

Near this Place
Lyeth the Body of CHARLES YATE, Efq.
who died the 11th of November 1738, aged 46.

He was one of his Majefties Juftices of the Peace, as likewife
Deputy Lieutenant of this County He difcharged with Juftice
and Equity to all, and with Honour and Reputation to Himfelf,
the Offices of a Magiftrate and a Chriftian His Authority
might have made him refpected whilft alive , but it
was the peculiar Sweetnefs and Affability of his
Manners, his great Kindnefs and Humanity
to all, his agreeable Chearfulnefs of
Difpofition, annexed to a virtuous mind,
which could alone render him fo
truly regretted when dead

Memoriæ Sacrum optimi Patris,
I Y

ON HANDSOME MARBLE MONUMENTS

Near this Place lie the remains
of HENRIETTA MARGARETTA-DOROTHEA
MILL, Elder Daughter of SIR RICHARD
MILL, Bart of Mattisfort, Hants, by
DOROTHEA, fecond Daughter of RICHd
WARREN, Efq of the Redcliffe, Somerfet,
who died 28 July, 1779, Æt 15

In Memory of ANNA MARIA EAST COURT,
of Shipton Moyne in the County of Wilts,
and one of the laft Defcendants of the
Ancient Family of YATE, of Arlingham,
Died 19th Day Sept 1783, æt 74
Wearied with Misfortunes, and a
Complication of Diforders,
Which fhe fuftained with that Patience,
the effect of true Religion,
She funk full of Honour, Piety and Virtue

On a Lozenge, Arms and Impalement of YATE
as above defcribed

Here lyeth MARY YATE, Widow
of CHARLES YATE, Efq Parents of JOHN
YATE, Efq. their only Son, both whofe
Virtues fhe highly efteemed as
giving her the greateft Confolation
during the many Years fhe furvived
them , hoping, through our Bleffed
Lord Jefus Chrift, for a joyful
Meeting in his heavenly Kingdom,
there to unite in Hymns of Praife
and Thankfgiving to our great and
Glorious Redeemer for Ever, Amen.
Died January 17, 1777,
Æt 77

ON FLAT STONES

Arms, Quarterly, 1ft and 4th, YATE, 2d,
BERATILY, 3d, Box, as above defcribed

Here refteth (in Hope of a better
Refurrection) the Body of that
prudent and pious Gentleman
RICHARD YATE, Efquire,
who, after an exemplarie Godlie
Life well finifhed, departed
in Peace, and entered into Blifs,
Nov 2, 1661, aged 78 Years

Here refteth the Bodies of two
Daughters of RICHARD YATE, of
this Parifh, Efq by ELIZABETH his Wife, who died,
JOYCE, March the 16th, 1689,
MARY, July the 18th, 1691,
Aged 14 Weeks, 5 Day

Arms and Quarterings of YATE, as thofe defcribed—impaling a lion rampant, for PRICE

Here lyeth
the Body of COLONEL RICHARD YATE,
Lord of this Manour,
who departed this Life the 17th day
of June, 1701, aged 41

Alfo the Body of
ELIZABETH the Daughter of MAJOR
THOMAS PRICE, of Glo'ft and Wife of
RICHARD YATE, of this Parifh, Efq
who departed this Life July 14, 1705,
Aged 40

I N

IN THE CHANCEL

ON A HANDSOME FLAT PYRAMIDICAL MARBLE MONUMENT AGAINST THE NORTH WALL

Arms, 2 flanches, on a fefs 3 crefcents, for HODGES;—impaling a goat, ftanding upon a child in a cradle on a mount, under an oak fructed, for DAVIES

In a Vault
near this Marble, are depofited the
Remains of the Rev THOMAS HODGES, A M
late Vicar of this Parifh   With him ended
the Male Line of an ancient and refpectable
Family, of Slowwe, in this Place
He died Feb 3, 1784, aged 29

ON A WHITE MARBLE MONUMENT AGAINST THE SAME WALL

Sacred be this Marble
to the Memory of Mr. JOHN HODGES,
Youngeft Son of
THOMAS HODGES, Gent of Slowwe,
in this Parifh,
who departed this Life July 10, 1780,
Aged 24

ON FLAT STONES

Hic jacet
RICHARDUS BUTLER,
Artium Magifter, necnon
hujus Ecclefiæ Vicarus,
qui obiit vicefimo feptimo
die Julii { Ætatis 73
Anno { Salutis 1732

Here lyeth the Body of ELIZABETH,
the Wife of RICHARD BUTLER,
Vicar, who departed this Life
April 24, 1727

Here alfo lyeth the Body of
MARY, the Daughter of RICHARD
and ELIZABETH BUTLER, who was
buried April the 1ft, 1726, ætat 17

Here refteth in Hope of a glorious
Refurrection, the Body of THOMAS BYCKE,
Gent who departed this Life March 19, 16 2,
Aged 47 Years

Alfo the Body of MARY, the Relict
of the aforefaid THOMAS BYCKE, Gent
who left this Life the 30th of Auguft, 1699,
Ætatis fuæ 70

ELIZABETH, Wife of WILLIAM BYCK,
Gent departed this Life the
9th of July, 1714, aged 44

THOMAS, the Son of WILLIAM BYCK,
Gent and ELIZABETH his Wife, died 2 Dec 1688

JOHN, Son of WILLIAM BYCK, and ELIZABETH
his Wife, died Auguft 14, 1706

THOMAS (the fecond), third Son of
WILLIAM BYCK, Gent died 28 March,
1694

MARY, the Wife of SAMUEL ROWLES,
of this Parifh, and Daughter of
RICHARD CHINN, of Newnham,
Mariner, who departed this Life
the 4th of March, 1730, aged 35

Alfo the faid SAMUEL ROWLES,
who departed this Life 9 Dec 1733,
Aged 44 Years

Sarah, Wife of the Reverend William Toye,
Vicar of this Parifh, died Dec 15, 1709,
aged 59

IN THE CHURCH YARD, ON TOMBS.

RICHARD CARTER Phyfician,
died 17 March, 1656
JOHN CARTER
died 19 June, 1690, aged 83
JOHN CARTER Jun
died Oct 26, 172 aged 52
ELIZABETH Wife of JOHN CARTER,
died 8 Jun 1730 aged 36
MARY the Wife of
WILLIAM CARTER
late of this Parifh, Gent
died 20 April 1692, aged 68
JONAS ROBERTS,
died April 1745 ætat 58
MARY his Wife
died Feb 20 1767, aged 67
THOMAS CARTER, Di
died Ji 1767, aged 71
RICHARD CARTER, Di
died 20 Nov m 1776 aged 64
RICHARD CARTER, Son of
the above RICHARD CARTER Di
died M 16 84 aged 56 Years

RICHARD CARTER, of Puckpoole,
died Jan 14, 1733, aged 55
JANE his Wife
buried 4 March, 1720, aged 30
GILES WILLIAM, and ELIZABETH,
their Children, died Infants
WILLIAM CARTER, of Puckpoole,
died Feb 27, 1743, aged 53
ELIZABETH his Daughter
died Oct 5 1734 aged 2
RICHARD SARA, WILLIAM SARAH,
and WILLIAM died Infants
SARAH, Daughter of GILES and
ANN CARTER died May 2, 1760
aged 2 Months

MARY Wife of WILLIAM CARTER,
died July 18, 1774 aged 48

JOHN CARTER, Yeoman,
died 27 Dec 1778, æt 78
SARAH, his Widow
died 18 March, 1786 æt 82
THOMAS their fecond Son,
died Oct 19, 1778 aged 42

THOMAS HODGES Sen
died 10 April 1705, aged 45
MARGARET his Wife
died 10 Nov 1 22 aged near 64
JOHN THOMAS, and MARY, their
Children died Infants

THOMAS HODGES
died 25 March 1729, aged 58
MARY his Relict
died 17 Jun 1 f aged 69
MARY ANN and MARGARET,
their Children, died Infants

Γ

RICHARD

RICHARD BUTT, of Overton,
who died   1700.

THOMAS, the Son of RICHARD BUTT,
who was buried   1698

Sacred to the Memory
of THOMAS HODGES, Gentleman,
who departed this Life
Feb 13, 1765, aged 41
Blest with an even Temper,
and in the Enjoyment
of a competent Fortune,
he lived without Reproach,
esteemed, respected, and beloved,
by his Friends, Acquaintance, and
Relations.
He discharged the Duties
of his earthly Station,
with Credit to Himself,
and to the general Satisfaction
of all who knew him

No Rhetoric adorns this humble Stone,
Praise when deserv'd, consists in Truth
alone

ELIZABETH COWLEY,
Relict of JOHN COWLEY,
late of Goffington, in the Parish
of Slimbridge, and one of the
three Daughters and Coheirs
of EDWARD NEEME, late of
Goffington aforesaid, who died
Jan. 20, 1743, aged 80 Years

WILLIAM FRYER, Sen
died Nov 27, 1735, aged 35
MARY his Wife
died Jan 28, 1742, aged 42.
WILLIAM, their Son, died an Infant.
MARY, their Daughter
died Dec 9, 1772, aged 46.
SARAH, Wife of WILLIAM FRYER,
died June 5, 1774, aged 49
WILLIAM, their Son, died
March 17, 1778, aged 15
WILLIAM FRYER died
April 27 1784
ANNA, second Wife of
WILLIAM FRYER.

MARY, Wife of JOHN ROWLES, Sen.
died 24 Jan 1759, aged 56.
JOHN ROWLES, died
April 10, 1780, aged 83.

JOHN ROWLES, Sen
died May 6, 1716, aged 45

ABIGAIL his Wife
died 6 August, 1716, aged 49.

ELIZABETH, Wife of HENRY BRETT,
late of the City of Bristol, and
Daughter of JOHN and ABIGAIL
ROWLES, of this Parish,
died 21 June, 1746, aged 44

MARY, the Daughter of
WILLIAM and JOAN CARTER,
and Wife of WILLIAM ALDRIDGE,
died 19 Nov 1729, aged 33

Hic jacet GULIELMUS LEIGHTON
(Mathesis), Filius THOMÆ & MARIÆ
LEIGHTON, qui obiit 28 Oct 1752,
Ætat suæ 46

RICHARD WEBB, Senior, RICHARD
WEBB, Junior MARY LEIGHTON, the
Wife of RICHARD WEBB, Junior,
the first Husband,
THOMAS LEIGHTON, the 3d,
and the Daughter of WILLIAM and
MARY BYCK, died March 28, 1741,
Aged 78.

THOMAS LEIGHTON, Gent.
died Dec 4, 1784 aged 84.

JOHN FRYER, of Overtown Yeoman,
died January 1, 1757, aged 62

MARY his Relict,
died May 17, 1767, Aged 66.

EDWARD SALE, Yeoman,
died June 13, 1784 æt 52

Two of his Children by MARY
his Wife, died Young

MARY, Wife of RICHARD THOMAS,
died June 6, 1756 æt 83

ON FLAT STONES.

SARAH, Daughter of WILLIAM BYCK,
died 2, Dec 1694 aged 34

ELIZABETH, Daughter of WM BYCK,
died January 1, 1676, aged 5

JANE, Daughter of WILLIAM BYCK,
died Jan 12, 1676, aged 20 Years

THOMAS LEIGHTON, Senior,
buried May 7, 1757

MARY, Daughter of THOMAS
and MARY LEIGHTON, buried
Sept 30, 1763

MARY, Relict of WILLIAM BYCKE,
Yeoman, died 11 June, 1701, aged 72.

WILLIAM BYCKE, Yeoman,
died Feb 2, 1671, aged 67

GILES HODGES, of this Parish,
died April 25, 1765, aged 65

ON HEAD STONES.

	Died	Aged		Died	Aged
Sarah, Daughter of Thomas and Sarah Watts,	18 Dec 1755	21	William Roberts, Yeoman,	27 July, 1774	38
Ann, Wife of Thomas Aldridge	6 Sept 1769	—	William Rasher	21 Nov 1783	62
Joan Wife of Thomas Carter, Sen	8 Dec 1724	60	William Aldridge	24 Mar 1769	72
Thomas Carter, Sen	11 July, 1740	80	Elinor his Wife	6 Aug 1774	75
Ann, Relict of Thomas George,	7 Apr 1762	63	Joseph Merry	8 Oct 1759	58
Dinah, Wife of John Harris, Daughter of William Paine of Westbury,	27 July, 1684	27	Mary his Wife	27 Jan 1765	70
Joseph, Son of John and Elizabeth Styles,	26 Feb 1757	33	Daniel Fryer	31 July, 1712	63
Mary their Daughter,	13 Feb 1760	35	Thomas Fryer, Jun	22 July, 1714	40
Charles Rowles	25 July, 1761	38	Thomas Fryer, Sen	27 Sept 1761	72
Thomas Rowles	26 Dec 1770	53	Elizabeth his Wife	27 Mar 1736	34
Charles Clark	3 Aug 1773	56	John Stiles, Sen	11 Feb 1739	38
Hannah his Wife	20 May, 1774	57	William his Son	2 Mar 1756	25
			Ann Bendall	15 Mar 1752	70
			Ann Watts	5 July, 1751	42

THIS parish lies in the lower part of the hundred of *Tewkesbury*, and in the deanery of *Worcester*, about two miles nearly east from *Tewkesbury*, and eleven miles north from GLOCESTER. It consists of rich meadow and pasture land, with a considerable proportion of deep arable.

The soil is chiefly clay, in some parts it is of a light sandy nature, and generally produces good crops of wheat, barley, and beans. There are likewise many orchards here, from the fruit of which good cyder and excellent perry are made.

The river *Caran* or *Carant* rises near the northern borders of this parish, and falls into the *Avon*, a little above *Tewkesbury*, and a small brook called *Turle*, after passing through the southern part of it, empties itself into the *Swilgate*, not far from that town. The road from *Tewkesbury* to *London* passes through it. The name of this place was originally *Eastchurch*, and it was so called from its lying to the eastward of *Tewkesbury*, but it is now written *Ashchurch*.

Several hamlets make a part of this parish, viz. 1 *Northway and Newton* 2 *Pamington* 3 *Iddington*, and 4 *Aston upon Carn* or *Hamman's Downs*, or *Home Downs* (so called from Robert Hamman, who formerly possessed a very considerable estate in this neighbourhood), and *Natton*, are places in the tithing of *Fiddington*. *Ashchurch*, which gives name to the parish, and in which the church stands, consists but of two farms, and is in the tithing of *Northway and Newton*.

In the hamlet of *Northway and Newton* there is a spring of mineral water, of much the same quality as that at *Cheltenham*. About forty years ago, a pump was erected over it, and endeavours were used by the inhabitants of *Tewkesbury* to make it a place of resort, but, from its vicinity to *Cheltenham*, they did not succeed. Many people, however, having lately found benefit from this water in scorbutic complaints, the plan is revived, and, it is said, a subscription has been proposed for building a pump room, &c.

CHARLES HAYWARD of *Quedgley*, Esq. has a considerable estate and manor in the hamlet of *Northway and Newton*. A good estate in the same hamlet belongs to ROBERT MORRIS, Esq.

LORD CRAVEN, to whom the manor of *Pamington* belongs, has a good estate in that tithing.

HENRY WAKEMAN, of *Beckford*, Esq. holds the manor of *Aston*.

MRS KEMBLE, the relict of THOMAS KEMBLE, Esq. holds, together with the manor, considerable property in the hamlet of *Fiddington*, as does JOHN MORRIS, of *The Sheephouse* near GLOCESTER, Esq. late High Sheriff of the county, who has a manor and good estate in this dale.

The church, which is dedicated to Saint ———, is a large ancient building, with battlements on the south side, and a handsome tower at the west end, containing six bells. On the north side there is a large aile, which was anciently called *Saint Thomas's Chapel*. In the window of the aile are the remains of some good painted glass, consisting of figures and devices. The living is a perpetual curacy, annexed to *Tewkesbury*, notwithstanding which, the incumbent, at the visitation, is styled the *Rector of Ashchurch*. The impropriation, as well as the patronage, belongs to JOHN PARSONS, of *Kemmerton*, Esq.

BENEFACTIONS

WILLIAM FERRERS, Esq. gave by will, in the year 1625, to be disposed of by the churchwardens of the parish of *Ashchurch*, with consent of such testator's kindred as should inhabit in the said parish, unto and amongst the poor people inhabiting within the said parish of *Ashchurch*, in annuity, or yearly rent issuing out of the manor of *Skellingthorpe*, in the county of *Lincoln*, the annual amount of which is ten pounds, seventeen shillings, and eight pence, and is paid by the governors of Christ Hospital, *London*. —See the inscription on his monument.

THOMAS HARRIS, citizen of *London*, gave by will (date not mentioned) to be distributed to such poor widows and housekeepers as are not upon the parish book, the interest of fifty pounds, vested in Nicholas Smithfield, of *Worcester*, Esq. the annual produce of which is two pounds ten shillings.

CHARLES PARSONS, of Breedon, Gent. gave by will, 30th December 17— to be distributed yearly, in the church, in bread or money, every Christmas-day, to such poor people as attend divine service in the said parish church of *Ashchurch*, an annuity or rent issuing out of land in *Northam*, in the parish of *Breedon*, in the county of *Worcester*. Thomas Mumford, of *Northam* foresaid, Yeoman, is owner of the lands out of which the annuity issues, and the annual produce is one pound.

Sir Robert Atkyn says, a house, and the church yard, and three ridge of land, worth two pounds, six shillings, and eight pence yearly, are given towards the repair of the church.

INCUMBENTS	PATRONS		INCUMBENTS	PATRONS
1703 Joseph Hatch,	——————		1746 Matt Bloxam, M A	John Parſons, Eſq.
1728 William Williams,	John Parſons, Eſq		1768 John Darke, M A	J Parſons, Eſq his ſon.

PRESENT LORDS OF THE MANORS,
Aſhchurch, and *Northway*
CHARLES HAYWARD, Eſq.

Pamington
LORD CRAVEN.

Fiddington
MRS KEMBLE.
JOHN MORRIS, Eſq.

Aſton upon Caran
HENRY WAKEMAN, Eſq

The following perſons were ſummoned from the hamlets of this pariſh by the Heralds in 1682 and 1683.

From *Fiddington*   From *Aſton*
Thomas Clutterbuck   William Dowdeſwell, Gent
From *Northway.*
Richard Darke, Gent

At the Election in 1776, Twenty-two Freeholders polled from this pariſh and its hamlets.

ANNUAL ACCOUNT OF MARRIAGES, BIRTHS, AND BURIALS, IN THIS PARISH

A D.	Mar	Bir	Bur	A D	Mar	Bir	Bur	A D	Mar	Bir	Bur	A D.	Mar	Bir	Bur
1781	4	25	7	1791				1801				1811			
1782	2	20	9	1792				1802				1812			
1783	2	14	8	1793				1803				1813			
1784	4	16	10	1794				1804				1814			
1785	4	17	18	1795				1805				1815			
1786				1796				1806				1816			
1787				1797				1807				1817			
1788				1798				1808				1818			
1789				1799				1809				1819			
1790				1800				1810				1820			

INSCRIPTIONS IN THE CHURCH

ON A MONUMENT AGAINST THE SOUTH WALL IS THE EFFIGIES OF AN OLD MAN, AT HALF LENGTH, HABITED AS A CITIZEN OF LONDON IN A LIVERY GOWN, AND HOLDING IN HIS RIGHT HAND A PAIR OF GLOVES, AND UNDER HIS LEFT IS A HUMAN SKULL, WITH THE FOLLOWING MOTTO SURROUNDING IT

Live well and die never,
Die well and live ever

Over the Image are the following arms viz On a bend cottiſed 3 Horſe ſhoes, a Creſcent for difference, Creſt—an Oſtrich, in the beak an Horſe ſhoe

MEMORIÆ SACRUM
WILLIAM FERRERS, Citiſen of London, ſecond ſonn of
ROGER FERRERS, of Fiddington Gent had 3 Wives, with
whom hee lived 50 Yeares moſt lovingly, and by whom
hee ſaw himſelf a happy Father and Grandfather, all
his Children dyed before him Hee preferred many of
his Brothers, of his Kindred, and of his Countrymen, and left
behinde him ſeveral Workes of Piety, As to the Poore
of this Place where hee was borne 10l per Annum
10 a Preacher in this Pariſh, and to the mending of the
Highways about Fiddington, To every one 5l
Yearly for ever Moreover he gave 30l yearly for
ever towards a free ſchool in Tewxbery, and 5l
per Ann to the Poore of that place, with ſeverall
Guiftes to the Poore, and other pious Uſes in and about
London Hee likewiſe gave large Legacies both
in Lands and Monyes to his 3 Grand Children,
Brothers, and Kindred Hee departed this Life the
26 Day of September, 1625, and lyes buried in Allhallows
Church, in Lumbard Street, London

THOMAS FERRERS, his Brother, and part Executor
with Love and Care built this ſmall Monument

ON A BRASS PLATE AGAINST THE SAME WALL.

Arms, Azure, 5 escallops in cross Or—Crest,
on a rock Argent, a falcon close Or

Memoriæ ROBERTI BARKER, Gener
Qui Phtisi Laborans, & cupiens
dissolvi, voti Compos fuit 3tio die
Martii Anno Dni 1671mo, ætatis vero
Suæ 40

ON MONUMENTS AGAINST THE NORTH WALL

Here lyeth the Body of JOHN
HAWLING, who departed this Life
the 2, Day of July, 1662   JOANE
his Wife died 2, March, 1678

Here lyeth the Body of MARGARET,
the Wife of RICHARD DARKE, Gent
of Aulston, and only Daughter
of   Wood, of   ,
, aged 18

Also MARGARET, the   of SAMUEL
Wood, who   this Life
the   Day of August, 1699

In Memory of
Mr WILLIAM HAYNES of Ashchurch,
Senior, who died in the Year 1654

Also of MARY his Wife, Daughter of
RICHARD DARKE of Aulston, Gent who
departed the 26 Day of Feb 1652

Also of WILLIAM HAYNES, the Son of Mr WILLIAM
HAYNES, Senior, who departed this Life the 20
day of May, 1721, aged 69 Years

Likewise MARY his Wife Daughter of
THOMAS SURMAN, of Tredington, Gent
who died March the 10th, 1719, aged 65

Arms, a cross moline—impaling a fess between 3
fleurs de lis

In Memory of GEORGE BANNISTER,
Senior, Gent who died March 6, 1734,
Aged 57

SARAH his Wife died 12 May, 1729, aged 56

ON FLAT STONES

Here lyeth the Body of ROGER
FERRERS, Gent who departed this
Life the 31st of Dec Anno Domini 1579

Here also lyeth the Body of THOMAS FERRERS,
Son of the aforesaid ROGER,
Citizen and Merchant of London,
who departed this Life 3 day of Dec
1636, being aged threescore Years.

In Memory of ELIZABETH CROSS,
late of Dixon, in this County
She died July 30, 1753, aged 56 Years.

Here lyeth the Body of JOSEPH
PENNELL, of Northway, who departed
this Life the 30th day of June, 1688,
Aged 45 Years

Here lyeth ROGER FERRERS, and ANN his Wife,
Who lived together a Godly Life,
They lived together some Twenty-four Years,
A Virtuous Life as doth appeare
The Almes that they have left behinde,
Their Souls with Christ in Heaven do finde

ROGER FERRERS, Gent deceased the first
day of Januarie, 1583   And ANNI his
Wife deceased the seaventh of February,
1605

CHARLES, the Son of WILLIAM and
MARY HAYNES (his Wife was of
Ashchurch) died 24 March, 1712,
Aged 24 Years

In Memory of BENJAMIN HAYNES,
of Ashchurch (Yeoman) He died May 17,
1762, aged 63 Years

Also ANN his Wife died June
9, 1760, aged 63 Years

Sacred to the Memory of
JOHN DOBBINS, Gent late of Tewkesbury,
in this County He departed this Life
July 26, 1773, aged 74 Years

Here also lieth the Body of
HENRY CLIFFTON, Gent Nephew to
the above JOHN DOBBINS, who
departed this Life Dec 18, 1779, aged 46

WILLIAM HAYNES, Gent
died June 2, 1771

FRANCES his Daughter, by ANN his
Wife, died 29 Feb 1772

MARY, Daughter of RICHARD and ANN
BEST, of Fiddington, died Nov.
4, 1771, aged 11 Years

Here lyeth interred the Body of
NICHOLAS SMITHSEND,
of Fiddington, Gent who departed this
Life the 8 Day of June, 1697, aged 82,
who lived comfortable and happy with
ALICE his Wife, 54 Years and upwards

ALICE his Wife departed this Life
the 16 day of June, 1697, aged 82

Here lyeth the Body of THOMAS
SMITHSEND, of Fiddington, Gent
Son of NICHOLAS and ALICE his
Wife, who departed this Life the
5 day of Nov 1724, aged 73

Also the Body of ELIZABETH
SMITHSEND, daughter of the above
named NICHOLAS SMITHSEND, who
departed this Life Feb 2, 1728, aged
85 Years and Seven Months.

Here lyeth the Body of NICHOLAS
SMITHSLND, of Walton Cardiff,
Gent who died Sept 16, 1727, aged 82

Also here lyeth the Body of THOMAS
SMITHSEND, Grandson of the above
said NICHOLAS SMITHSEND, who departed
this Life the 27 of Sept 1742, aged 1 Year
11 Months

NICHOLAS SMITHSLND, Gent
died 10 Aug 1746, aged 58.

Also here lies the Body of SARAH SMITHSEND,
Wife of the said NICHOLAS SMITHSEND
She died the 1, Day of March, 1782,
Aged 74 Years

ANNE, the Wife of NICHOLAS
SMITHSEND, of Walton Cardiffe,
Gent departed this Life 26 Dec
1723, aged 70

ELIZABETH, Daughter of NICHOLAS
and ANNE SMITHSEND, died the 23d
of April, 1734, aged 39 Years and 6 Months

ON A WHITE MARBLE GRAVE STONE

Arms, a bend wavy—impaling a cheveron between
3 griffons heads—Crest, a swan

Here lyes interred the Body of
THOMAS SMITHSEND,
late of TEWKESBURY, in the
County of GLOUCESTER, Gent who
departed this Life, in hopes
of a joyful Resurrection, the 17 of
May, 1717, aged 26 Years

This Stone is fixed here by his
Widow, in respect to his Memory

Also PAULINA, the Wife of
THOMAS SMITHSEND, died
October 28, 1735, aged 51

Here lyeth the Body of
THOMAS DOWDESWELL, of Smow, Gent
who departed this Life November
the 28th, in the true faith of Jesus
Christ, in hope of a joyful Resurrection, aged 62, Anno 1680

Arms, a Fess imbattled between 3 lions rampant —Crest, a Castle triple towered

Here lyeth the Body of MARY,
the Wife of NICHOLAS STEIGHT,
of Pannington in this Parish   She
died the 7 of March, 1756, aged 66 Years

Also the Body of the
Said NICHOLAS STEIGHT,
of Pannington, Gent. who
departed this Life the 9th of
Feb 1763, aged 80 Years

This Stone was erected at the Expence
of NICHOLAS SPICER STEIGHT, in Memory
of his Sister ANN STEIGHT, Daughter of
NICHOLAS and MARY STEIGHT, of Pannington,
Gent ob. Dec 3, 1763, æt 32

Here lies the Body of Mrs SARAH SHIELD,
Daughter of JOHN SHIELD, of Pannington,
who died 31 Jan 1712, aged 85

IN THE CHURCH YARD, ON TOMBS

RICHARD HAINES, of Natton,
died 22 February, 1671

JOHN HAINES, of Natton,
died Dec 6, 1694, aged 52

SARAH, the Wife of JOHN MORRIS,
of Natton, Gent died Sept 26,
1746, aged 75

JOHN HAINES died April 11,
1711, aged 70.

JOHN YEEND died
June 12, 1713, aged 49

MARY Wife of GILES PERRY,
died Oct 20, 1776, aged 24

JOHN ROWLES
died 4 Sept 1614

JAMES NIND, Senior,
died Sept. 27, 1727, aged 74

JAMES his Son,
died Nov 12°, aged 51

Also PRISCILLA, ANNE, SUSANNA,
Daughters of JAMES and MARY
NIND, were here buried

ELIZABETH, the Wife of JAMES NIND,
Yeoman, died 17 Jan 1707, aged 55

ON FLAT AND HEAD STONES

	Died	Aged
Henry the Son of Henry and John Weaver	28 Apr 1757	55
Ann the Wife of Henry Weaver, Sen.	21 Nov 1773	68
William Weaver	13 May 1741	77
Agnes his Wife -	22 Dec 1745	79
Thomas Heath, late of Tiddington	9 Nov 1783	51
his Wife	11 Aug 1763	19
William ... ... Eliz Stiles,	17 Jun 1778	5
... Wife of ... Bullock, late ... Walton Cardiff	7 Apr 1761	41
... ... Whitborn	12 Nov 1781	80
... Whitborn of Cheltenham	23 Oct 1770	35
Walton Weir	4 July 1757	32
John Weir	1 June 1715	14
... Pinnock	4 Dec 1754	67
... ...	15 Feb 1766	18
... ...	1 Mar 1741	61
Ann ... Wife of Thomas Weir	12 May 1761	1
... Wells	10 ... 1781	10
Mary ... his Wife	1 Nov 1713	61

	Died	Aged
Margaret their Daughter,	19 Feb 1733	5
Elizabeth their Daughter,	8 Oct 1759	5
Ann, the Wife of Samuel Afton, of Cheltenham Parfinep,	20 Feb 1771	40
Thomas Brotheridge	2 June 1772	7
Elizabeth his Wife	21 May 1780	74
Thomas Attwood, Senior, late of Tiddington,	11 Feb 1761	70
William his Son	3 Feb 1770	13
William Straley, of Walton Cardiffe,	17 July 1763	55
George Straley	3 Oct 1761	27
Susanna Wife of William Straley,	14 Jun 1782	73
Robert Townley	2 Aug 1765	61
Ann, the Wife of John Cull,	25 July 1711	30
Daniel Farmer -	6 Feb 1768	32
John Benton	28 Jul 1766	45
George Buck late of Tiddington,	12 May 1770	61
William Haines of Walton Cardiff,	2 Nov 1754	7
Mary his Wife -	6 Aug 1751	46

THIS parish lies in the upper division of the hundred of *Berkeley*, and in the deanery of GLOUCES-
TER, about eight miles fouthweft from *Tewkefbury*, and five miles north from GLOUCESTER. That
part of the hundred of *Berkeley* in which *Afbelworth* lies, is every way feparate, and at leaft fourteen or
fifteen miles diftant from the lower divifion. The land confifts of about two thirds arable, and one third
good meadow and pafture, the latter lie near the *Severn*, by which river this parish is bounded towards
the eaft. And, as part of *Corfe Lawn* is within the limits of it, there is a confiderable tract of common.
The foil is chiefly a light loam, in fome parts inclining to fand, in many places a whitish limeftone is
found no far below the furface.

The parifhioners formerly ufed to circumambulate their parish, and upon thofe occafions, it is faid,
they went s near as they could guefs to the **middle** of the *Severn*, which they confidered as the precife
bounds of t on that fide. This cuftom has been long difufed, nor is the circumftance of their going
on the river remembered by any of the prefent inhabitants.

A feaft, or wake, was ufually held here on the Sunday after *Saint Bartholomew's* day, but it has been
difcontinued about fifteen years, having been fuppreffed by the prefent vicar, foon after he was inducted
to the living.

In this parish are the following hamlets, 1 *Longridge End*, or rather *Long-Reach End*, from that part
of the parish being fituated at the end of a remarkable long reach of the river *Severn*. 2 *Knights Green*
3 *Napping End* 4 *White End* 5 *High Crofs* 6 *Wickeridge* 7 *Mare End*, all which are in the
tything of *Afbelworth*.

The manor belonged to the Abbey of *St Auguftine* in BRISTOL, 9 Edw II, and continued in that
Abbey till its diffolution, when it was granted, 34 Hen VIII, together with the rectory and advowfon
of the vicarage, to the Bifhop of that diocefe.

CHARLES HAYWARD, of *Quedgley*, Efq is the prefent leffee under the Bifhop, and holds a Court Leet,
and Court Baron. The impropriation, exclufive of fome of the great tithes, which belong to the vicar,
is likewife held by him. The principal part of the parish is the property of Mr HAYWARD.

The manor, or court houfe, a very old building, is now a farm.

In the MS already mentioned, in the poffeffion of the EARL OF BERKELEY, is the following account
of this place.

" *Afbelworth*, in Domfdei booke *Efcelunord*, and in the times of Richard I and of Kinge John, written *Effelewid*, is a manor and parish, not far from the city of GLOUCESTER, belonging to the Bifhop of
BRISTOLL.

" Anciently this manor was part of the great manor of *Berkeley*, and of *Berkeley herneffe*, and was, by
Robert, the fonne of Hardinge, given, among other manors, to the Abbot and Covent of the Monafterie of *St Auguftine's*, with whome it continued till the diffolution of that monafterie, 31 Hen VIII, and,
upon the King's erectinge of newe the Bifhoppricke of BRISTOLL, was defigned to bee part of the
poffeffions of the Bifhoppricke.

" The common, or derivation of the name of this parish or townfhip, take whether of thefe two wayes
you pleafe, either from the word *Weorth*, now fpoken *Woorth*, a bafe court or yard, fuch as is commonly
before the better fort of houfes, or from the Germane word *Werd*, which is a Poole.

" Of able men for the warres, between 20 and 60 yeares of age, 71. Of trayned fouldiers under
William Thorpe, Efq their captaine now, are 4, viz 2 corflets and 2 mufketts "

The living is a vicarage, and the church, which is dedicated to *Saint Bartholomew*, has an ifle on the
fouth fide, and at the weft end a good tower, with battlements, upon which is a ftone fpire of confiderable height. The tower contains fix bells. There is a chancel at the end of the ifle, as well as adjoining
to the nave, one of thefe belongs to the lord of the manor, the other to the vicar. The outfide of the
nave is covered with lead, the ifle with tile. This church is built in a plain ftyle, and though it hath the
appearance of antiquity, there is no peculiarity by which the era of it found tion may be determined.
From its vicinity to the *Severn*, the water of that river often flow in on it. At the time of the great flood,
November 1ft, 1770, it rofe to the height of four feet feven inches throughout the whole church.

The Vicarage houfe, which is fituated about half a mile northward from the church, is a general
ftructure, built with large pieces of timber very firmly, compacted together. It feems to have flood a long
age, and from its prefent appearance is likely to ftand feveral more.

Upon a Table in the Chancel is the following Memorial

" 17.. Mary ..., Duchefs of the Honourable Major General STEWAN, of Matfon, in the
county ... and widow and relict of WILLIAM HAYWARD, Efq formerly lord of this manor, hath devifed
one hearth ... and all south ses at rates, the intereft thereof to be applied to the education of two
poor children ... number of poor children of this parish, the children and teacher to be appointed by the vica
the cofts to the ... being which annuities are now vefted in the joint name of CHARLES HAYWARD,
Efq prefent lord of the manor and the Rev JAMES HAYWARD, the prefent vicar.

BENEFACTIONS, as returned, 1786.

A person unknown, time beyond the memory of man, the ufes not fet forth, but generally given to the fecond poor, gave land, the annual produce of which is fifteen pounds, thirteen fhillings, and nine pence It is now vefted in John Lane, as the furviving truftee, who is aged about 70

Mrs Margaret Hayward gave, by will, time not mentioned, the intereft for the education of four poor children, fifty pounds South Sea ftock

The Reverend Mr John Hayward gave, by deed, 1772, for the fame purpofe, fifty pounds in the fame ftock   The annual produce of both thefe fums is three pounds

Befides the above, the poor have a fhare of commonage in fuch parts of *Corfe Lawn* and *Haifield* as lie within this parifh

Incumbents	Patrons	Incumbents	Patrons
—— Thomas Meakins,		1716 John Harper, M A	Bifhop of Briftol
1595 Robert Harris (*Hanns* in the Regifter),	Queen Elizabeth	1724 Jofeph Gegg, M A	Ditto
—— Richard Thompfon,		1770 James Edwards, B.D.	Ditto
1671 Edward Tidkin (*Fidkin*),	King Charles		
1695 Charles Smith,	Bifhop of Briftol		
1700 Charles Smith, M A	Ditto		
The above from Sir Rob Atkyns			

Present Lord of the Manor,
Charles Hayward, Efq.

There does not appear to have been any perfon fummoned from this parifh, or its hamlets, by the Heralds in 1682 and 1683

At the Election in 1776, fix Freeholders polled from this parifh

Annual Account of Marriages, Births, and Burials, in this Parish

A.D	Mar	Bir	Bur	A D	Mar	Bir	Bur	A D	Mar	Bir	Bur	A D	Mar	Bir	Bur
1781	1	11	8	1791				1801				1811			
1782	6	9	10	1792				1802				1812			
1783	1	19	7	1793				1803				1813			
1784	—	5	8	1794				1804				1814			
1785	1	13	8	1795				1805				1815			
1786	1	10	9	1796				1806				1816			
1787				1797				1807				1817			
1788				1798				1808				1818			
1789				1799				1809				1819			
1790				1800				1810				1820			

The increafe of population is evinced by the regifter of this parifh, which has been kept with great regularity   It commences as early as 1566, from which time to 1786, a period of 220 years, the entries of baptifms are 2283, burials 1913   The inhabitants have increafed 370, averaged annually at 1½

INSCRIPTIONS IN THE CHURCH.
ON FLAT STONES

Here lieth buried the Body of Sophronia Pauncefoote, wife of John Pauncefoote, Gent She was charitable to the Poore, and Courteous to all People She loved her Hufband with much Reverence, and was kinde to her Children, and brought them up vertuoufly She had iffue by him 15 Children, of which fhe left living with him to the pleafure of God, 4 Sonnes and 5 Daughters She deceafed the XXVIII Day of Aug in the 5 Yeare of her Age, and in the Yeare of our Lord God 1615

Richardus Tompfonus, Vicarius hujus Ecclefiæ, Annis et pietate gravis, Vita defunctus non Minifterio jam climat mortuus
Anagr
Su fum, corda fi vi nos huic rapet
obiit 22 Decembris A Dom 1671

Matthew, the Son of Matthew Tompfon, by Jane his Wife, departed this Life Mai 21, 1709, Aged 37

Here

Here lyeth the Body of MARY LONGE,
Widow, lately the Wife of ANTHONY
LONGE, of this Parish, Gent to whom
Shee bare 3 Sons and one Daughter
She was formerly the Wife of ALEXANDER
READY, of Maysmore, in this County,
Gent to whom shee bare 4 Sons
and 2 Daughters She was the eldest
Daughter of John BRAY, late of Fifield,
in the County of Oxford, Esq She
died the 8th of January, Anno Dom
1674 This Stone was placed here
at the Charge of ELIZABETH her 2d Daughter
by the foresaid ALEXANDER READY,
whom shee left her sole Executrix

Here lyes the Bodies of
WALTER LONG, Gent
and JOANE his Wife Hee
was buried the 6th day Novem 1642,
Shee the 22 Day of July, 1640

Here lyeth the Body of
ELENOR, Daughter of
HUGH WILLIAMS,
late of Sandhurst,
first Love and last Wife
of WALTER LONG, Senior,
who died 14 November, 1631

WALTER LONG, Esquire,
deceased the 15 day of Ju

Here lyeth the Body of WALTER
LONG, of Beamonds, who departed
this Life the XI of Oct Aᵒ 1638

Arms, a Lion passant, on a Chief 3 cross Croslets

Beneath this Stone lieth
(in hopes of a joyful Resurrection)
the Body of EDMUND LONG, late
of the Parish of Stonehouse, in
this County, Mealman, whose Dissolution
was on the 2d Day of Jun
1752, in the 60 Year of his Age

Here lyeth the Body of JAMES
LYANS, of the Parish of St Mary
De Cript, in the City of Gloucester,
who died April 22, 1766, aged 39

Also here lieth the Body of MARY,
the Daughter of the abovesaid JAMES
LYANS by Mary his Wife, who died
Nov 1, 1766

Here lieth the Body of
ROBERT SLOPER, Gent
who departed this Life
November 23, 1664 aged 28

IN THE CHURCHYARD.

JOHN HOBBS
died Feb 12, 1747, aged 94
PEGGY his Wife
died March 14, 1755, aged 74
JOHN their Son
died March 26 1767 aged 54
ELIZABETH his Wife
died Nov 3, 1764 aged 48

ANN, Wife of WILLIAM ROBERTS, Jun
late of this Parish, Yeoman
died 11 May, 1717, aged 28

ANN, the Wife of
RICHARD BAYLEY,
died October 17, 1727, aged 63

RICHARD BAYLEY
died 3 Dec 17.. aged 5)

MARY, their only Daughter,
Wife of JOHN CHURCH of Norton,
died Feb 8 1715, aged 25

WILLIAM HILL, Yeoman,
died Nov 30 1683, aged

WILLIAM DRAPER
died Nov 5, 1749 aged 4.

MARY, Daughter of
THOMAS and ELIZABETH DRAPER,
died August 7, 1759, aged 4

MARGARET Wife of WM CLARK,
of Wick age in the Parish of Hasfield,
died June 4, 1768 aged 46

WILLIAM CLARK
died Aug 30 1765 aged 46

ON HEADSTONES

	Died	Aged
Walter Long	26 Feb 1751	65
Sarah his Wife	28 Aug 1754	68
William Voice	20 Apr 1746	68
John his Wife Daughter of Mary Eldridge Widow	17 Oct 1737	50
Helen Daughter of William and Mary Voice	1 Oct 1754	19
Stephen Colchester Gent	1 Nov 17..	72
William Colchester Nephew to the abovesaid Stephen	1 Nov 1761	0
John Lane, Yeoman,	14 Apr 1763	80
Jane his Wife	5 Feb 1717	72
Edward Middleton	15 Feb 17..	71
Margaret his Wife	17 Apr 1717	72
with his Son,	2 May 1725	77
Carpet(?) Img of the City of Gloucester but late of this Parish	2 Nov 1715	55
J M Clerk	22 June 1718	

	Died	Aged
William Alford	16 July 1653	—
Elizabeth his Wife	Aug 17..	—
William Alford the Younger	9 Apr 1667	—
Samuel Middleton	9 Mar 17..	28
Thomas his Wife	24 Jun 1771	71
Walter Jelf, Yeoman	8 Apr 1718	75
William Son of William and Elizabeth Cardie(?)	25 Oct 17..	22
Henry Jelf the like	20 Feb 17..	4
Jane Wife of John Robert Yeoman	15 Jun 1761	85
George Son of John and Jane Robert	23 Apr 176.	23
Joan Robert Junior	Apr 171.	51
Sarah Daughter of William and Mary Lane	— 1765	12
William Lane of the Parish of Hasfield Yeoman	Jun 1766	60
Joseph Jelf Senior	13 Sept 1749	53
Judith his Wife	10 June 17..	48

XVIII. ASTON BLANK,
OR
COLD ASTON.

THIS parish lies in the hundred of *Bradley*, and deanery of *Stow*, about four miles north from *Northleach*, and twenty east from Gloucester. It consists chiefly of arable land, the soil in general a strong clay, and usually produces good crops of wheat, barley, and oats, in some parts it is light and stony, and not so fertile.

The river *Winrush* bounds this parish towards the north, and the *Fofs Way* on the east. It received the epithet of *cold*, from its bleak situation. Sir Robert Atkyns supposes that it obtained the denomination of *Blank*, from a family of that name, who were formerly owners of it, but the word is undoubtedly derived from the French *Blanc*, White, and was applied to it because the snow usually lies longer on the ground here, than in any of the adjacent parts.

That the situation of this place is remarkably healthy, and conducive to longevity, may be concluded form the list of incumbents, there having been but three in possession of the living from the year 1667 to the present time, a period of 119 years, and the third of these still enjoys a good state of health.

At a little distance from the road that leads to *Bourton on the Water*, the remains of some ancient intrenchments are to be seen, which are either Saxon, or Danish. There is also a barrow of a considerable size near them.

A fair, or rather a wake, is annually held here on Easter Monday.

The estate, with the manor, which formerly belonged to the family of the CARTERS, and afterwards to Sir John DOYLEY, of *Chiffel Hampton*, in Oxfordshire, is now in the possession of Dr NEWCOMBE, the present Bishop of Waterford, who married a grand daughter of that Baronet.

The church, which is dedicated to *Saint Andrew*, has a tower at the west end, adorned with battlements, and containing five bells. It appears to be a very ancient building, and, from the height of its situation, is to be seen at a great distance.

The living is a vicarage, the impropriation of which formerly belonged to the Priory of *Malvern*, and is now the property of EDMUND WALLER, Esq

---

BENEFACTIONS.

GODDARD CARTER, Esq gave, by will, time not known, for teaching poor children, a rent charge upon his estate, of five pounds per annum, vested in the person who pays the charity.

A PERSON NOT KNOWN, nor the time when, nor how, the interest to be given to poor house-keepers, gave twenty pounds, vested in the overseers, the annual produce of which is one pound.

INCUMBENTS	PATRONS
1667 Edward Ifles,	King Charles II
17-5 Charles Badger, Cler	King George I
1748 John James, B A	Lord Chancellor Hardwick

PRESENT LORD OF THE MANOR,

Dr WILLIAM NEWCOMBE, Bishop of Waterford

The only person summoned from this place by the Heralds in 1682, and 1683, was

M BARNARD WINCHCOMBE

At the Election in 1776, only two Freeholders polled from this Parish

ANNUAL ACCOUNT OF MARRIAGES, BIRTHS, AND BURIALS, IN THIS PARISH

A.D	Mar	Bir	Bur	A.D	Mar	Bir	Bur	A.D	Mar	Bir	Bur	A.D	Mar	Bir	Bur
1781	3	6	5	1791				1801				1811			
1782	3	9	5	1792				1802				1812			
1783	—	4	4	1793				1803				1813			
1784	1	4	7	1794				1804				1814			
1785	—	6	5	1795				1805				1815			
1786				1796				1806				1816			
1787				1797				1807				1817			
1788				1798				1808				1818			
1789				1799				1809				1819			
1790				1800				1810				1820			

INSCRIPTIONS IN THE CHURCH

ON A FAIR MONUMENT OF FREE STONE AND MARBLE, AGAINST THE WALL NEXT THE CHANCEL

Arms, Azure, two lions combatant Or—impaling, Or, an escallop in chief Sable, between two bendlets Gules, for TRACY

In Memoriam
Cl. VIRI ÆGIDII CARTER,
Olim de Swell Inferiori in hoc Comitatu,
Armigeri, Qui probitate morum, fide et
pietate in divinis, necnon erga principem
infignis, inter paucos pia feneĉtute Vitam Claudens,
Deceffit Anno ætatis fuæ octogeffimo, vicefimo quarto die Martii,
Annoq, Dom. 1664

Et præivit octo ante menfibus Chariffima
ejus Uxor ELIZABETHA, honefta & fplendida
Familia de TRACY orta, quæ una cum illo Sex-
aginta annos Matrimonio vixit uterque, cœlef
tis regni, ne rurfus feparentur, participes

GILES CARTER was the eldest Son of JOHN CARTER,
of Nether Swell, in the County of Gloucester, Efq
his two Brethren being JOHN CARTER, of Charlton-
Abbats, and WILLIAM CARTER, of Brees Norton, in
Oxfordfhire He married ELIZABETH, the Daughter
of Sir PAUL TRACY, of Stanwell, and died without Iffue

ON A SMALL MONUMENT BETWEEN THE CHURCH AND CHANCEL

In Memory
of SAMUEL, the Son of JOSHUA ELLIOTT, Clerk,
and ELIZABETH his Wife, Daughter unto EDWARD
AYLWORTH, of Aylworth, in the County of Gloucester, Efq
Hee died Aug 1, 1667 Shee died Jan 27, 1672

ON FLAT STONES

BERNARD WINCHCOMBE, GENT
SUB CINERIBUS,
MANY YEARS LOYAL TO
HIS KING AND CHURCH,
MEEKLY SUBMITTED TO DEATH,
AND CAME TO THIS PLACE OF REST,
FEB 16, 1683, ÆT 71

In Memory of MARTHA, Daughter of
JOHN and ELIZABETH NORRIS
She died June 24, 1736, aged 10 Years

In Memory of ELIZABETH NORRIS,
who died Jun 26, 1763, aged 69 Years

IN THE CHURCH YARD.

ON HEAD STONES

	Died	Aged		Died	Aged
Isaac Troy	16 Mar 1711	57	Mary his Wife	2, Mar 1763	7
Jane Troy - -	9 Dec 1750	76	Job the Son	29 May 1719	54
Isaac Troy - -	26 Aug 1761	81	Thomas Taylor,	— Jun 1699	54
Sarah, Wife of John Draper, -	10 Aug 1752	66	Mary his Wife	— Dec 1726	81
Ann Wife of John Ticket, -	23 Nov 1772	59	John Taylor, their Son -	7 Sept 1736	83
Joseph Cork	1 Jun 1757	70	Mary, Wife of John Taylor	2 Dec 1758	86

XIV ASHTON,

XIX. ASHTON,
OR
COLD ASHTON.

THIS parish lies in the hundred of *Pucklechurch*, and deanery of *Hawkesbury*, two miles west from *Marshfield*, and about thirty four miles south from GLOUCESTER. It consists of about an equal quantity of pasturage and arable land, with some woodland. The soil is various, in some parts clay, in others sand, and in many places it is stony.

Five springs, viz. *Hemeswell*, *Bridewell*, *Romswell*, *Clintonwell*, and another large one rising in *Monkwood*, run through this parish, and empty themselves into the river *Avon*.

The name of this place being anciently written *Estone*, since corrupted into *Ashton*, probably was so called from its being the most easterly town in the hundred.

In the fields belonging to it stones are found which resemble the bill of a duck, not much unlike muscle shells, only rounder, and others are serpentine stones. Sir Robert Atkyns tells us that an extraordinary cavity in the earth was accidentally discovered here some short time prior to the beginning of this century, by a person at plough. He describes it as extending half a mile one way, and to a length that had not been ascertained, another way, and as having several funnels, or a kind of chimnies, which ascended towards the surface of the earth. No entrance to this subterraneous cavity remains at present, the same having been stopped up, to prevent accidents, nor has the design or use of it ever been found out.

Sir BEVIL GRANVILLE, who was mortally wounded at the battle of *Landsdown*, as mentioned in the parish of *Aston and Hick*, was brought to the Parsonage House of this place, where he died.

There is a feast held here on Whitsunday.

Hamswell is a hamlet in this parish, and formerly belonged to the Priory of *Bath*. It is now the seat of THOMAS WHITTINGTON, Esq; who has a good house here.

Turners Court is an old house, and had anciently a consecrated chapel in it, which is now appropriated to other purposes. It formerly belonged to the family of the STROUDS, but the present possessor is JOHN GUNNING, Esq.

The living is a rectory; and the church, which is dedicated to the *Holy Trinity*, was built about the year 1500, by THOMAS KEY, then rector of the parish. It is large and handsome, has an aile on the south side, a flat roof with battlements, adorned with pinnacles, and a low tower on the same side, in which are four bells. The Parsonage House, of a very antique appearance, was likewise erected by Mr. KEY, in the year 1509. The exact time is known from the images of two angels carved in stone, which are placed on the south side of it, some distance from each other; from the breast of either hangs a label of stone; on one is carved "A M 9," and on the other "1509."

BENEFACTIONS

WILLIAM WHITTINGTON gave by will, June 5, 1717, four shillings per ann. for the more comfortable subsistence of the poor, on St. Thomas's day and Good Friday, vested in the possession of a ground, called *Hewood* in *Hamswell* farm.

WILLIAM WHITTINGTON gave by will at the same time five pounds per ann. for teaching to read and write all the children of such poor inhabitants, which should not be of abilities to pay for their children teaching, vested in the teacher, who having power to enter and distrain for the same.

THE Inhabitants in the parish, in the year 1766, gave, by consent, a lane or common house for a school master, now occupied by......

INCUMBENTS	PATRONS	INCUMBENTS	PATRONS
1570 Ambrose Hunt,	Queen Elizabeth	1720 Ivan Jones, M A	John Bayley
1581 John Taylour,	Timothy Pebwall	1739 Sam Catwell, B A	John Whittington, Esq
1624 Thomas Blanchard,	—— Whittington		
1639 William Dunning,	King Charles I		
—— Andrew Cole,			
1666 Edmund Fido,	Wm Whittington		
The above from Sir Rob ATKYNS			

PRESENT LORDS OF THE MANORS

Of *Ashton*
WILLIAM GORE LANGTON, and }
JOHN GUNNING, } ESQRS

Of *Hamesold*
THOMAS WHITTINGTON, Esq.

The persons summoned from this parish by the Heralds in 1682 and 1683, were

The Heirs of Sir Robert Gunning, Knight,
William Whittington, Gent

At the Election in 1776, four Freeholders polled from this parish

ANNUAL ACCOUNT OF MARRIAGES, BIRTHS, AND BURIALS, IN THIS PARISH

A D	Mar	Bir	Bur	A D	Mar	Bir	Bur	A D	Mar	Bir	Bur	A D	Mar	Bir	Bur.
1781	—	5	4	1791				1801				1811			
1782	4	8	7	1792				1802				1812			
1783	1	8	8	1793				1803				1813			
1784	2	9	7	1794				1804				1814			
1785	1	5	2	1795				1805				1815			
1786				1796				1806				1816			
1787				1797				1807				1817			
1788				1798				1808				1818			
1789				1799				1809				1819			
1790				1800				1810				1820			

INSCRIPTIONS IN THE CHURCH.

IN THE CHANCEL

ON A BRASS PLATE IN THE OLD ENGLISH LETTER AGAINST THE NORTH WALL

Egregius Rector, Thomas cognomine KRIUS
Conditur hac celebri pertumulatus humo
Qui totum hanc sacram propriis ex sumptibus ædem
Condidit, summi motus amore Dei,
O sæcio concedat tali pro munere sanctis
Trinus et Unus et cælica regna Deus

ON AN ATCHIEVEMENT OVER THE DOOR ARE THE ARMS OF WHITTINGTON, Gules, 3 sets the p v Or in l Azure—Crest, a lion' head, couped, Sable

UNDERNEATH, ON AN OVAL MARBLE MONUMENT, IS INSCRIBED,

In token of
a Grateful Remembrance
To JOHN WHITTINGTON, Esq.
whose Ashes are here waiting aid,
who died Nov 11, 1713, aged 52

What his own kindred neglected,
SAMUEL CASWELL, Rector,
John Patron erected
this Stone,
1753

ON FLAT STONES

Beneath this Stone lies
interred the body of
R... of WHITTINGTON, Relict
of THOMAS WHITTINGTON, Sen.
of Beach, Gent deceased
she departed this Life the
27th of March, 17..
Aged 90 Years

Here lieth the Body of
MARTHA, the Wife of
Mr THOMAS BLANCHARD,
Rector of this Parish
She was buried the 20th of
August 1632

Corpus Elizabe-
thæ Fido Hic
Dormit Huma-
t m, 22 Novemb
Anno Dom 1667,
Ætatis suæ
nono
Ut Flos, fimul ac.
Lgreflus eft
Succiditur

Here lyeth the Body of
Thomas Whittington, of
Beach, in the Parish of
Bitton, Gent who departed
this Life the 15th of Jan 1736,
Aged 87 Years

Here lyeth the Body of
George, the Son of Thomas Whittington,
Gent and Rachel his Wife, of the
Parish of Bitton, died 22 Oct 1723,
Aged 19 Years.

Richard, Son of Thomas Whittington
and Rachel his Wife, aforefaid, died
the 20 day of June, 1733, aged 31 Years

Rachel Whittington, Spinster,
one of the Daughters of Thomas
Whittington, Gent and Rachel
his Wife, late of Beach, died the
25th day of May, 1761, aged 60 Years.

Here lyeth the Body of
Joyce, the Wife of Andrew
Cole, late Rector of this
Parish, who departed this
Life the 10 Day of Jan
Anno Dom 1689

Beneath this Stone lies the Body of
Elizabeth Whittington, Spinster,
one of the Daughters of Thomas
Whittington, Gent and Rachel his
Wife, late of Beach, in the Parish of
Bitton She departed this Life the
28 Day of March, 1767, aged 78 Year

IN THE BODY OF THE CHURCH

ON A MONUMENT AGAINST ONE OF THE PILLARS.

Arms, on a fefs, between three bucks heads,
couped, three fleurs de lis—Creft, out of a coronet,
a buck's head

Beneath
lie interred Evan
Jones, late Rector
of this Parish, and
Mary his Wife

Evan } died { Feb 4, 1738, } aged { 57
Mary }   { Dec 5, 1730, }   { 42

John Jones, their
eldeft Son, who died
Feb 20, 1740, aged 23

ON FLAT STONES

Here lyeth the Body of
Alice Whittington, of
Alveston, Spinster, the Daughter
of John Whittington, Gent
and Mary his Wife, who died
the 18th of Nov 1751, aged 57 Years

Here lyeth the Body of John
Whittington, Senior, of Latwick, in
the Parish of Swainwick, Gent who
died the 30th day of January, 1690,
Aged 80 Year

Also the Body of John Whittington
of Alveston, Gent Son of the aforefaid
John Whittington, who departed this
Life the 5th day of December, 1
Aged 5 Year

Here lyeth the Body of
Mary, Wife of John Whittington,
of Alveston, Gent who departed
this Life the 16th day of April, 1733,
Aged 80 Years.

Here lyeth the Body of Joyce
the Wife of John
who died

Here lyeth the Body of
Johane Osborne, of this
Parish, Widow, who died
the 26th day of Sept 1694

Beneath this Stone lyeth
the Body of
Robert Whittington,
of Beach, in the Parish of Bitton,
Gent who died the 9th of March, 1776
Aged 7

Also near this Place lyeth
the Body of Elizabeth, the Wife
Robert Whittington
who died the 3d of Auguft, 1
aged 7

In Memory of Ann the
Wife of William B
late of Mashfield who died
Feb 1, 1   aged 61 Years
and 11 Months

Here lyes interred the Body of
MARY, Daughter of SAMULL and
ELIZABETH BUSH, who departed
this Life the 17th of April, 174?,
Aged 14 Years

Also the Body of SAMUEL, Son
of WILLIAM and ANNE BUSH, late
of Marshfield, who departed this
Life Dec 23, 1783, aged 23 Years

In Memory of WILLIAM BUSH,
of this Parish, Senior, who departed
this Life Dec 5, 1711, aged 7?

Also MARTHA his Wife
She departed this Life May
3, 1733, aged 8?

And also in Memory of
ELIZABETH, the Wife of SAMUEL
BUSH of the Parish of Dyrham
She departed this Life
June 13, 1766, aged 73

Also in Memory of the
abovesaid SAMUEL BUSH,
who departed this Life
July 5, 1768, aged 76

Under this Stone
lieth the Body of DOROTHY,
Wife of GILES BUSH, of the
Parish of Bath Easton, Yeoman,
who departed this Life the
19th day of September, 1754,
Aged 5? Years

Also under this Stone
lyeth the Body of GILES
BUSH, of the Parish of Bath-
Easton, Yeoman, who died
the 10th day of April, 1758,
Aged 73 Years

AGAINST THE NORTH WALL

Near this Place lieth the Bodies of
PHILIP, JAMES, and SUSANNA,
Sons and Daughter of PHILIP
and DYONYSIA WEST, of this Parish.
PHILIP died May 11, 1739, aged
17 Years, 3 Months,
JAMES died Aug ? 1740, aged
20 Years, 10 Months
SUSANNA died Dec 9, 1738, aged
?, Years, 2 Months

Also near this Place lyeth the
Body of PHILIP WEST, Father of
the abovenamed Children, who
died Aug ?, 177?, aged ??

IN THE SOUTH AILE

ON FLAT STONES

Here lyeth the Body of
WILLIAM GUNNING the Elder,
who departed this Life
the 13th of January, 166?

Also here lyeth the Body of
ALICE WHITTINGTON, Wife
of JOHN WHITTINGTON,

[The rest covered by the Pews]

Here lyeth the Body of
AN?, Wife of WILLIAM
GUNNING, who departed
March the 21st, 1675

ON THE VERGE OF A FLAT STONE

Here lyeth the Body of
JOHN GUNNING, Son of WILLIAM GUNNING, who
departed this Life
the 24th of   , 1647

Here lyeth the Body of
WILLIAM GUNNING, who departed
this Life the 12th Day of February,
1704, aged 92 Years

Also here lyeth the Body
of ROBERT GUNNING, Brother
to the said WILLIAM GUNNING, of
this Parish, who departed
this Life the 25th Day of March,
Anno Domini 1711, aged 81 Years.

Here lieth the Body of ALICE
GUNNING of this Place, who departed
this Life the 10 Day of March, 1698,
Aged 80 Years

Also near this Place lyeth the
Body of JOHN GUNNING, of this
Parish, Senior, who died the 19th Day
of Dec. Anno Domini 1706, aged 86 Years

Here lyeth the Body of THOMAS
LEWIS, who departed this Life
the 1st Day of May, 1708

Also JOAN, the Wife of
THOMAS LEWIS, who died
the 17th Day of May, 1704

In Memory of ROBERT the
Son of ELIAS OSBORN, Soapmaker,
of the City of Bristol, who
departed this Life, the 3d Day
of March, 1717, aged 2, Years

Here lyeth the Body of
JANE, the Daughter of
WILLIAM OSBORN, who
died Dec the 5th, 167?

IN THE CHURCH YARD, ON TOMBS

CHRISTIAN the Wife of
SAMUEL JONES died the
26th of May 1726, aged 77

———

THOMAS DAVIS died
Jan 19 1737 aged 80

MARTHA his Wife,
April , 1720 aged 32

THOMAS, their Son
died 6 April, 1731, aged 3,

ELIZABETH his Wife
died 1 April, 1730
Aged 31

EDWARD SPENCER
died 4 Jan 1763, aged 71

EDITH, the Wife of
SAMUEL CASWELL Rector
of this Parish Church, was
baptized April , 1659,
married January 13, 170,
died December 13, 1749,
and lies buried here

JOHN GUNNING of Langridge,
Gent died July 12, 15
Aged 69 Years and lies buried here

JOHN WHITTINGTON, eldest Son of
THOMAS WHITTINGTON, Gent and
RACHEL his Wife, late of Beach
in the Parish of batton died
15 Oct 1766, aged 79

THOMAS WHITTINGTON Gent f
Beach in the Parish of Batton died
the 21st of January, 1747, aged 94

ANN WHITTINGTON second Daughter
of THOMAS WHITTINGTON Gent
and RACHEL his Wife, late of beach,
in the Parish of Batton died
the 4 Day of Oct 1783, aged 84

WILLIAM WHITTINGTON, second Son
of THOMAS WHITTINGTON, Gent and
RACHEL his Wife, late of Beach in the
Parish of Batton, died the 24th day
of March, 1777, aged 86

ON A MONUMENT AGAINST THE EAST WALL OF THE CHURCH

Near this Place
lies interred the Bodies
of EDMUND FISO late
Rector of this Parish,
and MARY his Wife,

He } departed this Life { 3 July, 1720.
She } { 4 Jan 1712

His } Age { 95
Her } { 66

———

ON HEAD STONES

	Died	Aged		Died	Aged
Edmund Gunning -	20 Mar 1744	39	William, their Son,	— Sept 1,72	10
Ann his Wife	11 Dec 1766	61	Joyce, Daughter of Samuel and Mary Mannings	8 Nov 1773	25
Elizabeth Wife of John Gunning, of Langridge, Gent	2 Apr 1712	—	Hannah, Wife of Thomas Mannings	6 Sept 17 4	41
Andrew, Son of Thomas and Elizabeth Camery,	16 Feb 1747	34	Abraham Stone Senior,	30 Apr 1743	55
Elizabeth, Wife of Thomas Camery,	21 July, 1759	81	Frances his Wife	2 Feb 1771	72
Thomas Camery -	28 Jan 1734	60	Ann their Daughter,	13 Oct 1740	19
Judith Taylor,	17 July, 1763	80	Ann, Daughter of William and Mary Wilton,	24 May, 1766	15
Thomas Emerson -	3 July, 1736	66	Elizabeth, Wife of William Wilton senior,	30 June, 1757	75
William Taylor -	5 Oct 1720		William Wilton	4 May 1767	66
Mary his Wife -	16 Mar 1765	89	Robert Palmer	4 Ma , 1771	4
Isaac Davis -	27 Nov 1785	65	Sarah his Wife	2 July, 1746	41
Mary his Wife	24 Jan 1782	64	Elizabeth his second Wife	17 Sept 1774	49
Isaac, their Son	10 Apr 1783	27	John Woodward	27 May, 1737	28
Ann, their Daughter,	30 June 17,7	28	Ruth, Wife of Nathaniel Bara,	5 Feb 1 79	40
George Taylor -	23 July, 1783	72	Thomas Bine	12 July, 1784	56
Sarah his Wife -	13 Nov 1767	56	Mary his Wife	2 Dec 1,0	17
Samuel Mannings -	14 Apr 1769	33			
Nicholas, Son of Nicholas and Grace Mannings, -	— May, 1772	1			

xx. ASTON SOMERVILLE.

THIS parish lies in the lower part of the hundred of *Kiftelgate*, and in the deanery of *Campden*, about four miles fouth from *Evefham*, in Worcefterfhire, and twenty miles north-eaft from GLOUCESTER. The land is chiefly arable, the foil dry, with a fmall proportion of land, which ufually produces good crops of wheat, barley, and beans. About the year 1740 the vales and common fields were inclofed.

A fmall brook runs through this parifh, and, after joining one that rifes near, falls into the *Avon* near *Feltham*. Petrified fhells, ferpentine ftones, and other foffils are frequently plough'd or dug up in the fields belonging to it.

In order to diftinguifh this from the other *Iftons*, or *Aftons*, the denomination of *Somerville* was added to it, the SOMERVILLE family being the poffeffors foon after the Conqueft, and with whom it ftill remains. The ancient feat belonging to them once ftood on the fouth fide of the church, and vestiges remained, but is now totally demolifhed.

The church, which is dedicated to Saint ————, is an old building, covered with tile. It hath a handfome tower, at the weft end, with battlements and pinnacles, in which were three bells, but being fplit, they were fome years ago taken down and fold, and a clock purchafed with the money. On one of them was caft the name of ROBERT SOVERVILLE, Efq. and the following Latin diftich.

"*Defi tuam fugiens, cum te Campana vocavit*
"*Aufis, nulli pigri, fit tibi Gauja Morae*"

There was an aile on the fouth fide of the church, which was the burial place of the SOMERVILLE family, but it is now wholly demolifhed. And on the eaft window of the chancel were their Arms Argent, 3 leopards faces in fefs, between 3 annulets Gules. Thefe, likewife, are now totally defaced. On the fouth fide of the church there is a niche in the wall, wherein is an ancient image, refembling a knight templar, fuppofed to reprefent one of the anceftors of the SOMERVILLE family.

The living, which was anciently in the gift of the abbey of *Evefham*, is a rectory.

No Benefactions to the poor

INCUMBENTS	PATRONS	INCUMBENTS	PATRONS
—— Anthony Hunt,		1714 John Moore, M.A.	—— Somerville, Efq
1615 John Davies,	Sir Wm Somerville	1723 Jhn Somerville, LL.B	Wm Somerville, Efq
—— Giles Collier,		1735 Thomas Edkin, A.B	Ditto
1642 Richard Davies,	King Charles	1752 John Reynold, A.M	Ditto
1692 John Parry, A.M		1774 Wm Somerville, A.M	Lord Somerville
The above from Sir ROBERT ATKYNS			

PRESENT LORD OF THE MANOR,

LORD SOMERVILLE.

No perfon was fummoned from this place by the Herald in 1634 and 1683, nor did any in Freeholder poll from it at the Election in 1776.

ANNUAL ACCOUNT OF MARRIAGES, BIRTHS, AND BURIALS IN THIS PARISH.

A.D	Mar	Bir	Bur	A.D	Mar	Bir	Bur	A.D	Mar	Bir	Bur	A.D	Mar	Bir	Bur
1784	1	4	1	1791				1801				1811			
1785		4	2	1792				1802				1812			
1785	—	—	—	1793				1803				1813			
1786	—	2	—	1794				1804				1814			
1786	—	5	3	1795				1805				1815			
1786				1796				1806				1816			
1787				1797				1807				1817			
1788				1798				1808				1818			
1789				1799				1809				1819			
1790				1800				1810				1820			

INSCRIPTIONS IN THE CHURCH

IN THE CHANCEL

ON A MARBLE MONUMENT

Arms a fefs between 3 lozenges—impaling, Gules,
a cheveron, between 3 mullets Argent, for FULWOOD

Near this Place lies the Body
of Mrs RIBECC PARRY, Daughter of
THOMAS FULWOOD, Gent
an ancient Family in Warwickshire, Wife of
JOHN PARRY, Rector, by whom he had
feven Sons and three Daughters,
five furviving, and with her, at, and
before her Death She died July 1, 1709, aged 71

Near this Place lies also the Body
of JOHN PARRY, A M Rector of this
Parifh , , Years In all which Time
he was a conftant and faithful Preacher,
Diligent and Careful in all other Offices
of his Calling He died June 29, 1714,
Aged 75 He was the beft of Hufbands,
and the beft of Fathers, and
kind and charitable to all

Mr. SAMUEL PARRY,
Citizen of London, died there
March 16 buried here March the
20th, 1700, aged 30 Years

Mr THOMAS PARRY,
Citizen of London,
died there the 24th, buried here
the 28th of November, 1700, aged 26.

When he was here laft,
In Health, a year paft,
In this Place he chofe,
His Bones to repofe,
God did him infpire,
He hath his Defire,
Difturb not his Duft,
He'll rife with the Juft

Mr BENJAMIN PARRY,
Goldfmith, and Citizen of London,
Died there, was buried here
the 26th of Jan 1702, aged 27 Years

Here lyeth the Body of REBECCA,
the dear and only Child of JOHN
PARRY, A M Clerk, and MARY his
Wife, who died at London, Oct. the
15, and was buried here the 19th,
1719, in the 3d Year of her Age

Here lyeth the Body of the
Rev Mr JOHN PARRY, Junior,
who for many Years difcharged
his Minifterial Office in the
Parifh of St James, Weftminfter,
with the utmoft Faithfulnefs
and Affiduity and was always
juftly efteemed for his fober,
honeft, and virtuous Behaviour
He died at Bath the 3d of
January, in the 73d Year of his Age,
and was buried here Jan 18,
MDCCXXXVII

Here lieth the Body of
Mr CHARLES SOMERVILE,
fourth Son of Rob SOMERVILE,
Efq who was buried July 24, 1681

IN THE BODY OF THE CHURCH

Here lyeth the Body of
ROBERT PARTRIDGE,
who died May the 28th, 1719, aged 51 Years

To the Memory of
THOMAS MALLONE,
who was many Years Servant to
ROBERT SOMERVILE, and } Efqrs
WILLIAM SOMERVILE, }
Lords of this Manour
He died July 4, 1718

THOMAS STAITE
departed this Life, Sept 4 1720,
in the , th Year of his Age

ON A BLACK MARBLE MONUMENT

To the Memory of the Reverend
JOHN REYNOLDS, Clerk A M
Rector of this Parifh 32 Years,
and Rector of Hinton on the Green,
in this County Died Oct 19, 1775,
Aged 57 Years

A Wit's a Feather, and a Chief's a Rod,
An honeft Man's the nobleft Work of God

And alfo of Joyce
his Wife, died April 19 1776,
Aged 63 Years

IN THE CHURCH YARD

ON HEADSTONES

	Died	Aged
John Son of Timothy Gibes	9 Dec 1724	42
William Bayzand	21 Dec 1775	40
Richard Bayzand	27 Dec 1749	58
Elizabeth his Wife	9 Jan 1775	77

ASTON SUBEDGE.

THIS parish lies in the upper part of the hundred of *Kiftgate*, and in the deanery of *Campden*, about two miles north-west from that town, and twenty-eight miles north east from *Gloucester*. It consists of nearly an equal proportion of arable and pasture land. In some parts the soil is clay, in others there is a mixture of sand, both of which generally produce good crops of wheat, barley, and beans.

The common fields were inclosed, by Act of Parliament, about the year 1775.

The greatest part of this parish belongs to WALWYN GRAVES, Esq the Lord of the manor, and the manor house, which is the only one worthy of notice, is now a farm.

The living is a rectory, and the church, which is dedicated to *Saint Andrew*, is a small building, consisting of a nave only, without any steeple, and appears to have been founded before the Conquest.

BENEFACTIONS

The LAND-OWNERS, at the inclosing of the fields in 1771, set out about five acres of furze land for the use of the poor for firing, which is vested in the churchwarden and overseer for the time being, and the annual produce is two pounds, ten shillings.

INCUMBENTS	PATRONS	INCUMBENTS	PATRONS
1607 Thomas Fawfet, M A	Christopher Crag	1724 Daniel Slater, M A	Rich Morgan, Esq
——— Thomas Sellers,	———————	1750 Benj Field, M A	Thos Fletcher, Gent
1675 Francis Mason,	King Charles II	1782 Thomas Lloyd, M A	Lord Harrowby
1636 John Bloxam, B A	Walter Savage, Esq		
The above from Sir ROBERT ATKINS			

PRESENT LORD OF THE MANOR,

WALWYN GRAVES, Esq

There was not any person summoned from this parish by the Heralds in 1682 or 1683

At the Election in 1776, Four Freeholders polled from this parish

ANNUAL ACCOUNT OF MARRIAGES, BIRTHS, AND BURIALS IN THIS PARISH

A D	Mar	Bir	Bur	A D	Mar	Bir	Bur	A D	Mar	Bir	Bur	A D	Mar	Bir	Bur
1781	1	7	3	1791				1801				1811			
1782	1	5	2	1792				1802				1812			
1783	1	5	2	1793				1803				1813			
1784	—	6	3	1794				1804				1814			
1785	—	6	2	1795				1805				1815			
1786				1796				1806				1816			
1787				1797				1807				1817			
1788				1798				1808				1818			
1789				1799				1809				1819			
1790				1800				1810				1820			

INSCRIPTIONS

INSCRIPTIONS IN THE CHURCH.

ON THE NORTH SIDE OF THE CHANCEL, AGAINST THE WALL, IS THE IMAGE OF AN OLD MAN, HALF-
LENGTH, IN A SCHOLASTIC DRESS, HOLDING A BOOK BEFORE HIM, AND UNDERNEATH THE FOLLOWING
INSCRIPTION

THOMAS FAWSET, Artium Magister, hujus Ecclefiæ quondam Recto ,
Vir fingulari Prudentia & Doctrina prædit haud vulgari Vita quantum humana
fr gilitas pariebat ir integerrimus   In Ministerio quod per 40ª plus minus annos,
exercut fidelis & laboriofus Impotentibus baculum, i idiger tibus
promt arium, ægrotantibus medicina, omnibus fuavis, affabilis, lof, tis,
Qui ex agro Eboricenfi unde traduxit originem, fœliciter huc adve tus
dierum plenus, Chriftum anhelans farcinam carnis hic depofu t,
27° Aprilis, 1636

ON A SMALL MONUMENT

JOHN BLOXAM, Rector
of this Parifh thirty-eight Years,
was born in this Parifh ,
and buried in this Chancel,
the 25th of April, An Dom 1724,
Aged 76 Years

Here lyeth he Body of
MARY, the Wife of Mr JOHN UNDERHILL,
who departed this Life the
22d of December Anno Dom 1675,
Ætatis fuæ 45

Here refteth the Body of
MARGARET, the Wife of RICHARD
BUMPAS, Jun who was
buried April 27, 1684

IN THE CHURCH YARD.

ON HEAD STONES

	Died	Aged
Richard Bumpas -	23 Nov 1754	55
Mary, Daughter of Richard and Mary Bumpas,	28 Aug 1748	23
Elizabeth, the Wife of Richard Bumpas, of Wefton Subedge,	25 Feb 1761	73
June, the Wife of John Coldicoat, of Ilmington, and Daughter of Richard and Elizabeth Bumpas,	4 Jan 1758	35
Mary, Daughter of William and Mary Bloxham,	9 July 1769	30
Mary, Wife of Jofeph Wheatly,	27 Jun 1775	58
Jofeph Wheatly -	3 May, 1743	66
Ann his Wife	16 Nov 1759	72
Samuel Wheatly	16 June, 1720	85
Margaret his Wife	24 Oct 1711	80
Samuel Wheatly, of Wefton,	20 Apr 1727	36
Peter Hums -	3 Dec 1708	71
Mary his Wife	8 June, 1775	77
Nathaniel Smith	22 Feb 1781	64

XXII. ASHTON UNDER HILL.

ONE part of this parish lies in the hundred of *Tibbleston*, and the other part in the upper division of that of *Tewkesbury*, and in the deanery of *Campden*, about seven miles north west from *Winch-combe*, and seventeen north-east from GLOUCESTER. It consists of pasture and arable land, nearly in in equal proportion of each, and likewise of many orchards, from which good cyder is made. The soil is chiefly of deep clay, with a small part on gravel, and some sandy.

In the year 1773, an Act of Parliament passed for inclosing the common fields, which has been carried into execution. This parish was included in the same Act with that obtained for *Beckford*, to which it lies adjacent.

It probably was called *Ashton*, from its easterly situation to *Beckford*, for in Doomsday-book it is named *Fston*, and the addition of *Under Hill* was given to it, like that of the foregoing parish, upon account of its situation on the declivity of a hill.

A small manufacture of bed-ticks, sheeting, table linen, &c is carried on here.

Lord TYRCONNELL, the Rev Mr HIGFORD, of *Dixton*, and HENRY WAKEMAN, of *Beckford*, Esq are the chief proprietors of the lands in this parish.

The living is a vicarage, annexed to *Beckford*, and the church, which is dedicated to *Saint Barbara*, has the appearance of great antiquity, except the chancel, which, being much decayed, was rebuilt in the year 1624 by Sir JOHN FRANCKLYN, of *Willesdon* in *Middlesex*, Knight, then Lord of the manor. It has a small aile on the north side, and a handsome tower at the west end, wherein are five bells. At the time the Act for inclosing the common fields passed, the impropriation belonged to Lord TYRCONNEL, but lands were then allotted in lieu of tithes.

No Benefactions to the poor.

INCUMBENTS	PATRONS	INCUMBENTS	PATRONS
1674 James Badger, M A.	Jonath Blackwell, Esq	1762 Rich Andrews, B A.	Thos Branch and W Jones, Gent
1677 Labeus Lunne, M A	Bened Wakeman, Esq		
1718 Prideaux Sutton, M A	Charles Parsons, Gent	1766 Lionel Kirkman, M A	Eliz Nelson, Widow, and Thos Ramell
1724 John Harper, M A	Ditto		
1759 John Moseley, M A	Thos Branch and W. Jones, Gent	1768 Joseph Biddle, M A	Ditto.

PRESENT LORD OF THE MANOR,

LORD TYRCONNEL

The following persons were summoned from this place by the Heralds in 1682 and 1683

John Ashton, Gent
William Sambach, Gent

At the Election in 1776, twenty seven Freeholders polled from the two divisions of this parish

ANNUAL ACCOUNT OF MARRIAGES, BIRTHS, AND BURIALS, IN THIS PARISH

A D	Mar	Bir	Bur	A D	Mar	Bir	Bur	A D	Mar	Bir	Bur	A D	Mar	Bir	Bur
1781	1	16	5	1791				1801				1811			
1782	2	1		1792				1802				1812			
1783	1	8	1	1793				1803				1813			
1784	3	13	9	1794				1804				1814			
1785	—	15	7	1795				1805				1815			
1786				1796				1806				1816			
1787				1797				1807				1817			
1788				1798				1808				1818			
1789				1799				1809				1819			
1790				1800				1810				1820			

INSCRIPTIONS

INSCRIPTIONS IN THE CHURCH

ANNE, the Wife of WILLIAM HIGFORD,
Esq died January the 11th, 1709

Also the Wife of Mr CHARLES HIGFORD,
who died Sept 8, 1738

Here lieth the Body of BRIDGET
SAMBACH, late Wife of JOHN SAMBACH,
Gent who died the 5th day of Feb 1689.

Here lieth the Body of JOHN SAMBACH,
Gent. who departed this Life the
12th Day of April, 1668

Also of WILLIAM SAMBACH, Gent
who was buried the 15th of March,
1711, aged 55 Years

Mrs MARY BUSTEEN lieth here
Aged 77 She was brought from
London, and buried here, the 19th of May, 1738,
Ten Feet deep under the Communion Table

ON A ROUGH STONE, PLACED IN THE SOUTH
WALL, ARE THE FOLLOWING LINES, SUPPOSED TO
BE FOR ONE OF THE SAMBACH FAMILY

Reader, what needs a Panegyrick's Skill,
A Limner's Pencil, or a Poet's Quill,
They are but miserable Comforters,
When badd ones die, that paint their Sepulchres,
And when the Life in Honours is spent,
The naked Name's a Marble Monument
To keep from rotting, Piety and Almes
Doe farr excell the best Ægiptian Balmes,
Then, whosoe're thou art, this Course is full
Live, live thyselfe, both Tombe and Epitaph

A noris ergo posuit I S
April 8, ANNO DOM 1651.

Here lieth the Body of
MARY STOAKES, the Wife of
THOMAS STOAKES, who departed
this Life the 8th of Jan 1677

Here lyeth the Body of
THOMAS STOAKES who departed
this Life the 2d of Aug 1684.

Here lyeth the Body of
URSULA, the Wife of WILLIAM
SAMBACH, Gent who departed
this Life the 20th day of May, 1706

Here lyeth the Body of
ELIZABETH STOAKES, who was buried
the 7th day of January, A D 1663

ELIZABETH, Daughter of
WILLIAM HIGFORD, Esq
died March 4, 1710

ANNE BALDWIN, the Wife of
RICHARD BALDWIN lieth here
the 3d day of August, A D 1651

MARY, the Wife of BERNARD BALDWIN,
Gent died the 8th day of Nov 1723.

STEPHEN BALDWIN Gent
died Feb 19, 1780, aged 86 Years

RICHARD, the Son of THOMAS
BALDWYN, died Feb 23, 1692,
Aged 20

In Memory of Mrs ELIZABETH
BALDWIN who departed this Life
March 27, 1754, aged 58

Here lyeth the Body of SUSANNA
BALDWYN, Widow, who departed
this Life the 7th of October, 1693

Also the Body of RICHARD
BALDWYN, who departed this
Life the 22d of July, 1721, aged 64.

Also the Body of MARY, the
Wife of RICHARD BALDWYN, who
died July 10, 1742, aged 79

FRANCES, Wife of JOHN
BALDWIN Gent died 28 May,
1773, aged 71

In Memory of JOHN, Son of
JOHN and FRANCES BALDWIN, Gent
who departed this Life Sept
2, 1761, aged 21 Years.

JOHN BALDWIN, Gent
departed this Life Sept 13, 1769,
Aged 75

Here lyeth the Body of
MORGAN COWARN, Gent
who departed this Life
the 24th of August, 1688

Also HESTER, the Wife of
MORGAN COWARN, Gent who
departed this Life the
24th of August, 1688

Here lyeth the Body of
Mr BERNARD BALDWYN,
who departed this Life
the 14th day of March 1712.

IN THE CHURCH YARD

ON HEAD STONES

	Died	Aged		Died	Aged
John Hayes	24 Mar 1723	77	Lydia his Wife	1 Nov 1764	8
Edward Field, Yeoman,	15 Ap 1768	61	Thomas Son of Thomas and Martha Morris,	2 Feb 1756	
Sarah his Wife, Daughter of Henry			Elizabeth Wife of Benj Brant,	3 June 1741	
	25 No 1733	3	Benjamin Esther	13 Jan 1756	72
Henry	8 May 1729	56	Henry Dyer	31 May 1705	
Sarah his Wife	8 Apr 1763	81	Elizabeth his Wife	4 Nov 1777	
John Higch, Gent	11 Oct 1760	33	Isaac Byand	21 June 1761	
Sarah his Wife	6 Mar 1766	3	Hannah his Wife	9 Apr 1755	51
John	15 Apr 1663	44	Mary, Wife of Henry Dyer	2 May 1755	52
	13 Dec 1753	53	John Proctor	6 June 1684	5
Thomas	11 No 1766	55	Hannah his Daughter, Wife of		
Hester his Wife	12 Oct 1757	55	Moore	23 Apr 1753	6
Benjamin their Son,	26 June 1773	25	Benjamin Brant,	2 Oct 1737	
Thomas	1 Dec 1750	70	Benjamin his Son	13 May 1751	40
	1738	62	Elizabeth, Wife of William Stoaks,	29 Aug 1757	
	July 1 40				
	16 June	11			

XXIII   AVENING

XXIII. AVENING.

A PARISH fituate in the hundred of *Longtree*, and deanery of *Stonehouse*, more than two miles fouth of *Minchin Hampton*, three miles north of *Tetbury*, and fourteen fouth of GLOUCESTER. *Avon* rivulet, rifing from a collection of fprings at *Afton Hill*, continues a winding courfe through this parifh, to which it forms a boundary, and, paffing from *Woodchefter* to *Rodborough*, joins the *Stroudwater* at *Dudbridge* Avening probably owes its name to this ftream, "Ing," in the Danifh language, implies a low, meadow ground, and for that reafon has obtained much as a termination to the names of villages in *Lincolnfhire* The greateft extent of the parifh is nearly feven miles, and its greateft breadth which lies between the towns of *Tetbury* and *Minchin Hampton*, does not exceed a mile and an half A proportion of three fourths of it, is applied to tillage, the remainder confifts of pafturage, with 400 acres of woodland, chiefly beech The foil is, in general, light. Strata of ftone lie within a foot of the furface in many places, in which great quantities of anomiæ, and other foffil fhells, are to be difcovered

The benefice is a rectory, valued at 24l in the King's books, and the church, according to Ecton, dedicated to *Saint Mary* But the feaft, or revel, being kept on the feftival of the *Holy Crofs* (Sept 14), and the following Sunday, confirms a report, prevalent in the parifh, that the church was fo dedicated, and not to the *Holy Virgin* It is conftructed with a tranfept, a low tower in the middle, in which are five bells and a fmall ifle annexed to the nave, which is appropriated to the DRIVERS, of *Afton* The ftyle of its architecture is evidently that of the Norman era, apparent from the pillars, windows, and mouldings Tranfepts are unufual in this county, and it may be conjectured, that as the adjacent church of *Minchin Hampton* has ever had the fame patrons and ground form, they are coeval in the time of their erection WILLIAM the Conqueror granted the advowfon to the nunnery of *Caen*, in *Normandy*, at the fuppreffion of the alien priories, it was appropriated to that of *Sion*, in *Middlefex*

The property of the manor of *Avening* was vefted in the patrons of the advowfon, till the general diffolution of religious houfes, and the confequent difperfion of their revenues ANDREW Lord WINDSOR received it from HENRY VIII THOMAS Lord WINDSOR, his lineal defcendant, fold it to SAMUEL SHEPPARD, Efq in the laft century, in whofe family it ftill continues The right of prefentation, even living, though occafionally alienated, has been ever vefted in the Lords of the Manor EDWARD SHEPPARD, Efq the prefent poffeffor, refides at *Gatcomb Park*, where he has built an elegant modern edifice The park is not wholly in this parifh, the houfe and gardens being within the limit of *Minchin Hampton*

Nearly

Nearly midway between the church and the village of *Afton*, stands the ancient manor houfe. Francis Boughton, Efq is the prefent inhabitant His lady, the eldeft daughter of the late S Sheppard, Efq is maternally defcended from John Lord Bruges Baron Chandois, of *Sudley*, whofe feventh fon, Henry Brydges, Efq was a refident in this parifh, and of whofe monument in the church, an engraving is annexed

A large tumulus, or barrow, in a field adjoining to *Gatcombe Park*, is faid to have been thrown up during the wars of the Saxons and Danes On the fummit is placed a huge fragment of ock, evidently a fepulchral monument, which has been known for ages by the name of *Tingle Stone*

Of the two hamlets belonging to this parifh, *Nailfworth* and *Afton*, the former is a confide able village, a mile and an half weft of the church The elliptic arch of a window is there fhewn in a ruinous building, which is reported to have been a chapel for the fervice of this populous diftrict, in which the manufacture of cloth has been long eftablifhed, and is ftill continued by gentlemen of reputation

Afton, fo called from its eafterly fituation, bears nearly an equal diftance from the village of *Avening* This place, with the extenfive farm of *Loefmore*, was inherited for many generations by the family of Driver, a refpectable name, now extinct, excepting in very remotely collateral branches The relief of the laft Mr Driver fold thefe eftates to Mr Beresford, of whofe executors *Afton* was purchafed by Edmund Estcourt, Efq and now poffeffed by Thomas Estcourt, of *Shipton Moigne*, Efq and *Loefmore* (a reputed manor, the privileges of which have never been allowed) by Mr Sloper, whofe fon, George Sloper, Efq of *Tetbury*, fucceeded to this eftate

The Parfonage houfe, which, by the non-refidence of former rectors, had fuffered confiderable dilapidations, has been repaired and improved by the prefent incumbent

---

BENEFACTIONS

John Driver, late of *Afton*, in the parifh of *Avening* Efq gave, for ever, to bind out poor children apprentices, fifty pounds, vefted in George Sloper, of *Tetbury*, Efq the annual produce two pounds ten fhillings

Elizabeth Coxe gave, to bind out poor children apprentices, one hundred pounds, vefted in Edmund Cripps, of *Avening*, Efq the annual produce four pounds.

Elizabeth Coxe gave, to teach poor children to read, and find them books, fifty pounds loft by the infolvency of the perfon in whofe hands the money was once vefted

S Afton

SAMUEL SANDFORD, late of LONDON, gave, for ever, to teach fix boys to read, and when they can read their primer, and fay their catechifm, to be cloathed, and put away, and then the like number to be taken in, taught, and cloathed, in like manner, the management whereof is left entirely to SAMUEL SHEPPARD, Efq. and his affigns, two hundred pounds, vefted in Mrs. ANN CLUTTERBUCK, of *Hyde*, in the parifh of *Minchin Hampton*, daughter and executrix of the faid SAMUEL SHEPPARD, Efq. the annual produce forty pounds fourteen fhillings

AMBROSE WEBB gave, to be laid out every Chriftmas, in four-penny loaves, and to be diftributed among poor widowers and widows, four pounds, vefted in *Avening* parifh

ANN BURCH, of *Afton*, in the parifh of *Avening*, gave two pounds, to be laid out at the fame time, and in the fame manner, vefted in *Avening* parifh the annual produce of this and the aforegoing fum is fix fhillings and eight pence

RICHARD CAMBIDGE gave, at the difcretion of the overfeers, twenty pounds, vefted in WILLIAM BUCK, the annual produce of which is one pound

JOSEPH BROWNING, of the tything of *Nailfworth*, gave by will, to be laid out in tenements, land, &c vefted in WILLIAM SMITH, but in difpute, the annual produce one pound

INCUMBENTS	PATRONS	INCUMBENTS	PATRONS
—— William Buck,	——————	1728 Philip Sheppard, M A.	W Sandford, Gent
1609 William Hall,	Hen Pigot, and Thos. Hall	1769 Rob Salifbury Heaton, M A	Thos Gryffyn, Efq. and Edm Clutterbuck, Gent
—— William Hall,		1774 Thos Chamberlayne Coxe, M A	Edw Sheppard, Efq.
1664 Rob Frampton, D D afterwards Bp of Gloucefter, 1680, deprived by K William, for refufing to take the oaths	Philip Sheppard, Efq	1779 NathThornbury,LL.B.	Nath Thornbury, Gent
1685 George Bull, D D afterwards Bifhop of St David's, 1705	Ditto		
1705 John Swynfen, B D	Queen Anne.		

The above from Sir ROB ATKYNS

PRESENT LORD OF THE MANOR,
EDWARD SHEPPARD, Efq.

The following perfons were fummoned from this place by the Heralds in 1682, and 1683

John Driver, Gent
Mr William Hall, Cler
The Heirs of Mr. William Windowe

At the Election in 1776, fifty-one Freeholders polled from this Parifh

ANNUAL ACCOUNT OF MARRIAGES, BIRTHS, AND BURIALS, IN THIS PARISH.

A.D	Mar.	Bir	Bur	A.D	Mar	Bir	Bur.	A.D.	Mar	Bir	Bur	A.D	Mar	Bir.	Bur.
1781	19	24	11	1791				1801				1811			
1782	10	25	19	1792				1802				1812			
1783	8	24	11	1793				1803				1813			
1784	3	22	19	1794				1804				1814			
1785	10	23	23	1795				1805				1815			
1786				1796				1806				1816			
1787				1797				1807				1817			
1788				1798				1808				1818			
1789				1799				1809				1819			
1790				1800				1810				1820			

INSCRIPTIONS IN THE CHURCH

ON MONUMENTS IN THE NORTH CROSS AILE

Arms, Argent, a cross Sable, charged in the centre with a leopard's face Or

HERE LYETH THE BODY OF HENRY BRIDGES,
ESQUIOR, SON TO JOHN LORD CHAVNIOS,
BARON OF SHEVDLEY, WHO DEPARTED THIS LIFE
THE 24 DAY OF JANVARI ANNO DOM 1615

Arms,

Arms, Party per chevron Sable and Ermine, in
chief two boar's heads couped Or

In Memory of
SARAH, the Wife of WILLIAM
SANDFORD, of Stonehouse, Gent
and Daughter of SAMUEL ADAMS,
of this Parish, Clothier, who died
the 17th day of February Anno Dom 1722

―――――

In Memory of
REBECCA, wife of SAMUEL RODWAY,
who died August the 8th, 1738,
Ætatis 46

Also of JOHN, their Son,
who died August 5, 1737,
Aged 24

In Memory also
of the aforesaid
SAMUEL RODWAY,
who died August 1, 1757,
Aged 64 Years

Also in Memory of CHARLES, Son
of the above SAMUEL and
REBECCA RODWAY, who died
April 25, 1761, aged 41

In Memory
of THOMAS BAILEY, who departed this Life
July 5, 1763, aged 76

Also
of GRACE, the Wife of THOMAS BAILEY
She departed this Life Nov 13, 1762, aged 63

Likewise WILLIAM, their Son
He died Sept 14, 1760, in the 29th year of his age

Also of THOMAS SMITH,
who died May 3, 1776, æt 50

Also of SAMUEL and ELIZABETH, Son and
Daughter of THOMAS and LETHEL SMITH,
who died in their Infancy

―――――

Arms, a cross, in the first quarter an eagle
displayed

In Memory of RICHARD WEBB,
of this Parish, Clothier,
who died August 19, 1712, aged 78

Also of RICHARD, his Son,
who died June 11, 1748, aged 60 years

―――――

ON A FLAT STONE IN THE NORTH CROSS AILE

JOHN SEAGER, of Chevenage,
died Feb 3, 1755, aged 47

WILLIAM, the Son of the
said JOHN SEAGER, who
died April 19, 1757, aged 25

―――――

IN THE CHANCEL

ON A MONUMENT ON THE SOUTH SIDE

Arms, a chevron, between three mullets.

In quod Morti cessit
ROBERTI BROWNE, PHARMACOPŒI,
De Oppido STROUD, in Agro GLOCESTRENSI,
Juxta Exuvias ELIZABETHÆ, MATRIS,
THOMÆ FRATRIS, CHIRURGI,
ELIZABETHÆ CLEMENTS, SORORIS,
GUILIELMI HALL, A M AVUNCULI,
Subtus jacet depositum,
Die quinto JULIJ
ANNO ÆTATIS 59°,
ÆRA CHRISTIANA 1730°
Animam in Manus DEI effudit

ON A MONUMENT ON THE NORTH SIDE

Near this Place lie the Remains
of Mr GEORGE FILLICHER,
of this Parish, Clothier,
A dutiful Son, a loving Husband,
A tender Father, a sincere Christian,
A Man of the strictest Integrity
in all his Conversation
He died April 6, 1762, aged 43

MARY, his disconsolate Widow,
erected this small Monument
to his Memory

―――――

ON FLAT STONES

Here lies the Body of
MARGERY BECK, the Daughter
of WILLIAM BECK, Puritan
of Avening, Anno Dom 1695

―――――

Here lyeth the Body of
WILLIAM BECK, Rector of
the Church of Avening,
who deceased the first Dec
Anno Dom 1603

JOHANNES SWINNEN Staffordiensis,
Sacræ Theologiæ Baccalaureus,
Hujus Ecclesiæ
ob Viginti & Duos Annos
Rector,
Nat Aug 14, 1664,
Denat Apr 21, 1736

In Memory of REBECCA, Relict
of the Rev JOHN SWINNEN
late Rector of this Parish who
departed this Life April 1730
in the 8 Year of her Age

Here lieth the Body of ELIZABETH,
Daughter of GEORGE BULL, D D
Rector of this Church, who departed
this Life Decem 29, 1690

GEORGE, the Son of GEORGE
and RACHEL BULL, died Feb 19, 1702

MARY, 5th Daughter of WILLIAM HALL,
departed this Life the 11 May, 1683,
Æt 23°

Here resteth the Body of
WILLIAM HALL, Rector of this
Church, who departed this Life
the 9 day of Novem 1683, aged 74

Arms, as before described

Here lyeth the Body of
SAMUEL SANDFORD, late of
London, Merchant, who departed
This Life the Ninth day of April,
Anno Dom 1710,
in the Sixty-eighth Year of his Age

Here lyeth the Body of
MARY, the wife of WILLIAM GYDE,
Clothier, and eldest Daughter
of SAMUEL and MARY KINN,
of this Parish, who departed
this Life the 10th day of October,
1693, aged 45

WILLIAM GYDE, Clothier,
who departed this Life 27 April, 1708,
Aged 63

Here also lyeth the Body of
DANIEL GYDE, late of this Parish,
Clothier, who departed this Life
the 22d Day of Dec 1752, aged 69

MARGARET, Relict of the above
DANIEL GYDE She departed this Life
23 Oct Anno Dom 1773, aged 90

Also the Body of WILLIAM GYDE, Jun
the Son of DANIEL and MARGARET GYDE,
who died March 26, 1728, aged 17

ON MONUMENTS IN THE SOUTH CROSS AILE

Arms, party per pale indented two lions com
batant,—impaling a chevron engrailed, between
three crabs

To the happy Memory of
JOHN DRIVER, Gent who
deceased June the 12th, Anno 1681,
in the 85th year of his Age

And also
ELIZABETH his wife, who deceased
January 28, A Dni 1675, aged 73 years,
They having lived together 52 Years

Resurrectionem expectantes gloriosam

Arms, as above

CAROLUS, filius natu maximus
JOHANNIS DRIVER, Gent
obiit 20 die Januari,
Anno Dom 1636, æt 50

MATTHEUS, ejusdem JOHANNIS natu
secundus, olim Colleg Omnium
Animarum in Oxon Socius, postea
Conliliarius id Legem, obiit XXVIII
die Januarii, Anno Dom 1661, t 27
Refurrectionem Corporum
expectans gloriosam

Arms, as before,—impaling, Per chevron, a
crecent counterchanged

Beati miserecordes   quandam ipsi
Misericordiam   consequentur

M S
JOHANNIS DRIVER, Gen JOHANNIS, Filii tertii, qui,
mortuis CAROLO et MATTHÆO fratribus, in Paterne
hæreditate satis ampla (sine cujus quam invidia)
Successit
Vir omnibus quibus notus erat desideratissimus ut poté
φιλοξενο φιλανθρωπο,, nemini inimicus, amicis
amicissimus, demum in pauperes et egenos beneficentia
exemplar illustrissimum,
obiit nonas Januarii A D MDCLXXXVII,
Ætatis LI

UNDER THE ABOVE IS THE BUST OF A MAN, WITH
A CIVIC CROWN IN ONE HAND, HIS OTHER ON A
DEATH HEAD AND BENEATH THE FIGURE IS THE
FOLLOWING INSCRIPTION

Hoc Monumentum
in honorem Conjugis optime
de se meriti suique immortalis in ipsum
Amoris quilecunque testimonium
propriis sumptibus erexit
ELIZABETHA, Vidua

Arms on a lozenge, as before

To the Memory of
DOROTHY, Daughter of JOHN DRIVER, Jun
of Aston, Gent who died Jun 14, 1665,
Aged 14 Years and a half

And also
of JOHN his Son who died Oct 16, 1655,
aged one Year

ON FLAT STONES

JOHN DRIVER, Gent
died Jan 5, Anno Dom 1687

WALTER DRIVER,
died the of July,

JOAN, the Wife of ROBERT
DRIVER, of Forwood, died 6 Nov 1746

ROBERT DRIVER, of Forwood, Gent
died April 25, A D 1671

DOROTHY, Daughter of
ROBERT DRIVER, of Forwood,
died July 28, 1749

NATHANIEL DRIVER,
of Afton, Efq died 17 Apr 1693,
in the 53d year of his Age

DOROTHY, Daughter of JOHN
DRIVER, Gent died Jun 14, 1685

In Memory of ROBERT DRIVER,
who died March 29, 1751, aged 77 Years.

In this Chapel are interred
JOHN DRIVER, of Afton, Gent
who died Dec 6, 1725,
CHARLES DRIVER, M D
who died Auguft 21, 1740, aged 57,
MARY, Daughter of CHARLES
DRIVER aforefaid and MARY
his Wife, who died Nov 29, 1740, aged 19
Alfo MARY, the Wife of the faid
CHARLES DRIVER,
who died Jan 21, 1742, aged 65

Here lieth the Body of
RACHEL DRIVER, Widdow of
NATHANIEL DRIVER, Efq
She died the 26th of Dec 1700, in
the 51ft year of her age

JANE, the Wife of WILLIAM WINDOW,
died April 30, 1678

THOMAS DAVIS, of Hampton,
died 28 September, 1746

IN THE CHURCH YARD, ON TOMBS.

JOHN HUMPHRIS,
died May 8, 1764, aged 69 Years
CHRISTIAN, Relict of
JOHN HUMPHRIS,
died Aug 12, 1764, aged 76

JOHN HARRIS,
died April 10, 1738, aged 84

THOMAS, his Son
died July 3, 1739, aged 30

DINAH, Daughter of
THOMAS HARRIS,
died July 19, 1731, aged 17

THOMAS HARRIS
died March 29, 1750, aged 67

EDWARD COUCHER
died April 15, 1755, aged 62
ANN his Wife
died Nov 9, 1754, aged 63

THOMAS EARLE,
of Hampton, Maltfter,
died July 9, 1759, aged 63
ELIZABETH his Wife
died May 16, 1731, aged 35

SAMUEL KINN,
of this Parifh Clothier,
died April , 1701, aged 77

BARTLEE SMITH
died Nov 2, 1736, aged 27

THOMAS SMITH
died Nov 7, 1714, aged 78

ANN, Daughter of
EDWARD ADAMS,
died 23 Oct 1663

More Infcriptions for this Family, but
fo obliterated they could not be made
out

JOHN SPARROW,
late of Stroud Victualler,
died 26 Nov 1762, aged 50

ON HEAD STONES

	Died	Aged		Died	Aged
Thomas Hill	— Dec 1752	77	Henry Lucas -	1 June, 1754	70
Bridget his Wife	14 Dec 1753	87	Thomas, Son of William and Elizabeth Lucas,	28 Feb 1756	21
Joanna, Wife of Richard Blackwell,	12 Jan 1767	31	William Gleed	25 May, 1774	46
John Pavey	23 June, 1753	35	Benjamin Hopkins Yeoman,	15 Oct 1742	72
William Pavey -	22 Oct 1767	63	William, Son of John and Mary		
John Pavey	6 Sept 1764	75	Hopkins of Chevenage,	22 Aug 1745	28
Thomas Lerley -	16 Aug 1760	51	John Howard -	7 July, 1745	42
Richard James - -	—— 1751	2	John Stafford	25 Sept 1713	47
Sarah his Wife	—— 1728	49	Robert Howard - -	13 Apr 1757	32
Bridget, the Wife of William Green,	6 Nov 1706	—	Mary his Wife	10 Mar 1 ,	50
William Choudfley	8 Jan 1766	59	Berjman Hill -	7 Mar 1749	43
William Ovens	17 Apr 1751	35	Sarah his Wife	3 Jun 17	61
Mary, the Wife of William King,	17 Dec 1750	61	Hannah, Wife of William Avery,	4 Nov 1747	45
Richard James -	—— 1723	41	Thomas Hudd	— July 1746	64
Sarah his Wife	—— 1751	72	John Hudd	17 July, 1744	62
John Cull	1 Apr 1750	58	Matthew Saunders of Minchin		
Thomas his Son	1 Mar 1774	18	Hampton	7 Mar 1725	34
Sarah Wife of Robert Ind, -	21 Sept 1751	60	Matthew Saunders -	26 Dec 1723	67
William Lilley -	22 Aug 1749	80			
Elizabeth his Wife	3 May, 1731	20			

THIS place is a tything in the parish of *Henbury*, but as there is a church belonging to it, in which and the church yard are many inscriptions and, as it is no farther dependant on that parish, than by paying tythes to the vicar thereof, having distinct parochial officers, separate rates, &c &c it may not be improperly placed here in its alphabetical order

Aust is situated upon the banks of the *Severn*, in the hundred of *Henbury*, and deanery of BRISTOL, five miles south-west from *Thornbury*, eleven miles north from BRISTOL, and about twenty miles south-west from GLOUCESTER, and lies at the distance of eight miles from *Henbury* church It consists chiefly of pasture, meadow, and marsh, land, the whole not exceeding one fourth part The soil in general is clay, or stiff loam

The name of this place was anciently *Austre Clive*, i e the Southern Cliffs, or Rocks on the South Side of the River, near which the church and houses of the hamlet are situated

Under, and near the cliff, a considerable quantity of alabaster is found, in pretty large and small pieces, some falling from the side or the cliff, some thrown up by the force of the tide, which is here sometimes very violent That this cliff formerly extended further is manifest, the channel of the river *Severn* frequently changes its course, sometimes running on this, sometimes on the opposite side, which occasions the increase and decrease of land (as will be noticed under *Berkeley*), and contributes to render the navigation of the *Severn* difficult and dangerous. The alabaster found at *Aust* is rented by Mr THOMAS PEARCE, of *Berkeley*, and applied to various uses

Out of the cliff have been taken the grinding teeth of some animal, supposed to be those of an elephant They were nearly as large as a man's fist, and their colour, by lying so long on the ground, was black

There is a Passage here across the *Severn* to *Beachley*, a hamlet in the parish of *Tiddenham*, about two miles over with a Passage house on each side, at which are good accommodations for travellers It is called the Old Passage, in order to distinguish it from the New Passage, which lies not far from *Redwick*, in the same parish, about three miles nearer the mouth of the river

CAMDEN thinks this place peculiarly memorable from the following incident "King EDWARD the " Elder, lying at *Aust Clive*, invited LEOLIN, Prince of Wales, then at *Bethersley* (probably now *Beach-* " *ley*), to a conference about some matters in dispute between them, but LEOLIN refused whereupon " EDWARD passed over to him, which so affected LEOLIN, that he leaped into the water, and embraced " the boat King EDWARD was in, saying, Most wise King, your humility has conquered my pride, " and your wisdom triumphed over my folly Mount on that neck, which I have foolishly exalted " against you, and enter into that country, which your goodness has this day made your own' Then, ' taking him on his shoulders, made him sit on his Robes, and did him Homage"

The following Memorandums are entered in the Register of this Parish

" 1687 March, 2d day, the river of *Severn* did overflow over the walls from *Aust* to *King-Road*, " and flooded the levels high as the Great or the Large Pool"

" 1688 Feb 8 day, it came over again

" 1(8) Mar 3d day, at night there was a great earthquake "

' 1703 Novem 7 day, at night there happened a very blusterous storm, which caused the *Severn* " to overflow the sea walls, and all the marsh from *Aust* to *King Road* It flowed, the same time, from ' the Passage to Compton, and all *Almondsbury* marshes were under water'

The manor of *Aust* in the Conqueror's days, was in TURSTIN, the son of ROLF After him it passed through many hands and it settled for some time in the family of the CASES It was afterwards purchased by Sr ————— CASE whose widow gave all her estates between her three surviving daughters From one of them it descended to the SMITHS, and sold by the late Sr JARRIT SMITH to the Rev STEEN ————— and ————— who married Mrs DOROTHY WILSON, Widow, the present possessor of it, and ————— on the principal part of the tything, belongs

Mr ————— BERROW to whom the *Passage* of *Aust* belongs, has a good estate here

Mr ————— possesses the principal house in this place, together with an estate

After the church living of *Henbury*, and the church, which is dedicated to ————— , con ————— handsomely painted and covered with lead at the west end a handsome tower, with ————— of five bells and a clock Service is performed in it once a month ————— and on the other Sunday, lectured agreeably to the endowment of ————— mentioned in the Benefaction The Rev Mr WILLIAM TREMAN is the ————— who is appointed by the lady of the manor, and the most respectable inhabitant, ————

BENEFACTIONS.

John Baker, 30 Dec 1706, gave by will, for such poor housekeepers as do not receive alms, the sum of twenty shillings in bread, yearly, for ever And ten shillings to the vicar of *Henbury*, or his curate, for a sermon to be preached in the chapel of *Aust*, on the feast-day of *Saint John the Evangelist*, yearly, for ever, charged on lands in the tything of *Aust*, and vested in William Osborne, of *Kington*, in the parish of *Thornbury*

Lady Elizabeth Astry, in 1707, gave by deed, for divine service to be performed every Sunday in the chapel of *Aust*, for ever, an annuity, or yearly rent charge of twenty pounds, charged on lands at *Aust*, and vested in Edward Sampson, of *Henbury*, Esq

PRESENT LADY OF THE MANOR,
Mrs Dorothy Wilmot, Widow.

The only person summoned from this place by the Heralds in 1682 and 1683, was Mr Churchman

At the Election in 1776, three Freeholders polled from this tything

ANNUAL ACCOUNT OF MARRIAGES, BIRTHS, AND BURIALS IN THIS PARISH

AD	Mar	Bir	Bur	AD	Mar	Bir	Bur	AD	Mar	Bir	Bur	AD	Mar	Bir	Bur
1781	1		2	1791				1801				1811			
1782	—	4	2	1792				1802				1812			
1783	2	4	2	1793				1803				1813			
1784	3	2	3	1794				1804				1814			
1785	3	2	2	1795				1805				1815			
1786				1796				1806				1816			
1787				1797				1807				1817			
1788				1798				1808				1818			
1789				1799				1809				1819			
1790				1800				1810				1820			

INSCRIPTIONS IN THE CHURCH.

ON A MONUMENT IN THE CHANCEL

Arms, Barry wavy of six Argent, and Azure, on a chief Gules, three bezants

In this
Vault underneath
is deposited
all that was mortal of
Sir Samuel Astry, Knt
Coroner and Attorney of the King's Bench,
from the 29th Year of King Charles the IId,
and so continued till the 3d Year of
Queen Anne, descended from the
ancient Equestrian Family of
Astry, in the County of Bedford,
and Lord of this Manor
He married Elizabeth, only Daughter
and Heiress of George Morel, of Henbury,
in this County, Gent
by whom he had two Sons, Luke
and Saint John, and four Daughters,
Elizabeth, Diana, Anne, and Arabella
He died the 22d of September,
1704, in the 73d Year of his age
Which said Elizabeth, in Memory
of her dear Husband, erected
this is a Monument of her
Love and Grief

Also Luke Astry, Esq
Son as abovesaid, who died
the 7th of May, Anno Dom 1751,
in the 28th Year of his age

AGAINST THE NORTH WALL IN THE BODY OF THE CHURCH

Here lyeth the Body of
Mary, the second Wife
of Robert Churchman, of
this Parish, who departed
this Life the 14th day of
January, 1709, in the 60th Year of her age

Near this Place also lieth
the Body of Robert Churchman,
Son of this Parish, who departed
this Life the 29th of September, 1716,
Aged 64 Years and 6 Months

ON A MARBLE MONUMENT
In Memory of
Capt Henry Churchman,
late of the City of Bristol,
whose Remains lye interred
near this Place
He departed this Life
the 3d Day of May,
One Thousand Seven Hundred and Sixty two,
Aged 59 Years

ON A MONUMENT ON THE SOUTH SIDE
In Memory of
The Rev Mr John Wall, late of this Place,
Minister of the Manor called Thornbury in this County,
and Deputy Chaplain to the 9th Regiment of Foot
He died at the Plymouth, after two taken,
in the Year 1762, aged 49 Years

ON FLAT STONES

Under this Stone lieth the Body
of the Rev Mr WILLIAM PIERCE, some
time Rector of Littleton, and Vicar
of Elberton, who died Jan 8,
1733, aged 55

Here lieth the Body of JANE,
the Wife of RALPH BAKER,
who departed this Life the 4th
day of August, in the 44th
Year of her Age Anno Domini 1701

Alse ANNE his Daughter
who died the 3d day of Nov
Anno Domini 1701, aged 18

Here lyeth the Body of
JOHN BAKER, of the City of
Bristol, Mercer, Son of
RALPH BAKER, of Aust,
died Nov 29, 1713, ætat 26

ELIZABETH BAKER, died the
16th of Feb, 1761, aged 68 Years

Here lieth the Body of
RALPH BAKER, of Aust,
Yeoman, who departed this
Life Sept 24, 1728, aged 74 years

Here lyeth the Body of
JANE PHILLIPS, of this Parish,
who was buried in 1711,
Aged near 80 Years

Here lieth the Body of
HENRY HARRIS, of this Parish,
who departed this Life Aug 15,
1711, aged 36 Years

| I H | 1683 | I A | R A | R S |
| I H | 1680. | 1657 | 1597 | 1618 |

ON AN ATCHIEVEMENT ARE THESE ARMS

Azure, fretty Argent, on a fess Gules, three
leopards faces Or, on a canton the arms of ULSTER
—impaling, two bars, on a chief two pales The
above atchievement was put up in 1771, on the decease of Dame ANNE, widow of Sir ROBERT CANN,
Bart and daughter of HENRY CHURCHMAN, of
this Place

IN THE CHURCH YARD, ON TOMBS.

ALICE, Wife of JOHN CAPEY,
of this Parish, died Dec 28, 1747,
Aged 72

JOHN CAPEY, of this Parish,
died Dec 2, 1724, aged 37

Arms, two bars, on a chief two pales.

Here lies interred
the Remains of
Mr HENRY CHURCHMAN,
of this Place, who died
January 9, 1755,
aged 75 Years

JOHN BAKER, of this Parish, Yeoman,
died Oct 5, 1701, aged 76

JANE the Wife of HENRY CHURCHMAN,
Nauta, died 30 May, 1732, aged 48

Dame ANN CANN
died 10 April, 1771, aged 62

MARY PRIGG of this Parish,
Widow and Relict of Mr SAM PRIGG,
late of Westerleigh, in the
County of Gloucester

And also
SAMUEL and ELIZABETH,
their Son and Daughter,

SAMUEL died 31 Dec 1743

MARY died Feb following, and

ELIZABETH the 21 of the same Month

Mr WILLIAM WHITCHURCH,
of this Parish, Yeoman,
died Aug 25, 1781, aged 84

HESTER his Wife
died 11 March, 1769, aged 73

MARGARET WALTERS, of this Parish,
died May 24, 1780, aged 72

THOMAS LANE, of this Parish,
died 12 March, 1757, aged 56

EDWARD WALTERS, of this Parish,
died Nov 3, 1775, aged 47.

WILLIAM HARRIS, Sen
died Jan 26, 1776, aged 50.

JOHN BAKER
buried Sept 26, 1653

ON HEADSTONES

	Died	Aged		Died	Aged
William Harris - - -	25 Dec 1755	64	William Hickes	19 Dec 178	25
John his Son - - -	12 July, 1735	26	John Phillips -	10 Apr 1741	45
William Wilcox, Son of Jms Fow-			Richard Frier - -	11 June, 1724	69
ler, of this Parish, Widow,	19 May, 1764	32	Hannah his Wife	24 Oct 1724	75
Mary, Wife of John Jenkins, of Inst,			Katharine, Widow of William Har		
in the Parish of Olveston, -	16 Sept 1768	75	ris, and Wife of John Bright, -	10 Dec 1753	62

L I E S in the Hundred of *Bledislow* and *St. Briavel's*, and *Forest* deanery, nearly three miles south east from *Newnham*, and fifteen south west from GLOUCESTER. A proportion of nearly two thirds of this parish affords excellent pasturage, including commons which are applied to that purpose. The soil adjoining the river is a strong clay, but the upland parts are of a lighter nature.

The river *Severn* forms a boundary to the parish of *Awre* on the east side, a small rivulet divide it from *Newnham*, on the north, another, called *Lynch Brook*, on the south, and its limits on the west, are closed by the forest of *Dean*. Two streams become considerable at *Blakeney*, which, passing through the parish, join the *Severn* at *Bream's Pill*.

Of the etymology of the name of this village, the more general conjecture is from *Aure Yellow*, in the British, confirmed by the colour of the sands. Some have referred it to the surname of GILBERT DE AWRE, who is said to have accompanied WILLIAM le Conqueror. No such name occurs, either in the roll of *Battle Abby*, or *Scrcen*, so that it appears more probable that he adopted the name of the possession.

The living is a vicarage, endowed by donation, with the great tithes of the parish, formerly appropriate. The church, which is dedicated to *Saint Andrew*, consists of a nave of considerable length, with an aisle of the same dimensions, and a strong embattled tower, containing six bells. The aisle is divided from the body by large round pillars and elliptic arches unornamented, apparently prior to the foundation of a chantry in this church, by WILLIAM DE CHILTENHAM 33 EDW III 1360. The patronage which formerly belonged to the priory of *Lantony*, is vested in the Haberdashers Company, of the City of LONDON.

This parish is so extensive, as to include five Tythings, with distinct manorial Rights *Awre*, in which the Church stands. *Haglow* at the distance from it of nearly a mile, nearly south. *Bledifloe* about the same distance north west, which gives a Name to the Hundred. *Lea* or *Ley*, square nearly two miles south west, and *Blakeney*, two miles farther in the same direction. *Gatcombe* a small village in this parish, but not considered as a hamlet to it. *Hayes* and *Poulton Court* are occupied mansion houses.

The village of *Awre* is not so considerable as that of *Blakeney*. The manor was held by family named AWRE, and continued their property almost two centuries, from the reign of King John to the latter part of that of King EDW III. The corporation of GLOUCESTER, are the present proprietors and belong to the Blue-coat Hospital of that City. The purchase was made with the money left by Sir THOMAS RICH Bart. for the foundation and support of the Charity.

The estate belonging to them is divided into five farms.

The ancient mansion in this tything, said to have been the residence of GILBERT DE AWRE, and reported by Sir R. Atkins to be remaining, is now totally dilapidated. A reputable Family of that name have been long settled here, and are still inhabitant. The held house and estate, formerly the property of JOHN TRIPPER, Esq. his descended to Messrs. HOOPER, CADCAN and TRIPPER, in right of their wives, his grand daughters, and coheirs. At *Hocedand*, the seat of the family of HOPKINS, the Arms of the Tudors, Kings and Queens of *England*, are emblazoned in fresco on the wall of a common parlour, and on either side this precept of St. Paul (Rom xiii) "Let every Soul be subject to the higher "powers, in the Saxon character, from whence it has been thought, that HOPKINS, the builder of STEPHENSON, was of this house, a supposition more easily made than supported. It has been intimated that STEPHENSON was likewise a native of this Parish. ROBERT STEPHENSON Gen. held a considerable estate in 1570, but of this family no sepulchral Monuments remain at *Awre*.

The *Severn* is here nearly two miles broad, though but a little high water, and does not exceed half a mile. Opposite the church lies the bar of sand, called the *Noose* which renders the Navigation extremely hazardous for vessels of any considerable burden. Formerly vessels would venture to pass without a Pilot, and even now the same assistance is sometimes thought necessary. The difficulty is occasioned by the frequent shifting of the sands and it presents a singular appearance. The *Noose* is large, but about a year since. At the Lent assizes, 1752, held at GLOUCESTER, a hundred was presented against the commons, and found by the grand jury.

There is a large common near the river in the tything of *Awre*, on which the right of Pasturage is exercised by the proportion of lands or tenements of the inhabitants. It is called the *Hoe*.

The situation of this parish being so near the River, the lower or marshy parts are subject to inundation from the irruption of the Tide. A short time before the death of King CHARLES II it flowed over the highest part of the Sea Wall, and, if we may depend on tradition at one place in an uninterrupted perpendicular. The inhabitants, from the general state of the air in such situations, are subject to intermittent and inflammatory disorders. Near, opposite *Bream's Pill*, the Hagloe crab, the fruit of which has long engaged the attention of the curious, it being peculiar to the Severn, and indeed a tree of a particular nature, begins to form that bear, or head, which has a particular season of the year, and the quality it is in.

with tremendous violence, for twenty or thirty miles in the country, ... these ... ..., when, ...
immersed in ... seem to have motion, are found ... Sand

Bledisloe was a Member of the Manor of *Awre* ... the time of ... ... belonged to WIL-
LIAM, the son of BADRON, and was afterwards held by the BASSETTS ... ... afterwards Manor
... the property of ROBERT BOX, Esq ... ... a *Hegloo* ... ... now ...
verted into a farm, was the ancient residence of the BASSETTS. There remained, to ... instance de-
picted in one of the windows the Crest, or Cognizance, of that Family ... ...,
coloured, holding in his right hand ... ... cleft at one end, and in his left ... ... proper

A large ancient House in this Tything, in which the first of the HOWICKS were formerly settled,
is now in the possession of Mr W. MARSHALL. THOMAS BARROW, of *Luton*, Esq is lord of the
hundred of *Plasto*, appoints the chief constable and holds Courts Baron, and Leet

Luton duo *Lee* is likewise a distinct Manor, being parcel of the Dutchy of *Lancaster*, it was once vested
in the COOKES, of *Highnam* Sir CHARLES BARROW, Bart is the present lord MATTHEW ADEANE,
Esq is possessed of a large Estate in this tything, with a handsome house, in which he resides *Little*
ham was also, in ancient times, a member of the manor of *Awre*

The village of *Bledisloe* is situate on the turnpike road leading from *Chepstow* to GLOUCESTER, about
twelve miles from the former and fifteen from the latter, and three and a half from *Newnham* on the
South It consists of sixty houses Two fairs for cattle are held annually on the 12th of May, and
the 12th of November

GEORGE SAVAGE, Esq is Lord of the manor of *Blakeney*

Poulton Court, an ancient Mansion, with a private Chapel, now totally demolished, descended from
the POULTON'S to the BRIDGEMAN'S Here is a reputed manor, which was sold by SAMUEL BLACKWELL,
Esq to Mr JAMES THOMAS of *Oatfield* in this parish, from whom it passed by inheritance to JOHN
BIRKIN THOMAS Esq the present Proprietor

Near *Blakeney*, in a ground called *Church Croft*, it is said that the church was intended to have been
founded, but that the part which had been built in the day was removed during the night to the present
situation This ground was a few years since examined by the proprietor, Mr ADEANE In his research "he found several large clumps, consisting of various stones, tiles, and mortar, strongly cemented
"And about two feet from the Surface, a Foundation nearly as many deep, which consisted of four semi-
"circular walls 12 or 13 feet in diameter, the ends of which intersected and crossed each other, with two
"square rooms irregularly connected with the other Building, in one of which were found a number of
"square Bricks for pavement, from seven to twelve or fourteen Inches, some whole, and some broken
"A quantity of rubbish of the same kind was intermixed with the Ruins

A good old House with a considerable estate is the property and residence of Miss MARY A'DEANE,
which lies in the hamlet of *Blakeney*

The Chapel was a small ancient structure, consisting of a Nave only till the year 1748, when we are
informed by a memorandum on the front of the Gallery, "that it was enlarged by Subscription, a new
"aisle and Chancel being added, the Nave lengthened, a new Pulpit erected and the whole neatly pewed
"Mr MATTHEW A DEANE and Mr ROBERT BOX acting Trustees" It is dedicated to *All Saints*, and
annexed to *Awre* The officiating Minister is styled the Chaplain or Assistant Preacher of the Chapel of
Blakeney Baptism is performed here, but Marriages and Sepulture at the mother Church

The Assistant Minister was for many Years nominated by the Patrons to serve the chapel of *Blakeney*,
who applied the Profits of the Impropriation, one part in augmentation of the vicarage of *Awre*, and the
other for his Provision In 1693 they divided the parish as respecting the impropriate Tythes, into two
nearly equal parts, the divisions of *Awre*, and *Blakeney*, which were appropriated as abovementioned
In this state it continued till a few years since the Tythes were resumed by the patrons, and granted in
Lease to the Vicar, subject to the payment of the Assistant Preacher's Salary from 50l to 100l a year The
present Vicar of *Awre* has been lately presented to the Chapel of *Blakeney*, but such Union is entirely at
the option of their respective Patrons

Sir ROBERT ATKINS says, "*Gatcombe* was heretofore a Port of considerable Trade, and *Pomerton* was a
"large town in this Parish, but now both are wholly ruined" Whatever was the state of *Gatcombe* when
Sir ROBERT wrote this account, it has been for some Years past a Port of consequence of an extensive
trade to Ireland, and most of the Ports of this Kingdom In a large Yard in this Place a great number
of Vessels are built Of *Pomerton* not the smallest traces are now extant, nor from the oldest Inhabitants
can any certain Intelligence of it to be collected

BENEFACTIONS

Mr RICHARD HART gave by will, 1670, to ... out of such poor persons ... not chargeable to the
parish fifteen pound In 1707 the parish with some little addition of Money, purchased a house in
Blakeney, called the *Church House*, which is let at four pounds, fourteen shillings, and six pence, per ann
and this after deducting expences of Repair, is distributed according to the directions of the Will

Mr THOMAS ... gave by will, 1771, the interest to be disposed of yearly on *Saint Thomas's*
day, in bread among the poor people of the tythings of *Blakeney* and *Etloe*, at the direction of the church
wardens thereof to pounds the annual produce of which is ten shillings and had in whom vested

Mr JAMES ... gave by will, 1745, to be disposed of on *Saint* ... ass day, yearly among the
poor people of the tythings of *Plusterdine*, and *Etloe* in this Parish, at direction of ANN BERRIDGE, of
————, in the county of *Hereford*, the estate and the church warden ... ... Parish clothes of which
There

There are three cottages, but by whom, or when given not known, in two of them the poor live, and the third is let at one pounds five shillings per ann which is given to the poor

There is a piece of land, but by whom, or when given not known, it formerly produced four shillings per ann but, owing to the inundations of the *Severn*, now produces nothing

Sir Robert Atkyns says, a house and tenement in *Awre*, together with a small parcel of meadow by the *Severn*, were given towards the repairs of the church

INCUMBENTS	PATRONS	INCUMBENTS	PATRONS
1670 James Whiting,	———	1720 Thomas Lane, M A	Haberdashers Company, London
1677 Charles Chapman,	Daniel Andrews		
1707 Rob Maxwell, M A.	Haberdashers Company, London	1721 Herman Morse, M A	Ditto
		1765 John Sergeant, Cler	———
The above from Sir ROBERT ATKYNS		1750 Chas Sandiford, M A	Rural Dean

Assistant Preachers at the Chapel of *Blakeney*

——— Nicholas Billingsley,		1749 Edmund Asheton,	———
1688 Richard Mantle,	Haberdashers Company, London	1754 J C Hitchcock, M A	———
		1762 John Sergeant, M A	———
1727 John Beale, D D		1763 William Arnos,	———
1744 Roynon Jones, M A	Haberdashers Company, London	1785 Chas Sandiford, M A	Haberdasher Company, London

PRESENT LORDS OF THE MANORS

Of *Awre*,

The MAYOR and BURGESSES of the City of GLOUCESTER

Of *Etloe* Dutchy,

Sir CHARLES BARROW, Bart

Of *Bullow*,

ROBERT BOY, Esq

Of *Poulton*,

JOHN BARKLY THOMAS, Esq

The following persons were summoned from this parish by the Heralds in 1682 and 1683

From *Awre*,

Richard Trippet, Gent.

From *Blakeney*,

Thomas Barrow, Esq
John Jones, Gent
John Barrow, Gent
Mathew Buck, Gent
George Barrow, Gent
Mr Billingsley, Clerk
Capt William Jones
Major Gainsford

At the Election in 1776, Forty Freeholders polled from this parish and its tithings

ANNUAL ACCOUNT OF MARRIAGES, BIRTHS, AND BURIALS, IN THIS PARISH

A D	Mar	Bir	Bur	A D	Mar	Bir	Bur	A D	Mar	Bir	Bur	A D	Mar	Bir	Bur
1781	1	13	26	1791				1801				1811			
1782	1	6	20	1792				1802				1812			
1783	1	8	24	1793				1803				1813			
1784	—	4	20	1794				1804				1814			
1785	—	12	23	1795				1805				1815			
1786				1796				1806				1816			
1787				1797				1807				1817			
1788				1798				1808				1818			
1789				1799				1809				1819			
1790				1800				1810				1820			

INSCRIPTION

INSCRIPTIONS IN THE CHURCH
ON MONUMENTS IN THE CHANCEL

ON THE SOUTH SIDE

Arms, a lion rampant between feme of crofs croflets, fitchy —impaling, a chevron between three leopards faces, for JORDAN

To the happy Memory
of Mrs. ELIZABETH BRABOURNE, late Wife
of Mr ROBERT BRABOURNE, Preacher
of God's Word, at Peterftow, in the
County of Hereford, who deceafed
July the 27th, A D 1699

And alfo
of Mr SAMUEL JORDAN, Minifter of
this Parifh, who died lamented April
the 28th, A D. 1670
Whofe Wife, out of her tender
Affection to her Mother and Hufband,
erected this Monument

ON THE SAME SIDE

Arms, a fefs in chief a label of three points
Creft, a demi lion

Near this Place lyes buried
JOHN BYRKIN, of Hagloe, Gent
who died Oct 31, 1740, aged 56.

Alfo MARGARET his Wife, Daughter
of Mr ANSELM NASH She died
January 24, 1748, aged 47.

ON THE NORTH SIDE, A HANDSOME MONUMENT
OF WHITE AND VARIEGATED MARBLE

Arms, a lion rampant.

Sacred to the Memory
of ANN, the beloved Wife
of MATT A DEANE, of Elloe, in this Parifh, Gent
in whom were happily united all the moral
and focial Virtues that render amiable
the Mother, Wife, and Friend She refigned this
Life, in hopes of glorious Refurrection,
May 20, 1771, in the 65th Year of her age

JOHN, their Son, of the City of Briftol, Merchant,
died 6 April, 1756, aged 25

ANN, their Daughter, died Feb 18, 1759, aged 17

Alfo MARGARET, their Daughter,
who lived efteemed, and died lamented,
Dec 3, 1784, aged 47

ON THE SAME SIDE

Arms, Ermine a chevron —impaling,
a greyhound trippant

In Memory of MARY, the Wife of Mr JOSEPH
JONES, Chirurgeon, Daughter of Mr ANSELM NASH,
of this Parifh, was buried Jan 3, 1721, æt 21

And alfo THOMAS, their Son, aged two Weeks

Alfo JOANNA, by MARGARET, his fecond Wife,
Daughter of JOHN TRIPPET, Gent of the Field
Houfe, in this Parifh, was buried Dec 31, 1724,
aged fix Weeks

Alfo JOHN, TRIPPET, JOHN, BENJAMIN, JAMES,
and RICHARD, their Sons, and ANNE and
MARGARET, their Daughters, who all died Infants

JOSEPH JONES, of Newnham, Surgeon,
died the 29th of May, 1755, aged 60

ON A HANDSOME WHITE MONUMENT, NEAR THE FOREGOING, ARE THESE ARMS, AND INSCRIPTION

A bend ingrailed between three gryphons heads erafed

Reverendi admodum vin JACKMAN MORSE, A M
Quod potuit mori hic fubtus depofitum eft Floruit In
Com Glocef de Huntley, Rector, et per 44 annos hujus
Parœciæ Vicarius Pietat charit fide Conftant præclarus
Omnibus charus, nemini noxius, corpore folutus 5° Jan
1765, æt 75 Ecclefiæ nœrorem Theologis exemplar,
relinquens Virtutis veræ cuftos rigidufque Satelles,
Habuit uxorem ANNAM eximiæ pietatis & vitæ bene
merentis, cujus reliquiæ in eodem tumulo fuit recondit æ,
14 Aug 1773, æt 75, juxtaque paternos cineres requiefcunt
corpora EDWARDI, ABRAHAMI, MATTHEI, et ANNÆ,
Tres filios fuperftates reliqueæ

ON FLAT STONES

Here refteth the Body of
CHARLES CHALMAN, Vicar of
this Parifh, who died the
8 March, Anno Dom 17

Here refteth the Body of
SUSANNA, the Wife of
CHARLES CHALMAN, Vicar
of this Parifh, who died the
April Anno Dom 1

Here lyeth the Body of   , the
Wife of John Wintle, of Nible, in this
Parish of Awre, who died
the 28th of March, 1635,
Daughter to Richard
Worgan of Clowerwall

The Reverend
Mr John Sargeaunt, late
Vicar of this Parish, died
Aug 8, 1780, aged 48

In Memory of Abraham,
Matthias, and Sarah, Sons and
Daughter of the Rev Mr Jackman
Morse, who were here interred

Abraham,	Dec 4, 1748,	aged	25
Matthias,	Dec 19, 1748,		12
Sarah,	Sept 11, 1732,		2

In Memory of the Reverend
Mr Edward Morse,
Son of the Rev Mr Jackman Morse,
late Vicar of this Parish,
who died July 29, 1767,
Aged 47 Years

Here lyeth the Body of Charles
Bridgman, of Poulton's Court, Esq
who departed this Life 6 April, 1646,
and left behind him four Sons and a
Daughter

Here lyeth also the Body of Charles
Bridgman, Esq, died
March the 8th, Anno Dom 16

In Memory of Mary Birkin,
youngest Daughter of John Birkin,
of Hagloe, Gent who departed this Life
the 22d July, 1733, aged 24 Years

Here lyeth the Body of
John Gise, Esq Son of Sir William Gise,
of Elmore, Knight, who deceased
the 6 Day of August, 1664

Here also lyeth the Body of
Mr Tyart Brown, left this Life
June 18th, 1737, in the 70th Year of her age

In Memory of Thomas He線, of this
Parish, who departed this Life 1 Nov
1696, aged 16 Years

Also Mary, his Wife,
died 20 May, 1735, aged 60 Years

Also Thomas Hering, their Son who
died 23 April, 1740, aged 45 Years

Also Elizabeth, their Daughter,
died 15 March, 1764, aged 72 Years

ms, is on the Monument for John Birkin

Here lyeth the Body of
Charles Birkin, of Hagloe, in this
Parish, Regarder, who died Feb.
the 15, 1656

Also the Body of John Birkin,
of Hagloe, Regarder, who died Feb 9, 1690.

Also in Memory of Richard Birkin,
Of Hagloe, Gent who was here interred,
Nov 6, 1732, aged 73 Years

James Thomas
died 3d May 1780, aged 50.

In Memory of John Birkin,
of Hagloe Gent who was here
interred Oct 31, 1740, Aged 56

Also Elizabeth, the Wife of
Robert Box, Gent eldest Daughter
of the above John Birkin, Gent
She died the 29th of August, 1751,
Aged 30 Years

Margaret, second Wife of
Joseph Jones, and Daughter of
John Trippet, of the Field House,
died Oct 4, 1776, Aged 73 Years

Here lyeth the Body of
Cathoren the Wife of John White,
who died the 3d day of Sept 1656

Also the Body of Anselm
Nash of this Parish, who died
the 3 Jan Anno Dom 1706 æt sua 46

Also the Body of Rose the
Wife of Andrew Nash, who
died 23 October 1730 æt sua 60

Arms, a buck's head caboshed —Crest, a demilion.

In Memory of Richard Blanch,
Son of John Blanch, and Grandson
of Jasper Blanch of Taftington, in
this County, who died Jan 10, 1712,
Aged 50 Years

Also of Anne, Daughter of Richard and
Margaret Blanch, of Idoe, died an Infant

Also Jasper Blanch, Grandson of
the above named Jasper who died
March 12, 1742, aged 8 Years

Also of Margaret Blanch, who
died December 15, 1748, aged 16 Years

Margaret Adian Blanch,
died 1765, aged 55 Years

Richard Blanch died
1771, aged 74 Years

Mary Bubb, Mother of
Mrs Mary China,
Buried Aug the 21st, 1755, aged 70

To the Memory
of the Barrows

In Memory of William Sadler
of this Parish, who died May
the 3d, 1743, aged 96 Years

Also

Alfo of ELIZABETH, Wife of WILLIAM
SADLER, fhe died Feb 3, 1727,
Aged 56 Years

Alfo ELIZABETH, the Daughter of
John and ELIZABETH SADLER, fhe died
Auguft 1, 1740, aged three Weeks

And of GEORGE their Son, who died
an Infant

Alfo in Memory of JOHN SADLER,
who departed this Life 10th of April,
1786, aged 76 Years

Here lieth the Body of WINIFRED
STIRLING, Daughter of Mr
JOSIAH MARSHALL, Minifter,
departed this Life April 12,
1714, aged near 32 Years

Here lyeth the Body of Mrs MARY
MARSHALL, the Wife of Mr JOSIAH
MARSHALL late of Procelter, who
departed this Life Sept 15, 1716,
aged 71 Years

MARGARET CHINN, Mother of the
under named GOUGH CHINN buried
here the 27th Nov 1714, aged 84

GOUGH CHINN, of Sempfie, in
this Parifh, Gent died Feb A D
1758, Æt 86

MARY, his Wife, died Nov 30, 1724,
Aged 21

MARGARET an only Daughter, who
married JAMES ADEAN of London,
Druggift, died November 1743, and
left iffue one Daughter

Alfo the Body of JAMES ADEANE, Gent
of Sempfly in this Parifh, who
departed this Life Jan 2, 1772, aged 70 Years

Here lyeth the Body of
ANN Daughter of MATTHEW
ADEANE of Idoe, who died
Oct 15, Anno Dom 1685

Alfo the Body of Theo ADEANE,
of Idoe, Mariner, who died
the 1ft of May, 1718

Alfo the Body of JOHN ADEANE,
of the City of Briftol, Wine Cooper
who died Nov 1 1714, aged 7 Years

Here refteth the Body of
RICHARD ADEANE of this Parifh
who departed this Life 19th of June

Alfo the Body of
JAMES ADEANE, of this Parifh,
who departed this Life the
21ft of September, An 1783, aged

Here alfo lie the Remains of
CHRISTIAN BAYLEY, fome time Wife
of the abovenam'd JAMES ADEANE
of Netherall whofe were interred
the 11th day of October 1755, aged 84

Here lyeth the Body of RICHARD
TRIPPET, late of the Field Houfe,
who departed this Life the 13th
of April, Anno Domini 1627

Alfo here lyeth the Body of
CHARLES, the Son of the faid RICHARD
TRIPPET, who died 19th Oct 1632

Here refteth the Body of
ELIZABETH the Wife of RICHARD TRIPPET,
of the Field Houfe, Gent Daughter to
Captain JOHN CLIFFORD, of Frampton,
who departed this Life the
17th of January Anno Dom 1695,
Ætatis fuæ 40

Here refteth the Body of
CHARLES the Son of RICHARD TRIPPET,
of the Field-Houfe, Gent who departed
this Life 22d of Feb 1696, Æt fuæ 24

Here lyeth the Body of
RICHARD TRIPPET, of the Field-Houfe, Gen
who departed this Life Jan 30, 1710, Æt fuæ 63

Art is a greyhound trippant

Here refteth the Body of RICHARD,
the Son of RICHARD TRIPPET of the Field
Houfe, Gent who departed this Life,
May 8, in the Year 1695, aged 9 Years.

In Memory of JOHN TRIPPET of the
Field-Houfe, Gent who was here buried
March 13, 1735, in the 57 Year of his Age

Alfo here refteth the Body, of
JOANNA, the Daughter of
TRIPPET, Gent and Daughter of
ROBERT of Kingfwood,
in the County of Wilts, fhe departed
this Life in the Year 1719, aged
40 Years

Alfo MARY her Daughter, who lie an Infant

Here lyeth the Body of
JOHN ADEANE, late of
Gent one of the Coroners of
this County, who departed
this Life the 24th of Auguft,
leaving behind him GRACE
his Wife, by whom he had
Sonnes and two Daughters

Here lieth the Body of GRACE,
the Relict of JOHN ADEANE,
of Idoe, Gent who departed
Auguft 20, Anno Dom 1656

MATTHEW ADEANE of Idoe, Son of
MATTHEW ADEANE of Idoe, died
1657 aged 18 Year

ROBERT ADFANE, of Etloe,
departed this Life the 31ft of Aug 17-7, aged 70

JOAN, the Wife of the abovefaid
ROBERT ADFANE, and Daughter
of MATTHEW DRIVER, of Hagloe,
who died the 11th Day of December, 1714, aged 45

Alfo the Body of ANNE ADFANE,
Daughter of MATTHEW ADFANE,
of Etloe, Gent who departed this
Life the 18th Day of Feb 1759, aged 17

In Memory of
WILLIAM PRESBURY, of this Parifh,
who died Nov 16, 1767, aged 68

Alfo in Memory of
ELIZABETH PRESBURY, Widow of
the above WILLIAM PRESBURY,
who died Oct 16, 1776, aged 70

ROBERT PRESBURY, then Son,
died Jan 4, 1779, aged 44

Here lieth buried the body
of ANNE, the Wife of THOMAS
SALTANGE of Purkeney, who
died the 2d of March, 1632

IN THE BODY OF THE CHURCH

ON THE SOUTH SIDE

Arms, two bars, a chief indented

In Memory of
Mr RICHARD HYMAN, of Hagloe in this
Parifh, whofe Body was interred near
this Place March the 21ft, in the Year of
our Lord 1736, and in the 60th Year of his Age

Alfo in Memory of Mr NATHANIEL
HOPKINS, of this Parifh, who departed
this Life Jan 15, 1749, aged 52 Years,

To the Memory of BETTY, the Daughter
of the late Mr NATHANIEL HOPKINS by
MARY his Wife, who was buried
April 25, 1749 aged 7 Years

This Monument
was erected in Gratitude to the Memory
of the deceafed by his Kinfman and Executor
Mr NATHANIEL HOPKINS

Near this Place lieth the Body of
MARY the Wife of Mr NATHANIEL HOPKINS,
who departed this Life May 26, 1748,
in the 25th Year of her Age

AT THE WEST END ON A HANDSOME NEAT
MONUMENT

Near this Place are the Remains of CHRISTIAN
Wife of KEITH BYAT, of the City of Briftol,
Innholder
She departed this Life Feb 9, 1774, aged 71
Having approached in due to several state of faithful Wife,
a tender Mother, and an affection to a friend

Joſeph their Son, late of the City of Briſtol,
Merchant,
died the 13th of April 1776, aged

ON FLAT STONES

In Memory of CALEB HULIN, of
this Parifh he died Oct 15, 1731,
Aged 59 Years

Alfo of ANN, the Wife of CUTTIMS GRIBER,
and Daughter of CALEB and ANN HULIN,
fhe died Aug 15, 1747, aged 30 Years

Alfo of MARY the Wife of CHARLES HOWELL
of this Parifh, and Daughter of
CALEB HULIN, who died Nov 25,
1765, aged 52 Years

In Memory of ANNE, the Wife
of CALEB HULIN, fhe died Jan
15, 1743, aged 59 Years

Alfo of ISABELLA, Daughter of
CALEB HULIN fhe died Aug 12,
1745, aged 28 Years

Alfo here lyeth the Body of
THOMAS HULIN, Son of CALEB HULIN,
who died April the 3d, 1777, aged 48 Years

SARAH, the Daughter of
MATTHEW DRIVER, died 24 Feb 1654
Here lyeth the Body of JOHAN
the Wife of RICHARD DRIVER,
who died the 26th of April, 1660
JOHN DRIVER, of Hagloe, Gent
who here interred the 26th of Dec 1719, aged 86

Here lieth the Body of ISABEL,
the Wife of RICHARD HOOPER of
this Parifh who died the 5th of May, 1695
Alfo ELIZABETH, the Wife of
RICHARD BYRKIN, of Etloe,
and Daughter of the faid RICHARD
HOOPER, who died the 17th of Nov
1711, aged 29 Years

Here lyed the Body of
JOHN ADFANE, who died the 19th of January, 1606
Alfo the Body of JAMES ADFANE
who died the 29th of April 1720 his father
Alfo JOHN, his eldeft Son
who was buried Nov 16
1701, aged 66 Years

James, the Son of John
Adeane, died 27 Nov 1662

Here lieth the Body of Alexander
Trippet, who died 24 Dec 1656

In Memory of Sarah Bayley,
Wife of Theophilus Bayley, of
Blakeney in this Parish, who
Died March 13, 1729, aged 31 Years

Theophilus Bayley, of the
Same Place, died 25 July 1766, aged 63.

Richard Bayley, their Son,
Dec 15, 1772, aged 46

Here lyeth the Body of George
Buck, who died Nov 17, 1680

Also Sarah Ricketts died
24 Jan 1768, aged 62

George Buck died 31 March,
1784, aged 36 Years

Here lieth the Body of
Matthew Buck who died
15 Dec 1684

Also Rachel Buck died
2 Jan 1708, aged 4,

Also John Buck died
1769, aged 78

Also John Thomas Dancey,
of the Parish of Barkley,
who died 26 Oct 1785 aged 38

In Memory of Edward Warren,
Anno Dom 1611

Joseph, the Son of John and Mary
Warren, died Oct 9, 1737, aged 23
This Stone was laid at the Expence
of Richard Warren

Here resteth the Body of Isabel,
the Wife of John Butler, of this Parish
Who departed this Life the 18th of June,
1712, aged 70 Years

Also of John Butler, of the Woodfield
in the Parish of Awre, who died
the 22d of April, 1721, aged 76

Also of Abigail, the Daughter
of George and Dinah Brain, of the
Woodfide, who died December
1, 1765, aged 32 Year

Here lyeth the Body of George Brain
of the Woodfield Gent who departed his
Life ... Ap 173. aged 61 Year

Also the Body of Dinah his Wife,
and late Wife of Arthur Lane,
who departed this Life 21 June, 1761
Aged 63 Years

Here lyeth the Body George Keddick

Also of George Keddick,
who died Sept 14, 1681

Here lieth the Body of John Hyman,
who died May 26, 1684

Also Elizabeth, Wife of Richard
Hyman, lately deceased, who
died 31 Aug 1712, aged near 80 Years.

Also the Body of Mr Richard
Hyman, of Hagloe, who died
March 18, 1736, aged 59 Years

Here resteth the Body of Eleanor,
Wife of John Hyman, of Hagloe,
who died Oct 1 1660,

Also Richard Hyman, who
died 22 Dec 1701, Ætat sua 69

Here lyeth the Body of John Powles,
who departed this Life, 17 March, 1711

Also Elizabeth, Wife of John Powles,
and late Wife of John Charles,
of this Parish, who died Nov.
23, 1758, aged 74 Years

Stephen Powles died
25 May 1771, aged 67

Here resteth the Body of
Abigail, the Daughter of
John and Elizabeth Charles,
of this Parish, who died June
9, 1748, aged 28 Years

Here resteth the Body of William
Read, who died the 11th of June 1699

Ann, Wife of Richard Rider,
and Daughter of William Read,
was buried here

Also here lyeth the Body of
John Charles of this Parish
who died Jun 24, 1760, aged 70 Years

In Memory of Richard How,
Clerk of this Parish, who was buried
March 5, Anno Dom 1728

Also of Mary, his Wife who was
buried August 3, 1734, aged 60 Years

Also of Isabel, their Daughter, who was
buried Oct 12, 1735, aged 13 Years

Also here lieth the Body of Thomas How
Son of the above Richard and Mary How
of this Parish, who died Feb 23, 1750 aged 51

Likewise here resteth the Body of
Mary, the Wife of Thomas How,
who departed this Life 1 Apr 1
1751 aged 5 years

Here lyeth the Body of
Mr Walter Bayley
Mariner, of the City of Bristol,
who died 14 Jan 1715, aged

Her

Here lieth the Body of
Mrs Ann Bayley, Wife of
Walter Bayley, Mariner,
of the City of Bristol, Daughter of
Richard Adlane, of this Parish,
who departed this Life 21
Nov 1712, aged near 49

Alexander Bayley, of this Parish,
who died much lamented,
April XII Anno Dom MDCCXXIX
Ætat suæ LIX

John and William, his Sons, by
Sarah his Wife, died Infants,

Here resteth the Body of Sarah,
the beloved Wife of Alexander Bayley
of this Parish, who was Daughter
of Richard Byrkin of Hagloe, Gent
who died June 7, 1732, in the 40th Year of her age

Also in Memory of Hannah Bayley,
the Daughter of Alexander Bayley
of this Parish, by Sarah his Wife,
who departed this Life the 22nd Day
July, 1774, aged 48

In Memory of Richard Rider
of this Parish He died May 9,
1750, aged 33 Years

Hannah, Wife of William Rider,
of this Parish, and Daughter of
John Charles She died Oct
28, 1764 aged 35 years

In Memory of Mary, Wife of
Richard Rider, of this Parish, who
departed this Life Jan 29, 1757, aged 60

Here lyeth the Body of
Isabel, the Wife of Alexander Bayley,
Mariner, who departed this Life
August 23, 1722, aged 44

Alexander their Son died an Infant

Ruth Wife of John Bayley, died A D 1683
Deborah, Wife of George Philpott,
died Nov 14, 1683

Jonathan Bayley, of this Parish,
died May 25, 1724, aged 63

Mary, Wife of John Phillips
died Nov 1, 1742, aged 48 Years

In Memory of Richard Higgins,
of this Parish, who died Feb 14,
1727, aged 83 Years

Also Eleanor, his Wife,
died June 3, 1725, aged 61 Years.

Also Mary, their Daughter,
died Oct. 17, 1738, aged 36 Years

Also in Memory of Samuel Evans,
of this Parish, who died
Feb 17, 1776, aged 74.

Elizabeth, his Wife
died Nov 7, 1779, aged 83

In Memory of John Higgins
of this Parish, who died Feb
16, 1766, aged 83 Years

In Memory of George Keddick
who died June 15, 1731, aged 70 Years

Also in Memory of John,
Son of John and Elizabeth Hopkins,
and Grandson of the said George
Keddick, who was here interred
Feb 21, 1739, aged 16 Years

Beneath this Stone lieth the Body
of Joseph Prestbury, of this Parish,
and Son of Joseph and Ann Prestbury,
who departed this Life Jan.
the 31st, 1782, aged 43

[*Another Flat Stone for the* Keddicks *not legible*]

In Memory of John Butler,
who was buried Nov 21, 1732,
Aged 48 Years

William Butler died Aug 25, 1741
Aged 30 Years

Also Mary Wife of John Stephens,
of this Parish, died Aug 24,
1758, aged 71 Years

Also in Memory of Ann,
the Daughter of William and
Abigail Powell, of this Parish,
who died Feb 24, 1785, aged 24 Years

[*More ancient Inscriptions for the* Butlers *not legible*]

There are several flat stones in the Porch covered
with morter, belonging to the Drivers of Hagloe,
formerly a respectable Family of this Parish

IN THE CHURCH YARD, ON TOMBS

John Lane
died April [illegible], 1726, aged 51

Sarah his Wife,
died [illegible], 17[illegible] aged 60

William Jenkins,
of Hunthall, died Oct 3, 1765, aged [illegible]

Isabella, his Wife,
died Oct 11, 1765 aged [illegible]

ANNE, the Wife of JAMES HYETT,
of the Box, died Feb 20, 1707,

JOHN, Son of JAMES HYETT, died Nov 9 1711
JAMES HYETT, only Husband of the
said Anne, was buried 10 May, 1722

JONATHAN HIGGINS,
died 30 Aug 1771, aged 49

ELIZBETH JONES,
died 8 Feb 1779, aged 64

WILLIAM JAMES, of Hagloe
died Dec 22, 1773, aged 27

Mr JOHN WARREN
died 17 Dec 1746, aged 63

Mrs MARY WARREN, his Wife,
Daughter of RICHARD JENNINGS,
died 26 Jan 1775, Aged 92

WILLIAM CUPITT,
died March 23, 1717, aged 39

MILBOROUGH, his Wife,
died 17 Feb 1746, aged 73.

With several of their Children

RICHARD CUPITT, of Gatcomb,
died 8 March, 1771, aged 55

ELIZABETH, Wife of RICHARD BROWN,
died Oct 9, 1749, aged 38 Years

JOHN, Son of JOHN and
ELIZABETH BROWN, was buried
24 May 1743, in the 30th Year of his age
Mr RICHARD BROWN,
died August 9, 1784, aged 73

JOHN BROWN
died 5 Dec, 1731, aged 52

WILLIAM BROWN,
died 8 April, 1733, aged 64

ELIZABETH, Daughter of
JOHN and ELIZABETH BROWN,
was buried 30 June, 1712, aged 4

ELIZABETH, Wife of JOHN BROWN,
died June 9, 1742, aged 54 Years

MARGARET, the Wife of
RICHARD WHITE, of Blakeney,
died Feb 1, 1780, aged 67

PETER, Son of RICHARD,
and MARGARET WHITE, of Newnham,
died Dec 1769, an Infant

MARY, their Daughter,
died an Infant

RICHARD, their Son
died an Infant

JAMES STOCKS
died Aug 30 1748, aged 75

ANN, Wife of JAMES STOCKS,
died March 24, 1730, aged 70

ANN, second Wife of JAMES STOCKS,
died May 23, 1742, aged 28

SARAH, Wife of THOMAS HAYWARD,
of Blakeney, in this Parish,
died 13 July 1762, aged 24

JOHN HOPKINS
died 26 June, 1731, aged 55

RICHARD, and JOHN, his Sons
by ELIZABETH his Wife, died young.

JOANNA, Wife of RICHARD HOPKINS,
died May 7, 1676

ELIZABETH, Wife of JOHN HOPKINS,
died Feb 15, 1767, aged 76

RICHARD HOPKINS
died Jan 30, 1675

NATHANIEL, his Son,
died 19 Jan 1700, aged 54

SARAH, Wife of NATHANIEL HOPKINS,
died 14 May, 1716

RICHARD BYRKIN
died Sept 16, 1747, aged 38

WILLIAM READ, Jun
died 9 May, 1725, aged 55]

ELIZABETH, his Wife,
died 28 Feb 1724

EDWARD MAN
died 12 Feb 1729, aged 48

EDWARD MAN
died Nov 16, 1777 aged 54

CHARLES AWRE
died Nov 2, 1711

CHARLES AWRE
died Feb 16, 1724, aged

MARY AWRE
died Sept 22, 1737, aged 57

CASLANDRIA, Wife of the above
CHARLES AWRE, died May
10 1717, aged 78

JOHN AWRE
died 6 July, 1765, aged 56

ANNE, the Wife of JOHN AWRE,
died 10 April 1761, aged 53

CHARLES, their Son,
died 10 Jan 1775, aged 21

GILBERT and THOMAS, Sons of JOHN
and ANNE AWRE, both died Infants

JANE, Wife of JOHN JANE
died Oct 16, 1714, aged 54

RICHARD

RICHARD MATTHEWS
died April 28, 1768, in the 35th Year of his age.

THOMAS, Son of ELIZABETH
and THOMAS SMITH, died Nov 5, 1753,
Aged near 16 Years

CHRISTOPHER SMITH was buried
June 15, 1752, aged near 26 Years

ELIZABETH SMITH, their Daughter,
buried 19 Dec 1753, aged 24

THOMAS SMITH
died Oct 17, 1758, aged 61

ELIZABETH, his Wife,
died 3 April 1769, aged 75

CHRISTIAN, Wife of
ROBERT SAUNDERS, of Hayfield,
died Aug 9, 1765, aged 54

ROBERT SAUNDERS
died 11 Feb 1770, aged 63

THOMAS, his Son,
died Oct 28, 1768, aged 29

JANE, the Wife of PHILIP MORGAN,
died Sept 5, 1754, aged 42

ANNE, Wife of PETER BRENT
of Gatcombe, in this Parish,
died 22 Aug 1756, aged 44

HANNAH, Wife of
WILLIAM FRANCIS
died April 16, 1757, aged 5

ANNE, Wife of THOMAS WADE,
died April, 171-, aged -

THOMAS WADE
died Oct 15, 1750, aged 60

JOHN WADE
died Sept 23, 1773, aged 73

ELIZABETH, his Wife,
died Feb 23, 1777, aged 73

CATHARINE, the Wife of CHARLES BROWN
died May 8, 1729, aged 43

Also RICHARD JENNINGS
died Oct 20 1758, aged 42

CHARLES BROWN
died Oct 9, 1743, aged 60

SARAH, Wife of RICHARD JENNINGS,
died 15 Sept 1760, aged 55

ON HEADSTONES

	Died	Aged
John Pray	5 May, 1756	31
William Pray	20 Dec 1761	35
John, son of John and Elizabeth Saunders,	11 Sept 1785	31
Anne, Wife of George Marshall,	10 Oct 1776	44
John, Son of Walter Marshall,	2 July, 1756	24
William, Son of Richard and Ann Wilks,	4 May, 1749	21
Margaret, Wife of William Hicks,	1766	
Ann Wife of Philip Hutton,	7 Mar 1722	33
Daniel Worgan	11 Feb 1694	51
James Webb	18 Dec 1729	46
Elizabeth Wife of James Webb, and late Wife of Thomas Wood,	16 Jan 1775	9
Richard Webb	17 Nov 1775	65
Thomas, Son of Richard Webb, by Mary his Wife,	22 Dec 1774	22
John Son of Richard and Mary Webb,	29 July, 1752	26
Mary, Wife of John James,	8 Sept 1762	29
Betty Wife of Thomas Brown,	6 July, 1784	44
Sarah Wife of John Spring,	3 June, 1742	42
Fran is their Son	14 Aug 1749	16
Esther, Wife of Thomas Rudge,	16 Oct 1754	64
Mary Wife of William Eaton,	14 Jan 1753	68
John Pooling	10 Nov 1754	63
Philip Glanonbury	20 Nov 1775	63
John Shaw, of Blakeney son	24 Dec 1743	65
Charles Merrick of Newnham,	8 June 1757	45
Mary Wife of Charles N ly,	4 Aug 1752	5
Charles N ly	6 Aug 1764	56
William Capit, of Coombe	11 June 1717	47
Thomas his Son	17 Sept 1717	8
James Capit, of Coombe	1 Feb 1761	
William Capit, of Coombe	17 Apr 1752	66
his Wife	18 Nov 1761	78
Ann Wife of Philip Smith,	25 Oct 1741	
Philip Smith	11 Jan 1719	61
Hazel Relict of James Markham	3 Sept 1760	53
John Barton, Relict of Richard Pyke, late of Hayfield,	10 Nov 1680	—
Jane Barton	16 Apr 1698	—
John son of John and Mary Smith of Nibley,	21 Mar 1741	9
Martha, Wife of John Byll	Oct 1750	
William Fox	May 1758	—
Joel Wife	5 Dec 1715	—
John Wood	23 July 1760	

	Died	Aged
Richard Lovell	2 Dec 1723	63
Joseph Prickett	12 June, 1756	75
John his Wife	13 Nov 1763	85
Mary Brown	7 Feb 1719	46
Abraham Hayward	9 June, 1748	70
Jane, Wife of George White	5 Nov 1751	45
Thomas, Son of Richard and Margaret White, of Blakeney	7 July, 1760	15
Mary Wife of John White of Blakeney	1 Dec 1756	7
Ann Hardwick	1 Feb 1758	21
Elizabeth, Wife of Edward Price of Blakeney	11 Apr 1752	41
William Bacon	8 May 1759	60
Ann, Wife of Philip Moss	4 Apr 1761	62
John, their son	1 Feb 1759	50
Richard Son of Richard and Margaret White	Dec 1724	1
John White of Jennings	7 Apr 1756	
John Hayward	Jan 1760	5
Elizabeth Daughter of Richard and Elizabeth Phelps	6 Nov 1756	16
Susannah their Daughter,	June, 1751	19
Mary Hicks	Jul 1719	—
Richard Wood	Feb 1752	—
Thomas, Son of John Parrow	1 June, 1768	—
Andrew the son of Richard and Ann Haskins	Apr 1758	52
Elizabeth Wife of John Hayward,	6 Dec 1757	
Matthew Adams of Nibley	4 Mar 1752	62
John son of John and Mary White of Blakeney	Sept 1751	
William Nest	16 Dec 1753	55
Elizabeth, Wife	18 Sept 1759	
John Hickin	3 Jul 1754	
Elizabeth Wife of John Hickin	6 Mar 1752	5
Anne Wife late of William Price late Hickin	28 Sept 1751	
William son of Richard and James of Blakeney,	June	—
Richard their father,	July 1752	46
William James	May 1752	6
William his Son	May 1752	
Mary Daughter of William and Mary Price	Oct 1752	4
Mary Wife of William James late Wife of John Price	Oct 1752	

ON HEAD STONES.

	Died	Aged
William Craduck, Son of John Craduck, of Stonehouse, by Sarah his Wife,	1 May, 1780	26
William Craduck	30 Apr. 1761	62
Margaret his Widow	23 Dec 1774	67
Elizabeth, their Daughter,	13 June, 1765	30
Walter Cadogan	28 Apr 1723	—
Jane his Wife	14 Dec. 1729	48
Jonathan Cadogan	8 Nov 1765	60
Mary his Wife	12 May, 1773	65
Thomas, their Son,	13 June, 1752	19
Reuben Ayres	29 July, 1761	71
Rev Mr William Evans, A. M.	31 Jan. 1761	48
Ann, Wife of Jonathan Hatton,	17 Aug 1759	66
Joseph, Son of William and Eleanor Matthews, was murdered	26 Mar 1782	36
Eleanor, Wife of William Matthews,	18 Dec. 1782	72
Mr John Hayward	2 Jan 1760	75
Elizabeth his Wife	1 Nov 1742	36
Thomas Adeane, of this Parish, Son of John Adeane, of Millen, Gent	5 Mar 1714	33
Mary, Wife of Thomas Adeane,	9 Jan 1731	51
John Meiser	2 Oct 1668	—
John Grining	8 May, 1685	—
Elizabeth, Wife of Charles Higgins,	15 May, 1714	—
Elizabeth, Wife of William Smart	18 Aug 1761	38
Josiah Smart, of Nibley, in this Parish,	23 Mar 1764	68
Mary his Wife	15 Jan 1784	80
Sarah, Wife of John White, Daughter of Josiah and Mary Smart,	20 Aug 1769	27
Betty, Wife of Charles Howell,	29 Nov 1753	39
Mary, Wife of Thomas Wade,	28 Feb 1714	—
Richard Wade	14 Mar 1729	26
Mary, Wife of Thomas Brown	26 Jan 1752	18
Mary, her Daughter, by Thomas Wade,	5 Apr 1753	28

	Died	Aged
Anne, Wife of Richard Jennings,	10 Feb. 1748	80
William, Son of William and Eleanor Matthews,	16 Aug 1731	16
John, Son of Richard and Ann Barrett, of Gatcombe, was drowned in the River Severn,	1 Feb 1775	14
Mary Wintle	10 Aug. 1759	21
William Cox, of Hagloe,	5 May, 1760	57
Edward Hill	29 May, 1784	44
Joseph Son of Joseph Whetstone,	1 Apr 1749	23
Mary, their Daughter,	2 Apr 1754	25
Jonathan Pritchard	2 Jan 1772	49
Elizabeth his Wife	12 Sept 1770	31
Richard Craft	19 Sept 1766	75
Catharine his Wife	7 Nov 1764	68
Margaret Yemm	19 Feb 1782	53
Thomas Gwilliam	29 Sept 1749	57
Catharine his Wife	21 Dec 1759	77
William Pritchett, of Alveston, in this County,	16 Apr 1749	21
John Parrey	4 Apr 1749	36
George Keddick	2 Jan 1759	48
Isabella his Wife	22 Aug 1765	58
Margaret, Wife of William Beddis,	14 Nov 1742	43
William, Son of William Beddis	9 Oct 1745	6
Isabel, Daughter of William Beddis,	14 Aug 1757	20
Mary late Wife of William Beddis,	5 Mar 1776	68
William Beddis	17 Nov 1780	73
Anne, Wife of George Hayford,	7 Jan 1768	50
Anne, Wife of John Terrett, of Etloe, in this Parish,	6 Oct 1726	52
John Terret, of Etloe,	9 Jan 1709	61
Joanna, their Daughter,	9 Oct 1730	21

XXVI.   BADGEWORTH.

THE Boundaries of this Parith are formed by *Brimsfield* on the Laft, by *Staverton* on the Weft, by *Cheltenham* on the North, and by *Brockworth* on the So th Si le   It is comprifed within the Hundred of *Dudfton* and *King's Barton*, and the Deanery of *Winibcombe*   The Diftance from GLOCESTER does not exceed five Miles on the Weft, nor fix North eaft from the Town of *Cheltenham*   Of Tillage and Paft nage the Portions are nearly equal, the foil is univertally a ftrong Clay   The Parithioners claim a general Right in a Common of fome hundred Acres   A fmall Stream, rifing in the upper Divifion of the Parith, joins the Severn near *Sandhurft*

The Living is a Vicarage, the impropriate Tythes of which are vefted in the *Principal and Fellows of Jefus College*, *Oxford*, for the Support of a School in *Abergavenny*, out of which 16l a e annually paid by that Society to *Chrift's College, Cambridge*, in lieu of Tythes belonging to them

The Church is dedicated to the *Holy Trinity*   On the North Side of the Nave and Chancel, is a Chapel dedicated to *Saint Margaret* (the legendary *Saint Plagius*), which appears to have been erected in the middle Ages   The Door and Windows are in the moft finifhed Norman Style   The fame ornamented Mouldings are on the Infide of each   on the Outfide, the Ellipfes of the Windows are fupported by two Figures repeated throughout, a crowned Head, and that of a Knight, with a Cafque and Gorget of net Wire Work, peculiar to the Norman Aara   Of the painted Glafs, with which thefe Windows were ornamented, a fmall Figure only of Chrift remains in an upper Compartment   No Arms are left which might afcertain the Founder   The Tower, of confiderable Height, which has Battlements of fret Work, contains fix Bells

The Manor of *Badgeworth* is the Property of WILLIAM CATCHMAND GWINNET, Efq by Inheritance from the late Mrs CHISTER, in compliance with a hot Will, he affumed her paternal Name, 1782

Bentham and *Hunt's Court* form a private Manor, which was for many Years the Poffeffion of the Family of HYNSON, it was purchafed by CHARLES HUNT, of *Gloucefter*, Efq   The prefent Proprietor is his grandfon BENJAMIN HYRIT, of *Painfwick*, Efq   *Little Shurdington* is likewife a Hamlet to *Badgeworth*   A very handfome Houfe, called *The Greenway*, of the Architecture of the laft Century, has been long the Refidence of the Family of LAWRENCE   WILLIAM LAWRENCE, Efq is the principal Landholder of this and the annexed Parith of *Great Shurdington*   The ancient Family of EDWARDS, fettled in this Hamlet, became extinct in the right Line by the Death of WILLIAM EDWARDS, Efq 1774   On his Demife, the Eftate, which had long been in the Family, devolved to his Daughters and

G 1   Cohens,

Coheirs, MARY, the Wife of ROBERT LAWRENCE, Esq and ANNE, first married to Mr BLANCH, secondly, to Mr SAMUEL WALBANK In another Hamlet, called *Little-Witcombe*, a good House and and Estate, the former Property of the STEPHENS's, of *Lypiatt*, is now that of DODINGTON HUNT, Esq The Manor-house of *Badgeworth* is situate in the Parish of *Great Shurdington*, the Intermixture of the Boundaries is peculiarly vague, and distinguished only by the Memory of the oldest Inhabitants

----

B E N E F A C T I O N S

HENRY WINDOW gave by Will, Dec 13. 1734, Twenty five Pounds a Year to a School master and School-mistress, &c.

GILES COX gave by Will, Oct 6, 1620, for the Relief of poor Householders in several Parishes not receiving Parish Relief, of which *Badgeworth* is one, the Proportion of which Parish, when the Estate neats 50*l* a Year, is 6*l*. subject to Land tax and Repairs, amount 1044*l* annual Produce 60*l*

WILLIAM MILES gave by Will, 1654, to the second poor, a Rent Charge of 1*l* 6s 8*d*

KATHARINE TALBOT gave by Will, 4 May, 1698, to the second poor, a Rent Charge of 4*l*

TALBOT BARKER gave by Will, 13 Feb 1719, to be distributed in Bread, a Rent Charge of 5*l*

WILLIAM STANBY gave by Will, in 1704, to apprentice Boys, a Rent Charge of 5*l* subject to Land tax.

Besides the above to the Poor,

LITTLETON LAWRENCE, of this Parish, gave a Purple Pulpit Cloth and Cushion, with a Cover of the same, for the Communion Table

BENJAMIN HYETT, Esq of *Hunt's Court*, in this Parish, gave in the Year 1757, the Tapestry, and Two Tables of Commandments annexed to the Altar, which Tapestry was an Altar Piece in the Cathedral Church of GLOUCESTER

INCUMBENTS	PATRONS	INCUMBENTS	PATRONS.
1572 Richard Kee,	George Huntley	1720 Thos Clement, M A.	Sir W Dodwell, Knt
1596 William Stedman,	William Horwood, Esq	1745 JohnChapone,LL.B	Thos Tracey, Esq and
—— Robert Lawrence,	——————		Mary his Wife
1689 Mark Trinder,	Paul Dodwell, Gent	1759 J Baghott Delabere,	Thomas Tracey, Esq
The above from Sir ROBERT ATKYNS,		M A	
		1779 Charles Bishop, Cler	Mary Tracey, Widow.
		1780 Anth Freeman, M A	The same

PRESENT

PRESENT PROPRIETORS OF THE MANORS.

Of *Badgeworth*,
WILLIAM CATCHMAYD GWINNET, ESQ.

Of *Hunt's Court*,
BENJAMIN HYETT, ESQ.

The following Persons were summoned from this Parish by the Heralds in 1682 and 1683

William Lawrence, Esq
William Randall, Sen
George Gwinnet, Gent

James Cartwright, Gent
—— Hynson, Gent

At the Election in 1776, Forty Freeholders polled from this Parish.

The Register of this Parish has its first Entry in 1559 Since the Year 1721 the Baptisms and Births of *Great Shurdington* are included

ANNUAL ACCOUNT OF MARRIAGES, BIRTHS, AND BURIALS, IN THIS PARISH

A D	Mar	Br	Bur	A D	Mar	Bir	Bur	A D	Mar	Bir	Bur	A D	Mar	Bir	Bur.
1781	3	20	14	1791				1801				1811			
1782	3	17	12	1792				1802				1812			
1783	2	10	7	1793				1803				1813			
1784	2	13	8	1794				1804				1814			
1785	4	20	12	1795				1805				1815			
1786	1	15	11	1796				1806				1816			
1787				1797				1807				1817			
1788				1798				1808				1818			
1789				1799				1809				1819			
1790				1800				1810				1820			

INSCRIPTIONS IN THE CHURCH.

ON A MONUMENT ON THE SOUTH SIDE OF THE CHANCEL

Arms, Azure, a Chevron Or, between three Suns proper, for HYNSON,—impaling, Per Pale,
a Lion rampant, for ROBERTS

Piæ Memoriæ
Dum charioris sui mariti GULIELMI HYNSON, Armigeri,
Columnam erigere studet ELIZABETHA
(Filia unica Hæresque Loidii ROBERTS, Generosi,)
Mœrens Relicta
Ipsa mœrore languida, & lugente morbo correpta
sævioribus Fatis succubuit, eademque Urnâ
Commistos Conjugum Cineres deponi Jussit
Moribunda
Quotquot eorum norint Pietatem Charitatem
Amicitiam Probitatem ergaque Proximos amorem
Nunquam finant hæc marmora conspici
Lachrymis orba

Obiit ${\text{Ille 10 Aug} \atop \text{Illa 25 Dec}}$ An Sal ${1667 \atop 1670}$ ætat suæ ${44 \atop 41}$

ON A MARBLE TABLET WITH A PYRAMID

Arms, Argent, a Cross raguly Gules, for LAWRENCE

Reader

Let this Marble be a Monitor to the Living, as well as a Memorial of the Dead, and, when thou readest the Name of
LITTLETON LAWRENCE, Esq
be instructed not to place thy Confidence in the most corporeal Excellencies, which, like his, must undergoe the Deformity of Corruption. And let his Virtues excite thy Imitation, particularly his parental Affection, inflexible Honesty, and christian Benevolence, which, through a stedfast Faith in thy Redeemer, will advance thee to a Life immortal, and full of Glory

He died the 5th Day of April, 1740, aged 54

ON AN ORNAMENTED FREESTONE TABLET IN THE NORTH AILE

Arms, Azure, a Cheveron, between three Spear Heads Argent, points embrued, for GWINNETT,—impaling, Or, on a Fess Gules, three Cheslrooks of the first, in chief three Martlets Sable, for BROWNE.

M S
prope hic jacet
SARA GWINNETT,
uxor cara casta pia prudens & frugalis
GEORGII GWINNETT, Gent
Et filia tertia JOHANNIS BROWNE, olim de Tirley,
in Com Gloc Gen

Obiit 27 July, Anno ${\text{Ætat } 71^{\circ} \atop \text{Salut } 1717}$

IN

IN THE NAVE, ON A MARBLE SARCOPHAGUS WITH
AN URN AND PYRAMID

Arms, Quarterly, 1st and 4th, GWINNITT,
2d and 3d, on a Fess, between three Boars Heads
couped, a Lion paſſant, for GOUGH

Near this Place is interred
GEORGE GWINNETT GOUGH, Eſq
who departed this Life the 27th Day of May, 1756
Deſcended on his Father's Side from an ancient
Family of the GWINNETTS, in North Wales,
who came to ſettle in this Pariſh in the
Beginning of the Reign of Queen Elizabeth
His afflicted Mother, Daughter of
JEREMY GOUGH, of London, Eſq
erected this Monument in Memory of her
moſt beloved and truly worthy Son

ON FLAT STONES IN THE CHANCEL,

A Croſs of Calvary within a Bordure, the only
remaining Inſcription, " NORWOODE "

Arms, HYNSON,—impaling, a Lion rampant

Here lyeth the Body of MARY,
the Wife of THOMAS HYNSON, who
departed the 16th Day of Nov. 1643, aged 47

Depoſitum
GULIELMI HYNSON, Armiger,
Qui obiit
8º die Octobris,
1686

Requieſcat in Pace

Here lyeth the Body of THOMAS
HYNSON, of this Pariſh, Eſq
who departed the 1ſt Day of Dec 1649

ELIZABETH HYNSON
died April 2, in the Eighteenth
Year of her Age, 1720

Arms, Or, a Fess imbattled, between three Catherine Wheels Sable, for CARTWRIGHT;—impaling,
Gules, a Croſs engrailed Argent, in the dexter Canton a Lozenge of the laſt, for LEIGH

Here lieth the Body of SARAH,
the late Wife of JAMES CARTWRIGHT,
of this Pariſh, Gent who departed
this Life the 12th Day of March,
1675, aged 28 Years

Arms, HYNSON

THOMAS, the Sonne of WILLIAM
HYNSON, of this Pariſh, Eſq
died the 2d of March, 165-

ANN HYNSON, Daughter
of Mr WILLIAM HYNSON,
was buried Sept 2, 1679

Dulcibella
GULIELMI LAWRENCE, Armigeri,
Conjux ſecunda
Obiit Mar 28, An Do 17
Ætatis ſuæ 78

Arms, LAWRENCE,—impaling, Fretté a plain
Croſs, for MARTIN

H S E
GULIELMI LAWRENCE, Armigeri,
ex antiqua Laurentiorum in Agro Lancaſtrienſi
Familiâ longo ſanguine prognati
Triſtes Exuviæ
Ad ſublimiorem locum magiſque cineribus
e meliori luto compoſitis idoneum
una cum Uxore Filioque unico dilectiſſimis
(ſi fata fuerent aliquando transferenda)
& in Sacello
juxta proprias Ædes altè extruendo
quod ipſe Sibi, Suis, & Pauperibus, dum in vivis
eſſet, pro ſingulari ſuâ pietate deſignaverat.
Solenni ritu religioſe deponendæ
Sed O quam inanes hominum Curæ
Qui Sacra finxerit Ædificia,
Qui Marmora monte conceperat
humili ſub hoc Lapide meliora meritis abſconditur
nec jam removendus
Antequam ſolutis terræ compagibus ad vitam
reſurrexit novam & immortalem
Obiit Auguſti 29º, Año Domi, 1697,
Ætatis ſuæ 63

ANNA
GULIELMI LAWRENCE, Armigeri,
Conjux Chariſſima
Obiit Jun 12, An Dom 1691,
Ætat ſuæ 41

GULIELMUS LAWRENCE,
GULIELMI LAWRENCE, Armigeri,
Filius unicus
Obiit Mar 3, Año Dom 1691,
Ætat ſuæ 23º

In Memory of ANTHONY, the Son
of JOHN EDWARDS, of this Pariſh,
who was buried 18 Sept 1709, aged 19

In Memory of RICHARD SOLLACE,
late of the Pariſh of Coleſbourne,
Gent who departed this Life
the 2d of June, 1702, aged 74

JANE, the Wife of RICHARD SOLLACE,
Gent was buried the 20th Day of
April 1705, aged 84

In Memory of MARY ELLIOTTS
who died Auguſt 13, 1737,
Aged 77

Alſo of MARY MILLS, Daughter of
MARY ELLIOTTS, who, after ſhe had
ſpent 76 Years, in the regular
Diſcharge of her Duty toward
God and her Fellow Creatures,
departed this Life the 7th of April,
1766

CATHARINE, the Wife of JOHN EDWARDS,
of this Pariſh, Gent departed
this Life the 16th of April, 1700, aged 71

JOHN EDWARDS, of this Parish, Gent
departed this Life Aug 2, 1692, aged 64

ISAAC EDWARDS, of this Parish, Gent
departed this Life May 9, 1730, aged 57.

Here resteth the Body of JOHN
EDWARDS, of this Parish, Gent.
who was b ried 13 Sept 1728,
aged 66 Years

ON FLAT STONES IN THE NORTH AILE

Here lieth the Body of SARAH,
eldest Daughter of GEORGE GWINNETT,
of Great Shurdington, Gent
who died 12 Nov 1695, aged 18

Also the Body of GEO GWINNETT,
of Great Shurdington, Gent
He departed this Life Aug 20, 1730,
aged 44 Years

Here lyeth ELIZABETH, the third
Daughter of GEORGE GWINNETT, of
Great Shurdington, Gent
Nat 1 Sept 1680,
Ob 16 Jan 1682

HANNAH, the second Daughter of
GEORGE GWINNETT, Gent died the
10th of June, 1697, æt 18

Here lyeth the Body of
WILLIAM LAWRENCE, Esq
Obit 28 Aug
Anno $\begin{cases} \text{Salutis} \\ \text{Ætatis} \end{cases} \begin{cases} 1682 \\ 88 \end{cases}$

Here lyeth the Body of ROBERT
LAWRENCE, Vicar of this Parish,
who departed this Life the 26th
Day of June, Anno Dom 1689

Near this Place lieth FRANCIS, the
Wife of ROBERT LAWRENCE, who was
buried the 25th of Sept Anno Dom 1684

Also in Memory of FRANCES, the
Daughter of ROBERT LAWRENCE, Vicar,
and Wife of RICHARD HAYWARD Gent
who was buried the 1st of Oct 1728,
aged 74 Years

Here lyeth the Body of MARK
TRINDER, Minister of this Parish
31 Years, who died Oct 29, 1720,
aged 68

Also HANNAH his Wife, by whom
he had 20 Children She died
Nov 23, 1720, aged near 47

Unus Amor suis his natorum cum sobolesque,
Area sepulchralis continet una duos

He e lieth the Body of
Mrs DOROTHY TROTMAN, Widow
of Mr EDMUND TROTMAN, of Witney,
in Oxfordshire, who was buried
June 28, 1729, aged 74 Years

In Memory of ANNE, the Wife
of WILLIAM EDWARDS, of this
Parish, Gent who died July 14, 1761,
aged 56.

Also in Memory of the above named
Mr WILLIAM EDWARDS, who
departed this Life Sept 4, 1774,
aged 81

M I
died in December 1715, in her 8th Year

In Memory of RICHARD EDWARDS,
of the City of Gloucester, Gent
Son of ANTHONY and MARY EDWARDS,
who departed this Life June 20, 1743, aged 59

In Memory of ANTHONY EDWARDS,
Son of this Parish, Gent who died
Dec 18, 1734, aged 80

Also in Memory of MARY, Wife
of ANTHONY EDWARDS, who departed
this Life June 5, 1737, aged 80

JOHN, the Son of ANTHONY
EDWARDS, Gent was buried
Feb 15, 1687

ANN WALBANK,
ob 7 Martii, 1779,
Æt 41

IN THE NAVE

Here lyeth the Body of SARAH
CARTWRIGHT, the Daughter of
JAMES CARTWRIGHT, Gent who
deceased the 5th of November, 1669

Here lie the Bodies of CHARLES
and ELIZABETH, Children of
ANNE CARTWRIGHT, of this Parish
He died March 2, 1670.
She November 21, 1675

- - - - - - -

Here lyeth the Body of
JAMES CARTWRIGHT, of this Parish,
Gent who departed this Life the
15th of February, 1667

- - - - - - -

In Memory of SARAH
CARTWRIGHT, late Wife of
JAMES CARTWRIGHT, of this Parish,
who departed this Life the 20th Day of Dec
1658

IN THE CHURCH YARD, ON TOMBS.

RICHARD GWINNETT, Gent died the 18th of October, 1675

GEORGE GWINNETT Gent died February 28 1723

RIC GWINNETT Fil 1° Gent ob 16 April, 1717, Anno Ætat 42

GEORGE B[illegible]CK of Heydon died May 29, 1738, aged 40 Years

MARY, the Daughter of GEORGE and MARY BICK, died May 1, 1743, aged 11

ANN, the Wife of JAMES OAKEY, died March 24, 1766, aged 61

ANN Daughter of WILLIAM and ELIZABETH OAKEY

ANN, Wife of GILES STEDMAN, died March 28, 1741, aged 2[illegible]

MARY, Wife of GILES STEDMAN, Senior, died July 14, 1757, aged 69

JOHN STEDMAN died Feb 5, 1755, aged 68

GILES STEDMAN Junior, died March 29, 1766, aged 58

THOMAS HALLING, of this Parish, died May 11 1729, aged 63

JONE his Wife died March 21, 1732, aged 64

WILLIAM HALLING, Senior, of this Parish, Yeoman, died Jan 14, 17-4, aged 64

THOMAS HALLING, Son of RICHARD VICAR HALLING, died March 20, 1732, aged 7 Years.

In Memory of ELIZABETH, the Wife of WILLIAM STAITE, of Stoke Orchard, who died the 10th of April 1,61, aged 43

WILLIAM BUBB, of Little Witcombe, died Oct 18, 1760, aged 77

JOHN BUBB, of Little Witcombe, died in Dec 1705 aged 84

JOAN his Wife deceased Sept 17, 1687, aged 60 Years

Also of JOHN BUBB, of Little Witcombe, their Son, who died March 1722, aged 76

In Memory of JOHN BUBB and ELIZABETH his Wife of Little Widcombe He died [illegible] 16[illegible] She May 6, 1620

Here was buried under this Tombe,
John Bubb by Name of Little Witcombe,
Who of all Flesh did goe the Waye,
In the Month of August the 4th Daye
The next Year after him, the Month of Maye
Elizabeth Bubb could no longer stave
But to her Husband she would goe,
The six and twentieth Day why [illegible]
But ever with him to take a Part,
Of those sweet Joyes in Heaven prepar'd,
Who now expect the Joyes to come,
To their Souls and bodies at the Day of Dome

THOMAS PITT Son of HENRY BUBB, Yeoman and MARY his Wife, of Bentham in this Parish by an unhappy Accident died the [illegible]th of Sept [illegible]6[illegible], in the 9th Year of his Age

JOHN BUBB died Feb 8 1[illegible], aged 16

ELIZABETH Wife of JOHN LOVE, of Stoke Orchard died Dec 25th, 1775 aged [illegible]6

ELIZABETH Wife of WILLIAM STAINSBY, Minister, died Feb 28, aged 78

JOHN EDWARDS, of this Parish, died Sept 1[illegible], 1728, aged 67

SARAH, the Wife of JOHN EDWARDS, died July 1, 1731 aged [illegible]9

CATHARINE EDWARDS, Daughter of JOHN EDWARDS, died Feb [illegible] [illegible]41, aged 61

HANNAH Wife of JAMES OAKEY, and Daughter of RICHARD and MARY JOYES, died March 6, 1[illegible]60, aged [illegible]

RICHARD JOYES died August 27 1768, aged 60

MARY, Wife of RICHARD JOYES, died May 8, 1786 aged [illegible]0

WALTER BRONWYCH, Gent died April 10, Anno Dom 159[illegible]

ANNE his Wife died May 1 Anno Dom [illegible]

[illegible] died April 1[illegible], [illegible]4[illegible]

R[illegible] [illegible]E died Sept [illegible] 1[illegible] aged 6[illegible]

[illegible] his Wife died Sept 14, 17[illegible] aged 6[illegible]

BEATA, Daughter of THOMAS and BEATA LAWRENCE, died [illegible]

WILLIAM RASTLE Senior Yeoman, died May 24, Anno Do[illegible] 17[illegible]

MARGARET, Wife of WILLIAM RASTLE, Senior died Nov 4 [illegible]4[illegible]

THOMAS LONG, [illegible] by an unhappy Accident, departed his Life March 24 17[illegible] aged [illegible]4

ELIZABETH the Wife of [illegible], died Nov [illegible], 17[illegible] aged [illegible]

JOHN SAUTELL, Yeoman, of [illegible] in this Parish died April [illegible] 1[illegible] aged [illegible]

SARAH Daughter of JOHN SAUTELL, Junior, and MARY his Wife died June 14 1761 aged 4 Years 8 [illegible]

MARY Wife of JOHN SAUTELL died Oct 2, 1781 aged 4[illegible]

ELIZABETHA ANTONII EDWARDS hujus Parochiæ 17[illegible], Gen uxor obiit Dec [illegible] Anno Dom [illegible], Ætatis suæ 71

Ipse etiam ANTONIUS hic obdormit [illegible], qui obiit Decembris 24°,

Anno { Ætatis 79 / Salutis 1760

ON A TABLET AGAINST THE NORTH WALL

Near this Place Lieth the Body of THOMAS LAWRENCE Yeoman He departed this Life May 10 [illegible]7[illegible], aged 66

Also in Memory of BEATA Wife of the above THOMAS LAWRENCE She departed this Life March [illegible], 17[illegible], aged 7[illegible]

AGAIN THE [illegible] WALL

In Memory of [illegible] STAITE late of Stoke Orchard who died Oct [illegible], 1774 aged 67 Years

ON HEAD STONES

	Died			Aged
Elizabeth Godwin	21	June	1,65	80
John, Son of Joseph and Ann Pitt,	14	May	177	2
Elizabeth, Wife of John Wilcox,	14	May,	1743	-
Michael Swift - -	22	Nov	1726	[illegible]
William Swift, Senior,	22	Aug	17[illegible]7	7
William Swift Junior -	3	Nov	1,27	40
Mary, Wife of William Swift, Senior,	1	Sept	1731	,6
John Hoidship -	14	Aug	1708	49
Charles Ellis -	21	July,	1691	—
John his Son	20	Aug	1728	47
John Bliss -	—	Dec	1766	51
John Coles, of Norton,	2	Dec	1754	39
Thomas Bick, Senior	15	Mar	1731	63
Susanna, Wife of John Bick, -	11	Oct	174[illegible]	62
John Bick	16	Sept	175[illegible]	81
Thomas Venfield	21	Sept	1756	56
Sarah his Wife - -	2	July,	1758	6,
Charles Cox - -	27	June	175[illegible]	37
Margaret, Wife of Francis Hill,	10	Mar	1758	,2
George Boyce, of Brockworth,	2	June,	17[illegible]	3,
William Killmaster	9	Nov	1733	3,
William Robbins	7	Oct	1,4	25
John Harris, of Little Witcombe	15	Nov	176,	4
Elizabeth, Wife of John Shill,	1[illegible]	Oct	1,[illegible]	48
Edmund Blizard - -	[illegible]	J[illegible]	1728	60

	Died			Aged
William Taylor, Senior	[illegible]0	Dec	[illegible]00	
Elizabeth, Wife of Benjamin Baldwin	3	Mar	17[illegible]1	[illegible]
John Bishs	19	Aug	1708	
Richard Bishs -	[illegible]	Mar	1,54	46
William Drinkwater -	27	Mar	1,55	
Thomas Benfield	2	N[illegible]	17[illegible]	[illegible]
Joseph Turner -	19	Oct	[illegible]	[illegible]
Elizabeth his Wife -	2	J[illegible]	[illegible]7[illegible]3	[illegible]
Sarah their Daughter	[illegible]	Au[illegible]	7[illegible]	[illegible]
Mary Wife of John Coker	1	M[illegible]	[illegible]	
Hester their Daughter -	1[illegible]	M[illegible]	[illegible]5	24
Mary Wife of William Hopkins,	5	Ap	17[illegible]8	[illegible]
Sarah, Wife of William Harman of Ebley, in the Parish of Randwick,	4	M[illegible]	17[illegible]	2[illegible]
John Harris	[illegible]	J[illegible]	[illegible]	84
Richard Hall[illegible] -	8	[illegible]	[illegible]	
William Bennett -	[illegible]5	[illegible]	[illegible]81	-
John Kane	—	M[illegible]	[illegible]5	[illegible]0
Mary his Wife	3	[illegible]	1[illegible]	[illegible]
Ann Wife of Thomas Bick's,	7	[illegible]	[illegible]	[illegible]
John Roberts	1	O[illegible]	[illegible]9	[illegible]
Joan Wife of John Andrews by an unhappy Accident departed this Life	[illegible]	May,	17[illegible]0	64

SITUATE in the Hundred of *Grumbald's Ash*, and Deanery of *Hawkesbury*, is distant from *Tetbury* nine Miles on the South-east, six North-east from *Sodbury*, and twenty-six South from GLOUCESTER. This Parish, with that of *Little Badminton*, is nearly included within the Boundary Wall of the Park and Warrens of his Grace the Duke of BEAUFORT, a Circumference of ten Miles. The Soil is chiefly productive of Corn, with a considerable Extent of Pasturage.

The Benefice is a Vicarage, once an Appendage to the Priory of *Lylshall*, in *Shropshire*. The Lands are consequently free of impropriate Tythes. The Vicarage has been augmented by Benefaction of the noble Family of BEAUFORT, its certified Value is stated by Ecton at 13'. The ancient Church, dedicated to *Saint Michael*, was rebuilt at the sole Expence of his present Grace HENRY Duke of BEAUFORT, from a Design of Mr EVANS, of *London*, and has given Place to one of singular Elegance, which was consecrated October 9, 1785. A Nave, with two Ailes and a pinnacled Tower, containing three Bells, form a compleat Structure. The Symmetry and Lightness of the Elevation is perfectly Grecian. Its uniform Plainness beautifully relieves, and prepares the Eye for Ornaments so finished and appropriate, as those with which it is decorated within. The Roof of the Nave is supported by six Pillars of the Italian composite Order, the Cieling of the Ailes is formed by four small Domes, the whole of Stucco, exquisitely wrought. The Pews are of Dutch Oak, in a new Style, and over the Altar is a Picture by C GHEZZI, of "CHRIST disputing with the Doctors." A more superb Display of Marbles, or more correctly disposed, few Places can exhibit. The Approach to the Altar is made by Steps of Jasper and Verd antique. The Pavement of it is composed of a great Variety of Marbles of mosaic Work, in the Centre of which, the Arms and Supporters of BEAUFORT of considerable Dimension, are emblazoned, and inlaid, Parts of which consist of Lapis Lazuli. HENRY, third Duke of BEAUFORT made this Collection during his Travels in *Italy*. In large Recesses on either Side the Communion Table, are Monuments on which the whole Skill of the elaborate RYSBRACK seems to have been exerted.

The Manor, comprising the whole landed Tenure of the Parish, appears to have been possessed by few Families. EDRIC, a Saxon, held it at the Conquest. Soon after it was vested in the knightly Family of BOTELER, who made it their Residence, and from NICHOLAS BOTELER it descended by Purchase to THOMAS SOMERSET, third Son of EDWARD Earl of WORCESTER, created Viscount SOMERSET, of *Cashell*, in *Ireland*.

On the Scite of the ancient Mansion, a magnificent Edifice was founded by the first Duke of BEAUFORT, soon after his Accession of Honour, and Departure from his Castle of *Ragland*, in *Monmouthshire*, rendered uninhabitable by the Ravages of the Civil War, and the memorable Siege it sustained against CROMWELL.

A House so situated cannot but command that Air of Grandeur which results from so extensive a Domain, the Effect of which is greatly heightened by many Avenues of stately Trees, one of which, terminated by an Artic Building, called *Ilb Gratel Lodge*, extends for nearly three Miles.

In the Picture Gallery the original Portraits of the princely Family of SOMERSET, descended from JOHN of GAUNT, are arranged in the following chronological Series:

1 John of Gaunt, Duke of Lancaster	8 ... and Somerset, fourth Earl
2 John de Beaufort, Earl of Somerset	9 Henry Somerset, first Marquis of Worcester
3 Edmund de Beaufort, Earl of Mortain, and Marquis of Dorset	10 Edward Somerset, Earl of Glamorgan, second Marquis
4 Henry de Beaufort, Duke of Somerset	11 Henry Somerset, first Duke of Beaufort
5 Charles, first Earl of Worcester	12 Henry Somerset, second Duke
6 Henry Somerset, second Earl	13 Henry Somerset, third Duke
7 William Somerset, third Earl	14 Charles Noel Somerset, fourth Duke

The Gardens and Pleasure Grounds are delineated by Kip, in the view, engraved for Sir Robert Atkyns's History of this County, abounding with the "Topiary Works," green Statuary and Labyrinths of Yew Trees, but these have long since yielded to the Requirements of the modern Mode of Gardening.

The Village of *Badminton* contains more than few or Houses. A large Building was erected for charitable Purposes by MARY Duchess Dowager of Beaufort, Esq. A Road was appropriated to the Vicar for the ...

B E N E F A C T I O N S

MARY Dutchefs of BEAUFORT by Will, 171_, gave in annual Salary of 1_l_ for a School mafter to teach Children to read and write, arifing from Lands vefted in his Grace. At the fame Time an Almshoufe for three poor Men, and three poor Women, under the Appointment, Direction, and Government of the Duke (whofe Servants are to be preferred) with a weekly Allowance of 2s 6d each

INCUMBENTS	PATRONS	INCUMBENTS	PATRONS
—— Ralph Bifhop,	Queen Elizabeth	—— John Hottman,	John Horton in
1599 William Cable,	Nich Boteler, Efq	—— Thos Franklyn, M A	Marquis of Worcefter.
—— Gilbert Maffey,	Sir George Ivey	—— Atkinfon,	Duke of Beaufort

For many Years paft, the Duke's domeftic Chaplains have officiated as Minifters
The prefent Chaplain is the Rev ROBERT PENNY, D D Rector of *Cromhall*, in this County

PRESENT LORD OF THE MANOR,
HIS GRACE HENRY DUKE OF BEAUFORT.

No Refident in this Parifh was fummoned by the Heralds in 1682 and 1683

The Regifter of *Badminton* is one of the moft ancient, not only in this, but in any County It has many Entries of the BOTELERS, and one as early as 1538, from which Period, to 1599, they are made in one Manufcript.

It appears from an Extract of this Regifter, 1654, that, in purfuance of an Act of Parliament, JOHN WINBOW was appointed Regiftrar of this Parifh The Appointment is figned by NATHANIEL POWER, Minifter, and fix Inhabitants

The following is a literal Tranfcript of the Regifter, relative to the Foundation of the new Church

"The old Parifh Church at *Great Badminton*, which was very ruinous, was begun pulling down Tuefday March 4, 1783, and on Tuefday April 22, 1785, the firft N E corner Stone was laid by HENRY, fifth Duke of BEAUFORT, and the fame Time laid by his eldeft Son HENRY CHARLES, Marquis of Worcefter The Foundation of the new Church was put back farther towards the Eaft, than the old, fo that the Tower of the new Church now ftands where the Chancel ftood before

"It was finifhed the latter End of September, 1785, and on Sunday the 9th of October, 1785, it was confecrated by SAMUEL Lord Bifhop of GLOUCESTER, attended by his Chancellor, EDWARD COOKE, Efq

"The Church Yard of *Little Badminton* was confecrated the fame Day, having been enlarged for the Ufe of both Parifhes

"October 16ᵗ 1785

" BEAUFORT,
" WORCESTER,
" C H SOMERSET,
" R PENNY, D D
" T BRYAN,
" ISAAC HATHERELL, } Church Wardens
" THOMAS WEBB,
" THOMAS WATTS,
" ROBERT BENNETT, } Inhabitants "
" JAMES DOWDING,

ANNUAL ACCOUNT OF MARRIAGES, BIRTHS, AND BURIALS, IN THIS PARISH

A D	Mar	Bir	Bur	A D	Mar	Bir	Bur	A D	Mar	Bir	Bur	A D	Mar	Bir	Bur
1781	2	16	10	1791				1801				1811			
1782	—	14	10	1792				1802				1812			
1783	6	14	5	1793				1803				1813			
1784	3	18	4	1794				1804				1814			
1785	4	19	4	1795				1805				1815			
1786	5	17	8	1796				1806				1816			
1787				1797				1807				1817			
1788				1798				1808				1818			
1789				1799				1809				1819			
1790				1800				1810				1820			

INSCRIPTIONS IN THE CHURCH

In the Rees on the right Hand of the Altar, on a Base, a Sarcophagus of black Marble, on ... is a Statue, as large as Life, of the second Duke of Beaufort, in his ... , holding a Medallion with a female Bust in basso relievo, near him the third Duke in a Roman Dress and Attitude standing ... Coronet and Scroll, with the motto ... ... by two Genii in Relievo on the Pyramid

SACRED TO THE MEMORY

Of the High, Puissant and most Noble Prince,
HENRY SOMERSET,
Second Duke of Beaufort,
Marquis and Earl of Worcester,
Earl of Glamorgan,
Baron Herbert, Lord of Ragland,
Chepstow, and Gower,
Baron Beaufort, of Caldecot Castle,
Lord Lieutenant of the Counties of
Southampton and Gloucester,
And City of Bristol,
And Custos Rotulorum,
And Lord Warden of New Forest,
Captain of her Majesty's Honourable Band
of Gentlemen Pensioners,
And One of the Lords of her Majesty's
Most Honourable Privy Council,
Knight of the most Noble Order of the Garter,
who died the 24th Day of May, 1714,
in the 30th Year of his Age

On the Pedestal, the Arms of BEAUFORT in the
Garter, Quarterly France and England within a
Bord ... compone Pearl and Sapphire

And
of Lady RACHEL NOEL, his second Wife,
Second Daughter and Coheir to
WRIOTHESLEY BAPTIST NOEL,
Earl of Gainsborough
She died the 13th Day of Sept. 1709

And also
Of HENRY SOMERSET,
their eldest Son,
Third Duke of Beaufort, &c.
who died issueless
the 24th Day of Feb. 1745,
in the 37th Year of his Age
Was succeeded in Honour and Estate
by his only Brother
Lord CHARLES NOEL SOMERSET,
Fourth Duke of Beaufort

Arms of BEAUFORT as before —impaling,
Topaz, fretty, Ruby a Canton Ermine, for NOEL

IN THE LEFT RECESS

On a Pedestal, a Statue as large as Life, standing, in a Roman Garb, and in the Attitude of public speaking, a Cherub reclining supports the Coronet on a Cushion
On the Pyramid
Arms, Beaufort as before,—impaling, Ruby, a Chevron Ermine, between ten Crosses, patee, Pearl, for BERKELEY

(The following Epitaph was composed by Doctor King, late Head of St Mary Hall, in the University of Oxford)

H. S. E.
Princeps illustrissimus
CAROLUS NOEL SOMERSET,
Dux de BEAUFORT,
Qui a vetusta praepotentum Anglorum oriundus
Splendore ... variatam prosperavit,
Locupletando ... quicumque is nisi ...
P... fortunae ...
Ac tentatam ... fastidiivs,
... que publici amoris non testis,
Tum in re ... um temporum iniquitas,
Incrementum ... virtute excoluit,
fait ... publicae bonum futurum
Dignus ... honores
... bene excellentissimum
... propter ... opium,
Cum ... Carolum nulli ...
... virtute ornamentis confirmant
... ...
Dux populus suam
Cum ... ... tuit honorem ...

Nam domesticarum ...
Ac cuncti honestissimae vitae officia
Dulcissime fovens ...
Maritus fidelissimus,
Pater optimus,
Amicus certus & constans
Hospes comitatus & iucundus
Accident ... Oxoniensis praesidium,
Literarum omnium patronus
Ipse eruditissimus
In ... um Lab ... nomen ...
Nihil quod patriae & reipublicae ... amicum,
Tremens illi ... vultus decoris ...
... Laudabilis virtute cum compensavit
Ut honor ... domerendis non valde ...
Uxorem duxit
ELIZABETHAM, filiam JOHANNIS PORTMAN, de
Stoke Gifford, in agro Gloucestriae Armigeri,
foeminam primariam, ... divino dignissimam
Ex qua ... filios quinos, famulam ... ,
Sunt ... spe praeclarum ... quinque nobis
Quem incolumem tege Deus,
Ut nobilissimi in dominam,
Principe ... illustrissimi
Luminis ... morte liberet ... ,
Avuli ... ... restituit fortunae & ... ta
Finis, ... qua familiaris!
Obiit Atlantico dolore confectus
Die 8 Octobris 1756, ... anno ...

F f

V SA

ANNA, fila natu maxima, quæ nupta fuit CAROLO COMPTON, Comiti de NORTHAMPTON, ob 16 Mail, 1763

ELIZABETHA, fecunda innupta, ob 10 Maii, 1760

HENRIETTA tertia, Dño WATKINS WILLIAMS WYNNE, Baronetto, nupta, ob (fine prole) 24 Julii, 1769

MARIA ISABELLA, ultima, CAROLO MANNERS, Duci de RUTLAND, nupta

IN A RECESS AT THE WEST END OF THE SOUTH AILE, WAINSCOTTED WITH MARBLE, THE FLOOR MOST BEAUTIFULLY VARIEGATED, THE CYPHER AND COGNIZANCE OF BEAUFORT IN MARQUETRY, A LARGE TABLE TOMB, THE SLAB AND BASE OF WHICH ARE OF BLACK MARBLE, ON THE SIDES THE FOLLOWING INSCRIPTIONS AND ARMS

BEAUFORT,—impaling, Ruby, a Lion falient, between three Crofflets fitchy topaz, for CAPEL.

MARY, Widow to HENRY Lord BEAUCHAMP, maryed HENRY Duke of BEAUFORT, and by him had thefe Children,

ELIZABETH, buried att Raglan,
HENRY, att Windfor,
EDWARD, att Raglan,
another HENRY, att Raglan,
CHARLES Lord Marquis of WORCESTER, att Raglan,
Lord ARTHUR SOMERSETT, maryed MARY, Daughter to
Sir WILLIAM RUSSELL, Baronett,
MARY, maryed to JAMES Duke of ORMONDE,
HENRIETTA, firft maryed to HENRY HORATIO Lord
OBRIAN, now to HENRY Earle of SUFFOLK and BINDON,
ANNE, maryed to THOMAS Earle of COVENTRY

Arms, Topaz, on a Pile Ruby three Lions of England, between fix Fleurs de Lis Sapphire, for SLYMOUR,—impaling, CAPEL, as before

MARY, eldeft Daughter of ARTHUR Lord CAPELL, maryed firft to HENRY Lord BEAUCHAMP, Son to WILLIAM Duke of SOMERSET, and by him had thefe Children,

FRANCIS, buried at Hadham,
MARY, at Bedwin,
WILLIAM Duke of SOMERSET, at Bedwin,
ELIZABETH, Countefs of AILSBURY, at Ampthill,

To the moft Noble MARY,
Dutchefs of BEAUFORT,
Relict of the moft Puifant Prince,
HENRY Duke of BEAUFORT,
Daughter to the Right Honourable ARTHUR
Lord CAPELL (who was murdered
by the Rebells in the Year 1648),
Departed this Life January
the 7th, 1714, in the 85th Year of her Age

On the South Side are the BEAUFORT Arms, Supporters, and Creft

---

ON FLAT STONES IN THE BELLFRY

Hic jacet CAROLUS PRICE,
Illuftriffimo Domino HENRICO Duci
de BEAUFORT dum vixit a Secretis,
Cui quinquaginta novem annorum
fpatio pervigili operi &
induftria in agendo Servitium se præbuit
perquam fidelem obiit 11 die
Februarii Anno Domini 1703,
Ætatis fuæ 79

Requiefcat in Pace!

Arms, Quarterly, 1ft and 4th, a Lefs between three Birds, 2d and 3d, Ermine, on a Bend, engrailed, three Roundels —Creft a Bird

Here lyeth the Body of JOHN LOCKWOOD, Gentleman of the Bed Chamber for above Forty Years to the Moft Noble HENRY, the firft Duke of BEAUFORT, who departed this Life March 2), Anno Dom 1720, Ætatis 90

IN THE CHURCH YARD

Here refteth the Body of MILLICENT, the Wife of ROGER STOCKERSTON, who deceeded this Life the 11th Day of Feb Anno 1647, Ætatis fuæ 50

Here refteth the Body of Mr JOHN HUMFREYS of the Town of Northampton, who was buried the 2d Day of March Anno Dñi 1697

Arms,

Arms, in a Lozenge, Per Pale three Lions
rampant

D O M
Sub hoc Lapide
Refufcitationem juftorum præ-
ftolantur exuviæ MARGARETÆ,
filiæ fecundo genitæ ARTHURI
PROGER, de Badminton, Generofi,
Ancillæ honorariæ præcellentiffimæ
Heroinæ LLENÆ Comitiſſæ Ormon-
diæ & Oſſoriæ
Defponfata fuit EDVARDO MOLLI-
NEUX, Vectenfi Armigero, è clientela
nobiliſſima DI THOMÆ Vicecomitis
SOMERSET
Sed deſtinatas vellunt nuptias
Inopinato fatum vulnere
Sponfo Fido fuperftite,
Qui amantem deflens VIRGIN M
Hoc Marmor curatus pofuit,
Obiit vi die Menſis Augufti

Anno { reparationis humanæ MDCXXXVI
      { ætatis fuæ XXVI

On a Flat Stone of grey Marble, was the Figure
of a Knight in Brafs, and out the Verge, in old
black Characters, the following Infcription

Filius ejus RADULPHUS
BOTTLER, Miles Dominus

At the Feet of the Figure, on a Shield, a Lion
rampant

Here lyeth the Body of SAMUEL THORP,
late Servant to the Right Honourable Lord
Marquiſſe of WORCESTER, who departed
this Life upon the 13th Day of October,
Anno Domini 1682,
Ætatis fuæ 55

In Memory of
THOMAS SHILWAY,
late Yeoman to his Majefty,
who departed this Life
the 25th of Nov 1756,
aged 56 Years

Here lyeth at the Right Hand of her Father
ARTHUR PROGER, Gent ANN his eldeſt Daughter,
late Wife of GEORGE RUSSELL, of Acton Turville,
who departed this Life the 30th Day of October,
Anno 1643

Here lyeth the Body of
JOHN SMART, who departed this
Life the 9th Day of April, 1729, aged 70

RUTH his Wife
died Feb 1 , 1720, aged 82

Here lyeth the Body of ELIZABETH
MUDD, Wife of CHARLES MUDD, Gent
who departed this Life the 31ſt of
May, 1743, in the 81ſt Year of her Age

ON HEAD STONES

	Died	Aged
Elizabeth Wife of Thomas Lee,	19 Feb 17 ,	55
Jam Son of Thomas and Eliz en Lee	17 Aug 1779	2
Thomas Pool, late Coachman to his Grace the Duke of Beaufort	18 Feb 17 5	55
Mary, Daughter of Martha and Smart Poach	27 Sept 1770	1
Thomas his Son	14 Mar 1 7	
Smart Poach their Father	30 May, 1775	62
Henry Tuck	1 Mar 1657	—
John Linley	22 Sept 176 ,	—
Sarah Wife of John Linley	9 June, 1663	
Mary, Wife of Had South,	13 Aug 1678	32
James Bishop	12 May 1763	26
Mary his Wife	6 Mar, 1760	27
Elizabeth, Wife of William Te nell,	, June ,	21
Sarah Wife of Robert Warren,	18 Dec 1691	63
Richard Phillips	30 Mar 1 1	74
William Will m	5 June 1 43	100
William Harden	8 Dec 1743	
Hefter his Wife	21 Mar 1 11	56
Jane Wife of Thomas Watts,	12 Dec 1 37	79
Thomas Jones	23 Feb 1 0	15
Elizabeth Wife of Jonathan Lee, Daughter of William and Martha Younge,	9 Feb 1765	24
Heſter, Wife of Robert Somers,	14 ch 1 80	43
George, Son of Thomas and Sarah Watts,	5 Dec 1723	73
Thomas Fowler	16 r 1 44	64
Ann Wife of Thomas Hogar	13 Feb 1733	
Margaret their Daughter Wife of John Hort		
Elizabeth, third Wife of John Hort	June 1775	
Elizabeth, Wife of William Hort,	Nov 17 ,	43

	Died	Aged
Ann Wife of Thomas Hort,	5 Dec 1738	44
Thomas Hort	25 Dec 1763	60
Thomas Roach	6 Mar 1780	62
Francis Lincoln Yeoman departed this Life at Badminton Purv	22 June, 1780	42
Ifabel, Wife of Richard Philpot and Daughter of William and Martha Liney,	7 Aug 1765	8
Joan, the Wife of Thomas Roach	3 Oct 1746	67
Thomas Roach their Parish Guardian to Robert Venn	10 Nov 1748	80
Robert Venn	13 Feb 1665	
Mary Daughter of Thomas and Joan Roach	4 June, 1764	63
Henry Wife of John Sullivan	31 Mar 1731	32
Another and John their Children		
Elizabeth the Wife of Jean Sullivan,	23 Jan 1 4	2
William Arthur	41 Mar 1 59	58
Ann his Wife	5 Dec 1779	64
John their Son	21 Apr 1769	21
William Reynolds	11 Feb 1742	1
John M Thruſh	6 Dec 40	45
Mr Jane Appleton Houſekeeper to John Gaitch Duke Beaufort and Servant to his Grace the Duke Beaufort	1 Feb 1728	65
Sarah Wife John Birth Smith	1 Mar 1726	13
Hannah Barrett	17 Apr 1	6
Jane Barrett her Husband	4 Feb 1740	40
Mary Jordan, Jane, and John their Children, died infants		
Lot Bennett	1 Apr 176 ,	9
Andrew Bennett	6 Oct 1	1
James Bennett	3 Apr 1768	0
Edward Day	6 Oct 1739	43

XXVIII. BADMINTON PARVA.

A Hamlet of the Parish of *Hawkesbury*, contiguous to *Great Badminton* on the North West, is entirely included within the Park of his Grace the Duke of Beaufort. The Soil, which is light, consists solely of arable Lands, which contribute to the Parish Rates of *Hawkesbury*.

The Church appears to be of ancient and rude Architecture, it is a double Building, supported in the Middle by very low Pillars, and was much dilapidated but has since been repaired, and Divine Service occasionally performed. *Hawkesbury* claimed it as a Chapel of Ease, but, since the Year 1750, an Agreement took Place, and an Order was issued, that it should be annexed, as to ecclesiastical Concern, to the Parish of *Great Badminton*. On the Building of the new Church there, the Burying Ground was enlarged and re consecrated, and applied to the common Sepulture of both Places.

The Property, both of Manor and Impropriation, has been always joined with that of *Great Badminton*, but no House of Consequence at present remains.

A Revel was once held on the Anniversary of the Patron Saint (Michaelmas Day), which has been long disused.

No Benefaction to the Poor, Freeholder, nor Herald's Summons belong to this Hamlet.

PRESENT LORD OF THE MANOR,
HIS GRACE HENRY DUKE OF BEAUFORT.

INSCRIPTIONS IN THE CHURCH

RICHARD FRANCOM, of this Parish,
Yeoman, died April 2, 1732, aged 70.

DOROTHY his Wife
died Nov 7, 1747, aged 78

FRANCIS FRANCOM, of this Parish,
died Nov 20, 1754, aged 64

SARAH, the Wife of FRANCIS FRANCOM,
died August 1, 1764, aged 80

SAMUEL, Son of FRANCIS and SARAH
FRANCOM, died May 21, 1764, aged 56

ELIZABETH, the Wife of ISAAC COURTIER,
died 18 Dec 1735, in the 84th Year of her Age.

Near this Place lies interred
the Body of ISAAC COURTIER, late of
London, Son of THOMAS and ANNE
COURTIER, who departed this Life
the 6th Day of March, 1746, in the
33d Year of her Age

Also the Bodies of JOHN and ELIZABETH,
Son and Daughter of ISAAC and ELIZABETH
COURTIER, who departed this Life,
JOHN, 11 May, 1715, aged 24,
ELIZABETH, 16th July, 1711, aged 27

IN THE CHURCH YARD

ON HEAD STONES

			Died	Aged
William, Son of Jonathan and Elizabeth Lovelock,	-	-	20 Aug 1784	
William Roach	-	-	23 Mar 1761	61

XXIX BAGINDON

XXIX. BAGENDON

IS an inconfiderable Parish as to Extent, conftituent of the Hundred of *Crowthorne* and *Minety*, and the Deanery of *Cirencefter*, from which Town it is diftant of about three Miles on the North, and fourteen nearly South-eaft from GLOUCESTER. The Soil is light, and ftony, but, on the arable Lands, which are in the far greater Proportion, artificial Graffes are cultivated with fingular Succefs.

A Rivulet, rifing near *Likfton*, after paffing through this Village, joins the *Churn*, at a Place called *Barrow's Bridge*. Of this Hamlet many Names are recorded, and various Etymologies offered, yet fuch as are readily rejected, as fanciful and vague. This Parish, indeed, affords very little Matter for the Inveftigation either of the Naturalift, or Antiquary. On its South weft Borders, the Veftiges of the *Irmin Street* Way are ftill to be traced. This confular Road extended from the Town of *Southampton* to that of *St David's*, in the County of *Pembroke*.

The Living is a Rectory, and the Church, which is of uncertain Antiquity, is dedicated to *Saint Margaret*. It has a Nave with an aifle on the North Side, and a low Tower, containing two fmall Bells. The Advowfon was originally vefted in the Chantry of the *Holy Trinity* and *Saint Mary*, in the Church of *Saint John the Baptist*, in *Cirencefter*. JOHN YOUNG, as Chaplain thereof, prefented in 1403. At the Suppreffion of Chantries it was appropriated, with the Manor and its Appurtenances, to Sir JOHN THYNNE, 3 EDW VI 1551, and has fince belonged to his Defcendants the Vifcounts WEYMOUTH.

To this Parish no Benefactions have been made.

INCUMBENTS	PATRONS	INCUMBENTS	PATRONS
1679 Thos. Poulton, M A	Lord Vifc Weymouth	1737 Pickering Rich, M A	Lord Vifc Weymouth
1713 Wm. Huntington, M A	The fame	1761 Tim Meredith, M A	The fame

PRESENT LORD OF THE MANOR,

The Right Honourable THOMAS Lord Vifcount WEYMOUTH.

No Perfon refident in this Parish was fummoned by the Heralds in 1682 and 1683, and, at the Election in 1776, there appeared to be but one Freeholder.

The firft Notice in the Regifter bears Date 1630.

ANNUAL ACCOUNT OF MARRIAGES, BIRTHS, AND BURIALS, IN THIS PARISH.

A D	Mar	Bir	Bur	A D	Mar	Bir	Bur	A D	Mar	Bir	Bur	A D	Mar	Bir	Bur.
1781	1	4	2	1791				1801				1811			
1782	2	6	—	1792				1802				1812			
1783	2	2	2	1793				1803				1813			
1784	1	4	1	1794				1804				1814			
1785	3	3	3	1795				1805				1815			
1786				1796				1806				1816			
1787				1797				1807				1817			
1788				1798				1808				1818			
1789				1799				1809				1819			
1790				1800				1810				1820			

INSCRIPTIONS IN THE CHURCH.

Arms, Frettè Sable, on a Chief three Mullets.

In Memory of
WILLIAM HUNTINGTON, M A.
of Merton College, Oxon
and Rector of this Parish
for 24 Years. He died Dec
30, A D 1737
He was the third Son of
DENNIS HUNTINGTON,
Vicar of Kempsford for 25
Years, who brought up to
the University three Sons
This was erected by ANNE
his Widow

Near this Place are deposited
the Remains of GILES PARSLOE,
who departed this Life Sept 15, 1728,
aged 40

Near the same Place are interred
the Remains of EDITH his Wife,
who departed this Life March 5,
1758, aged 64

In Memory of MARY POULTON,
the Wife of THOMAS POULTON, Rector
of this Parish, who departed this Life
March 8, 1709, aged 80

Here resteth the Body of
THOMAS POULTON, Rector of
this Parish, who departed this
Life Aug 30, 1713, æt 81

In Memory of EMM, the
Wife of THOMAS GUEST
She died Dec 14, 1762, aged 70

IN THE CHURCH YARD

ON HEAD STONES

	Died	Aged
Ralph Olliffe	20 Feb 1769	33
Francis Ashmead	12 Dec 1770	70
Thomas Hill	18 Aug 1761	69
Joan his Wife	3 Dec 1748	40

xxx. B A R N S L E Y,

OR, as it is mentioned in the Pedigree of the Family of BOURCHIER, *Berdesley*, is situate on the great Road from *Bath* to *Oxford*. It is one of those Parishes by which the Hundred of *Brightwells Barrow*, and Deanery of *Fairford* are formed. The Distance from GLOUCESTER is eighteen Miles Eastward, and from *Cirencester* about four Miles on the North-east. The Soil is various, the arable Lands are exceeded in Quantity by the Pasture, both of which are applied to the Feeding of large Flocks of Sheep. The Inclosure of the common Fields was first undertaken in 1762. In this, and the contiguous Parish of *Bibury*, are Strata of Free-stone, of an excellent Quality, large Quarries of which have produced a confiderable Property.

The Benefice is a Rectory in the Peculiar of *Bibury*. The Church consists of a Nave and North Aisle, and a small inelegant Tower with three Bells. There is a Tradition, that this Church was founded by Sir EDMOND JAME, of *Fairford*, who is said to have built an Inn in the Village, for his Accommodation on his Journey to *Rendcombe*, the Building of which Church, at his own Expence, he was at that Time fuperintending. This munificent Knight was Lord of the Manors of *Fairford* and *Rendcombe*, in the Beginning of the fixteenth Century. It is, however, no unfair Conjecture, that the original Structure confifted only of the prefent Nave, the Tower and Aisle bearing marks of a much more modern Erection.

The Manor was long held by the BOURCHIERS, from whom it devolved by Marriage to HENRY PIRROT, Efq who built the prefent Manor-houfe, called *Barnfley Park*, a fome Diftance from the Village. It is a fumptuous Edifice in the high Italian Style, where, in a very magnificent Saloon, are frefco Paintings by the beft Mafters. The Park is extenfive and well planted. On the Death of Mrs CASSANDRA PERROT, the laft Coheir in 1778, it became the Poffeffion of JAMES MUSGRAVE, Efq

The ancient Refidence of the BOURCHIERS ftands in the Middle of the Village, but is now much dilapidated. The Rectory houfe is convenient and well fituated.

———————————

B E N E F A C T I O N S.

Mr WILLIAM WISE gave by Will, 1774, for the Ufe of the fecond Poor, 125*l.* in the Confolidated 3 per Cent. Annuities, the annual Produce of which is 6*l.*

INCUMBENTS	PATRONS	INCUMBENTS	PATRONS
1573 Nicholas Morris,	Thomas Bourchier	1696 Robert Payne, M A	Rob Payne, Sen Efq
15.. Robert Awood,	The fame	1739 Simon Prief B A	Wm Leigh, Efq
..9, Robert Haw,	Wm Bourchier, Efq	1744 William Walker, Ll D	Wm Leigh, und Thos
1..1 Nath Allworth,	The fame		Perrot, Efq
——— John Leigh,	———	1761 Chrift Golding, D D	Cafflandra and Martha
16.. Charles Caird..,	Wm Bourchier, Efq		Perrot, Spinfters
16.. John Stubbs, M A	Wm Bourchier, Efq	1764 Peter Senhoufe, D D	The fame
1696 Thomas Conftable,	The fame	1767 Charles Coxwell, M A	The fame

PRESENT LORD OF THE MANOR,

JAMES MUSGRAVE, Efq

The only Perfon fummoned from this Place by the Heralds in 1682 and 1683, was

William Bourchier, Efq

At the Election in 1776, Three Freeholders polled from this Parifh

The firft Entry in the Regifter occurs in 157.

ANNUAL ACCOUNT OF MARRIAGES, BIRTHS, AND BURIALS, IN THIS PARISH.

A D	Mar	Bir	Bur	A D	Mar	Bir	Bur	A D.	Mar	Bir	Bur	A D	Mar	Bir	Bur
1781	5	11	8	1791				1801				1811			
1782	—	7	3	1792				1802				1812			
1783	2	7	4	1793				803				1813			
1784	2	9	2	1794				1804				1814			
1785	—	5	4	1795				1807				1815			
1786				1796				1806				1816			
1787				1797				1807				1817			
1788				1798				1808				1818			
1789				1799				1809				1819			
1790				1800				1810				1820			

INSCRIPTIONS IN THE CHURCH.

ON A WHITE MARBLE MONUMENT, AGAINST THE NORTH WALL IN THE CHANCEL

Arms, Azure, a Chevron Or, between three Martlets Argent, a Crescent for Difference, for BOUR-CHIER,—impaling, a Cross between four Leopards Heads jessant, for HULBERT

Hic propè situm est
quod mortale fuit ELIZABETHÆ,
Uxoris præstantissimæ BRERETONI BOURCHIER,
de Barnesley,
in Agro Glocestriensi, Armigeri,
Filiæ unicæ THOMÆ HULBERT, de Costham,
in Agro Wiltoniensi, Generosi, & ANNÆ, Uxoris ejus
Enixa Gemellos
Filiam primogenitam ELIZABETHAM, Filiumque,
haud illâ minorem natu BRERETONUM,
(qui paucorum tantum dierum luce fruebartur
in partu, obitu, & sepultura penè individu,)
decem deinde mensibus non per tus elapsis,
magna imbecillitate Corporis fracta,
Obiit   } 1691,
2° Novembris Anno } ætatis suæ 22

ON ANOTHER MARBLE MONUMENT AGAINST THE SAME WALL

Arms, Azure, a Chevron Or, between three Martlets Argent, for BOURCHIER,—impaling, Argent, two Bars Sable, for BRERLTON

In Memory
of SARAH BOURCHIER,
Widow of WILLIAM BOURCHIER, M A
late Rector of Hatherop, in this County,
and Daughter of ROBERT BRERETON,
of Cirencester, Gent
This Monument was erected
by SUSANNAH RICH,
her God daughter and sole Executrix,
as a grateful Acknowledgment
of her great Beneficence
She departed this Life June 28, 176,
aged 93

Near this Place
are deposited the Remains
of the said Mr BOURCHIER
who died Feb 7, 1 05

And also those of MARTHA,
their only Child, who died
Apr. 6, 176, aged 0,

ON FLAT STONES

Arms three Bezants, on a Chief crenelle, three Harts,—impaling, three Pears, on a Chief a Lion issuant, for PERROT

Hic jacet, refurgendi spe,
RICHARDUS PAYNE, A M
Hujus Ecclesiæ per 42 Annos
Rector
Pastor vigilans,
Cujus Virtutibus nec obstitit
Seculi pravitas,
Nec celavit Loci obscuritas,
Literatus erat, Pius, & Benelus,
Suavitate morum, dum vixit,
Omnibus Charus,
Mortuus verum merito desideratus
Decessit Die 16° Aug Anno Domini 1 .,
ætatis suæ 74

Near this Place lieth the Body
of Mrs ANN PAYNE his Wife,
who died the 4th Day of December,
in the Year of our Lord 1,4
aged Years

Ne op aqui   presumpees
Terr   Text e
    sason oi the m Rel qui se perit
hr s F eha Rec oris d gn fh u
    Lhon s Constable   A M
Vm prud ntis & Theolog cord ti,
    on atoris upotent s & Ch i i
    prum   idelitatis utem clel u,
   c n & A t ol se   is
    p er m   ke n o h
vord   pa t vtico per multos n i
Labo r s patientia t eam decet)
    n mau s dile ffa i u Je i
Anim i plam t nde n exfpir t
De ienh Augufti   o,
    { Etat   72
i no {
    { Doann 1696

An   Lat n In cup on fel A Al
    the Wit of Thomas Constable,
    gi eatl obliterated   She die Oct   ,
    16 9

Pra intifia e matron e
Cl us orta no lib us tum un n t m
    corp ris o m t ffiine
    ven ib lis V m Magift Stephani
    Constabl Rector s m per Paroch e
    inter W l one res t utm voc m Val
    on an   n non Eccl fie Su sburentis
    Prebend in   & Uxoris dile tiffim i
    perpetua m Memori colenda
    Ma ftre Sarab Constabl
    Hic repo untur Exuvie
    T um multo ci for defer it Anim fed
    depon t fibi reduc cim X lorio r
    indicandas, & cum beate beand m
    eter um pietatis ideoque fpe plena
    obut Jun 7, a o vi x re giboliahr
    ti mie tat 72,
    L i que X iana 1688

[The Infer pt n is mu l ob iterated]

Ar   m a Lozenge Gules a Cro
engr iled Arg t m i dexter C n u
a Loz nge d e L e

In fen r y of
Mrs Irypt na Leich,
Daugh er to
Theo hilus Leich, Efq
    h s firf Wite
Th   A ith Crave
    Sone Heiress to
S   William Craven
    of Len h Wick,
    Worcef er fh e
    She depatted this L e
    on Good Fri ly,
    ab t nin e of the Clock
    i tt e Mo n ng
    the 23 t of M ch,
    1 43,
    ag ed 62

Here lieth the Body of
John Le ich, Rector of Barnf ley,
who died the 11 th of June, 1634

Refurgam

Here lieth the Body of Mrs Kat arine
Master, Relict of Wil iam Master,
of th Pa ifh o Ampney Cruci s
Gent who (after a pious Life of 73 Years)
depart d this Life Feb 3, 1692

  e a en, an Infant Daug er (he
   o o he Twins) of
Br   t on Bou h r Efq
ra Elizab r h s W e
dep rt d this Life th   10th
and wa b ried h re the 19th,
    of Ja   16 0

Br   ton, an Infan Son (he
yo   er of the Twins of
B reton Bourchier Efq
and Elizabeth h Wife,
depar ed his Life th 10th
and was buried here the 11 th,
    of Jan 1690

Her lieth the Body of Mrs
R ecca Brereton, Daughter
of Martha
Wife of William B
Barnesley, Efq who died
    the
    Anno 1669

[The ref obliterated]

IN THE CHURCH YARD

Against the North Wall of the Church

This Stone is erected to the
Family of Wise s 17 4 who w is
buried b eath

ON HEAD STONES

	Died	Aged		Died	Aged
William Ad ns, Senior	7 Aug 171)	7	Eliz beth, Wid of oan Moulder,	Sep 162	66
Alice s Wite	2, July, 1720	75	Sarah Larfer	Aug 17 9	65
F d Allowr, Senior	13 Oct -5	7	Mary, Wife of Robert Poole	21 May, 1 6	4
Ann the Wife ol Ri hard Allaw y	3 Apr 17 5	—	S th, Wife of John Moulder	5 Ju 71	5
Mary the Wife of Richa d Allaway Senior,			George Jin man,	Dec 1754	
John thon Allaw y	1 D c 17 8	61	Henry P er	6 Nov 17	77
Cha les Mo , Senior	May 1742	18	Mary Wife of Henry L rk r	4 June 17 5	38
Rich rd Norris	1 Apr 1 28	67	Thomas L e er	9 Aug 17 0	63
Thom s obbar	17 Aug 64	3	Thomas Griffin	1 May 1774	83
William Philip e	1 Aug 1 6	63	Mary his Wif	5 Nov 17 1	6
William B rand Senior	27 Mar 17 8	7	Robert Poole	31 Mar 175	57
Sarah his Wife	9 Mar 1729	85	Mary his Wife	May 1 64	48
John Moulder Senor	-7 July, 17 1	64	Sarah then Daughter	12 Mar 1776	1
S ah is on	10 July 17 5	6	William Dike Junior	5 May, 1751	28
S ufanna, Wife of John Moulder of W hall,	4 Feb 1731	5	Richard Prid man	15 Sep 17 5	1
John Mo lder for me Per Yea es nom,	13 Mar 175	8	William Cripps	1 Jul 1 1	61
			Betty his Wife	30 Oct 1 81	5
	7 Mar 176	73	Ann, Wife of Cole t Cripp	1 176	6
			Mar, Widow of Richard Norris,	3 Mar 17 9	9

THE ancient Confular Way, called by the Saxons, *Irmin Street*, on the Site of which the Road from Gloucester to London is formed, leads through this Village. It is a conftituent Parish of the Hundred of *Dudston* and *King's Barton*, and lies eight Miles South of *Cheltenham*, and two only on the East from Gloucester, in which Deanery it is comprised.

The whole Extent of the Parish is about a Mile fquare.

Churcham terminates it on the North, *Matfon* on the South, *Upton St Leonard's* on the Eaft, and on the Weft the Hamlet of *Wootton*. The Pafture Land exceeds the Arable by a Proportion of two Thirds; the Soil of which is in general a light Gravel. Several Streams pafs through this Parish, on which Mills are erected. One hundred Acres of Meadow Land on the Banks of the Severn, two Miles diftant from any Part of the Parifh, are appropriate to it and give Right of Commonage.

The Living is an endowed Curacy, with all the Privileges, in that Part of no great Value. The Impropriation, with the Manor and Fee of the whole Parish, was confirmed to the Abbey of Gloucester by William the Conqueror, when Serlo prefided as Abbot. At the Suppreffion, it was given by Henry VIII to his newly erected Chapter of Gloucester, and it now conftitutes a Part of their Revenues. No Eftate in the Parish is free Land, but held under the Dean and Chapter by Copy, or Leafe. The Church, imbattled Tower, and a very narrow Aifle, which refts on the Arches of the Nave, were added to an ancient Chapel by Abbot Parker about the Year 1500. Two Efcutcheons are over the Door of the Tower, one defaced, on the other, a Stag at Gaze between three Phœons, for Parker.

The Chapel, now uſed as a Chancel, has a fquare Turret which is covered with an ornamental Pinnacle, in which were Bells; at the other End of the Roof ftands a Crofs patee encircled, which was the Badge of the Knights Hofpitalers of *Saint John of Jerufalem*. The old Font, which is cancelled, was lined with Lead, and is of confiderable Dimenfions. Some Efcutcheons and rude Sculpture on it, but the Arms are deftroyed.

In Proof of its great Antiquity, it has been obferved, that Fonts of the earlieft Date were capacious enough to admit of the total Immerfion, according to the Canon of the Church.

The Patron Saint is *Saint Lawrence*. In the Tower are five modern Bells. The Roof of the Nave was ceiled 1730, the Pews and Communion Table, &c are neatly carved, and were erected in 1750, at the Expence of 200l bequeathed by Mrs Whitehead, for that Purpofe.

The Manor was held in Leafe by Sir Thomas Stephens, of *Little Sodbury*, in this County. The Family of Johnson were Leffees nearly a Century. The three Daughters and Coheirs of the late William Johnson, Efq fold it to John Morris, Efq 1782, who is the prefent Leffee and with it holds a very confiderable Eftate.

BENEFACTIONS.

Giles Cox, of *Abload's Court*, in this County, gave by Will, Oct 6, 1620, to poor Houfekeepers, who do not receive Alms of the Parifh, a Sum of Money, wherewith an Eftate has been purchafed at *Upton St Leonard's*, the annual Produce of which is 1l 10s vefted in feven Truftee.

Mrs Mary Wright gave by Deed (Time unknown), for the Maintenance of a Charity School, re-vefted in the Dean and Chapter of Gloucester, the annual Produce 5l

The Living being only a Curacy, by the Appointment of the Dean and Chapter of Gloucester, the Names of the Curate do not occur in the Books of the Regiftry of the Diocefe.

The prefent Curate is the Rev John Longden, M A

The Summons of the Herald in 1682 and 1683, was directed to one Perfon only of this Parifh, viz

John Marfhall Gent

The Regifter commences with Baptifm in 1651

Annual Account of Marriages, Births, and Burials in this Parish.

A D	Mar	Bir	Bur	A D	Mar	Bir	Bur	A D	Mar	Bir	Bur	A D	Mar	Bir	Bur
1781	4	11	9	1791				1801				1811			
1782	2	11	7	1792				1802				1812			
1783	3	16	11	1793				1803				1813			
1784		6	5	1794				1804				1814			
1785	1	10	8	1795				1805				1815			
1786	1	13	9	1796				1806				1816			
1787				1797				1807				1817			
1788				1798				1808				1818			
1789				1799				1809				1819			
1790				1800				1810				1820			

INSCRIPTIONS IN THE CHURCH

ON THE SOUTH SIDE OF THE CHANCEL

ON A SMALL MARBLE MONUMENT, WITH A
TABLET PENDANT FROM A PYRAMID

Arms, Argent, a Bend Sable, on a Chief of the
second three Woolpacks of the first, for JOHNSON,
— impaling, Party per Bend, Ermin, and Ermines
a Lion rampant Or, for EDWARDS

Near this Place
are interred the Remains of
WILLIAM JOHNSON, Esq who departed
this Life the 1st Day of March,
1749, aged 56 Years

And also of ELIZABETH, Wife
of the said WILLIAM JOHNSON, and
Daughter of ANTHONY EDWARDS, of
Little Shurdington, Esq who
died the 20th Day of Oct 1773, aged 68 Years

ON A PLAIN MARBLE TABLET

Arms, JOHNSON — impaling, Argent, on a Bend
cotised Sable, three Annulets Or, for SELWYN

Sacred to the Memory
of BEATA JOHNSON Sister to his Excellency Major
Gen SELWYN, late Governor of Jamaica, and Wife
of WILLIAM JOHNSON, Esq of Bowden Park, in
the County of Wilts to whom she bore eleven
Children, and after living sixty Years as a
Christian ought to live, she died, as a Christian
would wish to die, Nov 9, 1722

Near this Place lieth also interred the said
WILLIAM JOHNSON, Esq who departed this Life
January 19, 1729
Also
Near the Entrance of this Chancel lieth the Body of
WILLIAM JOHNSON, Esq Son of the said
WILLIAM and BEATA, who died March 1, 1749,
aged 56 Years

ON A SMALL TABLET IN THE NAVE

To the virtuous Memory
of ANNE, the beloved Wife of
ROBERT GREGORY, of the Parish of Barnwood,
who died March 28, 1732, aged 57

IN THE SIDE AISLE

ON A SARCOPHAGUS ATTACHED TO THE WALL,
A CHERUB RECLINING ON AN URN WITH A PYRA
MID OF GREY MARBLE

Arms, Azure, a Fess Argent, between three
Flowers de lis Or, for WHITEHEAD —impaling
JOHNSON, as before

Near this Place lie the Remains of
ELIZABETH WHITEHEAD,
Daughter of WILLIAM JOHNSON, Esq
and BEATA his Wife,
Relict of MANASSETH WHITEHEAD,
of the City of Bristol, Esq
She died on the 15th Day of May, 1756,
aged fifty-five Years
Her Liberality to this Church, the kind
Legacies she bequeathed to many
distressed Widows, and her charitable
Benefactions to the Infirmaries of
Gloucester and Bristol, give the
best Testimony of her Benevolence, and will
most effectually recommend her Example,
and perpetuate her Memory

AGAINST THE WALL

Arms, a Stag standing at gaze, between three
Pheons, within a Bordure engrailed, charged with
Roundlets

Near this Place resteth the Remains
of
RICHARD, the Son of JOHN PARKER, Gent
Also of
JOHN, Son of the said RICHARD PARKER, Gen

RICHARD } died A D { 1632,} aged { 64
JOHN } { 1694,} { 70

Also ELIZABETH, Wife of the
Rev THOMAS PARKER, M A
who died April 7, 1755, aged 29 Years

ON A FLAT STONE

Here lyeth the Body of ANNE,
the Wife of RICHARD HAYWARD,
who departed this Life the
25th Day of January, 1666

IN THE CHURCH YARD

ON TWO FREESTONE TABLETS AGAINST THE TOWER

Near this Place
lieth the Body of ANN, the Wife
of WILLIAM BUBB, of this Parish, Yeoman
who departed this Life the 5th of April,
1731, aged 45
Also in Memory
of JOHN their eldest Son,
who deceased April 28, 1729,
aged 20 Years

JEREMIAH their youngest Son
died Nov 18, 1728, aged 9 Weeks

In Memory of
REBECCA Daughter of
WILLIAM and HESTER CHURCH,
who departed this Life March 4
1771, aged 2 Years

ELIZABETH their Daughter
died an Infant

O

ON TOMBS

JOHN MANFIELD, of this Parish, Yeoman,
departed this Life Nov. 2,
1698, aged 70

MARGARET his Wife
died July 5, 1720, aged 72

SARAH, Wife of RICHARD DRINKWATER,
and Daughter of JOHN and MARGARET
MANFIELD. She died May 12, 1729,
aged 38

SAMUEL MORRIS, of this
Parish, Yeoman, died Feb 8, 1753,
aged 55

Also HESTER his Wife
died August 18, 1750, aged 61

JOHN, SAMUEL, and ELIZABETH, their
Children, died Infants.

HESTER, Wife of THOMAS GWINNETT,
died Feb 20, 1771, aged 46

JOHN MORRIS, of this Parish,
Yeoman, died Feb 9, 1771, aged 45

WILLIAM WATKINS, Sen. of this Parish, Yeoman,
died Feb 27, 1727, aged 54 Years

SARAH his Wife
died Nov 12, 1743, aged 73 Years

WILLIAM WATKINS, Jun. of the
Hamlet of Wotton, in the Parish of
St. Mary de Load, Yeoman, died
the 3d of May, 1753, aged 44 Years

SARAH, Wife of the above said
WILLIAM WATKINS, died 12 May,
1753, aged

WILLIAM their Son
died Feb 3, 1743, aged 11.

REBECCAH their Daughter
died Nov 6, 174-, aged 4

MARY, Wife of JAMES RIDER,
of Brockthrop, and Daughter of
THOMAS BISHOP, of Hucklecote,
in the Parish of Church Down, Yeoman
She departed this Life July 7, 1733,
aged 27

Here lyeth the Body of Mr WILLIAM
MILLS, of this Parish, and his
beloved Wife ANNE, by whom he
had seven sonns and one Daughter,
Wife of MICHAEL BINGLEY, of Upton,
his second Wife was the Daughter
of Mr ROBBINS, of Matesdon.
This Tomb was erected by Mrs
ESTHER MILLES, Daughter of Mr THOMAS
MILLES, of the City of Gloucester

In Memory of THOMAS, the youngest
Son of Mr WILLIAM MILLES, of the
City of Gloucester, who enjoyed the Estate,
as did also ELIZABETH his Daughter.

JOSEPH WINGATE, of this Parish,
died July 2, 1760, aged 64

WILLIAM his Son
(by Eleanor his Wife) died
August 28, 1760, aged 11

JANE, the Wife of JOSEPH WINGATE,
died Dec 28, 1771, aged 82.

AARON, Son of AARON
and ANNE BICK, of this Parish,
died Oct 24, 1739, aged 1 Year and 12 Days

THOMAS DAY, Yeoman,
late of this Parish, died
January 1, 1770, aged 65

ANN DAY, Relict and Wife
of THOMAS DAY, died Feb 2,
177-, aged

ON HEAD STONES

	Died	Aged
... Wife ...	20 Jan 1743	46
Elizabeth Wife of Samuel Perkins	15 June 1751	80
Daniel Wingate, Junr.	5 May 1745	50
John Witt	9 Jan 1760	16
Thomas Poole	3 July 1730	70
Hannah ...	... 2	47
John Witt	Dec 17	
... his Wife	Sept 1	
..., Wife of ... Wilks	1 Nov 1730	63
...	6 Oct 1743	33
...	8 Nov 1748	55
... Wife of John Gay	9 Nov 1731	76
George Creed	15 Jan 1710	55
... Wife of George Creed	Dec 1714	5
... Wife of ...		
...	4 Nov 1734	4
...	5 Sept 1730	56
... his Son	Nov 1750	10
... their Children		
...		
...	7 Dec 1741	52
... Robert	7 ... 1757	62
...	3 June 1751	10
...	4 Apr 1771	1
... Witt	5 Nov 1730	
William ... Yeoman	1 Jan 1760	63
William Ellis	17 Jan 1767	9

	Died	Aged
Elizabeth, Wife of Arthur Ullett,	22 Feb 1750	64
William Jordan	7 Mar 1754	
Mary, Wife of Richard Jordan	5 Jan 1760	55
Mary, Wife of Edward Hudd	2 Sept 1755	9
William Baldwin, of Redmarley D'Abitot, in the County of Worcester,	5 May 1758	5
Thomas Gwinnett, Junr.		
Samuel Gwinnett, of the City of Gloucester, Innholder	6 Dec 1751	9
Rev. Jonathan Godfrey, Clerk	3 Dec ...	
Hannah Deane	4 Apr 1730	6
... of Upton Brook of this Parish,	27 ... 1741	
Thomas Witt	6 Feb ...	
Ralph, Wife of Thomas Witt	26 Jan 1755	85
Katharine, Wife of Charles Witt	1 July 1752	59
James Coffey	26 Nov 1753	42
Jane, Wife of Joseph Coulston,	6 Nov 1753	76
Joseph Coulston,	3 Mar 1767	77
John the son of Joseph and Jane Coulston	... Dec 1759	3
... their Son	25 Oct 1752	1
Richard the son of William and Elizabeth Coulston	8 Sept 1758	16
Mary the ... of Richard Dabnell and Daughter of Thomas Lazar,	19 Dec 1765	52
Mary, the Wife of Samuel Cook,	15 Oct 1761	9

XXXII. BARRINGTON MAGNA.

THIS is a frontier Parish on the *Oxfordshire* Side of the County, in the Hundred of *Slaughter*, and Deanery of *Stow*, six Miles East from *Northleach*, and twenty six from the City of *Gloucester*, in the same Direction. An intmixed Portion of the County of *Berks*, of uncertain Extent, is within the Limits of this Parish.

The arable Lands are the more frequent, but on the Banks of the River *Windrush*, which takes its Course through this District, there are many Meadows, which are rich and extensive.

The Soil is a Mixture of Clay and Gravel. Durable Free stone is found here, which has been used in Buildings of Consequence.

The Intercourse between this and the adjoining Parish of *Little Barrington* was occasionally obstructed by the River, till the Erection of a long Causeway by THOMAS STRONG, of *Taynton*, Freemason.

The Living is a Vicarage, the Impropriation of which belonged to the Priory of *Llantony*, in *Wales*, and was granted, with the Manor and Tythes of the Demesnes to JOHN GYSE, the Ancestor of the present Sir JOHN GUYSE, But in Exchange for *Apley Guise*, in the County of *Bedford*.

The Church appears to have been built about the Beginning of the Reign of HENRY VII, and is dedicated to Saint Mary, a Portrait of whom, in painted Glass, still remains in one of the Windows. It has a Nave, one Aisle low enough to admit of a Row of Windows above it, and an embattled Tower containing six Bells. An Effigy of a Man in Armour, with a Ruff, and his Sword girt on his right Side, is extended under the furthest Window of the Aisle. The Monument of Captain EDMOND BRAY, of whom an Anecdote is recorded by Sir R. ATKYNS, is wanting for this Peculiarity.

On the Rafters of the Nave is this Date, "1511."

The Manor passed by Purchase to CHARLES Lord TALBOT, Lord Chancellor, from the Family of BRAY, in whom it had been vested for many Generations. He built the present Mansion in 1738, and after which Period, the old House was destroyed by Fire. The elegant Structure is in the Doric Style, its Situation is extremely good, on an Eminence about 200 Yards above the River Windrush. The Grounds are judiciously laid out, and give a true Idea of the *Ferme ornée*. The Circumference of the Park, which is well planted, is little less than three Miles.

A Bird's eye View of the old House and Domain is preserved by Sir R. ATKYNS. The Delineation of it is impicturesque as they are, and totally void of Perspective, become invaluable as faithful Representations of many capital Residences which in the Course of one Century are non in existence.

Lord Chancellor TALBOT lies interred at *Barrington*, but, is yet, no Monument erected to his Memory.

M m

B I N I

B E N E F A C T I O N S.

THOMAS STRONG, of *London*, Freemason, gave 5*l* the Interest of which to be distributed to the Poor on Saint Thomas's Day

WILLIAM MATTHEWS, of *London*, also gave 5*l* the Interest to be given to the Poor, on the same Day.

JOHN TAYLER gave an annual Rent Charge on Lands at *Milton*, of 1*l*

JOHN BRADLEY, M A of Corpus Christi College, *Oxford*, Vicar of this Parish, built the Parsonage-house at his own Cost, 1691

INCUMBENTS	PATRONS	INCUMBENTS	PATRONS
1604 John Hicks,	King James I	1730 James Stiles, B A	Paul Talbot
1664 Benjamin Griffin,	King Charles II	1750 James Pitt, B A	Mary Countess Talbot,
1684 Thomas Lambe, Cler.	The same		Rich Frankland,
1689 John Bradley, M A	I Hungerford, Esq		and Fred Frank
The above from Sir ROBERT ATKINS.			land, Esqrs
		1784 John De la Bere, M A	Mary Countess Talbot

PRESENT LADY OF THE MANOR,

Right Hon CECIL DE CARDONNEL (in her own Right) BARONESS DINEVOR.

The Persons summoned from this Place by the Heralds in 1682 and 1683, were

Reginald Bray, Esq
John Greyhurst, Esq

At the Election in 1776 Eleven Freeholders polled from this Parish

The earliest Date in the Register occurs in 1547

ANNUAL ACCOUNT OF MARRIAGES, BIRTHS, AND BURIALS, IN THIS PARISH

A D	Mar	Bir	Bur	A D	Mar	Bir	Bur	A D	Mar	Bir	Bur	A D	Mar	Bir	Bur
1781	2	23	8	1791				1801				1811			
1782	5	17	8	1792				1802				1812			
1783	—	13	12	1793				1803				1813			
1784	1	12	11	1794				1804				1814			
1785	1	17	9	1795				1805				1815			
1786				1796				1806				1816			
1787				1797				1807				1817			
1788				1798				1808				1818			
1789				1799				1809				1819			
1790				1800				1810				1820			

INSCRIPTIONS IN THE CHURCH.

ON AN ELEGANT MARBLE MONUMENT IN THE NORTH AISLE, ARE THE FOLLOWING ARMS, AND UNDERNEATH, THE FIGURES OF AN ANGEL LEADING WITH HIS RIGHT HAND A GIRL, AND WITH HIS LEFT A BOY. OVER THE ANGEL IS THIS VERSE.

"If unto you, in Flower the Angels do behold the Father which is in Heaven."

Arms, Quarterly, 1st and 4th, Argent, a Chevron, between three Eagles Legs à la Quise, Sable, for BRAY, 2d and 3d, Vaire, 3 Bendless, Or, quartering, 2d and 3d, Or, a Gryphon Segreant Azure

Motto, Quod tibi hoc alteri.

This Monument was erected by EDMUND BRAY, Esq and
FRANCES his Wife, in Memory of their dear Children JANE and EDWARD
She died of the Small pox, at her Aunt CATCHMA's in Gloucester,
on Monday the one and twentieth Day of May, 1711, in the eighth
Year of her Age, much lamented, her extreme good Qualities
having engaged the Affection of all that knew her
He died upon Christmas Day, 1720, of the Small pox at the
Royal Academy, at Angiers in France, in the fifteenth Year
of his Age, so much esteemed for his good Sense and fine Temper,
that every Gentleman of the Academy (Foreigner, as well as Briton)
seemed to rival each other in paying just Honours to his Memory,
and the Beauties of his Person were equal to those of his Mind.
The Freestone Effigies is for Captain EDMUND BRAY, whose
Father REGINALD BRAY was buried at Lynch, but most of
the underwritten (Descendents from him) lie here interred,
viz. REGINALD his Son, Sir GILES his Grandson, REGINALD his Son,
and REGINALD his Grandson, who dying before Sir GILES, the Estate
came to Sir EDMUND BRAY, the youngest Son of Sir GILES
He married FRANCES, one of the Daughters and Coheiresses of Sir
WILLIAM ASHCOMB, of Alvescot, in Oxfordshire
And by her had five Sons, viz. REGINALD, GILES, EDMUND, JOHN,
and ASHCOMB, and two Daughters, ANN and MARY.
REGINALD died of the Small pox Dec 23, 1688, EDMUND was
bred to Arms, and died Major to Sir HARRY JONES's
Regiment of Horse, at the Siege of Maestrick, of the Small pox,
GILES, JOHN, ASHCOMB, and MARY all died also of the
same fatal Distemper to this Family, ANN died an Infant
the last named REGINALD married JANE, Daughter and Heiress
of WILLIAM RANTON Esquire of Sutton, in Berkshire, and by
her he had six Sons, viz. GILES, REGINALD, WILLIAM
the present EDMUND, REGINALD, and WILLIAM, and nine
Daughters, FRANCES, BARBARA, JANE, ANN, MARY, CATHERINE,
FRANCES, MARGARET, and ELIZABETH. GILES died of a
Consumption in Oxford, REGINALD died young, WILLIAM died
of the Small pox, the second REGINALD was bred at St John's
College, in Oxford, and died greatly lamented Octr 3, 1717
The second WILLIAM died upon the ninth of April, 1720 He was
many Years a Lieutenant Colonel of Horse
here bred in Flanders and was universally esteemed in the
Army In the last Parliament of King George he was
chosen for Monmouth He was a true Patriot a good Soldier,
a faithful Friend, and a kind Brother FRANCES died
of the Small pox, 16 , MARGARET died 17 , CATHERINE
died 17 , ELIZABETH died 17 , BARBARA, JANE, ANN, MARY,
and the second FRANCES are yet living.

ON A MONUMENT AGAINST ONE OF THE PILLARS.

Arms, Party per Chevron Azure and Ermine,
in chief two Eaglets displayed, Or,—impaling BRAY

Near this Place lies interred
the Body of JAMES STEPHENS,
Efq (who married BARBARA,
Daughter of REGINALD BRAY,
Efq and JANE his Wife) he dyed
the 1ſt of May, 1692,
aged 68

Near him lye alſo the Bodyes
of JOHN and JAMES STEPHENS,
Sons of the ſaid JAMES and
BARBARA JOHN dyed the 28th
of October, 1688, aged two
Months, JAMES dyed the 22d
of November, 1695, aged
five Years

ON FLAT STONES.

Arms, two Chevronels, on a Canton an Eagle
diſplayed

Here lyeth the Body
of PHILIP PARSONS,
Doctor of Phyſick, and
Preſident of Hart Hall,
Oxon
Deceaſed the firſt of May,
1653

HESTER, the Daughter
of JOHN BRADLEY, and
MARGERY his Wife, was
here buried July 5, 1694

IN THE CHURCH YARD, ON TOMBS.

HANNAH, the Wife of
RICHARD MINCHIN,
died 21 May, 1768, aged 38.

WILLIAM MINCHIN, Sen
died April 18, 1758, aged 74.

MARGARET, the Wife of
WILLIAM MINCHIN,
died July 4, 1773, aged 84.

RICHARD PATRICK,
Grandſon of WILLIAM MINCHIN,
died May 24, 1748

THOMAS BRIDGES, Jun
died May 5, 1738, aged 70.

ILEANOR, his Wife,
died Oct 27, 1766, aged 75

THOMAS BRIDGES, Senior,
died Dec 25, 1726, aged 85

ELIZABETH his Wife
died Oct 24 1720, aged 59

CHARLES SIMONS,
died June 10, 1753, aged 72

KATHARINE his Wife
died May 10, 1762, aged 80

ELIZABETH, the Wife of
EDWARD ROGERS, of
Witney Park,
died July 1, 1764, aged 49

HENRY ADAMS
died Aug 4, 1707, aged 86.

CATHAM his Wife,
died Feb 20, 1709.

HARRY ADAMS
died Aug 13, 1717.

JOSEPH HARRIS,
died June 2,, 1767, aged 60.

MARGARET his Wife
died 31 May, 1770, aged 62.

THOMAS, their Son,
died March 28, 175,, aged 15

JANE, their Daughter,
died May 1, 1769, aged 2,

ROBERT PARTIN,
buried Feb 3, 1742, aged 72

JOAN his Wife,
buried Nov 21, 1718

JOHN, their Son,
died May 13, 1783, aged 70

JOANNA his Wife
died July 9, 1784, aged

ON HEAD STONES

	Died	Aged
John North	3 Oct 1754	90
Martha his Wife	26 July, 1742	75
Richard Jenner	6 Feb 744	42
Elizabeth Wife of John Long, of Witney,	18 June, 1762	52
William Minchin	7 Nov 1762	—
Sarah the Wife of William Minchin,	14 Apr 1760	45
Elizabeth, Wife of William Minchin,	19 Oct 1702	—
Gabriel Sharp	28 May, 1707	—
Ann his Wife	15 Dec 1716	84
Benham Sharp	9 June, 1731	70
Katherine his Wife	20 Sept 17-7	53
William Sapway	12 Jun 1746	68
John Hook	30 Dec 172-	31
George, Son of William and Ann Bridges,	24 June, 1711	21
Peter Harris	24 May, 175?	87
Mary, Wife of John Harris,	16 Oct 17-1	55
Mary, Wife of John Harris,	7 Nov 1712	—
John Cockerell	20 May, 1739	66
Hannah his Wife	29 July, 1739	73
Daniel Lidridge	16 Apr 17?3	—
Bethia, Wife of John Lidridge, Senior,	2 Mar 1736	55
Mary, Wife of Thomas Simons	22 Sep 1715	—
Thomas Simons, Senior,	16 Apr 1703	—
Ann, Wife of Vincent Simons,	29 Feb 1703	—
Mary, Wife of Vincent Simons,	7 Mar 1700	—
Vincent Simons,	20 Sept 1758	89
Mary his Wife	27 June, 1748	68
Ann, Daughter of Thomas and Jane Bals,	2 July, 17-+	32
Elizabeth, Daughter of Walter and Elizabeth Hurst, of Farford,	16 Apr 1752	73
Robert Matthews	14 July, 1720	66
William his Son	12 Oct 173+	31
Mary, Wife of Isaac Hemming, and Daughter of Thomas and Sarah Matthews,	7 July, 1773	31
John Patten	4 Mar 1712	82
Robert Patten	11 Jun 1751	86
Judith his Wife	17 May, 17_5	—
Richard Day, Junior,	11 June, 173?	55
Eleanor Wife of Richard Day,	5 Sept 1706	67
Richard Day,	5 July, 1721	81
John Day,	17 July, 1746	67
Thomas Day,	26 Jun 1747	74
Mary, Wife of Thomas Day,	14 July, 1751	65
William Peto	20 June, 1770	46
Thomas Hemming	24 Apr 1705	7
Ann his Wife	9 Nov 1750	64
Sarah, Wife of William Minchin,	4 Apr 1760	45
Thomas Sharp	5 June, 1710	7
Elizabeth Sharp, his Sister,	2 Jun 1753	69

AGAINST THE CHANCEL WALL

	Died	Aged
John Matthews	21 Dec 1777	84
Sarah his Wife	6 Jun 1758	57
Ann, Son of Vincent and Sarah Matthews,	8 Sept 1760	49
Vincent, Son of Vincent and Sarah Matthews	4 Feb 1775	39
Christian, the Wife of John Puteridge, and Daughter of John and Esther Simons,	1 Aug 1756	5
Thomas Hemming,	19 Apr 1765	72
Daniel Hemming,	11 Jun 1756	73
Hester Hemming,	5 Feb 1711	—

XXXIII. BARRINGTON PARVA,

ADJOINING to *Great Barrington* on the North eaſt, is a ſmall Pariſh, through which the *Wind-ruſh* continues its Progreſs into *Oxfordſhire*, where it joins the River *Iſis* The Soil and the Pariſhes which ſurround it, are nearly the ſame

The Benefice is a Vicarage, the Great Tythes, prior to the Reformation, were included in the Impropriation of *Great Barrington*, which was an Appendage to the Priory of *Llanton*, They are now Part of the Eſtate of GILES GREENAWAY, Eſq to whom, or the Incloſure of the Common Fields, Lands were aſſigned in Lieu of Tythes

The Church is a low Building, in the ground Form reſembling that of the adjacent Village, the Tower embattled, and containing three Bells It may be conjectured that it is coeval with, and erected at the Expence of the Convent to which they both belonged, they have likewiſe the ſame Patron Saint The great Door is conſtructed with Saracenic Mouldings, Pilaſters, and Capitals, and gives a good Specimen of that Style

The Manor was long held by the Family of GREYHURST Of them it was purchaſed by JOSEPH ELLIS, Eſq and reſold to GILES GREENAWAY, Eſq

BENEFACTIONS.

A Meſſuage or Tenement, containing one Yard Land, late in the Poſſeſſion of CATHARINE HALL, Widow, and another Meſſuage or Tenement, being a Sheep Houſe, late in the Occupation of ROBERT TRINDER, were made over Jan 7, 1719, to Feoffees, in Truſt for the Uſe and Benefit of the Pariſh, for Reparations of the Church, for the Uſe and Relief of the Poor and Impotent, and for ſuch other charitable Uſes as the Feoffees, Churchwardens, and ſubſtantial Inhabitants, ſhall think fit This Donation annually produces 30*l*

JOHN GREYHURST, Gent gave by Will 5*l* the Intereſt to be applied to the Schooling of one poor Boy of *Little Barrington*

JANE DORSET gave by Will 5*l* the Intereſt to be annually given to the Poor

INCUMBENTS	PATRONS	INCUMBENTS	PATRONS
1571 Fulk Jones,	Queen Elizabet	1728 Alex Saunders,	King George II
16.. Lewis Jones,	King James I	17.. Jo.. Ely,	The ſame
1669 William Caldwell,	King Charles II	17.. Wm Gooderough, M A	The ſame
167. Samuel Torrent,	The ſame	1769 Benjamin Boys, M A	King George III
16.4 Thomas Lane	The ſame		
	The above from Sir Rob Atkyns		

PRESENT LORD OF THE MANOR,

GILES GREENAWAY, Eſq

No Diſtinction between the Pariſhes of each *Barrington* was made in the Summons iſſued by the Herald in 1682 and 16..

At the Election in 1776 ſeven Freeholders polled to this Place

The Regiſter begins in 16.. and contains ſome Entries, which are deſcriptive, relating chiefly much to the Character of a former Incumbent

" The Proclamation of King JAMES II or him, thanſgiving to his Majeſty wordehis deliverance " were headed by JAMES SCOTT formerly, Duke of *Monmouth* and his party, at Court, together with " the Service appointed for that Day, were read and performed in the Church, as in Duty bound on the " 27th of July, 1685 " THOMAS LANE Vic

Regiſter were conſtantly intended to the Period of his death and after to the date of a page Rec.. with Notices of the Inhabitants But they were in the ſtyle of the preſent incumbent in the Opinion of the ſociety in View

16.. Buried on Oct. 6, 1695, I paid my Brother for a of the Church in Gold taking in Charge O.. L.. J.. A. N Vic

ANNUAL ACCOUNT OF MARRIAGES, BIRTHS, AND BURIALS, IN THIS PARISH

A D	Mar	Bir	Bur	A D	Mar	Bir	Bur	A D	Mar	Bir	Bur	A D	Mar	Bir	Bur.
1781	1	6	3	1791				1801				1811			
1782	—	—	2	1792				1802				1812			
1783	1	4	4	1793				1803				1813			
1784	2	5	5	1794				1804				1814			
1785	—	3	5	1795				1805				1815			
1786				1796				1806				1816			
1787				1797				1807				1817			
1788				1798				1808				1818			
1789				1799				1809				1819			
1790				1800				1810				1820			

INSCRIPTIONS IN THE CHURCH

IN THE CHANCEL

ON A VERY HANDSOME OBLONG MARBLE TABLET
ON THE NORTH SIDE

Arms, Argent, a Fefs indented Azure.

Here lies
JOHN GRAYHURST, Gent
who was
Impropriator of this Parish,
and eldeft Son of
JOHN GRAYHURST, Gent.
By ANNE his Wife,
who was the Daughter of
THOMAS CHADWELL,
formerly of this Parish, Gent
deceafed

Here alfo lies SARAH, the wife of
the abovenamed JOHN GRAYHURST
He died Auguft 26, 1730, aged 67
She died October 8, 1739, aged 69.

As alfo here lies WILLIAM GRAYHURST,
Gent Nephew and Heir of the firft
mentioned JOHN GRAYHURST, Gent
who died Oct 24, 1749, aged 49

ON A FLAT STONE

Mr THOMAS LAMB,
Vicar, was buried
December 20, 1702

IN THE CHURCH YARD, ON TOMBS.

JOHN MITCHELL and
MARY his Wife
She died June 7, 1731, aged
He died April 18, 1747, aged 6,

JOHN and THOMAS MITCHELL,
died in a good old Age

JOSEPH BEAUCHAMP and
URSULA his Wife They were
buried Feb 28, 726
He aged 71, and fhe 73, Years

THOMAS WILKINS
died July 3, 1706,
aged 60 Years

Jane his Wife buried
Nov 17, 1720

ANNE his fecond Wife
buried July 19, 1721

JOHN PROSSER, Senior,
died July 10, 1706, aged 64 Years

ELIAS his Son
died Feb, 1706, aged 31

JOHN Son of JOHN BROWN, Junior,
died June 9, 1717, aged

THOMAS HEMMING Clothier
died Auguft 18, 1
aged 44 Years

THOMAS HEMMING Senior,
died July 10, 1
aged Year

FRANCES Wife of JOSEPH LARGE
and Relict of THOMAS HEMMING,
died May 31, 1, aged

On a Stone placed against the Porch, between four Figures, representing the Persons, Father and his Son, Mother and her Daughter, mentioned in the following Inscriptions

By Order of
WILLIAM MURY, Carpenter,

This done in Memory of
the late Family of the TAYLERS,
of this Parish

Near this Place lyeth the Body
of WILLIAM TAYLER, Senior,
who was buried May 4, 1699,
aged 45 Years

And also WILLIAM TAYLER, Junior,
who was buried Oct ,, 1702,
aged 21 Years

Also ELIZABETH TAYLER, the Wife
of WILLIAM TAYLER, who was buried
the 28th of January, 1726,
aged 78 Years

MARY, the Wife of WILLIAM MURY,
Daughter of WILLIAM and ELIZABETH
TAYLER, departed this Life Nov
the 11th, 1733, aged 49 Years,
4 Months, and 6 Days

O N   H E A D   S T O N E S

	Died	Aged
Thomas, Son of John and Eleanor Jenner, of Mayshill, in the Parish of Mayley Hampton, in this County,	12 July, 1740	33
Mary, Wife of John Stephens,	2 Feb 1745	54
John Stephens	4 June, 1769	85
Sarah, Wife of James Smith,	24 July, 1706	—
James Smith	— Nov 1718	—
Edward Stephens, Junior,	——— 1718	—
Richard Hemming	4 Nov 1746	75
Richard, Son of Richard and Ann Hemming,	21 Mar 1729	20
Anne, Wife of Richard Hemming, Senior,	30 Sept 1751	77
Thomas, Son of Richard and Ann Hemming,	8 Oct 1742	28
John Smith	13 Sept 1776	73
Mary, Wife of Edward Mulls,	25 Mar 1784	67
John their Son	1 Apr 1784	29
Mary Hyatt, Daughter of Anthony and Hannah Hyatt,	28 Sept 1776	31
Richard Hathaway	2 Jan 1774	53
Elizabeth his Wife	8 Nov 1771	71

XXXIV. BATSFORD,

ANCIENTLY written *Beceshore*, is a small Parish in the upper Part of the Hundred of *Kiftf gate*, and in the deanery of *Campden*, from which Town it is distant four Miles on the South-east, and twenty eight North east from the City of GLOUCESTER.

The Proportion of arable Lands is small. The Soil varies with the Situation, light and sandy or a heavy Clay.

The Living is a Rectory, with Glebe Lands unusually extensive, which were allotted to it in the Reign of Queen ELIZABETH, when a general Inclosure of the waste Lands was completed.

The Church is dedicated to *Saint Mary*. It is a small Structure, perfectly modern and neat, without a tower. It was repaired and embellished in the year 1774.

In ancient Writings this Church was denominated, *Capella de Bacheford*, and was under the peculiar Jurisdiction of *Bleckley*, in the County of *Worcester*, where the Inhabitants had a Right of Sepulture, and still acknowledge Mortuaries claimed by the Vicar of that Parish.

From the Family of CROKER, and a few intermediate Possessors, the Manor passed to that of FREE-MAN about the beginning of the present Century, who were considerable Landholders in this Parish, in the Reign of HENRY VII.

THOMAS EDWARDS FREEMAN, Esq; the lineal Descendant, and present Lord of the Manor, has an elegant Mansion, inclosed by a Park and Plantations of great Beauty, and correct Taste.

Of this Family was THOMAS FREEMAN, of *Magdalen College, Oxford* mentioned by WOOD, in his " *Athenæ Oxonienses*," as flourishing in 1614 the most celebrated Epigrammatist of his Time.

This Parish, which is almost entirely the Property of Mr FREEMAN, is intersected by a small Rivulet which joins the *Evenlode*. It extends to a spot of Ground, which is marked by an ornamented Pillar, as forming the Boundary of four Counties, of *Oxford* on the East, *Gloucester* on the West, *Warwick* on the North, and a detached Part of *Worcester* on the South Side. Here is a small Roman Entrenchment nearly entire.

BENEFACTIONS

Mrs ANN FREEMAN gave, in 1728, by Will, the Interest of 50l. for reading Prayers, and doing other Duties, on Christmas Day, Good Friday, and every other Holy Day, and also educating the Children.

INCUMBENTS	PATRONS	INCUMBENTS	PATRONS
1608 Henry Cook,	Mary Sheldon	1732 Rev. Jones, M A	Chr Ch Coll Oxford
—— Thomas Easton,	Thos Harrington, Esq	1746 Thos Burton, D D	The same
1643 Edward Purefoy,	————	1757 Edw Smallwell D D	
—— John Easton,	John Hide, Esq	Lord Bishop of St	The same
1689 John Wilson, M A	Antony Simbach, Esq	Davids	
The above from Sir Rob Atkyns			

PRESENT LORD OF THE MANOR

THOMAS EDWARDS FREEMAN, Esq

The only Person summoned from this Place by the Heralds in 1682 and 1683 was

John Freeman, Esq

At the Election in 1776 four Freeholders polled from this Place

The Population returned Dr. in 1502

ANNUAL ACCOUNT OF MARRIAGES, BIRTHS, AND BURIALS, IN THIS PARISH

A D	Mar	Br	Bur	A D	Mar	Bir	Bur	A D	Mar	Bir	Bur	A.D	Mar	Bir	Bur.
1781	—	2	3	1791				1801				1811			
1782	—	2	1	1792				1802				1812			
1783	2	—	—	1793				1803				1813			
1784	1	5	1	1794				1804				1814			
1785	1	3	3	1795				1805				1815			
1786				1796				1806				1816			
1787				1797				1807				1817			
1788				1798				1808				1818			
1789				1799				1809				1819			
1790				1800				1810				1820			

INSCRIPTIONS IN THE CHURCH.

ON A WHITE MARBLE MONUMENT

To the Memory of
SARAH WHITE,
Who, through a long Course of Years,
proved herself an Example (most worthy Imitation)
of strict Honesty, and unshaken Fidelity,
that her many faithful Services might be long remembered,
THOMAS EDWARDS FREEMAN, Esq
caused this Marble to be put up near the Place
where she was buried March 8, 1762

ON A HANDSOME MONUMENT OF WHITE MARBLE

To the Memory
of the Right Hon. RICHARD FREEMAN,
Lord High Chancellor of Ireland,
and ELIZABETH his Wife,
Daughter of Sir ANTHONY KECK

MARY, Wife of WALTER EDWARDS, Esq
their only Child

ANNA, Daughter of RICHARD MARSHALL, Esq.
second Wife of the said Lord Chancellor FREEMAN

RICHARD FREEMAN, Esq their only Son

And ANNA their Daughter

MARGARET ELIZABETH FREEMAN,
and WALTER EDWARDS FREEMAN, Esq
eldest Son of the abovenamed WALTER EDWARDS,
by MARY his Wife

This Monument is dedicated by
THOMAS EDWARDS FREEMAN, Esq
in — Son of the said WALTER EDWARDS,
Anno Dom 1756

Underneath are these Arms

Quarterly 1st and 4th, Azure, three Lozenges
Or, for FREEMAN 2d and 3d, Party per
Bend Ermine and Ermines, a Lion rampant Or,
for EDWARDS

ON A HANDSOME MARBLE MONUMENT.

In Memory
of
ELIZABETH, Daughter of
WILLEY REVELEY, of — by Wiske,
in the County of York, Esq

The truly affectionate, beloved,
and much-lamented Wife of
THOMAS EDWARDS FREEMAN, Esq
A most sincere Christian
in Faith and Practice
She died October 26, 1781, and was buried
in the Family Vault near this Place

MARY (Daughter of JOHN CURTIS, of Butcomb,
in the County of Somerset, Esq deceased)
Wife of THOMAS EDWARDS FREEMAN, Junior, Esq
died the 2d of February, 1782,
and was buried in the Family Vault
Conjugal Love endeared her to her very
affectionate Husband,
Natural Love—to her tender Brothers,
Innate Goodness of Disposition, with accomplished
Manners, fixed the Esteem of every Acquaintance

An Infant only Daughter (at an Age which
happily knows no Grief on Loss of Friends),
survived her fond and very attentive Mother

ON A FLAT STONE

Here lie
the Remains of
HENRY JONES,
A M
interred Nov 29, 1746

On

On a neat marble Monument in the
Chancel

Arms, a Crofs between four Rofes.

To the Memory of
the Rev Thomas Burton, D D.
Rector of this Parifh,
Prebendary of Durham,
and
Archdeacon of St Davids,
who died July 1727,
in the fifty feventh year of his Age,
and lies interred, by his own Direction,
in the adjoining Church Yard
The Soundnefs of his Faith
was evinced by the beft of Proofs,
the Exemplarinefs of his Practice
The ferious, friendly, and affectionate Attention,
with which he confcientioufly difcharged
every Branch of his minifterial Function,
engaged the Hearts, and influenced the Manners
of all his People

Thankful for the good Things of this Life,
which the Providence of God
had amply beftowed upon Him,
he employed them to Purpofes
of real Ufefulnefs
He was a Friend, a Father to the Poor,
a generous, indulgent Mafter
to a faithful and obfervant Houfhold,
a Lover of Hofpitality,
and a chearful Promoter
of every focial, every liberal Affection
Juftice, Humanity, Benevolence, and Charity,
marked the Character
of
this excellent Man,
whofe Life was fo uniformly good,
That Death, though fudden, found him not
unprepared

Bleffed fhall that Servant be,
whom his Lord when he cometh
fhall find fo prepared

IN THE CHURCH YARD

ON A FLAT STONE

Here lyeth the Body of
Thomas Burton, D. D
Rector of this Parifh,
whofe Monument is in the
Chancel

XXXV.   B A U N T O N,

BAUDINTON, or *PENNINGTON,* as it appears from the moſt ancient Evidences This ſmall Village lies in the Hundred of *Crowthorne* and *Minety,* and the Deanery of *Cirenceſter,* from which Town it is only two Miles diſtant on the North

The Boundaries of this Pariſh are made by the River *Churn* on the Weſt, and the great Roman *Foſs* Road on the Eaſt

The Situation being high, the Soil is conſequently barren and ſtony, and admits of a very ſmall Portion of Paſturage The Common Fields, by an Act of Incloſure granted in 1776, were aſſigned to the Proprietor of the Eſtate, which includes the Fee of the whole Pariſh

The Benefice is a perpetual Curacy, the Impropriation of which was originally an Appendage to the Abbey of *Cirenceſter,* and remained ſuch till the Suppreſſion of Monaſteries, when it was granted to the Family of GEORGE, from whom it deſcended, by Purchaſe, with the Manor and its Demeſnes, to the MASTERS, of *Cirenceſter,* about the cloſe of the laſt Century

The Church is a ſmall mean Building, conſiſting of a Nave only, which affords no Veſtige which might aſcertain its Antiquity The Inhabitants were formerly buried at *Cirenceſter* In the Year 1625, at the Requeſt of JOHN GEORGE, Eſq then Proprietor of *Baunton,* a Burial Place was conſecrated by Dr GODFREY GOODMAN, Biſhop of GLOUCESTER

No Benefactions to the Poor.

CURATE	PATRON
Joſeph Chapman, M A	Thomas Maſter, Eſq

The Succeſſion of Curates is not recorded in the Regiſtrar's Office of this Dioceſe

PRESENT LORD OF THE MANOR,

THOMAS MASTER, Eſq.

At the Viſitations of the Heralds, in 1682 and 1683, the Perſons ſummoned, were

James George, Eſq
William Poulton, Clerk

At the Election in 1776, no Freeholder appeared from this Pariſh

ANNUAL ACCOUNT OF MARRIAGES, BIRTHS, AND BURIALS, IN THIS PARISH

A D	Mar	Bir	Bur	A D	Mar	Bir	Bur	A D	Mar	Bir	Bur	A D	Mar	Bir	Bur
1781	—	5	1	1791				1801				1811			
1782	—	3	—	1792				1802				1812			
1783		2	—	1793				1803				1813			
1784	1	3	3	1794				1804				1814			
1785	—	3	2	1795				1805				1815			
1786				1796				1806				1816			
1787				1797				1807				1817			
1788				1798				1808				1818			
1789				1799				1809				1819			
1790				1800				1810				1820			

INSCRIPTIONS IN THE CHURCH

ON A FLAT STONE

ANNO DOMINI 1627,
THE XXX DAY OF APRIL,
CATORN DAVES WAS
BURILD HEAR, THE
FIRST BURIED IN THIS
CHURCH

ON A MONUMENT AGAINST THE NORTH WALL

In Memory of
HENRY STEPHENS,
who died April 10, 1768,
aged 58 Years

Also of CATHARINE his Wife,
who died May 2,, 1769, aged 58 Years

And also of CATHARINE and
ELIZABETH their Daughters
CATHARINE died Dec 15, 1774,
ELIZABETH died July 26, 1780,
Both aged 37 Years

ON FLAT STONES

Here lyeth the Body of
HENRY STEPHENS, of this
Parish, who died March 17,
In the Year of our Lord 1728,
ætatis suæ 65

Also in Memory of
ELIZABETH his Wife,
who died Sept 6, 1725,
ætatis suæ 56

In Memory of
DORCAS, the Wife of
THOMAS STEPHENS,
who died Dec 21, 1754,
aged 28 Years

Also of THOMAS, their Son,
who died May 27, 177-,
aged 17 Years

In Memory of
WILLIAM WAKEFIELD Yeoman,
who died Dec 3, 1719, aged 53

Quam religiose vixit Virgo pia,
Quam inculpate conjux casta,
Quam pie obiit puerpera Maii,
16,6, ætatis suæ 22

ELIZABETH, sole Daughter and
Heire of JOHN GEORGE, Esq and
ELIZABETH his Wife, and late Wife
to RICHARD WHITMORE, of Nether
Slaughter, Esq with her dear
Child resteth here in peace
waiting for the Resurrection
of the Body, and the Life everlasting

Ornata bonitate Morti,
nos nostrique virtus
Post lachrymas tamen
tamen vivit

IN THE CHURCH YARD

ON HEAD STONES

Robert Hancock, Senior,	-	-	
Thomas Hancock	-	-	
Robert Pearce	-	-	
Eleanor his Wife	-	-	
William Williams, Senior,	-	-	
Jane his Wife	-	-	

XXXVI. BECKFORD.

A PARISH in the extensive Vale of *Fresham*, and conftituent of the Deanery of *Campden*, fix Miles North weft from *Winchcombe*, and fifteen from GLOUCESTER on the North eaft. An ancient Landmark, called *Twoleftone*, ftill remains in this Parifh, and gives Name to the Hundred, in which the greater Part of it is contained, the Hamlet of *Didcote* only being in the upper Part of the Hundred of *Tewkfbury*. The Soil, which is applied in nearly equal Portions to Arable and Pafture, confifts in general of a ftrong Clay. By an Act paffed in 1773 the common fields were inclofed.

The Brook *Carart*, which rifes in the adjacent Parifh of *Afhton Underhill*, continuing its Courfe through this Diftrict, joins the *Avon* near *Tewkfbury*.

The Priory of *Beckford* was a Cell to the Monaftery of *Saint Margaret and St Barbara in Normandy*. It was founded by ROBERT FITZ HAMON, and endowed with the Manor, and the greater Part of the Parifh, and at the general Suppreffion of Alien Priories was granted by HENRY VI to his newly founded College of *Eton in Berkfhire*.

The Family of WAKEMAN held thefe Poffeffions early in the feventeenth Century, which have defcended to HENRY WAKEMAN, Efq. The Manfion-houfe, which is of ample Dimenfions in the old Tafte, has been for Ages the Refidence of this refpectable Family.

The Church (according to Leton) is dedicated to *Saint John the Baptift*. It has a Nave only, between which and the Chancel, ftands a lofty Tower of good Architecture, in which are fix bells. This was once terminated by a Spire Steeple which becoming dangerous by Decay, was totally removed in the Year 1622. The Saxon Style prevails through the whole Building, over the North Door is in it a curious Hieroglyphic and attached to the North Side of the Chancel is a fmall Structure, probably defigned for an Oratory.

The Benefice is a Vicarage, the Impropriation of which belongs to Mr WAKEMAN, who had the Tythes of *Beckford*, *Grafton*, and *Didcot*, before the general Inclofure, when proportionate Lands were affigned to him. The Patronage is now vefted in the prefent Incumbent, to whom likewife certain of the new Inclofures are appropriate.

In this Parifh are four Hamlets, *Beckford*, *Didcot*, *Grafton*, in which is a confiderable Eftate, belonging to the Earl of TYRCONNEL, and *Bengrove*, from the Tythes of which, two Pounds are annually due to the Crown.

Over the Entrance into the Chancel is this Infcription

" This Chancel was furnifhed with Seats for a School at the Charge of Mr JONATHAN and Mr ISAAC
" BLACKWELL, anno Dom 1656 R I."

BENEFACTIONS

The Land, called *The Comb Farm*, produces about nine Pounds yearly, was given by an unknown Benefactor for the Ufe of the Poor.

INCUMBENTS	PATRONS	INCUMBENTS	PATRONS
1573 Gerard Currington,	Matthew Parker Archbifhop of Canterbury	1718 Prideaux Sutton, M A	Charles Parfons, Gent
1576 Gerard Currington,	Queen Elizabeth	1724 John Harper M A	The fame
1577 Ralph Wedder,	Humphrey Coningfby, Efq	1755 John Moteley, M A	Thomas Branch and Will Jones, Gent
1585 Richard Pernichew,	Sir John Tracy	1761 Richard Andrews, B A	The fame
1590 William Brickwell,	John Wakeman	1766 Lionel Kirkman, M A	Elizabeth Nelton and Thomas Ruffel
— Edward Waren	—		
1674 James Butler, M A	Jonath Halfwell, Efq	1768 Jofeph Biddle, M A	The fame
1677 James Towne M A	Jared Wakeman, Efq		
The Governors of King's College			

PRESENT LORD OF THE MANOR,

HENRY WAKEMAN, ESQ

The following Perſons were ſummoned from this Pariſh by the Heralds in 1682 and 168,

Madam Wakeman,
John Wood, Gent
Edward Freeman, Gent.
William Freeman, Gent

At the Election in 1776, eight Freeholders polled from this Pariſh

The Regiſter commences with Burials 1538.

ANNUAL ACCOUNT OF MARRIAGES, BIRTHS, AND BURIALS, IN THIS PARISH

A D	Mar	Bir	Bur	A D	Mar	Bir	Bur	A D	Mar	Bir	Bur	A D	Mar	Bir	Bur
1781	2	20	9	1791				1801				1811			
1782	3	11	3	1792				1802				1812			
1783	1	10	16	1793				1803				1813			
1784	2	13	6	1794				1804				1814			
1785	4	12	1	1795				1805				1815			
1786				1796				1806				1816			
1787				1797				1807				1817			
1788				1798				1808				1818			
1789				1799				1809				1819			
1790				1800				1810				1820			

INSCRIPTIONS IN THE CHURCH

IN THE CHANCEL

ON A BLACK AND WHITE MARBLE MONUMENT AGAINST THE NORTH WALL

Arms, Vert, a Saltire wavy Ermine, for WAKEMAN,—impaling Argent, a Chevron between three Talbots Heads eraſed, Sable, for HALL.

D O M

Mortale Spolium RICHARDI WAKEMAN, Armiger Illuſtribus genere
Et preclare parentibus Odoardo & Mar church hoc tegit Saxum
Qui Sacramento fidei ad extremum belli aleam iterum reddidit
Per uni Regis ſecutus tuit, domum tandem redux dexero in integritis?
Recuſo in Riſtra & Lironce unus Romanorem conſul am exemplo
Gumineam facile colonis omnibus facher reiſtheina penute
Coronam praripuit

Sed I heu! brevis parenti Agri huic,
prid Kal Sept Anni puerunt
CIƆIƆCIXII ex ipſa etatis meridie praceps in Occaſum ruit
Ægre per quam extincti tulere dehiderium Amici propinqui, Serores,
Juſtes Liberi, ſed omnium acerrime ANNA conjux moratiſſima,
Qua parentum viri dehideratiſſimi, memoria ane hitee late
Marmori charecteribus, (pallam ipſe avaquem inferum)
Premuit

O N   F L A T   S T O N E S

Arms, a chevron between three Thorn Leaves, for THORNTON, impaling, Parti per Chevron three
Lions paffant, for LUNN

En! quæ fecundum D Jefu expectat epiphaniam,
Pulchra, modefta, chara ELIZABETHA THORNTON,
Quæ
Parentes LEBBEUM LUNN, Ecclefiæ hujus Paftorem,
Fideliffimam Uxoremque ipfius ELIZABETHAM,
Et conjugem ROBERTUM THORNTON, A M de Staunton,
In Agro Wigornienfi, triftes reliquit, & infelices,
Sept 4° Anno { Dom 1706
              { Ætat fuæ 29.

Depofitum
JOHANNIS HARTER, A M
Hujus Ecclefiæ Vicarii,
Qui
Munere fungendi
Quam opes cumulandi
femper ftudiofior
fuit
Natura debitum reddidit
A D 1764,
Ætat 71

Arms, Parti per Cheveron three Lions paffant, for LUNNE,—impaling, a Fefs nebulé, charged
with three Hare's Heads couped, for HAREWELL

H S I
Præftantis Ingenii Vir
Reverendus LEBBEUS LUNNE, A M.
Hujus Ecclefiæ Paftor indefeffus
Parochiæ pacificus,
Vivus Exemplar
et Mortuus Defiderium,
Obiit die Septimo
Septembris
Anno
Minifterii fui in hac Ecclefia 41°,
Ætatis fuæ 73,
Domini noftri 1718
Hic etiam Dilectiffima LEBBEI, Vidua,
Sepulta eft ELIZABETHA LUNNE,
Erga Deum Pietatis erga proximos
Benevolentiæ exemplar non vulgare,
Morbo corporis diutino oppreffa
Lectoque per quinquennium affixa
In Patientia poffedit animam
Et tandem Deo reddidit
Oct 10, 1733, et 78

John Morris, of Benprove,
died the 15th Day of May, 1656,
aged 74

JOHN MORRIS died
16 Feb 1703, aged 27.

SAMUEL, Son of JOHN
and SUSANNA MORRIS,
died March 14, 1703, an Infant.

JOHN MORRIS, Gent
Son of JOHN and SARAH MORRIS,
died June 24, 1740, aged 39 Years

Arms, a Chevron between three Crescents

M C 1728

F H 1749

IN THE CHURCH YARD, ON TOMBS

Arms, Argent, on a Fess Azure three Lozenges
Or, in chief a Lion issuant Gules, holding a Lo
zenge, for FREEMAN

Here lyeth the Body of
WILLIAM FREEMAN, of this Parish, Gent
who was buried April 20, 1694,
aged 31 Years

Here also lyeth the Body of
ELIZABETH, the Daughter of
BERNARD BALDWIN, of Ashton Underhill,
Gent Relict of the aforesaid
WILLIAM FREEMAN, who was buried April 1739,
aged 80 Years

In Memory of
WILLIAM FREEMAN, Son of
WILLIAM and SARAH FREEMAN,
of this Town, Gent who departed
this Life the 14th Day of Nov 1764,
aged 42

In Memory of MARK TRINDER,
Son of the Rev Mr TRINDER
of Bidgworth, who was buried
Jun the 20th, 1725, aged 31 Years

Also of MARY his Wife, Daughter
of WILLIAM FREEMAN, of this Parish,
Gent who was buried Sept 28, 1750,
aged 63

In Memory of ELIZABETH GARSTON,
Daughter of RICHARD PAXTON,
of Toring, in the Parish of Kedminy
Dalton, in the County of Worc
Gent and Relict of JOHN GARSTON,
late of Stanton, in the said County,
Gent who died the 4th of July,
1756 in the 73d Year of her A

To his wife is here interred JOHN, the
son of WILLIAM and SARAH FREEMAN,
Senior who departed this Life Ma
the 11th 1755 aged 27

MARGERY NEWMAN, buried
February 2, anno Domini 1655,
in the 79th Year of her Age
This Monument was erected
by DANIEL and SEPTIMUS NEWMAN,
two of her Nephews, her Executors

In Memory of
RICHARD ROBERTS, of Grafton,
in this Parish, Gent aged 55 Years

And MARY his Wife, aged 31 Years

He was buried March 5, 1746,
and she was buried Feb 19, 1727

In Memory of
Mrs ANNE WOODWARD, Sister of
Mrs MARY ROBERTS, Daughter of
RICHARD WOODWARD, of Lekington,
in Worcestershire, Gent aged 46
She was buried June 5, 1739

ISAAC ROBERTS of Grafton, was
buried Sept 14, 1721, aged 60 Years

Mr EDMUND COLLINS late
of Somerton, in the County of Oxford,
who departed this Life Aug 17, 1765,
aged 72

Dorothy the Wife of JOHN NIND, Sen
of Grafton, in this Parish died the 18th of Feb
1765, aged 72 Year

JANE RANDALL this Parish,
was here buried Ma 5, 1658

ON HEAD STONES

	Died		Aged
John Price, late of Beckford, - - - -	26 Nov	1754	69
Elizabeth his Wife, Daughter of William Freeman, Gent. of Beckford,	13 Apr	1762	76
Also three of their Children			
Ann, Wife of Daniel Dobbins, -	18 June,	1754	36
Mary, Wife of William Barnes, - - -	29 Jan	1762	42
Susannah, Wife of William Wilks, - - -	21 July,	1754	32
William Grove - -	24 July,	1768	73
Richard, Son of Richard and Hannah Tombs, - -	11 Jan	1766	8
Thomas Coison - - -	11 May,	1758	79
Richard Roberts - - - -	6 Apr	1713	68
Elizabeth his Wife - - - -	13 Oct	1704	69
Thomas Ridler, Yeoman, - - -	1 Jan	1761	78
Anthony Barnes -	12 Mar	1766	74
Susanna, Wife of Edward Hale, and Daughter of William and Elizabeth			
Freeman, - - -	22 Feb	1715	44
Edward Hale - - - - -	6 Mar	1758	42
William their Son - -	———	1736	23
Thomas Ward, of Grafton, in this Parish, Yeoman, -	4 July,	1775	73
Simon Skey, of Grafton, in this Parish, Yeoman, -	12 Jan	1771	74
Elizabeth, Wife of Richard Roberts, -	13 May,	1701	77
Dorothy, the Wife of William Nind, Senior, of Grafton, in this Parish,	18 Feb	1765	72
William Nind, Senior, - -	26 June,	1775	86
Lydia, Wife of William Nind, late of Grafton, in this Parish, -	23 Feb	1781	49
Thomas Yates - - -	16 Mar	1777	75
Sarah his Wife - - - - -	31 July,	1777	80
Richard Wilkes - - - -	1 June,	1775	28
Daniel Dobbins - - -	13 June,	1770	56
Samuel Dobbins - - -	15 June,	1773	69
Jane, Wife of Thomas Brotheridge, - -	6 June,	1776	45
Nicholas Langston, late of Grafton, in this Parish, - -	26 Sept	1779	68
Mary his Wife - - - -	12 May,	1759	45

XXXVII. BERKELEY.

SITUATE in the North west Part of the very extensive Hundred to which it gives Name, and included in the Deanery of *Dursley*. The Town is sixteen Miles distant from GLOUCESTER on the South-west, five westward from *Dursley*, seven from *Thornbury* on the North, and one from the River *Severn*, with which there is a navigable Communication for Vessels of forty or fifty Tons burthen. The Tide flows up this narrow Channel round the Castle Gardens nearly a Mile beyond the Town. The Soil varies from a stiff Clay to a rich Loam, and is applied with very small Exception to Pasturage. The Hundred and its Vicinity, comprehending the Vale for twenty or thirty Miles in extent, is particularly celebrated for making the Cheese, called Single and Double Gloucester, the best Sorts of which is exceeded in no County whatever for Quality and Flavour. From some Orchards in this Parish good Cyder is made, particularly of the Pippin.

The following Extracts are made from the valuable Manuscripts of Mr Smyth beforementioned, communicated by the Earl of BERKELEY.

" *Berkley*, in the Book called Domesday, written *Berch la*, and in the Saxon Tongue *Beorceular*. " The Place I heere describe is the Burgh, or Burrough, or Mercate Towne of *Berkley*, and the Castle " adjoining thereto, holden of the King by Knight's Service in Capite, and is at this the Head or " principall Place of the Baronie of *Berkeley*, the present Inheritance of GEORGE Lord BERKELEY, 1639. " Of this Towne the Booke of Domesday hath only thus, *Ibi unum Forum in quo mane ibi 17 Denars, & " reddunt Consuem in firma*.

" In this Towne, a Markett is holden each Tuesday, by the Grant of Kinge Henry Seconde, made " in the first Yeare of his Raygne to ROBERT, the Sonne of ROBERT FITZHARDINGE, and his Heires, " whereby the Kinge granted to him, to have in his Manour of *Berkley*, *Unam liberam* *mercatum* *cum* " *libertatibus qua ad Mercatum pertinent, quacunque die septimanæ voluerit* : *Et tam cum proprius Mone- " tario suo*, *viz* A free Markett with all Liberties to a Markett belonging, what Day of the Weeke " him best liked, and Money there of his own stampinge, or Coinage, whereof Freddus was " chosen, and soe continueth to this Day. Yet it was apparent by this Booke of Domesday, that there " was a Market in the Time of William the Conqueror, and before, in the Time of Edwarde the Con- " fessor, if *Forum* signify there a Markett. But I find no that the Lords of this Markett Towne, had " any Fayre here, before that THOMAS Lord BERKELEY, fourth of that Name, did in the 18th of K. " RICHARD Seconde, obtaine of that Kinge, to have one there holden on the Vigil and the Day of the " Invention of Holy Crosse, called Holy Rood Day in May, with all Liberties and Customs apperteyn- " inge, which soe alsoe continueth to this Day, contenting themselves with their Fayres formerly ob- " tained in their Townships of *Wootton*, *Dursley*, *Newport*, and *Cambrige* within the Hundred of " *Berkeley*, the Reason whereof seems to have beene, for that in Times forative and flourishinge, as of " those former Ages were, the Lords of this Towne, would not draw such a Concourse of People of all " Sorts as, then the way to *London* were soe frequented, accustomorily resorted to all their " to meete to their Castle Gates, whereby soe important a Peer might by their Opposites suddenly and " easily have lyn surprised. Which Name alsoe, of *Burgh* or *Baroe* doth so inform us Saxon, " that the Place is anciently fortified, the Prints whereof are in some Places yet descried done or " washed out, the Name also of *Lockfast Brooke* yet remaininge, leaving from *Hame*, over the further " Ewe or Water, so neeth to imply, as much.

" The Towne of *Berkley* is seated on an Hill, and Hill Side there have of the greater streete " or Main Street, viz *High Street*, *Salter Street*, *Mary Brook Street*, alias *Milbrook Street*, *Canonbury- " this Yongars Street*, and *St Michaels Lane*, with divers other, whose Houses are for the most parte " from some of Edwardes *Cottesswold Hills*, the Land of Peace, the River severn, mightie Corne Crops " so ever Power remarkable for Eminence.

" The Towne itselfe was so much decayed in the Reigne of King Henry the third and Edward the " fourth through the great Incursions, Strife and Sieges that found, and in their Castle alsoe " betweene Thomas BEAUCHAMP, Earl of *Warwicke*, and his Wife, Cohires to them Coron and " *Horse Street*, and some others, are not nowe to be found, other Lands allso and under Land " beloved of Elms, which declare that such they were, and that out of Knights which laid so many " valued and added to the Lord as now come downe to 10 per Annum confirmed to the said. " Hoste alsoe to this Day and in many old Deeds called *New Land* but whether " *Lockley*, an old Towne, was seated to it, or whether in Part of this Land, as yet, is un- " certaine.

" The Towne underlyeth the Government a Mayor, and his Brethren, such as have byn M...
" But there is never any other Incorporation, but by Prescription, nor ever had any Burgesse in Par-
" liament, which I have much sought after, yet dyvers Grants have very anciently byn made to them,
" by the Name of the Burgesses and Merchants of *Berkely*, their Heires and Assigns by which were
" MAURICE Lord BERKELEY, in 46 HEN. VI. released to them all Exaction and Cryme of Toll, and all
" Kinds of Privilege of Toll, which he had, or might demand of them. And THOMAS Lord BERKE-
" LEY Father of the said Lord MAURICE, granted to the Burgesses, about 20 HEN. to have Common
" of Pasturage without the Towne, as they were wont to have, and that no Attachments should be made
" in the Burrowe of *Berkeley*, but by the Reeve or Bayley of the Burrough. But however Affairs have
" gone of old, the Inhabitants may be said at this Day, to have *Nomen sine Re*, and may rather boast
" of their Market Townes Antiquity, than the Towne of their Ability or Government amongst them-
" selves."

From the Date of this Account to the present Time, an Interval of nearly two Centuries, few Alterations have taken Place, either as to the Appearance or Extent of the Town (and though here are
few good Houses, it may be in general considered as a regularly built). The Forms of a Corporation
are continued, but their Privilege is merely nominal, excepting the Receipt of certain Tolls of inconsiderable Amount.

In the same Manuscript are preserved the following Records relative to the Church

" The Parish Church seated in this Towne, answereth in greatness to the huge Extent of the Parish,
" built at first as it seemeth with Aptness and Relation to the greatness of the Lord's Demaine Lands,
" and his Numbers of Tennancies within the Limits thereof, which, from the Place called *Phawmere's*
" *Bridge*, by *Hurst*, which parteth it from *Sumbridge* Parish, to the further end of *Hill*, this *Hill*, next
" *Oldbury*, which parteth it from *Thornbure* Parish, is eight Miles in rich and fruitful Soile, and from
" the midst of *Seveane* (acrosse the former Length to *Maston* and *Sowthwine* Bridges, in *Nibeie*, which
" parteth it from *Wootton*, to which Church *Nibley* is a Chappel), yet as many more. Wherby it
" may seeme there was a good Cause for the Abbots of S. *Augustin*, by *Bristol*, for their building of
" eight Tythe Barns of noe mean greatness, for the Inning of the Tythe Corne thereof, which yet there
" continue. As the Tythe Barn of *Cinonbury*, of *Hicke*, of *Hame*, of *Stone*, of *Hill*, of *Oldmester*,
" and *Bradstone*. Within the Limits of which Tythe Birne of *Hame*, a Custom hath anciently pre-
" vailed, to pay three Pence in Money for the Tythe Hay of every Acre mowed, and not in Kinde.
" Which received a Resolution accordingly, in a Suite between HOOPER and MALLET in 38th ELI-
" ZABETH.

" The Church and Advowson of this Parish with its Chapels was, by ROBERT, the Sonne of HAR-
" DING, the first Lord BERKELEY, in the Time of Kinge HENRY Seconde, given amongst others to
" the Monestary of St *Augustine's* aforesaid at his first Foundation thereof, which the Abbots of the
" Convent, shortly after found Means with the Bishop of *Worcester*, and an Incumbent of their owne pre-
" ferринge, to appropriate with others.

" The Appropriation of the Church, as to the Vicaridge which is presentative, belongs to the Dean
" and Chapter of *Bristol*, of newe erected in 38 HEN. VIIIth, being therein made one of the ten Deaneries
" then by that King founded and endowed anewe. Of which Church the blessed Virgin MARY was
" the tutelary Saint, to whom the same was dedicated, and under whose Protection it remained, as divers
" Deeds doe showe.

" The Lady KATHERINE BERKELEY the Widow of THOMAS, the third Lord of that Name, who died
" 35 EDW. III. and, in the Daye of her Husband's Grandchilde and Heire, in 8 RICH II. found a
" Chantry in the said Parish Church for a Chaplen, and his Succession perpetually, to pray at the Altar
" of St *Peter* for the good Estate of herselfe, and of THOMAS, then Lord BERKELEY, and the Lady
" MARGARET his Wife, endowinge the same with divers Land, and Tenements in *Breadly*, *Bradley*,
" and *Hurst*, Manors. For which there an Inquisition founded on a Writ of *Ad quod Damnum*, re-
" maininge in the Tower of *London* in 7 RICH II. the officer had the King's Licence for that alienation in
" Mortmaine, and thereupon had a Confirmation from the Bishop of *Worcester*. And from that the
" Actu was called St *Andrew's Chantry*, till the Dissolution thereof. This VICount of which Church
" Lord BERKELEY her now is, receiveth from the King's Receiver yearly Chief Rent or free Shil-
" ling, as his wife his Ancestors have done since he found are thereof. In his Church noe THOMAS
" Lord BERKELEY, temp. EDW. III. founded another Chantry, which was called St *Mary* or *Our*
" *Lady's Chantry*, endowinge the same with divers Lands and Tenements, rent of which Grant Lord
" BERKELEY her now is, receiveth of the King's Receiver as Chief Pencion yearly, held in his Suc-
" cellor ever and since the foundinge thereof, though the Land hath bee long since sold, as is his
" Grante.

" In this Church was also another Chantry, founded temp. EDW. III. endowed with Lands and
" Tenements for the Maintenance of a Priest, &c.

" The Lord of the Manour anciently used to pay Peter's Pence to the Bishop of *Worcester* 16 s.
" yearly and sithe the same to the Bishop of *Rome* which, being a part of the entire Year, thereupon
" the Land came into the Hand of EDW. II on account of the Rebellion of MAURICE Lord BERKE-
" LEY, the Bishop was sued to have the appointment him to be anciently behad, as the Record in
" the Tower of *London* doe showe.

WILL...

James Lord Berkeley

Thomas

Lord Berkeley 1361

WILLIS mentions a Chantry in this Church, called *Brakenbury Chantry*, of which JOHN HAROLD was Incumbent and had a Pension in 1553, of 4l. annually, probably the last rected by Mr SMITH (See *ante, v. p* 40)

The Rectory is a Vicarage, in the Presentation of the Earl of BERKELEY, the Chapter of Bristol having imputed their Right, by Act of Parliament, to GEORGE first Earl of BERKELEY, in Consideration of an Exchange of the Advowsons of *Berkeley* and *Hinton*, for that of St *Mary*, of *Stoke Bardolph*, in the County of *Nottingham* But the Impropriation is retained by them

The Church consists of a Nave, two Aisles, and a Chancel, all of considerable Dimensions The Stile of the Architecture is that of the Age of ROBERT FITZ HARDING, who was most probably the Founder The Nave is divided by six low Arches on either Side, but the whole Structure seems to have been altered from its first Form, by repeated Reparations It was refitted and pewed 1732

The Tower, which contains six Bells, is at some Distance from the Church It was erected about thirty Years since, on the same Spot where the ancient Tower stood, to which several religious Buildings were attached, called the *Nunnery Chapel* In the MSS of D PARSONS at Oxford, it is said, that "there was an ancient Church dedicated to our Saviour and his Saints, upon whose Wall was written the "Apocalypse in Latin It was joined to the old Tower" It is asserted, that the Castle occupies the Site on which that Nunnery was built, which was suppressed by the fraudulent Practices of Earl GODWIN in Saxon Times, but it appears that there was a subsequent Foundation for Nuns, of a smaller Extent

On the Base of the Windows of the South Aisle are three cumbent Figures, with Latin accounts at the Feet of each, these do not exceed a Yard in Length *

Between the Nave and South Aisle, on an Altar Tomb, are the Effigies of THOMAS Lord BERKELEY, and CATHERINE his second Lady, sculptured in Alabaster His Lordship is represented in the Armour of the 14th Century, charged with the Family Bearings, and the Lady with a Head dress of extraordinary Shape and Size This Baron died in 1360, before which Time the Nobles of this Family were interred in the Conventual Church of St *Augustine*, now the Cathedral, at *Bristol*

The Font is square, very capacious, and lined with Lead It is supported by one large, and four smaller Pillars a Form of the highest antiquity.

On a beautiful Gothic Skreen of carved Stone, which divides the Choir, or Chancel, from the Nave, the subjoined Arms are emblazoned, being the different Alliances of the Noble House of BERKELEY

  1   Or, three Lions passant guardant Azure, semée of Hearts *Fitz-Harding*.
  2   BERKELEY
  3   Gules, a Lion rampant Argent *Mowbray*
  4   Sable, a Lion rampant Argent, ducally crowned Or *Segrave.*
  5   Azure, Crusile, and a Lion rampant, Or *Bruce*
  6   Gules, three Lions passant guardant Or. *Brotherton.*
  7   Azure, three Garbs Or *Blondeville*
  8   Checquy Or and Azure *Warren*
  9   Gules, a Lion rampant, between three Cross Crosslets fitchy Or *Capel.*
 10   Barry of   Or and Azure
 11   Gules, an Inescutcheon of *France*, within an Orle of Lions of *England*
 12   Argent, a Chevron Gules, between three Bull's Heads couped Sable *Boleyn*
 13   Argent, a Cross Moline Gules *Uvedale*
 14   Azure, three Quatrefoils, in chief a Boar passant Or *Massingbeard.*
 15   Quarterly, Or and Gules, a Bend of the last *Beauchamp, Baron of Bedford.*
 16   Chequy Or and Azure, within a Bordure Gules, Billette Argent
 17   Azure, a Chief indented Ermine *Butler*
 18   Argent, on a Bend Sable, three Roses of the first *Carey Lord Hunsdon*
 19   BEAUFORT
 20   Azure, three covered Cups Or *Butler*
 21   Ermine, on a Chief Sable, three Crosses patee Argent *Waringham*
 22   Quarterly *France*, *England*, *Scotland* and *Ireland* within a Bordure compone Argent and Azure the Argent charged with Roses proper *Pole*
 23   Chequy Or and Azure, on a Chief Gules, a Plume Argent   *Drax*

In the South Wall of the Chancel is joined the *Sacellum*, or little Chapel, erected by James Lord Berkeley about the Year 1450 On the Outside it is ornamented, embellished in the very richest and costly Stile, the Arms and Cognizances of the Family interfixed with the Ornaments on the several Shields peculiarly elegant and simple, consisting only of a Lover over the Entrance large and small

The Figure of St *George* subduing the Dragon is affixed to one of the Pinnacles The Communication with the Chancel is made by a low fretted Arch, under which is an Altar Tomb of Alabaster, on which recline two Figures of an old and young Master Aimont, the Arms of Berkeley on the Corners of Mail, Collars of a military Order round both their Necks, the Mitre, their Cognizance, under the Heads and a Lion couchant under the Feet of each The Arms on the Chancel side are charged with a File of three Lambeaux, for Lord THOMAS, the Grandson

---

* These are called by Dr PARSONS the Children of THOMAS Lord BERKELEY, viz THOMAS MAURICE and ISABEL who died in their Infancy Some Antiquaries, however, have conjectured that they are habited in female Apparel, as purposely attired as for Nuns

ON the Side of the Tomb, within the Chapel, are two Rows of Compartments of Tabernacle Work, containing Figures of Knights, Lecclesiastics, and the BERKELEY Arms inclosed within Quatrefoil, wrought in the most finished Sculpture of that Day.

This Monument was erected for JAMES, the fifth Lord BERKELEY, and THOMAS his Grandson, but no Inscription remains. The several other Memorials will be noticed in Order.

Of the Castle Mr SMYTH has the following Notices

' In the Southest End of the Towne is seated the Castell of *Berkeley*, a great Part whereof was built
" out of the Ruines of the Nunnery, which stood in the same Place, which was demolished by the Pre-
" of Earle GODWN, in the Time of EDWARD the Confessor. The buildinge of this Castell was by
" Kinge HENRY the Seconde, in the Time of K. STEPHEN, whilst the said HENRY was Duke of No-
" *rmandie*, as plainly appears by a Deed of the said Duke HENRY's made to ROBERT, the Sonne of
" HARDING, wherein the Duke dothe acknowledge to have covenanted with the said ROBERT, to build
" for him this the Castle according to the Will of the said ROBERT, and then gave his Oathe to per-
" forme the same, and also did joyne other Noblemen with the Duke. The Words whereof in the original
' Deed are, *Et pono firmare ibi Castellum secundum voluntatem ipsius* ROBERTI *Et Ego per sacramentum affiави*
" *et idem affirm'* RICINALDUS *Comes Cornubie*, &c. And to see this Building the better performed, the said
" Duke HENRY, it long before the Death of K. STEPHEN, came in Person to *Berkeley*. Howbeit it is
" certain that this first Building, the Castle contained no more than the innmost of the three Gates, and
" the Buildings within the same, for the two utmost Gates, and all the Buildings belonging unto them
" first the Keepe, were the Addition of Lord MAURICE, eldest Sonne of the Lord ROBERT, in the
' latter End of K. HENRY Seconde, and of Lord THOMAS, the seconde of that Name, in EDWARD II
" and of Lord THOMAS, the third of that Name, in 18 EDWARD III. And as for the greate Kitchen
" (great indeed) standing without, but adjoyninge to the Keepe of the Castle, it was the Worke of K.
" HENRY Seventh, at his first Entrance into Possession thereof, about the ninth Yeare of his Reign,
' shortly after the Death of WILLIAM Marques BERKELEY, who had conveyed the same amongst other
" to that King. In this Castle were of late Years (not yet wholly ruined or deformed) two beautiful
" Chapels or Oratories, endowed with divers Privileges from the Bishops of *Rome*. The one of them
" but at the Castle called the Keep, with a goodly Well of Water under it. The other at the
" upper End of the great Hall Staires, leading to the great Dyninge Chamber. and for the decent
' keeping of the Ornaments thereunto belonging, divers Allowances were by the Lords yearly made, as
" directed. Accompte and Deeds in the Evidence House in this Castle appears. MAURICE Lord BER-
" KELEY the 4th of that Name, in the 38 EDW. III. obtained of Pope URBANE Seconde, by his full
' Bull and Power that to the End his two Chappels, the one of our *Lady* the *blessed Virgin*, the other of
" *Saint John the Baptist*, founded in the Castle of *Berkeley*, might be renewed, and frequented with due
" Reverence, for the Yeres of Pardon and Release of the Pennance enjoyned, to every one who should in
" the said Chappels in the festival Days of the Yeare, hear Masses, or say kneeling three Ave Maries,
" or should give any Vestments, or Chalices, or any other Aids of Charitie to the said Chappels. And
' who soever shall there pray for them that obtained these Pardons, and for the Life and good Estate of
" the Noble Lord MAURICE de BERKELEY, and the Lady ELIZABETH his Wife, and for their Chil-
" dren, and for the Soule of the Lord THOMAS his Father, being in Purgitory, shall bee allso releast at
" certaine Days of the Pennance enjoyned them. And this Faculty, Grace, or Instrument for the In-
' dulgences, was also under the Seales of eleven of that Popes Cardinals, perhaps allso somewhat the
' rather procured by that Lords Wisdome, through the great Scisme of three Popes at once, that then
' raigned in the Church.'

From these Evidences it is apparent that the Castle was originally founded in the Reign of King STE-
PHEN, and has continued with one Alienation only, of short continuance, the Baronial Residence of this
noble Family, during the Lapse of more than six Centuries.

' Barony to Mr Madox, was Knight Service in baronel, that is knight Service or great Land
" created into a barony, or made a Barony at its first Creation, every Nobleman as her by the Te-
" nure a noble to his military Duty limited only to Service within the Kingdom but his very
" person to serve at the Command of his King, and not truly in his own Person, but was
' bound a Number of Knights as he was able to maintain, by the several Fees of which his Barony was
" composed. The spiritual Barons allso though exempted from personal Service, were required to send
" their leudal ordinary Tenants in Proportion to the Number of Feuds represented, when summoned by
" the King.

Lord LYTTLETON'S Hist. HENRY II. vol. II. p. 89.

In the same Exchequer in the second Year of King RICHARD I. MAURICE de BERKELEY is called the
of the Knights Fee, in the second Levy, upon the Ransom of the King, ROBERT his
son Maurice doth keep, was levied of and five Knights Fee
In the same year ROGER de BERKELEY paid 15l and 7 each for his Knights Fee
Ex. Inter Rot. Scaccer fol. XLVIII. ad Sept. Ric. I. Annis Regn 2d, 6th, 9.

MSS. DODSWORTH, Bodl. Lib. vol. XI.

The Same doth attain the Wealth and Territory of this noble Family at this Day, but it appears
in this some in the County only

In the MS Collections of the late Mr PRYNNE, from which Extracts are with great Candour permitted by the present Possessor D'ANSTON HUNT, Esq it is stated "that Robert Lord BERKELEY, "an Adherent to the Empress MAUD, was taken Prisoner by King STEPHEN and treated with the "greatest Indignities at his own Castle Gates, for refusing to deliver it up" This proves that the Castle was in a defensible State early in the Reign of STEPHEN Here the second Edward's ended an inglorious Reign having been given up with this Castle to the MORTIMERS by THOMAS Lord BERKLEY, who was afterwards honourably acquitted by his Peers of being accessary to his Death In the Contentions of York and Lancaster this Castle had no Share but it suffered greatly from the disputed Title to its Possession, between the Heir of the Barony, and RICHARD BEAUCHAMP, Earl of Warwick Mr PRYNNE mentions, that "In 1416, the Earl of Warwick, lay before the Castle with an armed Force fully determined to lessen it, but was diverted from his Purpose by the Intercession of the Bishop of Worcester, and the neighbouring Gentry It sustained at this Time several Sieges, which were as frequently raised After Lord Warwick's Decease, his Heirs preferred their Claims in Suit that continued a Century and a Half, during which Period, their Partizans wearied by the tedious Process of the Law, had frequent Recourse to the Decision of the Sword Mutual Reprisals were made till the Dispute was finally adjusted by Combat on Nibly Green, when the Claim of WILLIAM, first Lord BERKLEY, was confirmed by the Death of THOMAS Lord LISLE, whom he defeated in the Field

COLEFIT, in his Military Government of Gloucester, edit 1645, informs us, that, during the grand Rebellion, "Berkely Castle was held for the King by a Scottish Captain, and subdued till the Country" He speaks of frequent Incursions and Skirmishes but of no regular Siege only, by MASSIE, with two Troops of Horse and 200 Musketeers The Castle was not taken Colonel VEALE is mentioned as the newly made Governor of Berkly Castle, p 68 Whatever Buildings were demolished it is most probable they were between the outer Gate and the present Structure, where sentinels and that these were less considerable than they are represented to have been

The present Form of the Castle approaches nearer to a Circle than to any other Figure The great Gate leads, under a lofty, Pile of Building connected with the Keep on the left Side, into an irregular Court, about one Hundred and forty Yards round The Keep the Walls of which are remarkably lofty and massive, resembles the Form of a Roman D, flanked by three semicircular Towers, besides that in which the great Stone Staircase is contained which is square, and has a small Room, in which King EDWARD is said to have suffered The whole is rudely inhabited One Peculiarity is remarked by LELAND in his Itinerary Sed non sit it in Mole eget Terra, though certainly on the highest Ground in the Castle It is on the Inside sufficiently capacious to have admitted of the Chapel Mr SMYTHE records, the Well of which only is preserved The Entrance into it is made by an arched Door-case of finished Sanctity, call the Muniment Room The Barbican, or, as it is commonly called, Thorpe's Tower, is the straight Part of the Keep, by no means roomy It may be conjectured, that the large Aperture partly filled up by a comparatively low Wall is where the ancient Gateway stood, and that the Towers founded by the Duke of Normandy could add to this Structure only

When the Castle in some Measure ceased to be reckoned a Military Strong Hold, and became the capital Residence of the Barony, numerous Edifices of Convenience were erected the Dates of which are distinctly marked in the foregoing Manuscript Of these the Hall, built in the Reign of EDWARD the Third, is a lofty Room, 48 Feet in Length and 31 Breadth with four Windows on the North Side of Norman Architecture No Arms, painted Glass, Armour, nor any other Gothic Ornaments, are preserved Of the same Era is the Chapel of St MARY adjoining, noticed by Mr SMYTH, the Dimensions of which are 30 Feet by 24, the Windows are with two spacious Niches, formerly used as private Oratories

In the various Apartments of the Castle many original Family Portraits are arranged, chiefly of the STRATTON Branch, which were the bequest of the last Peer of that Name GEORGE Baron BERKLEY, 1616, by COUNTESS JACSON 2 the Queen of Bohemia, by the same Master This curious Portrait is marked in the Corner with a Celestial Crown, and Motto, "Then This" In a Cabinet Room, executed from the Wall, are ten [?] valuable Miniatures

No 1 MAURICE Lord BERKLEY, 1518
2 KATHERINE Wife of MAURICE Lord BERKLEY, 1518
3 THOMAS Lord BERKLEY, 1523, Brother of MAURICE
4 THOMAS Lord BERKLEY, 1534
5 HENRY Lord BERKLEY, 1551
6 Lady JANE his second Wife, Daughter of Sir MILES STANHOPE
7 THOMAS BERKLEY, who died before his Father Lord HENRY, who was succeeded by his Grandson GEORGE Lord BERKLEY, 1616, whose Portrait before noticed completes the Series for one hundred Years

* In SHAKESPEARE who is known to have consulted the most authentic Chronicle of his Day, useful Perkins thus recorded, during the Commotion which conducted the Government the last Years of the Reign of RICHARD II

NORTHUMBERLAND "How far is it to Berkley Edward Poor
Keeps good York there, with his Men of War?
Percy There stands the Castle by yon Tuft of Trees,
Mann'd with Three Hundred Men, as I have heard
And in it are the Lords of York, Berkeley, and Seymour
None else of Name and noble Estimate
BY RICHARD II Act II Scene 3
This was the fourth Lord THOMAS, who afterwards pronounced the Deposition of the King in Parliament 1399

A State Bed is here shewn, with a Date, 5.0 the Pils of the *Corinthian* Orders of the y gilt

The *Grecian* Orders were about this Period first intro't cain into *England*, and very sparingly uted, excepting in the internal Ornaments of Houses, or the most splendid Furniture

The Foundation and outward Walls on the South-east Side are many Feet below the Level of the Court, and are supported by Buttresses of impregnable Strength and Thickness

In surveying this proud Monument of antient Splendor and Magnificence, the very Genius of Chivalry seems to present himself, amidst the venerable Remains, with a Sternness and Majesty of Air and Feature which shew what he once has been, and a mixture of Disdain for the degenerate Posterity that robbed him of his Honours

Amidst such a Scene, the manly Exercises of Knighthood recur to the Imagination in their full Pomp and Solemnity, while every patriot Feeling beats at the Remembrance of the generous Virtues which were nurled in those Schools of Fortitude, Honour, Courtesy, and Wit, the Mansions of our antient Nobility

Of the Parks and Chaces enumerated by *Leland*, and in Mr. Smyth's Papers, all are converted into Farms, excepting *Micklewood Chace*, and *Whitcliffe Park*, some Furlongs distant from the Castle. It contains the highest ground in the Parish, and commands an extensive View of the *Severn* and *Bristol Channel*, is extremely well wooded, and reputed to be five or Seven Miles in Circumference

The Fishery of the River *Severn*, for a great Extent, is one of the Manerial Rights of the Earl of *Berkeley*, which, however, is in several Instances superseded by an exclusive Privilege, annexed to certain Lands, situate on the Banks of the River, the Channel or Current of which is the Property of the Inhabitants in general

In this Parish are Four very large Districts or Tythings all of which have distinct Officers, removing Proportion from one to the other, and act as separate Parishes, for which Purpose, Vestries are held weekly at *Berkley*

1 The *Borough* The principal and most respectable Families of Property settled here are, Raymond, Hicks, and Jenner, the ancient Family of Weston is extinct in the right Line

2 *Alkington*, in which are *Newport* (Two Farms annually were established in this Hundred, by Thomas Lord Berkeley, on the 7th of *July* and 2 of *September*, who founded a Chantry to the Honour of *St Maurice*, 17 Edw. III 1344, in the Chapel of *Newport*), *Hoodfield*, *Huntingford*, *Hook*, *Boversworth*, *Goldwick*, and *Raghag*, which are severally possessed by the Families of Hicks, Coxon, Co, and Port

3 *Ham*, which includes *Pedington*, late the Property of Thomas Hicks, Esq. *Clapton*, *Bowen*, which contains *Blanbury Farm*, held by Gee, and an Estate by Pottinger

4 *Hinton*, wherein are *Hosfield*, reputed a Manor, held with a considerable Estate, by Daniel Lysons, M.D. which formerly belonged to the Family of Thorpe. The tradition, that the Tenure of this Manor is by military Service and a Tower in *Berkeley Castle* called *Thorpes Tower*, is without Foundation. *Sanger*, long held by an old Family of the same Name, in which also is another Estate belonging to Woodward, *Hinton*, *Hilcot*, and *Breadstone*, in which various Estates are possessed by the Families of Names Pennell, Fust, Cheltenham, Adey, Hebbledin, Croome, Coxon, and Nash. At *Purton* the present Lord Berkeley has made a Decoy Pool on a large plan, being the only one in this County Stove will be mentioned in its station. *Ores*, is a distinct Parish

---

B E N E F A C T I O N S.

To the Borough

In 1625, John Attwood gave by Will Lands to the Value of 18l. 10s. *per ann.* to be disposed of to the Profit and Advantage of the Poor of this Borough

In 1656 Thomas Morris bequeathed by Deed Land for the Relief of the poor Inhabitants of this Parish, thereby Value then at about 4l.

In 1650 John Maurice devised by Will Land the annual Produce of which is 5l. to be distributed amongst the poor of this Borough

—— also a House and Mault... Tenement with Land to the Poor of this Borough the yearly Value of which is 3l. and 10s. inhabited by them

—— Mr. Townsend left by Will a Mault... Tenement and Land, the Issue and Profits of which are 2l. Annually to be disposed of for and towards the Relief of the poor Inhabitants of this Borough

—— Thomas Gainer devised by Will for the Relief and Maintenance of the Poor of this Parish the several Annuities then out of Land The Tything Barn of Ham containing the Sum of 5l. Annually to the Poor of this Borough

In 1720 Thomas Horton Esq. gave Land to the Value of 1l. 6d. *per Ann.* to be laid out in Bread among the Poor of this Borough, who do not receive Relief from the Overseers

In 1724, BRIDGET VICK left by Will, to be distributed to the poor Widows and Housekeepers of this Borough, not receiving Relief from the Overseer, Lands to the Value of . . . .

In 1728, ELIZABETH BEVAN devised, by Will, Land, the annual Produce of which is to be distributed in Bread amongst the Poor of this Borough, who do not receive Relief from the Overseer.

RICHARD LYLLP, late of the City of Bristol, Consequent to the Will of his Brother JOHN LYLLP, Gent (both Natives of this Parish), in the Year 1750, gave an Estate, situate in the Tything of Ham, for the following Uses, as appears by a Deed enrolled in Chancery in the Year 1751, ... Thirty Shillings, to be equally divided between the Clerk and Sexton of the Parish Church of Berkeley, for . . . . the Bell, and attending Divine Service, as herein after directed. The remaining Part of the yearly Profits to be divided between the Ministers of Berkley, Cam, Hutton and the Coxhall, Lectworth, Derly, and Thornbury, for reading Morning Prayer, and preaching Sixteen Sermons annually in this Church on the following Days, and during Lent, on the following Subjects:

1. The Lent Fast
2. Against Atheism and Infidelity
3. The Catholic Church
4. Excellency of the Church of England
5. The Defence of the Divinity of our Saviour
6. Baptism
7. Confirmation
8. Confession and Absolution
9. Error of the Church of Rome
10. Against Enthusiasm and Superstition.
11. Restitution
12. Attending Public Worship
13. Frequenting the Holy Communion
14. Repentance

Sermons on the first Seven Subjects to be preached in the first Year beginning . . . . 1750, and on the remaining other Seven in the following Year in the . . . . the five given . . . ever. One of the said Sermons to be preached by each of the above-mentioned Ministers on their Monday in Lent, Four of other Ten by the Minister of Berkley, and the remaining Six by the respective Ministers of the other Parishes aforesaid, on the first Monday in every Month . . . . within the Compass of the Year.

To the Tything of Alkington.

In 1718, THOMAS HORTON, Esq; gave Land to be yearly let, and the Produce thereof to be distributed in Bread amongst the Poor of this Tything, who do not receive Relief from the Overseer.

In 1724, Mrs BRIDGET VICK bequeathed Land, the Issues and Profits to be yearly disposed of to the Widows and poor House-keepers of this Tything not receiving Relief from the Overseer.

In 1728, Mrs ELIZABETH BEVAN devised, by Will, the sum of 13s. yearly issuing out of Lands, to be distributed in Bread amongst the Poor of this Tything, who receive no Relief from the Overseer.

In 17.. THOMAS PARKER left . . . . to the poor . . . . of Land.

To the Tything of Ham.

In 1718, THOMAS HORTON, Esq; devised Land, the annual Produce whereof to be distributed amongst the Poor of this Tything who do not receive Relief . . . . . .

In 1724, Mrs BRIDGET VICK gave, by Will, to poor Widows and Housekeepers of this . . . . Land, the Issues and Profits of which to be yearly disposed of . . . .

In 1728, Mrs ELIZABETH BEVAN gave, by Will, Land, and the Value thereof to be distributed in Bread to the Poor of this Tything who receive no Relief from the Overseer.

In 1650, Mr JOHN MARTIN bequeathed to the Poor . . . . Land, the annual Profits whereof to be distributed to the Poor of this Tything.

Mr EDWARD . . . . left, by Will, the Sum of . . . . and . . . . of, both Support of the Poor of this Tything.

To the Tything of Hinton.

Mr THOMAS PARKER gave, by Will, to the Poor of this Tything, the . . . . out of Lands.

In 1718, THOMAS HORTON, Esq; gave, by Will, the Produce whereof . . . . . . to be distributed in Bread amongst the Poor of this Tything who do not receive . . . .

In 1724, Mrs BRIDGET VICK devised, by Will, to the poor Widows . . . . of this Tything, Land, the annual Profits whereof . . . .

In 1728, Mrs ELIZABETH BEVAN gave, by Will, to the Poor of this Tything who do not receive Relief from the Overseer, Land, the Issue and Profits of . . . .

INCUMBENTS	PATRONS	INCUMBENTS.	PATRONS

John Trevifa, who tranflated the Bible, was prefented to the Vicarage of *Berkeley*, by *Thomas* fourth Lord *Berkeley*, who was an eminent Patron of Literature. *Trevifa* died in the Year 1409.

INCUMBENTS	PATRONS	INCUMBENTS	PATRONS
157, John Norbrock,	Queen Elizabeth	1728 Ralph Webb, M A	Earl of Berkeley
1586 William Green	William Sprint	729 Stephen Jenner, M A	The fame
1639 Thomas Tucker,	——	1755 Geo Cha Black, M A	The fame
—— Edward Chetwynd,	——	17,8 Henry Knox, M A	The fame
1618 Richard Siffin, M A	Chapter of Briftol	1771 Aug Thomas Hupfman,	The fame
—— Jerome Gregory,	Earl of Berkele,	1773 David Williams, LL B	The fame
1691 Henry Head, M A	The fame	1774 Jane Cooper, B A	The fame.
The above from Sir Rob Atkyns		178, Aug Tho Hupfman, Clk	The fame

PRESENT LORD OF THE MANOR,

The Right Honourable FREDERICK AUGUSTUS Earl of BERKELEY

At the Vifitations of the Heralds, in 1682 and 1683, the following Perfons were fummoned from this Place and its Tything

From *Berkeley*	From *Ham*
George Earl of Berkeley	Walter Lloyd
Richard Siffin, Clerk	Francis Jay
From *Alkington*	From *Hamfallow*
Jofeph Yeomans	Daniel Lyfons
From *Breadftone*	John Morfe
John Nelme	John Clutterbuck
From *Hinton*	
Edward Saniger	

At the Election in 1776, One Hundred and Eleven Votes were found in this Parifh and its Hamlets

The earlieft Entry in the Regifter bears Date 1598

ANNUAL ACCOUNT OF MARRIAGES, BIRTHS, AND BURIALS, IN THIS PARISH

A D	Mar	Bir	Bur	A D	Mar	Bir	Bir	A D	Mar	Bir	Bir	A D	Mar	Bir	Bir
1781	20	67	57	1791				1801				1811			
1782	20	74	39	1792				1802				1812			
1783	6	50	46	1793				1803				1813			
1784	13	28	50	1794				1804				1814			
1785	15	48	51	1795				1805				1815			
1786	16	47	26	1796				1806				1816			
1787				1797				1807				1817			
1788				1798				1808				1818			
1789				1799				1809				1819			
1790				1800				1810				1820			

From the above Extract it appears that the Increafe of Population during the laft fix Years amount to 71

INSCRIPTIONS

INSCRIPTIONS IN THE CHANCEL.

On an Altar Tomb of Alabaster, two Cumbent Figures, the Man in Armour, with the Trunk Cognisance at his Feet, the Woman in her Coif, &c. with a Lion couchant. The following Inscription is on a Table under the Cornice, the Family Arms excepted.

Arms, Quarterly, 1st, Ruby, a Chevron between ten Crosses patée Pearl, for Berkeley, and Gules, three Lions of England a Label of three Points Argent, and Gules a Lion rampant Azure, &c. .... force of crofs Gules, a Lion rampant Or, 5th, Sable a Lion rampant Argent, 6th Quarterly, Or and Gules, a Bend of the second, 7th Barry of fix Or and Gules, 8th Gules a Lion rampant Azure, 9th Gules, a Cross Or, and Azure, 10th, Gules, &c. ... Azure, within an Orle of Lions of England, 11th, Or, a Bend for ... Gules.

Here lyeth the Body of Sir Henry Berkeley, Knight
Lord Berkeley, Mowbray, Segrave, and Bruse, Lord Lieutenant
of the County of Gloucester, who departed this Life the 26th Day
of November in the Year of our Lord God 1613, having
Day to he accomplished the Age of Fourscore Years.
He first married Katharine, Sister to Thomas Howard, Duke
of Norfolk, by whom he had Three, Thomas, Mary, and
Francis, Thomas, being a Knight of the Bath, married
Elizabeth, only Daughter and Heire into Sir George
Carey, Knight, Lord Hunsdon, Mary, the eldest Daughter,
was married unto Sir John Zouch, Knight, and Frances
the second Daughter, unto
Sir George Shirley, Baronet.
He secondly married Jane, the Widowe of Sir Roger
Townshend, Knight, yet living, by whom he had no Issue.

ON A MARBLE TABLET.

Arms, Berkeley, as before described, —impaling, Topaz fretty, Ruby, a Canton Ermine, for Noel.

H. S. E.
Carolus Comes de Berkeley, Vicecomes Dursley,
Baro Berkeley de Berkeley Cliff Mowbray, Segrave,
Et Bruce, e Nobilissimo ordine Balnei Eques
Vir talis genus quod spectat & P... os usquequaque Nobilis
Ut longo, si quis alius Procerum stemmate census,
Meritis etiam tum nihil illis pr... dignioribus natus
Siquidem a Gulielmo III. ad ordines statum Belgii
Ablegatus & Plenipotentiarius Extraordinarius
Rebus, non Britannie tantum sed totius f. Europe
(Tunc temporis præcipuum innuis) per annos V. manibus
Quam richer diligentia, tide quam integritate,
Evalidos fues, Lector, quod, supra de Patre,
In Maritimum ordinem adhibitum muter.
Tum a Juncturibus ordinis & Rege Guliet. & Anna Regina,
Et Proceribus Hibernia secundus,
Comitatuum Civitatumque Glocest. & Bristol. Domino Locum
Summi & Glocest. Custos Rotulorum Urbis Glocestr... que
Seneschallus, Ann... fort de Bristol Gubernator,
Gardianus Forestae de Dean
Designatus de Juncturum, immania multæ ad Romani Imperator cum
Cum Potestate Extraordinaria Plenipotentiale,
Quo minari Prefectura erat (præ meritis)
Obijt, ... tuo co post widerat
Sed ut illa idan... præcipuos fontes ...
Homo verus Habing... et vel in diem veritate,
Obijt Venetiaus Rei... dem tutiorais, Ipsa
Die Decimum octavum Januarii,
Æternum aure... aque et Superbus,
In Chriftum implens, obdorm...
annos ... Carolus... mitur... anni
Natus VIII. April Anno MDCXLIX. denatus
XXIV. Septembris MDCC... coth... MXII.

ON A PLAIN TABLET

To the perpetual Memory, of the moſt
vertuous and pruden Lady, ELIZABETH
Lady BERKELEY, the Widdove of Sir THOMAS
BERKELEY, Knight, Sonne and Heire of HENRY
Lord BERKELEY, GEORGE Lord BERKELEY, her
only Sonne, hath in this Chipple of his
Anceſtors in a dutiful Acknowledgement
of her pious Life and Death, conſecrated
this Inſcription for a Memorial of her
vertue who leat this Life at her Houſe
at Cranford, in the County of Middleſex,
the 25th Day of April, Anno Domini,
1675,
where, according to the Direction of her
Will, ſhe hath buried

IN THE CHANCEL

Arms, Or, two Bars Azure, in Chief a Lion
paſſant of the laſt

M S

JEREMIÆ GREGORII, hujus Eccleſiæ Vicarii,
Qui obiit XV Kal Feb A D MDCXC æt XL
Immaturum ejus mortem bonis omnibus
Quibus notus erat, ingenti luctu
Proſequentibus,
Quippe vir fuit cum ſtatura tum gratia
Dotibus ornatiſſimus, moribus ſuaviſſimus,
Acri ingenio, memoria admiranda præpotenti,
In concionandi facundia, et quod
Caput eſt, exiia pietate, qua magna non modo
Locutus eſt, ſed et vixit
Poſtquam per XV Annos Cirenceſtriæ Paſtorali
Officio ſumma diligentia functus eſt huc
Receſſit, ut laboribus ingentis oppidi, quibus
Nemo unus ſuffecerat, tandem reſpiraret,
Sed huic finis fero, ſiquidem phthyſi
Infanabili contracta, intra paucos
Menſes hic ſanctam animam
Expiravit

Arm, Gules, ſeme of Croſs Croſſes fitchee,
a Lion rampant Or, charged with a Creſcent,
Sable for Difference, being the yonger Branch
of the Family of Hopton, of Hopton Caſtle, in
the County of Salop

In Memory of
[...]aret Daughter of WILLIAM HOPTON,
of Can Gent by ELIZABETH his Wife,
Daughter of THOMAS CAM, of Newport,
in this County Gent who deceaſed
Auguſt 30, 1696

In Memory
of [...] Daughter of WILLIAM HOPTON,
of Can Gent who died March the 17th, 1737

Here lieth the Body of WILLIAM HOPTON,
[...] 6th Day of September,
Anno Domini 16[...]

In Memory
of the Rev Mr EDWARD SMITH, A M
who died Auguſt the 9th, 1774,
aged 80

MARY his Wife died March 15, 1765,
aged 70

The Rev Mr EDWARD SMITH,
their Son, died June 8, 1777
aged 46

Two of their Children died Infants

Alſo their Daughter
Mrs ELIZABETH SMITH,
died Sept 21, 1781,
aged 48

Arms, in a Lozenge, a Croſs quarterly quartered, in the firſt Quarter an Eagle diſplayed, for
WEBB

In
Memory of HESTER WEBB,
Daughter of JOHN WEBB,
late of Proceſter, in this
County, Gentleman, who departed
this Life the 14 Day of
December, in the Year of our
Lord 1736, aged 5 Years

ON A SARCOPHAGUS AND URN

Arms, Pendant from the Pyramid, an Eagle
diſplayed, for WISTON

To the Memory of
GEORGE WISTON, Eſq who died 26 July, 17[...]
aged 6 Years

Alſo
WILLIAM WISTON, Eſq who died OЄt 15, 17[...],
aged 5 Years

On a mural Monument

Arms, a Crofs coupee between Four Fleur de lis, for JENNER,—impaling, a Chevron between Three Unicorn's Heads couped, for HEAD

In Memory of
The Rev Mr STEPHEN JENNER,
late Vicar of this Parish, who died
December the 9th, 1754, aged 52 Years.

Also of SARAH his Wife,
who died October the 10th, 1754,
aged 46 Years

O N   F L A T   S T O N E S

Arms, as before emblazoned

Here lyeth the Body of WILLIAM HOPTON,
of Cam, in this County, Gent who departed
this Life, 26 June, 1671, aged 35 Years

Here also lieth the Body of ELIZABETH,
his Daughter, who died 30 Aug   6, aged 33

Also here lieth the Body of ELIZABETH
HOPTON, his Wife, who departed this Life
5th January, 1714, aged — Years

———

Arms, HOPTON, as before

Near this Place lies the Body of
JOHN HOPTON, of Littleton upon Severne,
in this County, Efq who departed this
Life A D 1681   Also the Body of
ANNE his Wife, who died in December,
A D 1713   Also the Body of WILLIAM
HOPTON, Efq Son of the faid JOHN, who
died in April 1713

Here also lieth the Body
of JOHN HOPTON, Efq Son of the
faid JOHN, who departed this
Life March the 15th, 1727, aged 48.

———

ANNE HOPTON

———

Arms, Hopton, as before

Hic jacet
GULIELMUS HOPTON, Armiger,
Stirpe et moribus vere generofis,
Amicorum fideliffimus, et bello
Per triginta fere Annos Dux latignifimus
Ob XV Aprilis Anno Dom MDCCXV.
Ætatis L annorum

———

Arms, HOPTON, as before

Here lieth the Body of
THOMAS HOPTON, of Bristol, Efq
who departed this Life Decem 5, 1718,
aged 73

Also here lieth the Body of ELIZABETH his
Wife, who departed this Life Nov 18, 173,
aged 67

———

Arms, Two Bars, each charged with Three
Mullets for HOPTON

JEREMIAS HOPTON, Gen
Redditus et proventus pranobilis,
Et dignffimi GEORGI Comitis
De BERKELEY Regi a directionibus
Confiliis, in ardui hac fua
Baronia Receptor generalis,
Prepropero fato John XXXI.
Lugentibus vicinis omnibus,
Præcipus, præfertim uxore Maria,
Filia JHANNIS HOUSTON, CAROLO
Primo Divæ memoriæ Regi
Efcuyer d'efcuyrie, quæ
Conjugalis amoris ergo
Hoc monumentum
Ei impofuit.

Hic etiam jacet fepulta Maria uxor
Ejus, quæ poftea nupta fuit WALTERO
LLOYD, Gen Hic e vita
Difceffit XV die Aug
MDCCXIV

———

Arms, Three Eftoiles iffuant from as many
Crefcents

RICHARDUS SAFFIN, A M
Ecclefiæ Anglicanæ Prefbyter per annos
XXI Vicarius de Berkeley fidus et
Orthodoxus, hic una cum Filio ejus
Richardo trium Septimanarum Infantulo
Requiefcit in Pace
Obiit   Infans Janu 1   anno   1679
RICHARD   Pater Junii 16   1690, æt 53
FRANCISCA Filia GULIELMI HOPTON,
De Oldley, Gen Vidua Mærens
Pofuit

———

In Memory of
ELIZABETH, the Wife of EDWARD
LICKNELL of Hopton, in the County
of Middlefex Gent (Daughter
of the Reverend Mr HENRY HEAD
A M late Vicar of this Church,
and Prebendary of Bristol)
who died June 6, 1730, aged

Also of MARY HEAD Daughter
of the faid Mr HEAD, died
March 18, aged

Arms, as before

In Memory of
the Reverend Mr HENRY HEAD,
late Vicar of this Parish and Prebendary
of Briston, who died May the 18, 1720,
aged 6_

Also of EDWARD, his Son, aged 4 Months

Also of MARY, his Wife, who died Dec 1,
1739, aged 75

Also of HENRY JENNER, their Grandson
and Son of STEPHEN JENNER, now
Vicar of Birkley, who died May
the 12th, 1736, aged a Year and a Half.

SARAH HAYWARD, Widow, and
Daughter of the Rev STEPHEN JENNER,
died May 13, 1765

STEPHEN JENNER
SARAH JENNER
1751

Here lyeth the Body of JANE, the
Wife of JOHN MORSE, of Wickes Elm, Gent
the daughter of WILLIAM CLARK, of
Stanford, in the County of Somerset,
Esq who departed this Life January
7th, Anno Domini 1671

FRANCES, their Daughter, July 29, 166_

And THOMAS, their Son, was buried
April the 7th, 1668

Here lyeth the Body of SARAH, the
Wife of JOHN MORSE, of Wickselme,
Gent the Daughter of THOMAS WHEATE,
of Glympton in the Hole, in the County
of Oxford, Esq who was buried Dec
the 1st, 1683 And THOMAS, then
Son was buried September 1, 168

Here lyeth the Body of NICHOLAS MORSE,
of Wickselme, Gent who was buried
the 17th Day of November, 1729, aged 47

Also SARAH, his Daughter, was here
buried April the 17th 1725, in the 6th Year
of her Age

Here resteth the Body of THOMAS
____ of Wantwell, who departed
this Life the 28th Day of February An Dm 167
Viram bonendo _____

In Memory of the Rev Mr
EDWARD SMITH A M who died
Aug 9, 1774, in the 51st Year of his Age

Also of MARY his Wife,
who died March 1, 176_ in the
51st Year of her Age

In Memory of
Mr ____ ____ who died
Sept ____, ____, 48 Year

Here resteth the Body of
SARAH the Wife of THOMAS SMITH,
of Wantwell, who departed this Life
May the 2, d Anno Dom 1675,
aged 76 Years

Here resteth the Bodies of
JOHN CLUTTERBUCK,
of Hinton, Yeoman, and ELIZABETH
his Wife, who were buried (viz.)
JOHN, May the 5th, 1678
ELIZABETH, Feb 16, 1699

Arms, Three Elm Trees eradicated

Here lyeth the Body of
WILLIAM NELMES, of Briston, Esq
Eldest Son of JOHN NELMES, of Breadstone,
in this Parish Esq who died the
18 Day of April, 1745, aged 65

Arms, Three Elm Leaves

In Memory of JOHN NELMES,
Esq of Breadstone in this Parish,
who died September the 10th, 1719, at true 6_

Here also lyeth the Body of MARY, his
Wife, who died the 30th of September, 1729
aged 66

Arms, as before

Here lyeth the Body of
SAMUEL NELMES, of the City of Bristol,
Gent Son of JOHN NELMES, of Breadstone,
in this Parish, Esq who died the 2_ Day of
October, 1754, aged 50

Arms, as before

Here lyeth the Body of SUSANNA
NELMES, Daughter of JOHN NELMES Esq
by MARY, his Wife, who died Feb 9,
1733, aged 56

In Memory of THOMAS CLARK, Son of
THOMAS CLARK Gardiner to the Right
Honourable Earl BIRKELLY who is
here interred the 4th Day of July, 174_
aged One Year

And also MARY Daughter of the
said THOMAS CLARK and MARY his Wife
who died February ____ ____ 175_ ____

Also the Body of the said MARY
CLARK, who ____ ____ ____ ____
in the 69 Year ____ ____

In Memory of ____ ____
____ Churchwarden of this Parish,
who died ____ 176_ ____ in the ____ ____,
aged ____ Year

And also ____ ____ in N____ and
the Wife of JOHN MASTERS of this Town,
Surgeon ____ ____ ____ ____ ____ in
the ____ Year of ____ ____

Arms, Quarterly, 1ft, an Eagle displayed 2d,
3 Fleurs-de-Lis in Pile, 3d, fix Lioncels rampant,
4th, Webb as before

In Memory of
CHARLES WESTON, of Berkeley, Efq
Eldeft Son of PHILIP WESTON, Efq
deceafed, and great Grandfon of
Sir RICHARD WESTON, Late of Weſton Hall,
in the County of Stafford Knight, who defcended
if a very ancient Family in that County,
who died Sept 4, 1724,
aged 64

Alfo in Memory of the Rev
Mr JOHN WESTON, A B Vicar of Strichenoine,
in this Diocese, and 4th Son of the above named
CHARLES WESTON, who died June 2, 1739,
aged 25 Years

Alfo of THOMAS WESTON, Gent 5th Son
of the faid CHARLES WESTON who died
June 8 1740, aged 24 Years

Arms, Quarterly, 1ft, WESTON 2d, Irton,
in chief three Roundlets 3d, fix Lioncels rampant,
4th, fix Fleurs-de-Lis in Pile

Here lieth the Body of
JANE, the Relict of CHARLES WESTON,
Efqr of Berkeley, Efq
who dyed the 10th Day of December,
in the Year of our Lord 1742, aged 61 Years

Here lieth the Body of CHARLES WESTON,
the eldeft Son of CHARLES WESTON, of
Berkeley, Efq who was buried the 10th
Day of April, 1748, aged 49 Years

Alfo of SARAH WESTON, of
Berkeley, who died Nov 21, 1753

Here lieth the Body of WILLIAM TRYE,
late of New Park in the Parish of Berkeley,
Gent who departed this Life April
the 14th, Anno Domini 1675, æt fua 59

In Memory of the Rev
Mr HENRY KNOX, A M late Vicar
of this Parish who died Dec 24, 1770,
aged 75 Years

ON A MONUMENT AGAINST A PILLAR BETWEEN
THE NAVE AND NORTH AISLE

In Memory of
JAMES BAYLEY, of this Town, Mercer,
who died the 8th Day of May, 1712

Alfo of ELIZABETH his Wife, the eldeft
Daughter of OSANDER WEBB, of Dudfley
Mercer, who died the 9th Day of August,
1727

ON FLAT STONES IN THE NAVE

Arms, two Chevronels between three Cronels,
for FREME, —impaling, a Bend compone, on a
Chief three Mcallops — With the Figure of a Lawyer
in Brafs, holding a Heart, infcribed Mercy

Hic jacet Corpus WILLIELMI FREME,
cujus animæ propitietur Deus & animarum
omnium fidelium & Sanctorum, pro tua
fuorum Contende initiare per angufam port.

In Memory of
ROBERT MARKLOVE, of this Town,
Mercer who departed this Life
the 10th of Dec 1755 aged 30

ROBERT his Son
died Feb 6, 1756, aged 5 Years and 8 Months

In Memory of ANN the Wife
of ROBERT MARKLOVE, of this Town,
Mercer, who departed this Life
Jan 15, 1731, aged 34

ANN, his Daughter, died an Infant

ROBERT MARKLOVE, of this Town,
Mercer died July 30, 1743, aged 44

In Memory of THOMAS FRYER, of
Newport in this Parish, who died
August 2, 1759 aged 41 Years

Here lieth interred the Body
of ANNE, the Wife of JOHN PAXTON,
of this Town Alderman, who
died March 8, 1770, aged 54 Years

ANN, the Daughter of JOHN
PAXTON, died Oct 29 1758,
aged 10 Years and 11 Months

SARAH, the Wife of
JOHN PAXTON, Jun of this Town,
died Nov 11, 1784 aged 30

THOMAS, Son of THOMAS and MARY
CUNOCK, of this Town, died
June 1, 1777, in his Infancy

Here lieth the Body of
WILLIAM HARVEY, Gent who
departed this Life March 21, 1696

THOMAS HOOPER,
Feb 6 1711

In Memory
of MARY JENNER, of Clapton,
who died August 14, 1758,
aged 57

Here lieth the Body of
JOHN PARTARRIDGE, who died
Feb 17, 1687

MARY the Wife of JOHN PARTARRIDGE
was buried Oct 7, 1680

ON MONUMENTS IN THE SOUTH AILE

Arms, Gules, a Fess wavy, between three Fleur-de-lis Or, Crest, a Buck's Head couped Or

To the pious Memory
of THOMAS HICKES, of
Pedington, in this Parish, Gent.
who departed this Life
February 9, 1766,
aged 52 Years

Also of ELIZABETH his Wife,
who died December 6, 1772,
aged 83 Years

In Memory
of ELIZABETH, the Wife of
HENRY JONES, of this Parish, Esq
who died Oct 26, 1769,
aged 28 Years

In Memory of
ANNA, the Wife of WILLIAM JENKINS,
of the Stock, who died Dec. 3,
1778, aged 47

Also ELIZABETH, their Daughter,
died Nov 11, 1781, aged 24

Near this Place
lies the Body of
WILLIAM RAYMOND, Gent
youngest Son of GEORGE RAYMOND,
of Yeat, in this County, Esq
who died Oct 7, 1736,
aged 71

MARY his Wife
died Nov 19, 1745, æt 76

In Memory of
THOMAS HOOPER,
of Clapton in this Parish, Gent
who died Feb. 6, 1744,
aged 64 Years

ON FLAT STONES IN THE SOUTH AILE

Here resteth the Body of
WILLIAM ATWOOD,
of Woodford, Gent who
departed this Life the 3d
of October, 1707, æt sua 48

Here lieth the Body of WILLIAM LAWRENCE,
of Bradston, senior, Gent who was
buried the 12th Day of May, 1683

Also the Body of WILLIAM LAWRENCE,
Gent who was buried the 18th Day of June,
1725, in the 83d Year of his Age

Here lieth the Body of EDWARD
LAWRENCE, of Berkeley, who was buried
here the 10th Day of September, 1679

Also of MARY his Wife,
who was buried the 10th Day
of February, 1693

Here lieth the Remains of
Mr JOHN WHITEHOUSE, of
Gainsborough, who departed
this Life the 11th of Oct 1786,
aged 24 Years

In Memory of
ELIZABETH SMETHYMAN,
Wife of ROWLAND SMETHYMAN,
and Daughter of Mr WILLIAM JENKINS,
of the Stock, who was buried the
10th of June, 1759, aged 27 Years

SARAH SMITH, of Heathfield,
in this Parish, died December
the 9th, 1764, aged 77 Years

Here lieth the Body of Miss
CHARLOTTE HARRY, of Cheltenham
She died at Newport, in this Parish,
in her Way from Bristol, April
21, 1774, aged 13

To the Memory of Mr WILLIAM
JENKINS, of the Stock, in this Parish,
Mariner, who died Feb 21, 1766, aged 78

Also ELIZABETH JENKINS,
Wife of the abovesaid Mr WILLIAM
JENKINS, senior, of this Parish,
died May 6, 1707, aged 72 Years

ANNA JENKINS,
1778

Here resteth the Body of
GEORGE BENCE, of Pedington,
Yeoman, who was buried
the 2d Day of March, 1693

Also ELIZABETH his Widow,
died Dec 1, 1699, aged 72

Underneath this Stone lieth the
Remains of WILLIAM PICK, of London,
who died Oct 8, 1782, aged 53

Here resteth the Body
of WILLIAM HATTING, of Saniger, in the
Parish of Barkeley, and County of Gloucester,
who departed this Life Nov 18, 1673,
ætat sua 63

Here lieth the Body of GILES
RAYMOND, of this Town, Gent
who departed this Life Oct 16, 1773,
aged 70 Years

ELIZABETH, Daughter of
CHRISTOPHER and DOROTHY RAYMOND,
of Bristol ob Sept 16, 1730,
aged 60

IN THE NORTH AILE

ON A PLAIN TABLET AGAINST THE WALL

To the Memory of
HANNAH, the Wife of JOHN JOYNER,
of this Town, who departed this
Life Oct 1, 1779, in the 69th Year
of her Age

Also in Memory of the said
JOHN JOYNER, who departed
this Life Jan 15, 1781, aged 62

ON FLAT STONES

In Memory of WILLIAM HARVEY,
of the Day House, in the Parish of Hill,
who was buried Oct. 19, 1732, aged 36

Here lieth the Body of
JOHN SMITH, of Wanswell, Gent
who departed this Life
Aug 17, 1679, ætat suæ 30.

ON FLAT STONES BETWEEN THE NORTH AND SOUTH DOORS

Arms, three Leopards Faces ducally crowned,
Crest, a Hind's Head gorged with a Coronet

In Memory of
FRANCIS JAYE, of this Parish, Gent
who was here buried the 15th of March,
1736, in the 70th Year of his Age

Also of
ELIZABETH his Wife, who was here buried
the 11th of June 1709, aged about 40

Also of
ANNE JAYE, their Daughter, who was
here buried the 18th of March, 1736

Also of CHARLES JAYE, their eldest Son,
who died in 1692, in his infancy

Also of CHARLES JAYE, Gent
Brother of the said FRANCIS, who was here
buried Nov 8, 1707, aged 46

Arms, as before

To the Memory of FRANCIS JAYE, Gent
second Son of FRANCIS JAYE, Gent
who was here buried Nov 25, 1713,
in the 23d Year of his Age

Also of
THOMAS, another Son of the said
FRANCIS, who was buried in
Dec following, in the 7th Year of his Age

Also of
CHARLES JAYE, Gent the only surviving
Son of the said FRANCIS JAYE, who was Steward
to JAMES Earl of BERKELEY, and died in
London, and was buried in the Chapel
of the Broadway, Westminster, Nov 6, 1725,
in the 25th Year of his Age

CHARLES JAYE,
Gent

Arms as before.

To the Memory of
CHARLES JAYE, some time of Darking,
in the County of Surrey, but afterwards
of the Parish of Berkeley, a Gentleman
descended from an ancient Family in
the County of Southampton, who was
here buried July 6, 1657

Also of
FRANCIS JAYE, Gent only Son of the
said CHARLES JAYE, who was here buried
Nov 2, 1685, in the 52d Year of his Age

Also of MARTHA his Wife, who was
here buried Jan 9, 1713, aged 75

Also of ELIZABETH their Daughter,
who died in March 1727

CHARLES BEVAN, of this Town,
was buried July 24, 1734,
aged 56 Years

JOHN HOOPER, of Clapton,
died Sept 20, 1685.

THOMAS HOOPER, of Berkeley,
Yeoman, died July 18, 1724,
in the 79th Year of his Age.

Here resteth the Body of THOMAS
HICKES, of Pedington, Clothier, who
departed this Life February 15,
anno Dom 1674 aged 60 Years
his Wife, was buried
August 20 1693
Both waiting a joyful Resurrection

Here lieth the Body of ANNA, the
Wife of WILLIAM PEARCE,
senior, who departed this Life the 1st Day
of February, anno Domini 1703

Here lieth the Body of WILLIAM PEARCE,
of Woodford, who departed this Life
the 25th of August, anno Domini 1720,
ætatis suæ 78

THOMAS HICKES,
Feb 9, 1746

ELIZABETH HICKES, 1772

Here resteth the Body of ROBERT FIELD,
of New Parke, Yeoman, who was buried
Nov 25, 1717, ætatis suæ 70

In Memory of his Son
ROBERT FIELD, of Ham, buried
Feb 1718, aged about 30

SARAH, Relict of ROBERT FIELD,
of Ham, buried March 17, 1775,
aged 6

In Memory of
HENRY HICKES, Son of THOMAS HICKES,
of Pedington who died Dec 7,
1773, in the 11th Year of his Age

Also of HARRIOT his Daughter
who died May 1, 1778, aged 13

O N

ON FLAT STONES AT THE WEST END,
UNDER THE GALLERY

Here lieth the Body of
WALTER BEAVAN, of the Parish
of Berkeley, who was buried
Feb 24, 1711, aged 43.

Alfo JANE, the Wife of WALTER
BEAVAN, who was buried
March 13, 1728, aged 62

Here lyeth the Body of
JOHN SUMMERS, of Berkeley, Alderman,
who was buried April
26, 1709, aged 75

Here lieth the Body of
TIMOTHY BEAVEN, of
Berkeley, Alderman,
who deceafed July 29,
1676, ætat 35

Here lieth the Body of
WILLIAM BEAVAN, of Berkeley,
Alderman, who was buried
Feb 3, 1708, aged 34.

Here lieth the Body of MARY,
the Wife of LAWRENCE NOIT,
of Gloucefter She died the 29th
Day of April, 1707

Here refteth the Body of
JOANL, the Wife of RICHARD
ARCHARD, of Greenftreet, who
deceafed Oct 23, anno 1681

Here refteth the Body of
RICHARD ARCHARD, of Greenftreet,
who deceafed Nov 5, 1665

Alfo of five of his Sons and one
Daughter, viz RICHARD, THOMAS,
WILLIAM, JOHN, WILLIAM, and KATHERINE.

Alfo the Body of AGNES, the
Daughter of RICHARD ARCHARD,
of Greenftreet, who died Nov 20, 1710

Alfo ELIZABETH ARCHARD, of Ham,
Widow, who was buried Oct 4, 1690,
ætatis fua 67

In Memory of JOSEPH MINETT,
of Baynham, in this Parifh, Yeoman,
who died Feb 22, 1712, aged 69

MARGARET his Wife
died Oct 30, 1768, aged 69.

Here lieth the Body of
ELIZABETH the Daughter of
JOHN TIPPETTS, of Kitt s Green,
Clothier, who was buried the
4th of Jan 1709

Alfo of ROBERT his Son,
who died Jan 4 1723,
both in their Infancy

Here lieth the Body of
ANN, the Wife of RICHARD ARCHARD,
of Greenftreet, who died
Feb 3, 1688, with
ANN and ELIZABETH their Children

Alfo the Body of RICHARD
ARCHARD, the Son of RICHARD
ARCHARD, of Greenftreet, who
was buried Nov 9, 1715, ætat 29.

In Memory of JOHN HEATHFIELD,
of Bevington, in this Parifh,
who died April 23, 1770,
aged 75 Years

Here lieth the Body of RICHARD ARCHARD,
of Greenftreet, Yeoman,
who was buried Feb 21, A D 1712,
aged 54.

Alfo here lyeth the Body of
SARAH his Wife, who was
buried the 7th Day of Sept 1737,
in the 69th Year of her Age

Here lieth the Body of THOMAS CAM,
of Newport, Gent who
died the 30th of October, 1673,
aged 43 Years

Alfo here lyeth the Body of
THOMAS GWYNN Gent Grandfon
to the faid THOMAS CAM, of Newport,
Gent who died April 20, 1720, aged 33

Alfo the Body of Mrs MARY GWYNN,
the Wife of RICHARD GWYNN, of
Swanfey, in Wales, Gent and
Daughter to the abovefaid THOMAS CAM,
of Newport, Gent who died
the 7th of Sept 1720, aged 53

Here lieth the Body of JAMES
CLUTTERBUCKE, of Hinton, who was buried
the 16th of June, 167.

WILLIAM and THOMAS his Brothers
were buried the laft of March, 1675

EDITH, the Daughter of THOMAS
CLUTTERBUCKE, of Hinton, was buried
the 29th of Dec 1728, aged 17

ESTHER his Daughter
was buried Jan 30, 1732, aged 19

EDITH CLUTTERBUCK, of Hinton,
Widow, died March 29, 173

FORTUNE CLUTTERBUCKE, of Hinton,
Widow, was buried Aug 2, 1684

JOHN, Son of THOMAS CLUTTERBUCKE,
of Hinton, died in 1697 an Infant

THOMAS CLUTTERBUCKE of Hinton, Yeoman,
died March 22, 1713 aged 47

JOHN BLISS, of the Boxtree,
departed this Life Nov 8, 1696,
ætatis suæ 67

SAMUEL BLISS, of the Boxtree, Tanner,
Son of JOHN BLISS, died the
8th of April, 1707, æt 40.

ELIZABETH, the Wife of
JOHN BLISS, died the
December, 16
ætatis suæ 57

IN THE CHURCH YARD, ON TOMBS

THOMAS SMYTH,
of Stinger, was buried
Nov 7, 1720, æ at's suæ 45

SARAH his Wife
died Dec 10, 1757, aged 76.

JOHN SMYTH, of Clapton
died Dec 11, 1686, aged 35.

MARY his Wife
died July 18 1707, aged 58.

MARY SMITH of Heathfield
in this Parish, Spinster
died May 16, 1745, aged 7

MARY the Wife of
THOMAS JENKINS, of Heathfield,
died July 19 1702 aged 38

JOHN SMITH,
of the City of Bristol, Joiner
died Jan 31, 1763, aged 4

JOHN his Son,
died Jan 22, 1754, aged 5 Months

JONATHAN PINNETT,
of Hinton in this Parish, Yeoman,
buried Jan 7, 1708

ANNE his Wife
buried Dec 27, 1687

JOHN their Son
buried Ap 9 1736

WILLIAM WARE
of Wolghalton in this Parish
died July 5, 1776, aged 73

SARAH, the Wife of JOHN WARE,
died March 1, 1756, aged 6

ANNE the Wife of WILLIAM WARE,
died Nov 4, aged 61

JOHN, the Son of WILLIAM WARE
and ANN WARE
died June, aged a Year and
8 Months

Ann Pelchey on Ye head and
here Chthers Heads crthd,

JOHN STUMP, of Betocky Yeoman,
died Aug 2 1742, aged 3

MARY Root of the above JOHN STUMP
died Sept 13 1758, aged 60

JOHN, their Son died Ap 30, 170,
in his Infancy

JOHN STUMP, their
died April 9 1772, aged 4

THOMAS TAYLOR
of Prior's Wood, in this Parish,
died Sept 6 1762, aged 42

RICHARD PICK, of Hinton in this Parish
Tanner, died Dec 23, 1720, aged 49

JOHN his Son,
died May 23 1738, aged 24

SARAH his Daughter
died Aug 13, 1774 aged 15

ARTHUR HOOPER
died 1722, aged 69

JANE, the Wife of ARTHUR
HOOPER, of Clapton, senior,
buried Jan 15, 1724, aged 57

KATHERINE HOOPER
the Widow of ANTHONY HOOPER,
of Clapton jun or was buried
July 7, 1663

ARTHUR HOOPER
buried March 7, 1675

WILLIAM KING,
Alderman of this Town,
was buried May 18, 1763,
aged 69

SARAH his Wife
died Jan 27, 1767, aged 76

WILLIAM, their Son,
was buried June 2 1724 aged 9 Months

JOHN KING of Clapton,
in this Parish, Yeoman,
died Jan 4, 1748, aged 75

MARY his Wife
died June 29, 1766, aged 67

JOHN KING,
died April 7 1766, aged 6

ELIZABETH his Daughter
Wife of JOHN WARNER of Cambridge,
died Dec 7, 1732 aged 39

In Memory of three Children
of WILLIAM KING of this Town

WILLIAM was buried Feb 1, 17
aged 1 Year 7 Month

ELIZABETH was buried April 19, 17
aged 1 Year 6 Weeks

WILLIAM was buried Feb 176
aged 5

THOMAS HOOPER of Clapton Yeoman,
was buried Jan 10, 1705, aged 47

ELIZABETH his Wife,
Daughter of JOHN MORE of Stone
was buried Oct 30, 1694 aged 36

MARY, the Daughter of
THOMAS HOOPER was buried
March 31, 1695

WILLIAM HOOPER, of Clapton, senior,
was buried Nov 30, 1754, aged 5

ELIZABETH his Wife
died July 1, 1726 aged 63

WILLIAM HOOPER of Clapton,
in this Parish, died April 7, 1754,
aged 38

MARGARET his Wife
died Oct 16 1716 aged 65

MARY HICKES, Daughter of
NICHOLAS HICKES, of Pedington,
Yeoman, died Oct 18, 1718 aged 5

NICHOLAS HICKES
of Pedington Yeoman,
was buried Oct 18, 1715, aged 65

MARY his Wife
died Oct 1, 1713 aged

SARAH NEAL, Relict of
JOHN NEAL, of Iron in this Parish
and Daughter of Niece of Hickes
of Pedington died Ap 2 1714,
aged 64

HANNAH Relict of WILLIAM NEAL
of Kingshill, in the Parish
of North Nibley
and Daughter of Neal's Heir,
of Pedington in this Parish
died Dec 4 1741 aged 6

JANE and ELIZABETH, common
Daughters of JOHN and NICHOLAS NEAL,
died in her Infancy

JOHN PICK of Ham, Tanner,
died April 1, 1717, aged 4

ELIZABETH his Daughter,
buried April 2, 1761

MARY PICK Widow of
JOHN PICK of this Tanner,
died Jan 6, 1755 aged 85

RICHARD PICK of Ham Tanner
died April 14, 1720, aged 6

SARAH his Wife
died Jan 14, 1711 aged 51

their Son
died July 28 1788 aged

MARY Wife of JOHN PICK
of Alkington in this Parish
died Dec 14, aged

JOHN, their Son died in Infancy
a few Months

JOHN their Son aged Sixteen
Years died Feb 15
aged Weeks

JOHN Ham and Frances Reed his
Son, died Ap 2 aged 15

HESTER the Daughter of
RALPH PEARCE, died Sept. 7, 1721,
aged 9 Years

WILLIAM his Son, died Oct. 8, 1732,
aged 18

RALPH PEARCE of Alkington, in
this Parish, Yeoman died
Sept. 17, 1742, aged 65

HESTER, Relict of the above RALPH
PEARCE, died Dec. 8, 1753, aged 72

JOANNA the Wife of
JAMES MANNING, Tanner,
Daughter of WILLIAM RAYMOND, in
this County, Esq died
Dec. 26, 1761, aged 50

JAMES MANNING, of this Parish,
died Sept. 24, 1763, aged 51

ELIZABETH, the Daughter of
WILLIAM KEMBLE, of Cirencester
Gent. and Wife of THOMAS MANNING,
of this Parish, Tanner,
died June 18, 1767, aged 56

MARY MANNING
was born July 21, 1708 aged 65

THOMAS MANNING
of Berkeley Sadler
was buried Dec. 25, 1732, aged 28

JOANNA the Daughter of
JAMES MANNING, of Israel's, Tanner,
was buried June 8, 1745, aged 3 Month

JOHN BAYLEY, of Ham Senior,
died July 23, 1681

ELIZABETH his Wife
buried June 4, 1682

ANN his Daughter,
buried in 1679

MARY was buried Dec. 29, 1692

ELIZABETH was buried July 13, 1683

EDWARD BAYLEY, of Ham,
died April 19, 1671

SARAH his Wife
died Jun 14, 1699

JOHN BAYLEY, of Ham, Yeoman,
died Sept. 17, 1715, aged 41

ELIZABETH his Widow
died March 19, 1766, aged 89

Mr JOHN HITTER
died March 17, 1740, aged about 30

Mr GEORGE JEAN,
of this Town, Officer of Excise
died June 13, 1738, aged about 5

In Memory of their sons and Daughters
of SAMUEL CHERRINGTON, of this
Parish, died as followeth

Sarah died Oct. 1, 1719, aged 1 Year

... died Jun 1, 1740, aged 3 Weeks

Samuel died Feb. 1, 1741, aged 3 Weeks

Charles died Mar. 11, 1742,
aged 9 Week

John died June, 1749,
aged 8 Years

SAMUEL CHERRINGTON
died Feb. 4, 1766, aged 55

SARAH his Wife
died Oct. 1, 1768, aged 63

WILLIAM TILEY, of Bevington,
in this Parish,
died July 17, 1731, aged 82

Four of his Children as follows

SARAH, Feb. 25, 1754 aged 9

ANN, May 1765, aged 15

WILLIAM and THOMAS died Infants

ROBERT COLE, of Oakley,
in this Parish, Yeoman
died April 6, 1781, aged 66

JOSEPH TYLER, of Berkeley, Mercer,
died Feb. 7, 1695

HESTER his Wife
died Nov. 26 1699

JOHN SMITH, of Ham Tanner,
died Nov. 21, 1690, aged 56

ANN his Wife
died Nov. 23, 1687

Under and near his Tomb, are buried
their sons and Daughters of JOHN
TYLER, of Berkeley, Mercer

JOHN Dec. 21, 1678, aged 1 Year

HESTER, July 9, 1677, aged 13 Days

RICHARD, July 23, 1683 aged 1 Year

THOMAS Oct. 19, 1685 aged 1 Year

THOMAS Oct. 6, 1689 aged 1 Year

MARGARET, Aug. 29, 1703,
aged 2 Years

THOMAS NELME, of Ham,
buried Dec. 3, 1722 aged 59

THOMAS NELME, junior,
died June 28, 1698

MARGARET Daughter of JOHN NELME,
of Ham, buried March 6, 1693

WILLIAM, Son of JOHN NELME,
of Ham, buried Oct. 11, 1693

THOMAS Son of THOMAS NELME,
junior, buried Dec. 2 1698

JOHN NELME of Woodford Yeoman,
Son of JOHN NELME, of Ham,
buried Aug. 20, 1697

JOHN NELME of Hill, Yeoman,
buried Sept. 1, 1685

ELIZABETH the Daughter of
THOMAS NELME, of Ham,
buried March 19, 1687

ELIZABETH NELME, of Ham Widow,
buried Jan 11, 1721, aged 61

THOMAS NELME, of Ham Yeoman,
buried July 11, 1693, aged 32

THOMAS NELME
died Feb. 1, 1715

SARAH the Wife of ARTHUR DARCEY,
of Middleton, the Daughter of Hinton,
died Dec. 21, 1761 aged 80

DANIEL PICE of Stone, in
this Parish, died Jan. 17, 1718, aged 58

SARAH his second Wife
died July 1, 1763 aged 66

ELIZABETH, Wife of Benj. COTTON,
died April 2, 1768 aged 68

BENJAMIN COTTON,
died April 9, 1769, aged 61

Mr WILLIAM HAWKES, of Berkeley
V D M died Dec. 16, 1726, aged 58

ANN, the Wife of WILLIAM HAWKES,
V D M died Oct. 5, 1721, aged 62

JOHN, Son of Mr WILLIAM HAWKES,
V D M died an Infant, June 19, 1727

JOHN CROOME, of Breadstone, Yeoman,
died May 5, 1753, aged 68

JANE CROOME, Relict of JOHN CROOME
died June, 1739 aged 70

MARY the Wife of JAMES CROOME
of Breadstone, Yeoman,
died March 9, 1679

Also three Sons and one Daughter of
JOHN CROOME, of Breadstone, Yeoman

MARY died Feb. 2, 1678,
aged 1 Month

RICHARD died Sept. 19, 1718,
aged 3 Years and 6 Months

JAMES } of Bristol, { Jul 11, 1701
THOMAS } { Jun 1, 1741

RICHARD CROOME of Breadstone
Yeoman, died Sept. 28, 1742

SARAH his Wife
died July 1, 1760 aged 43

MARY, the Wife of FRANCIS PECK,
of Newnham Tanner
died Feb. 6, 1766, aged 39

JOHN MARTIN of Blakeney Ham,
in this Parish, died Dec. 6, 1720,
aged 58

MARY his Wife, Daughter of
DANIEL HOPTON of Bevington
in this Parish, died May 10, 1737,
aged 42

HANNAH Wife of
WILLIAM NEALE, of this Town,
died April 1, 1723, aged 42

MARY WATTS of Mobly, in the
Parish of Hinton, in this Parish,
died Sep. 14, 1783, aged 63

PETER SUMMER, of this Parish,
buried July 13, 1707, aged 42

JANE his Wife
buried May 31, 1711, aged 7

PETER, their Son
was buried Nov. 1, 1715, aged 2

ROSE, their Wife
was buried at Greenwich, in the
County of Kent, Aug 13, 1711

JEREMIAH,
buried at Greenwich May 5, 1710

HANNAH, Wife of the above said
RICHARD VIZER
died Feb. 15, 1711, aged 87

RICHARD, Son of RICHARD VIZER
died Sept. 20, 1711 aged 61

DANIEL another of their sons
died Aug. 10, 1712 aged 18

John, Son of RICHARD and MARY
Esthope, Mariner, of Bridgenorth,
in the County of Salop, died
June 10, 1767 aged 38

RICHARD Son of WILLIAM and ANN
Esthope. Nephew to the above said
JOHN ESTHOPE died June 10, 1767,
aged 5

They were both drowned near
Purton Passage

NATHANIEL WILLIS, of this Town,
died Nov 15, 1730, aged 9

Other Inscriptions on this Tomb obliterated

GILES HYETT, of Sanger,
was buried Jan 1, 1719 aged 71

ANN the Wife of GILES HYETT,
of Sanger junior, buried
Jan 15, 1719, aged 71

THOMAS BEVAN, of Berkeley, Alderman
buried 1, 1663

WALTER his Son, buried June 9, 1684

ALCE the Wife of THOMAS BEVAN,
was buried April 9, 1684

ARTHUR BEVAN, of Berkeley, Alderman
buried May 6, 1721, aged 5

ELIZABETH Wife of ARTHUR BEVAN,
buried Dec 2, 1721

THOMAS LARGE,
Five Times Mayor of this Town,
died Feb 5, 1663, aged 7

THOMAS WITTS, of Newport,
in this Parish, died June 16, 1771
aged 6

MARY his Wife
died Aug 28, 1758, aged 50

ANTHONY WILTSHIRE, of Newport,
buried June 13, 1653

Also SARAH his Wife,
buried June 13, 1733, aged 71

SARAH Wife of GEORGE ROBERTS,
of Ross, died July 17, 1747, aged 29

BETTY, Daughter of THOMAS
WITTS ..., of Newport,
died Dec 4, 1749
aged 3 Years and 3 Months

SARAH LUTTY, Widow
was buried Feb 1, 1710 aged 77

JOHN ANDREWS
was buried April 1, 1726, aged 37

JOHN WATTS, of this Town, Alderman,
died Nov 3, 1718 aged 52

MARY in his Wife
died March 7, 1718

ANNA the Wife of
... of this Town
died March 5, 1683 aged 8

ANNE, the Wife of
THOMAS ... of the Town
died Jan 21, ... aged 31

ELIZABETH his Daughter,
died June 9, 73, aged 14

SARAH LUTTY
died May 11, 1730 aged 30

MAURICE, the Son of
MAURICE SMITH, of this Town, Mercer
died Jan 30, 1762, aged 23

DANIEL SMITH Esq
Daughter of MAURICE and
ELIZABETH SMITH, of this Town,
died April 19, 1780, aged 4

MAURICE SMITH, of this Town
Mercer, died Jan 13, 1746 aged 63

ELIZABETH his Wife,
died Jan 27, 1775 aged 70

THOMAS SMITH of Berkeley, Mercer,
died May 7, 1685 aged 29

MARY his Wife,
died April 10, 1734, aged 76

WILLIAM SANTER,
of Froggitt, Yeoman,
died Jan 17, 1704

RICHARD SMITH
of Froggitt, senior
buried May 9, 1683

EDITH, the Wife of
JOHN SMITH, of Froggitt,
buried May 17, 1699, aged 27

PETER CLUTTERBUCK,
of Bucketts Hill, in this Parish, Yeoman
died Jan 27, 1777 aged 66

RICHARD TRAYMAN,
of Berkeley, buried Feb 3, 167

ANN his Wife
buried April 2, 1685

JOHN their Son
buried March 11, 1670

DANIEL PICK, of Kings Hill, in
the Tything of Hinton, in this Parish,
Yeoman, died March 14, 1732
aged

MARY, Relict of the aforesaid DANIEL
PICK, died Jan 16, 1782 aged 60

DANIEL their Son
died June 26, 1751, aged 4

SARAH, Wife of THOMAS RICKETTS,
of Breadstone, in this Parish,
died April 7, 1771 aged 30

ELIZABETH CARR of Ledington in
this Parish, Widow of CHRIS CARR
of the Hill, in the Parish of Meir at
Valence, died May 1, 1693 aged 53

ELIZABETH her Daughter,
died May 4, 1667

RICHARD their Son,
was buried July 26, 1700 aged 17

CHRIS CARR of Ledington,
in this Parish, Clothier,
Dec 22, 1737 aged 73

BETTY the Wife of JOHN THOMAS,
of the Parish of Kimbridge,
died March 18, 1716 aged 33

SARAH their Daughter
died Dec 26, 16
aged Years and 7 Months

MARY Daughter of JOHN and
... THOMAS of the Parish
of Wotton ... died Jan 1, ...
aged 4 Months

ELIZABETH, wife of JAMES PHILLIPS,
of Breadstone in this Parish, Yeoman
died Aug ..., 1750 aged 60

JAMES PHILLIPS, the aforesaid
died Jan 15, 1733, aged 72

JAMES, their Son
died Aug 9, 1715, aged 10

THOMAS PHILLIPS of Breadstone,
Yeoman, died June 20, 1755, aged 72

HESTER his Wife
died Feb 7, 1756, aged 60

Also six Children of THOMAS PHILLIPS,
of Breadstone in this Parish

	Died	Aged
THOMAS,	Feb 5, 1730,	Years
JAMES,	Dec 25, 1736,	7 Weeks
HENRY,	April 7, 1733,	3 Years
THOMAS,	Feb 2, 1735,	15 Years
HESTER,	Nov 30, 1736,	
And PETER,	Nov 14, 1746,	15 Years

JAMES PHILLIPS of Haresfield
late of Breadstone in this Parish,
Yeoman, died Sept 12, 1779 aged 52

HESTER his Wife, Daughter of
JOHN and MARY LOWELL, of Arlingham,
died Sep 11, 1762, aged 34

MARY Daughter of JAMES and
ELIZABETH PHILLIPS died Aug 13, 1765,
aged 4 Years

JOHN JONES, of Whitewall Court,
junior, in this Parish, Yeoman
died April 4, 1771, aged 65

ELIZABETH his second Wife,
died April 27, 1737, aged 36

Arms Argent a Fess Nebulee between three ... stopped ...

MARY, second Daughter of
WILLIAM ... Esq
died Feb 1, 1669, aged 1

GEORGE JONES, Esq
died July 1, ... aged 3

JAMES BARTY, of Clapton, Yeoman,
died Oct 10, 1651, aged 46

ELIZABETH his Wife
died Sept 13, 1655

ELIZABETH the Wife of JOHN PHILLIPS,
of Kingwood Daughter of WILLIAM
OLLIFFE of Woodford in this Parish,
died March 21, 1751, aged 47

WILLIAM OLLIFFE of Woodford,
in this Parish, died April 12, 1761,
aged 66

MARY his Wife
died May 9, 1776, aged 74

WILLIAM PEARCE of Lower Wick,
in this Parish, Yeoman,
died Aug. 29, 1738, aged 36

ELIZABETH his Wife,
died May 20, 1744, aged 40

ELIZABETH, their Daughter,
died Nov. 22, 1737, aged 9 Weeks

ELIZABETH, another Daughter,
buried at Tortworth

MARY Daughter of
JOHN MEESE PEARCE of Lower Wick,
by ELIZABETH his Wife died Dec. 5,
1761, aged 3 Years and 10 Months

THOMAS PEARCE of Lower Wick,
in this Parish, Yeoman
died April 29, 1728, aged 58

THOMAS his Son,
died May 13, 1714, aged 7 Weeks

ELIZABETH, Relict of the
said THOMAS PEARCE
died Jan. 2, 1736-7, aged 56

In Memory of two Daughters
of RICHARD and MARY ANDREWS,
of Alkington in this Parish,
who died viz.

ANNE May , 1741, aged 8

SARAH, May 1771, aged 3

JOHN PAYNE of this Town, Mercer,
died March 18, 1743, aged 54

ESTHER, the Daughter of
EDWARD SANIGER of SANIGER, Gent.
was buried Aug. 16, 1692

EDWARD SANIGER, of Saniger Gent.
was buried Dec. 3, 1739, aged 48

SUSANNA Relict of EDW. SANIGER,
Gent. died May 14, 1744 aged 56

JANE Daughter of EDWARD SANIGER,
of Saniger, Gent. died June 15, 1735,
aged 24

EDWARD SANIGER, of Saniger senior,
Gent. died July 16, 1689

ESTHER Wife of EDWARD SANIGER,
of Saniger, Gent.
died June 13, 1693

WILLIAM HUNTLEY of Wanswell, in
this Parish, Gent. was buried
Jan. 1718

Joseph Wife was buried Nov. 21737

EDWARD their son was buried
F1 1699

THOMAS HUNTLEY, of Newport
in this Parish, died Feb. 14, 1722,
aged 63

Anne his Wife
died May 18, 1718

Thomas their son,
died Nov. 1723, aged 60

STEPHEN BEARLEY of Newport
in this Parish, died March 7, 1772,

ELIZABETH, the Wife of JOHN PEARCE,
of Kitt's Green, in this Parish, Gent.
died Sept. 21, 1777, aged 72

MARY, their Daughter,
died Nov. 8, 1761, aged 15

WILLIAM CORNOCK of Goldwick
Yeoman, died March 3, 1696, aged 40

HESTER his Wife
died Aug. 1, 1728 aged 70

ELIZABETH CURNOCK, of this Town,
Spinster, died June 2, 1762 aged 19

JOAN CURNOCK her Sister, late of
this Town, Spinster died May 13, 1765,
aged 1

NICHOLAS CORNOCK, of Goldwick,
died Oct. 26 1653

ELIZABETH his Wife
died Oct. 6 1676

WILLIAM CORNOCK, of Goldwick
Yeoman, died April 5, 1708 aged 55

MARY CORNOCK Widow of WILLIAM
CORNOCK, of Goldwick,
died Jan. 25, 1761, aged 68

NICHOLAS CORNOCK of Woodford,
died June 4, 1700

ANNE Daughter of WILLIAM CORNOCK,
of Wick, senior died Nov. 20, 1691

SUSANNA, the Wife of
WILLIAM CORNOCK of Oldbury upon
Severn, in the Parish of Thornbury,
died June 23, 1761, aged 64

NICHOLAS CORNOCK, of Blanchworth,
in this Parish died Nov. 30, 1755,
aged 57

MARY his Wife
died April 6, 1760, aged 73

JOHN CORNOCK, of Bristol Wine Cooper,
died June 23, 1719 aged

NICHOLAS Son of NICHOLAS and
MARY CORNOCK of Blanchworth,
in this Parish died Nov. 30, 1759

WILLIAM, their Son,
died July 4, 1749
aged 6 Years and 21 Weeks

HESTER STINCHCOMBE, Daughter
of NICHOLAS and MARY CORNOCK,
died March 10, 1702 aged 2

RICHARD CORNOCK their Son,
died March 16, 1755, aged

NICHOLAS CORNOCK of Breadstone
in this Parish Yeoman,
died Nov. 4, 1683, aged 44

MARY CORNOCK of Codrick in
this Town, aged Oct. 22, 1765, aged 50

NICHOLAS CORNOCK of Codrick
died Nov. 30, 1733 aged 6

WILLIAM CORNOCK of Oldbury upon
Severn, died Nov. 9, 1777, aged 66

NICHOLAS CORNOCK his son
died June 3, 1770 aged 4

JOHN MAYO, of Crawles, Yeoman
died Nov. 19, 1718, aged 63

ANNE, the Daughter of JOHN MAYO
of Crawles senior,
was buried June 24, 1710 aged

ALICE the Wife of JOHN MAYO,
of Crawles senior who died
June 19, 1720, aged 58

JOHN MAYO of Breadstone
in this Parish died Aug. 1, 1733
aged 51

ELIZABETH Relict of JOHN MAYO,
died July 21, 1766 aged 84

MARGARET Wife of WILLIAM
HOPKINS of this Parish, died
Oct. 16, 1770 aged 40
ROBERT their Son,
died Feb. 13, 1776 aged 6

BETTY, their Daughter
died Feb. 14, 1770 aged

EDWARD LUCAS of this Town, Gent.
died Dec. 28, 1714, aged

MARY his Wife
died June 13, 1714 aged 16

EDWARD LUCAS, their son
died June 14, 1749 aged 40

MARY Daughter of EDWARD LUCAS,
of this Town died May 18, 1743,
aged

MARTHA Relict of the Rev.
Mr. WILLIAM LUCAS A.M.
late Rector of Cormington in the
County of Essex and Vicar of
Hill in this County died
May 1, 1749, aged 7

JAMES and JOHN LUCAS died Infants

WILLIAM BAYLY, of this Town
was drowned July 30, 1712, aged 32

SARAH his Wife late Wife of
JOHN MILLARD died Oct. 16, 1765
aged 96

JOHN WILLIS
died Dec. 9, 1759

JOHN, the son of WILLIAM BAYLY,
of Lower Wick was buried
Jan. 1756

CHARLES LIFFILL
died June 1717
MARY his Daughter
died March 1, 1761

ON HEAD STONES

	Died	Aged
John Rich.d, of Bu.e s in the ..	5 Dec 17.8	70
Mary his Wife	12 Feb 17..	0
.......s W.. of Pi.e .re in	7 Apr 17..	8.
..rh.t...	4 Ma. 15	58
Ja.. Son of William Hoo.er, of	1. De 17.	1
Thom. G..rd of O. s Town	N.. 8	.5
Da..l G..ner	1 Jun 1759	..
Lau.. le Wi.e of Thos. G..rd of this Tow. Md.n.	4 Feb 175.	.7
John Fr..man of Ham	9 Aug 1.6	14
Ar.. Hooper of Capt.. .. s	.. Mar 1.2	05
Joan Hoop. of Clapt..	Ma. ,5	.
M..aret h. Wife	 694	—
..ho.. Latter of Clap.. Yeoma.	3. Febru..	77
Hetter his Wife	17 Feb 1.55	..
Jose.h Pearce	10 Dec 16..	..
Thomas Hooper, of Clap..	17 Feb 17.4	43
S..h his Wife	1 Feb 1771	77
...abeth War.. .n	8 May 1.4.	55
Elizabeth .e. Widow	6 Ma, 17..	.
J..kn.. of B..ington	15 Ma. 17..	.
Ar..Kit.. of Clapton	.. Oct 1772	81
I.bell h. Wife	6 Sept 177.	69
William their Son	4 July, 176.	30
Arthur Kit.. Son of .. h.r K.. of Clap..	1. Oct 1780	39
..ary, W..e of R.ch..rt ..ck of Ha. ..t	1. Jun 1.4.	51
Thom. Clu.. of Ham t.. ..dh, Yeom..	. Sept 1766	53
Mar..ret their Dau.h..	5 Dec 1754	49
William Hoo.. of Ham	2 Apr 1706	4.
Mary his Wid.. l.te Wife of ..	7 Dec 1759	62
Ann. W..e of John Mart. Daughter of William Ho.. h..	11 Jan 1777	4.
W..m Son of this Town	15 Feb 176.	5
Ann. ..	21 Jan 1768	64
William Frazey	16 Feb 1749	40
Mary his Wife	7 June 174.	4.
Joseph Vi..go	1 Feb 174.	.
Joh. s Son	16 May 7.1	.
W.m.. his Son	.. Dec 1763	4
...as Den.ing of his Town, .leman	10 Aug 17.2	86
Jan. the Wife of Thomas R.y.ond, of Berkeley, Mercer	2 May 1718	73
Jane th. Wife of John Rogers Mercer	1 Sep 1736	44
Charles Ponton, of Ham, .. of	2 July 1.0.	.
Thomas Ponton, of Ham	24 Jan 1739	—
Jane, late Widow of .. h Wal.. of Ham	25 Apr 1747	—
William Porting, of Ham	2 Sep 1744	10
Sarah his Wife	14 May 7.7	35
S..a Varnham, of his Town, Widow	8 Nov 17.4	65
James Son of John and Elizabeth Dyer	8 Mar 1773	.
Daniel Edward, of Coom in the Parish of Wotton under edge	7 Apr 17.6	58
John Edwards of this ..	17 Apr 17..	5.
Jane Hu.. of this Town Widow	3 Feb 1779	3.
Edward Phillip of Ham	1 Jun 1753	47
Jane Phillips of Ham	1 Sept 174.	.
John Aul..y, of this Town, Aldeman	9 Aug 1764	55
Rachel Carver	5 June 174.	55
Joseph Cole, Son of James Cole of Tadington	2 Aug 17.0	34
.. s Cole of .. t.. in this Pa..	Feb 17.2	6.
..er.. Wife	16 Dec 1735	—
Chan.. his Son	4 Au. 17.7	74
Joseph Cole o. Ham	14 N.. 17.1	8.
J..e his Wife	19 June 1751	69
J..k he.. Ham ..	4 May 1.6.	70

	Died	Aged
Litely Clark, of this Town, Sadler	3 July 18..	2.
John Bishop, of this Town	18 May 1772	55
Judith his Wife	4 Jun 17.8	55
Paul their Son	23 Jun 1768	0
Hester their Daughter	1 June 1770	14
Paul Bishop, of Sanger	5 Nov 17..	43
Martha his Wife	4 Dec 17..	38
John Hofer, of this Town, Stone Cutter	7 Nov 1.	42
Hannah, Daughter of Edward Hofier, by Mary his Wife	5 Dec 1747	32
Edward his Son by Margery his Wife	11 Jun 1759	6
Rachel Daughter of John Merman of Hinton	12 Dec 1757	3
John Merman, of Hinton	11 June 1729	—
William Browning of Halmore	9 Sept 175.	.
Elmer, Wife of George Dix	17 Apr 1761	53
George Dix	15 May 1761	63
William White, of this Town	7 Aug 1761	44
John Gooding	23 July 1762	26
Chillion, Daughter of the abovesaid William White	4 Mar 177.	10
Richard White, late Groom to the Right Hon Earl of Berkeley	10 Sept 777	5.
John the Son of William Millard, of Halmore	6 June 1766	28
Bett, Wife of Samuel Pegler, of Wicks Elm	15 May 1772	38
Daniel Hile, of Breadstone	1 Jun 1762	50
Edward Browning, of Bevington	10 Oct 1758	39
Mary his Wife, late Wife of John Davis	24 Mar 1751	55
Catharine, Wife of Thomas Sanger, of this Town, and Daughter of Edward Cotton, of Ash under hill in this County	9 Sept 1778	32
James Cotton Son of Edward Cotton of Ashton under hill in this County	1. Apr 1768	16
George Neale of this Town	16 June 1757	40
Betty his Wife, late Wife of James Hurt	1 Jun 1762	44
Anthony Smith, of this Town, Alderman	19 Mar 1748	80
..ny his Wife	5 Jun 732	60
Thomas his Son	1 Apr 1769	—
Margaret a Daughter	Jun 1.07	55
Thomas Denn, of his Tow. Butcher	6 Dec 1.06	44
Joan .. of Thomas and Ruth Denning	19 Dec 17..	8
Hester, Wife of Thomas Hurt Daughter of Thomas and .. Denn		
	13 Feb 17.	64
Samuel Lassecate	5 Oct 17.1	6
Sarah his Wife		
Esther Wife of Thomas Rouse of the Tow.	17 Jun 17.	5.
Mary Wife of Thomas Pollard	2 Oct 17..	..
John .. his ..	11 June 1761	6.
..pick.. l.te	11 Feb 17.6	1.
.. h his Wife	4 Oct 17..	5.
.. th his Wife	6 Oct 174.	50
Hester N.c.ms of Wo..d in the Parish of Hill	15 July 1779	66
Hannah his Wife	3 Aug 1782	4.
Mary Wife of Nicholas Cole of Scotland in the Parish of Hill, Yeoman	1. Apr 1768	1.
Nicholas Cole	13 Oct 17.	1.
Joseph Son of J.. Cole of Ham	Ma. 17.	.
John Son of John Cole and Han.. h his Wife	. May 17.	.
John Mary his .. na.	. Ma. 1.	5
William Bully of Ham ..	11 Nov 1.	.
Mr. Jane Hill of ..		
Samuel his Wife	.	.

ON HEAD STONES

	Died	Aged		Died	Aged
Charles Hurt late Huntsman to the Earl of Berkeley	7 June, 1784	36	Ann his Wife, Daughter of Edward and Ann Gaftrell of this Town	27 July, 1777	55
Ann Daughter of Joseph and Sarah Knight of this Town	26 Nov 1770	24	John Watts, of Wanfwell in this Parish	25 Mar 1775	84
Joseph Knight, of this Town	22 Feb 1781	62	Mary his Wife	27 June, 1781	
Sarah his Wife	2 Jan 1785	84	George Watts of Mobly in this Parish, Junior	7 Sept 1750	41
with their Daughter	26 Sept 1785	—	Elizabeth his Wife	8 Ap 1750	40
John Litch of Swancey in this Parish	3 Apr 1748	55	George Watts of Alkington, fenior	7 Oct 1721	45
Daniel Litch of his Town	9 Nov 1746	59	Elizabeth his Wife	11 Feb 1750	72
Sarah his Wife	7 Apr 1762	62	Edward their Son	9 Oct 1716	—
Thomas James, of Clapton	20 Feb 1773	44	Urfulla Watts, of Alkington	4 Nov 1734	3
Mary Wife of John Jelfs	24 Jan 1775	22	Thomas Watts	28 Apr 1736	27
Larking of Ham in this Parish	2 Nov 1765	68	Elizabeth, Daughter of George and Elizabeth Watts	8 Sept 1778	65
William Turner of this Town	16 June, 1772	55	Ann Wife of Peter Summers of this Town	24 Dec 1738	31
Barbara his Wife	1 Aug 1750	54	Henry Summers of this Town, Mercer	9 Apr 1773	82
Thomas, Son of William Terrer	2 Dec 1763	20	Martha his Wife	1729	39
John Summers, of Wick Elm in this Parish	5 Aug 1746	54	Elizabeth their Daughter	1731	19
Ann his Relict	15 July, 1776	81	Ann their Daughter died in London	13 Oct 1768	38
William King of Ham, Yeoman	8 Feb 1769	74	Sarah their Daughter	26 Nov 1769	51
Mary, Daughter of William and Mary Smith, of Hinton in this Parish	17 May, 1758	22	John Packer Mercer	18 Oct 1728	31
James Everett, of Hinton, Yeoman	20 Dec 1759	73	Mary Williams	11 Oct 1711	
Mary his Wife	29 Nov 1754	52	Sarah Daughter of Samuel Packer, of this Town, Mercer	6 June, 1772	35
Sarah his Daughter	31 May, 1757	22	John Hyett of Sanger	15 Feb 1719	12
Daniel his Son	10 Oct 1760	23	Ann his Wife	Sept 1735	13
Daniel Everett of Hinton	3 Oct 1760	30	William Lewes of the Heath in this Parish	Dec 1749	52
Venetia, Wife of Benjamin Son Daughter of Arthur and Sarah Dorney	21 Dec 1755	32	John Lewes, of Wick	12 Aug 1710	71
Henry Heathfield, of Bevington, Yeoman	11 Jan 1723	66	Sarah his Wife	Aug 1694	71
Hannah his Wife	May 1697		William Attwood of Newport in this Parish	Apr 1744	2
Sarah Relict of Henry Heathfield	1 Feb 1753	55	Giles Dur of Oldbury in the Parish of Thornbury	23 Oct 1762	65
Richard Gwynn, of this Town, Alderman	1 June, 1740	40	Hannah his Wife	1 Mar 1745	40
Mary Widow of Thomas Stump, of this Town	5 Aug 1734	84	Betts their Daughter	6 Nov 1755	21
Sufanna, Daughter of the aforesaid Thomas and Mary Stump, and Relict of Richard Gwynn	11 May, 1753	58	John Watts, of this Town Baker	2 July, 1740	25
Timothy Pead, of the Heath in this Parish	27 Aug 1731	56	William Neal, of this Town, Alderman	7 Sept 1755	
Daniel his Grandson	11 Aug 1757	25	Elizabeth his Wife	5 Sept 1736	52
John Pead, of this Parish	1733		John Neal, of this Town, Alderman	7 Oct 1748	61
Sufanna his Wife	2 Mar 1762	57	Jean his Wife	31 Jan 1740	45
Ann Wife of Robert Clark	24 July, 1753		Christian, Wife of Thomas Neale, of this Town	16 Feb 1759	7
Thomas their Son	17 Nov 1759	—	Thomas Neale	15 Jan 1741	21
Sarah Daughter of Thomas and Mary Clark	20 Sept 1761	17	George their Son	May 1743	6
Thomas Nicholas, of Wanfwell in this Parish	Apr 1744	5	George Son of William and Jean Neale	21 Jan 1770	17
Mary his Wife late of Inft in the Parish of Olveston	11 Nov 1762	50	George Watts, of Oldbury	14 Apr 1751	
Thomas Nicholas, of Inft in the Parish of Olveston Son of Thomas Nicholas, of Wanfwell in this Parish	30 Sept 1758	3	Sarah Gaftrell of Hinton in this Parish	2 Apr 1777	5
Levin Nicholas, of the Inft in the Parish of Weftbury on Severn Son of Thomas Nicholas, of Wanfwell	19 Oct 1755	1	Hannah her Daughter	26 Dec 1759	1
Sufha, Widow of Daniel Hopton of Bevington in this Parish	16 Feb 1741	65	Robert, Son of William Clark, of Hinton	12 Nov 1769	3
Daniel Hopton of Olveston Son of Daniel and Sarah Hopton, of the Town	28 Aug 1724	8	George Phillimore Son of Daniel Phillimore Son of this Parish	6 Dec 1745	4
Daniel Hopton, of Bevington	23 Mar 1761	32	William James, of this Town junior Cordwainer	Jan 1741	6
Daniel Hopton of Bevington fenior	11 May, 1720	55	Richard Jones and William Jones	Jan 1740	1
John Hobby of this Town	2 May, 1720	67	Richard Watkins of Berkeley Cordwainer	4 May 1742	22
Elizabeth his Wife	25 May, 1718	49	Elizabeth his Wife	June 1770	55
William Hobby, of Bevington	7 Aug 1681		William three Sons	8 Mar 1756	3
Ann his Wife	11 Feb 1703	—	James his their Son	8	3
William Hobby of Heathfield	23 July, 1730	55	Nathaniel Cole	21 Aug 1763	28
Jean Hobby of Hill	11 Feb 1711	55	John Sutton, of this	1 Jan 1743	16
Joseph Hobby	6 Jan 1755	56	Mary his Wife	11 Jun 1738	68
Edward Cole of his Town	25 Feb 1744	6	John Sutton of this Town in this Parish Yeoman	5 Apr 1763	16
Ann his Wife	2 Feb 1744	1	Ann his Wife	21 Oct 1757	63
Ann Webb	19 Jan 1745		James Ruftell of this Town, Alderman	24 Mar 1755	41
			Sarah his Wife	Nov 1720	73
			John Ruftell of this Parish	Dec 1726	70
			Mary his Wife	5 Nov 1725	50
			John Cole	19 May 1740	50
			Sarah his Wife	28 Mar 1705	65

ON HEADSTONES

	Died	Aged		Died	A
J— their Daughter	5 Jan 1739	23	Ann, Daughter of Charles Trotman of Breadstone	13 Sep 1 9	0
Arthur Snelcombe, or Swanley	29 July 1740	5—	Hester, Wife of Charles Trotman, of Breadstone	M— 1 66	24
John Rickets	15 Dec 1754	34	Daniel Thayer of Preedstone	2 May 176;	47
Katharine his Wife	11 Nov 1777	52	Elizabeth Wife of Peter Griffon	1 F— 1—	1
Maurice Sanger, of Breadstone	28 Sept 176—	86	Joseph Dorney, of Clipton	19 Mar 1 68	50
William Coxley of the Parish of Strinbridge	8 Apr 1758	54	Thomas his Brother	3 Apr 169	5
Ann his Wife	2 Apr 1775	37	Hannah his 1st Wife	6 May 174	26
Michael Gibbons Padar, of the Town Apothecary	9 May 1758	60	Martha his 2d Wife	16 May 1765	13
William Cowley, of Saniger in this Parish, Yeoman	29 Dec 1777	71	Joseph his Son, by Martha his 2d Wife	10 Nov 176	9
George Hall	7 Feb 1772	67	Elizabeth Daughter of Thomas Dorney, by Hannah his 1st Wife	2 M— 17—	1
Charles Hall of this Parish, Mason	14 Jan 1709	44	William Browning of Pedington in this Parish	1 June 1786	0
Elizabeth his Wife	26 Aug 1759	86	Thomas Hillier of Prior Wood was drowned in the River Severn Mar 1777 and buried here May 2, following		0
Ann, Wife of Samuel Hopton	4 Feb 1773	43			
Hannah Wife of Arthur Dowell, of this Town	22 Aug 1778	45	Edward Sanger, of Pedington in his Parish	31 Aug 176	0
William Ridler, of Halmore in this Parish	25 Nov 1785	55	Mary his Wife	6 Mar 175	
Mary his Wife	17 Apr 1762	52	Richard Rutter, of Pedington	31 Oct 175	0
George Wood, of this Town, Schoolmaster	17 May 1744	40	Mary his Wife	7 Apr 174	
Richard Smith of Riddleford in the Tything of Hinton	20 July 1783	48	Thomas Wickham, or Butler Son of Thomas Wickham of Newport	9 Sep 17—	
Richard Cornock, of this Parish	14 Jan 174—	53	James Wickham of this Town	14 Jun 176	
Ann his Wife	25 Sep 1729	47	Mary his Wife	11 Mar 17	
Hester, Daughter of Richard Cornock	14 Jan 1756	16	William Wickham of the St kin his Parish	1 Jun 69	
James his Son	11 1756	19	Sarah his Wife	17 Sep 1	
Thomas his Son	20 Apr 1743	20	John Hardlow, of this Town Alderman	5 Aug	65
Edward Cornock, of this Town, Carpent	4 Apr 1768	74	John Burton of Pedington	1 Jun 181	75
Sarah his Wife	5 Jul 1755	67	Elizabeth his Wife	9 Nov 17	
William Wakefield	7 Jun 1732	5—	Thomas Colvin of Pedington	9 Nov 17	
John Pearce, of Hinton Yeoman	3 Dec 1782	62	Richard, Son of Thomas and Betty Wooliche of the J	— May 178	
John Oldland, of the Davlord in the Parish of Hill, Yeoman, late of Halmore in this Parish	4 Feb 1768	60	Betty Wife of Thomas Wooliche, of this Town	5 Apr 181	
Sarah his Wife	6 Oct 1780	76	John, Son of Thomas and Hester Hill	11 Jun 175	
Robert Pearce, of Hinton in this Parish Yeoman	10 Aug 178;	4	John Crump of Clipton	21 Nov 176;	
Elizabeth his Wife	4 Apr 1765	9	Elizabeth his Wife	13 Oct 1	
William Pearce, of Hinton	21 Feb 1760	00	Nancy Daughter of Charles Green	9 Sep 1 0	
Martha his Daughter Wife of Anthony Jenkins of this Town	5 Aug 178		Hannah his Wife	21 Jun 1	5
Sarah Wife of Timothy Collin Daughter of Robert and Elizabeth Pearce of Hinton, in this Parish	19 May		Richard Andrews Thomas Miller the Parish Yeoman	— Sep 17	4
John Smith, of Riddleford in this Parish	18 Apr 174	6	Mary Wife of Joseph Pig and Daughter of Daniel Hatley of Newport	1 Dec 1 7	
Ann his Wife	13 Oct 17		William Price, of Upper Wick in this Parish	N—	
John Hall of this Town, But her	5 Jun 17	40	Mary his Wife	— Jun 17	
Sarah his Wife			Thomas Cole of Lower Wick this Parish	— C— 1 6	
George Trotman, of Lower Wick in this Parish	5 Feb 175		Elizabeth Wife of Thomas Cole of London her husband	4 Jun 175	
Sarah his Wife	15 Sept 14		Mary Wife of the Parish		
Daniel Deane of Breadstone	3 Aug 176	45	Elizabeth Daughter dill, of Upper Wick this Town		
Aaron Cook, Son of Aaron Cook of Riddleford in this Parish	11 Feb 1761	6	Mary Wife Richard Nelmes Richard Nel and wife of Richard Jefferis Wick in		5
Charles Cook, of Hinton in this Parish	6 Oct 176;		Samuel Anderson Son of M Blacksmith	Nov 2	8
Mary Wife of John Hall of T—	1 Apr 1737	36	Samuel Anderson son of the Parish	Mar 1	51
John Hall of Halmore in this Parish	6 Jun 176;	41	Mary his Daughter	Mar 1	16
John Hall, of Halmore in the Parish Wife	17 Jun 1743	5	George Burnet of Lower Wick in this Town	Oct	
Joseph Wife of John Jones of T— Parish	4 Dec 1740	4	Mary his Wife	1 Apr 1	
J— Martin of C— Parish	9 Apr 175		Jane Daughter of Hill	9 Apr 17 4	

ON HEAD STONES

	Died	Aged		Died	Aged
A d, W e o Henry Jobins of Hertsfie'd this Parish	22 Oct 1772	72	Hannah, Daughter of Thomas and Susanna Andrews -	12 Dec 1771	2,
Henry Johns of Ireland	18 Jan 1775	72	William Burly, of Newport in this Parish	18 Feb 1753	46
Hen y their Son	17 Dec 1771	,0	Ann his Wife -	25 Dec 1756	42
L son th ir Son	3 May, 1736	27	Susanna Pope, of the Heath in this Parish	15 Mar 1782	48
William Dunn of Clapton, Son of William Dunn, of Ham in this Parish	23 Apr 1767	44	Edward Pope, of the Heath in this Parish, Yeoman -	29 Mar 1775	69
Henry, Son of Nathaniel and Mary Long of this Town	22 Aug 1780	3,	Elizabeth, Wife of Richard Clark, of the Heath in this Parish	12 May, 1784	45
Nathaniel Long, of this Town, Blacksmith	3 June, 1757	45	Mary Pope, of the Heath -	28 Oct 1763	66
Mary, Wife of Francis Long, of this Town	25 Dec 1784	4,	John Pope, of the Heath -	25 Apr 1742	40
Thomas Graiton of Breadstone	23 Jan 1732	50	Edward Son of Walter Knight, of Billow in this Parish -	14 Jan 1730	14
William Knight, of this Town, Blacksmith	11 June, 1741	34	Walter Knight, of Breadstone, Son of Walter and Sarah Knight, of Billow in this Parish	18 Nov 1785	40
Mary his Wife, late Wife of Nathaniel Long	2 Apr 1776	61	Mary, Wife of Walter Knight, of Billow -	8 Aug 1740	23
Thomas, Son of Thomas and Naomi Andrews of this Town	9 May, 1785	15	William Edwards of this Parish	28 Oct 1732	—
Mary their Daughter -	26 Jan 1786	15	Martha his Wife -	15 Aug 1738	—
Thomas Andrews, of this Town, Blacksmith	6 Sept 1766	67	Mr James Reeves, late Steward to the Right Honourable the Earl of Berkeley	2 July, 1767	46
First his first Wife -	5 Sept 1729	29			
Susanna his 2d Wife -	19 Apr 1776	68			

ON A MALL HEAD STONE ARE THE FOLLOWING VER IS

Here lies the Earl of SUFFOLK's Fool,
Men call'd him DICKY PEARCE,
His Folly serv'd to make Folks laugh
When Wit and Mirth we e scarce

Poor Dick, alas ! is dead and gone,
What signifies to cry ?
Dickys enough are still behind,
To laugh at by and by

Buried June 16 17 8 aged 63

This Epitaph, we are credibly informed was composed by the celebrated Dean SWIFT, who had been Chaplain to the Earl of BERKELEY, who one of the Lords J riers of Ireland and whose Epitaph (written also by SWIFT) has be n given in p 159

XXXVIII. BEVERSTONE.

IN the Margin of LELAND's Itinerary there is the following Note.—"There is a Quarre of good "Stone at Beverstan, unde Nomen ex conjectura."

Another Etymology is from Bupe ꝼtan (Stone tower), which was its more ancient Name. The Distance of this Village from GLOUCESTER is Twenty Miles, from Tetbury Two, it lies in the upper Extremity of the Hundred of Berkeley, and the Deanery of Dursley. The Parish by a late Admeasurement was found to contain 2300 Acres, three fourths of which are Arable.

"Beverston, in the Booke of Domesday written Beureslan, a Name derived (as may bee conceived) "from the greate Blewe Stones wherewith this Place aboundeth, more than any other Township or Place "of this Hundred, wherein the CONQUEROR, and before him K. EDWARD Confessor had in Demesne "Ten Hydes of Land. The Township being a Member or Parcell of the greate Mannour of Berkeley, "was by Kinge HENRY Seconde, given amongst many other inferior Mannors to ROBERT, son of HAR-"DING, when he first created him a Baron of this Realm, to holde by Knight Service in capite, as the "Tenure continueth to this Day." MSS. SMYTH.

A Market on Monday weekly was granted, with an annual Fair for three Days, at the Assumption of Our Lady, by King EDWARD I. in the Twenty first Year of his Reign, to JOHN AT ADAM, to be held here, but these have long been discontinued, the present Village consisting only of few Houses.

The Church, dedicated to Saint Mary, has a Nave, one narrow Aile, with a smaller one belonging to the Lord of the Manor, and an embatled Tower. The Impropriation and Advowson of this Church, and the annexed Chapelry of Kingscote, were, with the other Churches of Berkeley Harness or Lordship, given to the Convent of St. Augustin at Bristol, by their Founder ROBERT FITZ HARDING. D. PAR-SONS &c. "it was carried from thence by the GOURNAYS, of whom ANSELM DE GOURNAY, in I Ed-"WARD I. gave it to the Abbey of St. Peter in Gloucester." With them it continued till their sup pression, when the Advowson was vested in the Crown, and the Benefice endowed by HENRY VIII. In the great Window of the Chancel are the Arms of BERKELEY, which was probably built by THOMAS lod

Lord BERKELEY, in the Reign of EDWARD III. To the South Wall of the Tower is affixed, on the Outside, a Figure in Relief of an Ecclefiaftic holding a Crofier, which appears to have been a fepulchral Monument.

The Manor, after having been inherited from the BERKELEYS, by the GOURNAYS, GAUNTS, and AP ADAM, returned to them in 1331, being purchafed by THOMAS Lord BERKELEY. In the 29th of ELI ZABETH, Sir JOHN BERKELEY fold it to Sir JOHN POINTZ. It foon after became the Property of the knightly Family of HICKES, who are the prefent Poffeffors.

The Æra of the original Foundation of *Beverftone* Caftle is not diftinctly known, and the military Hiftory of it is equally obfcure. We find in WILLIAM of MALMSBURY (lib. VI. p. 77), that "in the Year 1048 a folemn Convention was held here by Earl GODWIN and his Sons, under Pretence of affifting King EDWARD the Confeffor againft the Incurfions of the Welfh. In the 11th Year of HENRY III. MAURICE DE GAUNT was profecuted by the King for having fortified his Caftle without the royal Permiffion, the "*Licentia crenellare*." It then became a Military Fortrefs, and was probably much dilapidated during the Barons Wars, for, when purchafed by THOMAS Lord BERKELEY, Additions were made to it fo confiderable, as to render it in Effect a new Structure.

LELAND has the fubjoined Memorandum concerning it, Itinerary, vol VI p 68.

" THOMAS Lord BARKELEI, as olde Syr WILLIAM BARKELEI told me, was taken Prifoner in *France*, " and after recovering his Loffes with Frenche Prifoners, and at the Battle of *Poyters*, buildid after the " Coft of *Beverftan* thoroughly, a Pile at that Time very pretty." This Circumftance is confirmed by Mr. SMITH, who fays further, that " it is doubtlefs a Pile of as ancient Buildinge, as any at this Day ftandinge in the Hundred, many Yeares, yea, many Ages, more ancient than that of *Berkley*, which is full kept in goode Repaire, and oftentimes the Dwellinge Houfe of the Lorde thereof. Belonginge to this ancient Caftell was a Coneftabulary, or Office of Conftable, related to THOMAS Lorde BARKELEY, '*Totum Jus & Clamitum de, & in Officio Coneftablariae Caftri de Beverftan*,' which hee held for Terme of Life, by Grant from THOMAS AP ADAM immediately on the faid Lord's Purchace it was agreed for the Lord BERKELEY to fettle in that Office one of his own Servants, of whofe Fidelitie he might bee the more affured."

It appears that the Caftle was ufed only as a Manfion houfe, till the grand Rebellion in 1643, when it was feized for the King, and befieged by Colonel MASSIE with 300 Foot, and 80 Horfe. Of this Siege, and the fubfequent Surrender, a minute Account is given by CORBET, in his "Military Government of " Gloucefter, p. 61, 62.

The

The most considerable Remains of this ancient Fabric are a very large square Tower, formerly flanked by four small octagonal Turrets, two of which are totally destroyed. Of the Rooms yet to be traced, the most perfect is the Chapel, 33 Feet by 25, which has a beautiful arched Roof, a Gothic Window, and on the right Side of the Altar, a Shrine of two Compartments of Tabernacle Work, with a Lavatory, a Closet, 12 Feet by 10, in which is a Confessional, and over it a Prison of the same Dimensions, the Floor once covered with Lead, Parts of which remain inserted in the Side Walls. The lower of two Angles adjoined to the N W Side of the Castle, was appropriated solely to military Purpose. It has Three Stories, or Divisions, the Floors were of solid Beams of 8 Inches in Thickness. In the uppermost of these, is an Aperture of about 2 Yards square, 32 Feet from the Level of the Dungeon, through which the Prisoner was let down into it. This dreadful Abode is not more than 9 Feet square, to which there is no Entrance, but by a dark Passage excavated through the Wall, and 7 Feet from the Ground.

The curious Investigator of the Punishments inflicted on Prisoners of War, in those Days of Barbarism, would hardly find a Dungeon more systematically horrid, than this at *Beverstone*. Beside these, are several very spacious Apartments, the Windows and Chimney Pieces of which are in the Style of the 16th Century, so altered for Convenience, when inhabited as a private House.

The Castle was destroyed by Fire soon after the Siege. A large Dwelling house built within the Walls was burnt down about a Century past, and that which was rebuilt, is the present Farm house. The Moat, which is partly filled up, was 200 Yards in Circumference, over which was the outer Gate, the Ruin of which remain. The whole has a venerable Effect, and, from its elevated Situation, is conspicuous at a great Distance.

One of the 12 Chaces and Parks belonging to the Barony of *Berkeley* was situate at *Beverstone*. The Foundations of the Stone Inclosure are frequently met with at a small Distance from the Castle, extremely massive and spacious.

" About a Mile from *Beverstone* standeth *Cawkett Farm*, which belonged to the Abbey of *Kingswood*,
" where is a Barne 130 Feet long, which will hold 900 Loads of Corn, where in the South Part is in-
" scribed Anno Dni' M CC perpici Abbatis XXIX ' PARSONS's MSS

No Benefactions to the Poor.

INCUMBENTS	PATRONS	INCUMBENTS	PATRONS
1554 William Jennings,	Queen Mary	1711 John Swynfen, B D	Queen Anne
—— Thomas Purcy,	——	1728 Thomas Savage, M A	King George II
1617 Rich. Hall,	Henry Pool	1760 Allen Bathurst, LL. B.	King George III
1684 Andrew Needham,	King Charles II.	1767 Chas. Jasper Selwyn, M A	King George III.
The above from Sir ROBERT ATKYNS			

PRESENT LORD OF THE MANOR,

MICHAEL HICKES, Esq

The only Person summoned from this Place by the Heralds in 1682 and 1683 was
Sir William Hickes, Bar.

At the Election in 1776 Two Freeholders polled from this Parish

The first Entry in the Register is of a Baptism in 1563

ANNUAL ACCOUNT OF MARRIAGES, BIRTHS, AND BURIALS, IN THIS PARISH

A D	Mar	Bir	Bur	A D	Mar	Bir	Bur	A D	Mar	Bir	Bur	A D	Mar	Bir	Bur
1781	1	3	4	1791				1801				1811			
1782	—	4	1	1792				1802				1812			
1783	—	2	2	1793				1803				1813			
1784	1	2	4	1794				1804				1814			
1785	—	1	5	1795				1805				1815			
1786	3	5	1	1796				1806				1816			
1787				1797				1807				1817			
1788				1798				1808				1818			
1789				1799				1809				1819			
1790				1800				1810				1820			

INSCRIPTIONS IN THE CHURCH

ON FLAT STONES IN THE CHANCEL.

In spe Beatæ Resurrectionis
Posita sunt hic Reliquiæ
Viri admodum Reverendi
ANDREÆ NEEDHAM,
A. M. hujus Ecclesiæ, necnon
adjacentis Capellæ de Kingscote,
per annos ter novem Pastoris,
qui satur dierum, & maturus
Cœlo, huic Mundo placide nec
invitus valedixit sexto Die Augusti,
Anno { Salutis nostræ MDCCX
{ Ætatis suæ LXIX

ANNA NEEDHAM, Vid: obiit sexto
Die Jan Anno Domini 1726,
ætatis 86

SUB HOC SAXO REQUIESCIT
CORPUS RICHARDI HALL, HUJUS
ECCLESIÆ RECTORIS, QUI POST-
QUAM IN HOCCE TRIGINTA
OCTOQUE ANNOS HONESTE
AC FIDELITER MUNERE
SACERDOTALI PERFUNCTUS,
ESSET MORTALITATEM
DEPOSUIT
VICESIMO DIE AUGUSTI,
ANNO DOM 1684,
ÆTATIS SUÆ 73

JACET CORLS
MAGISTRI RICHARDI HALL,
RECTORIS ISTIUS
ECCLESIÆ, OBIIT
30 JUNII, 1638

Here lieth the Body of
MARY the Daughter of
ANDREW NEEDHAM, Rector of
Beverstone, and ANNE his Wife,
who departed this Life the
9th Day of September, 1703,
in the 23d Year of her Age

Here resteth the Body of
WILLIAM, the Son of ANDREW NEEDHAM,
Rector of this Parish,
and ANN his Wife,
who departed this Life
Nov 21, 1692

Here lieth SIBELLA, the
Wife of JAMES CORNELIUS Clerk,
Daughter of ANDREW NEEDHAM,
Rector of Beverstone,
and ANN his Wife, who departed
this Life Nov 29, 1700

ON THE VERGE OF A FLAT STONE, IN OLD CHARACTER

Here lyeth the Body of
CATHERINE PERRY, Wife of THOMAS
PERRY, Minister of the Word in
this Place, who died the 18 Day
of December, in the Year of our Lord,
1694, and of her Life the 67th

IN A SMALL CHAPEL ON THE NORTH SIDE

THOMAS CROOME
died Sept 13, 1716, aged 48

ANN, the Daughter of THOMAS
and SARAH CROOME, died an Infant

SAMUEL, the Son, and MILLICENT
and SARAH, the Daughters of
THOMAS CROOME and SARAH his Wife

SAMUEL was buried Jan 22, 1704-5, aged 4 Years

MILLICENT, the same Day, aged 2 Years

SARAH, the 31st of January, 1704-5, aged 5 Years

ON A BRASS PLATE, UNDER AN ARCH IN THE SOUTH WALL

In Memory of
ELIZABETH BRIDGES, Widow,
who, after a long Pilgrimage of
93 Years here on Earth, departed
this Life the 11th of July,
Anno Dom 1693

ON PLAIN TABLETS AT THE WEST END

In Memorie of SARAH, the
Daughter of JOHN SHIPWAY
and CATHARINE his Wife,
who departed this Life
May 4, A D 1703, æt 12

In Memory of JOHN SHIPWAY,
who departed this Life July 7, 1711,
ætatis suæ 48

Also of CATHARINE the Wife
of the said JOHN SHIPWAY
who departed this Life
January 29, A D 1718, æt —

In Memory of ESTHER, the
Wife of LEWIN TUGWELL
She died July 8, 1759,
aged 40

Also of THOMAS their Son,
who died March 15, 1750,
aged 15

Underneath lie interred
the Remains
of WILLIAM TUGWELL,
and of LEWIN his Brother,
both of this Place

WILLIAM died Sept 27, 1763, aged 58

LEWIN died Feb 7, 1776, ætat 69

IN THE CHURCH YARD, ON TOMBS

John the Son of Daniel
ew, died Nov ... 17 , aged 7,

A... the Daniel Brown
wife... Jan 5, 7 , aged 1

Elizabeth, the Wife
Daniel Brown
died July 6, 7 , aged 7

Thomas Brown
b... Jan 15, 17 8 , aged 6

Daniel Son of Daniel Brown,
... that died April 19, 17 9 ... 8

John Brown
died Oct 17 aged 6,

Al... Elizabeth Brown ...
... August 6 1 , aged 58

John Ingram
died July 25, 174 , aged 51

Elizabeth the Wife
John Skidway
died Dec ... 4

Elizabeth Wood
Wife of Timothy Wood
died March 1 164

John Heavay
die April 1 175 , aged 8
Also Jane the Wife John Heavay
and ... Hannah ,
died January 2 1749
aged 9 Years

Robert Drew
of Newinton Bushpath,
died Dec 11 170 , aged 84,

Dorothy his Wife
died Dec 11, 74, aged 89

Sarah Relict of
John Ingram
died Sept 21 17 1, aged

Mary Wife of
William Drew of Dimsey,
died Dec 1 17 8, aged 34

Isaac their Daughter
Hannah and Sarah their ...

... died their ...
died Dec 15, 17 , aged

ON HEAD STONES

	Died	Aged		Died	Aged
	8 July, 17	6	His the Wife	1 Sept, 175	6
his Wife	Aug 1,7	85	Dorothy Drew	June 1 4	45
the Daughter of Thomas Tho			Elizabeth Noe	1 Aug 1	
... and of John Noe	Aug 1		... their Daughter and Wife of		
... Daughter John property			John Church	July 175	
Thomas ... the Wife	19 April	9	Susanna, Daughter of John and		
John ... his Daughter	July 1	1	... Susanna Church	Jan 10	
... John William Noe	March 175		Mary Wife of Daniel John 1		
... his Grandson	Feb 1 58	12	... and	1 Jan, 17	
his Grandson	1 May 1	4	Richard Brown senior	8 Aug 16	
... the 1 July	1 July,	46	Mary his Wife	Aug 1	
No. Noe of Newington	1 Dec 17	1	his their Deceased	1 Sept 1	
...	1 Nov 1	7	William Drew	1 Oct 1	

XXXIX. BIBURY.

AT the Time of the great Survey made by the CONQUEROR, *Bechebury* (the modern *Bibury*) gave Name to a Hundred, which contained " *Aluredingtune, Berebuy, Aldesarde,* and *Painstie,*" all of which are now included in the Hundred of *Brightwells Barrow*, and the Peculiar of *Bibury*

II Distance of his Village, which is situated on the great Road from *Bath* to *Oxford*, is from Gloucester Twenty, and from *Cirencester* Seven Miles on the Left Of the Soil, which is ... equally high the greater Part is tilled, excepting the Meadows on the Banks of the *Colne*

The Benefice is a very extensive Vicarage with the Chapel of *Winson* annexed The Impropriation is granted to the Abbey of *Osney*, near *Oxford*, about the Year 1130 From Mr PENNANT's MSS collect, " that Contest between Thomas PACKHAM Bishop of *Worcester* (who had made the Endowment), and the Convent, is adjusted by Pope ALEXANDER III by the following Composition That the Abbey should pay annually Three Pounds to the Church of *Worcester*, the Bishop of which relinquished an exclusive Privilege of appointing one Canon at *Osney* so that in Twenty Years Age is presumed to pay them to the Church " The Peculiar of *Bibury* is of ancient Establishment I terms expressly give to be frequently contested by the Diocesan, of providing its own Chaplains whom employed Parishioners in the Right before received

It also was admitted by LANE and Archbishop of *Canterbury* in the time Centre, who exempted other from Adverse as to these Dioceses of *Worcester*, episcopal Visitation ... This Custom demand obtained immemorial

The Church is a question monument of the Architecture of the middle Ages is erected, much bears character by the Conventual Priory The Tower, which is embattled ... contains Six Bells ... To Build the Nave ... when he added Two Aisles, and the Chancel, the Property of as Impropriator ESTCOURT CRESSWELL, Esq The colossal Picture of St George ... time ... by on the South Wall is now totally defaced He was no Patron of ... in honour of the St Mary or St Michael is not positively known

... Abbey of *Osney* the Manor of *Bibury Osney* was granted to the Clergy of ... with the Rights of the Impropriation and Peculiar, to ... Severalty ... having been obtained by JOHN DUDLEY Duke of ... Sir THOMAS SACKVILLE of the Family of the Earls of ... of the last Century, from whence before came the ... Daughter was the Mother ... at Petworth

The Manor-house is spacious, in the best Style of the Age in which it was built, the Date (1623) still remaining over the Porch, with the Arms of the Founder Sir Thomas Sackville.

The most picturesque Landscape Painters have scarce imagined a View truly the more beautiful than which forms the Front Prospect of this venerable Building: being situated on an easy Eminence, it commands the River *Colne*, and the Hills above it covered with ... Wood of the most variegated Foliage, which, contrasted with the barren Downs on the Summit, completes a Scene perfect in its Kind.

In this Parish are four Districts, or Hamlets, *Bibury*, of which ... two Tythings *Osney*, and *Northumberland*, *Arlington*, *Ablington*, nearly a Mile further, on the Court of the River *Colne*. The Family of *Coxwell* of very respectable Ancestry, have long possessed this Manor, with a competent of Lands. Their ancient Residence, erected in 1590, has lately had considerable Additions, both of ... and Convenience, from the present Owner, the Rev. Charles Coxwell, M.A. Hewson, which has its Chapel, but no Monuments of Consequence. The Manor is vested in Charles D'Oyley ... and a considerable Estate in the Family of Howse.

When the Act for the general Inclosure was passed in 1760, the Parish was exonerated from Tythes requisite Proportions of the Waste Lands (which were mutually extensive) being allotted to the Impropriation and the Vicarage.

B E N E F A C T I O N S.

Hugh Westwood gave by Will, 1559, for four of the most impotent and poor Men of *Bibury*, for Maintenance, Clothing, and Firing, and who are lodged in his Alms house a Rent Charge, payable out of Lands in *Ampney Peter*, *Holy Rood Ampney*, and *Ashbrooke*, the annual Produce of which is 18*l*.

John Smithier gave by Will, 1621, for Four Widows, if possible, in *Bibury*, 10*l* vested in the Hands of the Churchwardens, being borrowed for the Use of the Church, 1691, the annual Produce ...

Thomas Tawney gave by Will, 1676, for the Use of the Poor of *Bibury*, 50*l* lent to the Church of ..., 1754, annual Produce 2*l* 10*s*.

Mrs. Catharine Sackville gave by Will, 1750, for the use of the Poor of *Bibury*, 100*l* vested in the Hands of her Niece, Mrs. Ann Crisswell, the annual Produce 4*l* 10*s*.

A Church House has been given, but it is dubious when ... it appears, however, by Deed of Feoffment, dated 1719, to be given for the Purpose (as expected) of the Reparations and Amendments of the King's Highways in the Parish of *Bibury*, and in Sustentation and Maintenance of the poor Men and Women inhabiting and dwelling in the Parish of *Bibury*. It has several Tenements occupied by the Poor of *Bibury*.

INCUMBENTS	PATRONS	INCUMBENTS	PATRONS
1268 Gilbert Cann,	Abbey of Osney	1457 Thomas Willycote,	Abbey of Osney
1301 Richard Garmyn,	The same	1533 William Tawney,	The same
1330 Thomas Dowcton,	The same	1551 William Sheldon,	King Edward VI
1331 Thomas De Minsford,	The same	1553 Harry Willis,	Hugh Westwood
1336 Nicholas De Hondford,	The same	1558 Lewis Guyse,	The same
1357 John Camden,	The same	1561 Robert Bag,	John Bag
1442 Peter Oxenford,	The same	1585 David Rice,	Queen Elizabeth

In above from Mr Prynne's MSS

INCUMBENTS	PATRONS	INCUMBENTS	PATRONS
1599 Richard Jennings,	John Coxwell	1721 Thomas Piker, M.A.	Thomas Bider, Esq
1608 John Rundle,	Sir T. Sackville, Knt	1757 Will Somerville, M.A.	Geo Somerville, Esq
1611 Benj Wymington, M.A.	Rich Westwood, Esq		
1673 John Vining, D.D.	Rich Sackville, Esq		
	From Sir Robert Atkyns		

PRESENT PROPRIETORS OF THE MANORS.

Of *Bibury*, *Osney*, and *Northumberland*, with ...

LASCOURT CRISSWELL, Esq.

Of *Arlington*   Of *Hewson*

CHARLES COXWELL, M.A.   CHARLES D'OYLEY, Esq.

From this Vestry, and its Hamlets, the Persons summoned by the Herald in 1682 and 1682 were

Sir William Coventry, Knight,
John Coxwell, Esq.
William Hill, Gent.
John Vining, D.D.

At the Election in 1776, Seven Freeholds appeared from the Parish and its Hamlets.

The first Notice in the Register is ...

... Religion was deprived by Queen Anne ... ...

A

AN EXACT ACCOUNT OF MARRIAGES, BIRTHS, AND BURIALS, IN THIS PARISH

A.D.	Mar	Bir	Bur	A.D.	Mar	Bir	Bur	A.D.	Mar	Bir	Bur	A.D.	Mar	Bir	Bur
1781	7	7	7	1791				1801				1811			
1782	3	30	12	1792				1802				1812			
1783	4	24	15	1793				1803				1813			
1784		23	8	1794				1804				1814			
1785	7	6	16	1795				1805				1815			
1786				1796				1806				1816			
1787				1797				1807				1817			
1788				1798				1808				1818			
1789				1799				1809				1819			
1790				1800				1810				1820			

INSCRIPTIONS IN THE CHURCH

ON A NEAT PYRAMIDICAL MONUMENT OF SIENA MARBLE, ON THE NORTH SIDE THE CHANCEL, IS THE FOLLOWING INSCRIPTION

Arms, in a Lozenge, per fess embattled Argent and Sable, six Crosses patty counterchanged, for WARNSFORD. On an Escutcheon of Pretence, Quarterly Or and Gules, a Bend vaire, for SACK-VILLE

Near this Place
lieth interred the Body of
ELIZABETH WARNSFORD, Relict of
EDMUND WARNSFORD, Esq.
She was eldest Daughter of
HENRY SACKVILLE, Esq. late of this Place
She departed this Life the 13th of May 1756,
to the inexpressible Grief of her Family and
Acquaintance, g[...]
S[...]r of[...]

ON A MARBLE MONUMENT ON THE NORTH SIDE THE CHANCEL

Arms, in a Lozenge, Quarterly Or and Gules,
a Bend vaire, for SACKVILLE

Near this Place
lieth interred the Body of
KATHARINE SACKVILLE, youngest Daughter
of HENRY SACKVILLE, Esq. late of this Place,
She departed this Life Sept[...], 1760
She [...]

ON A MARBLE MONUMENT AGAINST ONE OF THE PILLARS

Arms, Argent a Bend wavy Sable, between
[...] Cock Gules, for COSWELL

Underneath
[...] the Body of John Coswell, Esq.
[...] Alderman of this Parish
[...] he departed this Life August [...] 16[...]
in his 70th Year
He left behind him a Widow
she continued to the end of her [...]
and [...] Children

Near this Place lieth
the Body of Mrs MARY COSWELL,
Relict of JOHN COSWELL, Esq. of Ab[...]
She died March 15, 1767, aged 93
Her character is and example
D[...] of [...] and [...]
D[...], [...] her no less deserved,
esteemed in her Life-time, but
regretted at her Death, by all her
Relations and Acquaintance

AGAINST A PILLAR IN THE NORTH AISLE
Sacræ Memoriæ
[...] Reverendi BENJAMIN
WARNSFORD, in Arte Magistri
[...] Vicarii [...]
Mortem [...] Februar
Cœlum [...]
Julii 5, 17[...]

ON THE STONES

Arms of COSWELL

[...] Memoriæ
CAROLI COSWELL [...] Aldermani [...]
Parochiæ [...] JOHANNIS COSWELL
de Ab[...]n Generosi [...]
qui obiit [...] XVI Anno Domini
1[...] [...] XLII

Al[...] COSWELL [...]

Piæ [...] Memoriæ
[...] Cos[...], Aldermani Civitat
Coswell de Ab[...]n Generosi, qui obiit
M[...] XI[...] Anno Domini [...]
ætatis suæ XXX

Hic Sacræ Memoriæ
MARIÆ COSWELL Filiæ tertiæ
JOHANNIS COSWELL de Ab[...]
& ANNÆ uxoris ejus, quæ obiit
XXIII Anno Domini 1[...] ætatis suæ XII

[...] Memoriæ
[...] XVII Februarii hoc complet[...]
JOHANNIS COSWELL & ANNÆ Generosi
& ANN[...] [...] qui obiit [...]
Julii [...] Anno Domini 1[...] LXXX

Piæ & eternæ Memoriæ
CATHARINÆ COXWELL, Filiæ natu
Maximæ JOHANNIS COXWELL, de Ablington
Generoſi, & ANNÆ uxoris ejus, quæ
obiit Julii XX, A D 1707, ætat ſuæ LV

CATHARINA COXWELL,
Filia natu Quinta JOHANNIS
COXWELL, de Ablington, Arm
obiit Maii 19, 1765,
ætatis ſuæ 17

Arms on a Feſs between three Swans Necks
eraſed and ducally gorged, three Cinqueto ls

In Memory of
the Rev THOMAS BAKER, M A
late Vicar of this Church,
who departed this Life
November 8, 1759,
aged 63

Near him he interred his two Daughters

JANE, June 26, 1747

LUCY MARIA, Dec 31, 1749

Alſo
ELIZABETH BAKER his Siſter,
June 26, 1747

M S
ANNÆ, Uxoris Chariſſimæ
THOMÆ BAKER,
Hujus Eccleſæ Vicarii,
quæ Tabe correpta obiit
Decimo ſexto die Martii,
Anno Domini 1734

Here lyeth the Body of
Mrs EDITH LAMBERT,
Relict of Mr ANTHONY LAMBERT,
of Coln St Aldwins
She departed this Life the
5th Day of Nov Anno Dom 1762.
ætatis ſuæ 56

Here lieth the Body of
RICHARD MATTHEWS, of Winſon,
who departed this Life the
19th Day of Auguſt, A D 1600

Here lieth the Body of
JANE MATTHEWS, Daughter of
Mr RICHARD MATTHEWS, deceaſed,
who was buried the 16th of June, 1688,
aged 25 Years

And likewiſe the Body of ANNE,
Daughter of Mr RICHARD MATTHEWS,
and Grand daughter of Mr RICHARD
MATTHEWS aforeſaid, who was buried
July 1, 1688, aged 7 Months, odd Days

Here lies the Body of
JOHN MATTHEWS, late of Winſon, who
departed this Life the 14th Day of
December 1707, in the 53d Year of his Age.

GEORGE VANNAM, M A
Rector of Bibury Rocks,
died Nov 27, 1716, aged 37

JOHN VANNAM, D D
Vicar of Bibury,
died July 14, 1721, aged 84

ELIZABETH HICKS
Daughter of Dr VANNAM, and Wife of
ROBERT HICKS, Eſq of
Comb in the County of Gloucester,
died July 30, 1720, aged 44

Sacred to the Memory of
GEORGE HALL, Son of WILLIAM HALL,
and HESTER his Wife, who died
Nov 29, 1771, aged 55

Sacred to the Memory of WILLIAM
HALL, of Arlington, Gent who died
Sept 23, 1739, aged 67
Alſo of HESTER his Wife, who died
March 17, 1767, aged 80
Sacred to the Memory
of RICHARD HALL, Son of
WILLIAM HALL, Gent and
HESTER his Wife who died
Feb 26, 1781, aged 58

IN THE CHURCH YARD, ON TOMBS

EDMUND TENFANS,
of Barnſley in this County, Gent
He departed this Life the
9th of Nov 1762, aged 64

ROBERT PANCKRIDGE
died July 7, 1723, aged 4

ELIZABETH, Wife of
WILLIAM DAY Clerk,
died Aug 1, 1734, aged 25

RICHARD WINSTANLEY,
died June 6, 1705, aged 3
... his Wife
died June 6, 1771, aged 59

Mr JOHN HESTER junior,
died Feb 28, 1711, aged 61
JOHN HESTER ſeno,
died Ju 5, 1711, aged 67
MARY his Wife
died Dec 5, 1722, aged 65

THOMAS WILKINS
died Jan 30, 1723, aged 78

JOAN his Wife
died Feb 17, 1732, aged 81

MOSES and AARON,
Sons of THOMAS WILKINS

Moses died at Bengal in the East Indies
the 13th of Dec 1713, aged 38

AARON died at Sierra Leona, on the Coast of
Africa, the 17th of May, 1722, aged 39

RICHARD MARCHANT
died Dec 1, 1675

ELIZABETH his Wife
died Sept 11, 1692

JOHN SKUCE
died April 17, 1727, aged 5,

THOMAS SKUCE, Father of JOHN
aforesaid, died Feb 22, 1700

WILLIAM SKUCE
died Sept 20, 1774, aged 85

ANN his Wife
died Nov 16, 1782, aged 68

JASPER WARREN
died March 17, 1684
ROBERT his Son died Oct 5, 1712.
ROBERT, the Son of
ROBERT and ANNE WARREN,
died Nov 17, 1739, aged 54
ELEANOR his Wife
died March 15, 1736, aged 52

JOHN BRINDLE
died April 19, 1753, aged 63
MARY his Wife
died July 18, 1762, aged 72
SAMUEL their Son
died Feb 16, 1741, aged 15

ROBERT BRINDLE
died April 18, 1776, aged 85

JOHN MARCHANT
died April 4, 1742, aged 74.
MARY his Wife
died Sept 30, 1727, aged 64.
THOMAS their Son
died Feb 21, 1730-1, aged 29
LEONARD their Son
died April 6, 1771, aged 72
MARY his Wife
the Daughter of ROBERT and
JANE BOULT, died June 21,
1773, aged 73

O N H E A D S T O N E S

	Died	Aged
Robert Boult, senior	31 Dec 1729	83
Jane his Wife	21 May, 1738	81
Jane, their Daughter	6 Feb. 1763	66
John Brindle	5 Oct 1771	—
William Brindle	4 Mar 1772	49
William Freeman	7 Nov 1762	85
Thomas Freeman	5 Nov 1781	6
Thomas Morley Freeman his Son	11 June, 1781	0
Thomas Jackson	3 Mar 1747	77
Ann his Wife	14 Mar 1757	70
Sarah, their Daughter	3 May, 1731	4
John Jelfton	11 Aug 1780	68
Mary his Wife	9 June, 1765	55
Anne, their Daughter	12 June, 1774	6
John Chatters, late of London	3 Dec 1771	20
Richard Porter	15 June, 1760	65
Sabina Porter, Daughter of Richard and Sabina Porter	4 Mar 1763	24
Robert Marchant	10 Dec 1771	55
Thomas his Son, by Mary his Wife	12 Dec 1771	3
Elizabeth, Daughter of Thomas and Elizabeth Marchant	20 Nov 1746	51
Elizabeth, Wife of Thomas Marchant	15 Aug 1753	50
John Marchant	29 May, 1755	56
Elizabeth Skuce, Daughter of William and Ann Skuce	8 Sept 1772	22
Mary, their Daughter	17 Aug 1778	50
John Stevens	11 Apr 1773	4
Ann, John his Wife	25 Oct 1775	
Jane his	4 Feb 1756	76
Ann his Wife	24 Apr 1771	50
John Powell, junior	1 Apr 1736	75
Thomas his Son	9 Aug 1716	4
Samuel Powell	1 Dec 1756	10
Henry Robins, junior	26 Mar 1765	55
Mary, their Son	15 Jun 1765	5
William Hall, senior	Nov 1733	65
Mary his Wife	— June	1

BICKNOR CHURCH.

FIGURES IN BICKNOR CHURCH

XL. BYKENOR ANGLICANA,
OR
BICKNOR ENGLISH.

SO denominated to diftinguifh it from *Welfh Bicknor*, which lies on the oppofite Shore of the River Wye, in the County of *Monmouth*, formerly within the Limits of the Principality of *Wales*. This Parifh belongs to the Hundred of *St. Briavel's*, and the *Foreft Deanery*, it is diftant three Miles on the North from *Celford*, and nineteen on the Weft from GLOUCESTER. The Lands applied to Pafture and Tillage are nearly equal, excepting fome fertile Meadows on the Banks of the *Wye*, which is the Boundary of this Parifh on the Weft. The foil confifts of Lime-ftone, of which the Style-Cyder is the peculiar Produce, and Strata of Coal, feveral Mines being worked for the Supply of the Vicinity.

A Promontory of great Height is formed by the fantaftic Courfe of the *Wye* (the *Vaga* or the Ancients), which, though but a few Hundred Yards acrofs, has a Circumference of three Miles. This romantic Spot has been cultivated with great Judgement and Tafte by the Poffeffor Mr. WYRALL.

The Living is a Rectory. The Church, which has *St. Mary the Virgin* for its Patron Saint, confifts of a fpacious Nave, two Aifles, and a low embattled Tower at the Weft End, containing five Bells. On either Side the Chancel, is a private Chapel, appropriated to the Sepulture of the ancient Families of WYRALL and MACHEN. The former of thefe are defcended from MATHEW WYRALL, who occurs as High Sheriff of his County in 1299, and have enjoyed extraordinary Privileges and immunities in the Royal Foreft of *Dean*. The MACHENS trace their Ancestry fome Generations before THOMAS MACHEN, who was thrice Mayor of GLOUCESTER, and died in 1614. On the Site of the Church the Remains of a Fortrefs are ftill to be traced, the Moat which furrounded it is in many Parts perfect. The Church either efcaped the Demolition of the other Fabric, or was founded with its Materials. But of this no Authentic Record is preferved, unlefs it is inferred merely as a Tradition. On *Chapel Hill*, in the South-weft Part of the Parifh, the Ruins of an Oratory were vifible within the Memory of Man.

The two Figures in the annexed Engraving are diftinguifhed neither by Infcriptions nor Arms. It is probable, that they were intended for fome of the ancient Families here fettled. Whether the upper Figure be an Ecclefiaftic, or Female, is left to the Decifion of more intelligent Antiquaries. The Figures of Men are almoft without Exception with Armour, in the Age in which thefe appear to have been fculptured.

The Manor was for a Hundred and Twenty Years Parcel of the Priory of Deir Herefts of *Clartly*. In the laft Century it paffed to BENEDICT HALL, of *High Meadow*, Efq; and was inherited by his Son and by THOMAS Lord Vifcount GAGE, the moft confiderable Proprietor. The Manor-houfe is there, and occupied.

Bicknor Court-houfe, which has been rebuilt, is the Refidence of GEORGE WYRALL, Efq; the prefent Reprefentative of that Family. *Eaftbatch Court*, for modernized, is the Property of the Relict of the late Benedict Lewis MACHEN, Efq. The Eftates annexed to thefe, and that on *Chapel Hill*, belonging to WILLIAM LEWIS, Efq; are the moft valuable, independent of the Manor.

This Parifh claims the Rights of Commonage, and other Privileges of the Foreft of *Dean*, which fhall be fpecified in the Account of *St. Briavel's*.

At *Pceton* eftablifhed a Family of the fame Name, who bore, Argent, on a Chief Azure, three Boars heads, in Or. But there are no Memorial of them remaining.

BENEFACTIONS

A Tenement and Garden, now ufed as a Poor-houfe, Two Acres and a Perch of Land, with Two Acre of Coppice Woodland, and 5s a Year, payable out of the Eftate of THOMAS CORE, were vefted in truft from Mifs Mary WYRALL, furviving Truftee under a former Deed, on the 5th Day of January, by a Deed in Truft, the Rents and Profits to be received by the Churchwardens for the time being, and to be employed by them toward the better Relief and Maintenance of the poor People of the Parifh. Whereas the Land, and been given, is unknown, in the preceding Deed are all. Thefe are now vefted in WILLIAM BISSET, and the annual Produce of 6l. exclusive of the Pasture and 7s. a Year when the Coppice Wood is cut.

KNERAM Lewis, given, by Will Feb. 3, 1711, to be diftributed in Bread to the poor Parifhioners, time with Leave of Deceafed, 10s. a Year, payable out of his Eftate and to be held in reference Tourth.

INCUMBENTS	PATRONS	INCUMBENTS	PATRONS
1592 Thomas Hofper,	William Mackland	1710 Rich. Mantle, B A	Will Hodges, Gent
1599 Humph y Smart,	Earl of Effex	1728 Rich Lloyd, M A	The fame
—— Thos Godwyn, J L B	——————	1731 John Beale, B A	Will a n Hodges, Efq
1699 William Hughes,	——————	1744 Jas Meredith, M A	Sam Whitmore, Miles
—— Samuel Harris, M A	Thomas Leyfter, Efq		Oatridge, M les Beale,
The above from Sir ROBERT ATKYNS			and Trugge, Gents
		1777 Morgan Evans, Clerk,	Will Anne, and Jane
			Jones
		1760 Duncombe Pyrke	John Davis, D D.
		Davis, M A	

The Advowfon is now vefted in the Provoft and Fellows of Queen's College, Oxford

PRESENT LORD OF THE MANOR,
The Right Honourable WILLIAM HALL Lord Vifcount GAGE

The Perfons fummoned from this Place by the Heralds in 1682 and 1683 were,
Jeptha Wyrall, I fe
Edward Machen, Efq

At the Election in 1776, Thirteen Freeholders polled from this Parifh

The firft Notice in the Regifter bears Date 1720

ANNUAL ACCOUNT OF MARRIAGES, BIRTHS, AND BURIALS, IN THIS PARISH

AD	Mar	Bir	Bur	AD	Mar	Bir	Bur	AD	Mar	Bir	Bur	AD	Mar	Bir	Bur.
1781	4	14	9	1791				1801				1811			
1782	4	21	14	1792				1802				1812			
1783	3	9	10	1793				1803				1813			
1784	3	8	12	1794				1804				1814			
1785	8	16	16	1795				1805				1815			
1786	7	12	7	1796				1806				1816			
1787				1797				1807				1817			
1788				1798				1808				1818			
1789				1799				1809				1819			
1790				1800				1810				1820			

INSCRIPTIONS IN THE CHURCH

ON A PLAIN STONE MONUMENT AGAINST THE SOUTH WALL IN THE CHANCEL

Memoriæ Sacrum
Joan a nior iti pudem Uxons
THOE T GODWYN, H B hujus Eccle Rectors,
Boti, Pucntel progator bons
Collopio um in Agro Dortetenn
Honeftie non minus in specta ımila
Genwynosorem in Agro Herefordenf,
Fxime ntinctque gloria familias,
S nce feminei decus non exiguum,
Vns charam ri tio, d li teque amiti in,
Nec expreffen animi on defleti mortu as,
Cui, 4 fouri ni videbit n poft a
fub vidgarl fise ra procul ame pebho,
honel se ani peali tur et atee
non n tturi o te re quam labens exercuit,
ed feredi hujc cunt.
mai o que on lon e i puort,
obut Aur i Iepida Aug 19,
Anno Domini 1671

ON A LS STONE IN THE CHANCEL

In Memory of the Remains of
ANN the late Wife of JAMES MEREDITH,
Rector of this Parifh, who was
interred the 17th Day of April, 1776

Alfo in Memory of the abovenamed
JAMES MEREDITH, Clerk who,
after a Refidence of 33 Years in this
Parifh, as Rector of the fame, died on
the 2d Day of May 1777, at Highgate,
Middlefex and was there interred,
aged 72 Years

In Memory of ELIZABETH, late Wife
of the Rev. JAMES MEREDITH,
Rector of this Parish, who died Dec. 17, 1753

MARTHA MEREDITH his Daughter,
interred June 6, 1759, aged 23

CATHARINE his Daughter Oct. 12, 1767

ANN his Daughter, Wife of RICHARD TARRETT,
died June 9, 1777, aged 30

In Memoriam MARIA, Uxoris
RICHARDI MANTER, hujus Ecclesiæ
Rectoris, quæ mortem obiit 29
Septembris, Anno Domini 1716,
Annoque ætatis suæ 63

Etiam in Memoriam RICHARDI MANTEL,
hujus Ecclesiæ Rectoris,
qui mortem obiit 2 Die Martij, Anno Dom. 1727

SIBILL, the Wife of JOHN PARKER, Gent
was buried March 15, 1632

MARY, the Daughter of JOHN PARKER, Gent.
died March 17, 1632

Here lieth the Body of SARAH,
the Wife of WILLIAM WYRALL,
younger Son of JEPTHAH WYRALL,
who departed this Life Jan. 4, 1705

Here lyeth the Body of
GEORGE WORRELL, Son of WILLIAM
WORRELL, Esq. who departed this
Life the 13th Day of March, 1702

Præn... est Joh... nen Atant,
...
A shot...

ISIBIL, the Daughter of
SIMON KING of Frampton on Severne,
deceased March 5, 1631

JOHN, Son of STEVEN VANNAM
and MARY his Wife, died Nov. 2, 1630

In Memory of MARY, Wife
of WILLIAM AMBERY, of Stowfield, Gent
She died May 3, 1779, aged 56

In Memory of CATHARINE,
Daughter of JAMES MEREDITH, Clerk,
Rector of this Parish, who died the
12th of October, 1767

In Memory of MARY,
the Wife of THOMA MANTEL,
who departed this Life January
the 9th, Anno Domini 1719,
in the 30th Year of her Age

Here lyeth the Body of THOMAS
GODWYN, Barones of the Law,
Rector of Inglish Bicknor
Prebendary of Hereford, Son of THOMAS
GODWYN, Doctor of Divinity, and Curate
of Hereford, Grand child to FRANCES
Lord Bishop of Hereford, and Great
Grand child to THOMAS GODWIN, Lord
Bishop of Bath and Wells, who
deceased the 17th Day of November, 1669,
in the age 51

ON FLAT STONES IN THE
MIDDLE AILE

Here lieth interred the Body of
Mrs. ELIZABETH SNOWELL, who departed
for Life June 23, 1700

Here lieth the Body of HANNAH
the Wife of RICHARD GODWIN, who
departed this Life Jan. 16, 1695

RICHARD GODWIN died Jan. 28, 1697

Here lieth the Body of BRIDGET,
the Wife of EDWARD PRICE, who
died July 7, 1725

Here lies the Body of JOHN TIRLITT
of this Parish, who died the 28th Day
of March, 1746, aged 63 Years

IN WYRALL'S CHAPEL
ON FLAT STONES

Here lieth the Body of
GEORGE WYRALL, Esquire,
who married BRIDGET, the
Daughter of GEORGE MANTEL
of Durham Hamme, and had
Issue, WILLIAM, JAMES,
GEORGE, ANN, and MARY, here
lived 70 Years, and died
the 5th of June 1709

Here lieth the
Body of GEORGE
WYRALL, the Son of
WM WYRALL, Esquire,
and had Issue WILLIAM,
DENNIS, GEORGE, JENKIN,
and ELIZABETH, MARY,
JANE, JANE, BRIDGET,
CATHERINE, and ALICE,
was buried the 5th of May, 1648.

Here lieth the Body of
GEORGE, the eldest Son of
JEPTHAH WYRALL, Gent
who departed this Life the 8th
Day of April, 1716, aged
13 Years

Here lyeth the Body of
JONATHAN, the youngest
Son of JEREMIAH WYRALL,
who departed this Life
the 7th Day of December,
Anno Domini 1714,
aged 13 Years

And of
BARBARA,
the Wife of
RICHARD DAVIS, and a
Daughter of JEREMIAH
WYRALL
the elder. She dyed
the 16th of Feb 1744,
aged 50 Years

IN MACHEN'S CHAPEL

ON A MARBLE MONUMENT IS THE FIGURE OF
AN ANGEL RESTING HIS RIGHT ARM ON THE ME-
DALLON OF EDWARD TOMKINS MACHEN, ESQ
AND UNDERNEATH THE FOLLOWING ARMS AND
INSCRIPTION

Arms, Gules, a Fefs Azure, between three Pelicans Heads erafed Or, for TOMKINS,—in paling
Three Eagles Heads erafed

In a Vault adjacent, reft the Remains of
EDW. TOMKINS MACHEN, of Faftbatch Court, Efq.
who exchanged Time for Eternity, April 10,
in the 72d Year of his Age, of Redemption 1778
Through Life,
Honour, and Integrity,
Goodnefs of Heart, and foundry of Judgment,
Sincerity in Friendfhip, and firmnefs in Religion,
invariably characterized
he Gentleman the Friend, and the Chriftian,
to the Memory of whom
this fhort, but true Recital is infcribed
by his affectionate Relict,
HANNAH

ON FLAT STONES

Here lyeth the Body of IMMANUEL, the
Son of Son of EDW. MACHEN, Efq and MARY
his Wife, who departed this Life the 6th Day of
Auguft Anno Domini 1698
And a Spread Eagle

Here lyeth interred the Body
of EDWARD, the eldeft Son of
RICHARD MACHEN, of Faftbatch
Court Efq who departed this Life
April 6, 1755, aged 5

---

ry, the Daughter of
RICHARD POWELL, Gent
of October 11, 1658

ANN, another Daughter,

Here lyeth, in hopes of a joyful
Refurrection, the Body of MARY, Wife
of EDW. MACHEN, Efq who departed
this Life Aug 13, Anno Dom 1707

JOHN MACHEN, the Son of EDW.
MACHEN and MARY his Wife, who
died April 1691

Alfo MARY, the Daughter of
RICHARD MACHEN, Gent and MARY
his Wife, who died April 30, 1709

And alfo the Body of MARY MACHEN,
late Wife of RICHARD MACHEN, Efq
who died May 12, A D 1751

To the Memory of MARY,
Relict of RICHARD MACHEN,
of Faftbach Court, Efq who
deceafed Jan 5, 1677
Refurgam

Alfo RICHARD, the Son of
RICHARD MACHEN, Gent
and MARY his Wife, who
died Feb 18, 1708-9

Here lyeth the Body of
RICHARD MACHEN the elder,
who departed this Life
the 10th Day of October, in the
Year of our Lord 1673
He married with MARY
CHARLETT, Daughter of
JOHN CHARLETT, Doctor of
Divinity, and had Iffue
13 Sons and 4 Daughters

And alfo here lieth the
Body of JOHN MACHEN, Gent
the Son of RICHARD MACHEN,
Efq by MARY his Wife,
who departed his Life the
1ft Day of May, Anno Dom 170

Here lieth the Body of JUDITH BROWNE,
Widow of JOHN BROWNE, late of this
Parifh, Gent and Daughter of RICHARD
MACHEN, Efq who departed this Life
the 5th of February, Anno Dom 1739

IN THE CHURCHYARD, ON TOMBS

JOHN JORDAN
died April 10, 1610

EDMUND JORDAN
died Nov 2, 1641

BENEDICK JORDAN
died Aug 1, 1661

Arms, a Lion rampant, between Eight Cross
Crosslet fitchy, for JORDAN, —impaling a Chevron,
between Three Lions Heads erased, for HALL.

ANN HALL, Widow,
died Dec —, 1708, aged 88

ANN, Wife of JOHN LELAND,
Gent Daughter of JOHN JORDAN,
by ELIZABETH his Wife,
born March 16, 1695,
and buried Oct 25, 1718

Mrs ELIZABETH JORDAN
died Sept 22, 1749, aged 81

Arms, Gules, a Chevron Or, between three
Cross Crosslets, and in Chief a Lion passant Argent,
for WYRALL,—impaling, on a Fess Three Mullets pierced, between Three Martlets, for BROWNE.

JEREMIAH WYRALL, Gent
died Feb 12, 1762, aged 43

MARTHA, Wife of
JEREMIAH WYRALL, Gent
died Jan 28, 1779, aged 82

WILLIAM BROWNE
died May 11, 1695, aged 79

WILLIAM BROWNE
died Sep —, 1693

JOHN BROWNE the elder
died Nov 15, 1719

RICHARD BROWNE, Gent
died Oct —, 1747, aged 63

MARY, Daughter of
RICHARD BROWNE, Gent
died Sep 20, 1754, aged 25
He Life was an instructive Proof
the Piety reconciles attended with Moderation,
not Contradicts with Levity,
to attain Pleasure becontentedly without Prejudice,
in doing Hope without Presumption
a severe Charity without Ostentation,
attending Christian Virtue
to as the span of Years
to make it perfect

RICHARD TRIGGE, Gent
died Dec 25, 1687

MARY his Wife
died Nov 30, 1728

RICHARD TRIGGE, Gent
died April 17, 1744

JANE the Wife of
THOMAS MARSHALL,
died July 8, 1712

THOMAS MARSHALL
died May 28, 1714, aged 92

MARGARET, the Wife of
GEORGE MARSHALL
died June 4, 1730, aged 41

GEORGE MARSHALL
died Sept 16, 1735, aged 66

JOHN POTTER
died Feb 8, 1729, aged 60

MARY his Wife
died March 13, 1733, aged 60

MARY, then Daughter,
Wife of RICHARD WYSHAM, junior,
died Jan 29, 1773, aged 73

JOAN TAYLOR
died Dec 18, 1730, aged 56

ALICE, Wife of WILLIAM AMBERY,
died June 13, 1737, aged 43

WILLIAM AMBERY
died May 15, 1753, aged 60

ANTHONY, then Son,
died March 20, 1771, aged 37

JANE, Wife of ANTHONY AMBERY,
died March 15, 1770, aged 74

WILLIAM HADDOCK
died Aug 10, 1738, aged 90

DOROTHY his Wife
died July 15, 1756, aged 65

WILLIAM BENNETT
died July 11, 1761, aged 72

MARY his Wife
died Jan 6, 1755, aged 78

ON FLAT AND HEAD STONES

	Died	Aged
Mary Elizabeth Brown	3 Oct 1781	—
Elizabeth, Wife of Joseph Ambery	1 Oct 1782	51
Mary, Wife of William Marshall	6 May, 1731	44
Richard Godwin	23 June, 1746	73
Elizabeth his Wife	27 Apr 1727	—
Providence Potter Hillersland	14 Aug 1749	72
Elizabeth his Wife	17 Nov 1760	82
John Hodges	19 Mar 1748	72
Hannah Lane his Daughter by Jane his Wife	11 June, 1747	35
Jane his Wife	5 Jan 1751	77
George Wintle, of Joyford	18 Apr 1732	43
Elizabeth his Wife	2 Mar 1736	62
Ann, Wife of George Wintle, of the Scrowls	18 Mar 1784	67
George Wintle, of the Berry	16 June, 1778	57
William Preece, of Whorthorns in the Parish of Newland	19 July, 1782	77
James Preece	17 May, 1771	71
Elizabeth, Wife of James Preece	5 Dec 1761	71
William Birt	23 Oct 1784	26

BISLEY CHURCH

MONUMENT OF A KNIGHT TEMPLAR IN BISLEY CHURCH

CONCERNING the Etymology of this Name, various have been the Conjectures

In Domesday Book, amongst others, an annual Rent is specified, as due to the Manor, of Two Quarts of Honey (2 Sext Mell) This Circumstance is singular, and seems to confirm the Idea, that this Parish derived its Name from *Bees*, so many of them being here cultivated, as to render their Produce of Consequence to the Demesne

The Parish of *Bisley* is so considerable as to Extent, as to be from the most accurate Computation from Twenty to Twenty-five Miles in Circumference The Village, which has been considered as a Town, since the Grant of a weekly Market, and Two annual Fairs, by King JAMES II lies in the Centre of the Hundred, which receives its Name from it, and is distant four Miles on the East from *Stroud*, Nine Westward from *Cirencester*, and from GLOUCESTER Ten on the South It is constituent of the Deanery of *Stonehouse*

This being the last Parish of that Division of the County called the *Cotswold*, the Land is extremely uneven, and the Soil various The Hills are Woodland, or tilled, the Vallies, which are very frequent, afford good Pasturage, watered by many Rivulets, from the Confluence of which the *Stroudwater* River is formed About the Year 1730, the Commons were measured, with an Intention of Inclosure, and the Number of Acres was ascertained to be 700, prior to which, they were much more extensive, and even at that Time, than now The Establishment of the Manufacture of Cloth introduced many new Inhabitants, who availed themselves of an undisputed Settlement on the Waste Lands A detached Village, on the Declivities of the *Great Common*, consists of these Cottages, to which, long Possession has given a prescriptive Right These are collectively called the *Lynches* A Tradition prevails, that this Place was anciently covered with Beech Wood, as Privilege of cutting Wood is stated in old Terriers of the various Estates This cannot be readily credited, for it is well known, that Beech, the spontaneous Produce of the Soil, is not easily eradicated, especially if the Ground be not applied to Tillage

The Benefice is a Vicarage, the Impropriation of which, once belonging to the College of Westbury, is now possessed by the Hon THOMAS COVENTRY BULKELEY In 1660, when *Stroud* was separated from *Bisley* is to Parochial Affairs, it appears, by the Endowment made by REGINALD BRYAN, Bishop of Worcester, a Copy of which is preserved in the Registry of that Diocese, "that the Tythe of all "the Corn and Hay belonging to the Impropriation, and all Tythes of Lamb and Wool, with Ob- "lation, Offerings and all privy Tythes, and the full Tythes of the Glebe, were allotted to the "Vicar" These Rights, whether dormant from Custom, or compromited by a temporary *Modus*, cannot be ascertained for the Vicarage The Church is dedicated to *all Saints*, and is spacious and handsome It has a Nave and Two Aisles When it was re-pewed in 1771, a fresco Painting was discovered, of about Ten Feet square, against the North Wall, of "ST MICHAEL subduing the Fallen Angels," in very lively Colours, but it was immediately defaced The Arches, which divide the Nave from the South Aisle are not correspondent with those on the opposite Side Under a Window is a finished Figure of a Knight Templar, of which an Engraving is annexed, On the Battlements on the Outside, are the Arms of MORTIMER, and CLARE, and these Characters, ❦ ❦ ❦ The Joints of the Roof, which is of Timber Frame, are ornamented with the Cognizance of the Houses of YORK and STAF- FORD These Circumstances seem to prove that this Aisle, at least was built in the Reign of Ed- ward IV The Steeple, which is a clumsy Obelisk, though so conspicuous as to serve as a Landmark, contains Six Bells, and over the Chancel Door is a Gothic Pediment in the best Style of that Time A large House now dilapidated, belongs to the Impropriation There is said to have been a Chauntry in this Church, but of the Revenues there is no Account The Chauntry House and Land in *Pydry* were appendant to the College of *Westbury upon Trim*, near *Bristol*

The MORTIMERS, Earls of MARCH, were Lords of this Manor for nearly three Centuries, when it devolved to Edward Duke of York (afterwards King EDWARD IV), the Heir general of that Family THOMAS MASTER, D D held it in the beginning of the last Century, and about the End of it, it passed by Purchase from Sir ROBERT ATKYNS, Knight, to the Family of STEPHENS, of *Lypiat*, the last of whom, JOHN STEPHENS, Esq died in the Year 1776 His Nephew, THOMAS BACHOFF DE LA BERE, Esq is the present Possessor

In this Parish are Nine Tythings, or Districts, which have their separate Tythingmen In 1760, a very populous Village The most considerable of these, called *Higgins Court* was long held by the DENS, who (as it appears from the Register) were settled here in the Reign of EDWARD VI formerly

...ded in the Family of MILLS   2 *Chalford*   The greatest Part of the Valley, called *Chalford Bottom*, belongs this Tything   On the River which passed through it many Mills are erected, and employed in the Manufacture of Cloth   the most ancient of these coeval with the more general Introduction of that Manufacture into this County about the Year 1500   It is held by Lease under *Corpus Christi College*, Oxon   For the Service of this populous District, a very neat Chapel was founded by Subscription 1722   The Stipend of the Minister is supplied by the Inhabitants   W TAYLOR, Esq dying in 17__, devised the Interest of 50l after the Death of his Mother Mrs HESTHER TAYLOR, as a farther Support   This Village, which, from the excessive Acclivity of the opposite Hills, is truly romantic, contains many handsome Houses, one of which has been long the Residence of the Family of BLACKWELL   It has been compared, by Travellers of Taste, to the Valley in which the *German Spa* is situated   Its Waters, though possessing no medicinal Quality, have extraordinary Powers of Petrifaction   The general Effect of the Prospect has suffered much by the great navigable Canal, now completing, from the *Severn* to the *Thames*, which is conducted through the whole of it   Nature, no where more luxuriant, is subdued to Art   3 *Througham and Grove*, belonging, for many Generations, to the Family of SMITH, now extinct   The present Proprietor is the Relict of the late MARMADUKE BERDOE, M D   Of this Estate are large Quarries of Tile   4 *Bidfield*, to NICHOLAS WEBB, Esq   The Claim of a separate Manor is disallowed   5 *Tunly and Dinneway*, in which the Family of HANCOX have an ancient House and little where are preserved the compleat Furniture and Apparel of the Age of Queen ELIZABETH   Of 6 *Oakridge*, 7 *Burgage*, 8 *Avenage*, and 9 *Steanbridge*, there is nothing worthy Remark

At *Ferris's Court* the STEWARTS were settled, for one of whom is the first Inscription in the Church   They were of the YIOMANRY of *England*, a respectable Order of Men, who, from the Practice of consolidating small Farms, are hardly known in these Days   Sir R ATKYNS has retained the Tradition from CAMDEN, that the celebrated ROGER BACON was a Native of this Parish   That Honour is claimed by other Places, on clearer Evidence

---

BENEFACTIONS.

Mr THOMAS BUTT gave by Will, 1688, for Bread to the Poor, and a Sermon on Easter Monday, Land vested in the Churchwardens, the annual Produce of which is 1l 10s

Mr WALTER RIDLER gave by Will, 169_, to such as do not receive Alms from the Parish, the Sum of 300l the annual Produce of which is 15l, charged on the Estate of SAMUEL NISBITT, Esq of *Harescomb Gloucestershire*, and disposed of by the Minister and Churchwardens

Mrs JOAN RIDLER gave by Will, 171_, for the same Purpose, the Sum of 300l which is vested and disposed of in the same Manner as the former

Mrs MARY RIDLER gave by Will, 171_, for teaching Children to read, 100l the annual Produce 5l, and it is vested in the Minister and Churchwardens

Mr SAMUEL ALLEN gave by Will, 1734, to cloath Five Widows, a House and Land, vested in the Minister and Churchwardens, the annual Produce of which is 6l 2s

Mr WILLIAM WISE gave by Will, date not mentioned, for Linen Cloth to the Poor, 60l vested in the Minister and Churchwardens the annual Income 3l

Mrs _____ gave by Will, date not mentioned, for the same Purpose, 80l laid out in Land, with 50l supplied by the Parish, vested in the Minister and Churchwardens the annual Produce __

Mrs _____ gave by Will, 173_, for clothing and teaching Ten Boys to read and write, Land, vested in NATHANIEL WISE, Esq the annual Produce of which is 23l

A Fund for Repairs of the Church, and other pious Purposes, vested in Sixteen Feoffees, Eight now living, the annual Produce of which is 47l 5s the Time of the Donation and the Donor unknown

Besides the above, the following Charities are mentioned in the Table of Benefactions

17__ Mr THOMAS ROGERS, Blackwell Hall Factor, gave in Money 25l

17_9, CHARLES COX, Esq Dean Spratt 10l 10s

17_5 THOMAS RANDELL, of *Gloucester*, Esq Cloth and Bread 5l

Mr R__ Mr RICHARD BUTTER, Vicar of *Bringham*, in Bread

[footnotes, badly faded:]

A liberal Education of a Bishop TANNER before King EDWARD VI may be allowed an exhibition, a ...

...

INCUMBENTS	PATRONS	INCUMBENTS	PATRONS
—— Robert Amond,		1716 Stephen Phillips, B A	King George I
1572 John Lightfoot,	Queen Elizabeth	1740 Stephen Phillips, M A	King George II
1588 Christopher Windle,	The fame	1782 Edw Hawkins, M A	King George III
—— John Sedgewick,			
—— Daniel Lawford,			
1641 Richard Britton	King Charles I		
1679 Joseph Lodge, M A	King Charles II		
1681 Isaac Prieft, M A	The fame		
From Sir Robert Atkyns			

PRESENT LORD OF THE MANOR,

THOMAS BACHOTT DE LA BERE, Eq.

The Perfons fummoned from this Place by the Heralds in 1682 in 1683 were

Thomas Chitterbuck, Gent   William Rudle, Gent
William Freeman, Gen   Mr Prieft, Clerk,
Edward Townshend, Gent   William Hancox, Gent
Robert Poole, Gent

At the Election in 1776 One Hundred and Four Freeholders polled from this Parish

The Register commences with Baptifms in 1548 From that Period to 1598 it is our Minuter remarkably fair fuppofed to have been copied by CHRISTOPHER WINDLE, then Vicar During the grand Rebellion it was kept with fingular Care and Exactnefs

ANNUAL ACCOUNT OF MARRIAGES, BIRTHS, AND BURIALS, IN THIS PARISH

A D	Mar	Bir	Bur	A D	Mar	Bir	Bur	A D	Mar	Bir	Bur	A D	Mar	Bir	Bur
1751	9	157	67	1791				1801				1811			
1752	56	54	77	1792				1802				1812			
1753	23	107	97	1793				1803				1813			
1754	17	83	114	1794				1804				1814			
1755	13	113	123	1795				1805				1815			
1756	13	108	94	1796				1806				1816			
1757				1797				1807				1817			
1788				1798				1808				1818			
1789				1799				1809				1819			
1790				1800				1810				1820			

INSCRIPTIONS IN THE CHURCH

IN THE CHANCEL

A PORTRAIT IN STONE, IN THE DRESS OF THE TIMES HOLDING A BOOK

Arms Argent a Chevron Sable in Chief a Pattée cinded Gules for Freame —impaling, a Chevron between Points, in Chief Three Croffes Pattée Azure for Lewis

M S

GULIELMI FREAME, Generofi
DOMO DE FREAME de Epney, Armiger,
Alter oriundo Ebo,
Caput in superco Chrifti in Amico Joviata,
fumma Benevolentia effecti,
Ut permanerent fui debiteri relique ct
Annoriet vite liber
Feb 10ᵐᵒ, Anno { Eis fur 54,
{ Domini 1696

Arms Azure, a Lion rampant between Eight Four de Lis Or, —impaling, Chevron between Three Spear Heads

Juxta hunc lapidem

Requiefcit quod mortue eft

ROBERTI POOLE, de Browns Hill, Junipenti,

Qui vitam hunc de mortuae

Quinto die Martii,

Anno Dom MDCXX,

etatis fuæ LXXX

Pie Memorie Church Soceri

SARA CROME, de Minchin, Generofa,

Hoc ponit Monumentum

Arms, a Cross Moline, between Four Bars of
Wheat,—impaling, on a Fess between Three
Martlets, Three Annulets

Here lies the Body of
THOMAS FREAME, of Lypiate, Esq
who departed this Life the 5th Day
of January, 1659

M S
Viri Reverendi D SIMONIS PRIEST, A M
Coll Regin Cant olim Alumni hujusque
per Annos 24 Ecclesiæ vigilantissimi
Pastoris, qui Morte heu crudeli nobis
abreptus est Julii 16 A D 1715, æt suæ 61.

Hic inta 4 etiam Liberorum,
qui posuerunt Mortalitatis exuvias
obiit

ELIZABETHA, Apr 26, 1712,

ISAACUS, Junii 9, 1685,

MARTHA, Sept 5, 1719,

MARIA, Sept 29, 1714.

Porro juxta Sacrum hoc Altare
MARTHÆ, sororis Domini SIMONIS PRIEST,
ANNÆQ REYNOLDS, Viduæ, cineres
Sepultæ jacent, quarum hæc ævi jam
prægnata decedit Feb 9, A D 1706,
ætatis suæ 103, illa Jan 10, A D 1686

Mortem quoque ELIZ uxoris D SIMONIS PRIEST
(cui Amoris nexu indissolubili
conjuncta fuit), nos fulmine una cum
teneris orbis (proh dolor) ciatis
lacrymis patheticè lugemus!
Obiit Domini 1723,
Aprili 13 Anno ætat suæ 69

Near this Altar lieth the Body
of ESTHER, the Wife of the Rev Mr
ISAAC PRIEST who died in Child-bed
December the 5th, 1734

The Rev SECUNDUS ISAAC PRIEST
was buried June 24, 1757, aged 62

Arms, a Chief vaire, for JAYNE,—impaling,
on a Chevron between Three Eagles Heads erased,
Three Trefoils slipped, for KILL

In a Vault underneath this Monument
are deposited the Remains of
WILLIAM JAYNE, eldest Son of
THOMAS JAYNE, of this Parish, Gent
who died the 29th Day of July, 1735,
aged 14 Years

Also SARAH, the Wife of the
said THOMAS JAYNE who died
March 30, 1744, aged 9

Also THOMAS JAYNE, the youngest Son
of the said THOMAS JAYNE, who
died the 1st of Oct 1745, aged 8

Also Jane, the Wife of HENRY JAYNE,
of this Parish, Gent who died
Dec 2, 1758, aged 50

Also Sarah the Daughter of Henry Jayne
died June 10, 1760, aged 50

ON A NEAT WHITE MARBLE MONUMENT OVER
THE DOOR

Arms, a Sword in Pale, between Two Lions
rampant adorsed

Underneath the outside of this Door lie
interred the Remains of WILLIAM TAYLOR,
of Chalford Bottom in this Parish Esq who filled
the Office of High Sheriff in the Year 1742, and
was an acting Justice of the Peace for this County
He died the 30th of May, 1749, aged 64

Adjoining to the same Grave, in a new Vault
lie deposited the Remains of WILLIAM TAYLOR,
of Hurst Coll Oxon only Son and Heir of the said
WILLIAM TAYLOR, by HESTER his Wife
He died the 24th of October, in the Year 1773,
aged 27 Years
greatly regretted, being a Gentleman of the most
promising Hopes and Expectation, and highly
esteemed by all his Neighbours and Acquaintance
The said HESTER TAYLOR, his disconsolate Mother,
out of Pious Regard to her Husband and Son,
erected this Monument

Arms, Per Chevron Azure and Argent, Two
Falcons rising Or, for STEPHENS

Underneath
this Monument are
deposited the Remains of THOMAS STEPHENS, Esq
Barrister at Law, Steward of the Sheriff's Court,
and Deputy Town Clerk of the City of Bristol,
younger Son of THOMAS STEPHENS, of Over Lypiat
Esq whom in several Parliaments served as Knight
of the Shire for this County, and was Lord of this Manor
His great Candour and Benevolence &c
entitled him to the Esteem of all that knew him
and he was not only an Ornament to his Profession,
but also to the worthy and ancient Family
from whence he descended
He died greatly lamented the 7th Day of December,
in the Year 1745, aged 46 Years.

ON BRASS PLATES NEAR THE DOOR

Near this Place lies the Body
of WILLIAM POOLE, Clothier, who died
Jan 5, 1739 40, æt 67

Near this Place lie the Remains
of WILLIAM ROBERTS, of Chalford, Gent
who died Aug 9, 177 , aged 49 Years

ON FLAT STONES

THOMAS CLUTTERBUCK, Esq
departed this Life July 21, 1655,
aged 46 Years

M S
RICHARDI BRITTON,
Qui
Hinc instituendo Ecclerum per Septem &
Triginta Annorum ſeries Pastoris erat
Qui Vigilantissime præfectus est,
obiit, Dec 9th, A D 1679, æt 56

Here reſteth the Body of S[...]AH
the Wife of RICHARD B[...]TTON, Paſtor
o this Church, who deceaſed Auguſt 1[...],
1071, [...] his Age 54

Here lieth the Body of ANN
WATKINS, the Mother of John WATKINS,
hich lieth under this Tombe,
and Wife of John WATKINS of
Todenhore, who departed the 9th
of Auguſt, Anno Domini 1664

IN THE NAVE

On a ſtill FLAT STONE, and the Figure of
a Woman, Six Sons, and Five Daughters in
Brass. On a Plate the following Inscription
in old Characters.

Pray for the Soule of Kateryn Shewell late
the Wife of Thomas Shewell, which Kateryn
deceſed the [...]th Day of January the Yere of
our Lord M[...]
On whoſe Soule Jheſu have Mercye   Amen

Arms, TAYLOR, as before

In Memory of THOMAS TAYLOR,
of this Town, Gent who died Sept
2[...], 1[...], in the 58th Year of his Age

Arms TAYLOR, as before

Near to this Place,
in the Church Yard, oppoſite
the Porch Door, are depoſited the
Remains of Mr WILLIAM TAYLOR, late
of Ch[...]ord Hill in this Parish Cloſier,
who died Nov [...]4, 177[...] in the
70th Year of his Age

John alſo his eldeſt Son lies buried in
the ſame Place. He died Nov 1,
1760, [...] 24

Mrs TAYLOR, Relict of the ſaid WILLIAM TAYLOR,
out of a pious Regard to the Memory of her
worthy Husband and Son, erected
this Monument

To the Memory of
HANNAH the Widow of
JOHN PANTING who died
December 14 17[...], aged 25 Years

Arms, Two Saltires in Pale, Creſt, a Lion
rampant

In Memory of theſe, Parents
JOHN MILLS, of this Parish, Gent
died Feb 3 Anno Domini 1718
HESTER his Wife died Nov 10, A D 1701

Arms on a Bend, Three Owls

Near this Place
lieth the Body of
SCHOLASTICA SAYLL, the Wife of
Mr WILLIAM SAYLL, of Ch[...]ord
Bottom, who departed this Life
Jan 18, 175[...] aged 5[...] Years

Alſo Two of their Children namely,
SAMUEL and RICHARD

SAMUEL died Aug 20 175[...],
aged 13 Months

RICHARD August 31 175[...],
aged 6 Weeks

JOHN, their Son, died Nov 9, 1752,
aged 6 Years

Arms, a Chevron, between Three Ploughs

In the North Iſle of the Church near the Remains of a much loved
Wife, Father, and Mother, lie thoſe of THOMAS SMART, Esq of Gray
in this Parish, who bearing with Fortitude, and the moſt engaging
Goodneſs and Cheerfulneſs diſcharged all the Offices of this Life,
exchanged it for Immortality on the 6th of December in the Year
of our Lord 1745, and in the Sixty third Year of his Age

There alſo lie the Bodies of his Son WILLIAM and Two [...] the
former died in his Infancy the latter on the [...]th of April, 1[...] aged 11

This Monument, with the Juſteſt ſenſe of Affection Gratitude and
Duty was erected to their Memory by their ſurviving Brothers RICHARD and SAMUEL Esq

The abovementioned THOMAS SMART, Esq and [...] were another
Son of the Name of RICHARD, elder Brother of theſe WILLIAM
THOMAS and RICHARD, who died very young and are buried at
DONSBORNE ROUSE

ON BRASS PLATES AGAINST
THE PILLARS, &c

In Memory of THOMAS BUTLER,
Son of JOHN BUTLER, of Rockwood,
Clothier who departed this Life the
2d Day of March, Anno Dom 1688,
and his Body resteth in the Middle
Alley of this Church, near this Place
He gave to this Parish 30s. per Ann
for ever, that is to say, to the Minister
for preaching a Sermon on Easter Monday,
and 20s. to the Poor, to be disposed of
in small Bread, according to the Discretion
of the Churchwardens, the same Day, yearly

Here lieth interred the Body of ANN, the
Wife of JOHN MOORE, the youngest Daughter
of JOHN HANCOX, of the Manor of Lunley

Also DINAH, who was borne the first
Friday in Lent, Anno Dom 1597,
and departed this Life the 7th of April,
Anno Dom 1649

In Memory of WALTER HANCOX,
of Dense in this Parish, who
departed this Life March 22, 1742-3,
aged 65 Years

In Memory of MARTHA, Daughter
of JOHN MILES and wife of JOSEPH LAWRENCE,
who died Feb 1, 1734, aged 72

DEBORAH MILES, her Sister,
died March 23, 1734, aged 71

ON PLAI SIONES

Intombed here lieth the Body of
NATHANIEL RIDLER, Clothier who departed
this Life April 5, 1655

Here resteth the Body of THOMAS
RIDLER, the Son of NATHANIEL RIDLER,
of Chalford Clothier, who departed
this Life April 5, Anno Dom 1689

NATHANIEL RIDLER of Chalford,
ob ...

ELIZABETH Wife of NATHANIEL RIDLER,
of Chalford, ob ...

Near this Place the Son of
NATHANIEL RIDLER ... of Chalford,
ob May 1, ...

Here resteth the Body of JOANE RIDLER,
the Daughter of NATHANIEL RIDLER,
of Chalford, Clothier, who departed
this Life Oct 4, Anno Dom 1714

In Memory of MARY, the Daughter
of NATHANIEL RIDLER, of Chalford, Clothier,
who departed this Life the 17th Day of
August, Anno Dom 1715, aged 42 Years

She gave One Hundred Pounds to her
Sister JOAN Three Hundred Pounds,
and her Uncle WALTER Three Hundred
Pounds to the Poor of this Parish

Near this Place lieth the Body of
THOMAS ILLS, of Oxbridge, who died
March 28, 1714, aged ...

Also in Memory of ANNE, the
Wife of WILLIAM DIAND, and Grand
daughter of THOMAS ILLS, of this Parish,
who died the 9th of January, 1741, aged ...

Near this Place lie
interred the Bodies of WILLIAM BUTT, of
Chalford, Clothier, and CHRISTIAN his Wife
Also of WILLIAM BUTT, their Son,
who departed this Life Oct 23, 1732,
aged 45 Years
And Also of ANNE his Daughter,
who died Oct 12, 1744, aged 5 Weeks

ANN, Wife of THOMAS SMART,
of Troughan, obiit Oct 24, 1710

THOMAS SMART Generosus,
obiit 24 die January, A D 1725,
ætatis suæ 75
SARA SMART, Vidua ob July 25,
1736, ætatis suæ ...

THOMAS SMART, late of Troughan,
Gent ob Dec 16, 1716, aged 60

ESTHER, the Wife of JOHN MOORE the Elder
and Daughter of JOHN CRIPPS, of Cirencester,
died March 1, 1652

THOMAS BATT of this Parish
Clothier buried Oct 2, 17 .. aged 72

SUSANNA, Wife of WALTER HANCOX,
departed this Life Sept 16, 1653

WILLIAM HANCOX of Dense,
obiit Dec 17, 1617

NATHANIEL HANCOX, of this Parish,
born Jun 14, 1675, died Jun 24,
1701 aged 25 Years and two Days

In Memory of MARY the Daughter of
EDWARD ... who departed
this Life May 9, 1725

IN THE PORCH

HENRY TWISSELL, of Oakridge,
obiit Nov. 11, 16_7

In Memory of the following Persons buried near this Place

A.D.		Aged
16_6, June 14, THOMAS TWISSELL, of Chalford, Clothier, died	-	40
1696, Nov. _, ISABEL his Wife, Daughter of ROBERT HOLLOW, of Great Witcombe		78
1734, THOMAS TWISSELL, their Son, of Oakridge Farm	-	87
1702, MARY his Wife, Daughter of ROBERT RIDLER, of Quarhouse, Clothier	-	49
169_, Two ROBERTS, their Children		
1712, April 1_, WILLIAM, their Son	-	34
1734, Aug. 23, The Rev. THOMAS TWISSELL, their Son, Rector of Wool Bedding, Sussex		56
1749, March 15, JOHN TWISSELL, their Son, died in the Year of his Age	-	77
1702, Also SARAH their Daughter	- - - -	7_

IN THE CHURCH YARD, ON TOMBS

ON A BRASS PLATE AGAINST THE
SOUTH SIDE OF THE CHURCH

Also, On a Tomb between Three
Fir-llop, a Mullet Gules, a Dexter
lion, holding, as it were by

Here lyeth the Body of ANN, the
Wife of ED___ FARRANT of the Parish
of Stroud, Clothier, and Daughter of
Mr ___ C___, died Feb 4th,
1_ ___ his Wife, who was
___ died ___ Day of June 1744,
aged 30 Year

Also in Memory of RICHARD their Son

——— SAUN___ of this Par___h,
died Feb 8 1702

D___ RALPH his Wife
died Jun 18 1713

——————

JOHN KR___
died O___ _ 17_3, aged 51

D___ ___ Keturah ___ his Friend,
died April ___

N___ ___ Wife
died He___

___ of ___ ___ Children

R___ ___

M___ his Daughter
March 1_, ___

——————

JOH. S___ of his ___
of this Parish, died ___

JOSEPH BENNETT
died Dec 24, 1724, aged 63

MARY his Wife
died Feb 16, 1753 aged 84

JOSEPH their Son
died Feb 2, 17 59, aged 60

RALPH RANDELL,
of this Parish, Clothier,
died Jun 17, 17_7 aged 52

MARY his Wife
died Sep 16, 1750, aged 51

RICHARD BUTT of Chalford in this
Parish, died June 12, 1741, aged 78

ANNE his Wife, Daughter of
Mr SAMUEL SAUNDERS of Tetbury,
died Feb 10, 1750, aged 6_

——————

JOHN FREEMAN,
of this Parish, Clothier,
died ___ 51, _

JOAN his Wife
died June 7, 1672

ROWLAND their Son
died May 6, 1713

——————

THOMAS FREEMAN
of Druisham in this Parish
died Oct _, 1735 aged _

ELEANOR his Wife
died June 30, 17__, aged _

THOMAS FREEMAN
died Oct _ 1720 aged _

FRANCES, Wife of WILLIAM FREEMAN
of the ___ died ___,
died June _, ___ aged __

ROBERT ___ of their ___
died Nov _ 1712 aged 5_

ANNE his Wife
died Nov _ 1731 aged 6_

JOHN JONES
died January _, 1762, aged 7_

MARY his Wife
died Nov 12, 1750, aged 56

ANNE, Wife of JOHN TURNER JONES
died June _, 17__, aged _

WILLIAM ALLEN of this Parish
died March 17 1725 aged 84

ELIZABETH his ___
died Oct _, 1711, aged 73

FAITH, the Wife of THOMAS CAPNER,
of this Town, died June 10, 1756
aged 3_

MARY, Wife of THOMAS CAPNER
Dec _ 17__, aged 62

SARAH, Daughter of WILLIAM ALLEN
died June 11, ___ aged 29

ELIZABETH, Wife of RICHARD CHAND___
___ ___ Daughter of
WILLIAM ALLEN died April _ 1716,
aged 51

ON FLAT STONES

THOMAS HERRAN
died Feb _ 17__

ELIZABETH his Wife
died ___

JOHN FREEMAN
died May 1_, ___

___ died ___

___ their Son
___

MARTHA, Wife of THOMAS FREEMAN
died Dec _, 17__, aged _

JOHN FREEMAN
died April _, 17__, aged _

Elizabeth, Wife of Richard Coke, of Stroud, died Feb 3, 1764, aged 81

William Gurner, died Oct 10, 1735, aged 71

William his Son died Nov 26, 1755, aged 65

Samuel Damsell, senior, died April 3, 1720, aged 58

Ann, the Wife of Samuel Damsell, died Aug 6, 1737, aged 89

Ann their Daughter died June 2, 1724, aged 19

Elizabeth, Daughter of Sam Damsell, of this Parish, died March [illegible] 172[illegible]

Sarah, Daughter of William Carner, died Oct 16 1715

Mary, Wife of Isaac Restell, died Feb 24 175[illegible], aged 57

James Pantin of this Parish, Baker, died Nov 29, 1765, aged [illegible]

Sarah his Wife died Feb [illegible]3 1760, aged 63

Thomas White, Son of Francis and Sarah White, Yeoman of Stroud, died March 12, 1767 aged 21

Esther, Wife of Isaac Restell, of this Parish, Baker, died Dec [illegible], 175[illegible], aged 45

Ann, Wife of Isaac Restell, died May [illegible] [illegible]

Francis Arthur, junior Mal[illegible] [illegible] Lypiatt in the Parish of Stroud, died June 14, 1750, aged 26

Elizabeth Wife of Walter Hancox, of Frampton in the Parish of Sapperton, died March 23 1723

Grace Wife of Peter Clissold, de[illegible] 18 June, 17[illegible]

Peter Clissold died April [illegible], 175[illegible], aged 88

Susanna his Wife died Sept [illegible] 1762, aged 76

Ann, Wife of Samuel Bucknell, of this Parish died Oct 19, 1774 aged 35

Francis Franklin died Sept 1[illegible], 176[illegible] aged 60.

John Stephens died May 1[illegible], 1758, aged 76

[illegible] his Wife [illegible] [illegible] [illegible] of Bisley, [illegible]

[illegible] Daughter [illegible]

[illegible] died [illegible]

[illegible]

George Smart, Yeoman, died Sep 17 1707

Nathaniel Cook of this Parish, Clothier, died Feb 13, 1760, aged 55

Johannes Gould, Generosus, June 10 1712

Elizabeth Wife of Will Moreton, of the Parish of Rodborough, died Jan 8 1773, aged 70

Elizabeth Batt died Feb 25, 17[illegible]9

Roger [illegible], Clothier, died May 29, 1711

Eleanor his Relict died Aug 16, 1711

William Watkins Clothier, of the Parish of Stroud, died Jan 1, 1767, aged 68

Catherine his Wife died April 22, 176[illegible] aged 78

John Berriman, Yeoman, died March [illegible], 1[illegible]4[illegible], aged 56

John Lacy died May 6, 171[illegible], aged 2[illegible]

Mary Wife of John Bidmead, August 25, 173[illegible], aged 49

Jeremiah Bidmead died April 1[illegible], 1743

[illegible] his Wife died Oct 22, 1739 both aged 78

Timothy Cox of this Parish Yeoman, died Sep 14 Sept 17[illegible]7, aged 44

John Winston died March 7, 1755, aged 89

Catherine his Wife died Nov 24, 1[illegible]33, aged 59

Thomas Bartlett, of this Parish, died Nov 21, 1781, aged 68

John Aldridge died April 24 1737 aged 67

Jane his Wife died April 21, 1713 aged 36

Jane their Daughter died Sept [illegible], 1736, aged 30

Jane the Wife of Peter Clissold, died Nov 11, 176[illegible], aged [illegible]

William Bullock of Stroud in this County, died May 1[illegible] 17[illegible]2, aged 78

Ann his Wife died Oct 14, [illegible], aged [illegible]7

John [illegible], of this Town Cooper, [illegible]

Thomas [illegible] of this Town Yeoman died March [illegible] aged [illegible]

[illegible] Wife [illegible] Clissold, died [illegible] 1785 aged 50

James Kibble, who lived a Servant to John Stephens of Lypiatt 20 Years died March 9, 17[illegible], aged [illegible]0

Alexander [illegible], late [illegible] to John Stephens, Esq died Dec 18, 17[illegible], aged 51

Sarah, Daughter of John Keen, died July 22, 1747, aged 23

Thomas Blanch, Yeoman, died Oct [illegible], 1783, aged 41

John Cox of this Parish, died April 21 1769 aged 51

Betty his Wife died Sept 7, 1772 aged 5[illegible]

Hannah Wife of Daniel Cook, of this Parish, Yeoman died Nov 14, 1770, aged 83

Richard Pecker died January [illegible], 1707

Mary Wife of Edmund Lightbick, died March 2 1728, aged [illegible]9

William and John, Sons of John and Eleanor Morse

William died June 10, 1730 aged [illegible]

John died Nov 10 1731, aged 19

William and Thomas, Sons of John and Eleanor Morse

William died July 16, 171[illegible]

Thomas died Oct 6, 17[illegible], aged [illegible]

Mary, Wife of John Nash, of Brown's Hill in this Parish, Clothier, died Dec 10, 173[illegible], aged [illegible]

Sarah their Daughter and Wife of William Parham of Chalford, Clothier died March 2 17[illegible]3

Isaac Nash their Son died Jul 2, 1734

Elizabeth, Daughter of John Nash, of Brown's Hill, Clothier, died May 2[illegible], 1[illegible]1, aged [illegible]2

John, Son of John Nash, of Brown's Hill, Clothier, died Feb [illegible], aged [illegible]

Roger Batt was buried Sep [illegible] 1740, aged [illegible]0

Martha his Wife died March [illegible]

[illegible] died Sept [illegible] 17[illegible]4 aged 41

Sarah Wife of [illegible], of the [illegible]

[illegible] of Bisley died [illegible] 12 [illegible]5 aged [illegible]

Nathaniel Clissold, of Bisley, died June [illegible] 176[illegible] aged [illegible]

Rebecca, Daughter of Jos Clissold died [illegible] 17, 17[illegible]

John Clissold
died Dec -, 1686.

George Rogers, of Buslage,
Clothier, died May 27, 1757, aged 37

Elizabeth, Wife of Thomas Clissold,
died June 16, 1688.

Thomas Rogers, of Cattswood in
this Parish, Gent died
Feb 14, 1759, aged 35

Hester Wife of Thomas Smith,
of this Town, died
April 17, 1771, aged 47

Ann, Wife of Richard Rogers,
of Toadsmoor, died
Aug 13, 1727, aged 76

Anna Brown, Widow and Relict
of Mr Robert Brown, late of Stroud,
Apothecary, and Daughter of
Thomas Rogers of Cattswood
in his Parish Gent died
June 9, 1760, aged 74

William Tollson, of this Parish,
Yeoman, died June 1, 1783,
aged 60

John Wyatt, of Stroud,
died March 28, 1763, aged 49

Daniel Wyatt of Avnash in this
Parish died Sept 19, 1783 aged 42

Walter Sewell
died March 8, 166-

Thomas his Son
died Feb. 2, 1694

Joan his Wife
died Sept -0, 1714

Jane, Daughter of Thomas Showell,
of Ferris Court, Yeoman,
died Oct 1764 aged 32

John Sewell
of Ferris Court in the Parish of Stroud,
Yeoman died Jan 5 1780, aged 45

John, the Son of John Sewell,
died Dec 10, 1751 aged 23

Mary, Wife of John Sewell, junior,
died Dec 5, 1783 aged 51

Jane, the Wife of William Smart,
died Feb 20 1762, aged 23

Andrew Smart
buried Oct. 14 1681

Elizabeth, Relict of John Stratford,
died April 9, 1761 aged 52

John Stratford, late of this Parish,
Yeoman, died Dec 20, 1773, aged 57

Stephen Nibiett,
died March 21, 1771, aged 67

Martha his first Wife
died Jan 3, 1758, aged 55

William Turner
died Feb 7, 1714, aged 79.

Elizabeth his Daughter
died March 31, 1703

Sarah Wife of William Turner,
died June 6, 1737, aged 76

John, Son of William
and Sarah Turner,
died May 14 1721, aged 21

Thomas Dowell
died Sep 1, 1664

Judith his Wife
died Oct 31, 1673

Alice, Wife of James Lowell,
died Jan 1 1719 20

Edward Gregory, of this Parish,
died June 13, 1759, aged 59

Martha his Wife
died Feb 26 1761, aged 57

Henry Mason, of Bisler,
died June 27, 1767, aged 72

Ruth his Wife Daughter
of Richard Chew, died Dec 6, 1755,
aged 46

Benjamin Grazebrook, of this Town,
died July 7, 1758, aged 62

Ann his Wife
died April 4, 1763, aged 70

Benjamin Neale, of this Parish,
Yeoman died Feb 1, 1776 aged 81

Mary, Relict of Benjamin Neale,
died July 31 1782, aged 73

Thomas Keene
died Aug 3, 1752, aged 73

Mary his Wife
died Feb. 9 1750, aged 78

ON HEAD STONES.

	Died	Aged		Died	Aged
William, Son of William and June W. of this Parish	20 July, 1781	17	Elizabeth their Daughter	28 Jan 1778	61
Ann, Daughter of Thomas and Ann Windsor	2, Jan 1787	13	Sarah, Wife of Thomas Bartlet	26 Jan 1761	14
Anthony Bidmead	10 May, 1751	93	Thomas Vaughan	20 June, 1769	72
Martha his Wife	1 Apr 1720	60	Mary his Wife	19 Jan 1	60
Martha, Wife of William Biddle	15 May, 1760	52	Charles Denman	17 Apr 1760	76
Daniel Davis of this Parish	18 May, 1748	53	John Seed	28 Apr 1765	5
Ann his Wife	15 Feb 1761	69	Elizabeth his Wife	13 Feb 1752	66
Richard Davis	8 May, 1762	48	Edward Seed	16 Jan 1743	1-
Matthias Welch, of this Town	8 July, 1769	74	Thomas Ween	- May, 1737	61
Elizabeth his Wife	30 Dec 1758	68	Hester his Wife	22 Jan 1756	58
Hannah their Daughter	25 Dec 1751	36	Ann Wife of James Innell of Hampton	21 July, 1704	40
Thomas their Son	17 June, 1759	35	Joan Wife of John Ricketts, Clerk, of Stroud	18 Jan 1738	85

XLII.   B I T T O N.

THE River *Avon* divides this Parish from the County of *Somerset* on the South, which is situate in the Hundred of *Langley* and *Swineshead*, and the Deanery of *Hawkesbury*. Its Distance from BRISTOL is Six Miles on the East, and Thirty eight on the South from GLOUCESTER. By the last Perambulation it was found to have a Circumference of Thirty Miles.

The Soil in general consists of Loam, or strong Clay. The Pasture Lands exceed the Arable in a Proportion of Two Thirds. The Fossil Productions are Coal, and Iron Ore, in very large Quantities.

Of this Parish, the far greater Part is within the Limits of the Forest of *Kingswood*, where are Coal Mines of extreme Depth, and in the other Division of it are erected Furnaces for smelting of Copper Ore, and other Metallic Preparations, for which very spacious Buildings were erected about Thirty Years since. The River *Boyd*, passing through this District to join the *Avon*, is particularly serviceable to these Manufactories.

The Benefice is a Vicarage annexed to the Prebend of *Bitton*, in the Collegiate Church of *Salisbury*, by Virtue of which the Prebendary is Patron. The Impropriation, which is Part of its Endowment, is in Lease to THOMAS EDWARDS FRELMAN, of *Batsford*, Esq.

The Church has a very long Nave, and a small North Aisle, formerly a Chantry, which has an Entrance from the Porch. On the Left, are Two small Figures of Ecclesiastics, cumbent, about Four Feet long, evidently intended for some of the officiating Priests of this Chantry. On the other Side are *subsellia* of Four Compartments, under Pediments and Quatrefoils. This Aisle is a Dormitory used by the Families of BARR and NEWTON, for the former of whom are no remaining Memorials. This Chapel is said to have been founded and endowed by JOHN BARR, in the Reign of EDWARD IV. The Chancel externally appears to have been the most ancient Part of the Structure. The Inside was commodiously pewed, and modernized in 178. The Tower, which contains Six Bells, is lofty, embattled, and pinnacled, in the lightest Gothic Style, erected in the 15th Century. It is remarkable, that in Countries where the Materials of Architecture naturally fail, the Piety of our Ancestors supplied the Deficiency by Masonry more sumptuous and embellished.

Bitton comprises three very extensive Hamlets. *Bitton*, the Manor of which has been successively inherited by the Families of BROUNT, BARR and CRADOC otherwise NEWTON. Sir JOHN NEWTON, Bart. the last of this Line, lies buried in a Chapel in the Cathedral at *Bristol*, in which are sever sumptuous Monuments erected to that Family. He entailed the Manor, and a great Estate, on Sir JOHN NEWTON, of *Lincolnshire*, who was included within the Limitations of the Patent of the Baronetage. *Barrs Court*, their ancient Seat, notice This CAMDEN, is now in Ruins. *Highfield*, another dilapidated Mansion, is held, with a considerable Estate, by ———— DRUMMOND, M. D. &c. 2. *Hanham* is, without Doubt, a Place of the highest Antiquity. From the Remains of Trenches, and other Fortifications on the Roman Plan, it has been thought to be the Scite of the Station *Abone* mentioned in the Itinerary of *Antoninus*, as being distant (XV *Mill. pass.*) from *Aquæ Solis*, the modern *Bath*. The Translator is evidently misplaced, for by no Computation of Distance could *Hanham* be reckoned Fifteen Miles from *Bath*, as stated in the Itinerary. The *Abone* of *Antoninus* is by others confidently placed at *Alvington* as mentioned in the Account of that Parish. The Manor of *Hanham* was appropriate to the Abbe of *Keinsham*, in the County of *Somerset*. It is now vested with the most considerable Estate, in the Family of CRESSWICKE. The Grove, once held by the Priory of *Farley*, in *Wiltshire*, was lately the Property of CHARLES BRAGGE, Esq. and is now in the Possession of JOHN WILLS, Esq. In the Hamlet is a small Chapel, which is divided by low Arches. *Oldland* has likewise a small Chapel, appendant to *Bitton*, and is served by the same Minister. Baptisms are performed at it, but at *Oldland*, Sepulture only. The WOODWARDS hold Lands in this Hamlet. *Bitton Court*, to call the honourable in Possessor, is at present in the Estate of Dr. JOHN WARREN, Lord Bishop of *Bangor*. *Barrs Court*, *Hanham*, *Oldland*, and *Upton Cheyny*, and *Bitton* are subject to the Jurisdiction of the Honour of *Gloucester*.

Iter XIV. Villa and Gallevan. "Venta Silurum, m.p. IX. Abone IX. Trec. IX. Aquæ sol. VI. m.p.
GALVEN. The Gabion.
The various Commentators on this Itinerary, have obscured, rather than cleared the Matter by grounding their Opinions on mere Conjecture.

BINI

BENEFACTIONS

To *BITTON*.

Mrs ELIZABETH WARNE, by Deed, dated 1656, gave to the Poor of the Hamlet of *Bitton*, 10s to be distributed on the 3d of May, which is vested in the Vicar of *Bitton* for the Time being

Mr BRICE SEED, by Will, 1682, gave to the second Poor, Land, to the Value of 1l 10s per Ann vested in the Churchwardens and Overseers

Mr SEED (lapsed in 1769) gave to the second Poor, to be distributed at Christmas, a Rent Charge of 1l 12s payable out of *Culley Hall* Estate, vested in Lieutenant RICHARD WILLIAMS

—— UNDERHILL gave to the second Poor, to be distributed at Christmas, 10s per Annum, vested in THOMAS EDWARDS FREEMAN, Esq

A Person, or Persons unknown, gave to the second Poor, at Christmas, the different Sums of 9s 2s and 7s out of the Rent of Three Houses, without *Lawford's Gate*, *Bristol*, in the Possession of JOHN WOODWARD, Mr LAND, and Mr HORSLER

Unknown, gave to the second Poor, at Christmas, 1l 6s 4d out of the Rent of a House in *Tucker Street*, *Bristol*, in the Possession of Mr GARRAT

Besides the above Benefactions to the Poor of the Hamlet of *Bitton*, as given in the Returns,

Mr FREEMAN gave 2l for ever, for Four Sermons, to be preached every Year

THOMAS EDWARDS FREEMAN, Esq gives, out of an Estate at *Bitton*, 1l very, for Two Sermons, on Whit Monday and Tuesday.

To *OLDLAND*

Mrs ELIZABETH WARNE, by Deed, 1656, gave to the Poor, to be distributed annually, on Michaelmas Day, 1l, vested in the Hands of the Vicar of *Bitton*

Mr ROBERT KITCHEN, late Alderman of *Bristol*, gave to the Poor, to be distributed annually, on Good Friday, 10s, vested in Lieutenant RICHARD WILLIAMS

Mr THOMAS, in 1667, gave 1l extraordinary, upon every Rate made for the Relief of the Poor of *Oldland* This is entered in the Donation Table at *Oldland* Chapel, but never known to have been paid

Besides the above to the Poor,

Mr ARTHUR FARMER, late Alderman of *Bristol*, gave 6l per Annum, for a Sermon to be preached the first Sunday in every Month.

Mrs ELIZABETH WARNE gave 1l for Two Sermons to be preached on Michaelmas Day

To *HANHAM*

Mrs ELIZABETH WARNE gave, by Deed, 1656, to the Poor of *West Hanham*, to be distributed on the 1st of April, 10s per Annum, vested in the Vicar of *Bitton*

RICHARD JONES, Esq by Will, dated 1696, give to Sixteen Poor Families 4l to be distributed annually on the 10th of December, vested in Mrs QUICK

Mrs ELIZABETH WARNE likewise gave, with the above, 10s annually, to a Sermon to be preached on the same Day

INCUMBENTS	PATRONS	INCUMBENTS	PATRONS
573 William Sprint,	John Sprint	1714 Joseph Stockwell, M A	Prebend of *Bitton*
—— Lewis Evans,		1715 John Eade, B A	The same
1664 John Burnley,	Andrew Atwood	1719 Robert Eyre, M A	The same
—— Richard Towgood, M A	Prebend of *Bitton*	1724 Richard Barry, M A	The same
1671 Edward Parker, M A	John Seymour, Esq	1768 Charles Elwes, M A	The same
The above from Sir ROB ATKINS			

PRESENT LORDS OF THE MANORS,

Of *Bitton*,
MICHAEL NEWTON, Esq

Of *Hanham Court*,
HENRY CRESWICK, Esq

At the Visitations of the Heralds, in 1682 and 168 , the following Persons were summoned from this Place and its Hamlets

From *Bitton*	
John Tindall, Esq	Richard Jones, Esq
William Beech, Gent	James Creswicke, Esq
Samuel Bavey, Gent	Sir Richard Hart, Knight
From *Hanham*	From *Oldland*
Dame Mary Newton, Widow	Sir John Newton, Bar
	James Woodward, Gent

At the Election in 1776, Forty-seven Freeholders appeared from *Bitton*, Thirteen from *Hanham*,
and from *Oldland* Twenty

The earlieſt Entry in the Regiſter bears Date 1572

ANNUAL ACCOUNT OF MARRIAGES, BIRTHS, AND BURIALS, IN THIS PARISH

A D	Mar	Bir	Bur	A D	Mar	Bir	Bur	A D	Mar	Bir	Bur	A D	Mar	Bir	Bur
1781	35	123	99	1791				1801				1811			
1782	35	124	73	1792				1802				1812			
1783	43	148	116	1793				1803				1813			
1784	46	181	96	1794				1804				1814			
1785	39	100	88	1795				1805				1815			
1786	47	103	88	1796				1806				1816			
1787	41	135	114	1797				1807				1817			
1788				1798				1808				1818			
1789				1799				1809				1819			
1790				1800				1810				1820			

INSCRIPTIONS IN THE CHURCH

ON A MONUMENT AGAINST THE NORTH WALL,
IN THE CHANCEL

Arms, Gules, Two Wings conjoned in Lure Or.

Memoriæ Sacrum
JOHN SEYMOR, militis,
Comit Gloucest

Qui non minus illuſtris animi dotibus
excelluit, quam præ illuſtri & nobili ortu claruit,
mortem obiit Novembris 17, anno epochæ
Chriſtiana 1663

AGAINST THE SOUTH WALL

Here lyeth beneath this
Place, the Body of JOHN
BURNLIE, Vicar of Bitton,
and Preacher of the Word of
God who deceaſed
the 22d Day of May,
Anno Domini, 1627

*In the Chancel are ſeveral obliterated Inſcriptions on
Flat Stones, for the Family of* WHITTINGTON

IN THE BODY OF THE CHURCH.

ON MONUMENTS AGAINST
THE SOUTH WALL

Arms, Quarterly—1ſt, a Lion rampant, for
Jones, 2 Azure, a Stag's Head erboſhed Or, 3
Argent three Acorns Azure 4 Sable, a Croſs
colore . . . tilled Or, between Four Martlets Argent,
. . . on a . . . savary, between Three Water bougets,
Three Croſs Croſſes, 6 as the Firſt

Near this Place
lyeth the Body of ARTER, the Wife
of RICHARD JONES, of Hanham, Eſq

Alſo
the Body of CATHARINE BETHELL,
Widdow, one of the Daughters of
Sir FRANCIS NORREYES, Knight, who
died June 3, 1692, aged 44 Years

Likewiſe the Body of
RICHARD JONES, of Hanham, Eſq.
who died January 27, 1697,
aged 87 Years

In his Vault at Oldland's Chapel
lies the Body of THOMAS TRYE,
of Hanham, Eſq Grandſon of the abovenamed RICHARD JONES, Eſq who
departed this Life Nov 23, 1728,
ætat 59

Arms, Parti per Pale an Eagle diſplayed

Neere to this Place lieth
buried the Body of FRANCIS
STONE, who departed this Life
December 9, in the
Year of our Lord 1641

Alſo by him
lieth buried his 3 Sons, JOHN
FRANCIS, and EDMOND   JOHN
was buried July 7, 1647
FRANCIS was buried May 2,
1658   EDMOND was buried
September 4, 1656

Neere to this Place lieth buried
the Body of BRIDGET, the Wife
of FRANCIS STONE, the elder
She died May 3, 1655

ON A MONUMENT AGAINST THE NORTH WALL

Arms, Parti per Pale a Lion rampant

In Memoriam STEPHANI ROSEWELL, Gen
qui vitam obiit 28 die Feb 1650

ON A BRASS PLATE AGAINST THE SAME WALL

Near this Place lieth the Body
of JANE HOLLISTER, Daughter
of EDWARD HOLLISTER, of Upton Cheney,
Gent by MARY his Wife, and Niece
to WILLIAM SEEDE, of Cullyhall, Gent
and KATHARINE his Wife, who
departed this Life the 23d Day of Oct 1716,
aged 11 Years, 8 Months, 1 Week,
and 5 Days

ON FLAT STONES.

EDWARD, the Son of EDWARD and ELIZABETH
PARKER, died May 27, 1741, aged 29 Years

SARAH, Wife of JOSEPH PARKER,
died September 5, 1745, aged 25 Years

Also the said JOSEPH PARKER,
died Jan 16, 1778, aged 70.

MARY, Wife of RICHARD PARKER, Gent
died Aug 18, 1764, aged 53 Years

Also Seven Children of
the said RICHARD and MARY are
interred near this Place

Also the said RICHARD PARKER
died Nov 7, 1770, aged 56 Years

Here lyeth the Body of WILLIAM, the
Son of HENRY WEARE and MARY his
Wife, who departed this Life the 30th
Day of July, Anno Domini 1700

Here lyeth the Body of PHILIP WEARE,
the Son of HENRY WEARE and MARY his Wife
who departed this Life the 24th of January,
Anno Domini 1707, ætatis suæ 14

Here resteth the Body of MARY WEARE,
the Daughter of HENRY and MARY WEARE,
who departed this Life the 5th Day of
May, 1712, aged 37 Years

Here lyeth the Body of HENRY WEARE,
of this Parish, Gent who departed this Life
the 21st of March, 1720, aged 77 Years

Also the Body of MARY, Wife of
the said HENRY WEARE, ob Sept 11, 1757,
aged 88 Years

In Spe Resurrectionis,
Hic jacet Corpus FRANCISCI CRESWICKE,
Armig qui obiit 18 Jan 1732, ætatis suæ 89

Ac etiam Corpus MARIÆ Uxoris ejus, ætat 58

Ac etiam Corpora JOHANNIS, GALFRIDI, FRANCISCI,
& MARIÆ, CRESWICKE, Filii & nata FRANCISCI
& MARIÆ,

Nec non Corpus HENRICI CRESWICKE, Armigeri,
qui obiit
Vicesimo sexto die mensis Julii, Ann Dom 1744.

Et enim infra jacet Corpus HELENÆ, Uxoris
HENRICI CRESWICKE, Armigeri, obiit vicesimo
secundo die Junii 1757, ætatis suæ 46

ON THE VERGE OF AN OLD STONE, THE
FOLLOWING FOUR LINES

Here lyeth the Body of
JOHN BURGIS, of this Parish, Gent who departed
this Life the 10th Day
of October, Anno Dom 1697, aged 84 Years

Beneath this Stone,
secure from Storm or Tempest, rests at Peace,
the Body of Captain SAMUEL ALDEN, native
of New England He was bred to the Sea
Service from his Youth, in which dangerous
Employment, by the Providence of GOD, he
was so successful as never to meet with an Accident
After a Passage in Life of 45 Years,
he launched into Eternity, Oct 10, 1757
To whose Memory this Stone is erected by
his truly afflicted Widow
EDITH ALDEN

Also underneath lieth the Body of EDITH,
Wife of the above Captain SAMUEL ALDEN, and
late Wife of Mr GEORGE WILLIAMS, of the Parish
of St James in the City of Bristol She left this
Life on Nov 29, 1773, aged 55 Years

Here lyeth the Body of WILLIAM, the Son of
WILLIAM MARTIN, of the Parish of Long Ashton
in the County of Somerset, who departed this Life
in the 83d Year of his Age, Anno Domini 1710

He also lieth the Body of EDITH his Wife,
who departed this Life April 10, 1714,
in the 86th Year of her Age

Here lyeth the Body of Mrs SARAH DUNN,
Wife of Mr TOBIAS DUNN, of Hinham in the
Parish of Bitton and County of Gloucester, who
departed this Life October the 29th, Anno Dom
1719, aged 65 Years, 2 Months, and 2 Weeks

Also here lyeth the Body of ANN DUNN, Daughter
of Mr FRANCIS DUNN, Woolen Cooper in the
City of Bristol, and Granddaughter to the said
SARAH DUNN and departed this Life March 13,
Anno Dom 1719 aged 16 Months

Also here lieth the Body of Mr TOBIAS DUNN,
of the Parish who departed this Life
March 29, Anno Dom 1721, aged 72 Years

In Memory of Mr LDMUND WARD,
late of Nevis, one of the Leeward Islands in the
West Indies, who was killed by a Fall from his
Horse, as he was passing through this Parish,
on the 20th of June 1784, aged 33

Here lyeth the Body of Mrs MARY WORNELL,
of Hanham in this Parish who departed this Life
May 17, 1721 aged 60 Years

Also here lyeth the Body of ELIZABETH BATT,
Sister to the above-named MARY WORNELL,
who departed this Life March 17, 1733,
aged 81 Years

Here lyeth the Body of MARY, Wife of
NICHOLAS WORNELL, Yeoman,
who was buried Feb , 1699,
aged 61 Years

Here also lyeth the Body of NICHOLAS WORNELL,
Yeoman, who died June 19, 1711,
aged 67 Years

IN THE NORTH CHAPLL.

ON MONUMENTS

Arms, Quarterly, 1st and 4th, Argent, on a
Chevron Azure, Three Garbs Or 2d and 3d, Ar-
gent, Two Thigh Bones in Saltier Sable, for NEW-
TON

Here lyeth the Body of
Sir JOHN NEWTON, Bart
Thrice Burgess of Parliament,
a most loving Husband,
careful Father, and faithful Friend,
pious, just, prudent,
charitable, valiant, and beloved of all.
He was born June 9, A D 1626,
being the Son of THOMAS NEWTON,
of Gunwarby in the County
of Lincoln, Esq
and died May 31, A D 1699
He married MARY, the Daughter of
Sir JERVASE EYRE,
of Rampton, in the County of
Nottingham, Knight
They lived happily all their Time
together, which was 55 Years,
by whom he had Issue
Four Sons and Thirteen Daughters
This Monument was erected
at the Charge of his youngest Son
GERVAS NEWTON, Esq

Arms on a Lozenge, per Chevron Sable and
Or, Three Eagles displayed, counterchanged, for
STRINGER, — impaling NEWTON

Piæ Memoriæ
Dom
ELIZABETHÆ STRINGER,
obiit Ludlinio
Primo die Feb,
Anno Dom 1699
Sepulmon quiriivi non pauibus æquis

ON FLAT STONES.

Arms, on a Lozenge, as before

Here lyeth the Body of Dame
MARY NEWTON, Widow and Relict of
Sir JOHN NEWTON, late of Barr's Court, Bart
by whom he had Four Sons and Thirteen Daughters
She died Nov 23, 1712, in the 85th Year of her Age

Here lyeth the Body of
Mrs ELIZABETH STRINGER,
Daughter to Sir JOHN NEWTON,
Baronet, and Dame MARY
his Wife, and Wife to FRANCIS
STRINGER, of Sutton upon Lown
in the County of Northumberland,
who died . .

Here lyeth the Body of ELIZABETH,
the Wife of JOHN WHITTINGTON,

. .

. .

Here lyeth the Body of DOROTHY, the Wife of
FRANCIS WOODWARD, of this Parish, Gent
and youngest Daughter of the Honourable
Sir JOHN NEWTON, Bart who departed this Life
the 16th Day of October, 1712, who had
Issue 8 Sons and 3 Daughters.

Here lyeth the Body of the said FRANCIS WOODWARD,
of this Parish, Gent who departed this Life
Dec 12, 1730, in the 60th Year of his Age

And also here lyeth the Body of JOHN, Son of JOHN
and ELIZABETH WOODWARD, and Grandson of
FRANCIS and DOROTHY WOODWARD, who departed
this Life May 29, 1741, aged 11 Years

Beneath this Stone lies the Body of
JOHN, Son of JOHN WOODWARD, Gent who died
May 29, 1741, aged 8 Years

Also in Memory of ANNE, Wife of NEWTON
WOODWARD, of this Parish, Gent who died
June 28, 1743, aged 50 Years.

Also Five Children of the above NEWTON WOODWARD,
by ANNE his second Wife

	Died	Aged
FRANCIS BERKELEY,	Mar 25, 1750,	12 Months
ANN,	May 20, 1750,	6 Years
MARY,	May 31, 1754,	3 Months
THOMAS,	Mar 21, 1758,	19 Months
FRANCIS	July 16, 1764,	12 Years

In Memory of DOROTHY their Daughter, who died
July 15, 1775, aged 15 Years

Also the Body of NEWTON WOODWARD, Gent
who died Dec 9, 1778, aged 79

ON THE VERGE OF A FLAT STONE

Here lyeth the Body of FRANCIS, Son of
FRANCIS and DOROTHY WOODWARD, Gent
of this Parish, Grandfon of Sir JOHN NEWTON,
Bart. who was buried September 7, 1701

Here lyeth the Body of GERVES, the Son of
FRANCIS WOODWARD, Gent by DOROTHY his Wife,
Daughter to Sir JOHN NEWTON, deceafed,
who departed September 6, 1702

Here alfo lyeth the Body of RICHARD; the Son of
FRANCIS WOODWARD, Gent by DOROTHY his Wife,
who departed November 11, 1703

Here alfo lyeth the Body of FRANCES, Daughter of
FRANCIS WOODWARD, Gent by DOROTHY his Wife,
who departed the 18th Day of Auguft, 1705

IN THE CHURCH YARD, ON TOMBS.

CHARLES BARRY,
the youngeft son of the
Rev. RICHARD BARRY, fenior,
Rector of Upton Skidmore
in the County of Wilts,
and Brother of the Rev.
RICHARD BARRY late Vicar
of this Parish, died the 2d
Day of Dec. 1768 aged 64

MOSES STRANGE
died Aug 31, 50, aged 86.

HANNAH his Wife
died Aug 28, 1752, aged 69.

MOSES STRANGE, junior,
died March 14, 1765, aged 63

JONAS SEEDEN
died May 29 1752, aged 59.

MARTHA his Wife
died April 6, 1767, aged 70

WILLIAM THOMPSON fenior,
died Dec. 1755, aged 58

JANE his Wife
died Sept 28, 1742, aged 55

WILLIAM, Son of
WILLIAM and JANE THOMPSON,
died Jun 2, 1740, aged 24

WILLIAM TREBODY, their Son in Law,
died June 9 1744, aged 43

JANE his Wife
died Aug 13, 1739, aged 22

SAMUEL Son of
WILLIAM and ELANOR BUSH,
died Oct 1744, aged 6 Years

GILES their Son died Dec 29, 1745,
aged 2.

WILLIAM BUSH,
late of Beach in this Parish,
died April 21, 1744, aged 77

ELANOR his Wife
died July 6, 1759, aged 66

JOHN their Son
died June 1760, aged 34

WILLIAM his Son
died Jan 1788, aged 65

JOHN FLOWER
died July 24 1725, aged 43

JOHN his Son
died Dec 10, 1738, aged 29

MARY FLOWER, Widow,
died Dec 22, 1763, aged 76

WILLIAM BARTON
died in August 1759

SUSANNA, Wife of WILL YORBERRY,
and Daughter of JOSEPH ROSEWELL,
died Feb 5,

JOAN, Wife of JOSEPH ROSEWELL,
died Sept 3, 1734, aged 87 Years

BRICE SEED, Gent
died Feb 26, 1682

MARTHA his Wife
was buried Sept. 1, 1653

WILLIAM SEED, Gent
died April 9, 1739, aged 77.

SARAH, the Wife of
JOHN SEED, died
Sept 22, 1714, aged 64

ANN, Wife of THOMAS LAMB,
and Daughter of JOHN SEED,
died Aug 18, 1776, aged 36

JOHN SEEDE, junior,
died Feb 29, 1776, aged 25

WILLIAM SEEDE, Son of JOHN SEEDE,
brightfmith, of Briftol,
died July 4 1772, aged 25

THOMAS HOLDIN, Yeoman,
died in the Year 1732 aged 55

MARY his Wife
died May 6, 1743, aged 68

ELIZABETH the Wife
of JAMES FRANCIS died
Jan 11 1767, aged 93

JOHN BUSH
died the Day of 1711

SAMUEL BUSH Gent
died Aug 4, 1751, aged 62.

ABIGAIL ATWOOD
died July 21, 1702, aged 73

EDWARD HOLLISTER,
of Upton in this Parish, Gent
died March 10, 1734, aged 58

Alfo ABIGAIL HOLLISTER,
Daughter of ABIGAIL ATWOOD

Alfo WILLIAM ATWOOD, Son
to ABIGAIL ATWOOD

JOSIAS, Son of JOSIAS
and MARTHA ROBBINS,
died Feb 6, 1750, aged 26

PENELOPE their Daughter
died May 15, 1751, aged 21.

JOSIAS ROBBINS, fenior,
died July 11, 1730, aged 41.

FRANCIS GOODMAN,
of Upton Cheney, Gent
died April 3, 1747, aged 77.

JOHN GOODMAN, Father
of the faid FRANCIS GOODMAN,
buried May 2, 1698, aged 73

ELIZABETH his Wife
Daughter of ADAM
BAYNSHAM, of Yate, Efq
died May 11, 1711, aged 90

ELIZABETH, Wife of
FRANCIS GOODMAN, Gent
died Dec 15, 1761, aged 90

ELIZABETH Wife of
GEORGE HARRINGTON Grand-
Daughter of FRANCIS GOODMAN,
died Jan 23, 1743, aged 28.

JOHN ATKINS, Yeoman,
died July 26, 1716, aged 60

MARTHA, Wife of WILLIAM ATKINS,
of Upton in this Parish, died
Feb 4 1767, aged 72

WILLIAM ATKINS
died July 1, 1774, aged 78

JOHN BENNETT,
late of London, Gent
died Nov 1, 1769, aged 50

THOMAS BRYANT, of Clifton,
died Jan 24, 1773, aged 50

ROGER

ROGER HARDING, Yeoman,
died Nov 13, 1718

ROGER, the Son of
ROGER and MARTHA HARDING,
died in May 1710

MARTHA, Relict of ROGER HARDING,
and since Wife of HARRINGTON DAVIS,
died Sept 25, 1746 aged 65

JOHN SEYMOUR
died Nov 4, 1763, aged 53.

MARY his Wife
died May 6, 1773, aged 68

JOHN FLOWER, Yeoman,
died April 5, 1761, aged 77

JOHN FLOWER, Yeoman,
Son of GEORGE and REBECCA FLOWER,
of Kelston, died
May 7, 1763, aged 46

ANN, the Daughter of
LAMORACK and SUSANNA FLOWER,
died July 30, 1730

ELIZABETH FLOWER, Spinster,
Daughter of the above,
died March 6, 1744, aged 64

JOANNA FLOWER, Spinster,
Sister to the above ELIZABETH,
died Jan. 23, 1753, aged 65

ELIZABETH, Wife of
JOHN FOORD, Tanner,
died Aug 27, 1684

GEORGE FOORD
died Aug. 30, 1700, aged 41

JOHN HARRINGTON, Gent
died Oct 16, 1714 aged 41
BETTY, Wife of GEO HARRINGTON,
Yeoman, died Sept 15, 1773 aged 69.

ANN, Daughter of JOHN
HARRINGTON Gent by
MARY his Wife, died
Jan. 7, 1774, aged 66

GEORGE HARRINGTON, Gent
died Feb 14, 1781, aged 77

JOAN, Daughter of
WILLIAM and MARGARET NUTT,
died Jan 21, 1702

MARGARET Wife of WILLIAM NUTT,
died Dec 7, 1714, aged 67

JOHN, Son of JOHN NUTT
Grandson of WILLIAM NUTT,
died Oct. 29, 1725, aged 16

WILLIAM NUTT
died March 8, 1727 8, aged 90.

THOMAS, Son of JOSEPH
and MARY LONG and Grandson of
THOMAS and MARY DAFTER,
died Feb 7, 1761, aged 41

MARY BARTLETT,
Daughter of JOSEPH and MARY LONG,
died Oct 15, 1760, aged 46

RICHARD DAVIS of Oldland
in this Parish died June 20, 1725,
aged 85

SARAH, Wife of RICHARD
DAVIS, died Sept 6, 1671

ELEANOR, Wife of the said
RICHARD DAVIS, died
May 12, 1696

JOSEPH LONG, Son of
JOSEPH and MARY LONG,
died Oct 13, 1759, aged 43.

CHARLES BROOKS
died Jan 12, 1759, aged 86.

ANN his Wife
died Jan 18, 1740, aged 68
They lived 44 Years a married Life

SAMUEL their Son
died April 22, 1757, aged 55.

SAMUEL BAILEY
died Aug 3, 1751, aged 60.

SAMUEL HAINES
died Jan. 16, 1770, aged 60.

POYNTZ FOX
died Feb 14, 1732, aged 67

JOANE his Wife
died Feb. 28, 1762, aged 94

JOHN SMITH
died Jan 6, 1763, aged 68

JOHN SMITH the elder,
died March 5, 1717

ANNE his Wife
died April 2 following.

JOHN PINKER, Yeoman
died June 22, 1768, aged 44

MARY his Wife
died Oct 7, 1769, aged 64.

JAMES, Son of
JOHN and MARY PINKER,
died Oct 3, 1756, aged 3,

ISAAC STOUT
died Dec. 21, 1737, aged 58

MARY his Wife
died June 12, 1745, aged 65

JOHN PINKER, senior,
died Sept 19, 1764, aged 71

MARY his Wife
died Feb 5, 1773, aged 73

JOHN STIBBS, Yeoman,
died Oct. 3, 1765, aged 56

ISAAC LEONARD Yeoman,
died Oct 20, 1783, aged 57.

JACOB COX, of the out Parish
of St Philip and Jacob,
died Sep 8, 17   aged 69.

JOSEPH, Son of THOMAS JONES,
died April 16, 1638

CATHARINE Wife of GABRIEL JONES,
died March 8, 1734, aged 84

ELIZABETH, Wife of JACOB COX,
died Oct 22, 1737, aged 65

SAMUEL COX
died Feb 16, 1746 aged 31

SAMUEL, Son of SAMUEL and
ELIZABETH COX, died
Dec 9, 1768, aged 22

ELIZABETH Wife of SAMUEL COX,
died July 2, 1752, aged 51

JOSEPH WHITTICK
died in May, 1733, aged 7

ABRAHAM WHITTICK, Gent
died March 9, 1744 aged 79

SARAH, Wife of ABRAHAM WHITTICK,
died Oct 17, 1747, aged 65

ON HEADSTONES.

	Died	Aged		Died	A
Martha, Wife of John Barnes	9 Apr 1755	33	Christian, Wife of John Thomas, of the Parish of St Stephens, Bristol	13 July, 1782	25
Thomas Barnes	13 Mar 1754	51	George Fry	1 July, 1780	7
John, Son of Abraham Whittuck	3 June, 1731	36	George Foot	20 Oct 1753	6
Mary, Wife of Thomas Barnes, jun and Daughter of Abraham Whittuck	27 Apr 1743	38	Thomas his Son, by Mary his Wife	10 July, 1760	60
			Mary, Wife of George Foot	30 Aug 1751	
Hannah, second Wife of Thomas Barnes	6 Dec 1777	61	Sarah, Wife of Mark Tanner	2 June, 17	4
Robert Nott	24 Feb 1733	75	Thomas Sweet, of the Parish of St George	31 Oct 1781	6
Lydia, Wife of George Nott	2 Feb 1749	40	Margaret his Wife	26 June, 1780	53
George Robbins	26 Aug 1774	73	Dorothy his second Wife	14 May, 1770	6
Leighton Adlington	13 May, 1763	50	Henry Sweet, of this Parish	2 Sept 1761	58
Susanna his Wife	11 Nov 1777	68			

Robert

	Died	Aged
Robert Fox	29 Sept 1739	44
Elizabeth his Wife	10 Jan 1768	63
Robert son of Richard and Elizabeth Williams	— Oct 1739	30
Elizabeth their Daughter	11 Dec 1730	19
Richard Williams senior	11 Mar 1755	71
Jane his Daughter	8 Jan 1748	19
Samuel Bailey	5 Sept 1760	14
Elizabeth Wife of Samuel Bailey, senior	15 Apr 1761	61
Sarah, Wife of Samuel Brooks	4 Feb 1776	81
John Palmer	18 Feb 1778	37
Arthur Palmer	22 Nov 1759	60
Ann his Wife	1 June 1757	57
Francis Tippett, of Oldland	9 Oct 1743	36
Samuel his Son	21 June, 1763	28
Jane Wife of Joseph Paynter,	15 Feb 1761	30
George Wilmot	7 May, 1777	69
Edward Wilmot	16 Mar 1758	70
Jane his Wife	27 Dec 1771	70
Isaac Jeffers	15 Mar 1758	83
Elizabeth his Wife	17 July 1762	66
Stephen Tippett	3 June, 1767	76
Sarah his Wife	13 Feb 1764	66
Stephen Tippett, junior	4 Nov 1756	51
Ann his Wife	2 Aug 1761	32
Stephen Tippett the youngest	19 Nov 1781	2
Richard Bailey	23 Jan 1754	62
Mary, Wife of Thomas Bailey, senior	15 June 1768	68
Thomas Bailey her Husband	15 Nov 1775	78
Elizabeth, Wife of Thomas Bailey, junior	5 Mar 1768	23
Jane Wife of John Tippett	11 Dec 1777	6
Francis their Son	29 May, 1779	30
Samuel Potter	17 June, 1777	62
Ann his Wife	9 Nov 1775	60
Thomas Potter	30 Jan 1779	66
Mary his Wife	9 Oct 1763	36
Samuel Potter, senior	17 May 1739	67
Henry Bright	8 Dec 1757	60
Richard Wilson	6 June, 1768	56
Thomas Cruddy	13 Jan 1774	75
Jane his Wife	11 Aug 1782	78
Thomas Son of John and Sarah Nash	3 Feb 1760	25
Rachel Daughter of John and Sarah Nash	30 Mar 1774	34
Sarah, Wife of the said Joan Nash	20 Aug 1774	66
John Nash	24 May, 1759	75
Elizabeth his Wife	2 May, 1760	65
Richard Williams	13 Oct 1749	60
William, Son of William and Mary Prince	10 Mar 1755	23
Mary Wife of William Prince	15 Jul 1763	66
Samuel Brain	11 Sept 1756	56
... Brain late of Bath	20 May 1756	60
William Bence	8 Oct 1757	26

	Died	Aged
Mary first married to the above William Bence, late Wife of James Brimble	6 Aug 1781	51
William Barman	18 Aug 1727	49
Sarah his Wife	19 Feb 1733	7
Charles Sweet	18 Oct 1762	9
Jane Wife of John Phillips	7 Jan 1767	15
John Robbins, senior	20 Feb 1717	61
John Robbins	14 Sept 1774	45
William Williams, senior	23 Feb 1747	60
Ann Newman	5 Sept 1759	19
Grace, the Wife of Thomas Newman	6 Nov 1759	53
Thomas Newman	19 Nov 1757	75
John Evans	7 Mar 1744	28
William Langman	1 Apr 1785	54
Joyce his Wife	2 July, 1781	67
Sarah, Wife of William Simpton	19 Oct 1775	72
William and Sarah (twins), Son and Daughter of William and Sarah Harding, both born in one Hour { William	5 Jan 1762	0
Sarah	17 Jul 1762	0
Mary, Wife of Roger Harding, senior	1 Aug 1751	67
Roger Harding, senior	5 Apr 1759	74
Roger Harding, junior	6 June, 1765	49
Joan his Wife	16 Apr 1747	55
Thomas Gunning, senior,	6 Oct 1747	56
Mary his Wife	17 Feb 1748	56
Sarah Wife of John Ford, of Peach	17 Jan 1775	60
Elizabeth, Wife of William Thompson	1 Jan 1768	49
Mary, Wife of James Thompson, junior	4 Jan 1766	18
James Thompson, senior	23 Dec 1757	50
John his Son	16 Nov 1755	6
Ann Wife of James Bush	2 July, 1773	5
George Smith	11 Apr 1755	70
Helen his Wife	13 Feb 1743	74
Henry Smith	17 Sept 1757	72
Sarah his Wife	10 July, 1760	56
Thomas Strange	15 July, 1756	53
Joseph, Son of Thomas and Mary Strange	6 May, 1768	18
William Teat	7 Jan 1751	70
Sarah, Wife of Francis Hobbs	26 July, 1774	53
John Lovelock, Yeoman	6 Oct 1751	75
Elinor Wife of James Querman	15 Nov 1751	49
James Querman	16 Nov 1785	56
William Ferris	11 June 1766	71
Elizabeth his Wife	3 Dec 1770	74
Isaac Carter, of the Out Precincts, Bristol	5 May 1770	57
William Britten, Yeoman	21 Nov 1771	43
Joan Britten, Yeoman	5 Sep 1744	70
Thomas James, senior	11 June 1757	80
Ann his Wife	25 Mar 1751	91
Mary, Wife of Benjamin Tucker	7 Mar 1751	71

INSCRIPTIONS IN OLDLAND CHAPEL IN THIS PARISH

IN THE NORTH AISLE

Here lyeth the Body of
Mr Thomas Woodward, Grandson
of Mr Thomas Woodward,
who departed this Life Oct
26, 1728, in the 50th Year of his Age.

IN THE SOUTH AISLE

Here lyeth the Body of
James Shatford, of Hanham,
who departed this Life
Aug 14, 1746, aged 69 Years

Also here lyeth the Body of
Susanna, the Wife of the above
James Shatford, who departed
this Life Jan 24, 1762, aged 70 Years

Also the Body of
Ann Christopher, Sister-in-law
to the above James Shatford,
who departed this Life
July 20, 1745, aged 42 Years

Here lyeth the Body of
George Bush, senior, of this Parish,
Yeoman, who departed this Life
May 4, 1722, aged 70 Years

Also in Memory of
Samuel Ivans, of the Parish of St George,
who lies buried here   He died
March 11, 1765, aged 57 Years

Also the Body of Joan,
Wife of the said Samuel Evans,
and late Wife of George Godfrey
She died June 5, 1774, aged 62 Years

Here lyeth the Body of
Ann, Wife of William Humphris,
of this Parish, who departed
this Life Jan 5, 1720

Here also lyeth the Body of
William Humphris, of this Parish,
who departed this Life April 1, 1727,
aged 72 Years

In the North Side the Chancel are the
following Arms

Or, a Bend Azure, for Trye,—impaling, Argent, a Wyvern Sable, Crest, a Buck's Head caboshed Gules

---

IN THE CHAPEL YARD, ON HEAD STONES

	Died	Aged
Nicholas Palmer		55
Francis Waters	27 Apr 1777	62
Dorothy, Wife of Samuel Edwards	2 July, 1768	51
Samuel Edwards aforesaid	5 May, 1773	59
Mary, Wife of William Lewton	24 Oct. 1772	66
John Lewton, senior, of Hanham	13 June, 1772	80
Hannah his Wife	5 Oct 1740	43
Sarah, Wife of John Lewton, junior, of Hanham	28 Sept 1767	43
Elizabeth, Daughter of James and Jane Lewton, of Cliffton	19 July, 1784	28
Samuel Morgan	10 Mar 1779	27
William Clark	22 June, 1772	66
John, Son of William Clark	21 Aug 1782	20

XLIII. BLAISDON.

A SMALL Parish in the Hundred of *Westbury*, and the *Forest* Deanery, situate Four Miles on the East from *Mitchel Dean*, and Nine from GLOUCESTER on the West. The Soil is various, though chiefly of Clay, applied, in nearly equal Portions, to Tillage, Pasturage, and Woodland, with many very fruitful Orchards. A small Rivulet, intersecting this Parish, joins the Severn at *Westbury*. *Blaisdon*, in 1281, was not returned as a distinct Parish, or Village, by the Escheator, but as appendant to *Longhope*, " *cum Hamletto de Blethesley* ' The Village of *Blaisdon* is considerably less than before the great Fire, which happened on the 7th of July 1699, and is recorded on a Table in the Church the Amount of the Loss, delivered on Oath, was 4210*l* 16*s* 9*d*

The Living is a Rectory, and the Church, which is dedicated to *Saint Michael*, consists of a Nave only, with an embattled Tower, low and massive, which contains Five Bells. The Right of Advowson is alternately vested in the Families of HAYLE and WADE

The Manor was given to the Abbey of *Flaxley*, in this County, by the DE BOHUNS, Earls of *Hereford* Sir ANTONY KINGSTON received it at the Dissolution from the King. From his Descendants it passed to the WADES, who are the present Proprietors, with other Claimants

The Family of MARTIN were anciently among the principal Inhabitants Lands are still distinguished by their Name At *Standley* the BULLOCKS obtained an Estate in the Reign of ELIZABETH, which is now held by WILLIAM BULLOCK, Gent

BENEFACTIONS.

Two Tenements, inhabited by the Poor, the annual Value 2*l* , the Donor, and Time of Donation unknown

INCUMBENTS	PATRONS	INCUMBENTS	PATRONS
1570 Thomas Cooke,	Rob and Rich Kerle	1705 Bendy Grove, B A	Thomas Wade, Esq
—— William Mayo, M A	——————	1728 John Jelfe, Clerk,	Ann Hayle, Widow
The above from Sir ROBERT ATKYNS		1778 John Morse, B A	John Wade, Esq

CLAIMANTS OF THE MANOR,

JOHN WADE, Esq ——— JONES, Gent
——— RICHARDSON, Gent ——— CHINN, Spinster.

No Person was summoned from this Parish by the Heralds in 1682 and 1683

At the Election in 1776, Nine Freeholders polled from this Parish

ANNUAL ACCOUNT OF MARRIAGES, BIRTHS, AND BURIALS, IN THIS PARISH

A D	Mar	Bir	Bur	A D	Mar	Bir	Bur	A D	Mar	Bir	Bur	A D	Mar	Bir	Bur
1781	2	5	8	1791				1801				1811			
1782	—	4	8	1792				1802				1812			
1783	1	6	2	1793				1803				1813			
1784	1	10	4	1794				1804				1814			
1785	2	8	3	1795				1805				1815			
1786				1796				1806				1816			
1787				1797				1807				1817			
1788				1798				1808				1818			
1789				1799				1809				1819			
1790				1800				1810				1820			

3

INSCRIPTIONS IN THE CHURCH.

ON A MONUMENT IN THE CHANCEL

Beneath are deposited
the Remains of JOHN BOUGHTON, of Flaxley,
late of Broad Oak, Merchant
He departed this Life July 4, 1767,
in the 67th Year of his Age

In Memory alfo of ANNE his Wife,
who died May 29, 1741, aged 45 Years

Near this Place likewife were interred
their Daughter and Son, ANN and WILLIAM,
the former of whom died Sept 29, 1751,
the latter, Auguft 28, 1755,
both at the Age of 23 Years.

OVER THE CHANCEL DOOR

REBEKAH, the Wife of ROBERT KIRKE,
was buried Jan 20, 1653

ON ANOTHER MONUMENT IN THE CHANCEL

The Remains of
THOMAS BULLOCK, late of this Parifh,
formerly of the City of Ghent,
Merchant, who died March 7, 1784.
He gave by Will 20l to be diftributed
amongft the Poor of this Parifh

ON FLAT STONES

ANNE HAYLE, Widow and Relict
of ROBERT HAYLE, of this Parifh, Gent
buried Dec 5, 1736, aged 60.

Here refteth the Body of
WILLIAM MAYO, Rector of this
Parifh, who was buried May 26,
Anno Dom 1705

WILLIAM his Son, by MARY
his Wife, was buried Sept 10, 1695

A fecond WILLIAM their Son
was buried Sept 11, 1696

MARY their Daughter was
buried in the Year 1692

Here lyeth the Body of ROBERT
KIRKE, fenior, who departed this
Life Nov 16, 1658

And of ANNE his Wife, who
departed this Life Jan 18,
Anno Dom. 1675

IN THE BELLFRY

In Memory of GEORGE MARTEN, fenior,
who was buried Jan 19, 1669

In Memory of GEORGE MARTEN, junior
He was buried Oct. 23, 1712, aged 60.

Here refteth the Body of DEBORAH,
the Wife of GEORGE MARTEN, junior, who
departed this Life Nov 5, 1735, aged 79

WILLIAM MARTEN, Son of GEORGE and
DEBORAH MARTEN, died a Bachelor
Dec 10, 1757, aged 66.

In Memory of
WILLIAM MARTEN, of this Parifh,
who died June 20,
aged near 40 Years

Alfo here refteth the Body of HENRY,
the Son of WILLIAM MARTEN,
of this Parifh, by ELIZABETH his Wife, who
departed this Life April 26, 1768, aged near 26

IN THE CHURCH YARD ON TOMBS

EDWARD BULLOCK, of Standly,
died Dec 21, 1764 aged 62
Alfo in Memory of ANNE his Wife
who died Jun 11, 1781, aged 69
EDMOND, Son of EDMOND BULLOCK,
of Standley, Mar 12, 1757, aged 20

GEORGE the Son of EDMOND BULLOCK,
of Standley died in his 36th Year, 1766
SAM. WINTLE Son of SAM WINTLE,
buried Mar 1, 1742, in his 27th Year

ROB. HAYE. died June 4, 1679 at 61
MARGARET, Wife of ROBERT HAYLE
fenior, died Jul 16, 1706, aged 93

JOHN HAYE died Feb 8, 1689, æt 32
ROB HAYLE died Jan 30, 1714 æ 29

Here are depofited the Remains of a
virtuous Woman, in the Age of 84 Years,
MARGARET, Daughter of I HAMPTON,
of Bofeley, Merchant, and Wife of
GEORGE BULLOCK, of Standly
fhe died Feb 15, 1757

Here refteth the Body of EDMOND
BULLOCK, of this Parifh, who departed
this Life May 25, 1697

Alfo the Body of GEORGE BULLOCK,
who died Dec 10, 1710

THOMAS HART, fenior,
died Sep 13, 1751 aged 59
JANE his Wife
died May 23 1782, ag d 89
SARAH, Wife of THOMAS HART,
died April 1, 176 , aged 55

JONATHAN WINTLE
died July 30, 1773, aged 67

WILLIAM TRIGG fenior
of the Parifh of Weftbury died
May 26, 1778, aged 60

HANNAH, the Wife of GEO MARTEN
and Daughter of WILLIAM JONES,
who died March 8, 176 aged

ON FLAT AND HEAD STONES

	Died	Aged		Died	Aged
Mary Wife of Jofeph Boughton, of Flaxley	1 May 173,	61	Jofeph Morrice	8 Aug 1762	20
Jofeph Boughton	5 May 1749	67	Mary his Wife	26 Oct 1 8	
Richard Hart, fenior	7 Aug 1713	66	William Harper, fenior	1 Mar 174	
Richard Hart, junior	14 Dec 1746	51	John Boughton late of the Spout, in this Parifh	1 Mar 175	
Jane the Wife of William Hayle of Longhope, and Daughter of Geo Marter, of this Parifh	16 Dec 1741	55	Margaret his Relict	11 Jun 1 56	5
			John Boughton	4 Nov 17	
			Jofeph Boughton	30 Apr 1751	

BLEDINGTON,
OR
BLADINGTON,

IS bounded on the Eaſt by the River *Fuenlode*, which divides this County from *Oxfordſhire* The Pariſh is conſtituent of the Hundred of *Slaughter*, and the Deanery of *Stow*, from whence it is diſtant Three Miles on the South-eaſt, and from GLOUCESTER Twenty eight on the Laſt The Soil is mixed, of Clay and Gravel The Arable Lands are exceeded by the Paſture Some of the Common Fields are incloſed, by Act of Parliament, obtained in 1770, with theſe Reſtrictions, "That the *Far* " *Heath*, and *Cow Common*, do remain uncloſed, and that a Portion of Furze, or Heath Ground, not " exceeding Six Acres, in the *Home Heath*, be veſted in the Churchwardens and Overſeers of the Poor, " in Truſt, for raiſing Fuel for the Uſe of the poor Pariſhioners" It is computed that the Terrier of the whole Pariſh is compriſed in rather more than 1500 Acres

The Impropriation belonged, with other Lands, to the Abbey of *Winchcombe*, and afterwards to that of *Eveſham* At the Diſſolution, it was made a Part of the Revenues of the newly erected Chapter of *Chriſt Church* in *Oxford*, who have ſince preſented to the Vicarage. The Leſſee of the Impropriation is AMBROSE REDDAL, Eſq

The Church is dedicated to *Saint Leonard* It is built in a good Style, with a double Row of Windows on the North Side, which are ornamented with Portraits of Saints, and the firſt Biſhops and Martyrs with Legends on Scrolls Attached to the Chancel was a Chantry, on the Window of which, now totally ob literated, was inſcribed, " 𝕺rate pro 𝕬nimabus 𝕹icholas 𝕳obbes, et 𝕬gnetis 𝕌xoris ejus' There is an Aiſle on the South Side, and a Tower, containing Five Bells

The Manor, and principal Eſtate, paſſed from the Abbey of *Winchcombe*, Utica in *Normandy*, and *Eveſham*, to the Family of LEIGH, being granted, at the general Diſſolution, to Sir THOMAS LEIGH, 7 EDW VI It was purchaſed of his Deſcendants, the Heirs of JAMES LEIGH, Eſq in 1771, by AM BROSE REDDAL, Eſq.

No Benefactions to the Poor.

INCUMBENTS	PATRONS	INCUMBENTS	PATRONS
——— William Herbert, Clerk,	———————	1730 Penyſton Haſtings, Cle	King George II
From Sir ROBERT ATKYNS		1738 John Ingles, B A	Chriſt Church, Oxf
		1758 Robert Richards, Clerk,	The ſame
		1763 Henry Browne, M A	The ſame
		1780 Thomas Horne, B A	The ſame

PRESENT LORD OF THE MANOR,

AMBROSE REDDAL, Eſq

The only Perſon ſummoned from this Place, by the Heralds in 1682 and 1683 was
William Lord, Gent

At the Election in 1776 Eleven Freeholders polled from this Pariſh

The only remaining Regiſter bears Date 1760.

ANNUAL ACCOUNT OF MARRIAGES, BIRTHS, AND BURIALS, IN THIS PARISH

A D	Mar	Bir	Bur	A D	Mar	Bir	Bur	A D	Mar	Bir	Bur	A D	Mar	Bir	Bur
1781	1	9	6	1791				1801				1811			
1782	—	9	4	1792				1802				1812			
1783	3	6	4	1793				1803				1813			
1784	1	6	10	1794				1804				1814			
1785	—	3	5	1795				1805				1815			
1786	1	7	6	1796				1806				1816			
1787	1	6	3	1797				1807				1817			
1788				1798				1808				1818			
1789				1799				1809				1819			
1790				1800				1810				1820			

INSCRIPTIONS

INSCRIPTIONS IN THE CHURCH.

Here lyeth the Body of Mr
WILLIAM HERBERT, Clerke, and
Minister of this Place, who
departed this Life the 28th Day of
October, Anno Dom 1709,
aged 55 Years.

Also here lyeth the Body of
MARY HERBERT, Relict of the abovenamed Mr WILLIAM HERBERT, who
departed this Life Aug 10, 1731,
aged 80 Years

Here lyeth interred the Body of
SARAH, the Wife of JAMES RICHTON,
of this Place, and Daughter of
THOMAS and ANNE PHILLIPS, of
Cornwell in the County of Oxford,
who departed this Life January
the 17th, 1719-20, aged 32 Years.

In Memory of ELIZABETH, the
Wife of JOHN CATLING, of Blockley
She departed this Life April 17, 1753,
aged 80 Years

Here lies interred the Body of
FRANCIS MACE
who departed this Life
June 7, Anno Dom 1717,
aged 62 Years.

IN THE CHURCH YARD, ON TOMBS

ANNE, the Wife of
CHRISTOPHER ROSE, of this Town, and
Daughter of the late JOHN GUY,
She died Sept 22, 1723, aged 44

CHRISTOPHER ROSE
died Feb 12, 1732, aged 52

JOHN CORBETT, of Burford,
died Aug 8, 1746, aged 46.

AGNES, the Wife of
Mr JOHN GRAYHURST,
buried Oct 9, 1704

JOHANNES GRAYHURST, Gen
ob 24 Decembris, 1720, æt 83.
He was elected one of his Majesty's Coroners for
this County, in the Year 1676, which Office he
executed 37 Years, and then weakened by old Age
resigned it

The Rev JOHN INGLES,
Vicar of this Parish,
died Dec VIII, MDCCLVII,
aged LXII

JANE his Wife
died July XXV, MDCCLVII,
aged LXXVI

ON HEAD STONES.

	Died	Aged
William Pegler - - - -	30 Jan 1741	82
Elizabeth his Wife - - - -	— Apr 1754	71
John Pegler - - - -	8 Feb 1775	55
William Stow - - - -	10 July, 1754	41
Thomas, Son of John and Ann Andrews, Gent -	19 Apr. 1762	31
Thomas Andrews - - - -	4 May, 1716	64
Joannah, Wife of Thomas Andrews -	9 Apr. 1749	77
Ann, Wife of John Andrews, and Daughter of Haines Woodman, of Clapton	16 Aug 1743	36
John Andrews, senior - - -	15 May, 1702	73
Thomas Baker - - - -	17 Sept 1727	60
Thomas Baker, senior - - -	5 Mar 1743	72
Thomas, Son of Thomas and Mary Baker -	31 Aug 1747	45
Sarah, Wife of Thomas Baker - -	5 Jan 1775	76
William Baker, of Lineham	16 Sept 1774	69

BLOCKLEY

CHURCH

THE original Division of Counties, and particularly the arbitrary Detachment of certain Parishes from the main District, is accounted for by their being Parcels of some great Seignory belonging to Baronies, Bishoprics, or Abbies * This Reason is applicable to *Blockley*, which has been, for Time immemorial, a manerial **Appendage** to the Bishops of *Worcester*, although totally insulated by Parishes of the Counties of *Gloucester* and *Warwick*. As it has been for some Centuries the only Place of Sepulture for several adjacent Villages, it claims our Notice in this "SUPPLEMENTARY *History* of GLOUCESTER-"SHIRE"

Blockley lies in the **Eastern Division** of the **Hundred** of *Oswaldeslow* in the County of *Worcester*, and gives Name to a rural **Deanery**. It is situate between *Chipping Campden* on the North, and *Stow on the Would* on the South, and is distant from *Worcester* Twenty-six, and from GLOUCESTER Twenty seven Miles The Soil admits both of Pasture and Arable of good Qualities The River *Evenlode* intersects the Parish, and affording copious, and constant Supplies of Water, gave Encouragement to the Establishment of Silk Mills Of these the first was erected by HENRY WHATCOTT, Silk-throwster, in the beginning of this Century.

The Benefice was a Rectory till appropriated, in 1327, by THOMAS COBHAM, and endowed with the Tythes of Hay, Wool, and Lamb, by JOHN THORESBY, Bishops of *Worcester* The Instrument of Endowment is still subsisting in the Registry of the Diocese, and bears Date at *Blockle*, 20 Sept 1352 When the Inclosure of the Hamlets of *Draycott* and *Paxford* was completed in 1772, adequate Lands were allotted to the Vicarage. The Peculiar is exempted from the Archdeacon's Visitation, and claims Mortuaries from the Parishes of *Bourton on the Hill*, *Morton in Marsh*, and *Batsford*, in this County, and *Stretton super Fosse* in *Warwickshire*. In 1440 the Inhabitants of *Stretton* petitioned for a Right of Sepulture at their own Chapel, which was not granted. They pleaded the Prevention of Floods, and the Distance from the Mother Church Dugdale recites a Contention with the Rector of *Stretton* on this Account † By a Bull of Pope JULIUS II the Parishioners of *Morton* were permitted to bury in their own Chapel, "propter interposita Montium Juga, præcipue brumali Tempore." The Impropriation is held, in Parcels, by Lease of the Bishop of *Worcester* The great Tythes of *Northwick* and *Draycott* are granted to the Family of RUSHOUT, those of *Paxford* to FIELD and FLETCHER, those of *Aston Magna* to THOMAS BUND, Esq of *Worcester*, and of *Ditchford* and *Dorn* to the Vicar, for Twenty one Years, renewable every Seven, by the Permission of the Bishop

The Church is dedicated to *St Peter and St Paul*, consisting of a spacious Nave, and North Aisle, of the Architecture of the middle Ages The Chancel, of the Saxon Style, is probably the same Structure that is described in DOMESDAY Book. In 1724, the old Tower was taken down, and the present was finished in 1728, by THOMAS WOODWARD, who designed and conducted the Building, which is of modern Gothic The Contribution, which was supplied solely by the Parish, under the Auspices of the late Sir JOHN RUSHOUT, Bart amounted to 519l 19s 8d ½ by which the Expence was defrayed. In the Chancel, on large flat Stones, are curious Portraits in Brass, of former Incumbents A Chauntry, in Honour of the Virgin, was founded in this Church by JOHN DE BLOCKELLI, 1375

The Manor was an Appendage to the See of *Worcester*, prior to the Conqueror's Survey; it was also an episcopal Residence, from whence many Deeds were issued, and where Consecrations were performed ‡. WALTER DE CANTILUPO died at his Palace here in 1235, and HENRY WAKEFFIELD in 1395 § Fairs were obtained by former Bishops, and these were extended to Sixteen Days, in the Course of the Year, by EDWARD I at the Request of GODFREY GIFFARD, 1275 Two annual Fairs are now held, on the Tuesday after Easter Week, and on the 10th of October The ancient Manor house has been long deserted by the Bishops, and the Manor granted in Lease to the Family of CHILDE, who settled here in the Year 1320, 13 Edw II from whom it passed, by Purchase, to that of RUSHOUT (of noble Extraction from the Barons De Rushault in Picardy), in the Reign of CHARLES II.

* HEARNE's Antiquarian Discourses
† History of Warwickshire, p 509
‡ THOMAS's Survey of Worcester, p 107
§ WHARTON's Anglia Sacra, p 496.

In

In this Parish are Seven Hamlets. 1 The Township of *Blockley*, a populous Village 2 *North-wick*, the ancient Manfion of the CHILDS, was new modelled in 1730, by the late Sir JOHN RUSHOUT, Bart from a Defign of the celebrated Earl of BURLINGTON From its prefent Poffeffor, *Northwick* has received fuch Improvements in the Houfe, Pleafure Grounds, and Park, as to entitle it to a Place amongft the beft Specimens of modern Art and refined Tafte 3 *Dorn* It has been thought that a Roman Station once occupied the Site of this Hamlet This Conjecture is confirmed by the Difcovery of many Coins, of the debafed Metal of the Lower Empire The *Fofs Road* leads through it The principal Proprietor of *Dorn* is THOMAS EDWARDS FREEMAN, Efq 4 *Ditchford*, the fole Property of the Right Hon CHARLES HENRY DILLON LEE, Nephew and Heir of the Right Hon GEORGE HENRY LEE, the laft Earl of *Litchfield* 5 *Paxton*, 6 *Afton*, and 7 *Draycott*, where Efftates are held by the Earl of GAINS-BOROUGH, and the Family of POPE Three Chapels are faid to have been founded for the Service of thefe Hamlets, no Veftiges of which remain at this Time

---

B E N E F A C T I O N S.

In the Year 1702, the Right Reverend Father in God WILLIAM Lord Bifhop of WORCESTER cieled and beautified the Chancel

In 1703, the Church was new paved by the Contribution of the principal Inhabitants of the Parifh, and the Chancel by the Minifter

In 1706, Mrs ELIZABETH MARTIN, Wife of FRANCIS MARTYN, of *Upton Old*, gave a large Silver Plate for the Communion Table

In 1707, Dame SARAH SHORE gave a Communion Table Cloth and Damafk Napkin

A New School Houfe was erected and given for the Ufe of a School in this Town, by ERASMUS SAUNDERS, D D Vicar

Mrs MARY CARTER gave the Sum of 100*l* the yearly Ufe of which to be laid out for teaching poor Children at *Blockley*, and for buying Books for the Poor of *Blockley* and *Campden* The above Sum was depofited in the Hands of the Parifh Officers of *Blockley*, which they employed in Building a Work-houfe, or Houfe of Maintenance of Poor, and annually pay the Intereft of 4*l* per Cent which is applied to the Purpofes abovementioned

Mrs JANE CROFTS bequeathed the Sum of 3*l* 10*s* per Ann towards cloathing and buying Books for the poor Children taught at the School in *Blockley*

Mr PERKINS, of *Drayton* in the County of *Middlefex*, gave the Sum of 400*l* the Intereft of which to be made Ufe of in cloathing the poor old People and Children of the Parifh

FRANCIS MARTIN, Efq gave 100*l* the Intereft of which, for teaching poor Children at the Charity School for ever

By a Benefactor unknown, half a Meadow in *Blockley*, called *Church Meadow*, and other Lands, to the Value of 4*l* per Ann was given towards the repairing of the Church for ever

In 1732, the Right Hon ELIZABETH Countefs Dowager of NORTHAMPTON, Sifter to Sir JOHN RUSH-OUT, of *Northwick*, Bart gave, to the Parifh Church of *Blockley*, the following Set of Communion Plate viz Two large Silver Flaggons, Two Silver Chalices, Two Salvers, One large Difh, and One Plate, the Weight of the whole, 164 Ounces and 16 Pennyweights. She gave alfo a fine Damafk Table Cloth, with Six Napkins

GODDARD CARTER, of *Afcot* in the County of *Oxford*, Efq by his Will, dated the 9th of November, 1723, gave 10*l* a Year, out of his Lands in *Upton Old*, to teach poor Children, living in the Parifh of *Blockley*, to read, write, and fomething of Arithmetic, and 10*l* a Year out of the fame Eftate, for Cloathing the pooreft old People of the Parifh of *Blockley* The Owner or Owners of the faid Eftate to appoint the Perfon who fhall teach the Children, and alfo what poor Perfons fhall be cloathed and with what Cloathing, and that a full Account, in writing, under their Hands, be delivered to the Inhabitants yearly, in the Eafter Week, when they fhall meet to choofe Church Wardens, how they have difpofed of the faid Charities

Mr

Mrs. Martha Scattergood, Daughter of the Rev. Mr. Scattergood, formerly Vicar of this Parish, by her last Will, bearing Date August 2, 1753, gave to the Town of Blockley 100l to be disposed of as the Minister and Churchwardens shall think best for the Benefit of the Poor. Which said Will of the said Mrs. Martha Scattergood was proved in the Prerogative Court of Canterbury, on the 29th Day of May, 1754, and the Legacy paid by her Executors to the Right Hon. Sir John Rushout, Bart. in June 1756, with 3l. Interest, the whole Sum, amounting to 103l. was invested in the 3½ per Cent. Bank Annuities, 1756, and purchased 110l. Stock, which stands in the Name of Sir John Rushout, Bart. of Northwick in this Parish.

Mrs. Anne Martyn left by her Will, bearing Date May 1, 1737, 5l. to the Poor of Blockley, the Interest of which was to be disposed of as Mrs. Elizabeth Martyn, her Mother, should direct. The Interest is applied, pursuant to the Direction of the said Mrs. Elizabeth Martyn, for the Instruction of poor Children in reading, knitting, and sewing.

Mrs. Elizabeth Martyn, who died in the Year 1747, left by her Will another Sum of 50l. to the Churchwardens of the Parish of Blockley with Part of the Interest of which they are directed to buy yearly a Ton of Coals, for the Use of the Charity School in Blockley Church Yard, and with the Remainder to buy Cloaths, as far as the same will extend, for the poor Children taught in her Daughter Anne's Charity School.

Incumbents	Patrons	Incumbents	Patrons
——————,	Bishops of Worcester	1572 Thomas Wilson,	Nich. Bullingham
		1586 Henry Daniel,	Edmund Freke
1242 Vincent de Bergavenny,	Walt. de Cantilupo	1627 George Durant,	Henry Parry
1270 Lucian de Cormeilles,	Nicholas de Ely	1653 Giles Collier,	(See Vacant)
1279 Philip de Croft,	Godfrey Giffard	1678 Francis Phipps,	James Fleetwood
1291 William Gransend,	The same	168 Sam Scattergood, M A	The same
1320 Benedict Paston,	Thomas Cobham	1696 Thomas Turner, M A	Edw. Stillingfleet
1349 John Devalve,	John Thoresby	1700 William Lloyd, D D	William Lloyd
—— Richard Culey,		The above were communicated by Browne Willis,	
1419 Walter Aston,	Philip Morgan.	Esq and are inserted in the Register	
—— John Clerke,			
1455 John Bell,	John Carpenter	1705 Erasmus Saunders, D. D.	William Lloyd
1465 Philip Warthim,	The same.	1724 Michael Biddulph,	John Hough
1489 William Neele,	John Alcocke	1727 William Byrch LL D	The same
1540 Robert Holdsworth,	Hugh Latymer	1742 Rich. Congreve, M A	The same
1552 Dominick Maton,	Nicholas Heath	1761 Charles Jasper Selwyn, M A	James Johnson
1562 John Freeman,	Edwin Sandys		

Present Lessee of the Manor,

Sir John Rushout, Bart.

The Register commences with the Year 1538, and has been kept with laudable Exactness.

Annual Account of Marriages, Births, and Burials, in this Parish

A D	Mar	Bir	Bur	A D	Mar	Bir	Bur	A D	Mar	Bir	Bur	A D	Mar	Bir	Bur
1781	8	46	40	1791				1801				1811			
1782	9	42	33	1792				1802				1812			
1783	11	47	19	1793				1803				1813			
1784	11	42	36	1794				1804				1814			
1785	8	52	31	1795				1805				1815			
1786	17	51	26	1796				1806				1816			
1787	6	41	26	1797				1807				1817			
1788				1798				1808				1818			
1789				1799				1809				1819			
1790				1800				1810				1820			

INSCRIPTIONS

INSCRIPTIONS IN THE CHURCH.

IN THE CHANCEL.

ON A BRASS PLATE

𝔅enedictus 𝔇eus   𝔅enedictus 𝔇eus
Orate pro anima Magistri Willi Neele quondam
Vicari hujus Ecclesie, & Rectoris Ecclesie de Bur-
ton sup' Aquam, qui obiit VIII die Augusti, Anno
Domini DCE, cujus anime propicietur Deus.
Amen

ON A LARGE BLUE STONE IS A BRASS FIGURE,
REPRESENTING A PRIEST IN HIS SACERDOTAL
ROBES, IN A KNEELING POSTURE, HIS FACE
TOWARDS THE NORTH. OUT OF HIS MOUTH PRO-
CEEDS A LABEL, WITH THESE WORDS.

Unica spes vitæ mihi Virgo.

OVER THE HEAD HAS BEEN A FIGURE OF THE
VIRGIN AND THE CHILD JESUS, NOW DESTROYED
BEFORE THE PRIEST ARE CUT THE OUTLINES OF
A CHALICE, AND UNDERNEATH THE FOLLOWING
VERSES.

Insignem gravitate virum gemino decoratum
Stole gratum, semper pietat ad opera primum,
In cineres versum duroque sub marmore pressum,
Plangite, vosque sonet sit tibi vita Deus.

ROUND THE MARGIN OF THE STONE, THE FOL-
LOWING INSCRIPTION.

Hic jacet Magist Philippus Wartham, quond' Vicarius Ecclesie de Blockley, qui obiit in Crastino
Sancti Bartholomei A D MCCCCLXXXIIII
cujus Anime propicietur Deus Amen.

ON A BLUE FLAT STONE, ANOTHER FIGURE OF
A PRIEST IN HIS ROBES, KNEELING UNDERNEATH
IS THE FOLLOWING INSCRIPTION.

Quisquis eris qui transieris Sta' per lege plora
Sum quod eris, fueramque quod es pro me precor ora.

In Memory of HANNAH, the
Wife of MELCHIOR GUY DICKENS, Esq
who died Oct 20, 1752, aged 46

And of FREDERICK WILLIAM GUY DICKENS,
Clerk, who died Sept 15, 1779, aged 50

AGAINST THE NORTH WALL.

Arms, Argent, a Cheveron between Three
Saltires rightly Sable. Motto,

Virtus propter se.

A MARBLE MONUMENT SUPPORTED BY CORIN-
THIAN PILLARS, WITH THE EFFIGY OF A MAN IN
ARMOUR, KNEELING

Arms, on Three Escutcheons; 1st, Gules, a
Chevron Ermine, between Three Eagles close Argent,
for CHILDE. 2d, CHILDE,—impaling, Argent, a
Lion rampant Purpure, crowned Or, for FOLIOT 3d,
CHILDE,—impaling, Argent, a Chevron between
Three Scaling Ladders Sable, for JEFFERIES

GULIELMUS CHILDE, Filius & Hæres
GULIELMI CHILDE, Armigeri,
defuncti, religiose posuit, 1615

N B. *By the Register it appears that* WILLIAM
CHILDE *was buried Nov 2, 1601*.

ON A MONUMENT, CONTAINING THE EFFIGIES OF
A MAN AND WOMAN, IN A KNEELING POSTURE,
IN THE DRESS OF THE TIMES

Arms, CHILDE, as before.

UNDER THE MAN

Hic requiescit secundum Domini
Adventum fœliciter expectans
GULIELMUS CHILDE, Arm qui (dum vixit)
Amicus suit & hospitalis Piis & Honestis.
Promissis constans, inopia laborantibus
Misericors, & spem ferens,
obiit 9 Die Decembris, Anno Dom 1633,
ætatis suæ 80

UNDER THE WOMAN

Hic requiescit secundum Domini
Adventum fœliciter expectans
ELIZABETHA, Uxor Charissima GULIELMI
CHILDE, Arm una filiarum GULIELMI BABINGTON,
Militis, de Kiddington, in Com Oxon,
Quæ post 46 Annos in conjugis
Fidelissime expletos,
obiit 9 Die Novembris, Anno Dom 1662,
ætatis suæ 64.

ON A MURAL MONUMENT, IN WHICH IS THE
EFFIGY OF A WOMAN RECLINING, AT FULL
LENGTH, IN THE DRESS OF THE TIMES

Arms, CHILDE,—impaling, Azure, on a Fess
wavy Argent, a Cross patée Gules, in Chief Two
Estoiles Or, for JENKINSON

In Memory of ANNE MARY, Daughter to
Sir ROBERT JENKINSON, of Wilcott in the
County of Oxford, Knt and Wife to THOMAS
CHILDE, of Northwicke in the County of
Worcester, Esq

         Positum est.

OVER SIXTEEN VERSES IN ENGLISH

Epitaphium fecit ipsa *Paulo* ante obitum, qui
accidit 11 Die Feb 1659.

On a Tablet

Arms, Sable, Two Lions paſſant within a Bordure engrailed Or, on a Canton, the Arms of Ulſter, for RUSHOUT,—impaling, Argent, a Frett Sable, and a Canton Gules, for VERNON

Sir JAMES RUSHOUT, Bart
and ARABELLA his Wife,
Daughter of Sir THOMAS VERNON.

AGAINST THE SOUTH WALL

Arms, Quarterly, per Feſs indented Azure and Or, in the firſt Quarter a Lion paſſant guardant of the ſecond, for CROFT,—impaling Azure, ſemé of Fleur de Lis a Lion rampant guardant Or, for BEAUMONT.

In Memory of EDWARD CROFT,
of Northwick, Gent

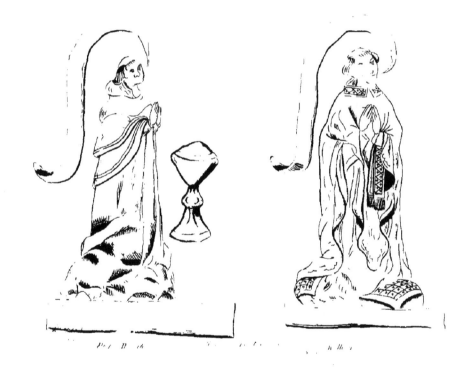

is born 1631, died 1698
J. J. MOORE Fecit

MARIA Mater Chariſſima

INSCRIPTIONS IN OLDLAND *CHAPEL IN THIS PARISH*

IN THE NORTH AISLE

Here lyeth the Body of
Mr Thomas Woodward, Grandson
of Mr Thomas Woodward,
who departed this Life Oct
26, 1728, in the 50th Year of his Age

IN THE SOUTH AISLE

Here lyeth the Body of
James Shatford, of Hanham,
who departed this Life
Aug 14, 1746, aged 59 Years

Also here lyeth the Body of
Susanna, the Wife of the above
James Shatford, who departed
this Life Jan 24, 1762, aged 70 Years

Also the Body of
Ann Christopher, Sister-in-Law
to the above James Shatford,
who departed this Life
July 20, 1745, aged 42 Years

Here lyeth the Body of
George Bush, senior, of this Parish,
Yeoman, who departed this Life
May 4, 1722, aged 70 Years.

Also in Memory of
Samuel Evans, of the Parish of St George,
who lies buried here   He died
March 11, 1765, aged 57 Years

Also the Body of Joan,
Wife of the said Samuel Evans,
and late Wife of George Godfrey
She died June 5, 1774, aged 62 Years

Here lyeth the Body of
Ann, Wife of William Humphris,
of this Parish, who departed
this Life Jan 5, 1720

Here also lyeth the Body of
William Humphris, of this Parish,
who departed this Life April 1, 1727,
aged 72 Years

IN THE NORTH SIDE THE CHANCEL ARE THE
FOLLOWING ARMS

Or, a Bend Azure, for TRYE,—impaling, Argent, a Wyvern Sable, Crest, a Buck's Head caboshed Gules

IN THE CHAPEL YARD, ON HEAD STONES

	Died	Aged
Nicholas Palmer		55
Francis Waters	27 Apr 1777	62
Dorothy, Wife of Samuel Edwards	2 July, 1768	51
Samuel Edwards aforesaid	5 May, 1773	59
Mary, Wife of William Lewton	24 Oct 1772	66
John Lewton, senior, of Hanham	13 June, 1772	80
Hannah his Wife	5 Oct 1740	43
Sarah, Wife of John Lewton, junior, of Hanham	28 Sept 1767	43
Elizabeth, Daughter of James and Jane Lewton, of Cliffton	19 July, 1784	28
Samuel Morgan	10 Mar 1779	27
William Clark	22 June, 1772	66
John, Son of William Clark	21 Aug. 1782	20

XLIII. BLAISDON.

A SMALL Parish in the Hundred of *Westbury*, and the *Forest* Deanery, situate Four Miles on the East from *Mitchel Dean*, and Nine from GLOUCESTER on the West. The Soil is various, though chiefly of Clay, applied, in nearly equal Portions, to Tillage, Pasturage, and Woodland, with many very fruitful Orchards. A small Rivulet, intersecting this Parish, joins the *Severn* at *Westbury* *Blaisdon*, in 1281, was not returned as a distinct Parish, or Village, by the Escheator, but as appendant to *Longhope*, " *cum Hamletto de Bletbesder* " The Village of *Blaisdon* is considerably less than before the great Fire, which happened on the 7th of July 1699, and is recorded on a Table in the Church the Amount of the Loss, delivered on Oath, was 4210*l* 18*s* 9*d*

The Living is a Rectory, and the Church, which is dedicated to *Saint Michael*, consists of a Nave only, with an embattled Tower, low and massive, which contains Five Bells The Right of Advowson is alternately vested in the Families of HAYLE and WADE

The Manor was given to the Abbey of *Flaxley*, in this County, by the DE BOHUNS, Earls of *Hereford* Sir ANTONY KINGSTON received it at the Dissolution from the King From his Descendants it passed to the WADES, who are the present Proprietors, with other Claimants

The Family of MARTIN were anciently among the principal Inhabitants Lands are still distinguished by their Name At *Standley* the BULLOCKS obtained an Estate in the Reign of ELIZABETH, which is now held by WILLIAM BULLOCK, Gent

---

BENEFACTIONS.

Two Tenements, inhabited by the Poor, the annual Value 2*l*, the Donor, and Time of Donation, unknown

INCUMBENTS	PATRONS	INCUMBENTS	PATRONS
1570 Thomas Cooke,	Rob. and Rich Kerle	1705 Bendy Grove, B A	Thomas Wade, Esq.
— William Mayo, M A	———	1728 John Jelfe, Clerk,	Ann Hayle, Widow.
The above from Sir ROBERT ATKYNS		1778 John Morse, B. A.	John Wade, Esq

CLAIMANTS OF THE MANOR,

JOHN WADE, Esq ——— JONES, Gent
——— RICHARDSON, Gent ——— CHINN, Spinster

No Person was summoned from this Parish by the Heralds in 1682 and 1683

At the Election in 1776, Nine Freeholders polled from this Parish

ANNUAL ACCOUNT OF MARRIAGES, BIRTHS, AND BURIALS, IN THIS PARISH

A D	Mar	Bir	Bur	A D	Mar	Bir	Bur	A D	Mar	Bir	Bur	A D	Mar	Bir	Bur
1781	2	5	8	1791				1801				1811			
1782	—	4	8	1792				1802				1812			
1783	1	6	2	1793				1803				1813			
1784	1	10	4	1794				1804				1814			
1785	2	8	3	1795				1805				1815			
1786				1796				1806				1816			
1787				1797				1807				1817			
1788				1798				1808				1818			
1789				1799				1809				1819			
1790				1800				1810				1820			

3

INSCRIPTIONS

INSCRIPTIONS IN THE CHURCH.

ON A MONUMENT IN THE CHANCEL

Beneath are deposited
the Remains of JOHN BOUGHTON, of Flaxley,
late of Broad Oak, Merchant.
He departed this Life July 4, 1767,
in the 67th Year of his Age

In Memory also of ANNE his Wife,
who died May 29, 1741, aged 45 Years

Near this Place likewise were interred
their Daughter and Son, ANN and WILLIAM,
the former of whom died Sept 29, 1751,
the latter, August 28, 1755,
both at the Age of 23 Years

OVER THE CHANCEL DOOR.

REBEKAH, the Wife of ROBERT KIRKE,
was buried Jan 29, 1653

ON ANOTHER MONUMENT IN THE CHANCEL

The Remains of
THOMAS BULLOCK, late of this Parish,
formerly of the City of Ghent,
Merchant, who died March 7, 1784
He gave by Will 20l to be distributed
amongst the Poor of this Parish

ON FLAT STONES

ANNE HAYLE, Widow and Relict
of ROBERT HAYLE, of this Parish, Gent
buried Dec 5, 1736, aged 60.

Here resteth the Body of
WILLIAM MAYO, Rector of this
Parish, who was buried May 26,
Anno Dom 1705

WILLIAM his Son, by MARY
his Wife, was buried Sep 10, 1695

A second WILLIAM their Son
was buried Sept 11, 1696

MARY their Daughter was
buried in the Year 1692

Here lyeth the Body of ROBERT
KIRKE, senior, who departed this
Life Nov 16, 1658

And of ANNE his Wife, who
departed this Life Jan 18,
Anno Dom. 1675

IN THE BELLFRY

In Memory of GEORGE MARTEN, senior,
who was buried Jan 19, 1669

In Memory of GEORGE MARTEN, junior
He was buried Oct 23, 1712, aged 60.

Here resteth the Body of DEBORAH,
the Wife of GEORGE MARTEN, junior, who
departed this Life Nov 5, 1735, aged 79

WILLIAM MARTEN, Son of GEORGE and
DEBORAH MARTEN, died a Bachelor
Dec 10, 1757, aged 66.

In Memory of
WILLIAM MARTEN, of this Parish,
who died June 20,   ,
aged near 40 Years

Also here resteth the Body of HENRY,
the Son of WILLIAM MARTEN,
of this Parish, by ELIZABETH his Wife, who
departed this Life April 26, 1768, aged near 26

IN THE CHURCH YARD

EDWARD BULLOCK, of Strudley,
died Dec 21, 1764 aged 62
Also in Memory of ANNE his Wife
who died Jan 11, 1781, aged 69
EDMOND, Son of EDMOND BULLOCK,
of Strudley Mar 12, 1757, aged 20

GEORGE, the Son of EDMOND BULLOCK,
of Strudley died in his 36th Year, 1766

SAM WINTLE, Son of SAM WINTLE,
buried May 11, 1774, in his 7th Year

ROBERT HAYLE died June 4, 1679 æt 61
MARGARET, Wife of ROBERT HAYLE
senior died Jan 16, 1706, aged 93

JOHN HAYLE died Feb 8, 1689, æt 32
ROD HAYLE died Jan 30, 1714 æt 29

Here are deposited the Remains of a
virtuous Woman, at the Age of 84 Years,
MARGARET, Daughter of THOMAS HAMILTON,
of Boseley, Merchant, and Wife of
GEORGE BULLOCK, of Strudley
She died Feb 1, 1757

Here resteth the Body of EDMOND
BULLOCK, of this Parish, who departed
this Life May 5, 1660,

Also the Body of GEORGE BULLOCK,
who died Dec 10, 1710

ON TOMBS

THOMAS HART, senior,
died Sept 11, 1731 aged 51
JANE his Wife
died May 5, 1782, aged 89
SARAH, Wife of THOMAS HART
died April 1, 1783, aged 55

JONATHAN WINTLE
died July 30, 1773 aged 67

WILLIAM TRIGG senior
of the Parish of Westbury died
May 26, 1778, aged 60
HANNAH, the Wife of GEORGE MARTEN,
and Daughter of WILLIAM TRIGG
who died March 8, 1776 aged

ON FLAT AND HEAD STONES

	Died	Aged		Died	Aged
Mary, Wife of Joseph Boughton, of Tanley	21 May 1763	61	Joseph Morrice —	8 Aug 1762	21
Joseph Boughton	5 May 1733	67	Mary his Wife	26 Oct 1762	
Richard Hart, senior	7 Aug 1733	65	William Hart, senior	21 Mar 1759	
Richard Hart, junior	14 Feb 1730	51	John Boughton, late of the Spout, in this Parish	1 Mar 17	
Jane the Wife of William Hayle, of Longhope and Daughter of George Marten, of this Parish	16 Dec 1744	55	Margaret his Relict	12 Jun 1760	5
			John Boughton	1 Nov 17	
			Joseph Boughton	30 Apr 177	

BLEDINGTON,
OR
BLADINGTON,

IS bounded on the Eaſt by the River *Fuemode*, which divides this County from *Oxfordſhire* This Pariſh is conſtituent of the Hundred of *Slaughter*, and the Deanery of *Stow*, from whence it is diſtant Three Miles on the South-eaſt, and from GLOUCESTER Twenty eight on the Laſt The Soil is mixed, of Clay and Gravel The Arable Lands are exceeded by the Paſture Some of the Common Fields are incloſed, by Act of Parliament, obtained in 1770, with theſe Reſtrictions, ' That the *Lay* " *Heath*, and *Cow Common*, do remain unincloſed, and that a Portion of Furze, or Heath Ground not " exceeding Six Acres, in the *Home Heath*, be veſted in the Churchwardens and Overſeers of the Poor, " in Truſt, for raiſing Fuel for the Uſe of the poor Pariſhioners " It is computed that the Terrier of the whole Pariſh is compriſed in rather more than 1500 Acres

The Impropriation belonged, with other Lands, to the Abbey of *Winchcombe*, and afterwards to that of *Eveſham* At the Diſſolution, it was made a Part of the Revenues of the newly erected Chapter of *Chriſt Church* in *Oxford*, who have ſince preſented to the Vicarage The Leſſee of the Impropriation is AMBROSE REDDAL, Eſq

The Church is dedicated to *Saint Leonard* It is built in a good Style, with a double Row of Windows on the North Side, which are ornamented with Portraits of Saints, and the firſt Biſhops and Martyrs with Legends on Scrolls Attached to the Chancel was a Chantry, on the Window of which, now totally obliterated, was inſcribed, " 𝕺rate pro 𝕬nimabus 𝕹icholai 𝕳obbes, et 𝕬gnetis 𝕌xoris ejus" There is an Aiſle on the South Side, and a Tower, containing Five Bells

The Manor, and principal Eſtate, paſſed from the Abbeys of *Winchcombe*, Ut in *Normandy*, and *Eveſham*, to the Family of LEIGH, being granted, at the general Diſſolution, to Sir THOMAS LEIGH, 7 Edw VI It was purchaſed of his Deſcendants, the Heirs of JAMES LEIGH, Eſq in 1771, by AMBROSE REDDAL, Eſq.

No Benefactions to the Poor

INCUMBENTS	PATRONS	INCUMBENTS	PATRONS
—— William Herbert, Clerk, From Sir ROBERT ATKYNS	——————	1730 Penyſton Haſtings, Clerk	King George II
		1738 John Ingles, B A	Chriſt Church, Oxf
		1768 Robert Richards, Clerk,	The ſame
		1763 Henry Browne, M A	The ſame
		1780 Thomas Horne, B A	The ſame

PRESENT LORD OF THE MANOR,
AMBROSE REDDAL, Eſq

The only Perſon ſummoned from this Place by the Heralds in 1682 and 1683 was
William Lord, Gent

At the Election in 1776 Eleven Freeholders polled from this Pariſh
The only remaining Regiſter bears Date 1763

ANNUAL ACCOUNT OF MARRIAGES, BIRTHS, AND BURIALS, IN THIS PARISH

A D	Mar	Bir	Bur	A D	Mar	Bir	Bur	A D	Mar	Bir	Bur	A D	Mar	Bir	Bur
1781	1	9	6	1791				1801				1811			
1782	—	9	4	1792				1802				1812			
1783	3	6	4	1793				1803				1813			
1784	1	6	10	1794				1804				1814			
1785	—	3	5	1795				1805				1815			
1786	1	7	6	1796				1806				1816			
1787	1	6	3	1797				1807				1817			
1788				1798				1808				1818			
1789				1799				1809				1819			
1790				1800				1810				18			

INSCRIPTIONS

INSCRIPTIONS IN THE CHURCH.

Here lyeth the Body of Mr
WILLIAM HERBERT, Clerke, and
Minifter of this Place, who
departed this Life the 28th Day of
October, Anno Dom 1709,
aged 55 Years.

Alfo here lyeth the Body of
MARY HERBERT, Relict of the abovenamed Mr WILLIAM HERBERT, who
departed this Life Aug 10, 1731,
aged 80 Years

Here lyeth interred the Body of
SARAH, the Wife of JAMES RIGHTON,
of this Place, and Daughter of
THOMAS and ANNE PHILLIPS, of
Cornwell in the County of Oxford,
who departed this Life January
the 17th, 1719 20, aged 32 Years.

In Memory of ELIZABETH, the
Wife of JOHN CATLING, of Blockley
She departed this Life April 17, 1733,
aged 80 Years

Here lies interred the Body of
FRANCIS MACE
who departed this Life
June 7, Anno Dom 1717,
aged 62 Years.

IN THE CHURCH YARD, ON TOMBS

ANNE, the Wife of
CHRISTOPHER ROSE, of this Town, and
Daughter of the late JOHN GUY,
She died Sept 22, 1723, aged 44

CHRISTOPHER ROSE
died Feb 12, 1732, aged 52.

JOHN CORBETT, of Burford,
died Aug 8, 1746, aged 46

AGNES, the Wife of
Mr JOHN GRAYHURST,
buried Oct 9, 1704

JOHANNES GRAYHURST, Gen
ob 24 Decembris, 1720, æt 83.
He was elected one of his Majefty's Coroners for
this County, in the Year 1676, which Office he
executed 37 Years, and then weakened by old Age
refigned it

The Rev JOHN INGLES,
Vicar of this Parifh,
died Dec VIII, MDCCLVII,
aged LXII

JANE his Wife
died July XXV, MDCCLVII,
aged LXXVI.

ON HEAD STONES

	Died		Aged
William Pegler	30 Jan	1741	82
Elizabeth his Wife	— Apr	1754	71
John Pegler	8 Feb	1775	55
William Stow	10 July,	1754	41
Thomas, Son of John and Ann Andrews, Gent	19 Apr	1762	31
Thomas Andrews	4 May,	1716	64
Joannah, Wife of Thomas Andrews	9 Apr	1749	77
Ann, Wife of John Andrews, and Daughter of Haines Woodman, of Clapton	16 Aug	1743	36
John Andrews, fenior	15 May,	1702	73
Thomas Baker	17 Sept	1727	60
Thomas Baker, fenior	5 Mar	1743	72
Thomas, Son of Thomas and Mary Baker	31 Aug	1747	45
Sarah, Wife of Thomas Baker	5 Jun	1775	76
William Baker, of Lincham	16 Sept	1774	69

BLOCKLEY

CHURCH

BLOCKLEY.

THE original Division of Counties, and particularly the arbitrary Detachment of certain Parishes from the main District, is accounted for by their being Parcels of some great Seignory belonging to Baronies, Bishoprics, or Abbies * This Reason is applicable to *Blockley*, which has been, for Time immemorial, a manerial Appendage to the Bishops of *Worcester*, although totally insulated by Parishes of the Counties of *Gloucester* and *Warwick* As it has been for some Centuries the only Place of Sepulture for several adjacent Villages, it claims our Notice in this " Supplementary *History of* Gloucester-" shire "

Blockley lies in the Eastern Division of the Hundred of *Oswaldeslow* in the County of *Worcester*, and gives Name to a rural Deanery. It is situate between *Chipping Campden* on the North, and *Stow on the Would* on the South, and is distant from *Worcester* Twenty-six, and from Gloucester Twenty-seven Miles The Soil admits both of Pasture and Arable of good Qualities The River *Eventode* intersects the Parish, and affording copious, and constant Supplies of Water, gave Encouragement to the Establishment of Silk Mills Of these the first was erected by Henry Whatcoti, Silk throwster, in the beginning of this Century.

The Benefice was a Rectory till appropriated, in 1327, by Thomas Cobham, and endowed with the Tythes of Hay, Wool, and Lamb, by John Thoresby, Bishops of *Worcester* The Instrument of Endowment is still subsisting in the Registry of the Diocese, and bears Date at *Blocle*, 20 Sept 1352 When the Inclosure of the Hamlets of *Draycott* and *Paxford* was compleated in 1772, adequate Lands were allotted to the Vicarage. The Peculiar is exempted from the Archdeacon's Visitation, and claims Mortuaries from the Parishes of *Bourton on the Hill*, *Morton in Marsh*, and *Batford*, in this County, and *Stretton super Fosse* in *Warwickshire* In 1440 the Inhabitants of *Stretton* petitioned for a Right of Sepulture at their own Chapel, which was not granted. They pleaded the Prevention of Floods, and the Distance from the Mother Church. Dugdale recites a Contention with the Rector of *Stretton* on this Account † By a Bull of Pope Julius II the Parishioners of *Morton* were permitted to bury in their own Chapel, " *propter interposita Montium Juga, præcipue brumal Tempore* " The Impropriation is held, in Parcels, by Lease of the Bishop of *Worcester* The great Tythes of *Northwick* and *Draycott* are granted to the Family of Rushout, those of *Paxford* to Field and Fletcher, those of *Aston Magna* to Thomas Bund, Esq. of *Worcester*, and of *Ditchford* and *Dorn* to the Vicar, for Twenty-one Years, renewable every Seven, by the Permission of the Bishop

The Church is dedicated to *St Peter and St Paul*, consisting of a spacious Nave, and North Aisle, of the Architecture of the middle Ages The Chancel, of the Saxon Style, is probably the same Structure that is described in Domesday Book: In 1724, the old Tower was taken down, and the present was finished in 1728, by Thomas Woodward, who designed and conducted the Building, which is of modern Gothic. The Contribution, which was supplied solely by the Parish, under the Auspices of the late Sir John Rushout Bart amounted to 519l. 19s. 8d ½ by which the Expence was defrayed In the Chancel, on large flint Stones, are curious Portraits in Brass, of former Incumbents A Chauntry, in Honour of the Virgin, was founded in this Church by John de Blockley, 1375.

The Manor was an Appendage to the See of *Worcester*, prior to the Conqueror's Survey; it was also an episcopal Residence, from whence many Deeds were issued, and where Consecrations were performed ‡. Walter de Cantilupo died at his Palace here in 1236, and Henry Wakefield in 1395 § Fairs were obtained by former Bishops, and these were extended to Sixteen Days, in the Course of the Year, by Edward I at the Request of Godfrey Giffard, 1275 Two annual Fairs are now held, on the Tuesday after Easter Week, and on the 10th of October The ancient Manor house has been long deserted by the Bishops, and the Manor granted in Lease to the Family of Childe, who settled here in the Year 1320, 13 Edw II from whom it passed, by Purchase, to that of Rushout (of noble Extraction from the Barons *De Rushault* in *Picardy*), in the Reign of Charles II.

* Hearne's Antiquarii in Discourses
† History of Warwickshire p 599
‡ Thomas's Survey of Worcester p 107
§ Wharton's Anglia Sacra, p 496

In this Parish are Seven Hamlets 1 The Township of *Blockley*, a populous Village 2 *Northwick*, the ancient Mansion of the CHILDS, was new modelled in 1730, by the late Sir JOHN RUSHOUT, Bart from a Design of the celebrated Earl of BURLINGTON From its present Possessor, *Northwick* has received such Improvements in the House, Pleasure Grounds, and Park, as to entitle it to a Place in one of the best Specimens of modern Art and refined Taste 3 *Dorn* It has been thought that a Roman Station once occupied the Site of this Hamlet This Conjecture is confirmed by the Discovery of many Coins, of the debased Metal of the Lower Empire The *Foss Road* leads through it The principal Proprietor of *Dorn* is Thomas Edwards Freeman, Esq 4 *Ditchford*, the sole Property of the Right Hon Charles Henry Dillon Lee, Nephew and Heir of the Right Hon George Henry Lee, the last Earl of *Litchfield* 5 *Paxton*, 6 *Aston*, and 7 *Draycott*, where Estates are held by the Earl of GAINSBOROUGH, and the Family of Port Three Chapels are said to have been founded for the Service of these Hamlets, no Vestiges of which remain at this Time

---

B E N E F A C T I O N S.

In the Year 1702, the Right Reverend Father in God WILLIAM Lord Bishop of WORCESTER cieled and beautified the Chancel

In 1703, the Chancel was new paved by the Contribution of the principal Inhabitants of the Parish, and the Chancel by the Minister

In 1706, Mrs ELIZABETH MARTYN, Wife of FRANCIS MARTYN, of *Upton Old*, gave a large Silver Plate for the Communion Table

In 1707, Dame SARAH SHORE gave a Communion Table Cloth and Damask Napkin.

A New School House was erected and given for the Use of a School in this Town, by ERASMUS SAUNDERS, D D Vicar

Mrs MARY CARTER gave the Sum of 100l the yearly Use of which to be laid out for teaching poor Children at *Blockley*, and for buying Books for the Poor of *Blockley* and *Campden* The above Sum was deposited in the Hands of the Parish Officers of *Blockley*, which they employed in Building a Work house, or House of Maintenance of Poor, and annually pay the Interest of 4l per Cent which is applied to the Purposes abovementioned

Mrs JANE CROFTS bequeathed the Sum of 3l 10s per Ann towards cloathing and buying Books for the poor Children taught at the School in *Blockley*

Mr PERKINS, of *Drayton* in the County of *Middlesex*, gave the Sum of 400l the Interest of which to be made Use of in cloathing the poor old People and Children of the Parish

FRANCIS MARTIN, Esq gave 100l the Interest of which, for teaching poor Children at the Charity School for ever

By a Benefactor unknown, half a Meadow in *Blockley*, called *Church Meadow*, and other Lands, to the Value of 4l per Ann was given towards the repairing of the Church for ever

In 1732, the Right Hon ELIZABETH Countess Dowager of NORTHAMPTON, Sister to Sir JOHN RUSHOUT, of *Northwick*, Bart gave, to the Parish Church of *Blockley*, the following Set of Communion Plate viz Two large Silver Flaggons, Two Silver Chalices, Two Salvers, One large Dish, and One Plate, the Weight of the whole, 164 Ounces and 16 Pennyweights She gave also a fine Damask Table Cloth, with Six Napkins

GODDARD CARTER, of *Alscot* in the County of *Oxford*, Esq by his Will, dated the 9th of November, 1723, gave 10l a Year, out of his Lands in *Upton Old*, to teach poor Children, living in the Parish of *Blockley*, to read, write, and something of Arithmetic, and 10l a Year out of the same Estate, for Cloathing the poorest old People of the Parish of *Blockley* The Owner or Owners of the said House to appoint the Person who shall teach the Children; and also what poor Persons shall be cloathed and with what Cloathing, and that a full Account, in writing, under their Hands, be delivered to the Inhabitants yearly, in the Easter Week, when they shall meet to choose Church Wardens, how they have disposed of the said Charities

Mrs. Martha Scattergood, Daughter of the Rev. Mr. Samuel Scattergood, formerly Vicar of this Parish, by her last Will, bearing Date August 2, 175, gave to the Poor of Blockley, and to be laid out as the Minister and Churchwardens shall think best for the Benefit of the Poor; which last Will of the said Mrs. Martha Scattergood was proved in the Prerogative Court of Canterbury on the 9th Day of May 1754, and the Legacy paid by her Executors to the Right Hon. Sir John Rushout, Bart. in June 56, with 3l. Interest, the whole Sum, amounting to 103l. was invested in the 3¼ per Cent. Bank Annuities, 1756, and purchased 110l. Stock, which stands in the Name of Sir John Rushout, Bart. of Northwick in this Parish.

Mrs. Anne Martyn left by her Will, bearing Date May 1, 1737, to the Poor of Blockley, the Interest of which was to be disposed of as Mrs. Elizabeth Martyn, her Mother, should direct. The Interest is applied, pursuant to the Direction of the said Mrs. Elizabeth Martyn, for the Instruction of poor Children in reading, knitting, and sewing.

Mrs. Elizabeth Martyn, who died in the Year 1747, left by her Will another Sum of 50l. to the Churchwardens of the Parish of Blockley, with Part of the Interest of which they are directed to buy yearly a Ton of Coals, for the Use of the Charity School in Blockley Church Yard, and with the Remainder to buy Cloaths, as far as the same will extend, for the poor Children taught in her Daughter Anne's Charity School.

Incumbents	Patrons	Incumbents	Patrons
	Bishops or Worcester	1572 Thomas Wilton,	Rich. Billingham
		1586 Henry Daniel,	Edmund Ficke
1242 Vincent de Bergavenny,	Walt. de Cantilupo	1627 George Durant,	Henry Parry
1270 Lucian de Cormeilles,	Nicholas de Ely	1653 Giles Collier,	(See Vacant)
1279 Philip de Croft,	Godfrey Giffard	1673 Francis Phipps,	James Fleetwood
1291 William Grinefund,	The same	1683 Sam. Scattergood, M A	The same
1320 Benedict Paston,	Thomas Cobham	1696 Thomas Turner, M A	Edw. Stillingfleet
1349 John Devalve,	John Thoretby	1700 William Lloyd, D D	William Lloyd
── Richard Culey,	────	The above were communicated by Brown Willis,	
1419 Walter Aston,	Philip Morgan	Esq. and are inserted in the Register	
── John Clerke,			
1455 John Bell,	John Carpenter	1705 Erasmus Saunders, D D	William Lloyd
1465 Philip Warthim,	The same	1724 Michael Biddulph,	John Hough
1489 William Neele,	John Alcocke	1727 William Byrch, LL. D	The same
1540 Robert Holdsworth,	Hugh Latymer	1742 Rich. Congreve, M A	The same
1552 Dominick Maton,	Nicholas Heath	1761 Charles Jasper Selwyn, M A	James Johnson
1562 John Freeman,	Edwin Sandys		

PRESENT LESSEE OF THE MANOR,

SIR JOHN RUSHOUT, Bart.

The Register commences with the Year 1538, and has been kept with laudable Exactness.

ANNUAL ACCOUNT OF MARRIAGES, BIRTHS AND BURIALS, IN THIS PARISH

A D	Mar	Bir	Bur	A D	Mar	Bir	Bur	A D	Mar	Bir	Bur	A D	Mar	Bir	Bur
1781	8	46	40	1791				1801				1811			
1782	9	42	33	1792				1802				1812			
1783	11	47	19	1793				1803				1813			
1784	11	42	36	1794				1804				1814			
1785	8	52	31	1795				1805				1815			
1786	17	51	26	1796				1806				1816			
1787	6	41	26	1797				1807				1817			
1788				1798				1808				1818			
1789				1799				1809				1819			
1790				1800				1810				1820			

INSCRIPTIONS

IN THE CHANCEL.

ON A BRASS PLATE

Benedictus Deus   Benedictus Deus
Orate pro anima Magiſtri Willi Neele quondam
Vicarii hujus Ecclesie, & Rectoris Ecclesie de Burton ſup Iquam, qui obiit VIII die Auguſti, Anno
Domini MCX, cujus anime propicietur Deus
Amen

ON A LARGE BLUE STONE IS A BRASS FIGURE,
REPRESENTING A PRIEST IN HIS SACERDOTAL
ROBES, IN A KNEELING POSTURE, HIS FACE
TOWARDS THE NORTH OUT OF HIS MOUTH PROCEEDS A LABEL, WITH THESE WORDS

Unica ſpes vitæ mihi Virgo.

OVER THE HEAD HAS BEEN A FIGURE OF THE
VIRGIN AND THE CHILD JESUS, NOW DESTROYED
BEFORE THE PRIEST ARE CUT THE OUTLINES OF
A CHALICE, AND UNDERNEATH THE FOLLOWING
VERSES

Inſignem gravitate virum gemino decoratum
Scole gradum, ſemper pietat ad opera primum,
In cineres verſum duroque ſub marmore preſſum,
Plangite, voſque ſonet ſit tibi vita Deus.

ROUND THE MARGIN OF THE STONE, THE FOLLOWING INSCRIPTION

Hic jacet Magiſt Philippus Wartham, quond' Vicarius Ecclesie de Blockley qui obiit in Craſtino
Sancti Bartholomei A.D MCCCCLXIIII
cujus Anima propicietur Deus Amen.

ON A BLUE FLAT STONE, ANOTHER FIGURE OF
A PRIEST IN HIS ROBES, KNEELING UNDERNEATH
IS THE FOLLOWING INSCRIPTION,

Quiſquis eris qui tranſieris Sta per lege plora
Sum quod eris, fueramque quod es pro me precor ora.

In Memory of HANNAH, the
Wife of MELCHIOR GUY DICKENS, Eſq.
who died Oct 20, 1752, aged 46

And of FREDERICK WILLIAM GUY DICKENS,
Clerk, who died Sept 15, 1779, aged 50.

AGAINST THE NORTH WALL

Arms, Argent, a Cheveron between Three
Saltires raguly Sable Motto,

Virtus propter ſe.

A MARBLE MONUMENT SUPPORTED BY CORINTHIAN PILLARS, WITH THE EFFIGY OF A MAN IN
ARMOUR, KNEELING.

Arms, on Three Eſcutcheons; 1ſt, Gules, a
Chevron Ermine, between Three Eagles close Argent,
for CHILDE 2d, CHILDE,—impaling, Argent, a
Lion rampant Purpure, crowned Or, for FOLIOT 3d,
CHILDE,—impaling, Argent, a Chevron between
Three Scaling Ladders Sable, for JEFFERIES

GULIELMUS CHILDE, Filius & Hæres
GULIELMI CHILDE, Armigeri,
defuncti, religioſe poſuit, 1615.

N B *By the Regiſter it appears that* WILLIAM
CHILDE *was buried Nov.* 2, 1601.

ON A MONUMENT, CONTAINING THE EFFIGIES OF
A MAN AND WOMAN, IN A KNEELING POSTURE,
IN THE DRESS OF THE TIMES

Arms, CHILDE, as before.

UNDER THE MAN

Hic requieſcit secundum Domini
Adventum fœliciter expectans
GULIELMUS CHILDE, Arm qui (dum vixit)
Amicus fuit & hoſpitalis Piis & Honeſtis.
Promiſſis conſtans, inopia laborantibus
Miſericors, & ſpem ferens,
obiit 9 Die Decembris, Anno Dom 1633,
ætatis ſuæ 80.

UNDER THE WOMAN

Hic requieſcit secundum Domini
Adventum feliciter expectans
ELIZABETHA, Uxor Chariſſima GULIELMI
CHILDE, Arm una filiarum GULIELMI BABINGTON,
Militis, de Kiddington, in Com Oxon,
Quæ poſt 46 Annos in conjugis
Fideliſſime expletos,
obiit 9 Die Novembris, Anno Dom 1662,
ætatis ſuæ 64.

ON A MURAL MONUMENT, IN WHICH IS THE
EFFIGY OF A WOMAN RECLINING, AT FULL
LENGTH, IN THE DRESS OF THE TIMES

Arms, CHILDE,—impaling, Azure, on a Feſs
wavy Argent, a Croſs patée Gules, in Chief Two
Eſtoiles Or, for JENKINSON

In Memory of ANNE MARY, Daughter to
Sir ROBERT JENKINSON, of Walcott in the
County of Oxford, Knt and Wife to THOMAS
CHILDE, of Northwicke in the County of
Worceſter, Eſq
Poſitum eſt

OVER SIXTEEN VERSES IN ENGLISH

Epitaphium fecit ipſa *Paulo* ante obitum, qui
accidit 11 Die Feb 1659.

ON

OF A TABLET

Arms, Sable, Two Lions paſſant within a Bordure engrailed Or, on a Canton, the Arms of Ulster, for RUSHOUT,—impaling, Argent, a Frett Sable, and a Canton Gules, for VERNON.

Sir JAMES RUSHOUT, Bart
and ARABELLA his Wife,
Daughter of Sir THOMAS VERNON.

Sir JAMES, born 1676, died 1705.

His Wife, born 1679, died 1705

Sir JAMES their Son, born 1701,
died 1711

AT THE EAST END OF THE NORTH AISLE

A sumptuous MARBLE MONUMENT OF THREE COMPARTMENTS, TWO OF WHICH ARE FINISHED WITH PEDIMENTS, AND THE MIDDLE ONE WITH A PYRAMID ON THESE ARE ARRANGED THE FOLLOWING BUSTS OF SIR JAMES RUSHOUT, BART SIR JOHN RUSHOUT, BART. AND ELIZABETH COUNTESS OF NORTHAMPTON, BY RYSBRACK, AND OF LADY ANNE RUSHOUT, AND DAME ALICE RUSHOUT, BY MOORE

IN THE FIRST COMPARTMENT

Arms, RUSHOUT, as before,—impaling, Sable, a Lion paſſant Or, between Three Helmets Argent, garniſhed Or, for COMPTON

The Right Hon Sir JOHN RUSHOUT,
Treaſurer of his Majeſty's Navy,
was born 1685, died

And

the Right Hon Lady ANNE COMPTON
his Wife, fourth Daughter of
GEORGE Earl of NORTHAMPTON,
and one of the beſt of Women,
was born 1695, died 1766.

IN THE MIDDLE COMPARTMENT

Arms, on a Lozenge enſigned with an Earl's Coronet, for COMPTON,—impaling RUSHOUT

The Right Hon ELIZABETH,
Counteſs Dowager of NORTHAMPTON,
third Daughter of
Sir JAMES RUSHOUT and ALICE his Wife,
was born 1683, died 1750

All are depoſited in an adjoining Vault

IN THE THIRD COMPARTMENT

Arms, RUSHOUT,—impaling, Barry, of Six Or and Azure, in Chief Three Mullets of the ſecond, for PITT

Sir JAMES RUSHOUT, of Northwick, Bart
his Majeſty's Ambaſſador to Conſtantinople,
was born 1644, died 1698

And

ALICE PITT his Wife, the only
Child of EDMOND PITT, of Harrow
on the Hill in Middleſex, Eſq
was born 1651, died 1698
J. F. MOORE fecit

AGAINST THE SOUTH WALL

Arms, Quarterly, per Feſs indented Azure and Or, in the firſt Quarter a Lion paſſant guardant of the ſecond, for CROFT,—impaling, Azure, ſemé of Fleur de Lis a Lion rampant guardant Or, for BEAUMONT

In Memory of EDWARD CROFT,
of Northwick, Gent.

And of JANE his Relict,
who (as a laſting Teſtimony
of her Piety and Charity)
bequeathed 3l 10s per Ann to the Uſe of
the Poor of this Pariſh for ever
They were both interred in their
own Seat, near the uppermoſt Pillar
in this Church He died Feb 20, 1706,
aged 61
She Oct 18, 1711, aged 49
And this Monument
was, of pious Gratitude, erected by
Mr ROBERT CUBBERLEY

ON A SMALL NEAT MARBLE MONUMENT

Arms, Sable, a Chevron Ermine, between Three Bulls Heads caboſhed Argent, for SAUNDERS.

To the Memory of
ERASMUS SAUNDERS, D D.
Vicar of this Pariſh
who, by the Piety, as well of his Life as Writings,
endeavoured to promote Religion and Virtue,
and
who, by his Prudence in ſecular Affairs,
improved the Value of his Living
His eldeſt Son ERASMUS SAUNDERS, D D
erected this honorary Monument,
A D 1771

Arms, Azure, Two Liars combatant Or, for CARTER,—impaling, Gules, a Chevron vaire between Three Creſcents Argent, for GODDARD

Memoriæ Sacrum
EDVARDI CARTER, de Upton Old,
Armigeri, Legum Angl Profeſſoris
Viri
tanta pietate in Deum O M beneficentiâ erga
Pauperes fidelitate adverſus amicos Juſtitia atque
candore in omnes, ut digniſſimus plane ſit qui poſteris
ad imitandum proponatur, obiit 27 Die Febr
An Dom 1667, ætatis ſuæ 45

EDVARDUM juxta ſita eſt
MARIA CARTER, EDVARDI & MARIA, filia natu
minor, eximie pietatis virgo, utriuſque Parentis
virtutum amula, qua dum Bathoniæ ſanitati corporis
operam dedit, ſalutem æternam conſecuta eſt
25 die Junii, Ann Dom 1675, ætatis ſuæ 19
Marmor hoc ſepulchrale poſuit
MARIA CARTER, EDVARDI Conjux,
MARIA Mater Chariſſima

ON BRASS PLATES AND FLAT STONES

M S.
Francisci Martin, de Upton Old,
Armigeri,
Qui cum negotio Mercatorio, apud
Londinates, felici industriâ honeftate
vere infigni per aliquot incubuiffet
annos feceffit feculo
Et huc in Patriam reverfus, ut ad
æterna tempeftive fe accingeret,
inter bona quæ fecit opera perpetuum
centum librarum reditum pofterorum
beneficio in hac Parochia pie dedit,
& a pofteris inviolabile perpetuo etiam
fibi dari hoc fepulchrum obnixe
obteftatur.
Huj is voti & amoris ergo, Monumentum
hoc mœftiffima fua Conjux Elizabetha
pofuit
Ob $\begin{cases} \text{An æt } 75 \\ \text{An Dom } 1713. \end{cases}$

In Memory of
Mrs Anne Martyn,
youngeft Daughter of Francis Martyn,
late of Upton Old in this Parifh, Efq
by Elizabeth his third Wife,
whofe early Death,
on the fixth Day of May,
in the Year of our Lord 1727,
in the 24th Year of her Age,
was greatly lamented
As an Inftance of her pious
and charitable Difpofition,
fhe gave, by her laft Will, the
Sum of Fifty Pounds,
for the Ufe of the poor Children of this Town ,

the Intereft thereof,
yearly, to be applied
in teaching them to read and write,
and inftructing them
in the Principles
of the Chriftian Religion

Arms, on a Bend cottifed Three Cinquefoils, in
Chief an Annulet;—impaling Two Bars between
Three Mullets

The Remains of Elizabeth,
Relict of Francis Martin, Efq
of Upton Old
She departed this Life
on the 9th Day of May, 1748,
aged 82

In Memory of
James Baxter, of Hanging Afton,
who departed this Life
Auguft 13, 1741, aged 48

Anne, Daughter of
John and Mary Barns,
died June 27, 1742, aged 23 Years

Christian Widdows,
of Northwick, departed this
Life the 9th Day of January, 1698,
ætatis fuæ 82

IN THE CHURCH YARD, ON TOMBS.

Joane, the Wife of Thomas Wilkes,
died April 12, 1720, aged 71

In Memory of Richard Wilkes
and Elizabeth his Wife

She died Nov 7, 1769, aged 75
He died March 5, 1771, aged 83

Thomas their Son died Auguft
28, 1724, aged 3 Years 10 Months

Frances their Daughter
died July 31, 1728, aged 2 Years

Alfo Thomas Wilkes
died Oct 18, 1721, aged 18

Richard Wilkes
died March 5, 1771, aged 83

Elizabeth his Wife
died Nov 7, 1769, aged 72

Mr Robert Strong
died Feb 3, 1780, aged 57.

John Dawson
died July 14, 1734, aged 76

Hefter his Wife
died Nov 28, 1734, aged 84

Letticia their Daughter
died July 18, 1712, aged 24

John Pengree, Gent
late of Upton Old in this Parifh,
died Dec 27, 1768, aged 60

Elizabeth his Wife
died Feb 22, 1782, aged 76.

John their Youngeft Son
died July 31, 1769, aged 18.

Beneath

Beneath this Stone
are depoſited the mortal Part
of ELIZABETH, the Wife of GEORGE
PENGREE, junior, of London, Merchant,
who departed this Life Oct 14, 1772
aged 22 Years

FRANCIS WHEATCROFT,
of Ditchford in this Pariſh,
died Feb 10, 1784, aged 68

MARY his Wife
died Nov. 8, 1783, aged 66

Mr THOMAS FOX
died Aug 4, 1776, aged 83.

MARTHA, Daughter of
THOMAS and JANE FOX,
died Nov 3, 1746, aged 15.

Mrs JANE FOX, Relict
of Mr THOMAS FOX,
died Nov 3, 1778, aged 85.

RICHARD ROBERTS,
of Paxford in this Pariſh,
died July 7, 1782, aged 72.

SARAH, Wife of THOMAS
WHATCOTT, died Dec 14, 1773,
aged 77

THOMAS WHATCOTT
died March 9, 1786,
aged 84

ON HEAD STONES.

	Died		Aged
Thomas Wells, of Draycot	6 Feb	1763	70
Elizabeth his Wife	25 Mar	1783	83
Frances, Wife of James Gilſon	5 May,	1776	48
John Lloyd	4 Apr	1785	74
John Keen	5 Sept	1772	48
Sarah, the Wife of John Keen	— Feb	1745	61
Sarah, Wife of Richard Smith	3 May,	1743	22
William Etheridge	29 Nov	1776	65
Mary, Daughter of William and Elizabeth Etheridge	8 May,	1773	16
Richard, Son of William and Elizabeth Etheridge	19 Apr.	1780	25
John Charles, of Eſton in this Pariſh	2 May,	1750	73
Samuel Charles, ſenior, of Aſton	24 Oct	1724	77
Samuel Charles, junior	25 Sept	1727	44
Mrs Ann Charles, Relict of Samuel Charles, ſenior	12 June,	1740	84
Sarah Gifborn	13 June,	1784	79
Sarah Manſell	21 Jan	1766	63
Mary, Daughter of Thomas and Grace Hartwell, of Aſton Magna	1 Dec.	1758	70
William Ruſſell, of Aſton	13 Oct	1727	58
Mary his Wife	25 Mar	1756	76
William Meadows	30 Dec	1704	69
Mary Charlwood	51 Sept	1710	24
Elizabeth Bradley	29 Nov.	1758	65
Ann, Wife of Robert Dyde, of this Town	4 June,	1770	33
Robert Dyde	14 Feb	1779	47
Thomas Dyde	17 Oct	1781	87
William Dyde	21 Sept	1781	42
Robert Warner	28 Sept	1709	56
Elizabeth, Wife of John Marſhall, of Aſton Magna	11 June,	1769	66
John their Son	8 July,	1775	40
William Marſhall, Son of John and Elizabeth Marſhall	17 June,	1736	36
John Wheatcroft, of Draycot in this Pariſh	14 Oct	1729	47
Mercy his Wife	18 Apr.	1765	77
Ann, Wife of Joſeph Prew	22 May,	1736	46
John Bennet, of Draycot	1 Mar	1753	52
Thomas Wmd, of Draycot	22 Jan	1764	74
John Brun	11 Sept	1775	80
Ann his Wife	31 Aug	1767	60
Martha Manſell their Daughter	8 Sept	1771	30
John Phillips, of Dorn	4 Apr	1746	46
Mary his Wife	4 June,	1764	63
Thomas Wheatcroft, of Paxford	24 Apr.	1754	32
Sarah, Wife of Robert Holtham, of Paxford	14 Dec	1782	48

7   Samuel

O N   H E A D   S T O N E S

	Died	Aged
Samuel Cormell, late of Ebrington	19 Jan. 1760	44
Eleanor, Wife of Thomas Hill, of Paxford	30 Nov 1707	92
Francis Robbins, of Paxford	10 Aug 1748	75
Mary his Wife	25 Aug. 1738	70
William their Son	31 Oct 1755	57
Thomas Robins	7 Apr. 1742	48
Thomas Hands, of Paxford	31 Oct 1774	72
Eleanor his Wife	27 Nov 1767	72
Harry Taplin	27 Jan 1777	75
Philadelphia, Wife of John Read	5 Jan 1776	40
Elizabeth Robins, Wife of John Robins	5 Sept 1769	72
John Patterson, of Northwick	28 June, 1778	52
Susanna his Wife	27 June, 1778	61
Elizabeth, Wife of Richard Clark	13 Feb 1780	84
Richard Churn	4 Jan 1777	80
Alice his Wife	20 Jun 1767	70
William their Son	18 Dec 1747	28
William Trotman	29 Apr. 1772	46
Mary, Wife of Thomas Trotman	30 Oct. 1781	55
John Gibbs	30 Oct 1711	54
Richard Roberts, of Paxford	4 Apr 1721	37
Elizabeth his Wife	21 July, 1761	77
Jane their Daughter	14 Sept 1749	37
Elizabeth, Wife of James Sharp, of Paxford	20 Nov 1775	65
John Wallington	6 Nov 1762	57
John Figgures	21 Nov 1781	67

OF this Parish nearly equal Parts are included in the Hundreds of *Tewkesbury* and *Westminster*, but the whole in the Deanery of *Winchcombe*. It is situate in the great Vale of *Gloucester*, from whence it is distant more than Six Miles on the North East, from *Cheltenham* Four, and from *Tewkesbury* Five Miles, on the South. The Soil is universally a very strong Clay, and the greater Part of the Lands Pasture, with a considerable Tract of Coppice Wood. A Rivulet, called the *Chelt*, passing through the Parish, joins the *Severn* at *Wainload Hill*.

The Living is a Chapelry, in the Peculiar of *Derhurst*, and is annexed to *Staverton*, with the Vicarial Tithes. The Abbey of *Tewkesbury* held the Impropriation which has descended from various Possessors to the Family of *Arkel*. St *Mary Magdalen* is the Tutelar of the Church. It is a long Building, without an Aisle, apparently very ancient, with a low slated Tower. With Consent of the Abbot of *Tewkesbury*, in 1469, the Church Yard was consecrated for Sepulture.

Amongst the early Possessors of this Manor, were the Barons DE FERRARS of *Coartley*, and BEAUCHAMPS Earls of WARWICK. Of the Earl of CRAVEN it was purchased by the Family of LOCK in 1657, the last of whom bequeathed it to the Rev. EDWARD FORD.

LELAND noticed, " at *Boointune* a fayre Minor Place with a Park." The House was probably newly built at that Time. It is evidently of the first Style of Building which prevailed, when Castles were no longer necessary for the security of Residence. It is surrounded with a Moat, and in a Field adjoining is an Oak of very extraordinary Growth, and of Three Centuries standing*

The Parish contains Three Hamlets. 1 *Barrow*, which received its Name from a Hill, which appears like an artificial Tumulus in so level a Country. 2 *Heydon*, Part of which belongs to *Staverton*. The reputed Manor of *Heydon* was held by the Abbey of *Westminster*, and is now the Estate of THOMAS DOWDESWELL, Esq. as Lessee under the Dean and Chapter of that Church. Several medicinal Springs, of a saline Quality, are at *Moredon* in this Hamlet. 3 *Withy Bridge*. At *Butler's Court*, Lord CRAVEN possesses a reputed Manor, and holds a Court, with a large Estate. The Family of PEARCE were Proprietors of considerable Lands in *Heydon* in this Parish. *Bodington Moor* is a Lot Meadow, the Property divided by Mears, and commonable after the Hay is off, containing about One Hundred Acres, entirely of Pasture. The Court of the Honour of GLOUCESTER anciently claimed the Jurisdiction of this Parish.

INCUMBENTS	PATRONS	INCUMBENTS	PATRONS
1681 Daniel Griffith, M A	Wm Earl of Craven	1715 John Herbert, M A	Dorothy Lock, Widow
1682 James Christmas, M A	The same	1723 Nicholas Fenn, LL D	John Lock, Esq
1690 Thomas Hayward, M A	The same	1730 Thomas Buckle, M A	The same
	The above from Sir ROBERT ATKYNS	1758 Henry Wyndowe, B A	John Lock, Esq
		1772 John Kipling, M A	Mary Lock

PRESENT LORD OF THE MANOR,

The Reverend EDWARD FORD

The Persons summoned from this Place by the Herald's in 1682 and 1683 were,

William Leech, Gent

——— Barret, Barrister at Law

At the Election in 1776, Three Freeholders polled from this Parish

*The Dimensions of the *Bodington Oak*. " The Stem is remarkably collected and close at the Root; the Sides of its Trunk being more collected than those of large Trees in general. Its Circumference is Twenty Paces; measuring with a Rule it is more than Eighteen Yards. At Three Feet high it measures Forty two Feet; and at its smallest Dimensions it is Thirty six Feet round. From the Ground to the Top of the Crown of the Trunk is Twelve Feet; and the greatest Height of its Branches Forty five by Estimation. The Stem is quite hollow, being near the Ground a perfect Shell, forming a capacious Room; near it in one part Ten Feet in Diameter: the Loftiness contracts and forms a natural Dome, to that no Light is admitted but at the Entrance which is a small Aperture on one Side. It is still perfectly alive and fruitful." *Practical Treatise on Planting*, &c. p 513, ed 1785,

A D	Mar	Bir	Bur	A D	Mar	Bir	Bur	A D	Mar	Bir	Bur	A.D	Mar	Bir	Bur
1781	1	4	1	1786				1791				1796			
1782	—	1	—	1787				1792				1797			
1783	2	—	—	1788				1793				1798			
1784	—	4	8	1789				1794				1799			
1785	3	3	4	1790				1795				1800			

INSCRIPTIONS IN THE CHURCH.

Near this Place
lyeth the Body of WALTER BUCKLE,
youngeft Son of RICHARD and ANNE
BUCKLE, of this Parifh, who departed
this Life May 11, 1729, aged 31 Years

Alfo MARY, the Wife of THOMAS ROGERS,
of the City of Gloucefter, Baker, Daughter
of JOHN and JOAN BUCKLE, of this Parifh
She died Feb 14, 1736, aged 68 Years

Alfo ELIZABETH, Wife of SAMUEL VERNUM,
and Relict of ROGER LONE, Yeoman, and
Daughter of RICHARD and ANNE BUCKLE,
interred April 1, 1746, æt. 45

Near this Place lieth the Body of
RICHARD BUCKLE, of this Parifh, who
departed this Life Dec. 29, Anno Dom 1707,
aged 55 Years

And of JOHN, eldeft Son of
RICHARD and ANNE BUCKLE, who was buried
Aug 6, 1712, aged 29 Years

And of RICHARD, fecond Son of the abovefaid
RICHARD and ANNE BUCKLE, who was
buried May 25, 1713, aged 27 Years.

Alfo ANNE BUCKLE,
Relict of the abovefaid RICHARD BUCKLE,
who was buried June 29, 1727,
aged 66 Years

Alfo of WILLIAM BUCKLE, and MARY,
Wife of JOHN MEWS, youngeft Son,
and fecond Daughter of
THOMAS and JOAN BUKIE, of Cheltenham

WILLIAM } died { Sept 14, 1742, } aged { 14
MARY } { 21, 1743, } { 27

Here lyeth WILLIAM LEECH, the eldeft Son of
WILLIAM LEECH, the younger, of Bodington, who
was buried Nov 9, } Domini 1680.
Anno } ætat 28

Here lyeth SAMUEL LEECH, the youngeft Son of
the faid WILLIAM LEECH, who was buried the
11 of January, } Domini 1680
Anno } ætat 8

Here lyeth the Body of ELIZABETH, the Wife
of WILLIAM LEECH, the younger, who departed
this Life May 1, } Domini 1684
Anno } ætat 56

Here lyeth the Body of SAMUEL DIPPER, who
died Dec 31, 1700

Alfo SARAH his Wife
who died June 21, 1698

WILLIAM LEECH, the elder, of Boddington,
Yeoman, who departed this Life Sept 16,
Anno { Domini 1678.
{ ætatis 76

In Memory of RICHARD BUCKLE,
of this Parifh, Yeoman, who departed
this Life 31ft Day of Dec
Anno Domini 1708,
aged 55 Years

IN THE CHURCH YARD.

ON A TOMB

HENRY PEARCE, Yeoman, of Haydon Farm
in this Parifh, died July 30, 1723, aged 74

Alfo near this Place lie HENRY PEARCE
his Father - - buried 1685
RICHARD his Brother - 1690
MARY his firft Wife 1694
THOMAS his Brother - 1696
JOAN his Mother - - 1698.

SARAH HARDMAN his Niece - buried 1702
MARY his Daughter, by his laft Wife - 1705
WILLIAM HARDMAN his Nephew - 1705
JOHN PEARCE his Nephew - 1720

SARAH, late Wife of HENRY PEARCE,
buried Feb 23, 1748, aged 74

SARAH GARDNER, Daughter of HENRY
and SARAH PEARCE, buried
Aug 23, 1727, aged 27

ON HEAD STONES

	Died	Aged			Died	Aged
Mary, Wife of William Lord, of Barrow in this Parifh	Mar 1773	55		Armel Miles junior	8 July 1761	5
Anne Miles, Junior, of Boddington				Anne his Wife	23 Nov 1757	41
Abel	9 Oct 1761	85		Armel Miles	1 Oct 1711	6

XLVII BOURTON

BOURTON ON THE HILL.

A PARISH divided between the Hundreds of *Tewkesbury* and *Westminster*, about Five Miles from *Stow* on the North, an equal Distance on the South from *Campden*, and Twenty-eight Miles from GLOUCESTER. The Soil is of a light Clay, admitting chiefly of Pasture, with extensive Sheep walks. The Village of *Bourton* is pleasantly situate on an Eminence, on the great Road from *London* to *Worcester*.

Here are Two distinct Manors, each included within the Hundreds before stated. Of these, the former constituted a Part of the Revenues of the Abbey of *Westminster*, and was continued to the Chapter when established by HEN. VIII. The Family of BATESON have been the Lessees for successive Generations. The other Manor passed from the Lords WENTWORTH, to Sir NICHOLAS OVERBURY, about the Close of the 16th Century, whose Son, the celebrated Sir THOMAS OVERBURY, was a Native of *Bourton*, and succeeded to the Estate. Few Parts of our History are better known than the Memoirs of this accomplished and unfortunate Courtier †. His Heir was a Nephew of the same Name, who is likewise mentioned by WOOD as an Author ‡. In 1680 the Family of POTHAM became Proprietors, who were succeeded by the BATESONS, the present Possessors. Another Estate is held by JOHN HEAD, Esq. in Right of his Wife, sole Heir of the Family of HARWARD.

The Benefice is a Rectory in the Deanery of *Campden*, with the Chapel of *Morton in Marsh* annexed, once in the Peculiar of *Blockley*, and still subject to the Payment of Mortuaries. A great Part of the Tythes of *Morton* are appropriated, and belong to WILLIAM BATESON, Esq. The Church is dedicated to *St. Lawrence*, and is a massive and capacious Edifice. It consists of a Nave, Two Aisles, and a low Tower, in which are Six Bells and a Saint's Bell. The Parishioners obtained Permission to bury in their own Cemetery in 1542.

No Benefactions to the Poor.

INCUMBENTS	PATRONS	INCUMBENTS	PATRONS
—— George Marsh,	——	1707 Austin Goodwin, M A	——
1577 James Beck,	Richard Palmer, Esq	The above from Sir ROBERT ATKYNS.	
1583 James Beck,	Queen Elizabeth		
1617 Nicholas Cartwright,	Sir Nicholas Overbury, Knight	1733 Daniel Kemble, D D	
		1761 William Mayd, Clerk,	Thomas Kemble, Esq
1637 Giles Oldisworth, M A §	——	1768 Matthew Bloxham, M A	The same
1645 Nicholas Oldisworth		1784 Joseph Martin, M A	Margaret Kemble
1673 Richard Watkins, D D	Sir Th Overbury, Knt.		

* WOOD says at *Compton Scarsen* in the Parish of *Ilmington*, co *Warwick*.

† Sir THOMAS OVERBURY was the eldest Son of Sir NICHOLAS OVERBURY, of *Bourton on the Hill*, by MARY Daughter of GILES PALMER, of *Ilmington* in the County of *Warwick*, born in the Year 1581. He became a Member of *Queen's College*, *Oxford* in 1595. Three Years after he entered at the *Temple*, and studied the Municipal Law. On his Return from his Travel, he conciliated the strictest Confidence of Sir ROBERT CARRE, Knight of the Bath, and the Favourite of King JAMES I by whose Interest he was knighted at the Coronation in 1602, and his Father Sir NICHOLAS was made one of the Justices of the *Marches* of *Wales*. Sir THOMAS having given the most steady Opposition to CARRE's Connection with the Countess of ESSEX he fell a Victim to her implacable Revenge, being poisoned by her Procurement, during his Confinement in the *Tower* for having contumeliously refused an Ambassage to the Court of *Russia*, which he declared to be "a Kind of honourable Grave." He died in 1613 aged 32. WOOD, in his ATH OXON vol I p 331, stiles him "a most accomplished Person, which the Happiness of his "Pen, both in Poetry and Prose, doth declare, who in Judgement and Learning excelled most of his Age." He gives the following, A count of his Writings. 'A Wife, being a most exquisite and singular Poem on the Choice of a Wife,' printed in the Author's Life time. 2. "Characters, or witty Descriptions of the Properties of sundry Persons." This is the first of this Species of Essay Writing that appeared in *England*. MONTAIGNE'S Essays had been approved in *France*. Other Publications were attributed to him, but their Authenticity is suspected.

‡ Sir THOMAS OVERBURY Knight the Nephew and Successor of the former was the Author of several controversial Tracts. He died at *Quenton* in this County in 1680. The intelligent and ingenious Editor of the "British Topography" mentions, 'A true and perfect Account of the Examination, Confession, Trial, Condemnation, and Execution of JOAN PERRY and her 'Two Sons, for the supposed Murder of WILLIAM HARRISON, Gent being one of the most remarkable Occurrences, which 'hath happened in the Memory of Man, sent in a Letter by Sir T O (THOMAS OVERBURY), of *Bourton*, to T S (THOMAS 'SHIRLEY), M D in *London*.' Lond 1676, 4to. To the Title he adds the subjoined Account of the Occasion of his Letter 'Mr HARRISON had been carried out of the Kingdom, and after a few Years Absence returned. JOHN PERRY, the Servant, 'was thought to have been out of his Senses his Mother and Brother denied the Fact to the last though the old Woman was 'made to suffer first in Compliance with the vulgar Prejudice, that by her Skill in Witchcraft she prevented her Sons from 'confessing. HARRISON's Transportation is supposed to have been brought about by his eldest Son, who might suppose that 'the Ruffians had killed him, and so prosecute the Innocent to prevent a Discovery. He succeeded his Father both in his Estate, 'and Place of Steward of Lord CAMDEN, at *Campden* and by his Misbehaviour in it created the Suspicion against him. 'This Event is said to have occasioned the Law to prevent any Persons being executed, except the dead Body of the Person supposed to be murdered be first found." *British Topography* vol I p 379. It is further remarkable, that Mr HARRISON at his Return refused to give any Account of himself, or the Occasion and the PERRY his Servant (who is thought to have been insane) persevered in accusing his Mother and Brother to the last.

§ WOOD Ath Oxon p 737

PRESENT LORD AND LESSEE OF THE MANORS,
WILLIAM BATESON, Esq

At the Visitations of the Heralds, in 1682 and 1683, the following Persons were summoned

Sir Thomas Overbury Knight,   Michael Rutter, Esq
Alexander Popham, Esq   John Dumbleton, Gent
———— Bateson, Esq   John Gibbes, Gent

At the Election in 1776, Five Freeholders polled from this Parish

The first Notice in the Register bears Date 1568

ANNUAL ACCOUNT OF MARRIAGES, BIRTHS, AND BURIALS, IN THIS PARISH

A D	Mar	Bir	Bur	A D	Mar	Bir	Bur	A D	Mar	Bir	Bur	A D	Mar	Bir	Bur
1781	1	8	2	1786	2	10	5	1791				1796			
1782	3	10	8	1787	2	11	4	1792				1797			
1783	1	12	9	1788				1793				1798			
1784	2	7	4	1789				1794				1799			
1785	2	12	2	1790				1795				1800			

INSCRIPTIONS IN THE CHURCH

ON A MARBLE MONUMENT AGAINST
THE SOUTH WALL

Arms Chequy Or and Azure, on a
Bend Sable, Three Eagles displayed Or,
on an Escutcheon of Pretence Azure, a
Chevron Ermine, between Three Lions
rampant, and as many Altars Or, for
SMITH

In Memory of
KEMPE HARWARD, Doctor in Physick,
who died January 1, 1713,
aged 66 Years

And of ALTHAM HARWARD, who died
February 20, 1733,
aged 20 Years

This Monument is erected by
LUCY HARWARD, as the last and only
remaining Testimony of filial Duty
and Regard to her Father and
affectionate Remembrance of her Brother

ON A WHITE MARBLE MONUMENT

Arms Quarterly, 1st and 4th, Argent
Three Bats Wings erect Sable, on a Chief
Gules a Lion passant of the Field, for
BATISON 2d Argent, a Fefs Gules in
Chief Three Fortemixes, for D'EVEREUX,
3d, Sable, a Bend vaire on a Can on Argent
a Wolf's Head couped Gules, for
CLIFFE, 4th as the 1st

To the Memory of
ROBERT DEVEREUX BATESON, Esq
Son of
WILLIAM BATESON, Esq

of this
Parish He married ANNE, second
Daughter of ALLEN CLIFFE of
Mathon in the County of Worcester,
Esq by whom he left Issue Two
Sons, WILLIAM and ROBERT,
and one Daughter, ANNE He died
the 23d of Oct in the Year of our Lord
One Thousand Seven Hundred Thirty
and Six in the Forty fifth Year of his Age

This Monument was erected to
his Memory, by his equally loving,
and beloved Widow ANNE BATESON

ON A MONUMENT AGAINST ONE OF
THE PILLARS

Arms in a Lozenge Argent, on a
Chief Gules, Two Stags Head, cabossed
Or, for POPHAM

Near this Place is interred
the Body of BRILLIANA, the
Wife of ALEXANDER POPHAM,
of this Parish, Esq

Also that of her third Daughter,
LÆTITIA POPHAM

B P ⎱ died ⎰ Sept 12, 1698.
L P ⎰   ⎱ Oct 17, 1738.

ON FLAT STONES.

Here lyeth the Body of
JOSEPH CORSEY the sonne of
MYLES CORSEY who died
July 24, Anno Dom 1624.

Here lyeth the Body of
WILLIAM the Son of CHARLES JAMES,
by SARAH his Wife,
who departed this Life
Feb 25, 1741, aged 27 Years

Also the Body of CHARLES JAMES
who departed this Life Dec 30, 1752,
aged 72 Years

And also SARAH his Wife, who died the
23d of May, 1752, aged 74 Years

In Memory of JOHN GIBBS,
who departed this Life Oct 17, 1747,
aged 74 Years

Also of ELIZABETH, Wife of JOHN GIBBS,
who departed this Life Jan 29 1721
aged 42 Years

WILLIAM, the Son of the Rev
WILLIAM MAYO and ANN his Wife,
who departed this Life Dec 1, 1760,
aged 18 Years

The Rev WILLIAM MAYO Rector of
this Parish departed this Life
Dec 21, 1767, aged 47 Years

IN THE CHURCH YARD

ON HEAD STONES

	Died	Aged		Died	Aged
Thomas Hayward -	24 Oct 1750	48	Edward Stephens	21 June, 1763	58
Thomas Gibbs	14 Aug 1750	45	Rose, Wife of William Cole -	18 June 1782	28
Hewor, Daughter of William and			Edward Stephens -	26 Feb 1766	39
Ann Powell	21 Dec 1743	47	Richard Mokeky	7 Sept 1743	81
Thomas Edwards	23 May 1775	23	Mary his Wife -	30 June, 1758	60
Joseph, Son of Walter and Ann			John Bread	13 July, 1738	7
Powell	4 Oct 1770	33	Ann, Wife of Thomas Rawlings	2 Jan 1763	48
Walter Powell	19 Feb 1771	62	John Cook -	29 May, 1753	77

T. Pennell del.   Wormleaton to Meadow sculp.

XLVII. BOURTON ON THE WATER.

BY which Name it is distinguished from the other *Bourton*, with a Reference to its Situation. This Parish lies in the Hundred of *Slaughter*, and the Deanery of *Stow*, from whence the Distance is nearly Four Miles South, and Twenty one from GLOUCESTER on the East. The Soil of the high Grounds is light, and applied to Tillage, and in the Vallies are many fertile Meadows, the whole in a Circumference of Ten Miles. An Act for Inclosure of the common Fields was granted in 1773.

The Village of *Bourton* has peculiar Advantages of Situation. The Houses, though detached from each other, form a long Street, arranged on either Side the River, which is a Confluence of Streams, Thirty Feet wide but not distinguished till it reaches the Village of *Bourton*, and receives its Name. The Prospect is much too regular to be very picturesque, but it affords a perfect Idea of Cultivation and Convenience. From Ruins and Foundations frequently discovered, the Village has certainly been more extensive.

The Benefice is a Rectory, the Advowson of which was formerly vested in the Priory of *Kirkham*, co. *York*. The old Church, dedicated to *St. Lawrence*, measured 120 Feet by 22, with a Tower in the Middle, of singular Construction, and the highest Antiquity. On the same Site the modern Structure was begun in 1784, for which Purpose 500l. were bequeathed by SARAH YATES, Spinster. The Plan given by WILLIAM MARSHALL, Architect, has not, as yet, been completed. The Base of the Tower (now at the West End) is of a rustic, the Corners decorated with Ionic Pilasters, and the whole finished by a Balustrade, Urns, and a Cupola. The exterior Appearance of the Church is plain, on the Inside it is ornamented with a Colonade of the Ionic Order, and neatly paved. The Aisle, projecting on the South Side, is appropriated to the Inhabitants of *Clapton*, the Chapel of which, with that of *Lower Slaughter*, is annexed to the Rectory. A Chauntry was founded here in Honour of the Virgin *Mary*, the last Incumbent of which, MARK SAUNDERS, received a Pension.*

The Abbey of *Evesham* in *Worcestershire* were the earliest Proprietors of the Manor. EDMOND Lord CHANDOS held it in the Reign of ELIZABETH, and in that of CHARLES I. Sir THOMO was Lord, from whom, and many intermediate Possessors, it devolved to the Family of INGRAM, of came St. *Aloys's*, in 1764. The Manor house is large and commodious, and in the Village are many of that Description, with Estates, belonging to the Families of MOORE, COLLETT, VERNON, ANSTIS, and SNOOKE. *Nethercote* is the only Hamlet, it was formerly vested in the Abbey of *Evesham*, and purchased of the COLLETTS, by the Family of PALMER.

The great Roman Road passes within a few Furlongs of the Village, and near to it the same Distance from the Road is a Camp of a quadrangular Form, inclosing Sixty Acres, proved to have been a Roman

Station, by the Discovery of Coins and other Vestiges   On this Spot a Court Leet for the Hundred of *Salemanſbury*, now of *Slaughter*, is annually held   The following Names of Places conſtituting that Hundred occur in Domeſday Book " *Scloſter, Weſberie, Oundon cum Berew, Scireburne, Malgereſberie, Riſin-* " *ton*, and *Newetune* "

B E N E F A C T I O N S.

Mr ANTHONY COLLETT gave by Will, 1719, for the Inſtruction of Ten poor Boys, the Sum of 10*l* per Ann charged upon his Eſtate

Mr WILLIAM MOORE, 1768, demiſed the Sum of 5*l* per Ann in Aid to the above Charity, which is now in Chancery

Mrs JANE FARREN, 1779, left the Sum of 10*l* per Ann for apprenticing a poor Boy, charged upon her Eſtate

Mrs DOROTHY VERNON, 1761, bequeathed the Sum of 540*l* to be diſtributed amongſt the Poor of this Pariſh, *Lower Slaughter*, and *Clapton*, which is now in Chancery

A the Incloſure of this Pariſh, 1773, Eight Acres of Land were allotted for the Uſe of the Poor.

INCUMBLNTS	PATRONS	INCUMBLNTS	PATRONS
1574 Nicholas Band,	Queen Elizabeth	1720 Richard Vernon, LL B	Henry and Caroline Vernon
1575 Robert Antold,	The ſame		
1584 William Symondes,	The ſame	1753 William Vernon, M A	Dorothy Vernon, Spinſter
1585 Thomas Morland,	Giles Lord Chandos		
1589 John Innes,	The ſame	1781 William Hunter, M A	Charles Vernon
—— Robert Wright *, D D	———	1782 Edward Vernon, Clerk,	Edward Vernon Clerk
1622 Thomas Temple, D D	———		
1649 Antony Palmer †, M A	Appointed by Parliament		
1667 George Vernon, M A	Richard Cockes, Eſq		
The above from Sir ROB ATKYNS			

* ROBERT WRIGHT was elected Fellow of Trinity College, Oxford 1581, Chaplain to Queen ELIZABETH, in 1613 he was appointed the firſt Warden of Wadham College, by the Founders DOROTHY WADHAM, but reſigned his Office ſoon after, not being permitted to marry He was conſecrated Biſhop of Briſtol in 1622, and tranſlated to Litchfield and Coventry in 1632
                                                                                Wood's Catalogue of Biſhops, vol II p. 634

† ANTONY PALMER was born at Great Comberton, co Worceſter admitted Fellow of Balliol College 1640 He is painted by the ſevere Pencil of A Wood, with the ſtrongeſt Tints of party Zeal being appointed a Commiſſioner for ejecting ſcandalous Miniſters by the Parliament, and adopting the virulent and unprincipled Meaſures His Writings were frequent in Support of his religious Tenets and his Duty The Goſpel New Creature which was publiſhed in 1658, is the moſt approved of his Productions He died in 1678 The high Eſteem in which his Memory is held by his Followers, contraſts but the extreme ſeverity with which the Royaliſts have marked his Character It may be candid to determine from ſuch oppoſite Deſcriptions that he was a Man of ſtrong Parts, enterpriſing and undaunted in the Execution of what he thought his Duty and it is but juſt to allow that no Part of his private Life could in this way ſubject him to the Inquiry

PRESENT LORD OF THE MANOR,
THOMAS INGRAM, Efq

The Perfons fummoned from this Parifh by the Heralds in 1682 and 1683, were
John Venfeld, Gent
Chriftopher Trinder, Gent and
Anthony Collett, Gent

At the Election in 1776, Thirty-fix Freeholders polled from this Parifh

The earlieft Entry in the Regifter bears Date 1654

ANNUAL ACCOUNT OF MARRIAGES, BIRTHS, AND BURIALS, IN THIS PARISH

AD	Mar	Bir	Bur	AD	Mar	Bir	Bur	AD	Mar	Bir	Bur	AD	Mar	Bir	Bur
1781	9	12	5	1786	6	15	12	1791				1796			
1782	10	28	11	1787	7	7	12	1792				1797			
1783	4	20	18	1788				1793				1798			
1784	6	12	6	1789				1794				1799			
1785	9	19	15	1790				1795				1800			

It may be neceffary to remark, that in this Parifh is a numerous and refpectable Congregation of Proteftant Diffenters

INSCRIPTIONS IN THE CHURCH

ON A HANDSOME MARBLE MONUMENT ON THE NORTH SIDE OF THE CHANCEL

Arms, Or, on a Fefs Azure Three Garbs of the Field, for VERNON,—impaling, Argent, on a Chevron Sable, Three Mafcles Or, between Three Pellets, each charged with a Martlett of the Field, for PRATT

In hoc Cancello cuntumulantur Reliquæ
Reverendi Viri GEORGII VERNON, A M
Hujufce Paroch necnon de Sarfden, in Com Ox
Rectoris, vere pii,
Et ELIZABETHÆ, Viduæ, plurimum mœrentis,
Non longo tamen intervallo fejunctæ,
Ille enim obiit 17 Dec 1720, æt 83,
Illa 1 Aprilis, 1724, æt 80

Propè jacent duo filii
THOMAS, Infans, deceffit Sept 10, 1670

RICHARDIS, LL B hujus Paroch poft Patrem
Rector, Indigentiæ tacite munificus,
obiit Feb 18, 1752, æt 78

Hoc, in cariffimorum Memoriam,
DOROTHEA VERNON, P P

ON A MARBLE GRAVE STONE

Here lieth the Body of
DOROTHY VERNON, who
died March 6, 1764,
in the 78th Year of her Age

ON A MONUMENT AGAINST THE SOUTH WALL

In Memory of
ANTHONY COLLETT, Gent
who lies at the Entrance of this Seat
His Charity and Zeal for his Religion
furvives in a Donation of Ten Pounds
yearly, for the inftruction of Twelve
poor Boys in the Principles of the
Church of England, who deceafed April 7,
1719, aged 45 Year

IN THE SOUTH AISLE ARE THESE ARMS

Quarterly, ft and 4th, Argent, on a Fefs Sable, between Three Towers Gules, a Lion paffant Or — 2d and 3d, Argent, a Fefs florette Gules, between Three Cornifh Choughs proper Creft, a Tower Gules

IN THE CHURCH YARD, ON TOMBS

THOMAS CLARK, Yeoman,
died Sept 24, 1755, aged 71

MARY, Relict of THOMAS CLARK,
died Jan 19, 1744, aged 83

MARY CLARK
died April 7, 1772, aged 82

HANNAH, Daughter of
THOMAS and MARY CLARK,
died Sept 22, 1717, aged 19

Arms, on a Fefs, between Three Towers, a Lion paffant,—impaling, a Fefs between Three Birds

ANN, the Wife of JOHN JORDAN, Efq
died March 18, 1722 3, aged 42

JOHN, the Son of JOHN and ANN JORDAN,
was buried June 24, 1701

JOHN JORDAN, Gent
died Jan 6, 1774, aged 59

Mr John Rooke,
bured April 20, 1700

Mary, Wife of Henry Collett,
died Dec 25, 1737, aged 58.

Anthony Collett, Son of
Mr Henry Collett,
died Sept 14, 1732, aged 16

Anthony Collett, Gent
died Nov 2, 1682, aged 50

Henry Greene
died Jan 11, 1665

Giles his Son
died March 22, 1685

William Matthews
died Nov 24, 1696

Margaret his Wife
died March 1, 1702

John Matthews
died Sept 17, 1703

John Humphris, of Lower Swell,
died Oct 7, 1748, aged 65

Ann, the Wife of
James Tilling, died Jan 21, 1766, aged 65

James Tilling, late of Tangley Farm
in the County of Oxford,
died Mar 24, 178,, in the 67th Year of his Age

ON HEAD STONES

	Died	Aged		Died	Aged
Ann Wife of Joseph Burford	29 Sept 1781	52	Frances, Wife of William Slatter	29 Aug 1779	62
John Rose -	23 Sept 1742	42	Elizabeth, Wife of John Slatter	16 Apr 1777	54
William Rose -	8 Jan 1765	89	Thomas Peacy	10 Mar 1765	103
Thomas Rose -	5 Jun 1767	54	William Collett, of Lower Slaughter		
Elizabeth his Wife	25 May, 1765	54	ter	1 Mar 1705	5
Elizabeth, Wife of Edward Rose	———— 1738	—	Richard Collett	6 Aug 1765	59
Edmund their Son -	———— 1758	—	Hannah, Wife of John Collet	1 Dec 1763	3
Samuel also their Son	June 1753	52	Jane Farrin	30 Oct 1783	82
Mary Wife of James Taylor	21 Nov 1714	43	Frances Baynes -	10 Ap 1759	70
Joseph Son of Joseph and Elizabeth			Ann Baynes	17 Mar 1774	
Pain	10 June, 1764	4	May Baynes -	4 June, 1767	—
Joseph Pain	5 Sept 1742	59	Thomas Akerman -	23 Sept 1759	4
Elizabeth his Wife -	11 Feb 1750	58	Susanna his Wife	1 Oct 1759	83
Elizabeth Daughter of Joseph Pain	14 May, 1757	47	William, Son of William and Eliza		
Sarah, Daughter of James and Ann			beth Akerman -	6 Feb 1757	35
Pain	5 Feb 1753	24	John Akerman	6 Oct 1780	5
Catharine Wife of William Tombs	5 Sept 1755	82	Henry Akerman -	3 June, 1770	41
William Tombs	7 Aug 1728	67	Joseph Son of William Hill, Gent		
Elizabeth their Daughter -	28 Aug 1723	26	and Hester his Wife	2 July, 1765	53
William Akerman -	7 Aug 1704	8	William Phillips	7 May 49	50
Thomas his Son -	17 Feb 1742	25	Mary his Wife	12 Mar 1765	51
Jane Wife of William Akerman	9 July, 1755	71	Thomas Edwards -	17 Jun 1764	62
William Matthews	Sep 1746	76	Jane his Wife	1 Mar 1760	53
Ann his Wife -	12 Feb 1775	55	Thomas their Son	19 July 1776	20
William Tombs	20 Nov 1751	37	Thomas Lambert	13 Nov 1760	60
Mary his Wife and late Wife of			Elizabeth his Wife -	14 Jun 1749	60
Richard White	10 Aug 1751	73	Thomas their Son -	11 Nov 1761	39

XLVIII. BOXWELL.

A considerable Plantation of *Box Wood* upon an Eminence, from whence issues a copious Stream of Water, furnishes the Etymology of this Name. This Parish lies in the Hundred of *Grumbald's-Ash*, distant from *Wootton Under Edge* about Four Miles on the East, and Twenty South from GLOUCESTER.

The Soil is light, and applied in a Proportion of Two-thirds to Tillage, and the remainder Meadow and Pasture. The Lands produce an excellent Breed of Sheep. A System of Agriculture, more judicious or successful than that which is in Use in this Parish, has been no where adopted.

The Benefice is a Rectory in the Deanery of *Hawksbury*, with the Chapel of *Leighterton* annexed. The Church (now under compleat Repair) is a low Building, dedicated to St. ..., consisting of a Nave, one small Aisle on the North Side, and an octangular Turret forming a pointed Cupola in the Middle. The Form and Height of this Structure, on Comparison with other Specimens of the same Architecture in this County, is evidently of the Erection of the early Part of the Fourteenth Century. About that Period, the Abbey of *Walsingham* in *Norfolk* presented to the Rectory.

Of the Manor, the First Proprietors were the *Abbey* of *St. Peter* in *Gloucester*. Prior to the Dissolution of Monasteries, they shared it with the Family of HUNTLEY, who were the Lessees of those Lands which they did not hold in Fee. In the Reign of ELIZABETH, that Moiety belonged to the celebrated Sir WALTER RAWLEIGH, which was soon after passed to the HUNTLEYS, who are now the sole Proprietors of Estates in *Boxwell*. An ancient Mansion near the Church has been for many Generations their manorial Residence.

LELAND * retains a Tradition of there having been a Nunnery at *Boxwell*, which was destroyed by the Ravages of the *Danes*. It was never re-established. Foundation Stones, which have been discovered, fix the Site of this Building in a most romantic Valley, between the Church and Hill abovementioned, the Declivities of which are cloathed with a Plantation of Box, containing Fifteen Acres of the most flourishing Vegetation, and singular at least in this County. It produces a considerable Income, and is included within a free Warren of Forty Acres anciently chartered. The Rivulet which rises here, forming a small Lake below the Wood, has a pleasing Effect, and afterwards, in Confluence with others, joins the Severn below *Berkeley*.

Leighterton, or *Laterton*, is a Hamlet of greater Extent than *Boxwell*, to which Rectory it belongs, but has separate parochial Officers and Rates. The Chapel is small, with a very low embattled Tower. It has been lately repaired, and pewed in a decent Style. All the Land in this District are inclosed, and possessed in nearly equal Portions by several Proprietors, of whom are the Families of SHIPLAND, WARE, MORSE, BINNEY, VENN, and HOLBROW, Successors to the ancient Freeholders of the Name ... LYS, DREWE, FORDE, and HEAVIN.

Near the great Road from GLOUCESTER to BATH, is a Tumulus, or Barrow, of considerable Dimensions. About a Century since, it was opened and investigated by Mr. HUSSEY, who also discovered three small Vaults, in which were Urns filled with Ashes, but no Coin or other Roman Antiquities. In the *Warren* were lately found a small Quantity of Roman Coin, some human Bones, with Stones discoloured, as by Fire.

No Benefactions to the Poor.

INCUMBENTS	PATRONS	INCUMBENTS	PATRONS
1541 Edward de Boxwell,	Abbey of Gloucester	1727 Richard Hun... , M A ...	
1576 Antony Hayward,			Warner Hyg...
1588 Robert Woodruff,	Walter Osborne	1726 William Holmes, D D L ...	Warner, ...
1640 Richard Coxe			Arnold, M A ...
1688 Wykes Huntley, LL B	Matthew Huntley, LL...		Horner ...
The above from Sir ROBERT ATKYNS.		...8 Samuel Arnold, M A ...	
		17... Rich Huntley, M A ...	

PRESENT LORD OF THE MANOR,
The Reverend RICHARD HUNTLEY, M A

The Persons summoned from this Place by the Heralds in 1682 and 1683 were,
Matthew Huntley, Esq
———— Lyte, Gent

At the Election in 1776, Six Freeholders polled from this Parish

The First Date in the Register of *Leighterton* occurs in 1548   In that of *Boxwell*, in the Year 1582

ANNUAL ACCOUNT OF MARRIAGES, BIRTHS, AND BURIALS, IN THE PARISH OF BOXWELL AND
CHAPELRY OF LEIGHTERTON *

A D	Mar	Bir	Bur	A D	Mar	Bir	Bur	A D	Mar	Bir	Bur	A D	Mar	Bir	Bur
1781	—	3	6	1786	3	2	5	1791				1796			
1782	—	4	2	1787	—	5	4	1792				1797			
1783	2	3	3	1788		3	3	1793				1798			
1784	—	3	1	1789				1794				1799			
1785	1	2	10	1790				1795				1800			

INSCRIPTIONS IN THE CHURCH.

ON MONUMENTS AGAINST THE PILLARS.

In Memory of
ELIZABETH, only Daughter of
RICHARD GLASS, A M
late Vicar of Purton, Wilts,
and ELIZABETH his Wife,
born August 30, 1740,
died February 17, 1757,
aged 17 Years

In Memory of
ELIZABETH JOHNSON,
(Widow of T Johnson, of
Newcastle upon Tyne, Gent)

And of MARY HUNTLEY,
Daughters of
MATTHEW HUNTLEY,
late of this Place, Esq
and ELIZABETH his Wife

E J born May 28, 1695,
died Nov 1, 1775

M H born August 25, 1698,
died July 2, 1765

ON FLAT STONES

Here resteth the Body
of SYLVESTER, the Wife
of GEORGE HUNTLEY, Esq.
who departed this Life
the 25th Day of February,
16
Daughter and Heir of
EDWARD WAKE, of Wells, in
the County of Somerset, Esq

Here lieth the
Body of GEORGE
HUNTLEY, Esq
who died on
the Life the fifth Day
of July 16 6

Here resteth the Body
of Mrs. FRANCES HUNTLEY,
who departed this
life the 1st Day of
August, 1661.

Also in Memory
of ANNE HUNTLEY,
Wife of RICHARD HUNTLEY,
Rector of this Parish,
and Daughter of
NICHOLAS BAKER,
of Nettleton,
in the County of Wilts, Esq
who died December 2, 1782,
aged 48 Years

ROUND THE VERGE OF A FLAT STONE

Here lyeth the Body of
MATTHEW HUNTLEY, Esq
who was buried the 3d
Day of October, 1663

ON THE SAME STONE

Under this Stone likewise
lies interred the Body of the
Reverend Mr RICHARD HUNTLEY,
late Rector of this
Parish, and of Castlecombe,
Wilts, who departed this Life
April 1, 1728, in the
39th Year of his Age

Also
Here lieth the Body
of ANNE HUNTLEY,
Widow
of the said RICHARD HUNTLEY,
and Daughter
of HENRY LEE, of Dane-John,
in the County of Kent, Esq
She died { June 18, 1761
          { Aged 77, Years

* And do appoint that ... were ... ed of ... Truth ... in the most authentic and ancient Records it is fixed Pa
... aged de Leomin.

1   800

Sub hoc reconduntur
tumulo cineres GEORGII
HUNTLEY, Armigeri,
qui dum inter vivos
esset et esset vitam
agebat, qua nullo
præeunte morbo subito
finita vigesimo 2d die
Octobris anno ætatis
suæ 20m sexto Obiit
Anno Dom M DCLXXIX

Here resteth the Body
of LIZABETH, late Wife
of MATTHEW HUNTLEY,
Esq who departed this
Life the 21st day of November
Anno Dom 1684

Here lyeth the Body of ELIZABETH,
the Wife of MATTHEW HUNTLEY,
Esq who departed this life the
3d Day of July,
Anno $\begin{cases} \text{Domini, 1713,} \\ \text{Ætatis suæ 50} \end{cases}$

Here lyeth the Body of
MATTHEW HUNTLEY, Esq.
who departed this Life the
16th Day of August
Anno $\begin{cases} \text{Domini 1713,} \\ \text{Ætatis suæ 58.} \end{cases}$

Here lyeth the Body of
Mrs MARY LEE, Daughter of
HENRY Lee, Esq of Dane John,
in the County of Kent,
who died May 12, 1742,
Æt suæ 57 Years

H S S
Cineres RICHARDI CHANDLER, Arm
Patris ELIZABETHÆ Uxoris MATTHEI
HUNTLEY, Arm Obiit 4 die Mar,
Anno $\begin{cases} \text{Domini 171,} \\ \text{Ætati suæ 49} \end{cases}$

Omnibus equidem bonis viris vero,
quam maxime lugendus obiit
In rebus etenim gerendis se
virum præstitit honestissimum
Fidemque semper tenuit inviolatam
In literis fuit et modum veritatis,
Pietate nulli secundus, maximi
erga omnem sinceritate et integritate,
summa erga Deum reverentia et submissione
se gerebat

Here lyeth the Body of ELIZABETH
CHANDLER, Relict of JOHN
CHANDLER of London,
Merchant, and Mother
of ELIZABETH the Wife
of MATTHEW HUNTLEY,
Esq who departed this
Life the 22d of August 1729,
in the 76th Year of her Age

SAMUEL HUNTLEY, filius
2dus WILKES HUNTLEY, LL B
hujus Ecclesiæ Rectoris,
et MARIÆ uxoris ejus,
habet corpusculum suum
hic reconditum XXV°,
die Jan An Dom 1689

Here lyeth the Body of
ROSE HUNTLEY, Daughter of
MATTHEW HUNTLEY, Esq
and ELIZABETH his Wife, who
departed this Life the 13th
Day of January,
Anno $\begin{cases} \text{Domini, 1714,} \\ \text{Ætatis suæ 23} \end{cases}$

Here lyeth the Body of MATTHEW,
Son of MATTHEW HUNTLEY, Esq
and ELIZABETH his Wife of this
Place, who departed this Life
the 5th Day of January, 1711,
aged 18 years and six Weeks

Here lyeth the Body of RICHARD, Son
of RICHARD HUNTLEY, Esq and ANNE his Wife,
who departed this life the 7th Day of
May, A D 1720, aged 7 Months

Here lyeth the Body of FRANCES HUNTLEY,
Daughter of MATTHEW HUNTLEY, of
this Place, Esq who was buried
the 4th Day of July Anno Dom 1640

Here lyeth the Body of
ELIZABETH, Daughter of RICHARD
HUNTLEY, Esq and ANNE his Wife,
who departed this Life the 4th
of January, Anno Dom 1720,
aged 2 Years and 4 Months

Here lyeth the Body of ALICE WINSMORE,
Wife of JOHN WINSMORE, of Wedmore,
in the County of Mid Esq Daughter
of MATTHEW HUNTLEY, of this Place, Esq
who died on Monday the 2d Day of
September, Anno Dom 16,,
Ætatis suæ 23

Here lyeth the Body of ELIZABETH,
Daughter of MATTHEW HUNTLEY,
Esq and of ELIZABETH his Wife
who departed this Life of 2 Months
old on the 3d Day of May, 1691

Here resteth the Body of EDMUND HUNTLEY,
Gent youngest Son of MATTHEW HUNTLEY, of
this Place, Esq who departed this Life the
10th Day March, Anno Sal 1661 æt suæ 28

Also here lyeth the Body of
WILLIAM, Son of WYKES HUNTLEY,
who died July 5th 1728, aged 44 Years.

Here lyeth the Body of the
Reverend Mr WYKES HUNTLEY,
Rector of Boxwell and Leighterton
38 Years, who died the 27th Day
of January, 1726, aged 71 Years

Here lyeth the Body of
the Rev Mr SAMUEL HUNTLEY,
who departed this Life
Oct 13, 1737, aged 46 Years.

Here lyeth the Body of RUTH WATTS,
Widow, Relict of RICHARD WATTS, of
London, Citizen, who departed this Life
the 15th Day of May, 1700,
in the 75th Year of her Age

Here lyeth the Body of
Mrs ELIZABETH SMITH, who departed
this Life April 1, 1711,
aged 58

IN THE CHURCH YARD, ON TOMBS

In Memory of
PAUNCEFOOT MILLER, of this
Parish, Yeoman, who was buried
April 6, 1706, aged 80 Years

Also of ELIZABETH his Wife
who was buried Aug 9, 1699,
aged 47

Also of ANN his second Wife,
who was buried Aug 12, 1712,
aged 80

As also of WILLIAM, the Son of
PAUNCEFOOT MILLER and ANN
his second Wife,
who was buried March 16, 1732,
aged 60

Also of HESTER his Wife,
who was buried Oct 15, 1754,
aged 81

This Tomb is erected
to preserve the Memory of
RICHARD MILLER, Son of
WILLIAM MILLER and HESTER
his Wife, who was buried Aug 28, 1775,
aged 76.

Also of ELIZABETH his Wife,
who was buried Feb 9, 1770,
aged 58

To the Memory of
WILLIAM MILLER, Esq
Son of RICHARD and ELIZABETH MILLER,
who died Jan 6, 1781,
aged 40 Years

Also of Mrs HESTER MILLER,
his Sister, who died July 20, 1781,
aged 36

And also of RICHARD MILLER,
Esq their Brother, who died
March 13, 1782,
aged 39

Sub hoc tumulo honorifice
sepultum
placide quiescit Corpus RICHARDI COXE,
hujus Ecclesiæ necnon Capellæ de
Leighterton Rectoris, qui postquam
in hisce annos quadraginta octo curis pastoralibus

anno ætatis 74, undecimo
die Augusti, Anno Dom 1688
Candide lector, ipsum sequere et currite Christum.

ON A FLAT STONE

In Memory of MARY SMITHFIELD,
Daughter of RICHARD SMITHFIELD,
of Bath Easton in the County of Somerset, Esq
who died March 10, 1754,
aged 73 Years

O N   H E A D   S T O N E S.

	Died	Aged
John Longford	26 Sept 1752	8
Daniel Baker, of Oakſey	25 Oct 1751	39
Sarah Baker	13 Jan 1739	39
Elizabeth Heaven	24 Apr. 1771	23
Richard Davis, ſenior	4 Feb 1758	74

L E I G H T E R T O N.

IN THE CHURCH YARD, ON TOMBS.

ROGER DREW, ſenior, Yeoman,
died July 17, 1675

JOHN DREW, Yeoman,
died April 10, 1756, aged 24

HESTER, Daughter of WILLIAM DREW,
died Jan. 2, 1710, aged 22

MARY, Wife of WILLIAM MORSE,
of the Pariſh of Kingſcote,
and Daughter of JOHN and JOAN DREW,
of this Pariſh,
died April 28, 1785, aged 55.

WILLIAM DREW
died Nov 27, 1713,
aged 54

SARAH his Wife
died April 29, 1718,
aged 63

WILLIAM BUCKINGHAM
died Nov 10, 1772,
aged 69

SARAH his Wife
died March 28, 1785,
aged 82

ELIZABETH, late Wife of
WILLIAM TURNER,
of Petty France, died May 9, 1781,
aged 47

ANNA HOLBOROW, Wife of
WILLIAM HOLBOROW,
died Jan 7, 1760,
aged 69

WILLIAM HOLBOROW, Yeoman,
died May 1, 1773,
aged 75

WILLIAM HOLBOROW, ſenior, Yeoman,
died Dec. 11, 1749,
aged 65

WILLIAM HOLBOROW, junior,
died Feb 26, 1749,
aged 31

SARAH, Daughter of
WILLIAM and ANN HOLBOROW,
and Wife of JOHN COX, Yeoman,
died March 14, 1744,
aged 31

DANIEL HOLBOROW,
Son of WILLIAM and ANNA HOLBOROW,
died May 31, 1767,
aged 40

SAMUEL HOLBOROW, Yeoman,
Son of WILLIAM and ANN HOLBOROW
died June 4, 1762,
aged 35

ANN, Relict of
WILLIAM HOLBOROW,
died Oct 29, 1762,
aged 79

ANN HOLBOROW, Spinſter,
died Jan 9, 1774,
aged 55

RICHARD SARGENT, Yeoman,
died Oct 31, 1765,
aged 62

ELIZABETH his Wife
died March 7, 1765,
aged 56

RICHARD, Son of RICHARD SARGENT,
died Oct 19, 1760,
aged 23

FRANCIS FRANKCOM, Yeoman,
died Dec 27, 1761,
aged 55

HENRY FOORD
died Aug 12, 1660.

JOHN FOORD, Yeoman,
died March 21, 1713,
aged 78

ANNA his Wife
died Sept. 25, 1721,
aged 69

JAMES FOORD
died March 1, 1732,
aged 77

ANN, Wife of
CHRISTOPHER CLARK,
formerly Wife of HENRY FOORD,
died June 27, 1673

O N H E A D S T O N E S

				Died	Aged
Ann, Wife of Samuel Witts, of Tresham	•	•	•	19 Aug 1765	42
Hester, Wife of Robert Player	•	•	•	2 Mar 1764	30
James, Son of John and Mary Clark	•	•	•	13 Aug 1742	17
Elizabeth, Wife of Allin Walker	•	•	•	9 Dec 1747	43
Allin Walker, Yeoman	•	•	•	4 June, 1759	62

The Church & Castle of St Briavel

XLIX. ST. BRIAVEL'S*, OR ST. BRULAIS'.

THIS Place does not occur in the great Survey made by the Conqueror, either as giving Name to a Hundred, or a diſtinct Pariſh. The preſent Hundred of *St. Briavel* was at that Time included in that of *Weſtburie*, and the Pariſh a Hamlet to *Newland*.

The Diſtance of this Village from *Coleford* is Five Miles on the South, and Twenty five from Gloucester, of the Soil the greater Part is Woodland, with nearly equal Portions of Arable and Paſture. It varies with the Situation, of Sand or Clay. The Orchards produce the beſts Sorts of Cyder peculiar to the Foreſt Diviſion. The Circumference of the Pariſh is Twenty Miles, in which are Four Thouſand Acres of Commonable and Foreſt Land. The Scoria, or Cinders of Iron, are frequently found in large Quantities a few Feet beneath the Surface, which proves that ſome of the Royal Foundeneries were eſtabliſhed here.

The Benefice is a Chapel ſ er lowed with Vicarial Ti hes, annexed to *Tydney* in the *Foreſt* Deane y, the Impropriation and Advowſon of which belong to the Dean and Chapter of the Cathedral of *Hereford*.

The Church conſiſts of a Nave and a Tranſept. In the Nave are appendant Two ſmall Aiſles over which the Roof is continued, theſe are divided by two Rows of Pillars, on the North of h S r cene, on the South of early Norman Architecture. The Roof of Timber Frame was covered with a modern Cieling and Cornice, about Thirty Years ſince. In the Tranſept is a ſmall Arcade, or Receptacle for Holy Water. The Tower is low, maſſive, and embattled, of hewn ſtone, and exhibits with the whole Structure, the Marks of every remote ... It is dedicated to St. Mary.

The Caſtle of *St. Bria* ... was once of the higheſt Conſequence in this ... enjoying ...

[lines heavily degraded and largely illegible]

beautiful, than what occur in any other Tract of equal Extent in the Kingdom. Two Views of the Castle are published, one by NATH BUCK in 1730, the other by FRANCIS GROSE, Esq in 1775, in their Collections of the Antiquities of Britain

MILO FITZ-WALTER, Earl of *Hereford*, founded the Castle of *St Briavls* in the Reign of HENRY I to curb the Incursions of the *Welsh*. It continued in that Family, about a Century, when it was forfeited to the Crown, by whom its Constables have been since appointed *

CONSTABLES OF THE CASTLE OF *ST. BRIAVEL*

YEAR	REIGN	CONSTABLES
1215,	17 King John,	John de Monemouth
1260,	44 Henry III.	Robert Waleran
1263,	47 Henry III	John Giffard (Baron)
——,	———,	Thomas de Clare
1282,	12 Edward I	William de Beauchamp, Earl of Warwick
1289,	19 Edward I	John de Bottourt (deprived)
1291,	21 Edward I	Thomas de Everty
1298,	27 Edward I	John de Handeloe
1300,	29 Edward I	Ralph de Abbenhalle
1307,	1 Edward II	John de Bottourt (restored)
1308,	2 Edward II	William de Staure
1322,	15 Edward II.	Hugh Le Despenser, senior
1327,	18 Edward II.	John de Nyvers
1327,	20 Edward II	John de Hardeshull
1341,	14 Edward III	Roger Clifford (Baron)
1491,	14 Richard II	Thomas de Woodstock, Duke of Gloucester
1436,	14 Henry VI	John Duke of Bedford
1459,	38 Henry VI	John Tiptoft, Earl of Worcester
1466,	6 Edward IV	Richard Neville, Earl of Warwick.
* *	* * *	* * * * *
* *	* * * *	* * * * *
1612,	9 James I	Henry Earl of Pembroke
1632,	10 Charles I	Philip Earl of Pembroke
1660,	1 Charles II	Henry Lord Herbert of Raglan (Duke of Beaufort
1706,	5 Queen Anne,	Charles Earl of Berkeley
1710,	9 Queen Anne,	James Earl of Berkeley
1736,	8 George II	Augustus Earl of Berkeley
1755,	27 George II	Norborne Berkeley, Esq (Lord Bottetourt)
1766,	6 George III	Frederic Augustus Earl of Berkeley

That the Village was formerly more extensive, appears from Ruins frequently discovered, and of its Privileges as a Royal Vill, or Borough, we are informed by the following Extract from the Archives of the Cathedral Church of *Hereford*

" 2 John II The King grants a Market to be held every Week upon Tuesday, and a Fair Three " Days at each of the Feasts of the Annunciation and St Michael, in his Manor of *St Briavel*

" 12 John II The King commands his Sheriff to proclaim the said Markets at the said Seasons

" 26 John III The King, at the Request of GUIDO DE BRYAN, grants to the Burgesse of the Town " or Vill of *St Briavel*, a Freedom and Exemption from all Toll, Pontage, Paviage, Murage, Pickage, and Pontage, and all other Customs of the like Sort, throughout the Realm

To these, now obsolete Immunities, is added a Claim of immemorial Usage, of a Right of Common in a Wood called *Hudnalls* and its *Purlieus*, confined solely to the Inhabitants of the Parish. It lies South west from the Village, on the Banks of the *Wye*, in the Form of a Crescent, six Miles round and one broad. Their Claim was contested, but confirmed to them, on Petition, by CHARLES II A tradition prevails that this Benefaction was obtained by the Wife of one of the Earls of *Hereford* on the same capricious Condition as Lady GODIVA procured Privileges for the Citizens of *Coventry*. It is certain, that one Penny is annually contributed by every Parishioner to purchase Bread and Cheese, which given on Whitsunday to every Claimant, is a Condition of the Charter

The Hamlet of *Brockwear* on the *Wye* is partly in this Parish, from whence there is a navigable Communication with BRISTOL, for the Conveyance of Timber, Iron, and the other Produce of the Forest of *Dean*

* CAMDEN reckons *St Briavel's Castle* but gives rather a History of its first Founders from the Annals of GIRALDUS. In Topographic Description of it CAMDEN, Edit GIBSON, vol I p 70

At *Bafwear* the Family of CATCHMAY were feated in 600   The ancient Manfion houfe was rebuilt in 1755 by JAMES ROOKE, Efq who married the Heir of that Family   It is now poffeffed by Major General JAMES ROOKE, Knight of the Shire for the County of *Monmouth*

Hillfbury has been vefted in the Family of GOUGH for many Generations   They are of a *Britifh* Extraction, and trace their Defcent from Sir MATHEW GOCHE, or GOUGH *, who ferved in *France* under King HENRY V   By a Marriage with one of the Coheirs of WILLIAM WARREN, they inherited this and other confiderable Eftates   A Plate of the Monument of WARREN and MARIANA CATCHMAY his Wife is annexed

Aylfmere belonged to the Family of BOND, the Coheir of which, the Relict of ——— PROSSER, is the prefent Poffeffor   CHARLES EDWIN, Efq has a confiderable Eftate in this Parifh, long held by the Family of HATHEWAY   befide thefe, the remaining Property is nearly equally divided

---

B E N E F A C T I O N S

JOHN GUNNING, Efq Time when, or for what Purpofe given not mentioned, gave Land, vefted in CHARLES EDWIN, Efq the annual Produce of which is 5*l*

Mr WILLIAM WHITTINGTON gave, by Deed, 1625, for Poor Widows' Land, vefted in the Hands of Truftees   the annual Produce of which is 3*l*   He likewife gave Land to the fame Value for placing out Apprentices

Mr WILLIAM HOSKINS gave for the Poor, Land vefted in Mr EDWIN HOSKINS, the annual Produce of which is *l*

Mr JOHN BRABAN gave for the Poor, Land vefted in Mr JAMES DAVIES, the annual Produce of which is 2*l*

Mr WILLIAM WHITTINGTON, befides the above Benefactions to the Poor, gave 1*l* 6*s* 8*d* for Four Sermons, one to be preached every Quarter, and 1*l* for ever, for adorning the Church

INCUMBENTS	PATRONS	INCUMBENTS	PATRONS
1681 John Evans, M A.	Dean and Chapter of Hereford	1712 Thomas Gwillam, M A	Dean and Chapter of Hereford
1690 Daniel Pilfworth, M A	The fame	1726 Robert Breton, M A	The fame
1694 Thomas Mathews, M A	The fame	1769 John Evans, M A	The fame
		1783 Charles Morgan, M A	The fame

PRESENT LORD OF THE MANOR, AS CONSTABLE OF THE CASTLE,
The Right Hon FREDERIC AUGUSTUS Earl of BERKELEY

At the Vifitations of the Heralds, in 1682 and 1683, the following Perfons were fummoned
Sir William Catchmay, Knight,   Edmund Bond, Gent
William Gough, Efq   William Morgan, Gent

At the Election in 1776, Thirty-four Freeholders polled from this Parifh

The firft Date of the Regifter occurs in 1660, in which are many Inftances of the Longevity of the Inhabitants   In 1767 Five Perfons died whofe Ages amounted to 450 Years

ANNUAL ACCOUNT OF MARRIAGES, BIRTHS, AND BURIALS, IN THIS PARISH

A D	Mar	Bir	Bur	A D	Mar	Bir	Bur	A D	Mar	Bir	Bur	A D	Mar	Bir	Bur
1781	3	12	16	1786	—	11	10	1791				1796			
1782	1	18	5	1787	—	18	4	1792				1797			
1783	2	17	7	1788				1793				1798			
1784	2	13	15	1789				1794				1799			
1785	2	17	6	1790				1795				1800			

* The Refpect in which he was held by his warlike Countrymen is expreffed by a Monkifh Rhyme
" Mortc Matthei Goche—Cumbria clamitat Oche "
Itin W DE WORCESTER, Edit NASMITH, p 357

INSCRIPTIONS IN THE CHURCH.

In the Chancel is a large Mural Monument semi canopied, on which are the Effigies, of painted Freestone, of a Man and Woman in a reclining Posture. On a Compartment beneath, are the Figures, in Relief, of Three of their Children kneeling, and an Infant lying on a Cushion. Upon a Pediment, supported by Two Corinthian Pillars, are the Figures of Faith, Hope, and Charity, between which is a Shield, bearing the Arms of Warren, Checky Or and Azure. There is no Inscription on the Monument, but it was erected to the Memory of William Warren and Mariana Catchmay his Wife, who died in the Reign of Queen Elizabeth.

ON FLAT STONES

Arms, two Bars, on a Canton five Billets in
Saltire

Here lieth the Body of
William Catchmay, Esq; eldest Son
of Tracy Catchmay, Esq; of Bigtware,
by Barbara his Wife. He departed
this Life March 29, 1743, aged near 42

Here lyeth Elizabeth, Daughter of
Sir William Catchmay, Knight,
by Dame Eleanor his Wife,
who departed this Life the 23d of
August, 1731, aged 84 Years

Here lyeth the Body of Tracy
Catchmay, Esq; who married
Barbara, the Daughter of Reginald
Bray, of Barrington Esq; by
whom he had Issue, William,
Tracy, and Jane. He died the 30th
Day of November, 1706

And also the abovenamed
Barbara, who departed this Life
Jan. 23, 1740 1, aged 75

Here lyes the Body of Tracy
Catchmay, Esq; youngest Son of
Tracy Catchmay Esq; by Barbara
his Wife. He departed this Life
Feb 17, 1731, aged 51 Year

Hic jacet quod reliquum est
Edward Jones, A M
late Here Prebendum,
nec non de Lidney
Vicarii vigilantissimi, & ad
beneficentiam propensissimae
Obiit 1 Die Junii, 1681, æt 64

Hic jacet Edvardus Jones, juxta
jacentis filius natu quintus, obiit
Die DEgMI *, Anno ætatis 1681.
24 *

Here lyeth the Body of Thomas James,
of Soylwell in the Parish of Lidney, Esq;
eldest Son of Thomas James, of
Lidney who departed this Life the 14th
Day of July, Anno Domini 1702

Here lyeth Elizabeth, the Daughter
of Thomas James, of Warrens Esq.
who departed this Life the . Day
of Nov 1715

Here lyeth the Body of
Jane, Widow and Relict of
William James, of Soylwell, Esq.
also deceased. She died the
17th Day of May, 1728, aged 64.

Here lyeth the Body of
Richard James, Esq; of the
Inner Temple, fourth Son of
Thomas James, Esq; Son of
Edward James, Esq; whose
Bodies lie under this Stone
He departed this Life in London
Dec 18, Anno
aged 28 Years

Here lyeth the Body of Thomas
James, Son of William James,
Gent. who departed this Life
May 20, 1694,
aged 16 Months

Here lyeth the Body of
William Jones, Esq; who
departed this Life the 5th Day of
April, 1727

* Sic

ON A MARBLE MONUMENT AGAINST THE SOUTH
WALL IN THE CHANCEL

Arms, a Chevron, between three Millinks.

Near this Place
lies interred the Remains of
WILLIAM JAMES,
of Soilwell in the Parish of Lidney,
in the County of Gloucester, Esq
obiit Feb 6, 1741,
ætatis 46

Also FRANCES,
Daughter of the above WILLIAM JAMES, Esq
by ANN his Wife,
obiit Jan 26, 1766, æt 23

This Monument was erected
by the above Mrs ANN JAMES

Also ANN, Wife of the above
WILLIAM JAMES, Esq
who died November 20, 1784, æt 73

ON A FLAT STONE.

Arms, On a Chevron three Chessrooks, between
three Rooks Crest, a dexter Arm embowed,
holding a Pistol

Here lyeth the Body of JAMES ROOKE,
Esq of Bigsweare He departed
this Life June 16, 1773,
aged 89 Years,
who married JANE, the Daughter of
TRACEY CATCHMAY, Esq Surviving
Issue by her, JAMES, JANE, and BARBARA

IN THE MIDDLE AISLE.

ON FLAT STONES

Arms, Quarterly, 1st and 4th, Paly of six,
Gules and Argent, on a Chevron Azure, three
Cross Croslets Or, for CARPENTER, 2d and 3d, three
Estoiles and a Chief vairè

Here resteth, in Hopes of a glorious
Resurrection, the Body of ELIZABETH,
the Daughter of WILLIAM CARPENTER,
of Hewersfield, Gent by ELIZABETH
his Wife, who died Jan 21, 1720,
aged 47 Years

In Memory of WILLIAM CARPENTER,
Gent who departed this Life
Jun 23, 1680

Also the Body of MORRIS CARPENTER,
Gent who departed this Life
Feb 25, 1741, aged 81.

ELIZABETH, Wife of WILLIAM
CARPENTER, of Hewersfield,
Gent. who departed this Life
March 20, 1722,
aged 73 Years

ELIZABETH, Wife of WILLIAM
CARPENTER, Gent died Nov 16,
1712, aged 82

ELIZABETH, Daughter of WILLIAM
and ELIZABETH CARPENTER, died
March 18, 1744, aged 78

Also of ANNE, Relict of THOMAS
CURTIS, of the City of Bristol,
and Daughter of WILLIAM and
ELIZABETH CARPENTER, Gent who died the
23d of April 1753, aged 77

Here lyeth the Body of
JANE, the Wife of JAMES DAVIES,
Clerk, who departed this Life
the 1st Day of June, 1752
aged 29.

Also here lyeth the Body
of JAMES DAVIES, Clerk, who
departed this Life Jan 19,
1781, aged 74

FRANCES, the Wife of GEORGE MAN,
Junior, of Brockweare, and
Daughter of WILLIAM CARPENTER,
of Huersfield, Gent died
December 3, 1720, aged 38

ALICE, Wife of WILLIAM WHITTINGTON,
Gent who left this Life the
4th of October, 1625

Here lyeth the Body of
RICHARD BYRKIN, Gent who
departed this Life 22d Day of
July, 17 9, aged 55 Years

Also SARAH, Daughter of
EDWARD MACHIN, Esq by ANNE
his Wife, Grand Daughter of the
above named RICHARD BYRKIN,
who departed this Life the 3d of June,
175?, aged 33

Here lyeth the Body of THOMAS
BYRKIN, of this Parish, Gent
who departed this Life the 17th Day
of September, 1748, aged 48.

MARY, the Wife of THOMAS
BYRKIN, Gent died December 16,
1757, aged 55 Years

Here lyeth the Body of MARY,
the Wife of WARREN JANE, Gent.
and Daughter of EDWARD MACHIN, Esq.
who died January 6, 1745, aged 20

Here lyeth MARY, Wife
of JOHN JANE, who died the
6th of September, 1629.

Here resteth the Body of
EDWARD BRABAEN, of St Briavel's,
who died January 25, 1660

ELIZABETH, his Wife, died the
17th day of October, 1688

Also here lyeth the Body of
ELIZABETH, the Wife of THOMAS
BYRKIN, who died May 14, 1714

Also ANN, Relict of EDWARD
MACHIN, who departed this Life
the 20th of July, 1760, aged 61

Here lyeth the Body of   . ..
Wife of RICHARD BYRKIN,
Gent who departed this Life,
June 14, 1729, aged 55 Years.

Here lyeth the Body of ELIZABETH,
the Relict of JAMES DAVIES, Clerk,
who died May 12, 1781, aged 70

Here lyeth the Body of
CHRISTOPHER THORNE, who departed
his Life, December 2, 1704

MARY, his Daughter by
MARY his Wife, died July 27, 1724

On A MARBLE MONUMENT AGAINST THE
GALLERY AT THE WEST END OF THE CHURCH

Near this Place lie the Remains of WILLIAM
WORGAN, late of Dunklins, who died March 24,
1781, aged 61

Also near this Place lie the Remains of ELIZABETH,
the Relict of the above WILLIAM WORGAN,
who died October 13, 1782, aged 61 Years

IN THE NORTH AISLE AGAINST THE WALL.

Arms, as before

RICHARD CATCHMAY,
one of the Trustees
of WILLIAM WHITTINGTON,
1625.

ON A FLAT STONE

Here lyeth the Body of WILLIAM
MORGAN, of Mork, who departed
this Life the 20th Day of January, 1708

Also the Body of ELEANOR, the Wife
of WILLIAM MORGAN, who departed
this Life the 16th Day of September,
A D 1726

IN THE SOUTH AISLE AGAINST THE WALL

Arms, Azure, three Boars Heads couped
Argent, for GOUGH

WARREN GOUGH, Esq.
one of the Trustees of
WILLIAM WHITTINGTON,
1625

ON A MONUMENT AGAINST THE WALL.

In Memory of ALEX THORNE,
who departed this Life
Jan 20, 1704-5, aged 92 Years.

ON FLAT STONES

CHRISTOPHER THORNE, of Mockbrook,
died Aug 4, 1732

MARY his Wife
died Nov 10, 1749

Here lyeth the Body of TRYPHOSA
GRIFFITH, Wife of JOHN GRIFFITH,
late of the City of Bristol, who
died Dec 24, 1744, aged 50 Years

Also here lyeth the Body of
JOHN GRIFFITH, late of the Cinder Hill
in this Parish, who died
Aug 19, 1779, aged 80

IN THE CHURCH PORCH

Here lyeth the Body of
JONATHAN GRIFFITH,
of this Parish, who departed
this Life March 9, 1744, aged 56 Years

JOHN, Son of JONATHAN and
MARY GRIFFITH, died Feb 28, 1738

MARY, Wife of JONATHAN
GRIFFITH, died Jan 5, 1778,
aged 78

WARREN GRIFFITH
died May 18, 1743, aged 94 Years

IN THE CHURCH YARD, ON TOMBS.

MARY Wife of JAMES KING,
died Dec. 25, 1781, aged 64.

JAMES KING died
March 16, 1782, aged 66

LAWRENCE HIGGINS
died Jan. 20, 1780, aged 36

MARGARET, Widow of
FRANCIS GEORGE, of Hewelsfield,
died March 7, 1765, aged 78

KEDGWIN HOSKINS,
late of Platwell in the Parish of
Newland, Gent died May 27, 1764,
aged 56.

ELIANOR HOSKINS, Spinster,
died April 5, 1747, aged 37

KEDGWIN HOSKINS, Gent
late of Stow Grange, died
April 18, 1743, aged 69

ALICE, the Relict of KEDGWIN
HOSKINS Gent aforesaid, died
August 10 1756, aged 83

Hic jacet Corpus JOHANNIS ROBERTS,
spe Resurrectionis ad novam vitam, qui
obiit 20 Die Junii, An 1720, at 76

Hic etiam Depositum est Corpus
ELIZABETHÆ, Uxoris JOHANNIS
ROBERT, quæ ex hac vita discessit
1 Die Junii, Anno Dom 1720, ætit 69

Hic jacet Corpus JOHANNIS ROBERTS,
filius JOHANNIS & ELIZABETHÆ
ROBERTS, de St Briavel, qui
decessit ex hac vita 23 Die Martii, 1754,
ætatis 61

THOMAS ROTHERY
died May 23, 1731, aged 80.

ANNE his Wife
died May 11, 1760, aged 79

THOMAS their Son
died Jan 22, 1745 aged 34

MARY their Daughter
died April 12, 1772, aged 62

DEBORAH, Relict of
RICHARD GODWIN, Gent
died Jan 25, 1772, aged 54

DEBORAH, Wife of
EDWARD BARROW, Gent.
died July 15, 1760, aged 84

RICHARD GRIFFITH
died Jan 1, 1730, aged 80

ELIZABETH BUTLER Daughter of
JOHN WORGAN, of this Parish, deceased,
and Wife of MATTHEW BUTLER of the
City of Westminster Gent one of
the Messengers of the Chambers in
Ordinary to King CHARLES the First,
and to his now Majesty King CHARLES
the Second, died Jan 5, 1668, aged 50

HENRY WORGAN
died Oct 5, 1687

HENRY Son of EDWARD
and MARY WORGAN died
Dec 28, 1721

EDWARD WORGAN of the Roads,
died Aug 12 1734

WILLIAM his Son
died June 8, 1747, aged 57

JOHN HUMPHRYS, Gent
Son of THOMAS HUMPHRYS, late
of Penywyllt in the County of Hereford,
Esq died Feb , 782, aged 51

H S E
ANNA Uxor GULIELMI GOUGH,
filia JOHANNIS DOUGLAS, Militis
Jan 4, 1669

CATHERINA, Uxor GULIELMI GOUGH,
(Nepotis GULIELMI & ANNA)
Filii CHRISTOPHORI POUNTLEY Arm
ob Oct 18, 1672,

Superstes CATHARINA
GULIELMUS GOUGH, de
Willsbury Gen
obiit Dec 27 1773 æt 84

Arms as before

JACOBI GOUGH, de Pasterstull, Gen
qui ob 7 Julii, Anno { Salt 1691
{ Æt 79

Ac etiam
CAROLI GOUGH, de Willsbury, Gen
qui ob 27 Oct Anno { Salutis 1728
{ Ætatis 67.

ANN the Wife of
ALEXANDER THORNE,
died June 14, 1679

CHRISTOPHER BLUNT
died March 24, 1752, aged 36

THOMAS BERROW
died March 25, 1726, aged 78

THOMAS, Son of THOMAS BERROW,
died June 17, 1702, aged 25

ALICE, the Wife of THOMAS VEALE,
died April 8, 162

JOHN CLOSS
died Sep 22, 1775, aged 65

WILLIAM FLOID, of Redhouse, Gen
died Nov 6, 1733, aged 51

MARY his Wife
died Sep 18 1760, aged 80

his son their Son
died April , 17 , aged 37

SIBILL Wife of WILLIAM
CONSTANT, died Sept 13, 1764,
aged 68

JOHN CONSTANT
died June 14, 1775, aged 80

JOHN MILTON
died Dec 9, 1761, aged 71

his Wife
died March 11, 175 aged 51

O

ON FLAT AND HEAD STONES

	Died	Aged
John Barrow, of the Hoggins	9 Aug 1717	—
William Son of William Barrow, of the City of Bristol	15 Dec 1745	—
Edward Barrow	11 Feb 1725	—
Edward Barrow, of Dunkley	26 Nov 1760	75
John Cretwick	20 Nov 1759	38
Thomas Dale	28 Dec. 1623	—
Edward Dale, Son of John Dale, Yeoman and Maudlin his Wife	31 July, 1642	—
John, Son of Edward Dale	— Nov 1665	—
Elizabeth Dale, Widow	16 Feb 1667	—
Edward Dale	— 1671	—
Ann, Wife of Thomas Dale	23 Dec 1693	—
Thomas Dale	— 1707	—
Edward, Son of Thomas Dale	17 Sept 1709	—
Thomas Dale	20 Nov. 1735	61
John Gough	18 Jan 1711	—
James Gough	11 Apr 1712	—
George Gough, Esq	22 Sept 1765	82
Warren Gough, of Willsbury, Esq	15 Dec. 1636	—
Mary Daughter of William Gough, of Brook Hall Gent	7 June, 1725	13
Blanch Lewis, Daughter of George Gough of Huelsfield, by Mary his Wife, Daughter of William Warren, Esq	8 Nov 1641	—
John Ball	17 Dec 1759	59
Hannah his Wife	19 Apr 1735	35
William Ball	11 Aug 1759	56
Henry Dunn, Keeper of Park's End Lodge	22 Sept 1751	49
Mary his Wife	6 May, 1759	52
Elizabeth Daughter of Humphry and Mary Powell	2 Apr 1754	25
Henry Martin	20 Jan 1648	—
Thomas his Son	24 June, 1679	—
Thomas Martin	5 Feb 1715	—
Mary, Wife of Thomas Martin	4 Apr 1731	—
Thomas Williams	8 Dec 1757	55
Elizabeth his Wife	17 Oct 1765	70
Alexander Thorne	31 Mar 1708	—
John Griffith	30 July 1689	—
Mary his Wife	9 July, 1723	—
Bryan Griffith	23 Apr 1748	76
Mary his Wife	1, Apr 1757	—
Robert his Son	31 Dec 1740	32
Alice Wife of Thomas Martin, formerly Wife of Bryan Griffith	29 Mar 1679	—
Henry Worgan	13 Nov 1698	—
William Tylor	4 Sept 1662	—
Matthew Morse	25 June, 1738	—
Dorothy Morse	30 Dec 1760	75
Mary, Wife of William Evans	17 Nov 1780	45
William Gough	27 May, 1715	—
Barbara Wife of George Lewis	8 Feb 1682	—
George Lewis, of Landogoe	8 Jan 1703	—
William George of Skenfrith	2 July, 1725	—
Francis George, of Hewelsfield	3 June, 1752	66
Anselm Morton	2 July, 1745	78
Robert Phillips	29 Sept 1762	80
William Phillips, of the Lower Meend	26 Aug 1730	47
Richard Prichard	11 Jan 1716	43
Mary, Daughter of Joseph and Mary Constant	22 Aug 1721	—
Susanna Wife of James Allen, who lived but 10 Days after him	30 Dec 1728	—
Ann Wife of Thomas Allen, of Hoggins	4 May, 1761	19
Rebecca, Wife of Richard Jennings	17 Sept 1785	34
Thomas, Son of John and Sarah Clofs	18 Mar 1784	28
William Court	19 Mar 1782	74
Samuel Court	14 Oct 1784	43
William Court	24 Apr 1777	42
Sarah, Wife of William Court	20 May, 1773	72
William Pritchard, late Cattle keeper	13 Sept 1771	53
Robert, Son of John and Ann Griffiths	4 Jan 1782	30
Francis Jones	8 Mar 1781	60
William Holt	7 July, 1776	52
Mary, Daughter of James and Mary King	7 Sept 1772	24
James their Son	21 Mar 1765	23
Hannah, Wife of William Halliday	17 June, 1775	26
James Williams	20 June, 1766	56
Henry Barrow	25 Jan 1777	56
Mary, Wife of John Jones, of Elwood	29 Mar 1781	24
Charles Thomas	10 June 1774	67
Mary his Wife	28 Mar 1784	82
Sarah, Wife of George Thomas	19 Feb 1773	34
Anne, Wife of William Chamberlaine	6 May, 1714	—
Simon Culter	21 Dec 1776	54

L. BRIMPSFIELD,

IS a Parish of small Extent, situate on that Ridge of Hills which bounds the *Cotswold* Division towards the Vale of GLOUCESTER, distant about eight Miles from that City on the South-west, nearly five North from *Painswick*, and is included in the Hundred of *Rapsgate*. The Soil is chiefly light, and Arable, the Woodlands are likewise considerable.

Of the Living, which is a Rectory in the Deanry of *Stonehouse*, the Advowson was once vested in the Priory of *Brimpsfield*, a Cell to the Abbey of St STEPHEN DE FOUNTENAY in *Normandy*. The Founder is not known, it shared the Fate of the Alien Priories, at their Dissolution by HENRY V, and was afterwards granted by EDWARD IV to the Collegiate Church at *Windsor*.

Near the Village stands the Church, which consists of a Nave without Aisle, or Transept, and a small Tower in the Middle embattled. It is dedicated to St *Michael*.

The Manor was given by the CONQUEROR to OSBORNE GIFFARD as the Reward of his military Services. This Family had much Power in *Normandy*, and were made of the greater Barons of this Realm soon after the Conquest, when WALTER GIFFARD was created first Earl of BUCKINGHAM, with almost the whole of that County, by Tenure *in Capite* of the King.

The Date of the Foundation of the Castle cannot be ascertained with Precision, but is most probably as early as when *Brimpsfield* became the Seat of the Barony. It is thought to have been of the usual Form of the Strong-holds of that Æra, of one very large square Tower, and four smaller ones at the Angles [+]. A Ditch, or Moat, of about 300 Yards round a Rampart, now covered with a close Thicket, is all that remains to mark the Scite of this Edifice. Of the Buildings not the smallest Vestiges are left—*et iam per ire Ruina*. We find in an ancient Chronicle, that the utter Demolition of the Castle was effected by the Army detached for that Purpose by EDWARD II in his March from *Cirencester* to *Worcester*. It was then held by JOHN GIFFARD, who was a strenuous Partizan with the Barons against the SPENCERS [†]. Though the Office of Constable of the Castle was granted, with the Manor, by EDW. III to MAURICE BERKELEY, it should seem rather a Restoration of its Privileges, which were escheated to the Crown, and a Liberty of re-building it, than a Proof that it was in a defensible State at that Period.

The Title of "GIFFARD OF BRIMPSFIELD" being a Barony in Fee, connected with seven others, is now borne by the Right Honourable CHARLES TALBOT Earl of SHREWSBURY, by Inheritance from the Family of SPENCER, of *Blockmore*, who married the Heir of GIFFARD. Summoned to Parliament June 5, 1308.

CONSTABLES OF THE CASTLE of *BRIMPSFIELD*

YEAR	PRINCE		CONSTABLES
—— ,	—————— ,		Elias Giffard
—— ,	—————— ,		Thomas Giffard
—— ,	—————— ,		Elias Giffard (deprived)
1216,	18 John,		Bartholomew Peche
1216,	1 Henry III		Elias Giffard (restored)
1240,	53 Henry III		John Giffard
1299,	27 Edward I		John Giffard [†]
1322,	15 Edward II		Hugh le Despencer, the younger
1327,	1 Edward III		John Maltravers
1341,	14 Edward III		Maurice Berkeley [‖]
1349,	22 Edward III		Lionel Duke of Clarence
1382,	5 Richard II		Edmond Earl of March

---

* The Castle is noticed by Sir R. ATKYNS, p. 298, edit. 1712.
† Vide his Account of Ancient Castles.
‡ DICIT JOHANNES GIFFARD ligas Regis cum Armis versus WILLIAM tendente spectavit. Undecies, Rex, Labientiam ad liberationem versus Castrum dicti JOANNIS properavit, & *funditus demolitus est.* GIFFARD. Collect. vol. I. p. ‖ FERINIM SYSTEM WARI evertit ex Castello de *Brimsfield,* alias *Bremsfield,* quod in Custodia est Joannis GIFFARD. VIII. III. p. ...
‖ ELIAS GIFFARD was seized of nine Knight's Fees in the County of *Wilts.* Lib. Niger, secund. edit. HEARNE, p. ...
JOHN GIFFARD founded Gloucester Hall in *Oxford* 1283, to found a ... for active Services, to be educated by the Abbey of Gloucester, which Privilege was afterwards extended to the whole County.
... Being detected and taken Prisoner at the Battle of *Boroughbridge,* he was brought to *Gloucester* and executed ... Anno 1322. HOTLIN 1nc ... p 331.
• He was Second Son of Maurice, and Brother of Thomas Baron BERKELEY.

Year	Reign	Constables
——,	————,	Roger de Mortimer
1425,	3 Henry VI	Edmond de Mortimer
——,	————,	Richard Earl of Cambridge
——,	————,	Richard Duke of York
1460,	38 Henry VI	Cicely Dutchess of York

Upon her Deceafe, 1495, 10 Henry VII it paffed to the Crown, and was afterward granted, in Jointure, to the unfortunate Q. Katherine of Arragon. King Edw VI gave it to John, firft Lord Chandos, from whofe Heirs it was transferred to the Family of Sandys early in the laft Century, by them it was fold to Dr John Gilbert, Archbifhop of York, whofe Daughter is the Lady of the prefent Proprietor.

The Park was a chartered Inclofure of 200 Acres, which with the old Manor-houfe, fince rebuilt, is now occupied as a Farm. Troome Rivulet, which rifes here, is the Source of Stroudwater.

The Fair and Markets procured for this Village by the Duke of Clarence have been long difcontinued.

Crudle Green is a Hamlet in this Parifh, the principal Eftates of which belong to the Families of Taylor and Walbank.

That Part of Birdlip Street which lies on the right Hand of the great Fofs Road from Glocefter to Cirencefter is alfo within the Limits of Brimpsfield. This moft romantic Spot is thus flightly remarked by Leland † "Comming from Glocester to Cirencefter, almoft yn the myddle Way between, wher "the Wood tyleth and the Campayne Countre towards Cotefwold appereth, the fayre old Way made by "the Britons ys very evidently feen, and foe goeth as ftrayte as a Line to Cirencefter and fro thens to "Bath." From an immenfe Declivity the rich Vale of Glocester is expanded to the View, and terminated by the blue Mountains of Malvern, which relieve the extreme Flatnefs of the other Parts, and give a fupremely beautiful Effect to the whole. The moft ftriking Feature in the Landfcape is the great Confular Way, called by the Saxons Irmin Street, which leads from the Bafe of the Hill to the City of Glocester in a right Line of fix Miles extent. This, though certainly unpicturefque, gives fome Idea of the Mafters of the World, whofe public Works could be thus compleated, without the Prefervation of private Property.

Hazel-hanger, a Woodland of 100 Acres, is attached to the Manor.

The Site of the Priory is ftill fhewn, and it is reported, that certain fmall Members of Architecture, with Tracery of exquifite Gothic Workmanfhip, have been formerly difcovered.

B E N E F A C T I O N S.

The Sum of 20 l. the Time and Perfon both uncertain, but fuppofed to be fome of the Sandys Family, was given for the Benefit of fuch poor Perfons as are not relieved by the Parifh, which is vefted in the Hands of Samuel Niblet, Efq; Banker, in Glocester; the annual Produce of which is 1 l.

Thomas Bicknell, 1750, left by Will, for the Benefit of fuch poor Perfons as abovementioned, 1 l. per Annum for ever, payable out of his whole Eftate, vefted in Thomas Bridges, of Winjon in this County, who has hitherto refufed to pay the Legacy.

Incumbents	Patrons	Incumbents	Patrons
1585 John Turner,	John Billingham, Bifhop of Gloucester	1710 Hambury Sandys, M A	William Sandys, Efq
1691 James Smith,	Giles Lord Chandos	1726 Thomas Chamberlayne Coxe, M A	Charles Coxe, Efq
1616 John Martin, M A	Sir Wm Sandys, Knt	1745 John White, M A	Imma Gilbert
1671 Henry Hook,	John Guyse, Efq	1777 James Parfons, M A	Lord Judge 1666
From Sir Robert Atkyns		1785 William Metcalfe, M A	The fame

Prefent Lord of the Manor,

The Right Honourable George Lord Vifcount Mount-Edgcumbe and Valletort.

The only Perfon fummoned from this Parifh by the Herald in 1682 and 1683, was William Sandys, Efq.

At the Election in 1776, Thirteen Freeholders polled from this Parifh.

The earlieft Entry in the Register bears Date 1710.

In the Itinerary of William de Worcester, written about 1470 p. 98. "Brimpsfield Parke in Glocester, per 8 Miliaria Anglicana a Gloucester. Apud Coerecim prope apud Tewkesbury hic prope fuerit caftrum." Vide Worcester edit Nafmith p. 65.

ANNUAL ACCOUNT OF MARRIAGES, BIRTHS, AND BURIALS, IN THIS PARISH

A D	Mar	Bir	Bur	A D	Mar	Bir	Bur	A D	Mar	Bu	Bur	A.D	Mar	Bu	Bur.
1781	—	12	7	1786	1	6	4	1791				1796			
1782	1	7	5	1787	2	7	7	1792				1797			
1783	—	9	8	1788				1793				1798			
1784	—	8	7	1789				1794				1799			
1785	2	8	3	1790				1795				1800			

INSCRIPTIONS IN THE CHURCH

ON FLAT STONES IN THE CHANCEL

Here resteth the Body of
Mr John Martin, Master of Arts,
the Minister of Brimpsfield,
who departed this Life July 24,
Anno Dom 1656

Here also lieth the Body of
Mary, the Wife of the above
Mr John Martin, who left
this Life October 28,
Anno Dom 1672

Arms, two Lions passant per Pale

Under me lieth interred the Body of
Humphry Taylor, of Caudle Green in this
Parish, Gent who departed this Life
July 14, 1745, in the 85th Year of his Age

Also Mary his Wife,
who departed this Life
June 16, 1752, aged 70

Elizabeth Taylor
died March 23, 1771, aged 51

Hannah Taylor
died March 12, 1776, aged 60

William Taylor, Gent
died July 5, 1787, aged 68

In Memory of William Lawrence,
of this Parish, Gent He departed
this Life March 19, 1708 9,
aged 78 Years

Also Mary his Wife She died
December 14, 1701, aged 59 Years

And also Mr Isaac Lawrence,
of Stony Hill in this Parish
He departed this Life May 27,
Anno Dom 1759, aged 82 Years

Also Elizabeth his Wife
She died May 12, 1757,
aged 67 Years

Arms, on a Chevron, between three Escallops,
three Fleurs de Lis

In Memory of
Matthew Walbank, of this Parish, Gent
who departed this Life August 2,
Anno Dom 1721

Also of Hester, the Wife of
Matthew Walbank, Gent
died September 5,
Anno Dom 1729, aged 75

IN THE CHURCH YARD ON TOMBS

Richard Welch, Gent
lived the Faith of a Minister
in the Parish London son of
William and Margaret Welch,
of this Parish,
died Jan 5, 1771, aged 26

William, son of William and
Margaret Welch, of this Parish,
buried Nov 8, 1759, aged 16 Years

Hannah Welch, Daughter of
William and Margaret Welch,
Grand daughter of Walter and
Priscilla Long, died Aug 17, 1743,
aged 4 Years and 3 Months

Walter Long, Yeoman,
died Oct 6, 1748, aged 70

Priscilla his Wife
died Dec 27, 1753, aged 77

Walter Long, son of
of the Lord of Hudlip, Yeoman,
died May 7, 1743, aged 71

Jane his Wife
died May 2, 1714, aged 44

Walter their Son died an Infant

The third Walter Long of
the Lord at Hudlip Yeoman
died Oct 31, 1756 in the
65 Year of his Age

Ann his Wife
died May 10, 1766, aged 86

RICHARD HAYWARD Yeoman,
died June 27, Anno Dom 168

MARY his Wife
buried May 15 1696

EDWARD HAYWARD Yeoman,
died May 28, 174?, aged 64

JOAN his Wife
died July 19 , aged 80

EDWARD HAYWARD, Yeoman,
died May 20 1717 æt 60

ELIZABETH the former Wife of
EDWARD HAYWARD
died Sept 18, 280 æt 48

RICHARD HAYWARD fenier Yeoman,
died March 3, 1700, aged 89

ALICE his Wife
died Jan 26 1703, aged 86

EDMUND BISHOP of Birdlip
died Dec 22, 1751, aged 78

HESTER his Wife
died March 30 1762, aged 68

SARAH, Wife of ISAAC BISHOP
died April , 1774 aged 39

RICHARD DANCER
died July 1, 1759, aged 5—

Also RICHARD his Wife
died Sept 10, 175?, aged 45

WILLIAM LAWRENCE, Gent
died March 11, 1743, aged 76

JOHN HAYWARD
died Aug 19, 1783, aged 48

JOHN HAYWARD
died April 3 777, aged 77

MARY, Daughter of JOHN
and MARY HAYWARD died
Oct 28, 1781, aged 5?

EDWARD HAYWARD
died Sept 8, 1784 aged 59

MARY his Wife
died July 8, 1775, aged 4—

SARAH WINNING, Relict
of THOMAS WINNING of
Highworth Wilts, Daughter of
of ISAAC and ELIZABETH LAWRENCE,
of Stony Hill in this Parish
died July 3, 1763, aged 55

ON TWO TABLETS AGAINST
THE CHURCH

JOSEP JORDAN,
of this Parish, Yeoman,
died March 8 1773,
aged 63

JOHN LIMBRICK, fenior,
of this Parish
died June 20 1759,
aged 73

JANE his Wife
died Dec 11, 1774,
aged 87

HESTER, Wife of
JOHN LIMBRICK,
died Nov 12 1784,
aged 46

O N   H E A D S T O N E S

	Died	Aged		Died	Aged
William Potter	7 Feb 17,	70	William Bird	7 Jan 174	53
Sarah Kilmaʃter	21 Jun 1777	5—	Elizabeth his Wife	—— 1768	58
Giles Ball —ger late of Witcombe	3 Nov 1774	84	Suʃanna Wife of John Bird	15 Nov 1747	
Rachel his Wife	2 Jan 1776	85	Also Mary his Wife	15 July, 170	34
Robert their Son	6 June, 1778	63	Also Elizabeth his Wife	23 Feb 175	6
Samuel Jordan Yeoman	12 Nov 1765	86	George Durrett	5 Feb. 1743	4?
Katherine his Wife	3 Nov 1741	81	Mary, Wife of George Durrett	1 May, 1766	73
John Pinchin	15 Sept 1719	55	Rachel, Daughter of George and Mary Durret	18 Aug 1758	26
Biggs Hamblin, youngeʃt Son of Anthony and Lucilla Hamblin, of Birdlip	10 Apr 17—2	23	Robert Meek Cent of the City of London, died March 12 1769 aged 23 and in that early time of Life had viʃited both Eaſt and Weſt Indies		
William Hamblin, of Birdlip in this Parith	13 Oct 1753	47	Owen Osborn	10 Apr 1765	47
Mary his Wife	19 Sept 1753	50	Mary his Wife Daughter of Edmund Biʃhop of Birdlip	9 Oct 17—8	4—
Sarah, Wife of Peter Herbert and Daughter of William Hamblin of Birdlip, died (Cowes Mar 2) 1777 aged 5—, and lies interred at Aberdeen			John Arkill	1 Sept 1762	5
James Field	8 Nov 1734	55	Hester, Daughter of John and Sapphira Arkill, and Wife of Daniel Stockwell	8 Sept 1761	
Henry Welch of Candle Green in this Parith	— Feb 1711	64	Henry Curtice of his Parish, Yeoman	6 Mar 761	
Katherine his Wife	5 Feb 17,0	71	Ann his Wife	13 Jun 1765	
Elizabeth their Daughter	26 Apr 7,8	4	Hester Daughter of Joseph and Hannah Jordan	, Apr 1765	
John Athard of Candle Green	15 Apr 777	1	Robert Mason	6 Feb 17—	
Richard Bird junior	19 Apr 1741	55	Elizabeth Relict of Robert Mason	Mar 177	
Jane Hayward, second Wife of Edward and ay 1d	2 May 1729	0	Mary Webb Widow		
David Humtin, a Chriſtian	14 Aug 173	2	William Hayward Yeoman	19 Nov 750	
Mary his Wife	5 Dec 1778	77	Mary Hayward, Wife of John Hayward	6 Aug 178	
John Sadle of Candle Green, Yeoman	1 Dec 1764	8,	William their Son	Apr 17	
Mary his Wife	2 Dec 1737	52	Ann their Daughter	13 June, 176	
Nathaniel Biddle	30 Nov 1746	70	John Son of Edward Hayward Yeoman	1 Oct 1711	
Eʃther his Wife	5 Apr 1752	77	Mary, Wife of John Hayward, Yeoman	July, 170	
Sarah, Wife of John Biddle Yeoman	25 Oct 1755	45	Ann, Wife of Philip Hayward Philip Hayward and John and Mary Hayward	30 Mar 176	
Benjamin Biddle of Candle Green	15 Dec 1759	6	George Son of William Lawrence Gent	28 May 71	
Mary Martha Durrett, Wife of Thomas Orkill	19 July 1761	0	Also Mary Wife of Geo Lawrence	11 Feb 17,	6
Jane Biddle of Candle Green	9 Mar 1779	7	Jeremiah Hooper	13 July, 7,	6
Mary his Wife	27 Aug 1752	51	Martha his Wife	11 Oct 175	6
William Chance the devoted Son of Edward Chance Hollow'd and	13 July 1754	42	Ann, Wife of Thomas Cutter and Daughter of Jeremiah Hooper	5 Nov 1767	5
Hannah Relict of Walter Chance	30 Apr 1781	66			
Thomas Biddle of Candle Green	3 Sept 176	53			
William Son of William and Eliza — inbd	7 Nov 171—	6—			

LI. BROADWELL, or BRADWELLE,

WHICH lies in the North-east Extremity of the County, is a Parish seven Miles in Circumference, in the Hundred of *Slaughter*, distant from *Stowe* (in which Deanery it is comprised) about two Miles and from GLOUCESTER twenty six. The far greater Part of the Lands are Arable, in very extensive common Fields, as yet uninclosed by Act of Parliament. The Soil, which is of Clay, produces in general great Quantities of Corn.

The Living is a Vicarage, annexed to *Adlestrop*, of which the Advowson, and Part of the Impropriation, was held by the Abbey of *Evesham*, who presented to it in 1402, in the last Century it was vested in the Family of LEIGH. The Church is dedicated to *St Paul*, it is a decent Building, with one Aisle on the South Side, and an embattled Tower. A small Dormitory joins the Aisle, appropriated to the Family of HODGES, in which is a decayed Monument to the Memory of ROBERT HUNKS, Esq who died 1588, with these Arms, " Quarterly, 1st and 4th, Gules, on an Inescutcheon Argent, three Mullets " Sable, within an Orle of Bezants, 2d and 3d, Or, on a Chevron Sable three Goats passant of the " Field." In the Church-yard are several very ancient Tombs, the Inscriptions on which are so defaced, as to baffle the Researches of the Antiquary. The Arms " a Fess dancette," for CHADWELL, and " a " Lion rampant, in chief three Escallops," for CLUTTERBUCK, are still to be distinguished.

The earliest Proprietors of the Manor were the Monastery of *Evesham*, and the Fraternity of KNIGHTS TEMPLARS in the Reign of HEN III, afterwards, the great Families of DE BEAUCHAMP, DE CLINTON, and HASTINGS, possessed it. It passed, at the Suppression, to the BASKEVILES, and, about 1610, was purchased by the Family of HODGES. Their ancient manerial Residence was re-built, in 1757, in the modern Style, by the late Dr. THOMAS CHAMBERLAYNE, Dean of BRISTOL, who was connected with them by Marriage.

The largest Estate, formerly vested in the CHADWELL's, now belongs to the Family of DAWE. In the last Century, a Mansion-house and competent Estate belonged to the SELWYNS, a Branch of the MATTESDEN Family, since sold to the SHUTES, from whom it is inherited by WILLIAM LENTHAL, Esq of *Bessil's Leigh*, to *Oxford*.

A Rivulet takes its Rise from a considerable Spring which gives Name to the Village, and continues its Course to the *Evenlode*.

No Benefactions to the Poor.

Sr ROBERT ATKYNS says, that three Houses, a Piece of Meadow, and some Land in the common Field, were given for the Repair of the Church.

INCUMBENTS	PATRONS	INCUMBENTS	PATRONS
1511 Thomas Bambroke,	——————	1717 Theophilus Leigh, M A. The same	
1570 Richard Willet,	Walter Baskevylle	1763 Thomas Leigh, LL B James Leigh, Esq	
1599 Thomas Tidmarsh,	Eliz Baskeville		
———— Richard Johnson,			
1675 Augustin Mutin,	——————		
1696 Edward Wake, M A	Theoph Leigh, Esq		
1699 Henry Brydges, M A	The same		
The above from Sir ROBERT AIKYNS			

PRESENT CLAIMANTS OF THE MANOR,

The Right Honourable HENRY FOX STRANGEWAYS, Earl of ILCHESTER, and MARY LEIGH, Widow, Sister and Heir of the late HENRY DANVERS DOUGHTY HODGES, Esq.

The Persons summoned from this Place by the Heralds, in 1682 and 1683, were
Danvers Hodges, Esq   John Tidmarsh, Gent
Jasper Selwyn, Esq   William Chadwell, Gent

At the Election in 1776 Eleven Freeholders polled from this Parish.

The

The Regifter commences with the Year 1697.

ANNUAL ACCOUNT OF MARRIAGES, BIRTHS, AND BURIALS, IN THIS PARISH

AD	Mar	Bir	Bur	AD	Mar	Bir	Bur	AD	Mar	Bir	Bur	AD	Mar	Bur	Bir
1781	2	3	3	1786	1	3	9	1791				1796			
1782	—	6	4	1787	—	7	7	1792				1797			
1783	2	9	5	1798				1793				1798			
1784	3	1	3	1789				1794				1799			
1785	—	7	7	1790				1795				1800			

INSCRIPTIONS IN THE CHURCH.

AN ALABASTER MONUMENT AGAINST THE NORTH WALL IN THE CHANCEL, IN WHICH ARE TWO FIGURES KNEELING, WITH A CHILD, IN THE DRESS OF THE TIMES, ON A TABLET THE FOLLOWING INSCRIPTION

Arms, Quarterly, 1ft and 4th, Or, an Eagle difplayed Sable, for WESTON, 2d and 3d, Argent, on a Chief Azure five Bezants.

In obitum generofiffimi Viri HARBERT WESTON, qui
religione erga Deum, charitate erga proximum,
& erga omnes diffufa benevolentia, &c. Anno Domini
1635, ætatifque fuæ 30, extremos expiravit halitus,
unicum relinquens filium NATHANIELEM, adhuc
fuperftitem in pretiofi huju anime is memoriam
ELEANOR WESTON, uxor ejus, dum ixit, chariffima,
Filia JOHANNIS BRAY, de Limeld in gio Oxon,
Armig hoc eternum amoris mon ta itum cum
lachrymis & luct i perp o pofuit

ON A MARBLE MONUMENT IN THE SOUTH SIDE OF THE CHANCEL

Deo Op Max Sacrum,
Hic prope jacet
quod fuit Mortale
RICARDI JONSONII,
Philologi, Philofophi, Theologi,
Non e multur
Prefbyteri Ecclefiæ Angl
quondam Reverendi
Rectoris Bridwelli,
multum defideratidi,
qui ad plures obiit
VIII kal Mart,
Anno falutis MDCLXXIV
ætatis LXXII

Mæftus amico pofuit JOANNES CARTWRIGHTUS,
de Aynho, Arm

ON FLAT STONES IN THE CHANCEL.

C H S E
Hic jacet MARIA, eruditiffima viri (Ohcet)
RICARDI JONSONII, Ecclefiæ Ecclet
(Dum vixit) Rectoris, conjux
ducentiffima qui obiit Septim
Calend, obiit is LXXII
Anno q Domini MDCLXXVI

Quiefcit hic venerandus ille
RICARDUS JONSONIUS, cujus
Me qui
vivis migravit octavo cal Mart
ætatis 72, Anno Dom 1674

Here lyeth the Body of
SARAH MARTYN,
Daughter of AUGUSTIN MARTYN,
formerly Rector of this Place
fhe died Oct 2, 1724,
in the 60th Year of her Age

Hic jacet,
in fpe Beati Refurrectionis,
MARIA
Filia GEORGII LEIGH (Caroli Regis & Martyris
in exercitu Equitum Turmæ Prefecti),
Filii natu fecundi GULIELMI LEIGH,
de Longborough, Militis,
Uxor AUGUSTINI MARTYN, hujus Ecclefiæ Rectoris,
juxta recondita,
ex quo
liberorum trium, JOANNIS, GEORGII, & AUGUSTINI,
Filiarumque fex, ELIZABETHÆ, MARIÆ, JUDITHÆ,
SARÆ, REBECCÆ, & MARTHÆ,
Mater facta eft
A quorum plurimis
Sobolem numerofam confpexit & felicem,
Vixit orbata marito Annos 21
Supremum diem obiit 28 Octobris,
Anno { falutis } 1718
      { ætatis } 82

M S
Reverendi viri AUGUSTINI MARTIN, hujus Ecclesiæ
per Annos viginti duos Rectoris diligentissimi,
qui Oxoniæ in Collegio Orielensi bonis Literis
feliciter incubuit, quarum fructus tulit vita
in e t simul u leniter fluens nullis avaritiæ
fordidis aut malarum artium labe fœdata,
fiquidem domum hospitibus cujuscunque ordinis
femper paravit
Et cum per totius vitæ cursum pacis & charitatis
ftudia coluiffet in omnes perhumanus & facilis
omnibus uti meruit carus, hoc in loco multa
cum pace & laude requievit,
Anno ætatis 65,
obiit Aprilis 12,
Anno falutis 1697

Pofuit MARIA MARTIN,
mœrens Vidua

In Memory of
Mrs JUDITH SELWYN,
Widow and Relict of JOHN SELWYN,
late of this Place, Gent
who departed this Life the
12th of October, 1718, æt 56

ANN, the Wife of CLIFTON RUDING,
youngeft son of WALTER RUDING, Efq
of Weftcoats, near Leicefter,
died October 24, 1774,
aged 33 Years

IN THE BODY OF THE CHURCH

THOMAS BARKER, of Broadwell
in the County of Gloucefter, Gent
born Febr 17, 1664, died Auguft 3, 1710
The Hufband of MARY, the Daughter of
GILES DISTON, of Sherthampton in the County of
Oxford, Gent by whom he had one Son,
Lieutenant THOMAS BARKER, only Son of
THOMAS and SARAH BARKER,
and Grandfon of THOMAS and MARY BARKER,
who died May 22, 1761
aged 39 Years, lyeth buried here

MARY BARKER, late Wife of
THOMAS BARKER, of Broadwell,
Gent died June 20, 1756,
in the 80th Year of her Age

CATHARINE BARKER, Daughter of
THOMAS and SARAH BARKER,
died May 1, 1753,
aged 23 Years

THOMAS BARKER,
eldeft Son of Lieutenant THOMAS BARKER
and ANN his Wife, died
Sept , 1775, aged 23 years

MRS SARAH BARKER,
Widow of Mr THOMAS BARKER,
died Feb 5, 1700, aged 72

F B Daughter of R and F BARKER,
born Aug 29, 1709,
died Aug 3, 1710

In Memory of Mrs MARTHA COLLIER,
Wife of Mr SAMUEL COLLIER,
of this Place, Gent who departed this Life
April 10, 1720, æt 30

Alfo of JOHN and JOHN, their Sons,
who died Infants

ON A MONUMENT IN THE SOUTH AISLE

Here lies interred ANTHONIE HODGES, Gent
and MERRIAL his Wife, Daughter of WILLIAM
CHILDE of Northwycke in the Countie of Worcefter, Efq by whom he had two Sonns, WIL-
LIAM, who married ANNE, Daughter of Sir WIL-
LIAM LEIGH, of Longborough, Knt and DONNE,
who married ELIZABETH, one of the Daughters
and Coheirs of JOHN D'ANVERS, of Slakerfton in
the Countie of Leicefter, Efq as alfo three Daughters, ELIZABETH, married to RICHARD EVANS, of
Chaftlton in the Countie of Oxford, Efq MARY,
married to ABEL GOWER, of Boulton in the Countie of Worcefter, Efq and GRACE, married to
JOHN CARTER, of Charlton Abbots in the County
of Gloucefter, Efq the faid WILLIAM HODGES,
and DONNE HODGES, and ANTHONY HODGES, Son
and Heire of WILLIAM, by the faid ANNE his
Wife, lie here buried alfoe

ANT. HODGES		1643
MERRIAL HODGES		1670
WILLIAM HODGES	obiit Anno Dom	1644
ANT HODGES, jun		1652
DONNE HODGES		1662

DANVERS HODGES, e Medio Templo, Armiger,
pofuit hoc fepulchrale Monumentum
Anno Dom 1703

ON FLAT STONES IN THE SOUTH AISLE

Arms, Or, three Crefcents Sable, on a Canton
Gules, a ducal Coronet of the field, for HODGES

Here lies interred the Body of
DANVERS HODGES, Efq
Barrifter at Law,
and Bencher of the Middle Temple
He died June 2, 1721,
aged 68 Years

Here alfo interred the body of
ELIZA DANVERS
DANVERS HODGES, Efq
who died June 15, 1774,
aged years

Here lies interred ELIZABETH,
the Widow and Relict of DONNE
HODGES, Gent who lived a long,
pious, and peaceable Life, and
died lamented the 11th Day of
Nov MDCCVII

Also here lies the Body of
Miss ANN DOUGHTY, who departed
this Life August 3, 1746

Here lies interred ELIZABETH
HODGES, youngest of the two
Daughters of DONNE HODGES, Gent
by ELIZABETH his Wife, Daughter
of JOHN DANVERS, Esq
who departed this Life the
15th of May, A.D 1714, aged 55

In Memory of PETER NEVE LEIGH,
second Son of the
Rev PETER LEIGH, of the Westhall
at Highleigh in Cheshire, and
MARY his Wife, who died
March 10, 1777, aged 20 Years.

Here lies the Body of DONNE HODGES,
of Broadwell, Gent the Son of
ANTHONY HODGES, Gent buried
February 16, A D 1662,
who left his beloved Wife ELIZABETH
four Sons and two Daughters,
DANVERS, ANTHONY, RICHARD, JOHN,
MERRIAL, and ELIZABETH

Here also lyeth MARTHA,
Daughter of JOHN HODGES, Gent
buried Oct 23, 1723, in the 19th
Year of her Age, amiable for her
Beauty both of Mind and Person

Likewise here are deposited the
Remains of MARY, Wife of THOMAS
CHAMBERLAYNE, D D Dean of Bristol,
Daughter of the aforementioned
JOHN HODGES,
A Woman adorned with every Christian Grace
and Virtue, and an Ornament to her Sex,
but was called hence on Feb 11, 1757,
æt 56, to the unspeakable Grief of her
Husband and all that knew her.

Also here lyeth the Body of the
abovenamed THOMAS CHAMBERLAYNE, D D.
Dean of Bristol, who departed this Life
Sept 15, 1757, aged 74

AGAINST THE SOUTH WALL ON AN ATCHIEVEMENT
THESE ARMS

Quarterly, 1st and 4th, HODGES, as before, 2d
and 3d, two Bars, between three Mullets, for
MARTIN.

IN THE CHURCH YARD.

ON HEAD STONES

	Died		Aged
Richard Jacques	3 Oct	1756	50
William Jacques	12 Jan	1764	79
John, Son of Richard and Ann Jacques	22 Oct	1783	53
Hannah, Wife of John Jacques	2 Mar.	1780	39
Elizabeth Jacques	24 Feb	1711	67
Moses Jacques	24 Mar	1776	66
Martha his Wife	24 Dec	1776	68
Sarah, Wife of Thomas Shuery	12 Oct	1759	74
Joseph Rose	31 Oct	1764	86
Judith his Wife	13 May,	1743	69
James Rose	29 Sept	1784	30
Moses Guy	19 Oct	1748	84
Anne his Wife	27 Aug.	1755	84
Thomas their Son	17 Jan	1771	61
Moses their Son	13 Feb	1760	48
John Guy	7 Sept.	1761	62
Mary his Wife	28 Oct	1769	63
John their Son	15 Apr.	1782	49

LII. BROCKWORTH,

OR, as it is ſtyled in Domeſday, *Brocowordinge*, is a ſmall Pariſh in the Hundred of Dudſton and King's Barton, ſeven Miles South-eaſt from *Cheltenham* and four from Gloucester on the South, ſituate near the great *Foſs Road* It extends nearly three Miles but in Breadth no where exceeds one The Soil is of a ſtiff fertile Clay, and the greater Portion of Land cultivated as Paſture.

The Living is a Vicarage in the Deanery of *Hereford*, the Impropriation of which was anciently in the Priory of *Llanthony* In the Reign of Q. Elizabeth it belonged to Robert Dudley, Earl of Leicester, but has ſince been the Property of the Family of Guiſe. The Church which is built to Cross conſiſts of a Nave and North Aiſle, with a low Tower in the Middle fitted in a certain form, which is ſupported by two heavy Saxon Arches

Before the Reign of King JOHN the Manor was poſſeſſed by the Family of CHANDOS, but on the Confirmation of the Foundation of the Priory of *Llanthony* it was granted to them, and formed Part of their Revenues till the Suppreſſion In 1541 to King exchanged this Manor and its Appurtenances with JOHN GYSE Eſq for thoſe of Aſton Grey and Bourton, and Horton Grey in the County of *Oxford* A ſmaller Manor, with a Wood of 300 Acres called *Bedley*, was antiently of SIR LAWRENCE DE CHANDOS by the Abbey of *St. Peter* in Gloucester when JOHN PALMER was Abbot, 44 HEN. III. now held by Leaſe under the Dean and Chapter of Gloucester by JOHN MORRIS, Eſq

The Family of THEYER poſſeſſed the only Eſtate of Conſequence independent of the Manor at preſent *Couper's Hill*, a Hamlet in this Pariſh, now belonging to JOHN TOWNSEND, Eſq Of his Family was JOHN THEYER, who is noticed by WOOD as an eminent Antiquary. A good Eſtate, Part of the Manor, has been held for many Generations by the Family of JONES A ſmall Brook, riſing here, falls into the *Severn* near *Sandhurſt*

BENEFACTIONS

WILLIAM MILLS, 1614, gave by Will, for the Uſe of the Poor, Lands now rented by Mr JONES, of *Deerſhurſt*, the annual Produce of which is 8s

GILES COXE, Oct. 6, 1620, gave by Deed, for the Uſe of poor Houſeholders of ... Pariſh Relief, Land now veſted in Mr WHITCOMBE, of *Upton St. Leonard's*, the annual Produce of the Land is good

INCUMBENTS	PATRONS	INCUMBENTS	PATRONS
1575 Richard Swery,	John Gyſe, Eſq	1713 John Lawrence, B. A	Sir John Guiſe, Bart
1590 John White,	William Gyſe, Eſq	1725 William Jane, M. A	The ſame
1610 James Clifford,	The ſame	1730 John Wall, M. A	Sir John Guiſe, Bart
1615 John Somers, M. A.	Sir Chriſt Guiſe, Bart	1746 George Wall, M. A	He ſame
	The above from Sir ROBERT ATKYNS	1757 John Cheſter, M. A	Sir John Guiſe, Bart

PRESENT LORD OF THE MANOR,

The Honourable and Right Reverend SHUTE Lord Bishop of SALISBURY, in Right of his
Lady, Sister and Heir of Sir WILLIAM GUISE, Bart

The Persons summoned from this Place by the Heralds in 1682 and 1683 were,

Sir John Guise, Bart
———— Jones, Gent

At the Election in 1776, Ten Freeholders polled from this Parish

The First Date in the Register is in 1559

ANNUAL ACCOUNT OF MARRIAGES, BIRTHS, AND BURIALS, IN THIS PARISH *

A D	Mar	Br	Bu	A D	Mar	Bir	Bu	A D	Mar	Bir	Bur	A D	Mar	Bir	Bur
1781	1	13	6	1786	1	7	12	1791				1796			
1782	—	10	5	1787	1	15	12	1792				1797			
1783	—	5	8	1788				1793				1798			
1784	4	9	2	1789				1794				1799			
1785	1	10	—	1790				1795				1800			

INSCRIPTIONS IN THE CHURCH.

IN THE CHANCEL

ON A WHITE MARBLE MONUMENT ON THE NORTH SIDE, CONTAINING, OVER THE TABLET, THE BUST
OF SIR CHRISTOPHER GUISE, BART WITHIN A WREATH OF BAY LEAVES.

Arms, Gules, seven Lozenges, 3, 3, and 1, conjoined vure on a Canton Or, a Mullet pierced
Sable, on an Inescutcheon the Arms of ULSTER, Crest, a Swan issuant from a ducal Coronet

Hic sittu est ille Honorabilis
CHRISTOPHERUS GUISE, in hoc Agro Gloucest
Miles ac Baronettus, necnon ab utroque
praelustrium proavorum sanguine
longissima serie perinsignis, vir erat
non vulgariter eruditus, indolis per-
acutae, memoriae tenacis, ii genii
vividi, judicii perquam subacti, hinc
propter eximias dotes, fidem, fortitu-
dinemque provinciae suae praefec-
tus alter a Regio diplomate con-
stitutus est, unde postquam fidelis
ille primota legi, patriae, sibi suisque
satisfecisset, & interiores provinciae
suae comitatus urbem Gloucestriae
circumjacentes ab urbis servitudine
perai aqua iniquisque civium privile-
giis emancipasset immunesque,
posteris reliquisset, sub æra MDCLXX
æt 53. Heu! nimis propera inter sua!
Pretiosa cujus memoriae unicus filius
ac haeres JOHANNIS GUISE, Miles
ac Baronettus, hoc Monumentum
parentavit

---

* From an Account taken in 1563, it appears that there were 30 Houses, and 253 Inhabitants MSS SNELL

Arms,

Arms, Argent, a Crofs raguly Gules, for
LAWRENCE

SUSANNA, the Wife of
Mr JOHN LAWRENCE, died May 1, 1724,
aged 33

SUSANNA his Daughter died
Jan 25, 1715, aged 4

EDMUND his Son, and DIANISIA
his Daughter, died Infants

Arms, Quarterly, 1 Ermine, a Saltire Gules,
for JONES, 2 Sable, a Lion rampant i guardant
Or, 3 Argent, a Lion rampant Sable, debruited
by a Bend Gules, 4 Paly, of fix Or and Gules,
a Lion rampant Sable, 5 Paly, of fix Or and
Gules

In Memory of JOHN JONES, Gent
who departed this Life
March 30, 1747, aged 36

In Memory of WILLIAM YOUNG,
of Wootton, who departed this
Life August 29, 1762,
aged 50 Years

Also of MARY his Wife,
who departed this Life March 21 1777 aged 64

Here lyeth the Body of
WILLIAM LONG, deceas
ed the 2d of June, 1595

JOHN LONG
died Nov 24, 1783, at 77

In Memory of ELEANOR,
the Wife of JOHN JONES, of
Cooper's Hill in this Parish Gent
who departed this Life
June 12, 1719, aged 37 Years

Also of JOHN JONES, of Cooper's Hill,
Gent who departed this Life
July 4, A. D. 1726, aged 54 Years

In Memory of THOMAS TERRET,
of this Parish, who departed
this Life March 1, 1710, aged 67

Also of MARY his Wife who
died in the Year 1672, aged 21

WILLIAM their Son was buried
Jan 13, 1701, aged 24 Years

SARAH their Daughter died
August 23, 1744, aged 69 Years.

In Memory of Mrs   RY,
the Relict of the Rev Mr JOHN
SOMMERS, late Rector of this
Parish, who departed this Life
December 3, 1722,
aged 74 Years

IN THE CHURCH YARD.

ON A MONUMENT AGAINST THE CHURCH

Under this Monument lie interred
the Remains of ELIZABETH LONG,
Relict of WILLIAM LONG,
of this Parish, Gent She departed this Life
February 3, 1766,
aged near 79 Years

Near this Place also lie the
Remains of THOMAS their Son,
who was buried May 27, 1702,
aged 3 Months.

ON TOMBS.

JOHN KING
died March 20, A D 1688

ELIANOR his Wife
died Jun 1, 1695

JOHN LONG, fenior,
died June 14, 1732, aged 65

Also SARAH his former Wife
died July 1, 1706, aged 29

WILLIAM, Son of WILLIAM JONES,
of Cooper's Hill, Gent who died at London,
and was buried there 1769, in the
26th Year of his Age

JOHN LONG, of Little Witcomb in
the Parish of Badgworth, Gent
died March 26, 1779, aged 76

SARAH, Relict of JOHN JONES,
of Cooper's Hill in this Parish, Gent
Sifter to the abovefaid JOHN LONG,
died Feb 5, 1776, aged 71.

WILLIAM LONG
died April 21, 1717, aged 42
GEORGE LONG
died June 2, 1650
ALICE his Wife
died August 9, 1629

THOMAS WITTS, Yeoman,
was buried Dec 30, 1718, aged 88
ANNE his Wife
was buried Jan 14, 1719, aged 88
GILES their Son
died June 7, 1693, aged 29
MARGARET, Wife of
RICHARD BALDWIN, Yeoman,
and Daughter of THOMAS and ANN
WITTS, died October 13, 1735,
aged 71

JOSEPH BALDWIN, Junior, Yeoman,
died June 17, 1700, aged 61

PRISCILLA his Wife
died May 13, 1737, aged 46

WILLIAM her Son
died June 5, 17,, aged 15

JOHN their Son
died Oct 11, 1,58, aged 14

MARGARET, Wife of RICHARD HILL,
died Oct 17, 1781, aged 76

BENJAMIN their Son
died April 29, 1787, aged 36

WILLIAM YATES, of this Parish, senior,
died Jan 11, 1779, in the 62d Year of his Age

WILLIAM, eldest Son of
WILLIAM and MARY YATES,
died April 5, 1777, aged 33

HENRY YATES, senior, Yeoman,
died March 1, 1700, aged 80

MARY his Wife
died Nov 11, 1700, aged near 80

MARY their Daughter
died Aug 16, 1715, an Infant

SARAH their Daughter
died June 23, 17-7, aged 18.

THOMAS YATES, of the City of Gloucester,
Son of WILLIAM and MARY YATES,
died Feb 20, 1770, aged 5,

HENRY, the Son of
HENRY YATES, junior, by,
ELIZABETH his Wife,
died May 29, 1715, aged 20

THOMAS SMART, of the City of Gloucester,
died June 6, 1762, aged 44

MARY his Wife
died Feb 12, 1767, aged 8

RICHARD BALDWIN
died Feb 10, 174, aged 70

THOMAS BALDWIN
died Nov 25, 1777, 18t

PRUDENCE, the Wife of Thomas Baldwin
died Nov ,, 1770, aged

RICHARD YATES
died May 2,, 17 , aged 7

ELIZABETH, Rich of this city,
late Wife of Thomas Yates
died in April , 7 , aged

MOSES YATES
died Apr 15, 17 2, aged 5

O N   H E A D   S T O N E S

	Died	Aged		Died	Aged
William, eldest Son of William and Mary Hone	24 July, 1745	70	Richard Turner, of this Parish, Yeo	21 Nov 172,	87
Henry Turner	7 Feb 176,	—	Grace his Wife	25 Apr	
Richard Hone	16 Dec 171	57	Robert Hyett	5 , , 17	
Elizabeth his Wife	— 1715	68	Mary his Wife	16 A , 17	
Clement Hillier	— Ja 1710	76	Thomas Vizer	15 Apr 17	
Sarah, Wife of Jona Curtis	29 Nov 1,20	32	Elizabeth his Wife	Dec 17 ,	7
Richard Hill	Aug, 1717	4,	William Chapman, sen	11 , 177	6
John Kendal	16 July, 173,	70	Elizabeth, Wife of William Chapman	, , 17 ,	4
William Organ	17 June, 1731	65	Mary, Wife of Giles Vizard	— 17 ,	6
Elizabeth, Wife of William Chapman	— June, 173,	47	Joan, Wife of Richard Turner	— 17 ,	6
Mary, Wife of William Derrett	— Oct 1726	61	James Wood	17 ,	51
James Colchick	19 Mar 17,	79	William Derrett		
Rebekah his Wife	21 Feb 17	8,	Mary his Wife		
Mary, Wife of James Wood	16 Ma 174,	51	George Bredies	, ,	
Benjamin, Son of William Togwell	30 Oct 175,	1	William, eldest Son of William and Mary Hone	July 17	
William Togwell	29 Oct 1760	51	Benjamin, Son of William and Prudence Baldwin		
Friend his Wife	17 Oct 172,	—	Thomas Chille, of Churcham,	, ,	
Betty their Daughter	19 May, 172,	15	George Buck	, ,	
George Hone	1 Jun 173,	36	Jane his Wife	, ,	
George Hone	21 Sept 1738	6	Ann, Wife of William Cottle	, ,	
Sarah, Wife of George Hone	20 May, 1749	60	Ann, Wife of Thomas Atkins	— Nov 5	
John Taylor	— Aug, 1751	64	Hannah their Daughter	, ,	
Anne, Wife of George Cooper	13 Sept 1,21	41	Daniel Atkins	— May,	
Mary, Wife of John Faulkes	21 May, 1752	60	Elizabeth his Wife	15 Apr 17	
Jane, Wife of George Tuck	5 May, 174,	31			

LIII. BROCKRUP,

OR

BROCKTHORP.

THE fame Broco, or Broc, in *Saxon* Times, appears to have given Name to this, as to the preceding Parish.

Brockrup is situate in the Hundred of *Dudston* and *King's Barton*, six Miles distant North from *Stroud*, three from *Painswick*, and four from GLOUCESTER on the South-east

The Soil is in general a stiff Clay, and the Lands Pasture, excepting on the Foot of the Hill, where the Strata naturally becomes more light It includes about 500 Acres.

The Living is a Vicarage, in the Deanery of GLOUCESTER, the Impropriation of which belonged to the Abbey of *St Peter*, founded there, and is now vested in the Dean and Chapter, charged with certain annual Payments to the Vicarage, which is farther augmented by Queen ANNE's Bounty The Church is an ordinary Building, dedicated to *St Swithin*, with one Aisle, and a low slated Tower, and contains nothing curious or interesting

The Manor was given to the Abbey of GLOUCESTER by ADELINE, Widow of ROGER DI IVORI, in 1103, and at the Suppression was annexed to the NEW SEE, by the Founder King HENRY VIII The Family of WOOD were Lessees for many successive Generations, and inhabited the ancient Court house, now converted into a Farm

We are informed by CORBET, p 70, that a considerable Skirmish happened at *Brockthorp Hill*, in which the Parliament Forces received great Detriment, and the Life of Governor MASSIL was much endangered

---

BENEFACTIONS.

GILES COX, Gent 1620, devised by Will for the Relief of poor Householders not receiving Alms, of several Parishes, of which *Brockthorp* is one, an Estate, which when it produces 50*l* per ann this Parish is to receive 2*l* subject to Taxes and Repairs, the annual Produce is now 1*l* 10*s* The Trustees are Sir RICHARD SUTTON, and Sir JOHN GUISE, Barts SAMUEL HAYWARD, HOWE HICKES, BENJAMIN HYETT, ROBERT CAMIBEL, and THOMAS MEE, Esqrs DANIEL LYSONS, M D RICHARD ROGERS, and MARTIN BARRY, Clerks

INCUMBENTS	PATRONS	INCUMBENTS	PATRONS
—— Roger Wheeler,		1700 Thomas Pugh, B A	Dean and Chapter of
1570 Richard Tyrell,	Walter Jones		GLOUCESTER
1583 Richard Smith,	Dean and Chapter of	1708 Richard Collins, Clerk,	The same
	GLOUCESTER	1727 Jeremiah Bett, Clerk,	The same
1613 James Bridshawe,	The same	1753 Richard Done, M A	The same
1618 Whithar one Massinger,	The same	1740 William Howlett, M A	The same
1559 George Venn,	The same	1751 William Done, B A	The same
1691 John Henges, B A	The same.	1754 John Newton, M A	The same

PRESENT LESSEE OF THE MANOR,
ANNE BUSBY, Spinster

At the Visitations of the Heralds, in 1682 and 1683, the only Person summoned was
Rowland Wood, Esq

The whole Parish is held by Copy or Lease under the Church of GLOUCESTER

The Register begins in 1618

ANNUAL ACCOUNT OF MARRIAGES, BIRTHS, AND BURIALS, IN THIS PARISH.

A D	Mar	Bir	Bur	A D	Mar	Bir	Bur.	A D	Mar	Bir.	Bur.	A.D	Mar	Bir	Bur.
1781	1	6	2	1786	1	5	2	1791				1796			
1782	2	7	2	1787	—	4	1	1792				1797			
1783	2	2	3	1788				1793				1798			
1784	—	3	3	1789				1794				1799			
1785	—	3	1	1790				1795				1800			

INSCRIPTIONS IN THE CHURCH.

ON A BRASS PLATE

Here lyes the Body of RICHARD WOOD, Gent
who, after a Pilgrimage of 52 Years,
furrendered his Soule into the Hands of his
Redeemer, Menfe Junii, Anno Dom 1598

Here lyeth the Body of THOMAS
WESTERDALE, Son and Heyre unto
CHRISTOPHER WESTERDALE, Gentleman,
deceafed the   Day of March, 1590

ON A TABLET AGAINST THE NORTH WALL "

In Memory of GEORGE VENN,
Minifter of this Parifh above 35 Years,
who died March 8, 1694, aged 87

Also of ANNE his Wife
who died May 7, 1693, aged 80

Here lieth the Body of SARAH,
the Wife of SAMUEL COLLIER, of
the Parifh of Harefcomb, who
departed this Life July 17, 1783,
in the 41ft Year of her Age

IN THE CHURCH YARD.

ON TWO TABLETS AGAINST THE CHURCH

In Memory of THOMAS SMITH,
of the Parifh of Whaddon, Yeoman,
who died April 2, 1723 aged near 57

SARAH the Daughter of THOMAS
and SARAH SMITH died
April 12, 1759, aged 9

In Memory of HESTER, Relict of
ISAAC WELLS, fenior, of this Parifh,
Yeoman She died Auguft 3, 1759,
aged 90 Years

Alfo five Children of MESHACH
CHARLTON, of the City of Gloucefter,
by ABIGAIL his Wife, Grand children
of the abovefaid

ON TOMBS

THOMAS BROWNING
finifhed his Courfe
Auguft the 1ft 1634

JOHANE BROWNING,
Wife of THOMAS BROWNING, Yeoman,
died March 16, A D 1643

THOMAS BROWNING, the Younger,
died October 6 1669
ELIZABETH his Wife
died October 6, 1668

JOHN WIXMAN
died November 6, 1666.

THOMAS WINSTON
died July 23, 1632

JOHN WINTLE, Yeoman,
died March 31, 1684, aged 32.
John his Son died an Infant

JOHN SMITH, Yeoman,
died Sept 22, 1712 aged 85
ROBERT SMITH, fenior Yeoman,
died Jan 3, 1747, aged 81
JANE his Wife
died Dec 1, 1734 aged 60.
SUSANNA the Wife of
JOHN SMITH Yeoman,
died March 27, 1697

ROBERT SMITH, Yeoman
died Sept 14, 1752, aged 56
MARY his Wife
died March 5, 1753, aged 55

CALEB WELLS
of the City of Gloucefter, Apothecary,
Son of ISAAC and HESTER WELLS,
of this Parifh, died March the
21ft, 1740, in the 29th Year of his Age

ISAAC WELLS, fenior,
died Auguft 15, 1744, aged near 60

EDWARD PENNELL,
of the Parifh of St Catherine
in the City of Gloucefter
Gardener, died March 2, 178-, aged 63

MARY, Relict of
JOHN COPNER, of the
Parifh of Harefhield,
died Feb 11, 1769 aged 84

ON FLAT AND HEAD STONES

	Died	Aged		Died	Aged
Robert Payne	July 1647	—	James Son of Richard and Hannah Bull	14 June, 17	12
John Payne	-	-	Thomas only Son of Thomas and Edith Spilman	9 June, 1762	
Olive the Wife of John Payne	23 Jan 1732	75	Thomas Spilman, of this Parifh Yeoman	18 Nov	
Olive their Daughter	1 May, 1713	55	Griffith his Wife	11 Nov	
Richard Son of John Payne	17 May, 1743	63	Mary Wife of James Partridge	24 Oct	
Elizabeth Daughter of Samuel Vail of Celthrop and Wife of Henry Houle	5 Oct, 1749	1	John Organ, Yeoman	27 Jun, 17	
Jane Wells	4 Nov, 1713	6	Mary his Wife	21 Sept	
Mary, Wife of John Wells, Yeoman	- Oct 1718	70	Charles Organ of the Parifh Yeoman	12 Aug, 1726	
Mary, Wife of Daniel Organ of this Parifh, Daughter of Thomas and Abigail Beckwith Harefcomb	23 May 1733	55	John Son of Robert and Mary Smith	2 May 1783	53
			William Clofe	24 Aug 17	
Thomas Spring	24 Apr 1757	64	Elizabeth, Daughter of Robert Smith, Yeoman	7 June, 17	4

LIV BROMESBERROW

LIV. BROMESBERROW.

THIS Parish, which is nearly eight Miles in Circumference, is situate on the Confines of the County of *Worcester*, at the Western Extremity of the *Malvern* Hills, and contains Part of the ancient Chace. It is included in the Hundred of *Botloe*, and is distant from *Newent* six Miles on the North-east, and fourteen North-west from GLOUCESTER. The greater Portion of the Lands are tilled, of a red sandy Soil, with little Variation, which are most productive of the inferior Sorts of Grain, particularly of Rye. On the Banks of the *Glynch*, by which Rivulet the Parish is intersected, are many fertile Meadows.

The Benefice is a Rectory in the *Forest* Deanery. The Church, which is dedicated to *St. Mary*, is an ancient Structure, though from late Reparations it has externally a modern Appearance. It consists of a Nave only, with a Tower at the West End embattled. A Burial Chapel, which adjoins the Chancel, was built in 1725, by WALTER YATE, Esq. and appropriated to his Family, who have been frequent and judicious Benefactors to the Church, which is decorated in a Style of singular Neatness and Propriety.

The Succession of the Property of the Manor since the Year 1325, 18 EDW. II. is authenticated by Court Rolls extant, and continued to the Year 1779. Prior to that early Period, the Account of it is interrupted and unsatisfactory. In 1321 considerable Privileges were granted, with the Manor, to WILLIAM DE WHITEFIELD *. A collateral Branch of the knightly Family of BROMWICHE, of *Castle Bromwich*, co. *Warwick*, became Possessors in the Reign of RICHARD the Second, and continued for several Centuries. It appears from the Title Deeds, that it was vested in Trust for the Use of ISAAC BROMWICH, Esq. in 1632 †. It was purchased early in this Century of EDMUND BROMWICH, Esq. by JOHN HYETT, Esq. of GLOUCESTER, and soon after sold by him to WALTER YATE, Esq. who had acquired large Estates in this and the contiguous Parishes. His Father RICE YATE ‡, Esq. became possessed of a capital Mansion, called *Hook-house*, in 1660. WALTER YATE, Esq. by his Will, dated in 1744, bequeathed his Estates in the Counties of GLOUCESTER, *Worcester*, and *Hereford*, to JOHN YATE, Barrister at Law, for six Years, and after the Expiration of that Term to JOHN YATE, only Son of CHARLES YATE, Esq. of *Arlingham*. Upon their Demise without Issue the Manor and other Estates devolved to the Heir at Law, ROBERT DOBYNS §, Esq. of *Evesbatch Court* in the County of *Hereford*, who pursuant to the Will of WALTER YATE, Esq. assumed by Act of Parliament in 1760 the Name and Arms of YATE. He re-built *Hook-house* in a very elegant Style, the modern Name of which is *Bromesberrow Place*. This Edifice was compleated by the late ROBERT GORGES DOBYNS YATE, whose Son and Heir is the present Lord of the Manor, and Patron of the Church.

The *Brook End*, the ancient Inheritance of the Family of STONE ||, now belongs to SAMUEL STONE, Esq. who is settled in *Ireland*. The *Grove House* and *Russel's End* have been long vested in the Family of BROOKE. Beside these, are two Estates possessed by the Right Hon. Lord SOMERS, and the Relict of JOHN NANFAN, Esq. but the greater Part of the Parish is held with the Manor.

* "Rex concessit WILLIELMO DE WHITEFIELD liberam Warennam in *Bromesberrow* in com. GLOUC. ita quod nullus intret [illegible] WILLIELMI." Rot. Cart. [illegible] In the Reign of PHILIP and MARY the Lord of *Bromesberrow* was entitled to the Privilege of the adjacent Chace of *Malvern*, being a free Suitor at the Court of *Hanley*, co. *Worc.* and Chace of *Great Malvern*, with the Abbot of *Pershore*, Prior of *Great Malvern*, the Earl [illegible] and other Persons of Consequence.

† By Indenture of Feoffment, Sep. 18, 1632, ISAAC BROMWICH of *Hampton upon Severn*, and THOMAS YATE, of *Arlingham*, Esqrs. on the one Part, and Sir ROBERT POINTZ, Knt. of *Iron Acton*, and SAMUEL [illegible] of *Didmarton*, Esq. on the other Part, it is witnessed that [illegible] at the Request and by the Appointment of the said ISAAC BROMWICH did grant to the said Sir R. POINTZ, &c. all that the Manor of *Bromesberrow*, with the Advowson thereof, to hold in Trust for the sole benefit of the said ISAAC BROMWICH. [illegible] 1671, ROBERT BROMWICH, Esq. conveyed the Manor in Trust to RICE YATE, Esq. and others for Purposes mentioned in the Deed. ABSTRACT OF TITLE DEEDS.

‡ The very ancient and respectable Family of YATE were seated at *Arlingham* in this County in the Reign of King JOHN. About a Century after JOHN YATE became Lord of the [illegible] by Marriage with [illegible] Coheir of JOHN BERKELEY. RICE YATE, Esq. was of a younger Branch of that Family settled at [illegible] *Carmarthen* [illegible] Coll, built [illegible] *Longe* [illegible] which still [illegible] Name of [illegible].

§ The Family of DOBYNS were anciently opulent, and long established at *Evesbatch Court*. Their Representative ROBERT DOBYNS, Esq. was Heir General of WALTER YATE, Esq. being [illegible] CATHERINE YATE.

|| [illegible] the Family of STONE have been established at *Brook End* [illegible] in [illegible] but [illegible] quartered [illegible].

 BENE

B E N E F A C T I O N S.

TO THE POOR

Rev WILLIAM STONE, Rector of *Eastnor*, gave, 1701, by Will, for instructing annually one poor Child in the English Tongue and the Church Catechism, yearly five Pounds

THOMAS ECKLEY, Gent 1716, devised 50*l* by Will, for teaching poor Children, and binding them Apprentices

WALTER YATE, Esq 1744, left by Will 30*l* vested in the Rev HENRY GORGES DOBYNS YATE, the Income to be annually distributed on *St Thomas's* Day, with a Preference to the necessitous Tenants of his own Estates

CATHERINE YATE, Widow of RICE YATE, Esq 1710, devised 30*l* to produce a yearly Rent of 1*l* 10*s* to be distributed to the Poor, vested in the Relict of the Rev WILL HAYWARD, of *Tewkesbury*.

Ten Pounds, vested in ——— HAYWARD, Widow, the Donor and Time of Donation uncertain.

TO THE CHURCH

WALTER YATE, Esq built the Altar Piece in 1725   The Reading Desk and Pulpit were erected in the Year 1750   ROBERT GORGES DOBYNS YATE, Esq built the Gallery, gave the Tiles, and presented the Parish with 105*l* for re casting the Bells, and increasing their Number to six   The Sum of 122*l* 17*s* 6*d* raised by Assessment, was expended on the Repairs of the Church, under the Direction of Mr YATE in 1773   A new Set of crimson Velvet Furniture was added in 1783

INCUMBENTS	PATRONS		INCUMBENTS	PATRONS
1403 John Berston,	——— Bromwiche		1620 Christoph Stock, B A	Sir Richard Tracy, Bart
1467 Thomas Eikins,	Thomas Bromwiche		1674 Richard Eaton,	Robert Bromwich
* * * * *	* * * *		1708 Rich Eaton, jun B A	Walter Yate, Esq.
1562 Thomas Horwell,	John Bromwiche		1745 Robert Harden, M A	John Yate, Esq
1567 John Cheynynge,	Sir John Bromwiche.		1771 Will Hayward, M A	Robert Gorges Dobyns
1583 James Price,	John Bromage.			Yate, Esq
1591 Henry Hopper,	John Bromage			
——— Thomas Higgs,			1781 Henry Gorges Dobyns	
1607 John Stock,	Richard Stone		Yate, I L B	The same

PRESENT LORD OF THE MANOR,

WALTER HONYWOOD YATE (a Minor).

The Persons summoned from this Parish by the Heralds in 1682 and 1683, were

Robert Bromwich, Esq and
Rice Yate, Esq.

At the Election in 1776, Seven Freeholders gave Votes from this Parish.

The Register commences in 1558, and contains Notices of some remarkable Weather, particularly of a Comet in 1680, ' The Tail of which was like the Blade of a Sword, and when getting to the West " reached almost, if not altogether, to the Zenith " Its second Appearance, in 1682, was not so formidable

ANNUAL ACCOUNT of MARRIAGES, BIRTHS, AND BURIALS, IN THIS PARISH

A D	Mar	Bir	Bur	A D	Mar	Bir	Bur	A D	Mar	Bur	Bur	A D	Mar	Bir	Bur
1781	3	13	3	1786	2	5	3	1791				1796			
1782	2	14	1	1787	1	5	3	1792				1797			
1783	3	12	9	1788				1793				1798			
1784	2	5	10	1789				1794				1799			
1785	—	10	11	1790				1795				1800			

INSCRIPTIONS

ARMS ON ATCHIEVEMENTS IN THE CHANCEL:

1st Azure, a Fefs, and in Chief two Mulletts Or, for YATE,—impaling, Argent, a Crofs Sable, for WALL

2d YATE as before, quartering, Gules, a Cheveron between ten Croffes patee Argent, for BERKE-LEY, 3 Gules, a Stag's Head cabofhed Or, for Box, 4 Argent, a Lion rampant Sable, for PRICE, over all, on an Efcocheon of Pretence, Sable, a Crofs between four Rofes Argent, for BARNESLEY

3d As the fecond.

4th Quarterly, 1 YATE as before, quartering, Azure, a Chevron between three Annulets Or, for DOBYNS, 2 YATE, 3 BERKELEY, 4 Box,—impaling, quarterly, 1 Argent, a Chevron between three Hawks Heads erafed Azure, for HONYWOOD, 2. Argent, a Chevron Gules, charged with three Talbots paffant of the Field, for MARTIN, 3 Sable, three Goblets Or, within a Bordure of the 2d, for BUTLER, 4 Sable, two Bars Or, and a Chief Argent, for FROGNOLD.

5th As the fecond

INSCRIPTIONS IN THE CHURCH

IN THE CHANCEL

ON A HANDSOME MONUMENT

Arms, Quarterly, YATE, BERKELEY, Box, as the 1ft

H S I

RICIUS YATE, Armiger,
Generofa de ftirpe olim & etiamnum Arlinghamiæ vigente
oriundus,
Quam
Per Conjugem CATHARINAM
(THOMÆ WALL, de Lentridge, Armig Filiam),
duplici fobole,
GUALTERO et CATHERINA,
feliciter propagatam,
Ampliatâ etiam infigniter re familiari
impenfius ornavit
Virum rebus gerendis natum
Oftenderunt,
In foro pacis publicæ tutela,
In campo militaris peritia,
In negotiis civilibus egregia prudentia,
In officiis humanitatis fedula fidelitas,
In diffidiis vicinorum dirimendis fagacitas exercitatiffima
Demum
Poft tot exintlatos in vita negotiofiffimâ labores
Sept 8, A D 1690, ætat 67
Virum fortiffimum unico et inopinato ictu proftravit
Apoplexia
I nunc, amice fpectator,
et quantillum contra mortem valeant illa Mortalia
Opes robur ingenium
ferio ! nec fero
Meditare

ON AN OVAL TABLET BENEATH THE ABOVE

CATHARINA, filia præfati RICII YATE,
fepulta fuit apud Ivefbatch in com
Hertford, 11° Jan Anno Domini 1757,
ætat 84 Matrimonio tradita fuit
imprimis ROBERTO DOBYNS, Arm
& 4 liberos fufcepit, ROBERTUM,
GULIELMUM, CATHARINAM, & MARIAM,
poftea Confortem thalami fumpfit
ROBERTUM UNITT, Gen fed nullam
produxit fobolem

Arms, YATE, BERKELEY, BOX, and YATE,
as before.

RICE YATE, Efq
died Sept 8, 1690

Arms, as above,—impaling, Argent, a Crofs
Sable, for WALL

CATHARINE, the Wife and Relict of
RICE YATE, Efq died the
19th Day of March, 1710 11

In Memory of HARRIOTT HAYWARD,
an Infant, Daughter of WILLIAM HAYWARD,
Rector of Bromefberrow, and ANN his
Wife She was buried July 13, 1777

Hic depofitum eft Corpus
ROBERTI HARDEN, M A
Florurt aliquando
In Coll Hertford, Oxon.
Socius & vice principalis
Poftquam hujus Parœciæ
nec non Evefbatch in Com Hereford,
Per annos complures Rector
Obiit Anno 1771,
Menfis Januar Die 12,
ætatis Anno 57.

IN YATE'S BURIAL CHAPEL*

ON A HANDSOME MARBLE MONUMENT

Arms, YATE as before defcribed

In Memory of JOHN YATE, of the Inner Temple,
London, Efq Barrifter at Law, fecond Son of
RICHARD YATE, of Arlingham in the County of
Gloucefter, Efq He married JANE, one of the
Daughters of WILLIAM BARNESLEY, of the County
of Hereford, Efq and Relict of JOHN VANHAM, of
Bibury in the County of Gloucefter, Efq
He died May 29, 1749, aged 47 Years

Alfo JANE his Wife, who died Feb 3, 1748,
aged 58 Years

JOHN YATE, Efq only Son of CHARLES YATE,
Efq died unmarried at Arlingham,
May 24, 1738, aged 28 Years

ON A HANDSOME MARBLE TABLET

Arms, Quarterly, YATE and DOBYNS,—impaling
HONYWOOD.

ROBERT-GORGES DOBYNS YATE, Efq.
died May 26, 1785, aged 33
He married ANNABELLA-CHRISTIANA,
only Daughter of WILLIAM HONYWOOD, Efq
of Malling Abbey in the County of Kent,
and Sifter to Sir JOHN HONYWOOD, Bart
By whom he had two Sons, WALTER HONYWOOD
and ROBERT-GORGES-DOBYNS,
and three Daughters, ANNABELLA-CHRISTIANA,
CAROLINE-ELIZABETH, and ANNA-MARIA,
who died an Infant

ELIZABETH, youngeft Daughter of
ROBERT-DOBYNS YATE, Efq by ELIZABETH,
Daughter of RICHARD GORGES, Efq of Lye
in the County of Hereford,
died June 15, 1784, aged 19 Years

ON FLAT STONES

Arms, YATE,—impaling, Or, a Fefs Wavy, be
tween fix Billets Sable, for DOWDLSWELL

ELIZABETH, the Wife of
WALTER YATE, Efq
died April 26, 1710, aged 25
She was Daughter of CHARLES DOWDESWELL, Efq
of Forthampton in this County

Arms, YATE, in a Lozenge

KATHARINE, Daughter of
WALTER YATE, Efq and
ELIZABETH his Wife,
died May 2, 1713, aged 5

Arms, YATE as before

WALTER YATE, jun Efq
died June 28, 1738, aged 28 Years

Arms, YATE as before

Here lieth the Body of
WALTER YATE, the elder, Efq
late of Hook houfe in this Parifh,
who died December 12, 1744, aged 76
He was Lieutenant Colonel of the Militia,
a Deputy Lieutenant, and a
Juftice of the Peace for this County

ROBERT-GORGES DOBYNS YATE, Efq
lies interred beneath this Stone

---

* Two Banners, borne by the family of YATE are preferved in this Chapel the firft infcrib d 'Religio Proteftantum "Lex Angliæ Libertas Parliamentorum' On the fecond, a dexter Arm vambraced iffuant from a Cloud holding a Sword Motto ' Ora & Pugna Jehovah pravit & juvabit "—The prefent Incumbent has fhewn the good Tafte which he has purfued the Study of Antiquities by preferving fome curious painted Glafs and arrangement in the Window of this Chapel The Defign confifts of a Device a Hand holding a Palm Leaf, and thefe Arms repeated throughout " Party per Pale Azure and Gules on a Chevron Argent between three Palm Trees of the Third a Rofe between two Lions proper flipped " [...] which had belonged to the Family of CHAPMAN and is this Time to the YATES

4

ANNA-MARIA,
Daughter of
ROBERT GORGES DOBYNS YATE, Efq
and of ANNABELLA-CHRISTIANA his
Wife, died May 3, 1783,
aged near 3 Years.

ARMS, YATE, quartering DOBYNS, BERKELEY,
and BOX,—impaling, Argent, a Whirlpool proper,
for the knightly, and once noble, Family of GORGES

Here lieth the Body of
ROBERT-DOBYNS YATE, Efq
late High Sheriff of this County,
and a Juftice of the Peace for the fame,
and the County of Hereford
He departed a Life well fpent, on the
10th of Jan 1766, aged 38 Years

Alfo RICHARD-GORGES,
fecond Son of ROBERT-DOBYNS YATE, Efq
and ELIZABETH his Wife, was buried
near this Place on the 20th of April, 1762,
aged near 6 Years

JOHN YATE, Efq 1749

JANE, the Wife of JOHN YATE, Efq 1748.

RICHARD GORGES DOBYNS YATE, 1762.

ON A COARSE STONE AGAINST THE SOUTH WALL,
IN CAPITALS

ELIZA STOCK,
the Wife of CHR STOCK, who departed
this Life Anno Dom 1621, December the 15

ON A FLAT STONE IN THE BODY

In Memory of
JOHN STONE,
of Brown's End in this Parifh, Gent
and ELIZABETH his Wife
She died March 16, 1713,
aged 28 Years
He died Auguft 3, 1742,
aged 62 Years

Here lieth the Body of
MARY NANFAN, Sifter of the
above JOHN STONE, and Relict of
GILES NANFAN,
Rector of Birts Morton
She died Jan. 23, 1767,
aged 84 Years

ON A FLAT STONE IN THE BELFRY

Here, in Hopes of a joyfull Refurrection,
lyes interred the Body of
Mrs. ANN CARN, Relict of
Mr FRANCIS CARN,
Cytizan and Diftiller of London,
By whom fhe left one Son and one Daughter
She was the third Daughter of
WILLIAM STONE, of the Brook End
She departed this mortal Life
the 12th Day of April,
in the 57th Year of her Age,
and in the Year of
our Lord God MDCCXXI.

IN THE CHURCH YARD.   ON TOMBS

The Rev Mr RICHARD EATON,
late Rector of this Parifh, after the
diligent Labour of 36 Years, fell afleep
Jan 30, 1708, aged 73.

ELIZABETH, the youngeft Daughter
of the Rev Mr RICHARD EATON,
late Rector of this Parifh,
died March 20, 1708,
aged 22

ROBERT his youngeft Son died in
the innocency of Childhood

THOMAS HILL, Gent junior,
Son of THOMAS HILL, Gent of
Little Longridge, by SARAH his Wife,
died April 23, 1777, aged 54

JAMES, the Son of THOMAS HILL, Gent
by SARAH his Wife,
died June 14, 1766, aged 41

SARAH, Wife of THOMAS HILL, fen Gent
of Little Longridge, died March 1, 1770,
aged 84 Years

THOMAS HILL, fenior, Gent
Hufband of the abovementioned,
died April 22, 1785,
aged 89

MARGARET, the Wife of
JOSEPH HILL,
of this Parifh, Gent
died Dec 29, 1773,
aged 36

RICHARD their Son
died in Infant.

In Memory of THOMAS HANKINS,
of Bromefberrow Heath in the Parifh of Dymoke,
in the County of Gloucefter
He exchanged Time for Eternity
the 10th Day of April, 1785,
aged 62 Years
A Man of an unexceptionable Character
through all the different Relations
of
Hufband, Father, and Friend.

O N

O N   H E A D   S T O N E S

	Died	Aged
Hannah, Wife of Benjamin Fisher	17 Feb. 1752	36
Benjamin Fisher	4 Feb 1762	82
William Radway, senior	16 July, 1718	43
William Radway, junior	22 Oct 1736	31
John Weale	25 Sept 1718	55
Ann, Wife of John Weale, senior	28 Oct. 1752	63
Benjamin, Son of Benjamin and Margaret Hope	4 May, 1761	27
Elizabeth their Daughter	2 June, 1762	30
Richard Belcher	26 Jan 1729	50
Mary his Wife	2 Jan 1738	51
Thomas their Son	29 Aug 1755	29
Catharine, Wife of John Gilding	27 Aug 1718	61
William Pewtris	11 June, 1720	42
Elizabeth his Daughter	25 Mar 1739	27
Esther, Wife of the late William Pewtris	29 Sept 1747	68
Lleanor their Daughter	22 June, 1745	26
John Taylor, late of Redmarly Dabitot	17 June, 1777	63
Ann Hill, Wife of the late John Hill, of the Lower-house, Donnington, Herefordshire, and Daughter of Richard Brooke, Gent of Rufferfland, and Alice his Wife	18 July, 1783	69
John White	5 Nov 1729	50
Joseph Hill	29 June, 1716	55
John Hankins	6 Aug 1757	58
Mary his Wife	1 Nov 1756	62
John Stone	— Dec 1695	—
Elizabeth his Wife	2 Aug 1690	—
Abel Tayler	3 July, 1766	36
John Baker, late of Redmarley	7 Mar. 1717	70
Mary, Relict of John Baker	6 Mar 1728	74
Robert Dobbins, of Redmarley	14 Mar 1729	37
Deborah, Relict of Robert Dobbins, Chirurgeon, of Redmarley	11 June, 1734	39
Hester their Daughter	26 Apr 1734	25
Deborah, Wife of Richard Brooke, and Daughter of Robert and Deborah Dobbins	21 May, 1719	61
John Nubbery	11 Oct 1770	63
Joseph Balding	15 Mar 1781	34

LV. BUCKLAND,
OR
BOKELOND.

SIR ROBERT ATKYNS, to whose Opinions in Matters of Antiquity we willingly accede, reports that the *Saxons* held their Lands by two Kinds of Tenure, by oral Tradition, and written Evidence. The one they termed *Folk Land*, the other *Boc Land*, and from the latter of these this Parish derives the Etymology of its Name * It lies in the upper Division of the Hundred of *Kiftsgate* six Miles West from *Campden*, and twenty four Eastward from GLOUCESTER The Terrier of the Parish contains 1600 Acres, applied in nearly equal Portions to Pasture and Tillage, the Soil universally a strong Clay The Situation of the Village is sequestered and rural, and the Landscape pleasingly diversified with Groves of various Trees

The Living is a Rectory in the Deanery of *Campden*, but one Moiety of the impropriate Tythes are vested in the Lord of the Manor, and the Demeine Lands are exempted The Church was probably built by the Abbey of GLOUCESTER, in the Style of the fifteenth Century It consists of a Nave, two Aisles, and an embattled Tower, at the Angles of which are grotesque Figures of flying Dæmons, as Water Spouts. The Inside appears to have been fitted up at the same Time In the East Window of the Chancel, are three Compartments of beautiful painted Glass, executed with such brilliancy of Colouring, and correctness of Outline, as to prove their having been done, when the Art had gained its utmost Perfection † The Window, in which they are contained, has a Date on the Outside 1585 They must have been taken from some other Place

KINRED, King of the *Mercians*, gave the Manor, and the Fee of the whole Parish, to the Abbey of GLOUCESTER, who are recited as being the Possessors in Domesday Book At the Suppression it was exchanged for Lands in *Yorkshire*, by Sir RICHARD GRESHAM, Lord Mayor of *London*, 1536 One of the Coheirs of Sir THOMAS GRESHAM (who so eminently promoted the Interests of Learning and Commerce by his Foundations of *Gresham College* and the *Royal Exchange*) was married to Sir JOHN THYNNE, the Ancestor of the noble Family of WEYMOUTH

The Manor-house is large and low, in which a few incomplete Suits of Iron Armour are still preserved.

The Rectory-house was built about the Year 1520 The Hall has a lofty Roof of Timber-frame, and in one of the Windows are these Arms, "Azure, a Sword in pale point in base Or, between two Keys "in Saltire of the second" Abbey of GLOUCESTER A Device of a Tun with the Grift of a Tree issuant from it On a Label, ' **Will Grafton, Rector**," dispersed are Figures of Birds, holding Labels, inscribed, "**In no'ine Jesu**"

The Hamlet of *Laverton* is more populous than *Buckland* Its old Chapel is now converted into Tenements for the Poor There are no Proprietors of Lands distinct from the Manor

---

* In Confirmation of this Conjecture it appears, on consulting the *Fuller*, that there are few Counties which have not a Parish called *Buckland*

† The Subjects of these Delineations have been mistaken They represent one of the Sacraments of the Romish Church, and not the Abbot of GLOUCESTER holding his Court The first Compartment is the Ceremony of Baptism which consists of six Figures a Priest epiropally habited with a Crosier, and a Woman holds the Child upon the Fore Ground, in the Gothic holds the Book behind is another Woman with a Child Another Priest in a Surplice the Godmother lynx in her Hand The second Compartment is the Office of Matrimony containing seven Figures the Persons joined according to the Custom of the Times with a Purse at his Girdle, the Bride has a Venture of Ermine Lining and hold a Glove the Priest is joining Hands and reading the Ceremony Beyond are several Figures old and young stretching one of which holds a Pair of Gloves The third Compartment is the Extreme Unction, or last Figure the fare is principally habited he for the appears as before with his attendant Priest the dying Person reclines in the Fore Ground behind are four Figures in Consolation, one in the Attitude of commanding Attention Mr WALPOLE in his Anecdotes of Painting Vol I 51 observes that the first painting in staining Glass were settled at Coventry about the Close of the fifteenth Century by some of whom these might have been probably executed

B E N E F A C T I O N S.

HENRY FREDERICK THYNNE, Efq gave by Deed, in 1707 or 8, for the Education of thirty Boys in the Parifh of *Buckland*, and for the Education of certain Children in the Parifh of *Chipping Campden, Glouceſter-ſhire*, Lands veſted in the Lord of the Manor of *Buckland* for the Time being, the Right Hon Lord TRACEY, the Rector of *Buckland* for the Time being, the Vicar of *Campden* for the Time being, THOMAS EDWARDS FREEMAN, of *Batsford*, Efq, THOMAS EDWARDS FREEMAN, junior, Efq, WILLIAM BATESON, of *Bourton on the Hill*, Efq; R MARTIN, of *Pebworth*, Efq; the annual Produce of wʰⁱᵍʰ is 105*l* The Salary to the Maſter of *Buckland* School is 25*l* a Year If any Surplus after the Payment of the Maſters of both Schools, and the Repairs of certain Premiſes to the Charities belonging, to be employed in cloathing and apprenticeing poor Children of the ſaid Pariſhes at the Diſcretion of the Truſtees

INCUMBENTS	PATRONS	INCUMBENTS	PATRONS
1515 William Grafton,	ABbey of St. Peter in GLOUCESTER	1714 Trethreway Tooker, B A	Guardians of Thomas Thynne, Eſq.
1570 William Wingfield,	Sir John Thynne	1746 John Martin, M A	Ld Viſc Chedworth
1591 John Maltbee, B A	John Thynne, Eſq	1776 Robert Vanburgh, M A	Lord Viſcount Wey-mouth
1636 William Gare, M. A			
———— Gardiner, D. D	James Thynne, Eſq	1784 Anthony Dauvert, B A	The ſame
1693 Richard Smart, M A	The ſame		

PRESENT LORD OF THE MANOR,

The Right Honourable THOMAS Lord Viſcount WEYMOUTH.

The Perſons ſummoned from this Place by the Heralds in 1682 and 1683 were,

James Thynne, Eſq
———— Gardiner, D. D
———— Wheeler, Gent

At the Election in 1776, Three Freeholders polled from this Pariſh.

In the Regiſter, which begins in 1539, is an Account of the Plague which raged here in 1606, by which the Rector JOHN MALTBEE loſt ſix Children in the Space of one Month

ANNUAL ACCOUNT OF MARRIAGES, BIRTHS, AND BURIALS, IN THIS PARISH

A D	Mar	Bir	Bur	A.D	Mar	Bir	Bur	A D	Mar	Bir	Bur	A D	Mar	Bir	Bur
1781	—	17	3	1786	1	10	12	1791				1796			
1782	—	13	5	1787	2	8	9	1792				1797			
1783	1	11	6	1788				1793				1798			
1784	1	12	7	1789				1794				1799			
1785	1	5	9	1790				1795				1800			

INSCRIPTIONS IN THE CHURCH

IN THE CHANCEL

ON AN ATCHIEVEMENT OVER THE LAST WINDOW

Quarterly, 1ſt, Barry of ten Or and Sable, for BOTTEVILLE, alias THYNNE, 2d, Argent, a Lion rampant Gules, for   , 3d, Or, on a Feſs Gules three Bezants, in chief a Greyhound currant Azure, for EYNNES, 4th, Quarterly, Gules and Ermine, on the 2d and 3d three Piles of the 1ſt, over all, on a Feſs Azure, three Bezants, for GATACRE, 5th, Barry of ſix Or and Sable, in chief two Pallets of the 2d, over all, an Ineſcocheon Gules, charged with three Barrs Ermine, for BURLEY, 6th, Sable, a Chevron, between three Leopards Faces Argent, for BIRKH *(all Shropſhire Families)*, 7th, Argent, a Chevron Ermine, between three Mullets Sable, for GRESHAM, 8th, as the 1ſt

ON A BLACK and WHITE MARBLE MONUMENT
AGAINST THE SOUTH WALL

Arms , Quarterly, 1ft and 4th, Barry of 10 Or
and Sable for THYNNE; 2d and 3d, Argent, a
Lion rampant Gules, for

Here lyeth the Body of JAMES THYNNE, Efq
Son of Sir HENRY FREDERICK THYNNE, Bart.
and MARY, Daughter of the Lord Keeper
COVENTRYE, a Man of exemplary Virtue and
Charity, beloved and valued by his Equalls,
bleft and pray'd for by the Poor After fome
Legacies to his Relations, his whole large
perfonal Eftate he bequeathed to pious Ufes,
and his Lands to his Nephew THOMAS THYNNE,
who erected this Monument in Gratitude to his
Memory He died March 15, 1708-9, aged 66

ON FLAT STONES

Subtus jacet
RICHARDUS SMART, M A
hujus Ecclefiæ Rector,
obiit 8 die Martii,
Anno Dom 1713,
ætatis fuæ 61

Here lyeth the Body of ANN SMART,
Niece to the above RICHARD SMART,
who died July 4, 1754, aged 73.

Memoriale hoc deplorari
Adolefcentis JOHANNIS MALFBÆI, Art Bac
hujus Ecclefiæ Rectoris Filii feptimi,
qui obiit Nov 16, 1627, ætatis
hæc pene infculpfit I M

RICHARD WHITE
departed this Life Jan 20, 1683

JOHN WHITE,
of Laverton, departed this Life
the 22d of February, 1716, aged 63

SARAH WHITE, Wife of
JOHN WHITE, departed this Life
Sept 8, 1727, aged 72

MARY, Daughter of JOHN WHITE
and SARAH his Wife,
died March 22, 1738, aged 50 Years

JOHN WHITE, Gent
died May 13, 1747, aged 52

JANE WHITE
died Auguft 31, 1765, aged 71

WILLIAM WHITE, Son
of JOHN WHITE,
died Sept 29, 1727, aged 34 Years

Alfo SARAH, Daughter
of JOHN and JANE WHITE,
died Jan 11, 1731, aged 8.

ELIZABETH WHITE
died Nov 19, 1743, aged 14.

THOMAS WHITE,
late of Laverton, Gent
died Sept 14, 1682, aged 42.

HENRY WHEELER, Gent.
the eldeft Son of THOMAS WHEELER, Gent
of Laverton, died Dec 6, 1681,
aged 45 Years

JOHN FOSTER,
late of the Parifh of St. Margaret,
Weftminfter,
obiit Oct 6, 1733

ALICE, the Widow of THOMAS FOSTER, Gent.
died March 21, 1707, aged 71

THOMAS FOSTER, Gent
died April 5, 1694, aged 67

MARY, Daughter of
THOMAS FOSTER,
obiit June 1711.

JOHN BAYZAND, Gent.
died June 22, 1752, aged 53.

ABIGAILE, Wife of JOHN BAYZAND, Gent.
died Nov 10, 1756, aged 59

JAMES FOSTER, Gent
died June 3, 1708, aged 84.

RICHARD BAYZAND, of Laverton,
died April 15, 1728, aged 68.

Alfo MARY, the Wife of
RICHARD BAYZAND,
died April 12, 1700, aged 35

MARY, Daughter of
JOHN BAYZAND,
died Feb. 7, 1726, aged 4 Years,

ELIZABETH, Daughter of
JOHN BAYZAND,
died June 9, 1730, aged 2 Years.

JOHN BAYZAND,
Son of JOHN and ABIGAIL BAYZAND,
died Oct 27, 1758, aged 37

CALEB COOPER
departed this Life March 6, 1720,
aged 48 Years

ON A SMALL STONE IN THE CHANCEL .
I M.
for JOHN MARTIN, late Rector.

IN THE CHURCH YARD, ON TOMBS.

THOMAS GLOUCESTER, alias WORKMAN, Lavertoniæ in hac Parochiâ
Incola & Indigena,
Honeſtis inibi Parentibus natus, Avorum & Atavorum longa retro ſerie,
Plurimis
Animi Corporis & Fortunæ Bonis exornatus, numerosâ
Beatus prole, quinque filiis & totidem filiabus,
Humo in pace obdormit,
Anno { Domini 1658
      { Ætatis 58

MARGARETA, Uxor THOMÆ GLOUCESTER, alias WORKMAN,
Hic in contiguo Dormientis, ROBERTI HARRIS, Peborthiæ filiæ,
Mulier
Omnibus omnium Virtutum Ornamentis (præſertim Mulierum)
Cumulatiſſima,
Exuvias fœliciſſime depoſuit,
Anno { Ætatis ſuæ 74
      { Domini 1675

Arms, Gules, three Clarions Or, for GRANVILLE

Colonel BERNARD GRANVILLE,
Son to BERNARD GRANVILLE, Eſq
and Grandſon to Sir BEVIL GRANVILLE,
who was killed in Landſdowne
Fight, lies here interred, died in
the 53d Year of his Age, on the
8th of December, 1723

THOMAS FREEMAN, ſenior,
of Laverton in this Pariſh,
died October 5, 1714, aged 44.

ESTHER his Wife
died June 23, 1748, aged 75

MARY, Wife of THOMAS FREEMAN, junior,
died Auguſt 15, 1754, aged 22.

O N H E A D S T O N E S

	Died	Aged
William Powell	31 Mar 1700	66
Richard Freeman of Laverton	12 Mar 1701	66
Humphry Parrott	13 Apr. 1774	84
Mary, Wife of Humphry Parrott	14 Jan 1759	75
Alſo Robert and Mary Smith, Father and Mother of the above Mary Parrott		
Thomas Richardſon	3 Nov 1739	38
Elizabeth, Wife of John Cook	25 Oct 1733	36
John Cook, junior	5 Jun 1745	26
William Pitman, of Laverton	6 July, 1784	44
John Richardſon	18 May, 1785	70
Thomas Gibſon, of Laverton	18 June, 1770	64
Robert Gibbs, of Laverton	10 Apr 1770	60
Jane his Wife	17 May, 1780	57
Francis Price, Gent	8 May, 1731	54

LVI. BULLEY,

LVI. BULLEY,

OR, as it is written in Domesday, *Bullege*, is a small Parish in the Hundred of the Dutchy of *Lancaster*, about seven Miles East from *Mitchel Deane*, and five westerly from GLOUCESTER.

The Arable and Pasture Lands are nearly equal. The Soil varies from a very deep Clay to a light Marl, and is very fertile.

The Living is a Chapelry, annexed to *Churcham*, the Impropriation and Advowson of which are vested in the Dean and Chapter of GLOUCESTER. The Church, according to Leron, is dedicated to *St Andrew*. It is a small plain Building, without Aisle or Chancel, with a low Spire at the West End. What Traces of Architecture remain are of very heavy *Saxon*.

The Manor was held in the Reign of HEN. III by the family DE MUSGROSE, since which Period it has had very many intermediate Possessors, and was purchased in this Century by the Family of HYETT. Other considerable Estates belong to JOHN FENDALL, and WILLIAM MONEY, Esqrs and the Rev Mr BURGESS, besides whom there are several Freeholders.

No Benefactions to the Poor.

INCUMBENTS	PATRONS	INCUMBENTS	PATRONS
1673 Abraham Gregory,	Dean and Chapter of GLOUCESTER	1733 John Whinfield, M A	Dean and Chapter of GLOUCESTER
1679 Thomas Thatch, M.A	The same	1753 Edward Sprikes, M A	The same
1725 Robert Bull, D D	The same	1776 James Edwardes, B D	The same
1730 Peter Gully, M A	The same	1765 Thomas Parker, M A	The same.

PRESENT LORD OF THE MANOR,

BENJAMIN HYETT, Esq

The only Person summoned from this Place by the Heralds, in 1682 and 1683 was

Jeremiah Hooper, Gent

At the Election in 1776 Twenty three Freeholders polled from this Parish

ANNUAL ACCOUNT OF MARRIAGES, BIRTHS, AND BURIALS, IN THIS PARISH

A D	Mr	Bu	Bur	A D	Mu	Br	Bur	A D	Mu	Br	Bur	A D	Mu	Br	Bur
1781	4	—	—	1786				1791				1796			
1782	1	—	—	1787				1792				1797			
1783	—	—	—	1788				1793				1798			
1784	—	—	3	1789				1794				1799			
1785	1	5	1	1790				1795				1800			

INSCRIPTIONS IN THE CHURCH

Here lyeth the Body of
JOHN CRUMP, Yeoman,
who died Anno Dom 161

Underneath this Place lieth the Body
of JEREMIAH HOOPER, of this Parish,
who died Dec 4, 1705,
aged then 67 Years

IN THE CHURCH YARD, ON TOMBS.

RICHARD READ,
died April 15, 1769, aged 75.

ANN his Wife
died July 8, 1751, aged 63.

RICHARD their Son
was buried Dec 14, 1751, aged 27

ANN, the Wife of
THOMAS BAKER, and
Daughter of RICHARD READ,
died March 7, 1783, aged 61

THOMAS DREW, of Churcham,
died July 28, 1778, aged 28.

JANE SIMMONS
died Feb 24, 1785, aged 74

WILLIAM HARDWICK, junior,
died July 17, 1737

MARY his Wife
died May 27, 1761

ON HEAD STONES

	Died	Aged
Jeremiah Hooper	6 May, 1726	60
Mary his Daughter	14 Aug 1728	26
Ann his Wife	2 Feb 1756	80
Jeremiah Hooper, senior	2 May, 1693	90
Elizabeth, Relict of Jeremiah Hooper	17 Feb 1697	72
Edward, Son of Jeremiah Hooper	16 Feb. 1759	26
Mary, Wife of Thomas York, Daughter of Jeremiah Hooper	1 July, 1772	31
Richard Read, senior	14 Dec 174	60
Jane his Wife	12 Nov 1724	62
John Smith, late Clerk of Churcham	20 Sept 1762	69
Mary his first Wife	27 Mar 17 1	
Thomas Smith	— Dec 1775	42
Thomas, Son of John and Hester Young	9 June 1761	18
Giles Capner	— — 1	66
William Young, senior	17 Sept 7 1	6
John Thomas	12 Jan 1760	57
Confidence his Wife	17 Nov 1	69
Mary their Daughter	1 Apr 1756	
John their Son	19 Oct 1763	27
John Ready, Gent	25 Jun 1695 6	—
Elizabeth his Wife	1 Dec 1701	—
William, Son of William and Sarah Lodge	20 Apr 1750	33
Thomas Mechin, of Churcham	6 Aug 1770	79
Robert Stephens	13 Oct 1722	46
Anne his Wife	16 Aug	—
Robert Merrick	8 May, 1707	—
William his Son	15 May, 1707	—
Robert his Son	18 May, 1707	—
Elizabeth, Wife of Robert Merrick	8 May, 1729	—
Elizabeth their Daughter	23 Oct 1737	—
Richard, Son of John and Ann Merrick	8 Jan 1744	—
Ann, Wife of John Merrick	4 Nov 1770	56
John Merrick	15 Nov 1772	67

C A M

LVII. CAM, OR CAME,

LIES in a Valley in the Hundred of *Berkeley*, and is nearly five Miles in Extent Its Distance from *Dursley* is one Mile only, from *Berkeley* five on the East, and fourteen South westward from GLOUCESTER. In an accurate Terrier lately made, this Parish was found to contain more than 3000 Acres, of which the far greater Portion is Pasture, with many large and fruitful Orchards The Amount of all the Commonable Lands is 280 Acres

The Village, including *Upper* and *Lower Cam*, which are divided by a Rivulet of the same Name, is extensive and populous, the poorer Inhabitants being generally employed in the Manufacture of Cloth

In the MSS of Mr SMYTHE, before cited, are the subjoined Notices of the Parish of *Cam*, being a Member of the Barony and Hundred of *Berkeley*

" *Came*, in Domesdei Booke *Camma*, wherein WILLIAM the CONQUEROR had six Hydes of Lande in
" Demesne, and eleaven other Hides of Land there, which were, as I conceive, in Tenent's Hands,
" such as Copyholders for Lives, there at this Day are, and such Lands as since that Tim have byn
" enfeoffed to divers Men, and given in Tayle by the Lords of this Manor It is a goodly and large
" Parish, divided bie a preatty, little, sweete River, running through the middest of it, into two Parts,
" *Upper Came*, or *Upthorpe*, and *Lower Came*, or the *Nether Towne* Upper Came comprehendeth
" *Ashmead* and *Churchena*, and *Lower Came* comprehendeth *Drenel*, *Clenanger* commonlie pronounced
" *Clinger*, whereto may be added *Stinchcombe* and *Snytend*, and *Halmes*, a Minor of 100l per annum, or
" thereabouts, the Inheritance of GEORGE Lord BERKELEY, and Parcell of the Baronie holden by Knight's
" Service, *in capite*, containinge in the entire Compasse of itselfe at least five Miles, beside the Villae
" of *Stinchombe* and *Snytend* A Townshipe toe evenlie partaking of Hill and Vale, with an wholesome
' Aire to both, and so equally furnished of Timber and Wood for Building, Fire, and all Boones in
' Husbandrie, with Arable, Meadow, and Pasture Ground, for the Feed and Breed of all Sorts of Cat
" tell with Fish, Fowle, Perry, Cyder, and the like, that it would abundantlie suffice for the Main
" nance and Well beinge of its own Inhabitants without Supply from any other any needful Thing
" which the Hart of Man would moderately desire "

The Benefice is a Vicarage, or rather a Curacy, endowed in the Deanery of *Dursley* The great Tythes were appropriated to the Abbey of *St Peter* in Gloucester an 1361, to which it became

stipendiary Cure, with a Pension of 13l 6s, 8d to the Curate serving at the Altar, who was bound to account to the Abbot for all Oblations received By Charter of HEN VIII the Bishop was obliged to augment the Stipend of the Vicar, but since, by the Piety of Bishop GOODMAN in 1660, sixty Pounds annually are allotted from the Impropriation for the Vicar's Salary * The Impropriate Tythes have been long vested in the Family of ESTCOURT, as Lessees under the Bishop of GLOUCESTER

The Church is dedicated to St Mary, but we are informed that it was more anciently to St George, whose Image, carved in Wood, stood in the Porch, and was conveyed to Colnbrooke in the Reign of EDW VI where it gave Name to the great Inn It consists of a spacious Nave, two Aisles, with a lofty and light Tower, embattled and pinnacled, at the West end It is conjectured, that the greater Part of it was erected by THOMAS Lord BERKELEY, who founded a Chantry here, 14 EDW III 1341, and whose armorial Ensigns were painted in the Windows, and still remain upon an Escocheon affixed to the Tower

The Manor is parcel of the Barony of Berkeley, and was included in the original Grant from King HENRY II to ROBERT FITZ HARDING, in whose noble Descendants it has been vested to the present Time The best Estate (independent of the Manor) was held for several Generations by the Family of HORTON, originally of the County of Hereford, and passed from them to the HADLEYS by Inheritance Another Estate is possessed by the Family of PHILLIMORE

The Hamlets are enumerated in the Extract from Mr SMYTH's MSS Lorenge Farm belongs to the Parish of Stanley St Leonard, having been given to the Priory by THOMAS Lord BERKELEY, temp HEN III but the Land tax of it is charged with this Parish Cam River, on which several Mills are erected, has its Source near Owlpen, and joins the Severn at Frampton Pill " Long Downe and Pike ' Downe are two great Hills, the one representing a Sugar Loaf, the other a Barne, parted only by the " Highway " MSS PARSONS The Form of these is peculiarly artificial, but no Vestiges of Encampments are to be traced, nor has any Discovery of that Kind been as yet made

---

B E N E F A C T I O N S.

CHRISTOPHER WOODWARD gave by Will, for the Poor in general, an Annuity, issuing out of the Lands of Lord CLIFFORD, the annual Produce 10s

THROGMORTON TROTMAN gave by Will Oct 30, 1663, an Annuity, issuing out of an Estate directed by the Will of the Donor to be purchased for this and other Purposes, towards building an Alms-house, and towards the Maintenance of it, or towards a Stock for setting poor People to Work, or yearly

* PARSONS, ut supra.

distributed

diſtributed among the Poor, as the Company, or who they ſhall appoint thereto, ſhall think fitting; or any other Way, for the Benefit of the Poor, as they ſhall appoint, veſted in the Company of Haberdaſhers in *London*, the annual Produce of which is 30*l* out of which 6*l* per annum is deducted by the Company for the Land Tax

RICHARD HICKES gave by Will, March 2, 1711, to be paid annually for ever to ſuch poor Perſons as do not receive Pariſh Alms, veſted in Truſtees, the annual Produce 10*l* 11*s* 8*d*

NATHANIEL HICKES gave by Will, Sept 18, 1724, an Annuity, iſſuing out of Freehold Lands, veſted in Truſtees, the annual Produce 5*l*

MARGARET TROTMAN and ELEANOR TROTMAN gave by Deed, Dec 16, 1727, an Annuity, iſſuing out of Freehold Lands, 10*l* out of which the Land Tax is deducted, the Sum of 6*l* Part of this Charity to be given annually to ſix poor Widows, not receiving Pariſh Alms, 1*l* each, and the remaining 4*l* thereof to be annually given away in Bread, both upon St Thomas's Day, for ever, veſted in PACKER OLIVER

FRANCES HOPTON gave by Will, March 11, 1730, in Lands, for erecting and maintaining a School for ever, for the Education and Benefit of ten poor Boys and ten poor Girls, till they arrive to the Age of ſixteen Years, the annual Produce 50*l*, veſted in the Rev Mr BENIAMIN WEBB

INCUMBENTS	PATRONS	INCUMBENTS	PATRONS
1515 ———	Abbey of GLOUCESTER	1654 William Harding,	Biſhop of GLOUCESTER
* * * * * * * * * * * *	1664 John Barnſdale,	The ſame.
1569 Richard Smith,	Biſhop of GLOUCESTER	1708 Edward Turner, Clerk,	The ſame
		1717 Daniel Capel, B A	The ſame
1582 Hugh Parſons,	The ſame	1737 Peter Senhouſe, M A	The ſame
1598 John Churchman,	The ſame	1763 Benjamin Webb,	The ſame.
1620 William Smith,	The ſame		

PRESENT LORD OF THE MANOR,

The Right Honourable FREDERIC-AUGUSTUS Earl of BERKELEY

The Perſons ſummoned from this Pariſh by the Heralds in 1682 and 1683, were

Robert Trotman, Gent.   Edward Hill, Gent
John Trotman, Gent   John Trye, Gent

At the Election in 1776, Twenty-eight Freeholders gave Votes from this Pariſh.

The firſt Entry in the Regiſter bears Date in 1569 The earlier Parts of it are ſingularly accurate, and contain Liſts of all the parochial Officers from 1599 to 1685, and a Statement of the Population from 1569 to 1679, ſince which it appears to have been conſiderably encreaſed

ANNUAL ACCOUNT OF MARRIAGES, BIRTHS, AND BURIALS, IN THIS PARISH

A D	Mar	Bir	Bur	A D	Mar	Bir	Bur	A D	Mar	Bir	Bur	A D	Mar	Bir	Bur
1781	5	15	7	1786	12	21	21	1791				1796			
1782	4	23	9	1787	6	31	17	1792				1797			
1783	5	18	13	1788				1793				1798			
1784	4	16	19	1789				1794				1799			
1785	7	28	19	1790				1795				1800			

INSCRIPTIONS IN THE CHURCH.

IN THE CHANCEL.

Hic jacet in occiduo cinere
GULIELMUS HARDINGE,
In artibus Magiſter, Theologus tam Doctrinâ
Quam pietate eximius, concionator fœliciſſimus,
Paſtor fidelis, maritus amantiſſimus, parens
indulgens, poſt varia ſtudia, quibus fideliter
nec infœliciter incubuit, inſtinctu & impulſu
Spiritus Sancti, monitu & hortatu amicorum,
ordines ſacros implexus, & curæ paſtorali
hujus Eccleſiæ Cumæ indutus anno ſui Jeſu
1654, Decanumque Durſlæ Ruralis Decanus,
vitæ officiis & omnibus curis,
Morte exitus die Dominico
mane ultimo Februarii, Anno
Domini 1663, ætat. 39
In Memoriam hujus Reverendi Viri,
Chara pater & pia uxor DOROTHEA
Hoc poſuit Monumentum

To the Memory
of the virtuous and religious Mrs DOROTHY HARDING, Daughter
of Mr ANSELM SANDFORD, of Stanley, Gent. and mournful Widow
of the Rev Mr. WILLIAM HARDING, Minifter of this Parifh
She departed this Life, at her Houfe in the
City of Gloucefter, on the 1ft Day of March,
in the Year of our Lord 1702, and of her Age 68

Near this Place lieth the Body of EDWARD TUR-
NER, Vicar of Cam, and alfo fometime Vicar of
Durfley In both thefe Places, among other good
Deeds, for which his Zeal was eminent, he procured
a Charity School He died Feb 13, 1717, aged
44 Years, leaving a mournful Widow and nine
young Children to the all fufficient Care of Providence

HESTER his Daughter died March 19, 1717,
aged 3 Years 10 Months

[The above Infcription was againft the South Wall,
and that of Mr HARDING in Brafs againft the North
Wall, but both are removed or demolifhed]

ON A MONUMENT AGAINST THE NORTH WALL

Arms, a Battle axe, between three Pellets, for
MORSE, impaling a Chevron, between three Anchors, for HOLDER.

In Memory of
NICHOLAS MORSE, fenior, of Downhoufe,
who died in Auguft 1770, aged 68 Years

Alfo of ANN his Wife,
who died May 24, 1784, aged 75 Years

Alfo three Children by ANN his Wife –

ANN died Jan 23, 1734, aged 11 Days

NICHOLAS died Feb 5, 1752, aged 13 Years.

JOHN died July 15, 1778, aged 43 Years.

Arms, Ermine, on a Chief indented Gules,
three Eftoiles Or

In Memory of ANN, Daughter
of MATTHEW ESTCOURT, Efq and
LYDIA his Wife She was
buried Oct 19, 1747,
aged 9 Years

ON TRANSIONS

Here refteth the Body of
JOHN HARDING, who departed this
Life the 15th Day of July, 1702,
at his Age 42

Here lieth the Body of
ALICE, the Wife of JONATHAN WOODWARD, fenior,
who departed this Life
the   Day of January, 1689,
at his Age 70

LYDIA, late Wife of JONAH OKES,
departed this Life Feb 22, 1712

LYDIA their Daughter died in 1712

Arms, Vert, a Fefs dancette Ermine

CORNWELL SOMERS, Armig
obiit Junii Quinto,
Anno Salutis MDCXCIX,
ætat LXV.

ON A HANDSOME MARBLE MONUMENT, BETWEEN
THE CHURCH AND CHANCEL

Arms, Quarterly, 1ft and 4th, per Pale, a
Chevron engrailed, between three Lions ram..,
for HOSKINS, 2d and 3d, on a Cheveron, between
three Owls, three Mulletts, for HILL, on an
Efcutcheon of Pretence, Gules, a Fefs vaire, between three Pelicans Heads erafed Or, for MA-
CHEN

In a Vault near this Monument are interred the
Remains of LEWIS and HARRIET, Son and Daughter of LEWIS HOSKINS, late of Pantee in the County
of Monmouth, but now of Durfley, Efq and ELI-
ZABETH his Wife

LEWIS, died Aug 10, 1762, aged 2 Days

HARRIET, died May 24, 1772, aged 5 Years

Alfo of ELIZABETH HOSKINS, Spinfter, Sifter of
the aforefaid LEWIS HOSKINS, who died
November 2, 1770, aged 45 Years.

ON MONUMENTS IN THE
SOUTH AISLE

Arms and Impalement as before

Sacred for ever be the Memory
of Mrs MARY MORSE, Wife of THOMAS MORSE,
of Durfley, Gent who died Oct 26, 1764,
aged 60 Years
She was a Pattern worthy of Imitation,
in the Exercife of her Duties of Religion,
and in the regular Difcharge of the moft
important Offices of Life, which endear the
Wife, the Mother, and the Friend
The abovementioned THOMAS MORSE Gent
a moft affectionate Hufband, Father, and Friend,
and an exemplary honeft Man, exchanged this
Life for a better, Jan 23, 1781, aged 74

Arms, Argent, on a Bend cottifed Sable, three
Annulets Or, for SELWYN

In Memory of three Children, viz
WILLIAM, WILLIAM, and SARAH, of
JASPER SELWYN, of this Parifh, Gent
and ELEANOR his Wife, whofe Remains
were in this Aifle depofited,
the 1ft on the 18th of Sept 1726,
the 2d on the 1ft of July, 1727,
and the 3d on the 22d of Dec 1730

Arms

Arms, three Barrs, and in Chief three Cinquefoils, for PHILLIMORE;—impaling, Argent, on a
Fefs Sable, three Cinquefoils of the Field, between
three Lozenges Gules, for PURNELL.

To the Memory of
JOHN PHILLIMORE, Gent.
who died the 27th of Feb 1762,
in the 60th Year of his Age

Alfo of ELIZABETH his Wife,
who departed this Life the
15th of Sept 1764, aged 62 Years

THOMAS, the Son of THOMAS MORSE,
of Wick's Elm, Gent. was buried
the 29th Day of Jan 1696

In Memory of NICHOLAS,
the Son of NICHOLAS MORSE, of
Downhoufe, who died April 12, 1733,
ætatis fuæ 80

ON A TABLET AGAINST ONE OF THE PILLARS

Before this Place lies the Body of
THOMAS STRATFORD, Vicar of this Parish
25 Years. He died March 1, Anno Dom. 1707,
ætatis fuæ 64.

Alfo before this Place refts the
Body of SARAH, Wife of THOMAS STRATFORD,
Vicar here, Daughter of
HENRY HAM, fometime Rector of Sadbury
in this County, and after
Rector of Much Waltham in Effex

Alfo of SARAH their Daughter

The Mother died the 18th of May, 1705;
The Daughter died the 11th of Aug 1702.

ON FLAT STONES IN THE MIDDLE AISLE

Here refteth the Body of JOHN A WOOD,
Phyfician, who departed this Life
the 4th Day of Feb Anno Domini, 1704,
and in the 9 th Year of his Age

Here refteth the Body of JOHN HILL, Gent
who died the 9th Day of June, 1676,
ætatis fuæ 34

Here refteth the Body of ELIZABETH,
Relict of JOHN HILL, Gent
who died the 14th Day of Auguft, 1737,
ætatis fuæ 86

To the Memory of ELIANOR,
the fecond Wife of EDWARD HILL, Gent
who died June 6, 1669

EDWARD HILL, Gent
died May 1, 1695, in the 80th Year of his Age

ON A FLAT STONE, BETWEEN THE MIDDLE AND
NORTH AISLES

In Memory of Mrs ELIZABETH FORTUNE,
Relict of Mr WILLIAM FORTUNE, of
North Nibley, who died Dec 3, 1754, aged 84

As alfo of Mrs MARY PHILLIMORE,
Daughter of the faid Mrs. ELIZABETH FORTUNE,
and Relict of Mr JOHN PHILLIMORE, of Upthiop,
who died Nov 10, 1769, aged 77

ON A MARBLE MONUMENT IN THE NORTH AISLE

Arms, Argent, a Crofs between four Rofes Gules,
for TROTMAN.

In Memory of
EDWARD TROTMAN, of the Steps in this
Parish, Gent and MARGARET his Wife
He was buried May 10, 1638, in the Church Yard,
near this Aifle, and covered with a Tomb-ftone,
and fhe was buried in this Aifle the 22d Day of
October, 1663.

Alfo in Memory of NICHOLAS TROTMAN, Gent
(Son of the aforefaid EDWARD TROTMAN) and ANN
his Wife, whofe Remains were in this Aifle depofited

His January 22, 1706.
Hers July 2, 1705.

Alfo in Memory of CHARLES, EDWARD, ESTHER,
ANN, and ELEANOR TROTMAN, immediate
Defcendants from the faid NICHOLAS and ANN

The Remains of

CHARLES,		March 16, 1681.
EDWARD,		April 6, 1720
ESTHER,	were in this	Dec 14, 1662
ANN,	Aifle interred,	Dec 8, 1702
ELEANOR,		Dec 24, 1728

MARGARET deceafed Feb. 8, 1746

ROBERT TROTMAN, Gent deceafed
October 20, 1759, aged 73 Years

ON A SMALL TABLET IN THE NORTH AISLE

Near this Place lieth the Body
of JOHN, the Son of RICHARD and SARAH OSBOR
who departed this Life Jan 2, 1714,
aged 9 Months

ON FLAT STONES.

Here reft the Body of
NICHOLAS TROTMAN, of this Parish, Gent.
who departed this Life the 20th Day of
January, Anno Dom 1706

ANN his Wife died
June 30, Anno Dom 1705

ANN, Daughter of NICHOLAS TROTMAN, Gent.
died the 3d Day of December, 1702

ROBERT TROTMAN, Gent
died Oct 20, 1759, aged 73

IN THE CHURCH YARD

On Tablets against the Church

In Memory of Mr Stephen Workman,
late of this Parish, Clothier, who was
near this Place interred, the 4th of November 1737,
ætat 70

Also three of his Children by
Elizabeth his Wife died Infants

Elizabeth his Wife, and Relict
of William Baine, died the
20th of March, 1770, aged 57 Years

In Memory of John Carpenter
and Hannah his Wife
She died December 26, 1733, æt 62
He May 24, 1741, æt 67

Also of Daniel Shirmur and Mary
his Wife, Daughter of the said John
and Hannah Carpenter He died
July 22, 1743, æt 49, and
she June 2, 1767, æt 68

Likewise three of their Children, who died,
Elizabeth, November 30, . , æt 22,
Mary, Dec 18, 1746, æt 26,
and John, January 26, 1754, æt 26.

Near this Place are deposited
the Body of William Fowler,
of this Parish, Gent who departed
this Life July 13, 1740, aged 36 Years

And also Elizabeth his Wife
Daughter of John and Mary Phillimore,
who departed this Life Jan 27, 1770,
in the 64th Year of her Age

In Memory of Nathaniel,
Son of Thomas Hickes, of this Parish, Clothier

And also of Elizabeth his Wife, whose Remains
were underneath deposited in one Grave
His April 26, } MDCCXXVIII
Hers May 12, }

Near this Place lieth the Body of
Mr Joseph Twemlow, of Durfley,
Minister of the Gospel, who departed
this Life the 22d of August, 1740, aged 67

Mrs. Mary Twemlow, Relict of
the above Mr Joseph Twemlow,
died March 24, 1759, aged 89

ON TOMBS

Daniel Phillimore,
of Upthrop Clothier,
died July 25, 1726,
in the 52d Year of his Age

Elizabeth his Wife
died May 6, 1737, aged 70

Eleanor, Wife of
John Phillimore, of
this Parish, Clothier,
died June 13, 1691

Josiah Phillimore
was buried Dec 25, 1730,
aged 62

Elizabeth his Wife
was buried May 3, 1738,
aged 63

John Phillimore, senior,
of this Parish, Clothier
died July 21, 1738, aged 73

John Phillimore,
of Upthrop in this Parish, Clothier,
died April 17, 1753, aged 57

Mary his Wife,
Daughter of Mr Stephen Jenner,
of Slimbridge, by Mary his Wife,
died June 8, 1736, aged 39

Samuel their Son
died May 10, 1752, aged 16

M John Phillimore,
of Draycots Mill,
died, unmarried, Dec 5, 1741,
aged 45

William Turner
died June 16, 1777 aged 74

Sarah, Wife of William Cowley,
of Hurst Farm in the Parish of
Slimbridge, died May 26, 1781,
aged 27

Two of their Sons died Infants

Robert Long,
of Durfley, Baker,
died June 10, 1764, aged 48

Robert his Son
died March 26, 1773, aged 16

Thomas Gunn, Clothier
died Sept 29, 1731, aged 59

Ann, Relict of Thomas Gunn,
died April 16, 1738, aged 84

Ann, Wife of Joseph Long,
died July 9, 1748, aged 54

James Partridge
died Feb 21, 1751, aged 64

Ann his Wife
died Nov 10, 1768, aged 80

John their Son
died Feb 11, 1742, aged 19

Mary, Daughter of
Samuel and Elizabeth Phillimore,
died Sept 21, 1751, aged 14

Mary, the Wife of John Foard,
Baker, of Eastington in this
County, died Oct 29, 1773,
aged 44

John Foard, of Eastington
Baker, died Sept 23, 1780, aged 57

Hannah their Daughter
died August 22, 1777, aged 3 Years.

Thomas Tindall,
Baker, died March 30, 1761
aged 67

Sarah his Wife
died August 3, 1749, aged 54

Benedict Perratt
died April 11, 1711, aged 74

Rebeckah his Wife
died July 12, 1711, aged 74

William their Son
died Dec 5, 1685

Peter Perratt
died Jan 12, 1706, aged 84

THOMAS HUGHES
died May 30, 1765, aged 88

MARY his Wife
died August 28, 1747, aged 69

ROBERT HUGHES, Cloth-drawer,
and ANN HUGHES, Son and
Daughter of the above THOMAS
and MARY HUGHES.

ROBERT died April 20, 1760, aged 52
ANN, Feb 1, 1781, aged 7,
GEORGE, another Son, died an Infant

ELIZABETH, Wife of
TIMOTHY COLLENS,
of Oldbury upon Severn in
the Parish of Thornbury,
died Oct 14, 1709.

SARAH MORSE
died May 23, 1767, aged 69

WILLIAM, Son of JOHN MORSE,
died Oct 20, 1711.

ELIZABETH, the Wife of
JOHN MORSE, Gent
died March 10, 1749, aged 77

JOSEPH PACKER
died August 19, 1703, aged 65

JOSEPH his Son
died April 22, 1723, aged 24

JOHN PACKER
died June 24, 1731, aged 58

CHRISTIAN his Wife
died May 18, 1727, aged 43

JOHN PACKER, junior,
died Sept 13, 1765, aged 54

Also SARAH, the Wife
of JOHN PACKER, senior,
died Dec 1 1759, aged 84 Years.

Mr EDWARD TROTMAN, the elder,
late of Eastwood, Sonn of
Mr RICHARD TROTMAN,
of Poole Court in Worcestershire, by
CATHARINE his Wife,
Daughter of EDWARD TYNDALE,
Esquire He was born the of
October, 1545, and died the 9th
of June, 1637

ANNE, the Wife of EDWARD TROTMAN,
Daughter of RICHARD WATS, of
Stroud, by MARY his Wife,
Daughter of JOHN HALL, of
Woodchester Court
She was born the 28th of April, 1557,
married the 20th of Jan 1575,
and of her good Life made
a godly End the 4th of Nov 1635

EDITH, Wife of JOHN SELMAN,
died Sept 3, 1614

EDWARD TROTMAN, the younger,
Son of NICHOLAS TROTMAN and
CISLY his Wife, of Breadston,
died May 9, 1638, aged 72.

THOMAS HICKES, Clothier,
died April 22, 1747

DANIEL TROTMAN
died July 25, 1769, aged 39

RACHEL, the Wife of THOMAS CAM,
died April 14, 1759, aged 36

THOMAS, Son of THOMAS
and RACHEL CAM, died the
20th of April, 1773, in the
22d Year of his Age

JOHN DAVIS,
of Ashmead, Gent
died Sept 16, 1757, aged 73

Also two of his Sons
by ELIZABETH his Wife

THOMAS died August 31, 1748,
aged 21

JOHN died Dec 1, 1750,
aged 26

ELIZABETH, the Wife of
JOHN DAVIS, of Ashmead, Gent
died Sept 7, 1769,
in the 80th Year of her Age

———— WOODWARD
was buried here

SARAH his Wife
died Oct 6, 1704

MARY their Daughter
died Jan 19, 1739

SARAH their Daughter
Wife of JOHN ROACH,
died Nov 23, 1746

JOSIAH Son of JOSIAH and
SARAH ROACH,
was buried here

JOHN WOODWARD, Clothier,
died October 11, 1704.

THOMAS POPE,
Son of THOMAS and
DOROTHY POPE, late
of this Parish, Clothier,
was interred Feb 14, 1718 19

DANIEL FOWLER, Clothier,
was interred Feb 7, 1747,
aged 78

DANIEL FOWLER, junior,
was interred Sept 18, 1740,
aged 33

BARBARA his Wife
was interred Dec 28, 1741,
aged 71

ELIZABETH FOWLER,
only Daughter of
DANIEL FOWLER,
of this Parish, Gent
died Feb 6 1735,
in the 21st Year of her Age

DANIEL HICKES,
of this Parish, Son of
DANIEL HICKES,
of London, Merchant
His Remains was here
deposited May 12,
1715

RICHARD HICKES, Clothier,
Son of THOMAS HICKES,
was interred here
May 22 1711,
aged 64

WILLIAM HICKES, Clothier,
Son of THOMAS HICKES,
was interred here
Nov 19, 1707,
aged 58

ON HEAD STONES.

	Died	Aged
Thomas Phillimore -	25 July, 1757	48
Ann his Wife -	22 July, 1758	64
Hannah their Daughter -	10 Dec 1734	—
William Hill -	5 June, 1756	56
Lydia his Wife -	30 June, 1756	53
Sarah, Daughter of William and Hannah Davis -	18 Mar 1781	27
Sarah, Wife of William Harding, and Daughter of Mr. John King, of Woodchester -	14 Apr. 1757	44
Samuel Harding -	27 Feb 1768	68
Esther his Wife -	20 Aug 1738	—
William Dainty -	4 Nov 1777	43
Thomas Butcher -	28 Nov 1758	50
Ann his Wife, Daughter of Stephen Hankes -	7 Feb 1740	40
Olive their Daughter, Wife of Benjamin Millard, of Dursley -	27 Feb 1783	44
James Trull -	10 Sept. 1722	38
Grace his Wife -	27 June, 1759	—
Isaac Bendall -	12 Sept. 1769	74
Joanna his Wife -	22 Dec 1757	72
Hannah, Wife of Daniel Bendall, of this Parish, senior -	1 Jan 1787	61
William Hitchings -	1 July, 1774	40
John Summers, of this Parish, Schoolmaster -	24 May, 1765	57
Olive his Wife -	24 May, 1751	44
Hester Grimig, Daughter of John and Mary Warlick -	14 July, 1763	23
John Parslow -	19 May, 1768	57
Catherine his Wife -	2 Mar 1777	78
Susanna Rider -	2 June, 1769	64
Hannah, Wife of Edward Rider	22 May, 1784	53
John Bendall -	20 Sept 1763	40
Rachel, Wife of William Champion	3 Oct 1763	54
Daniel Minett -	27 May, 1767	60
Mary, Wife of Jonathan Cutts	2 July, 1710	—
Jonathan Cutts -	0 Nov 1728	52
Hannah, Wife of Jonathan Cutts	22 June, 1763	74
Samuel Cutts -	28 June, 1778	55
Daniel Foord -	19 May, 1755	62
Mary his Wife -	18 Oct 1756	66
Daniel Tyndale -	30 Dec. 1753	61
Margaret, Wife of Daniel Tyndale	25 Feb. 1732	34
Jane, Wife of Robert Seaborn	25 Jan. 1763	62
John Millard -	12 Apr 1737	81
Hester his Wife -	11 Mar. 1739	84
William their Son -	22 Apr 1767	78
Elizabeth, Wife of Joseph Millard	30 July, 1777	33
John Millard -	11 Feb. 1779	63
Samuel his Son -	24 July, 1767	22
Daniel Millard -	22 Apr. 1780	74
Richard Parker -	24 Aug. 1762	47
Daniel Trotman -	11 Aug. 1773	50
Jane Hersfield -	19 July, 1769	45
Richard Harper -	25 Aug 1726	59
Hannah his Wife -	2 May 1755	84
John their Son -	31 Aug 1726	27
Peter their Son -	26 Sept 1733	22
Eleanor their Daughter -	25 Dec. 17—	31
William Cam, of this Parish, Chandler -	21 June, 1783	69
Charles Cordy -	9 Aug 1724	78
Bridget his Wife -	14 Sept. 1790	86
William their Son -	5 May, 1779	59
Ann, Wife of William Cordy	28 June, 1781	66
Mary their Daughter -	10 June, 1781	31
Thomas Stiff, junior -	8 July, 1757	26
Samuel Stiff -	19 May, 1758	22
Joseph Cornock -	22 Mar. 1770	75
Sarah his Wife -	6 Sept. 1774	77
Nathaniel Jenner -	20 Apr. 1743	43
Ann his Wife -	20 Apr. 1755	65
Susanna their Daughter -	5 Mar 1757	27
Mary, Wife of Nathaniel Jenner	30 Nov 1760	56
Beata Wife of Nathaniel Jenner	16 Feb. 1781	60
William Keen -	10 Aug. 1780	62
Mary, Wife of Thomas Greening	15 June, 1758	65
John Baglin, of Slimbridge	19 Jan 1722	36
John Bendall, of Slimbridge	10 Dec. 1764	65
Elizabeth his Wife -	18 Apr 1764	68
Elizabeth, Wife of John Baglin	28 Aug. 1724	70
John Harding -	22 Aug 1746	50

CAMPDEN.

LVIII. CAMPDEN,
OR
CHIPPING CAMPDEN,

IS a fmall Market Town, included with its Parifh in the Hundred of *Kiftefgate*, twenty Miles diftant from *Tewkefbury* on the Eaft, ten from *Stow* Northwards, and from GLOUCESTER twenty-eight, in the fame Direction inclining to the Laft

The Soil is various, and the Portions of Arable, Pafture, and Sheep Downs, nearly equal Each of thefe is confiderable, the Parifh having a Circumference of fifteen Miles, or more

The Town is fituate in a fertile Valley, furrounded with cultivated Hills, and extends the greater Part of a Mile in Length, of one Street only, proportionably broad, and in general commodioufly built Of the Antiquity of its Eftablifhment, it is recorded, that in the Year 689, the Kings of the *Saxon* Heptarchy held here a folemn Convention to confult about a Treaty with the *Brittons* † But the Æra of its moft flourifhing State, was the 14th Century, when it became a moft crowded Mart for Wool, and the Refidence of the moft opulent Merchants, who exported it to *Flanders*, then the Seat of the Manufacture of Cloth, for the general Supply of *Europe* By thefe, many capacious Dwelling Houfes were erected, of which we may judge by one only, now remaining It is ftated, in the Preamble of the Charter granted by King JAMES in 1605, that *Campden* was an ancient Vill, and originally incorporated ‡ The Corporation of the new Borough is required to confift of two Bailiffs, and twelve capital Burgeffes or Affiftants, twelve Inferiors, from whom the Bailiffs are to be chofen, and a Steward learned in the Law In their Court of Record, held every fourth Friday in the Year, Actions of Debt, Trefpafs, &c not exceeding the Sum of 6*l* 13*s* 4*d* arifing within the Borough and its Liberties, are decided Four Fairs are kept annually on *Afh Wednefday*, and the Feftivals of *St Andrew*, *St George*, and *St James*, with a weekly Market on Wednefday The Emoluments of two of thefe are appendant to the Manor, the former Privileges of which are fecured by a fpecific Refervation in the prefent Charter The public

---

* From ceapan, to buy It is to be remembered that entire *Saxon* Words remained long in common Ufe in our Language And in other Etymology in Queftion *Chepynge* is ufed as a Market Place in WICKLIFFE's Bible, Matt x 16 and in CHAUCER for Market Town Knight's Tale, l 2002 " The *Chepynge* brenning withe the blake Smoke " that is, " the Town on fire " WARTON'S *K llington*, p 21, Note
† CAMDEN'S *Britannia*, edit GIBSON, vol I p 281
‡ Sir R ATKYNS, p 313, where it is copied at large

By Him

Buildings, the Court and Market Houfes ftand in the middle of the Street   The firft is probably as an-
cient as any in the Town, the other was built by Sr Baptist Hickes in 1624, at the Expence of 90ʳ
From various Caufes the magifteral Power is at prefent much declined, the Corporation defective both in
Number and Police, and the Merchandize and Manufactures of early Days totally loft.

The Living is a Vicarage, the Chief of its own Deanery, and of the Impropriation, the earlieft Proprietors were the Abbey of Chefter, afterwards confirmed to the Chapter of the new See by Henry VIII
1542   It is now a Part of the Manor and its Eftates   Edward Lord Noel annexed the Great
Tythes of Hinfryth, co Dorfet, to this Vicarage in the Reign of Charles I

Upon an eafy Eminence above the Town, ftands the Church, which is dedicated to St James   It is
a Structure perfectly fymmetrical, confifting of a fpacious Nave, two Aifles, at the Laft End of which are
two Chapels, formerly Chantries, that of the South is appropriated as a Dormitory to the noble Families of Hickis and Noel   The Tower, which with its Pinnacles is 120 Feet high, is light to the
greateft Degree and has a Chaftenefs in its Ornaments peculiar to the moft refined Gothic Style, of which
the whole exhibits a fingular Specimen   To the Munificence of the Merchants abovementioned, it is
reafonably conjectured, that this beautiful Edifice owes its Erection   feveral of whom are here interred
with brafs Figures and Memorials   The Effect on the Infide is deftroyed by Pews irregular and mif-
placed   None of the painted Glafs is preferved, with which moft of the Windows were ornamented, but
in an old Cheft, is fhewn a Cope of crimfon Velvet, femée of ducal Coronets and Eftoiles, and on the

* In a Letter from a celebrated Antiquary, dated at Oxford, Nov 22, 17--, are the following Remarks
    That the Church is not of an elder Date, the Style of the Building plainly decribes   and that it was built in the Time I
have fixed the following Obfervations make it very probable   The old Stone Coffin lately difcovered by taking down fome
Windows in the Chancel   I am men A.h in the Wall, in which was found Pieces of Apparel, not quite perifhed, Sir
" .our   ce of all which I fend you an Account and you informed me they were of the Age of K Edw III   And indeed
" it in upon viewing the Arch obliged me to fix on a particular Circumftance that it was intact when the Church was built
" The old Log, or old Seats made of Plank of Oak curved were undoubtedly of the Age I have fixed, as the were thai
" Coat of Arms carved on the Embofsment of Wool Merchants who lived in this Place at the very Time I mention   but
" it was born to make good for my Purpofe is a beautiful and well preferved Marble for William Gr vill of
" Campire, who died 1401   On the Grave   and his Wife Joan, Daughter of Sr John Thorneborough   he reprefented
" in Full Length, in two Niches, of various, neatly dained   Now the Embellifhments of thefe brafs Portico   and his
" beautiful basso infaid in the Stone correfponds exactly with the interlaced Work over the Door, at the Weft End, and the
" Bell   Work, and the Pinnacles of the Tower   I not this a plain Indication that Grevill either built or contributed
" the Erection of the Tower   Such Circumftances in fimilar Cafes have been frequently allowed to determine fuch doubtful
" Benefactions   And on this I am inclined to think the Town a Benefactor   towards the Building the North Aifle from
" Independence on the fecond Door appears for the seal of himfelf, his Wife, and Parliaments "

Border the Portraits of Saints curiously embroidered. Four Chantries were founded in this Church, which had competent Endowments *

Few Manors have had a fuller Series of Possessors than what are enumerated of *Campden* by Sir Robert Atkyns. Of these, the principal were the great Barons De Someri, Clare, De Audli, and Stafford. Queen Elizabeth found it vested in the Crown, and granted it to the Family of Smith, of whom it was purchased by the famous Sir Baptist Hickes, created Viscount Campden 4 Car. I. 1628, with Remainder to the noble Family of Noel, who have been the subsequent Lords. Early in the last Century, upon his Purchase of the Manor †, Sir Baptist built a most sumptuous Mansion, with Accompanyments of correspondent Magnificence, which was destroyed by Fire, during the Civil Wars, by the Command of Baptist Lord Noel, that it might not be seized by the Parliamentary Forces and used as Barracks ‡. This disinterested Conduct proved in the Sequel unnecessary, as the Enemy approached not nearer than *Warwick*. From an accurate Plan and Elevation still extant, it appears to have been an Edifice in the boldest Style of that Day §. It consisted of four Fronts, the principal toward the Garden, upon the grand Terras, at each Angle was a literal Projection of some Feet with spacious Bow Windows, in the Centre a Portico with a Series of Columns of the five Orders (as in the Schools at *Oxford*), and an open Corridore. The Parapet was finished, with Pediments of a capricious Taste, and the Chimneys were twisted Pillars, with Corinthian Capitals. A very capacious Dome issued from the Roof, which was regularly illuminated for the Direction of Travellers during the Night. This immense Building was enriched with Frizes and Entablatures most profusely sculptured, it is reported to have been erected at the Expence of 29000l. and to have occupied, with its Offices, a Site of eight Acres. Part of a Wall, discoloured by Fire, and the two Banquetting Houses which terminated the Terras, are the Remains most worthy Notice, of this magnificent Pile. Beside these is the grand Entrance adjoining the Church yard; composed of two low Pavilions, connected by a Skreen, with Pediments of a Form which defies Description. Without Doubt, the munificent Founder employed the most eminent Architect that Age afforded, but whom it is not known. A sameness of Style pervades the Hospital, and other public buildings, which he gave for the Benefit of the Inhabitants of *Campden*, all of which are distinguished by his armorial Ensigns.

There are four Hamlets in this Parish. 1. *The Borough*. 2. *Broad Campden*, a populous Village, with a dilapidated Chapel. 3. *Brunton* or *Berrington*, Tradition informs us, that a great Battle was fought here between the *Mercians* and *West Saxons*, and that it received its Name from the Barrows or Tumuli in which the Slain were deposited. The Lands were given for the Support of *St. Catherine's* Chantry at *Campden*. 4. *Westington* and *Combe*.

These Hamlets, excepting the *Borough*, have a Right of Commonage in common Fields of some Hundred Acres extent. The only Estates of Consequence, exclusive of the Manor, are held by Sir John Rushout, Bart. and the Family of Cotterell.

In the Reign of King James I. 1610, Robert Dover, a Man of heroic Spirit instituted Olympic Games, and distributed Prizes ‖. The Scene of these manly Diversions has been since called *Dover's Hill*, to which an incredible Concourse of every Rank annually resorted on the Thursday in Whitsun Week, but the Novelty has long ceased, as did the Rewards with the Institutor, and the Festival is now but rarely frequented.

Dr. Robert Harris ** was born at *Campden* 1578, and became President of *Trinity College, Oxford*, during the Interregnum. His Character is given by Wood, with his usual Acrimony.

* "1 *Stratford's*, or *St. Catherine's* said Chantry, whereof Part 11 Error was held Incumbent, and had a Pension "Issue of 6l. 2 *St. Catherine* second Chantry, of which Christopher Laxeir was the last Incumbent and received a "Pension of 5l. 3 A Chantry called Our Service, dedicated to the *Holy Trinity*, whereof Thomas Mortimer, the last In- "cumbent, had a Pension of 6l." *Valor*.

† Idem. Abus circa triumph. battery, tradi aureas tour." *Vide Mon. Exon.*

‡ In the Inscription on Baptist Lord Noel's Monument he is called 'The eminent Loyalty to King Charles, "notwithstanding, his inestimable Losses in his Estate, spoil and sack of several of his Houses, beside his burning of that "noble Pile of Campden." *Corpus Dil. Com. Glouc. in Vol. III. p. 86.*

§ In the Possession of Lord Gainsborough, the Heir Male, descended from Sir ——

‖ The best Poets of the Age contributed a commendatory Verse in honour of this Celebrity, which were collected in one Volume, entitled, 'Annalia Dubrensia, Lond. 1636, 4to. Of this Book and the Institution, We express the following Account. "These Corpus I Game were solemnly continued to our own Time of an Year for thirty Years together, by one R "nert Dover, in Account of *Brimble Head* or *Brimbud*, Son of John Dover of ——— who from full of Antiquity, and of a generous free, and public Spirit dedicated unto Recreation King James I the Inhabitants of *Gloucestershire*, where that Games should be revived. In some Parts of IJ. the Name of the County did not want "to that King a Person of a most generous Spirit did, to encourage Dover, give him Suits of the old King's old Cloaths, "with a Hat and Feather, and ruff, purposely to grace him and make public the Solemnity. Upon which ceremony there "Person, well mounted and accoutered, and so directed his motion of these Games, frequented by the Nobility and Gentry for a "out whose came by 3 Miles to them, and till the finally Rebellion rose many by the Preciseness, which gave a Stop to "their Proceedings, and spoiled all that was precious and precious elsewhere. The Verses of the Poets, called Annalia "Dubrensia, were composed by several Wits, some of which were then of the best of the Nation." *Ath. Ox. vol. II. p. 91.*
"The late ingenious Mr. Somerville, Author of the Chace, wrote a mock heroic Poem, called 'Hobbinol', or Rural "Games. The Scene of Action is placed at *Dover's Hill*, and the Poem opens with a Invocation to the Sovereign Muse.

** Vide Ath. Ox. vol. II. p. 246, and Last vol. II. p. 71, where a Story is related and his his Descent. Dr. R "Harris was a profound Loyalist, which his Epitaph on which notwithstanding he is styled 'Prince's commended hand. "But the Restoration ensuing, Baxter attacked the Praise and condoled to be contested in the Latin Copy of Wood's History, "and Antiquities of the University of *Oxford*. William Durham, M. A. published the Life of Dr. Harris in 1662, with "Other Anecdotes of Dr. Harris and in the Works ——— Life of Barnet 1st, p. 246, and in the Life of A. Wood, vol. II. "p. 330, col. 1, 2."

B E N E F A C T I O N S.

JOHN VEREBY, Efq about the Year 1486, gave Lands, the annual Produce of which now is 80*l*. for the Maintenance of a free Grammar School, and Poor of *Campden*

Other Lands, to the Value of 40*l* per Annum, given for various Charities, the Time and Perfon unknown

JAMES THYNNE, Efq 1707, devifed Lands to the Amount of 80*l* per Annum for a Blue Coat School, and other Charities

GEORGE TOWNSEND, Efq 1682, left by Will, Lands to the yearly Value of 6*l* 12*s*, 4*l* of which to be applied to the Support of a Children's School, the Remainder to be diftributed in Bread to the Poor

GOOPER and AUSTIN, 1628, gave by Will, 3*l* 15*s* per Annum, iffuing out of Leafehold Lands

Sir BAPTIST HICKES, 1629, gave for an Alms-houfe for fix poor Men and fix poor Women, Lands to the Value of 140*l* per Annum, vefted in the the Earl of GAINSBOROUGH, who appoints to the Charity

Mr BLACKLEY, 1670, gave 2*l* 12*s* per Annum, to be diftributed in Bread amongft the Poor

Mr FREEMAN, 1642, demifed by Will, 2*l* 12*s* annually to be given in Bread to the Poor

ENDYMION CANNING left by Will, 1683, 20*cl* one for the Ufe of the Poor, the other for Town Stock

EDWARD JOHNSONS, 1724, by Will, gave 50*l* the Intereft of which to be applied in Cloathing the Poor

Sir BAPTIST HICKS demifed by Will (fuppofed in the Prerogative Court), for the Ufe of the Poor of the Hamlet of *Berrington*, 500*l*

The Rev HENRY HICKS, 1708, gave by Will, 70*l* for buying Books, and Cloathing the Poor

Mr SAVAGE, 1656, gave four 5*l* to be fet out without Intereft for the Ufe of poor Tradefmen of *Chipping Campden* for four Years, they finding proper Security for the fame.

Mrs TAINTON gave 2*l* 12*s* per Annum, for Bread to the Poor.

Lord NOEL gave alfo the like Sum for the fame Purpofe

INCUMBENTS	PATRONS	INCUMBENTS	PATRONS
1472 Nath Hatford,	———————.	1709 Thomas Manfell, M A	Baptift Earl of Gainf-borough
—— John Jennings,		—— Nathaniel Wefton,	Baptift Earl of Gainf-borough
1616 Robert Lilly*,	King James		
1636 William Bartholomew †,	Edward Lord Noel		
1660 Henry Hickes ‡,	Baptift Vifc Campden	1743 William Wefton, M A	The fame

PRESENT LORD OF THE MANOR,
The Right Honourable HENRY Earl of GAINSBOROUGH.

At the Vifitations of the Heralds, in 1682 and 1683, the Perfons fummoned from this Parifh and its Hamlets, were,

From *Chipping Campden*,

John Eden,
Samuel Horfeman, } Burgeffes.
Robert Taylor,

From *Combe*,

Thomas Godwyn, Gent

From *Broad Campden*,

—— Wills, Gent

From *Berrington*;

John Godwyn, Gent
—— Hickes, Gent.

At the Election in 1776, Sixty Freeholders polled from this Borough and its Hamlets.

The Regifter commences with a Baptifm in 1610 In the fubfequent Entries the Names of the Sponfors are recited, till the Year 1645 During the Rebellion it was kept with unufual Accuracy

---

* An Uncle of the celebrated WILLIAM LILLY the Aftrologer   LILLY's Life, p 2

† In the early Part of his Life he was fufpected of being addicted to the Doctrines of the Prefbyterians, which he afterwards renounced and publifhed a Sermon on the Reftoration, entitled, "The ftrong Man erected by a ftronger than He, fhewing how he ftrong Man Satan is caft out of the Palace of the Heart, and the Lord's Chrift poffeffed thereof, with fome Application to "the prefent Judgment of the late Ufurper, Satan's Confederate, out of the Royal Palace, and the Lord's Chrift King CHARLES "the fecond poffeffed thereof" London, 1660, dedicated to JULIANA Vifcountefs CAMPDEN In this Publication, as well as the Title of it, the Author, though he violently combats the Principles, retains the Phrafeology of the Fanatics See WALKER's Sufferings, &c

‡ He was born at *Shipfton upon Stour*, co *Vigorn*, 1632, the moft florid Preacher of his Time He publifhed a Sermon on the Death of JULIANA Vifcountefs CAMPDEN in 1680, printed at *Oxford* 1681; thirty Copies only As a Specimen of his Panegyric on her Virtues, "That her Doors were without any tall Porters, her Tables fpred twice a Day, fo furnifhed that they were "to others, what her Confcience was to herfelf, a continual Feaft God, that provided her Plenty, provided her Guefts "and what fhe gave to Hunger, fhe gave to Heaven Sermon, p 19

ANNUAL

ANNUAL ACCOUNT OF MARRIAGES, BIRTHS, AND BURIALS, IN THIS PARISH

AD	Mar	Bir	Bur	AD	Mar	Bir	Bur	AD	Mar	Bir	Bur	AD	Mar	Bir	Bur
1781	21	55	41	1786	14	39	57	1791				1796			
1782	9	37	45	1787	10	51	30	1792				1797			
1783	11	45	46	1788				1793				1798			
1784	11	44	38	1789				1794				1799			
1785	12	39	40	1790				1795				1800			

INSCRIPTIONS IN THE CHURCH.

IN THE CHANCEL.

ON THE NORTH SIDE IS A MONUMENT, CANOPIED, WITH THE FIGURE OF A MAN IN FREE-STONE, LYING IN ARMOUR, WITH TWO WIVES AND FIFTEEN CHILDREN KNEELING, *viz.* SEVEN SONS AND EIGHT DAUGHTERS, AND THE FOLLOWING ARMS AND INSCRIPTION.

1ſt, Sable, a Fels, between three Saltires Or, for SMITH, Creſt, two Serpents entwined proper, 2d, SMITH,—impaling, Gules, on a Chevron Argent, three Bar Gradels of the Field, for THROCKMORTON.

Hic jacet ſepultus vir vere Chriſtianus THOMAS SMITH, Armiger, quondam Manerii de Campden Dominus, a pueritia ſua aulicus, qui ſuo tempore fuit e conſiliis Regis ac in Wallia, biſque vicecomes Comitatus Gloceſtriæ, ac juſtitiarius pacis quidem comitatûs ubique a conſentaneus, qui habuit duas uxores, primam ELIZABETHAM, Filiam & Heredem Juſtaine Fitz-Audin, Argenti,

2. KATHARINAM, filiam Georii THROCKMORTON, Militis, ...

filius & filiabus

qui obiit die   Anno Dom 1533

Arms, a Croſs engrailed between four Pellets, each charged with a Pheon, for FLETCHER.

Prope hunc lapidem quicquid
Mortale fuit THOMÆ FLETCHER,
Villæ hujuſce, Gen eſt depoſitum,
Qui obiit die Martii 15,
Anno Dei Salvatoris noſtri 1746,
ætatis ſuæ 67
Vir fuit S. S Religionis Chriſti
Doctrinarum non ignarus, fideique
Orthodoxæ, quamvis indignus,
Aſſertor ſincerus

Near this Monument lyeth the
Body of JOHN MARTIN, Mercer,
who departed this Life September 22, 1757,
aged 57 Years

Alſo the Body of ELIZABETH his Wife,
who died March 18, 1761,
aged 68 Years

ON MONUMENTS IN THE NORTH AISLE

In Memoria GULIELMI ATKINS, Lapidarii,
cujus reliquiæ juxta hunc locum
ſunt depoſitæ, qui in ſpem beatæ
Reſurrectionis, animam expiravit decimo octavo die
Junii, Anno { Ætatis 62
{ Salutis 1729

MARY, Wife of WILLIAM ATKINS,
departed this Life
October 29, 1747, aged 73 Years

Magiſter Robertus Titius,
Son . . . diſtinct ace eject . . .
Vir ſummi genus, gravis, veteranus
Quem ſpem genui Glaceſtrenſis, natus
Aliam Mare Coventrigiæ, tandem demum
Patto concludentigi exet beantei ter . . .
Undeq̃ ſique ſum ſixit factis, ſith quod
Cæleſti dolores recriſhont futurum in vita
fecerunt vi in ludorum ter impedito atii
XX dies ſoluo) prorſus illictiſſimum
Qui tandem xantii 5 XX annorum huc locui tiorbus,
Tribus optima ſuperi hominum funeri ſe ſentens
Superſtitem ſua dulciſſimis quis perimſilſet
filiis cælo te puntus eſt ;
Natura conceſſit X al die Octobris, 1636,
& ætatis ſuæ 54
Legatum hæc perpetui amoris monumentum
Amantiſſima pariter ac meſtiſſima conjux
HONORA LILLY luges poſuit

In Memory of
HENRY MINORS,
who departed this Life
Feb 1, 1729, aged 25

I ege, Spectator ! & Luge !
Hoc enim fub lapide in pulverem
percolatur vir fummo ingenio & pietate,
GULIELMUS BARTHOLLMEW, A M
& Co'l Trin Cantabr
Primitias annorum & minifterii EDVARDO
Vicecomiti CAMPDEN, Clariffimo Heroi
fœliciter dicavit, cui in Ædibus Brokianis
e facris fuit
Mox in hujus Ecclefiæ vicarii fuccenturiatus
viginti-quatuor per annos, negotio animarum
incubuit, omnium cum amore, laude, admiratione
Orator eximius, Malleus Sectariorum, Orthodoxæ
Religionis Ecclefiæ Anglicanæ partium Carolinarum,
peffimis licet temporibus, intrepidus affertor.
Moriens
Todem in tumulo quo SUSANNAM, filiolam olim
condiderat mortalitatis fuæ exuvias voluit recondi

Obiit illa Sept 3, Anno Dom. 1642, ætatis fuæ 3
Obiit ille Oct 11, Anno Dom 1660, ætatis fuæ 56

ON MONUMENTS IN THE SOUTH AISLE

Arms, a Talbot paffant, in chief two Annulets
for TAYLOR

To the Memory of
Mr CHARLES TAYLOR,
late Citizen and Skinner of London,
who died March 18, 1718-19,
in the 59th Year of his Age,
whofe Remains are depofited
near this Place
This Monument was
erected by ANNE his Wife,
as a Teftimony of her fincere
Love and Regard

SUSANNA, Wife of WILLIAM TAYLOR,
died July 30, 1785, aged 53

IN VISCOUNT CAMPDEN'S CHAPEL

TWO BANNERS, WITH THE FOLLOWING ARMS

On the 1ft Quarterly, 1ft and 4th, Ruby, a
Fefs wavy, between three Fleurs de lis Topaz, for
HICKES, 2d and 3d, Gules, a Chevron Ermine,
between three organ Refts Or, for

On the 2d 1ft, Topaz, fretty Ruby a Canton
Ermine for NOEL, 2d, Gules, a Lion rampant,
femee of Crofs Crofflets fitchy Or, for HOPTON, of

Hopton Caftle, 3d, Azure, three Boars Heads
couped Or, between nine Crofs Crofflets fitchy Argent, for HEVIN, 4th, Argent, two Pipes in Pile,
between nine Crofs Crofflets fitchy Gules, for
DOWNTON, 5th, Gules, three Bars Or, for ST
OWEN; 6th, Argent, a Lion rampant Azure,
within a Bordure engrailed Sable, for TYRELL (all
Shropfhire Families)

A VERY STATELY ALTAR TOMB, ON A RAISED
SLAB OF BLACK MARBLE, THE EFFIGIES RECUMBENT OF BAPTIST LORD VISCOUNT CAMPDEN AND
HIS LADY IN THEIR ROBES OF STATE AND CORONETS THE CANOPY IS SUPPORTED BY TWELVE
PILLARS OF EGYPTIAN MARBLE, AND FINISHED
WITH PEDIMENTS AND TABLETS †.

Arms, HICKES, quarterly, as on the fecond
Banner, Creft, a Buck's Head erafed, Supporters,
two Bulls Argent, armed Or, Motto, " Nondum
" Metam " 2d, HICKES,—impaling, Gules, a
Fefs, between eight Billets Or, for MAY.

ON THE FIRST TABLET

To the Memory of her dear deceafed Hufband
BAPTIST Lord HICKES Vifcount CAMPDEN, born
of a worthy Family in the City of London, who,
by the Bleffing of God on his ingenious Endeavours, arofe to an ample Eftate, and to the aforefaid
Degree of Honour, and out of thofe Bleffings difpofed to charitable Ufes, in his Life-time, a large
Portion, to the Value of 10,000 Pounds, who lived
religioufly, virtuoufly, and generoufly, to the Age
of 78 Years, and died Oct 18, 1629.

ELIZABETH Vifcounteffe CAMPDEN,
his dear Confort, borne of the Family
of the MAYS, lived his Wife in all Peace
and Contentment the Space of 45 Years,
leaving iffue by her faid Lord and Hufband
two Daughters, JULIANA, married to EDWARD
Lord NOEL, now Vifcount CAMPDEN, and
MARIA, married to Sir CHARLES MORRISON, Knt
and Baronet, hath pioufly and carefully
caufed this Monument to be erected as a
Teftimony of their nuptial Love, where
both their Bodies may reft together,
in Expectation of a joyful Refurrection

ON THE SECOND TABLET

Ad Terram CAMPDENICAM
Campdena fælix, poffides largas opes;
corpus patroni, quæ recondis, optimi,
dominum potentem prædus, & qui addidit
iftis honorum flofculos terris novos
Domino fepulchrum præbens, ille ædibus
decoravit amplis, hortulis nitidis, ignum
tuum, nec ædem negligi eft paffus Dei,
fed indigentes forte fuftinuit pia
vivo voluptas, mortuo fac fis quies
Hic et pudicam quæ focia vitæ fuit
tenes matronam, corpus hoc geminum fove
refufcitandum, & contegas almo finu

A LARGE MURAL MONUMENT * REPRESENTING A CABINET, THE FOLDING DOORS OF WHICH ARE OPENED, AND BEAR FULL INSCRIPTIONS IN A NICHE WITHIN ARE THE STATUES, IN PARIAN MARBLE, OF LORD NOEL AND LADY JULIANA, AS LARGE AS LIFE, STANDING IN THEIR WINDING SHEETS, BETWEEN ARE THE

Arms, NOEL impaling, HICKS On one Side, as on the first Banner, on the other, as on the second, on the Pediment the NOEL Arms and Supporters

This Monument
is erected to preserve the Memory and Pourtrait of the Right Honourable
SIR EDWARD NOEL Viscount CAMPDEN,
Baron NOEL of Ridlington, and Hicks of Ilmington, a Lord of heroic high Parts and Presence He was a Knight Baneret in the Wars of Ireland, being young, and then created Baronet, Anno 1611. He was afterwards made Baron of Ridlington, the other Titles came unto him by right of Dame JULIANA his Wife, who stands collateral to him in this Monument, a Lady of extraordinary great Endowments both of Virtue and Fortune This goodly Lord died at Oxford, whither he went to serve and assist his Souverain Prince CHARLES the First, and so was exalted to the Kingdom of Glory,
8 Martii, 1642

The Lady JULIANA,
eldest Daughter and Coheire of that Mirror of his Time
SIR BAPTIST HICKS Viscount CAMPDEN.
She was married to that noble Lord who is here engraven by her, by whom she had BAPTIST Lord Viscount CAMPDEN, now living (who is blessed with a numerous and gallant Issue)

HENRY, her second Son, died a Prisoner for his Loyalty to his Prince

Her eldest Daughter, ELIZABETH, was married to JOHN Viscount CHADWORTH

MARY, her second Daughter, to the very noble Knight SIR ERASMUS DE LA FONTAINE

PENELOPE, her youngest Daughter, died a Mayd

This excellent Lady, for the pious and unparalleled Affections she retained to the Memory of her deceased Lord, caused this stately Monument to be erected in her Life time, in September Anno Dom 1664

On a Scroll,
" JOHN MARSHALL Sculp Lond fecit "

ON A MURAL MONUMENT † THE BUST OF LADY PENELOPE NOEL IN A VANDYKE DRESS

Arms, on a Lozenge quarterly, as on the second Banner

To the most exquisite Model of Nature's best Workmanship, the richest Magazine of all divine and moral Virtues,
PENELOPE NOEL
Having added to the Nobilitye of her Birth a bright Shine of true Noblenesse, the exemplare sweetnes of her Conversation, her Contempt of earthly Vanities, and her zealous Affections towards Heaven, after 22 Years Devotions, commended her Virgin Sowle into the Hands of its true Bridegroom Jesus CHRIST May 17, Ann 1633 Over whose pretious Dust here reserved, her sad Parents EDWARD Lord NOEL Viscount CAMPDEN and the Lady JULIAN his Wife dropped theyr Tears, and erected this Marble to the deare Memorie of thevr invaluable Losse

Superata tellus Sidera Donat

ON A MURAL MARBLE MONUMENT THE BUST OF LADY ANNE NOEL IN THE DRESS OF THE TIMES

Arms, Topaz, fretty Ruby a Canton Ermine, for NOEL, —impaling, Pearl, on a Fess Sapphire three Lozenges Topaz, for FIELDING

To the sacred Memory of Lady ANNE NOEL, second Daughter of WILLIAM Earl of DENBIGH, who was married to BAPTIST NOEL, eldest Sonne of EDWARD Lord NOEL, and HICKES Viscount CAMPEDEN Shee changed this Life for a better the 24th of March, in the Yeare of Salvation 1636 Shee had Issue by her said Husband, three Sonnes, the eldest, CHARLES, also the second, CHARLES, and the third EDWARD, which three Sonnes deceased before eyther of them accomplished 2 Yeares,

---

ON LARGE BLUE FLAT STONES, WITH BRASS FIGURES

Arms, Sable, on a Cross with a Bordure engrailed Or, five Pellets, a Mullet for Difference, for GREVEL

Hic jacet Willielmus Grevel, de Campeden, quondam Civis London e flos Mercatorum Lanae totius Angliae, qui obiit primo die Mensis Octobris, Anno Domini Milesimo CCCCI

Hic jacet Mariana, Uxor praedicti Willielmi, quae obiit decimo die Mensis Septembris, Anno Dom. Milesimo CCCXLI quorum animabus propicietur Deus Amen

Hic jacet Willielmus Welley, quondam Mercator istius Ville, qui obiit LW die Aprilis, Anno Dom MCCCCL e Alicia Uxor ejus, quorum animabus propicietur Deus Amen

---

Hic jacet Johannes Letherard, quondam
Mercator istius Ville,

Anno Dom ƧCCCCLXIIJ & Johanna Uxo-
cjus, &c.

Hic jacet Johannes Barker quondam Burgensis
hujus ... or ... XIX die Mensis Aprilis, Anno
Dom ƧCCCCLXII cujus anime propicietur
Deus ... et Domino confeso

Upon this Stone is the Figure of a Cross, at
the Bottom is inscribed, Memento, and on
each Side, Jesu Merci   Mary Help

A full male & seal, with the Figures of
a Man, his three Wives, and thirteen Children, the following Inscription

Orate pro Animabus Wilhelmi Gibbys, Alicie,
Margarete, & Mariane confort ... sue, qu quidam
Wilhelmus, obiit XIII die Mensis Ja-uarii,
Anno Domini Millesimo CCCCLXXIIII
Quorum animabus propicietur Deus, Amen

On small Fillets of Brass

Jhu Merci   Lady help

ON OTHER FLAT STONES

Arms, FLETCHER, as before,—impaling, Argent, three Bats Wings erect two and one Sable,
on a Chief Gules, a Lion passant of the Field, for
Batson

Here lyeth the Body of ELIZABETH,
the Wife of Nicholas Fletcher, of this
Parish, who departed this Life the
19th Day of September, 1709

Beneath this Stone, at their joint Request,
are deposited the Remains of Thomas Fletcher,
Gent and Dorothy his Wife
She, the last survivor, died July 22, 1769,
aged 87 Years

Next to the Bones of her Ancestors are
deposited the Remains of Elizabeth Fletcher,
whose Patience, though various Tryal,
astonished many of her Acquaintance,
but with Cheerfulness she resigned herself
into the Hands of her Creator 1774,
aged 58 Years

In Obedience of the Call of his Heavenly
Father, after 30 Years spent in this Place
with Skill in an Apothecary, on the
13th Day of Sep. 1777 departed
John Fletcher, Gent   This Tribute was paid
to his Memory by his afflicted Widow
E F

Edward Johnston, Gent
departed this Life December 6, 1774,
aged 55 Years

Jane, late Wife of Edward Johnston, Gent
died Feb 26, 1733, aged 23 Years

Here lyeth the Body of
Elisha Yarnold, Gent
who departed this Life
January 20, 1710, aged 75
Also his Sister
Mrs Margaret Yarnold, Spinster,
who died May 29, 1720,
aged 79 Years

Mrs Susanna Cooper,
the Wife of Mr Robert Cooper,
of Pebworth, senior, eldest Daughter
of Mr John Gooding, of Comb
She departed this Life
6th of Feb 1710, in the 84th Year of her Age

Here lyeth the Body of
Mr William Hankes, interred
July 29, Anno 16 ,

Margaret, the Wife of
Robert Hilron, of Weddington,
died June 10, Anno Dom 165-

Nathan Izod, of Westington, Gent
departed this Life July 2-, 1716, in the
60th Year of his Age

Anne his Wife
died Sept 13 Anno Dom 175-
in the 64th Year of her Age

Sarah, Wife of William Izod,
of Weddington, died March 5, 1722, aged 19

William Izod, Gent
died June 27, 175-, in the 57th Year of his Age

Nicholas Field, Surgeon,
died Jan 15, 1786

Mary, the Wife of John Humphries,
died April 16, 1716, aged 63

George Combes
died Aug 1, 1726, aged 62

Elizabeth Wife of Edward Woodward,
died July 23, 1768, aged 76

Claudius Gascoyne
died Jan 15, 1714, aged 5-

Martha, the Wife of Claudius Gascoyne,
died March 17, 1730, aged 7-

Hazlewood Wells
and Lydia his Wife
She departed this Life April 18, 1731, aged 66

Thomas Taylor
died Nov 13, 1744, aged 88

Jane his Daughter
died Aug 21, 1770, aged 62

Anne his Daughter
died Dec 8, 1782, aged 71

Arms, HICKES as before

H S E
Dominus HENRICUS HICKES,
Collegii S S Trinitatis apud Oxonienses, alumnus,
gradu Magiftri in Artibus ibidem infignitis,
Ecclefiæ Parochialis { de Stretton Rector,
{ de Campden Vicarii,
Utriufque per Annos tantum non quinquaginta
Paftor fidelis,
Ecclefiæ Anglicanæ veræ Apoftolicæ
Filius Orthodoxus,
Et contra omnes Adverfarios
Tam pfeudo Catholicos quam nuperos novatores
Intrepidus Vindex
Hic etiam reconditæ funt Reliquiæ
MARIÆ,
Domini GULIELMI BARTHOLOMEW,
Hujus Ecclefiæ olim Vicarii,
Et explorate in Regem fidelitatis Viri
Filiæ,
Et prædicti HENRICI Conjugis
Diem fupre { Illa Dec 23, A D 1701, æt 62.
mum obiit { Ille Jan 11, 1708, æt 78

CHARLES TAYLOR
died Aug 18, 1742, aged 45

THOMAS PAIN
died Aug 8, 1749, aged 62

ANDREW SIMKINS, Son of JOHN SIMKINS,
died Feb 6, 1726, aged 77

ELIZABETH ROUND,
Daughter of JOHN SIMKINS,
died June 13, 1734, aged 82

ELIZABETH, Wife of RICHARD SMITH,
died June 29, Anno Dom 1733

ROBERT SMITH
died June 25, 1742, in the 48th Year of his Age
JANE, the Wife of ROBERT SMITH,
died March 19, 1772

THOMAS PHIPPS
departed this Life July 3, 1722, aged 60
MARY his Wife
died Aug 14, 1754, aged 76.

MATTHEW PHIPPS
died Oct 4, 1705, aged 50
ANN his Wife
died Aug 28, 1774, aged 56

HENRY PEART,
of Blandon in the County of Oxford,
died June 2, 1671

JOHN SCOTT, Gent
died Aug 28, 1779, aged 67.
ELIZABETH his Wife
died Sept 21, 1780, aged 57

Mr WILLIAM YATE, fenior,
died May 13, 1680, aged 60.
MILLICENT his Wife
died May 1, 1660, aged 30
Also Mr BENJAMIN GOLD
died April 7, 1746, aged 74

Mr WILLIAM YATE, junior,
died November 3, 1689, aged 41
Also Mr CHARLES YATE,
the 4th Son of Mr WILLIAM YATE,
died March 28, 1690, aged 29

MILLICENT, the Daughter of
Mr WILLIAM YATE and MILLICENT his Wife,
died July 24, 1685, aged 29
Also ELIZABETH LANE,
Grand daughter of Mr WILLIAM YATE,
died March 29, 1711, aged 34

ANN WALKER, Wife of SAMUEL WALKER,
lies here interred by
her firft Hufband CHARLES TAYLOR
She died March 31, 1757, aged 54.

IN THE PORCH

RICHARD DARBY
died Dec 20, 1776, aged 78
MARY his Wife
died Feb. 18, 1783

IN THE CHURCH YARD

ON TABLETS AGAINST THE CHURCH

ANDREW STUARD
died May 15, 1716, aged 73

SAMUEL BALLARD
died July 8, 1710, aged 46
ELIZABETH his Wife
died July 10, 1744, aged 73

Depofited beneath this
the Body of MARY PALMER,
who died Nov 8, 1780, aged 84

EDWARD WHITEHEAD
died Nov 23, 1781, aged 60

ON TOMBS

THOMAS FLETCHER, Gent who, after more than 30 Years spent in a Profession he dignified, died in the 62d Year of his Age truly lamented, as by the Poor, to whom he was a private Benefactor, and in Distress, Counsellor and Friend, obiit Dec 4, 1766.

THOMAS WOODWARD
died Aug 4, 1746, aged 76

RICHARD, Son of EDWARD and ELIZABETH WOODWARD, died June 2, 1755, aged 3

EDWARD WOODWARD
died March 4, 1766, aged 69

DAVID IRELAND
died March 27, 1762, in his 92d Year

SARAH his Wife
died April 3, 1760 aged 84

WILLIAM FREEMAN
died May 12, 1754, aged 88

MARGERY his Wife
died Jan. 12, 1757, aged 61

ANN JAMES
died Nov 20, 1700 aged 81

JOHN ROBERTS
died Dec 5, 1761, aged 52

SARAH his Wife
died 12 Feb 1750, aged 60

MARY their Daughter
died May 1759 aged 8

RICHARD TOMES
died Oct 1, 1783, aged 40

ON HEADSTONES

	Died	Aged		Died	Aged
William Saunders	14 Apr 1719	64	Samuel Smith	27 Apr 1720	66
Mary his Wife	4 Mar, 1729	83	Sarah his Wife	10 Nov 173	6
Mary, Wife of Job Barret	28 Oct 1750	61	Thomas Muteley	20 Mar 1715	66
Samuel Cecil	24 Oct 1759	73	Ann his Wife	24 Sept 1705	60
James Izod, of Broad Campden	27 Aug 1762	68	John Hancock, of Broad Campden	21 Aug 1729	39
Elizabeth his Wife	10 Jan, 1740	39	Ann his Wife	18 Feb 1741	31
Ann, Wife of John Allen, Grocer	24 June, 1764	36	Nicholas Taylor	9 Apr 1733	42
M. John Allen	8 Mar 1773	52	Mary Wife of Robert Pickerill, Daughter of Francis and Elizabeth Taylor	1 May 1734	39
John Thompson	1 May, 1762	18			
Sarah his Wife	7 Jun 1763	65	William Bradwey, of Paxford	14 Mar 1751	
Susanna, Wife of Richard Smith	6 June, 1764	2	Robert Hands	2 Feb 1755	
Catharine, Wife of Thomas Russell	16 June, 1764	71	Robert Hands	26 Jun 1758	
Thomas Russell	2 Nov 1776	71	John Tomes	29 June 1740	4
George Jelfs	2 Jan 1742	52	Mary, Daughter of John and Mary Tomes	6 July 1755	
Sarah his Wife	4 June, 1772	52			
Elizabeth his Wife	3 Nov 1790	76	Thomas Wilton	10 Sep 1705	
Thomas Holtham	10 June, 1735	63	Edward Wilton	7 Jun 1752	12
Mary his Wife	9 May, 1749	77	Mary Wife of Benjamin Ansel	18 1743	5
William Perrin	25 Aug 1762	62	Elizabeth, Wife of Benjamin Ansel	21 Oct 1751	
Ralph Dutton	27 Feb 1754	73	Benjamin Ansel	2 Nov 1761	73
Mary his Wife	30 May, 1751	76	Ann White	3 Jul 1760	
Henry Darby	21 Jan 1768	73	William White of Broad Campden	5 Nov 1755	
Catherine his Wife	26 Dec 1749	65	Edward Williams	1 Jun 1753	71
Sarah, Wife of John Darby	18 Oct 1761	42	Mary Abbit	26 Apr 1755	51
John Darby, Son of Henry and Catharine Darby	3 Sept 1770	59	Nicholas Ballard	11 Jun 1756	
John, Son of Thomas Keen	17 Sept 1755	18	Hannah Wife of William Ordway		
John Chandler	17 Jan 1757	58	William Ordway		
Mary, Wife of Lewis Harrison	15 Oct 1762	61	Mary, Wife of William Randell		
John Loe	27 Nov 1757	78	Elisha their Son		
Jonathan, Son of Jonathan and Catharine Hulls	27 Aug 1783	21	Mrs Elizabeth Wife Relict of Robert Wife, Gent of Aston Magna		
John Truby	13 Feb 1782	71	Richard Keyte		
Eleazer Tomes	11 Feb 1746	76	Alice his Wife		
Elizabeth his Wife	18 Apr 1752	85	Samuel their Son	2 Mar 1780	37
Thomas their Son	9 Nov 1733	21	Elizabeth their Daughter Wife of William Dyer		
Mary their Daughter	8 Apr 1742	2	Elizabeth Wife of Robert Fletcher		
Richard Hemmin	2 Apr 1742	39	Robert Fletcher	7 July 1765	71
Stephen Davis, of Broad Campden	25 Nov 1725	25	Mr Thomas Davis Writing Master of the Free School in this Town	18 May 1777	58
Rebekah his Wife	8 May 1750	82	John Allen	6 Sep 1785	49
Susan Kind	30 July 1751	39	Richard Aden	6 May 1750	64
Anthony Stanley	7 Oct 1729	66	Elizabeth his Wife	4 June 1750	65
Elizabeth his Wife	1 Nov 1741	61	John Atkins	3 Mar 1755	55
Frances their Daughter	20 Oct 1741	42	Susanna his Wife	30 Oct 1705	54
Ann, Wife of Thomas Hulton	15 Mar 1759	0	John Howse		50
Mary, Wife of Thomas Atkins	19 Sept 1773	25	Mary his Wife	5 Sept 1750	76
Ann Wife of John Atkins	21 Apr 1760	33	Elizabeth their Daughter	21 July 1763	9
John Plevden	Oct 1757	5	William Howse	27 Aug 1784	17
Elizabeth his Wife	7 Mar 1724	75	Ann Reed Daughter of Anthony Ansell	23 May 1763	18
Martha their	20 Sept 1766	41	Ann, Wife of Anthony Ansell	9 Mar 1777	
John, Son of Thomas and Susanna Mevns	27 Feb 1771	27	Ann, Wife of Thomas Holtham	31 Apr 1753	10
Thomas Mevn	13 June 1776	75	Mary Wife of Holtham Gent	4 May 1765	45
Martha his Wife	7 Apr 1751	60	Henrietta Wife of William Johnston, Surgeon		

IT is probable that the *Saxon* Name of this Place was Leophn-eye, or *Churn* Water, on which Riv let it is situate. In Domesday Book, where it occurs *Cernei*, it was usual to soften the old *Saxon* Appellations, and to adapt them to the *Norman* Pronunciation, from which Cause, they are not always sufficiently discriminated, and various Errors have arisen

Cerney North is so called from the Point of Distance it bears from *Cirencester*, and in Distinction to another Village, which lies in the opposite Direction It is one of the Parishes, by which the Hundred of *Rapsgate* is formed, in the *Cotefwold* Division of the County, distant four Miles from *Cirencester*, seven South westerly from *North Leach*, and from GLOUCESTER fourteen on the West The Extent of it is nearly six Miles, the Breadth less than three, of a light Soil chiefly tilled, with many Meadows on the River's Side The Village, on every Approach to it, forms a pleasing and highly cultivated Landscape, the Acclivities upon which it is built being easy and picturesque

The Benefice is rectorial GILBERT DE CLARE, Earl of GLOUCESTER and HERTFORD, presented to it in 1315 Some Years since, it was vested in the Families of GUISE, or COXE, but the Right being disputable, it was sold to the Master and Fellows of *University College*, *Oxford*, by mutual Agreement of the Parties The Rectory-house is commodious and well situated, and the Glebe Lands unusually extensive

The Church belongs to the Deanery of *Cirencester*, and is dedicated to *All Saints* It has a Nave, a Transept, and a slated Tower, not inelegantly finished All the Windows of the Transept were once decorated with painted Glass There are still several mutilated Figures of Saints and Martyrs, but one only perfect Representation of the Crucifixion, with the two MARYS, and a Man praying, with a Label, " **Te precor, Domine, falbum me fac**," but the Inscriptions to pray for the Souls of WILLIAM WHYT-CHURCHE and JOHN BYCOTE, mentioned by ATKYNS, are destroyed, and the Effigy of the Priest (supposed to be of THOMAS FEREBY) was removed on the Re-building of the Chancel about a Century ago The Pulpit is of Stone, with beautiful Gothic carving, and in the Church-yard are the Shaft and Base of an ancient Cross

Of the Manor (after the Defection of GISLEBERT, who was settled in it by the CONQUEROR), the DE CLARES were the earliest Possessors, to them succeeded the STAFFORDS, who held it for several Centuries It then passed to various Proprietors till it was vested by Purchase in the noble Family of BATHURST

A handsome House and Estate belonged for many Generations to the Family of RICH, by whom they were sold to THOMAS TYNDALE, Esq * Another Estate is held by the Family of KIMBER

Two Hamlets are annexed to this Parish 1 *Woodmancote*, which is a part of the Estate of the Family of GUISE, 2 *Calmsden*, which in the Reign of King RICHARD II belonged to Sir SIMON BURLEY, knight Banneret, and on his Attainder was escheated to the Crown, but restored to his Heirs in 1405, 4 HEN IV † It forms a joint Manor with *Woodmancote*, independent of the great Manor, and was claimed as such by the late Sir WILLIAM GUISE, Bart

On the Downs, which are commonable, annual Horse Races were long established, as respectable as any provincial Assembly of that Kind The imperfect Vestiges of a Roman *Specula*, or Outpost, with Circumvallations, are here to be traced, and a Lachrymatory of a blue vitrified Substance was formerly discovered.

No Benefactions to the Poor

INCUMBENTS	PATRONS	INCUMBENTS.	PATRONS
1315 ——————,	Gilbert De Clare	1684 John Coxe,	King Charles II
—— Thomas Fereby ‡,	Humphrey Ld Stafford	From Sir ROBERT ATKYNS	
1575 Philip Pritchard,	Richard Brydges, Esq	1736 Thomas Chamberlayne	
		Coxe, M A	Sir John Guise, Bart.
—— Samuel Rich, D D	——————	17 John Coulton, B D	University Coll Oxf
1683 John Coxe,	Richard Pool, Esq	1780 John Alleyne, B D	The same

* Of whose Family, some Account is given under "CHARLTON."
† See Hollinshed's Chron vol II p 464
‡ He died in 1519, and was buried in the Chancel ATKYNS

PRESENT LORD OF THE MANOR,

The Right Honourable HENRY Earl BATHURST

The Persons summoned from this Place by the Heralds, in 1682 and 1683, were

Thomas Rich Esq
Samuel Rich, D D

At the Election in 1776 Ten Freeholders polled from this Parish

The most ancient Register bears Date 1567

ANNUAL ACCOUNT OF MARRIAGES, BIRTHS, AND BURIALS, IN THIS PARISH

AD	Mar	Bir	Bur	AD	Mar	Bir	Bur	AD	Mar	Bir	Bur	AD	Mar	Bir	Bur
'81	2	25	5	1786	6	17	6	1791				1796			
'82	4	22	11	1787	2	14	7	1792				1797			
1783	3	12	9	1788				1793				1798			
1784	2	15	11	1789				1794				1799			
1785	2	17	9	1790				1795				1800			

INSCRIPTIONS IN THE CHURCH.

ON MONUMENTS IN THE SOUTH AISLE

Arms, Quarterly, 1st and 4th, per Pale Sable and Gules, a Cross Botonè fitchy, between four Fleurs de lis Or, for RICH, 2d and 3d, Azure, a Cheveron Or, between three Martletts Argent, for BOURCHIER

Here lyeth the Body of THOMAS RICH, Esq one of the Masters of the High Court of Chancery, who married ANNE, one of the Daughters and Coheirs of THOMAS BOURCHIERE, of Barnesley, Esq by whom he had ten Sonnes, THO WILL EDW SAM JO ROB EUSTACE, HEN ARTH and CHA and five Daughters, BRIDGET, who married JO HOW, Bart MARY, who married GILES DOWLE, Gent and ANNE, and ANN, who died young, who departed this Life Oct 27, 1647

Arms, RICH is above —impaling, Azure, on a Bend, between three Leopard's faces Or, three Martlett Gules, for NOTT

In Memory of THOMAS RICH, Gent Obiit March 1704 5

Also SUSANNA his Wife, Daughter of EDWARD NOTT, of Braidon in the County of Wilts, Esq obiit Oct 1700, who had Issue five Sons and four Daughters, THOMAS, SEWSTER, EDWARD, JOHN, and ROBERT,

ELIZABETH, ANNA MARIA, LUCY, and SUSANNA Erected by ROBERT RICH their youngest Son

ON A BRASS PLATE

SUSANNA PERRY died Oct 20, aged 14 Years, 1089, and here was buried

ON AN OVAL MARBLE FLAT STONE:

E T obiit 28 Jun. at 17 Mense, 1775.

ON A MONUMENT IN THE NORTH AISLE

Near this Place lie the Bodies of RICHARD PAINTER, senior, and JOYCE his Wife, Daughter of PHILIP and PRUDENCE STOCKWELL He died Aug 14, 1749, aged 75 Years

She died Dec 1, 1757, aged 85 Years

Erected by RICHARD PAINTER their youngest Son

ON

ON FLAT STONES IN THE NAVE

Here was interred the Body of
ROBERT BROAD,
who died Oct 7, 1753,
aged 66 Years

Also ELIZABETH his Wife
died Feb , 1756, aged 65

Also of three of his Children
ROBERT died Sept 16, 1753,
aged 32

MARY died Nov 20, 1743,
aged 21

SARAH died Nov 6, 1753,
aged 25

Here rests the earthly Part
of THOMAS TYCOTT of Woodmancott,
who departed this Life
Sept 6, 171 , aged 60

ON A FLAT STONE IN THE CHANCEL

Here resteth the Body of
Mr WILLIAM CHERINGTON,
late of Calmelden in the Parish of
North Cerney, who departed
this Life May 7, 1721,
ætat suæ 80

IN THE CHURCH YARD, ON TOMBS

WILLIAM CHERINGTON
died April 19, 1696

ELEANOR his Wife
died Feb 19, 1656

GEORGE CHERINGTON
died March 3, 1739, aged 54

SARAH CHERINGTON, senior,
died Oct 28, 1760, aged 76

RICHARD JORDAN
died Oct 17, 1669

MARGERY his Wife
died Jan 17, 1698

MARY, Wife of DANIEL STOCKWELL,
buried Feb 21, 1730, aged 60

DANIEL STOCKWELL
died Nov 7, 1740, aged 60

PRUDENCE, Daughter of
JOHN and HESTER STOCKWELL,
and Wife of JOHN GARDEN, of
Minchinhampton in this County,
died March 30, 1777, aged 40

THOMAS TYCOTT
died Sept 17, 1750, aged 75

HENRY BALDWIN, senior,
died Aug 25, 1727, aged 79

ELEANOR his Wife
died March 14, 1738, aged 79

HENRY their Son
died Sept 8, 1756, aged 79.

BEATA his Wife
died Nov 11, 1773, aged 82

GEORGE their Son
died Oct 18, 1736, aged 13

ANN, Wife of JOHN BLAKE,
Daughter of HENRY and BEATA BALDWIN
died Dec 7, 1785, aged 56

RICHARD STEPHENS,
of Woodmancott in this Parish,
died Nov 2, 1718, aged 69

MARY, Wife of ROBERT STEPHENS
died in Childbed with two Babes,
April 18, 1782, aged 32

WILLIAM, Son of
RICHARD and ANNE STEPHENS,
died Jan 12, 1754, aged 5

O N

ON FLAT AND HEAD STONES.

	Died	Aged
William Eycott	16 July, 1748	38
Beata his Wife	20 May, 1776	62
Ann, Wife of John Haines	19 July, 1764	60
Margery, Wife of Robert Townsend	5 May, 1784	37
William, Son of William and Elizabeth Griffith	22 Jan 1774	35
William Painter	24 Nov 1742	62
Richard Eycott, of Woodmancott, Yeoman	6 Nov 1702	45
Bridget his Wife	12 Sept 1730	74
John Bryan, of Woodmancott, Yeoman	6 Apr 1766	56
Ann, Daughter of John and Elizabeth Bryan	21 Mar 1778	26
Thomas Bryan, of Woodmancott	28 June, 1783	42
Sarah, Wife of Joseph Eycott	11 Nov 1755	77
Joseph Eycott	20 Apr. 1735	63
Joseph his Son	9 Mar 1734	20
Mary, Wife of James Millar, Daughter of Thomas and Betty Stephens	7 Oct 1758	29
Robert Stephens, senior	9 Jan 1742	89
Mary, Wife of Robert Stephens	21 Mar. 1736	84
George Cherington	17 Apr 1780	38
Henry Guest	6 Dec 1734	70
Hannah his Wife	19 Mai 1708	29
Thomas Broad, of Woodmancott	18 Jan 1701	—
Hester his Wife	11 Aug 1708	—
Thomas Broad	14 Feb. 1761	77
Mary his Wife	29 June, 1764	85
Mary Hawkins, Widow	29 Mar 1728	65
Edward Fry	25 Dec 1759	61
William Eldridge	17 Apr. 1729	88
Judith Lovesy	3 Apr 1761	49
Giles Radway	18 Mar. 1760	57
Josias Corbet	15 Sept. 1727	75
Jane his Wife	5 May, 1727	76

LX. CERNEY SOUTH

IS situate on the River Cerney in its Course from a Concept's town the Thames at Cricklade, co. Wilts and is comprised in the Hundred of Crowthorne and Minty, four Miles from Cirencester, and from Gloucester twenty-one on the South-east.

Its Pasture Lands exceed the Arable by a very considerable Proportion, and the Produce of these is greatly improved by their being annually laid under Water, by an artificial Immersion, a Mode of Agriculture practised with singular Success in this Parish. Further from the River, the Soil is of a light Gravel. The Circumference is more than ten Miles, including 600 Acres of Common Fields.

The Living is a Vicarage, the Advowson of which was given to the Abbey of St Peter in Gloucester, by Walter, Sheriff of Gloucester, in the Reign of Henry I. It was appropriated to them in 1307, 1 Edw. II by Adam de Orliton, Bishop of Hereford, and confirmed to the Bishops of Gloucester, at the Dissolution, 33 Hen. VIII by the Charter of Erection of that See. The Family of Hiox have been the Lessees for several Generations. The early Norman Style pervades the whole Structure of the Church, which is in the Deanery of Cirencester, and dedicated to All-hallows. It contains a Nave, an Aisle on the North, with a low Tower and Spire. In the Chancel is a very curious Lavatory, with a Canopy of Gothic Foliage exquisitely carved for that rude Era.

The Effigies of a Man and his Wife remain in the Church-yard, they are said to be of William Cutts, a Benefactor to the Parish, a Deed relating to which Benefaction is extant, dated the year 1450, and the Head-dress of the Woman appears to be of that Century.

From Time immemorial three distinct Manors have been claimed and held in this Parish, the most valuable of which belonged to the Priory of Llanthony in 1287, the Possession of Matilda Empress By Richard, re-stated in the Charter of Confirmation by King John. At its Suppression it was granted to William Fitz-Williams, Lord of Southampton, and his Heirs. The Family of Wye afterwards possessed it, from whence it received the Name of Wye's Manor. The Ancestors of the present Proprietor John Jones, Esq. purchased it in 1677. Having been Parcel of a religious Foundation, it is consequently exempted from Tythe.

The Second, which is of the greatest Extent, was held for some Centuries by the great Barons Dr St Amand and their Heirs. Of Sir Nevil Pointz it was purchased by Sir Edward Kerns, it has been since called St Kerns' Manor, and is the joint Property of the Families of Jones and Wyatt in different Portions.

On the Dissolution of the Dean and Chapter of Bristol, the King endowed them with a third Manor, situate in this Parish. The former Lessees were the Family of Drew, they were succeeded by Thomas Best, Esq. who has built a handsome modern House, and since Effects annexed to the Manor.

Cerney Tyle, or Tile, is the only Hamlet in which remain many Freeholders of various Property.

The considerable Canal, by which the Junction of the Rivers Severn and Thames will be effected, is conducted through the whole of this Parish.

BENEFACTIONS

William Cutts gave by Deed June 2, 1450, Houses and Land for the Use and Relief of the Poor of the Parish of South Cerney, and for Repairs of the Church and also for the Repairs of the King's Highways within the said Parish, which have been always applied by the Trustees in such Proportions to each of the foresaid charitable Uses, as they in their Discretion have thought proper, the annual Produce is 1l. 6d.

* In Cerney is situated an ancient Approp....... Preface an Instance ..... The Style and Tenure of the Deed Foregoing were not always steady, but The Pope, the Ordinary's Opposition to such prevailing, and ...... to the Appropriation of these charitable Defence or rather more than the ... of Cler....
See Cerney ... Wilts ... Kerneton ... Net ...

The Church as those of the several Parishes commemorated by Leland. The Cerney the Duke of Norfolk, which are preserved ... History, as Herald, th...... cut of the ...... mon

John and Thomas Jones, by Deed, June 22, 1726 gave the Sum of ... annually, a Thing out of Land, towards apprenticing a Boy of the Parish of *South Cerney* ... by the Nomination of the Heirs o the said John Jones, subject to a Deduction of all ... every the Taxes, Assessments, and Rates as well parochial as parliamentary, charged or to be charged, on the said annual ... of the said Annuity to be paid if any Suit, Action, or Suit ... to recover ... Arrears, or ... Taxes to be disbursed ... only the P Chapmen of ... the ... of the P ... of P Jones.

William M ... by Will Jan 1, 17 ... the Sum of ... per annum, out ... Land to such as are Poor of the Parish of Sou ... Cerney ... as shall not be ... holy maintained at the Expence con ... old Poor, for relieving the Term of twenty Years ... to the Relief res ... ceive, to be laid out in Bread, and distributed to them ... on Cert'in Days ... by such Person or Persons ... to ... Will, from Time to Time being the said Term of twenty Years, been in Possession of, ... titled to, the Rents and Profits of his ... old Estate.

Thomas Bush, Esq. gave by Deed, March 1 1740, to ... Apprent ... ships of Boys on ever ... Easter Monday, the Sum of ... per annum to be paid to the Churchwardens or Overseers.

Incumbents	Patrons	Incumbents	Patrons
	Bishops of Glouces- ter	1702 Alex Stanhope, M.A. Edward Fow	J ... Sir Robert Atkins
1577 William Whitebrook,	Richard Cheyney,	1728 George Parrett	A John Whitcce
1583 Richard Harpe,	John B ... l m	1741 Francis Waldron Clear ... s ...
1586 Richard Clar ... ngton,	... Jones, Esq.	1758 Arthur Jones M A James Johnson
16... Thomas Sa ... ry, Dunc	John Patchett		

Present Proprietors of ... ors,

Of A ... ins Manor,	Of W ... 's Manor	Lessees of the C ... ...
John Jones, Esq.	John Jones, Esq.	The Heirs of Thomas Bush, Esq.
——— Weare, Gent		

It does not appear that any Paten was summoned from the ... of Henry the Third in 1682 and 1683

At the Election in 1776, thirty nine Freeholders polled at South Cerney including Eisey Myst

The Register commences with the Year 1584

ANNUAL ACCOUNT OF MARRIAGES, BIRTHS, AND BURIALS, IN THIS PARISH

AD	Mar	Bur	Bur	AD	Mar	Bur	Bur	AD	Mar	Bur	Bur	AD	Mar	Bur	Bur
1781	7	15	13	1786	7	20	18	1791				1796			
1782	15	12	14	1787	6	14	18	1792				1797			
1783	8	15	15	1788				1793				1798			
1784	4	15	10	1789				1794				1799			
1785	9	16	15	1790				1795				1800			

INSCRIPTIONS IN THE CHURCH

In ... Isaac Jenkins mo ... bath erected ... to ... the four ... of Gabriel Jenkins, qui mort ... buried in ... this ... no texto anno trans ... August ..., ... o Dom 1651

On a handsome Marble Monument, with a Pyramid ... Sarcophagus ... Genius holding a S ... ... on an Urn, on the Py ramid, a Bust within a Wreath of Oak

Arms Argent, a Horse ... rampant Sable, in Chief three Cross's ... Gules, for ... Bush — Impaling On three Bulls Heads ... Sable barbed Gules, for Butt

This Monument is erected to perpetuate the Me mory of Thomas Bush, Esq. late of Cirencester, and Mary his Wife

He died Sept 29, 1750 aged ... She Oct 5, 17... aged 58

... s ... ... a ... Compl ... of the Peace ... ... Wife ... ... Adm ... ... to ... ... the Qu ... three Qu ... ... Comm ... ... with ... ... of ... Cond ... ... Year of G ... ... Uniform ... ... D ... his Office ... ... to ... led ... ... to die ... ... be ...

On a ... Stone

Here lieth the Body of Mary Jones, the Wife of Richard Jones, and Daughter of Thomas R ... n ... n, of Cerney Wick, who departed this Life in the 73d Year of her Age, and was buried the ... th Day of Nov, Anno Dom 1687

IN THE CHURCH YARD, ON TOMBS

RICHARD, the sole Son of RICHARD MATTHEWS,
of this Parish (who married ELIZABETH MENDEN,
by whom he had Issue five Sons and ... Daughters),
died 11 Sept Anno Dom 1683, aged 1 57.

MARY, Wife of Farmer JOHN JONES,
died April 20, 1695, aged 5

JOHN MILES
was buried May 17, 1702, aged 19
JOANNA his Wife
was buried Dec 9, 1731 aged 80
THOMAS MILES
was buried Nov 8, 1718, aged 45.
MARY his Wife
was buried Feb 19, 1759, aged 63
MARGARET their Daughter,
buried Nov 25, 171 , 1 57
SARAH, Daughter of THOMAS and ANN MILES,
died Apr 24, 1760, aged 1
MARY MILES
died March 29, 1754, aged 4
SARAH MILES
died Nov 17, 1702, aged 52
THOMAS MILES
died June 6, 1757, aged 51
ANN, Wife of THOMAS MILES,
died Jan 2, 1762, aged 62
ELIZABETH, Wife of JOHN MILES,
died Aug 25, 1772, aged 46.
JOHN MILES
died Dec 26, 1782, aged 69

CRISTOPHER HINTON
died July 30, 1722, aged 60
MARY his Wife
died Oct 30, 1729, aged 62
THOMAS the Son
died Feb 16, 1720, aged 1 50
B IA Wife of THOMAS HINTON,
died July 7, 1740, aged 35
HENRY their Son
died June 1726
I MP D their Son
died July 172
MARY the Daughter
died May 1, 1731
THOMAS HINTON, late of Twerton Wiltshire,
died Jun 28, 1795, aged 37

MARY HITCHINS
died Jun 31, 1754, aged 70
SARAH HITCHINS
died Jun 25, 1760, aged 38

GRACE, Wife of ROWLAND TAYLOR,
died July 20, 1751, aged 30

THOMAS MOSS
died Dec 1753, aged 83
RACHEL his Wife
died Oct 2, 1751, aged 76
WILLIAM MOSS
died Feb 19, 1771, aged 75
JOAN his Wife
died Feb 24, 1765, aged 70
THOMAS their Son
died Apr 12, 1729, aged 6
JOHN STONE MOSS
died Oct 5, 1751, aged 21
RACHEL, Wife of HENRY ELDRIDGE,
died Feb 7, 17
JOHN, Son of HENRY ELDRIDGE,
buried March 5, 1751

HENRY COLE
died Jan 1756, aged 6
his Wife
died Jan 1779, aged 77
WILL M their Son
died June 1761, aged 59

THOMAS the Son of JOHN JONES, Yeoman,
died Aug 2, 1707 aged 5
ANN his Wife
died July 2, 1695, aged 60

JOHN, the Son of THOMAS JONES,
died June 24, 1662, aged 5
RICHARD Son of the forsaid JOHN JONES,
died Oct 30 1670 aged 58

ELIZABETH, Wife of JOHN RANDELL,
died April 2, 1768, aged 7
ELIZABETH their Daughter
died Sept 9, 1773, aged 3
WILLIAM, Son of JOHN and ANN RANDELL,
died April 15, 1746, aged 1
ANN, Wife of JOHN RANDELL
died Apr 17, 1765, aged

EDWARD WALL
died April 5, 1 aged 5
SARAH Wife of EDWARD WALL,
died Feb 9, 1 , aged 82
ELIZABETH, Wife of EDWARD WALL, junior,
Daughter of HENRY and AMY COOK,
died Jun 15, 1756, aged 6

WILLIAM HASKINS
died Sept 30, 1761, aged 2
WILLIAM HASKINS senior,
died Sept 17, 1753, aged 50
ANN, Daughter of WILLIAM and ANN HASKINS,
died May 5, 1705, aged 17
WILLIAM, Son of WILLIAM and MARY HASKINS,
died Dec 17, 1779, aged 21

O N   H E A D   S T O N E S

	Died	Aged
William Hinton	14 Mar 1737	36
Margaret, Wife of Thomas Hinton	13 July, 1727	70
Elizabeth, Wife of Thomas Rigby	20 Oct 1741	78
Henry Paren	1 Jan 1759	62
William Cook	19 Aug 1728	67
Thomas Portlock, of Wick in this Parish	2 May, 1747	67
John, Son of Thomas and Alice Portlock	28 Feb 1756	41
Mary, Wife of John Portlock	2 Mar 1766	58
Esther, Daughter of John and Mary Portlock	17 Feb 1758	19
William Harrison	20 Mar 1728	75
Richard Harrison	6 Jan 1743	78
Susanna, Wife of Richard Harrison, senior	8 Apr 1750	59
Henry Cook	3 Mar 1713	
William Haskins, senior	17 Sept 1743	80
Ann his Wife	6 Nov 1741	75
Ann their Daughter	28 May, 1705	7
Sarah, Wife of Matthew Johnson	20 Aug 1754	73
Sarah, Daughter of John and Grace Stephens	20 Sept 1753	27
Elizabeth, Wife of Thomas Jasper	9 July, 1746	58
Susanna, Wife of William Millard	23 Aug 1751	36
William Stephens	2 Mar 1752	75
Jane, Wife of William Stephens	25 Jan 1748	53
Anne, Wife of William Simmons	24 May, 1755	59
Anne, Wife of Humphry Jasper	—— 1683	——
Joseph Moulder	1 Apr 1756	80
Mary his Wife	20 Jun 1755	78
William Davis	9 May, 1753	77
Rachel his Wife	5 Oct 1749	67
William Davis	5 Oct 1749	63
James Davis	23 June, 1781	67
Mary Bramble	17 May, 1729	79
Eliza, Wife of George Bramble	10 July, 1709	45
Jane, Wife of Joseph Pearce	8 Feb 1755	59
James Morris, senior	31 July, 1724	65
Susanna his Wife	—— Dec 1742	70
Jane their Daughter	4 July, 1752	50
John Weeks, senior	27 Jan 1747	75
Elizabeth, Wife of William Stephens	22 Feb 1749	85
Mary, Wife of John Millard	28 Dec 1775	50
Sarah, Wife of William Cook	24 Mar 1776	79
William Ford	3 May, 1771	72
Dinah his Wife	26 May, 1767	70
Thomas Fitchew	24 June, 1780	69
William Ford	9 Nov 1779	71
Humphry Jasper	2 Feb 1757	52
Alice his Wife	8 Sept 1770	63
Thomas Mots	6 May, 1777	23
Elizabeth his Wife	23 July, 1776	28

IN Domesday Book *Cirvelde* This is comparatively a small Parish, in the upper Division of the Hundred of *Grumbald's Ash* (anciently *Bacheflaues*), five Miles distant from *Sodbury* Northwards, three on the South west from *Wotton-under Edge*, and twenty three in the same Direction from the City of GLOUCESTER.

The Soil is of Sand and Lime-stone, chiefly applied to Pasturage, with a small Portion of Arable. The Circumference of the Parish includes nearly six Miles, and is divided from *Kingswood* by a Rivulet which unites with the *Severn* near *Berkeley*.

The Benefice is a Rectory, endowed with annual Payment of 20*l* out of *Micklewood Chace* in Lieu of Tythes. The Advowson has been long vested in the Family of TYNDALE.* There is nothing peculiar or striking in the Structure of the Church, which is dedicated to St *James*, it consists of a Nave, a South Aisle, and a low Tower of ordinary Architecture at the West End. In the Windows are Fragments of painted Glass, but no Subject is perfect, excepting the Holyrood.

The Manor was possessed by the MASSEYS in the Reign of HENRY the Third, by Intermarriages, the Family of LE VEEL became alternately Proprietors. CATHARINE, Daughter of Sir JOHN CLIVEDEN, and Relict of Sir PETER LE VEELE, of *Charfield*, brought the Manor to the BERKELEYS, by her second Marriage with THOMAS Baron BERKELEY in the Reign of EDWARD the Third. About the Commencement of the last Century, the Family of HICKES were Lords, to whom it devolved by successive Purchases from the TRACYS, BAYNIONS, DUTTONS, and THROCKMORTONS of *Tortworth*. It is now vested in the Nephew and Heir of the last RICHARD HICKES, Esq and is claimed by Jurisdiction of the Court of the Honour of GLOUCESTER. Amongst the chief Proprietors of Estates are the Right Honourable Lord DUCIE, and the Families of CULLIMORE and PULLEINE.

Tafarn Bach is a small Inn in this Parish where Courts are held. This ancient British Name has excited the Notice of several Antiquaries, from the rare Use of entire Appellations, either Saxon or British, though most are derived from those Languages by expert Etymologists.

No Benefactions to the Poor.

INCUMBENTS.	PATRONS	INCUMBENTS	PATRONS
1574 Francis Heydon,	Edward Heydon	1710 Edward Pilsworth, B.A	John Biddle, Clerk
1577 Evans Powell,	Queen Elizabeth	1724 John Tyndale, M A	N Hickes, Esq
1610 Richard Powell,	Sir W Throckmorton	1747 Josiah Bennett, B. A.	Will Tyndale, Gent.
——— Daniel Pilsworth,		1749 William Tyndale, B A	Bp of GLOUCESTER
1685 Charles Pilsworth,	Daniel Pilsworth	1763 Richard Tyndale, M A	Will Tyndale, Gent.
1700 Nicholas Hickes, B D	Edward Pilsworth		
From Sir ROBERT ATKYNS			

PRESENT LORD OF THE MANOR,

JOSEPH WALTON, ESQ.

The Persons summoned from this Parish by the Heralds in 1682 and 1683, were

Nicholas Hickes, Esq
Samuel Witchell, Gent
Daniel Pilsworth, Gent

---

* The Family of TYNDALE were settled originally in *Northumberland* in the Reign of RICHARD II and as we collect from BROMFIELD's History of *Norfolk*, they had ample Possessions in that County. Some of them having taken an active Part in the *Lancastrian* Cause, migrated to *Stinchcombe* in this County, and, as it appears from the Register of *North Nibly*, bore for Concealment the Name of HUTCHINS or HITCHINS, but resumed their own in the Reign of HEN. VII.

" WILLIAM TYNDALE, who was deservedly styled the English Apostle, was the first who translated the New Testament out of the original Greek. This Translation was printed in 1526 without the Translator's Name. Three or four Years after, he published a Translation of the Pentateuch from the original Hebrew, and intended to have gone through the whole Bible. The first Impression of the Testament that gave Umbrage to the Popish Clergy was bought up at Antwerp in 1527 by Order of TONSTALL then Bishop of LONDON, and soon after publickly burnt in *Cheapside*. The Sale of this Impression enabled the Translator to print a larger and more accurate Edition. He was burnt for a Heretic at *Filford* near *Bruflels*, 1536.

At *Magdalen Hall Oxford*, of which he was a Member, there is an ancient Portrait of him, which is engraved in HOLLAND's Heroologia. GRANGER's Biography, vol 1 p 97. WOOD's Athen. FOX's Martyrs.

At

At the Election in 1776, Eleven Freeholders gave Votes from this Parish.

The Regifter has its firft Entry in 1587, and is continued in a very fair Manufcript

ANNUAL ACCOUNT OF MARRIAGES, BIRTHS, AND BURIALS, IN THIS PARISH

A D	Mar	Bir	Bur	A D	Mar	Bir	Bur	A D	Mar	Bir	Bur	A D	Mar	Bir	Bur
1781	1	16	7	1786	6	3	5	1791				1796			
1782	1	3	5	1787	—	11	4	1792				1797			
1783	1	8	7	1788				1793				1798			
1784	—	6	4	1789				1794				1799			
1785	2	8	7	1790				1795				1800			

INSCRIPTIONS IN THE CHURCH.

ON MONUMENTS IN THE CHANCEL

Mortis Tropheum
de corpore Joſannis filii Arthuri Hickes,
de Charfield, in Artibus Magiſtri, nec non
Medicinæ in Academia Oxon alumni,
qui licet mortis fugandæ aut ſaltem ſallenuæ
apprime eſſet peritus,
fato tamen, de humano genere triumphanti
inopinato devictu, ſuccubuit,
Septembris 21°,
Anno Dom 1684,
ætatis ſuæ 28

Here lyeth the Body of JOHN, the Son
of ARTHUR HICKES, of Charfield, who
was buried the 8th Day of Oct 1684, æt 26

Arms, Gules, a Fefs wavy, between three Fleurs
de lis Or, for HICKES   Creſt, a Bucks Head
couped Or, gorged, with a Chaplet Vert

Hic requieſcit inter
paternos cineres corpus diu
morbis fatigatum DANIELIS HICKES,
generoſi, qui Wottoniæ per multos
annos vixit, Briſtoliæ vero
poſtremos finivit, & in hac villa
quâ primum vitam ſuſcepit
mortuum ſepeliri juſſit
Obiit 23 Januarii, 1713, ætat ſuæ 58

ON FLAT STONES

Here lyeth the Body of
RICHARD HICKES, of Charfield
Clothier, who ended this Life
the 27th of Auguſt, A D 1664

Here lyeth the Body of
MARGARET, the Wife of
RICHARD HICKES, of Charfield, Clothier,
who departed this Life the
26th Day of April, Anno Dom 1670

Here lyeth the Body of
NICHOLAS HICKES, of Wickwar,
Clothier, who departed this Life
the 19th of February, 1669.

his Relict
departed this Life the
10th of November, 1695.

In Memory of
the Rev Mr JOHN TYNDALE,
late Rector of this Pariſh,
who departed this Life
March 3, 1746,
aged 49 Years

Alſo
the Rev WILLIAM, Son of the aboveſaid
JOHN TYNDALE, Rector of this
Pariſh, who departed Feb 23, 1763,
æt 37 Years

Alſo
WILLIAM, Son of the above WILLIAM,
who died in his infancy

Alſo
WILLIAM his ſecond Son
died May 16, 1766, aged 8 Years

Here lyeth the Body of
Rev THOMAS LODER, A M.
late Rector of Little Sodbury
and Hiſelton,
born in this County,
who departed this Life
Jan A D 1750, ætatis ſuæ 54

Alſo of MARY TYNDALE his Siſter,
Relict of the Rev JOHN TYNDALE,
Rector of this Pariſh, who ſuddenly departed
this Life the 2d Day of May, A D 1764
æt 64

Here lyeth the Body of
DANIEL HICKES, Gent late of
this Pariſh, and Inhabitant of the
City of Briſtol, who departed this Life
Jan 23, 1713, aged 58 Years

Here

Here lies the Body of
MARY LODGE, Relict of THOMAS LODGE,
late Rector of Newington Bagpath,
who died Jan 18, 1736, aged 69

Here lyeth the Body of
WILLIAM BISHOP, who departed
this Life Feb 25, A D 1739-40,
aged 49 Years, and
Minister of Kingswood
in the County of Wilts
Twenty-four Years

In Memory of
ELIZABETH PILSWORTH,
Relict of the Rev Mr DANIEL PILSWORTH,
Rector of this Parish,
and Daughter of Mr JOHN Iscorn,
of the City of Exon,
Merchant and ELIZABETH his Wife,
was here interred March
22, 1687 Likewise ELIZABETH
PAYNARD, Relict of Mr JOHN
PAYNARD, of the City of Here
ford, Draper, and Daughter
of the said Mr DANIEL PILSWORTH,
who died Feb 25, 172., aged 68

As also DANIEL PAYNARD, Apothecary, Son of the said JOHN
and ELIZABETH PAYNARD, who
departed this Life Sept 26, 1748,
aged 50 Years

M S S D P
Hic acquiescunt cineres Reverendi
nuper viri DAN PILSWORTH, hujus
Ecclesiæ Rectoris, necnon Pastoris,
qui ut cœlum introiret carnem
exuit 29° die Nov Anno Dom
1684°,
ætatis 65

In spe beata Resurrectionis
infra jacent cineres Reverendi
admodum viri EDVARDI PILS-
WORTH hujus Parochiæ Rectoris
Vita decessit decimo nono die
Mensis Septembris, A D 1724, suæ 33

Here resteth the Body of
ISABELLA, the Wife of
Mr CHARLES PILSWORTH,
Rector of this Parish, and
was here interred April 20, 1688,
ætatis suæ 32

Also ELIZABETH, Daughter of
Mr EDWARD PILSWORTH,
late Rector of Charfield,
and ELIZABETH his Wife,
was here interred Jun 12, 1728

Here lieth the Body of
WILLIAM, Son of JOHN Ross,
of Charfield, Gent who
departed this Life the 2d of April, 167

WILLIAM TYNDALL,
1735

ON FLAT STONES IN THE NAVE

Here lieth the Body of
NICHOLAS HICKES, Gent
who departed this Life the 19th Day of March,
Anno Dom 668

Here lieth the Body of
ANNE HICKES, the Wife of NICHOLAS HICKES,
of Charfield, Gent
who departed this Life the
17th Day of
Ann Don .

Here lieth the Body of
JUDITH HICKES, Wife of NICH HICKES,
buried the Day of Apr

Here lieth the Body of
JUDITH the Wife of RICHARD HICKES,
of this Parish, who was buried March 17, 1687.

RICHARD HICKES, of this Parish,
was buried March 6, 1745,
aged 61 Years

Also SARAH, Relict of the said
RICHARD HICKES,
who died May 21, 1757

ON FLAT STONES IN THE SOUTH AISLE

Here lieth the Body of
WILLIAM ROACH, of this Parish,
who departed this Life
the 6th of March, 1729,
aged 56

To the happy Memory of
WILLIAM ROACH,
who behaved himself agreeably in all
the Relations of Life and
died June 29, Anno Dom 173-,
aged Years

Under this Stone lyeth the
Body of ..., the Wife of
BENJAMIN Herr.. of Wir..r,
and Daughter of WILLIAM and
ELEANOR ROACH, of this Parish,
who departed this Life the
th Day of November, 1. aged 26 Years

Joseph her Son died an Infant

Also here lieth the Body of
ELEANOR ROACH, Widow,
who departed this Life
under the 1. 173., aged Years

Here lieth the Body of
JOHN ...NG, Gent
died ...ber 164,
b ... Years.

ON A MONUMENT IN THE SOUTH AISLE

Arms, a Bezant, between three demi Lions rampant, for BENNET;—impaling three Roaches nayant, for ROACH

In Memory of
the Rev JOSIAH BENNET, B A
and
Master of the Grammar School
in Wickwar
He died February 20, 1756,
aged 48

Also of ELEANOR his Wife,
who was Relict of
Mr THOMAS GRIFFIN, of Cromhall,
and Daughter of
Mr WILLIAM ROACH, of this Parish
She died June 13, 1758,
in the 60th Year of her Age

And likewise JOSIAH their Son
died Nov. 6, 1759, æt 21

IN THE CHURCH YARD

ON A TABLET AGAINST THE CHURCH
Here lieth the Body of
CHARLES HICKES, of Wickwar, Son of
RICHARD HICKES, of this Parish,
Clothier, who died Oct 7, 1702,
aged 42 Years

ON TOMBS

WILLIAM MORTON, senior,
died Nov 30, 1760, aged 79
MARY his Wife
died May 15, 1750, aged 69

WILKINS STOCK senior,
died May 15, 1683, aged
WILKINS STOCK, junior,
died Aug 18, 1708, aged 25
ANNA, Wife of WILKINS STOCK, senior,
died Dec 1, 1702, aged 43

ARTHUR COX
died Dec 10, 1711, aged 50
SARAH his Wife
died Jan 23, 1737, aged 81
JOHN COX,
of the Parish of St Augustine in Bristol,
died May 14, 1743, aged 47

SARAH, late Wife of DANIEL PRICE,
died May 14, 1743, aged 38

JOHN DOWNS, late of Watsome
in the Parish of Kingswood,
died March 1757, aged 50
HANNAH his Wife
died Oct 13, 1756, aged 44

JOHN SHIPWAY,
of Frampton Cotterel,
died March 7, 1744, aged 73
REBECCA his Wife
died March 7, 1722, aged 48
JOHN SHIPWAY, senior,
died May 24, 1707, aged 77
THOMAS, the Son of JOHN SHIPWAY,
buried June 24, 1748, aged 47
JOHN his Son died June 26, 1730.
ANNA, Wife of DANIEL DEVERELL,
of Wotterleigh, and Daughter of
JOHN SHIPWAY,
died Dec 19, 1765, aged 59

HUGH PARNELL
died March 21, 1757, aged 88
SARAH his Wife
died Dec 25, 1759, aged 59

Buried　　Aged
ANNE PARNELL, Sept 2, 1771, 63
NICK PARNELL, Aug 3, 1775, 77
WILL PARNELL, July 4, 1772, 52
MARY PARNELL, Feb 24, 1777, 65
EDW PARNELL, May 4, 1778, 60
MARGARET PARNELL, Mar 1, 1782, 68

MARY, the Wife of
JOHN CROOME, of Kingswood,
died Sept 7, 1763, aged 52
MARY CULLIMORE,
Widow of JOSEPH CULLIMORE, of
Tortworth, died July 21, 1744, aged 63
SARAH, Wife of SAMUEL HALLIDAY,
died Dec 22, 1702, aged 70
JOHN HALLIDAY their Son
died July 8, 1692, aged 51

NICHOLAS FOWLER
died Dec 19, 1767, aged 54.

THOMAS WATTS, senior,
of the Parish of Kingswood,
died Sept 23, 1745, aged 62
ST ANNA his Wife
died Sept. 29, 1742, aged 64
Also THOMAS and WILLIAM, Sons of
THOMAS and ANN. WATTS, junior
THOMAS died Feb 1, 1768,
in the 20th Year of his Age
WILLIAM died July 1, 1769,
in the 21st Year of his Age

WILLIAM HICKS
was buried Sept 17, 1719, aged 47
SARAH his Wife
was buried June 30, 1729, aged 42
RICHARD their Son
died June 30, 1747, aged 31

JOHN PICK
died June 13, 1737, aged 73
MARY his Wife
died Nov 24, 1756, aged 68
ELIZABETH their Daughter
died March 28, 1735, aged 26
WILLIAM their Son
died March 6, 1731, aged 19

RICHARD MAYO
died Dec 20, 1626, aged 55

Sub hoc Tumulo
novissimum Domini adventum præstolantur exuviæ mortalis THOMÆ WITCHELL sen. de hac Parochia, Pannificii, qui obiit Junii die vigesimo tertio, annoque Domini 1712, ac ætatis suæ 76

M S.
THOMÆ WITCHELL, hujus Parochiæ Generosi qui fato cessit vicessimo quarto die Januarii, anno 1720, ætatis suæ 24
SARAH, the Wife of
THOMAS WITCHELL, of this Parish, and Daughter of ARTHUR PROUT, of Cromhall, Yeoman,
died Dec. 12, 1696, aged 25

SAMUEL, Son of SAMUEL WITCHELL,
died April 23, 1686
ELIZABETH, Daughter of THOMAS
WITCHELL, died Jan 6, 1674
MARY Daughter of THOMAS WITCHELL,
died March 5, 1690, aged 15
SARAH, Wife of RICHARD WARREN,
of Bristol, and Daughter of
THOMAS WITCHELL, senior,
and ELIZABETH his Wife,
was buried July 11, 1730, aged 46.

JOHN WITCHELL
died June 16, 1756, aged 57
ANNE his Wife
died March 26, 1764, aged 59
JOHN their Son
was buried Sept 30, 1757, aged 23

ELIZABETH, Wife of
THOMAS WITCHELL, senior,
died March 8, 1735, aged 77
ESTHER, Daughter of
THOMAS WITCHELL, senior,
died Nov 17, 1745, aged 59

ANNE, Daughter of THOMAS WITCHELL,
was buried Nov 9, 1699, aged 21

ON HEAD STONES

	Died	Aged		Died	Aged
Anne, Wife of Thomas Harris	29 Sept 1748	62	Josiah Millman		
Thomas Harris her Husband	9 Dec 1765	80	Martha, Daughter of William Fowler	4 Jan 1764	20
Thomas their Son	7 Feb 1755	45	Sarah, Daughter of Joseph Hicks	31 Jun 1766	15
William Pain, of Wickwar	11 May 1761	40	Mary Wife of Daniel Tyler, of		
Sarah his Wife	4 May, 1767	44	Kingswood	24 July, 1756	52
Joseph Downs, of Wickwar	13 Feb 1754	34	Sarah, Wife of Thomas Drew,		
Mary his 1st Wife	9 Dec 1723	30	Daughter of John and Hannah		
Anne his 2d Wife	21 Oct 1738	40	Dowls	17 Feb 1771	40

4

LXII

LXII. CHARLTON ABBAT'S,
OR
CHARLINGTON,

IS one of the fmaller Parifhes, in the lower Divifion of the Hundred of *Kiftefgate*, from *Cheltenham* diftant five Miles on the North-eaft, two Southward from *Winchcombe*, and fixteen North eafterly from the City of GLOUCESTER. Of the Soil the greater Part is tilled, and varies from Clay to a lighter Strata on the Bafes of the Hills. The additional Name was given for Diftinction from *Charlton King's*, with Reference to its moft ancient Poffeffor, the Abbey of *Winchcombe*. When the CONQUEROR'S Survey was taken, they were the Lords, and continued till the Diffolution, and at the Difperfion of their Revenues, this Part of them was granted by King EDWARD VI to the Family of BRUGES, of *Sudley* *. The TRACEYS, of *Todington*, foon fucceeded, from whom it as foon devolved to the Family of CARTER, who have held it for feveral Generations, and it was bequeathed by the laft EDWARD CARTER, Efq to the prefent Proprietor. To the Manor is annexed the Fee fimple of the whole Parifh. The large manerial Houfe, long the Refidence of the CARTERS, is dilapidated and occupied as a Farm.

The Church or Chapel was a ruinous Structure, but has been refitted on a very fmall Plan for occafional Service. The Impropriation has been, with few Exceptions, held with the Manor, and is charged with the Maintenance of a Curate, who is merely a Stipendiary, and not inftituted by the Bifhop. Many of the Parifhioners preferve a Right of Sepulture at *Winchcombe*.

———— AYLWORTH, Efq bequeathed 800*l* to purchafe Land for the Augmentation of feveral fmall Livings, of which this is one, and receives annually about 5*l* for its Proportion of the Benefaction.

This Parifh contains nothing worthy the Attention either of the Foffilift or Antiquary. Two Rivulets have their Rife here, one of which, after a long Courfe, joins the *Severn*, and the other the *Thames*.

No Benefactions to the Poor.

The Series of Curates is neceffarily imperfect, none of them occurring in the Books of the Regiftrar of this Diocefe.

OFFICIATING MINISTERS.	PATRONS
——— John Taylor, Clerk,	Edward Carter, Efq
1776 John Weekes Bedwell, B A	The fame

PRESENT LORD OF THE MANOR,

FRANCIS PYM, ESQ

The Perfons fummoned from this Place by the Heralds in 1682 and 1683 were

John Carter, fenior, Efq
John Carter, junior, Gent

The Regifter commences fo late as 1727, probably when the Chapel was repaired.

* MSS PRYNNE

ANNUAL ACCOUNT OF MARRIAGES, BIRTHS, AND BURIALS, IN THIS PARISH.

A D	Mar	Bir	Bur	A D	Mar	Bir	Bur	A.D	Mar.	Bir	Bur	A.D	Mar	Bir	Bur
1781	2	4	1	1786	—	4	4	1791				1796			
1782	1	3	1	1787	—	3	1	1792				1797			
1783	—	3	2	1788				1793				1798			
1784	—	4	2	1789				1794				1799			
1785	1	1	—	1790				1795				1800			

INSCRIPTION IN THE CHURCH.

ON A PLAIN TABLET AGAINST THE NORTH WALL.

In Memory of JANE, the Wife of EDWARD AKERS,
of Goldwell She died Sept. 12, 1754, aged 52.

Also in Memory of EDWARD AKERS,
who died May 1, 1777, aged 77.

IN THE CHURCH YARD.

JOHN HALL died March 14, 1788, aged 80.

ELIZABETH his Wife died August 21, 1758, aged 58.

KING

CHARLTON KING'S,
OR
A S H L E Y,

WHICH laſt Denomination more peculiarly belongs to an inſulated Manor, held in Fee-farm of the great Lordſhip of *Cheltenham*, than to the whole Pariſh, and is therefore not ſeparately recited in Domeſday Book, but included in that Manor, under the Title of " Terra Regis "

The Diſtance of this Village from *Cheltenham*, in which Hundred it is contained, is one Mile on the Eaſt, eleven from GLOUCESTER in the ſame Direction, and ſeven from *Winchcombe* on the South The Soil is compoſed both of Clay and Sand, and is ſingularly fertile, it is applied in nearly equal Portions to Paſture and Tillage, and conſiſts of 3000 Acres

Of the Benefice, which is an endowed Curacy, the Stipend of 40*l* annually is charged on the Impropriation, by a Decree in Chancery 1624, 1 CHARLES I when the Appointment was veſted in *Jeſus College*, Oxford, ſubject to certain Reſtrictions (which ſhall be explained in the Account of *Cheltenham*), and the impropriate Tythes granted to Sir WALTER RYDER, under whom the Earl of ESSEX makes his Claim No Glebe belongs to the Impropriation, and an immemorial Cuſtom has obtained for every Landholder to incloſe and hold in ſeveralty, according to the Reſolution in Sir MILES CORBET's Caſe

The Church is built with a Tranſept, and an embattled Tower in the middle, is ſpacious, but of plain Architecture To its firſt Erection the Abbey of *Cirenceſter* were probably large Contributors, as it appears from their Regiſters, pp 61, 230, 231 " That the Chapel of *Charlton King's* was dedicated, " and made ſubject, to the Mother Church of *Cheltenham*, by WILLIAM Biſhop of *Hereford* in 1190, by " Indulgence of Pope INNOCENT III and then given to the Abbey of *Cirenceſter*, at which Time it " gained parochial Rights " It forms a Part of the Deanery of *Winchcombe*, and has the *Virgin Mary* for its Patron Saint Though at the CONQUEROR's Survey, the Manor of *Eſhley*, or *Aſhley* be not ſeparately noticed, its Exiſtence is proved by authentic Records almoſt immediately ſubſequent to that early Period WALTER DE ESHELEY lived in 1246, 30 HEN III The Families of COKESEY and GREVILLE † poſſeſſed this Manor before the 16th Century, when Sir EDMUND TAME, Knight, gave *Rendcombe* in Exchange for it to Sir EDWARD GREVILLE In 1542 it was held by the Families of WELLS and PALMER.- In 1608 GILES GREVIL and WALTER PALMER were the Owners of it It was purchaſed by JOHN PRYNNE, Eſq collaterally related to the celebrated WILLIAM PRYNNE ‡, in 1697, of the MITCHELLS, ſince which Time the original Eſtate is very conſiderably encreaſed, and was bequeathed by the laſt WILLIAM PRYNNE, Eſq to DODINGTON HUNT, Eſq. who had married ELIZABETH his only Daughter and Heir

The cuſtomary Lands in the Pariſh of *Charlton King's* are held under the Manor of *Cheltenham*, in which, notwithſtanding, are ſeveral, appendant ſolely on the Manor of *Aſhley*

---

* MSS PRYNNE

† " Sum hold Opinion that the GRAVILLES came originally in at the Conqueſt The eldeſt Houſe is at *Drayton*, two Miles " of *Banbury* in *Oxfordſhire* Other GRAVILLES have purchaſed fayre Landes, and otherwiſe cum to Landes by Marriage of " Heires Generals " LLELAND, Itin vol IV, p 16 " LODOVICK GREVIL, the Son of WILLIAM GREVIL buried at Camp " *Iſn* in 1401, became poſſeſſed of *Drayton*, by Marriage of MARGARET, Daughter and Heir of GILES ARDEN " MSS

‡ The Family of PRYNNE were originally of *Allington*, co *Wilts*, and had Arms confirmed to them in 1588 WILLIAM PRYNNE, the Cenſor General of the Age he lived in, was born at *Swainſwick* near *Bath* in 1600, educated at *Oriel College*, *Oxford* and became Bencher and Reader of *Lincoln's Inn* about 1632 He died in 1669 having been never married Of his Induſtry Wood records that he publiſhed 173 Tracts and Pamphlets, many in Folio, and computes, that he wrote a Sheet for every Day of the laſt fifty Years of his Life The Subjects of theſe Publications were what he thought the Enormities of the Time their Merit is neceſſarily loſt with the Occaſion of them, but his Law Tracts are ſtill much eſteemed The Fortitude, with which he ſubmitted to the ſevere Penalties and corporal Inflictions levied on him by the Court, is an unqueſtionable Proof of the Sincerity with which he ſupported thoſe Principles he had undertaken to defend

About the Year 1737 JOHN PRYNNE, Eſq completed his Manuſcripts, and prepared them for the Preſs a Deſign which has never been completed They conſiſt of Collections chiefly emendatory of Sir R ATKYNS's Hiſtory of this County, by Collations of the moſt ancient Records, and authentic Evidences, with his Text, beſide many curious and intereſting Additions Mr PRYNNE purſued his laborious Inveſtigations, with that unwearied Induſtry and Arrangement, by which ſome Correctneſs can be acquired, and for which theſe MSS are equally ſingular and valuable We cannot but repeat our Obligations to DODINGTON HUNT, Eſq the preſent Poſſeſſor, for his very candid Communication of them

Some Years since the Manor House were built in a modern and commodious Style, but the Park and Pleasure Grounds being naturally low, did not admit of much picturesque Beauty. The present Proprietor has joined the superior Excellence of unimproved Art of Gardening when applied with real Judgment and Taste, in relieving the Flatness of some Parts by Objects with which the Distances are pleasingly broken, and giving to himself a delightful Prospect by widening and enlarging it. A Circuit of about two Miles is inclosed within the Park Pale, and it may soon be observed, that it wears a Face of Scenery beautiful and easy, such as its former Appearance could not have promised.

Besides the Manor and Estate of Ashley the more ancient Proprietors were the Families of PATES, PACKER, HICKS, and WHITHORNE, which Estates are now held by WHITHORNE and COOKE. Upon the River Cheu, which intersects the Parish, Mills are erected for grinding Corn.

BENEFACTIONS.

Certain Lands in the Parish of Charlton King's purchased by the Feoffees of the said Parish heretofore, with small Sums of Money left by different Persons to the Poor of the said Parish, also certain other Lands in the said Parish leased by the Feoffees, heretofore to JOHN PRYNN, Esq for a long Term of Years, amounting together to the yearly Value of 21l 1s which Sum is vested in the Hands of SAMUEL COOK, CHARLES HICKS, SAMUEL HICKS, THOMAS NETTLESHIP, WILLIAM BUCKLE, and WILLIAM GREVILLE, Feoffees in Trust for the Poor of the Parish, and is directed to be applied in the Manner following: 10l of the Money to bind out yearly two Apprentices, a Christmas Gift of 2l 10s yearly, to be disposed of to such Poor of the Parish as the Feoffees and other Inhabitants upon St Thomas's Day shall agree upon and think fit to receive the same, the remaining Part to pay the Payments upon the said Lands, and if any poor Person be sick or lame, or any other extraordinary Occasion that may happen to any of the poor Inhabitants, then the remaining Part to be employed towards their Relief.

GRACE BINTON late by Will, 1700, the Sum of 12s a Year, issuing out of Lands, to buy two poor Women Linen, vested in the Feoffees abovenamed.

WALTER MANSELL bequeathed by Will the like Sum of 12s a Year, payable out of his Estate, for the Use of such poor Persons as the said Feoffees think proper.

SAMUEL COOPER devised by Will, 1743, Lands to the Value of 10l a Year, for the putting of six poor Children of this Parish to School for two Years only, and at the End of that Time six others, and so continue changing at the End of every two Years, the remaining Sum to buy Fuel and Cloaths for six poor Men and Women of this Parish, as the said Feoffees shall from Time to Time think proper to bestow the same, but on such Persons only as receive no Relief otherwise from the Parish.

The Register's Books do not give a regular Series of the officiating Ministers. The Bishop of this Diocese appointed, till the Agreement took Place between the Impropriator Sir BAPTIST HICKS and *Jesus College, Oxford*, 1624.

OFFICIATING MINISTERS	PATRONS	OFFICIATING MINISTERS	PATRONS
1675 William Wynne, M A	Jesus College, Oxf	1776 John Weekes Bedwell, B A	Oriel College, Oxf
1712 David Gwynne, B D	The fire	1783 John De la Bere, M A	Queen's College,
—— John Jones, M A	The same		Cambridge

PRESENT LORD OF THE MANOR,
Or *Ashley* in *Charlton*
DODINGTON HUNT, Esq

At the Visitations of the Heralds, 1682 and 1683, the Persons summoned from this Parish were,

Giles Greville, Gent	Robert Backhouse, Gent
Alexander Packer, Gent	Lynett Pates, Gent and
Theophilus Brereton, Gent	Conway Whithorne, M A and B M

At the Election in 1776, Thirty Freeholders polled from this Parish.

The Register has its first Date 1539, and is fairly written.

AN ANNUAL ACCOUNT OF MARRIAGES, BIRTHS, AND BURIALS, IN THIS PARISH

A D	Mar	Bir	Bur	A D	Mar	Bir	Bur	A D	Mar	Bir	Bur	A D	Mar	Bir	Bur
1781	4	10		1786	4	15	27	1791				1796			
1782	7	14	11	1787	3	25	12	1792				1797			
1783	4	17	9	1788				1793				1798			
1784	1	17	13	1789				1794				1799			
1785		6	19	1790				1795				1800			

* John Whithorne held Lands in *Charlton King's*, 10 Hen IV. We select the following from the Book in the Herald's Office. John Whithorne of *Charlton King's* died in 1590. Conway Whithorne his son was a Citizen of London, and served his Majesty King Charles I in the Garrison of *Worcester*. Conway Whithorne, the son of the abovenamed Conway Whithorne, was a Lieutenant under Colonel Bashmaker at *Aberystwith* Castle in Wales in 1645, was a Captain of Foot in the King's Service at the Surrender of *Bristol* in 1643, and served under King Charles II at the Battle of *Worcester* in 1651, he was entered of *Pool's College*, Oxford, proceeded M A and L M, and became Rector of ... in *Yorkshire* ...

INSCRIPTIONS

INSCRIPTIONS IN THE CHURCH.

IN THE CHANCEL

ON A MONUMENT AGAINST THE NORTH WALL

Arms, in a Lozenge, quarterly, 1st and 4th, Argent, two Bars Sable, for BRERETON, 2d and 3d, Sable, on a Bend Argent, three Lozenges of the 1st, for CARRINGTON, in the Centre a Crescent Gules, for Difference

THEOPHILUS and HESTER BRERETON, buried near this Place, had five Daughters and four Sons, of whom six are deceased

THEOPHILUS
SUSANNA   } who died { in this Parish
SUSANNA
BRIDGET   }   { at Gloucester
ROBERT   { at Sea

THEOPHILA BRERELTON, who was borne May 4, 1674, and died Feb. 28, 1709, and is buried in the Chancel, at whose Request this little Monument was erected for the Memory of her and her deceased Friends

ON A BRASS PLATE OVER THE DOOR

SAMUEL COOPER, of this Parish, Gent died May 13, 1743, who by Will gave to the Trustees undernamed, and to others, Successors, his Trustees for ever the Rent of his Grounds in the same Parish called Cutham Butts and Battle Downs, for buying Books, and teaching six poor Children of this Parish to read two Years, at the End of which Time six others to be chosen by the said Trustees, with the privity of the Churchwardens, the overplus to provide Fuel, and cloth six aged or infirm poor Persons, not receiving Alms of this Parish

Trustees {ROBERT GALE,
          EDMUND WELCH, } Gentlemen
          EDWARD GALE, }

ON FLAT STONES

The mortal Parts of ELIZABETH and THOMAS, the Wife and Son of ALEXANDER PACKER, junior, Gent which rest here in the 11th Day of March Anno Dom 1651

SARAH Wife of JOHN PRYNN, died January 25, 1720

KATHERINE, the Wife of JOHN PRYNN, departed this Life Nov 25, Anno Dom 1717

Here lieth the Body of MARY, the Daughter of SAMUEL and SUSANNA STORER, Gent She died June 17, 1733, aged 31 Years

ELIZABETH, Daughter of SAMUEL and SUSANNA STORER, died April 1755, aged 5

Here lieth the Body of SAMUEL COOPER Gent who departed the Life May 13, 1743, aged 61 Years

Arms, BRERELTON, as before

Here lieth the Body of THEOPHILUS BRERETON, senior, Gent who was interred on the 5th Day of March, Anno Dom 1688, aged 60

HESTER his Wife died March 14, 1707, aged 63

Arms, Azure, a Bend Or, for TRYE

Lapis hic sepulchralis condit Laudes BRANDON TRYE, Gen Johannæ mater GULIELMI TRYE nuper de Hardwick, Arm. mortem obiit 5° non Septembris,

Anno {Salutis MDCCXXVIII
      {Ætatis XXVIII

Et JOHANNIS TRYE LONGFORD X Mensium III Dierum, in unum Ob 5° kal Mau, MDCCXXX.

IN THE NORTH WING

ON A HANDSOME MARBLE MONUMENT

Arms Or, a Cross ingrailed Azure, between three Scallops Gules Crest, a demi Eagle displayed, for PRYNN

Here under lie the Remains of Mrs ELIZABETH PRYNN, the Wife of WILLIAM PRYNN, Esq and eldest Daughter of THOMAS RIDLER, Esq of Edgeworth in the County of Gloucester, Esq who departed this Life March 5, 1771, aged 51 Years

Also of Mrs ELIZABETH HUNT, Daughter of the abovenamed WILLIAM PRYNN and ELIZABETH PRYNN, who was married to DOMINGTON HUNT of the Inner Temple, London, Esq and departed this Life August 10, 1772, aged 24 Years and six Months

ON FLAT STONES

Mrs MARY PRYNN Relict of JOHN PRYNN Clerk, died June 2, 1760, aged 65

JOHN PRYNN, Clerk, died May 11, 1743, aged

Here lieth the Body of
JOHN PINN, Efq; who departed this Life
the 20th of Feb. A. D. Do. 1736,
aged 7

ELIZABETH PINN
died June 9, 1744,
aged 25 Years

KATHARINE PINN
died June 29, 1745,
aged 72 Years

Arms, a Crofs lozengy, between four Rofes,
for PACKER

Here lieth the Body of
WINIFRED Wife of JAMES INGRAM, Gent.
and Daughter of ALEXANDER PACKER,
and DOROTHY his Wife, who departed his Life
March 26, 1694, aged 23 Years

Here lieth the Body of
CARTWRIGHT, Son of WALTER and MARY BUCKLE,
who was buried Dec. 23, 1707,
aged 17 Years and 6 Months

Here lieth interred the Body of
JOHN WHITE He died Jan. 16, 1751,
aged 22 Years

IN THE SOUTH WING

ON A PLAIN STONE AGAINST THE WALL

Hic jacet Johannes Pates,
Magifter artis ingeniique Largitor,
nec minus medicinæ quam
theologiæ ftudiofus,
qui annis quadraginta circiter
ingenue peractis
fummum naturæ debitum he
qu m æquanime perfolvit
Jan. 11, Anno Dom. 1646

To the Memory of ANNE the Wife of
WALTER COOPER and Sifter to the faid
John Pates who refigned her Soule
to the Hands that gave it
April the 27th, Anno Dom. 1647

ON FLAT STONES

Here lieth buried EDITH PATES,
late the Wife of RICHARD PATES, Gent.
who departed this Life Sept. the 2d,
Anno Domini 1650

---

a poor honeft Gentlewoman,
died on the fecond of April, 1
aged 60 Years

---

the Wife of Linfeil PATES Gent.
Daughter of FRANCIS NORWOOD Efq.
died July 17, 1650

Here lieth the Body of
THOMAS PATES, Gent. who ended his Life
Feb. 23, 1727, aged 44 Years

WILLIAM PATES Yeoman,
died Nov. 15, 1771, aged 55 Years

ELIZABETH his Wife
died May 14, 750, aged 72 Years

Here lieth the Body of
CATHARINE, Relict of Linfeit PATES Gent.
of WILLIAM KECK and John BATTEN, Yeoman
She was buried April 5, Anno Dom 1729

LINSETT PATES Gent.
died April 10, 1685

FRANCES, the Wife of THOMAS PATES, Gent.
buried Nov. 16, 1755, aged 76

EDWARD GRIST, Yeoman,
was buried on the 11th of April, 1768, aged 6

MARY his Wife
died October 16, 175-, aged 59

RICHARD, Son of LINSETT PATES, junior, Gent.
died April 12, 1707, aged 25

JOHN MARSTON Clerk,
died Jan. 17, Anno Dom 1643

Alfo MARY his Wife,
who departed this Life the 16th of the
fame Moneth and Yeare

Here lyeth the Body of
ELEANOR, Daughter of EDWARD BEDFORD,
Vicar of Prefbury, Relict of RICHARD PATES
and Wife of WALTER NICHOLLS, who
died Feb. 11, 1738 in the 44th Year of his Age

SAMUEL COLLETT
buried Sept. 30, 1601

GILES ATKINS, Gent.
died April 9, 1629

ANNA, Wife of SAMUEL WHITHORNE,
died Jan. 5, 1721

ANN, Wife of JOHN WHITHORNE,
late of this Parifh, Daughter of
JOHN BEAL of Temple Guiting, Gent.
died Dec. 30, 1727, aged 86

SAMUEL WHITHORNE, Gent.
of this Parifh, obiit 23 Dec. 1739, aged 61

ANNA, Wife of RICHARD OVERBURY
and Daughter of SAMUEL WHITHORNE,
Gent. died Dec. 11, 1766, aged 55 Years

IN THE SOUTH AISLE ON FLAT STONES

SARAH, the Wife of
WILLIAM WINDT, of Temple Guting, Clerk,
and Daughter of HENRY MASON, of Ham, ...,
was buried August 29, 1723,
in the 40th Year of her Age

WILLIAM BUCKLE, of Ham in this Parish,
died April 9, 1726, aged 65
MARY his Wife
died June 15, 1737, aged 79

WILLIAM MOULDER
was buried Sep. 5, 1681, aged 23

JOE MOULDER
was buried April 2, 1702, aged 69

THOMAS MOULDER
was buried April 4, 1741, aged 85.

JOHN MOULDER, Yeoman,
died April 2, 1762, aged 6,

ISABEL, Daughter of
WALTER and MARY BUCKLE,
buried May 11, 17 8, aged 56

IN THE NAVE

ON A SMALL MARBLE TABLET AT THE WEST END

Underneath lye the
Remains of JOHN GALE senior,
and his Wife
He died the 2d of Feb 176,.
She died the 13th of Sep 1766,
each aged 46 Years

ON FLAT STONES

Here lieth the Body of Mrs MARY BARNARD,
Widow heretofore of TIMOTHY CARTWRIGHT,
of this Parish, buried Aug 26, 1699, aged 94

ISABEL, the Wife of THOMAS PUCKET, and
and Daughter of TIMOTHY CARTWRIGHT
of this Parish, died Dec 7, Anno Dom 171,,
aged 81

SARAH, heretofore Wife of RICHARD MANSELL
and Daughter of SAMUEL MANSELL,
died May 29, 1664

late Wife of SAMUEL MANSELL,
died May 1, Anno Dom 60 4

CATHERINE PUCKET
died February 17 8, aged 61

JANE, late the Wife of JOHN STILES,
died Dec 14, 164

Also the Body of JANE, the
Wife of ANTHONY WILL of this Parish,
Daughter of SAMUEL MANSELL,
and Grand daughter of the aforesaid
JANE STILES, who died April 4, 1657, aged 61.

ANTHONY WILL
died Sept 4, 1697, aged 81

THOMAS ASHMEAD
died Anno Dom 1663

ELIZABETH his Wife
died Anno Dom 1665

SUSANNA, Wife of
SAMUEL STOFER,
died Nov , , aged 48.

SAMUEL STOFER, Gent
died March 1 , 1711, aged 20

SAMUEL STOFER, Gent
died June 21, 171 , aged 51

CHARLES HICES
died March 23, 1751, aged 63

SUSANNA his Wife
died June 1, 17 5, aged 45

IN THE CHURCH YARD   ON TOMBS

Arg Per Pale Sable and Gules, a Cross botton Or, ... hy, between four Fleurs de lis Or, Impaling, on a Chevron, between three Boars Heads couped

In Memory of Mrs MARGARET RICH,
Daughter of EDWARD RICH, of Dowdeswell, Esq
she was buried Sept 2, 169

JOHN HOLDER, junior,
died May 16, 169 , aged 26

JOHN DANEY, Yeoman,
died Oct 5, 1699, aged 65.

... heretofore the
Widow of JOHN DANEY, Yeoman,
died Sept , 17 0 aged 8

THOMAS ASHMEAD, senior,
died Jan , 16 6, aged 63.

THOMAS ASHMEAD
died June 8, 17 5, aged 59

ANN his Wife
died Feb 25, 1761, aged 69
THOMAS their Son
died Jan 2, 1 , aged 5
GILES ASHMEAD,
Grandson of THOMAS ASHMEAD,
died March 2, 165, aged 4

THOMAS BETTS, Yeoman,
died Jan 9, 17 , aged 7
ANN his Wife
died April , 170, aged

C... WHITHORNE,
of Tewkesbury, Son of
JOHN WHITHORNE, formerly of this Parish,
and MARGARET his Wife,
died April 16, 1710, aged 67

SAMUEL and SARAH, Son and Daughter of
SAMUEL WHITHORNE, by SARAH his Wife
SAMUEL died in Oct 1711.
SARAH died Oct 11, 1717

SAMUEL WHITHORNE, junior,
died July 16, 168, aged 26

SAMUEL WHITHORNE, senior,
died Dec 16, 1708, aged 88

JOYCE his Wife
died April 18, 1707, aged 83

ANN GREGORY, Widow,
died June 14, 1717, aged 85

RICHARD WAGER
died Sept 12, 1661

ELIZABETH, Wife of WILLIAM BELCHER,
died March 1, 1762 aged 63

WILLIAM their Son
died Dec 30, 1758, aged 32

WALTER HICKS, of this Parish,
who served his Majesty King CHARLES the First,
a Commission Officer in his Army,
died Dec 12, 1698, aged 85

FRANCES his Daughter
died April 8, 1722, aged 25

WILLIAM MANSEL, Yeoman,
died Nov 18, 1732, aged 72

ON HEAD STONES

	Died	Aged		Died	Aged
Robert Gale, Constables born July 16, 1, 1 and died August 27			Thomas Ballinger	5 Mar 18	
			Rebecca this Wife	1 Jan 1,73	50
Robert Gale an Ancestor of the said Robert was born in the Year 1606, and died in the 65th Year of his Age			Sarah Wife of William Westmancote	20 June 1,52	50
			William Westmancote	20 Oct 1760	70
			Thomas Simmons	27 July 1,6	57
			Sarah his Wife	4 Sept 1,66	72
Anne, Wife of Stephen Boulton	9 Mar 17	30	John Sollis	18 June, 1767	50
Anne, Wife of John White	17 Sep 176	8	Thomas Sollis	23 July 17,8	55
Father, Wife of William Wood	7 June, 176	76	William Sollis	3 Apr 1744	52
Edward Gale, Yeoman	7 Dec 1,50	—	Samuel Broad, Yeoman	24 Oct 1751	66
Sarah, Wife of William Tombs, Daughter of John Gale	14 Mar 1,29	51	Hester his Wife	19 Apr 1752	6
Thomas Hill	11 May, 178	56	Ann, Wife of Richard Bendall	2 Sept 1,66	40
Edith his Wife	20 Aug 1770	50	Stephen Lennard	13 Apr 1778	74
Robert their Son	12 Mar 1770	15	Edith his Wife	1 Dec 1760	84
Thomas Peer	29 July 1,79	72	John Prince	24 July 1784	7
Susan Wife	1, June, 177,	7	Hester his Wife	25 Mar 1772	5
Jane Wife of Richard Pitts	20 June, 176	66	Elizabeth their Daughter	5 Sep 1768	16
William Johnson	— 1712		John Kent	13 Apr 1,6	57
Thomas Gardener Yeoman	24 July 17,0	5	Elizabeth his Wife	12 Nov 1762	57
Ann his Wife	10 July, 1,50	83	Jane Wife of Edmund Barrows	20 Feb 1771	7
Richard Newman	30 Mar 1747	43	Mrs Elizabeth Cooper, many Years Housekeeper to William Prinn, Esq	16 Dec 1781	68
Joyce, Wife of John Pink, Daughter of Edward and Hester Greenwood	7 June, 186	49	Izael, Wife of Robert Gale junior Gent	6 Apr 1757	35
Edward Greenwood	15 Dec 175	74	Robert Gale, Gent	14 Feb 1784	73
Hester, Daughter of Edward and Hester Greenwood	2 June, 1764	4	John Tutts	18 Apr 175,	7
	21 Sep 1,71	28	Nicholas Tutt	5 July, 177,	7
William Smith	2 Aug 1,66	52	Martha his Wife	2 July, 1778	7
Mary his Wife	15 Oct 1766	66	Thomas Tutt	4 Mar 1,64	76
Mary, Relict of Edward Delme, aged 85 or old	28 June, 1,76	84	Elizabeth his Sister, Wife of William Webb of Moreton Valence	26 Dec 1753	0
and Susan	2 May, 1,05	68	John Ballin	19 Dec 1,86	70
his Wife	13 Oct 1,65	42	Ann his Wife	4 June 1,86	68
Wife of Edward Delme	17 May, 1,51	55	William their Son	24 June, 175	1
Jane Py her Mother	— 1,82	87	Peter and Mother	26 Nov 1,52	0
Wife of William Belcher	1 Mar 1,6	63	Ann Daughter of Richard and Elizabeth Mutte	11 May, 1,53	0
Yeoman	30 Dec 1,58	32	Mary Wife of Anthony Mutte	4 Feb 1,0	70
	2, Mar 1755	48	Thomas Gale Son of George Gale and Eliz the his Wife, Daughter of Walter Hicks	8 July, 1698	—
John Lawrence	17 May 17,1	1	John Hodges of this Parish	13 Jan 1,3	
	10 Sep 7, 0	3			
	1 Jan 1,60	72			
Yeoman	3 Jan 17,1	82			
Wife	15 Apr 1,7,	90			

LXIV. CHEDWORTH,

WHICH lies in the upper Extremity of the *Cotefwold*, is a Parifh of more than ordinary Extent, including a Circumference of twelve Miles, in the Hundred of *Rapfgate*. It is diftant from *Northleach* four Miles South weft, feven Northward from *Cirencefter*, and nearly feventeen on the South eaft from the City of *Gloucefter*. The Soil, which is light, is almoft univerfally tilled, with fome Meadows near the *Colne*, which forms a Boundary on the South-eaft, and the Commonable and Woodlands are likewife confiderable.

The Benefice is a Vicarage, endowed with a third Part of all Tythes, and Glebe Lands of an unufual Proportion. In the Commencement of the fifteenth Century the Carthufian Priory of *Bethlehem* at *Sheene* in *Surrey* held the Impropriation jointly with the Advowfon. After the Suppreffion it became the Property of Hugh Westwode, Efq. who, in 558, invefted the Provoft and Fellows of *Queen's College, Oxford*, with the Right of perpetual Advowfon, and fettled the Impropriation (fubject to an annual Charge of 16s 2d to the Crown), for the Foundation of a free Grammar School in the Town of *Northleach*, the Mafter of which is to be nominated by that Society.

It has been conjectured that the Church, which is of mixed Architecture, was erected at the Expence of the Priory, as there was a Figure with an Infcription for JOHN IVES the Prior, in one of the Chancel Windows. Sir R ATKYNS, who records this, gives no farther Information, and the whole is now totally obliterated and defaced. Befide this Evidence in favour of the Conjecture are an Infcription in 1461, and a Date 1485, ftill remaining, which Periods were during their Poffeffion of it.

The Structure confifts of a Nave and North Aifle with a low embattled Tower. The Pulpit of carved Stone is in the fame mafterly Style, and of the fame Æra, with the *Roftra* in the Divinity School at *Oxford*, which are fo defervedly admired.

The Manor was, at the Time of the Conqueft, Parcel of the Demefnes of the Crown. In 1133 it was granted by WILLIAM RUFUS to HENRY DE NEWBURG, the firft Earl of *Warwick*. From his Defcendants it paffed to the BEAUCHAMPS, was inherited by the NEVILLES, and remained a Part of the immenfe landed Property of the Earls of *Warwick*, during five Centuries. King HENRY VII obtained it fraudulently from CICELY Dutchefs Dowager of WARWICK. In 1548 it was given to JOHN DUDLEY*, Earl of *Warwick*, as having been anciently annexed to that Lordfhip. Early in the laft Century it was purchafed of the TRACEYS, of *Todington*, by the knightly Family of HOWE, who were created Barons of *Chedworth*, by Patent, bearing Date May 12, 1741, 14 GEORGE II.

On a Spot of Ground, called *St. John's Afh*, was a Chapel dedicated to that Saint, now totally dilapidated.

About the Year 1760 the Veftiges of a *Roman* Bath were difcovered at *Iftercombe*, near the *Wood Barton* in this Parifh. There was a Spring and other neceffary Appendages. Moft of the Bricks were very legibly marked " ARVIRI," defcribing probably by connected Initials the Titles of the Legion, which were ftationed here, within two Miles of the great *Fofs* or *Confular* Road. The Tumulus has been found to contain great Quantities of human Bones, a Mode of Sepulture peculiar to the *Britifh* or *Saxon* Times.

BENEFACTIONS.

In the Reign of RICHARD II fome Perfon unknown gave by Deed, for the Repairs of the Church, and Maintenance of the Poor, Lands and Cottages, the annual Produce of which now is 9l 2s 8d, vefted in the Churchwardens.

Hugh Westwood, Efq. gave by Will, May 1, 1549, the Sum of 13s 4d annually, for the Ufe of the Poor, payable out of the Impropriation for ever.

*Afterwards Duke of NORTHUMBERLAND.

INCUMBENTS	PATRONS	INCUMBENTS.	PATRONS
————————,	Abbey of Lyra in Normandy	* * * * * *	* * * * * *
	Abbey of Lvesham	1682 Jeffry Wall, M A	Queen's College, Oxf
1413 ————————,	Priory of Sheene	1743 Philip Brown, M A	The same
1489 ————————,	The same	1744 James Rawes, B A	The same
* * * * *	* * * * * *	1759 George Dixon, D D	The same
—— Edward Bracegirdle,		761 Richard Bolton, D D	The same
1602 George Bevan,	Jonn Reynoldes	1765 James Rawes +, B D	The same
1602 Nathaniel Aldworth,	Queen Elizabeth	1785 Benjamin Gridale,M A	The same.

PRESENT LORD OF THE MANOR,

The Right Honourable JOHN Lord CHEDWORTH

The only Person summoned from this Place by the Heralds in 1682 and 1683 was
Richard Howe, Esq

At the Election in 1776, Sixty three Freeholders polled from this Parish

The Register has its first Entry in 1653, and is continued with great Regularity

ANNUAL ACCOUNT OF MARRIAGES, BIRTHS, AND BURIALS, IN THIS PARISH

A.D	Mar	Bir	Bur	A D	Mar	Bir	Bur	A D	Mar	Bi	Bur	A D	Mar	Bir	Bur
1781	11	22	12	1786	6	26	23	1791				1796			
1782	6	24	17	1787	5	22	13	1792				1797			
1783	7	24	16	1788				1793				1798			
1784	6	19	17	1789				1794				1799			
1785	6	16	17	1790				1795				1800			

I N S C R I P T I O N S   I N   T H E   C H U R C H

I N   T H E   C H A N C E L

ON A NEAT MARBLE TABLET

Sacred to the Memory of
the Rev JAMES RAWES, B. D
sometime Fellow of Queen's College, Oxford,
and 35 Years Vicar of this Church
He died May 30, 1785, aged 68 Years

ON TWO PLAIN STONE TABLETS

In Memory of THOMAS ROGERS,
of this Parish, Yeoman, who died
Nov 19, 1742, aged 83

DENNIS, the Wife of THOMAS ROGERS,
died April 7, 1748, aged 78

NICHOLAS, the Son of NICHOLAS
and SARAH TURK, died Aug 11, 1741,
aged 11 Month

JOHN, the Son of THOMAS ROGERS
and DENNIS his Wife, died Aug 19, 1724,
aged 21 Years

ON FLAT STONES.

Here resteth the Body of
THOMAS HILL, senior,
who departed this Life Feb 25, 1696,
aged 97

RICHARD, the Son of GEOFFRY WALL, Clerk,
and DOROTHY his Wife, departed this
Life the third Day of July, 1717, in the
20th Year of his Age

Here lieth the Body of
DOROTHEA, Daughter of the Rev M GIM
Rector of Withington,
and Wife of GEOFFRY WALL, M A
Vicar of this Church
She died July 13 Anno Dom 1723,
aged 63

GALFRIDUS WALL, A M
hujus Ecclesiæ
circiter Annos LXI Vicarius,
obiit Maii 25°, Anno Dom MDCCXLIII, æt 88

MARY ARTHUR their Daughter
died Jan 13, 1723, aged 40 Year

ON A BUTTRESS

Hic jacet in Tumba Ricardus Selp, et Elinort
uxor ejus qui obiit 12 die Mensis Maii, Anno Dom
1461, cujus animæ propicietur Deus

IN THE CHURCH YARD, ON TOMBS.

EDMUND HAINES, Yeoman,
died Aug 11, 1701, aged 54

ALICE his Wife
died Feb 7, 1715, aged near 73

ANN DICHE, Widow,
died July 2, 1742, aged 68

HANNAH, Wife of GILES COATES,
Land Surveyor, died May 7, 1775, aged 67

THOMAS DRAKE
died March 7, 1714-5, æt 81.

PRISCILLA his Wife
died in the Year 1692

SARAH, Wife of ROBERT SLY,
died May 22, 1743, aged 81

SARAH their Daughter,
Wife of JOHN MIDWINTER,
died March 17, 1731, aged 26

JOSEPH, Son of ROBERT and SARAH SLY,
died Oct 25, 1708, aged 23

NICHOLAS TURK
died June 6, 1757, aged 59

JOHN TUFFLEY, Mason,
died Feb 13, 1760, aged 72

ON HEAD STONES

	Died	Aged
Thomas Clappen, of Halling in this County	3 Jan 1779	47
John Tuffley, Yeoman	30 July, 1732	74
Edward Sanfum	27 Nov 1779	96
Mary, Relict of Edward Sanfum	4 Aug 1780	71
Thomas Coates	- Jun 1779	82
Ann, Wife of John Harding	8 June, 1772	67
Hannah, Daughter of Edmund Haines, and Wife of Edmund Hooper	6 Mar 1768	37
Matthew Robins	8 Aug 1742	56
Sarah his Wife, Daughter of Francis and Ann Adams	22 Feb 1741	61
Deborah, Daughter of William and Elizabeth Clark, of the Parish of Cowley	28 Oct 1736	24
William Child	8 Apl 1762	88
Ann his Wife	10 Nov 1746	68
John Blackwell, of this Parish, Yeoman	11 July, 1702	47
John Massey	24 Nov 1758	65
Catharine his Wife	Oct 1761	68
Edith, Wife of Joseph Robbins	24 Sept 1724	—
Richard Peachey, of this Parish, Yeoman	11 Mar 1731	63
Charles Ballinger	20 June, 1763	64
Sarah his Wife	9 May, 1753	71
Giles Robbins	2 Apl 1768	74
Mary Robbins his Niece	26 Mar 1765	26
Richard Robbins	23 Apl 1769	70
Mary his Wife	9 June, 1773	76
Charles Blackwell	9 Nov 1754	84
Mary his Wife	5 Nov 1717	40
Thomas their Son	15 Dec 1755	42
Giles their Son	29 Sept 1767	66
William Rundell	16 Feb 1774	29
Mary his Sister	11 Apl 1767	77
Richard, Son of John and Bridget Wilson	9 Aug 1759	23
John Wilson	27 Dec 1772	80
John his Son, by Bridget his Wife	30 Jan, 1742	10
Joseph Wilson, Junior	15 Nov 1676	82
Mary his Wife	4 Dec 1725	48
Mary Waite	22 Feb 1759	30
Robert, Son of Joseph and Mary Sly	15 June, 1764	45
Richard Turk, Yeoman	15 Oct 1779	87
Mary his Wife	3 Nov 1780	74
Charles Turk	27 May, ——	54
Sarah Turk	6 Feb 1757	24
Giles Curtis	5 June, 1781	61
Mary, Wife of Giles Curtis	15 Jun 1770	37
Charles Jark	7 June, 1751	63

	Died	
Henry Gold, senior, late of Stowell	21 Dec	1754
George Parfett	30 Dec.	1783
Simon Hathaway	28 Oct.	1777
Nicholas Turk, Yeoman	6 June,	1757
Sarah his Wife	3 July,	1768
Nicholas, Son of Nicholas and Elizabeth Turk, of Shipton Sollis	13 Mar	1769
Mary, Wife of Thomas Court, Daughter of the above Nicholas and Sarah Turk	30 Jan.	1782
Richard Turk, of Shipton Sollis	17 July,	1785
John Wright, alias Glover	15 Sept	1757
Edward Miles, of Shipton Olliffe	30 Jan	1756
Ann his Wife	24 June,	1767
Mary, Wife of Robert Radway	7 May,	1777
Anthony Crump, senior	17 May,	1759
Hester his Daughter	13 Apr.	1758
Esther Crump	3 Apr.	1774
William Day, of Northleach	15 Apr	1744
Anthony Crump, junior	24 Mar	1762
Edmund George	1 May,	1750
Sabina, Wife of Robert Roff, and Daughter of Fletcher and Mary Eltom	23 Oct.	1781
Betty, Daughter of John and Hester Miles	2 Feb	1762
Thomas Preston	17 Apr 1755	
Mary, Wife of Thomas Preston	26 Sept.	1773
John Stephens	22 Nov	1786

CHELTENHAM

LXV. CHELTENHAM,
OR
CHILTHAM,

A NAME derived from the Rivulet *Chilt*, on which it is situate.

The Parish of *Cheltenham* lies in the Eastern Extremity of the great Vale of Gloucester, from which City it is distant ten Miles, nine South from *Tewkesbury*, and six from *Winchcombe*. It is the Chief of its own Hundred, over which it still exercises certain Manerial Jurisdictions. The Soil, in so wide a Circumference is ten Miles, admits of great Variety, from a loose Sand to Clay or Loam, the whole of extraordinary Fertility. The Arable Lands exceed 1900 Acres, the Pasture 1500, and as yet no general Inclosure has taken Place.

In the early Centuries, *Cheltenham* [*] had obtained the Privilege of a Market and Fairs, but the precise Period of the Grant is not known. The Town consists of one principal Street, extended to a Mile in length, and formerly not remarkable for commodious Buildings, or other Advantages, excepting those of Situation, which is considerable, it being entirely protected from the North-east by that immense Amphitheatre formed by the *Cotswold* Hills. These terminate abruptly within the Distance of two Miles, in a bare Rock of a white granulated Stone.

Upon the Discovery of the Medicinal Spring, in the beginning of the present Century, and its Efficacy being proved, and generally known, *Cheltenham* became a Place of great Resort, and frequented by the first Ranks in Society. To this Circumstance it owes its present Appearance, and, as the first Cause has increased in the opinion of the Public, it has gained various Acquisitions of Improvement and Con-

* "*Chintham* there a fair, havenge a Markett. It belonged to the Abbay of *Cirnesly*, now to the Kinge. There a Brooke on the South side of the Towne." LELAND, Itin vol IV. 179.

4 N

venience Buildings, peculiar to these Situations, of public as well as private Accommodation, have been so frequently and judiciously erected, as to make this a very respectable Specimen of a *modern* Town, and perhaps the Improvement of our old Towns, is amongst the most successful Inventions of this Age It does not appear that this Town was ever incorporated, but it possessed various and peculiar Privileges within its own Hundred, which in the Lapse of Time are in general become totally obsolete and disused *

The Benefice is an endowed Curacy † King Henry the First in 1133 gave the Impropriation to the Abbey of Cirencester, which was confirmed to them by Pope Celestine in 1289 It has ever included

* MSS Prynne

† The Particulars are taken from a very curious Manuscript written in 1624 in the Possession of John De la Bere, Esq of Cheltenham on which he has with great Politeness, suffered Extracts to be made Two Letters are added to on the Lords Salisbury and Verulam as elucidating the Subject is being original and shewing what was the official Style of the Day

To Mrs Elizabeth Bacshott

" After my hearty Commendations Having received from my Lord the Bishop of Gloster a Complaint against you, in " Behalfe of the Inhabitants of Cheltenham that whereas by Covenante contained in your Lease of the Impropriation, you " were bound to minister by your own Castles and Charges two distinct Chaplains and two Deacons, for the Service of God, " ministers in of his People in his Churches there you have notwithstanding mainteyned only two reading Minister there " .... the Allowance of but ten Pounds a Yeere, to the Scandle of the Church of God and the defrauding of his Majesty's " .... of the spirituall Food ... their Soule Although I might tell you to strict Accompte for the same, to answer the " breach of your Covenant I have, notwithstanding, thought good for this Tyme to let you know, by this my Letter, the " Complainte and .... and doe require you, either to reforme that Abuse perfectly, by allowing the two Chaplains " compounded by mee with the Knowledge and Allowance of my Lord Bishop there or to make your speedy Repaire unto " me if ... ... to these ...... but Reasons you may have to continue such an Abuse whereof ... be let, it is implied I shall be " unwilling to think in Conscience ... unles you speedily to reforme And so do I commend you to God, expecting a performance " As witcheth you mean to pacifie him ... From the Court, 16 April, 16.. Your loving Friend,

                                                                                                    " R Salisbury "

To Mistress Bacher

" After my hearty Commendations Whereas you retyred by Covenante with me to find two fit and different Chaplains " and ... Deacons, to ... me ... another Non-Resident, for the Churches, and Furtherance of Cheltenham and Charlton " Kings ... whereby ... that ... were bound to end me by vertue of your Lease, granted to me by Queen Eliza- " beth ... the ... the Inhabitants of the said Families that you have notwithstanding, defrauded them not also at " ... ... and laid ... Non ... laity ... ought by Covenant to provide at your own Charge but have " ... upon them .... spiritall Food ... their Soules allowing yeerly unto two Curates only 20 Although you have " ... ... evil unto Non-residence breach of your Covenant by allegation comeing yet I have through the breach " seen I ... ... with you ... therefore ... require you quickly to reforme the said Abuse, by allowing unto the .. " ... ... demanded by his Majesty or his Auditor their report of your reckoning to another Other " ... ... service that either other and to part and either I owe and have " ... ... in his Court of Complaint in the Exchequer ...... except me, your Courtesy " ... ... Court ... to the ..... Bury, 13 Nov 16.. Your loving Friend,

                                                                                                    " Fran Verulam "

the Parish of *Charlton Kings*, with its Chapel, as an Appendage. At the Dissolution of Monasteries it reverted to the Crown, and was granted in Lease to Sir HENRY JERNINGHAM, 22 May, 1560, 2 ELIZABETH, on the 10th of May, 1592, 35 ELIZABETH, to WILLIAM GREENWELL, on the 15th of February following, to RICHARD STEPHENS, and on the 17th of February 1597, to Sir FRANCIS BACON, Knight, for forty Years, in Consideration of 75*l* 13*s* 4*d*. ELIZABETH BADGER, or BAGHOTT, Widow, held under the last mentioned Lessee. In 1609, on Information to HENRY PARRY, Lord Bishop of GLOUCESTER, that the Stipend allowed to two reading Ministers, and two Deacons, was but 10*l* and [illegible] a Year to each; the Bishop came to *Cheltenham*, and preached, but the Impropriatrix continuing obstinate, a Petition was presented to Lord SALISBURY, then Secretary of State, that a Chaplain might be appointed for either Parish. By the Mediation of THOMAS STEPHENS, Esq; Attorney General to Prince CHARLES, it was compromised for the Time, the Sub-Lessee allowing the privy Tythes for Payment of the Stipends. But, the Covenants being again infracted, the Parishioners petitioned the Lord Chancellor BACON, the Lessee of the Crown, stating, that by the allowing only 20*l* to two Chaplains, and refusing to supply the Sacramental Bread and Wine, 6000 Communicants were deprived. The Attainder of Lord VERULAM prevented the due Effect of this Remonstrance, and a farther Application was made to the King, with Reference to the Diocesan, and Lord Keeper WILLIAMS. In 1624, when the Impropriation was granted to Sir BAPTIST HICKES, a Decree in Chancery was obtained, by which the Impropriator is bound to allow a Salary of 40*l* each, to the officiating Ministers of either Parish. This Arrangement being made, Sir BAPTIST invested the Principal and Fellows of *Jesus College, Oxford*, with the Nomination, subject to the subjoined Restrictions, which are copied from an authentic Manuscript.

"The Parties recommended by the College must be sufficient preaching Ministers, Masters of Arts "of two Yeares standing at the least, and unmarried Persons.

"The College, upon any Avoydance of either of the said Churches, to present to the Heire of the "Lord CAMPDEN three of the Fellowes, and he to nominate and elect whom he pleaseth. If, after such "Presentment made, the Heire shall not within six Weekes elect out of the Persons so presented, the "Nomination for that Turne shall be in the College; and, on the other Side, if the College present not "within two Moneths, the Heire shall name for that Turne. None to be elected by the College, or "presented by the Heire, but Fellowes of the College, and they to continue but six Yeares at most, "unles by a new Presentment and Election. The sayd Ministers to preach once every Sabbath, not to "be absente both together, to have no other Benefice, and to remaine unmarried.*" The Impropriation is now vested in the Right Honourable WILLIAM ANNE-HOLLES, Earl of ESSEX, and JOHN DE LA BERE, Esq.

The Church, which is very spacious, consists of a Transept and two Aisles, a Tower in the Middle, finished by a lofty octagonal Spire, and containing eight musical Bells. Part of the ancient Rood Loft is preserved, and in the North Transept is a circular Window, about fifteen Feet in Diameter, with beautiful and singular Ramifications. In the Chancel is a very curious Lavaratory, resembling an external Pinnacle, and, from which it may be collected, the Style of Architecture is that of the Middle Ages. The ancient Cross in the Church-yard remains nearly entire.

Of the Chantry founded here in Honour of the *Virgin*, to whom likewise the Church was dedicated, the last Incumbent was THOMAS BALL†, who received a Pension. Another Chantry was dedicated to *St Catherine*.

In Domesday Book this Manor occurs under the Title of "Terra Regis," and had formerly belonged to King EDWARD the CONFESSOR, who had charged it with a yearly Payment of 9*l* [illegible] and [illegible] for the King's Dogs. It afterwards paid 20*l* and 16*s* in Lieu of the Bread, and was rated to contain 8½ Hides ‡, about 850 Acres. WILLIAM LONGESPEE, Earl of SALISBURY, enjoyed this Manor in 1219, 3 HEN. III. In 1415 it was taken from the Alien Priory of *Montburg Lyschamp* in *Normandy*, and granted to the Nunnery of *Sion* in *Middlesex*, by King HENRY V. It afterwards passed to Sir MAURICE BERKELEY, Grandson of THOMAS Baron BERKELEY, the Re-founder of *Beverston* Castle. Upon the general Dissolution of Monasteries it reverted to the Crown, from which it was never entirely alienated till the Sale of it, by King CHARLES the First. This Conjecture is formed on the clearest Evidence. The Lease of the Manor was confirmed to WILLIAM NORWOOD, of *Leckhampton*, Esq; on the 27th of May, 1590, 32 ELIZ. from which we collect that he had a prior Possession of it. About the Year 1618, CHARLES, then Prince of WALES, deputed his Surveyor, JOHN NORDEN §, Esq; to make a Return of his Manor of *Cheltenham* and its Dependencies, after which he agreed to sell the Lordship to certain [illegible] for the Sum of [illegible] at [illegible] Payments ‖, levied on the Tenants of the Manor, in Consideration of the Recognition and Adjudication of their ancient Copyhold Custom. The Act of Parliament by

* MSS. [illegible]

† WILLIS.

‡ "A Hide, or Carucate, of Land, [illegible] which one Man could cultivate in a Year."

BLOMEFIELD's *Norf.* vol. I. p. 3[illegible]

§ JOHN NORDEN [illegible] in the Reign of JAMES I. [illegible] which he "received [illegible] and chorographical [illegible] at all [illegible] and [illegible] published [illegible] [illegible] Speculum Britanniae [illegible] GRANGER's Biography, [illegible] of [illegible] Worc. [illegible] vol. I. p. [illegible]

‖ The first Agreement [illegible] ADAM NEWTON, Knight and Baronet, Treasurer "and Receiver General [illegible] the Prince [illegible] the Manor of *Cheltenham* [illegible] "for Confirmation [illegible] Copyhold [illegible] said Manor, the [illegible] Money of "[illegible]"

[illegible] the Expence of passing [illegible]

which

which the Agreement was ratified, was passed in 1625, to which GILES GREVILLE, Esq the Lord of the Manor of *Aſhley* in *Charlton King's*, assented, and received a proportionate Consideration from the Tenants of his Manor These Covenants were finally settled in 1628, 3 CHARLES I and in that, or the following Year, the Manor was sold by the Feoffees to JOHN DUTTON, of *Sherborne*, Esq who held his first Court June 3, 1629 In his Descendants it has been vested to the present Possessor, who was ennobled on the 20th of May, 1784, 24 GEO III by the Title of Baron SHERBORNE, of *Sherborne* in this County

The leading Distinctions and Peculiarities of the Tenure, is confirmed by the Act of Parliament, are hese " That the Descent of customary Lands shall be henceforth as by common Law, saving, " that there shall be no Co-heirship, but the eldest Female shall inherit solely That the Husband surviving the Wife, shall not hold by Courtesy, and that the customary Lands shall pass by Surrender, " in open Court, before the Steward, or out of Court, before two customary Tenants "

The Free Grammar School * was established and endowed by RICHARD PATE, of *Minſterworth*, Esq in 1574 By an Indenture between him and the President and the seven Senior Fellows of *Corpus Chriſti College*, *Oxford*, dated October 6, 1586, it appears, that Queen ELIZABETH, in Consequence of her granting Lands and Messuages appendant to the Manor of *Cheltenham*, in free Socage, subject to the annual Rent of 19*l* 18*s* 1*d* ¼ for the Foundation of the School and an Hospital, was to be styled " The " Foundress," and the Nomination of the Head Master to be vested in the said President and Fellows, in Default of Heirs, which has since happened The present Head Master is the Rev HENRY FOWLER, M A In 1682 GEORGE TOWNESHEND, of *Rowell*, Esq bequeathed eight Exhibitions to *Pemb ok College*, *Oxford* for Youths educated in this County, two of whom are sent from this Seminary The Hospital founded at the same Time has received far her Benefactions. The annual Income of PATE's Endowment was 73*l* 19*s* 4*d* as appears by the Rental dated 1583

The greater Part of the Town consists of Burgage Tenures under the Manor These now pass by Lease and Release as other free Lands, the Grant by "Copy being destroyed by a Verdict in Ejectment, brought to ascertain the Mode of passing them about the Year 1717. To these the Right of Commonage in the *Marſh* of about fifty Acres, is solely appendant.

Nearly 1260 Acres are included in the Town Hamlet; beside which, are three others belonging to this Parish 1 *Arle* *Arle Court* originally belonged to a Family of that Name, from whom it passed by Inheritance to the GREVILLES, and from them to the LYGONS, a Branch of the *Worcesterſhire* Family It was afterward the Property of Sir FLEETWOOD DORMER, Knt The Honourable JOHN YORKE, third Son of PHILIP, late Earl of HARDWICKE, is the present Proprietor, in Right of his Lady, ELIZABETH, Daughter and Heir of REGINALD LYGON, Esq Attached to this ancient Structure was a Chapel, now destroyed, on a Beam of which was a Date 1250. Here likewise is a medicinal Spring 2 *Alſtone* Of this District the Proprietors are the Principal and two Senior Fellows of *Jeſus College*, *Oxford*, in Trust, for certain Exhibitions, JOHN DE LA BERE, THOMAS WHITE, and RICHARD CRITCHETT, Esqrs 3 *Weſtal*, *Naunton*, and *Sandford*, form the third Hamlet, the former is the sole Property of JOHN DE LA BERE †, Esq between whom, DODINGTON HUNT, Esq and the Families of WOOD and HIGGES, the others are divided In 1779 JOHN DE LA BERE, Esq purchased of the Earl of Essex, and GEORGE Lord Viscount MALDEN his Son, all the Tythes and Glebe of *Weſtal*, *Naunton*, and *Sandford*, with the rest of his own Estate in *Alſtone* Mr. PRYNNE mentions a Priory in *Cheltenham*, of which a Part was inhabited by the Lessee of the Impropriation ‡ In PATE's Rental several Messuages are specified, as formerly belonging to the Chantry of *St Catherine*, and others to that of *St Mary*

---

* The Master of this School is required to be a Master of Arts, and thirty Years of Age, and when superannuated is entitled to the first Vacancy in the Hospital, with the additional Stipend of two Pence weekly This Provision is however, worded with some Delicacy " It hee will accept of the Roome of a pore Man ' Statutes MSS That Queen ELIZABETH was considered as Foundress is farther proved by the subjoined Title Page " Anglorum Præma ab anno 1387, uſque ad Annum 1578 summatim perſtricta, Authore CHRISTOPHERO OCKLANDO, Scholæ *South warkenſis*, dein *Cheltenamenſis* post a jam ſicut " Magiſtate fundatæ, Moderatore Londini, 1582," 8vo

† Of the Family of DE LA BERE, a more particular Account will be given under "CLEVE '
The very curious Portrait, of which an Engraving is annexed was certainly done soon after the Introduction of Painting in Oil into this Kingdom The Invention is ascribed to JOHN VAN EYCK in 1400, but Mr WALPOLE supposes, says "Anecdotes of Painting," vol I p 45, that the Art has been practised in *England* prior to that ... probably his Picture would strongly confirm his Opinion The Event which conferred such high'd Honour on this Family happened in 1445 and his been a received Tradition, that this Picture is nearly of equal Antiquity Sir RICHARD personally rescued the King from the most imminent Danger on that Day of Triumph and was afterwards in 1456 Escheator of the King, having been High Custos, or Sheriff of the County of *Hereford* from the Year 1465 to 1473, an Instance of unlimited Confidence Fuller's Worthies p 43 In RYMER's Fædera vol VII p 345 (1393 5 RICH II) " Beddicus & concilio ... the Soldan " burſes, banneretto Calidum de *Fine de Laneter*, co *Karmarthen*, quod RICHARDUS DE LA BERE Chivaler, ... " farther Limit pro Termino vitæ suæ ' This ascertains the Time of his Death and we collect from Leland, that very lately p..., that he was buried in the Church of Black Friars in the City of *Hereford* founded by Edw III When the Licence for fortifying was certified in 1480 Record was made of this Picture, it is said " to be curiously painted and for its great Value " preserved MSS Coll Arm In Lelands Collectanea vol IV p 214, another Sir RICHARD DE LA BERE is mentioned as having ... erected a banneret at the Battle of *Stoke* in 1486 Fuller, in his Worthies p 46 confirms this Circumstance and the Reward of his Attachment to King Henry VII But STOWE in his Annals p 472 asserts that he was created at the Coronation of that Prince h

Noted from FANNER's Notitia Monaſtica, p 144, and said to have been founded in 800, but is really only that founded by PATE, and his Continuator STEVENS

The Portrait of Sir **Richard De la Bere** ....
.... for Edward the Black Prince at the battle of Crecy 1347
....

....

The Medicinal Spring, fo juftly celebrated and frequented, was firft known in 1716, but to what Accident the Difcovery of it may be attributed, it may be now too late, or unneceffary, to enquire It rifes in a Meadow, a few Furlongs diftant from the Town, on the South Side, about fix Feet beneath the Surface It was foon after inclofed and fecured by the Proprietor, and attracted the Notice of the Faculty, by fome of whom analytical Experiments were made, and its Properties afcertained * Various Treatifes have been publifhed, and Opinions fupported, which are fomewhat contradictory, as to the conftituent Particles The moft received Definition of it is, that it may be termed " a neutral, purgative, " chalybeate, Water," efficacious to a very eminent Degree in thofe Diforders which are peculiar to the natural Habit and Conftitution of Englifhmen Of the Progrefs of his falutary Fountain to its prefent State of Celebrity, fome Account will be expected In the Year 1721 it was firft leafed out for 61*l* per Annum, and a fmall Pavilion erected over the Well In 1738 HENRY SKILLICORNE, the Proprietor, built a commodious Room for the Reception of the Company, and the Avenue of Trees leading from the Church was planted after a Defign of the late NORBORNE BERKELEY Lord BOTETOURT The Length of this Vifta is 190 Yards, the Breadth 7, and the Space between each Tree about four Yards. Subfequent to thefe, many additional Improvements have taken Place, and fuch as render it equal to moft Reforts of the Kind The Fee of it, with a confiderable Eftate, ftill remains in the Family of SKILLICORNE Upon an eafy Eminence above this Spot, the prefent Earl FAUCONBERG has built an elegant modern Edifice, in the Attic Style, which in the Summer of 1788 was honoured with the ROYAL RESIDENCE † During which, a Well was ordered to be funk at a fmall Diftance from the Manfion-houfe, for domeftic Ufes At the Depth of about fifty Feet a Spring was difcovered, and is found by Analyfis to poffefs all the fpecific Medicinal Qualities of the other, and to be much more copious This fortunate Circumftance will enable the Proprietor to give a more conftant Supply for the Service of the Company, the Chemifts who extract Salts, and for Exportation

---

B E N E F A C T I O N S.

RICHARD PATE gave by Will, 1574, for the founding and endowing a free School, and Hofpital for fix poor Perfons, Lands, to the Value of 31*l* 18*s* ‡ per Annum, vefted in *Corpus Chrifti College, Oxford.*

THOMAS GEORGE, 1620, bequeathed by Will the Sum of 6*s* 8*d* per Annum, viz 3*s* 4*d* to the Poor, and 3*s* 4*d* to the Minifter for a Sermon

JOHN WALWIN by Will, 1627, left Lands, the annual Produce of which now is 2*l* 10*s* to be diftributed amongft the Poor, vefted in the Churchwardens

Several Donations in Lands were given in 1667 for the Ufe and Maintenance of the Poor, the annual Produce of which now is 22*l*, vefted in the Churchwardens, and is fubject to Taxes

GEORGE TOWNSEND, 1682, by Will, towards the Support of eight Scholars at *Pembroke College, Oxford,* two of which to be elected from *Cheltenham* School, left 8*l* per Annum, the annual Proportion of this Donation is uncertain, depending upon the Number of refident Scholars

He alfo gave Lands, the annual Produce of which now is 4*l* for teaching poor Children to read, vefted in Mr LUCAS

And alfo 5*l* per Annum for the apprenticeing of poor Boys, vefted alfo in Mr LUCAS

Rev WILLIAM STANLEY, 1704, left by Will, Lands, for the apprenticeing of poor Boys, the annual Produce of which is 3*l* 10*s*, vefted in the Minifter

LADY CAPEL, 1721, by Will, gave a Portion of 105*l* to fupport a Charity School, the yearly Sum thence arifing is 8*l*, vefted in Mr NETTLESHIP.

GILES COX, by Deed, 1727, gave for teaching poor Children to read and write, or to apprentice a poor Boy, Lands to the Value of 4*l* per Annum, vefted in ——— Cox, Spinfter

---

* The firft Analyfis of this Water was made by Doctors GREVILLE and BAIRD in 1721 About the Year 1740 Dr SHORT, in his Treatife on Mineral Waters, declares this to be a " neutral, purgative, chalybeate, Water," and gives it the Preference to any of that Defcription in *England* In 1741 CONRADUS HIERONYMUS BENKENBURG, of *Leyden,* publifhed his Examination in the Philofophical Tranfactions " No 461 p 630, in which he confutes the Idea of its containing any chalybeate Particles In the fame Number this Opinion is confirmed by Mr CROMWELL MORTIMER Dr LUCAS, in his Effay on Waters, Part II calls it " faline, bitter and flightly vitriolic," and " certainly impregnated with Steel " It has been found that by " mixing a few Drops of the Infufion of Galls, as 12 to 2 Ounces, that it inftantly ftrikes a pale, but vivid Purple and on † Evaporation, to certain in a Gallon eight Drams of nitrous Earth with two Drams of an alkaline Earth, that it confifts " of a large Quantity of calcareous Nitre (to which it owes its cathartic Qualities), a light Sulphur, and a volatile Steel It " is not affected by alkaline Spirits, but ferments with Acids

Dr SMITH, in his Effay (edit 1786), obferves, ' that the Spring is fuppofed to yield thirty five Pints in an Hour, a com " paratively fmall Quantity '

Other Writers on this Subject are, Drs LINDEN, RUSSEL, FOTHERGILL, and HULME

† In Commemoration of this Event, Medals have been ftruck, exhibiting the Profile of his prefent Majefty Legend, " GEORGIUS III DEI GRATIA " Reverfe, Royal Efcutcheon enfigned with the Crown Legend, " CHELTENHAM, JULY 12, ' 1788 ' The Exergue is very deeply engraved

‡ The Endowment of the Hofpital only

OFFICIATING

Officiating Minister	Patrons		Officiating Ministers	Patrons
—— Richard Walker,	——	1692	Luke Williams, B D	Jesus College, Oxf
1624 Richard Brooke, B D	Toby Packer	1709	Henry Heafe, M A	The fame
1624 John Inglish, D D	Bp of Gloucester	1716	Humphrey Lloyd, M A	The fame
* * * * * * *		1716	—— Maurice, M A	The fame
1660 Maurice Roberts, M A	Jefus College, Oxf	17	George Stokes, M A	The fame
1662 —— Bowen, M A	The fame	1734	Edmond Meyrick, M A	The fame
1669 Henry Maurice, B D	The fame	1740	Thomas Morgan, B D.	The fame
16-- —— Lloyd, M A	The fame	1754	Jones Reid, D D	The fame
1673 Rith Weld, B D	The fame	1767	John Lloyd, B D	The fame
1688 Kenrick Puleltone, M A	The fame	1773	Hugh Hughes, B D	The fame

PRESENT LORD OF THE MANOR,

The Right Honourable JAMES Lord SHERBORNE

The Perfons fummoned from this Parifh by the Heralds in 1682 and 1683, were

St Fleetwood Dormer, Knight,   —— Ludlow, Gent
The Heirs of William Prynne, Efq   Walter Ireland, Gent
The Heirs of Thomas Packer, Gent   George Roberts, Gent
Edward Wright, M D   Edward Mitchell, Gent
John Ellis, Gent   Samuel Arrowfmith, Gent.
Ralph Weld, B D   William Roberts, Gent
George Stunning, Gent   William Freme, Gent.
John Jones, A x

The Regifter commences in 1660

ANNUAL ACCOUNT OF MARRIAGES, BIRTHS, AND BURIALS, IN THIS PARISH

A D	Mar	Bir	Bur	A D	Mar	Bir	Bur	A D	Mar	Bir	Bur	A D	Mar	Bir	Bur
1781	18	35	46	1786	16	56	43	1791				1796			
1782	13	44	42	1787	18	69	50	1792				1797			
1783	20	55	51	1788				1793				1798			
1784	19	57	44	1789				1794				1799			
1785	13	53	50	1790				1795				1800			

INSCRIPTIONS IN THE CHURCH.

IN THE CHANCEL

ON A COARSE STONE AGAINST THE EAST WALL.

THE SAD MEMORIAL OF JOHN ENGLISH, DOCTOR IN DIVINITY, TO JANE HIS MOST DEARE WIFE, DAUGHTER TO THE HONOURABLE ELIZABETH LADY SANDYS BARONESS DE LA VIN COMIT SOUTHTON, FROM WHOM HE WAS DIVORCED BY 18 WEEKS CLOSE IMPRISONMENT, WHICH SHO E AFTER CAUSED HER DEATH ON AUGUST 8, 1643. TO MARY HIS SECOND DAUGHTER, WHO DECEASED OCT 25, FOLLOWING

SIC CRESCIT ET VINS, ET DISSOLVET CRESCENS,
IN CONJUX AC MOESTUS PARENS   I L
QUI MUNDO SUSPIRANS, ET COELUM ASPIRANS,
INDESINENTER CLAMAT
BONI JESU, ESTO MIHI JESUS
SIS MIHI, O JESU, SIS JESUS (CHRISTI) MEORUM!
SI FELIX SALVTOR OF MANKIND,
"THIS ——— MILE A —— MINE
ASPIRANS OR IT,
SIC ASPIRANS EXPIRAVIT,
EXPIRANS EXPIRAVIT,
JOHANNES INGLISH, SANCTE VERITATIS STUDIOSUS,
OBIIT ANNO CHRISTI   AMEN

ON A LARGE BLUE FLAT STONE, THE EFFIGIES IN BRASS, OF A MAN IN HIS JUDGE'S ROBES AND COIF, HIS WIFE, THREE SONS, AND SEVEN DAUGHTERS, INSCRIPTION ROUND THE MARGIN REMAINING [*].

"𝕾𝖑𝖔𝖚𝖌𝖍𝖙𝖊𝖗, 𝖜𝖍𝖎𝖈𝖍𝖊 𝖂𝖎𝖑𝖑𝖎𝖆𝖒 𝖉𝖊𝖈𝖊𝖘𝖘𝖎𝖉 𝖙𝖍𝖊 𝖝𝖎 𝕯𝖆𝖞𝖊 𝖔𝖋 𝕸𝖆𝖗𝖈𝖍𝖊, 𝖎𝖓 𝖙𝖍𝖊 𝕴𝕴𝕴𝕴 𝕽𝖊𝖗𝖊 𝖔𝖋 𝖙𝖍𝖊 𝕽𝖊𝖎𝖌𝖓𝖊 𝖔𝖋 𝕶𝖎𝖓𝖌𝖊 𝖍𝖊𝖓𝖗𝖞 𝖁𝕴𝕴𝕴"

ON A PLAIN FREE STONE MONUMENT

Arms; on an Inefcutcheon, a Lion rampant, for BLOMER

Near this Place lies the Body of JOSEPH ARKEL, who departed this Life Oct 1, 1699, aged 79 Years

Also FRANCES, Wife of the abovefaid JOHN ARKEL, and youngeft Daughter of HENRY BLOMER, late of Cowley, Gent who exchanged this Life for a better March 23, 1720, aged 73

[*] This Monument was erected for WILLIAM GREVILLE, of A le Court in this Parish, who was one of the Juftices of the Court of Common Pleas, appointed in that Office by Henry the Seventh. In Leland's Itin. vol VI p 622. "The Heir of the Lord now lyving, is married unto the Heir of Sir WILLIAM GREVILLE, a Judge, and a Man of Law."

ON A HANDSOME PYRAMIDICAL MONUMENT OF WHITE AND VARIEGATED MARBLE

Arms, three Demi Lions

Beneath this Monument are deposited
the Remains of HENRY STURMY,
who departed this Life Oct 24, 1772,
aged 51 Years

ON A PYRAMIDICAL MARBLE NEAR THE ABOVE

Arms, a Chevron between three Pheons an
Escutcheon of Pretence, a Cross.

In Memory of BAPTIST SMART, M D
late of this Parish, who, after a long and painful
Illness, departed this Life (at the Hot Wells, Bristol)
Dec 20, 1772, in the 63d Year of his Age,
and lies interred at Clifton

ON A NEAT MONUMENT OF BLACK AND WHITE MARBLE

Arms, Quarterly, 1 an Eagle displayed, 2 a
Bend, 3. Paly of six, 4 a Chevron between three
Leaves

To the Memory of KATHARINE,
the Wife of WILLIAM P A'COURT,
of Heytesbury in the County of Wilts, Esq
who departed this Life on the 23d Day of
Sept 1776, in the 32d Year of her Age
The strictest Honour and Virtue,
Elegance of Manners, Integrity of Heart,
and Delicacy of Sentiment, endeared her to a select
Circle of Friends and Acquaintance,
she was cherished as an only Child by an
indulgent Father,
beloved from her Infancy by a tender Husband,
in whose Arms she died an unnatural Death,
effected by Poison,
administered by the Hands of a cruelly wicked
Livery Servant,
whose Resentment at being detected in Theft,
prompted him to perpetrate this
horrid and execrable Crime

ON A BRASS PLATE NEAR THE VESTRY DOOR

Arms, a Bend between two Dolphins —impaling,
on a Less, three Escallops

Here lyeth the Body of ELIZABETH,
the Wife of WILLIAM FRENCH, Gent
and Daughter of the Rev JAMES INGRAM, D D
formerly Rector of Whittington in this County
She died the last of his fourteen Children on the
10th of Sept in the 65th Year of her Age,
and in the Year of our Lord 1727

Also the Body of MARGARET, the Daughter
of the abovesaid ELIZABETH FRENCH
She died March 15, 1729, aged 44

ON FLAT STONES

MARY, the Daughter of JOHN WHITHORNE,
of the City of Gloucester, departed this Life
Nov 10, 1700, aged 22 Years.

ROBERT OWEN
died June 4, 1721, aged 30

MARGARET, Wife of JOHN HAYES,
and Relict of ROBERT OWEN, and Daughter
of the aforesaid JOHN and MARY WHITHORNE,
died Oct 13, 1769, aged 84.

JOSEPH NICHOLLS, of this Town, Gent
died December 14, 1730, aged 39

WALTER IRELAND, Gent
was buried July 25, 1692

RICHARD, Son of the abovenamed WALTER,
died in April 1715, aged 24

HESTER, Wife of the abovenamed
WALTER IRELAND, died Sept 13, 1729,
aged 78

Three of their Children, viz WALTER,
MARY, and HESTER, died Infants

ANNE HILL, Daughter of
THOMAS and ANNE WATERS,
died Oct 24, 1765, aged 80

Mrs ANNE HIGGES, Daughter of
THOMAS HIGGES, Gent sometime of Cheltenham,
who deceased August 1, 1620

THOMAS HARTLEBURY
died June 24, 1767, aged 65

SARAH, the Widow of WILLIAM HOWLETT,
of Winchcomb, and Daughter to
LAWRENCE HIGGES, of this Town,
departed this Life December 22, 1694.

JOHN HOWLETT, Son of
WILLIAM and SARAH HOWLETT,
died May 17, 1708, aged 15

THOMAS HIGGES, of Sandford,
was buried March 21, 1679

MARY HARTLEBURY, the Daughter of
THOMAS and ANNE WATERS,
died May 7, 1740, aged 56

BERNARD HIGGES, Gent.
died Jan 25, 1648.

ELIZABETH his Wife
died June 29, 1672

THOMAS WATERS, Gent.
died July 7, 1686

ANNE his Widow
died Aug 16, 1720, aged 64.

Mrs ELIZABETH FIELD
died April 15, 1784, aged 60.

WILLIAM

WILLIAM PRYNNE, Gent
died November 12, 1080, aged 61.

ELIZABETH, the Daughter of WILLIAM PRYNNE,
Gent died November 18, 1657

Also ANNE, who died (his Widow and Relict)
on the 20th of August, 1697, aged 69

JOHN, Son of JAMES ETHERIDGE,
died July 27, 1696,
aged 3 Years and 7 Months
ANNE ETHERIDGE
died Jun 9, 1774, aged 45.

WILLIAM COOK
died April 4, 1752, aged 60
HESTER his Wife
died Feb 16, 1767, aged 30
WILLIAM their Son
died Dec 7, 1745, in the 20th Year of his Age

Hoc Tumulo Conduntur Cineres
BRIGITTE PETTY,
Reverendi ELIÆ PETTY,
de Shipton Sollers in hac Diocesi,
olim Rectoris
Relictæ
Obiit 26 Die Aprilis, Anno Dom. 1717.
WILLIAM PETTY
died July 10, 1749, aged 53.

EDMUND WALWEYNE, Gent.
died February 17, 1617
GEORGE STURMY, Mercer,
died July 19, 1711, ætat suæ 85.
HESTER his Daughter
died April 21, 1723

HENRY STURMY
was buried Dec 31, 1676

ALICE, Daughter of GEORGE STURMY, Mercer,
died June 1, 1715

ALICE, Relict to Mr EDMUND GINES,
Citizen of London, and second Daughter to
EDWARD JOHNSON, Mercer in this Town,
died May 6, 1694.

Mrs MARY GINES
deceased in London Feb , 1714, aged 31.

ANNE WANLEY BOWES, Wife of
GEORGE WANLEY BOWES, Esq of Thornton Hall
in the County of Durham,
and Daughter of JAMES HUTTON, Esq
of Maske in the County of York
died Sept 1, 1761, in the 49th Year of her Age

IN THE NORTH TRANSEPT.

ON A HANDSOME MONUMENT.

Arms, Azure, ten Billetts, 4, 3, 2, 1, Or, on
a Chief of the last a Demi Lion issuant Sable, for
DORMER,—impaling, Argent, two Lions passant
Gules, for LYGON

Hic juxta sita est
CATHARINA
FLEETWOODI DORMER, Equitis Aurati, Sponsa,
JOHANNIS LYGON, de Arle Court, Armigeri,
Ex ELIZABETHÆ Uxoris filia,
Utriusque Parentis Hæres unica,
cujus Familia in Agro Wigorniensi
per trecentos & amplius annos
Floruit, & adhuc fœliciter floret
A tanto licet genere oriunda nobilique nuptæ
Stirpem tamen & Conjugem,
Utrosque antea illustres,
Morum sanctitate illustriores reddidit.
Maritum si non Patrem, Hæredem scripsit
Hæc illum moriens amplo Patrimonio
Ille hanc amissam hoc Monumento decoravit.
Decessit Februa 3,
Anno { Ætatis 72
{ Domini 1678.

JOHANNES LYGON, supradictus, obiit 1644.
Filius unicus RICARDI LYGON,
de Maddersfield, Arm ex secundis
Nuptiis cum MARGARETTA, Filia
JOH TALBOTT, Militis, ex stirpe Comitum Salop.æ.
Affinis etiam fuit Baronibus
de Berkly Castro, aliisque Proceribus;
& per Uxores suas Hæredibus
quorum Insignia superne
depinguntur.

[ON THE ATCHIEVEMENT MENTIONED IN THE
INSCRIPTION, ARE THE FIFTEEN FOLLOWING
COATS OF ARMS, WITH THE NAMES ANNEXED

1 LYGON as before
2 Gules, a Fess Or, in chief two Mulletts Argent, for BRACEY
3 Azure, on a Bend Or, three Bars dancette
Gules, for MADERSFIELD
4 Argent, fretty Gules, for HARFLEET
5 Or, a Cross pierced Azure, for DECORS.
6 Gules, three Lions passant Argent, for GIF-
FORD
7 Gules, a Fess between six Martlets Or, for
BEAUCHAMP
8 Parti per Pile Or and Gules, three Roundlets
counterchanged, for ABTOT
9 Argent, on a Fess Azure, three Fleurs de lis
Or, for UFFLET
10 Argent, a Bend between six Martlets Gules,
a Crescent for Difference, for FURNEVAL
11 Or, a Lion rampant, per Fess Gules and
Sable, for LUTOT
12 Or, a Fret Gules, for VERDON.
13 Sable, on a Cross within a Bordure engrailed
Or, five Pellets, for GALVIT
14 Or, a Bird riding Vert, within a Tressure
Sable, for ARLE
15 Argent, a Chevron Azure, between three
Garbs Or, banded and stalked Vert, for SOUTHEY]

On

ON A SMALL STONE AGAINST THE SAME WALL

Near this Place
lies interred the Body of
Mrs LLEANOR ONION,
who departed this Life
April 25, 1728.

ON A NEAT MARBLE MONUMENT AGAINST ONE OF THE PILLARS

Arms, a Chevron between three Fleurs de lis, for HUGHES, on an Efcutcheon of Pretence, Argent a Crofs Sable, charged in the centre with a Leopard's Face Or, for BRIDGES

In a Vault near this Place lie interr'd
the Remains of ELIZABETH HUGHES, Wife of
THOMAS HUGHES, Efq of this Town, and
Daughter and Coheir of HARRY BRIDGES, Efq
of Keynfham Abbey in the County of Somerfet,
Having filled all the Relationships of this Life
with Honour to herfelf, and Pleafure to others,
fhe departed this Life on the 14th of Nov 1750,
aged 58
ever to be regretted whilft Virtue, Benevolence,
and Charity, are efteemed by Mankind.
She bore a long and painful Diforder with a Patience,
Refignation, and Fortitude which nothing
could have infpired but the Piety of her whole
Life, and a firm Reliance on thofe Rewards
hereafter, which are promifed to the Exercife
of fo much Goodnefs here

ON FLAT STONES

Here lyeth the Body of JOHN LYGON,
of Arle Court in the County of Gloucefter, Efq
who departed this Life the 21th Day of Sept 1664

MARY, the Wife of JOHN BUCK,
of Lincoln's Inn, London, Efq who died
Jun 14, 1716, aged 41 Years

I H
I H
MIS MARY PACKER
died the 21ft of March, 1765, aged 66 Years

Arms, Gules, a Crofs Lozenge Or, between four Rofes Argent

THOMAS PACKER, the Son of LODOWICK PACKER,
of this Town, Gent departed this Life
Nov 16, 1705, ætatis fuæ 38

KATHERINE his Wife departed this Life
the 1ft of March, 1736, aged 70

THOMAS PACKER, of this Town, Gent
died the 14th Day of June, 1709

LODOWICK, Son of THOMAS PACKER, Gent
died May 20, 1703

SUSAN PACKER died July 27, 1704

LODOWICK PACKER, Gent Proctor of the
abovefaid Town, who died Auguft 31, 1750,
aged 19

EDWARD PACKER, Gent
died Feb 22, 1709, aged 8

Mrs ELIZABETH his
departed this Life May 1, 1715, aged 83.

Mrs KATHERINE PACKER, junior,
died the 4th of June, 1749, aged 49

Mrs ELIZABETH PACKER,
died March 17, 1750, aged 68

Mrs ANNE GREGORY
was buried the 10th of March, 1664

THOMAS GREGORY, the Son of
FRANCIS and HESTER GREGORY, of Alfton,
departed this Life the 2d of Nov 1709,
aged betwixt 3 and 4 Years

Arms, a Dove flanding on two Serpents entwined,
holding in the beak an Olive branch

To the Memory of WILLIAM SLOPER, Gent
who departed this Life Dec 20, 1715

Alfo of JOHN ATTWAY, late Mercer of this Town
who married ELIZABETH, Daughter of the above
WILLIAM SLOPER He departed this Life
July 17, 1777, aged 85 Years

MARTHA ATTWAY died Sept 5 1788

Arms, Or, a Bend Azure, for TAYLER,—
impaling, Paly of fix a Bend, for LONGFORD

Lod in Tumulo conduntur cineres
ELIZABETHÆ, GULI TRYE, Arm Filiæ,
necnon JOH LONGFORD Uxoris
Maxime chari, prei, cariffæ,
& JOHANNIS & ANNÆ,
filii filiæque prædicti JOHANNIS & ELIZAB

ANNA		29 Nov 1733,		1 meaf
ELIZAB	ob	15 Jan 1735,	æt	30
JOHAN		27 Mar 1736,		2 ment

JANA LONGFORD ob Mar 30, 1731, æt 0

MARTHA, Wife of ROBERT SNOW, Efq
of the City of Waterford in the Kingdom of Ireland
died Auguft 27, 1772, aged 35

ELIZABETH, Daughter of the
Rev Mr GEORGE COOKE
was buried Nov 1, 1751, aged 5

Here lieth the Body of GILES HARVEY,
Chirurgeon, who departed this Life
the 11th of January, 1704

GEORGE VERNON, Efq Merchant, of London,
died Sept 13, 1700, aged 7 Years

Here

Here lyes interred ELIZABETH, late Wife of
Mr GABRIEL CURLL, of Buttermore in the
County of Wilts, Gent and Daughter to the
Rev Mr ROGER POWELL, Rector of Moreton
in the County of Hereford, who, by means of
Grace, lived a prudent and pious Christian,
a just and generous Neighbour,
a firm and faithful Friend,
and, in Hopes of Glory, died in Peace
the 23d of Oct 1734, aged 36.

THOMAS SARGEAUNT,
a Native of Tunton,

Also ELIZABETH his Wife,
of Newent, both in this County.
He } dyed { Oct 24, 1741 } aged { 64
She }   { April 1, 1742 }   { 63.

EDMUND COTTON,
who was born at Hereford,
here buried Dec 29, 170
aged 37 Years

SARAH, the Wife of THOMAS ASHMEAD,
Mercer, died Aug 5, 1703, aged 69.

THOMAS ASHMEAD, Mercer,
died March 21, 1706, aged 71.

Also ANN his late Wife
Daughter of GEORGE STURMY,
died April 8, 1710.

RICHARD COOMBE, of Alstone,
died Jun 14, 1719, aged 80

JANE his Wife
died Dec. 15, 1716, aged 84

ELIZABETH, Wife of JOHN BENFIELD,
was buried the 6th of May, 1679.

Here lieth interred in a Vault the Body of
the Rev Mr STEPHEN CULL, Son of
STEPHEN and ELIZABETH CULL, of
Climperwell in the Parish of Cranham,
who died the 25th of December, 1760,
in the 65th Year of his Age

JOHN BENFIELD, Architect,
died June 23, 1766, aged 54.

Mrs ANN BENFIELD, Relict of
the above JOHN BENFIELD
She died March 5, 1783, aged 82.

HARRIOTT, the Daughter of
ROBERT SNOW, Esq by MARTHA his Wife,
who died April 30, 1771,
aged one Year and eight Months

RICHARD ANDREWS, Gent
died Aug 27, 1743, aged 46

HANNAH his Daughter
died June .. 1751, aged 2 Years

JOHN ROYDON HUGHES,
Son of THOMAS HUGHES and
ELIZABETH his Wife, who died on
the 1st of Feb. 1771, the Day he was
six Months old

REBECCA, Wife of the
Rev ANTHONY FREEMAN, departed this Life
April 24, 1773, aged 37 Years

WILLIAM, Son of THOMAS and ANN HINDE,
died March 1, 1770, aged 4 Months.

ON FLAT STONES IN THE NAVE.

RICHARD BECKETT
was buried May 4, 1713, aged 23

SARAH, Relict of JAMES BECKETT, senior,
died August 3, 1728, aged 76.

HENRY, the Son of HENRY and ELIZABETH
SKILLICORNE, died April 7, 1738,
aged 2 Years, 9 Months, and 3 Days

HENRY SKILLICORNE, the Father,
died October 14, 1763, aged 83

EDITH, Wife of ROBERT COX, senior,
died Sept 2, 1713, aged 30

ROBERT COX, senior,
of this Parish, Gent who departed this Life
March 4, 1759, aged 77

EDWARD, Son of the above
ROBERT and EDITH COX,
died July 3, 1767, aged 60.

EDWARD BARKMAN SMALLPEECE,
Son of JAMES and HESTER his Wife,
obiit May 30, 1710

GEORGE SMALLPEECE, Son of
JAMES SMALLPEECE and HESTER his Wife,
obiit 20 die Junii, 1707

Also THOMAS, another Son,
was here buried Jan 31, 1709.

HENRY AKERMAN, Gent
departed this Life July 4,   .   .

MARY, the Wife of the abovesaid
HENRY AKERMAN, Gent and Daughter of
DANIEL CHESTER, of this Town,
died the 9th of January, 1746,
aged 60

Mrs ANN HARVEY
died Jan 28, 1783, aged 73

ON MONUMENTS IN THE SOUTH AISLE AND TRANSEPT.

Near this Place lieth the Body of
CHRISTOPHER BAYLEY, M A
in Corpus Christi College, Oxford, who lived Master
of the Free School in Cheltenham 32 Years,
and deceased April 13, 1654

In Memoriam
Piæ Virginis
IUDITHÆ IONESIÆ (*Jones*),
ROBERTI, & ELIZABETHÆ,
Prolis Unicæ
unice Parentibus dilectæ
Vixit Annos XXI,
Præmissa Anno Domini
MDCLXXVIII,
Decemb XVII

In Memory of MARY GALLOWAY,
who departed this mortal Life
April 14, 1747, æt suæ 61.

In Memory of
THOMAS BENFIELD
He died June 8, 1766, aged 56.

ANNE, Wife of THOMAS BENFIELD, junior,
died June 18, 1741, aged 49

Also SARAH CHESTER,
Sister of the abovesaid ANN,
died Jan 21, 1765, aged 75.

Arms, Per Pale Argent and Gules, a Lion
rampant Sable, for ROBERTS

In Memory of
WALTER COX, of Alstone in this Parish, and
SARAH his Wife, as also of WILLIAM ROBERTS,
Gent who married SARAH their only Child,
and whose Family lie interred near this Place

WALTER COX deceased Aug 24, 1682, aged 57.

SARAH his Wife, April 11, 1688, aged 57

WILLIAM ROBERTS, Dec 11, 1706, aged 67.

SARAH his Wife, April 27, 1719, aged 68

Their Children deceased		A D	Æt suæ
SARAH	⎫	Sept. 5, 1679,	4
THOMAS	⎪	Sept 25, 1679,	7
SARAH	⎬ ROBERTS,	Sept 29, 1699,	17
COX	⎪	Jan 16, 1702,	31
WILLIAM	⎭	May 11, 1715,	29.

ON AN ELEGANT WHITE MARBLE MONUMENT

Arms, Or, three Quaterfoils pierced Gules, a
Chief vairé, for D'EWES,—impaling, Azure, a
Bend Or, cottised Argent, between six Martlets of
the second

Near this Place lie the Remains of ANNE, Wife
of BERNARD DEWES, Esq Daughter of JOHN DE
LA BERE, Esq who with great Beauty of Person,
and elegance of Accomplishments, united the more
valuable Endowments of a sensible, virtuous, and
pious Mind, adorned and recommended by the
most amiable sweetness of Manners and Disposition
Her early loss will be long and severely lamented
by her Friends, and in a particular Manner by her
afflicted Husband, who with the deepest regret in-
scribes this Marble to her Memory She left two
Children, too young to be sensible of their great
loss, and died August 13, in the 30th Year of her
Age, Anno Dom 1780

ON FLAT STONES

MARY, the Wife of RICHARD HYETT, of Alstone,
Gent eldest Daughter of JOHN BROWNE, of
Church Down, was here buried, near
eight of her Children
She departed this Life April 12,
Anno { ætatis suæ 43,
{ Domini 1705

The above RICHARD HYETT,
was here buried August 14, 1704,
aged 67

JOHN, Son of the said RICHARD HYETT,
December the 21st, Anno Dom 1707,
in the 13th Year of his Age

CATHARINE, the Wife of
TOBY STURMY, of this Town, Mercer,
Daughter of RICHARD HYETT, of Alstone, Gent
died Dec. 28, 1711, in the 23d Year of her Age.

In a Vault lie the Remains
of MARTHA APPLEGARTH, Relict of
JOHN APPLEGARTH, late of Dowdeswell, Gent.
She was interred the 29th of January, 1763,
aged 88

MARY GREGORY, Relict of RICHARD GREGORY,
Daughter of TOBY STURMY,
died Sept 17, 1775, aged 66

JOHN HARCOURT, Esq
of Dany Park in the County of Brecon,
died Oct 2, 1781, in the
65th Year of his Age,

LITITIA SARAH MARIA,
Relict of the above JOHN HARCOURT, Esq
died Dec 27, 1785, in the
56th Year of her Age.

EDWARD JOHNSON
departed this Life the 16th of May, 1670

MARY, Relict of the abovesaid EDWARD JOHNSON,
deceased Sept 5, 1705, aged 81

JOSEPH UPTON, of Cheltenham, Gent
who married the eldest Daughter of
the abovesaid EDWARD JOHNSON,
died March 28, 1720, at 80

MARY his Wife
died January 20, 169-

JOS-, Son of HENRY ST LEGER
and MARY his Wife, deceased
March 20, 1696, aged 15

MARTHA, Sister of the abovesaid Jo-
died June 20, Anno Dom 1705, aged 2-

C--- PUGET, Gent
buried the 17th of October, 1718

THOMAS S LEGER, Esq,
died June 5, 1725, aged 75

JOHN BECKET, late of the
Parish of Bishop' Cleeve in this County, Gent.
was here interred the 21st Day of August,
Anno Dom 1728

Hic jacet JOHANNES filius WILLIELMI BECKIT,
Armiger, qui obiit 11 Die Augusti, 1717,
Anno ætatis primo

Hic jacet WILLIELMUS, filius CAROLI MOUNT,
Gent qui obiit 1 Die Nov 1725,
Anno ætatis primo

Hic etiam inhumatur CAROLUS
MOUNT junior, qui Anno quinto
Die Aprilis, 1728 Anno
ætatis sui diocedenno

Hic est kondit HEN SAWYER,
filius HEN SAWYER, Gent qui obiit
die Junii ætatis suæ 1st, 1737
M S in 1740   W S an 1747

MARY BECKIT, Widow,
buried Sept 24, 1683

JOHN BECKIT, of the Inn,
buried Dec 22, 1684

Mr JOHN BECKIT, of Woodmancote,
buried August 30, 1689

JAMES BECKETT, junior,
died Jan 12, 1715, aged 77

FRANCES OWEN
Hic conditur m--r
Oxon--- Artium
Cheltenhamiæ Doctor
Hic non d-- June depula
Oc 9
Pape-ens celu hedic era Janua

Jan --- Wife of the abovesaid
Francis Owens died the 8th Day
of April --- 1741

In Memory of two Sons of JAMES BECKETT, junior

JOHN   } buried { Aug 4, 1700.
JAMES }   { July 3, 1710

FRANCES BECKETT, Daughter of
JAMES BECKETT, of Alstone,
died Dec 17, in the 16th Year of her Age

Mr THOMAS PATE, Son to Mr JOHN PATE,
was buried May 20, 1651

Mrs MARY PATE, Widow,
was buried January 2, 1684

JOHN PATES, Gent
deceased April 10, 1685, aged 56

FRANCES, Wife of the abovesaid
JOHN PATES, Gent died July 27,
Anno Dom 1702, aged 73

PATES, Son of JAMES BECKETT, of
Alstone, Grandson to the abovesaid
JOHN and FRANCES PATES,
died Dec 29, 1719, aged 15

HENRY WILLIS, Gent
died in the Year 1742, aged 62

JANE his Wife
died Feb 1, 1769, aged 8-

Also two of their Sons, RICHARD and JAMES

Mrs ANNE CARNOLL, late of Hayles,
died May 12, 1699, in the 83d Year of her Age

Mr HENRY CARNOLL her Husband
lyeth in the Chapel at Hayles

The Rev Mr R ROGERS, youngest Son of
Mr WILLIAM ROGERS, of Dowdeswell, M A
of Pembroke College Oxford, Master of
the Free School of Cheltenham for above
13 Years, ended his Labours on New Year's
Eve 1701, aged 37 Years and 8 Months

Also in Memory of
ELIZABETH MATTHEWS Daughter of
THOMAS ROGERS and REBEKAH his Wife,
of Dowdeswell, who departed this Life
April 20, 1758, aged 72

ANNE PACKER Widow,
buried the 13th of October, 1662

Near to this Place lieth four sons
of THOMAS PACKER, of Alston, Gent

JOHN   }   { Feb 16, 1691
GEORGE } was { Apr 22, 1694
JOSEPH } buried { Oct 1, 1695
LODOWICK }   { Apr 12, 1697

ANNE, Wife of EDWARD MITCHELL, Gent
was buried Dec --, 1691

Ann,

Arms, Argent, a Chevron Sable, in Chief a Bar
engrailed Gules, for FREME,—impaling, a Chevron
between three Roundletts, in chief three Crosses
Patee fitchy, for PATE

MARY, Relict of WILLIAM FREAME, of Bisley,
Gent Daughter of THOMAS PATE,
of this Town, Gent by MARY his Wife,
who also lies buried here
The said MARY departed this Life April 5, 1699,
aged 67

Near unto whom lieth the Body of Jo PATE,
of Alstone, Gent Son of the said
THOMAS and MARY, also THOMAS,
RICHARD, BARNABAS, and REBEKAH,
Children of the said JOHN PATE, Gent.

The Rev Mr EDMUND MERRICK
died May 27, 1740, aged 55.

EDWARD MICHELL, Gent
died Sept 23, 1727, ætat suæ 73

MARY, Wife of the said EDWARD MITCHELL,
Sister of SAMUEL COOPER, Gent.
died July 21, 1695, aged 25

ANNABELLA, also the Wife of the abovesaid
EDWARD MITCHELL, departed this Life
April 16, 1728, ætatis suæ 60

JOHN, Son of the abovesaid EDWARD MITCHELL,
Gent (by the abovesaid MARY his Wife,)
died Oct 6, 1730, ætatis suæ 36

MARY, Wife of the Rev Mr GEORGE STOKES,
Daughter of the above EDWARD MITCHELL,
died Jan 7, 1778, aged 75 Years

MARTHA her Daughter,
Wife of THOMAS JORDAN,
died Jan 9, 1777, aged 44 Years.

Arms, Argent, a Chevron engrailed Sable,
between three Fleurs de lis Gules

In spe Beatæ Resurrectionis
Lapis hic suppositur denotet
RICARDUM WOOD, filium natu
Maximum ROLANDI WOOD,
Armigeri, de Brockthrop, Gloc.
Qui Anno { Dom 1682, } Morbillis Corruptus,
{ Ætatis 16, }
expiravit Sept 24

Mis JOYCE BANNISTER, Widow,
was buried Jan 20, 1691.

RICHARD BANNISTER, Gent.
died November 22, 1680

MARY, Wife of RICHARD BANNISTER,
was buried Nov 27, 1696

Arms, Ermine, on a Fesse three Escallops.

Unto the Memory of
JOHN INGRAM, Gent
who being 14 Years old on the
30th of March, changed his Life
for Death, in the Year of our Lord 1690.

ANNE, late Wife of EDWARD MITCHELL, Gent
who was the only Daughter of JOHN CARTER, of
Charlton Abbotts in this County, Esq
died November 30, 1691, aged 43

EDWARD MITCHELL, Gent only Son of
the above written ANNE, by the Body of
the above written EDWARD MITCHELL,
died Aug 17, 1698, in the 14th Year of his Age.

HENRY LANE, of Sandford,
was buried April the 9th, 1632

RICHARD LANE, Glover,
was buried Oct 13, 1646.

MARGERY, Wife of WALTER LANE,
buried Jan 31, 1676.

Arms, SLOPER, as before

ELIZABETH, Wife of WILLIAM SLOPER, Gent.
and Sister of EDWARD MITCHELL, Gent
died Jan 26, 1694

ELIZABETH, Wife of JOHN ALLWAY,
Daughter of the abovesaid WILLIAM SLOPER,
was buried Jan 15, 1752, aged 55

Also WILLIAM, Son of the above
WILLIAM SLOPER, Gent
died Feb 23, 1765, aged 70

IN THE CHURCH YARD, ON TOMBS

WILLIAM Son of JOHN PARKES,
born August 10 1693,
died April 1, 1720

PATIENCE the Wife of
THOMAS NETTLESHIP,
and Daughter of JAMES PARKES,
of Cheltenham, who was born
May the 1st 1687,
and died Dec 6, 1738

THOMAS NETTLESHIP
died April 2, 1762, aged 76

Also MARY and ANN, Daughters of
THOMAS and MARY NETTLESHIP
MARY died Sept 9, 1769, aged 43
ANN died April 7, 17.., aged 8

JOHN PARKES
was buried April 7, 1714, aged 54

Also JOHN and MARY,
his Son and Daughter, by
MARY his Wife
JOHN was buried April 24, 1712,
aged 23
MARY was buried July 17, 1714,
aged 17

MARY Wife of JOHN PARKES,
died Feb 24 1732, aged 60

MARY, Daughter of the
Rev RICH PARKES and ELIZ his Wife,
died June 24 1752, aged 23.

WALTER COX, senior,
died Feb 24 174., aged 67.

SARAH his Wife
died Sept 2, 1727, aged 58

SARAH, Wife of JOHN JONES,
of Tewkesbury Butcher, and Daughter
of WALTER COX,
died Oct 14, 1742, aged 52

WALTER COX, junior
died Dec 5, 1749, aged 47

THOMAS

THOMAS COX, senior,
died March 10, 1697, aged 76

Mrs MARY COX
was buried Dec 2, 1690

THOMAS COX, junior,
died June 24, 1684

MARY, Wife of JOHN COX,
died Sept 18 1768, aged 58

JOHN COX
died Dec 7, 1779, aged 69

THOMAS COX
died Dec 24, 1726, aged 61

ANN his Wife
eighth Daughter of THOMAS PUCKET,
of Uckington, died Sept 6, 1727,
aged 66 Years

ROBERT COX, junior, Gent
died Dec 6, 1759, aged 54

ANNE his Wife
died May 1, 1764, aged 56

GILES COX, Gent
died June 27 1777, aged 55

JAMES WOOD
died August 19, 1709 aged 75

HANNAH his Wife
died Aug 20, 1723,
aged 68 Years and 11 Months

THOMAS their Son
died April 14 1772, aged 90

WILLIAM WOOD
died Dec 23, 1745, aged 56

SARAH his Wife
died Jan 27, 1765

WILLIAM their Son
died Nov 1, 1754 aged 31

JOHN ELLIS senior,
died July 6, 1665

GUY his Son
died Dec 28, 1670

JOHN Son of GUY ELLIS,
died Oct 28 1691

DANIEL, the Son of
WILLIAM and ALICE ELLIS,
died April 24, 1751 aged 50

MARY their Daughter
died March 23, 1760 aged 77

JOHN TAYLOR
died Oct 15, 1766 aged 80

MARY his Wife
died April 9, 1773, aged 77

MARY their Daughter
died March 10, 1774 aged 60

ELIZABETH, Wife of JOHN DOBBINS,
of this Town Maltster and
Daughter of JOHN CART Yeoman,
and ELIZABETH his Wife, of
Purton Court in Churchdown,
died March 10, 1755, in the
6th Year of her Age

ELEANOR, Wife of JOHN HARTNELL,
of the City of Bristol, Maltster,
died Dec 9 1749 aged 65

ANN CURTIN their Daughter
died Dec 7, 1751, aged 16

MARY Wife of JAMES JOHNSTON,
died June 23, 1715

MARTHA, 2d Wife of JAMES JOHNSTON,
was married Jan 4, 1734, aged 45

HENRY MASON

FLEA or his Wife
died Feb 10 1694, aged 78

JOHN their Son
died June 2, 1712, aged 71

WALTER Son of
HENRY MASON the elder,
Maltster of Cheltenham,
died June 3, 1700 aged 51

MARGARET, Wife of ROB. FRAMPTON,
died March 1, 1716, aged 44

ELLEN, Wife of JOHN COLLETT,
died Oct 20, 1679, aged 51

JOHN COLLETT
died Jan 6, 1663, aged 59

BETTY Wife of THOMAS COLLETT,
died March 18 1782, aged 50

THOMAS WILLS
died April 17, 1758, aged 54

MARY his Wife
died Jan 23, 1761, aged 91

JOHN MACHIN
late of Seabridge in Staffordshire, Gent.
died April 21, 1701, aged 70

Hic jacet GULIELMUS BUCKLE,
Armiger, Filius maximus natu
GULIELMI BUCKLE, Armigeri, de
Chacely Obiit 28 Aprilis 1752 æt 6,

Hic etiam jacet DIANA BUCKLE
GULIELMI ejus uxor, quæ obiit
undecimo die Decembris,
1738, ætatis Anno 75

DIANA ROBELLA GREEN,
youngest Daughter of JAMES GREEN,
Esq and DIANA his Wife,
died Dec 7, 1765,
aged 3 Years, 7 Months, and 2 Days

Mrs HANNAH HUGHES,
Wife of JOHN HUGHES,
Druggist in London,
died May 23, 1752, æt 47

JOHN HUGHES aforesaid
died Feb 1, 1767

FRANCIS WILLS of Alstone
was buried June 16, 1750, aged 68

SARAH his Wife
was buried May 4, 1764, aged 62

JOHN WHITE, of Alstone
died Sept 4, 1778 aged 54

ANN his Wife
died Dec 1, 1781 aged 6

WILLIAM SLATER
died Aug 20, 1749, aged 60

ELIZABETH his Wife
died May 31, 1744, aged 51

JOHN PRUEN
died Dec 2 1756, aged 45

SARAH his Wife
died Feb 25, 1742 aged 32

JOHN SMITH and SARAH,
their Children died young

Mr RICHARD ELEROUGH,
late of London Father of
ELIZABETH PRUEN late Wife to
THOMAS PRUEN one of the
surviving Sons of JOHN and
SARAH PRUEN,
died Feb 22, 1711 aged 76

(N.B. The above ELIZABETH, Wife
of THOMAS PRUEN died in the Year
1763, aged 30, and was buried at St
Ann's, Soho London)

GILES ASHMEAD, of the Moores,
died in the Year 1682

MARGARET his Wife died in 1670

MARY their Daughter
died Jan 9 1673, aged 63

THOMAS ASHMEAD, of the Moores,
was buried Apr 1, 1713, aged 62

THOMAS his Son
died May 2, 1775, aged 67

ETHELBERT PERKES,
late of this Town
died Dec 9, 1766, aged 9

ANTHONY PERKES,
Son of the said ETHELBERT
and JOANNA his Wife
died July 17, 1729, aged 33

JOANNA Wife of
ETHELBERT PERKES aforesaid,
died Feb 16, 1755, aged 63

LAWRENCE their Son
died July 26, 1750, aged 28

Hic sit
cineres prater os corpus
suum sepeliri voluit
ETHELBERT PERKES A.M.
cum diutris Cœlone
in coratatu Vigorniensi,
Rector, obiit Anno
Domini 1781 ætatis 63

JOANNA, Daughter
of ETHELBERT PERKES
and JOANNA his Wife,
died Nov 6 1784, aged 60

SARAH, Wife of
THOMAS COX, Relict of THOMAS
ASHMEAD of the Moores,
died June 30, 1729, aged 55

SARAH ASHMEAD
Daughter of the deceased
SARAH COX
died April 10 1769, aged 65

FRANCES, Wife of
DANIEL COX,
died Oct 2, 1759, aged 66

JOHN JOSEPH KRUMER,
aged 5 Years,
The good and faithful Servant of
General VAN MOYSEN
He departed this Life
July 2, 1776

WILLIAM VERMAN BUCKLE MERMAN,
Esq died June 2, 1770, aged 10

SAMUEL HICKS
died March 23, 1789, aged 6

JOHN GREGORY of London, Gent
died Jan ., 179., aged 4 years

ELIZABETH, Wife of
JOHN ROGERS, Vintner,
late of Gloucester
died July 7, 1783, aged

JOHN GREGORY of A Tine
died March 23 1788, aged 74

JOHN POLE
died March 27, 1722, aged 44

MARY his Wif
died March 23, 1704, aged 91.

THOMAS their Son
died Oct 1., 1765, aged 54

JOHN their Son
died Jun 14, 1711, aged 4

JOHN their Son
died May 26, 1761, aged 46

CATHARINE Wife of WILLIAM POPE,
died Jun 27, 1746, aged 33

ELIZABETH their Daughter
died March 26, 1751, aged 6

ALICE, Wife of EDMUND GALL,
died Aug 11, 1683, aged 76

EDMUND GALE her Husband
died Dec 14, 1692, aged 80

ROBERT BICK,
Father of the said ALICE GALE,
was buried April 29, 1641

ELIZABETH, Wife of JOHN CART
Daughter of EDMUND and ALICE GALL,
died March 28, 1702, aged 63

ANNA, Wife of
WILLIAM SURMAN junior
died Jun 2, 1777, aged 34

SAMUEL ASTON, Junor
died April 20, 750, aged 10

SAMUEL ASTON, junior
died March 3, 1702, aged 1

THOMAS NEALE, of Alstone,
died May 26, 1774 aged 61

ANNE his Wife
died July 2., 1782, aged 64

WILLIAM NEALE, of Alstone,
died July 6 1717, aged 56

ELIZABETH his Wife
died June 11, 1761 aged 41

WILLIAM SURMAN junior,
died April 1702, aged 63

MARGARET his Wife
died Aug 26, 1773, aged 7

ANN their Daughter
died April 10, 1752 aged 7

ANN Wife of WILLIAM MEEKINGS jun
died Jun 19, 1718, aged 66

THOMAS their Son died an Infant.

WILLIAM MEEKINGS
died Jan 15, 1748, aged 77

ELIZABETH his Wife
died June 28 1718, aged 66

Two of their Children,
JOHN and ELIZABETH, died young.

NATHANIEL CHESTER Gent
died June 8 1697 aged 5

SARAH his Wife
died March 1, 1705, aged 60

NATHANIEL CHESTER D.D. their Son
died April 24, 1758, aged 78

SARAH NICHOLS their Daughter
died March 16, 1759, aged 59

JOHN IRELAND Gent
Grandson Robert his and NICHOLLS,
died Nov 20, 1775, aged 28

THOMAS GARDNER
died Oct 4 1716, aged 73

JOHN Son of
THOMAS and EDITH GARDNER,
died Feb 28 1780, aged 58

ELIZABETH his Wife
died March 1, 1763 aged

Also six Children of THOMAS and
EDITH GARDNER, viz.

EDWARD died June 5 1749,
aged 14 Months

ANN died Sept 6, 1764,
aged 13 Years

JAMES died Aug 21, 1766, aged 16

EDITH COX died May 23, 1767, aged 24

JAMES LAMBER died Dec 27 1770,
aged 5

MARY died Jun 24, 1772, aged 35

O N   H E A D S T O N E S

	Died	Aged
John Hopkins, Servant to the Right Hon Viscount Belleyre, died in his Lordship's Service	25 Jan 1766	27
O en Dodd another of his Lordship's Servants	8 Aug 1773	3
Mr John Ke till was drowned in th Cold 1 ith	29 Jly 1768	9
Catharine, Wife of Richard Nichols, and Daughter of W. Camuel, Esq	June, 1762	60
Giles Webb, junior, Gent	25 Nov 1757	68
Samuel Cook	1 Mar 1755	61
Jane his Wife, Daughter of William Sloper Gent	5 May, 1742	44
Mary Wife of Thomas Potter, and Daughter of and James Cock	26 Aug, 1765	7
Walter Hitchcoury, of Alstone this Parish, Gent	14 Nov 1745	83
Su h his Wife	—	—
Walter their eldest Son	—	45
Elizabeth their Daughter	—	17
Mary Relict of Walter Hartlebury Gent	31 Au 1756	67
Thomas Surman Gent	16 Dec 1766	70
Elizabeth his Wife	19 June, 1745	59
Hannah Wife of Samuel Surman	4 May, 17	60
Edmund Surman	1 Aug 1765	53
Frances his Wife	27 Nov 1742	45
William Upton	21 July 1765	42
William Gibbs	1 Apr 1745	67
Elizabeth his Wife	27 Jan 1756	
Martha Wife of John Crabb	25 Jan 1765	5
Sarah Wife of William Crabb	15 Dec 1740	27
Dorothy Wife of Bird Lizard, and Daughter of William Gibbs	13 Jan 175.	7
John Taylor Cook	24 Nov 1768	47
Hannah, Wife of James Botten	1 Aug 1769	63
Mr James Bott	2 Jun 1786	69
Ann Wife of Ralph Poulton	6 Jul 740	44
Ralph Poulton	5 Jan 1772	64

	Died	Aged
Anne Wife of Ralph Poulton Relict o William Keyte	23 May 1777	58
William Ward of Alstone	4 Mar 1744	46
Alice his Wife	17 Jul 1740	65
John Ward	24 Aug 1757	63
Joyce his Wife	6 Mar 1729	60
John Davis	1 Oct 1749	70
Ann his Wife	10 Dec 1755	80
Rebecca Wife of John Avens	14 Apr 1740	30
Mary Wife of John Williams	8 Apr 1757	31
Robert Harbert Bricklayer	2 Mar 1766	52
Mary his Wife	16 Nov 1710	57
James Carpenter Br Layer	16 Sept 1730	60
Elizabeth his Wife	7 Aug 1729	5
Thomas Cup ter Bricklayer	3 Sept 1742	7
Thomas Jervoise Collier Baker	— Aug 1765	52
Thomas Spencer	26 Nov 1756	65
Ann his Wife	6 Mar 1759	9
Arthur Spencer	22 Jun 1720	60
Edward Powell	20 Feb 1767	
Ralph Powell	7 Feb 1673	
Anne, Wife of Walter Goodrich, Daughter of John Powell of Frogmill	— Nov 1772	30
Elizabeth Powell	5 Mar 1717	65
Anthony Treward of Sandford an his Daughter	7 Jul 1612	71
Walter his Wife	13 Oct 1720	66
Martha his Wife	2 May 1751	66
Edward Son of Edward and Mary Ireland	6 Sept 1742	29
John Ireland	21 Jan 17	
Sarah his Wife		
Frances their Daughter	1 May 1710	16
Thomas White	3 Nov 1732	
Jane Wife of Samuel Sheward	4 Jul 1745	
Thomas Sheward	11 Nov 1751	
Mary his Wife	11 Dec 1759	
Elizabeth, Wife of Thomas Sheward	17 Apr 1758	5

ON HEAD STONES.

	Died	Aged
John Stroud, of Alſtone	1 Apr 1690	—
John Son of George Cufford, of Swindon	30 Sept 1738	76
Heſter his Wife, Daughter of John Stroud	21 Oct 1738	79
Edith, Daughter of Thomas Stroud, of Alſtone, late Wife of Thomas Sturmy, of Heydon	27 Apr 1742	33
Eleanor, the latter Wife of Thomas Stroud, of Alſtone	19 Oct 1681	56
Thomas Morris	26 Apr 1729	50
James Morris	26 Apr 1773	50
Elizabeth, Wife of Thomas Halling	16 Dec. 1726	25
Elizabeth, Wife of Edward Maſon	22 Jan 1755	32
John Major	1 Mar 1708	88
Elizabeth his Wife	29 Dec 1764	82
Mary their Daughter	11 Dec 1756	42
Elizabeth Wife of Benjamin Maſon	30 Nov 1768	—
Elizabeth Wife of Richard Maſon	23 Nov 1726	50
Robert Hyett of this Town, Maltſter	17 Feb 1714	—
William Hyett	16 June 1760	63
Margaret, Wife of William Hyett	10 Aug 1766	77
Walter Clevely	6 May 1736	56
Sarah his Wife	11 Nov 1741	55
Mary, Wife of John Pewtris, Daughter of Walter and Sarah Clevely	19 Jan 1750	39
Samuel Drinkwater	16 Jan 1730	79
Olive his Wife	26 Nov 1728	80
Walter Taylor	23 Mar 1761	49
Katharine, Wife of Valentine Smith	1 Sept 1710	60
Valentine Smith	28 Mar 1747	58
Heſter, Wife of Valentine Smith	13 Feb 1760	76
Mary Baker Mother of the ſaid Heſter	4 Apr 1743	84
Frances, Wife of Richard Peachy	11 Apr 1767	44
James Peachy	23 Nov 1770	37
Samuel Church, of Arle	2 July 1715	65
Samuel Church, of Alſtone	21 Dec 1723	24
Alice, Wife of Timothy Banes	18 May 1760	36
Edmund Clements	3 Aug 1767	40
Heſter his Wife	27 Nov 1769	4
John Robbins	26 Oct 1736	46
Richard Robbins	19 May 1784	57
William Kette	21 Nov 1746	29
William Hooper	30 June 1721	71
Frances his Wife	— Dec 1728	77
Richard Hooper	18 Dec 1745	65
Elizabeth his Wife	22 May 1734	35
John their Son	17 June 1734	20
Elizabeth their Daughter	7 Apr 1734	21
Sarah Wife of Richard Hooper	24 July 1775	55
John Clark of Alſtone	— Apr 1702	71
John Clark, Taylor	27 Aug 1739	55
Mary his Wife	13 July 1737	60
Amy, Wife of Anthony Clark	23 Jan 1714	70
Elizabeth, Wife of Thomas Clark	4 Feb 1720	54
Thomas Clark, Yeoman	19 Aug 1757	73
Thomas Clark his Son	15 Dec 1761	44
Elizabeth Wife of William Mills, Relict of Thomas Clark junior	3 Aug 1779	66
Richard Clark	27 July 1744	61
Elizabeth his Wife	13 Aug 1756	50
William Gregory of Alſtone	17 Nov 1746	74
Sarah his Daughter	14 Dec 1734	16
Martha, Wife of John Gregory	26 June 1751	32
Thomas Gregory	4 June 1732	32
Catharine, Wife of John Gregory	29 July 1695	—
Elizabeth Wife of John Gregory	23 Feb 1747	31
Elizabeth 2d Wife of John Gregory	16 Jan 1761	46
Frances Gregory	1 July 1761	30
Ann his Wife	9 Dec 1771	82
Elizabeth, Wife of William Gregory, ſenior	6 May 1772	63
John Mills of Hatherſfield	11 Oct 1749	22
Mary, Wife of Mathew Mills of Hatherfield	23 Sept 1758	68
Mary Wife of William Mills, ſenior	4 Mar 1675	65
Frances Wife of John Mills	23 Jan 1711	56
John Mills ſenior Maltſter of this Town	11 Nov 1713	56
Anne, late Wife of John Mills	12 Mar 1743	65

	Died	Age
Mary, Wife of Edward Mils	27 Jan 1775	74
William Major	11 June 1769	12
Eleanor his Wife	12 June 1707	90
Toby their Son	16 Apr 1726	60
Elizabeth his Wife	28 Apr 1724	5
Elizabeth Wife of William Freeman, Daughter of John and Hannah Nicholls	27 May 1776	3
Jane, Wife of Joseph Nicholls	5 May 1725	53
Joſeph Nicholls, ſenior	20 Oct	63
Ann, 1ſt Wife of Joſeph Nicholls, junior	1 Apr 1739	65
Mary, 2d Wife of Joſeph Nicholls, junior		
Edward Nicholls	13 June 1713	70
Elizabeth, Wife of Richard Nicholls	9 Nov 1752	4
Eleanor, Wife of Richard Nicholls	19 Jan 1715	51
Mary, Wife of Thomas Nicholls	26 Aug 1729	60
Elizabeth, 2d Wife of Thomas Nicholls	11 June 1749	58
Walter Nicholls	8 Oct 1724	72
Hannah his Wife	6 June 1714	57
Martha their Daughter	27 June 1714	16
William, Son of Walter Nicholls	1 Mar 1717	57
Henry Oakey	2 June 1758	76
Elizabeth his Wife	22 Dec 1728	45
Frances his 2d Wife	25 Mar 1731	72
Hannah, Wife of Robert Tanmore, Daughter of Walter and Hannah Nicholls	29 Apr 1744	66
Thomas Benfield, ſenior	12 Jan 1762	84
Ann his Wife, Daughter of Walter and Hannah Nicholls	15 Apr 1750	63
John Cherrington	27 June 1754	67
Mary his Wife, Daughter of Walter and Hannah Nicholls	23 Apr 1764	70
Edward Benfield	23 Jan 1754	51
Elizabeth his Wife	1 Jan 1777	70
Elizabeth, Wife of John Dobbins, ſenior	23 May 1769	80
Nicholas Dobbins	26 Sept 1726	64
Anne his Wife	3 Nov 1736	71
John their Son	20 Nov 1766	74
Thomas Dobbins	23 Sept 1745	59
Anthony Cheſtroe	4 Apr 1728	—
John Cheſtroe	7 May 1729	73
Margaret his Wife	20 Aug 1688	6
William Cheſtroe	21 Nov 1729	60
Anthony Cheſtroe	8 Oct 1773	76
Elizabeth his Wife	8 Dec 1770	73
Suſanna their Daughter, Wife of Watkins Hyett	6 Nov 1782	50
William Hughes	23 Dec 1766	66
Elizabeth Wife of William Hughes	2 Oct 1748	64
William their Son	— June 1756	29
Elizabeth, Wife of William Hughes, junior	— May 1766	45
Sarah Daughter of William and Elizabeth Hughes	4 Oct 1776	32
Guy Ellis of the City of Glouceſter, Ironmonger	8 Nov 1703	—
Anne his Wife	5 Feb 1715	58
William Ellis	8 Nov 1729	8
Alice his Wife	5 Sep 1741	61
Elizabeth their Daughter	4 Jan 1776	80
Joſeph Neale of Alſtone, Miller	4 Aug 1749	63
Anne his Wife	6 Oct 1748	70
Mary, Wife of Benjamin Neale	15 Oct 1723	27
Benjamin Neale	7 May 1722	60
Giles Jenkins	13 Dec 1749	73
Sarah his Wife	16 Aug 1744	3
Sarah his 2d Wife	13 Sept 1754	3
Joſeph, Son of Giles and Margaret Jenkins	16 May 1782	26
Sarah, Wife of Jonathan Jenkins	24 Dec 1724	83
Jonathan Jenkins	6 Jan 1769	76
Sarah Wife of King Dee	4 Aug 1757	35
Henry Teale	11 May 1726	3
Sarah Teale, Widow	30 Apr 1730	57

O N   H E A D   S T O N E S.

	Died	Aged		Died	Aged
Mrs, Wife of Henry Russell	27 Mar 1,6,	38	Mary Wife of Thomas Ricketts	28 Jun 1661	32
Henry Russell	3 Feb 1780	56	Nich his Godh ead	25 Oct 1741	74
Ann, Wife of Charles Russell	1 Sept 1761	29	Mary his Wife	13 Oct 1741	77
Sarah Cook	8 May 1746	80	Elizabeth, Daughter of Nicholas		
Margaret his Wife	15 May 17..,	77	Atherton, Relict of Richard Bliss,		
William Cook	7 Nov 85	74	and Wife of Thomas Dipper	16 May 1765	67
Hannah his Wife	1 Dec 1765	60	William Wills	20 Jun 1756	70
Thomas, Son of Matthew and Han			Elizabeth his Wife	21 Oct 1757	71
nah Cook of Mitchelde in this			Sarah, Wife of John Collins	21 Sept 1703	74
County	14 May, 1773	23	William Page	21 May 1709	58
Mary, Wife of Thomas Cotterill	5 Feb 1,65	49	Mary his Wife	30 Dec 1766	81
Thomas Cotterill senior	6 Nov 1728	96	Catharine, Wife of William Hud		
John and Axtell	—	—	man	1 June 1682	56
Mary his Wife	—	—	Daniel Keare	1 Jun 170	
Anne, Wife of Thomas Sandford,			Mary his Wife	8 Nov 686	—
of Heydon	3 Feb 1610	—	Richard Keare	Nov 1767	6,
John Sandford	30 Jan 1740	43	Sarah his Wife	1 Feb 1741	57
Sarah his Wife	2 Sept 1742	45	Owner Thomas Humphris, of Glou-		
Ann, Wife of John Sandford	1 July 1765	41	cester	6 May 1782	56
John Sandford	1 June 1750	55	Richard Humphris	5 Apr 1783	68
Mary his Wife	1 Jan 1760	37	William Sudman senior	24 Apr 1772	63
William Sandford or Axtell	7 May 1780	63	Margaret his Wife	6 Aug 1765	7
Elizabeth his Wife	25 Nov 1775	54	Ann their Daughter	10 Apr 1757	27
William, Son of Thomas and Ann			James Wills	1 Oct 1758	4
Wilks	15 July 1755	18	Mary, Wife of John Clutterbuck,		
Francis Edwards of Arle	21 Mar 1771	71	senior	1 Oct 1787	70
Jane his Wife	— May 1770	60	Hester their Daughter	5 Jun 1768	10
John their Son	4 May 1772	1	Thomas Newman	8 Sept 1774	70
Henry Edwards	5 Oct 1682	56	Mary his Daughter, Wife of Richard		
Bartholomew Edwards	15 June 1741	66	Cull	3 Nov 1773	56
Elizabeth his Wife	31 Dec 1741	71	Mary, Daughter of Richard and		
Richard Coules who married Ma			Mary Cull	16 Apr 176	15
ry, the Daughter of Henry Ed			Thomas Sone	1 Jan 76,	7
wards	4 May 1700	33	Ann his Wife	13 May 1765	68
John Cowling	— 1733	35	John their Son	11 June 1739	39
Thomas Overbul	21 Aug 1703	50	Thomas their Son	7 Aug 1770	52
Mary his Wife	10 Apr 74	36	Elizabeth their Daughter, Wife of		
Joan Kennett, Bricklayer	6 Aug 1790	40	William Jones	12 June 1785	34
John Kennett, bricklayer	23 June 1751	55	George Quittel	6 Jan 1774	77
Margaret his Wife	— Oct 1738	56	Jane his Wife	16 Feb 176	57
Mary Wife of Joseph Kennett,			Benjamin Jenson, Mason	10 Nov 1780	71
junior	27 Apr 1776	4	Susannah Wife	2 May 176	80
Daniel Chester	18 Jul 1733	70	Samuel Jackson	7 June 1769	66
Sarah, Wife of Daniel Chester	4 Apr 1744	66	Hester Jackson his Sister	1 Jun 1773	60
Anthony Chester, Citizen and Tal			Eliz Cox	1 Feb 1767	48
low Chandler of London	15 May 1731	65	James Jackson	21 July 1769	38
Joan Sturmy, Mercer	3 July 1734	61	Thomas Giles	6 Dec 1779	67
Susannah Wife	30 Nov 1731	6,	Ann his Wife	27 Dec 1770	60
Hester Sturmy	3 July 1759	36	John George Musician	26 Feb 1779	6,
Charles Wing	26 May 1710	54	John Frankel	28 May 1780	40
John Crowter	2 Sep 1729	40	Robert Latt	3 July 1709	5
John Weston, of Swindon	— Apr 1711	58	Nicholas Marchant, of Lship		
Mary his Daughter	2 Oct 1737	63	Cleeve	17 Jan 1754	27
John Hampton	Feb 1761	57	Mary his Wife	20 Nov 1758	65
Ann his Wife	15 Sept 1757	64	Musiah Dyke Schoolmaster	13 Apr 1778	61
Samuel Hampton Son	— Apr 1733	58	John Strutley Clerk of this Parish		
Thomas Hampton	27 July 4	5	32 Years	28 June 1717	50
Mary Wife of Henry Hampton	30 Nov 1737	28	Mary his Wife	23 May 1771	6,
Job Attie	5 Oct 1743	51	Henry Cooper of Arle	5 June 1743	57
Hannah his Wife	1 Apr 1747	53	John Cooper	5 Jun 1756	85
Samuel Ufe	— Dec 1	3	Mary Dunnerfield	11 June 1762	4
Ann, Wife of Samuel Hun	9 July 1715		Joseph Felton	21 Dec 1776	
Thomas Hun of Ludford	4 Apr 1	67	William Upton Butcher	21 Jun 1780	6
Sarah his Daughter	2 Nov 1743	57	Mary, Wife of Joseph Shppard	20 Dec 1787	
Thomas his Son	15 Nov 1738	67	Hester Fowke	10 June 1787	72
John Lawson	1 Sept 1712	5	John Baker	10 May 1713	3
Sarah his Wife	1 Oct 1753	72	Elizabeth, Wife of Samuel Kent	13 June 1713	
Sarah their Daughter	Feb 1716	23	James Crim	22 Apr 1720	64
Margaret Daughter of Thomas			Thomas Leech, Plumber and		
Luker	20 Aug 1725	—	Glazier	6 Oct 1755	
Richard Edwards Steward of Hall			Hannah his Wife	31 Oct 1761	91
in the Parish of Notton	23 May 1715	68	Ann Wife of Samuel Leech	11 Apr 1775	71
Ann Fletcher	1 Mar 1741	6,	John their Son	20 Apr 1771	7
Joan, Wife of Thomas Wills	7 Dec 1		Robert Hill, Apprentice to Rob		
Mary, Wife of Thomas Wills	15 Nov 1743	41	bin	1 Apr 1751	18
Thomas Wills	24 Jun 17	7	Thomas Hover	Dec 1787	21

O N   H E A D   S T O N E S

	Died	Aged		Died	Aged
James Bates	2 Sept 1776	38	Elizabeth, Wife of John Roberts	26 Nov. 1785	57
William Weaver	13 Feb 1764	74	John Page	29 May, 1773	71
Mary his Wife	23 Apr 1770	60	Mary, Wife of John Page	26 Aug 1769	47
Mary their Daughter	22 Jan 1780	33	James, Son of Davis and Mary Pearfon	29 Mar 1767	22
William Relly	24 Feb. 1777	61	Elizabeth, Wife of Richard Jones	1 Feb. 1749	55
Anne his Wife	25 May, 1765	63	Richard Jones	11 Oct 1757	59
Mary, Wife of James Gore	13 Sept 1774	27	William, Son of Joseph and Ann Brinyard	8 Feb. 1785	33
John Ballinger	20 Dec 1787	34	John Dowdeswell, senior	3 Feb. 1781	65
Elizabeth Young	25 May, 1779	22	Mary his Wife	30 Aug. 1768	53
Christopher Cook, of Alstone	28 July, 1779	70	Samuel Richards	21 July, 1774	66
Ann, Wife of Thomas Warder	28 Aug 1786	37	Mary his Wife	19 Mar 1753	44
John Blifs, junior	19 June, 1766	19	Mary Roper	26 Aug 1773	70
John Blifs, senior	30 Aug 1767	60	Richard Roper	29 June, 1779	47
Thomas Blifs	4 Sept 1776	27	Thomas Wilkins	7 Mar 1786	76
Daniel Haselton	5 Aug 1773	68	Mrs. Dorothy Hopkins	23 Nov 1783	83
Anne his Wife	14 May, 1780	73	Mrs. Frances Stevens	31 Dec 1779	87
Elizabeth, Wife of John Paine	2 Feb 1785	57			
Richard their Son	28 Apr 1768	6			
John Surman Paine their Son	12 July, 1769	18			
John their Son	6 Jan 1765	13			

CXI. CHERINGTON.

LXVI. CHERINGTON.

THIS Name has not varied fince the Compilation of Domefday, where it occurs *Cerntone*. The Parifh includes a Circuit of more than fix Miles, in the Hundred of *Longtree*, diftant from *Tetbury* four Miles on the North, three from *Minchin Hampton* on the South, and from GLOUCESTER fixteen on the South-eaft The Soil is light and ftony, and chiefly applied to Tillage, with about five Hundred Acres of Pafture Lands Fofhils are frequently difcovered, which are in general of the Bivalve kind About the Year 1740 all the Commonable Fields were inclofed and allotted. The Rivulet *Avon* has its Source here, and immediately forms a Lake of fome Acres extent, in a Valley, on the Acclivities of which the Village is pleafantly fituate

The Benefice * is rectorial, the Emoluments of which arife from a Farm of 330 Acres, appropriated to the Rector, at the Time of the general Inclofure, in Lieu of Tythes The Church, dedicated to *St Nicholas*, and included in the Deanery of *Stonehoufe*, contains a Nave and Semi-tranfept only, with a low embattled Tower It is apparently ancient, and in the Style of the Age of King HENRY the Second

In the Reign of EDWARD the Firft, this Manor was held an Appendage to the Dutchy of *Cornwall*, as of the Honour of *Wallingford*, by the Family of DE LA MERE, with whom it remained fome Centuries This Honour was transferred to *Ewelme*, co *Oxon*. by King HENRY VIII and held Jurifdiction of this, and feveral other Manors, which Rights are now vefted in the Crown Of the knightly Family of BAYNTON, it was purchafed by THOMAS STEPHENS, of *Lypiate*, Efq Attorney General to Prince HENRY, about the Year 1608 He bequeathed it to his third Son NATHANIEL STEPHENS, the firft of that venerable Family fettled at *Cherington*; from whom it defcended by the Heir female to JOHN NEALE, Efq of *Allefley*, co *Warwick*. Sir JOHN TURNER, Bart afterward purchafed it, and it was foon re fold to the Family of SMITH, of LONDON, who are the prefent Proprietors, with a Manor-houfe, Park, and a confiderable Eftate The other landed Property is vefted in the Right Honourable FRANCIS Lord DUCIE, and the Families of TAYLOR, and VAUGHAN, parcel of which Eftates belonged to th *Benedictine* Nunnery at *Godftowe*, co *Oxon*

On the 29th of March, 1644, a Skirmifh happened on *Charing Down* in this Parifh, between the Armies of the Royalifts under the Command of RALPH Lord HOPTON, and the Parliament's Forces under Sir WILLIAM WALLER, in which the former were defeated The Hiftorians of the Rebellion are filent concerning this Battle, and even CORBET, who is very minute as to what was done in this County in the early Part of thofe Diffentions, but flightly mentions, that fuch a Skirmifh had happened It is, however, traditionally afferted that many Perfons of Diftinction of the royal Faction were flain on that Day, amongft whom are recorded " JOHN Lord STUART, Sir JOHN SMITH, and the Colonels SCOTT, " MANNING, and SANDYS " But we collect from the " Loyalift's Bloody Roll †" (lately publifhed), that they all fell in an Engagement near *Alresford*, co *Hants*, and the Name of the laft is not to be found in that Lift, as having held a Commiffion

BENEFACTIONS.

ELIZABETH COCKS, formerly Widow of JOHN DRIVER, of *Afton*, gave by Will the Sum of 50*l* towards erecting a Charity School in *Cherington*, for the teaching poor Children to read, fay their Catechifm, and underftand the prime Offices of the Chriftian Religion

THOMAS STEPHENS, of the City of GLOUCESTER, Efq left by Will, 1721, for the better fecuring the faid Gift (by ELIZABETH COCK), and the Produce thereof for the Purpofes aforefaid, Land, to the Value of 5*l* a Year (fubject to a certain Rent of 4*s* a Year), 50*s* of which to be paid to the Schoolmiftrefs, and the Remainder to be employed in keeping the Premifes in Repair

* Subject to an annual Payment of 10*s* to the Rectory of *Avening*, according to ECTON.
† BRADWICK's Refpublica, p 132, 1787, 4to.

INCUMBENTS	PATRONS	INCUMBENTS.	PATRONS
1574 Thomas Wheeler,	Henry Baynton, Esq	1661 Joseph Trapp, M. A.	
1577 John Sell,	John Cooke	1698 Benjamin Piatt, B. A.	Edw Stephens, Esq
1575 Thomas Wulpy,	Henry Baynton	1700 John Trapp, B. A	The same
1593 Brian Harris,	Thomas Clarkson	1716 Nathan Hickham, Clerk,	The same
1610 Daniel Parker, B. D		1756 Samuel Lysons, M. A.	Daniel Lysons, M. D

PRESENT LORD OF THE MANOR,

SAMUEL SMITH, ESQ.

At the Visitations of the Heralds, in 1682 and 1683, the only Person summoned from this Parish was

Edward Stephens, Esq.

At the Election in 1776, Three Freeholders polled from this Parish

In the Register, which commences in 1568, is the following Entry

" Anno 1631, March 26° —Whereas upon the second Day of March, 1630, there was, under the
" Hand of the Parson and Church wardens, a Licence to eat Flesh in Lent to WILLIAM BAYLEY, who
" was then notoriously known to be sick, and whereas his Sickness lasted above a Fortnight. Now that
" his Licence is here entered in the Register Book, the 26th Day of March, 1631. Ita est, D. N.
" PARKER, Rector."

ANNUAL ACCOUNT OF MARRIAGES, BIRTHS, AND BURIALS, IN THIS PARISH

A D	Mar	Bir	Bur	A D	Mar	Bir	Bur	A D	Mar	Bir	Bur	A D	Mar	Bir	Bur
1781	1	9	4	1786	1	5	4	1791				1796			
1782	1	4	3	1787				1792				1797			
1783	1	8	4	1788				1793				1798			
1784	2	3	5	1789				1794				1799			
1785	—	3	9	1790				1795				1800			

INSCRIPTIONS IN THE CHURCH.

IN THE CHANCEL

ON A MONUMENT AGAINST THE NORTH WALL

Arms, three Cheval Traps.

M S

Viri Reverendi D JOSEPH TRAPP, A M
ædis Christi Oxon olim alumni, &
hujus ecclesiæ per annos 37 rectoris vigilantissimi
Cujus
(licet obscuro in loco positus fuerit)
dignæ sunt virtutes quæ posteris tradantur
Exımiæ ergo Deum pietatis,
in suscipiendo Presbyterio affectus propensissimus,
munificentia in pauperes pace quam par fuit
effusior,
in amicos fides & obsequium,
in universos benevolentia
Ingenio sane vividus & perspicax, eruditione
non mediocriter instructus,
summe humanus animi & modestus
In congressibus comis, humanus, facilis,
fervandae fidei probus intentus,
disciplinæ fideique ecclesiæ Anglicanæ tenax
Heu nimis cito vertimus vir eximie laudatissimo
(eruditus dum mihi quidem sed doctis & piis
heu nimium fit mi)
quod sit in hac totum nodo finitum invenerit,
de finito tempore primum fuit huius
Obiit Ann Dom 1608
Sit pace quiesco Et huic 61

ON A PLAIN TABLET:

M S

MARIÆ THEOPHILI QUINTIN, viri reverendi, ecclesiæ
Bristolliensis prebendarii, Tokenhamensis vero
in agro Wilton rectoris, filia natu minime,
quæ fuit
vultu et natura ad modestiam composita,
ingenio facili sed recondito,
virtutum omnium, præsertim Christianarum, exemplum
& ornamentum & exemplu,
temporis frugi, in rerum misericordiis perquam liberalis,
in verbis solum modo parca,
in S Scripturis versatissima,
in precibus publicis privatisque deurum
frequentior in flagrantior
Ecclesiæ Anglicanæ fidem & disciplinam temperatam
colui, veri illibati functio vere integrae
mores denique ex conscientiis (ut solet) manare
teerunam gaven,
patientia tulit spe simplex, et immortalitati deeditus,
ætatis suæ 34,
ann Christi 1695

1650
DANIEL PARKER,
facræ Theologiæ
Baccalaureus, hujus
Ecclesiæ Rector, post
mortem BRIANI HARRIS,
obiit anno 1610, Dec 1.

ON A FREESTONE MONUMENT

Underneath
lie the Remains of
THOMAS COXE, Yeoman,
who departed this Life
August 10, 1758, aged 64

Also THOMAS and MARY,
Son and Daughter of the above THOMAS COXE,
by SUSANNA his Wife

Thomas died August 28, 1761, aged 38

MARY died December 20, 1762, aged 41

Also ELIZABETH, the Wife of THOMAS COXE,
senior, departed this Life Sept 1, 1759, aged 69

SUSANNA, Wife of the first named
THOMAS COXE, Yeoman,
departed this Life Sept 13, 1766, aged 73

JOHN COXE, late of this Parish, Yeoman,
Son of THOMAS and SUSANNA COXE aforesaid,
died August 8, 1767, aged 51

In Memory of
JOHN RADWAY, of this Parish, and late of
Chavenage in the Parish of Horsley, Yeoman,
who died Aug 7, 1711, in the 43d Year of his Age

LYDIA, Wife of the above JOHN RADWAY,
died Nov 18, 1732, aged 72

ON FLAT STONES

DEBORAH, the Daughter of
DANIEL and DINAH PARKER,
and Wife to ROBERT GILMAN,
obiit 1665, April 22

DINAH, Daughter of DANIEL PARKER,
and Wife to FRANCIS CAM, Coroner,
obiit Oct 28, 1658

JOHN CAM, Gent
obiit Anno 16_2, aged 1,

ELIZABETH, Wife of JOHN CAM, Coroner,
obiit 14 Nov 1649

JOHN RADWAY
deceased April 18, 1669

JOHN RADWAY
died Jan 22, 1714

Mr JOSEPH ADAMS,
Son of Mr NATHANIEL ADAMS, of Avening,
died March 9, 1723, in the 49th Year of his Age.

JOHN COXE
departed this Life March 8, 1685

Mrs KATHARINE QUINTIN,
the Widow of Mr THEOPHILUS QUINTIN
Rector of Tokenham Wick in Wilts,
and Prebendary of Bristol,
was here interred Feb 2, 1696

THEOPHILUS, filius JOSEPHI TRAPP,
(hujus ecclesiæ rectoris) bimuli non jam
exacto moriens obiit Martii XII, MDCLXXXV
Læta beata Resurr spe
hic subter is obiit

Mr WILLIAM TAYLO
died July 29, 1729

Mrs MARY TAYLOR,
Widow of Mr WILLIAM TAYLOR,
departed this Life Nov 22, 1732

The Rev NATHANIEL HACKHAM,
who was 40 Years Rector of this Parish,
died May 5, 1756, aged 66

ELIZABETH HACKHAM his Wife
died March 11, 1724, in the 31st Year of her Age

IN THE CHURCH YARD.

ON A PLAIN TABLET AGAINST THE CHURCH

Underneath lie the Remains
of MATTHEW RADWAY and MARY his Wife
He died Feb 10, 1733, aged 61

MARY, Daughter of the above
MATTHEW and MARY RADWAY, and
Wife of WILLIAM WHITING, of this Parish,
died Aug 21, 1762, in the 65th Year of her Age

WILLIAM WHITING
died August 25, 1776, aged 82

THOMAS MILLIP,
of Aston, Yeoman
died July 11, 1766, aged 34

MARTHA his Wife
died June 28, 1771, aged 39

THOMAS, son of
THOMAS and MARTHA MILLIP,
died Oct 8, 1755,
aged 20 Years, 7 Months and 6 Days

GEORGE MILLER
died Sept 3, 1, 1 2 d 5

ON HEAD STONES

	Died	Age
George Driver	——— 1741	73
Mary, the Wife of George Driver	2 Apr 1730	59
Mary, Daughter of John and Alice Driver, of Ashton Keynes, Wilts	2 Dec 1761	24
Edith Wilkins, Daughter of George and Mary Driver	23 Dec 1758	60
Mary, Daughter of George and Mary Driver	1 May, 1779	79
Hannah Driver	12 Feb 1786	71
Dorothy, Wife of John Radway	15 Oct 1746	53
Bridget, Wife of Daniel Radway	20 Apr 1732	55
Daniel Wigmore	27 Nov 1762	62
Anne his Wife	2 Jan 1752	48
Thomas Dickes, Blacksmith	21 May, 1760	80
Mary his Wife	25 June, 1737	54
Mary, Daughter of Isaac and Rachel Dickes	20 Dec 1772	23
Edward Young	30 Jan 1769	83
Martha his Wife	23 Dec 1771	78
Mary, Wife of Thomas Young	10 June, 1772	29
Mary, Wife of Abraham Lovelock	30 May, 1766	42
William Fowler	29 Apr 1774	66
Elizabeth his Wife	1 Sept. 1782	77
Edward Coxe	1 Sept. 1753	52
Anne, Wife of Edward Coxe	8 Mar. 1744	32
Charles, Son of Edward Coxe	3 Aug 1760	9
John, Son of Edward Coxe	21 Dec 1768	19
Sarah, Wife of John Bowley	12 Apr 1771	67
Edward their Son	1 Mar 1771	41
William Bowley	22 Feb 1770	36
Dinah, Widow of Francis Payne	9 Nov 1742	28
John Whiting, late of this Parish, Carver	21 Apr 1777	51
William Whiting, Mason	16 Oct 1732	72
Elizabeth his Wife	7 May, 1740	77
Sarah, Wife of Thomas Fauter	20 Jan. 1758	78

CHURCH-DOWN

LXVII. CHURCH-DOWN,
OR
CHURCH-DENE,

CORRUPTEDLY "*Clofen*," lies in the Hundred of *King's Barton*, in the Vale of GLOUCESTER, four Miles distant from that City on the East, six Miles from *Cheltenham* on the West, and from *Teweſbury* nine on the South. The greater Portion of Lands is of Pasture, the Soil changes from a deep Clay into a heavy Sand, and comprises, by Computation, about 4000 Acres, 900 of which are common Fields, allotted, but is yet uninclosed.

Of *Churchdown Hill*, which approaches nearest to an oval Shape, the Circumference is almoſt four Miles, and the Height more than half of one. The Acceſs from the Baſe is eaſy and regular, nearer the Summit it breaks into many Irregularities of Ground, clothed with low Wood. The greateſt Area do not exceed a few Acres. Upon the higheſt of theſe Acclivities the Church is built, a Spot, moſt probably, in the earlieſt Times made ſacred by a Croſs. The laborious Piety of our Anceſtors frequently ſelected ſuch eminences for Conſecrated Buildings; and many Inſtances occur of Hermitages, Oratories, and Chapels, in the Situations of which, Convenience ſeems to have been as little conſidered as in this Place. The Hill riſing almoſt pyramidally, forms a bold and beautiful Feature in the Landſcape of the Vale, ſo widely expanded round it, of which it commands a moſt advantageous View.

The Benefice is an endowed Curacy, augmented by Benefaction of URSULA TAYLOR, Widow, and Queen ANNE's Bounty. The Tythes belonged to the *Auguſtine* Priory of *St Oſwald* in GLOUCESTER, and the Living was annexed as a Chapelry to the Church of *St Catherine* in that City. But, at the Diſſolution in 1543, the Impropriation and Advowſon were given to the Dean and Chapter of Briſtol, to appoint the Ieſſer, charged with the annual Payment of 20l. to the Officiating Miniſter. The

* Mr GILPIN, the moſt approved Critic of Landſcape, remarks "that the pyramidal Shape in a Mountain is at all times
"beſt: as it will be touched in the Mountain or in their Delineations the moſt pictureſque Forms. Mountains therefore, from
"a regular and attenuated Line, are often without groteſque Shapes, are leſs pleaſing." *Northern Tour*, vol. I. both p. 189. § 8.

2   Church,

Church, dedicated to *St Bartholmew*, has a Nave and North Aisle, and of the Date of the Tower the following Notice is engraven on the inside Wall : " This Bell hous was buyldede in the Yeere of our " Lorde God 1601 "

In 1053 Stigand Archbishop of CANTERBURY held this Manor, but in Domesday it is attributed to Thomas Archbishop of YORK, with whose Successors it remained till the 6th of EDW VI 1552, when it was heired to Sir Thomas CHAMBERLAYNE, otherwise TANKERVILLE, Knight, whose lineal De tenant is the present Possesso   The adjoining Parish of *Norton* owes Suit and Service to this Manor

On the Hamlets, which are four, *Hucclecote*, anciently *Uhelcote*, is the most considerable, and is situate on the lower Road   A House, on the Plan of an Italian *Loggia*, was built here about twenty Years since, by the late Sir WILLIAM STRACHAN, a Baronet of *Nova Scotia*, now belonging to the Family of TREWARD, of *Smith &* Others with Estates are held by the Families of ROGERS, COLCHESTER, HODGES, and PRICE, of GLOUCESTER   *Hucclecote* is separately rated and taxed

In the next Estate *Churchdown* was purchased in the last Century by the Family of WINDOWE, of GLOUCESTER, and retailed by them to the late R. ROGERS, Clerk   *Brickhampton* is a Part of the undi vided Estate of Sir ROBERT ATKYNS, now descended to the Representatives of his Co-heirs, EDMUND JOHN CHAMBERLAYNE, Esq and the Heir of the late THOMAS HORDE, Esq

The last Pinson and Elmbridge   The Property of these Hamlets, traditionally an exempted Manor, is vested in the Right Honourable WILLIAM Lord CRAVEN, and the Family of SINGLETON, of *Norton*

JOHN HARMAR, M A the most celebrated Grecian of his Time, was a Native of *Churchdown* about the Year 1595 educated at *Magdalen College, Oxford*, and appointed Regius Professor of Greek in that University   He died in 16,.   WOOD*, who speaks contemptuously of his Principles which were possibly Republican allow his extraordinary Learning Sir R ATKYNS calls him " a mere Scholar " in thread bare Cloaths," so justly does ROGER ASCHAM declare, that " Scholars live Nobody knows how, " and die Nobody knows where !"

* ATHEN OXON vol II p

BENEFACTIONS.

HENRY WINDOWE left by Will 1734, 20*l* a Year for eſtabliſhing a Schoolmaſter, and 5*l* a Year for a Schoolmiſtreſs

GILES COX left for the Uſe of poor Day Labourers and Widows who do not receive Alms, Money, the Amount of which is 6*l* 13*s* 4*d* per Annum

Mrs BLUNT gave for the ſame Purpoſe Land to the Value of 5*l* 5*s* per Annum

WILLIAM STANLEY left 3*l* per Annum, iſſuing out of Lands, for putting three Boys apprentice yearly

RICHARD HOLFORD bequeathed four Alms houſes, with three Acres and a half of Arable, and one Acre of Paſture Land, for the Uſe of four poor Widows of this Pariſh only, the annual Produce of which is 3*l* 10*s*

JEREMIAH MITCHELL, by Will, gave Land to the Value of 1*l* 4*s* per Annum, for the providing Bread and Wine for nine monthly Sacraments.

INCUMBENTS	PATRONS
—— Henry Wyndowe, Clerk,	
1772 John Evans, B A	Dean and Chapter of Briſtol

PRESENT LORD OF THE MANOR,
EDMUND JOHN CHAMBERLAYNE, ESQ

No Perſon was ſummoned from this Place by the Heralds in 1682 and 1683

At the Election in 1776, Twenty-five Freeholders polled from this Pariſh and its Hamlets.

The firſt Date in the Regiſter occurs in 1583.

ANNUAL ACCOUNT OF MARRIAGES, BIRTHS, AND BURIALS, IN THIS PARISH

A D	Mar	Bir	Bur	A.D	Mar	Bir	Bur	A D	Mar	Bir	Bur	A.D	Mar	Bir	Bur
1781	2	18	4	1786	3	20	12	1791				1796			
1782	3	20	6	1787	6	13	5	1792				1797			
1783	—	21	12	1788				1793				1798			
1784	2	9	11	1789				1794				1799			
1785	3	14	13	1790				1795				1800			

The annual Increaſe of Population has been ſeven, during the laſt ſeven Years

---

INSCRIPTIONS IN THE CHURCH.

ON A MONUMENT IN THE CHANCEL

Arms, Or, a Chevron Gules between three Lions Jambs eraſed and erected Sable, on a Canton the Arms of Ulſter, for AUSTIN,—impaling, Argent, on a Feſs double cottiſed Gules, three Griffins Heads eraſed Or, for DASHWOOD

Here lyes Sir ROBERT AUSTIN, Bart.
of Hall Place, near Dartford in Kent,
of an ancient Family
He was honeſt and generous
He died Sept 20, 1743, in the 43d Year of his Age.

ON FLAT STONES.

RICHARD HOLFORD
died March 30, 1655.

GILES MATTHEWS, late of this Pariſh,
died Sept 13, 17 , aged 73

JOSIAH LITTLE, of this Pariſh, Gent
died April 7, 1769, aged 79

JOHN, Son of JOSIAH and ELIZABETH LITTLE,
died Sept 30, 1777, aged 46

PHILIP THACHE
died March 10, 1737.

JOHN PRINSEP HAWKES,
Son of WM HAWKES, Eſq and SARAH his Wife,
died July 4, 1788, aged 3 Years 6 Months

THOMAS BISHOP, ſenior,
died July 7, 1714, aged 95

JOHN ROGERS, Gent.
was buried 6 Day of Feb 1633.

JEREMY BADGER MICHELL,
Son of JEREMY MICHELL,
died May 9,   aged 7

MARGARET his Wife
died Jan 3, 1755, aged 85

REBECCA, Daughter of
JOHN MANFIELD, of Bainwood,
Wife of THOMAS BISHOP, of this Pariſh,
died Oct. 5, 1713, aged 35

Here

Here resteth the Body
of John Danvers, the Son of
Richard Danvers, Esq
and Brother to Sir William Danvers,
who deceased January 16, 1616.

Beneath lie the Remains of
William Spencer, a Youth possessed of
every Quality which could excite
the Hopes, or engage the Affections of
Mankind, yet cut off by Death
in his earliest Bloom, at the age of
15 Years, the 11th of March, 1788.

IN THE CHURCH YARD, ON TOMBS.

Hoc sepulchro in diem resurrectionis
reconditur corpus Dom Joh Browne,
sen hujus paroch qui ex hac vita
migravit 21 Feb anno Dom 1689,
ætatis suæ 72

Hic etiam acquiescunt corpora
Catharinæ Annæ, Henrici,
natorum Domini Johannis Browne, sen
& Catharina uxor ejus Catharina
humata erat Martius 28,
Anna hujus Junii 20.
Henricus Julii 1, trosesdem An 1683

John Browne, of this Parish, Gent
died Oct 14, 1701, aged 36

Catharine, the Wife of
John Browne, of this Parish,
died May 27, 1694, aged 53

Aaron Bick
died Oct 17, 1748, aged 74

Anne his Wife
died July 2, 1749, aged 73

Valentine, the Son of
John Stratford, senior, and
Elizabeth his Wife
died August 18, 1706

Giles Viner
died March 26, 1723, aged 54

William Viner,
of Gloucester Grocer,
died April 13, 1779, aged 74.

John Cummin, of Pierton's Court,
Brother to Edward Cummin,
died Dec 23, 1706, aged 58.

Henry Wright, senior,
died Oct 8, 1663.

Jane his Wife
died May 3, 1667.

Edmund Wright,
died June 26, 1710, aged 57

Anne, the Wife of
Richard Halling,
was buried Oct 27, 1696, aged 53

William Blizard, Yeoman,
died Dec 29, 1776, aged 54.

William, Son of
William and Ann Blizard,
died   aged 28

Thomas their Son died an Infant

Elizabeth, Wife of George Long,
died March 11, 1777, aged 55

Thomas Mason
died Oct 26,   aged 57

Sarah his Wife
died June 7, 1772, aged 65

ON A FLAT STONE NEAR THE CHANCEL
WINDOW

Arms, Quarterly, 1st and 4th Azure,
a Fess counter embattled between three
Lions Jambs erect and erased Or, for
Windowe, 2d and 3d, Argent, a Chevron Sable, in chief a Bar engrailed
Gules, for Freme; on an Escucheon of
Pretence, per Chevron, Azure and Argent, in chief two Falcon's volant Or,
for Stephens

Here lieth Henry Windowe, Esq
who died March 21, 1745-6,
in the 63d Year of his Age

In this Vault is also deposited
the Body of Sarah, the Wife of
Henry Windowe, Esq of this Parish
She died Nov 7, 1759, aged 60.

ON FLAT AND HEAD STONES.

	Died		Aged
John Edwards, of Miserden	6 Apr	1754	90
Daniel Burrows, of Brickhampton in this Parish	27 July,	1763	52
Eleanor his Wife	15 Aug	1775	72
Elizabeth Wife of Richard Coopey	26 Dec	1755	50
John Herbert senior	28 Nov	1781	73
John Herbert, junior	11 June,	1746	15
Richard Coopey	19 Mar.	1769	63
George, Son of Richard and Mary Cook, of Wooton	9 Apr	1732	22
William Arkell	23 May,	1766	36
Joseph Bliss	19 Nov	1730	68
Joan his Wife	8 Mar	1737	65
Thomas Wilce senior	22 May,	1717	72
Martha his Wife	11 Jan,	1727	70
Thomas Wilce, junior	14 Feb	1735	43
Hannah Wilce of Thomas Wilce	26 Apr	1728	54
Giles Wilce	8 Mar	1754	64
Martha Daughter of Thomas Wilce, Wife of Giles Tuffley	16 May, 1768		53
Hannah, Wife of William Shaw	9 Mar	1752	62
John Vick	17 Oct	1763	28

	Died		Aged
Thomas Townshend	25 May,	1762	50
Susanna his Wife	29 Oct.	1765	49
Jeremiah Mann	11 May,	1745	62
Priscilla his Wife	2 Apr	1749	58
Jonathan Hone	17 June,	1763	32
Ann, Wife of John Greville	16 Nov	1765	50
Giles Chapman, of Hucclecote	9 May,	1767	55
Esther, Wife of Will Rose, Daughter of William Marchen	30 Nov	1709	27
Giles Little	— July,	1693	43
Thomas Little, Son of Josiah Little and Elizabeth his Wife	22 Dec	1767	36
William Low, late of Brockworth, Yeoman	3 June,	1770	61
Thomas Bamford	27 Apr	1772	34
Mary, Wife of John Tuffley, Clerk, of this Parish	14 Dec	1785	56
Nicholas Wranford, late of Up-Atherley	4 Jan,	1782	44
Hannah, Wife of John Sadler	19 Dec	1783	17
William Beale, late of Hucclecote	7 Mar	1773	49

LXVIII. CHURCHAM;

ORIGINALLY "*Hamme*," in Domefday, and other ancient Evidences *Churcham* and *Highnam* are the more modern Appellations, in order to diftinguifh the Places   This Parifh is divided between the Hundreds of *Weftbury* and *Dudftone*, eight Miles eafterly from *Mitchel Dean*, feven Northeaft from *Newnham*, and five from GLOUCESTER on the North weft   The Soil is principally of heavy and fertile Clay. The Circumference of the Parifh is more than eight Miles, in erfected by the Rivulet *Leadon*, in its progrefs to the *Severn*   Nearly equal Portions of Land are Pafture, and tilled, and in *Huntley Heath* the Inhabitants poffefs a joint Right of Comnonage, where is an extenfive Tract of Wood Land, exempted from Tythes, Part of the Eftate of Sir JOHN GUISE, Bart

The Living is a Vicarage in the *Foreft* Deanery, with the Chapelry of *Bulley* annexed   Both the Impropriation and Advowfon belonged to the Abbey of *St Peter* in GLOUCESTER, and were continued to the Dean and Chapter, upon their firft Eftablifhment

It is probable that the Church was built by the *Normans*, as it confift of one Nave or Pace only, a Mode of Architecture peculiar to them   It has a low Spire at the Weft End, and the whole has been lately very decently repaired   The Pews are thofe which were erected before the Reformation, a regular Arrangement of plain Benches, low and open, and without Diftinction   Pews, according to the modern Ufe, would have obftructed Proceffions, and other Ceremonies of the Romifh Religion   St Andrew is the tutelary Saint.

WOLFIN LE RUE, Conful of GLOUCESTER, in the Reign of CANUTE was Lord of "*Hamme*"   That Monarch, having expelled the Secular Priefts from the Abbey of GLOUCESTER, and introduced Benedictine Monks, the Refentment of WOLFIN prompted him to kill feven of them in the Year 1048. The POPE taking Cognizance of this Outrage, he was fain to make the ufual and only fatisfactory Atonement, and gave this Manor to increafe the Revenues of the Abbey   It remained with them till the Suppreffion, when it was granted to the Dean and Chapter, under whom it has been held by Leafe by the Families of CHAMBERLAYNE, BROWN, HARRIS, BARROW, and MONEY, in Succeffion

The Hamlets of *Highnam*, *Linton*, and *Over*, form one Tything in the Hundred of *Dudftore* and *King's Barton*.

1 *Highnam*   The Manors of *Highnam* and *Over* were likewife Parcel of the Abbey of GLOUCESTER King HENRY the Eighth fold them to JOHN ARNOLD, Efq of the County of *Monmouth*   THOMAS LUCY, Efq of *Charlcote*, co *Warwick*, by Marriage with the fole Heir of that Family, became poffeffed of them   His only Daughter was married to Sir WILLIAM COOKE, of the Family of COOKE, of *Giddy Hall*, co *Effex*, about the Year 1600   WILLIAM JONES, Efq of *Nafs* in this County, and HENRY GUISE, Efq of the City of GLOUCESTER, having married the Heirs Generals of this laft Family, one Moiety of thefe Eftates was inherited, and the other purchafed, by JOHN GUISE, created a Baronet Dec 10, 1783, 23 GEO. III.

The Manfion-houfe is well fituated, and contains feveral very fpacious and magnificent Apartments.* It was built during the Interregnum, from a Plan of INIGO JONES†, by WILLIAM COOKE, Efq who had borne a Colonel's Commiffion under CROMWELL, but was reconciled at the Reftoration, and was High Sheriff for this County in 1663   The old Manor houfe was garrifoned during the Siege of GLOUCESTER ‡, held by both Parties, and rendered uninhabitable by Fire   A private Chapel was
erected

---

* Thefe Apartments are embellifhed with many original Family Portraits particularly of General GUISE in a Roman Character painted by GERVASE HAMILTON at *Rome*   The General was highly efteemed by FREDERICK Prince of WALES, and collected Pictures for him in *Italy* during which Time he made his own fumptuous Collection which he at length bequeathed to *Chrift Church, Oxford* The Family Pictures were returned to the Heir at Law and a very fine MADONA, by TITIAN, is one of them   An original Portrait of CROMWELL, moft probably by R WALKER (to whom he moft frequently fate), given by the PROTECTOR to Colonel COOKE, and mother of the Portrait ALGERNON SYDNEY, by LELY   Befide thefe, is a Half length of Mrs JANE LANE, who conducted the Efcape of CHARLES II after the decifive Battle of *Worcefter*

† The Works of INIGO JONES (as it is obferved by Mr WALPOLE, vol II p 273) are not fcarce, and fome that bear his Name, are the Productions of his Scholars   FRANCIS CARTER ftudied under JONES, and was in high Favour with CROMWELL being Surveyor of his Works   JONES, dying in 1651, then quite fuperannuated, renders a Conjecture allowable, that CARTER is the Defigner of *Highnam Court*

‡ 'Mean while a great Power of the Welfh Army advanced towards GLOUCESTER, and fettled at *Highnam Houfe*, within two Miles of the City and began to intrench   The Governor (MASSIE) placed a Guard at the Bifhop's Houfe (*the Vineyard*) to keep them at a Diftance   Sir JEROME BRETT their Major General had the Confidence to demand the Town, but the Summon was received with Scorne from a Welfh Brigade and became ridiculous, when Prince RUPERT had been twice refuled   Immediately after the taking of *Malmefbury*, Sir WILLIAM WALLER bent his Courfe towards GLOUCESTER and laid his Defigne for the up fize of the Welfh Army   He gave Notice of his Advance unto Colonel MASSIE, with Directions in a ftudy to draw forth both Foot and Horfe before *Highnam*, and to keep them in continual Alarum, that they might not underftand his Approach   The Governor fo timed it according to the Intentions of the Poft drew forth both the Horfe and a Party of 500 Foot, brought up the Ordnance neere the Houfe, and kepte them in the Heat of Play till the Evening   At Night he left Guards to ride the Houfe, with fuch boldnefs and Confidence, that the Enemy durft not ftirre, nor a Spy
Heate

erected by the Family of COOKE, in which several of them are interred without Memorials The Park, Gardens, &c are extensive, and suitable to the Place   This District only is free Land, the Remainder of the Parish being held by Copy or Lease It claims a Right of turning two Horses into the mowing Grass in *Walham* Meadow, from the Festival of *St George* till the Hay be made

2 and 3   *Linton,* or *Lylton,* and *Over,* are the sole Property of Sir JOHN GUISE, Bart.

During the Civil War a Skirmish happened in this Parish in 1643, in a broad Lane near *Highnam,* in which a Captain and four Privates of the Republican Party were slain *. At *Churcham* the Parliament had a small Garrison †

B E N E F A C T I O N S

To the Parish of *Churcham* no charitable Donation has been made ; but to the Hamlets of *Highnam, Over,* and *Linton,* GILES COX, late of *Abloads Court* in this County, gave by Will, Oct 6, 1620, Messuages and Land , the annual Produce of which now is 1*l* 17*s* 6*d*

INCUMBENTS	PATRONS	INCUMBENTS	PATRONS
1673 Abraham Gregory,	Dean and Chapter of GLOUCESTER	1733 John Whinfield, M A	Dean and Chapter of GLOUCESTER
1679 Thomas Thatch, M A	The same	1753 Edward Sparkes, M A	The same
1725 Robert Bull, D D	The same	1778 James Edwardes, B D	The same
1730 Peter Gally, M A	The same.	1785 Thomas Parker, M. A	The same

PRESENT PROPRIETORS OF THE MANORS
Lessee of the Manor of *Churcham,*
WILLIAM MONEY, ESQ
Lord of the Manors of *Highnam, Linton,* and *Over,*
SIR JOHN GUISE, BART

The Persons summoned from this Place by the Heralds, in 1682 and 1683, were
William Cooke, Esq
Thomas Halsey, Gent

At the Election in 1776 Four Freeholders polled from this Parish and its Hamlets

The first Date that occurs in the Register, which is remarkably ancient and correct, is in the Year 1541

ANNUAL ACCOUNT OF MARRIAGES, BIRTHS, AND BURIALS, IN THIS PARISH

A.D.	Mar	Bir	Bur	A.D	Mar	Bir	Bur	A D	Mar	Bir	Bur	A D	Mar	Bir	Bur
1781	8	13	12	1786	4	15	13	1791				1796			
1782	6	17	10	1787	7	23	8	1792				1797			
1783	10	16	15	1788				1793				1798			
1784	4	10	11	1789				1794				1799			
1785	7	13	12	1790				1795				1800			

" steale out, although they lay 1500 stronge At Sunne-rising they had a fresh Alarme by our Ordnance, and were held to it
" by our Musket Shot This Morning their Horse issu d forth, attempting to force their Way through the Horse Guard,
" which they did, and put some of our Horse rashly charging and upon Disadvantage, to a disorderly Retreate , but coming
" up to a Foot Guard received a Repulse And to the Reliefe of that Guard, which was thought too weake, a Party was
" drawne from the Artillery and that againe by this Meanes much neglected, insomuch that at the same Instant the Enemy fell
" upon our Ordnance then like to be deserted, but were beaten backe by the gallantry of some few that kepte their Ground
" In this point of Action Sir WILLIAM WALLER came up and shot his warning Piece on the other Side which dashed the
" Enemy, and so revived our Men, that they ran up with Fury, stormed a Redoubt, and tooke in it two Captains and above
" thirty private Souldiers, which service had a maine Influence on the Surrender of the House Sir WILLIAM placed his Army
" to the best Advantage for Shew, and displaced the Colours of two Foot Regiments reduced to 150 Men, drewe neere the
" House, and made some few Shot with his Cannon After his Approach, not a Man of the Enemy was slaine or hurt yet
" the common Souldier would do any Thing but fight, when they were well fortified, and had a sufficient Magazine They
" founded a Parley and sent forth some Officers to treat, which had this Resulte, " that they should render the House and
" themselves as Prisoners and the Officers should have Respecte and Quarter according to their Quality   Upon the Returne of
" these Termes, some advised to break through which the common Souldiers utterly refused a d neglected the Advantage of
" a darke and rainy Night The Persons that treated dealt the second Time in a Kind of begging Way, but at last accepted
" the former Conditions, and gave up the Welsh Army into the Hands of Men quite spent with continuall Marches and
" Watchings Divers Persons of Quality were heere taken the most powerful Gentry of *Herefordshire* some of that in Scotland
" were stiled the ' Nine Worthies who in the first Opening of the great Breach affronted the Parlement with a scandalous
" Remonstrance Neere 1500 were led captive into GLOUCESTER as great a Number as Sir W WALLER s Army with the
" Garrison Forces, could rise unto ' CORBET, pp 27, 28   The Ensign or Banner borne by Colonel COOKE as described by
" PRESTWICH (p 67, Respub) was singular An armed Soldier on a Mount, holding in his left Hand a cocked Hat, or French
" Chapeau , in his right a Sword, with which he seems to be chopping it over his Head a Scroll inscribed, " Mi o
" quidd ita rotundus "
* CORBET, p 62
† CORBET, 1 79

7

INSCRIPTIONS IN THE CHURCH

IN THE CHANCEL

On a small Tablet of Stone inlaid and bordured with Alabaster, sculptured with Devices and Arms as follow

On four Efcutcheons 1 Gules, on a Fefs between three Billets Argent, three Lions paffant guardin Purpure, for Oldisworth, impaling, Giles, five Marlions Wings in Saltire Argent, for Porter, 2 Porter, impaling, Gules, a Chevron Ermine, between three Pheons Or, for Arnold 3 Arnold, impaling, Or, a Chevron between three Cinquefoils Azure, on a Chief Gules, a Griffin paffant Ermine, for Hawkins, 4 as the 1ft

Here lye buried near this Place the Bodies of Edward Oldisworth, Efq and Tace his Wife, Dowghter of Arthur Porter, Efq and of Alice his Wife, and Sifter to Sir Thomas Porter, Knight, which Alice was Dowghter of John Arnold, Efq and of Isabel his Wife, and Sifter to Sr Nicholas Arnold, Knight, which Isabel was the Daughter of William Hawkins, Efquier, the faid John, Isabel, and Sir Nicholas, being alfo interred in this
Church The faid Edward departed this Life the 8th Day of August, 1570, and the Tace the 6th Day of June, 1576, having had between them five Children, wherof two Sonnes, Arnold and Thomas, and three Daughters, Margaret, Anne, and Dorothy, of whom only Anne died yonge, in the Life of her Parents

Arms, three Crefcents, for Harris

In Memory of William Harris, who died the 14th of Nov, 1735, aged 8 Months

Also of Ebnezer Harris, who died August 3, 1738, aged 2 Years

Ebnezer Harris, fenior, Gent died Feb 4, 1741, aged 44 Years

ON FLAT STONES

Arms, on a Bend three Lion paffant

M S

Condidit hic Johannis Brown Ann civit Gloceftrie Aldermanni, ... et Ornamenta hujus materiae et Civium domini, qui poft ufum pretoris in civitate Glocet fuo tempore fummirupit cum gloria .... in poft exceptam .... &
.... et hic monumentabiles et pofuit exuvias primo die Septem anno Domini 1659,
ætatis 73

Arms, Harris as before

Chariffimi necnon affinibus nifce immifcet cineres Johannes Harris, gen filius neu maximus Johannis Harris, Arm (civitatis London clis quondam fenatoris longe digniffimi, hujus muneris per donationem Sare Browne, relict Johannis prædict Domini) obiit primo die Novemb

Anno { Salutis 1680,
{ ætatis 53

Arms, Harris,—impaling a Dolphin

Sifte, viato
Depofuit enim fub hoc marmore exuvias amabiles Sarah Harris uxor Thomæ Harris, gen hujus maneru domini, mulier
Inter fœminas præci riffima,
Inter uxores obfeq ientiffima,
Inter cœlicolas piiffima,
Inter vicinos munificentiffima,
Inter egenos tantum non prodiga,
Inter omnes chariffima
obiit
Et quos vivens venerata eft mo iens conjunxit cineres Johannis Johnson, hujus ecclefiæ paucis abhinc annis vicarii laboriofi

Illa } die { decimo } menfis { Maii 1665
Ille } { decimo tertio } { Julii 1675

In hac urna reconditi cineres Sare Harris, filiæ Thomæ Harris, hujus parochiæ generofi, quæ expiravit decimo fexto die Januarii, anno Domini 1679
Vixit fex feptimas & biduum

Thoma Prior, eccleficarum Gloceft quondam præbendar. .... Aprilis die XXI,
anno { Dom MDCLXXXV,
{ ætatis fue LXII

S H   H H
ob July 19, 1687, æt 6   ob Mar 2, 1684
                I H
          ob Apr 1, 1683

Thomas Greavilly, of this Parifh Gen died June 2, 1696, aged 6.

Clement Green, of this Parifh, died April 1, 1713, æt fue 6.

M S

CAROLI BARROW, filii THOMÆ BARROW, olim de
Awre & Fieldcourt, Arm qui per varios cafus
diu in India mercator, actus, hic tandem
humillima refurrectionis beatæ fpe requiefcit
Mar 3, anno Domini 1744,
ætatis 64

The Rev JOHN WHINFIELD, M A
late Vicar of this Parish,
died Oct 15, 1753, aged 57

CATHARINE WHINFIELD
died Feb 20, 1762, aged 70

O A BRASS PLATE INLAID IN A FLAT STONE

Here under lye the Bodyes of John Arnold and
Wife, which John deceafed the XII Day
of September MDXLVI, the firft Yere of our So
vereign Lord whofe Soules and all Chrif
tian Soules Jhus take to ....

IN THE CHURCH YARD ON TOMBS

Arms, a Bend three Boys Heads couped at the
Shoulders, each wrapped about the Neck with a
Snake, in Bafe as many Griffins Heads erafed of the
fuft, for MADDOCKS

CARTWRIGHT MADDOCKS
died June 8, 1729, aged 42

HANNAH, Wife of CARTWRICHT MADDOCKS,
died Jan 18, 1759, aged 75

THOMAS MADDOCKS
died April 8, 1760, aged 42

Arms, on a Bend between fix Crofs Crofflets
fitchy three Crofiers, for WEARE

ELIZABETH, third Daughter of
WILLIAM and MARGARET BAYSE, of Weftbury,
Gent and Wife of THOMAS WEARE, of Mannocks
in the County of Hereford, departed this Life
Sept 20, 1743, aged 63

MARGARET, Daughter of JOHN HOLDER,
of this Parish, Gent and Wife of
WILLIAM BAYSE, of Weftbury, Gent
died Oct 5, 1720, aged 68

MARGARET, fecond Daughter of
WILLIAM and MARGARET BAYSE, of
Weftbury in this County, and Wife of
THOMAS PROSSER, of Shenfith
in the County of Monmouth,
died July 13, 1750, aged 76

ANNE, Widow of THOMAS NORTH,
late of Newnham, Gent and Daughter of
WILLIAM BAYSE, late of Chafehill, Gent
by MARGARET his Wife,
died May 25, 1734, aged 67

JONATHAN GRIFFITH junior,
of the Parish of Minfterworth,
died June 21, 1749, aged 63

RICHARD CONSTANT
died May 1, 172-, aged 36

JOHN CONSTAN
died . 1,0-, aged 78

RICHARD GREEN
died Feb 19, 1651

ANNE his Wife
died Sept 11, 1676.

RICHARD GREEN
died June 27, 1767, aged 80.

ANNE his Wife
died Nov 30, 1735, aged 36

MARTHA his Wife
died March 22, 1780, aged 76

WILLIAM PRESBURY
died June 4, 1709, aged 40

JOHN PRESBURY, of this Parish, Yeoman,
died Dec 24, 1742, aged 49

HESTER, Daughter of JOHN and SARAH PRESBURY,
died June 12, 1756, aged 20

JOHN their Son
died Oct 1, 1765, aged 30

RICHARD SMITH, late of Churcham Farm,
died Sept 26, 1765, aged 46

SARAH, Widow of the above RICHARD SMITH,
died Jan 4, 1766, aged 60

Hic fubtus jacet cadaver CAROLI MONTACUE,
de Over in Parochia de Churcham
Obiit Dec 7, 171-, ætat 48

ANN, the Daughter of CHARLES MONTACUE,
and late Wife of SAMUEL GOODWIN, of this Parish,
died June 6, 1720, aged 64

---

* 1ft of King EDWARD the Sixth

JOB HULETT was buried
Oct. 31, 1765, aged 48

ESTHER his Wife
was buried Nov. 11, 1765, aged 35

JEMIMA their Daughter
buried Nov. 14, 1765, aged 15

JOHN their Son,
buried Nov. 19, 1765, aged 14

THOMAS their Son,
buried Nov. 19, 1765, aged 3

JOB HULETT
died Nov. 26, 1765, aged 96

ELIZABETH his Wife
was buried Dec. 1, 1747, aged 47

MARY their Daughter
died Nov. 24, 1727, aged 21

JAMES their Son
died May 11, 1733, aged 35

JOHN HULETT, of Pulley,
died April 10, 1781, aged 75

ELIZABETH, Daughter of
WILLIAM PARKER and ELIZABETH his Wife,
died Feb. 15, 1758, aged 17

GILES HALL, of the Parish of Slimbridge,
died August 20, 1758, aged 38

JOHN DREW
died Feb. 28, 1778, aged 59

JOAN his Wife
died March 8, 1771, aged 72

SARAH their Daughter
died Nov. 5, 1778, aged 39

ANN, Wife of JOHN PARRY, of Longao,
died Nov. , 1760, aged 29

NANCY their Daughter
died Jan. 17, 1772, aged 16

ROBERT ROWLES
died Aug. 12, 1784, aged 68

JAMES DRINKWATER, senior,
died May 17, 1729, aged 82

ELIZABETH his Wife
died May 22, 1729, aged 84

THOMAS DRINKWATER,
buried Jan. 1, 1727, aged 51

HESTER, Wife of
JEREMIAH HOOPER, of the Parish of Bulley,
died March 1, 1776, aged 80

MARTHA, Wife of JOHN FISHER,
died Aug. 1, 1755, aged 69

JOHN FISHER
died May 24, 1760, aged 76

ON FLAT AND HEAD STONES

	Died	Aged
Mary, Wife of Thomas Maddock,	31 Dec 1747	40
Mary, Wife of Francis Crump,	14 Sept 1761	24
Thomas Drew	4 Feb 1757	56
James Drew	17 Feb 1771	60
John Eldridge, of Over	19 Mar 1765	64
Hester his Wife	16 Oct 1705	66
John their Son	14 Aug 1767	34
Hester, Wife of Richard Driver, of Over	13 Jun 1776	35
William Long	3 Jun 1777	40
Edward Young	2 Dec 1750	26
John Cook, Blacksmith	25 Feb 1751	31
Thomas Presbury, of Gloucester, Glover	7 June 1745	49
John Montague, of this Parish, Innholder	10 Apr 1748	57
Mary his Wife	14 Feb 1716	72
Isbell, Wife of Thomas Hill	19 Aug 1769	60
Susanna, Wife of William Hulett, of Bulley	5 Jan 1786	21
Betty, Wife of William Hulet	10 Dec 1759	37
Thomas Viner	5 Nov 1763	52
Mary, Wife of Thomas Moye, of Highnam	20 May 1733	34
Samuel Goodwin, senior	22 Mar 1748	78
Ann his Wife	30 Nov 1711	49
Thomas, Son of Thomas and Mary Moye	8 July 1716	22
William Bury	27 May 1755	57
Thomas Branch, of Highnam	15 Oct 1751	76
Ann his Wife	1 Sept 1709	52
John Branch, late of Highnam	17 Oct 1718	—
Jane his Wife	5 Mar 1734	75
William Wingate	7 Apr 1715	54
Eleanor his Wife	1 May 1719	58
Dorothy, Wife of Richard Dwe	5 Oct 1765	14
William their Son	1 Nov 1765	19

3

ON

ON FLAT AND HEAD STONES

					Died	Aged
Matthew Hook, of the City of Gloucefter	-		-		31 May, 1759	45
Charles Goodman, late of Highnam		-		•	6 Nov 1771	5,
John, Son of Matthew and Elizabeth Hook	-		-		22 June, 1759	21
William Dobbs, of Weftbury	-		-	•	25 Apr 1755	62
William Griffiths, of Over	-		-	•	10 July, 1778	46
Elizabeth his Wife	-		-	•	18 Nov 1779	47
William Brown	-		-		16 Apr 1684	—
Mary his Daughter	-		-		—— 1681	—
Elizabeth, Wife of John Oakey, late of Weftbury	-		-		14 Feb 1780	76
Jane, Wife of John Gibbens	-		-		9 Apr 1751	7,
Samuel Vale, of Highnam	-		-		30 Apr 1754	69
Elizabeth his Wife	-		-		24 Dec 1762	73
Chriftopher Fawkes, of Highnam	•		-	-	16 July, 1745	43
Godfrey Stephens, of Highnam	-		-	-	5 Feb 1750	51
Mary, Wife of John Knight	-		-		14 Oct 1755	59
Margaret Hartland		-		-	11 Apr 1782	72
Francis Stephens	-		-	-	24 June, 1777	48
Ann Green	-	-	•	-	14 Mar 1783	50
Hannah, Daughter of Richard Anne Green		-		-	23 Dec 1761	,0
Caleb Rowbery	-		-		1 Jan 1732	70
John Underwood	-		-		28 May, 1769	21
Joseph Simmons	-		-	-	27 Dec 1779	5,
Mary his Wife	•		-		21 Feb 1752	34
Thomas Trigge	-		•		15 Apr 1755	8,
Elizabeth, Wife of James Hook	-		-		17 Oct 1783	74
James Hook	•		-		28 Apr 1786	63
Jane, Wife of William Sadler, of Gloucefter, Wheelwright		•			21 Nov 1762	47
William Sadler, of the City of Gloucefter		-			26 June, 1779	62
Ann Bellamy, late of the City of Gloucefter, Spinfter		•			2 Mar 1785	60
Mary, Wife of Samuel Bellamy	•		-		— July, 1782	40
Ann, fecond Wife of Samuel Bellamy	:		-		14 Aug 1785	35

CIRENCESTER

DIXTON   CIRENCESTER

LXIX: CIRENCESTER

HAS been distinguished from the remotest Period of this Kingdom, in the Time of our Subjection to the **Roman** Empire, as a large and magnificent City, and since the Conquest by the Normans, as a principal Vill or Borough, of which Description it still remains

The Borough is contained within its own Hundred, surrounded by that of *Crowthorne* and *Minety*, and is distant from **GLOUCESTER** seventeen Miles on the South east   The Arable, Pasture, and Woodland, are in equal Portions, of a light, and in some Parts a gravelly Soil, within a Circumference of four teen computed Miles, intersected by the River *Churn*

The Town, in its present State, is inferior to few provincial Boroughs, either in Extent, Situation, or commodious Buildings.   It consists of four chief, and seven less considerable Streets, within a Circuit of nearly two Miles   These have, excepting on the South Side, a very gradual Descent from the Centre, to the Extremities of the Town, and are healthy and open   Many Houses are unusually commodious and handsome, but dispersed in unfavourable Situations, which, if collected into one Street, would perhaps equal the Splendour of former Ages

The *Britons*, whose Cities, according to the best Authorities, were little more than a Collection of Huts secured by a Ditch or Rampart, possessed (according to B...) but twenty-eight that were dignified with this Appellation   In that Catalogue *Cirencester* is omitted, but in one subsequently made by **HENRY** of **HUNTINGDON**, it occurs under the Name of *Caer Cori*, though the whole Number be not increased

This may authenticate the Origin, but to the Romans it certainly owed its Foundation and its Consequence as a City; who were induced to fix on this Situation by the Meeting of the three great Roads, which were compleated by them †   Here they established a military Station of the first Importance, and making it the Metropolis of the Province of the *Dobuni*, it was thence called by **PTOLEMY** *Corinium Dobunorum*   **ANTONINUS**, in his Itinerary, states that *Durocornovium* (which all the Commentators allow to be *Cirencester*), in the 13th Iter, is distant from *Glevum* (the modern **GLOUCESTER**), fourteen Miles.   It is the fourth Station on the March from *Isca* (*Carleon*) to *Calleva* (*Henley upon Thames*, co *Oxon*), and is only once mentioned ‡

That the old City was encircled and defended by a Wall and Ditch, various Vestiges have sufficiently proved, which, beside the Suburbs, were more than two Miles in Circumference   **LELAND** in the 15th Century mentions that " A Man may yet, walking on the Bank of the *Churne*, evidently perceyve the " Compace of the Foundation of Towers sumtyme standing on the Wall   And neere to the Place wher " the right goodly Clothing Mylle was set up a late by the Abate, was broken downe the Ruine of an " old Tow , toward making of the Mylle Waulls, in the whiche was founde a quadrate Stone, fallen ' downe there, but broken *in aliquot Frustra*, wherin was a Roman Inscription, of the which, one " scantlie lettered that saw yt, told me, that he might perceyve POST MAX   Among divers " *Numismata* founde ther, **DIOCLESIAN's** be most surcll, but I cannot affirme the Inscription to have " be so dedicate on o hym   In the Middes of the old Towne, in a Medow was founde a Flore *de tessellis* " *versicoloribus*, and by the Towne *nostris temporibus* was founde a brossen Shank bone of a Horse, the " Mouth closed with a Pegge, the which taken out, a Shepird found it filled *nummis argenteis* § "   In the Year 1723 Dr **STUKELY** surveyed these Boundaries, and ascertained them to be of nearly the same Extent

The present Town occupies a Part only of the ancient Site, which lay on the East and South Sides, now cultivated as Gardens and Meadows ‖   In the later Ages, Discoveries which evince the former Grandeur of the Place have been more frequently made, or probably have been more in request, and

---

* Oppidum ... *Tessun* ... nt, quum filvas impeditas valo atque foffit num car ...
   ... Ax de Bell. Gallic. lib. V ... 1720
† The ... *regular Way*, the *Irmin* Street, and the *Roman* Street   F'k, on Roman ... FOSA D bj ... HEARNE
   ... *Gibson* v I p ...   LELAND, Itin v III p 16
* L... ASSER Itin ... p 15
‖ "... Medow Ground " LELAND ... V p C

better understood * About 1683 an Hypocaust was exposed, by removing the Surface about four Feet deep, in a Garden South of the Town, fifty Feet in Length, in Breadth forty, and six in Height. A great Number of Funnels were suspended by iron Bars, and the whole was paved, and supported by a Hundred Pillars of Brick. This was by common Conjecture a public Bath. In the Itinerary of Dr. Stukeley, very minute Accounts are given of Discoveries, of various Members of Roman Architecture, tessellated Pavements, Coins, and other Remains+ On a Stone lately in the Possession of Thomas Bush, Esq. was inscribed D M IVLIAL CASLAE CONIVGI VIX ANN XXXIII Upon another, dug up in *Watermore*, near the old City Wall D M P VICINAL CONIV near these were laid Urns, filled with Ashes, and Bones partly consumed. About fifty Years since, a Statue of Apollo in Bronze of eighteen Inches Height, was found, and presented by Thomas Master, Esq. to the University of *Oxford*, and deposited in the Bodleian Library. Portable Altars have been frequently met with. The most perfect and beautiful of the several Pavements, which the Removal of the Soil has brought to Light is that in the House of John Smith, Esq. in *Dyer Street*, discovered in 1783, of which a Representation has been published equally accurate and elegant ‡ Few Coins of great Scarceness or Value have as yet appeared, those known are chiefly of Antoninus, Dioclesian, or Constantine. Little Credit is due to the Tradition of that last Emperor's having been crowned here, and less to William of Worcester, in obscure Journalist of the 15th Century, who says, "Turris *Grosmont* ubi Rex Arturus coronabatur " jacet in Occidentali parte Villæ *Cirencestria* "

From the Departure of the *Romans* till the Establishment of the *Saxon* Heptarchy, *Cirencester* was not the Seat of any memorable Transaction, it was then included in the Kingdom of *Wiccia* §, afterward incorporated with *Mercia*, and between 577 and 656 was alternately held by the Mercians and West Saxons. King Ælfred in 879 having ceded to Godrun, or Gythurnus, a *Danish* Chief, the Kingdom of the *East Angles*, on Condition of his embracing Christianity, the Treaty was ratified at *Cirencester*, where they remained peaceably one whole Year || There is a Monkish Legend given by Gyraldus, that Godrun besieged the Town and burnt it, having tied Firebrands to the Tails of Sparrows, from which successful Stratagem the City obtained the Name of "Urbs Passerum "* In the Year 1020 King Canute, on his Return from *Denmark*, held a solemn Council here, by which Ethelwold was expelled his Dominions.

During the civil Dissentions which immediately followed the Conquest, the Castle founded here was held for the Empress Maud, by Robert de Mie lly, Earl of Gloucester, who summoned their Partizans to assemble at *Cirencester* in 1142, when they were defeated by King Stephen, and the Castle rased ++ But this Fortress being soon restored, the Constable of Simon de Montfort, Earl of Leicester, detached it from King Henry III who on gaining the Town, compleated the total Demolition of the Castle, in the first of his Reign, 1216‡‡ King Edward II kept his Christmas here in 1299

When the Crown was usurped in 1399 by Henry IV the unfortunate Richard being deposed and imprisoned, Edward Plantagenet, Thomas Holland and John Holland, Dukes of *Aumerle, Surrey*, and *Exeter*, and Thomas de Spencer, with John de Montacute, Earls of Gloucester, and *Salisbury*, attached themselves to the deposed King, and plotted his Restoration but the Conspiracy being discovered they were surprised at *Cirencester*, by the Townsmen, and beheaded, excepting *Aumerle*;

---

* "A fine Mosaic Pavement was dug up here in Sept 1723, with many Coins I bought a little Head which had been broken off to the Basso-relievo and seems by the Tiara of a very odd Shape, like Fortification Work to have been the Genius of the some D.   Masius which are in old Inscriptions, such like in Gruter, p 9   A Gardiner told me he had lately found   such like Images, I suppose one of the same " Stukeley's Itineraria Curiosa, who mentions further "Shafts of " the Pillars   feet long and the Cornices very handsomely moulded " A Part of a Pilaster, and the Capital of a Pilaster, we still preserve   This Pillar must have been at least twelve Feet long, beside the Capital and other Proportions

+ A few Years since these Discoveries were farther investigated, and have attracted the Notice of the Curious The most probable Conjecture, that it was an *Officina*, or Kiln where the *Tessera* were prepared, as there were many Ovens, or hypocausts   necessary for that Manufacture in which the Romans excelled

‡ This Drawing was taken in 1787 by Samuel Lysons, Esq. F S A and presented to the Society of Antiquaries, by whom it has been published   The Design consists of Laths and Sea Monsters   Animals of all Kinds (it is observed) are frequent subjects of Mosaic Work   The celebrated Pavement of the Temple of Fortune at *Præneste* supposed to be as old as Sylla's time, contains a Variety of Birds, Fishes, and Beasts with their Names superscribed   Another in the Ruins of the Temple of Hercules on the *Aventine* Mount at *Rome* engraved by Turretti, exhibits a Lion, a wild Boar, Stags, and an Elephant The beautiful one from *Alban* Villa, representing Doves in a Vale, described by Pliny, N t Hist XXXVI 25 is   red by the same Antiquary   And, not to go out of our own Country, the Pavement at *Woodchester* has an Elephant and   Boar   that at *Leicester* had Figures of Fish, and Dogs and Dolphins   one of those at *Hinton* had Orpheus surrounded   at the East *Stonesfield* Bath and several Birds   The Majority of these Designs are Emblems of Festivity, and therefore appropriated to the House of the *Triclinia* " We here so have the ingenious Mr Warton, *Addington*, p 59) to suppose with Tilears, that such Remains always point out the Habitation or Post of a Roman General   For present Part of four Hundred Years, the *Roman* occupied this Island in a State of Peace and Tranquillity as a Colony fertile and abounding in beautiful Studios is it have been inhabited by many *Roman* Adventurers, who migrated hither with their Families and built *Villas* in Country Seats where they lived in some Degree of Opulence and Elegance   Agriculture introduced Architecture   built *Houses* of Rank though have built Houses in the *Roman* Taste   Whenever we talk of the Romans in *Britain* we thought it nothing but Rapine and Hostility "

Lyceum no that, qua *breuior euo numerantur*, qua est in meridiana parte *Huic torum* "
                                                        After Money Gest Alfred, Anno 879

§ Saxon Chron v I p   Howel's Hist of Wales v III p 200
* *Civitas* a sexcenta *Cornix Passerum* to point per unam *Africanum* deduxit per obedientem civitatem, per p ducis * om *Horum* de comm tinctis hos evolando deduxit a " Joh W de Wyrcestre, p 279, ed Nasmith
++ Lysons the H v I p 29
‡‡ Gale on Chron v I p 285
§§ Saxon Chron p 2c

who

who was pardoned *   We fubjoin the Narrative of this Event from STOW's Annals, " The fame Day
" they came to *Cirencefter*, and on the twelvth Day late in the Eveninge, they there harbored with a great
" Number of Men of Armes, and many Archers   There they bruited that Kinge RICHARD was efcaped
" forthe of Pryfon, and that he was there with them, and to make their Wordes to have the more Cre-
" dite, they had gotten a Chaplein of King RICHARD's, called MAUDELEN, fo like to him in all Pro-
" portion and Favour, that one could unneth be difcerned fro the other   They put him in Armour,
" with the Crowne on his Helmet, fo as all Men might take him for King RICHARD   On the Morrow
" the People of the Towne miffliking their Proceedings fought againft them, and at length took the
" chiefeft of them, and led them to the Abbey there, and put them in a fure Chamber, under fafe Cu-
" todie   And on the Thurfeday the faid Lordes fearing the People, imagined how to efcape out of their
" Handes and caufed fome of their Servantes to fet Fire on certain Houfes of the Towne, thinking
" that therupon the People would departe from then, and feeke to ftaunch the Fire   But it chaunced
" contrary, for the People turned into marvellous rage againft them, runne upon them with a great Vio-
" lence, and drewe them into the Mercate Place, and there they beheaded the Dukes of *Lecefter* and
" *Surrey*, and the Earl of *Salfbury* +"   Edit. HOWES, p 324   The Wall and Gates were once in the
Reign, nor can it be accurately faid when they were totally demolifhed   At Length, in the Year 1754,
Parts were uncovered eight Feet in thicknefs, and three in Height, of hewn Stone, very ftrongly ce-
mented, but moft of thefe have been levelled

The military Hiftory of this Place ‡ records nothing from 1499 till the Year 1641, when the firft
forcible Oppofition was given to GEORGE Lord CHANDOS, then Lieutenant of the County, and executing
the Commiffion of Array   He received the greateft Indignities from the Populace, and narrowly efcaped
with his Life.   The Town was foon after garritoned by the Parliament, and on the firft of January in the
next Year, was befieged by the King's Forces, who continued two Days only, but returning with a
Reinforcement under Prince RUPERT, began the Affault on the fecond of February   CORBET gives
very circumftantial Detail of thefe former Proceedings, and adds that " the firft and maine Affault was
" made on a Houfe a flight Shot from the Towne, which was defended for in Houfe's Space by a Hun-
" dred Mufketeers againft two Regiments of Foot and a Regiment of Horfe, which were led on by the
" Prince, who at Length having drawne up their Mufketeers, and by Grenadoes fired the Barnes and
" Ricks, and fmothered the Guard, the Enemie's Horfe drove their Foote before them, and entered
" the Streets by maine Force, and poffeffed themfelves of the Garifon within two Houres, yet it coft
" them the Lives of many, amongft whom the Welfh men were reported to fuffer the greateft Slaughter
" Few of ours were flaine in the Fight, but many murdered after the taking of the Towne, eleven
" Hundred taken Prifoners, and at leaft two Thoufand Armes loft which the Country had there laid up
" as in a fecure Magazine   The miferable Captives were entreated with all Defpight and Contumely,
" Commanders and Gentlemen had no better Quarter than the common Souldiers, but were all thruft into
" the Church to be referved for a Triumph."

From another Account publifhed by Prince RUPERT's Chaplain we collect " that Colonel FETTIPLACE,
" who was the Governor, Captain WARNEFORD and JOHN GEORGE, Efq Member in Parliament for
" the Borough were amongft the Prifoners, and great Number of Arms were found in the Houfes, and
" drawn out of the River, to the Amount of 3000 "

Lord CLARENDON's Mention of this Siege § is equally minute, and confirms thefe Facts, though with
different Colouring, he confidered this Victory of the greateft Confequence to the Royal Party   From
this Time, to the Clofe of the Civil War, the Town was held alternately   After the Siege of GLOU-
CESTER, Lord Effex furprifed Sir NICHOLAS CRISP in his Quarters here, and captured 400 Horfe, with
Ammunition and Provifions   The firft Encounter attended with Bloodfhed in 1688 happened at *Cirencefter*   Lord LOVELACE on his March to join the Prince of Orange, was oppofed by Captain LORANGE
and his Son, at the Head of the County Militia, in which Engagement they were both flain.   Lord
LOVELACE was overpowered, and imprifoned at GLOUCESTER

A College, confifting of a Dean and Prebendaries, was eftablifhed at *Cirencefter*, in the early Saxon
Times, REIMBALDUS *, Chancellor to King EDWARD the CONFESSOR, prefided, and held large Eftates
in feveral adjacent Parifhes, which on his Death lapfed to the Crown

* Of this Confpiracy the following curious Account occurs in a Chronicle of *Malmefbury* preferved by LELAND   "Quidam
" de familia Regis Henrici IV jacebat una Nocte cum Meretrice *Londini* quae rogavit dominum tibi Vale Amice? qui implius
" te non videbo?   Et ille quafivit   Quare?   Qia & dixit   Con tra *Humeldune Caftra*, & Sarum, jacuit in infidiis in par-
" tibus de Aquilone Regem Archiepifcopum, & vos venientes de *Hund* occidunt   & Regem RICHARDUM reftituunt
" Et ille quafivit   Unde hoc nofti?   Et illa dixit Unus de familia eorum dormivit mecum   Hei nocte, qui hoc nofti dixit
                                                                                                  Collectanea v II p 310.
   " The Duke of Surrey and Title of Salfbury we encountered with, hard by *Cirencefter*, and over cum, and by and by
" heddid and quartered with each other, and their Quarters fent to LONDON in Sakkes   Ibid p 484
† RICHARD II Act II Scene VI
   BOLINGBROKE—" Good Uncle York, what lateft News we hear
      " Is that the Rebels have confumed with Fire
      " Our Towne of *Cirencefter* in *Gloucefter fhire*
      " But whether they be taken or flain we hear not "   Edit JOHNSON and STEEVENS
‡ CORBET's Military Government of GLOUCESTER, pp 8, 16, 17, 22, 25, 54, 71, 84
§ CLARENDON, Lib III p 12, Ed 8vo
‖ LELAND, Itin v II p 64
   * In the Book of the Church appears a Sepulchre Crofs of white Marble, is this   Hic jacet REMBALDUS Prefbyter, quondam
" hujus Ecclefiae Decanus, & tempore Edwardi Regis Angliae Cancellarius   LELAND, Itin v V p 62

King

King Henry I founded a Monastery for Canons Regular of the Order of St *Augustine*, and to the Priory of Reimpald added a more ample Endowment. The Structure was begun in 1117, and completed in 1127, the Conventual Church being dedicated to St *Mary* and St *James* * Of its Dimensions W DE WIRCESTRE has preserved these Notices "Consecratio duarum campanarum *Cirenceste* "feria quinta per 3 dies ante Festum. Sancti Lucæ. 1238 Longitudo magnæ Ecclesiæ ordinis Sancti "Augustini Canonicorum Regularium continet 140 gressus Latitudo navis dictæ Ecclesiæ continet cum "diabulis aliis 41 gressus, sive 24 Virgas, præter Capellam Orientalem Longitudo antiquissimæ Capellæ "Beatæ Mariæ in meridionali Ecclesiæ Abbathiæ à Coro continet 44 Virgas, cum una Ela ab antiquo in "nexa Latitudo 22 Virgas Longitudo Claustri 52 gressus Longitudo de "le Chapitre Hous," 14 "Virgas, Latitudo 10 Virgas, in finis sex fenestræ vitreatæ Dom Seynête *Amene* sepelitur in magna "Tumba Figura Militis, cum armis suis, *frette & tribus pellibus in Capite* † " LELAND, about fifty Years afterward, transmits the following Remarks " The Este Parte of the Churche of *Cirencester* Ab-"bay sheweth it to be of verie olde Buildinge The West Part from the Transeptum is but new Work "to speke of Ther is two Noblemen of St *Amands* buryed within the Presbyterie of *Cirenceshe* Abbay "Churche; and ther is buryed the Hart of SENTIA, Wife to RICHARD King of the *Romans*, and Earle "of *Cornewalle* ‡ "

A few Years after this Survey, upon the general Dissolution, the Abbey was destroyed We cannot account for that total Subversion which has Left no Ruins, but by supposing that the Materials were instantly sold and dispersed Mr WILLIS conjectures that the Site of this venerable Pile was in the North east Part of the present Cemetery The first House built by the Family of MASTER §, as delineated by Kip, is of the Age of Queen ELIZABETH, nor could it possibly have been the Abbots Lodgings, according to the Idea WILLIS has given of the Ground-plot of the Monastery The modern House, rebuilt in 1776 by THOMAS MASTER, Esq on the Foundations of the former, is large and handsome, with Environs on a suitable Plan The Site of the Abbey and its Appendages were granted 1546, 1 EDW VI to THOMAS Lord SEYMOUR, of *Sudley, in capite*, by Service of one Knight's Fee. Upon his Disgrace and Attainder it lapsed to the Crown, and in 1564, in the sixth Year of her Reign, Queen ELIZABETH conveyed it to RICHARD MASTER, M. D. one of her Physicians, who was the direct Ancestor of the present Possessor THOMAS MASTER, Esq Knight of the Shire for this County

By a Writ of *Inspeximus*, and Confirmation of the Endowment of the Abbey, by King EDWARD III the following Possessions are recited, which at the Suppression were valued at 1051*l* 7*s* 1*d* ¼ old Rents In this County twenty eight Hides, two Yardlands, and three Impropriations. In *Wilts* nine Hides and four Impropriations. In *Dorset* ten Hides In *Somerset* three Impropriations. In *Berks* nineteen Hides three Yardlands, and four Impropriations. In *Oxford* one Hide In *Bucks* one Rectory In *Northampton* two Benefices, beside the *Seven Hundreds* and the Town of *Cirencester* ‖ The Abbot was summoned to a Parliament at LONDON 1209, 49 HENRY III ** and to a Council at *Carlisle* 1307, 1 EDWARD II †† but had not obtained a Seat as a Baron till 1416, 1 HENRY V when the Mitre and Pontificals were granted by the POPE ‡‡ He had a Right of Coinage, and a Prison for Delinquents within his own Jurisdiction §§

SUCCESSION OF ABBOTS

A D		A D	
1117	Serlo Dean of Salisbury	1187	Richard.
1147	Andrew	1213	Alexander Neccham ‖‖
1173	Adam	1217	Walter
1183	Robert	1230	Hugh, or Henry de Bampton

* Anno 1127 dedicata est Ecclesia Canonicorum Regularium *Cirencestriæ* in honorem beatæ MARIÆ, a PARTOLOM TO "EXONIENSI Episcopo XIV die Novembris die Dominica, presente Domino Rege, qui eidem Ecclesiæ magnos redditus dedit
        LELAND, Collectanea, v III p 208
  This Order was instituted by AUGUSTINE Bishop of HIPPO. Their Habit, according to PETYOR VIRGIL, lib VII c and DUGDALE's *Warwickshire* p 162 was a white Coat and linen Surplice, under a black Cloak with a Hood covering the Head and Neck, which reached to the Shoulders, having under it doublet Breeches, white Stockings, and white Slippers, and when they worked out a black cornered Cap then Crown being shaven but not so much as other Monks
  † In W DE WIRCESTRE, pp 278, 279 ed NASMITH
  ‡ LELAND, Itin v II p 50
  § The Family of MASTER were anciently established in *Kent* RICHARD MASTER, M D proceeded 1562 a Fellow of All Soul's College, *Oxford* WOOD's Fasti, p 619 GEORGE MASTER his Son settled at *Cirencester* in 1570 King CHARLES I passed one Night at Sir WILLIAM MASTER's in his March from *Bristol* to *Oxford* in August 1643, and another on August 31 1644, in his Return from *Bath* Her Gro^{und} Coll Cur No 19 On the 27th of August, 1702, Queen ANNE lay at the House THOMAS MASTER Esq Par Register
  ‖   §
  ** EXCHEQUER Summons
  †† DODSWORTH's SPELMAN, p 211
  ‡‡ WILLIS's Mitred Abbeys
  §§ STEVENS Appendix, p 62
  ‖‖ ALEXANDER NECCHAM, born at St ALBANS, co *Herts*, and being desirous to become a Novitiate in the Abbey, applied to the Cenobite in these Words *Si vis veni, sin autem in autem* To which he received this Answer *Si bonus sis venias, Si nequam nequaquam* LELAND, Itin Min p 336 and CAMDEN, Rem p 160. "He was a frequent Writer both in Prose and Verse, as his MSS are preserved in the Abbey He died 1217, and was buried at *Worcester* '
                LELAND's Collectanea, vol IV p 158

A D	1238	Roger de Rodmerton		A D	1416	William Best
	1266	Henry de Munden			1429	William Wootton
	1281	Henry de Humptonel			1440	John Taunton
	——	Adam de Brokenbury			1445	William George †
	1319	Richard de Cherleton			1461	John Solbury, or Sodbury
	1334	William Herewarde			1478	Thomas Compton ‡
	1351	Ralf de Estcote			1481	Richard Clyve §
	1357	William de Marteley			1488	Thomas Afton
	1360	William de Dynton			1504	John Hakebourne ‖
	1363	Nicholas de Ampney			1522	John Blake **
	1394	John Leckhampton				

Appendant to Deeds executed by the Monaftery at different Times, the following Coats of Arms have been authenticated

1 Gules, on a Chevron Argent three Rams' Heads coupé Sable, attired Or

2 Gules, on a Chevron Argent three Rams' Heads affronté Sable, attired Or, in the dexter chief Quarter two Lions passant guardant Or

3 Per fess Or and Gules, in bend a Crofier Argent, within a Bordure Azure bezanté

The Benefice ‡‡ is a Vicarage without Glebe, but endowed with Oblations and all privy Tythes, excepting those of the Demefnes The Impropriation was vefted, soon after the Diffolution, in the Family of BOURCHIER, of Barnfley, and now belongs to the Right Honourable HENRY Lord BATHURST The Patron is the Right Reverend the Lord Bifhop of GLOUCESTER In 1708 a Houfe was purchafed for the Incumbent with various Benefactions It is the Chief of a rural Deanery

Of the firft Erection of the Church, dedicated to St John, a Structure fingularly magnificent and beautiful, we are led to make fome Conclufions from the Arms of Contributors and other Documents A Nave ‡‡, two Aifles, and five Chapels, befide the Chancel or high Choir, compofe this ftately Fabric

---

* WILLIAM BEST was the firft Abbot who obtained the Mitre and Pontificals about the Year 1416 His Succeffors fate in Parliament as Barons WILLIS, Mit Abb

† WILLIAM GEORGE received the Benediction from JOHN CARPENTER, Bifhop of Worcefter, at Perfhore, April 10, 1445, died 1461

‡ THOMAS COMPTON contributed to the Building the Parifh Church He died in 1481

§ Upon the Doorcafe of a Houfe near the Church is carved a Mitre between R A as being probably built during the Abbacy of RICHARD CLYVE, who died in 1488 As Abbot of Cirencefter he affifted at the Coronation of HENRY the Seventh and ELIZABETH his Queen, 1485 LELAND, Collectanea

‖ JOHN HAKEBOURNE, or HAYKEBORNE, was Prior of the College of St Mary of Augnftine Monks in Oxford He afterwards proceeded D. D and became Lord Abbot of Cirencefter WOOD's Fafti, vol I p 636 He was a great Benefactor to the new Parifh Church He was elected Abbot on the Refignation of his Predeceffor T ASTON, and died in 1522

** JOHN BLAKE, the laft Abbot, built two Fulling Mills at the Expence of 700 Marks, when the Manufacture of Cloth was firft introduced LELAND acknowledges his Courtefy, and the Information he received from him He refigned the Abbey to the King's Commiffioners Dec 29, 1539, 31 HEN VIII and accepted an annual Penfion of 2,ol RICHARD WOODWALL, 13l 6s 8d as Prior WILLIAM WARBOTT, Cellaret, 8l THOMAS FISHER, THOMAS HEDDE, JOHN RUSSEL, JOHN WALLE, WILLIAM MORE, RICHARD BOILE, JOHN STRAUNGE, THOMAS LOGGER, ANTHONY CHILCOLE, HENRY HAWKS, JAMES PLERGERN, and WILLIAM SMYTH, 6l 13s 4d each RICHARD LANE 5l 6s 6d WILLIS, ut fup

About the Year 1772 a small Brass Coin was found in the Abbey Garden, on one Side was a Coronet charged with three Rams Heads, part of the Conventual bearing with this Legend, ' AVE MARIA GRACIA PLEN ' on the Reverfe a Crofs flory between four Fleurs de lis, and G A It was certainly of the Coinage of BEST, WOOTTON, or GEORGE, but of which it cannot be pofitively faid

†† At the Suppreffion it was fettled by the Commiffioners " That WILLIAM PHILLIPS is affigned to the Vicarage and Cure " of the Parifh of Cirencefter, with the whole Tithes of Woolle, Lambe, Hey, Oblations Alterage and all other Profitts belonging " to the fame Churche The Tythes of the Domayne Landes, latelie being in the Occupation of the Late Abbot and Convent " there, only excepted Yeildinge therfore unto the King's Majeftie, in Confideration the fame Vicar fhalle be chargid with " the findinge of three Priefts befydes himfelfe to miniftre there, alfo fhalle fynd Wyke and Wax at his propre Cofts and " Charges yerelie 53s 4d And fo the faid Vicar fhall have a reafonable Living, and a conveynant Portion of the Profitts of the " faid Churche, the Quantitie of the Cure there duelie confidered

" ROBERT SOUTHWELL,	
" JOHN CARNA,	
" RICH GWINT,	Commiffioners '
" JOHN LONDON,	
" RYCHARD POWLITT,	
" WILL BURNERS	

WILLIS, Mit Abb ut fup

‡‡ " In nomine Ecclefiæ parochialis Sancti Johannis in Villa de Cirencefter, alias Cirencefter cum Choro conducit do Gruffus " Latitudo de te Ecclefiæ contnct cum duobus his do Gruffus Longitudo Comprehens contnct 7 Villas Latitudo Turris fue " Spera contnct 6 Vergas & dimid Itin W e Worcefter, p 277

There hath bene three Parochi Churches in Cirencefter whereof St Cecilie Church is clene doun, it was of late but a Chapell St Lawrence is ftandith, but as no Parochie Churche Ther is nowe but one Parochie Church in al Cirencefter, but that " is very fair He Body of the Church is at new Worke, to the which RUTHALL, Bifhope of Durram, borne and brought " up at Cirencefter, promifed much but preventid with Deth, gave nothing ' LELAND, Itin vol II p 51 But he meant the infide only

In a very auncient MS Ichnography is the following Statement of the Dimenfions of the whole Church

' Length 87 Feet, Breadth 84 Feet 9 Inches, including the Aifles Trinity Chapel Length 46 Feet 6 Inches, Breadth 18 " Feet 7 Inches St Mary's Chapel Length 47 Feet, Breadth 21 Feet St Katherine's Chapel Length 52 Feet, Breadth 12 " Feet 10 Inches Chancel or High Choir Length 47 Feet 6 Inches, Breadth 24 Feet 8 Inches St John's Chapel Length " 34 Feet, Breadth 24 Feet Jefus Chapel Length 12 Feet 6 Inches, Breadth 9 Feet 4 Inches, Height of the Tower 134 " Feet '

To these are added a Tower of great Height and Symmetry, containing twelve Bells, and a Porch of exquisite Gothic Masonry, all which deserve to be distinctly examined and described   The Nave is divided from
the Aisles by a double Row of five clustered Columns, well proportioned and light, over the Arches are an
equal Number of Windows, once ornamented with painted Glass   Affixed to the Capitals are Busts of Benefactors, with their armorial Ensigns, Initials, and Devices   On the North Side   1 A Cross encircled   2
On a Chevron three Rams' Heads affronte, Abbey of Cirencester   3 Quarterly, 1st and 4th, a Lion on pale
1a t between three Helmets, 2d and 3d, a Chevron within a Bordure charged with Roundlets, THOMAS
COMPTON, Abbot   4. A Device, with Initials R R , ROBERT ROWTHATE   5 A Device, with Ini-
tials H G , HUGH GARSTANG   6 A Cross engrailed between four Birds, on a Chief quarterly two
Roses stalked, impaled with the See of Durham, THOMAS ROWTHALE [*], Bishop of Durham   On the
South Side   1 ROWTHALE as before   2 A Crosier ensigned with a Mitre, I H , JOHN HASELBORNE,
Abbot   3 A Lion and Griffin combatant, TAME of Fairford   4 A Cross patonce, I P , JOHN
PRATTE, a Chantry Priest   5   Three Greyhounds current in Pale   6 Obliterated   Over the great
Window France (semee Fleur de lis) and England, in which were the following Delineations, now totally
destroyed   St George and St. Anthony, and the Arms of the Abbey   Berkeley, and a Chevron between
three Bulls passant   Between the Arches on smaller Escutcheons are the Emblems of the Crucifixion
In the North Aisle   1 and 2 defaced   3 Three Greyhounds in Pale   4 Quarterly, 1 a Fess between three Martlets,   2 a Lion rampant crowned,   3 as the second,   4 a Pile, BRUCES, of Sudley
5 Barry a Lion rampant, impaling Barry, over all an Escarboncle   6 BERKELEY of Rendcombe, impaling three Chevrons braced in base and a Chief, FITZ-HUGH

In the Windows   1 Sable, a Chevron between three Wolves' Heads erased Or   2 Argent, an
Escallop Gules, impaling, Azure a Chevron Gules, PRELATTE   In the South Aisle,   1 Device   2
Device, I M   , Device, I P , JOHN PRATTE   4 Bust of a Woman, Legend, " Alys Abenynge "
5 Device   6 Obliterated   The Windows of this Aisle are the most perfect   That on the right Hand
of the great Porch is in the best Preservation, and contains many Portraits of Saints, with Legends, purporting by whom these Embellishments were given.   Upon these the following Names are written :
" W Hampton, Johnes Hampton & uxor ejus, W Okyn & Johanna ur' ej. W Cclesbourne "
On others we read, " Johannes Rowthale, Marg & Alicia ur' ejus, Joh s Langele & Joh'nes Whyte "
A Device, with P G and the Arms, Azure, three Mascles Or, a Chief Argent, within a Bordure engrailed Gules, GARSTANG, are repeated in the highest Compartment of each Window, and externally on
the Buttresses in carved Stone   It is said, that in these Windows every Order instituted by the Romish
Church was delineated, from the Pope to the Mendicant, but an Investigation is now rendered imprac-
ticable by the Decay of Time, and the Rage of Fanatics   In the Chancel were Stalls prior to this Century,
when neat Pews were substituted   About 1673 these Arms remained on some of them   1 Abbey   2
A Fess between three Martlets, BRUCES   3 Sable, fiery, and three Bezants in Chief, ST AMAND
4 GARSTANG   5 Three Greyhounds current in Pale   Of the Chapels the most considerable, and probably the most ancient   is dedicated to the Holy Trinity   WILLIAM PRELATTE, buried there in 1462,
is said to have been " specialissimus Benefactor hujus Capelle,' and his Arms occur very frequently, but
this Building must have been more ancient than that Period   The Windows of this Chapel were once
most splendidly ornamented, particularly that at the East End, which contained five Portraits with Arms

1st Compartment   PETER King of Castile and Leon, Arms, Quarterly, 1st and 4th, Gules, a Castle
Or, 2d and 3d, Argent, a Lion rampant Gules   2 RICHARD PLANTAGINET, Duke of York, Arms,
Quarterly, 1st, England, 2d, Gules, a Cross Or, BIGOT, 3d, MORTIMER, 4th as 1st   3 THOMAS HOL-
LAND, Duke of Surrey, Arms, Quarterly, France and England, over all, a File of three Labels, nine
Bezants   4 RICHARD NEVILLE, Lord of Salisbury, Arms, Gules, a Saltire Argent, NEVILLE, quar-
tered France and England   5 Sir JOHN JENKLYATY, Knight   Arms, Azure, three Coronets Or, the
Head only of the Duke of York, very delicately penciled, is all that has escaped Demolition   Over the
Arches is carved a Phoenix, which was used is the armorial Bearing of the Borough   WILLIAM PAIN-
TER, the last Priest of the Chantry of this Chapel   received a Pension of 4l   The following Arms, con-
soling the paternal Coat of HENRY D'ANVERS, Lord of Danby, are emblazoned on small Escutcheons of
Stone   1 Gules, a Chevron between three Mullets pierced Or, for D'ANVERS,   2 Argent, on a Bend
Gules, three Martlets Or, winged Vert, for D'ANVERS,   3 Gules, two Bar Or, in Chief two Strips'
Heads erased of the second, for POPHAM,   4 Paly six, Argent and Azure, on a Bend Gules, three
Fleurs de lis Or, for RADLING,   5 Gules, a Chevron Ermine between ten Crosses pattee Argent, for
BERKELEY,   6 Gules, three Cross pattee Or, in Chief a Label of three Points, for ———— ,
Azure, a Fess between three Crosses pattee Sable, for GARNON,   8 Argent, a Cross Sable pierced in
the Centre, for ———— ,   9 Gules, three Chevrons Argent, for AVELY,   10 Chequy Or and
Gules, a Fess Ermine, or Thomey,   11 Azure, a Chevron between three Crescents Or, for BARKI-
THOLIS,   12 Per pale Or and Azure, over all a Bend nebuly Gule, for DANTISEY,   13 Argent,

                                                                                        . Chief

a Chief indented Sable, for BATTLEY, 14 Sable, six Swallows Argent, for ARUNDF, 15 Azure, a Bend Or, and Label of three Points, for CARMINOWE, 16 Ermine, on a Cross Gules five Mutlets Or, for LISTEROCKE, 17 Checquy Or and Azure, a Chief Argent jutte du fans, for COLESPELL, 18 Argent, fretty Gules, for BLACKAMISTER, 19 Gules, fretty Argent a Canton of the second, for HEWISH.

The Chapel of St. Mary retains no Veſtige of Antiquity. The Fees and Revenues, anciently annexed to the three Chantries founded in it, were very great, and are ſpecified in a Manuſcript preſerved amongſt Sir WILLIAM DUGDALE's Papers in the Muſeum at Oxford, amongſt which were the Impropriation and Advowſon of the adjoining Pariſh of Bagendon. THOMAS EDMONDES, the laſt Incumbent, received a Penſion of ƚ

St. Katherine's Chapel, it is conjectured, was founded by RICHARD OSMUND, whoſe Effigy in Stone is preſerved there. St. Katherine was canonized by Pope Pius II in 1461, which ſettles the Date, as it was cuſtomary to compliment the laſt made Saint in the Calendar with Dedications. Her Portrait, with the Symbols of her Martyrdom, is painted in Freſco on the Wall, and is ſtill in good Preſervation. The beautiful pendent Roof, moſt exquiſitely wrought with Devices, was added by Biſhop ROWTHALE and his Family. In the four Compartments of the Roof are I H Abbot HAKEBOURNE, I R THOMAS ROWTHALE, with the Cognizances of the Prince of WALES. The Arms of King HENRY the Seventh, within the Garter, 1508, are finely emblazoned.

In St. John's Chapel nothing remains worthy Notice.

The Chapel of Jeſus is an Incloſure of Iriſh Oak at the Eaſt End of the South Aiſle, affixed to which, are theſe Arms belonging to the neighbouring Gentry. 1 Argent, a Lion rampant guardant Gules, holding a Roſe in the dexter Jamb ſtalked Vert, MASTER. 2 MASTER, impaling, Sable, on a Chevron engrailed between ſix Croſſes pattee Or, three Fleurs de lis of the Field, each charged with a Pile, SMITH of Nibly. 3 On a Lozenge Argent, a Saltire Azure. 4 Sable, two Bars Ermine, in Chief three Croſſes pattee Or, BATHURST. 5 Argent, a Chevron between three Eagles diſplayed Sable, on a Chief, 1ſt, a Bend between two Martlets, 2d, RAYMOND. 6 Argent, a Chevron between three Stag's Attires Sable, COXE. 7 Argent, two Bars Sable, BRERETON. 8 Argent, a Bend wavy Sable between ſix fighting Cocks Gules, COSWELL. 9 Argent, on a Chevron Sable between three Oak Leaves proper, as many Bezants, on a Chief Gules a Sea Shell between two Anchors erect of the firſt, MONOUX. 10 Argent, a Croſs voided flory counterflory between four Mullets pierced Sable, ATKINS. 11 Or, a Feſs between three Wolves' Heads couped Sable, HOWE.

To the South Aiſle fronting the Market Place is attached a moſt beautiful Gothic Portal, of equal Height, and conſiderable Dimenſions. It was erected at the Cloſe of the fifteenth Century, by various Contributors, but chiefly at the Expence of Alice AVENING, the Aunt of Biſhop ROWTHALE, who gave 100 Marks *. The Ornaments externally are profuſely ſcattered, conſiſting of Friſes, with Figures of moſt grotesque and capricious Maſonry. In 1671 the great Chamber was applied to the public Uſes of the Borough for Veſtries and other Aſſemblies, by Licence of W NICHOLSON, Biſhop of GLOUCESTER.

By being thus minute in our Deſcriptions, we are enabled to adduce Proofs in Support of an Opinion reſpecting the Origin of this remarkable Edifice. In the Nave and Aiſles, ſuch is the Coincidence of Parts, that it would not have been poſſible to attain, had the Deſign been otherwiſe than original, or Additions made. That the Arms of Contributors are of different Dates, proves little, as they were the laſt Embelliſhments, made after the full Completion of the Plan in which every Benefactor, at various Times, might be included. The Tower was certainly built before 1416, as the Arms of France are ſeme Fleurs de lis on an Eſcutcheon affixed, which was laſt uſed by HENRY IV. WILLIAM DE WYRCESTER gives the Dimenſions of it in 1460. It is further to be remarked, that France is above is on an Eſcutcheon over the great Window of the Nave. In St. Katherine's Chapel the three Fleurs de lis only are emblazoned, which argues an Attention to heraldic Diſtinctions, and from theſe it may be fairly aſſerted that the Church was built early in the fifteenth Century. The Chapels (St. Katherine's at leaſt) were ſubſequent Additions for the Reception of Chantries. Of this Æra likewiſe are the open Battlements of the Tower. The Work on the Nave and the monſtrous Figures applied as Water Spouts, on it is perhaps ſingular that on the Parapet of the North Aiſle there is a regular Aſſemblage of Characters, habited as Minſtrels, with the double Pipes, Regals and other ancient Inſtruments of Muſic. One Figure, who appears to be the Judge Court is diſtinguiſhed by a Cap and Feathers, and holds a Scroll on which is inſcribed, in the Gothic Character " Be merrie."

The Manor very anciently included ſeveral Vills, and gave Name to a Hundred, the Limits of which were varied by the ſeveral Returns at different Periods. It was held by the Crown till the Reign of Richard the Firſt, who extended its Juriſdiction over ſeven adjacent Hundreds, with which he inveſted

the Abbey   When the Inhabitants had recommended themselves to King HENRY the Fourth by the Defeat of the Conspirators, they petitioned him to confirm to the Borough, the yearly Value of which was 14*l.* 4*s.* 8*d.* the Privileges and Immunities of a distinct Hundred, and to separate them from the Vill of Minct,   The Request being obtained, the out Parishes, with *Minety*, were named the "*Out Torne*," corruptedly *Crowthorne*   But this Settlement respected the Borough only, as the Abbey retained their manorial Rights, till the Alienation of the Revenues   Sir THOMAS SEYMOUR, Lord SEYMOUR of *Sudley*, procured the first Grant, which in 1554 was transferred to Sir ANTHONY KINGSTONE   In 1595 Sir JOHN D'ANVERS died seized of it, whose Son the Earl of DANBY sold it to HENRY POOLL, of *Saperton*   About 164, it descended by Heirs female to JAMES Earl of NEWBURGH   The Relict of his Son CHARLES Lord NEWBURGH sold the manerial Estate to Sir BENJAMIN BATHURST, Knight, in 1695, whose eldest Son ALLEN was created Baron BATHURST of *Battlesden*, by Patent dated Dec 31, 1711, 9 Q ANNE, and Earl BATHURST of *Bathurst*, co *Suffex*; Aug 12, 1772, 12 Gro III *

Lord DANBY, the Founder of the Physic Gardens in *Oxford*, and the Patron of INIGO JONES, most probably employed him in the House which he built here   It consisted of three Sides of a Quadrangle in the improved Style of the Age of King JAMES   The present Mansion was re built early in this Century, and though not grand is convenient, and the Rooms spacious and comfortable   Its principal Front of great Length, in the Attic Style, the Area in which it is inclosed, is surrounded by a very high Wall, covered with perennial Trees, so lofty, as to exclude every Communication with the Town   The other is finished by two Wings and a Portico, and commands a central View of the Avenue in the Park, terminated by a Column and colossal Statue of Q ANNE

In the Park so justly admired many hundred Acres are included, the more embellished Division of it consists of what is termed " a Belt," surrounding Plantations of Beech and Fir   Nearest the Wall, a continued Path serpentines under a close Covert, parallel to which, in more linear Directions, are Terraces, flanked by Plantations of Shrubs and Evergreens, and ornamented with several Buildings, which pleasingly mark the Distances, though in themselves neither sumptuous nor beautiful   An artificial Lake, some Acres in Extent, is certainly the most striking Feature in this cultivated Landscape, which is unavoidably deficient in Water, and Variety of Ground   The peculiar Praise of these Improvements is that which is due to priority of Design, which though they may decline a Comparison with those in a moderner and more correct Taste, were long considered as a first Specimen of an Art, the Invention of this Age, in which even it seems to have gained its utmost Perfection

The Borough and its Privileges are next to be considered

When the new Hundred was confined to the Borough only, the Abbey was exempted and included in the "*Out Torne*," as the Site and Precincts have since continued   Here are seven Wards, *Dyer Ward*, *Cricklade Ward*, *Castle Ward*, *Gosditch Ward*, *Dollar Ward*, *St Lawrence Ward*, and *Instrip Ward*   To each of these two Constables are annually assigned, and two High Constables appointed, who regulate the Borough and its Jurisdiction   In 1338 this Borough sent Representatives to a Council assembled by King EDWARD III   Queen ELIZABETH in 1571 added two Burgesses each for twelve Boroughs, to the Lower House, of which *Cirencester* was one   The free Burghers only obtained the Right of Election, in JAMES the First's Reign it was extended to all the Inhabitants, not chargeable to the Parish, and contributing to the Taxes, but in 1690 all Inmates or Lodgers were deprived, and in 1709 the Inhabitants of the Abbey Precincts were declared unqualified to give Votes

CATALOGUE OF BURGESSES

A D 1571	Gabriel Blyke, Thomas Poole.	A D 1585	Thomas Poole, junior, William Estcourt
1572	Thomas Poole, Thomas Strange	1586	Charles D'Anvers, Thomas Master.

* ALLEN BATHURST the eldest Son of Sir BENJAMIN BATHURST of *Paulet's Perry*, co *Northampton*, was born Nov 1684, educated at *Trinity College Oxford*, married July 6, 1704, CATHERINE (his first Cousin), Daughter and Heir of Sir PETER APSLEY, Knight, elected Burgess for *Cirencester* 1705, and created a Peer, with eleven others, Dec 31 1711   He was the warm Friend of Bishop ATTERBURY, against whose Attainder in 1723 he made a very memorable Speech   He was a strenuous Opponent to Sir ROBERT WALPOLE and his Administration   and his Speeches are recorded in the "History and Proceedings of the House of Lord "

In 174 he was sworn of the Privy Council   and in 1757 appointed Treasurer to his present Majesty, then Prince of WALES, and on the Accession 1760 he was continued of the Privy Council, but, declining public Offices, received a Pension of 2000   a Year   In 1772 he was advanced to the Dignity of an Earl his Son JAMES BATHURST having accepted the Seals, and being created Baron APSLEY of *l'l*   *   *   by Patent Jan 22, 1771   He died Sept 16, 1775, in the 91st Year of his Age   No Writer Rank ever knew better how to unite "*Otium cum Dignitate*"   To uncommon Abilities he added many Virtues   He was the *Maecenas* of the *Augustan* Age in *Britain*, and was courted by the *Literati*, not from Hopes   He preferred to the Close of his Life his natural Chearfulness and Vivacity   He delighted in rural Amusements, and is the Business of Planting as subservient to the united Purposes of Ornament and Utility had been his particular at all considered, he adopted this Idea with great Spirit and Judgement, and his natural and happy Temper permitted him to enjoy with philosophic Calmness the Shade of those Trees himself had planted   on his Park long before he was Edward

A D

A D 1588   Charles D'Anvers,
         Thomas Master
1592   Oliver St John,
         Henry Ferrys
1596   James Wroughton,
         Henry Powle
160   Richard Browne,
         Richard George
1603   Richard Martyn,
         Arnold Oldisworth
16   Sr Law Jones, Knt vice Martyn,
         Arnold Oldisworth
16   Sir Anth Mannye, Knt vice Jones,
         Arnold Oldisworth
1614   James Ratcliffe (Earl Newburgh),
         Thomas Rowe
1620   Sir Thomas Rowe, Knight,
         Thomas Nicholas
1623   Sir William Master, Knight,
         Henry Poole
1625   Sir Myles Sandys, Knight,
         Henry Poole
1625   Sir Nevil Poole, Knight,
         John George, Esq
1628   Sir Giles Estcourt, Bart
         John George, Esq
1640   Henry Poole,
         John George, Esq
1641   Sir Theobald Gorges *, Knight,
         Sir Thomas Fairfax *, Knight,
         John George, Esq
1653 †
1654   John Stone, of *London*,
         Nathaniel Rich
1656   John Stone,
         Nathaniel Rich
1658‡   John Stone,
         Nathaniel Rich
1660§   Richard Honour,
         John George
1661   Richard Honour,
         John George.
1678   Henry Powle,
         Sir Robert Atkins, Knight
1678   Henry Powle,
         Sir Robert Atkins, Knight
1680   Henry Powle,
         Sir Robert Atkins, Knight
1681   Henry Powle,
         Sir Robert Atkins, Knight
1685   Thomas Master,
         Charles Ratcliffe (Earl Newburgh)

A D 1688   Thomas Master,
         John Howe
1689   John Howe,
         Richard Howe
169   John Howe,
         Richard Howe
1698   Henry Ireton,
         Charles Coxe
1700   Charles Coxe,
         James Thynne
1701   Charles Coxe,
         William Master
1702   Charles Coxe,
         William Master
1705   Allen Bathurst,
         Henry Ireton
1707   Allen Bathurst,
         Henry Ireton
1708   Allen Bathurst,
         Charles Coxe
1710   Charles Coxe,
         Thomas Master
1713   Thomas Master,
         Benjamin Bathurst
1714   Thomas Master,
         Benjamin Bathurst
1722   Thomas Master,
         Benjamin Bathurst
1727   Thomas Master,
         Peter Bathurst
1734   Thomas Master,
         William Worldhouse
1741   Thomas Master,
         Henry Bathurst
1747   Thomas Master,
         Henry Bathurst
1748   John Coxe, vice Master
1754   John Dawnay
         Benjamin Bathurst
1761   John Dawnay,
         James Whitshed
1768   James Whitshed,
         Estcourt Cresswell
1775   James Whitshed,
         Samuel Blackwell
1780   James Whitshed,
         Samuel Blackwell
1783   Henry Bathurst (Lord Apsley), vacated on being made a Lord of Admiralty, re elected 1784
1784   Richard Master, vice Blackwell.

The Number of Electors has been stated to be 800, but, in a contested Election in 1768, 1488 Votes were given

The weekly Market is held on Monday, beside three annual Fairs on Easter Tuesday, July 18, and November 8, of great Resort

The Hospital of *Saint John*, founded by King HENRY I is particularized in the Account of Benefaction. The Trustees are the Vicar and parochial Officers, as settled by Inquisition 1635, 6 Charles I who elect the Paupers, and sign the Leases ‖

The Free Grammar School was established by Bishop Rowthall, with a competent Endowment. It appears that the Benefactions of Rowthall, being chiefly given for superstitious Purposes, were confiscated, and applied to the Poor, upon the Suppression. But 20l. a Year were granted from the Exchequer by Edw. VI. and confirmed by Queen Elizabeth, and 8l. a Year were assigned from the Chant. Money, by Decree of Chancery 1602, 1 James I. The Appointment and Visitation are vested in the Vicar and Parochial Officers. In some Instances the Lord Chancellor has nominated. The present Master is the Rev. John Washbourn, D. D.

Of the greater Part of the Parish Lord Bathurst and Thomas Master, Esq. are Proprietors, besides these; the principal Families of Property, and of the longest Establishment, are Small +, Cripps, and Selfe, with many others. The Seal used by the Borough is a Phœnix rising from her Ashes, in Allusion to the Conflagration in the Reign of Henry IV. His Grace the Duke of Portland is Baron of Cirencester by Patent April 9, 1689, 1 William and Mary ‡.

On the South Side of the Town are remarkable Vallations of Earth called the Querns §, near Cicely Hill, a Tumulus which was the Grismond's Tower before mentioned, and in a Field a few Furlongs from the Town, on the North east, another, which is known by the Name of Tar-borough. Such vague Descriptions have been given of the Design of these, that we cannot venture to ascertain it.

Within this Parish are five Tythings.

1. Spital-Gate Tything includes the Domain of the Monastery, to which was always added an Hospitium, or Receptacle for Strangers. There is likewise an Almonry Farm, both which compose the Estate of Thomas Master, Esq.

2. Hagold lies further from the Town, in the same Direction, and is a distinct Manor, held and claimed as such so early in the Reign of Henry III. Sir William Nottingham, who is buried in the Church, was seised of it 1 Richard III. 1484. It now belongs to the Families of Master and Cripps, and the Tithes were granted, as Part of the Abbey Estate, to the former.

3. Chesterton contains the greater Part of the ancient City, as may be inferred from the Name. Large Estates in this Tything were held by the Family of Lancey for several Centuries. Robert D'Oilé gave the Impropriation of Chesterton to the Convent of St. Peter in Gloucester in 1080, which was purchased by Lord Bathurst of Sir John Nelthorpe, Bart. between whom, and the Families of Master and Coxe, the other Property is divided.

4. Barton Farm and Tything, situate on the West Side of the Town, was originally the great Grange of the Abbey for the storing of their Corn Rents. In the Reign of Queen Anne it was vested in Sir Richard Onslow, Knight, Speaker of the House of Commons, who sold it to Lord Bathurst.

5. Oakley Tything (Achelie, or Querceburi) is further Westward from the Town, and is recited in Domesday as belonging to Roger de Laci. King Henry I. granted this District to the Abbey, as mentioned in the Charter, reserving only to himself his Hunting, and forbidding the Abbot to plough or till it. Thomas Lord Seymour received it at the Dissolution, from whom it passed to the Lords Danby, from them to the Pooles, of Sapperton. Sir Robert Atkyns soon after his Purchase sold it to Allen Lord Bathurst. The immense Plantations which were here formed under his Care, and which he lived to see flourish into Maturity, are a superb Memorial of his Taste. Ten large Avenues, or Ridings, meet in a Centre, from which the terminating Objects have a good Effect. Inclosed by the thickest Groves stands a Building called Alfred's Hall, an Imitation of a dilapidated Castle, rendered habitable by modern Additions. The Deception is now more likely to succeed, as the Ivy, Mosses, and other concomitant Features of Antiquity, are in the highest Perfection ||. The Similarity of Æglea, where King Ælfred made a Convention with the Danes, to Acheley, suggested the Idea to the late noble Owner, who so well knew how to improve it. In the various Parts of these vast Woodlands the Truffle, and other vegetable Productions are found.

                                                              BENT-

* I found in Leland that he (Rowthall) "in his Life he founded a free School at the Place of his Nativity and gave a House to ... for the Perpetual Maintenance of a Master, which School living, for the most Part flourished in good Sort, both educating them that have been famous both in Church and State." Wood's Athenæ Ox. vol. I. p. 565 ... is Skelwright, the most noted Poet, Orator, and Philosopher, of his Time, was educated there.
                                                                          Ibid. vol. II. p. 18
+ The Family of Smart are entered in the College of Arms, beginning with George Smart, of Cirencester, 1628. They ... one branch either in the Faith Register.
‡ ... Title Portland, vol. I. p. 139
§ ... examination, have been found to be replete with Skeletons, Urns, Lachrymatories, and Members of Roman ... by some suppose to have been the general Cemetery of the City, by others (Campus Mar ... for public Sport). I am ... of the ... on whence the City was built. Of Grismond's Tower Leland speaks ... "a Brick like a Windmill Hill in ... It." vol. V. p. 66. Camden, edit. Gibson, vol. I. p. 288
|| It ... Leland is a spacious Hall, with a vaulted Roof and Gothic Window. On Pediments over the Doors are these Inscriptions ...
... North Door, in Saxon copied from the Chron. Alfredi. ... "Saxon Chronicle," vol. II. p. 31 ...

BENEFACTIONS.

Dr WILLIAM CLARKE, late Dean of *Winchester*, having devised certain Lands and Tythes in the Parish of *Tillingham* in the County of *Essex*, in trust, among other Things, to augment ten small ecclesiastical Benefices with 30*l* a Year each, for ever

And Dr HENRY COMPTON, Bishop of *London*, and the Dean and Chapter of *St Pauls*, having the Nomination of six of those Benefices, declared they would assign this Charity to such Market-Towns as would settle an equal Revenue on their Minister, and the Inhabitants of the Town of *Cirencester*, with the Assistance of others, having raised the Sum of 613*l* 11*s* 8*d* by free Contribution, and with 600*l* of the said Money purchased an Annuity for their Minister of 30*l* a Year, charged on the Tything of *Oakly* in this Parish, the said Trustees then appointed *Cirencester* to be one of those Benefices to to be augmented, by an Instrument dated Jun 17, 1698, but, by a Deficiency in Profits of the Trust Estate from Inundations and other Accidents, the annual Payments to the respective Ministers from the first Commencement in 1699, have often fallen under, and sometimes exceed 1*l* a Year. The Surplus of the Money, 19*l* 11*s* 8*d* was given to the Minister towards defraying his Expences in settling the Augmentation. The principal Contributors to this laudable Benefaction were

Sir ROBERT ATKINS, junior, Knight, 100*l*
THOMAS MASTER, Esq 100*l*
Mrs BRIDGET SMITH, a Daughter to Sir WILLIAM MASTER, Knight, 100*l*
Mrs WINIFRED MASTER 50*l*
Mrs ANNE WILLIAMS 43*l*
Sir BENJAMIN BATHURST, Knight, 20*l*
Sir JONATHAN RAYMOND, Knight, 30*l*
Sir RICHARD ONSLOW, Bart 10*l*
Sir RICHARD HOWE, Bart 10*l*
JOHN WILLETT, Clothier, 20*l*
BERNARD BALLINGER 20*l*
JOHN COXE, Clerk, Rector of *North Cerney*, 10*l*
RALPH WILLET, Clerk, Rector of *Stratton*, 10*l*
ROBERT BRERETON, Gent 10*l*

The remaining Part was given by several Benefactors from 5*l* to 10*s* each

Till about this Time there was no Vicarage house, the Inhabitants first purchased a Lease of the present House, afterwards WILLIAM GEORGE, Esq gave the Quit rent of it, and in the Year 1708 Mrs REBECCA GEORGE his Widow gave the Lee of it for ever

For SERMONS, PRAYERS, and CATECHISING

1587 PHILIP MARNER gave 6*s* 8*d* for ever for a Sermon on the first Friday in Lent

1607 Sir GILES FETTIPLACE gave an Annuity of 20*s* out of Lands in *Fairington*, half for a Sermon on the 5th of November, and half for ringing on the same Day

JOHN COXWELL, Esq gave 20*s* a Year for two Sermons, in Christmas-tide and Lent

16 8 JEFFRY BATHE, Bailiff of this Town, gave 6*s* 8*d* for a Sermon on Ascension Day

16 7 Sir THOMAS ROWE, of *Cranford* in *Middlesex*, gave 2*l* for a Sermon or Prayers on the 13th of September for ever

1639 GEORGE MONOX Esq. a Native of this Place, who had been Sheriff of *London*, gave 8*l* a Year for a Sermon on the first Wednesday in every Month

1651 Mr MATSON, a Native of this Town, gave 10*s* for a Sermon on *St Andrew's* Day

169 JOHN MASTER, M D gave 200*l* one half of the Income of which to the Minister for the Time being, for ever, for reading Morning Prayers, the other half to the poor Housekeepers not receiving Alms

Mrs REBECCA POWLL gave 10*l* a Year for ever to the Minister, for catechising the Children, and for expounding the Catechism, and she also gave 2*l* a Year for to provide Candles and other Necessaries for the Service

NICHOLAS EDWARDS gave to the Minister the Interest of 5*l* for ever

Mrs HANNAH ASHWELL gave 10*l* the Interest whereof for a Sermon on the 30th of January for ever, but the principal Money is now lost, she also gave 10*l* more, the Interest of which to be divided between the Master and Parish Clerk, for a Psalm, with *Gloria Patri*, to be sung every Monday at Morning Prayers

"I ... ... upon Tenere, ... Son ... upon ... ... op huje ... ... on ge ...
" ... ... op *Taylingteynr*"

Upon ... ... the opposite Entrance, is this *Latin* Translation

" ... ... quod ... & GYTHBERT ... Roper, omnes *Angliæ* sapientes, & quicunque *in ham* incolebant Orientem ...
" ... ... in hoc ... ...
" ... ... Primo ... nostra lines id *Thamesin* evehunti, ...
" ... ... *Teydham* ... denique per ... ... viam *Teylingranam*"

FOR ORNAMENTING THE CHURCH, AND FOR THE EDUCATING AND APPRENTICING POOR CHILDREN

The large handsome Gallery on the North Side of the Church was built in the Year 1726, at the expence of the Right Hon ALLEN Earl BATHURST

The other Gallery at the Entrance of St. *Catherine's* Chapel was erected by Sir ANTHONY HUNGERFORD

The Organ was purchased with the voluntary Contributions of the Town and Neighbourhood

The two large Silver Flaggons, used at the Communion were given by LORD DYNES, Esq in the Year 1684

WILLIAM GEORGE, Esq and his Wife gave the two Plates for collecting the Offerings

Mr. ... gave the gilt Strainer for the Chalice, and Mrs. BRIDGET SMITH, and others, furnished the remainder of the noble Service of Plate with which this Church is accommodated

The best Bible and Common Prayer Book were given by THOMAS POWELL, Esq and his Wife

The marble Font was purchased by the Female Inhabitants of this Town

For the ornamenting and repairing the Church there is a Revenue of 67l 9s 4d a Year, arising chiefly from Houses in the Town (except a Close in the Tything of *Chesterton*), given by JOHN JONES, Esq and other Benefactors, about 22l of which are laid out in Repairs, and the Remainder is expended in Salaries, except 4l paid to the Minister, and 8l to the Master of the Free Grammar School, as directed by a Decree in Chancery in JAMES I

The said Grammar School was built and founded by Bishop ROWTHALE, the Master has a good House kept in Repair for him, and beside the 8l a Year beforementioned, Queen MARY endowed the School with 20l a Year out of the Exchequer, which Bounty was afterwards confirmed by Queen ELIZABETH

Here are two other Charity Schools

1 The *Blue* School was erected in the Year 1714, principally by the Benefice of THOMAS POWELL, Esq and REBECCA his Wife, but before that Time several Sums of Money had been given for teaching Children to read, which were then appropriated to the Establishment of this Charity. Mr POWELL, as in 1718, left to this School 15l a Year, and half the Profits of M'Kelyn's Ham in the Parish of Crudwell, and in the Year 1737 the Court of Chancery also appointed 20l a Year out of the Estate of Mrs POWELL his Widow, to make the School perpetual

2 The *Green* School was erected and endowed by virtue of the Will of Mrs. REBECCA POWELL, who died in the Year 1722, and an Estate for that Purpose. A School House was purchased at the Expence of near 1200l, but some Difficulties arising about the carrying the Will into Execution, the Court of Chancery decreed that 112l 6s a Year be applied to the cloathing, maintaining, educating, and bringing up twenty Boys in the Art of Stocking frame knitting, twenty Girls are also cloathed every Year, and are taught to read, and spin Worsted

Sir THOMAS ROWE, Knight, gave a Rent charge of 25l a Year out of Lands at *Meysey Hampton* in this County, 3l of which for a Sermon is already mentioned, the rest to put out poor Children of this Parish Apprentices, on the 13th of September annually, and once in three or four Years a Boy out of the Parish of *Rencombe*, if presented

Mr THOMAS PERRY gave 100l and his Son Mr TIMOTHY PERRY gave 12l which Sums were laid out in the Purchase of a Freehold Estate in the Parish of *Upton St. Leonard's* in this County

RICHARD GEORGE, Esq gave a Rent charge of 3l a Year out of a House in *Gloucester Street* in this Town

WILLIAM FORDEN, of *Ampney Crucis*, gave 20l

THOMAS POWELL, Esq gave 40l

JAMES CLUTTERBUCK, Citizen of *Exeter*, gave 100l

JAMES SHEWELL, Silkman, gave 10l

Mrs ELIZABETH EDWARDS in 1726 gave 100l

The Annual Produce of all which to be applied to the putting out poor Children Apprentices

HOSPITALS AND ALMSHOUSES

King HENRY I founded St. *John's* Hospital for three poor Men and three poor Women, who receive 1s 8d weekly

St *Laurence's* Hospital was founded by a certain LADY, of *Biggold* in this Parish, for a Master, with a Salary of about 2l a Year, and two poor Women, who receive 1s weekly

St *Thomas's* Hospital was erected by Sir WILLIAM NOTTINGHAM, who lived in the Reign of King HENRY IV and endowed it with a Rent charge of 6l 16s 8d a Year, out of an Estate in the Parish of *Tetbury* in this County, which is divided between four poor Weavers weekly

Mrs ELIZABETH BRIDGES in the Year 1620 gave an Alms house in *Dollar Street* for six poor Widows, and 1s each weekly for ever

JOHN MARSH gave two Habitations in *Gloucester Street* for two poor Widows

MONEY GIVEN, THE INTEREST WHEREOF IS FOR POOR CHILDRENS SCHOOLING

					£	s	d
1691	Sir RICHARD HOWE, of *Compton*, Bart	—	—	—	21	10	0
1614	JOHN COOK	—	—	—	5	0	0
16..	ANDREW SOLLACE, junior,	—	—	—	10	0	0
1638	THOMAS MALDEN	—	—	—	5	0	0

			£	s	d
1686	THOMAS ROGERS	— — —	5	0	0
1690	MARGARET SHEPPARD, from *London*, a Native of this Town,	—	5	0	0
	Mrs ELEANOR SOLIACE		5	0	0
1702	SARAH, Wife of PHILIP PAINTER,		2	0	0
1706	JOHN ROGERS, Clothier,		20	0	0
	JOHN BETTERTON, Baker,	—	5	0	0
1711	Mrs ELIZABETH DEACON	—	20	0	0
	Mr SIMON DEACON		30	0	0
1712	ELIZABETH, Wife of NICHOLAS EDWARDS,	—	20	0	0
	Mr THEOPHILUS BRERETON	—	10	0	0
	Mrs BRERETON his Mother	—	10	0	0
	Mis ANN WEARE	—	10	0	0
	Mr WILLIAM HILL, Clothier,	—	50	0	0
1713	MARY FELLING, Widow,	—	10	0	0
	ISAAC SMALL, Clothier,	—	10	0	0
1714	SARAH, the Wife of Mr JOHN PALLING,		5	0	0
	ROBERT BRERETON, Gent		10	0	0
1716	JONATHAN MILLINGTON	—	10	0	0
1717	Mr RALPH BRERETON, youngest Son of Mr ROBERT BRERETON,		50	0	0
	Mrs CATHARINE STEPHENS, Widow,	— —	5	12	6
	JOHN BANEFORD, as long as the Charity School continues,	—	1	0	0
	Mrs ANNE RUDGE		2	0	0
1720	Mrs ANN FOOT, of *London*, a Native of this Town,		20	0	0
	HOPEFUL VEECINES, of *Tetbury*, a Rent charge, yearly,	—	1	0	0
1721	Mrs ANN FORDEN		5	0	0
1722	THOMAS FERREBEE, Mercer,		5	0	0
1723	ANN, the Daughter of THOMAS DEACON, of *Elmsore*,		20	0	0
1724	MARY, Wife of RICHARD SHIRLEY,		5	0	0
1726	ELIZABETH, Daughter of Mr SHIRLEY,		5	0	0
1728	JOHN PALLING, Clothier,		20	0	0
1731	OLIVER St JOHN, Esq of *Soho Square*, *London*, upon visiting the Blue School in his Journey through this Town, and gave for its Support		50	0	0
	SAMUEL SLIFF, Esq	—	20	0	0
1747	ESTHER, the Widow of THOMAS MILLINGTON, for the Support of the said School	50	0	0
	RICHARD SHIRLEY	—	6	0	0
1752	ELIZABETH, Widow of RALPH WILLETT,	—	30	0	0

FOR THE RELIEF AND SUPPORT OF THE POOR

1587 PHILIP MARNER beforementioned gave one Tenement and two Gardens in *Abbot Street*, the yearly Rent 3*l* 13*s* 4*d* to be given to the Poor the first Friday in clear Lent, except 6*s* 8*d* for a Sermon on the Day aforesaid

1598 ALICE AVENING, Widow, gave a House in *Dollar Street*, the Rent 2*l* a Year, to be given to the Poor on Good Friday

JOHN WEOLLY gave the Rent of a House in *Gosditch Street*, since sold to Lord D'ANVERS, and an Annuity of 1*l* 6*s* 8*d* is affixed, instead of the same, on a House called the *Greyhound* in *Dyer Street*, the said Rent to be distributed to the Poor on Good Friday

1605 WILLIAM HOOPER gave a House in *Little Silver Street*, the Rent is 2*l* 4*s* and 2*l* whereof is to be given to the Poor on Good Friday by the Constables and Churchwardens, and the odd 4*s* to the Officers for their Pains

1615 Mr JEFFRY BATHE beforementioned gave a House in *Cricklade street*, Rent 2*l* a Year, whereof 6*s* 8*d* for a Sermon on Ascension day, and the Rest to the Poor

1632 Mr JOHN CHANDLER gave a Tenement in *Ciceley Street*, Rent 2*l* a Year, to be given to the Poor at May day and at Allhallows tide

1598 Mr HUMPHRY BRIDGES gave a House in *Cricklade Street*, Rent 2*l* a Year, the one half to be given to the Poor on Good Friday, the other at Christmas

1639 GEORGE MONOX, Esq gave all his Houses in this Town, being four in Number, now let at 23*l* 10*s* a Year, to be given to the Poor on St *Thomas's* Day, yearly, except 8*s* a Year for a Sermon on the first Wednesday in every Month, as aforesaid, and 6*s* 8*d* to the Minister, Churchwardens, and Constables, yearly, to expend as they shall think proper for their Pains in the Premises

1641 JOHN PAIN, late of this Town, butcher, gave one Messuage in *Dollar street*, Rent 3*l* a Year, 2*l* of which to be given to the Poor decayed Butchers of this Town, and the other 2*l* to the common Poor

1648 ROWLAND FREEMAN gave a yearly Rent charge of 2*l* out of a House and Garden, now incorporated into Lord BATHURST's Park, to be given to the Poor on Good Friday yearly

1702 WILLIAM GEORGE, Esq and REBECCA his Wife, gave six Houses and Gardens in *Love Lane*, for six poor Widows, whose Husbands had borne some Parish or Ward Office, and two Houses in *Cricklade Street*, one of them charged with 6*l* a Year, to buy the six Widows Gowns and Cloath at Christmas, and the Remainder to keep the Widows' Habitations in Repair

5 A

THOMAS

THOMAS POWELL beforementioned, who married the said REBECCA GEORGE, bequeathed the other Moiety of the Profits of *Maskelyne's Ham* to the Widows of those Alms-houses, to be equally divided among them, and the aforesaid REBECCA, Widow of the said THOMAS POWELL, gave an additional 1*l.* a Year to each of the said Widows, to buy Fireing

		£	s	d
1645	Sr HENRY PRATT, Bart of the City of *London*,	100	0	0
1639	Mr MONOX aforementioned, to buy Land, the Profits thereof to be given to the Poor on *St Thomas's* Day	100	0	0
1625	SAMUEL COXWELL, Gent	50	0	0
	WILLIAM BLOOMER, of *Hatherop*, Gent the Interest thereof to be given to the Poor on *St Thomas's* Day	40	0	0
	SUSANNA NEWPORT, Widow,	10	0	0
	ROBERT SLAMAN	6	13	4
1616	EDITH HOOPER	3	6	8
1621	JOHN DUTTON, of *Shireborne*, Esq.	5	0	0
	Mr ANDREW SOLLACE	5	0	0
1617	JOIN PRATT	6	0	0
	JANE EVANS	4	0	0
	THOMAS SERRELL, Haberdasher,	3	0	0
1618	THOMAS ARCHARD, *Meysey Hampton*,	3	0	0
	THOMAS KILDERMORE	5	0	0
	PHILIP CHANDLER	2	0	0

All the several Sums beforementioned, except 20*l.* Part of Mr BLOMER's Gift, was laid out to purchase Land at *South Cerney*, and also Mr CHAMBERS's 50*l.* was laid out in that Purchase, and 10*l.* Part of Mr BLOMER's Gift, was laid out in a House in *Gloucester Street*, which the Overseers dispose of to the Poor's Use.

		£	s	d
	THOMAS DAMSELL gave	100	0	0
	A Man who set up a Lottery in this Town	40	0	0
	THOMAS SHERMORE, of *London*,	20	0	0
	Mr JOHN STONE	20	0	0
	ROBERT GEORGE, Esq	10	0	0
	The Heirs of ROBERT STRANGE	10	0	0
	EDWARD PRATT, junior,	10	0	0
	The Lady of Sir GILES FETTIPLACE	5	0	0
	ANN ROBINS, Spinster,	5	0	0
1606	THOMAS SMITH	20	0	0
1615	JOHN MAY, of *Ampney St Mary*,	10	0	0
	ROBERT SLEECH, Butcher,	10	0	0
1626	Mrs ALICE GUNTER	2	0	0
	CHRISTOPHER HAYWARD	2	0	0
	EDWARD CHURCH	20	0	0
1602	The Rev HUGH ATWELL, of *St Tew, Cornwall*,	1	10	0
1699	Lady ATKINSON, of *Stowell*,	10	0	0
1673	THOMAS KIDDERMORE, junior,	5	0	0
1680	WILLIAM KIRBY, Citizen of *London*, a Native of *Cirencester*,	10	0	0
1679	JOHN OATES, Clothier,	10	0	0

JOHN COXWELL, Esq give 100*l.* the Interest of which to be given to the Poor on Passion Sunday Eve, in Lent, and on *St Andrew's* Day, except 1*l.* for two Sermons in Christmas tide and in Lent

1716 JOHN HEARD, Chirurgeon, gave 2*l.*

Rev Mr WM MASTER, second Son of Sir WM MASTER, give 50*l.* the Interest of which to be distributed at Christmas to poor decayed Householders, who receive no Parish Collection

1706 Mrs WINIFRID MASTER beforementioned give 60*l.* the Interest whereof to be given by the Minister on the 1st of March among such of the Poor as are constant Comers to daily Prayers, and frequent Receivers of the Sacrament

Mrs ELIZABETH EDWARDS, by Will, devised in Trust four Tenements in *Castle Street*, or letting them to be sold, and the clear Produce, with the further Sum of 50*l.* to be paid to, and placed out by the Minister and Churchwardens, and the Interest to be by them distributed yearly among four such poor Families as the Minister shall appoint, and in such Proportions as their Circumstances shall require, only to be 6*s.* yearly to the Minister, and 5*s.* to the Churchwardens for their Trouble therein. And accordingly, the said Tenements were sold for 60*l.* and the whole Sum of 90*l.* paid in the Year 1729, was directed by the Will, and that Sum, with the 100*l.* beforementioned, was laid out in the purchase of the Church Land

RICHARD NOTT give two Tenements to the Value of 3*l.* a Year to be given in Money to the Poor

17.. JANE OVERBURY give 50*l.* the Interest of which to be given to the Poor

1751 Mrs ELIZABETH CRIPPS gave by Will 500*l.* vested in the public Funds, Old South Sea Annuities, the Interest of which to be equally divided at Christmas between ten Widows, or old unmarried Women who do not receive Alms of the Parish

17.. JOHN DAY, Esq give by Deed, Land to the Amount of 47*l.* 11*s.* 3*d.* a Year, to be distributed yearly amongst old decayed Tradesmen, and old necessitous Persons of either Sex

Elizabeth Guerney left 20l. the Interest of which to be given to the Poor of the Presbyterian Persuasion.

Benjamin Guerney left 20l. for the same Purpose.

1642 Sir Anthony Hungerford, Knight, gave West Mead in Holy Rood Ampney, to buy eleven Coats for, and to give it each to so many aged and impotent Persons.

1603 Thomas Perry, senior, gave 20l. the Interest thereof to buy two Coats for two poor Men at Christmas.

1607 Edward King gave in Rents, issuing out of two Houses in Corwell Street, 2l. 9s. a Year, for Garments for two poor Men and two poor Women at Christmas.

1710 Ann, the Widow of John Rogers, Clothier, and afterwards Wife of Thomas Peters, Mercer, gave 20l. the Interest of which to buy Coats for two poor Men.

1711 Nicholas Edwards gave 40l. the Interest of which to buy Coats for two poor Men and two poor Women at Christmas.

Sarah, Wife of John Sutton, and afterwards Wife of John Humphries, gave 10l. the Interest to be laid out for poor Women at Christmas.

1737 Frances, the Wife of John Peek, in Behalf of her late Husband, gave 5l. to buy Linen for two poor Women of Cricklade Street.

Mrs Mary Chambers, of London, Daughter of Mr Monox, gave 50l. the Interest to buy Bread, to be distributed by the Minister amongst such poor Housekeepers as receive no Collection.

Mr Fettiplace gave 2l. the Interest to be given in Bread to the Poor on Ash Wednesday.

1711 Nicholas Edwards, Mercer, gave 10l. the Interest thereof to be given to the Poor.

1712 Elizabeth Edwards, Widow, gave 5l. to be disposed of in the same Manner.

1732 Isaac Tibbet, Father of the said Elizabeth Edwards, gave 20l. to the sole Benefit of the Poor of Castle Hard, to be distributed among them on the 4th of June by the Minister and Churchwardens.

INCUMBENTS	PATRONS	INCUMBENTS.	PATRONS
1530 William Phillippes,	————	1690 Joseph Harrison, B A	Bishop of Glou-CESTER
———— Thomas Carles, M A	Bishop of Glou-CESTER	1753 Samuel Johnson, M A	The same
1675 ———— Gregory, M A	The same.	1778 Martin Stafforde Smyth, M A	K George III

PRESENT LORD OF THE MANORS
Of Cirencester and the Seven Hundreds,
The Right Honourable Henry Earl Bathurst

The Persons summoned from this Borough by the Heralds in 1682 and 1683, were

Thomas Master, Esq
———— Gregory, M A Clerk,
Robert Brereton, Gent
Miles Sandys, Gent
William Freame, Gent
Edward Clutterbuck, Gent
Thomas Clutterbuck, Gent

Sir Robert Jocelyn Knight,
Ralph Willett, Gent
John Wood, Gent
James Cooke, Gent
George Bull, Gent
William Gegg, Gent
Thomas Earle, Gent

At the Election in 1776, One Hundred and Six Freeholders polled from this Parish.

The Register commences with the Year 1560, and is remarkably fair and regular.

ANNUAL ACCOUNT OF MARRIAGES, BIRTHS, AND BURIALS, IN THIS PARISH

A D	Mar	Bir	Bur	A D	Mar	Bir	Bur	A D	Mar	Bir	Bur	A D	Mar	Bir	Bur
1781	3	105	91	1786	34	70	89	1791				1796			
1782	30	98	79	1787	31	117	102	1792				1797			
1783	23	85	71	1788				1793				1798			
1784	51			1789				1794				1799			
1785	42	76	85	1790				1795				1800			

This Statement cannot ascertain the Number of Inhabitants, as there are three distinct Congregations of Protestant Dissenters.

INSCRIPTIONS

INSCRIPTIONS IN THE CHURCH.

IN THE SOUTH AISLE

On a blue Slab, with the Effigies of a Man and Woman

* Orate pro aiabus Will't Nottingham & Christine uroris ejus, qui quidem Will'mus obiit XXI die Novembris, Anno D'ni MCCCCXXVII Et previd' Christina obiit IV die Julii, Anno Dni MCCC-XXITU, q'i a'i abus p'piciet' Deus   Amen.

On a Stone near the above was anciently written,

Munde vale tibi de, fugiens me, dum sequerer te,
Tu sequris modo me, munde vale tibi de!

IN TRINITY CHAPEL.

On a blue Slab, the Effigy of a Man in compleat Armour, on the Pomel of his Sword

Arms, A Pile surmounted of a Chevron, round the Verge this Inscription

Hic jacet Richardus Dyxton, Armiger, qui obiit die Sancti Laurencii Martyris, Anno Domini MCCCCLXXVIII, cujus a i'e p'picietur Deus   Amen

---

On a Slab, the Figures of a Man, his Wife, and fourteen Children in Brass, on a Pilasier between him and his Wife is engraven the usual Diagram of the Trinity   On a Label, That to the Trinite for us pray, singe, or read

Hic jacet Robertus Pagge cum Margareta sibi sponsa prole fecunda
    Ultimus gratus fuerat mercator amatus
    Pacificus, plenis manibus subventor egenis,
    Ecclesiisque viis ornator, & his reparator,
    Mill' C quater X quater anno, sed Aprilis
    Octava luce mortem p' transit ipse
    Celi solamen Deus, illi conferat, Amen

On a Slab, the Representations in Brass, of a Man and his four Wives, two on either Side, round the Margin,

Hic jacent Reginaldus Spycer, quondam m'rcator istius ville qui obiit IX die Julii, Anno D'ni Will'mo CCCCXLII Et Margareta, Juliana, Margareta, & Joh'na, urores ejus quor' a i'abus p'piciet' Deus   Amen

---

On a large Slab, the Portraiture of a Man in Armour and his two Wives, one on each Side, with this Memorial

Hic sepeliuntur Will'mus Prelatte, Armiger, specialissim benefactor hujus capelle   Agnes, uxor Johannis Martyn, & Joh'na, filia & heres Ricardi de Cobyndon, relicta Johannis Twynyho, de Capsorde in comitatu Som', armigeri, urores ipsius Will'mi, qui quidem Will ni s prelatte, obiit in vigilia Ascensionis d'nice XXVI die Maii Anno D'ni MCCCCLXII, quor' a i'abus p'piciet' Deus.   Amen

---

IN JESUS CHAPEL

Under the Wall was this Inscription

Orate pro a'i'a Joh s Pratte, quondam capellani p'petue cantarie Beate Marie in eccl'ia S'ti Joh'is Baptiste Cirencestre' qui obiit A o D'ni MCCCCXX, cuj' a'i e p'piciet Deus   Amen

---

* We are enabled to give these Inscriptions as before the Mutilation from a Manuscript of Thomas Carter, M A. &c. d ed Dec B, 6 s obliging y communicated by the Rev. Mr Kunr

IN THE SOUTH AISLE

ON A SLAB, THE FIGURE OF AN ECCLESIASTIC IN BRASS, WITH THIS INSCRIPTION

Orate pro a'i'a D'ni Radulphi Parsons, quondam capellani p'petue cantarie S'cte Trinitatis in hac eccl'ia fundate, qui obiit XXIX die Augusti, Anno D'ni MCCCLXXXIII, cuj' a i e p piciet' Deus   Amen

IN ST. CATHERINE'S CHAPEL

Heere lyeth Thomas Pratte, Butcher, and Agnes his Wyfe, whiche Thomas dyed Nov 29, 1482.

IN TRINITY CHAPEL

ON A LARGE STONE WERE ENGRAVEN IN BRASS THE EFFIGIES OF A MAN, HIS TWO WIVES, AND EIGHT CHILDREN, WITH THIS MEMORIAL

Orate pro a'i'mabus Johannis Bennett, ac Agnetis uxoru' suar', qui quidem Joh'es obiit decimo nono die mensis Julii, Anno D'ni MCCCC, nonages' septimo qnorum a'i'bus   .

ON LABELS,

Sancta Trinitas unus De' miserere nob' !
Spiritus S'ce De' miserere nobis !
Fili redemptor mundi miserere nobis !

FORMERLY IN TRINITY CHAPEL

Hic requiescunt corpora Joannis Aveninge & Alice uxor' ejus, qui obierunt XIII die Aprilis, MCCCCCI

IN THE SOUTH AISLE.

ON A SLAB THE FIGURES OF A MAN AND WOMAN, UPON LABELS,

Merci God of my misdeede
Lady helpe at my most neede.

INSCRIPTION

Keepe gracious Jhu to endles Lyfe   At thy grete Dome wheze all schall appere.   Hughe Norys, Groc', and Johan hys Wyfe, nowe dede in the Grave and beryed here   Po' p'yers desyryng their Soules for chere, the I Daye of July, the Pere our Lorde God MCCCCCLXIX

FORMERLY IN TRINITY CHAPEL

Pray for the Soules of Johan George and Alice his Wyfe, who were buried here   which John deceassd the XIII th Day of Ocober MCCCCCLXII, and the said Alice deceassd the III d Day of May, MCCCCCLXII, and had four Sonnes and eight Doughters.

AT THE ENTRANCE OF ST MARY'S CHAPEL, ON A BRASS PLATE AFFIXED TO THE WALL, THE EFFIGY OF A MAN IN A BURGESS'S HABIT, WITH A CLOTHWORKER'S SHEARS, AND THIS INSCRIPTION.

In Lent by Will a Sermon he devised,
And yerely Precher with a Noble prysed,
Seven Nobles he did yeve, the Poore for to defend,
And 8 l to sixteen Men did lende,
In Cicester, Burford, Abyndon, and Tetburie,
Ever to be to them a Stocke yerelie
Philip Marner who died in the Peare 1587

IN THE CHANCEL

On a neat marble Monument

Near his Place resteth the Body of
Mrs Elizabeth Cripps, Wife of
Mr John Cripps, junior, who departed this Life
Feb 3, 1758, aged 41 Years

Also of Edward their Son, who died Feb 9, 1758,
aged 9 Years

And also of John and Henry their Sons,
both born Dec 3, and both died the 10th of the
same Month, in the Year 1743

To these are added
the Remains of the abovenamed Mr John Cripps,
who died May 7, 1771, aged 49 Years

H S T

Juxta chariffimum fratrem,
Vix ipfe fratri fi perftes,
Samuel Stiff, Johann & Eliz
Filius natu maximus,
Cui nil il unquam amicis defideratum
Præter ætatem diuturniorem
Dolemus, ut homines
Ut Chriftiani lætamur,
Optimis quippe conditionibus natus,
Annum agens vicefimum,
Cœlo maturus,
Vitam æterna caducam
Feliciter permutavit
D Feb 5, A S 1759

M S

Egregii juvenis
Radulph Willet Selfe,
Johannis & Elizabetæ Selfe, fil fecund.
Vultu honefta,
Pectore generofo,
Moribus placidiffimis,
Annum agens decimum fextum
Carus parentibus,
Carus præceptoribus,
Virtute quam annis maturior,
Diem obiit fupremum
XI cal Feb
MDCCLVIII

Vale, anima dulciffima !

Near this Place lies
the Body of John Selfe, Clothier,
To whom a moft kind and affectionate Hufband,
an indulgent and good Father,
a good Mafter, and a faithful Friend
He departed this Life on the 28th of Jan.
in the Year of our Lord 1763,
in the 56th Year of his Age

E S died July 29, 1766, aged 49 Years

Arms, Gules, three Chevronels Ermine, for
Stiff, on an Efcutcheon of Pretence Barry ten
Argent and Sable, on a Chief of the firft three
Lioncels rampant, for Willett

On a neat pyramidical marble Monument

In Memory of
Edward Wilbraham, Woolstapler,
who departed this Life Oct 10, 1771,
aged 60 Years

Also of Mary his firft Wife,
who died April 14, 1753, aged 57.

On an oval marble Tablet

In Memory of
Mrs Bridget Hughes,
who died March 19, 1774, aged 77 ;

Also Mrs Elizabeth Hughes,
who died July 5, 1776, aged 85,

Daughters of the Rev Mr Hughes,
late Rector of Coln St Dennis

On a square white marble Tablet

To the Memory of the
Rev Samuel Johnson, M A
fomet me Student of Chrift Church, Oxford,
one of the Vicars of Bampton,
and for more than 24 Years Minifter of this Parifh,
the laborious Duties of which he difcharged
with exemplary Zeal and Punctuality.
He departed this Life at Bampton
full of Faith,
March 9, 1784, aged 59 Years,
and lies buried with his Anceftors
at Laylock in the County of Wilts

ON FLAT STONES.

William Willis, Apothecary,
was buried here in April 1643

John Willis,
Grandchild of the faid William abovenamed,
departed this Life Nov 29, 1664

Mary, the Daughter of
William Willis and Esther his Wife,
was buried Jan 10, 1670

Catherine, Wife of Wm Willis, Apothecary,
was buried June 24, 1662

William Willis, fenior,
died Feb 10, 1680

Elizabeth Dowle, of Slymbridge,
died in the 18th Year of her Age,
was buried here Nov 5, 1698.

Here lie the Bodyes of Thomas Mou der
and Ann his Wife She deceafed
the 14th Day of June, 1676,
hee the 26th of Aprill, 1678

Arm,

Arms; on a Chevron between three Talbots a
Crescent, on a Chief crenelle three Martlets, impaling, six Roundlets, 3, 2, 1, and in Chief a Lion
passant, for BRIDGEMAN

M S
ROGERI BURGOYNE, M D
Qui post
Prudentem, piam, prosperam,
Facultatis medicæ
(Annos circiter viginti)
Administrationem
Tandem
Debilitato corpore
Subita sed non improvisa morte
Occubuit,
Decembris 21mo,
1674,
ætatis suæ 46

———————

FORMERLY NEAR THE STEPS WERE THE TWO FOL-
LOWING INSCRIPTIONS

H S
THOMÆ CARLES, A M,
De Cirencester Pastor, }
De Barnesley Rector, } Dignissi.
Utriusque ornamentum
Mortuus triste desiderium,
Vir
Integritate vitæ,
Suavitate morum,
Ingenii dotibus,
Concionandi venustate
Adeo insignis,
Ut non sine ingenti
Totius diocæseos luctu
Decesserit,
Oct. 7, Ann æt 50,
Dom 1675

———————

Arms, Argent, a Chevron Sable, in Chief a
Bar engrailed Gules, a Crescent for Difference, for
FREAME

H R I P
Deposita ossa subditi fidelis Anglicanæ,
Filii morigeri & artis chirurgiæ peritissimi,
GULIELMI FREAME, generosi,
Qui obiit Oct 24, A D 1678, ætat 58
Siste viator,
Mortuus loquor,
Audi,
Morte mea cecidi
Christi virtute resurgam
Ergo & tu.

———————

GEORGI LAWRANCE
died May 31, 1701

ANN his Daughter,
Wife of JOHN TIMBRELL, Mercer,
died Oct. 27, 1734, in the 34th Year of her Age.

Also two of their Children,
MARY died Aug 21, 1728;
HENRY died Aug 20, 1729

ISAAC LAWRANCE
died Oct 3, 1724, aged 4.

ANN his Wife
died Dec 25, 1738, aged 5.

ANN their Daughter
died April 22, 1754, aged 41

———————

ROGER LAWRANCE, Clothier,
died July 25, 1742, in the 34th Year of his Age.

Also SARAH his Wife
died June 11, 1767, aged 68

ANN their Daughter
died April 28 1779, aged 39

———————

WILLIAM LAWRANCE
died Feb 4, 1768, aged 69.

SARAH his Wife
died Feb 12, 1752, aged 6.

———————

JANE, Wife of WILLIAM JOHNSTON,
died March 24, 1708, aged 32

———————

SARAH WHITE
was buried Feb 8, A D 1691

———————

ANN, Wife of Mr CHRISTOPHER JOHNSTON,
of this Town,
died Nov 15, 1763, aged 75

Also ELIZABETH, Wife of the late
Mr ISAAC SLIMAN, of London,
died July 27, 1770, aged 76

———————

Underneath lie interred the Bodies of
JOHN PALLING, Clothier, and SARAH his Wife

He died April 30, 1728, aged 58.

She died May 27, 1714, aged 21.

Likewise ANN his second Wife
She died March 19, 1745, aged 65.

———————

HENRY TIMBRELL
died June 12, 1745, aged 75.

ALETHIA his Wife
died March 2, 1740, aged 64

———————

HENRY, Son of THOMAS and ELIZ COLEMAN,
died Jan 18, 1729, aged 12 Weeks.

ELIZABETH their Daughter
died Jan 8, 1735, aged 2 Years

THOMAS their Son
died Aug. 19, 1738, aged 7 Years.

THOMAS COLEMAN
died May 10, 1759, aged 59

ELIZABETH his Wife
died Nov 4, 1752

Sir Thomas Harrison, Knight,
Chamberlain of the City of London,
youngest Son of Joseph Harrison, Clerk,
late Minister of this Parish,
died Jan 2, 1763, aged 64

Dame Dorothea Harrison, Relict of
Sir Thomas Harrison,
died Jan 8, 1773, aged 71

ON MONUMENTS IN THE NORTH AISLE.

This Marble is placed here in Memory of
Mr John Gastrell,
who died the 18th of June, 1767, in his 45th Year,
and is buried in the North west Corner of
the Church-yard of St Mary le Strand in the County
of Middlesex
He was a Native of this Town,
and, after a liberal Education in Winchester School,
served in Apprenticeship in the Parish of
St Mary le Strand, where he was
soon after admitted to a Share of the Business,
and by Diligence, sweetness of Manners, and
unblemished Conduct,
obtained the Good will of all Ranks of People,
acquired a decent Fortune,
and bequeathed to his Relations and Friends,
with a clear Head and benevolent Heart
His Father Richard Gastrell, Gent
discharged the Office of Steward of the Manor of
Cirencester for many Years,
with proper Dignity, much Judgement, and great
Candour, was eminent and
justly esteemed as an Attorney and Conveyancer,
and remarkable for being more attentive
to the Advantage of his numerous Clients,
than to the Rewards which his Skill and Success
entitled him to expect or demand
He departed this Life the 27th of February, 1736,
aged 57,
and lieth interred in the Parish of Crudwell
in the County of Wilts

Near this Place lies
the Body of William Thompson,
of Applegirth in the County of Annandale
and Kingdom of Scotland,
who departed this Life
the 12th of March, 1705-6,
aged 48 Years

Near this Place lieth the Body of
Nicholas Edwards, Mercer,
who departed this Life August 13, 1711,
aged 31 Years

And also Elizabeth his Wife,
who departed this Life Sept 27, 1712,
aged 30 Years

And of their Daughter Elizabeth,
who died Nov 19, 1726, aged 21 Years

ON FLAT STONES

Jane, Daughter of Edward and Frances Lyne,
of Port Farm in this Parish,
died Nov 2, 1705, aged 11 Years and 9 Months

Also of Edward Lyne, of Port Farm,
who died July 7, 1771, aged 50 Years

Also of Mary Lyne,
who died July 29, 1772, aged 17

Charles and Anne, Son and Daughter
of Thomas and Ann Parsons,
he died Nov 6, 1715, aged 1 Year and 6 Months
she died Feb 2, 1716, aged 1 Year and 9 Months

Also Charles and Anne, Son and Daughter
of Thomas Parsons,
he died May 22, 1735, aged 9 Years and 8 Months,
she died Jan 21, 1731, aged 8 Years and 9 Months

In Remembrance of
Mary, the Daughter of George Hill,
who died Dec 25, 1743,
aged 24 Years

Likewise of Thomas his Son,
who died Aug 27, 1747, aged 25 Years

And also of Sarah, the Wife of George Hill,
who departed this Life
May 27, 1753, aged 64

George Hill
was underneath interred, the
11th of April, 1767, aged 79

Mary, Daughter of the abovenamed
George Hill by Mary his Wife,
the Daughter of Reuben and Martha Smith,
and Wife of the Rev John Collinson,
Curate of this Church,
died Nov 30, 1787, aged 32 Years

Isaac, Son of Nicholas Edwards,
departed this Life March 1, 1707

Nicholas, the Son of
Nicholas and Elizabeth Edwards,
departed this Life March 5, 1708

Isaac Tebrat, senior,
died Aug 14, 1692, aged 59

Also Susanna his Wife
died Nov 26, 1722, aged 89

James their youngest Son
died Feb 14, 1734, aged 57.

Jacob Tebrat, senior,
died Oct 12, 1728, aged 55

William Stone, junior,
of this Town, died Dec 6, 1724, aged 27

Ann Byam
died Oct 26, 1766, aged 41

Hester Arnold
died Jan 16, 1763, aged 27

MARY, Wife of JOSEPH COLEN,
died Aug 25, 1785, aged 71

ELIZABETH, Wife of GILES RADWAY,
died Sept 17, 1782, aged 49

WILLIAM WAIGHT
died Jan 14, 1738, aged 57

MARY, Wife of HENRY WAIGHT,
died Oct 10, 1764

JANE, the Wife of WILLIAM WILLIAMS,
died Feb 27, 1723, aged 57

Also WILLIAM WILLIAMS
died Oct 19, 1738, aged 61

THOMAS ROBBINS, senior,
died August 8, 1761, aged 69

MARY his Wife
died April 7, 1769, aged 69

IN THE NAVE

ON TWO NEAT MARBLE MONUMENTS AT THE EN-
TRANCE OF THE CHANCEL

Near this Place was interred
the Body of Mr JAMES CLUTTERBUCK,
who died June 30, 1722, aged 49.
He left to the Care of his Wife
Mrs SUSANNA CLUTTERBUCK a numerous Family,
which she brought up with parental Tenderness,
evincing her Affection for her Husband,
by a constant Attention to the Trust reposed in her,
till she departed this Life Feb 4, 1757,
in the 86th Year of her Age

Of their Children three died in their Infancy

EDWARD died April 17, 1728, aged 39.

SARAH   Dec 8, 1771,   68

WILLETT   June 24, 1773,   66

JAMES   Nov 26, 1776,   72

ELIZABETH, their youngest Daughter, having been
first married to Mr SOMERSET, Draper, of London,
and after his Death to Mr JOHN CRIPPS,
an Inhabitant of this Town,
died Feb 29, 1784.

To the Memory
of the Rev JOHN WILLETT,
only Son of JOHN and SUSANNA WILLETT,
Inhabitants of this Town
He was many Years Vicar of Wadhurst in Sussex,
and, among other exemplary Qualities, exhibited
a striking Instance of the goodness of his Heart
in his Attention towards his Twin Sister
Mrs SUSANNA CLUTTERBUCK,
who was left a Widow with six Children,
his tender Regard for their Welfare
ceased not but at his Death, which happened
Jan 30, 1742, in the 70th Year of his Age,

when his Remains were deposited in his own
Parish Church at Wadhurst
This, and the corresponding Monument,
were erected by the Executors of
Mrs ELIZABETH CRIPPS,
in pursuance of her Will

ON FLAT STONES

CUM JANA Uxore RADULPHUS WILLETT,
in dandis consiliis sapiens,
in expediendis negotiis promptus,
in communicandis litibusque prudens,
& in omnibus animi motibus
æquabiliter temperandis
supra modum felix,

Ob { Hic sepultus est,
     Hic Aug 23, 1692,   } annorum { 67
     Illa Sept 8, 1671, }   { 49

JOAN HANCOCK, the Widow of
GILES HANCOCK, senior, of Daglingworth,
died Jan 8, 1729

. Wife of LEBEUS HITYARD,
Daughter of GILES HANCOCK, of Diglingworth,
died June 11, 1748, aged 67

Arms, a Lion rampant, in Chief three
Escallops

Near this Place
are interred the Remains of
Mr JAMES CLUTTERBUCK, born Oct 11, 1673,
died June 30 1722,

And SUSANNA (Daughter of
JOHN and SUSANNA WILLET) his Wife
She was born June 11, 1671,
died Feb 4, 1757

Also
EDWARD their Son, born March 1 1689,
died April 17, 1728

JOHN their Son, born Oct 8, 1697,
died Nov 27, 1699

JOHN their Son, born Jan 21, 1700,
died July 2, 1701

MARY their Daughter, born Jan 1, 1711,
died Jan 11, 1711.

Mrs SARAH CLUTTERBUCK
died Dec 8, 1771, aged 68

Mr WILLET CLUTTERBUCK
died June 24, 1773, aged 66

SARAH, Wife of JAMES HEWES, Clothier,
was buried Feb 22, 1720, aged 67

JAMES HEWES, Clothier,
died Aug 23, 1732, aged 76

IN THE SOUTH AISLE

ON A MONUMENT AT THE WEST END

Hic prope situm est
Quod mortale fuit THOMÆ DEACON,
Oppidani utilis & amati,
Viri quidem scientis,
Necnon munere erga Deum & homines fungentis,
Multum deploratus obiit
4° Augusti anno {salutis 1661
{ætatis 46

Illi
(post annos circiter viginti novem
pura & sancta viduate elapsos)
accesserunt exuviæ MARGERIÆ,
ejusdem THOMÆ DEACON
uxoris præstantissimæ
Hæc mortalitatem exuit,
19th Maii, anno {salutis 1690
{ætatis 74

ON A WHITE MARBLE MONUMENT

Arms, a Lion rampant reguardant, for PENRY

Non procul hinc repositum quod
fuit mortale BRIDGIDIÆ
JACOBI SMALL, Filiæ natu maximæ,
inter landandas laude nonnullâ
dignæ matrimonio conjuncta fuit
JACOBO PENRY, de Aberkenny
in Agro Breconiensi, Clerico,
cui perperit ANNAM, Filiolam,
in eodem sepulchro contentam,
ob {hæc decimo
{Die Sept Anno Dom 1735.
{illi vicesi no quarto

ON A SQUARE MARBLE TABLET

Near this Place lieth the Body of
MARY GALE, Daughter of
THOMAS and ANN GALE
She departed this Life May 26, 1785,
aged 31 Years

ON A NEAT OVAL MARBLE

Near this Place rest the Remains of
SARAH, the Wife of TIMOTHY STEVENS,
who died Sept 4, 1784, aged 30

ON FLAT STONES

MARGARET HOOPER,
Wife unto HENRY HOOPER,
was here buried the 4th Day of March, 1601

ANNE, the Wife of WROTEN SPARROW,
died Dec 10, 1761, aged 60

ROBERT HOPKINS,
of Melksham in the County of Wilts,
was buried Dec 17, 1735, aged 82

THOMAS FORDER, senior,
died Feb 14, 1717-18, aged 50

AMY, the Wife of THOMAS FORDER, senior,
was buried Dec 28, 1734, aged 75

ANN, Daughter of THOMAS FORDER, senior,
died April 17, 1721, aged 36.

THOMAS FORDER
died Nov 22, 1753, aged 63
WILLIAM his Son
died Aug 8, 1754, aged 24

ANN, the Daughter of THOMAS FORDER,
died Feb 4, 1750, aged 29

JOHN, the Son of THOMAS FORDER,
died Oct 30, 1736, aged 16.

MARY, Wife of THOMAS FORDER,
died April 6, 1769

JOHN PEEK
was buried Jan 30, 1736
FRANCES his Wife
was buried July 5, 1759
Two of their Children, MARY and ELIZABETH,
died in their Infancy

SARAH, Wife of JOHN PEEK, junior,
died Nov 8, 1751, aged 40
MARY their Daughter
died Feb 7, 1752, aged 2 Years

SARAH FEWSTER
died July 24, 1730, aged 22.

Among the Remains of
WILLIAM EBSWORTH and ELIZABETH his Wife,
here are interred those of their Son
WILLIAM EBSWORTH and ABIGAIL his Wife,
with the Body of JOHN GRAYHURST,
Grandson to the said WILLIAM and ABIGAIL.

W E died July 13, 1684, aged 55.
E E died in 1716, aged 84.
W E died April 6, 1736, aged 74
A E died Dec. 24, 1738, aged 70.
J G died Nov 10, 1724, aged 14 Day

ISAAC, Son of JOHN MARSH,
died Feb 2, 1712, aged 1 Year 3 Months

JOHN BROWN, Soapboiler,
died April 12, 1713, aged 53.
MARY his Wife
died July 11, 1743, aged 66.
RICHARD BROWN, Soapboiler,
died Aug 2, 1762, aged 51

HOPKINSON PAINE, Clothier,
died Feb 3, 1642

ELIZABETH

ELIZABETH PAINE
died the 8th Day of January, anno Dom 1668

MARY PEARCE, the Wife of HENRY PEARCE,
Citizen and Merchant Taylor of London,
departed this Life in this Town of Cirencester,
on the 25th Day of November, in the
Year of our Lord God 1651,
ætatis suæ 23

JOHN CLEVELAND
died Feb 12, 1765, aged 95

SUSANNA his Wife
died Jan 9, 1735, aged 85

Their Children

MARGARET died Nov 16, 1781, aged 86
NATHANIEL died Dec 5, 1780, aged 83
ANN died Jan 1, 1782, aged 79
JOHN died Feb 1, 1788, aged 87

GEORGE SMALL
exchanged Frailty for Immortality,
the 11th Day of January, 1669

JAMES SMALL, senior,
died Oct 3, 168

MARY, Daughter of JAMES SMALL, junior,
was buried Dec 3, 1715

GEORGE SMALL
died July 24, 1738, aged 77 Years

MARY, Widow of JAMES SMALL,
died the 2d Day of May, 1703, aged 60

JAMES SMALL, Clothier,
died March 28, 1707

ANNE, Daughter of ISAAC SMALL, senior,
died the 30th Day of January, 1683

JANE, Wife of ISAAC SMALL, senior,
died the 27th Day of June, 1708.

JOHN SMALL
died Jan 28, Anno Dom   , aged 70

BRIDGET, the Wife of JOHN SMALL,
died the 12th Day of April, 1712.

ISAAC SMALL, senior,
died Feb 14, Anno Dom. 1713

ANNE, the Wife of JAMES SMALL,
died Oct 19, 1741, aged 52.

WILLIAM DEAN, senior,
was buried July 31, 1751, aged 59

In Tumulo sororis charissimæ JANÆ,
ux HEN GREENWAY, quæ obiit 9 Sept 1685

Et juxta illum ut videas, lector,
æque dilecti fratris & omnibus grati JACOBI
atque heu doloris 8° die post hujus Junii,
die   dominici 6 Aprilis, 1707.

Sepultus fuit ISAACUS SMALL,
vicarius de Kemble dignissimus

JOHN HOPKINS, senior,
died Aug 10, 1707, aged 72

ANN his Wife
died Jan 25, 1710.

JOHN HOPKINS
died Dec 28, 1778

JAMES HOPKINS
died May 2, 1780.

JOHN HOPKINS, junior,
died July 20, 1743, aged 76.

SUSANNA his Wife
died May 1, 1737, aged 57.

ANN HOPKINS
died March 17, 1771

MARY HOPKINS
died July 28, 1775

Mrs SUSANNA HOPKINS
died June 13, 1786

GABRIEL COOK, Gent
died Nov 22, 1697, ætatis suæ 81.

THOMAS MILLINSON,
died Dec 11, Anno Dom 1716

ELIZABETH his Wife
died Oct 8, Anno Dom 1734

ON FLAT STONES UNDER THE GAL-
LERY AT THE WEST END

Arms, a Cross between four Lions rampant

THOMAS DEACON
of Elmstree in the Parish of Tetbury, Gent
died Sept 30, 1723 aged 76

ANN his Daughter
died the 19th of Dec 1723, aged 36

ELIZABETH, the Wife of WILLIAM HILL,
died March 3, 1710, aged 77

ELIZABETH, the Daughter of HENRY TOWNSEND,
Clothier, of the Parish of Painswick,
was buried July 16, 1701, aged 7 Years 8 Months

HANNAH, the Wife of WILLIAM SELBY,
died Dec 28, 1766, aged 48

HENRY WHITTER
died Dec 24, 1729, aged 39

IN TRINITY CHAPEL

A Monument of white Marble, upon a Sarcophagus a weeping Genius between the Busts of Allen Earl Bathurst and Catharine his Lady, by Nollekins   Upon an Escutcheon the Arms, Quarterly, 1st and 4th, Diamond two Bars Ermine, in Chief three Crofses patee Topaz, for Bathurst, 2d and 3d, Pearl, on a Crofs Ruby five Efcallops Topaz, for Villiers   On an Efcutcheon of Pretence   quarterly, 1st and 4th, Barry of fix Argent and Gules, a Canton Ermine, for Apsley 2d and 3d, Gules, a Bend between two Efcallops Or, for Petre

Near to this Place are depofited the Remains of
Allen Earl Bathurst and Catharine Lady Bathurst

In the Legiflative and Judicial Departments of the great Council of the Nation he ferved his Country 69 Years, with Honour, Ability, and Diligence ; Judgement and Tafte directed his Learning, Humanity tempered his Wit, Benevolence guided all his Actions He died regretted by moft, and praifed by all, the 16th Day of September, 1775, aged 91	Catharine his Confort, by her milder Virtues added Luftre to his great Qualities , her domeftic Œconomy extended his Liberality , her judicious Charity, his Munificence , her prudent Government of her Family, his Hofpitality She received the Reward of her exemplary Life the 8th Day of June, 1768, aged 79

Married July the 6th, 1704

ON A SQUARE MARBLE TABLET

In Remembrance of
Mr William Turner, late of this Place, and of Catharine (for more than fifty fix Years) his entirely beloved Wife   He was the youngeft Son of the Rev John Turner, of Somerford Keynes in the County of Wilts and died Auguft 21, 1769, aged 76 Years She was the fecond Daughter of the Rev Joseph Harrison, more than 63 Years Minifter of this Parifh, and died four Months after her Hufband, and of the fame Age   They were a very humane and exemplary pair, acknowledged the moft high in every Difpenfation, and kept through Life the ferious Thought of Death

---

ON AN OVAL MARBLE TABLET

Near this Place reft the Remains of
Mrs Jane Nicholls, Daughter of
Mr William Turner, of this Town, deceafed
She died Dec 19, 1773, aged 47

Thomas, Son of Thomas and Jane Nicholls,
died June 19, 1782, aged 32.

ON FLAT STONES

Valentine Baily, fenior,
was buried Nov 1, 1712, aged 77

Charles Baily, his Grandfon,
died June 6, 1723, aged 7 Years.

Valentine Baily, junior,
died in Feb 1743, aged 62 Years

Elizabeth his Wife,
died Oct 3, 1741, aged 53 Years

Joyce, the Wife of William Hodges,
was buried September 23, 1733

John Turner
died Jan 5, 1773, aged 52

Mary his Wife
died May 19, 1773, aged 56.

Richard Scruton
died April 27, 1764, aged 55

Mary his Daughter
died May 18, 1764, aged 15

Mary, Wife of Richard Scruton,
died July 26, 1787, aged 68

IN ST MARY'S CHAPEL.

Under a Canopy on an Altar Tomb, the Effigies (recumbent) of a Man and Woman, in the Dress of the Times, carved and painted in Freestone

Arms , Argent, a Crofs Sable, charged in the Centre with a Leopard's Face Or, for Bridges

Here lieth the Bodies of
Humfry Bridges and Elizabeth his Wife
He dyed the 17th of April, 1598
Shee dyed the 6th of July, 1620
They had both Sonnes and Daughters
He gave 40s Yearly for ever
to the Poor of this Towne
She gave 6 Habitations for 6
Poore Widdowes, with 6s weekly
for ever

ON THE BASE OF A MURAL MONUMENT OF WHITE
MARBLE, THE EFFIGY OF A MAN SEMI RECUMBENT,
IN A LOOSE DRESS

Arms, Gules, a Lion rampant guardant O,
holding a Rose stalked Vert, for MASTER

Quos Deus conjunxit separat tantum non repudiat Mas

Memoriæ Sacrum
Fidissimi servi Dei, & regis subditi,
Patriæque amantissimi suæ,
GULIELMI MASTER, apud Corinios
Equitis aurati,
Qui martyrem regem mœrens martyr
Semimortuus vixit diu
Citius dominum secutus, in morbo paralytico
Restituisset firma fides.
Restituendi Regis insignissimi,
CAROLI Secundi,
Utcunque apud Vigorniam, fusi
Voti tandem, ac va icinu compos factus,
Tantique pignoris, justorum Resurrectionis,
Vitam mortalem ex uit, immortali Deo
Cœlitum choro gratias acturus
Anno 1661 (ætatis 61) mens Mart die 3
He married ALICE, one of the Daughters of
Sir EDWARD ESTCOURT, of Newton in the County
of Wiltes, Knight,
by whom he had Issue six Sonns and six Daughters
A Lady highly eminent both for her Partes
and Pietie, who having, by the Blessing of God,
passed through the Troubles of an intestine Warr,
and lived to see her Children bred up,
resigned her Soul to God, whose Body
lies here interred, waiting for the
Resurrection of the Just Sept 5, 1660

P H M
Filius unicus
In memoriam patris optimi,
THOMÆ MASTER, Armigeri,
In quo
Morum gravitas humanitate condita,
Animus pie liberalis,
Indolis vere generosa,
Quicquid demum aut virum probum
Aut ornatum decebat,
Summe emicuit
Virtutes has imitare lector,
Ut fias Deo & hominibus charus
Obiit A D 1680, æt 56.

Hic subtus depositum est
Quicquid mortale fuit
ELIZ MASTER, THO & ELIZ filiæ
Immortalem si requiras partem,
Ad patriam cœlestem rediit
Itineris terreni maculis
Quam minimum inquinata;
In quâ ingenii elegantia, gestus
Suavis, compositus decorus,
Omnes denique enituère virtutes,
Quibus indoles optima
Ad pietatem, prudentiam,
Et mores pudicos formata
Instrui & ornari possit,
Adeo ut licet ætas sit imperfecta,
Vita tamen illi perfecta,
Obiit Aug 15, A. D 1705, æt 16

M S
LIIZ MASTER, THO MASTER, AND VID
Et THO DIKE, de Horchin
In agro Suffexiæ, Arm filia,
Quæ se
Morum elegantia, integritatis pura,
Temporantia & modestia severa,
Candoris eximii, & pietatis sincera,
Omnibus imitanda in exemplum præbui
His animi dotibus accessit
Valetudo ad extremam
Senectutem integra
Quas si tibi contingant lector,
Summam huius vitæ
Felicitatem consequeris,
Et futuræ gloriæ expectes
Obiit Jan 28, A D 1703-4, æt 83

M S
ELIZABETHÆ, uxoris THOMÆ MASTER,
THOMÆ filii
Quæ (variola um morbo contracto)
Proxime a puerperio obiens,
Una cum infantulo
Hic jacet sepulta.
Ob nativam comitatem,
Ingenii elegantiam,
Singularem modestiam,
Omnesque alias quæ fœminam, uxorem,
Aut matrem exornant virtutes,
Maxime deflenda præsertim conjugi,
Cui, in solatium tanti doloris,
Et ad supplendas amicitiæ vices
(a fato solum dissolvendæ)
Infantes duos THO & ELIZAB
Charissima amoris pignora
Legavit, A D 1691, æt 26

ON FLAT STONES

ELIZABETH GREENWAY, Widow,
was buried April 7, 1666

MARY, the Daughter of JOHN GREENWAY,
was buried April 19, 1694

ABRAHAM, the Son of THOMAS DEIGHTON,
Citizen of London, died Aug 4, 1677

JOHN GREENWAY, senior,
died June 25, 1684, ætatis suæ 69

SARAH, the Daughter of JOHN GREENWAY,
departed this Life Sept 19, 1675

ALICE, the Wife of JOHN GREENWAY,
died Aug 22, Anno Dom 1693

MARGARET, the Wife of JOHN BRIDGES, Gent
Daughter of HUMFRY and ELIZABETH BRIDGES,
died February 21, 1652

JOHN GREENWAY
died July 31, Anno Dom 1700

MARY, the Wife of WILLIAM HINTON,
Soapboiler, died Aug 1, 1755, aged 27 Years

MARY their Daughter
died June 16, 1755, aged 13 Months

JOHN SMALL
died Nov 7, 1755, aged 62

IN ST CATHERINE'S CHAPEL

ON A VERY NEAT OVAL MARBLE TABLET

In Memory of
ALBERT EYLLS, late an Apothecary of this Town,
who died March 14, 1782, aged 5, Years,
and lies interred near this Marble

ON AN ELEGANT MONUMENT OF BLACK AND
WHITE MARBLE

Arms, On a Chevron five Horse-shoes, for
CRIPPS,—impaling three Talbots' Heads erased,
between semee of Cross Crosslets, for HALL

Near this Place lie the Remains of
Mr JOSEPH CRIPPS,
a person eminently distinguished
by many great and good Qualities
He was uniformly affectionate as a Husband,
prudently indulgent as a Father,
discreetly kind as a Master,
amiably free as a Friend,
in his extensive Business
he was able, upright, and successful
After the most earnest Endeavour to acquire,
at length he effectually attained,
that happy Frame of Mind, that Spirit of Resignation,
which rendered him superior
to the Changes and Chances of this mortal State,
to the repeated Attacks of a tedious and painful
Illness,
and to the Stroke of Dissolution
Obiit Mars 28 A D 1782, æt 53

ON FLAT STONES

RICHARD EYLES
died Dec 1, 1753, aged 53

MARY, Wife of RICHARD EYLES,
died Oct 10, 1755, aged 64

HENRY BADSEY
died March 26, 1738

SARAH his Wife
died Jan 8, 1758, aged 65

SARAH, Wife of JOSEPH JONES, Brazier,
departed this Life the 11th of February, 1689

Also Four of his Children

ELIZABETH EYCOTT
died June 16, 1775, aged 47

JONES EYCOTT her Husband
died May 1, 1779, aged 57

WILLIAM BURGE
died Feb 28, 1693

JOHN BURGE
died Dec 3, 1697

JOHN, the Son of JOHN BURGE,
died Dec 24, 1697

In Memory of
SAMUEL BURGE and MARY his Wife
They died March 10, 1727,
he aged 60, she 76

Wife of WILLIAM BURGE,
departed this Life Sept 4, 1663

SAMUEL BURGE, junior,
died Feb 19, 1728, aged 44.

THOMAS MILLINGTON, Cardmaker,
died Jan 12, 1727, in the 62d Year of his Age

ESTHER, the Wife of THOMAS MILLINGTON,
died Aug 14, 1741, in the 78th Year of her Age

JOHN SAUNDERS
died June 14, 1765, aged 45.

MARY his Wife
died Jan 7, 1780, aged 62.

SARAH, Daughter of
JOHN and SARAH BENGER, Yeoman,
died Nov 12, 1709, aged 4 Years

JOHN BENGER
died April 3, 1781, aged 66

SARAH his Wife
died Dec 8, 1777, aged 53

THOMAS their Son
died Feb 6, 1781, aged 29.

DOROTHY, Wife of GEORGE GLANVILL,
died March 26, 1725, in the 59th Year of her Age

GEORGE GLANVILL, Organist,
died Oct 17, 1760, in the 75th Year of his Age

ANNE JOHNSON, Widow,
died April 23, 1760, aged 62

T JOHNSON died March 23, 1762

ANTHONY CHANC
was buried May 21, 1667

KATHARINE CHANC,
one of the Daughters of ANTHONY CHANC,
died April 21, 165

JOHN OATES
died January 15, 1679

ELIZABETH, Widow of JOHN OATES, Gent
died June 4, 1728.

Mr SAMUEL PERRY
died Sept 26, 1701, aged 68

Arms, Azure, a Fess embattled Argent, between
three Pears Or, for PERRY

Mr THOMAS PERRY
died March 20, 1706-7, in the 75th Year of his Age

Mrs MERCY PERRY,
the Wife of Mr THOMAS PERRY,
was interred the 15th of June, 1668

ELIZABETH, the Wife of JOHN PRICE,
died March 29, 1734

Arms, on a Bend three Leopard's Faces.

Hic requiescit
ærumnarum portu & metæ salutis
quiequid terrestre fuit
THOMÆ KEMBLE, Gent.
ejus animæ
ad superos evolavit
14 cal Aug
annb ⎰ ætat sua 71
         ⎱ ara Christianæ 1710

ANNE KEMBLE, Daughter of
ANTHONY KIMBLE,
was buried December 14, 1733

WILLIAM KEMBLE, Gent
ob. Jan 22, 1745

THOMAS POWELL
died March 3, A D 1698 9

WILLIAM ELLIS
died Dec 13, 1727, æt 46

MARY his Wife
died Feb 1, 1746, aged 60

MARY, Wife of RICHARD BROWN,
died March 7, 1748, aged 37

ELEANOR, Wife of JOHN ELLIS,
died Oct 18, 1759, aged 39

UNDER TWO FIGURES IN BRASS

Mr JOHN GUNTER and ALICE his Wife,
being full as of Yeares, so of Pounty and
Charity, are gathered to their Fathers in Peace

She was here buried 18 Martii,
Anno Dom 1626, aged 86 Yeares

He was buried at Kyntbury in the
County of Berks, with the like Monument,
January 2, A D 1624, aged 89 Years

Jos PLAT, Ar corund. Gener & Exec hoc posuit

ELEANOR SOLLACE,
Daughter of ANDREW and ELLANOR SOLLACE,
died Dec 31, 1690, aged 31

ALICE, Wife of ANDREW SOLLACE,
departed this Life Oct 6, 1619.

MARY their Daughter
died Feb 12, 1633

ANDREW SOLLACE, Gent
died August 20, 1671, aged 55

ELEANOR SOLLACE
died June 21, 1682.

Mrs ANNE WARE
died April 25, 1711, aged 55

GEORGE, Son of GEORGE WEARE, Gent.
died the 7th Day of May, 1707

THOMAS, Son of GEORGE WEARE, Gent
by MARY his Wife,
died the 2d Day of December, 1718

JANE, Daughter of GEORGE WEARE, Gent
died August 11, 1717

MARY, the Wife of GEORGE WEARE, Esq
died July 7, 1749, aged 64

GEORGE WEARE, Esq
died Jan 2, 1754, aged 67

JANE KING
died May 14, 1707, aged 46

EDWARD TAYLOR
died February 5, 1699

EDITH TAYLOR
died February 21, 1706.

IN ST. JOHNS CHAPEL.

UPON AN ALTAR TOMB OF ALABASTER, CANO-
PIED OVER THE EFFIGIES OF A MAN AND WOMAN
KNEELING, IN THE DRESS OF THE TIMES UNDER,
IN RELIEVO, THE FIGURES OF THEIR TWO DAUGH-
TERS

Arms, on two Escutcheons, 1st, Argent, on a
Chevron Sable, between three Fig Leaves proper,
three Bezants, on a Chief Gules a Martlet, between two Anchors erect of the Field, for MONOX;
—impaling, Argent, on a Bend Sable, three Pears
Or, in the Point a Trefoil, for PERRY

2d, Vert, a Chevron undy, between three Griffins segreant Or, for   ,—impaling MONOX
as before

Memoriæ Sacrum

GEORGII MONOX, Armig Cirencestriæ nati, qui
(post plurimos annos in mercandizis laboriose & prudenter perimpleverat) ad gradum & dignitate officii
vicecomitus Londiniensis unanimi optimatum con-
fentu fuit vocatus, magnas denariorum fummas fe-
peribil locis in pios ufus legavit, & ut fingularem
amorem quo natale folum vivus amavit futuris fæ-
culis manifeftarat centum libras in percuriis nume-
ratis, & tenementa annui valoris viginti librarum pro
meliori hujus villæ pauperum fuftentatione, & lec-
tura hac ecclefia fingulis menfibus prædicanda in
perpetuum affignavit

MARIA uxor mœftiffima (ex quia
folas duas filias fuperftites fufcepit)
viro chariffimo pietatis amoris,
& obfervantiæ ergô pofuit
Dies mortis æternæ vitæ
natalis eft
obiit 26 die Junii,
anno falutis 1638,
ætat fuæ 66

ON FLAT STONES

THOMAS GROVES
died Sept 10, 1699

THOMAS, Son of
the abovenamed THOMAS GROVES,
died March 4, 1692-3

JOHN ARMES, of this Town, Cooper,
died Dec 9, 1751, aged 80

MARY his Wife
died in March, 1765, aged 82

SARAH their Daughter,
Wife of JOSEPH HARRIS,
of the Town of Buckingham, Mercer,
died in September, 1764, aged 45

WILLIAM ROWLES
was buried April 5, 1660

MARGERY his Wife
was buried Dec 6, 1664

WILLIAM ROWLES
Son of the abovenamed WILLIAM ROWLES,
died June 18, 1691

MARY, Wife of WILLIAM ROWLES, junior,
died June 7, 1696

MARGARET, Wife of
Mr PHILIP SHEPHARD, Citizen of London,
and Daughter to THOMAS ROGERS,
died October 7, 1690

JOHN ROGERS, Clothier,
was buried Nov 20, 1706

ELIZABETH, the Wife of THOMAS HAYNES
(Daughter of THOMAS ROGERS, Father of the
faid JOHN), died Auguft 13, 1685

Here lyeth the Body of
ANNE, the fecond Daughter of
Mr. ISAAC LAWRENCE and ANNE
his Wife, to whofe virtuous
Memory is this Infcription
She was firft the Wife of
Mr JOHN ROGERS, and afterwards of
Mr THOMAS PETERS, Natives of this Town
She departed this Life on Wednefday
the 29th Day of November, 1710,
in the 49th Year of her Age

The abovefaid Mr JOHN ROGERS,
died Feb 28, 1686

ROWLAND FREEMAN, Gent
departed this Life Anno Dom 1687

MERIEL, Wife of the faid
ROWLAND FREEMAN, Daughter of
ROBERT BERKELEY, Gent
departed this Life Anno Dom 1732.

ROWLAND FREEMAN, Gent
died June 3, 1747, aged 64.

MARGARET his Wife
died June 8, 1753, aged 79

Mrs FRANCES FREEMAN,
Daughter of ROWLAND FREEMAN, Gent
and MARGARET his Wife,
died Dec 16, 1768, aged 55

Alfo JOHN-LLOYD FREEMAN their Son
died an Infant

ANNE, Daughter of
THOMAS and ANNE FREEMAN,
died the 20th of January, 1702 3

ANNE, the Wife of THOMAS FREEMAN,
died the 13th Day of June, 1702

To the Memory of the Family of
EDWARD HOPKINS, which became extinct by the
Death of the Grandfon, the 38th and laft of
that Name in a lineal Defcent

The Father		June 13, 1711
The Son	died	Sept 12, 1713.
The Grandfon		July 31, 1713

SUSANNA

SUSANNA HOWSE
died June 5, 1759, in the 80th Year of her Age,
Wife of the late RICHARD HOWSE,
of Duntborn Roufe, Gent and
of the late Rev. Mr. NATHANIEL GWYN,
Rector of Daglingworth

ELIZABETH, the Widow of CHARLES STOCK,
Rector of King Stanley,
died in this Town, and was here buried
March 23, 1713, ætat fua 84

SARAH, the Wife of PHILIP PAINTER,
died the 20th of June, 1702

ANNE PAINTER,
Sister of PHILIP PAINTER,
died June 27, 1729

PHILIP PAINTER
died Jan 5, 1738, aged 67

MARY KEMISH, Spinster,
died Dec 9, 1749, aged 63

BARBARA KEMISH, Spinster,
died June 8, 1759, aged 72

JANE KEMISH, Spinster,
died Feb 21, 1760, aged 70.

THOMAS COX, Chirurgeon,
died Nov 27, 1714, aged 27.

THOMAS BROWN
was buried Dec 22, 1723

DANIEL ASHWELL
was buried May 4, 1744

THOMAS WEBB
died Sept 15, 1770, aged 49

MARY OLIVE,
Daughter of ROBERT and ELIZABETH OLIVE,
died Oct 30, 1701

ROBERT OLIVE
died March 8, 1735, aged 85

REBECCA MORRELL
died Nov 25, 1750, aged 23

JOHN STONE, Son of JOHN STONE,
Felmonger, of this Town,
died Sept 14, 1758

IN JESUS' CHAPEL

ON A MONUMENT OF MARBLE FINISHED WITH
THREE BUSTS

Arms, on three feparate Efcutcheons 1 Argent,
a Fefs Gules, between three Falcons Wings elevated
Azure, for GEORGES, 2 Gules, three Fleurs de lis
Or, on a Chief Argent, a Lion of the Field, for
. . . , 3 Parry per Fefs Or and Argent, a
Lion rampant Gules, for POWELL

To the lafting Remembrance
of
WILLIAM GEORGES, Efq
this Monument was erected
by
REBECCA his Relict,
who being afterwards married to
THOMAS POWELL, Efq
ordered that his Memory alfo should be
herein tranfmitted to Pofterity

WILLIAM GEORGES, Efq
was underneath interred June 18, 1707,
in the 81ft Year of his Age

By his Body is depofited that of
THOMAS POWELL, Efq
Sept 13, 1718, in the 67th Year of his Age.

To their Remains were added thofe of
REBECCA,
Nov 8, 1722, in the 80th Year of her Age,
whofe Bequeft out of the Eftate devifed
to her by W. G. and, at Lady-day 1728,
amount to 3500l. and 200l. a Year for erecting
and endowing a Charity School or
Schools in this Town

The other pious and charitable Gifts of
R. P. and alfo of W. G. and T. P.
are recorded in the
Catalogue of Benefactors to this Parifh

IN THE CHURCH PORCH

Under your Feet lyeth the Body of
WILLIAM CLETHEROW, Gent
in humble Penitent, who thought himfelf
unworthy of the lowest Place
in the Houfe of GOD
He departed this Life the 18th Day of Nov 1636

IN THE CHURCH YARD, ON TOMBS.

ON A LARGE RAISED TOMB

Arms, a Fefs dancette between three Cherubs
difplayed, for ADYE, 2 a Chevron between three
Croffes formee, for AINGE, 3 on a Chief indented
two Eagles difplayed, for DAY

Hunc tumulo mandati funt cineres
JOANNIS ADYE, Generofi,
Filii EDVARDI & ISTERÆ ADYE,
Quorum exuviæ juxta requiefcunt,
Innocui, probi, bonis literis imbuti,
Turbumque fugientis
Obiit 26° Martii, A D. 1745, ætatis fuæ 68

Hic etiam fepulta eft MARIA,
JOANNIS ADYE uxor chariffima,
Et EDVARDI FOYLE, de Somerford Keynes
in agro Wiltonienfi, Arm
Filia valde deploranda
De vita exceffit 24° Februarii, A D 1724,
ætatis fuæ 43

Idem quoque tumulus continet
Quicquid mortale fuit MARIÆ AINGE,
Uxoris RICARDI AINGE, de Lechlade in
Comitatu Gloceftrienfi, Generofi,
Et JOANNIS ADYE, fororis non indignæ
Obiit 30 Maii, A D 1744, ætatis fuæ 71

Confanguineorum affiniumque juxta exuvias
Voluerunt & fuas jacere
RICHMONDUS DAY,
de civitate Briftolienfi mercator eximius,
Vir juftitiæ pertinax fiduíque, ecclefiæ Anglicanæ
Difcipulus

Et MARIA, conjux ejus dilectiffima
Unicaque RICARDI & MARIÆ AINGE,
Et nequaquam impar filia,
Hos animo, pietate, morumque fuavitate pares
Annis plus quam quadraginta
Domefticas virtutes exercendo
Et amore mutuo peractis
Mors eodem fere tempore corripuit

Uxor à vitâ deceffit 29° Junii, A D 1738,
ætatis fuæ 63

Maritus a vitâ deceffit 19° Augufti, A D 1738,
ætatis fuæ 70

Hunc tumulum
Parentibus indulgentiffimis confanguineifque fuorum
Filius, nepos, juffit extrui
1739

Hunc tumulo mandati
funt cineres
JONAE ADYE, Generofi,
innocui probi bonis
literis imbuti,
turbumque fugientis,
q obiit .. II ... MDCCXLV,
ætatis fuæ LXVII

Matthew, son of
Thomas and Mary Hughes
died Oct 14 1744 aged ..

Elizabeth, Wife of
William Hinton,
Daughter of Thomas Hughes,
died Sept 1, 17..

Mary Wife of Thomas Hughes,
and Daughter of Thomas Fransham
of . the Town of Shitchorn Dorket,
died Jan .. 1734 aged 44

In Remembrance of
Thomas Hughes Son of the
John Hughes,
... Peers of Colin St Dennis
in this County
He died Dec 10 17.. aged 58

Edward Chetterles fenior,
died July 2 1701 aged 73

Mary his Wife
died Feb 3 1697 aged 6.

Lydia Carpenter
Grand Daughter
of .. and Mary Chetterles
died Sept 10 17.. aged ..

THOMAS HAYWOOD, Gent
died Feb 24, 1747, aged 43

A fo MARY his Wife
died Oct 16, 1738, aged 38

THOMAS HAYWOOD, junior, Gent
died Nov 5 1765, aged 38

SARAH his Wife
died August 3, 1783, aged 46

MARTHA HAYWOOD
died April 6, 1786, aged 61

OLIVE Wife of
MATTHEW CALVERT,
died Nov 14 1701, aged 39

JOHN GREENWOOD
died March 21 1763, aged 57

MARGARET his Wife
died Feb 21, 1755, aged 48

WILLIAM MILLINGTON, fenior,
died Nov 4 1740, aged 6

MARY his Wife
died Feb 10, 1724

WILLIAM MILLINGTON, junior
died Aug 16, 1749, aged 46

MARY Wife of John Reeve
Daughter of
William and Mary Millington,
died July 14, 1764, aged 64

OBADIAH ARROWSMITH, fenior,
died Sept 26, 1697, aged 54

OLIVE his Wife
was buried May 26, 1701

THOMAS ARROWSMITH fenior,
died July 12, 1757, aged 68

ANNE his Wife
died Sept 26, 1738, aged 75

OBADIAH ARROWSMITH
died March 3, 1773, aged 52

THOMAS ARROWSMITH
died July 2, 1755 aged 49

SAMUEL GIBBS, fenior
died Dec 6, 17.. aged 50

SARAH his Wife
died Dec 1, 1755, aged 50

SARAH STEEL, Daughter of
SAMUEL GIBBS fenior
died Jan 4, 1765, aged 57

JOHN RICHARDSON
died Nov 12 1768, aged 4

RACHEL his Wife
died Aug 15 1757 aged 44

RICHARD their fon
died July 11, 176. aged ..

MARTHA their Daughter
died May .. 1769 aged 18

EDMUND LANE
died Nov 5, 1770, aged 60

SARAH his Wife
died Feb 7, 1783, aged 78

ROBERT their Son
died July 10 1783, aged 38

Mr RICHARD GRIFFITH
died Dec 6, 1718

MARY his Wife
died July 3, 1718

ANN their Daughter
died June 9, 1733

MARY their Daughter
died Nov 7, 1762

ROBERT GRIFFITH
died Jan 9, 1735

MARY his Wife
died April 5, 1710

MARY Wife of
WILLIAM TAGGART,
died Jan 31, 1753, aged 65

JONATHAN MILLINGTON
died Aug 27, 1733, aged 42

MARY his Wife
died March 16, 1762, aged 58

WILLIAM BECKETT
died March 8, 1764, aged 7

MARY BECKETT
died Nov 6, 1739

JOHN GURNEE senior
died Feb 24 1754, aged 78

JOHN GURNEE junior,
died Aug 24, 1737, aged 63

SARAH, Wife of JOHN GURNEE, jun
died Aug 9, 1708, aged 40

JOSEPH their Son
died March 20, 1728, aged 20

JARVIS AUSTIN, senior
died July 24 1716, aged 60

MARY Wife of JARVIS AUSTIN, senior,
died Jan 26, 1741, aged 70

JARVIS AUSTIN,
died Sep 3 1754, aged 71

ELIZABETH Wife of JARVIS AUSTIN,
died Aug 25, 1749, aged 50

WILLIAM Son of
JARVIS and MARY AUSTIN
died March 28 1741, aged 15

ROBERT Son of
JARVIS and ELIZABETH AUSTIN
died July 25, 1741, aged 15

GEORGE WHITE
died Feb 5, 1763, aged 78

JOSEPH CANTER, junior,
died Dec 26, 1755, aged 47

SARAH his Wife
died March 1, 1765, aged 75

JOHN MARTYN
died May 19, 1768, aged 31

WILLIAM NEWCOMBE
died Feb 21, 1766, aged 71

Four of his Children died Infants

SAMUEL NEWCOMBE
died June 24, 1764, aged 8

Arms, Gules, a Chevron engrailed
Ermine between three Fleurs de lis
Argent, for Croome

ROBERT CROOME
died Dec 7, 1740 aged 63

MARTHA Wife of JAMES CROOME,
died March 1, 1772, aged 64

MARY, Wife of JAMES HILL,
died Nov 15 1784, aged 75

JAMES CROOME
died June 6, 1776, aged 61

RACHEL, Daughter of
JAMES and MARTHA CROOME
died May 4 1754, aged 7

CHARLES SMITH
died Dec 2, 1750, aged 47

ANN SMITH, Widow
died June 27, 1754, aged 7

ROBERT CROOME
died Feb 27, 1779, aged 73

ANN his Wife
died Sept 21, 1781, aged 61

ANN their Daughter
died Oct 31, 1774, aged 25

JANE their Daughter
died June 5, 1777, aged 15

ROBERT HANCOCK, Gent
died June 20, 1776, aged 69

JAMES HANCOCK
died June 15, 1783, aged 57

GRACE his Wife
died July 17, 1767, aged 57

MARY FOXM
died April 26, 1764, aged 11

SUSANNA RUTTER
died in March 1762, aged 47

JOHN TEMMS
died Jan 1, 1737, aged 59

SARAH TEMMS
died April 6, 1776, aged 80

WILLIAM HINTON
died Jan, 1715

ELIZABETH his Wife
died

MARY his second Wife
died

FRANCIS HEWER
died Feb 6, 1727, aged 56

CATHARINE, Wife of
FRANCIS HEWER,
died March 8, 1705

SAMUEL HEWER
died June 7, 1747, aged 77

EDWARD WILLIAMS senior
died August 6, 1728, aged 62

MARY his Wife
died May 16, 1744, aged 61

RICHARD SHERLEY
died May 21, 1747

MARY his Wife
was buried Nov 1, 24

ROWLAND TAYLOR
died Oct 5, 1753, aged 82

MARY TAYLOR
died May 19, 1750, aged 76

ROWLAND their Son
died June 17, 1714, aged

SARAH MAY
died June 29, 1758, aged 8

ROWLAND TAYLOR junior,
died Jan 1 1765, aged 43

ROBERT SALISBURY
died May 7, 1750, aged 63

HENRY his Grandson
died an Infant

WINIFRED Wife of
RICHARD FLETCHER
died Nov 8, 1767, aged 75

RICHARD FLETCHER senior,
died July 22 1782, aged 8

JOHN EVANS
died March 8, 1743, aged 63

BETTY his Wife
died July 1765, aged 72

RICHARD WAIGHT, senior,
died Sept 15, 1760, aged 76

PETTY his Wife
died Dec 24, 1745, aged 70

RICHARD WAIGHT
died Oct 18, 1760, aged 61

THOMAS WAIGHT
died Oct 23, 1772, aged 56

JOHN WHITLEY
died July 12, 1774, aged 53

HENRY TIPPER
died Aug 28 1786, aged 49

RICHARD ALLAWAY
died May 1, 1744, aged 37

THOMAS ALLAWAY
died March 8, 176., aged 7.

SARAH Wife of
THOMAS ALLAWAY
died Jan 1, 1778, aged 69

JOHN BALDWIN
died April 7, 1781, aged 6.

RICHARD HILLIER Clothier,
of this Town
died Dec 10, 1726, aged 43

MARGARET his Daughter
died Aug 21, 1736 aged 23

HANNAH, Daughter of
RICHARD HILLIER,
and Wife of Mr JOHN ASHMEAD,
Citizen of Gloucester,
died Feb 4, 1735, aged 36

HANNAH Wife of
RICHARD HILLIER,
died Mar 28, 1767, aged 82

SUSANNA their Daughter
died July 9, 1773, aged 51

ANTHONY HILLIER
died June 3 1749, aged 55

HANNAH his Wife
died Jan 9, 17.., aged 45

GEORGE CHLAM
died May 2., 1777, aged 5.

LAURA his Wife
died July 28 1735, aged 4.

ANDREW TURNER
died Sept 1 17.., aged 6.

MARY, Wife of
JOHN CO..
died Aug .. 18, aged 54

JOHN EDWARDS the elder,
of Barton Farm,
died Feb 9 1722, aged 8.

ALTHEA his Wife
died Nov 5, 1727, aged 81

JOHN their Son
died Nov 26, 1748 aged 70

RACHEL his Wife
died July 5, 1749, aged 60

ANNE Wife of
WILLIAM CHANDLER,
died Dec 13, 1719 aged 70

ANN their Daughter
died Aug 6, 1737, aged 20

WILLIAM CHANDLER
died March 6, 1732 aged 74

JOHN STONE
died July 1, 1744, aged 58

ANNA MARIA his Wife
died Jan ., 1758

WILLIAM STONE
died Sept 1, 1749 aged 24

JOHN HAIKES
died Feb , 1721, aged 69

JANE his Wife
died March 12, 1740, aged 80

DANIEL MASTERS junior,
died May 1, 1745, aged 38

ANN his Wife
died March 2, 1782, aged 82

JAMES their Son
died Nov 1, 1761, aged 37

THOMAS FRYER,
of Berkeley,
died July 2, 1765, aged 57

RICHARD PARSONS
died Dec 19, 1787, aged 63

ELIZABETH his Wife
died Aug 20 1763 aged 3.

THOMAS CROSLEY
died Feb 20 1745, aged 75

MARTHA his Wife
died May 10, 1740, aged 77

THOMAS CROSSLEY, junior
died Feb 1756, aged 50

DANIEL DAVIS
died June 23, 1782, aged 36

ANN SPARKES
died Aug t , 17.., aged 6

EDMUND FEREBEE,
of Dursley,
died July 22 1628

EDMUND FEREBEE,
Mercer, of this Town
died 22, 1687

JOHN PARSLOW
died Dec 5 1733, aged ..

MARY his Wife
died Sept 8, 1769, aged 5.

WILLIAM CHERRINGTON,
died June 16 1787, aged 61

SARAH CHERRINGTON
died May 1, 1780

JOHN JACOBS
died Jan 16, 1719, aged 51

CATHARINE his Wife
died March 28, 1768 aged 6.

BETTY JACOBS
died Nov 19, 1770, aged 4.

JOHN GREEN
died March ., 1754, aged 65

ANN GREEN
died April 20, 17.5, aged 6.

JOHN GREEN
died March 2 18., aged 6

ANN his Wife
died Nov 11, 18.., aged 64

ELIZABETH Wife of
THOMAS VAISEY,
died March 3, 1..., aged 58

THOMAS VAISEY, senior,
died March 8, 1780 aged 91

THOMAS CHERRINGTON, Son of
WILLIAM and ANN CHERRINGTON,
and Grandson of
THOMAS and ELIZABETH VAISEY,
died July 13, 17.., aged 17

MARY Daughter of
THOMAS and ELIZABETH VAISEY
died April 11, 174., aged 14

ELIZABETH, Wife of
THOMAS STRONGE,
was interred in the Church yard of
Coln St Aldwin's
She died May 30, 1758, aged 25

MARY Daughter of
Thomas and Elizabeth Stronge,
died Nov 23, 1776, aged 18

MARY Wife of
THOMAS STRONGE
died April 15, 1749, aged 29

THOMAS STRONGE,
many Years Surgeon and Apothecary
of this Place,
died Feb. 6, 1779 aged 53 Years

WILLIAM CHERLEY
died Feb 20, 1769

MARGERY, Wife of
JAMES CLUTTERBUCK,
late of Exon,
died March 1 1694

THOMAS JOHNSON
died July 11 1759 aged

SUSANNA his Wife
died Jan 4, 1767, aged 67

HANNAH their Daughter
died Dec 11, 1777, aged 54

MARY, Wife of
WILLIAM JOHNSON,
died Nov 12, 1780, aged 44

ANNE their Daughter
died July 1775, aged 12

TIMOTHY LEWIS,
late of this Place, Gent
died Dec 19, 1779, aged 49

CHARLES HANBURY LEWIS,
Son of TIMOTHY LEWIS,
died Jan 5, 1782, aged 20

THOMAS JENKINS
died July 7, 1780, aged 57

THOMAS PAGET
died August 28, 1788, aged 45

ON HEAD STONES

	Died	Aged		Died	Aged
Joseph Robbins	15 Sept 1785	66	Michael Hinton	— Dec 1761	—
Thomas Pew senior	11 Jan 1762	62	Susanna his Wife	— Mar 1774	—
Solomon Carter	18 Dec 1782	80	Joseph Whitmore	13 Mar 1772	16
Sarah his Wife	16 July, 1772	65	Benjamin Berkeley	9 July, 1769	75
Mary, Daughter of Solomon Carter	22 May, 1755	26	Ann, Wife of Edmund Welch	25 Feb 1760	66
Cues Coates	4 Oct 1763	74	William Orne	3 Oct 1756	
John Moore	2 Oct 1764	67	Mary his Wife	21 Jan 1762	74
Mary Wife of George Winstone	15 Mar 1786	63	Ann, Wife of James Ludlow	7 Nov 1786	75
Richard Radway, senior	5 Nov 1766	66	Hannah, Wife of Samuel Gegg	4 Mar 1784	7
Mary his Wife	17 Mar 1768	67	Robert Archer	7 July, 1757	75
Richard Radway	1 Oct 1711		Martha his Wife	16 Dec 1764	75
Edith his Wife	— 1739		Henry Saunders	15 Jun 1740	
Charles Freeman	5 Nov 1738	49	Susanna his Wife	8 Apr 1754	
Ann Wife of James Paget	14 July, 1785	41	Mary, Wife of Thomas Deighton	29 Apr 1773	78
Elizabeth their Daughter	23 June, 1785	13	Mary, Wife of Nathaniel Deighton	6 Oct 1760	76
Henry Paget senior	22 Mar 1785	84	Nathaniel Deighton	30 Sept 1785	80
Catharine his Wife	4 June, 1766	65	Anthony Mills	14 Aug 1759	54
George Richardson	10 May, 1758	42	Olive his Wife	20 Jul 1758	75
Robert Ratcliff	28 May, 1758	56	Mary Wife of Richard Fryer	12 May, 1758	31
Susanna his Wife	29 May, 1766	—	William, Son of Nathaniel and Hester Orton	21 Sep 1786	20
Priscilla Wife of Lawrence Edmunds	6 Jan 1769	49	Sarah their Daughter	21 Nov 1756	9
Lawrence their Son	4 Mar 1776	16	Sarah, Wife of Thomas Orton	29 June, 1784	8
Samuel Arundel	20 Mar 1774	74	Mary, Wife of John Athley and Daughter of Thomas Push	1 Oct 1772	49
Sarah his Wife	6 June, 1765	61	William Hatch, senior	27 Oct 1757	65
John their Son	12 Nov 1755	23	Ann his Wife	17 May, 1740	42
Elizabeth Wife of John Pew	9 May, 1771	50	Ann Sollice	— Jun 1755	26
Joseph Burton, senior	25 Sept 1777	50	Judith his Wife	7 June, 1765	76
Jane, Wife of William Lawrence	26 Feb 1776	80	Robert, Son of William and Ann Morie	24 Oct 1761	21
Mary their Daughter	16 Oct 1776	40	Ann, Wife of Joseph Tustin	21 May, 1757	46
George Doudn	10 Dec 1765	45	Susanna, Daughter of John and Jane Moysey	19 Nov 1766	24
William Lawrence	2 Apr 1774	45	Henry Ursell	27 Oct 1759	62
Nathaniel Merrett	7 Apr 1721	—	Elizabeth his Wife	11 Mar 1765	75
Sarah his Wife	27 Oct 1725	—	John Blake	11 Oct 1755	39
Samuel Carter	15 Aug 1766	65	Susanna, Wife of John Tuey	22 Mar 1749	26
Mary his Wife	30 Oct 1759	64	Gertrude their Daughter	6 Jul 1777	18
John Norris	7 Aug 1748	46	Jane their Daughter	26 Aug 1778	2
John Harding	26 Feb 1719		Gertrude, Wife of John Tully	18 Jan 1773	60
Timothy Stevens, senior	3 Apr 1744	64	Henry Ursell	12 May, 1785	72
Elizabeth his Wife	10 Feb 1746	69	Mary his Wife	12 Oct 1757	16
Betty, Wife of William Parsons	14 Dec 1774	55	William Stiles	12 Jan 1772	
Thomas Selby	12 Nov 1743	61	Sarah his Wife	22 Jun 1757	
Elizabeth his Wife	4 Feb 1758	80	Edward Combes	3 Jun 1742	
Mary Wife of Timothy Stevens	27 Apr 1774	29	Ann his Wife	19 Jul 1774	85
Robert Kilmister	3 Dec 1753	82	John Fryer	15 Jun 1757	17
Sarah his Wife	24 Apr 1715	42	Benjamin Baldwin	1 Jun 1754	
Joseph Carpenter	1 Jun 1783	58	Sarah Newcombe	6 Apr 1764	54
Thomas Carpenter	1 June, 1783	56	Elizabeth, Wife of James Smith	9 Mar 1751	63
Mary Wife of Thomas Carpenter	23 Aug 1765	28			
Richard Jacobs	12 Nov 1755	73			
Ann his Wife	18 Aug 1759	37			

JNO. CLAPTON

CLAPTON.

OF this Parish little can be said   It lies upon an Eminence in the lower Division of the Hundred of *Slaughter*, five Miles from *Stow* on the South weft, the fame Diftance in the oppofite Direction from *Northleach*, and twenty-three Eaftward from GLOUCESTER

The Soil is chiefly light, about 700 Acres, 100 of which are commonable, and the whole applied in equal Portions to Arable and Pafture

The Manor is diftinctly fpecified in Domefday Book   In the middle Centuries it was held by the Family of BRUGGE, or BRUCES, and was included in that of *Bourton on the Water*.   The Family of WOODMAN have long poffeffed it

Being a Chapel of Eafe to *Bourton*, moft of the Church Offices are performed there   A fmall Chancel was erected in 1670, and dedicated to *St. James*, in which only a Right of Sepulture is claimed by a few Families

The Property of the Parish is divided between the Families of WOODMAN, STEVENS, and WISE

No Benefactions to the Poor

PRESENT LORD OF THE MANOR,
PHILIP WOODMAN, ESQ.

There does not appear to have been any Perfon fummoned from this Place by the Heralds in 1682 and 168

It is conjectured that the Number of Inhabitants does not exceed 120, who are moftly regiftered at *Bourton*

INSCRIPTIONS IN THE CHAPEL.

IN THE CHANCEL

ON FLAT STONES.

JOHN WOODMAN
was buried April 29, 1700, aged 74.

PHILIP WOODMAN
died Auguft 15, 1773, aged 46

ANN, the Wife of PHILIP WOODMAN,
was buried Oct 25, 1699, aged 36

MARY KEARST, Wife of PHILIP KEARST,
died Jun 27, 1766, aged 53

IN THE NAVE

PRISCILLA WOODMAN,
Wife of PHILIP WOODMAN,
died Sept 15, 1763, aged 36

PHILIP, Son of PHILIP WOODMAN,
was buried Oct 3, 1693, aged 91

JOHN, Son of PHILIP and PRISCILLA WOODMAN,
died Nov 19, 1751, aged 7 Months

MARY, Wife of JOHN WISE,
died Dec 25, 1723, aged 51

JOHN WISE, fenior,
died May 28, 1756, aged 71

CATHARINE fecond Wife of
JOHN WISE Yeoman, of this Parish,
died Auguft 20, 1773, aged 76

JOANNA, Daughter of John and CATHARINE WISE,
died May 13, 1711, aged 5 Years, 3 Months
and 18 Days

MARY, Daughter of John and CATHARINE WISE,
died May 26, 1773, aged 44

JOANNA, Daughter of John and ELIZABETH WISE,
died Dec 26, 1794, in the 9th Year of her Age

STEPHEN REYNOLDS
died July 29, 1742, aged 5

THE NORTHERN DOOR-WAY

LXXI. CLEEVE EPISCOPI,
OR
BISHOP'S CLEEVE,

IS a Parish of extraordinary Extent and Fertility, the chief of its own Hundred, in the great Vale of Eafham. It is diftant from *Cheltenham* four Miles on the North, five South from *Tewkefbury*, and from *Glocefter* eleven on the North eaft

The Extent is feven Miles, the wideft part lefs than five, of a ftrong mixed Soil of Sand and Clay Some Hundred Acres of common Fields lie on the Summit and Acclivities of that Ridge of Hills which, breaking into bare Rock, from their Height and Whitenefs, are commonly called "*Cleeve Clouds*, and afford excellent Pafturage for Sheep Grain of the beft Qualities are produced by the arable Lands, which greatly exceed the others A fmall Brook forms a Boundary to this Parifh in its Courfe to the Carrot

To the Benefice, which is rectorial, in the Deanery of *Winchcombe*, are annexed very fingular Privi leges, an Exemption from Archidiaconal Vifitation, and from Epifcopal, excepting in every third Year, and a Power of granting Adminiftrations and recording Wills, reftricted to the fine a Parifh The Rec tory belonged to the See of *Worcefter* prior to the CONQUEROR's Survey In 1215, 16 King John, WALTER DE GRAY*, then Bifhop, appropriated it to the Prior and Convent of *Worcefter*, who, in the fame Year, leafed out the Tythes for forty Marks, and prefented ROBERT, a Monk, to the Vicarage GODFREY GIFFARD, Bifhop in 1269, 44 HENRY III, procured from Pope   this Impropri ation for the Term of his Life Bifhop CARPENTER †, in 1464, joining with WILLIAM CANNING, the

---

* 1215 WALTERUS DE GRAY, Epifc *Wigorn* dedit Priori & Conventui ecclefiam de *Clee* juxta *Lafham*, in proprios Ufus Reddidimus in firmam *Clevam* pro xl Marcis Dedimus ROBERTO Vicariam de *Clee*

WHARTON, Anglia Sacra, vol I pp 472 473

† GODWINI P afulcs

magnificent

munificent Mayor of *Briſtol*, in the Re eſtabliſhment of the College of *Weſtbury upon Trim* in this County, give certain of the Tythes as the Corps of a Prebend there, with the Advowſon, to the Vicarige   Upon the Suppreſſion the Great Tythes were reſtored, and the Privileges formerly exerciſed by the Biſhop confirmed to the Rectors

The Church, dedicated to St *Michael*, conſiſts of a Nave, Tranſept, and two Aiſles, in the moſt perfect Saxon Style   a Gothic Aiſle has been ſubſequently added   The Nave is divided from the Aiſles by heavy round Arches, which mark the Architecture much uſed in the Reign of HENRY III, the external Ornaments of the Door Cafes, and the whole Weſtern Front, ſeem to allow a Conjecture that it was built by the Abbey of *Worceſter*, when firſt granted them by the Biſhops   In 1696 the Spire fell on the Chancel, and cauſed ſuch Dilapidation as to leave us ignorant of their original Form   the whole Reparation amounted to 770*l* and was completed in 1700   In the Inſide of the Church are Specimens of the early Norman Mouldings, particularly in an Arcade, under which is extended a large Figure, with the Diſtinctions of a Knight Templar, erroneouſly ſuppoſed to repreſent GILBERT " the bold" Earl of CLARE and HEREFORD *.

The Rectory houſe is very ancient and ſpacious, and has received many Improvements, both of Taſte and Convenience, from the preſent Incumbent, in whom likewiſe the Advowſon is veſted.

With the Benefice, the Church of *Worceſter* was poſſeſſed of the Manor, but, in 1207, it was purchaſed of King JOHN by RANDULPHUS the Prior, with three others, for 100 Marks, which were afterward remitted by the King towards the Reparation of the Monaſtery †   Queen ELIZABETH, in the firſt Year of her Reign, 1558, reſumed it from the See, and in 1604, 2 JAMES I it was granted to PETER VAN LORE   The late Sir WILLIAM STRACHAN, a Baronet, of *Nova Scotia*, inherited it from his Father, and ſold it before his Death in 1776

---

* 1295 Die 7 Decembris, GILBERTUS de *Clare & Hereſia* Comes, obiit, & die 22° apud *Theokesbury*, cum patribus ſuis, eum GODFRIDUS Epiſcopus ſepelivit   WHARTON, Ang Sac vol I p 517

† " Acceſſit ad Regem RANDULPHUS, tunc Prior, rogans quatenus ei Libertat in in quatuor Maneriis donaret *Lindregge*, H " *and Stoke*, & *Cira*   Qui libertate donatâ & regali ſigno confirmati, centum etiam Marcas quas ei pro Libertate illa red " dere tenebamur ad Chriſtum & Othemas noſtras relaxandas, condonavit '   Ibid vol I p 480

The Temporalitie   Cure pertaining to the See of *Worceſter* were valued in the Reign of EDW I at 13/ 16 per annum In 1535, 26 HEN VIII at 5// 10s 9d including all its Dependencies   It is of the higheſt Valuation in the King's book Val U 6/

(i)

Of the four Hamlets, befide the Townfhip of *Cleeve*, the moft worthy Notice is

1 *Southam*, which obtained that Name from the Point of its Situation from the Church   This Manor was held of the Church of *Worcefter* by the DE BOHUNS, Earls of *Hereford*, for feveral Defcents, was inherited by the STAFFORDS, Dukes of *Buckingham*, and having merged in the Dutchy of *Lancafter*, was granted by King JAMES in 1608 to ROBERT CECIL, Earl of *Salisbury*, who in October 1609 fold all his Intereft in *Southam* to RICHARD DE LA BERE, of *Lincoln's Inn*, Efq. who dying without Iffue in 1635, left KINARD DE LA BERY of *Kinnerfley*, co *Hereford*, his Heir   The direct male Line of this venerable Family failing in KINARD DE LA BERE, Efq in 1735 he bequeathed this Manor and Eftate to his Nephew WILLIAM BAGHOTT, of *Prefbury*, Efq who, in purfuance of his Uncle's Will, affumed the Surname and Arms of DE LA BERE, and is fucceeded by his eldeft Son *

The very ancient Manfion at *Southam* was originally detached from the Manor, it is certainly the oldeft Dwelling-houfe in this County, and has been declared by able Antiquaries to be of as long ftanding, and to retain more of the original Form than any in the Kingdom   It is conftructed with two Stories only, without a Parapet   KINARD DE LA BERE, Efq married ELLEN, Daughter of Sir JOHN HUDDLESTONE, of *Melholme Caftle* in *Cumberland*, who built this Houfe, and was Sheriff of this County in 1501, 16 HEN VII by whom he was much refpected, and by that Connection the Family firft became poffeffed of it   Of Situation † it has fufficient Advantages, in Front an expanded Profpect of the Vale, clofed by the *Malvern Hills*, on the other Side, the moft picturefque Scenery of Woodland on the Bafe of the great Cliff, which rifes 630 Feet of perpendicular Height   Several of the Apartments deferve particular Inveftigation, one of the Halls, is paved with painted Bricks, the greater Part of which were removed from *Hayles* Abbey.   Upon thefe, frequently repeated are thefe Arms, Devices, and Names 1 Argent, a Lion rampant crowned Or, within a bordure Sable bezantee; RICHARD Earl of CORNWALL 2 Or, an Eagle difplayed Sable, borne by him as King of the ROMANS, the Founder of *Hayles* 3 ﬅel, and a Tun, for Abbot MILLION 4 Repeated, with the Pontificals. 5 Abbot ﬔorb 6 ﬓ. ﬖ ﬗ ﬕtephen ﬓagar, the laft Abbot 7 a Fefs humetee between fix Croffes botonne 8 *France* and *England*, with the Rofe of *Lancafter*, and Porteullis, King HENRY VII 9 An Eagle with two Necks Parti per Pale Sable and Ermine, GOODMAN 10 Quarterly, 1ft and 4th, Azure, a Bend Argent, cottifed Or, between fix Martlets of the laft, DE LA BERE, 2d and 3d, Gules, a Frett Argent, HUDDLESTONE.

Upon Efcutcheons affixed to a Chimney Piece of curious Gothic carving in Wood, the fubjoined Coats, quarterly of 8 1 DE LA BERE 2 Gules, a Chief counter compo'e Or and Azure, over all a Bend Argent 3 Azure, a Lion rampant crufule Argent, BREAUS, of *Gowr* 4 Paly of fix Argent and Sable, over all four Bars Gules, DE BARRY 5 Chequy Gules and Or, a Fefs Ermine, TURBERVYLE 6 Gules, three Chevronels Argent, JUSTIN AP GWRGANT 7 Paly of fix Or and Azure, over all a Bend Gules, PEMBRUGI. 8 Argent, two Bendlets and a Cinquefoil in Chief Gules   On fmall Efcutcheons 1 DE LA BERE, impaling, Gules, a Bend Ermine, for WALWEYNE 2 DE LA BERE, impaling HUDDLESTONE   In the Windows the Arms and Cognizance of King HENRY VII 2 Argent, a Bend between two Mullets pierced Sable, PIER   In the Apartments above, the fame are repeated with HUDDLESTONE and SEYMOUR   Painted in the Window of the great Parlour the quartered Efcutcheon of the Family, with the Cognizance granted them by EDWARD the Black Prince   Here too are fome handfome Portraits of the higheft Antiquity and Merit ‡   This is indeed one of the very few of the capital Refidences of the ancient Gentry, which have withftood the Decays of Time and Fortune, and remains flourifhing and unimpaired.

Haymes,

---

* The knightly Family of DE LA BERE accompanied the victorious WILLIAM, and obtained a Settlement at *Aunnefley*, co *Hereford* where they refided in great Splendour   CAMDEN, edit GIBSON, vol I p. 493   In the Courfe of the intermediate Century they were connected with the Families of DE HEVYN, BRIAN of *Brompton*, HARLEY, PEMBRUGE, BASON of *Kilpntle*, GAMAGE, PLUCANET, LUTHERVILE, ABRAHALL, DE BARRY, by whom, from the DE BOHUNE Earls of *Hereford*, through the Latimers, SCUDAMORE, and HUDDLESTONE, from which faid Connection they were induced to migrate into this County and to fettle at *Southam*   In 1433 Sir R DE LA BERE, Knight, with JOHN and RICHARD his Sons, were fummoned Knights of the County of *Hereford*   In 9 HEN III and from the 35th to 45th and in the 50th 8 RICH II and 19th, 8 HEN V 19 EDW IV 1 RICH III 8 HEN VII 2 HEN VIII the Sheriffs of that Province were fupplied from this Family   It fees Vomities, pp 44 45   In 1441 JOHN DE LA BERE, Dean of *Wells*, was confecrated Bifhop of St *David's*

† The accurate LELAND mentions *Southam* twice in the Courfe of his Itinerary   "Here dwelleth Sir JOHN HODLESTON, and "hath buildid a pretty Manour Place   He boughte the Land of one GOODMAN"—" *Southam* longd to one GOODMAN, now to "HUDDLESTON"   Vol VIII p 34   It is therefore evident that Sir JOHN HUDDLESTON, of *Melholme Caftle* in the County of *Cumberland* was the firft Builder, and that the Houfe was then internally fitted up in the Style in which it is now preferved   The View of it by KIP in Sir R ATKYNS's Hiftory is not faithful, feveral Alterations being there inferted, which were never effected

‡ The minuteft Defcription of thefe would require no Apology, we fhall not therefore hefitate to attempt it

No 1   A Man of advanced Age, holding a Halbert or ftaff of Office, his Chapeau ornamented with Jewels, in the Corner the Arms quarterly, ift, Chequy Argent and Azure, a Chief Gules   PALMER 2d, Argent three Herons Sable HERON, 3d, Argent, a Chev on between three Lions Heads erafed Gules   GARSHALL   4th, Quarterly, Argent and Sable, on a Bend Gules, three Heraldic Fleurs de lis of the firft   ROCLIFFE   WILLIAM PALMER, one of the Gentlemen Penfioners to King HENRY VIII and Porter of *Calais* ob S P 15   painted probably by ANDREW WRIGHT, then Serjeant Painter   WARTON, vol I p 99

No   King EDWARD the Sixth half Length Picture when very young, in a crimfon Robe of Sattin ermined, by HANS HOLBEIN

No 3   The fame, a full Length, when older   The Ground of this curious Portrait is formed by two Doric Pillars of Marble and a Curtain of green Damafk   The Drefs, a very ftiff Brown Brocade lined at the Edges of the Cloak   Upon the Left

5 G2   He

Haymes, in the Tything of *Southam,* was vested for several Centuries in the Family of LORANGE, who were first settled there in the Reign of EDWARD the Second, and claimed it as a distinct Manor. The last of this Family having been slain at *Cirencester* in 1688, the Estate was sold to Serjeant GOODINGE, *Custos Brevium* in the Court of *King's Bench.* It afterwards passed to the Family of STRACHAN, and was re-sold to THORNILOE, of *Worcester,* the present Possessor.

An elegant Mansion-house was built by Sir WILLIAM STRACHAN, which in a few Years was levelled with the Ground; and the Materials sold. *Brockhampton* is likewise included in this District

2. *Gotherington* is a Hamlet and exempted Manor, situate on the Hill. It was once appendant to the Priory of *St Augustine* in *Bristol.*

3 *Stoke Archer,* or commonly *Orchard,* lies South-westward of the Church, and has a small Part in the Hundred of *Tewkesbury.* It was many Centuries the Property of the BRUGGES, or BRYDGES, Barons CHANDOS of *Sudley,* the Manor and Estate is now vested in the Family of ROGERS, of *Dowdeswell.* The Chapel annexed to *Cleeve* is an inconsiderable Building.

4 *Woodmancote,* in the South-east Direction

Vestiges of military Transactions abound on the Hill, the Extremity of which is fortified by a deep Vallation of some Furlongs Extent. Tumuli are also frequent, one of which on Investigation was found to enclose a vast Quantity of human Bones, not entirely consumed, mixed with Earth of a very fine Quality. The general Supposition is in Favour of their having been raised in Consequence of an Engagement between the *Saxons* and *Danes*

B E N E F A C T I O N S.

An Acre of Arable Land, the annual Produce of which is 10s was given by some Person unknown, and which, according to the best Knowledge in being, was to be distributed amongst such poor Widows of the Township of *Cleeve* as do not receive Relief from the Overseers.

the Pillars, these three Inscriptions in English, Greek, and Latin, which seem to be a Version of the same Thought, and to have been long after, from the Style of their Composition;

" Arte hath not miste, but lively exprest,
The Shape of *England's* Treasur,
Yet unexprest, remaineth the beste,
Vertues above all Mesur "

The Greek is too imperfect for Transcription with Accuracy

" Exprimit Anglorum *Decus* en Pictura, sed illa
Munera virtutum nulla pictura dabit "

The following Proofs are adduced in Support of the originality of these Portraits

JANE SEYMOUR, the Wife of Sir J HUDDLESTONE, was the Aunt of the Queen of those Names, and ELLEN, the Wife of KINARD DE LA BERE, her first Cousin, beside this, PALMER (the first mentioned) was a Gentleman of the Houshold during the short Reign of King EDWARD VI

No 4, A Half length Figure of a Lady, remarkably fair, with bright auburn Hair, contemplating, a Book, an Urn on the Table, Dress, crimson Satin, sleeves flashed and puffed with white; to the Necklace of Gold the Medallion of a Man is ap pendant From the minute Description of her Person given by Sir T MORE, and DRAYTON in his " Heroical Epistles," this Portrait has been conjectured to be of JANE SHORE, an original of whom is preserved in the Provost's Lodgings at *Eton* College

No 5 GILES PALMER, Esq of *Lemington,* co *Warwick,* maternal Grandfather of Sir THOMAS OVERBURY, by Sir ANTONIO MORE

No 6 Sir THOMAS OVERBURY, Half length, an undoubted Original, by CORN JANSEN

No 7 The Wife of WILLIAM HOBBY, Esq the Daughter of JOHN HODGKINS, to whom the Abbey of *Hayles* was granted by Queen ELIZABETH

No 8 Her Daughter Wife, 1st of Sir NEVIL POOLE, 2dly, R. DE LA BERE, Esq 1622, æt. 33 These Portraits have the Peculiarity of Rings on the Thumbs of each

No 9 Sir JOHN HALES, of the *White Friars* in *Coventry,* of whom see DUGDALE's *Warwickshire,* p 123

No 10. DOROTHY his Daughter, Wife of MICHAEL RUTTER, Esq of *Quenton* in this County, ob 1662, æt. 31 An En graving taken from this Picture, was prefixed to a Sermon preached at her Funeral, by GILES OLDISWORTH, Rector of *Hourton on the Hill,* of which, and her Character, see GRANGER's Biog vol IV p 185.

No 11 Sir ROBERT PYE, a Colonel in the Parliament's Service, Half length in Armour, with a Medallion of General Lord ESSEX suspended by a Gold Chain See NOBLE's CROMWELL, vol II p 136

No 12 JOAN, Daughter of Sir JOHN HALES, of *Coventry,* and Wife of KINARD DE LA BERE, Esq by LELY

No 13 JOHN DE LA BERE her Son, by LELY

No 14 MARY, Daughter of Sir JOHN HALES, by LILY

No 15 JOHN STEPHENS, Esq of *Lypiate,* Recorder of *Bristol,* ob 1679, by LELY

No. 16 JOHN NEALE Esq of *Ailesly* and of *Aldborough Hatch,* co *Essex*

No 17 KINARD DE LA BERE Esq Knight of the Shire for this County from 1722 to 1727

No 18 HESTER his Wife, Coheir of JOHN NEALE

No 19 EDWARD STEPHENS, by DAHL Son of THOMAS STEPHENS, Esq of *Sodbury,* by ANN his Wife, the other Co he r See Memoirs of the NEALES NOBLE's CROMWELL, vol II p 36

There is sufficient Ground for Conjecture through what Families these Portraits have passed before they formed a Collection at *Southam* The two of King EDWARD the Sixth, and JANE SHORE, were probably the Property of Sir JOHN HUDDLESTONE, the Founder of the House, whose Connection with the SEYMOURS is already proved Those of the PALMERS, Sir THOMAS OVER BURY, and the RUTTERS, belonged to Sir JOHN HALES and, with his own Portrait, were brought to *Southam,* in Consequence of the Marriage of KINARD DE LA BERE and JOAN his Daughter, in 1650. The Intermarriages of the Families of NEALE, STEPHENS, and DE LA BERE, readily account for the Introduction of the other Portraits

INCUMBENTS

INCUMBENTS.	PATRONS.	INCUMBENTS.	PATRONS
1215 Robert,	Priory of Worcester	1672 Edm Bedingfield, M.A	Robert Cooke, Efq.
* * * * * * *	* * * * * *	1695 Robert Cooke, M A	Edmund Cooke, Efq.
1460 ————,	College of Weftbury.	1709 James Uvedale, M A	Rob. Uvedale, LL.D
1517 John Cleymond *, B D	Richard Fox. Bifhop of Winchefter.	1737 Francis Fitz-Edwards, M. A	Matth Lambe, Efq
1537 Seth Holland,	————,	1754 James Monteath,	Robert Coke, Earl of Leicefter
1548 John Parkhurft†, D.D	————.		
1574 Thomas Turner,		1756 William Reid, M.A.	David Reid, Efq.
1593 Peter Cockes,	Edm Hutchins, Efq	1778 Samuel Pickering, M A.	James Stuart Monteath, for Eliz. Reid, Widow
—— Robert Stubbes,	Voluorern Smith, M.D		
1612 Timothy Gates ‡,			
1660 Will Nicholfon ‡, D.D.	————.		

PRESENT PROPRIETORS OF THE MANORS.

Of *Cleve*,
—— THORNILOE, Spinfter.

Of *Stoke Archer*,
WILLIAM ROGERS, Esq

Of *Southam*,
THOMAS BAGHOTT DE LA BERE, Esq.

Of *Gotherington*,
Right Honourable WILLIAM Lord CRAVEN.

The Perfons fummoned from this Parifh and its Hamlets by the Heralds in 1682 and 1683, were

John De la Bere, Efq
Kinard De la Bere, Efq.
Thomas Lorange, Efq.
John Surman, Gent

Edmund Bedingfield, M A
Henry Collet, Gent
Thomas Holland, Gent
Francis Baker, Gent.

At the Election in 1776, Seventy-two Freeholders polled from this Parifh and its Hamlets.

The firft Date in the Regifter, which has been fairly kept, occurs in 1563

ANNUAL ACCOUNT OF MARRIAGES, BIRTHS, AND BURIALS, IN THIS PARISH

A.D.	Mar	Bir	Bur.	A.D	Mar.	Bir	Bur	A D	Mar	Bir	Bur	A.D	Mar	Bir	Bur.
				1786	6	32	24	1791				1796			
1782	5	46	27	1787	8	35	23	1792				1797			
1783	6	30	27	1788	12	34	19	1793				1798			
1784	8	34	21	1789				1794				1799			
1785	4	33	37	1790				1795				1800			

MONUMENTS IN THE CHURCH.

IN THE GOTHIC AISLE

A VERY SUMPTUOUS MURAL MONUMENT, CONSISTING OF A COVE, SUPPORTED ON EACH SIDE BY DOUBLE CORINTHIAN COLUMNS OF ALABASTER, FINISHED WITH PYRAMIDS, AND THE BASES EMBELLISHED WITH FIGURES OF THE CARDINAL VIRTUES IN BASSO RELIEVO   WITHIN THE COVE IS A TABLET UNINSCRIBED   BEFORE THIS, UPON A LARGE ALTAR TOMB, ARE THE EFFIGIES OF A MAN IN A SIR JEAN'S HABIT, AND A WOMAN IN THE DRESS OF THE TIMES   AROUND, ON SEPARATE ESCUTCHEONS, AND COLLECTIVELY UPON ONE, THE FOLLOWING ARMS

1 Azure, a Bend Argent, cottifed Or, between fix Martlets of the laft, for DE LA BERE   2 Gules, a Chief componè Or and Azure, over all a Bend Argent, for   . 3. Azure, a Lion rampant femee Crofs Crofflets Argent, BREAUS of Gower   4 Gules, on a Chief Argent, three Martlets Sable, for CHAPERNOUR   5 Paly, of fix Argent and Sable, over all four Bars Gules, for DE BARRY. 6. Paly, of fix Or and Azure, over all a Bend Gules, for PEMBRUGE   7 Checquy Gules and Or, a Fefs Ermine, for TURBERVYLE. 8 Azure, a Fefs unde, between fix Dolphins nayant Argent, for NEWMAN   9 Argent, two Bendlets and a Cinquefoil in Chief Gules, for   .

---

* JOHN CLEYMON born in Lancafhire, 1457, elected Prefident of *Magdalen College, Oxford*, in 1504, appointed Prefident of *Corpus Chrifti College*, and Rector of *Bifhop's Cleeve*, by the Founder Bifhop Fox, 1516, died Nov 19, 1537, and was buried in the Chapel of that College   In 1536 he founded certain Exhibitions in *Brazen Nofe College*, the Scholars of which are called CLEYMONDINES, one of which is eligible from *Bifhop's Cleeve*, co. GLOUCESTER   See Wood's Athen & Antiq Oxford, edit GUTCH, PP 315, 358, 395
† Confecrated Bifhop of *Norwich* in 1560
‡ Confecrated Bifhop of GLOUCESTER in 1660
‡ Memorials for COCKS, TURNER, and GATES, were deftroyed by the Dilapidations in 1696.

ON

ON SEPARATE ESCUTCHEONS

1. DE LA BERE,—impaling, Gules, a Bend Ermine, for WALWEYNE. 2 DE LA BERE,—impaling, Gules, a Fret Argent, for HUDDLESTON. 3 DE LA BERE;—impaling, quarterly, 1st and 4th, NEWMAN, 2d and 3d, Argent, two Bendlets and a Cinquefoil in Chief Gules, for . . . *

A CUMBENT FIGURE IN THE HABIT OF A NUN, FORMERLY PAINTED, SOME GOTHIC CHARACTERS REMAIN, SCARCELY LEGIBLE, AROUND THE SLAB †.

ON A LARGE BLUE FLAT STONE, AROUND THE EFFIGY OF A KNIGHT, WERE THESE ARMS AND INSCRIPTION, NOW DESTROYED

Three Piles meeting in Base, for BRYAN.

𝕬𝖗𝖒𝖎𝖌𝖊𝖗, 𝖖𝖚𝖎 𝖔𝖇𝖎𝖎𝖙 𝖚𝖓𝖉𝖊𝖈𝖎𝖒𝖔 𝖉𝖎𝖊 𝕸𝖊𝖓𝖘𝖎𝖘 𝕵𝖚𝖑𝖎𝖎, 𝕸𝕮𝕮𝕮𝕷𝕿𝕿𝕲. 𝕮𝖚𝖏' 𝖆'𝖊 𝖕'𝖕𝖎𝖈𝖎𝖊𝖙' 𝕯𝖊𝖚𝖘 𝕬𝖒𝖊𝖓.

INSCRIPTIONS IN THE CHURCH.

IN THE CHANCEL.

ON A LARGE MURAL MONUMENT

Arms, Ermine, an Eagle displayed Gules, armed Or, for BEDINGFIELD

H S I
EDMUNDUS BEDINGFIELD,
Ex æde Christi universitate Oxonii,
Olim alumnus & socius,
Ecclesiæ hujus parochialis rector,
Vir clarus ingenio;
In Divinis Scripturis eruditus,
Ecclesiæ Anglicanæ & fidei orthodoxæ
Assertor strenuus;
Et in extremis ecclesiæ miseriis et
Maxime fidus,
Concionator etiam ad ultimum assiduus,
In cujus memoriam
Optimo marito mœstissima conjux
Hoc monumentum posuit,
Obiit Feb 14, anno æræ Christianæ 1695,
sub anno ætatis suæ 55.
Duas habuit uxores,
Quæ juxta sitæ sunt.

ON TWO TABLETS ADJOINING

Arms, Azure, a Chevron between three Mullets Or, for CHETWIND.

MARIA CHETWIND,
in agro Staffordiensi,
Ob Mar 31, 1674

Arms, Ermine, a Cross engrailed Gules, for NORWOOD

CATHARINA NORWOOD,
Hujusce Comitatus,
Ob. Nov 14, 1711.

ON A SQUARE TABLET

In memoriam
JANÆ nuper uxoris JOHANNIS REED,
de Mitton, Armigeri,
filiæ & Cohæredis GEORGII HUNTLY,
de Frocester, Equitis Aurati
RICHARDUS REED, de Lugwardine,
in Comit Herefordiensis, Armigeri,
ex Mandato ultimo ELIANORÆ, Uxor'
suæ Filiæ, & Hæredis, predictorum
JOHANNIS & JANÆ posuit,
quæ JANA obiit in Puerperio, . die
. . . . . Anno Dom 1630.

ON FLAT STONES

Mr TIMOTHY GATES
was here interred Jan 22, 1660,
who had been Parson of Cleeve
neer upon 49 Years.

Arms, a Fret and Chief.

H S I
GULIELMUS CURWEN, Artium Magister,
Et Ecclesiæ etiam Anglicanæ &
Fidei Orthodoxæ
Assertor strenuus
Obiit Vir desideratus
24 die Martii,
Anno { Dom 1708-9,
{ Æt 62.

Here was buried the Body
of JOHN WETSON, M A.
and Curate Ob Sept 15,
anno Domini 1632.

---

* This Monument was erected by MARGARET, Daughter of JOHN NEWMAN, of Billington in the County of Worcester Gen the Relict of RICHARD DE LA BERE, of Southam, Esq who died in 1635, at the Expence of nearly 400l The Sculpture is in the boldest Style of that Age
† Of the Design of this Figure, a satisfactory Account cannot be easily given It is certainly in the Habit of a Religious; and was removed from Southam

Arms, a Cross Moline,—impaling, Checquy, in Chief a Rose

H S F
JACOBUS UVEDALE, A M
Hujus Ecclesiæ Rector digniſſimus,
Sacræ Scripturæ
Pro ſumma ſua Doctrina
Fidus Interpres,
Concionator
Gravis & diſertus,
Eximia erga Deum pietate,
Benevolentia erga omnes prope ſingulari,
Tanta erga Pauperes Charitate,
Ut Domus ejus
ΠΑΥΣΟΧΛΟΥ
Videretur
Obiit 27 die Martii, Anno Dom. 1737,
ætatis 54

Arms, Sable, a Chevron between three Stag's Attires fixed to the Scalps, Argent, for COCKS

Hic jacet
JOHANNES COCKS, nuper
Commenſalis Collegii
Pembrochiæ Oxon
Filius natu maximus JOHANNIS COCKS,
de Woodmancoat in hac Parochia, Generoſi,
Optime ſpei juvenis,
Natus XV kal Aprilis,
Anno Dom MDCCIV,
Donatus Idibus Decemb
A ino Dom. MDCCXXIV.

In Memory of JOHN COCKS, ſenior,
of Woodmancoat in this Pariſh, Gent
who departed this Life the 7th Day
of April, 1729, aged 60 Years.

And of MARY his beloved Wife,
who died Sept 25, 1746, in the
74th Year of her Age

JOHN FREEMAN, late of
Longwood in this Pariſh, Gent
died Dec 24, 1752, in the 85th Year of his Age

THOMAS MASTER, Gent.
died Nov 19, 1724, aged 71.

THOMAS his Son
died Jan 5, aged 26.

WILLIAM his Son died an Infant

THOMAS MASTER,
the Son of THOMAS MASTER,
of Woodmancoat in this Pariſh,
died March 29, 1754, aged 33

IN THE SOUTH TRANSEPT

ON A PLAIN TABLET

To the Memory of
THOMAS BEALE, Eſq
late of Swindon in this County,
who departed this Life
Aug 30, 1782, aged 48

Here lye the Bodys of THOMAS COCKS,
of Biſhop's Cleeve in the County of Gloucester, Eſq
and of ELIZABETH HOLLAND,
Daughter of ROGER HOLLAND,
of Dalton in Lancaſhire, his Wife.
He was buried Nov 20, 1601,
and ſhe the 26th Dec
Both lived to old Age, bleſſed with
ten Sons and ſix Daughters,
all the Sons living to be Men many
Years before the deceaſe of their Parents

THOMAS BEALE, ſenior,
died Dec 28, 1761, aged 48

MARY his Wife
died Nov 7, 1727, aged 52

JOHN, Son of THOMAS and MARY BEALE,
died Auguſt 12, 1742, aged 15

RICHARD STRATFORD
Son of THOMAS and MARY BEALE,
died alſo on the 13th of Auguſt, 1742

THOMAS BEALE,
of Stoke Orchard in this Pariſh, Yeoman,
died Jan 31, 1756, aged 58

MARY his Wife
died March 11, 1778, aged 79

WILLIAM ATTWOOD
died in April 1729, aged 44

ELIZABETH his Wife
died June 9, 1728, aged 50

JOHN their Son died in 1721, an Infant

IN THE SOUTH AISLE, ON FLAT STONES

RICHARD WEBB, ſenior,
of Biſhop's Cleeve,
died Nov 11, 1667, aged 83.

JARED WEBB his Son
was buried Oct 13, Anno Dom 1682

RICHARD WEBB, junior,
was buried April 6, 1704, aged 79

MARY his Wife
died Nov 2, 1697, aged 70

RICHARD, Son of RICHARD and MARY WEBB,
of Biſhop' Cleeve,
died June 2, 1775, aged 34.

ANTHONY, Son of RICHARD and MARY WEBB,
died May 14, 1776, aged 51

ANTHONY WEBB
died Jan 8, 17.., aged 60

RICHARD WEBB
died Anno Dom 17.., aged 76

MARY, Wife of RICHARD WEBB,
died Jan 18, 1773, aged 7.

IN THE NAVE,
ON FLAT STONES

Heare lieth the Bodie of CIPRIAN ATTWOOD, of Stoke Orchard, who departed this Life the 4th Day of April, Anno Dom 1674

Also here lieth ALICE his Wife, who lived together in Wedlock 60 Yeares, and departed this Life the 29th Day of August, Anno Dom 1666

JOMUND ATWOOD, Gent. of Bishop's Cleeve, died the 6th Day of Feb 1688, aged 68

THOMAS HOBBS, of Bishop's Cleeve, was buried Sept 22, Anno Dom 1710.

A. H
1720

MARY, Daughter of JOHN HOBBS, of Woodmancoat, Wife of WILLIAM HYDE, of Staverton, was buried July 26, 1754, aged 44

WILLIAM HOBBS, of Bishop's Cleeve, died Oct 5, 1726

HANNAH his Wife was buried the 8th Day of January, 1763, aged 82

EDWARD HOBBS died March 17, 1724

SAMUEL WARREN, Gent of Gotherington in this Parish, died Feb 20, 1736, aged 80

ELIZABETH his Wife died May 18, 1737, aged 70

THOMAS KITTERMUSTER, Gent died March 21, 1777, aged 76

FRANCES, the Wife of THOMAS KITTERMUSTER, Gent died June 25, Anno Dom 1750, aged 56

ON FLAT STONES
IN THE NORTH AISLE

FRANCES, the Wife of JOHN YEEND, of Afton upon Carrant in this County, and Daughter of THOMAS LORINGE, of this Parish, Gent by ANNE his Wife, died March 15, 1724, aged 60

EDWARD, the second Son of THOMAS LORINGE, Gent was buried the 3d of October, Anno Dom 167

MARY, Wife of THOMAS YEEND, and Daughter of PETER COCKS, Gent of this Place, who died July 2, 1742, aged 42

WILLIAM SURMAN, of Woodmancoat, was buried here June 30, 1712

T S 1732, aged 84

M S 1772, aged 87

ABIGAIL LORINGE, of Afton, died Oct 4, 1722

THOMAS SURMAN, the Son of WILLIAM SURMAN, of Woodmancoat, died the 1st of May, Anno Dom 1717.

HESTER, the Wife of SAMUEL WINSER, of Woodmancoat, died March 11, 1724

JANE, the Daughter of WILLIAM and HESTER SURMAN, of Woodmancoat in this Parish, died Nov 20, 1718, aged 1

IN THE CHURCH YARD, ON TOMBS

THOMAS KEYESS died Dec 24, 1753, aged 86

JOANNAH his Wife was buried Oct 1, 1720, aged 47

ELIZABETH their Daughter was buried Aug 27, 1763, aged 68

THOMAS their Son was buried Oct 18, 1727, aged 27

SARAH their Daughter died an Infant

JOHN, the Son of THOMAS and JOANNAH KEYESS, died June 25, 1717, aged 5

WILLIAM their Son died Sept 20, 1757, aged 24

SAMUEL their Son was buried Sept 23, 1777, aged 18

RICHARD HOBBES
the elder, of Cleeve,
died Dec 24, 1654
This Tombe was erected by
JOANE, the Wife of RICHARD HOBBES,
the Daughter of THOMAS ROGERS, Gentleman,
dwelinge in King Standly.

DAVID HOBBES
was buried June 15, 1667

ANN VICARIIS, the Wife of
WILLIAM VICARIIS, of the Hawe in the
Parish of Turley, and Daughter of
FRANCUM,
was buried Feb 8, 1650

Mr EDMUND SMITH,
of Brockhampton,
and MARY his Wife
She was buried the 1st, and he the 2d of March,
1690

Mr EDMUND SMITH,
of Cheltenham, Surgeon, their Son,
died Jan 9, 1743, aged 67

MARY his Wife
died the 2d of February following, aged 60 Years.

Mrs MARY ABLOT,
Sister of the above EDMUND SMITH, junior,
died Feb 16, 1739, aged 63

WILLIAM WAKE, Chandler,
died May 29, 1669

JANE, the Daughter of
WILLIAM WAKE,
was buried July 27, 1697

GILES FOWLER,
of Gotherington in this Parish,
died June 20, 1778, aged 60

ELIZABETH his Wife
died Oct 10, 1773, aged 42

WILLIAM KNIGHTS,
of Woodmancoit
died Oct 11, 1781, aged 75

ANN his Wife
died Nov 30, 1775, aged 62

JOSEPH their Son
died Jan 3, 1775, aged 28

THOMAS FOWLER the elder
died March 8, 1662

MARGARET his Wife
was buried Dec 5, 1637

SARAH, Wife of WILLIAM SHERIFF,
of Gotherington in this Parish,
was buried in the Year 1731.

WILLIAM SHERIFF
died July 2, 1726, aged 82

ELIZABETH, Wife of JOHN SHERIFF,
died March 21, 164

KINNARD SHERIFF
died March 29, 1771, aged 79

JOHN SHERIFF
died Nov 26, 1674

RICHARD, the Son of WILLIAM SHERIFF,
was buried in 1740, aged 58

DANIEL WASLEY,
of Stoke Orchard
died Sep 17, 1767, aged 41.

DANIEL WASLEY, senior,
died Feb 12, 1739, aged 61

MARY his Wife
died Anno Dom 1738

MARY their Daughter died an Infant

ON HEAD STONES

	Died	Aged		Died	Aged
John Ireland	3 May, 1729	74	William Trinder, of Southam	12 Nov 175	50
Mary, Wife of James Clune, of Gotherington	26 Jan 1748	39	Mary his Wife	6 Feb 1,4	70
			Thomas Trinder	14 Oct 157	50
Mary, Wife of William Hitt, of Teakesbury	10 Nov 1754	77	Ann his Wife	6 1 17,6	65
Thomas Barnard, of Elmston Hardwick	21 Dec 1769	74	Joan Leighton, of Gotherington	28 Sept 17	37
Thomas Barnard	19 Apr 1759	47	Eleanor, Wife of Richard Hodges, of Hucclecote in the Parish of Churchdown	7 June, 1755	65
Elizabeth his Wife	30 Dec 1764	53	Mary Wife of Thomas Holton	4 Oct 17, 3	8
Thomas Troughton, late of Stoke Orchard	21 Dec 1761	50	They were both Daughters of John Rutter of Alderton, Yeoman		
Joseph Troughton, of Stoke Orchard	13 Oct 1763	66	Joseph Porter	14 Sept 1,1	67
Benjamin Conner, of Stoke Orchard	9 Sept 1779	65	Mary his Wife	1 1 1	59
John Conner, of Stoke Orchard	11 Apr 1736	63	Allen Jenkins	Oct 1,6	
Mary his Wife	4 May 1748	71	William Jenkins	1 Apr 1	52
Andrew Bearne, senior	14 Dec 1758	64	Joan his Wife	19 Nov 1 5	86
Sarah Wife of Joseph Keeble	16 June, 1773	66	Sarah Wife of Thomas Wander, of Stoke Orchard	5 Jan 1 3	60
Thomas Read	6 July 1730	43	Simon Wander, of Stoke Orchard	6 18 11	
Mary his Wife	21 May 1744	57	Mary his Wife	3 May 1	60
William Read	12 July, 1770		Mary, Wife of Joseph Porter, Daughter of Richard and Mary Keeble, of Southam		
Elizabeth his Wife	17 Sep 1766	63			
Mary, Wife of William Trinder, of Joseph	18 Oct 1737	42		1 May, 1771	1

ON

ON HEAD STONES

	Died	Aged
Richard Keate -	10 Nov 1783	78
Elenor, Wife of William Maule	25 Aug 1736	86
Richard their Son	16 Sept 1754	60
Eleanor their Daughter	11 Jun 1748	70
Margaret their Daughter	24 Apr 1764	77
Joan, Wife of Thomas Newman, of Brockhampton -	2 Nov 1741	25
John Wilks	20 July 1738	78
Sarah his Wife -	2 Jan 1710	—
Frances his Wife -	21 Feb 1769	78
Ann Gooder, of Gotherington	6 Jan 1768	39
Elizabeth, Wife of Charles Fowler	8 Apr 1769	69
John their Son -	12 Nov 1756	29
Thomas Fowler	15 Apr 1726	76
Charles Fowler	8 Sept 1761	76
Thomas Potter	24 Nov 1747	53
Mary his Wife	8 Oct 1762	66
John Barnes of Woodmancoat	23 May 1779	87
Ann, Wife of Thomas Smith	20 Mar 1761	39
Jane, Daughter of John Barnes	19 Dec 1775	40
James Kittermaster -	21 Feb 1725	57
Elizabeth his Wife	25 Oct 1755	86
John Townshend	5 Sept 1707	31
Sarah his Wife -	25 Nov 1738	56
John their Son -	14 Mar 1770	64
Josiah Cook	22 Jan 1780	83
Rebecca his Wife	9 June 1749	40
Ann, Wife of Andrew Spencer, of Woodmancote	3 May 1757	78
Thomas their Son	10 Feb 1753	20
Elizabeth, Wife of Joseph Webb, of Southam	6 Jan 1776	74
Joseph Webb -	22 Dec 1777	82
John Eacott, of Southam	18 July 1770	52
John Wasley -	13 Mar 1774	66
Mary his Wife -	15 May 1767	57
Mary, Wife of Daniel Wasley	14 Nov 1783	81
Ann, Wife of John Whitmore, of Stone Orchard	6 July 1775	44
Esther, Wife of John Collett, of Southam	16 Nov 1784	66
Mary, Daughter of Thomas and Esther Witts	16 Nov 1784	32
Charlotte, Daughter of John and Mary Collett of Lower Slaughter in this County	13 May 1788	26
Thomas Collett, of Southam	5 Feb 1749	64
Mary his Wife	17 Apr 1755	60
Elizabeth, Wife of John Leech	17 Apr 1760	78
Mary, Daughter of John and Mary Leech	15 Oct 1762	78
Mary, Wife of William Leech, of Gotherington	23 Feb 1736	35
Elizabeth, Wife of William Leech	23 July 1773	46
Robert their Son	11 July 1760	80
Mary his Wife -	25 Mar 1739	83
William, Son of Robert and Mary Preston	14 July 1772	48
Samuel Windsor -	10 Dec 1757	83
Elizabeth his Wife	14 Mar 1773	74
Hester their Daughter, Wife of Samuel Cherington -	9 Mar 1780	50
William Ballinger, of Charlton King's	5 May 1780	72
William Potter, of Gambells in this Parish	5 May 1778	72
Mary, Wife of Richard Cull, Daughter of William and Mary Potter, of Gambells -	5 Apr 1780	47
John Leech -	4 Dec 1714	84
William Leech, late of Gotherington	21 Jan 1784	64
James Lawrence, of the Parish of Prescutt	12 Aug 1778	77
Betty, Daughter of James and Mary Lawrence, of the Parish of Prescutt	27 Jun 1759	6
William Fowler, of Gotherington	16 Jan 1780	80
Elizabeth, Wife of Thomas Roberts, of Gotherington	24 Feb 1781	77
Richard Fowler	28 Jan 1751	47
Jane, his Wife, afterwards Wife of Thomas Newman, of Southam	5 Feb 1758	58
Thomas Newman	13 Sep 1760	59
John Parker, senior	22 Sep 17	0
Ann his Wife -	13 Aug 1757	90
William their Son -	2 Oct 1729	21
Ann, Wife of Robert Webb	7 Apr 1749	43
Thomas Stafford -	9 Dec 1761	44
Ann, Wife of Josiah Cook	6 Feb 1760	43
Margaret, Wife of John Bayns	18 Feb 1754	64
Ferdinando Wilks	19 Feb 1769	68
Ann, Wife of Thomas Aston	1714	43
Susanna, Wife of Nicholas Tomlinson	26 Nov 17	60
John Tomlinson	2 Nov 1741	60
Ann his Wife -	26 Nov 1763	70
Pendock Harris	7 Dec 1751	58
William Ward, of Gotherington	30 July 1761	40
Ann his Wife -	3 May 1777	65
James Son of James and Sarah Potter	9 July 1777	32
Richard Son of Richard and Hannah Harford, of Southam	11 Oct 1785	3
Mary Wife of William Fowler	15 Dec 1733	69
Richard Fowler, senior	26 Mar 1740	83
Mary his Wife	31 June 1720	—
William Fowler	6 Apr 1744	61
William, Son of William and Mary Fowler	7 Mar 1721	1
Giles their Son -	21 Apr 1728	2
Meriel, Wife of John Potter, of Winnards	18 June 1741	88

Long on the Lord did wait:
I for the Lord did wait:
I left alive Children
And Grandchildren eighty eight

THE most ancient Records do not account for this additional Name as borne by any Family of Property in this Parish, and it is still used only in Distinction from *Ryon Clifford in Warwick-shire*, from which County it is divided by the River *Stour*. It lies in the upper Division of the Hundred of *Tewkesbury*, distant from *Campden* ten Miles on the North east, forty North from GLOUCESTER, and two only from the Town of *Stratford* upon *Avon*.

A Circuit of nearly five Miles is included within the Boundary, of a mixed Soil, composed of Sand and Clay, chiefly Arable. In 1780 a more general Inclosure took place, in pursuance of an Act of Parliament obtained for that Purpose.

The Living is a Rectory in the Deanery of *Campden*, the Advowson of which has been never detached from the Manor. The Church, dedicated to *St. Helen*, contains one Nave only, with a Tower of neat Gothic Workmanship at the West End.

With respect to the Descent of the Manor, in 1099, 12 WILL. RUFUS, ROGER DE BULLI or IULEI, conferred it on the Abbey of *St. Peter* in GLOUCESTER, who retained it in undisturbed Possession of it till the Suppression. It does not appear to have been disposed of before 1562, 4 ELIZ. when it passed by Purchase to CHARLES RAINSFORD, Esq. HENRY RAINSFORD, the last of that House, was a strenuous Partizan with King CHARLES the First, and as such compounded for 900*l.* for the Estate, which had been sequestered by the Commissioners of the Parliament. He soon afterwards, in 1649, sold this Manor to JOB DIGHTON, Esq. whose lineal Descendant is the present Possessor. Various Additions and Improvements have been made to the Manor house, which is pleasantly situate on the Banks of the *Stour*.

The manerial Estate comprises the greater Part of the landed Property of the Parish. Beside which, are those vested in the Families of PARRY and SPIERS.

Of the two Hamlets the more considerable is *Aylston*, that Part of it containing the Houses, with many Acres, the Tythes of which are appendant to the Rectory, lies in *Warwickshire*, in the Parish of *Atherstone*. It was once held by GILBERT DE CLARE, Earl of GLOUCESTER, as appears from the Escheator's Books in 1314, 1 EDW. II.

2 *Wincot* is divided between the Parishes of *Clifford Chambers* and *Quinton*, and was anciently appertinent to the great Manor of *Tewkesbury*.

This District is equally barren of Natural Curiosities, and Matters of Antiquarian Research, excepting a few Coins of the Lower *Roman* Empire lately discovered.

BENEFACTIONS

An Annuity of 10*l.* left by some Person unknown, payable out of an Estate (belonging to Mr. ED-WARD STANLEY) at *Alveston* in *Warwickshire*.

Four Houses in the Town of *Stratford* upon *Avon*, *Warwickshire*, the annual Produce of which is 12*l.* or 4*l.* for the Benefit of the Inhabitants of this Parish.

INCUMBENTS	PATRONS	INCUMBENTS	PATRONS
1099 ————,	Abbey of GLOUCESTER	1732 Rob. Goodhill, Clerk,	Francis Keyte Dighton
1668 John Silusbury,	————	1735 John Martin, M. A.	The same
* * * * * *	* * * * * *	1776 Stephen Nason, M. A.	Latter Dighton, Esq
1687 Christopher Smith,	William Smith	1787 John Brewer,	The same
1729 Rich. Dighton, Clerk,	Richard Dighton, Esq		

5 I

PRESENT LORD OF THE MANOR,
LISTER DIGHTON, ESQ

The Perfons fummoned from this Place by the Heralds, in 1682 and 1683, were

Henry Dighton, Efq   —— Owen, Gent
—— Watts, Clerk   —— Loggin, Gent

At the Election in 1776 Nine Freeholders polled from this Parifh and its Hamlets

The Regifter commences with a Date fo early as 1538

ANNUAL ACCOUNT OF MARRIAGES, BIRTHS, AND BURIALS, IN THIS PARISH

A.D	Mar	Bir	Bur	A.D	Mar	Bir	Bur	A.D	Mar	Bir	Bur	A.D	Mar	Bir	Bur
1781	2	8	6	1786	2	7	5	1791				1796			
1782	2	7	6	1787	2	8	5	1792				1797			
1783	2	5	9	1788				1793				1798			
1784	—	4	3	1789				1794				1799			
1785	1	7	9	1790				1795				1800			

INSCRIPTIONS IN THE CHANCEL.

UPON ATCHIEVEMENTS AGAINST THE WALL

1 Quarterly, 1ft, Argent, a Lion paffant between three Croffes patée fitchy Gules, for DIGHTON 2d and 3d, Azure, a Chevron between three Kite's Heads erafed Or, for KEITE 4th, is the 1ft,—im paling, quarterly, 1ft and 4th, Ermine, on a Bend Sable, three Eagles difplayed Or 2d and 3d Er mine, on a Fefs Sable three Mullets Or Creft, a Lion's Jamb Or, holding a Crofs patée ntchy Gules

2 Quarterly, 1ft and 4th, DIGHTON 2d and 3d, Azure, three Falcons Argent, ducally crowned Or On an Efcutcheon of Pretence, KEITE, as before

A MURAL MONUMENT, CONTAINING TWO FI-
GURES IN THE DRESS OF THE TIMES, KNEELING,
BETWEEN THEM THIS INSCRIPTION AND ARMS

1 Argent, a Crofs Sable, for RAINSFORD
2 Azure, an Eagle difplayed Argent, gorged with a Coronet, and beaked and membred Or, for WILCOTTS, of Wylcotts 3 Azure, an Eagle difplayed Argent, beaked and membred Or, for WYLLICOTES, of Great Tew, co Oxon 4. Sable, on a Chief Argent, three Lozenges Gules, for MOLLINS 5 Argent, an Eagle difplayed Gules, for HALL 6 Azure, a Chevron Ermine, between three Bucks trippant Or, for GREENE 7 Argent, a Chief indented Azure, for GLANVILE 8 Per Pile Or and Azure, a Chevron Ermine, for LYONS 9 Gules, on a Chevron Argent, a Cinque foil between three Gebs Or, for SCOCATHE 10 Argent, a Chevron between three Cinquefoils Gules for WAKEFED 11 Argent, a Chevron engrailed between three Lurillops Sable, for AR- DERBURG, or ARDERBOUCHE 12 Vaire Argent and Gules, on a Bend Sable three Boars Heads erafed Or, for PURCELL 13 Or, three Boar's Heads erafed Sable, muzzled of the firft, for BRE- WICKE 14 Argent, three Bendlets Azure, on a Canton Sable, a Lion paffant Or, for SURESALT 15 Or, three Chevronells braced in bafe Sable, on Chief Gules three Plates, for PRATTELL

Sir HENRY RAINSFORD,
of Clifford in the County of Glouceft, Knight,
(Son of HERBERT RAINSFORD, Efq)
died the of January, 6,
in the Year of his Age 36

He married ANN, Daughter and Coheyre
of Sir HENRY GOODER,
of Polfworth in the County of Warwick, Knight,
with whom he lived 27 Yeares,
and had Iffue three Sonnes

WILLIAM died

HENRY, married ELENOR,
Daughter and Coheire of ROBERT BOSWELL,
of Combe in the County of Southampton, Efq

and FRAUNCIS,

Henrico (huc dum nemo caput) Herct 1º,
Fil RAINSFORDE, Eq Aur Iufufq; diem
Vixit villa Domino, ingentis animi
Viro, nec ideo prudentia nec mitis minus
Ad honefta quæcunque nato, id meliora
Regreffo fratri Chariffimo
(& quod pulchrius)
Amico cum lætiffimi & luctuofiffima conjuge
Loromque (GULIEL Fil) GOODERES tunc vix
Damni & fuperftes, duo fui & fratris
Lachrymis indulget
Mœrentiffimæ
Mœrentiffimus P T
Nec minus exultat in Memoria exceffus
Uxor, fœmina
rum optima
Patre pietate Co
loni Virginis
Nec filia opti illud nomine
Meliora fimum quæ quod factura
virtutum,
Hæc res Goodere

On a brass Plate

Under this Stone lyeth the Body of
ELIZABETH, Daughter of HERCULES RAYNSFORD,
of Clifford in the County of Gloucester, Esq
married to EDWARD MARROWE,
Sonne and Heire of SAMUEL MARROWE,
of Barkeswell in the Countie of Warwick, Esq.
which ELIZABETH deceased Oct. 29, 1601.

Arms, RAYNESFORD quartered as before.

Here lyeth buried the Body of
HERCULES RAYNSFORD, Esquier,
Lord of this Mannor of Clifford,
who married ELIZABETHE PARRY,
Daughter of ROBERT PARRY, Esquier,
by whom, having Issue too Sonnes and on Daughter,
died the second Daye of August, Anno 1583,
in the Yeare of his Age 39

On Flat Stones

Here lyeth the Body of WILLIAM BARNES, Esq
Lord, whilst he lived, of Tilkton, alias Gidington,
in the County of Worcester,
which he give to his Nephew
WILLIAM BARNES, Esq
and of the Moiety of the Manior of Wincot
in this County and Parish,
(which he give to his Son in Law
Sir HENRY RAINSFORD,
Lord of the Mannor of Clifford)
He married, and having lived with her 36 Years,
died Sept. 24, 1622, aged 70

Here lyeth the Body of the
Reverend Mr. CHRISTOPHER SMITH
above forty Years Rector of this Parish,
who died April 22, 1720, in the
66th Year of his Age

Also CATHARINE his Wife
died A. D. 1737, æt 70

IN THE CHURCH YARD.

On Tablets against the Church

Underneath this Place lie the
Remains of ELIANOR, Daughter of
WILLIAM and MARY WALFORD.
She died Oct. 16, 1765, aged 39

MARY, Wife of JOSEPH BARNES,
died Dec. 22, 1763, aged 60.

JOSEPH BARNES
died June 27, 1777, aged 61.

On a Tomb

Here lyeth the Body of
Mr ROBERT CLARKE,
who departed this Life the
20th Day of May, 1683

ON HEAD STONES

	Died	Aged
Mary, Wife of Benjamin Barnes	28 Feb 1780	42
Ann, Wife of William Parker	12 June, 1747	55
Elizabeth, Wife of Robert Heritage	1 Apr 1744	66
Alice, Daughter of Richard and Ann Spiers	26 Feb 1748	
Richard Spiers	25 Mar 1775	69
Ann his Wife	9 Oct 1781	69
John Silvister	2 Nov 1766	52
Benjamin Silvister	23 Sept 1763	67
Mary his Wife	11 Nov 1756	78
Robert Morris	19 Sept 1737	63
Ursula his Wife	30 Sept 1736	49
Samuel Morris	12 Nov 1766	55
Thomas Knight	26 Jan 1738	59
John his Wife	25 Apr 1733	48
William, Son of William and Mary Spiers	51 May 1715	35
Elizabeth his Wife	3 May 1715	56

LXXIII. CLIFTON.

FEW Counties are found in the *Villare*, in which this Name does not occur, so demonstrative of its Situation This very beautiful Village is included in the lower Division of the Hundred of *King's Barton*, thirty-four Miles distant from GLOUCESTER, and one only from the City of BRISTOL The Soil consists of a thin Surface of red Earth on a limestone Rock, very unfavourable to Agriculture, no Part of it being tilled The Boundaries are not extensive *

A Situation so eligible as *Clifton*, with the additional Circumstance of its Vicinity to BRISTOL, induced many of the more opulent Inhabitants to select it for their Residence Upon the Brow of the Hill many elegant Edifices have been erected, which so frequently change their Proprietors, that to specify them would be needless Task The principal, built about twenty Years since by SIR WILLIAM DRAPER, now belongs to WILLIAM GORDON, Esq + Another Mansion has Environs cultivated at a great Expence, in the Taste introduced in the latter Part of the last Century, belonging to the Family of GOLDNEY, in which is a Grotto formed by marine and mineral Productions of such Rarity as to attract the frequent Notice of Travellers There are several detached Streets of Houses, applied chiefly to the accommodation of the Company resorting to the *Hot Wells*

The Benefice is a perpetual Curacy, in the Deanry of BRISTOL, without Tythes, but augmented by Queen ANNE's Bounty The Advowson anciently annexed to the Impropriation, was given to the re-founded College at *Westbury upon Trim*, by JOHN CARPENTER, Bishop of Worcester, in 1465 From the Family of HODGES the Impropriation has descended, by Purchase, to SAMUEL WORRALL, Esq and the Advowson to the present Incumbent

The Church consists of a Nave and two Aisles, re-built in 1654, long since the Tower, which is a Gothic embattled Structure, upon which, on two Escutcheons, are these Arms 1 Two Bars and 3 Roundlets in Chief 2 An Eagle displayed

The early Accounts of the Descent of the Manor are not satisfactory, Part of it belonged to the De CLARES and BEAUCHAMPS, Earls of *Gloucester* and *Warwick* The Family of CHIDIOC or CHADOCK likewise held it In 1480 BROKE, Lord Cobham was the Possessor ‡ In 1544 it was granted to Sir RALPH SADLER, whose Heirs sold it, about the commencement of the last Century, to the Company of *Merchants Adventurers* of the City of BRISTOL

For the very romantic Scenes || which are formed by the immense Acclivities of Rocks, on the East Side of the River *Avon*, and the salubrious medicinal Springs which issue from the Base of them, *Clifton*

---

* Metes and bounds of the Parish of *Clifton* " From *Rownham Passage* by the River *Avon* to the Chapel of *St Vincent*, and " from thence, by the River aforesaid, to *Walcams Slade*, and from thence to a Place called the *Hawrbins* and from thence to " Stone called the *Merestone*, lying between the Chapel of *Saint Lambert* and the King's Highway From thence by the aforesaid " Way to *Snowkeares*, from thence by the white Style, and then to *Deepstone* Style, and then to the Limekilns, and then by the " River *Avon* to the Passage aforesaid '   Par Register, fol [1538

+ The Area before this House is ornamented by an Obelisk and a Sarcophagus, bearing the following Inscriptions On the Obelisk, " GULIELMO PITT, Comiti de *Chatham*, hoc amicitiæ privatæ testimonium simul ac honoris publici monumentum posuit " G. DRAPER " Upon the base of the Sarcophagus, the Exploits of the 19th Regiment of Foot in the *East Indies*, are particularized, and the Names of 34 Officers recorded who were slain in Battle
" Siste Gradum si qua est *Britonum* tibi cura Viator '
" Siste Gradum, vacuo recotas inscripta Sepulchro
" Tristia sata Virûm, quos bellicus ardor *Eoum*
" Pro! Dolor! haud unquam redituros misit ad orbem
" Nec tibi sit lugere pudor, si forte tuorum
" Nomina nota legas, sed cum terràque marique
" Invictos Heroum animos & facta revolves,
" Si patriæ te tangit amor, si *Fama Britannum*
" Parce triumphales lachrymis aspergere lauros
" Quin si *Asiæ* penetrare sinus atque ultima *Gangis*
" Pandere claustra pares, *Indosque* lacessere Bello
" Ex his virtutem discas verumque laborem
" Fortunam ex aliis " —

Vocula *Clifton* cujus Dominus Villæ est N— BROKE dominus *Cobham*   ITIN W DE WYRCESTER, p 186

|| " The Scenery about *Clifton* is in a great Degree picturesque ; the River is cooped up between two high Hills both " of which are adorned with a rich Profusion of Rock, Wood, or Verdure Here is no offskip indeed, but as it is for " ground alone in one Picture, we are presented with a very beautiful one "   GILPIN's Tour on the Wye, p 9

has been most distinguished. These Rocks are composed of a Lime stone of a excellent Quality, with Lamina of vast Size, all lying in an oblique Position, extended for the Space of seve l Miles from these Clifts, the Classes of Botanists may be enriched with an infinite Variety of curious Plants, man of which are peculiar to this Soil * Internally the Chasms and Fissures of unfathomable Depth, the Sides of which are cloathed with a strong ferruginous Luth, upon which those fine Crystals generally called Bristol Stone † These, if large, are seldom clear. Before Pastes and other fictitious Jewels were brought to their present Perfection, Crystals collected here were held in great Estimation, as approaching nearest to the Diamond, both in Consistence and Brilliancy

Through this very wonderful Valley, the River Avon pursues a winding Course till it empties itself into the great Æstuary, about eight Miles distant from the Port of Bristol. The Tide generally rises to the Height of thirty Feet. In the remote Ages, a Gulph of so very artificial an Appearance is this, was

* The very rare Plants have been noticed and described by the first Botanists, GERARD, RAY, PARKINSON, PARLATORE, and HILL. They are likewise specified in CAMDEN's Brit. Edit. p. 290. Vol. I. and still more accurately in the Particulars which we adopt.

Alopecurus Incurvata Sea Hard grass By the River side —June to August
Alopecurus, Pratensis Bearded Fox tail grass St. Vincent's Rock —June to August
Anethum Foeniculum Fennel Below Coast —July and August
Antirrhinum Cymbalaria Ivy leav'd Toad flax Walls about Clifton —June to September
Aquilega Vulgaris Columbines St Vincent' Rock —June
Arenaria, Rubra Purple Sandwort, or Sea Spurry By the River side —June to August
Arenaria Tenuifolia Fine leav'd Sandwort The Foot of St Vincents Rock —June and July
Asparagus, Officinalis Common Sparagus Meadow below Cook's Hill —July and August
Asplenium Ceterach Spleenwort Common —May to September
Asplenium Ruta Muraria White Spleenwort, or Mule rue Common —June September
Arabis Stricta Rough Wall cresse On many Parts of the Rocks —March to May
Bryum, Extractorum Extinguisher Bryum Various Places on St Vincents Rocks —October to August following
Bryum Pomum Apple Bryum On the Rocks in Leigh Wood, rare —March and April
Bupleurum Tenuifolium Lean Throwwax or Hares ear In the Meadows below Cook's Hill —July and August
Carduus Acaulis Dwarf Thistle St Vincent Rock —July
Chenopodium Maritimum Sea Goosefoot By the River side —August
Chlora Perfoliata Yellowwort St Vincents Rocks and Leigh Wood —July
Cochlearia Anglica Sea Scurvy grass By the River side —May
Cochlearia Danica Venus Navelwort or Wall Pennywort St Vincents Rocks —June to August
Digitalis Purpurea Purple Fox glove Leigh Wood, and Coast's Hill —July
Erigeron Acre Blue Fleabane or blue Flabane St Vincent Rocks —July and August
Euphorbia Exigua Dwarf Spurge At the Foot of St Vincent Rock —July
Galeopsis Ladanum Red Dead Nettle, or Nettle Hemp St Vincent Rocks —June to August
Geranium Montanum Mountain Crane's bill Leigh Wood near Clifton Turnpike —July and August
Geranium Maritimum Sea Crane's bill By the River side —June and July
Geranium Sanguineum Bloody Crane's bill On St Vincents Rocks Common —July and August
Glaux Maritima Sea Milkwort or black Saltwort By the River side —June and July
Hippocrepis Comosa Tufted Horsehoe Vetch Near Cook's love —July
Hypericum Humifusum Trailing St John's wort Clifton Turnpike —June
Hypericum Androsaemum Mountain St John's wort Clifton Turnpike —July
Hypericum Pulchrum Elegant or Upright St John's wort St Vincent's Rocks, below Clifton Turnpike —July
Lithospermum Officinale Gromwell Leigh Wood —April and May
Lepidium Petraeum Mountain Pepperwort Various Places on St Vincents Rocks —April and May
Lepidium Ruderale Narrow leav'd Pepperwort, or Dittander At the foot of St Vincents Rock —June and July
Lichen Deustus Sooty Lichen The further end of St Vincent's Rocks —All the Year
Lichen Miniatus Cloudy Lichen With the above —All the Year
Lichen Polyrrhizus Dusky Rock, or fringed Lichen With the above —All the Year
Milium Lendigerum Shining Fox-tail grass Near the New Hot well —July and August
Menyanthes Exposita Primrose scented Hippophyes, yellow Menanthes, ground Nut In Leigh Wood —July
Ophrys Apifera Bee Ophrys St Vincent Rock, behind the New Hotwell —July and August
Ophrys Muscifera Fly Ophrys With the former —July and August
Ophrys Ovata Common Ophrys, or Twyblade Leigh Wood —May and June
Ophrys Spiralis Triple Ophrys or Ladies traces St Vincents Rock above the Hot well house —July and August
Ornithopus Perpusillus Bird's Foot Broad Walls near Clifton —May to August
Osmunda Spicant Spleenwort, Osmund Royal Below the Hot well in the Leigh Wood —August
Picris Echioides Rough Picris Below Cook's Folly —July and August
Pimpinella Dioica Sea Pimpernel or Burnet Saxifrage St Vincents Rock behind the Hot well House —May and June
Polypodium Dryopteris Branched Polypody In Leigh Wood, rare —June to September
Polypodium Fragile Brittle Polypody In Leigh Wood, with the former —June to September
Prenanthes Muralis Wall Lettuce, Ivy leav'd wild Lettuce with Prenanthes St Vincents Wood —July
Potentium Sanguisorbae Common Burnet St Vincents Rock —July
Potentilla Verna Spring Cinquefoil St Vincent Rock —May to end June
Rubia Peregrina Wild Madder St Vincents Rock and Leigh Wood —June and July
Scabiosa Columbaria Small Scabious St Vincents Rock —June and July
Scilla Autumnalis Autumnal Squill, or Star Hyacinth Near the Limekilns on Cook's Hill —August and September
Sedum Dasyphyllum Round leav'd Stonecrop St Vincents Rock, and Walls about Clifton —July
Sedum Rupestre Rockstonecrop The Road to Cook's Ferry —August
Sisymbrium Murale Wall Cabbage, or Wall Rocket Various places —May to July
Smyrnium Olusatrum Alexanders Near Cook's Hill —May and June
Solidago Virgaurea Goldenrod St Vincents Rock —August
Trifolium Officinale Birds foot Trefoil St Vincent Rock —June and July
Trifolium Subterraneum Dwarf Trefoil St Vincent's Rock —May
Tussilago Hybrida Honeywort Rough Lower Mudland Well behind the Hot well house —June
Veronica Spicata Spiked Speedwell Welsh speedwell on the Way to the Hot well —June to August
Veronica Hybrida Honey Vetch of St Vincents Rock from the Turnpike —March and April
Ulva Lactuca Lettuce Laver, Oyster Green On the Rocks of the River —September to March following

† An account of the stones, fossils, & found upon St Vincents Rocks would be too long. Bruton Observator.

5 K

of once removed by legendary Writers to the miraculous Agency of a Giant or a Saint * The
Summit was made sacred by the Foundation of a Chapel and an Hermitage, which were appendant
to the *Augustine* Monastery in BRISTOL They were dedicated to *St Vincent*, a *Spanish* Martyr + Not the
slightest Vestiges of these are now to be traced About half way down *Ghyston Cliff*, is a large Cavern,
called *Giant's Hole* or *Fox Hole*, which is said to have been connected by subterraneous Passages with the
Chapel ‡

The celebrated Well, so efficacious a Remedy in Cases of bodily Decay, was very anciently known,
although its Properties were but little explored, till the conclusion of the last Century § There are
beside several smaller Springs issuing from apertures in the Rock equally tepid.

In 1680, a signal cure was performed, and its virtues proclaimed The Spring was protected from
the irruptions of the Tide by a low Wall In 1690, the Corporation of BRISTOL increased the Buildings
and five Years afterward, the *Merchants Adventurers*, as Lords of *Clifton*, granted a Lease to Sir THOMAS
DAY, Knight, and other Citizens, who erected the *Hot-well* House, and various Accommodations for
the Company During the Interval between that and the present Time, so numerous and constant has been
the Resort, that some hundred Houses have been built, and disposed in a Square, Parades, and Streets of
considerable Extent

The Chapel in this District is appendant to the Church at *Clifton*, and supported by voluntary Contri
bution No parochial Offices are performed there

Upon *Clifton Hill* a circular *Specula* or Roman Outpost is readily traced Parallel Vallations are likewise on the opposite Hill These were connected by six others with *Olbury* and the *Trajectus* there, by
which means they were secured The Name of *Castrum Ostorii* or *Caer Oder* has been attributed to this
particular Encampment, and many Coins of the latter Roman Empire occasionally discovered, encou
rage the Conjecture ‖

B E N E F A C T I O N S.

1690 Mr AYLIFFE GREEN gave 20*l* to ceil the Church, 16*l* for the Communion Plate, 20*s*
yearly for a Sermon on Good Friday, and 20*s* to the Poor, in Bread, on the same Day for ever

1703 Mr CORNELIUS DENNIS, a Sojourner, gave 5*l* the Interest whereof is to be distributed amongst
the Poor, yearly, for ever

1716 Mr JOHN WICKHAM gave 5*l* for the Benefit of the Poor of this Parish for ever

1718 Mrs CATHARINE FREEMAN gave 20*l* the Interest thereof to buy Coals for the Poor of this
Parish for ever

1737 Mr CHARLES JONES, of this Parish, gave 20*l* the Interest thereof to be given in Bread to
the Poor, on the 2nd of February yearly, for ever

---

* " Sum thinke that a greate Pece of the Deepnes of the Haven from *St Vincents* to *Hungroad* hath been made by Hand, sum
fay that Shippes of very antient Tyme came up to *St Stephanes* Church in Bryghtstowe '   ITLAND Itin V, p. 94

† A D 1480 Rupis altissima de *Ghyston Cliffe* continet in altitudine 60 Brachia videlicet, de terra firma ad quadddam He
mitis, sun cujus Eccletia dedicata in honorem *Sancti Vincentii*

‡ The Hall of the Chappell of *Saint Vincent* of *Ghyston Cliffe* is six Yerdes long and the Brodeys six Yerdes The Lengh a
" of the Kytchen six Yerdes and the Brede 111, and from the Chapelle of *Synet Vincent* ys to the lower Water 40 Vethym And
" from the over Part of the main Grounde Lord of the and high Rok downe to the fayd Chappelle ben xx Vethym reckoned and
" proved and sie from the high mayn firm Lond of the fayd Rok downe to the lowest Water of the *Avon* is 60 Vethym and
" moche more proved by a joining Man of Smyths Occupation that sayd yt to me, hath both descended to the highest Rokke
" down to the Water syde "   ItIn W WYRCESTRE pp 142

‡ *Fox Hole* vocatur in tributes sen superius ito de *Ghyston* Cliffe super ripam de le Rokke altiorem, et valde periculo su sua
ad intrandum voluntate eo id tam Mare profunditatis 60 Brachiorum et ultra   Ibid p

§ Fons est ibidem, circa lowstitor ipad le blacke Rok in parte *Ghystone Cliffe* in profundo aqua, et est ita calidus sicut Lac vel
aqua *Badoum*   Ibid p

† *Amens* Well lying West of the City under *St Vincent* Rock and laved by the River, is soveregn for Sores and Scabs
to be washt in, and drunk of, to be either outwardly or inwardly applied Undoubtedly the Water thereof runneth through a
Stratum of Iron as appeares by the rutty ferruginous Tinge thereof, which it retaineth though boyled ever so much Experience
proves that Beer brewed thereof is wholfom and agreeth me against the Spleen   FULLERs Worthies, p 55 Bristol

This Water is frequently encipped the Attention of the Learned The specific Heat is ascertained to be more than three
fourthis of the Luminifclient When viewd in Glass, it is perfectly pellucid, sparkling, and abounding in Air bubbles, with
out Smell, and leaves a kind of Sopicity or Drynels on the Palate Upon Evaporation it is found to contain a leg, reddish
reemblng Pearls with a small Quantity of Marine Salts The exact Proportion is given by the following An
Of calcareous Earth combined with vitriolic Acid in the Form of selenite Drams or grains 8½ of calcareous Earth combined
with a duboius s Dwt a Grains 12 Of Marine Salt of Magnesia Dwts or Grains 5½ Of aca Salt Dwts o Grains
Two more it contains eight ounce Measures of elastic Air, beyond the Quantity retained by the calcareous Earth in to
Heat of boylng Water and two ounce Measures of Air equal if not superior to atmospheric Air in Purity Various Instances
of the curative Qualities of this water are adduced in the several Treatises of Drs KEIR, RANDOLPH, HIERVY, and
LURRY

Of its medicinal virtues it is observed that it mixes with Soap, with Oil of Tarter it becomes clouded Oals down
gives a purplish Tint Syrup of Violets turns it green and it slightly ferments with Acids

‖ Castellum situatum in fine terra non longe per quartam partem a diam de *Clifton Cliff*, ut dicitur Pleb is side to be
further a site et puto *di eine* Conjecturant per *Saxo anos vel Judeos*, vel per quendam *Giant* concatena in terra tenant
hib communicant in spicis trium congeriem unum unum lapidum spatium seminatorum, quod sibi videbatur fuisse ordinate
ad terram faciam proficient   ItIn W WYRCESTRE p 141

M

Mr JOHN GWYNNE, a Sojourner, gave 5*l* the Interest thereof to be diftributed among the Poor, yearly, for ever

Mr DAVID ROYNON gave 10*l* for the fame Purpofe.

1760 Mr ANTHONY OLIVER, of the City of Briftol, bequeathed 60*l* the Interest thereof to be applied for ever, in the following Manner, (viz) One Guinea for a Sermon to be preached on the 25th Day of June, and the Surplus to be laid out in Bread for the Poor of this Parifh

INCUMBENTS	PATRONS
——— John Hodges,	John Hodges, Efq
1740 Thomas Taylor, M A	John Hodges, Efq
1762 John Taylor, Clerk,	Thomas Taylor

PRESENT PROPRIETORS OF THE MANOR,

The Company of MERCHANTS ADVENTURERS of the City of BRISTOL.

The Perfons fummoned from this Parifh by the Heralds in 1682 and 1683, were

John Hodges, Efq	John Wickham, Gent
Thomas Goodman, Gent	John Whitington, Gent.
Ayliffe Green, Gent	

At the Election in 1776, Fifty-two Freeholders polled from this Parifh

The Regifter is a very fair Manufcript, commences in 1538, and has been fince kept with laudable accuracy

ANNUAL ACCOUNT OF MARRIAGES, BIRTHS, AND BURIALS, IN THIS PARISH.

A.D	Mar	Bir	Bur	A D	Mar	Bir	Bur	A D	Mar	Bu	Bur	A D	Mar	Bi	Bur
1781	27	54	58	1786	27	45	57	1791				1796			
1782	23	53	55	1787	25	58	38	1792				1797			
1783	25	68	55	1788				1793				1798			
1784	22	59	46	1789				1794				1799			
1785	22	63	29	1790				1795				1800			

INSCRIPTIONS IN THE CHURCH

IN THE CHANCEL

ON A WHITE MARBLE TABLET

Arms, Quarterly, first and fourth, Gules, on a Cheveron Ermine, between three Cinquefoils Argent, a Hurtefs Buckle Azure, between two Hurts, within a Bordure Or, Seme of Olive Leaves proper, for HAMILTON, fecond and third, Argent, a Fefs wavy between three Rofes Gules, leaved Vert, for BAILLIE

Hic fepultus jacet
JOHANNES HAMILTON, Vicecomitis de Binning Filius, Comitis de Haddinton nepos, Matrem habuit RACHAELEM, GEORGII BAILLIE, de Jervifwood, Armigeri, Filiam fecundam Puer optima fpei, et nimis fupra annos ingenio Praeditus, Deliciae Parentum,
Propinquorum omnium, Haud Formam praeftantiorem Terra tulit, haud Coelum, excepit pulchriorem animum,
Obiit Anno aetatis IV
Aerae Chriftianae MDCCXXX

ON A MARBLE MONUMENT.

In a private Vault under this Veftry are depofited the Remains of the Rev THOMAS TAYLOR, M A late a Prebendary of the Cathedral Church at Wells, Vicar of Congrefbury in Somersefhire, Rector of St Ewin's in the City of Briftol, and Patron, and 22 Years a faithful and able Paftor of this Parifh
Ob 16 April, 1762, aet 67

Alfo the Remains of Mrs ELIZABETH WARREN, a fincere Chriftian, The Wife of the faid Rev THOMAS TAYLOR, a Woman of a holy and devout Life
Ob 3 December, 1780, at 77

ON MONUMENTS IN THE NAVE.

Near this Place lies the Body of JOHN ROOS, who died 1704

Alfo the Body of MARGARET IVES, who died in 1705

Alfo the Body of MARGARET, the Wife of the faid JOHN ROOS, who died May 1, 1719

Hic juxta quiescunt
Reliquiæ LANGHAMI EDWARDS, A
Lximæ Pietatis Juvenis,
Quem
Vivum amarunt
Mortuum deflderant,
Omnes qui norunt
Cujus memoriam colens
Hoc Charitatis Fraternæ et Amicitiæ
Monumentum
Frater natu maximus
Mœrens pofuit
Obiit XXIX Die Apr
MDCCXXIX

Under the Chriftening Pew lie interred the
Remains of ELIZABETH, Daughter of
THOMAS POWER, of Badgnorth Court,
in the County of Somerfet, Efq by PENELOPE
his Wife, who departed this Life the 25th of
Auguft 1763, Aged 2 Years and 9 Months

In a Vault next the Pillar
lie interred the Remains of
WILLIAM ABRAM, of this Parifh,
who died January 1, 1760, Aged 50

Alfo of SARAH, the Wife of ROBERT BAYLEY,
and daughter of WILLIAM and SARAH ABRAM,
who died May 26, 1762
aged 22
Laftly in Piety and a fincere Chriftian

Near this Place lieth the Body
of Mifs ELIZABETH PROUDFOOT,
who departed this Life
the 19th Day of March, 1777,
Daughter of EDMUND PROUDFOOT, Efq
formerly an eminent Merchant in London

The Honourable
CHARLES HOWARD LESLIE,
fecond fon to the Earl of Rothes,
died on the 18th of April, 1762,
in the 15th Year of his Age.

ON FLAT STONES,
IN THE NAVE

ELIZABETHA, Uxor GEORGII IRISH nuper
de Parochia St Werburgæ, in Briftol,
(pofter hac Parochia) Gen
Ob 24 Die July, 1724.
Anno ætatis 6?

Prædictus GEORGIUS IRISH, natus fuit, in
Parochia de Banwell, in Com Somerfet,
20 Die Maii, 1652 Connorttis et
in Corn Street, in Briftol, a Menfe Mar 1,
1688, diq ad 29 Septembris, 1765
Ob 23 Die Maii

SARAH MARSH
1759

Alfo the Body of
THO COL MATTHEWS,
died after, 1769

Hic jacet Corpus
THOMA BENTLEY, LLD
Qui obiit XXIII Maii,
Anno 1742, æt 50

JOHN PARE, Efq
of the Ifland of Antigua,
departed this Life 13 July, 1757, aged 53.

RICHARD GOORE,
Son of CHARLES GOORE, of Liverpool,
Merchant, departed this Life
th 12th Oct 1739, æt 27

ESTHER, Daughter of THOMAS
and ESTHER AMOS, and EDWARD their
Son, died Infants

ESTHER, Wife of THOMAS AMOS,
died May 16, 1739, aged 61

DOROTHY, the Wife of WILLIAM GOODMAN,
of this Parifh, died March 23, 1704

Here lieth the Body of the Honourable
JOHN TALBOT,
fecond Brother of the Right Honourable
GEORGE Earl of Shrewfbury,
who departed this Life the 5th Day of April,
Anno Domini 1731, ætatis fuæ 26

ANN, the Wife of WILLIAM BAYLEY,
died Auguft 10, 1746, aged 43

WILLIAM BAYLEY,
died January 27, 1763, aged 59

Here lieth the Body of JOSIAH LITTLEPAGE,
of London, who came to drink the
Hotwell Water, for the Recovery of his
Health, but, in five Days after his Arrival,
died on the 31ft of January, 1712, aged 32

Here lie the Remains of EDMUND
ROGERS, and ANN his Wife, of this Parifh,
fhe died Oct 24, 1747, he the 21ft Dec 1754
Each in the 63d Year of their Age

ON MONUMENTS
IN THE NORTH AISLE

In a Vault near this Place is depofited, the Body
of MARY the Wife of PAUL FISHER, of this
Parifh, there to reft till it fhall be raifed in
Incorruption, and be united to her immortal
Soul in everlafting Life, thro' the Mercy of God
and Merits of Jefus Chrift
Oh Grave, where is thy Victory?
She died the 8th of January, 1755

Alfo the Body of
PAUL FISHER, who departed this Life
the 4th of Dec 1752, aged 72

In this Church are deposited the
Remains of ROBERT DINWIDDIE, Esq;
formerly Governour of Virginia, who departed
July 27, 1770, in the 78th Year of his Age.
The Annals of that Country will testify
with what Judgment, Activity, and Zeal he
exerted himself, in the Publick Cause, when the
whole North American Continent was involved
in a French and Indian War.
His Rectitude of Conduct in his Government,
his Integrity in other Publick Imployments,
add a Lustre to his Character, which was revered
whilst he lived, and will be held in remembrance
whilst his Name survives. His more private
Virtues, and the amiable social Qualities he possessed,
were the Happiness of his Friends and Relations,
Many of whom shared his Bounty.
All lament his Loss. As his happy
Dispositions for domestick Life were but
known to his affectionate Wife and Daughters
They have erected this Monument,
to the Memory of his Conjugal and Parental Love,
which they will ever cherish and revere
with that Piety and Tenderness he so greatly
merited.

———————

Arms .... ,between ....
....

Near this .... of MARY, the
loving .... Wife of GEORGE DAVIS,
of Docklington, in the County of Oxford, Esq;
after having borne a tedious consumptive Illness,
with resigned Christian Patience becoming the rest
of her Life, she submitted from all human
Scenes on May 19, 1750, in the 37th Year
of her Age, in the Village of Clifton,
where, at her particular Request, she was buried.
This Monument was erected by her afflicted
Husband, as the last Testimony of his most
unfeigned Affection for a
truly virtuous Wife, a fond Parent, and a
sincere Friend.

———————

Near this Place are interred the Remains
of ROBERT FILL, Esq; of London, who departed
this Life the 19th of May,
1759, aged 27 Years.

And also of Mr. MARTHA PERKINS,
Wife of Mr. JOHN PERKINS of London.
She died the 17th of February, 19, aged ...

———————

Here lieth buried Mrs. ANNE HAY,
of Chipping Barnet, in the County of Hertford,
who died the 9th of January 1761,
aged ... Years.
.... of Temper and Purity of Heart
rendered her belov'd in Life,
and sincerely lamented at her Death.

———————

Near this Stone are deposited the
Remains of Mrs. MARY COXE
who died Sept. 16, 1761, ...

Arms ....

Under ....
the Remains ....
Daughter of John Chudleigh ....
Governour of .... his Wife, M..........
.... Parish ....
.... together Child..........
of William Waters ....
.... Age was ....
....
Here..........
.... Tender..........
.... A

———————

Arms. Argent, a Pend .... Sable on a
round Buckle Or .... point of the .... or
a Lock displayed Or .... Sea .... in the
2nd Quarter, 3d .... Azure, a bend Or, 3 Gross Crossets Or, and Argent three trefoils, slipped
is 2, 4th ....

Here lieth,
In hopes of a blessed Resurrection,
the Body of MARGARET, the Wife
of ARCHIBALD STIRLING, of Keir,
in the County of Perth, Esq;
who patiently bore the Paines
of a tedious Illness and other
various Resignation, which .... other
.... her purity of Heart
and sincerity of Manners continuing,
died the .... of December, MDCCXLI
John Somervil this monument
by directions of her Husband.

———————

Arms. Sable, a Fesse betwixt four
.... Argent, and in Chief a Mullet for the Difference.

In the North Aisle, near this Monument,
lieth the Body of MARGARET MUNSTER, third
Daughter of FRANCIS MUNSTER, late of London,
Merchant, who liv'd to her forty third Year,
having proved herself a Pattern .... of
Imitation .... would many Years into
an over Compleated Life to a Period in which
was summoned into
the .... Part of December,
MDCCXXXII.

Also the Body of the said FRANCIS MUNSTER,
born Nov. 6, 1692, who died July ...,
Aged 85 Years and one Month.
.... who lov'd him, knew ....
.... Sister or of other Relations the
.... down or erected
.... their Bodies,
Francis Munster.

———————

Near this Place lie interred
.... and Wife of ....
of the Parish who died June the 6th, ...
aged 74.

Also .... and John Barton,
.... October the 9th, 1757, aged 9

———————

1

Here lieth the Body of JOHN BOWES, Son
of GEORGE BOWES, of Bowtham, near
the City of York, by FRANCES his Wife,
Daughter of Sir JOHN LEGARD, Baronet,
of Ganton, in the East Riding of York
Obiit Jan the 19th, 1721, aged 19 Years

To the Memory of THOMAS PRICE, Esq
of Gogerthan in the County of Cardigan,
who departed this Life Nov 7, 1737,
aged 46 Years

Near this Pillar lies the Body of
SARAH, Daughter of ROBERT WHARAM,
of Wentworth, in the County of York,
Gentleman, she departed this life the
first of Sept 1753, aged 30 Years

CHRISTIANA GORDON,
Daughter of Sir ROBERT GORDON, of Gordonstown,
in the Kingdom of Scotland, Bart.
The lovelieft of her Sex,
who, with all the Sprightliness natural at her Years,
possessed so great a Share of Prudence
and Judgment as to render her the Delight of
her Parents, and deservedly
the Favourite of her Acquaintance,
was interred near this Place,
26 March, 1759, aged 14 Years

ON FLAT STONES.

ANN WHITE,
died Sept 27, 1727, aged 27

JOHN WHITE, late of the City of Bristol, Vintner,
Brother to the above named ANN WHITE,
who died 11th day of May, 1728, aged 37 Years

Arms, Quarterly, 1st, A Lion Rampant, 2nd,
a Scaling Ladder in Bend between three Escallops,
3d, A Chevron between three Spears Heads, 4th,
fix Roundlets in Pile, and in Chief a Demi Lion
Isuant

Here lieth the Body of
LEWIS PRICE, late of Boverton, in the County of
Glamorgan, Esq who departed this Life
Sept 3, 1744, aged 32
He was the Eldest Son of FRANCIS PRICE,
of Erw-Wasted in the County of Carmarthen,
Esq and married ELIZABETH Daughter of
RICHARD LICE, of Boverton aforesaid, Esq
and Relict of EVAN LLYS, of the same
Place, Esq

ROGER BAYLY, of
the City of Bristol, Haberdasher,
died July 6, 1740, aged 50

THOMAS HUNGERFORD,
of the City of Bristol, Gent
Obiit Nov 16, 1741, aged 80

The Rev Mr GEORGE BURTON,
Rector of Radwinter, in Essex,
departed this Life March, 1723-4,
aged 52 Years

TOPP HEATH,
of Weston, in the County of Durham,
departed this Life Oct 19, 1756, aged 4-

DANIEL CHISTON,
of the City of Bristol, Merchant,
was born at Hereford, June 1712
Obiit the 4th Feb 1754

JOHN DARBY, of this Parish,
died 14 March, 1732, aged 30

ELIZABETH his Wife,
died 4 March 1733, aged 45

MARTHA Wife of JOHN PERKINS,
Citizen and Grocer of London
Obiit 17 Feb 1749, 40

ON MONUMENTS IN THE
SOUTH AISLE

To the Memory of SARAH POORE,
Daughter of JOHN and SARAH POORE,
of Portsmouth, who exchanged this Life for a
better, July 8, 1777, aged 28 Years

Here continue to waste,
His Soul having taken her Flight to Heaven,
the small Remains of JOHN POTT, Jun
who died of a Consumption
the 5th of January, 1779, aged 26
Young in Years, old in Virtue,
a Son second to none,
a Brother loving and beloved,
a Friend esteemed by all,
in Religion serene and sincere,
in Business steady,
in Conversation polite
Candour and Justice,
Humanity, Benevolence, and Courage
possessed his Soul
He lived with the Praises,
died with the Prayers,
of all those
whose Prayers or Praise
are of any Value,
and fell a Victim to honourable Death
This is not the vain Eulogium of fond ———
but the heart-felt Testimony of ————,
who, till this melancholy Period,
had enjoyed in this Small that Happiness
which Prudence ————
by Divine Grace ——— commandments
A like but proper Happiness
he wishes to every Life
Superior Merit is rarely ——

Here lies interred, in full Hope of a
glorious Resurrection, the Body of
Mrs MARGARET FERGUSON,
second Daughter of Sir JAMES FERGUSON, Bart.
one of the Senators of the College of
Justice in Scotland, she died Oct 9th, 1753,
in the 24th Year of her Age

———————————————

Arms, Two Lions passant.

To the Memory
of Mrs ELIZABETH BILLMAN,
Wife of WILLIAM BILLMAN, Esq of
the Island of
Barbadoes, and one of the Daughters of the
late JOSIAH DOTIN, Esq of the said Island,
who died in this Village on the 10th of August,
1763, in the 36th Year of her Age,
and the 17th of her Marriage, leaving four
Sons and two Daughters.
A Woman
uniformly and without Ostentation,
actuated by the great Principles of Virtue and
Religion, easy in her Desires and
Enjoyments by Prudence and a well disposed
Mind, secure against Temptation or Surprize
Tender is and Benevolence were seen in her
pleasing Countenance, an amiable Simplicity of
Manners in her Deportment,
and both shewed the constant influence of
Innocence
Quick to discover and acknowledge Merit,
yet indulgent to the Failings of Humanity,
she contemplated with Delight the Excellencies
of her Friends, and saw with Candour
their Defects
Insensible of her own Worth, she viewed
with partial Eyes
her Husband,
and give him the warm and active Affection
of a Heart which knew no Joy or Interest
unconnected with His
Let this Monument record
her Virtues, his Gratitude and Love

———————————————

Arms, Argent two Crescents in Base Sable, and
in Chief a Bear's Head couped Purpure, within a
Bordure Sable

Near
this Monument lies interred the Body of
Lieut Col ALEXANDER TENNANT,
of Horderwood, in Edinburghshire,
in whom
Courage, Honour, and Probity, joined with the
mildest Temper and gentle Manners, were
equally conspicuous
His Strength being wasted by Wounds
received in the Service of his Country
at Minden, Warburg and Campen,
he died at the Hot well,
Sept 17, 1763,
aged 49

———————————————

Near this Place lies interred
the Remains of HARRIOT HALL,
Daughter of Sir THOMAS HALL, Bart
of the County of Kent
She died here the 7th of Oct 1763
in the 24 Year

———————————————

JOHN WAUGH, of London Merchant,
died on the third, and ISABEL his Wife
on the twenty fourth of July,
MDCCLXXV
He in the 34th, and she in the 33d Year of
her Age
Their remains lie deposited in a Vault near
this Spot, A D 1770
Point Thomas Floor, Edinburgh his

———————————————

Hic situs est JOHAN PILGRIM, A B
Sac Coll John Corinth
Pietatis exempli, Literarum decus,
Quem
Nominate solenni decoravit
Mæcenas Holles Dux Novi Castri
Ob Jul 20, 1753 ætat 23

———————————————

Near this Place lies the Body of
JOHN LARBOURDI, Esq
who departed this Life the 21st of May, 1759,
in the 41st Year of his Age

———————————————

In Memory of
Mr CHARLES SUMNER,
youngest Son
of JOHN SUMNER, D D
late Provost of King's College, Cambridge
He died
in the 19th Year of his Age,
May 25 1773

———————————————

In their underment oned Vault
lie the Remains of Mrs ELIZABETH SMITH,
Sister to the two JANE and SOPHIA SMITH
who died April 26, 1780, aged 26 Years

———————————————

In a Vault underneath,
at the East End of the North Side,
inclosed with Brick work,
wherein is a Stone (with an Inscription)
signifying that here
lie the Remains of Miss JANE SMITH,
aged 16, and Miss SOPHIA SMITH,
aged 14, who both died the 27th April, 1772,
They were the Daughters of
SAMUEL BENNET SMITH, Esq Merchant,
of the Parish of
St John's, Southwark,
by ELIZABETH his Wife
Reader
if Innocence and Virtue
are worthy Remembrance,
then drop
an affectionate Tear
to their Memory

———————————————

In a Vault underneath
are deposited the Remains of
FRANCIS MARGARET STEVENSON,
Daughter of ROBERT and MARGARET STEVENSON
of Morton hall, Chiswick, in the County of
Middlesex, who died at Clifton
May 1, 1784, aged 7 Years 8 Months,
and 3 Days

———————————————

Sacred to the Memory of JANE, the Wife of
ROBERT BRENT, Esq of Plymouth,
who died on the 11th of July, 1781,
in the 26th Year of her Age
Her disconsolate Husband caused this
Monument to be erected to perpetuate her
Memory

JAMES ENGLL, Esq
Ensign of the 45th Regiment,
Obiit 13 April, 1785, ætatis 14 Years.
This Monument was erected by
his afflicted Father, who was
22 Years an Officer in the said Regiment

M S
Sacred to the Memory of
PRIOR, the third Son of the Rev FRANCIS SAY,
and DIANNA, his Wife, of East Hatley,
in the County of Cambridge, who departed
this Life August 2, in the 9th Year
of his Age, and in the Year of our Lord, 1787
His Remains are deposited in a Vault under
the Church

To the Memory of
LLEWLYN PIERREPONT, late an eminent Merchant,
of the City of London,
who died the 6th of April, 1787,
aged 36 Years
His Remains are interred in a
Vault underneath

In
the Vault of this Church are deposited
the Remains of the Rev JOHN STUCKEY
Son of JOHN STUCKEY, of Weston Down, who,
to commemorate his King,
and in Regard to his Virtue,
his Grateful and kind Men
hath raised this Monument
He finished an extensive Education at
Baliol College, Oxon
He was Master of dead and living Languages,
he was learned without Pedantry,
Religious without Ostentation,
and placed without Rigidity,
the World to him was all a Shade,
and Heaven his only Joy,
which he founded
On
the Life, Sufferings, and Death
of
JESUS CHRIST
He expired the 13th Day of Dec 178,,
at the Hot wells, near this Place,
with all possible Christian Fortitude,
and in a most pious Resignation
to the Omnipotence of God,
in the 30th Year of His Age
M DAWE

IN THE CHURCH YARD

ON TABLETS AGAINST THE CHURCH

Near this Stone lies
CATHARINE MURRAY,
Lady Rollo,
who died July 28, 1763

In a Vault beneath this Stone
lies interred the Body of the late
Rev LEWIS MASTERS, Doctor in Divinity,
President of St John's College,
in the University of Oxford,
who departed this Life 22 Nov 1774,
aged 76 Years

ON TOMBS.

MARY the Wife of CRAVEN LEWIS,
of St Pierre in the County of
Monmouth, Esq departed this Life
Aug 1, 1755

Sacred to the Memory of
CRAVEN LEWIS, fourth son of
CRAVEN LEWIS, of St Pierre,
in the County of Monmouth, Esq
who was unfortunately drowned in
crossing the Severn in a small Boat,
on Sunday the 6th of Nov 1715,
aged 16

CHRIS . . . . of the City of
Bristol, Merchant, died 2d of Feb
1752, aged 35

WILLIAM WAREHAM, of this Parish,
died June 4 1775, aged 41

RUTH, Wife of WILLIAM LANDON,
and late Wife of the said
WILLIAM WAREHAM,
died April 25, 1780, aged 47

JANE Wife of THOMAS BARRET,
died Apr 18, 1711, aged 55

THOMAS their Son died an Infant

JANE WILKINS,
died July 18, 1768, aged 84

THOMAS ELLIOTT,
died July 19, 1763, aged 5.

ELIZABETH BAKER LUNDON . . . .,
died Dec 31, 1760, aged 1

JAMES PEACE
of the Parish of St Mary Port,
Son of JOSIAH PEACE,
died July 1777, aged 3.

SARAH, the Daughter of THOMAS
LYNE, Esq of Hatton, near . . . . .,
died June 14, 1784, aged 5

MATTHEW PEACE,
of the Parish of St Philip and Jacob,
died May 13, 1745, aged 52

Also two Children by MARGARET
his Wife

MATTHEW PEACE,
of the Parish of St Philip and Jacob,
died July 13, 1742, aged 55

RACHEL, Wife of MATTHEW PEACE
died March 1, 1755, aged 60

REBECCA Wife of WILLIAM CAINS,
Daughter of MATTHEW and
RACHEL PEACE,
died March 9, 1761

Also four other Children
viz SARAH, SARAH, WILLIAM,
and JAMES

ANN Daughter of MATTHEW
and RACHEL PEACE
died July 1, 1718, aged 33

WILLIAM CAINS, Represent . . . .
of the said Parish of St Philip
and Jacob,
died Apr 16, 1761, aged

. . . . Regiment . . . . . .
died July 16, 1761, aged . .

HENRY LEWIS
died Feb. 4, 1755, aged 49

MARY his Wife
died Oct. 30, 1757, aged

SAMUEL NICHOLLS Jun.
died in November, ...

MARY Wife of SAMUEL LEWIS,
died June ...

... and ...
died July 6, ...

... Daughter of
SAMUEL and MARY ...
died Sept. ...

SAMUEL, Son of WILLIAM LEWIS,
died Nov. ...

... departed this Life May 4, 17...

... Son the second
... Years ...
died March 1, 7...

Mr. AMBROSE MAY,
late Quarter Master
to the ... Regiment of Foot,
who lost his Life in the Havana,
on the Island of Cuba,
died August 6, 17...
in the 53d Year of his Age

In Memory of
Mrs. CATHARINE TYSON,
late of Shifnal,
who came to Clifton,
this Tomb erected
by (I W) her affectionate Admirer,
as the last Testimony
of his unfeigned Love to a most
amiable and pious young Lady,
who possessed every Virtue
that adorned her Sex.

EVAN MORGAN
Sugar Refiner, of the City of Bristol,
died April 3, 17...

CHARLES ...
died ...

... COX
died March ...

JAMES KING
died May ...

... his Wife
died Oct. ...

... Wife of ...
... September ...
died Jan. 18, ...

ANN, Wife of WILLIAM MITCHELL,
of this Parish,
died August 31, 1751

NATHANIEL WATTS
late of the ...
died Dec. 28, 1755, aged 51

... CANN, Wife of Captain
WILLIAM CANN, in the Naval
... died July ...

JULIANA, Wife of SAMUEL WALKER,
died at ...
died ...

Arise, and ...
Free ...

... RICHARDSON, of this Parish,
died Jan. 8, 1755, aged 79

WILLIAM ..., of his Parish,
died ...

... died August 14, 7..., aged

... SOCERS
died Sept. ..., aged 40

EDWARD PAPPS, of this Parish,
died Nov. ..., 1755, aged 16

SUSANNA MARKHAM, Daughter of
EDWARD PARKER,
died August 16, 1755, aged 19

... Wife of THOMAS WOODALL,
died Nov. 19, 1754, aged 41

JOHN WOODALL
died Oct. ..., 1765, aged

... Son of
GEORGE ... of his Parish,
died ...

... DOLL,
died Nov. 2, 1756, aged 50

MARY WOODALL
died Oct. ..., aged 51

... Wife of
ROBERT ...
died July ... 1760, in the ... year of
her age

MATTHEW CLIFFORD,
of this Parish, Gent.
died Oct. 5, 17..., aged 40

ANN his Wife
died January ..., 17..., aged

... their son
died Nov. 19, ..., aged 4 Years
6 Months

ANN, Wife of PHILIP WILLIAM,
died August ..., 1765, aged 55

PHILIP WILLIAM
died June ..., 1752, aged 77

RICHARD EVANS, Surgeon,
died March 14, ...

... BROWN, of this Island,
... wright,
died ...

JOHN PEARSE, of the Parish of James,
... died Nov. ..., aged 55

DAVID ..., of this Church Parish,
died Oct. ..., 17..., aged 55

ANN his Wife
died Nov. ..., aged 54

JAMES HERD, of the Parish of St.
James,
died Jan. 13, aged ... Years and
... ...

MARY WOODRUFF, als C. ATRALL,
Daughter ... of the Parish of St. James,
died Aug. 5, 1755, aged 59

CHARLES JONES, of this Parish
died ...

JAMES, Wife of CHARLES JONES,
died Sept. ..., 1755, aged 6

... Wife ... died,
died June ..., 17..., aged 5

THOMAS CONSTANT, of the Parish of
James,
died August 6, 1758, aged 49

ANN CONSTANT
died ... April, 1776, aged

JAMES CLATERBY, Gent.
died ... 19, 17..., aged 35

... NATHANIEL
died 4 Jan. 1759, aged

POSTER, their son, died young

SARAH WILLOUGHBY
died April 4, 1766, aged 7

SARAH, Wife of JAMES HARRIS,
Mariner,
died Sept. 9, 1790, aged 30

MARY, Wife of JOHN FAVELL,
of the Parish of St. Augustine, Joyner,
died March 4, 1715, aged 28

JOHN FAVELL, her Husband,
died August ..., 1765, aged 69

ON FLAT AND HEAD STONES

	Died	Aged		Died	Aged
Mrs. ... Daughter of the Rev. ...	7 Jul. 17...	46	Ann, Wife of Charles Coney	16 May 1767	64
...			John Pollard	... Apr. 17...	
Walter Maber, ... of the ... Michael ...	21 Jan. 1771		Thomas Pollard his Brother	18 Dec. 17...	
...			... Brother of the late Thomas Pollard, M.D. ...		
... Cow ...	8 Sept. 17...		...	Mar. 1786	60
... of the Parish ...	14 Oct. 17...	5	Francis Marsha...	13 May 17...	
Esther, Wife of John ...	14 Oct. 17...	44	Mrs. John Marsh... of Jeffries Square, London		
Jane, Wife of John Turner	15 July, 17...	67		5 July 17...	

ON FLAT AND HEAD STONES

	Died	Aged		Died	Aged
Sir John Chalmers, late Captain in his Majesty's ... of ... respectable family of the County of Cork, Ireland	1 Jun 178?	59	John Chese	29 Aug 1771	5
Mons. Duval, Gent	1 Aug 1754		Ann ...	1 Oct 17?1	5
William Indrees, of this Parish, Victualler	June, 1782	5	John Lloyd, Attorney at Law	8 Apr 1713	5
Sarah his ...	5 Nov 1707	6	James Albert of St Augustine's Parish	21 July, 1755	5
Patrick Arthurs, of the Kingdom of Ireland ...	10 Apr 1774	—	Henry Vanburgh, Esq	19 Oct 1784	
Mary Colwell of ...	11 Mar 1778	5	Thomas Knight	1 Apr ...	?
Mary ... of Dublin	10 Aug 1778	1	John his wife	6 Nov 17?5	
John ... Carpenter of his Majesty's ship Nottingham ... drowned ... the Ho...	3 Dec 1778	24	Robert Adams	1 June 17?	
Henry Jones	8 Feb 1755	14	Ann his Wife	6 Aug 1?	
Martha Jones her Mother	3 Oct 1785	54	Jane ...	6 Jan ...	
John, son of Michael and Martha ...	3 Mar 1788	16	Mary ...	15 Aug 1755	
William Newton, of this Parish, Glassmaker	25 Oct 1786	65	Lucy, Wife of John Engers, of this Parish, Baker	12 Nov 1...	—
Mary, Wife of John Bedall	7 Aug 1785	5	John Cay	1 June 17?0	45
George Wright	4 Sep 1786	2	Susannah, Wife of James Wells of th Parish, at Augustin...	1 Feb 1782	14
Joseph, Son of William and Hester ...	2 May 1714	21	Elizabeth, Wife of Luke Guber	6 Sep 17?5	
John Delaine	22 Mar 17??	65	John ...	25 Nov 17?3	
... his Wife	23 Jan 1785	5	Francis Pipps	28 Jan 1771	54
Robert England, of Holborough	15 Dec 17?5	70	John Chisholm	6 Oct 1754	
Elizabeth, Wife of Edward Phillips	5 Aug 1754		Thomas Cumund	29 Oct 17??	
Richard Lund	21 Nov 1770	40	Mary his Wife	1 Apr 5	
Martha Jones of St Augustine's Parish	16 Dec 1787	6	George ... on	15 Nov 1755	
Jane Vedthropp, of ...	... Jan 1750		Martha, Wife of Samuel Garland	29 Mar 1754	54
Joseph Cousins	18 Feb 1765		Samuel Garland	5 Jul 17?5	
Henry Rogers	5 June 1765		Sarah, Daughter of George and ...binder	12 Aug 1761	14
Joseph, Son of Anthony and Elizabeth ...	4 Jul 1775	20	Robert Corp, Yeoman	6 Nov 17?3	6
Aaron Stilling, Shoemaker	31 Mar 1755	5	James Evans	20 Nov 1753	5
Elizabeth his Wife	12 June 1758	3	Elizabeth his Wife	6 Nov 17?5	
...	11 July, 1755		Joanna Walker	1 Apr 1774	
...	... Jan 17?5	4	Mary, Wife of John Hewfor	6 Aug 17??	
Michael Leek	... Jan 1745		Jane, Wife of Bernard Fitzpatrick	1 Sep 17?0	
... his wife	31 Mar 1745		... his Daughter	10 Feb 17?4	
... Ree	1 Jun 17??	49	Magdalen Williams	6 Jan 17??	5
Mary, Wife of William ...	... Oct 1755	—	Charles White	1 May, 1778	
... Luly	... Oct 1?	—	John Print	11 Nov 17?4	4
...	6 Nov 1?	—	William ...	6 Apr 17??	
Ann March the	July, 17?0		...		
John ... clerk, Yeoman	... Apr 17?5	5	...	1 June, 1782	
John Nell	7 ... 17??		Thomas ...	19 Feb 17?5	41
Joan ...			Ann, Wife of James Rustles, Gent	1 Dec 17?0	
...	1 ... 17?1		...	15 Dec 1754	
... Wife of ...	... Nov 17?1		John Keate	6 ... 17??	
...	... Nov 17?1		Stephen Sellars	17 ... 17??	
...	... Nov 1755		Thomas Line	... Apr 17	
... his Wife	6 July, 1755		Mary, late of William Wells Clerk on this Parish	1 Feb 1752	
...	... May, 17?0	4	Keturah Jones, Wife of William Jones, of ... Draper		
... Wife	...		Robert ...	19 Feb 17??	
...	5 Jan 175	70	Edward John W...	1 Dec 17??	

IS a Parish of ordinary Extent in the Hundred of *Berkeley*, six Miles North Eastward from that Town, three from *Dursley* on the North, and twelve on the South from *Gloucester*, and is bounded by the Hills of *Uley* and *Knapshill*. The Soil is heavy and fertile, and can it supplied to Pasturage.

The subjoined Account of this Parish extracted from the MSS. of John Smythe, Esq. in 1639, is given at Length, as indeed few places have undergone less variation of Property, though in other circumstances since that period.

" *Coaley* in Domesday Book . . . . a Parish and Manor whereof George Lord Berkeley is Lord,
" Part of his Barony of . . . . and holden by Knights Service *in Capite*, the Demesnes hereof con-
" sisted of fower Hides of Land as Domesday Booke sheweth. In the Hundred returns hereof,
" whereby the inhabitants are more distinctly known viz. . . . . As to
" this Parish of *Coaley* adjoineth the Parish of . . . . an ancient Parcel of . . . Possessions of the
" Abbot of *St. Peter's* in Gloucester, whose Convent there going . . . . Customes to be re-
" moved, and . . . to Lords Tennants of this Manor of *Coaley* and of his other Manor of *Uley*,
" next adjoining, for which Service the said Abbot, by his Cellarer, who . . . his Lord . . of *Matho*
" (a Cell to this Monastery . . . adjoining) to lett the Bulls and Boars of . . . said Manors,
" in Harvest time . . . the said Abbor complained to Thomas Lord Berkeley, the second of that
" Name, then Lord or . . . Manors, that to his great wrong and prejudice . . . . that Bull,
" fayning themselves Tennants to that Lord, Seriants and Baylifs to these his Manor . . when . . were
" not. Whereupon in 27 . . . . it was . . . . that in behalf of the . . . Lord, every one and
" Bayley of the said Manor should hold in short having a . . . under every Keeper . . . . Cotterer and
" Binder 2d. and every Raker . . . . said Convent . . . in Lieu of their Toll, which order I take till
" the Dissolution of that Monastery in the Time of King Henry VIII. or . . . thereto. In the 6th
" of Edw. III. 1333, there was an Agreement or Deed indented, between the said Lord Thomas and
" the said Abbot of St. Peter's, for . . . containing between their Tennants of *Coaley* and *Uley*, and
" for enclosing Part of the Fields of these Manors, which holds to this . . .

" The King is Patron of this . . . and whereof the Rectory and Appropriation is the In-
" heritance of John Brown, Esq. who purchased thereof in November . . . . from Morris and
" Phillips, who had the same from the King, by Letters Patent dated in September before, in
" Fee farm at 15 . . . yearly Rente; which Letters Patent to Wintersell and Price, their Heires, to
" shortly after sold the same to John Brown since the Father. Which Rectory or Appropriation is
" after the Dissolution of St. Peter's in Gloucester (to which it anciently belonged) granted to Sir
" Antony Kingston, and from him at time seen to the Crowne. It is holden now of the King, as
" of the Manor of *East Greenwich*, in free and common Soccage, and not in Capite.

" The which Church are dedicated to St. Bartholomew the Patron Saint thereof. On whose Feast
" day yet continue the such Concourse and Resort of People, that as hath the name of *Coaley* Fair
" day, whereto most know of Country . . . resort, and . . . a Booth or . . . up . . .
" It is no Grant or Letters from the Crowne, or otherwise than the Resort thereto of the old . . .
" Bretheren . . . of the Devotion and love of the Inhabitants both on that Day and on the Sundaie
" after, called Coaley . . . or the Wake day, which even now . . . in . . . in Fame and Flourishing . . .
" diminished and decayed.

" Of this Parish and . . . . . stone Have written of *Coaley* that if it were enclosed round from
" all other Soccage . . . Tennents . . . given it would abundantly suffice for the Habitation and Main-
" tenance of the Inhabitants, . . . no supply from other Hands, that the Minister of Arms could need
" only desire.

" The duty . . . Resort . . . accompanied in Part with the Luke accomplish, the Estern Part
" of the Parish . . . part . . . . whereof is called *Coaley*, where to be observed any Mound
" Meads discharge or discovery, and hence tumbling down, deserted, on a continual . . .

. . . .
. . . . . . Mill . . . .

" the Afternoon, what Time the Resorte is greatest, Langueth not in ... Delight to many of the ...
" Senalitie delighting them.

" Through this Town and Parish runne two pleasant Streames arising from the Foote of the fore...
" Hilles, that flowinge the... of many Yards asunder, before neither goe a Rice thro' ... part the play...
" of the Town, the other watering most of the... ordinance Inclosures, whereunder such Time...
" it summer white like Streit, from Came... a colt unto a certain Stones, retained by good ..., Per...
" wickes Oyster, and the like, of much Curiosi... Delight to lose upon, and to co...
" ... which Iniquites to unlose the greatest Sports of Nature, that ... ... the grete Paidou...
" ... of the Age, to have by sometime such much Curiosi... engendered in the Sea, and by the ... ...
" comvpon ... and in Places, and for to be shall times do nied."

These Notices not only faintly vol... mutely the Pr... of the Parish, but give to ...
pleasing Ketch of the parochial Customs of early Ages, which even in the late Century were...
declin... and are now mostly obsolete or supposed.

The Structure of the Church is plain, consisting of a Nave and North A... It appears that the
Tower, which is handsome furnished with tiered Battlements and Pinacles, was erected, probably,
by the Convent of Pears, in Gloucester for two Efeuch os in mon on other Side the Toore a...
Upon one a Gothic D inclosing the letter A, but this Initial will not apply to any of the Abbots. O...
the other a Cheveron defaced, Part of the Arms of Berkeley...

The Impropriation now belongs to the Rev John Go torth , M. A. by Purchase from the Farm...
of Minster to whom it is told under Decree of the Court of Chancery, from the Heirs of Hac...
court, who succeeded the Browns as about ... Years since.

To this Manor the far greater Part of the Parish is attached. Other Estates are held by the Families
of ... ..., ..., Matthews Vizard, Bulland, Underwood, Minet, Savage, Dis-
..., Roberts, and Corpor... of Gloucester.

B E N E F A C T I O N S

Mrs Brown ... lent an Annuity of 12s per Annum, inboc... of a House for the Use of the
Poor,

Houses and Land to the Value of 6l 14s 10d per Annum was given by some Persons unknown,
wards repairing the Church, and for the Relief of such Poor as do not receive Alms.

INCUMBENTS	PATRONS	INCUMBENTS	PATRONS
——— John Bromage,	———	1632 William Harding,	
1582 Thomas Pont,	Queen Elizabeth	1663 Richard Hall, A B	King Charles I
1608 Andrew Porter,	King James	1695 Henry Bond, LL B	King William II
1611 Richard Benchfield,	King John	1... Thomas Hornidge, Clk	King George II
——— Thomas Pho ,			

The present Lord of the Manor,

The Right Honourable FREDERICK AUGUSTUS, Earl of BERKELEY

The Persons returned from this Place both the Houses in 1685 and 165 , were

John Browning, Esq.   Stephen Bromage, Gent
John Bromage, Jun Esq

In ... 1730, Eleven Freeholders gave Votes for the Parish.

The Register commences with the Year 1580.

An Account of Marriages, Births and Burials, in this Parish

A...	...	...	A D	Mar	Bur	Bur	Lu	A D	M	Bur	Bur	A D	Mar	Bur
...			17.6	9	21	16		1791				1796		
...	21	...	18...	5	...	...		1792				179		
178			17...			10		179				179		
			17...					1791				17		
			17...					1795				18		

INSCRIPTIONS

INSCRIPTIONS IN THE CHURCH

IN THE CHANCEL.

ON A RAISED TOMB

Here lieth the Body of
RICHARD BROWNING, Gent
who died Dec 5, anno 1594

ON AN ATCHIEVEMENT ARE THESE ARMS AND INSCRIPTION

1st and 4th, Azure three Bars Wavy Argent, for
BROWNING, 2nd and 3d, Quarterly, Gules and Or,
a bend Argent, for FITZ NICHOL

In Memorie JOHANNIS BROWNING,
(hujus Pagi) Armiger, qui honore
ac opulenter vixit, posterosque copiose
curavit, et in hoc comitatu his vicecomitis officio fungebatur hoc factum est

Ob die 1 Decembris, Anno { Ætat 6,
{ Salutis 1674.

Non est mori, quod opto
Relinqui

ON FLAT STONES

STEPHEN BROWNING, Gent
departed this Life the 20th of Nov
Anno 1657

Arms, BROWNING as before, impaling Argent a
Fels couped Sable between three Lions passant
Gules, for CODRINGTON

JOHN BROWNING, Esq
Captain of the Youth of the Court,
deceased October 2 Anno Dom 1696,
aged 64 Years

Arms BROWNING as before, quartering Argent
a Bull passant Gules, for RIDLEY

JOHN, the second Son of
JOHN BROWNING of this Parish, Gent
died Feb 5, 1707, aged 6 Years and 4 Months

ELIZABETH Daughter of
the said JOHN BROWNING, Gent
died June 4, 1706, aged 3 Years and 6 Months

Arms BROWNING, impaling RIDLEY as before

ELIZABETH Daughter of
JOHN BROWNING Gent
by ELIZABETH his Wife, was born
Dec 7, 1699, aged 8 Weeks

Arms BROWNING, quartering RIDLEY as before

ELIZABETH Wife of JOHN BROWNING, Gent
departed this Life Oct 23, 1705, aged 32

Arms BROWNING only

JANE the youngest Daughter
of JOHN BROWNING Esq
ob Dec 27, 1727 in the 11th Year of her Age

Arms, CODRINGTON, as before

MARY Relict of JOHN BROWNING, Esq
Daughter of JOHN CODRINGTON, of Didmarton,
deceased the 18th Dec 1691, aged 59

CHRISTIAN the Wife of
JOHN BROWNING, deceased
August 24, 1637

Arms per Fess indented in Chief 3 Lioncels
quartering RIDLEY as before

SARAH the Wife of RICHARD RIDLEY, Gent
departed this Life June 2, in the 76th Year
of her Age, Anno Dom 1715

IN THE NAVE.

ON A BRASS PLATE NEAR THE PULPIT
1630.

I H   F M

LIE MANIBUS OMNIUM DANIELIS STAYNO,
verbi Dei præco, et artibus
Mori, Viri, ut quidem nobilium vixit,
integerrimi, multigenis eruditioni,
mari reque timendo rectoral in
Ecclesia huic Parochiali, cui
biennium et amplius præfuit,
femina et ad consumptas propre-
modum vixit diligenter, quond præ dicti
Coll Magdalen Oxonient been proe mente
qui, cui magno peculii incommodo,
et communi vicorum luctu, fuerum
tenerum communitavit, die XXIII
mensis Aprilis, anno salutis nostræ
MDCXXX Solute et patienter
Christum ipse mortalis immortale
prætium exemplum, placide
in Domino obdormificando
Mærens præcens
hoc posuit curavit,
RODERICUS STAYNO

ON A MONUMENT

Arms Gules three Greyhounds current in pale
Or, for HARDING

In Memory of MAURICE HARDING, Gent
and ANN his Wife,
he died Dec 23, 1718, aged 85 Years
She July 15, 1703, aged 66 Years

Likewise three of their Children

ELIZABETH, died June 2, 1695, aged 13,
MARY, died July 6, 1707, aged 13,
JOHN, died June 1, 1716, aged 33

In Memory also of ELIZABETH,
Wife of the said JOHN, who died May 23, 1722,
aged 46

In Memory also of JOHN, Son of the
said JOHN and ELIZABETH HARDING, Esq
who died May 29, 1727,
aged 7 Years

ON

ON FLAT STONES

WALTER OSBORNE, Gent
of this Parish, departed this Life
the 30th Day of August, 1677

ANNE the Wife of
WALTER OSBORNE, Gent
was buried Oct 23, 1680

IN THE NORTH AISLE.

In Memory of DANIEL OATRIDGE,
of this Parish, who was buried
the 4th Day of August, in the 73d Year of his
Age, 1703

In Memory of JOHN OATRIDGE,
of this Parish, Gent who died
April 26, 1734, ætatis suæ 79

Also of MARY his Wife,
who died June 22, 1712, æt 49

In Memory of HANNAH,
Daughter of JOHN OATRIDGE,
who died 22 June, in the 7th Year of her Age,
1704

In Memory of JOHN OATRIDGE,
of this Parish, Gent Son of JOHN
and MARY OATRIDGE, who died
June 28, 1749, ætatis suæ 64

ON A MONUMENT AGAINST THE NORTH WALL.

In Memory of MARY, the Wife
of MILES OATRIDGE, Daughter of JOHN WILKINS,
of Frocester, who died Feb 16, 1736,
aged 41

Likewise six of their Children

HANNAH died May 24, 1726, aged 11 Days

JOHN died May 27, 1727, aged 2 Weeks

JOHN died Jan 12, 1729, aged 2 Weeks and
5 Days

ROBERT died March 3, 1730, aged 2 Weeks and
3 Days

JOANNA died Dec 1, 1736, aged 4 Weeks

DANIEL died Nov 28, 1738, aged 16 Years
and 7 Months

Also in Memory of others of their Family,
now extinct

MARTHA Wife of THOMAS OATRIDGE, of
Tetbury, died Nov 11, 1754, aged 19,
and was buried there

MARY Wife of RICHARD CORY, of Frampton,
died Oct 15, 1759, aged 39, and was buried
there

MILES OATRIDGE, jun only Son remaining,
died May 12, 1770.

SARAH his Wife, Daughter of JOHN WILKINS
of Frocester, died July 22, 1767, aged 42,
and were both buried at Churchdown

JOHN their only Son died unmarried at Sea,
July 30, 1758, aged 28

The above MILES OATRIDGE, died Sept 14, 1774,
aged 80, and was buried at Hampstead,
in Middlesex

ELIZABETH Wife of JAMES ROSSIERE, died
18 Oct 1772, aged 57, and was buried at
Chichester in Sussex

ANN, Wife of MAURICE SAVAGE,
died May 20 1758, aged 71

IN THE CHURCH YARD, ON TOMBS

WILLIAM PARKER
died Oct 11, 1742, aged 68
MARY his Wife
died Sept 20, 1730, aged 58
DANIEL PARKER
died July 19, 1730, aged 57
ANNE his Wife
died Sep 29, 1722, aged 56
WILLIAM PARKER
died Nov 6, 1783, aged 68
JAMES the Son of WILLIAM and MARY PARKER,
died Oct 11, 1753, aged 31

SAMUEL FORD
died March 7, 1768, aged 51

JAMES JOYNER
died Dec 1, 1729, aged 47
ANNE his Wife
died Nov 26, 1723, aged 52
WILLIAM their Son
died Oct 28, 1767, aged 57
WILLIAM his Wife
died March 8, 1757, aged 71
WILLIAM JOYNER
died Oct 16, 1754
SARAH his Wife
died June 18, 1766, aged 77

MARY

MARY KNEE
died Dec 18, 1765, aged 78.

JOSEPH JONES
died June 2, 1769, aged 53

JOHN MABLITT, sen
died April 6, 1685, aged 50

JOHN MABBETT, jun
died March 13, 1711, aged 38

MARY his Daughter
died May 25, 1724, aged 21

RICHARD Son of JOHN MABBLTT, jun
died June 11, 1732, aged 34

MARTHA his Wife
died Feb 4, 1759, aged 69

Also RICHARD and THOMAS their Sons

RICHARD died April 7, 1776, aged 54,

THOMAS died Jan 19, 1758 aged 55

JOHN SAVAGE
died Jan 16, 1733, aged 73.

JANE his Wife
died June 24, 1743, aged 62

SARAH Wife of DANIEL SAVAGE,
died Aug 25, 1758, aged 45

DANIEL SAVAGE died Feb. 23, 1769, aged 78

Also two Sons

DANIEL died March 10, 1780, aged 38.

JOSEPH died May 21, 1786, aged 37

NATHANIEL UNDERWOOD
died April 19, 1766, aged 71.

MARY his Wife, Daughter of
NICHOLAS ISGAR, of Oldbury, in this County,
died Feb 24, 1757, aged 56

Left Issue two Sons and one Daughter
WILLIAM, NATHANIEL, and HANNAH

Also three Children of NATHANIEL and MARY
UNDERWOOD

NICHOLAS died Dec 10, 1733, aged 1 Year

MARY died May 9, 1744, aged 18

Also NATHANIEL, the Son of NATHANIEL
and ANNA MARIA UNDERWOOD,
died in his Infancy

WILLIAM BAILEY, Yeoman,
died June 20, 1756, aged 54

SARAH Wife of GILES BAILEY, Yeoman,
died April 10, 1754

ELIZABETH Wife of ANTHONY ROGERS,
and Daughter of GILES BAILEY, Yeoman,
and SARAH his Wife, died Dec 1735,
aged 27

GILES BAILEY, Yeoman,
died May 15, 1787

MICHAEL Wife of JOHN Cox,
and Relict of GILES BAILEY, Yeoman,
died April 1755, aged 74,

MARY Daughter of JOHN Packer
died Sept 15, 1741 aged 4

THOMAS Son of GILES Bailey
died March 1, 1730, aged 4

MARTHA, Relict of JONAS BUTCHER,
died May 15, 1775, aged 70

JONAH BUTCHER
died July 25, 1755

WILLIAM WILKINS, jun
died Jan 19, 1685, aged 5

WILLIAM WILKINS
died March 8, 1720

MARTHA, Relict of WILLIAM WILKINS,
died Feb 19, 1765, aged 84

WILLIAM WILKINS, their Son,
died Jan 23, 1738, aged 25

SUSANNAH his Wife, daughter of
NATHANIEL WILKINS, of Iron Acton,
afterwards Wife of DANIEL DANIEL Smith,
died Dec 23, 1755, aged 18

Likewise two Daughters of the said
WILLIAM and SUSANNAH

ANN died Nov 24, 1735, aged 1

MARTHA died Feb 5, 1775, aged 14

GILES PARTRIDGE
died Aug 19, 1695, aged 75

ANN, his Wife
died July 15, 1705, aged 91

JAMES PARTRIDGE
died Nov 14, 1731, aged 26

MARY his Wife
died Dec 7, 1719, aged 61

JOHN ANDREWS, Yeoman,
died Jan 30, 1716, aged 54

JOAN his Wife
died Sept 4, 1719, aged 58

RICHARD ANDREWS, Yeoman,
died May 24, 1737, aged 75

MARTHA his Wife
died June 23, 1748, aged 65

JOHN ANDREWS died April 11, 1755

SARAH his Wife, Daughter of COLE BERRY,
died Aug 30, 1759

WILLIAM WORKMAN, fen
died July 20, 1735, aged 58

WILLIAM WORKMAN, jun
died July 16, 1736, aged ... 36

RICHARD WORKMAN
died April 1?, 1759, aged 48

HANNAH his Wife
died June 11, 1758, aged 45

JOHN WOOD
died April 13, 1667

———

JOHN MERRICK of this Parish
died Jan 1?, 178?, aged 64

———

JOHN CAM, late of Afhley, in the County of
Wilts, died August 25, 1772, aged 51

———

SARAH Wife of THOMAS SMITH,
died July 5, 178?, aged 78.

———

THOMAS DANCER, Jun of this Parifh, fen
died Sept —— 1754, aged 54

ELIZABETH, Relict of THOMAS DANGERFIELD,
died May 21, 1755, aged 18

———

THOMAS BAILEY,
of Shipcrame, in the Parifh of Rockhampton,
died May 29, 1754, aged 54

MARY, Daughter of John and Mary BAILEY
died June 14, 1776, aged 23

———

SARAH, the Wife of SAMUEL LEONARD,
of the Parifh of Cam, died Augaft 178?,
aged 51

The above-faid SAMUEL LEONARD
died Sept 9, 1786, aged 62

———

ROBERT Wife?
died Auguft 2, 17?, aged ?

———

ON FLAT AND HEAD STONES

	Died	Aged		Died	A d
Sarah Daughter of James and Ann Joyner	9 Nov 1737	23	Anne, Wife of Thomas Whittard	8 Feb 176?	55
Also Samuel and James their Sons			Richard, Son of Richard Whittard	14 Jan 1?	
Samuel	24 O? 173?	20	Thomas, Son of Thomas Whittard		
James	12 Nov 174?	28	Milton	28 Sept 176?	
Edward Gunter	16 Aug 1747	48	Elinor Coopey		
Richard Haines	2? Sept 1766	63	Henry White, jun	2 Dec 173?	
Daniel, Son of Maurice Elliot	6 Nov 1739	25	Henry White, fen	1 May 174?	74
Richard Soul, of Frilington	5 Mar 1766	64	John Weight	1 July, 1737	
John his Son	3 Mar 1760	2?	Elizabeth Trotman	15 Mar 1746	
Mary Daughter of Richard and Mary Soul	Jan 17?		Joseph Savage	3 July, 176?	
John Barflow	30 Apr 1734	76	Sarah Wife of Joseph Swire	20 May, 1767	
Alice his Wife	15 Jan 1752	76	John Cam fenior	29 Apr 1745	56
Ann Wife of Richard Soul	30 Mar 1732	56	Sarah his Wife	6 Nov 173?	6
Richard Norton	2 June 1756	5	Thomas Cam	2 Jun 1794	
Deborah his Wife	17 July 1767	66		2 Jan, 176?	41
Thomas Smith, of Uley	17 Mar 1758	50	Hannah Wife of Thomas Thats	15 July, 1711	
Samuel Gabb	20 July, 1753	37	Sarah Wife of Ralph Reeve	17 May 179	
Mary, Wife of Samuel Gabb, of Wimfwell, in the Parifh of Berkeley	— Jan 1779	73	Daniel Ford	4 Dec 1729	
			Richard White	23 Feb 1756	65
Mary Daughter of Samuel Gabb, of Wimfwell	1 May 1761	12	Elizabeth his Wife	12 Sep 1763	65
Peter Smith	28 Apr 1743	47	Sarah Wife of William Howell	19 Mar 1738	
Mary his Wife	18 May 1743		Daniel Dangerfield	3 O 1746	23
John Terrell	4 Nov 175?	61	Elizabeth his Wife	9 May, 172?	
Mary his Wife	17 Apr 176?	70	Joseph Harold	Jan 60	
Letitia Pauley	19 July, 175?	—	Sarah his Wife	17 Jan 17	
Elizabeth his Wife	3 Sep 1714	26	Sarah their Daughter	—— 172?	
Sarah his Wife	27 Nov 1752		James their Son	—— 175?	
Daniel Tacker	1 July, 1726	47	Charles Ford	28 Feb 17??	
Mary his Wife, afterwards Wife of Daniel Dangerfield, fenior	30 Aug 176?	69	Elizabeth his Wife	12 May, 17??	
			Joseph Griffin	28 Ap ?	
			Joshua his Son	27 May, 173?	
			John, Son of William Bailey	1 Oct 175?	
			Mary his Wife	23 July, 156	61

THE same Name occurring in *Donegal*, IRELAND is needlessly mistaken in his Derivation of it from the Family of BERKELEY, who were Lords of it during three Centuries. It is there said to have belonged to DENA, a Thane of K. EDWARD the *Confessor*.

This Parish is nearly circular, and about five Miles across in the widest Part, divided between the Hundreds of *Rapsgate* and *Bradley*, four Miles South from *Cheltenham*, ten Northwestward from *Cirencester*, and from GLOUCESTER nine on the East. The Soil is light, and consists of Arable Woodland, and Pasture, but of the former in a far greater Portion. ✝ At the *Seven Wells*, near the great Road from GLOUCESTER to *Oxford*, the River *Churn* has it Source, and flows in a copious Stream through the Village, which is the first of a Succession of pleasant Hamlets, which are scattered on its cultivated Banks, before it reaches *Cirencester*.

The Benefice is rectorial, in the Deanery of *Stonehouse*, and anciently (1401) presented to a Chantry in the Church of *Beauvale*, in the County of *Nottingham*, and was itself in the Patronage of the Priory of *Little Malvern* in the County of *Worcester*.

There are good reasons to conclude, that the Church dedicated to *St Giles* was re-erected by THOMAS BERKELEY in 1339. It is certain, that he added an Aisle, and the Tower, and founded a Chantry in that Year. In the one his sepulchral Effigy still remains, and his Arms, "Arge on Fess between "3 Mulets Sable," are engraven in Stone upon the Buttresses, and repeated in the Windows of the Nave. Various Monuments of the Sculpture, of a remote Æra, are still undestroyed. Two cumbent Figures on either side the Altar, one of a Crusader, and of a Lady in the Dress of the 14th Century. A semi Effigy of a Knight holding an Escutcheon inclosed in a small Arcade, a cross-legged Female about a Yard in length, and many Slabs mutilated and broken, and robbed of their Brasses. These were doubtless intended to perpetuate the Memory of the Possessors of the Manor.

From the Date of the Conquest to the 8 EDWARD III. 1335, the De BERKELEYS were Lords, a Family nearly related to the Barons of the Castle. By Heirship it passed in 1405 to JOHN BRUGES, h Progenitor of the Barons CHANDOS of *Sudeley*. Soon after the Year 1608, it was purchased by the DUTTONS of *Sherborne*, and was given in Dower by JOHN DUTTON Esq with Lucy his Daughter, to Sir THOMAS POPE, Earl of *Downe*. It was re-purchased by PAUL CASTLEMAN, of *Beddington*, in the County of *Surrey*, Esq about the Year 1655, and sold in 1720 (the fatal *South-Sea* Year) by JONATHAN CASTLEMAN, Esq to the Father of JOHN HOWE, first Baron *Chedworth*, in which noble Family it is still vested.

Coberley Court. The Manor House, now in a State of Dilapidation, and about to be re-built as a Farm, is of great Antiquity. It was a large, low Building, with many spacious Rooms, Bay Windows, embattled on the outside, and a Quadrangle of Offices. IRELAND, in his Time, called it "the first rate House." The Domain includes the Property of the whole Parish.

Pinswell, the only Hamlet in the Hundred of *Bradley*, and in the Reign of EDWARD III. 1316, was held by ROBERT DE WALERAND as a distinct Manor, under the Abbey of GLOUCESTER, but in the later Courts it was consolidated with the other. Few Spots of Ground command a Prospect of greater Extent, from the Cotswolds of *Hereford* on one side, to the Downs of *Marlborough* in *Wiltshire* on the other, without Interruption.

No Benefactions to the Poor.

INCUMBENTS	PATRONS	INCUMBENTS	PATRONS
—— John Brooke,	Priory of Little Malvern	1755 John Tomkins,	Dorothy, Baroness Ched-
1559 Richard Wyatt,	Giles, Lord Chandos	M A	worth
1598 Lewis Jones,	——————	1761 Wil Haseldine, D D	The same
1651 Robert Rowden,		1771 Jn Arnold, Clerk	Hen Frrd Ld Chedworth
1712 John Brown, M A	Timothy Bourne, Gent	1778 Cha Coxwell, M A	The same
		1782 Wm Wright, LL B	John, Lord Chedworth

PRESENT LORD OF THE MANOR,
The Right Honourable JOHN Lord CHEDWORTH

The only Person summoned from this Place by the Heralds, in 168_ and 1683, was
Jonathan Castleman, Esq

At the Election in 1776, it does not appear that any Freeholder polled from this Parish

The Register commences with a Date so early as 1546

ANNUAL ACCOUNT OF MARRIAGES, BIRTHS, AND BURIALS, IN THIS PARISH

A D	Mar	Bir	Bur	A D	Mar	Bir	Bur	A D	Mar	Bir	Bur	A D	Mar	Bir	Bur
1781	2	3	2	1786	4	4	9	1791				1796			
1782	2	6	~	1787	2	6	3	1792				1797			
1783	2	1	1	1788				1793				1798			
1784	1	3	2	1789				1794				1799			
1785	3	6	4	1790				1795				1800			

I N T H E A I S L E

AFFIXED TO THE WALL A BLUE MARBLE, UPON WHICH WERE TWO FIGURES WITH CHILDREN
BENEATH, AND FOUR CORNER ESCUTCHEONS IN BRASS, NOW MUTILATED. UPON THE REMAINING
ESCUTCHEON,

Quarterly, 1 Argent, a Cross Sable charged in the Centre with a Leopard's Face Or, BRUCES—2
Or, a Pile Gules, Dr CHANDOS 3 Argent, 3 Fess between three Mullets Sable, BIRKETT of
Coberley, 4th as 1st,—impaling, quarterly, 1 Gules, a Chevron between three Bull's Heads cabossed
argent, BAYNHAM. 2 a Bend 3 Gutté 4 a Fess between six Cross Crosslets *

INSCRIPTIONS IN THE CHANCEL

ON FLAT STONES

RICHARD BRIDGES
died October 8, 1650

ELIZABETH, Wife of RICHARD BRIDGES,
was buried June 22, 1655, aged 85

Mr LEWIS JONES, Rector,
was buried July 29, 1651, aged 105

Mr JOHN BROOKE, Rector,
was buried June 17, 1598
ROBERT ROWDEN, Rector,
was buried Oct 17, 1712, aged 97

JOAN, the Daughter of Mr Robert Rowden,
was buried Oct 17, 1684, aged 23 Years
JOAN, the Wife of Robert Rowden Rector,
(who had Issue by him Sons and 2 Daughters)
was buried Jun 11, 1691, aged 77 Years

THOMAS ROWDEN, Gent
was buried Jan 28, 1664, aged 80 Years
MARY, Daughter of Robert Rowden,
buried Sept 18, 1655, aged 45
ROBERT, Son of Robert Rowden, Rector,
buried Dec 27, 1659, aged 3

ELIZABETH, Wife of THOMAS ROWDEN,
was buried May 19, 1662, aged 80

Arms, a Chevron between three Grimms Heads
erased

ELINOR, the Wife of EDMUND SMITH,
of Deerhurst Walton, Gent
buried April 17, 1695, aged 84

ELIZABETH, Wife of WILLIAM TRATMAN, Gent
and Daughter of ROBERT ROWDEN,
buried May 16, 1653

THOMAS TRATMAN, Gent
buried Dec 7, 1691

ROBERT BRIDGES
died August 2, 1653, aged 27 Years

THOMAS BRIDGES, Yeoman,
was buried Dec 12, 1704, aged 77

* This Memorial was placed for a Crispe Jones who by his Wife died Nov 2... Chedworth Baland ... in the Chancel ... raised three Markets ... Raphael Collins his Clerk ... Descendant of Eustace Baynham
Mr

Mrs ANNE BROWNE, Widow of
JOHN BROWNE, of Norton in this County, Gent.
and Mother of
Mr JOHN BROWNE, Rector of this Church,
died Jan. 7, 1718, aged 69

Mr JOHN BROWNE,
late Rector of Leckhampton and Witcombe,
and Son of Mr JOHN BROWNE,
Rector of this Parish,
died Oct 6, 1737, aged 33

SUSANNA ELIZABETH HICKES,
Daughter of HOWE HICKES, Esq
and MARTHA his Wife, and
Grand Daughter of Mr JOHN BROWNE,
Rector of this Parish,
died June 17, 1747, aged 1 Year and 23 Days.

JOHN BROWNE,
Rector of this Parish, and Vicar of
Longdon, in the County of Worcester,
died April 16, 1754, aged 85
Also ELIZABETH his Wife,
died December 24, 1766, aged 88

JOHN TOMKINS, Rector,
died Feb 2, Anno Dom 1764, aged 75

ON A FLAT STONE IN THE NAVE.
JOHN GOODALL
Servant to Mr CASTLEMAN's Family
between thirty and forty Years,
was buried here Nov 29, 1704, aged 56

ON A MONUMENT IN THE SOUTH AISLE

Arms, Azure, on a Mount Vert a Castle Or,
for CASTLEMAN, impaling, Argent, semee of Cross
Crosslets three Fleurs de lis Sable for BARFORD

In Memory of MARY, the Daughter of
JONATHAN BARFORD, Esq by ALICE his Wife,

Relict of PAUL CASTLEMAN, of Coberley, Esq.
All lying in this Vault,
and late Wife of THOMAS HORDE, of Coat, in the
County of Oxon, Esq
She departed this Life Tuesday May 21, 1717

CHARLES, the Son of
PAUL and MARY CASTLEMAN,
obiit, Sunday, August 27, 168?

In Memory also of
JANE, the Wife of
JONATHAN CASTLEMAN, of Coberley, Esq
who died July 4, 1712

And of
JANE,   } their
SUSANNA, and } Children, { Fr Sep 13, 1706
JONATHAN,   } who dyed { Fr Aug 19, 1709

A B }   { Sun Oct 7, } 1677
I B } ob {   }
P C }   { Fri Sep   } 1678

Arms, Argent, on a Chief Or, a Cornish Cough
proper for HORDE,—impaling BARFORD, as before

ON A FLAT STONE

Arms, on a Lozenge ensigned with an Earl's Coronet —Party, per pale Topaz and Sapphire, on
a Chevron between three Griffin's heads erased,
four Fleurs de lis, all counterchanged,—impaling,
Quarterly, Argent and Gules, in the second and
third Quarters a Fleur Or, for DUTTON

Here lyeth the Body of LUCY, Countess of Downe,
Wife of THOMAS POLE, Earl of Doane,
and Daughter of JOHN DUTTON, Esq
of Sherborne, in the County of Gloucester,
who had Issue only one Daughter, ELIZABETH.
She died April 6, 1656

EFFIGIES IN COBERLEY CHURCH

IN THE CHURCH YARD   ON TOMBS

JOHN WALKER, Yeoman,
died Jan 20, 174, aged 76.

ELIZABETH, his Wife,
died June 27, 1764, aged 88.

THOMAS BLACKWELL, Yeoman,
died March 6, 1721-2, aged 64

HESTER, Wife of THOMAS BLACKWELL,
died Dec 11, 1742, aged 64

JOHN MILLS, senior, Yeoman,
died Sept 21, 1728, aged 55

JANE, the Daughter of JOHN MILLS,
and MARY his Wife
died May 16, 1733, aged 27

JOSEPH MILLS, Yeoman,
died Nov 15, 1749, aged 58

THOMAS MILLS, Yeoman,
died Dec 5, 1753, aged 5.

ALICE, his Wife,
died Nov 15, 1743, aged 5

MARY, Relict of JOHN MILLS, junior,
died March 2, 176, aged 90

PAUL MILLS
of Bidfield, in the Parish of Bisley,
died Sept 14, 177, aged 67

JOHN MILLS
died July 25, 17, aged 75

THOMAS CHANDLER, Yeoman,
died Nov 17, 1746, aged 8

ELIZABETH, his Wife,
died August 17, 17 3, aged 2

ON HEAD STONES

	Died	Aged
Mary, Wife of Richard Lysully, senior, of Elstone	2 Nov 1774	
Mary their Daughter	1 Jun 1728	5
Henry Tuffly, of Chedworth, Yeoman	22 Oct 1 71	7
Anne, Wife of Paul Tuffley, Yeoman	1 Sept 17	6
Margaret their Daughter	25 Feb 1 51	1
Paul Tuffley, of this Parish, Yeoman	30 July, 177	65
Paul, eldest Son of John and Betty Tuffley	27 Dec 1759	2
Jane, Wife of Thomas Blandford, Yeoman	3 June, 1777	6
Joseph, second Son of John and Elizabeth Walker	1727	
Richard Musto	5 Oct 1755	80
Anne, Wife of Richard Musto	8 Nov, 1763	6
Anne, Wife of John Musto	31 Mar 1742	51
Anne, Wife of William Barnefield	7 Jun 1703	5
John Fox	25 Oct 1755	
Thomas Blandford	25 Aug 175	70
Elizabeth, Wife of John Wright	15 A 17	6
Elizabeth their Daughter	23 Feb 1 5	1
William Hews	15 Feb 175	6
Sarah his Wife	11 Mu 17	
John their Son	9 Se 175	2

LXXVI. COLESBOURN MAGNA

IS a small retired Village on the River *Churn*, in the Hundred of *Rapsgate*, six Miles South-East from *Cheltenham*, nine Miles North-West from *Cirencester*, and eleven from *Gloucester* on the East. The form of the Parish is nearly circular, the Soil light, and consisting of equal Proportions of Arable, Pasture, and Wood land

The Benefice is a restricted Rectory, claiming one third only of the whole Tythe. Two Portions called *Colesbourn Lebotte* and *Sampson* were given in 1137, by King *Stephen*, to the Priory of *Llanthony*, by the Constable of *Gloucester*, and are consequently exempt

The Church, dedicated to *St James*, lies within the Deanry of *Stonehouse*. It is constructed with a Transept, and a low embattled Tower at the West End, but contains nothing worthy remark

To the Church of *Worcester* the Manor is attributed in *Domesday* Book. In the gift Edward I it was transferred to the Priory of *Llanthony*. After the Dissolution it was holden 1650 of the heirs of Thomas Kemys. The Family of Higgs possessed it before 1608 and it was sold by them in 1680 to Philip Shepard, of *Hampton*, Esq. It became by Purchase, in 1770, the Property of Francis Lyne, Esq

The Manor House, a moated edifice, is situate at the Hamlet of *Rapsgate*, which gives Name to the Hundred in which the Parish is comprised. At this Denomination even in Lawrence mark the ancient Ground in the *Crickelade* Division of the County. To the Manor the greater Part of the Parish is annexed, beside which is an Estate belonging to the Family of Cove

Little Colesbourne is an insulated Manor appertenant to *Withington* long since purchased of the Ferrars tracts by the Family of Roberts. Here are the remains of a Chapel anciently endowed with Tythe of a considerable Value, but now consolidated with the Rectory of *Withington*

Part of the Estate of Samuel Bowyer, Esq at *Combend* is within the Limits of this Parish. In 1779 a Discovery was made of the Foundations of a Roman House in which the Passage 50 Feet in length and 14 broad, and in 1787 the Remains of another were discovered in the same Place, consisting of six Rooms in a parallel Direction, some of which had tessellated Pavements and a Hypocaust. Amongst the Ruins were found Tiles of a rhomboidal form, in which were the channels which conveyed heat, Fragments of Glass, Columns, and other Vestiges of a Roman Villa. The Site of these Remains faces the South about a Mile from the Roman Road

No Benefactions to the Poor

Incumbents	Patrons	Incumbents	Patron
1600 ———	Abbey of *Worcester*	— — Thomas Freeman,	———
———	Priory of *Llanthony*	1665 Amb. Freeman, M A	Bishop of Gloucester
———	Henry Fitz-Alan, Earl of Arundel	—— Joseph Wakes, M A	———
1650 Humphry Horton,	George Huntley	1713 Wm Alexander, M A	Philip Shepard, Esq.
1 Richard Griffith	Fobris Sandford	1720 George White, M A	The same
1680 Mathew Rote,	Thomas Higges	1747 Tim Millechamp, M A	Jos Shepard, Esq
		17 John De La Bere, M A	Francis Lyne, Esq

The Persons returned from this Parish by the Heralds in their Visitations

——— Cove, Gent   Cove, Gent

At the Election in 17,6, Six Freeholders polled from this Parish

The Register commences with an Entry in 1632

ANNUAL ACCOUNT OF MARRIAGES, BIRTHS, AND BURIALS, IN THIS PARISH

AD	Mar	Bir	Bur	AD	Mar	Bir	Bur	AD	Mar	Bir	Bur	AD	Mar	Bir	Bur
1781	2	8	2	1786	4	4	3	1791				1796			
1782	6	3	2	1787	1	3	2	1792				1797			
1783	2	7	2	1788				1793				1798			
1784	2	6	8	1789				1794				1799			
1785	2	3	6	1790				1795				1800			

IN   THE   CHURCH   ARE   THE   TWO   FOLLOWING   ATCHIEVEMENTS

1   Argent, a Chevron between three Bucks couchant Gules, for HIGGS, on an Escutcheon of Pretence Gules, a dexter Arm vambraced Or.

2   Ermine, on a Chief indented Sable, three Battle-Axes Argent, for SHEPPARD.

IN THE CHURCH YARD, ON TOMBS.

JOHN BROWN, of this Parish,
died April 1, 1760, aged 70.

MARY his Wife
died Jan 5, 1736, aged 39

RICHARD LIFFELLY
died April 11, 1711, aged 32

DEBORAH, the Wife
of THOMAS JONES,
died April 11, 1758, aged 78

ON   HEAD   STONES

	Died	Aged
Richard Preedon	11 May, 1739	60
Martha his Wife	5 Dec. 1703	82
Richard Preedon, senior	11 Feb. 1740	71
Hannah his Wife	21 Apr. 1772	65
Thomas their Son,	26 Mar. 1758	30
Edward Jane	15 Dec. 1737	33
Thomas Son of Thomas Preedon	12 May, 1752	24
Thomas Greenway	20 Aug. 1749	72
Jane Greenway	7 Sept. 1699	43
Thomas Cross	24 June, 1753	44

COLNE ST. ALDWYN'S

LXXVII. COLNE ST. ALDWYN'S.

THE River *Colne* gives Name to three Parishes which are situate on its Banks   *Colne St Aldwyn's,*
the most considerable, lies in the Hundred of *Brightwel's Barrow,* nine Miles distant from *Cirence /*
ter on the North east, eight South from *Northleach,* and twenty-five from GLOUCESTER in an Eastward
Direction   The Boundaries include nearly eight Miles, of a light Soil, changing to Clay near the
River, chiefly Arable, with many Meadows   A general Inclosure took place in 1770

The Living is a Vicarage in the Deanery of *Fairford,* the Impropriation of which was given in 1217,
2 HEN III to the Abbey of *St Peter* in GLOUCESTER, for Increase of Hospitality, by SYLVESTER
Bishop of *Worcester*   The impropriate Tythes, charged with 20/ a Year to the Vicar, are now held in
Lease under the Dean and Chapter of GLOUCESTER, to whom they were granted by their Charter of Confirmation 1541

By the Act of Inclosure, all Tythes, impropriate and vicarial, were abolished, and adequate Portions
of Land in the Common Fields were allotted to the Vicar, to whom the Stipend originally due from the
farmer, were to be continued

The Church, originally dedicated to *St Aldwyn,* but now to *St John Baptist,* has a Nave only, with
a Tower, on which were the Initials J G (for Abbot GAMAGE) and a Crosier on an Escutcheon   The
Battlements bear the Arms of the Abbey, and the De CLARE Earls of GLOUCESTER   By these the
Foundation is ascertained, the Architecture was of mixed Gothic and Saxon, but a general Reparation
was made in 1762, and the Church neatly pewed

In the early Saxon Times the Manor was given to the Abbey of GLOUCESTER, who retained it till
the Suppression, when it was added to the Revenues of the Dean and Chapter   The ancient Manor
House is inhabited by THOMAS INGRAM, Esq the present Lessee

Williamstrip, a Hamlet and distinct Manor, lies about a Mile Eastward from the Village   JOHN DE
HASTINGS possessed it in 13 1, 4 EDW III   In 1670 it belonged to HENRY POWLE, Esq Speaker of
the House of Commons, the . . . Sherston, Esq married his Daughter and Heir, and settled there in

1700

1700. Since that Period it has paffed by Purchafe through the Families of FORESTER, MACKWORTH PRAID, and BLACKWELL, to MICHAEL HICKES, Efq in 1784 The Manfion Houfe was built in the beginning of this Century, and has received many Additions and Improvements from its feveral fubfequent Poffeffors The Park Pale inclofes about feventy Acres

Upon the high Grounds, which rife in a picturefque Manner from the River, the Traces of the old *Ikenild* Way are ftill vifible

---

B E N E F A C T I O N S.

ELIZABETH FETTIPLACE, about the Year 1714, gave 20l the Intereft thereof for the Benefit of the Poor of this Parfh

CATHARINE LUTTON, 1714, gave a Rent Charge of 10l a Year, on Lands, to be annually diftributed by the Minifter and Churchwardens to the Poor of this Parifh, being Proteftants, viz a Coat to a poor Man, and a Gown to a poor Woman, and the Remainder in Bread

INCUMBENTS	PATRONS	INCUMBENTS	PATRONS
—— Henry Hind,		1727 John Lifield, Clerk,	Theophilus Partridge
1575 William Baird,	George Fettiplace		Fettiplace
1577 Thomas Symondes,	The fame	1775 Clem Headington, B A	Sir John Bridges, Knt
1591 Edward White	Queen Elizabeth		Dame Rebecca F
1618 Thomas Hountell,	John White		Wife, May Ellis
1673 Richard Hunt,	Giles Fettiplace		Thomas and Samuel
1703 George Hunt, M A	Heirs of Giles Fettiplace		Ingram, Efqrs
		1782 John Keble, M A	The fame

PRESENT PROPRIETORS OF THE MANORS,

Lefee of *Celne St Aldwyn's*, Lord of *Hamftrip*,

THOMAS INGRAM, Efq. MICHAEL HICKES, Efq.

The Perfons fummoned from this Place by the Heralds in 1682 and 1683, were
Henry Powle, Efq and
Giles Fettiplace, Efq

A f

At the Election in 1776, Eight Freeholders gave Votes from this Parish.

The Register commences with Baptisms in 1573

ANNUAL ACCOUNT OF MARRIAGES, BIRTHS, AND BURIALS, IN THIS PARISH

A D	Mar	Bir	Bur	A D	Mar	Bir	Bur	A D	Mar	Bir	Bur	A D	Mar	Bir	Bur
1781	1	8	9	1786	0	14	9	1791				1796			
1782	4	9	11	1787	2	13	12	1792				1797			
1783	2	12	1	1788	1	9	14	1793				1708			
1784	2	8	12	1789				1704				1799			
1785	3	12	5	1790				1795				1800			

INSCRIPTIONS IN THE CHURCH

IN THE CHANCEL

Arms*, 1st, Quarterly, 1st, Gules, two Chevronels Argent, for FETTIPLACE, 2d, Argent, three Torteauxes, for BESSILLES, 3d, Sable, a Lion pissant guardant Argent, crowned Or, 4th as the first.
2d, Quarterly, 1st and 4th, Azure, a Lion rampant between semee of Cross Crosslets Or, for POOLE, 2d and 3d, Argent, a Chevron Sable between three Bucks' Heads caboshed Gules

ON FLAT STONES

Arms, Azure, a Lion rampant between semee of Cross Crosslets Or, for POOLE

Here lyeth buried the Body of ANN POOLE, Gentlewoman, who deceased the 19th Day of August, 1658

HENRY POOLE, Esq
died the 2d Day of August, Anno Dom 1643

Here lies the Body of THOMAS CHURCH, Esq
Son of THOMAS CHURCH, of Tunstall in Shropshire,
and of THEODITA FETTIPLACE his Wife,
youngest Daughter of GILES FETTIPLACE, Esq
He departed this Life at Bath
the 1st of March, 1734, aged 57

ON FLAT STONES IN THE NAVE

Here lieth the Body of Mr THOMAS SMITH,
who departed this Life the 20th Day of November,
Anno Domini 1690

Here also lieth the Body of Mrs EDITH SMITH,
Relict of Mr THOMAS SMITH,
who was pious and devout towards God,
dutiful and obedient towards her Parent,
and faithful towards her Husband,
loving and affectionate towards her Relations,
and peaceable and most five toward all others

She departed this Life Oct 3, in
the Nativity of CHRIST 1721,
from her own 57

Also here lyeth the Body of
Mr THOMAS SMITH, the Son of
Mr THOMAS and EDITH SMITH,
who died March 2, 1711, aged 20 Years

Arms, a Chevron between three Lambs pissant
a Chief chequy

Here lieth the Body of Mr JOHN LAMBERT,
who was pious and devout without Superstition,
a faithful and dutiful Husband,
a tender and indulgent Father,
and a peaceable and friendly Neighbour
He died July 22, 1716, aged 88 Years

Also ELIZABETH, Wife of NIXON LAMBERT.
She was a tender and affection to Mother,
and a sincere Friend after living thirty seven
Years a Widow, she died Jan 31, 1774, aged 68

EDITH their Daughter
died May 1, 1776, aged 39

ELIZABETH, the Wife of Mr JOHN LAMBERT,
departed this Life June 30, 1729, aged 92

ELIZABETH, the Daughter of
Mr JOHN LAMBERT and ELIZABETH his Wife,
departed this Life May 10, 1724, aged 52

Mrs ANNE PARSONS,
Daughter of Mr JOHN LAMBERT and
ELIZABETH his Wife,
died June 9, 1745, aged 75 Years

Here lyeth JOHN MASSY, who was
of the Age of LXXXV Years, and
deceased the second Day of July, in the
XXXVIIIth Year of the Reign of
our most gracious Sovereign
Lady Queen ELIZABETH, Anno Domini 1596

Here lieth interred the Body of
ELIZABETH, Wife of THOMAS JONES
She deceased the 2d Day of July, 1628

* Erected to GEORGE FETTIPLACE, a Justice of South Wales, who died of the Plague in 1678

IN THE CHURCH YARD, ON TOMBS

ANTHONY LAMBERT, senior Gent
died Nov 8, 1737, aged 64

CATHARINE his Wife
died May 1747, aged 6,

SABINA their Daughter
died May 26, 1741, aged 21

ANN, Wife of GABRIEL GARDNER,
died Feb 23, 1777, aged 57

JACOT ALLEN
died Jan 22, 1731, aged 60

JANE his Wife
died April 21, 1747, aged 69

ELIZABETH their Daughter
died May 1, 1747, aged 29 Years

FRANCES their Daughter
died Oct 15, 1750, aged 44

ANTHONY LAMBERT
died May 14, 1769, aged 62

JOANNA the Wife of
ANTHONY LAMBERT,
died Jan 30, 1750, aged 43

RICHARD TOWNSEND,
Son of Rich and Eliz Townsend,
died April 17, 17__ aged 49

ELIZABETH Wife of Rich Townsend,
died November 24, 1714

FRANCIS SWEIT
died Sept 19, 1737, aged 58

MARTHA his Wife
died July 27, 1752, aged 55

Also three of their Children

JOHN TOMBS
died April 17, 1749, aged 15

JAMES TOMBS
died Nov 16, 1758, aged 54

FATHER his Wife
died August 13, 1729, aged 37

JOHN, Son of JAMES and ESTHER TOMBS,
died Nov 14, 1769, aged 49

JOHN LIPPETT,
Vicar of this Parish 48 Years,
was buried July 26, 1775, aged 75

REBECCA his Wife
was buried Feb 24, 1780, aged 8

JANE their Daughter
was buried March 25, 1767, aged 23

HANNAH their Daughter
died an Infant

RICHARD BRINSDON
was buried Dec 21, 1736, aged 71

ON HEAD STONES

	Died	Aged		Died	Aged
Henry Tombs	17 May, 1743	66	Sarah, Wife of William Tibbell,		
Elizabeth, Wife of John Tombs	28 Mar 1723	77	Daughter of John and Sarah Gardner	14 Oct 1771	24
Mary Daughter of John and Elizabeth Tombs	31 Dec 1708	—	John Son of John and Mary Gardner	9 Apr 1750	8
John Son of John and Elizabeth Tombs	30 Sept 1746	7	Ethel Jeffries	30 Jan 1767	74
Samuel Allen	27 Sept 1765	49	Elizabeth his Wife	3 Nov 1751	31
Mary his Wife	22 Apr 1767	46	Nixon Lamb	11 Oct 1736	36
William Jane senior	8 Dec 1760	76	Elizabeth his Wife	27 May, 172,	89
Edith his Wife	29 Apr 1753	75	John Gardner senior	5 Apr 1751	89
William Tuffley	31 Aug 1764	65	Amy his Wife	5 Aug 1745	8
Diana his Wife	7 Mar 1761	70	Priscilla Gardner	Jun 1711	—
William Tuffley	13 June, 1782	50	Giles Gardner	21 Feb 1746	—
Mary, Wife of Christopher Rose, sen	1 Apr 1750	24	Mary his Wife	14 Mar 1785	8
John Role senior	13 Apr 1761	48	Humphry Moulder	13 Nov 1746	77
Henry Knipe	21 May, 1753	—	Mary Wife of Humphry Moulder	15 Feb 1717	59
Michael Knipe, senior	3 Aug 1676	—	Thomas Burbridge	15 May, 1757	78
Joan Knipe, Widow	27 Aug 1679	—	John Tombs	17 Apr 1749	45
Ann Stratford	15 July, 1686	—	Henry Son of Henry and Mary Tombs		
Michael Knipe	27 July, 1695	—		30 Sept 1719	30
Elizabeth Knipe	14 Mar 1708	89	Richard Bartlett	1 Feb 1769	54
Margaret Green	29 May, 1722	—	Elizabeth, Daughter of John and Sarah Pool	15 Apr 1760	61
Thomas Green	8 Oct 1748	69	John Tombs	21 Dec 1712	
John Green, senior	24 Dec 1727	83	James Tombs	15 Aug 1725	81
John Green	18 July, 1767	85	Mary, Wife of John Freeman, Daughter of John and Esther Tombs of Queenington		
Frances Wife of Thomas Pugh	6 Jun 1775	13		2 May, 1787	64
William Cowper	28 Sept 1756	45	Joseph Wife of John Tombs	28 Mar 1747	6
Robert Radway	4 Mar 1759	53	Bartholomew Tombs	Mar 1767	6
Hannah his Wife	24 July, 1777	70	Elizabeth Tombs	14 Feb 1769	54
Robert Radway	7 Apr 1769		Elizabeth, Wife of Thomas Miles	15 Sept 1772	2
Thomas, Son of John and Elizabeth Norris, of Bourton on the Water	22 May, 1757		William Tombs	3 Dec 1777	
Mary Wife of Stephen Court	16 Aug 1762	5	Ann Wife of William Tombs	27 July 73	
Thomas Court	15 Mar 1723	58	William Tombs	5 Jun 1756	
Priscilla Wife of Anthony Lambert, of Coln Rogers	28 May, 1760	—	Elizabeth Wife of William Tibbals	4 Apr 1	0
Anthony Lambert senior late of Ablington in the Parish of Bibury	1 June 1757	67	Edith Wife of William Jones	9 May, 14	16
Ann Wife of John Bayns	1 Aug 172	37	Sarah Wife of William Tibbals	8 Oct 1	
Robert Cook	11 July, 1	43	Jane Wife of William Tibbals	8 Oct 1	
Hannah his Wife	22 Mar 17		Thomas Bishop	11 Feb 1	
William Jane John	2 May, 1		Ann Wife of George Coulter	20 June, 1	
Mary Wife of John Bradinton	20 Nov 1756	60	George Son of John and Sarah Coulter	5 July 1	
Ann Wife of Robert Essex	7 Feb 1769	56	John Coulter	6 Feb 1	
Judith, Daughter of John and Mary Wheeler	3 Nov 1741	21	Sarah Wife of John Coulter	1 June 1	
Thomas Knipe	4 Apr 1676	—	Samuel Bishop		
			Nicolas Bishop, Ivy and his Wife	2 July, 17	
			William Cole	5 Apr 172	5
			Andrew Milton	25 Apr 171	

LXXVIII. COLNE ST. DENNIS.

SO diftinguifhed as having belonged, at the Time of the Compilation of *Domefday*, to the Abbev of St *Dennis* in *Normandy*

This Parifh lies in the upper Divifion of the Hundred of *Deorhurft*, three Miles diftant from *Nortwleach*, feven from *Cirencefter* on the North, and twenty Eaftward from GLOUCESTER. The Soil is light, and chiefly tilled, and contains a Circuit of about fix Miles

The Church is a fmall Gothic Building without Ornament, with a low Tower in the Middle, fupported by pointed Arches

The Benefice is rectorial, in the Deanery of *Cirencefter* the Advowfon of which has been long vefted in the Family of HUGHES Two Parts of the Tythes of *Calcott* belonged to the Priory of *Llanthony*

This Manor, foon after the Conqueft, was annexed to the Priory of *Deerhurft*, a Cell to the Abbey of St *Dennis*, by whofe Mediation it was included in the Hundred, though widely detached from it

At the Diffolution of the Alien Priories it was granted, 7 Edw IV to the Abbey of *Tewkefbury*, and when the monaftic Revenues were difperfed by King HENRY the Eighth, fold in 1544, to WILLIAM SHAPRINGTON The Family of MASTER, of *Cirencefter*, afterwards held it, till it was tranfterred by Purchafe Confiderable Eftates, independent of the Manor, are held by the Families of D'OYLEY and HOWSE

Caldecote, or *Calcott*, is the only Hamlet

No Benefactions to the Poor.

INCUMBENTS	PATRONS	INCUMBENTS	PATRONS
—— Thomas Berrington,	Robert Weftwood	1737 Charles Hughes, M A	The fame
1596 Robert Hyett,	—— Smith	1742 Andrew Hughes,	John Piercy, Efq and
1675 John Hughes,	John Rogers and John Lord		the two foregoing
1726 Andrew Hughes, M A	John Spooner, Gent and John Read, Apothecary	1753 Charles Hughes, M A	
		1775 John Hughes, M A	Thos Cliffold, Clerk

PRESENT LORD OF THE MANOR,

LIONEL DARELL, ESQ

There does not appear to have been any Perfon fummoned from this Place by the Heralds in 1682 and 1683

At the Election in 1776, Nine Freeholders polled from this Parifh

The Regifter has its firft Date in 1561

ANNUAL ACCOUNT OF MARRIAGES, BIRTHS, AND BURIALS, IN THIS PARISH

A D	Mar	Bir	Bur	A D	Mar	Bir	Bur	A D	Mar	Bir	Bur	A D	Mar	Bir	Bur
1781	—	4	—	1786	2	2	3	1791				1796			
1782	2	1	2	1787	—	3	2	1792				1797			
1783	—	5	—	1788				1793				1798			
1784	—	3	2	1789				1794				1799			
1785	3	6	3	1790				1795				1800			

INSCRIPTIONS

INSCRIPTIONS IN THE CHURCH

ON A COARSE STONE IN CAPITA S

Heere lieth the Body of JOHANNE BURTON, third Daughter of RICHARD BURTON Minist, late of Bagin on who finished this mortal Life the two and twentieh Day of September, Anno Dom 1651

ON A TABLET

Near this Place wa interred the Corpse of JOHN BRIDGES, sen Nov 1, 1679
ELIZABETH his Wife, April 10 1678
JOHN BRIDGES his Grandson, Oct 14 1688
JOHN the Son of the abovesaid JOHN BRIDGES sen. April 19 1694
And WILLIAM his Son, Oct 1, 1701

ON A FREESTONE TABLET

Near this Place wa interred the Bodies of JOHN HOWSE and MARY his Wife He died May 1, 176, aged 87 She died Dec 13, 1743, aged 60
Also WILLIAM and RICHARD their Sons
WILLIAM died Oct 1, 748, aged 51
RICHARD died July 2, 1744, aged 31
SAMUEL READ their Grandson died Sept 15, 1747, aged 13

ON A MONUMENT

S I
JOHANNES HUGHT,
Illius Ecclesiæ Rector,
Qui obiit
Septimo die Octob
Anno Dom 1726, ætatis 78
MARIA HUGHES,
Filia ejus natu minor
Quæ obiit Sexto die Novembr,
Anno Dom 1724, ætatis 3

MARIÆ MATRIS
inter cineres,
H S I
Reverendus Vir
ANDREAS HUGHES, M A,
JOHANNIS HUGHES, M A
Filius,
Suorum Decus est Dolor
M H ob Maii Die 25,
Anno Dom 1707, æt 56.
A H ob Aprilis Die 18,
Anno Dom 1736 ætat 57

H S I
CAROLUS HUGHES, A. M
JOHANNIS filius,
Istius etiam Ecclesiæ Rector
Vir, si quis alius) fide prisca,
Moribus antiquis,
Obiit Maii die nono, A D 1742,
ætatis 49

CAROLUS HUGHES A B
CAROLI filius, viginti per annos
Istius Ecclesiæ
Rector, vir suis Caritiānus
Obiit Die Dec 5
Anno Dom 1774, ætatis 47

Sacred to the Memory of A S HUGHES
Relict of CHARLES HUGHES Rector of this Parish Daughter of
EDWARD PINE, of East Down in the County of Devon Esq
She died Feb 14 1768 in the 63e Year of her Age

In Memory of MARY THOMAS,
who died June 3, 1767, aged 73

ON A NEAT OVAL MONUMENT OF BLACK AND WHITE MARBLE

Arms, Gules, three Globe within a Bordure engrailed Or

Near this Place is deposited, in Hope of a Blessed Resurrection, the Remains of Sir BENJAMIN KEMP Bart who departed this Life Jan 25 1777, aged 67 Years

---

In Youth an excellent Scholar, and through Life an honest man
He was the only Son of a numerous Progeny of Sir ROBERT KEMP Baronet, of Gissing in Norfolk by a see and Lady a Miss BRAND, but her Family Seat is now at Ubbeston in Suffolk The above Sir ROBERT had four Wives, and fifteen Children The title descends to a Cousin, and the Estate to a Niece of the late Baronet, Miss KEMP, Daughter of the Rev Mr THOMAS KEMP This Marble is erected as an affectionate and grateful Tribute to his Memory by his Executrix and only surviving Sister Mrs SHORTER of Sevenoaks in Kent, youngest Daughter of the said ROBERT, and now the only surviving Child and Relict of DARELL SHORTER, Esq of Wadhurst in Sussex

ON A HANDSOME MONUMENT OF WHITE AND VARIEGATED MARBLE

Near this Place are deposited the Remains of JOHN KIRRALL, Esq who departed this Life May 1, 7 in the 73d Year of his Age
A Man highly esteemed and of the most amiable Disposition an impartial and humane Justice
He was descended from an ancient and honourable Family in the County of Kent
By his Wife ANNE Daughter of STEPHEN SPENCER, Esq
He had Issue two Sons and two Daughters,
Captain JOHN KIRRALL who fell at the Battle of Val in Flanders on the 3d of July 1747, aged 26
STEPHEN KIRRALL Doctor of Magdalen College, Oxford who died on the 10 of April 1747 aged 30
MARY KIRRALL married to the Rev Mr WINTER
JANE KIRRALL, now Widow of the Rev Mr CHARLES HUGHES late Rector of this Parish, and who dedicates this Monument to the Memory of her dear Father

---

IN THE CHURCH YARD, ON TOMBS

JEREMIAH HAWKINS
died Sept 12, 1761, aged 71

CATHARINE his Wife
died Nov 14, 1786, aged 84

JANE, Daughter of JOHN and ANN DAVIS,
died June 5, 1751, aged 51

ELIZA her eldest Daughter
died March 14, 1768 aged 64

ON HEAD STONES

	Died	Aged		Died	Aged
Sarah, Wife of John Adams	10 Aug 1729	51	Mary Wife of James Cook	9 Mar 17	
John Baldwin	29 Jun 1751	80	Sarah Wife of John Daly	3 Feb 17	
Robert Tombs	26 May 1762	67	Richard Day	9 Oct 17	
Joseph Davis	5 May 1752	82	Henry Day	8 Mar 1785 15	
John Collet	15 Mar 1766	5	Mary his Wife Daught of Joseph and Mary Hankinson		
Mary his Wife	10 Oct 17	36	Jane Davis	5 Aug 17	
Sarah Wife of John Polk, senior,	31 May 1767	44	Mary Davis	5 May 17	
John Davis	2 June 1740	82	Joseph Hankinson	2 Jun 17	
Ann his Wife	2 May 1746	70	Mary his Wife	8 Mar 17	
Elizabeth, Daughter of Joseph Craddock	17 09 14	14	John Hankinson	19 Mar 17	

LXXIX. COLNE ROGER'S.

FROM ROGER, Conſtable of GLOUCESTER, its moſt ancient Poſſeſſor, who, having been mortally wounded at the Battle of *Halliſon*, gave this Territory to the Monks of *St Peter* in GLOUCESTER in 1105.

It is a ſmall Pariſh in the Hundred of *Bradley*, ſeven Miles North eaſt from *Cirenceſter*, three and a Half from *Northleach*, and from GLOUCESTER twenty one on the Eaſt. It is divided by the River from *Colne St Denis*. The Soil becomes higher as further from the Meadows on the Banks of the River, and is principally applied to Tillage, compriſing, with extenſive Common Fields, about 1300 Acres.

The Living is a Rectory, endowed with forty eight Acres in the Common Fields, but with a twentieth Part only of the Tythes of the Demeſne Lands. The Dean and Chapter of GLOUCESTER obtained a Right of Preſentation when their Charter was confirmed at the Reſtoration, 1660, by King CHARLES II.

The Church is dedicated to *St Andrew*, in the Deanery of *Cirenceſter*, it is a ſmall and inconſiderable Building, conſiſting of a Nave only.

The Manor ſettled as beforementioned, was given to the Dean and Chapter of GLOUCESTER, 33 HENRY VIII (1542) and has deſcended from various Leſſees to JOHN CHALLONER READY, Eſq.

Pentrep, or *Pentlery*, is the moſt valuable diſtinct Eſtate, held by THOMAS COTTON, Eſq.

BENEFACTIONS.

The Rev. JOHN RATCLIFFE, D.D. Maſter of *Pembrok College*, *Oxford* gave by Will in 1785, for the Benefit of poor Children of this Pariſh, 100*l* in the three *per Cents*, by the Truſtees, the Dean and Chapter of GLOUCESTER.

INCUMBENTS	PATRONS	INCUMBENTS	PATRONS
1570 Nathaniel Huntford,	Roger Liggon, Eſq	—— George Duly	
1582 John Smith,	Chapter of GLOUCESTER	1694 Roger Ruſhile B.D.	Chapter of GLOUCESTER.
—— Thomas Tayler,	——	1707 Samuel Broad, LL.B	The ſame
1587 John Babington,	George Liggon and	1711 Chriſt Barnes, M.A	The ſame
	Henry Liggon	1728 Matthew Penny, D.D	The ſame
—— John Smith		1733 John Ratcliffe D.D	The ſame
1613 Thomas Hughes,	Michael Strange	1775 Hugh Price M.A	The ſame
1621 Thomas Hughes,	Robert Oldſworth, Eſq	1786 John Charnley, M.A	The ſame

The only Perſon ſummoned from this Pariſh by the Heralds, in 1682 and 1683, was

William Oldſworth, Clerk.

At the Election in 1776 two Freeholders polled from this Pariſh.

The firſt Entry in the Regiſter bears Date 1598.

ANNUAL ACCOUNT OF MARRIAGES, BIRTHS, AND BURIALS, IN THIS PARISH.

A.D.	Mar	Bi	Bur	A.D.	Mar	Bi	Bur	A.D.	Mar	Bi	Bu	A.D.	Mar	Bu	Bur
1781	1	1	—	1786	1	1	1	1791				1796			
1782		5	1	1789	—	5	1	1792				1797			
1783	—	4		1788				1793				1798			
1784	—	2	—	1790				1794				1799			
1785	—	—	4	1792				1795				1800			

INSCRIPTIONS IN THE CHURCH

ON FLAT STONES

JANE PLUMMAR, the Wife of
JOHN PLUMMAR, the Daughter of RICHARD CORTIS,
departed this Life Dec. 26, 1683

RICHARD, the Son of
Mr THOMAS and MARY MORSE,
died Sept. 26, 1717, aged 15 Months.

IN THE CHURCH YARD.

ON A SQUARE MARBLE TABLET AGAINST THE
CHURCH

Sacred to the Memory of
MARY, Wife of JOSIAH COOK,
of Cheltenham, Daughter of
JOHN and JANE MILLINGTON of this Place
She departed this Life Jan 1785, 51

ON A TOMB

JOHN MILLINGTON, senior,
died April 1, 1775, aged 80

JANE his Wife
died April 21, 1779, aged 71

ON HEAD STONES

Name						Died	Aged
Mary, Wife of Thomas Day	-	-	-	-		19 Ma. 1760	62
Richard, Son of Thomas ...			-	-		25 Sept 1705	21
John his Son				-	-	9 May 1735	17
				-	-	23 Mar 1752	77
					-	12 Mar 17..	79
				-	-	25 Sept 170.	
				-	-	.. Oct 17..	75
				-	-	29 Ma. 1777	8.
					:	17 Dec 1761	72

LXXX. COMPTON ABDALE

LIES in a small Valley, higher on the Course of the River *Colne* in the Hundred of *Br[illegible]y*, distant four Miles from *Northleac* on the West, ten from *Grenc[illegible]* on the North and seventeen from GLOUCESTER in a more easterly Direction. The Boundary includes about [illegible] Miles, of a light Soil chiefly Arable, and fertile in Corn.

The Living is a perpetual Curacy, the Stipend of which has been [illegible] Queen Anne's Bounty. The impropriate Tythes, with the Appointment of a Curate, originally belonged to the Priory of *St Oswald* in GLOUCESTER, and were granted at the Suppression to the Dean and Chapter of BRISTOL.

The Church is a small plain Structure, with a Nave and a North Aisle, divided by [illegible] pointed Arches. It is in the Deanery of *Cirencester*, and has *St Oswald* for its Patron Saint.

In *Domesday* the Manor is attributed to St [illegible] Archbishop of *C[illegible]*, but it appears that when the Temporalities of the See of *York*, were extended in [illegible], *Compton Abdale* was [illegible] to them. Sir THOMAS CHAMBERLAYNE obtained from King EDWARD VI [illegible] all the Archbishop's Lands [illegible] in the County of GLOUCESTER. About 1638 Sir RICHARD GRUBHAM [illegible] became possessed of it, and was [illegible] by his Nephew Sir JOHN HOWE, whose Descendants, since ennobled, have been the [illegible] Proprietors. The manerial [illegible] extends almost over the whole Parish.

The surrounding Hill have so sudden a Descent to the Village, that it is usually called *Compton in the [illegible]*.

No Benefactions to the Poor

OFFICIATING MINISTERS	PATRONS
17[illegible] Charles Pyge, M. A.	Dean and Chapter of BRISTOL
178[illegible] Charles Pyge, B. A.	The same

PRESENT LORD OF THE MANOR
The Right Honourable JOHN HOWE Lord CHEDWORTH

It does not appear that any Person was summoned from this Parish by the Heralds in 1682 and 1683.

At the Election in 1776 three Freeholders polled from this Parish.

The oldest Register now extant bears Date in 1720.

ANNUAL ACCOUNT OF MARRIAGES, BIRTHS, AND BURIALS, IN THIS PARISH.

A.D.	Mar.	Bir.	Bur.	A.D.	Mar.	Bir.	Bur.	A.D.	Mar.	Bir.	Bur.	A.D.	Mar.	Bir.	Bur.
1781	—	4	3	1786	1	7	1	1791				1796			
17[illegible]	—	7	[illegible]	1787	1	4	6	1792				1797			
1[illegible]	2	1	2	178[illegible]				179[illegible]				1798			
1[illegible]	2	4	[illegible]	1[illegible]				1794				1799			
1[illegible]	—	7	[illegible]	1790				[illegible]				[illegible]			

INSCRIPTIONS IN THE CHURCH.

John [illegible], died [illegible] 10, 1[illegible], aged [illegible].

[illegible] his Wife, died [illegible] 1[illegible], aged [illegible].

Thomas [illegible] of the Earth [illegible], died [illegible] 17[illegible], aged [illegible].

[illegible] his Wife, died [illegible] 2 [illegible] 17[illegible].

Thomas Y[illegible], died [illegible] 17[illegible], aged 61.

[illegible] Wa[illegible] Mary [illegible] 1[illegible], died [illegible] 8 [illegible].

[illegible], died Ma[illegible] 17[illegible].

IN THE CHURCH YARD.

ON FLAT AND HEAD STONES.

	Died	Aged
William Freeman	6 Au[illegible] 1[illegible]67	[illegible]
[illegible]	5 May 1[illegible]64	[illegible]
[illegible] his Wife	[illegible]	[illegible]
J[illegible]	15 [illegible] 17[illegible]	7
[illegible] his Wife		
Elizabeth [illegible] James Broom,		
[illegible]	6 Oct [illegible] 68	[illegible]
J[illegible]	5 Dec 17[illegible]	80
J[illegible] and Wife of James Pat[illegible]	9 June 1[illegible]	[illegible]
[illegible] of William Cook	13 Apr [illegible] 55	[illegible]

	Died	Aged
Thomas [illegible] and Mary		
[illegible]	17 June [illegible]75[illegible]	[illegible]
[illegible] of Thomas [illegible]	9 July [illegible]	[illegible]
William Y[illegible]	Nov 178[illegible]	[illegible]
[illegible] his Wife	2 Dec 1[illegible]	[illegible]
Joseph [illegible]	[illegible] Sep [illegible]	[illegible]
[illegible]	2[illegible] Sep [illegible]8	84
Susanna his Wife	2 June, 1777	77

LXXXI.

LXXXI. COMPTON GREENFIELD.

A PARISH of small Extent in the Hundred of *Henbury*, six Miles distant from the City of Bristol on the North west, nine South-west from *Thornbury*, and thirty three from GLOUCESTER in the same Direction. Upon the South Side the River *Severn* forms its Boundary. From its low Situation the Lands are chiefly Pasture, and the Soil heavy, the additional Name was given in Distinction to *Compton Eastward* in the Parish of *Henbury*.

The Living is a Rectory, with a considerable Glebe, in the Deanery of BRISTOL, originally detached from *Westbury* upon *Trim*.

The Church is small, with a low Tower. Vestiges of the Style of Architecture of the early Part of the 13th Century are still to be discovered. It was at that Time styled "*Capella de Cortone*," and was in the Presentation of RALPH BLOET, 1217, 18 JOHN. He was likewise one of the earliest Possessors of the Manor. In 1355, 28 Edw III it passed to Sir MAURICE BERKELEY, Knight, and continued with various of the Descendants, though with some few Interruptions, till the Reign of Queen ELIZABETH, 1570.

In the beginning of the present Century it was purchased by Sir THOMAS CANN, the Male Line of whose Family failing in 1765, by the Death of Sir ROBERT CANN, Bart. the Manor and principal Estate devolved to his Niece and Heir at Law, CATHARINE, Daughter and Heir of CHARLES JEFFRIES, of BRISTOL, Esq. and now Relict of Sir HENRY LIPPINCOTT, who was created a Baronet in 1778. Few Parishes are more deficient in what might attract the Notice of the Naturalist or Antiquary.

No Benefactions to the Poor.

INCUMBENTS.		INCUMBENTS.	
1609	John Odell, M A.	1683	William Stone, M A.
1619	John Green, M A.	1721	Walter Rainstrop.
1637	Christopher Collard.	1769	—— Durstone
		1770	James New, M A.

PRESENT LADY OF THE MANOR,
Dame CATHERINE LIPPINCOTT.

The Persons summoned from this Place by the Heralds in 1682 and 1683, were
Sir Robert Canne, Knight, and Richard Canne, Esq.

At the Election in 1776, Six Freeholders polled from this Parish.

The Register has its first Date in 1583

This Parish is so thinly inhabited as to supply few Articles for the Register. From the Year 1756 to 1783 seven Marriages have only taken place. Baptisms and Burials not more than one annually.

INSCRIPTIONS

ON FLAT STONES IN THE CHANCEL

MARY Wife of EDWARD BROWNE, of St Swithin in the Parish of Almondsbury in the County of Gloucester, Gent died the 6th Day of October, 1690, aged 61

Also five of their Children

The said EDWARD BROWNE Gent died Jan 16 1693, aged 7.

In Memory of EDWARD NASH, Esq who died May 3, 174, aged 60

ELIZABETH Daughter of JOHN RAINSTROP, of the City of Bristol, Merchant, and Niece of the Rev WALTER RAINSTROP, sometime Rector of this Parish, died Jan 14, 1729, aged 45

Also WALTER RAINSTROP, Brother of the above ELIZABETH, died Nov 9, 1784

Hic jacet Corpus RICHARDI CANN, hujus Parochiæ Generosi, defunctus Septembris Die 29, A D 1696, æt suæ 52

JAMES SEAGER, of the Parish of Henbury, died May 22 1731, aged

THOMAS Son of THOMAS SEAGER of the Parish of Henbury, died May 4, 173 , aged 21

ON A TABLET IN THE NAVE
Opposite this Monument lies the Remains of WILL PRICE, Taylor, Son of and SARAH TAYLOR of this Parish, who departed this Life June 9, 1782, aged 29 Years

ON A RAISED STONE IN THE CHURCH YARD

In this Vault rest the Remains of MARY RAINSTROP, who died Feb 21, 1765, aged 27
Likewise of SARAH CHAPMAN, of the City of Bath, died June 23, 1768, aged 28
Also of the Rev WALTER RAINSTROP, 45 Years Rector of this Parish,
and Father of the above MARY and SARAH, died Oct 9, 1769, aged 84

ON HEAD STONES

	Died	Aged
Grace, Wife of John Watkins, of Henbury	25 Sept 176	56
Charles Ockford, of Henbury	8 May, 1713	35

COMPTON PARVA

IS so diftinguifhed from *Long Compton* in the County of *Warwick*, an adjoining Parifh on the North *Oxfordfhire* forms all its other Boundaries Having been a Part of the Eftates of the Alien Priory of *St Dennis*, it was given to that of *Deorhurft*, and is one of the Parifhes belonging to that Hundred, unconnected with the main Territory It is diftant from *Morton in Marfh* four miles on the Eaft, fix from *Stow*, inclining to the North, and from GLOUCESTER thirty in the firft Direction Of the Soil the greater Part is light and applied to Tillage, with its Proportion of Pafture and Woodland comprifing by Computation, 1600 Acres, which includes a confiderable Tract of uninclofed and uncultivated Lands

The Living is a ftipendiary Curacy, which has been augmented by a Benefaction of 10*l* annually, by the celebrated Dr SOUTH, and the Intereft of 200 added by *Chrift Church College, Oxford*, who became invefted with the Tythes, upon their Foundation, by King HENRY VIII who transferred them from the Abbey of *Tewkefbury*, during the Period of whole Poffeffion it was a Vicarage

St Dennis is the Patron of the Church, in the Deanery of *Stow*, a very fmall and inconfiderable Structure

The Abbey of *Tewkefbury* obtained this Manor from King HENRY the Fifth, by Purchafe, when he diffolved all the Alien Priories, amongft the Cells or Dependants of which was *Deorhurft* In 1537 Sir THOMAS POPE *, Knight (appointed Treafurer of the Court of Augmentations in 1536), became the fole Proprietor, and upon his Eftablifhment of *Trinity College in Oxford* in 1555, he gave to the Natives of this Parifh an exclufive Preference, when Candidates for the Emoluments of his Foundation † By his Will, dated 1558, he bequeathed this Eftate to JOHN DODMER, the Son of his fecond Wife, who was the Relict of ROBERT DODMER, Lord Mayor of *London* in 1529 ELIZABETH his Daughter and Heir was the Wife of Sir ROBERT COTTON, Knight, 1608 A few Years after, it was purchafed by Dr WILLIAM JUXON, or JUXON, fucceffively Bifhop of *Hereford* and *London*, and at the Reftoration promoted to the Metropolitical See of *Canterbury* His Nephew WILLIAM JUXON, created a Baronet in 1662, was fucceeded by his Son, of both thofe Names, who died in 1739 without Iffue After his Demife his Relict was re-married to CHARLES Lord Vifcount FANE of the Kingdom of *Ireland*, and is the prefent Poffeffor The Manor-houfe was built by the Archbifhop, and has been fince modernized by his Defcendants

Upon a Point of Land in this Parifh is a Pedeftal with an Infcription purporting that it marks the Junction of the four feveral Counties of *Gloucefter, Warwick, Oxford,* and *Worcefter*, which Part of the laft mentioned is far diftant from the great provincial Diftrict

---

BENEFACTIONS

Dr WILLIAM JUXON, Archbifhop of *Canterbury*, left by Will 1662, 100*l* for the Ufe of the Poor of this Parifh, the annual Produce of which now is 5*l* 15*s*

INCUMBENTS	PATRONS
1630 John Maunder,	William Hayward
—— John Jones Clerk,	Chrift College, Oxford
1755 William Bake, Clerk,	The fame

* WARTON's Life of Sir T POPE, pp 181, 182, 183
† WOOD Antiq Oxon Edit CURCH, p 519
This, with other fimilar Privileges were fuperfeded by a Decifion of the Vifitor of the College in 1776, who fubjected all Claims fpecified in the Statutes of the Founder, to the Arbitration of the Prefident and his Majority of the Fellows of the College

WILLIAM JUXON, Son of RICHARD JUXON was born at Chichefter in Suffex, elected Fellow of St John's College, Oxford in 1598, and Prefident in 1626, and in the next Year Dean of Worcefter In 1633, confecrated Bifhop of Hereford, and in the fame Year tranflated to London He had the Honour and Happinefs (fays Wood) to attend King CHARLES the firft at his Execution, and it has been confidently faid, was the Author of the EIKON BASILIKE" "Afterward (continues the Oxford Hiftorian) " he retired to his Manor of Little Compton, co GLOUCESTER, where he fpent feveral Years in a devout and retired Condition, " and now and then, for Health's Sake, rode a hunting with fome of the neighbouring, and loyal Gentry" At the Reftoration in 1660 he was advanced to the See of Canterbury, and died in 1663, aged 81, leaving his Nephew Sir WILLIAM JUXON his Heir
WOOD's Athenae, vol II p 662

5 S   PRESENT

C O M P T O N P A R V A

PRESENT LADY OF THE MANOR,

The Right Honourable SUSANNA Lady Dowager Vilcountefs FANE

The only Perfon fummoned from this Parifh by the Heralds in 1682 and 1683 was
Sir William Juxon, Baronet

At the Election in 1776 one Freeholder polled from this Parifh

The Regifter begins in 1588

ANNUAL ACCOUNT OF MARRIAGES, BIRTHS, AND BURIALS, IN THIS PARISH

A D	Mar	Bir	Bur	A D	Mar	Bir	Bur	A D	Mar	Bir	Bur	A D	Mar	Bir	Bur
1781	2	9	6	1786	5	11	5	1791				1796			
1782	—	9	5	1787	2	7	3	1792				1797			
1783	4	5	3	1788				1793				1798			
1784	—	12	3	1789				1794				1799			
1785	3	5	1	1790				1795				1800			

INSCRIPTIONS IN THE CHURCH

ON FLAT STONES IN THE CHANCEL

Arms, Or, a Crofs Gules, between four Blackmoor's Heads couped at the Shoulders proper, the Arms of Ulfter, for JUXON —impaling, Barry of fix Or and Sable, for MARIOTT

Under this Stone lieth interred the Body of Sir WILLIAM JUXON late of this Place, Knight and Baronet, who died the third Day of February, 1739, in the 79th Year of his Age. He was the eldeft Son of Sir WILLIAM JUXON, Knight and Baronet alfo deceafed who intermarried with ELIZABETH Daughter of Sir JOHN WALTER, of Sariden in the County of Oxford, Baronet, alfo

deceafed Sir WILLIAM JUXON the Son intermarried with SUSANNA MARIOTT, youngeft Daughter of JOHN MARIOTT, late of Stufton in the County of Suffolk, Efq deceafed, but has left no Iffue whereby the Title is extinct

Mortale THOMÆ JUXON, Armigeri, qui Cœlum petiit 28° Feb Anno Domini 1643

ELIZABETHA PORY, uxor ROBERTI, Filiæ THOMÆ JUXON, Armigeri, Sacræ Pentiffima Animæ ad Sæcula In diem Redemptionis fub hoc marmore pofuit, Fœmini Chriftian Deceffit XV Kal Martii, Anno ætatis tricefmo ieceens exacto & a partu Deiparæ CIƆIƆCLII

Here lyeth interred the Body of the Rev JOHN JONES, who departed this Life the 10th Day of February, 1753, aged 57 Years

IN THE CHURCH YARD

ON HEAD STONES

	Died	Aged		Died	Aged
Mary, Wife of John Davis, of Chilleton Hill in the County of Oxford	16 July, 1777	48	Jane, Wife of Edward Rufhall	11 Feb 1769	75
			Mary, Daughter of Thomas and Jane Jordan	11 Feb 1775	45
John Cowley, of Little Woodford	18 Oct 1760	62	Thomas Davis	17 June 1759	70
Richard Shirley	21 Mar 1767	89	John Son of Richard and Mary Fletcher	13 July, 1747	31
Elizabeth his Wife	1 Feb 1764	81			
Henry Lyne	26 Sept 1743	65	Richard Son of Thomas and Elizabeth Walker	11 May 1761	35
Catherine his Wife	4 Mar 1759	71	Elizabeth Relift of Thomas Walker	19 May, 1759	67
John their Son	24 Apr 1747	35	Edward Rufhall	27 May 1765	75
Hannah, Wife of John Rufhall	9 May 1767	30	John Hanks	22 Apr 1749	71
Mary, Wife of Richard Jordan	12 Feb 1749	51	Elizabeth his Wife	29 June, 1751	5
Thomas Jordan	11 July, 1751	48			

THIS small Parish lies in the Hundreds both of *Kiftegate* and *Slaughter*, three Miles distant North-westward from *Stow*, eight from *Winchcomb*, and twenty-four from GLOUCESTER on the North east

The Soil is light, and very generally tilled, including, with the Common Fields, which were inclosed in 1779, a Circumference of about four Miles. In the Village, over a copious Spring, are the Remains of a very ancient Cross.

The Living is a Rectory in the Deanery of *Stow*, and prior to the Reformation was appropriated to the Abbey of *Winchcomb*, and granted to Sir THOMAS SEYMOUR in 1546. But the Impropriation has been since resumed, and the Glebe originally more than 100 Acres, was increased in its Proportion at the general Inclosure. An annual Payment of 3l. 13s. 4d. is likewise due from a Farm in the Hamlet of *Hinchwic*, divided between this and the Parish of *Bredon* in *Worcestershire*.

The Church, dedicated to St *Nicholas*, is a small Building, and contains nothing interesting or curious. It was once within the Peculiar of *Blockley*.

At the Time of the CONQUEROR'S Survey this Manor had several Proprietors. The larger Share belonged to the Temporalities of the Archbishop of *York*, and as such was conveyed to Sir THOMAS CHAMBERLAYNE, Knight. It has since had many successive Purchasers, at no very distant Periods, and is now held jointly by three Coheirs of the Name of COMLER, married to KNIGHT, HICKES, and DAVIES.

BENEFACTIONS

In 1779 five Acres of the general Inclosure were allotted to the the Poor to provide them with Fuel.

INCUMBENTS	PATRONS	INCUMBENTS	PATRONS
1573 Walter Kent,	Anne Croftes	1676 Robert Hill, M A	Henry Beard, Gent.
1628 Gilbert Drake,	————	1726 John Partridge, B A	Anne Cox
1663 Lewis Jones,	Henry Beard	177, William Baker, B A	Mary Hickes
1675 Edward Hales, M A	Edward Dudley, Esq	178? Henry Hodges, M A	William Ellis

PRESENT PROPRIETORS OF THE MANORS,
The Coheirs of ———— COMPLER, Esq.

There does not appear to have been any Person summoned from this Place by the Heralds in 1682 and 1683.

At the Election in 1776, only One Freeholder polled from this Parish.

The oldest Register extant bears Date so late as the Year 1717.

ANNUAL ACCOUNT OF MARRIAGES, BIRTHS, AND BURIALS, IN THIS PARISH

A D	Mar	Bir	Bur	A D	Mar	Bir	Bur	A D	Mar	Bir	Bur	A D	Mar	Bir	Bur
1781	—	4	—	1786	1	4	—	1791				1796			
1782	1		—	1787	—	2	2	1792				1797			
1783	2		3	1788	—	1	3	1793				1798			
1784	—	3	4	1789				1794				1799			
1785	—	1	3	1790				1795				1800			

* " A Watre runth at *Keylate* in *Cotefwold*, and thens to *Hinchwyte*, wherabout it renneth undre the Grownde "
LELAND, Itin. vol **V** p 1

Arms, a Salt re between femee of crofs Croffletts fitchy; impaling a Crofs.

H S E
ROBERTUS HILL, A M
Ecclefiæ hujus tantum non
Quinquaginta annos Rec ac
de Longborough Vicarius,
Qui quamvis utriufque curæ Paftor
optimus affidue incubuit fuæ
tamen ita profpexit ut cum venerit
Dominus licet fubcito vigilantem
invenerit & paratum
Obiit Maii 27, 1720, æt 75.

In Memory of
DOROTHY, the Wife of
the Rev. ROBERT HILL, Rector,
Daughter of JOSEPH WHETHAM,
of Longborough, Efq by whom
he had Iffue feven Sons and two Daughters,
three of which he here interred,
viz. JAMES and JOSEPH (Twins),
born Oct 9, 1681, and
DANIEL, born June 7, 1689,
the longeft of whofe Lives did not exceed 21 Days
She died in Childbed Sept 19, 1690, aged 34.

Arms; Gules, two Chevrons Argent, for HIDE.
Creft a Leopard's Head erafed.

Here lieth the Body
of MARY HIDE,
who departed this Life April 26, 1747, aged 97

HERCULES HIDE, Gent
died Nov. 8, 1719, aged 67

THOMAS, youngeft Son of
HERCULES HIDE,
died Sept 1, 1733, aged 13

SUSANNA, the Wife of
HENRY HASLUM, of Winchcomb,
Daughter of GEORGE HIDE, Gent
died July 15, 1732, aged 70.

Mr GEORGE HASLUM
Citizen and Apothecary in London,
died Aug. 11, 1741, aged 37

GEORGE STRATFORD, Gent
departed this Life Sept 4, 1720,
aged 84 Years

ELEANOR, Daughter of
Mr GEORGE STRATFORD,
died Auguft 29, 1721, aged 35

IN THE CHURCH YARD.
ON HEAD STONES

	Died	Aged
Cornelius Hall	10 Mar 1758	85
Edward Matthews, late of Cofcomb	4 June, 1761	50
Ann, Wife of Stephen Matthews	8 Jan 1749	73
Stephen Matthews, fenior	1 Feb. 1739	66
Mary, Wife of Stephen Matthews, junior	22 Aug 1755	38
Stephen Matthews, junior	25 May, 1707	63
Mary, Wife of Richard Humphris	10 Dec 1752	42

Arcade & Inscription against the Tower at Cotes

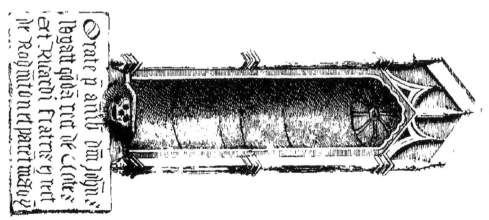

ONE of the frontier Parishes bordering on the County of *Worcester*, in the lower Division of the Hundred of *Westminster*, is four Miles distant Eastward from *Newent*, six South east from *Tewkesbury*, and about five North from GLOCESTER. The Soil consists chiefly of a strong red Clay, little more than one third Part of which is inclosed, equally applied to Tillage and Pasture, and each planted with Apple and Pear Trees of an excellent Quality. The Hops, which grow plentifully without Culture, prove that the Discontinuance of the Plantation of them, did not arise from the Deficiency of the Soil.

Corse Lawn, a Plain of most beautiful Verdure, is a Tract of commonable Lands of more than a thousand Acres, within the Limits of this Parish. Upon the Eastern Side is a Slope or Ridge, resembling an artificial Terrace, which extends for a few Miles, and gives an Effect to the Landscape highly picturesque. The two great Roads from *Worcester* and *Ledbury* to GLOCESTER become one, about the mid Way.

The Benefice is a Vicarage, endowed with the whole Tythes, within the Peculiar of *Deorhurst*. A very commodious House has been erected by the present Incumbent.

The Church, dedicated to *St Margaret*, consists of a Nave with two spacious opposite Porches, and a Tower at the West End finished with a low octogonal Spire. What remains to mark the Style of Building is evidently of Gothic.

It has been found in the earliest Records that two Manors have been ever separately claimed and held in this Parish. That of *Corse Chace* belonged in the early Centuries to the DE CLARES, DE SPENCERS, and BEAUCHAMPS, from whom, to the THROCMORTONS, who continued till the End of the last Century. WILLIAM DOWDESWELL, Esq. formerly Chancellor of the Exchequer, died possessed of it in 1775.

The manerial Jurisdiction of *Corse Lawn* was anciently appendant to the Abbey of *Westminster*, it was granted to the Dean and Chapter in 1543, 34 HEN VIII and continued to them in 1560, 2 ELIZ.

In this Parish are two Hamlets. 1 *Horridge*, which was held under the *Benedictine* Priory of the lesser *Malvern*, co *Vigorn* and was purchased with their other Estates by HENRY LEIGH 1546. 2 *Staynbridge*.

Corse Farm, the most considerable Estate was sold in 1648 by JAMES COOKE to MARK GRIME, of *Great Taye*, co *Essex*, of whom it was purchased in 1664 by RICH. YATE, of *Bromesberrow*, Esq. It was a few Years since transferred by Sale from ROBERT GORGES DOWNES YATE, Esq. to SAMUEL WILSON of GLOUCESTER, Gent. by whose Will it devolved in equal Portions to the Families of WILSON, of *Iovana*, Woon, &c. The *Buck Farm* was bequeathed to WILLIAM DOWDESWELL, Esq. Recorder of *Tewkesbury*, by RICHARD MORLEY, Esq. Others are severally held by the Families of HAWKINS, HILLS, CLARKE, and SEYMOUR.

The Rivulet *Glench* in its Course to the *Leden* forms a Boundary to this and the Parish of *Staunton* in *Worcestershire*.

B E N E F A C T I O N S.

Lands to the Value of 6*l* a Year were given by some Person unknown, for the Use of the industrious Poor not on the Parish Books, but it has of late Years been applied to the Parish Poor in general.

INCUMBENTS	PATRONS	INCUMBENTS	PATRONS
—— —— ——,	Priory of Deorhurst	1687 —— Proctor, M.A.	King James II
—— —— ——,	Abbot of Tewkesbury	1691 Charles Smith, B.A.	King William III
1590 —— —— Jones,	Queen Elizabeth	1716 James —— Clerk,	King George I
1—— —— Lambert,	King James I	1727 Joseph Gore, M.A.	King George II
1—5 —— —— Jones,	King Charles I	1769 Robert Gore, M.A.	King George III
1—— —— Pembertn, M.A	King Charles II		

PRESENT LADY OF THE MANOR,
BRID. DOWDESWELL, WIDOW.

The Persons summoned from this Place by the Heralds in 1682 and 1683, were
Thomas Browne, Gent and Thomas Pembrige, M A Vicar

At the Election in 1776 Seventeen Freeholders polled from this Parish
The Register commences with a Baptism in 1569

ANNUAL ACCOUNT OF MARRIAGES, BIRTHS, AND BURIALS, IN THIS PARISH

A D	Mar	Bir	Bur	A D	Mar	Bir	Bur	A D.	Mar	Bir	Bur	A D	Mar	Bir	Bur
1781	1	12	8	1786	1	13	5	1791				1796			
1782	1	9	3	1787	1	8	5	1792				1797			
1783	4	8	6	1788	2	5	5	1793				1798			
1784	2	6	3	1789				1794				1799			
1785	2	11	13	1790				1795				1800			

INSCRIPTIONS IN THE CHURCH

ON A MONUMENT ON THE SOUTH
SIDE OF THE CHANCEL

Arms, Sable a Cross Or charged
in the Centre with a Pellet for GRAILE

TIMOTHY GRAILE aged 1 Years,
set out by the Cape of Good Hope unto
the East Indies, Anno 1630
and passed by the Cape of Letter Hope
into Heaven August 12 1636

ELIZABETHA, Uxor EDMUNDI GRAILE,
Filium suum Charissimum secuta, per
Funder (optimæ spei caput) Jesum
In portum æterna foelicitatis appliquit
Februarii 13 Anno salutis 1638

EDMUNDUS GRAILE Generosus,
Huic Hospitio Medius Annos 35,

Feb 1 correptus obiit Septemb 24,
Anno Dom 1643 ætat 69
Et ab hujus Civitatis Ooidione
Memorabili Sep mina tcr it
Dogmatis Christiani & Galeni,
Integer ita conta e mavis,
Possidens coelos, pius, te furenti
Marte qui evit

Quæ supra Legis
Lector candide tribus Olim
Sveis Sepulch ebbu int thun i sub
Arcu jux a sellulus insculpta, & iam
Demum ped bis OLOEFEON terme tur ru
Hic nunc denuo de Novo in pristinam
Avorum suorum. Memoriam
THOMAS GRAILE Ezra filius, Nepos

EDMUND Rector Taringtoniæ, L.M Q
Posuit Anno Salutis MDCC
Ora, lege, & abi

To preserve this Mnoil of his Mo
ther's Relations, ROBERT GRACE Vicar
of this Church removed it hither from
the old Chapel of St Bartholomew's Hos
pital in Gloucester, on the Demolition of
that Structure in the Year 1750

ON A FLAT STONE

Here lyeth the Body of ROBERT JONES,
who deceased the XXth Day of October,
Anno Dom 1613

IN THE CHURCH YARD, ON TOMBS.

GEORGE KNOTSFORD
died the 10th of
in the Year of his Age 75,
our Lord 1702

MARY, the Wife of GEORGE KNOTSFORD,
died Dec 26, 1711, aged 63

CHARITY, the Wife of HENRY CLARKE,
and Daughter of the Rev Mr JOHN WALKER
(Minister of Ledbury) by SUSANNA his Wife,
died July 27 1774, aged 66 Years

ON HEAD STONES

	Died	Aged		Died	Aged
Hannah, Wife of Richard Line, of Huntsfield	14 Oct 1767	55	Sarah, Wife of John Fletcher	1 June 1697	—
William Hancock	8 Feb 1755	43	Richard Harding	1 Dec 1705	—
William Cattledine	Oct 1719	69	Mary his Wife	6 May 1700	63
Elizabeth his Wife	21 Jan 1732	42	Aaron, Son of Moses and Elizabeth Jones	23 Dec 1781	1
Sarah Wife of John Clarke	16 May 1756	20	Elizabeth Jones	1 Aug	
Jane, Wife of John Williams	6 Oct 1753	57	Edward Wadley	Jan 1 17	
Mary, Wife of Nathaniel Simmonds	29 Apr 1760	51	Mary, Daughter of John Merry, of Hartpury, and Ann his Wife	22 Dec 1713	
Mary Charvoe, Widow, of the Parish of Cleeve	15 May 1734	80	Edward Line	21 Apr 1714	
Samuel Line	25 Mar 1760	52	William, Son of Michael Wells	16 May 1711	21
Thomas Wadley	23 May 1747	54	William Young	4 Apr 1716	54
Elizabeth, Wife of Thomas Wadley	23 Mar 1731	24	William Hall	23 Apr 1710	60
David Mutlon	3 June 1705	58	George Stephens, late of Ashchurch	6 Mar 17	43
Mary his Wife, late Wife of Thomas Manning	13 Nov 1713	51	John his Wife	5 Oct	61
William Wilkes of the Parish of Tatenham in the County of Worcester	14 May 1765	46	William Son of William and Ann Webb	July 1716	
Mary his Wife	13 May 1764	65	Edward Spakes	6 Jan	54
Moses Jones	23 May 1721	68	Elizabeth Daughter of Nicholas and Sarah Nelms	29 May 17	
Mary, Daughter of Richard and Hannah Young	7 July 1785	20			

LXXXV.   C O T E S.

THIS Name was not confirmed till the Efcheator's Return in 128., o[...] T[...] In *Domefd[...]* the Parish is deferibed as confifting of three co[...]ed Vills, *H[...]t[...], [...] and [...]on*, and is thus noticed in the Itinerary of WILLIAM OF W[...] [...] *Villa [...]s [...]h [...]ons C[...]fe[...]or-*
"*titut Nomen, diftat per* iiiᵃ *Milliaria [...]y[...]re [...]ope ic [...] [...] way veil is B[...]oli [...]*"

In the early Centuries, when the upper Divifion of this County was a chin p[...]in [...]uncul[...]wated T[...]t of Land, this Village is faid to have furnifhed a Part of the gener[...]l Te co[...]mr[...]n, c[...] [...]ll a[...] to have been remarkable for the numerous and [...]eaut[...]ful Flocks of Sheep that [...]ere bred o[...]tue D[...]w[...] to the Exportation of fome of th[...] [...]th *Spa[...] [...]s* owe[...] a moft extenfive Commerce in Wool, of [...] Qu[...] y and Excellence produced in no o[...]her Climate. †

Cotes

---

* " Or entalis provinc[...] *Cl[...]efi* [...]ars Cellul[...]s attolitur qu[...] *Cotefu* [...]d die in [...]r[...] H[...] aura mfin[...] Gregu[...] Cop[...] Oves cer-
" vice pr[...] a & qu[...]di tco corpo[...] [...] La[...]re mo[...]llima & [...] [...]i[...]iga[...]o [...]pud omnes pr[...]tio "
R[...]e[...]r[...] Herm[...]nd[...] Put[...] Magn[...] edit 1661. 12 mo

† It m[...]y be pr[...]ba[...]l[...] interefti[...]g to f[...]me of our Reaxers to be informed of t[...] S[...]ition and Tre[...]ment adop[...]d b[...] [...]he Sheep [...]erds in [...]ya[...] The [...]hief [...]h[...]rater [...]he [...]tore re a[...]ive to that Subject is ful[...]joined [...]ast [...]ken from the Travels of the ingenious and accu[...]ate M[...] J[...]s[...] T[...]z[...]l[...] [...]r[...]os L[...]er V p 45

" O F   T H E   M E R I N O   S H E E P

" The Wool[...] f Sp[...]n[...] to [...] r[...]corde[...] [...]e [...]uch of our Commerc[...] wh[...] [...] [...] [...] It [...] s [...]en been faid that ther[...] fine
" Qu[...] y a[...]e [...]n a[...] [...]wi[...] to [...]ew *E[...]h[...] Sheep* f[...]tt[...] Sto[...], [...] p[...]e at [...] our Fl[...]s[...] the Second, or [...]c[...]ot[...]g to
" o[...]he[...], y [...] o[...]w[...] to [...]u[...]ll 1496, but wi[...]ut[...] e r[...]in to [...]am[...]s Inv[...]st[...] [...]r [...] [...]l [...]u[...] to r[...]re[...], and of [...]o
" lit[...]c[...] [...]nqu[...]e [...] I fhall e[...]t[...]re my[...]elf to f[...]eak of th[...]ir [...]e [...]l rel[...] t[...] [...]p[...]k[...] [...]n [...]s [...] o by the Name of *f[...]a[...] M[...]n[...]o,*
" (the Merino Fl[...]ck,) and d[...]fti[...] t[...]r[...]ee[...] an[...] M[...]h def[...] [...] conti[...] [...] [...] [...] [...] [...]d r[...]bas from [...]he Northern o[...]he[...] a[...]one a
" Pr[...]vince, to which they a[...]tri[...]ute [...]ha[...] peculiar [...]ne Qu[...]ity o[...] th[...]ir Wool, which [...]a[...] [...]e[...]d[...]r[...] [...]o famous a[...]l over
" Eu[...]ope

" There are two Sorts of Sheep in *Spa[...]* fome that have coar[...]e Wool [...]nd [...]re never r[...]moved o[...]t of [...]e Pl[...]ace to w[...]ich
" they be[...]on[...], and others th[...]t after fp[...]nd[...]g the Summer[...] in Le[...] [...]l[...] Mount[...]n[...] de[...]cend [...]n[...]e Winter o t[...]e m[...]lder
" [...]ro[...]n[...]s of *E[...]remadura* and *Andalufi[...]* [...]nd in the du[...]f[...] he[...]t of h[...]e Di[...]r[...]ts wh[...] g[...] b[...] the [...]ame [...] *M[...]r[...]e[...]* T[...]efe[...] e
" the Merino fheep, of which it is computed ther[...] are between [...]ur a[...]d f[...]v[...] M[...]l[...]on[...] [...] [...]he[...] [...]n[...] Th[...] [...]rd *Me[...]o* f[...]g
" nifies th[...] Governor of a Province The *Merino M[...]yor* [...]s al[...]s[...] th[...] fo[...]m[...] [...] a[...]d [...]pp[...]nte[...] [...]e [...]o[...]e [...]le[...] [...]e
" a [...]epar[...]te Jurifdiction over th[...] Flocks in *E[...]remadu[...]a,* whi[...] [...] [...]d[...]c[...]on V[...]r[...] [...]d t[...]ere [...]re [...]o [...]s [...] f[...]led a Merino
" M[...]nor

" [...]ach Flock confifts generally o[...] ten thoufand Sheep, w[...] a [...]M[...] v[...]rid[...] [...] [...]he d[...]r[...]ct[...] o[...] t[...]e moft h[...] [...]pt[...]e Man[...] well
" verfed in the nature of Pafture, as well as the Difeaf[...]s [...]nder [...]o th[...]s F[...]ck[...] Th[...] [...]ntr[...]l [...]r [...]er [...]on[...]ts ot [...] S[...]
" herds, a[...]d as many Dog[...] [...]ve of each to a Tribe Th[...] pr[...]ncip[...]l f[...]ephe[...]d has [...] [...]ho[...]se[...] of [...]e[...]e[...]o[...]n[...] [...]nd to t[...]e
" every Year The o[...]h[...]r f[...]rv[...]nts have 150 Re[...]ls for the fir[...]t Cl[...]s (at [...]u[...] [...]0 R[...]ls for t[...]e [...]ond [...] ([...] [...]d),
" 60 Reals for th[...] th[...]rd Cl[...]fs (13[...] 6d) a[...]d 40 Rials (9s) for th[...] other A[...]te[...]d[...]nc[...] be[...]des the[...] L[...]n[...]A[...]o[...]an[...] two
" Pounds of Bread [...]Da[...] w[...]th th[...] fame Quantity of an inf[...]r[...]or [...]or[...] for the Do[...]g[...] T[...]e[...] [...]ch[...]s[...] ar[...] p[...]mitted t[...] k[...]ep
" Goats and [...] [...]ew Sheep of which they h[...]ve the Meat, and th[...] L[...]mbs pr[...]vided [...] N[...]t [...]r[...] m[...]n F[...]h M[...]lk[...] [...]h[...]y
" may do wh[...]t they pleas[...] with the Milk [...]of which they fe[...]dom m[...]k[...] an[...] adv[...]n[...]a[...] In th[...] Mo[...]th of [...]p[...]l [...] f[...]t[...]v[...]l
" each Shepherd ha[...] 12 Reals given him (about [...] g[...]s) a[...] a Perquifit[...] pr[...]v[...]ous to h[...] J[...]urn[...]y

[...] Though thefe Flocks divide and [...]ep[...]r[...]te themfelves w[...] fe[...]er[...]l Pr[...]v[...]nc[...]s o[...] Sp[...]n, w[...]ll be un[...]ver[...]lly to t[...]l t[...] [...]r
" paffes in e[...]ch [...]h[...]r Go[...]ernm[...]nt being f[...]m[...]l[...]r a[...]d un[...]form Th[...] P[...]ces wh[...]re they [...]o [...]o f[...]ed [...]n th[...] [...]a[...]t o[...] th[...] S[...]mmer as
" [...]re in the *Montana* a[...]d *Mo[...]n[...]de [...]h[...]go[...]* in [...]he Summer[...] a[...]d [...] the Pro[...]in[...]e[...] o[...] *E[...]rem[...]du[...]a* in th[...] Winter [...] [...]e a[...]n[...] the
" h[...]ghw[...]rd of *E[...]rem[...]u[...]e,* the *Montana* as to the No[...]th[...] and t[...]e moft elev[...]ted P[...]rt of [...]p[...]in, *E[...]r[...]m[...]du[...]a* u[...]u[...]lly [...]th [...]o
" [...]me[...]ic Pl[...]ins, but th[...] *Montanu* is ent[...]rely w[...]hou[...] th[...]m

" Th[...] f[...]t C[...]r[...] of t[...]e Shepherd, in co[...]ing to th[...] Spot where they [...]re to fp[...]nd the Summer, is to [...]e to the Lab[...] is much
" It is the [...]well c[...]t for this [...]urp[...]fe they a[...]e pr[...]v[...]ded with twenty [...]ve Qu[...]n[...]l[...] for [...]ery th[...]u[...]nd H[...]ad, wh[...]h[...]re co[...]
" [...]m[...]d in l[...]fs th[...]n f[...]ve Months, but they [...]t [...]o[...]e on th[...]r [...]o[...]rney[...] on [...]n th[...] W[...]nter Th[...] M[...]th[...]d o[...] [...]v[...]ng [...]l[...]o th[...]m[...]s
" [...]t [...]n[...][...] the Shepherd pl[...]ces b[...]tt[...] o[...] t[...]ey th[...] St[...]nes [...]bo[...]t [...]re [...]e[...]p[...] d[...]t[...]nc[...] from e[...]ch o[...]h[...] t[...]e [...]r[...]w[...]n[...] m[...]ni[...]
" e[...]ch [...]ne [...]e[...] l[...]a[...]s his Fl[...]ck [l[...]wly thr[...]ugh the St[...]n[...]s a[...]d every She[...]p [...]k[...] up pl[...]t d[...]c[...] Th[...] [...] fr[...]que[...]tly [...]e[...]t[...]d,
" th[...] f[...]p n[...]t t[...] l[...] them fe[...]d o[...] th[...]fe Day[...] m [...]ny [...]p[...]t w[...]ere th[...] [...]v[...]l tim[...] [...]one W[...]en they h[...]v[...] e[...]ten th[...] [...]int[...] y ac
" [...]f[...]r [...]o[...]e [...]yall[...]v[...]ss Sp[...]ts, w[...]re from the cr[...]v[...]g[...] [...]h[...]y h[...]v[...] acqu[...]r[...]d, they dev[...]ur every th[...]ng[...] they meet w[...]th, and
" [...]etu[...]n [...]e [...]n to t[...] [...] w[...]th [...]edo[...]bled Ardour

[...] th[...] En[...] o[...] [...]uly e[...]er[...] [...]ephe[...]d d[...]tr[...]but[...]s the R[...]ms [...]m[...]ng[...] the E[...]es [...]ve or f[...]x b[...]e[...] [...]e[...]n[...] f[...]fh[...]rent f[...]r n hun
" d[...]ed E[...]e[...] Th[...] [...]ate [...]a[...]en out of Flocks, wh[...]re th[...]y are [...]ept ap[...]rt, a[...]d [...]f[...]er [...] pr[...]per [...]e[...]e [...]e[...]g a[...]d p[...]int[...]d f[...]om
" th[...] E[...]e[...]

[...] F[...]cha[...]s, [...]e [...]e[...]e[...]ter Qu[...]nt[...]ty o[...] Wool, th[...]u[...]h [...]ot [...]o f[...]n[...] as [...]he E[...]es f[...]r the F[...]ec[...] of the Ram[...] w[...]ll w[...]h
[...] twen[...]y [...]e P[...]unds a[...]d [...]t r[...]qu[...]re[...] f[...]x Fl[...]ec[...] of [...]e E[...]es t[...] p[...]o[...]c[...] the l[...]k[...] W[...]ght [...]h[...]h [...]p[...]y[...] r[...]a[...]on[...] h[...]r Ap[...]a
" k[...]own [...]y [...]h[...] fe[...]de[...] fr[...]m [...]he [...]e[...]h o[...] th[...] R[...]ms not f[...]ll[...]ng b[...]fore th[...] [...]qu[...]re[...] Y[...]ar[...] wh[...]le the E[...]es, fr[...]m [...]at[...]l[...]r[...]e[...]cy o[...] [...]ra[...]e,
" [...]r o[...]her [...]ufe[...] l[...]o[...] th[...]m [...]fter f[...]ve Years

" Ab[...]ut th[...] m[...]ddl[...] o[...] [...]p[...]mb[...]r th[...]y [...]re m[...]rk[...]d[...] wh[...]ch [...] done by r[...]bb[...]ng th[...]r l[...]ins w[...]th Oc[...]re d[...]lu[...]ed [...]n Water [...]ome
" f[...]y th[...] [...]h[...] in[...]orpor[...]te[...] w[...]th the Gr[...]ce o[...] the W[...]ol[...] a[...]d [...]orm[...] a K[...]nd o[...] V[...]rn[...]fh wh[...]ch [...]ec[...]r[...]s them from the Incle-
" [...]e[...]c[...] o[...] the W[...]ther, [...]o [...]t [...]s pr[...]t[...]n[...]d th[...]t the Mo[...]ftur[...] o[...] th[...] Ocr[...] k[...]ep[...] the W[...]ol f[...]t, a[...]d pr[...]v[...]nt[...] it[...] in t[...]e c[...]m[...]ng
" [...]d[...]r a[...]d [...]ry Qu[...]lity [...]t[...] cong[...]u[...]ng[...] m[...] th[...]t the O[...]re[...] in th[...] n[...]tur[...] o[...] an [...]b[...]rb[...]nt, [...]d[...] l[...]ck[...] up th[...] [...]x[...]e[...]s o[...]
" T[...]a[...]fp[...]rat[...]on wh[...]ch [...]o[...]ld [...]nd[...]r the W[...]ol[...] d[...]ng[...] a[...]d co[...]rfe

[...] T[...] c[...]u[...]te th[...] F[...]nd[...] [...]t [...]pt[...] n[...]t[...]r[...] th[...]t M[...]r[...]no Fl[...]ck[...] he[...] in th[...] t[...] M[...]ch [...]er[...] [...]a w[...]rmer Clim[...]te th[...] w[...]ol o[...] th[...] R[...]uth h[...]s
[...] [...]e[...]n g[...]e[...]t[...]y i[...]pr[...]v[...]d f[...]nce th[...]ir [...]ntr[...]d[...]ct[...]on Th[...] [...]ve a fre[...] [...]alt[...]y[...] thr[...]ugh[...] th[...]r l[...]b[...]ne[...], [...]d [...] m[...]st n[...]b[...]r[...] n the[...]r
[...] V[...]ll[...]g[...] b[...]t [...]re [...]y m[...]st pr[...]ve[...] m[...]ch [...]l[...]v[...]t[...]d [...]a[...]d[...] as l[...]e in th[...]r W[...]y the l[...]b[...]l n[...]nt[...] m[...]e th[...] [...]e[...] [...]e e[...]m[...]n
[...] ope[...]th [...]nery [...]e[...] wide, th[...]u[...]h which th[...]f[...] Fl[...]ck[...] a[...]e [...]bl[...]ged to p[...]f[...] r[...]p[...]dly, go[...]ng[...]t [...] t[...]m[...]s f[...]x or f[...]v[...]n L[...] [...] u[...]

Da[...],

Cotes included in the Hundred of Crowthorne and Mincty, three Miles distant from Cirencester Westward and eighteen South-eastward from Gloucester. The Soil consisting of nearly 1,500 Acres, is light and about a third very ill tilled, 400 Acres are in Cotes Wood, the Property of HENRY Earl BATHURST. The commons here, contiguous to the Parish of Rodmarton, are very extensive, the precise Boundaries of which, from Neglect of Perambulation, and Inattention to the ancient Mears, are now hard to be ascertained.

The Manor, in 1287, 15 Edw. I. was held by GILBERT DE CLARE, Earl of GLOUCESTER, and has therefore been since considered as subject to the Court of that Honour. About the middle of the fifteenth Century it was purchased of the Family of VERNON, by Sir WILLIAM NOTTINGHAM, from whom it passed to RICHARD POOLE, by Intermarriage with his Relict. Of his Descendants (in 1600) it was bought by Sir ROBERT ATKYNS, senior, Knight, and re-sold (in 1787) by his Heir General, to the Family of LOWIS, with the Demesnes and Advowson.

The Benefice is a Rectory, endowed with 85 Acres of Glebe, and 370 Sheep Pastures, and with the Tythes of a Farm in the Parish of Sapperton, upon which was a Chapel, in the Nomination of the Abbots

" Day, in order to reach open Spots less inconvenient, where they may find some good Pasture and enjoy some Repose. In
" such open Places they seldom exceed two Leagues a Day following the Shepherd and grazing as they move on. Their
" whole Journey, from the Mirana to the interior Parts of Estramadura, may be about one hundred and fifty Leagues, which
" they perform in about forty Days.
" The first Care of the Shepherds is to lead them to the same Places where they have been the Winter before, and where the
" greatest Part of them were eared. This is no difficult Task, for if they were not led there they will discover the Ground by
" the great Sensibility of their Organs, to be directed from that which is contiguous, or were the Shepherd to in-
" cord, they would find it no easy Matter to make them go further. The next Business is to order the Fold, which are made
" by fixing Stakes fastened with Rope, one to the other, to prevent their Escape and being devoured by the Wolves, for
" which Purpose the Dogs are stationed without. The Shepherds build themselves Huts with Stakes and Boughs, for the cutting
" of which, as well as for Fuel, they are allowed to lop off a Branch from every Tree. This Law is the Cause of so many
" Trees being rotten and hollow, which grow in the Places frequented by these Flocks.
" A little before the Ewes are to bear their Winter Quarters is the Time of their eaning, at which Period the Shepherds must
" be particularly careful, the better ones are separated from the others and placed in a less advantageous Spot, reserving
" the best Pasture for those that are fruitful, renewing them in Proportion to their Forwardness. The little Lambs are put into
" the richest Pasture, that they may improve the sooner, and acquire sufficient Strength to perform the Journey along with the
" early ones.
' In March the Shepherds have four different Operations to perform with the Lambs that were eaned in the Winter, the first
" is to cut off their Tails, the Fingers both of the Rump for Cleanliness; the Second is to mark them on the Nose with hot
" Iron, next they saw off the Tips of their Horns that they may not hurt one another when they are locked, finally they extend
" such Lambs as are doomed for Bell wethers to walk at the Head of the Tribe, which is not done without violence, by castrating
" by squeezing the Scrotum with the Hand, till the spermatic Vessels are twisted like a Rope, and they are in no further
" Danger.
" In April the Time comes for them to return to the Montana, which the Flock express with various Signs of their previous
" Movements and Restlessness, for which Reason the Shepherd is most Severe, very various and therefore people which often
" happens when proper care is not taken, and whole Flocks have sometimes strayed away out of their Leagues, where the Shepherd
" was asleep on these Occasions, they generally take the tenough Road to the sea, which they can follow.
" The first of May they begin to shear, unless the Weather is unfavourable, for the wet eastern part and doing so, others
" would farther in case of Dampness, and so to avoid which the Sheep are kept in covered Places till their tails are convenient,
" eminently, for this Purpose they have Buildings that will hold twenty thousand in a Time, which when kept so closely
" the Ewes are so delicate, that immediately after the shearing they were exposed to the chilling Air of the Night, they would
" certainly perish.
' One hundred and fifty men are employed to shear each thousand Sheep. Each Person is required to shear eight Sheep
" a Day, but it runs only five, not merely on Account of their Bulk and great Quantity of Wool, but from the tenderness
" ness of the paper, and difficulty to keep them quiet in a Random, for experienced that he is ready to fringe moved, which
" he finds the attention to the breed which they endeavour by such means and catches to keep him in Temper, and with much to those,
" and have very seldom him, they would engage men to him quiet and voluntarily induce them to proceed.
" On the shearing Day the Ewes are shut up in close Court, and from thence conducted under a quantity, which is a narrow
" Place, where they are kept precisely as possible that they may part productively, in order to them the Wool, and now it is
" with more care to the shearers. This is particular useful inspect to the Parts whose Wool is more valuable. The
" Fleece divided into three Sorts, the Back and Belly give the supreme, the Neck and side give the fine, and the breast,
" Shoulders, and thighs give the coarse Wool.
" The Sheep are then brought into other Three and marked extreme that those with a Tooth, which are destined for the
" Slaughter, and the believe led to a prize, if the other persons at a time, they are kept with Doors, till by Degrees
" they are accustomed to the Air. When the separation proceed the Winter being hurried away select of prefer their face
" Care never to take the first Places the sheep may find them a plenty, and at the vast Risk ever indeed with a
" distance to account with fire to Moderate, finding it necessary Occasion, must be obliged to march up another Spot

of R msy co Han's The T nes of the Demesnes belonged to the Abbey of Cirencester, and were so adjudged in 1463 In 1480 Richard Peachy, Rector, quitted his Claim to them to Richard Cervi, Abbot, Richard Vernon, Lord of the Manor, being a Party in the Indenture

The Church is in the Deanery of Cirencester, and dedicated to St Matthew To the Nave are attached one Aisle on the North, and a sepulchral Chapel, said to have been to appropriated by the Family of Nottingham The Tower, a neat Gothic Structure, 25 Yards in Height, was erected by John Wyatt, Rector, in the 14th Century Beneath a small vacant Niche the following Inscription is still legible " **Drate p' A ib' Dni Joha's Wigatt, quonda' hert de Cotes, & Richardi Fratris ej Rectis de Roomton et parce'tu' cor'm**" The Church was likewise externally beautified by him at the same Time, upon the Architrave of the Chancel Windows, ' **Wie nell fect Johes no're Wiyatt** The Approach to the Village on the North west is picturesque, from the beautiful Plantations of Beech Wood The chief Estate descended to the Coheirs of Edward Atkins, of See in this County, H j whose present Representatives are Edmund John Chamberlayne, Esq and Ann Horner, Spinster

In *Tarlton*, a Hamlet partly in this, and partly in the Parish of *Rodmarton* , a very considerable Estate is held by Charles Wesley Coxe, Esq

Trewsbury is another Hamlet, where are strong Vestiges of an Entrenchment, most probably one of the " *Castra exploratoria*" of the *Romans* But a modern, and greater Curiosity is the navigable Canal intended to join the Rivers *Severn* and *Thames*, the Line of which is conducted through the whole of this Parish, and the Aperture of the Tunnel, or grand subterraneous Passage, barely within the Limits of it This stupendous Work began in 1783, is now completed It pierces an immense Mass of Earth, in a Cylindrical Form, of a Diameter of 15 Feet, and is 3660 Yards in Length Shafts from one End to the other are sunk at the Distance of 30 Yards From each of these the Work was finished 15 Yards in each Direction some of these are left unclosed, to communicate Air The greater Part of the Tunnel is arched artificially with Brick or Stone, and in some Places the Strata of Rock support themselves, and, from the Surface of the Land to the Bottom of the Tunnel, the deepest perpendicular is 245 Feet These are Circumstances which prove it to be the most remarkable subterraneous Passage made by Art in the known World

---

B E N E F A C T I O N S.

William Partriter left by Will, about the Year 1680, 10l the Interest of which to be given to the second Poor, at Christmas
Rev William Tyndale, 1765, left 10l the Interest of which to be applied to the same Purpose

Incumbents	Patrons	Incumbents	Patrons
—— John Wyatt,		1600 William Master, M A	Sir Henry Poole.
1486 Richard Peachy,	Richard Vernon	1651 Will Mountsteven, M A	
15 Thomas Williams,		1678 Thos Careret, M A	Sir Robert Atkins
1574 Robert Vernon,	Sir Giles Poole	1720 William Tydur, M A	Will Tyndale Gent
1577 John Knight,	The same	1765 John Chamle, M A	John Selfe, Gent

PRESENT LORD OF THE MANOR,
JOSEPH TOMBES, Gent

The Persons summoned from this Place by the Heralds, in 1682 and 1683, were
Thos Careret, M A and
—————— King, Cur

At the Election in 1776, only one Freeholder polled from this Parish.

The Register commences with a Date so early as 1566

---

* In the Register of A marton 1676 is the following Entry " In the Windowe of the South Isle adjoining to the Chancell, " is in the Picture in the Glasse of one praying, in the Habit of a Minister *cum baculo pastorali* and underwritten Richar- " its Name which is broken by Children Perhaps he was both Cler of that Windoe There is also on the West " Side of the Tower, in Stones On the plumm' Richard Wyatt, & Richard de Roomton It may be that was the " Richard, which did, jointly with the Patron of Cotes to build this Tower The Intention, if recollected, could is uncertainly " equal, and then probably on Tradition

† Thomas Master Son of William Master, Rector of Cotes, near to a Meer site Town called Cirencester in Gloucester- " shire, was born at Cotes but descended from the gentle Family of the Masters, settled in that Town, instructed in Grammar " Learning by Mr Henry Fox, a noted Master in that Place, afterward opened for the University in Hylesley School, and " instituted perpetual Fellow of New College 1624, M A 1629 B D 1643 at which Time he commenced to print his Learning viz " educated civil Scholar, a several Artist and Linguist, a noted Poet, and a most Loyal Subject He published many Latin " Poems dedicated to Lord Herbert, of Cherbury his Patron The first matter thereof side, is dedicated to " his Father He was called over to and instituted such, Lord Herbert when he was Chancellor, Marshall for writing the Life of " King Henry VIII At length, being taken with a malignant Fever, he died thereof, to the relief very of all those that " well knew him, in December 1643, and was buried in the Chappel of New College " Wood Athenae, vol I p

ANNUAL ACCOUNT OF MARRIAGES, BIRTHS, AND BURIALS, IN THIS PARISH

A D	Mar	Bir	Bur.	A D	Mar	Bir	Bur	A D	Mar	Bir	Bur	A D	Mar	Bir	Bur
1781	1	6	3	1786	5	3	6	1791				1796			
1782	3	5	3	1787	0	9	4	1792				1797			
1783	7	3	3	1788	5	6	7	1793				1798			
1784	3	4	2	1789				1794				1799			
1785	6	9	8	1790				1795				1800			

INSCRIPTIONS IN THE CHURCH

ON FLAT STONES IN THE CHANCEL

GULIELMUS MOUNSTEVEN,
Annos 25 sedulus hujus
Ecclesiæ Rector,
per afflictiones ad Cœlum natus
Illuc obiit
17 Januarii Anno 1677
Cujus hic reponuntur cineres
beatæ Resurrectionis spes

RAFE MASTER
was buried 15 Day of June, 1624

MARGARET, the Daughter of
WILLIAM PARTRIDGE,
died Nov 3, Anno Dom 1658

ANNE Wife of WILL PARTRIDGE,
was buried the 20th of January, 1671

WILLIAM PARTRIDGE, Gent
deceased Feb 9, 1680

ELIAS CARTERET, Rector of this Parish,
died Dec 30, 1720, aged 68
PHILL CARTERET
died Oct 12, 1718, æt 66

IN THE NAVE

ON A TABLET
Erected to the Memory of
GILES TOMBS of this Parish Yeoman,
who died Aug 14, 1768, aged 62
Also four of his Children, namely,
HESTER, GILES, MARY, and ELIZABETH
HESTER died in June, 1752, aged 3
GILES died Aug 20, 1759, aged 2
MARY died Feb 1, 1767, aged 24
ELIZABETH died Feb 1, 1767, aged [illegible]

ON FLAT STONES

ELIZABETH, the Wife of
THOMAS COX, Yeoman,
died the 16th Day of Oct A D 1621

MARGARET GRIFFITH
departed this Life the 7th of Sept 1692.

WILLIAM TOMBS
died June 17, 1728, in the 55th Year
of his Age

JOANNAH, Wife of WILLIAM TOMBS,
was buried July 7 1736

Also WILLIAM TOMBS
was buried Jan 11 1728

THOMAS COX, Yeoman,
died June 7, Anno Dom 1622

Mrs BARBARA FRANKLYN, Widow,
died Nov 6 Anno Dom 16[illegible]

ELIZABETH, Wife of JOHN CURTIS,
Yeoman, died July 23, 1724, aged 7[illegible]

DOROTHY FRANKLYN
died Dec 9, 1738, in her 90th Year

JOHN CURTIS Yeoman
died Jan 16, Anno Dom [illegible]698

WILLIAM his Son
died August 11 1707

RICHARD his Son
died Aug 16, 1740, aged 60

GEORGE CURTIS
died May 15, Anno Dom 1[illegible]4

ESTHER Daughter of
WILLIAM and MARY [illegible]
died the 13th of Dec Anno Dom 1710

ANNE, the Wife of DANIEL DAVIS,
of Cirencester Woolstapler and
Daughter of THOMAS and ANNE HALL,
of this Parish
died Sept 18, 1768, aged 28

THOMAS HALL
died Jan 27, 1747, aged 51

ANNE, Widow of THOMAS HALL,
died March 1, 1771, aged 72

JOSEPH their Son
died June 8, 1745, aged 1 Year

ON FLAT STONES IN THE SOUTH AISLE

SUSANNA, the Wife of THOMAS PITT,
Yeom departed this Life Aug 29, 1708.

JANE late Wife of ROBERT BLISS,
died Dec 24, A D. 1698

JOSEPH their Son
died July 27 A D 1703

WILLIAM KING Gt
died Oct [illegible] A D 1661

MARY, Wife of GILES KING Gent
departed this Life Oct 14 [illegible]688

ON A TABLET IN THE NORTH TRANSEPT

Underneath lies the Body of
ELIZABETH CROSSLEY, Relict of
the Rev Mr [illegible] CROSSLEY,
some time Rector of [illegible]
Northamptonshire [illegible] departed this
Life Nov 20, 1738, ætatis [illegible]

IN THE CHURCH YARD, ON A TOMB

HANNAH, Relict of WILLIAM BROWN,
late of Fulton,
died Jan 9, [illegible] aged [illegible]8

MARTHA their Daughter
died Nov 6, 17[illegible], aged 17

BETTY, Daughter of
WILLIAM and ELIZABETH P[illegible]
died Nov 23, 1759, aged 5

ON FLAT AND HEAD STONES

	Died	Aged
Mary Daughter of Edward and [illegible]	1 Aug 1738	24
Thomas their Son	10 Oct 1728	25
Ann her Daughter	15 July, 175[illegible]	35
Thomas Son of John and Mary Hall	19 Oct 1783	14
John Thomas	20 Sept 1728	—
William, Son of Henry and Eliza Blackwell	8 Oct 1755	26
Mary Wife of John Blackwell	28 Oct 1737	41
Robert, Son of John and Mary Blackwell	2 May, 1758	26
James, Son of William and Jane Marshfield	12 July, 17[illegible]	2
Thomas Stevens	26 Apr 1751	44
Mary his Wife	28 Mar 1756	67
Mary Roberts	17 Feb 1755	—
Joseph Roberts	5 Feb 17[illegible]	2[illegible]
William Scott, of this Parish	5 Apr 17[illegible]8	[illegible]
Isabel his Wife	4 Sep 17[illegible]	[illegible]
Mary Smith	28 Mar 17[illegible]	5[illegible]

LXXXVI COWLEY

IS the fecond Village on the Courfe of the *Churn*, and has, in common with the *Cotefwold* Hamlets, an eligible Situation. Thefe little Villies fhew in general a fuperior Cultivation, contrafted with the large Tracts of Sheep Downs or Inclofures, which, though very fertile in Corn, are certainly barren of picturefque Beauty.

This Parifh is fituate in the Hundred of *Rapfgate*, five Miles South from *Cheltenham*, nine North-weftward from *Cirencefter*, and an equal Diftance from GLOUCESTER on the Eaft. The Soil is light, principally in Tillage, with a due Portion of Pafture, and more than 100 Acres of Woodland.

The Living is a Rectory in the Deanery of *Stonehoufe*, and in the Patronage of the King. The Church, dedicated to *St. Mary*, is a fmall ancient Structure, with a neatly finifhed embattled Tower at the Weft End, in which are fix mufical Bells, the fole Donation of HENRY BRETT, Efq. in 1730. Under a Niche in the Chancel is a recumbent Effigy, without Armour, and a Talbot couchant at the Feet.

With refpect to the Manor, it has ever been a Part of the Revenues of the Church. In *Saxon* Times it was given to the *Benedictine* Monks of *Perfhore* in *Worcefterfhire*, who retained it till 1543, 34 H. VIII, when it was granted to the See of *Weftminfter*, and confirmed to the Dean and Chapter in 1560, 2 Eliz. The Family of BLOMER were amongft the firft Leffees, from whom by Heirfhip to the BRETTS, the laft of whom, in 17.., fold it to SAMUEL HAWKER, of *Rodborough*, Efq. by whofe Heirs it was refold in 1781 to THAYER TOWNSHEND, Efq. It comprifes the whole Parifh under Leafes determinable by Lives. The Manerial Houfe was re-built about the Commencement of the prefent Century by the laft HENRY BRETT, Efq. and has been modernized and improved by the prefent Poffeffor.

The Hamlets of this Parifh are, 1 *Stockwell*, and 2 the North Part of *Ludlip*, already treated of under *BRIMPSFIELD.*

No Benefactions to the Poor.

INCUMBENTS	PATRONS	INCUMBENTS.	PATRONS
1598 Thomas Symondes,	Queen Elizabeth	1673 Nath. Tye, LL. D.	————
1619 Francis Turbervile,	Frances Baronefs Chandos	1717 Samuel Fowler, M. A.	King George I
163. Michael Bennet,	————	1724 Thomas Wells, M. A.	
1634 Ralph Roberts,	————	1763 John Brickenden, D. D.	King George III
16., James Ingram,		1751 Miles Cooper, LL. D.	The fame
1670 North Gregory, D. D.	King Charles II.	1785 St. Andrew St. John, DD	The fame

PRESENT LESSEE OF THE MANOR,

THAYER TOWNSHEND, ESQ.

There does not appear to have been any Perfon fummoned from this Place by the Heralds in 1682 and 1683.

At the Election in 1776, only One Freeholder polled from this Parifh.

The Regifter commences with an Entry in 1681.

ANNUAL ACCOUNT OF MARRIAGES, BIRTHS, AND BURIALS, IN THIS PARISH

A. D.	Mar	Bir	Bur	A. D.	Mar	Bir	Bur	A. D.	Mar	Bir	Bur	A. D.	Mar	Bir	Bur
1...	3	0	2	1786	1	10	3	1.61			1	1786			
1...	-	13	2	1.87	2	13	6	1..			1..	1...			
1...	3	11	1	1...				1793			1...				
1...	1	6	1	1...				1.14			1...				
1...		10		1...				1.15			1..				

INSCRIPTIONS IN THE CHURCH.

ON FLAT STONES

Here was buried under this Stone the Body of
GILES PLOMER, Gent
who deceased the 18th Day of March,
in the Year of our Lord 1624

WILLIAM RANDLL, of Cowley Farm, senior,
died Nov 19, 1690, aged 75

Here lyeth interred the Body of
that most virtuous Woman Mrs MARGARET BRETT,
Wife unto HENRY BRETT, Esq
who departed this Life the 18th Day of
October, 1645, aged 57

HENRY BRETT, Esq
departed this Life the 21st Day of March,
in the Year of our Lord 1674, and
in the 86th Year of his Age

ARTHUR, Son of HENRY BRETT, Esq
died March 5, 1683, aged near 11 Months

In Memory of
Dame HENRIETTA BROWNLOWE, Daughter of
HENRY BRETT, Lord of this Manor,
the Relict of Sir WILLIAM BROWNLOWE, of
Belton in Lincolnshire, Bart and late Wife of
HENRY MORGAN, of Bristol, Gent
who died August 19, 1718, aged 36 Years

GILES BLACKWELL,
of this Parish, Yeoman,
died the 27th Day of October, 1710, aged 44

JOHN BURBEN, Clerk,
died Nov 13, 1711, aged 72.

DOROTHY his Wife
died Aug 18, 1700, aged 72
John their Son died an Infant.

IN THE CHURCH YARD   ON TOMBS

WILLIAM RANDLE
was buried Dec 26, 1727, aged 75

MARY his second Wife
was buried July 31, 1728, aged 65

ROBERT BIGGS, Yeoman
died Dec 24, 1709, aged 38

EDWARD BIGGS,
of the Parish of Stroud, Clothier,
died Jun 20, 1755, aged 51.

RICHARD MILLS
died Feb 15, 1707-8, aged 78.

DANIEL MILLS, Yeoman,
died August 5, 1753, aged 52.

RICHARD MILLS,
of Stockwel in this Parish, Yeoman,
died Dec 2, 1733, aged 69

Thomas his Son, by MARY his Wife,
died Oct 7, 1743, aged 21

ON FLAT AND HEAD STONES

	Died	Aged
Richard Forte	15 Sept 1689	—
Jane, Wife of James Kibble, of the Parish of Stroud, Daughter of Richard Mills of this Parish	26 Sept 1766	59
Edward Randle Yeoman	16 Jun 1749	67
Margaret his Wife	15 Sept 1771	85
Ann, Wife of William Randle	12 Apr 1709	22
Thomas Cummins	16 Oct 1784	31
Bett, Wife of Samuel Scriven	21 Jun 1764	41
Edward Randle	15 Jun 1749	66
Thomas, Son of William Randle	21 Apr 1724	57
John Gibbens	22 May 1741	78
Frances his Wife	26 June, 1761	—
William Gibbens	27 May, 1730	65
Daniel Gibbens, of the Parish of Ashley	21 Nov 1750	55
Elizabeth his Wife	18 June, 1713	73

LXXXVII. CRANHAM, or CRONEHAM,

IS a small Parish in the Hundred of Rapfgate, eight Miles Southward from Cheltenham, and six from Gloucester on the South-east. The Soil is light and tilled, with very extensive Woodlands, lying upon the steep Acclivities of the Hills, which are unusually frequent in this District.

The Beech flourishes with great Luxuriance, and produces a considerable Income for Charcoal, and the Manufactures at Birmingham.

The Living is a Rectory in the Deanery of Stonehouse, and receives 1l 18s a Year out of Tibboth Farm, in Lieu of Tythes.

The Church, dedicated to St Jane, is built upon the Side of a very steep Hill, and consists of a Nave and South Aisle, but retains no striking Feature of Antiquity.

No mention being made of the Manor in Domesday, it is certain that it was included in the Barony of Brimpsfield, to which Place it adjoins. Hellias Gifford, becoming a Monk, conferred it on the Abbey of St Peter in Gloucester in 1165, when Hameline was Abbot. In 1167 an Exchange was made of it for eight Librats of Land at Willingswyke, co Hereford, but it soon reverted, and continued in their Possession till the Suppression*. At that Period it was divided. One Moiety, called an exempted Manor, was granted to the Dean and Chapter of Gloucester, the other was given in Jointure to Catharine of Aragon, the repudiated Queen of England. Upon her Death in 1556 it was transferred to Sir John Brydges, the first Baron Chandos of Sudley. William Sandys, Esq, purchased it about the Commencement of the last Century, and soon after sold it to his Uncle Sir William Sandys, of Misserden, of whose Descendants it was bought by Dr John Gilbert Archbishop of York, and was inherited by his only Daughter and Heir, the Lady of the present Possessor.

The great Manor claims the chief Estates. Overton Farm is vested in the Family of Davies, who became possessed of it in 1595, 37 Eliz. large Tracts of Wood-land still belong to Samuel Sandys, of Misserden, Esq and others to Samuel Hayward, of Wallsworth Hall, Esq at Upperwell. This Place is worthy Notice as being the first or that Confluence of Streams which form the River Froom, more generally called the Stroud-water. The mineral District, appendant to the Dean and Chapter of Gloucester, is held in Lease by Robert Morris, Esq of Barnwood.

No Benefactions to the Poor

INCUMBENTS	PATRONS.	INCUMBENTS.	PATRONS
From 1165 to 1532,	Abbey of St Peter in Gloucester	1676 Abel Hurt,	Miles Sandys, Esq.
		1677 William Hutton,	The same
		1689 Obadiah Dunn, M A	The same
—— Thomas Lane,		1739 Samuel Ridler, Clerk,	Martin Benson, Bishop of Gloucester
1585, John Bankes,	Giles Lord Chandos		
1590, Giles Randel,	The same		
—— Edward Judson,		1750 Will Walbank, Clerk,	John Gilbert, Bishop of Salisbury
1669 Benet Purv,	Miles Sandys, Esq		
1673 Edward Hiles,	Kennet Freeman	1785 Will Metcalfe, M A	Lord Edgecumbe.

PRESENT LORD OF THE MANOR,
The Right Honourable George Earl of Mount Edgecumbe

There does not appear to have been any Person summoned from this Place by the Heralds in 1682 and 1683

At the Election in 1776, Thirteen Freeholders polled from this Parish

The Register commences with an Entry in 1666

---

* This appears from a very beautiful MS. illuminated Rent er of the Abbey of Gloucester, in one Volume Folio, in the Possession of his Grace the Duke of Norfolk, at Holme Lacy, co Hereford

ANNUAL ACCOUNT OF MARRIAGES, BIRTHS, AND BURIALS, IN THIS PARISH

A.D	Mar	Bir	Bur	A.D	Mar	Bir	Bur	A.D	Mar	Bir	Bur	A.D	Mar	Bir	Bur
1781	0	4	4	1786	2	8	4	1791				1796			
1782	0	3	7	1787	1	6	7	1792				1797			
1783	1	1	2	1788	4	8	7	1793				1798			
1784	0	5	3	1789				1794				1799			
1785	2	9	5	1790				1795				1800			

INSCRIPTIONS IN THE CHURCH

ON MONUMENTS IN THE CHANCEL

Arms a Wolf salient, for Done

Here lieth the Body of OBADIAH DONE, Rector of this Parish 51 Years, who lived a pattern to his People, and to all who shall succeed them, and died much lamented May 20, 1738, in the 75th Year of his Age

Also of ELIZABETH his Wife who departed this Life July 24, 1748, aged 7?

Also in Memory of ELIZABETH the Daughter of OBADIAH and ELIZABETH DONE who was translated from this Life to a better Jan 18, in the Year of CHRIST 1732 and of her Age 37

Arms DONE as before —impaling Or, a Chevron Gules, and a Canton Ermine

To the Memory of the Rev. RICHARD DONE, M.A. late Vicar of Brookthorp,

and Minor Canon of the Cathedral Church of Gloucester, who having distinguished himself by an exemplary Diligence in performing the Offices of his own Station, and by an unwearied Readiness in tending Assistance to others, died much lamented on the 8th Day of June, A.D. 1740, aged 42

Also ELIZABETH ARNOLD, Daughter of RICHARD DONE, and Wife of the Rev. JOHN ARNOLD, who died Jan 19, 1758, in the 24th Year of her Age.

ON A PLAIN MARBLE TABLET

HALLIDAY DAVIES, Gent died Aug 3, 1753 aged 76 Years

MARTHA his Wife, Daughter of STEPHEN COLE, Gent died May 2, 1777, aged 6?

Their Son JOHN, in Respect to the Memory of their dear Parents, caused this Stone to be erected 1788

ON A MONUMENT IN THE SOUTH AISLE

Arms Per saltire four Lions-heads in Cross, for SADLER

In Memory of ELIZABETH the Wife of JOHN SADLER, of this Parish, who died the 30th Day of August 1744, aged 57 Years

Also in Memory of JOHN SADLER, of this Parish who was buried the 7th Day of October, 1765, aged 8?

ON A RAISED TOMB UNDER THE MONUMENT

To the Memory of JAMES SADLER, Gent who died in a good old Age being 75 Years old, and was gathered to his People, Nov 26, Anno Dom 1669

IN THE CHURCH YARD, ON A TOMB

WILLIAM NEWARK, Yeoman, died Jan 3, 1701, aged 88

DENIS his Wife died March 13, 1699, aged 85

WILLIAM NEWARK, Yeoman, died July 3, 1641

Mr SAMUEL NEWARK died July 10, 1753, aged 74

ON FLAT AND HEAD STONES

	Died	Aged
Ann, Wife of William Monk	12 Oct 1778	42
Anthony Jones	5 Aug 1716	54
Thomas Freame, Yeoman	9 Jan 1662	—
William Freame, of this Parish	29 July 1736	88
Thomas one of the Parish of ...		
by Clothier, son of William		
Freame of this Parish	27 Oct 1741	43
James Sadler	29 Dec 1727	63
Elliot Whittall	6 Nov 1748	25
Thomas Cottle, Yeoman	8 Mar 1756	65
Mary his Wife	12 Aug 1761	70
their Daughter	19 Sept 1742	—
... their Daughter	15 Jan 1745	22
... son of James ...		
...	7 Oct 1778	19
Anne Webb	7 July 1694	55
John his Wife	9 June 1726	—
Martha, Wife of John Webb, jun	8 June 1704	—
William Webb	19 Jan 1716	43
Hester Horlick	1 Apr 1768	70
Sarah, Wife of Peter Horlick	26 Sept 1784	60
James ... Yeoman	2 Oct 1759	57
Thomas Walker	5 Nov 1676	53
Anne his Wife	19 June 1708	—
Thomas Walker	6 Aug 1752	6
Mary, Wife of Thomas Walker	6 Feb 1725	40

	Died	Aged
Martha, Wife of Harry Moore, Gent	27 Oct 1785	55
Richard Powell	16 Nov 1681	—
Alexander Horlick	10 Sept 1657	84
Martha his Wife	14 Nov 1755	83
Martha their Daughter	— 1765	—
Daniel their Son	5 May 1785	2?
Nathaniel Hinton, Yeoman	1 Apr 1736	76
Ann his Wife	5 Feb 1750	70
Elizabeth, Daughter of Nathaniel Hinton	14 May 1737	2?
William Mills	25 Oct 1753	5?
John Son of John and Frances Weeks	5 July 1781	5
Nancy their Daughter	21 Oct 1771	1
William Cradle	8 July 1728	?
Mary his Wife	20 Mar 1765	74
Richard Bunckled	12 May 1731	51
Mary Bar child	5 June 1755	63
Thomas Crump	16 May 1759	—
Elizabeth his Wife	28 May 1716	86
Ann, Wife of Thomas Tanner	1 Apr 1700	—
Thomas Tanner	19 Aug 1710	6?
Walter Vernder	30 Oct 1718	6?
Eleanor his Wife	— 1760	—
Henry Webmore	5 Feb 1714	?
Ruth, Wife of William Sumer	31 May 1740	55
Jonathan, Son of John Sadler, Yeoman	14 May 1706	19

LXXXVIII. CROMHALL.

Of this Parish, in Mr Smyth's MSS is the subjoined Account

" *Cromhall*, alias *Cromhale*, in *Domefdey* Book in the Exchequer written *Cromale* A Manor and
" Parish long since parted in two, the one called *Cromhall Abbots*, from the longe since Possession of the
" Abbot of St *Augustin's* by *Bristoll*, to whom the Lord ROBERT, Sonne of HARDING, upon the
" firste foundinge thereof, amongst many other Mannors and Landes, giveth same, and to this Day is
" Parte of the Possessions of the Bishopricke of *Bristoll*, of newe erected by KING VIII, in the
" 34th of his Raigne, out of the Ruines of Part of that Monastery, and endowed with Part of the Pos-
" sessions, whereof this *Cromhall* was one and is now fetted by the Bishop for Life at 17l. Rente per
" Annum, which 31st Yeere of that Kinge, upon the Acte of Parlament which dissolved that and
" other Monasteries, was given to the Crowne And this Part of the Parish of *Cromhall*, called also
" *Abbot's Side*, in all Payments wherewith the whole Parish is charged, payeth an entire thirde Part,
" and consisteth of twelve Inhabitants, Payers, and Office-bearers, and hath a Leete for itself, and a
" Tything man, as doth as *Cromhall Lygon*

" The other Part of the Parish is called *Cromhall Lygon*, because the Family of the LYGONS were longe
" Owners thereof, and is now the Inheritance of Sir RICHARD DUCIE, Baronett, Sonne and Heire of Sir
" ROBERT DUCIE, late Alderman of *London*, who died 10 CAR I havinge before purchased the same
" of Sir HORATIO VEER, Lord of *Tilbury*, and the Lady his Wyfe, who, temp JAC I, purchased
" the same of Sir WILLIAM THROGMORTON, Baronett, Sonne of Sir THOMAS THROGMORTON, who died
" 6 JAC I, having in 38 ELIZ purchased the same of WILLIAM LYGON

" This Parish is Part of the *Hereness Nookes*, or Corners of *Berkley*, not adjoininge to any Side of
" the Mannor or Hundred of *Berkley*, and wherein WILLIAM CONQUEROR had two Hides of Lande, as
" *Domesdey* sheweth

" In all Payments to the Churche, Poore, or King, this of *Cromhall Lygon* beareth two thirde Partes.
" And to this Mannor is the Advowson of the Church belonginge, whereof Sir RICHARD DUCIE, by the
" Purchase of his Father, is Patron, and appendant to his Mannor Yet it was given to the Abbot of
" St *Augustine's*, by the said Robert or Harding, as in the originall Graunt thereof, which I have
" read, appeares but how or when it came backe to this Mannor, or from whom, I have not yet found
" The whole Parishe is within the Deanery of *Hockleburs*, as the Roll of Taxations in 20 EDW I
" sheweth, in the Tower of *London*

" The tutelary Saint of this Church to whose Protection in the Daies of our Great grandfathers it
" was committed, was St *Andrewe*, when on the Sunday followinge, the Wake or Feaste Day is holden,
" which the Age of Hospitalitie might still give rite to "

The Distance of this Village is nearly six Miles South-west from *Wootton Under Edge*, and from GLOU-
CESTER twenty three east by South The Soil, consisting of 3030 Acres, is chiefly Pasture, with extensive Woodland In *Cromhall Heath* (of 300 Acres) the Right of Commonage is equally claimed by
the adjoining Parish of *Tortworth* The Coal Mines were first sunk by the late THOMAS Lord DUCIE,
but afterwards discontinued, on Account of the frequent Intervention of Strata of Earth by which the
Project has been much hindered At present Lime Stone abounds upon the higher Lands, and employs the poorer Inhabitants, who prepare it, and supply the adjacent Country

The Benefice is a Rectory in the Deanery of *Hockleburs*, with about 50 Acres of Glebe the Advowson
of which is, by the late Hon. Matthew, the first Lord Ducie, to *Oriel College, Oxford*

What Traces of Antiquitie are in the Church the late Reparations have left undestroyed, are of the only
Aisle or Transept of the Nave, divided from the South Aisle by pointed Arches, in the eastern Window whereof the Arms Gules, a coloured patriall Argent, for Lygons, and Argent, on a Chevron sable three mullets Or Under an Arcade the figure of a Confessor of that family,
presumed to be one of the Lygons, which we erected in 1775 The Tower is evidently, of a non-
modern Construction

It appears that the Manor of *Cromhall Lygon* was originally vested in the BERKELEYS of *Beverstone*, prior to the 6th Year of HENRY the Sixth's Reign, 1428. Of the intermediate Poffeffors Mr SMYTHE has given an Account. Sir RICHARD DUCIE was succeeded by his Brother Sir WILLIAM DUCIE, created Lord Viscount DOWNE, of the Kingdom of *Ireland*, by King CHARLES the Second, who dying in 1677, without Issue, this Manor defended by Heirship to MATTHEW DUCIE MORTON, Esq of *Morton* and *Eagleton*, co *Stafford*, created Baron DUCIE June 13, 1720, 8 GEORGE I. which Patent was renewed April 27, 1763, 3 GEORGE III.

The Manor of *Cromhall Abbot's* was granted in 1543, to PAUL BUSH, the first Bishop of BRISTOL, " in puram & perpetuam Elymofunen," then valued at 17*l*. 3*s* 1*d* annual Rent. It was fold from that See in 1649 o RICHARD KIRRINGTON and ROGER COOK for 568*l* 0s 1½*d* restored to it in 1660, and now in Lease to FRANCIS Lord DUCIE.

At *Wood End* is a handsome modern Mansion house, with a competent Estate belonging to JOSEPH MATTHEWS, Esq. Other Estates of Consequence are held by the Families of HICKES, WEBB, and CODRINGTON.

Cromhall Park is more than two Thirds within the Boundaries of this Parish. It was enclosed by Sir WILLIAM DUCIE by Licence in 1660, and abounds in the most picturefque Forest Scenery, resulting from many striking Combinations of Wood and Water. The Vestiges of a perfect Encampment still remain, its vicinity to the old Road from the *Trajectus* at *Oldbury*, to *Aquæ Solis*, or *Bath*, and the Discovery of a teffelated Pavement, 18 Feet by 13, the Embellishment of the *Prætorian* Tent, confirm it to have been a Work of the *Romans*. There is a legendary Story of a Hermit of the early Ages of the Church, who retired to a Spot, still called *Anchorite's* Hill.

B E N E F A C T I O N S.

JOHN HICKES, Esq. Time unknown, left in Money 12*l* 10*s* for the Relief of five poor Housekeepers of the Parish of *Cromhall*, that do not receive Alms, the annual Produce of which is variable.

INCUMBENTS	PATRONS	INCUMBENTS	PATRONS
1148 ————,	Abbot of St Augustine's	1679 Abrah Gregory †, D D	Lord Visc Downe
* * * * * *	* * * * * * *	1684 Samuel Cordell, M A	The fame
1541 Will Jennings*, B D	————	1710 Allington Myles, M.A	Matthew Ducie Morton, Esq
1565 William Fleming,			
1576 John Wall,	Thomas Lygon	1734 Thos Woollen, M A	Oriel College, Oxford
1612 John Hault,	Sir Wm Throgmorton	1735 John Penn, M A.	The fame
———— Jonathan Pritchard,	————	1771 Robert Penny, D D.	The fame

PRESENT PROPRIETOR OF THE MANOR, LORD OF *Cromhall Lygon*, AND LESSEE OF *Cromhall Abbot's*,
The Right Honourable FRANCIS Lord DUCIE.

The Perfons fummoned from this Parish by the Heralds in 1682 and 1683, were

Abraham Gregory, D D
Robert Webb, Gent
Thomas Hickes, Gent

———— Stokes, Gent
John Howell, Gent

At the Election in 1776 twenty-one Freeholders polled from this Parish

The Regifter commences in 1654, with the following Entry

" NATHANIEL MASH is and ELIZABETH HORTON were married by GEORGE RAYMOND, Efq May
" 11, 1654. HENRY HARDING was then confirmed Regifter by Election, according to the Act of
" Parliament."

ANNUAL ACCOUNT OF MARRIAGES, BIRTHS, AND BURIALS, IN THIS PARISH

A D	Mar	Bir	Bur	A D	Mar	Bir	Bur	A D	Mar	Bir	Bur	A D	Mar	Bir	Bur
1781	9	13	10	1786	2	6	4	1791				1796			
1782	6	20	6	1787	2	12	10	1792				1797			
1783	5	24	10	1788	2	11	7	1793				1798			
1784				1789				1794				1799			
1785				1790				1795				1800			

* Appointed Abbot of Gloucester in 1541, died, Eliz 1565
† Prebendary of Gloucester

INSCRIPTIONS

INSCRIPTIONS IN THE CHURCH

ON MONUMENTS IN THE CHANCEL

Arms, Gules, a bend wavy between three Fleurs de lis Or, for HICKES

M S
Viri admodum venerabilis
NICHOLAI HICKES,
In facrofanctæ theologiæ
Baccalaurei,
Olim ecclesiæ
Mariæ Magdalenæ Collegii,
Oxoniæ focii, deinde
Ecclesiæ cathedralis
Cicestrensis prebendarii,
necnon de Charfield,
In agro Gloucestrensi, rectoris,
Qui postquam in sacris
Apprime & indefesse elaboravit,
in CHRISTO placide obdormivit
pridie iduum Septembris,
Anno redemptionis 1710,
ætatis suæ 75

Arms, HICKES as before,—impaling Sable, three Scallops in bend Argent, for WEBB

In this Chancel,
the Sepulchre for many Ages of the ancient
Family of HICKES, of the Court House in this
Parish, lie interred the Remains of
THOMAS HICKES,
who died January 11, 1726, aged ͵͵ Years

MARY his Wife died March 25, ͵͵9,
aged 69 Years

Also the following Children

MARY and RICHARD died in their infancy

JOHN died August 24, 1741, aged 36 Years

THOMAS, their eldest Son, died in London,
and was buried there

In filial Remembrance of her beloved Parents,
this Monument is erected by MARY,
only surviving Daughter and Heiress of the above
THOMAS HICKES and MARY his Wife,
Daughter of THOMAS WEBB, of Abbotside
in this Parish, Anno Domini 1͵͵͵

MARY HICKES died the 25th of May, 1783,
aged 70

ON MONUMENTS IN THE NAVE

Arms, HICKES as before,—impaling, Azure,
͵ ͵ as Or

Dedicated to the Memory
of ELIZABETH ANDREWS, Wife of JOHN ANDREWS,
Daughter of WILLIAM HICKES, of Bristol,
Grocer, ͵͵͵͵ ANDREW his Wife,
who departed this Life May 25, 1͵͵

Also WILLIAM ELLIOTT,
the Son of JOHN ELLIOTT, Clothier, and
SARAH his Wife, who departed this Life
the 6th of May, 17͵5, ætatis suæ 2͵͵

Also the said JOHN ANDREWS was
buried in the Chancel of this Church,
who departed this Life the 8th Day of
August, 173͵, in the 61st Year of his Age

Arms, WEBB as before

Near this Place lie deposited the
Remains of ROBERT WEBB, of Abbotside
in this Parish, who died the
25th Day of September, 1731, aged 41 Years

LUCIA his Wife,
Daughter of ROBERT ALLEN,
of Woodend in this Parish,
died the 3d Day of December, 1734,
aged 64 Years

ROBERT, eldest Son of the abovementioned
ROBERT and LUCIA WEBB,
died the 19th of August, 1762, aged 41 Years

CATHARINE, Wife of THOMAS, youngest Son of
the abovementioned ROBERT and LUCIA WEBB,
Daughter of JOHN LEWELLIN, of Bridgend
in the County of Glamorgan,
died the 7th Day of October, 17͵5, aged 61

ON FLAT STONES

ALINGTON, Son of
ALINGTON and ANN MILLS,
died Feb 3, 172͵, ætatis suæ 28

JOSEPH, Son of ALINGTON and ANN MILLS,
was buried March 26, 1696

The Rev Mr ALINGTON MILLS, M A
late Rector of this Parish, who died
the 14th Day of Feb A D 175͵, ætat 74

ANN, Wife of the late Mr MILLS,
died July ͵͵ 1742

Mr JONATHAN PRITCHARD,
Rector of this Church, departed this Life
March ͵5, 17͵͵, ætat suæ 61

The Rev Mr WILLIAM GODWIN, M A
late Minister of Stone, died the 5th Day of
April, 17͵6, ͵͵d ͵ Years

͵͵͵͵͵, Wife of ͵͵͵͵͵ ANDREWS,
died M͵͵ ͵ ͵ ͵, ͵͵d 6͵

ROBERT WEBB, of Woodend in this Parish, ͵͵
departed this Life the ͵͵th of April, 1͵
͵͵d ͵, Years ͵͵ ͵͵ ͵ ͵

A͵͵͵, the Wife of ͵ ͵͵ ͵ ͵ ͵ ͵ ͵ ͵
died the 17th D͵ ͵ ͵ ͵ ͵ ͵ ͵ ͵ ͵ ͵ ͵

Mrs JANE DARY
departed this Life Nov 4, 1760,
aged 65 Years

ROBERT ALIEN, of Cromhall,
was buried Jan 14, 1670.

ROBERT ALIEN, jun
died Oct 22, 1712, aged 51

SUSANNA, Wife of ROBERT WEBB,
was buried the 2d Day of . 1636.

ANNE, Sister to ROBERT WEBB,
died Oct 17, 1703, ætatis suæ 20.

RICHARD, Son of THOMAS WEBB,
of Cromhall Abbott's,
died April 22, 1714, aged 20

Mr JOHN PENN, M A
late Rector of this Parish,
died March 10, 1774, aged 66

ANN READ, Widow,
died in February 1720

Mrs ANNE HOYLE, Widow,
died Dec 9, 1708.

ELIZABETH, the Wife of
THOMAS HICKES, of Cromhall, senior,
departed this Life July 28, 1629

Mr THOMAS HICKES, of Cromhall, senior,
died March 22, 1707

Mr THOMAS HICKES, of Cromhall, junior,
died Nov 22 1724

MARTHA, Wife of THOMAS HICKES,
of Cromhall, senior died May 4, 1730,
aged 86

Also HESTER, the Wife of
AMBROSE MARKLOVE, senior,
and Daughter of THOMAS HICKES,
of Cromhall, senior,
departed this Life April 1, 1707

ANNE, Wife of THOMAS WHALTON,
and Daughter of THOMAS HICKES, senior,
died the 8th of April, 1762, aged 86

MARY MARKLOVE, Daughter of
Mr AMBROSE MARKLOVE,
and Grand daughter of Mr THOMAS HICKES, sen
departed this Life Oct 18, 1750, aged 51

JOAN, Wife of Mr ROBERT ALLEN, of Oxford
died March 21, 1685 aged 60 Years and 3 Months

Also MARGARET, the Wife of
ALEXANDER TOMES, of Abbotth le...
She lived a Widow 50 Years, ...
departed this Life the 5th of January 171
aged 64 Years, wanting 4 Days

ARTHUR, Son of ROBERT ALLEN,
was buried Jan , 1662

Arms, Quarterly, 1st, Argent, a Fess indented
Sable, between three Lions passant Gules, for Co-
DRINGTON, 2d, Sable, on a Bend Argent three
Roses Gules, barbed Vert, in the sinister Chief
Point a Chessrook of the second, for Small, 3d
as the 2d, 4th as the 1st

ROBERT CODRINGTON, Esq
departed this Life March 3, 1744,
in the 67th Year of his Age

ANNE his Wife
died June 1, 1761, aged 73

THOMAS BRUEEN the elder
was buried the 9th Day of March 1671,
aged 91 Years

MARY, the Wife of
RICHARD RIMER, of this Parish,
died the 27th of January, 1755, aged 89 Years

JOHN, the Son of
RICHARD and MARY RIMER,
was buried the 8th of September, 1756,
aged 41 Years

ARTHUR HICKES, of Cromhall,
died December 28, 1666

JOHN, Son of
RICHARD and ELIZABETH ANDREWS,
late of this Parish,
died Oct 16, 1784, aged 30

Mrs RACHEL CODRINGTON Spinster,
died Jan 4, 1750, aged 65

IN THE CHURCH YARD, ON TOMBS

WILLIAM SCOTT
died Oct 1776, aged 71
SARAH his Wife
died Feb , aged 15

THOMAS LORD
died Feb , 1700 aged
ELIZABETH his
died Oct 23, 1

H S E
Histerae Skey, filia unica
Thomae Griffin praedicti,
Uxor omnino placens Henrici Skey, A M
(Ecclesiae de Crinford agro Middlesex, Rectoris,
Scholae Wickwarensis Archididascali, &
Comitis de Berkele ... ...)
Cujus in se & suos amorem,
Virtutesque ha ad priscas in bilis,
Fide retinebit Memoria,
Cornix ... tatis
Obiit Jun ... , 1762, aetat 5)

Hic quoque recon tuntur
Anna & Esthera, filiae
Henrici & Elsith Skey

Anna obiit Sept 2 , 1748, aetatis 5

Esthera, Jan 2 , 176_, annum
vixilet Septuennis 5

His accessit
Elianora, cara ... umbilis hic Virgo
que phthisi confecta
Obiit Nov 1771, ae 15

Thomas Griffin
died May 18, 1692, aged 71
Mary his Wife
was buried March 6, 1684, aged 57
Predinel their Daughter
was buried Jan 28, 1669, aged 6
Robert Griffin
died Feb 10, 1716, aged 50
Esther his Wife
died May 16 171, aged 47
Esther their Daughter
was buried May 5, 1 6
Griffin their Son
was buried Jan 16, 1711

Juxta recond tutur cine es praedicti
Rev Henrici Skey, A M qui,
reperit i correst is ol ut octo die
Anno Dom 1775, ae 5)

Necnon Rev Thomas Griffin,
El gordea, qu ob it Mati secundo,
Anno Dom 177)

Tho s Griffin, Son o
K e and Esther Griffin,
died Sept 1 1728, aged 39
Elizabeth, the Wife of his Brother Robert
Su ered Aug 0, 17 — aged 7
Robert and William th Sons died Infan

John Griffin
died Jan 5, 1730, aged 57
Thomas Lancut, of Lo Thompson,
died July 1775, aged 7)
Alice his Wife
died Jan 7, 1 13, aged 41
A s their son
died April 3, 1 , aged 18

John Pick
died Aug 29, 1705, aged 55
Elizablth his Wife
died March 12, 1773, aged 70
Jos ph Pick
was buried March 13, 174 , aged 13
John Pick
died Sept 7, 1778, aged 69

Mathew Stinchcombe
died March 26, 1714
Thomas, the Son of
Mathew and Margaret Stinchcombe,
died April 26, 1713, aged 7
Matthew Stinchcombe, Baker,
died Aug 17 , aged 4

Thomas Stinchcombe, baker,
died Nov 6, 1746, aged 42
Margaret his Wife
was buried Oct 18, 17 , aged 76.
Mary, Wife of Thomas Stinchcombe,
died Aug 26, 1756, aged 53

Thomas Allen
was buried July 19, 1625
Margaret his Wife,
and his Widow 33 Year,
was buried July 2, A D 1658
Elizabeth, the Wife of
Robert Arnold,
died March 7, 1725, aged 70
Robert Arnold, junior,
died April 14, 1703, aged 27
Mr Richard Arnold,
died Nov 27, 1747, aged 60

Thomas Webb, of Buckover, Gent
died March 12, 1725, aged 5
Also to the Memory of Joseph Webb,
Thomas Webb, and Elizabeth Webb,
Grandfather, Father, and Mother, to the
abovesaid Thomas Webb

Mary Daughter of
Thomas and Mary Cox, of Thornbury,
died April 1, 1 9 aged 16
Thomas Cox, late of Thornbury,
died Jan 1, 1784, aged 53

Mary, Wife of Henry Mousell,
D ughter of Joseph Pick,
died March , 17 , aged 5
Henry Mousell
died Sept 4, 17 , aged 5
Joseph Pick of Rockhampton, Junior,
died Sept 1 , aged 5

Thomas Morris, of the Parish,
died March , 17 , aged 62
A his Wife
died June 17 1 aged 3
Thos their Son
died Oct 1 , 17 , aged 6

ON HEAD STONES

	Died	Aged		Died	Aged
John Knight -	2 Feb. 1703	70	Richard Croome	7 Jan 17..	..
Jane his Wife -	16 Oct 1680	52	John Croome -	8 Nov 1..	
Thomas Ford of Bristol, junior	12 Ap 176.	58	Ann his Wife	..	..
Sarah his Wife	12 June, 1760	30	John Croome, or Downing in the Parish of Mangotsfield	5 May, 1.0	
George Tanner, of Hal.. in the Parish of Herbury	21 Dec 1783	41	Charles Croome -	6 July, ..	
Elizabeth his Wife -	7 May, 1776	36	John Adds -	2. ..	
Betty, Wife of John Cook, of Sibland in the Parish of Thornbury	16 May 1783	53	Mary his Wife	2. Ju 1..	
Thomas Tanner, of this Parish	9 Nov 1784	47	Sarah, Wife of William ... Daughter of James and Sarah Pearce	10 Jun 17..	
Christian, Wife of James Goodman	6 Aug 1769	51	James, Son of James and Sarah Pearce	6 Aug 1..	
James Goodman - -	15 Apr 17.9	57	Anne, Daughter of James and Sarah Pearce, Wife of Christopher Denning	24 Nov 1767	
William Croome -	2 Jun, 1760	64	Sarah, Wife of James Pearce	9 Oct 17..	
William, Son of William and Sarah Baker -	27 Sep 1780	18	Mary Daughter of James and Sarah Pearce, Wife of John Fullin	6 Jul, 17..	
John Ford, of this Parish, Son of William Ford, of Falfield in the Parish of Thornbury	2 Sept 1768	71	James Pearce	2. O.. 1..	
Brice Webb of this Parish, junior	10 Nov 1729	25	Martha, Daughter of James and Sarah Pearce	3 Nov 1..	
Ambrose Marklove, of this Parish, Clothier	1 Mar 1689	59	Mary, Wife of Joseph Croome of Whitfield Farm in this Parish	5 May 1.4	
Ambrose his Son	26 May, 1708	30	Benjamin Woodward	2. July 17..	
Ambrose, Son of the late Ambrose Marklove -	27 May, 1734	33	Richard Punter	6 Feb 1..	
Winifred his Wife	17 Feb 1747	—	William Punter -	16 Jun 1..	
Ambrose their Son -	29 Sep. 1768	48	Elizabeth his Wife -	4 July 1..	
William Rogers	23 June, 1753	0	Mary Punter -	13 Jan 1.3.	
Ann his Wife -	19 Mar 1772	73	Richard Punter	9 May 17.0	
Mary their Daughter -	1 Aug 1753	21	Richard Heaven -	10 Feb 1..8	
Thomas their Son	11 Apr 1772	55	Sarah, Wife of William Scott	10 Feb 1..	
Elizabeth Wife of Richard Hayward of the Parish of Almondsbury, Daughter of Jacob and Mary Pick, of this Parish -	4 Feb 1783	31	Anne, Wife of Brice Webb	7 Sept 1..	

LXXXIX. DAGLINGWORTH

LIES in the Hundred of *Crowthorne* and *Minety*, in the *Cotefwold* Divifion three Miles North-weftward from *Cirencefter*, and fixteen in the precifely oppofite Direction from Gloucefter. The Soil is in general light and ftony, applied to Tillage, with a fmall Exception of Pafture and Woodland, within a Boundary of nearly fix Miles. To afcertain the Derivation of this fingular Name, is left to more experienced Etymologifts.

The Living, which is a Rectory in the Deanery of *Cirencefter*, was in 1499 in the Prefentation of the Abbefs of *Godftow*, co Oxon, and at the Suppreffion was referved to the Crown. It appears that the Church, which is a plain Structure of a Nave only, with a low embattled Tower, was erected at the Expence of the Nunnery.

In *Domefday* Book nothing is faid of this Manor, but in the Efcheator's Return of Vills in the Hundred of *Cirencefter* in 1281, 9 Edw I it occurs as including the contiguous Parifh of *Swaiton*. RALPH DE BLOET obtained a Grant of free Warren of this Manor at that Time, ftating that it had been held by his Anceftor in the Reign of Henry the Second. LIONEL Duke of CLARENCE held it in the 14th Century. The Family of BLOET regained the Poffeffion at his Death, and it paffed by Marriage in 1378, 2 Rich II to JAMES, afterwards Baron BERKELEY. In that Barony it continued till 1601, 44 Liz. when it was fold by HENRY Lord BERKELEY, to Sir HENRY POOLE, of *Saperton*, for the Sum of 1320*l*. With fome of the adjoining Eftates of POOLE and ATKINS, it was purchafed early in this Century by ALLEN Lord BATHURST. The Demefnes are not extenfive, the principal Proprietors of Eftates are the Families of HAYNES and HINTON.

The *Irmin Street* (*Via Vultaris*), or great Confular Road from Gloucefter to Cirencefter, paffes through this Parifh. This is one of the moft perfect public Works of the *Romans*, and ftill ferves its original Purpofe. Sufficient Veftiges of an advanced Poft from the grand Station at *Cirencefter* are difcovered in a Field near the Village.

Upon the Eaft Side of this Road is a fpacious Plain called *Dagham* Down, remarkable for a fingular Kind of Stone. It is found very near the Surface, upon a Bed of one black Earth, in detached Blocks of the moft grotefque Formation, with abundant circular Perforations of feveral Inches diameter, and delicately fmooth. The Confiftence of thefe is fo firm as to refift the Effects of Weather, and they are frequently of a large Size. When ufed as ornamental in ruftic Buildings they come to anfwer the leading Idea of that Order in a Manner not to be attained by anything artificial. On the fame Down is a Stone of a very clofe Grain, full of Petrifactions, and refembling the Marbles of *Derbyfhire*, when polifhed.

BENEFACTIONS.

JEREMIAH HANCOCK, by Will, 1730, gave 100*l* and WILLIAM BRITHA, Efq 35*l* for the religious Inftruction of the Poor, the annual Produce of both which now is 4*l* 10*s*

RICHARD SANDERS gave 5*l* for the Ufe of the Poor for ever

GILES HANCOCK, 1673, gave 5*l* for the fame Purpofe

JOHN HINTON 1773, likewife bequeathed 5*l* for the Ufe of the Poor

Other Donations, to the Amount of 20*l* were given, the Intereft of which is alfo applied for the Ufe of the Poor

Incumbents	Patrons	Incumbents	Patrons
1499 ————,	Abbefs of Godftowe	1723 James Kilner, M A	King George I
—— Richard Sanders,		1729 Jofeph Hinton M A	King George II
1617 Anthony Hovland,	King James I	1735 Jofeph Chapman M A	King George II
—— —— Humphry,		1776 Jofeph Chapman D D	King George III
1675 Nathaniel Gwyn,	King Charles II.		

* "… Pycott John & Heires JOHANNI Pcott de *Daglinworth* & *Ragland*, correfter to Jello. "Duci CLARENC, Manerium J. *Daglinworth* co Glouc …Clauf Rot 4 m 3

PRESENT LORD OF THE MANOR,
The Right Honourable HENRY Earl BATHURST.

The Persons summoned from this Place by the Heralds in 1682 and 1683 were
Giles Hancock, Gent. and Nathaniel Gwynne, Clerk

At the Election in 1776, Seven Freeholders polled from this Parish.

The Register commences in 1561

ANNUAL ACCOUNT OF MARRIAGES, BIRTHS, AND BURIALS, IN THIS PARISH

A D	Mar	Bir	Bur	A.D	Mar	Bir	Bur.	A.D.	Mar	Bir	Bur	A D	Mar	Bir	Bur
1781	1	10	4	1786	—	6	9	1791				1796			
1782	2	8	7	1787	3	9	6	1792				1797			
1783	—	4	6	1788	3	6	4	1793				1798			
1784	4	11	5	1789				1794				1799			
1785	2	6	4	1790				1795				1800			

INSCRIPTIONS IN THE CHURCH.

ON MONUMENTS.

Arms, a Lion rampant ducally crowned, between three cross Croslets for KING.

Erected by MARY WEBB Widow, 1731, in Testimony of her filial, conjugal, and parental, Affection,
To the Memory of
Mr THOMAS KING her Father,
who died Anno Dom 1710

Mrs ELIZABETH KING her Mother,
who died Anno Dom 1719

NATHANIEL WEBB her Husband,
who died Anno Dom 17-8

THOMAS WEBB her Son
who died Anno Dom 1708

KING WEBB her Son,
who died Anno Dom 1724

ELLANOR CHELKER her Sister,
who died Anno Dom 1717

ANNE HAINES her Grand daughter,
who died Anno Dom 1729

ANNE HINTON her Grand daughter,
who died Anno Dom 1739

To the Remains of these were added those of MARY herself
a Widow indeed, 1750, aged 82

Arms; three Crescents counterchanged for HAYNES —impaling, a Lion rampant, for EDWARDS

Erected by SARAH, the Widow of GILES HAYNES, of this Parish,
To the Memory of him,
her loving and beloved Husband,
who died May 3, 1743, aged 85 Years

The Soul of the abovenamed SARAH took its Flight from King Stanley to the Heavenly Mansions, and her Body was brought here to be interr'd Sept 4, 1751, aged 87

ON FLAT STONES

M S
NATHANIELIS GWYNNE,
Ecclesiæ hujus per annos prope 48
Rectoris, qui post longam
Valetudinem placide
in Domino obdormivit
Maii 30,
Anno { Domini 1723
{ Ætat 83

H. J
JANÆ,
JOSEPHI CHAPMAN,
Ecclesiæ hujus Rectoris,
Uxor,
Ob. 24 Junii, 1773, æt 52

IN THE CHURCH PORCH

Mr GILES HANCOCK,
ætatis suæ 71,
April 17, 1684

The Dissection and Distribution of
GILES HANDCOX,
Who to Earth bequeaths to Earth to Heaven his Soule,
To Friend his Love, to the Poore a Pound Dole,
To remain for ever, and be employ'd
for their best Advantage and Relief
in Daglingworth,
April the 9th, 1658

IN THE CHURCH YARD ON TOMBS

TIMOTHY WEBB senior
died Sept 2 172, in the 82d Year of his Age

DOROTHY his Wife
died Sept 8, 1687

DANIEL WEBB
died March 26, 1715, aged 35

TIMOTHY, Son of
DANIEL and SARAH WEBB,
died Jan 6, 1748, aged 4

ELIZABETH, Wife of TIMOTHY WEBB,
died June 16, 1757, aged 57

ELIZABETH Wife of WILLIAM WEBB,
and Daughter of DANIEL and LAMEY DAVIS, of Cirencester,
died Nov 27, 1780, aged 29

DANIEL and ELIZABETH their Children died Infants

THOMAS SMITH,
died March 11 766, aged 88

SARAH his Wife
died April 23 176, aged 80

ON FLAT AND HEAD STONES

	Died	Aged		Died	Aged
John Evans, senior	8 Sept 1 58	54	Mary Wife of William Healings of Cirencester	15 Nov 17,6	16
Joel, Son of John and Ann Evins	9 Apr 1766	27	John Haynes	8 Dec 1771	1
Thomas, Son of John Sidler of Bampsfield	6 Feb 17 0	31	Anne, Wife of John Haynes	10 Oct 1778	61
Hannah Sidler	30 Apr 17,1	14	John Ashmead	10 June, 1, 38	—
Richard Window	2 May, 1771	62	Ann his Wife	24 June, 1730	—
Anne his Wife	16 Jan 1762	71	John Ashmead, of Baret's Brook	14 May, 1741	16
William Cowley	8 Nov 1735	66	Richard Harris	7 Dec 17 2	60
Martha Wife of William Cowley	13 Oct 1728	55	Thomas Richardson, Minister, of this Parish		
Sarah, Wife of Giles Haynes	— Sep 1751	87	Ann his Wife	8 Dec 1771	62
John, Son of John and Ann Haynes	29 Nov 1757	13	Mary their Daughter	28 Nov 1761	67
Jane their Daughter	15 Nov 1758	21	Elizabeth, Relict of Thomas Webb, of Minchinhampton	1 Mar 175,	
Sarah, Daughter of John and Ann Haynes	3 Apr 1778	44	William Champion	21 Dec 17-3	
Elisabeth their Grand daughter	23 Apr 1779	27		24 Dec 17,	

XC DIAN

xc. DEAN MICHEL, or DENE MAGNA.

THOUGH the additional Name be generally supposed to have been given by the Tutelar *St Michael*, it will be found to be of *Saxon* original, from the Word *micl*, or *great*, in Distinction from the contiguous Parish of *Little Dean*. This Conjecture is confirmed by its Application in other Parts of the County

Michel Dean is a small Market Town, consisting of three narrow Streets very irregularly built, two of them diverging from the Extremity of the other, in the Form of a *Roman* Y Late in the Reign of HENRY VI the present Charter was granted for a weekly Market on Monday, and two annual Fairs, on Easter Monday, and the 10th of October These are now well frequented, and the Adjustment of Weights and Measures is settled by the Arbitration of an Officer, appointed by the Lord of the Manor, to whom certain Tolls are due The Town, evidently more considerable in former Times, is situate in a very deep Dell, surrounded, excepting on the North-east, by wooded Hills, on the great Road from GLOUCESTER to *Monmouth*, about eleven Miles on the West

The Form of the Parish is an irregular Circle nearly four Miles across in the widest Part Two thirds of the inclosed Lands are Pasture Being a Member of the Hundred of *St Briavel*, the Inhabitants are entitled to all the Immunities and Privileges of the Forest The Soil is most commonly of a deep red Clay Large Quantities of the *Scoia*, or Iron Cinders, are easily collected and sold It is long since the Manufacture of Pins flourished in the Town, and gave Place to that of Leather, which is now carried on to some Extent It is said that coarse Cloth was formerly made here

The Benefice is a Rectory in the *Forest* Deanery *, the Patronage of which has ever been connected with the Manor

* The *Forest* Deanery was originally Part of the Diocese of *Hereford* till the Erection of the See of GLOUCESTER The Archdeacon of *Hereford* visits every Summer, and the Chancellor of GLOUCESTER the other Part of the Year

The Ground Plot of the Church, dedicated to *St Michael*, is of a quadrangular Form, nearly equilateral, and confifts of a Nave, two Aifles on the North, and one on the South, to which adjoins the Tower, not embattled, but finifhed by a Spire 156 Feet from the Foundation, extremely light, and of truly beautiful Gothic Proportions   Early in this Century it received confiderable Reparations   In the Laft Window of the farther North Aifle are fome perfect Remains of painted Glafs, with which the Church was profufely decorated   In the higher Compartments is an Affemblage of female Figures with mufical Inftrumens, and, difperfed in other Panes, the Heads of Nobles and Ecclefiaftics of either Sex, delicately wrought   The whole Roof is of Oak Frame, and ftudded with Rofes and other Devices, of exquifite Carving   Dr Parfons fpeaks of Arms in the Chancel Window, " On a Fefs Gules, between three Birds, three Rofes Argent, " for   "   And in the great Weft Window, " Azure, on a Chief Argent, two Mullets Gules, for " "   ,—impaling Gules, a Chevron between three Bulls Heads affronte, for Baynham."

Of the man, mutilated Slabs*, once ornamented with fplendid Braffes, an imperfect one only remains, it is of Thomas Baynham, who died in 1444, the Founder of a Chantry dedicated to the *Holy Trinity* (the laft Incumbent of which was Henry Hooper), and moft probably a very munificent Benefactor to the whole Fabric   The two North Aifles are moft clearly of the Style of his Day

The Manor, foon after the Conqueft, was held by the Family of De Lacy, but with fome fubfequent Alienations to the Abbies of Gloucefter and *Porchefter*, as *Southwyle* in *Hampfhire*   To Perfons of the Name of De Den and Abenhall, the Family of Greyndour fucceeded, foon after the Commencement of the 14th Century   Sir John Greyndour, who was Lord of this Manor † in the Reign of Henry IV, was Sheriff of the County in 1405 and 1409, whofe official Seal was lately difcovered in the Old Houfe at *Dudley*   The Defcent of the Manor after this Period has been hitherto imperfectly defcribed   John Tiptoft, the accomplifhed and unfortunate Earl of *Worcefter*, having married Elizabeth, Daughter of Robert, only Son of Sir John Greyndour, became poffeffed of this Manor   Upon his Attainder and Death in 1471 it reverted to Alice the fecond Wife of Thomas Baynham already mentioned, and Daughter of William Walwayne, the Grandfon of Sir John Greyndour   In the Defcendants of

---

Thomas

THOMAS BAYNHAM it remained till about 1600, when it was fold to Sir ROBERT WOODRUFF From the Commencement of this Century it has been held by the Family of COLCHESTER The principal Estates are that annexed to the Manor, and one belonging to JOSEPH PYRKE, Esq

In a Wood upon a Hill about half a Mile from the Town is a subterraneous Passage communicating with the Church, concerning which many legendary Stories are told, but asserted with probability to have been in Feudal Times the Retreat of Outlaws who sought Sanctuary

---

BENEFACTIONS

JONATHAN PARKER bequeathed 200*l* to be laid out in Lands, the Profits of which to be applied in cloathing and apprenticeing some, or one Child yearly, the Produce is now 12*l* 10*s* a Year

RICHARD WALWIN left 20*l*, the annual Produce thereof 1*l* to be given to such Poor as are not on the Parish Book, on the Feast of *St John the Evangelist*

WILLIAM MORSE by his Will gave 100*l* with which Land has been purchased, the yearly Profits 6*l* 10*s* to be given to the Poor on Christmas Day for ever

WALTER LITTLE devised 15*l*, the annual Produce, 15*s* to be distributed amongst the Poor on the Feast of *St John the Evangelist*

ANDREW CREW likewise gave 10*l*, the Produce of which, 14*s* a Year, to be applied to the same Purpose

ROBERT STANTON bequeathed 6*s* 8*d* a Year, payable out of a Messuage, to be given to the Poor on the Feast aforesaid

JANE WALTER, 1760, left 20*l*, the Interest of which, is to buy Bibles for the Poor Inhabitants being Parishioners

Within these few Years a Charity School hath been established in this Town by voluntary Subscription, wherein upwards of fifty Children have been taught to read and write, which by a laudable Exertion of its Promoters, has produced a wonderful Reformation in the Morals of the rising Generation

INCUMBENTS	PATRONS	INCUMBENTS	PATRONS
—— William Austyn,	——	16-4 Thomas Andrews, M A	William Collins
1552 Edward Blennerhaffet,	——	16-9 Richard Hill, M A	Robert Pawling.
1574 Richard Petty,	Thomas Horn.	172, John White,	Maynard Colchester, Esq.
1587 Richard Petty,	Q Elizabeth	17-7 Richard Roberts,	The same
1592 Hugh Griffiths,	Thomas Baynton	770 William Parry,	The same
16-3 Richard Stringer, M A		17-3 John Harris, B A	The same

PRESENT LORD OF THE MANOR,
JOHN COLCHESTER, Esq

The Persons summoned from this Parish by the Heralds in 168_ and 1683, were

—— Nash, Gent	Charles W—er, Gent	Giles Tower, Gent
—— Morse, Gent	Thomas W—e, Gent	George Tower, Gent
Thomas Rudge, Gent	Thomas Gornery, Gent	Thomas W—ll, Gent
Richard Pyrke, Gent	William Merrick, Gent	Christopher Hatheway, Gent

At the Election in 17,0 Thirty four Freeholders polled from this Parish.

The Register commences with in Index in 16—

A—— Account of Marriages, Births, and Burials, in this Parish

A D	Mar	Bir	Bur	A D	Mar	Bir	Bur	A D	Mar	Bir	Bur	A D	Mar	Bir	Bur
175	5	15	13	1756	4	19	9	1791				1796			
17—		25	7	1757		18	8	1792				1797			
17—		17	11	1758	8	27	6	1793				1798			
1754		19		1789				1794				1799			
1755				1790				1795				1800			

IN THE FARTHER NORTH AISLE

A large blue Slab the Effigies in Brass of a Man between his two Wives in different Dresses, that on the left with a very singular Coif and Gloves. Over the Man's Head an Escutcheon (gone) with a Man and Crest. Four corner Escutcheons, three remaining, 1 Gules, a Chevron between three Bulls Heads caboshed Argent, so BAYNHAM, 2 a Fess surmounted of a noble inferted, for HODGE, 3 Quarterly, 1st and 4th, BAYNAM, 2d and 3d, on a Chief three Mullets,—impaling, Per Pale Or and Vert, twelve Guttes counterchanged, for GREENDOUR, and Crusuly a Fess, for   .

INSCRIPTIONS IN THE CHURCH.

ON A STONE AGAINST THE EAST WALL IN THE CHANCEL

Hic conditur fub terra RICHARDUS STRINGER,
Filius RICHARDI STRINGER, hujus Ecclefiæ Rectoris,
et ELIZABETHÆ uxoris, natus Deane Magna,
educatus fchola Collegialis Glocestrensis,
necnon morte peremptus, Aprilis 12,
Anno Salutis 1647, ætatis fuæ 15

ON A MONUMENT AGAINST THE SAME WALL

Ut fciant Posteri
Infra recondi caducum quod fuit
Venerabilis Viri RICHARDI HALL,
Hujus Ecclefiæ per Annos 44,
Et Ecclefiæ Abinghall Anno 37
Pastoris probatiffimi
Uxores duxerat JOANNEM & SARAM,
Quarum
Illa prope maritum hic fepulta jacet,
Hæc autem fuperstes amidum dolet.
Obiit
Anno { Domini 1722
       { Ætatis 72

In Memoriam etiam THOMÆ WORGAN,
Generofi qui hoc Monumentum
Erexit, & obiit Julii decimo die, 1721,
ætatis fuæ 40

Also SARAH, Wife of Mr RICHARD HALL,
deceafed in the Year 1729

Also MARY, Wife of Mr THOMAS WORGAN,
departed this Life Feb 11, 1746, æt 59

ON FLAT STONES IN THE CHANCEL

To the Memory of the painful
and faithful Preacher of God's Word,
both by Life and Doctrine,
Mr RICHARD STRINGER,
Master of Arts, and Rector of this Church
fifty-two Years, who went to be with
the Lord Jesus the 4th of February 1674,
in the 77th Year of his Age

Labor in terd, in Patria quies

JOAN, Wife of RICHARD HALL,
Rector of this Parifh, was buried
March 5, 1698, in the 42d Year of her Age

Ms AMY HALL
died Jan 18, 1706-7, in the 92d Year of her Age

THOMAS WORGAN, 1679

WILLIAM CALLOW, late of Deane Magna, Gent
departed this Life Nov 28, 1677, aged 61

MARY BARRETT, 1769.

ISABEL, Wife of WILLIAM CALLOW, Gent
died Dec 31, 1677, æt 74

Hic jacet Morale quod fuit
FRANCISCI ASHMEAD, qui obiit
15 Die menfis Februarii, A. D. 1729,
æ tatis fuæ 5.

SUSANNAH, Daughter of
FRANCIS ASHMEAD, Surgeon,
departed his Life April 30, 1743, aged 39.

HENRY PLATT, of this Town,
died June 17, 1762, aged 45.

ON A MONUMENT IN THE NAVE

Arms, a Chevron between three Palmer's Scrip

Underneath this Place are depofited
the Remains of Mr JOHN PALMER,
Joiner and Citizen of London
late of this Town, who died the
18th of June, 1782, æt 68
He was an affectionate Hufband and fincere Friend

ON FLAT STONES

WILLIAM HUGHES, of this Parifh, Gent
deceafed Feb 14, 1722, in the 46th Year of his Ye

WILLIAM, Son of WILLIAM and ANN HUGHES,
died June 8, 1712, aged 6

---

* The Memorandum is for THOMAS BAYNHAM, Efq who died in 1444 whofe firft Wife was MARGERY, Daughter of RICHARD HODGE, Knight, and his fecond Alice, Daughter of WILLIAM WALWYN

Hic jacet Corpus EDWARDI PARTRIDGE, fen
qui obiit decimo Die Jan Anno Dor 1691,
ætatis fuæ 82

Here lieth the Bodies of
DEBORAH and DEBORAH, the Daughters of
EDWARD MORSE, of this Town,
the eldeft departed this Life
the 14th, the youngeft the 18th,
of May, 1661

MARGARET, Daughter of EDWARD MORSE,
died Apr 19, 1680

Subter hunc
Lapidem reconduntur exuviæ ANNE, filiæ
JOHANNIS JELI, Rectori de Blaifdon, Comitatu
Gloucefttenfi, pc MARIA
Uxorem Spondit fuit
THOMÆ SARGEAUNT, de
Mitchel Deane, Com. ou prædicto,
Conjux amantiffima & felectiffim.,
Fœmina pia & prudens,
Amicis fidelis,
Indigentibus liberalis,
Quæ poft vitam viginti & quatuor
Annorum animam efflavit
Viceftmo fexto die Septembris,
Anno Salutis 1755

THOMAS RUDGE, of this Town,
departed his Life July 6, 1714, aged 28

SARAH, Daughter of JOHN and JOANNA RUDGE,
died Aug 14, 1752, aged 40

SARAH, Wife of THOMAS RUDGE,
died Oct 13, 1711, aged 2,.

ROBERT BROOKES, of this Town, Mercer,
died Feb 27, 1747, aged 54

ELIZABETH, the Wife of Mr WALTER RUDGE,
of this Town, Mercer, died Feb 4, 1675

Mr WALTER RUDGE
departed this Life Oct 4, 1689

Mr NATHANIEL RUDGE their Son
died Aug 30, 1775, aged 61

MARGARET, the Wife of SAMUEL BROOKES,
of this Town, Mercer, eldeft Daughter of
Mr NATHANIEL RUDGE,
died Oct 2, 1724, aged 33

ROBERT their Son
died Sept 28, 1724

WILLIAM RIDER, of this Town,
died in October 1714

JOAN his Wife
was buried Dec 2, 1679

SAMUEL DICKES
died Aug 14, 1751, aged 41

SAMUEL his Son, by JANE his Wife,
died Auguft 19, 1752, aged 11

ROBERT, Son of ROBERT RUSSEL,
died Dec 30, 1750, aged 31

SARAH, Daughter of JOHN and SARAH VOICE
died April 1, 1757, aged 11

ON A MONUMENT IN THE SOUTH AISLE

Arms, Gules, a Crofs Argent between four
Swords erect of the fecond, hilted Or, for HOLMES

This Monument was erected in
Memory of ELIZABETH, the Daughter of
THOMAS and MARY HOLMES, of the Parifh of
Llangarran, who departed this Life
the 5th of January, 1758,
aged Years

In Memory of MARY HOLMES,
who departed this Life the 15th of March 1765,
aged 61 Years

ON FLAT STONES
IN THE SOUTH AISLE

THOMAS BURCUM
departed this Life Sept 3, 1748, aged 35.

ROBERT AILLIAFT, of this Town, Cooper,
died July 5, 1773, aged 56

SARAH EDWARDS, of this Town,
was buried Aug 7, 1722, aged 69

IN THE BELFRY

THOMAS MORGAN, of this Town, Sadler,
died May 21, 1769, aged 32

THOMAS HUGHES
departed this Life May 27, 1755, aged 43

JOHN LANE
died the 20th of January, 1641

IN THE NORTH AISLES
ON MONUMENTS

To the Memory of BETTY, Wife of
FRANCIS LEWIS,
who died May 31, 1768, aged 28

Near this Place lie the Remains of
JOHN STEPHEN, who departed this Life
the 23d April, 1767, aged 58

Alfo the Remains of LACY his Wife,
who died Jan 1, 1773, aged 70

Near this Place alfo lie the Remains of
SARAH, the Wife of JOHN STEPHENS,
of his Town, Currier,
who departed this Life Dec 26, 1779, aged 43

Near

Near this Place lie the Remains of
WILLIAM CROSS, of this Town, Mercer,
who departed this Life Feb 8, 1734, aged 38

Also ELIZABETH his Wife
She departed her Life May 27, 1754, aged 64

SOPHIA, the Daughter of
WILLIAM and ELIZABETH CROSS,
died in her Infancy

Also ELIZABETH, the Wife of WILLIAM CROSS,
of this Town, Mercer,
departed this Life, with her Son,
July 27, 1776, aged 35.

Arms, Per Pale, three Saltires, for LANE;—
impaling, on a Fels three Cheflrooks and in Chief
three Martlets, for BROWNE.

Near this Place
lie the Remains of WILLIAM LANE, Gent
who died May 7, 1748,
aged 63

Also of ELIZABETH his Wife,
who died April the 1st, 1753,
aged 66.

They refigned this Life,
with well grounded Hopes for a better,
having given to the World fuch well known
Examples of the confcientious Difcharge
of the Duties refpectively incumbent upon them,
as need not Praifes,
but deferve Imitation

Arms, Argent, a Chevron between three Dolphins embowed Sable, for SARGEAUNT,—impaling,
on a Fefs three Mullets and a Canton, for PYRKE.

In Memory of EDWARD SARGEAUNT, of
Hart Barn in the Parifh of Longhope
in this County, Gent
who deceafed July 24, 1698,
aged 92 Years

Also of ANNE his Wife,
who deceafed June the 21ft, 1653.

Also JOHN, Son of EDWARD SARGEAUNT, Gent.
who died April 19, 1720, aged 80 Years

Also ANNE his Wife, Daughter of
THOMAS PURY, of Tainton, Gent
died March 20, 1727, aged 83 Years.

ELIZABETH, Wife of HENRY YEARSLEY,
departed this Life Feb 15, 1754, aged 70

Likewife WILLIAM BARRON,
Apothecary and Surgeon of this Town,
died April 20, 1767, aged 44

HENRY YEARSLEY, of this Town,
died the 30th of October, 1767, aged 77

ON FLAT STONES

MARY, the Widow of JOHN SARGEAUNT, Gent
deceafed in the Year of our Lord GOD 1671

Also EDWARD, Son of JOHN SARGEAUNT, Gent
died Oct 14, 1690, aged 30

Mr SAMUEL SARGEAUNT, Son of
JOHN and ANN SARGEAUNT, Gent
died April 1, 1757, aged 72

ELIZABETH, the Wife of ROBERT SARGEAUNT
of this Town, Gent paid the Debt of Nature,
Feb. 22, 1721, aged 41

ISABEL, Wife of EDWARD SARGEAUNT,
died April the 3d, 1753

ELIZABETH, Daughter of the faid EDWARD,
died May the 10th, 1753

WILLIAM, Son of JOHN SARGEAUNT,
of Hart Barn, Gent. and ANNE his Wife,
died March 23, 1734

RICHARD, another Son,
died Dec 6, 1738

ANNE their Daughter
died Dec 8, 1738, Infants.

MARY, Relict of WILLIAM SARGEAUNT,
of Hart Barn, Gent departed this Life
Dec 7, 1735, aged 59 Years.

WILLIAM SARGEAUNT, of Hart Barn
in the Parifh of Longhope,
died May 3, 1752, aged 33.

ELIZABETH, Wife of THOMAS BOWER, Gent.
deceafed October 3, 1639.

ROBERT SARGEAUNT, of Hart Barn
in this County, Gent.
died Jan 19, 1732, aged 55

MARY, Widow and Relict of
the above ROBERT SARGEAUNT, Gent
died Jan 3, 1776, aged 78

THOMAS TOMKINS, Gent
departed this Life the 5th of June, 1711.

Also ELIZABETH, the Wife of
THOMAS TOMKINS, Gent
Daughter of EDWARD MACHEN, Efq.
died the 19th of Dec 1712

EDWARD MACHEN, Efq.
died May 2, 1708.

ANN TOMKINS, Grand Daughter of
EDWARD MACHEN, Efq
died April 19, 1708

HENRY HAWKINS, of English Bicknor,
died Feb 27, 1745, aged 28.

SUSANNA, Wife of THOMAS BUTCHER.
died July 5, 1706, aged 24.

JOHN, the Son of JOHN GREEN,
of this Town, by ELIZABETH his Wife,
died June 22, 1735

Also JOHN GREEN, senior,
died Feb 7, 1750, aged 44

MARY their Daughter
died Jan 8, 1737

JOHN BUTCHER, of this Town,
died July 21, 1714, in the 36th Year of his Age.

MARY MORGAN, Widow,
died Sept 25, 1708, aged 79.

TIMOTHY MORGAN
died Aug 15, 1746, aged 76

CHARLES, Son of JOHN COLLINS,
by SARAH his Wife,
died Jan 11, 1751, aged 8.

MARY, Wife of GILES TOWER,
died Nov 10, 1682, aged 31

ELIZABETH, Wife of GILES TOWER, junior,
died Nov 28, 1711, aged 35.

GILES TOWER
died June 28, 1719, aged 73.

GILES TOWER, junior,
died June 15, 1755, aged 77

SARAH, Wife of JAMES RUDGE,
and Daughter of GILES and ELIZABETH TOWER,
died March 2, 1765, aged 58

ELIZABETH, Wife of THOMAS PERKINS, senior,
late of the Hay in the Parish of Aston Ingham,
and Daughter of GILES and ELIZABETH TOWER,
died Nov 6, 1779, aged 75

ELIZABETH, Wife of HENRY YEARSLEY,
was interred Feb 17, 1754.

HENRY YEARSLEY, of this Town,
died Oct 30, 1767, aged 77

ANN, Relict of JOHN ALDRIDGE,
died May 9, 1776, aged 40

NANCY, Relict of the above JOHN ALDRIDGE,
was buried Nov 17, 1781, aged 33

JOHN their Son died an Infant

JOHN BARROW
died Feb 28, 1750, aged 43

JOHN MORGAN, of this Town, Sadler,
died July 27, 1766, aged 62

ANNE his Wife
died March 30, 1783, aged 84.

SUSANNA, Wife of WILLIAM MEYRICK,
died April the 13th, 1678

WILLIAM MEYRICK
died July 6, 1697

SUSANNA their Daughter
died Dec 26, 1702

ROBERT GABBETT
died March 24, 1646.

ELIZABETH his Wife
died Oct 26, 1659

HANNAH, Wife of Dr POWELL,
departed this Life Dec 25, 1711, aged 70

SARAH, Wife of WILLIAM PEARCE,
died August 14, 1746, aged 23

JOHN, Son of WILLIAM PEARCE,
died Dec 20, 1726.

Here lieth the Body of
RICHARD PYRKE, of the Dunstan, Gent
Son of ROBERT, who lyeth with his
Father in Abbinghall Chancel
The said RICHARD left Issue,
RICHARD, JONATHAN, LAZARUS, ANNA, and
ELIZABETH

Here also lyeth MARY his Daughter,
who married with THOMAS WILKINS, Gent
and died March 3, 1722.

THOMAS WALLIN, junior,
died January 1, 1698

WILLIAM GIBBS
was buried March 1, 1728 9,
aged 59

ELIZABETH his Wife
was buried April 6, 1729, aged 61

PYRKE NATHANIEL LLOYD,
died Feb 2, 1739, aged 3

JAMES LLOYD
was buried August 28, 1752, aged 22

JAMES LLOYD, senior,
died Dec 26, 1770, aged 74

MARY, the Daughter of
HENRY and ELIZABETH LEWIS,
Surgeon of this Town,
died Dec 16, 1739

ANNE their Daughter died March 10, 1739

Mrs ANNE HUNTRIDGE, Grandmother of the
aforesaid MARY and ANN LEWIS,
who departed this Life June 7, 1740, aged 69.

THOMAS TURBERVILL
died April 14, 1728

THOMAS BRADLEY
died Jun 11, 1693, aged 59

WILLIAM

WILLIAM COXE
died August 14, 1657.

ELIZABETH, Wife of THOMAS RUDGE,
died February 4, 1675

THOMAS WALLIN
died Oct 29, 1695, aged 64

ELIZABETH, Daughter of
GEORGE and CATHARINE GIBBS,
died August 4, 1751.

ELIZABETH LANE, Widow,
died January 26, 1692

REBECKAH LANE her Daughter
died Nov 17, 1694

THOMAS, Son of THOMAS MERRITT,
of this Town, Baker,
died April 24, 1739, aged 28.

JONATHAN, Son of JONATHAN RUDGE,
by CATHARINE his Wife,
was buried Dec 19, 1726, aged 31

ON FLAT STONES
AT THE WEST END

WILLIAM BANNISTER,
of this Town, Yeoman,
died March 31, 1716, aged near 64

THOMAS PACEY
died April 5, 1731, aged 44.

MARY PACEY
died July 19, 1735, aged 64

THOMAS PACEY, of this Town, Blacksmid,
died Sept 7, 1724, aged 70

WALTER PACEY
died May 17, 1762, aged 76

JANE PACEY
died March 17, 1729, aged 77

SARAH PACEY
died Feb 6, 1749, aged 56

IN THE CHURCH PORCH.

ANN, Wife of ROBERT PEARCE,
Relict of WILLIAM BOSSOM,
died May 17, 1780, aged 68.

THOMAS BARNARD, junior,
died May 15, 1774, aged 26.

SARAH his Wife
died April 15, 1772, aged 33

IN THE CHURCH YARD, ON TOMBS

DANIEL PLATT, of this Town, Glover,
died July 6, 1737

CHARLES GIBBONS, senior,
died April 5, 1741, aged 58

SUSAN his Wife
died March 4, 1760, aged 77

WILLIAM, Son of
WILLIAM and ELIZABETH LODGE,
died June 6, 17.., aged 20

THOMAS BOSSOM of this Town,
died Nov 30 1749, aged 79

EDWARD, Son of
MARGARET WILLIAMS,
died March 7, 1716, aged 29

JAMES BULLOCK,
late of this Town, Butcher,
died October 5, 1736, aged 49

MARY Daughter of
JOHN BULLOCK
by SARAH his Wife,
of the Parish of Minster worth,
died Oct 11, 1764, aged 3

ON FLAT AND HEAD STONES

	Died	Aged		Died	Aged
Sybil Edwards	28 Aug 176.	51	Thomas Wyden	11 Jun 1747	—
Thomas Mitchell	15 Jan 1695	70	Mary his Wife	31 May, 178.	—
John Knight, of the Parish of Ab			Mary Rudge, Widow	3 Apr 17.0	14
bingh..l	17 Mar 1763	62	Thomas Bossom	— 1706	—
Mary his Wife	5 Nov 1798	78	Sarah, Wife of James Baldwin	8 May, 1723	6.
Mary, Wife of John Leonard	14 Apr 194	—	Thomas Robe ts	4 Apr 1712	—
Thomas, their Son	23 Dec 17.5	37	Thomas Roberts	22 Apr 1740	4.
Mary, Wife of John Harding, Daugh			Mary, Wife of Thomas Roberts	24 Jan 17.7	5
ter of John and Mary Leonard	19 Oct 1782	57	Joan Meek, Widow	20 Jun 17.1	8
Betty, Wife of Henry Hithes, Daugh			John Leonard, of this Town	22 May, 1784	76
ter of John and Mary Leonard	11 Sept 1787	36	Charles Walden	15 Dec 1755	36
John Morgan	7 Mar 1755	56	Margaret his Wife, late Wife of Ri		
Mary, Wife of John Morgan	2 Dec 1755	75	chard Knight	1 Jan 1759	54
Sarah Andrews Hartland, Daughter			Thomas Lane	12 Feb 1708	—
of Miles and Eliz Hartland	26 Jan 1773	7	Jane his Wife, afterwards Wife of		
Benjamin their Daughter	1 Jun 1763	3	Thomas Castle	29 Jan 17.0	9.
Abigail, Wife of Benjamin James	6 Feb 1743	—	Henry Harley	12 May 17.1	62
Jane Wife of Thomas Griffiths	3 Jun 1786	57	Sarah his Wife	25 June, 182	62
John Griffiths	— 1750	14	James Dowle	20 Dec 1758	5
Elizabeth his Wife	— 1760	60	Sarah, Wife of James Dowle	21 Sep 1767	63
Mary Griffiths	7 Nov 1751	62			

XCI. DENE PARVA, or LITTLE DEAN.

OF this Parish the early Records are exactly the same, as of its adjoining, *Michel Dean*, from which it was originally separated It is of an oval Form, one Mile in Breadth, and one Mile and a half in Length, of a deep fertile Soil, chiefly Pasture, three Miles South from *Michel Dean*, and twelve from GLOUCESTER on the West

The Village is large and well peopled, the poorer Inhabitants are employed in a Manufacture of Nails In the midst of it is a very curious Market Cross, around the Shaft of which is a low octangular Roof, which is then finished by a Pinnacle of fine Gothic Workmanship, with Niches and Effigies, on a small Scale There are two annual Fairs

The Living is an Impropriation annexed to *Newnham*, given to the Hospital of *St Bartholomew* in GLOUCESTER, and now held by the Mayor and Burgesses as Trustees It is leased to the Incumbent for 8*l* a Year, to whom all other Tythes are due

The Church, dedicated to *St Ethelbert*, consists of a Nave and North Aisle, with a Chantry parallel to the Chancel, and a Spire of exact and elegant Proportions The Windows of the North Aisle and Chantry exhibit very rich Remains of painted Glass Twice repeated are, " Or, a Fess between six Roses ' Gules,' the augmented Bearing of the Family of ABENHALL, by one of whom this Chantry was founded in 1412, 13 HEN IV GEO OF POMFREY, the late Priest, retired with a Pension of 4*l* The ancient Sacerdotal Vestments of Velvet, embroidered with the Portraits of Saints, are now used as a Covering for the Reading Desk

In *Domesday* Book no mention is made of the Manor, and it appears for the most Part to have been held with *Michel Dean* Yet, a distinct Manor was granted to the Abbey of *Flaxley*, and confirmed to Sir ANTHONY KINGSTONE at the Suppression 1545 RICHARD BRAYN purchased the principal Estate in 1573 15 ELIZ and in the next Century it was transferred to the Family of BRIDGEMAN Upon their Removal to *Prinknash*, it was sold to the Ancestor of the present Proprietor, JOSEPH PYRKE, Esq The chief Manor was vested in the Family of HEANE in 1608 Jac of whom it was purchased in 1670, — CARL. by JOHN PARKER, Gent of *Hasfield* whose Daughters and Coheirs, in 1730, resold it to MAYNARD COLCHESTER, Esq an Ancestor of the present Possessor The Families of ABRAHALL and SKIP are possessed of other Estates

In this Village was a very memorable Skirmish during the Civil Wars †

The House of Correction, now erecting here in pursuance of an Act passed in 1784, for the *Forest* Division, is built in a Style of singular Propriety, and evinces the superior Skill of the Architect

---

BENEFACTIONS

THOMAS BARTLEM, 1714, gave by Will a House and Garden, value 1*l* 5*s* a Year, to be distributed in Bread to the Poor
EUSTACE HARDWICK bequeathed two Closes of Land, the annual Produce of which 9*l* to be applied in cloathing the Poor (after deducting 10*s* for a Sermon, and the Expences of cleaning, net 8*l* 10*s*)
JANE WALTERS, 1760, gave 20*l* for Bibles, for the Poor of this Parish

---

* THOMAS MARSHALL Rector of *Lincoln College, Oxford,* endowed certain Scholarships with a Rent Charge of 1*l* per Annum, issuing from the Manor of *Little Dean* Wood's Ath vol II p 592 Ant q Oxon p 231
† " The Enemy had another Guard at *Little Dean,* either the Governor commanded a Party of Horse to beat those Quarters " which he fell upon at *Plays,* These Horse found the Enemy disquieting in the Towne and upon the Enemies refusall of them to " peace, insulting towards the Garrison, which the Troopers observing, disliked and set together with them in the Towne " where they tooke about twenty Men Decr into which Guard, Lieutenant Colonel Congreve was entered Novr " and one Captain Wigmore with a few private Soldiers were surrounded in his House by the Rebels of our Hor " These had accepted Quarter, ready to surrender themselves, when one of their Company from the House killed a Trooper " which forced up their heat that they broke in upon them and put them all to the sword which Accident this House was " not to be forgotten that expressed in one House an extreme Cruelty in the parts of Mercy and the Sense of our " Congreve died with these Words, ' Lord receive my Soul ' but were near dying not our Party not more " more deeply requiring at the last stroke, it changed it Deane Town
COLONEL Massy Governour Letters of 1643 p 40

7   DENE MA

DOROTHY PYRKE, 1760, left 200*l* the Interest of which to be distributed as follows, viz 4*l* 10*s* for a School and Books, 1*l* 1*s*. for a Sermon on Good Friday, and the Remainder for Linen Garments for the Poor, the annual Produce now is 7*l*.

Present Officiating Minister, BENJAMIN WEBB, Clerk.

The former Series will be inserted under *NEWNHAM*, to which the Curacy is annexed

PRESENT PROPRIETORS OF THE MANORS,

Of Part lying towards the Forest,	Of the Chief Manor,
Sir THOMAS CRAWLEY BOEVEY, Bart	JOHN COLCHESTER, Esq.

The Persons summoned from this Parish by the Heralds, in 1682 and 1683, were

Thomas Pyrke, Gent	William Braine, Gent
Christopher Braine, Gent.	John Braine, Gent
Euseby Hardwick, Gent.	Miles White, Gent

At the Election in 1776 Twenty-nine Freeholders polled from this Parish.

The first Entry in the Register bears Date 1684

ANNUAL ACCOUNT OF MARRIAGES, BIRTHS, AND BURIALS, IN THIS PARISH

A.D.	Mar	Bir	Bur	A D	Mar	Bir	Bur	A D	Mar	Bir	Bur.	A.D	Mar	Bir	Bur.
1781	4	22	12	1786	4	26	9	1791				1796			
1782	—	20	8	1787	7	20	26	1792				1797			
1783	2	17	12	1788	4	23	13	1793				1798			
1784	4	20	10	1789				1794				1799			
1785	7	18	11	1790				1795				1800			

INSCRIPTIONS IN THE CHURCH.

THE FOLLOWING ARMS AND INSCRIPTION WERE ON A MONUMENT ON THE SOUTH SIDE THE CHANCEL, NOW ENTIRELY DEMOLISHED:

On a Fess three Mulletts and a Canton, for PYRKE,—impaling, a Cross, and in the dexter chief Point a Rose

Ad posteros suos.
Virtus honor tituli, nec opum possessio certa,
Virtus sola decus, mens bona divitiæ
O quicunque domum cupias nomenque tueri,
Nomen amare pius disce domumque Dei
H S I
THOMAS PYRKE, Armiger,
Qui
Usque adeo in verbis fidem,
in poculis sobrietatem,
Et in hoc comitatu justiciarius,
Pacem publicam conservavit,
Ut tandem ævi satur
Ann. ætat LXXII, April IX, A D MDCCII
In pace decessit
Uxore DEBORA tribusque filiis diu antea
Praemissis, & in ecclesia de Abbenhall, una
Cum progenitorum stirpe sepultis
Ejus Memoriæ
NATHANIEL, filius hæresque,
Hoc monumentum gratus parentavit.

ON A NEAT MONUMENT OF VARIEGATED MARBLE, WITH A SARCOPHAGUS AND URN

Arms, PYRKE as before,—impaling, Azure, a Fess, and in chief two Mullets Or, for YATE

Here lie the Remains of
THOMAS PYRKE, Esq
one of his Majesty's Justices of the Peace,
a Verdurer of the Forest of Dean,
and Deputy Constable of the Castle of St Beevil,
all which Offices he discharged with
Honour and Integrity
He married DOROTHY, Daughter of
RICHARD YATE, of Arlingham, Esq
By whom he had four Sons
and two Daughters,
THOMAS and CHARLES, two of his Sons,
are interred in this Church,
NATHANIEL and MAYNARD,
BRIDGET and DOROTHY,
in the Parish Church of Abbinhall
He died March 2, 1752, aged 65

Mrs PYRKE caused this Monument
to be erected, out of her great Affection
and Regard to the Memory of
so good an Husband

ON

ON FLAT STONES
IN THE CHANCEL

ELIZABETH, the Wife of THOMAS PYRKE, Esq
departed this Life Oct. 12, 1679

After many long and heavy Afflictions
for the Loss of her Husband and six Children,
Here resteth, in hopes of a glorious Resurrection,
the Body of DOROTHY PYRKE, Wife
of THOMAS PYRKE, Esq
of this Parish, second Daughter of
RICHARD YATE, Esq
of Arlingham in this County
She deceased the 24th of January, 1762,
aged 76 Years

ELIZABETH, Wife of DUNCOMBE PYRKE, Gent
who died October the 16th, 1729

MARY YOUNG, Late of the Grange
in the Parish of Flaxley
in the County of Gloucester, Widow
of JOHN YOUNG o
Ley in the Parish of Westbury, Gent
and Daughter of LEWIS PYRKE,
of Little Dean, Esq
who departed this Life Feb. 7, 1731, aged 78

MARY Mother of the said MARY YOUNG,
second Wife of the said THOMAS PYRKE,
who departed his Life Mar. 17, 1668

Mr CHARLES PYRKE,
Son of THOMAS PYRKE, of this Parish, Esq
by DOROTHY his Wife,
died the 9th of April 1754, aged 23

ROWLAND HUNT
departed this Life the 23d of October, 1610.

Here resteth DEBORAH,
Uxor THOMAS ROD, de Newton prope
Hereford, Gen & filia GULIELMI ROWLES,
de Cockshoote in Newnham, Gen
Obiit III die
Augusti, { A.D. 1657
{ Aetatis XXVII

Here rests MARIA, uxor
GULIELMI ROWLES, de Cockshoote in
... cum prole quindecim
MARIAM, uxorem
Stapleton prope Bristol, Gen
ELIZABETHAM, uxorem GULIELMI
SEDDON ORE, de Glouc. Gen &
DEBORA, nuper uxorem THOMAS ROD,
de Newton prope Hereford,
Gen obiit XXVI
Die Octob. Anno { Domini 1687
{ Aetatis 62

Here lyeth also the Body of
WILLIAM ROWLES, of the Cockshoote,
late the Husband of the aforesaid
MARY, who departed this Life
the .. Day of August, A.D. 1692,
aetatis suae 71.

JOHN HAWKINS, Gent
deceased Febru 19 o, 1623

In Memoriam reverendi rius
JOHANNIS WISE,
Huius ecclesiae per annos 14 insti,
Viri pius, probus, integer, pluribus
Pauperibus ultra facultatem benignus,
Satis diu, cum pene octogenarius
In coelo migra
JOANNA prole
Uxor dum in ... matque,
Mater tum ex optim is filiis ...
Qui te ... in libellos perit & obie vit,
JOHANNEM MAGE LLAM, & JACAM,
reconditur hic
Interpret rib morti um clamant expecta s.
Abiit hic or, & po ...
Ob { Ille Die 19 16.. } cum { 79
{ Illa Ale 22, 65 } { 57

Filius JOHANNES, ecclesiae de Newr a vicarius,
Pietatis ergo, & in fui ficium ponit

H S I
FESTATUS HADWICK,
de Dean Pury in com Glouc Gen
Filius JOHANNIS, de Hadwick
prope Bromyard com Hereford, Gen
qui obiit 6 Mar. 70,
circiter circum aetatis anni

Hic jacet
MARIA,
Illa FESTATI HADWICK, Gen
per Mat am conjunctissimo,
Filia m Domini GEORGII PRATT,
de Coleswall, com Bere Baron
per Ma cam tiam filii
Domini HENRICI HOBART,
de Alderm aston, com Bere Baron
Quae obiit
1 Augusti, Anno Dom 1694,
aetatis 12

THE FOLLOWING ARMS AND INSCRIPTION WERE
IN THE NAVE AGAINST THE SOUTH WALL, BUT
ARE NOW UTTERLY DESTROYED

Sable, ten Bezants, 4, 3, 2, 1, and on a Chief
Argent, a Lion passant Sable, for BRIDGMAN

Here resteth the Body of
CHARLES BRIDGMAN, Esq
and Justice of the Peace,
who died the 27th of December,
1643

ON FLAT STONES

THOMAS MORSE
deceased the 14th Day of June,
Anno Domini 1614

JOAN Wife of THOMAS MORSE,
deceased the 1st Day of June,
A.D. 1615

In Memory of JAMES HARRIS, Gent
Keeper of Latimer Walk, in his Majesty's
Forest of Dean in the County of Gloucester,
which Office he held upwards of thirty Years,
and executed it with Honour and Integrity
He departed this Life
the 10th of January, 1761,
aged 60 Years

Also in Memory of
CATHARINE his Wife,
who departed this Life March 2, 1747 8,
aged 47

ON FLAT STONES IN THE NORTH AISLE

Arms, a Mullet, and in Chief two Crescents.

GEORGE BARRON, Clothier,
departed this Life August 3,
Anno Dom 1707

Also the Body of NICHOLAS,
the Son of GEORGE BARRON, Gent
who departed this Life Feb 14, 1702

Also MARGERY, Daughter of
GEORGE BARRON,
who deceased May 24, 1705

Here resteth the Body of
.. . PEMBRUGE, of
. . in the County of Hereford,
who departed this Life the 26th of May, 1688,
ætat suæ 87

FRANCES, the Wife of
RICHARD STAFORD, Daughter of
THOMAS DAVIS, of the Bourne
in the Parish of Stroud, Clothier,
deceased the 19th Day of June,
A D 1656

JOHN CHANNAN, Gent
departed this Life June 22, 17 ,
aged 79 Years, 5 Months, and 24 Days

Arms, Azure, on a Fess, between three Bugle
Horns stringed Argent, a Hemp Buckle Gules

KIFORD BRAINT, senior,
departed this Life Dec 5, 1705.

IN THE CHURCH YARD, ON TOMBS.

PHILIP ROBINSON, senior,
died April 16, 1712 aged 66

HENRY, Son of
PHILIP ROBINSON,
died Dec ., 1712.

SARAH, Wife of the above
PHILIP ROBINSON,
departed this Life Sept 13, 1730,
aged 94

JOHN ROBINSON,
Son of the above
PHILIP and SARAH ROBINSON,
died Sept 14 1767, aged 69

JANE, Wife of
JOHN ROBINSON,
died May 17, 1766, aged 53

PHILIP ROBINSON
died Dec 9, 1711, aged 37

MARY his Wife
died January , 1691

JANE, Wife of
JOHN ROBINSON,
of Little Dean Cross, Gent
died May 17 1768, aged 53

JOHN ROBINSON,
of Little Dean Cross, Gent
died Feb 1, 1764, aged 71

PHILIP ROBINSON, Gent
died Feb 3, 17 aged 4

JOHN ROBINSON his Brother
died Sept 4, 1785 aged 76

MARY Wife of
THOMAS TAYLOR,
of this Parish and
Daughter of RICHARD LONGSTRETH,
of Frampton upon Severn,
died Sep 26, 1741, aged 35

THOMAS TAYLOR,
of this Parish,
died Oct 16 1764 aged near 76,

AMY Wife of
THOMAS HOLES,
died April 4, 1772, aged 38

NATHANIEL MALIE,
Father of the above AMY HOLES,
died Feb 16 1774, aged 3

THOMAS HOL
died April 24, 1767 aged 57

WILLIAM JAMES
died June 1, 1762 aged 90
He was Clerk of this Parish forty seven
Years

ANN, Wife of
WILLIAM JAMES,
was buried May 4, 1760, aged 68

THOMAS PACKER,
of this Parish,
died Dec 2, 1779 aged 73

WILLIAM PACKER
died Aug 1, 1786 aged 8.

SAMUEL SLEET,
of this Parish Surgeon
died March 29 1747, aged 69

MARY Wife of
JOHN SLEET Carpenter
was buried Nov 1 1 and 5

SUSANNA Daughter of
JOHN SLEET and MARY his Wife,
died in August 1 , aged 15

JOHN SLEET
died Nov 5, , aged 64

LUCY Wife of
JOHN SLEET
of Little Dean Cross
died June 1 1 , aged 51

SARAH Wife of
JAMES SLEET
was buried July 6, 1764, aged 18

A. M LEAN
died May 1 1761 aged

Mrs SARAH ARTHUR
died Feb 21, 1720-, aged 72

Mr RICHARD BROWNING her Nephew
died May 17 1719, aged 35

WILLIAM ABRAHALL
died Mar 7, 174

DOROTHY his Wife
died Jan 1, 1742 aged 60

ISABELL Wife of
AARON WIKS of the
Parish of Hanton,
Daughter of
THOMAS and ELIZABETH ABRAHALL,
of this Parish,
died Dec 7, 1771 aged 41

ELIZABETH Wife of
THOMAS ABRAHALL
of this Parish
died May 26, 1766 aged

THOMAS ABRAHALL
died Jan 10, 17 aged 61

MARY ABRAHALL junior,
died 31 7 aged 4

MARKEY ABRAHALL senior,
died Oct 24, 1775, aged 75

MARY his Wife
died Jan 3, 17 , aged 71

JOHN BAN
of the Parish of Newnham
died Nov 6 6 , aged 62

of
ROBEN
died Feb 12 87 aged 63

JOHN their son
died Dec 31, 1 aged 29

ROBERT PYRKE,
late of Newnham, Gent
died May 13, 1780,
in the 44th Year of his Age.

JOHN PYRKE Gent
Brother of the above
ROBERT PYRKE
died Sept 2 177 ,
in the 31st Year of his Age

Arms six Lions rampant 3, 2, 1,
for SAVAGE

Here are deposited
Remains of
ELIZABETH SAVAGE
Wife of Gentleman and
Quartermaster HENRY SAVAGE,
late of the
Hon East India Company Military,
died Aug , 1767, aged 33

THOMAS WILMOT,
of this Parish,
died July 2, 1780 aged 58

WILLIAM OKEY
died March 2, 1774 aged 72

ELIZABETH his Wife
died May 10, 1775, aged 81.

Mrs MARY Widow of
Mr SAMUEL KENNSTON,
of London Merchant
died July 22, 1765 aged

Mrs KATHERINE SKIPP,
Daughter of
SAMUEL and MARY STEVENS,
and Wife of
GEORGE SKIPP, Gent
of the Grange
in the Parish of Flaxley,
departed this Life Dec 8, 1772,
aged 50

GEORGE SKIPP, Esq
of the Grange
in the Parish of Flaxley,
of a very ancient
Family of that Name
in the County of Hereford
and lineally descended from the
Right Rev JOHN SKIP,
Lord Bishop of Hereford,
in the Reign of
King Edward the Sixth,
Son of
RICHARD SKIP,
of Donington Hall
in the County of Hereford Esq
and of MARY his Wife,
Daughter of
THOMAS , Esq
of this Parish
He died May , 1782, aged 85

ON HEAD STONES

	Died	Aged		Died	Aged
William Pearce	11 Sep 1769	77	Elizabeth his Daughter	14 Apr 1771	14
Elizabeth Wife of William Phillips	19 Aug 1759	63	Sarah, Wife of James Bennett, Daughter of Richard Stiles	20 Apr 1794	22
Ann, Wife of William Baldwin	14 Aug 177	57	James Bennett	24 July 1765	57
Henry Robinson	17 Nov 1707	—	Ann Hovey	21 Dec 1764	58
Henry Robinson	21 Jan 1715	56	Thomas Hobbs	2 July 175	65
Alice, Wife of James Drew	2 Apr 1788	59	James his Wife	3 July 17	50
James Drew	26 May 1747	62	Abigail Adams	3 July 1741	82
George his Son	1 Mar 1747	27	William Trigg	8 Sept 1743	22
Thomas Ward	16 Jan 1750	54	Frances, Wife of Joseph Williams	25 June 1781	64
Elizabeth his Wife	6 May 1750	58	Samuel Trigg	6 Jun 47	57
John Ward	27 Dec 1	—	John Trigg, junior	14 Jan 1728	80
Elizabeth Wife of John Trigg	23 May 1757	60	Abigail his Wife	31 Mar 1732	80
Anthony Ward	16 May 1751	1	Hannah, Wife of Thomas Wood	5 Dec 1760	37
John Cuitt	23 Feb 1727	65	Ann his second Wife	31 May 176	47
Elizabeth his Wife	8 Mar 1756	65	James Oxard	7 May 1741	33
Sarah Wife of Richard Cuitt	11 Dec 1746	45	Ann his Wife	3 Dec 1750	76
Elizabeth Wife of William Pickes	2 Apr 1759	35	James Morgan		
John Cuitt	1 Aug 1764	2	Ann, Wife of James Morgan	10 Apr 1752	82
Ann their Daughter	21 Aug 1750	62	Thomas, Son of James and Mary Morgan	7 May 1760	1
Robert Bryle	7 Oct 1741	15	James Morgan, junior	7 June 1773	77
John his Wife	14 Jan 1769	76	Ann his Wife	7 July 176	76
Elizabeth Wife of Anthony Bryn	22 Apr 1784	78	George Morgan	5 June 1746	33
Richard Wood junior	26 Nov 1787	45	James Very	1 Jun 17	34
Ann, Wife of Richard Stiles	3 Nov 171	—	Elizabeth Wife of Thomas Brynham, of the Parish of Flaxley	27 May 1783	80
William Mayfield	23 Sept 1727	55			
William Williams	18 May 1745	54			
	1 June 1780	55			

O N   H E A D   S T O N E S

	Died	Aged		Died	Aged
John Thomas	13 Oct 1757	47	David Price	9 May, 1752	64
Esther, Daughter of John and Elizabeth Thomas	22 Jan 1766	22	Sarah Steel	1 June, 1768	70
William Higg.	6 Oct 1752	65	William Smith	5 Mar 1756	31
Mary his Wife	2 Jan 1763	58	Jacob Broben	19 Oct 1748	5
Sarah his Second Wife	10 May 1782	72	Mary Broben, of Newnham	8 Apr 1751	46
William Whetstone	14 Apr 1748	65	John Broben	8 Jan 1753	70
Mary, Wife of Thomas Wood, Daughter of William Whetstone	18 Dec 1757	2,	John Reynolds, one of the Keepers of the Forest of Dean	in May, 1740	47
John Charles	7 May, 175,	6-	Ann his Wife, Daughter of Desborough Bridges, of Slimbridge, Gent	17 Oct 1756	68
Anthony Packet	30 Oct 747	66	Thomas Jones	27 Nov 1766	80
Thomas Moore	27 May, 1781	62	Ann his Wife	24 Dec 175,	6-
John Morgan	28 July, 1781	61	Thomas Webb	19 Jan 751	7c
William, Son of William and Mary Foxle of Longhope	2 Apr 1759	33	Rebeckah his Wife	4 Sep 1757	57
Ann Stephens	23 Feb 1769	13	William Howell	3 Aug 1765	60
Mary, Wife of Joseph Wooley	17 Feb 17-5	2,	Samuel Young	11 Jan 1787	3
Gives Clarke	5 Jan 1723	—	Elizabeth his Wife	22 Jan 1761	61
Mary his Daughter	6 July, 1727	—	Jane Hale	9 Oct 1763	67
Jonathan Packer	1 July, 17-1	67	Audrey, Wife of William Brooke	30 Aug 1756	5,
Gabriel Packer	14 Mar 1739	7.	Richard Brooks	15 Jun 1756	,
Margaret his Wife	8 Mar 1759	88	William Moore	25 Apr 1762	57
Mary their Daughter	20 Mar 1759	50	Elizabeth his Wife	2 July, 1761	7,
Samuel Packer	20 Mar 1746	32	Thomas, Son of William and Elizabeth Moore	6 Dec 1780	16
Margaret Packer	7 May, 1767	65	Beata Mountjoy	19 Nov 1745	60

FOREST OF DEAN.

THE Origin of Forests in *England*, as an Appendage to the Crown, was certainly prior to the Conquest. CANUTE, in the first Year of his Reign, issued a Law prohibiting his Subjects from hunting with the Royal Inclosures. It is therefore probable that William the Conqueror found many in his new Dominions †, and was more jealous of this than of any of his Prerogative, and more imperious to extend it. His Successors, HENRY II, RICHARD, and JOHN, depopulated whole Counties to enlarge their Forests. These Boundaries were in 1300, 28 Edw. I restored to their ancient Limitation as ascertained by Perambulations. New Laws for Forest Government were enacted, and confirmed by Parliament in the celebrated "*Charta de Foresta*."

The Forest of *Dean* is situate in the western Part of the County, between the navigable Rivers *Severn* and *Wye*. The Quantity of Land belonging to the Crown, within the latest Perambulation, is about 23,015 Acres, exclusive of Freehold Property. In different Parts, and County, containing about 2000 Inhabitants, and 1798 small Inclosures, amounting to 158 Acres belonging to the Forest, but occupied by Cottagers. As the whole Forest is extra-parochial, and are exempted from Rate and Tax, have unlimited Right of Pasturage, beside the Access to the Wood and Timber, and the Privilege of taking Mines.

The early Records abound in Accounts of Perambulations. In 1215, 9 H. III one was made on the Petition of the Monks of *Flaxley*, including the Additions in the uniform Reigns, which in 1300, 28 Edw. I were disafforested, and called *Purlieus*. This Second was confirmed by Parliament in 1325, 3 Edw. III.

Although numerous Grants are still extant of Lands and Immunities within the Verge of the Forest, they seem not to be limited to our present Purpose, as being much altered in their Usage, or of Lands restored. No Lease had obtained effect, from the Crown of the Rambies prior to 1611, 9 Jac. I who granted to WILLIAM HERBERT, Earl of *Pembroke*, the whole Soil, at the annual Rent of 2133l. 6s. 8d. for 12 Years. In 1623 the same were again granted to Lord Conway and Nicholas Naisson, and WILLIAM BELL, who became the Lessees, in Consideration of 1500l. (Jac. 20, 1623), and who then covenanted that their Lands should remain in its Jurisdiction † to the King. King CHARLES, upon his Accession in 1625, transferred the same to the Lessees, at a Consideration not specified, in the eighth whole Term (1 Hy. 10, 1634) in the first Year and held at Gloucester, and a Report made concerning the Metes and Bounds. About the Years after, and Sir John Wintour, of *Lidney*, offering to become the Purchaser, in Consequence Survey returned by the Commissioners, stating that the Forest contained 23,021 Acres. After disafforesting the whole, the King ratified the Purchase by his Letters Patent, dated March 31, 1641, for the Sum of 106,000l. to be paid by Instal-

* "Volo, ut omnis liber Homo prohibeatur suo Licentia tenere, & velle in parcis suis, super eas foris suas Chacet eorum.
"Sciatur omnis mea aliquan cum habere parcus boscis. Decante de Foresta. by John Manwode, 1583) p. 1
† "The resident Forest men in *England* at this Day, the *New Forest* in *Hampshire* that satisfie the Conqueror...
* These Perthi ei months should reflect *Laws* where then acommon enter man, which subjected their ground. His own Records, to unmore in all their Forests in England, and as warrant their Lands the Foresta Counts. to the Man
" The recorded unlimited rude more favourable than ever were enacted. *Charta de Foresta* made to after Henry III.
† The ancient Limits of *Flaxley*, included in Name *Flaxley* Abbey to the use the Forest Perambulation...
* Ca. 9. with *Naisson Denison* and *Wintour* ... the Dean Wood should have been cleared and the Purchase of Iron... the Reason had in the Forest of the Dean had Vessels were particularly this Reason cleared with People...
§ ... an ten subjoined to the Order of twelve thousand as the Letters now preserved in Record Office.

6 D

ment, and a fee firm Rent of 1950l. 12s. 8d. for ever. The Coal Mines and Quarries of Grindstone only were excepted, having been leased for 31 Years to Edward Tiringham in 1637 at 30l. a Year.

In 1656, Cromwell, in his Military Parliament, declared the Patent of Sir John Wyntour, who had been a zealous Royalist, null and void. He reafforested 18000 Acres, and expelled and destroyed the Cabins of 400 beggarly People, who subsisted by the Waste of the Timber.

Upon the Restoration of Charles II, 1660, Sir John Wyntour regained his Patent, and entered on Possession, and upon Surrender of his former Charter a new Agreement was made, and he was indemnified by a Grant of 30,000l. from the Treasury. It appears that he took undue Advantage of his Privileges, as a Complaint was laid before the Council in 1663, " that Sir John Wyntour had 500 Cutters " of Wood employed in *Dean* Forest." An Order of Council, dated July 20, was accordingly issued to prohibit a farther Devastation.

Sir Charles Harbord, a very active Surveyor of the Crown Lands, procured an Act of Parliament to be passed in 1668, 20 Car. II. by which it was ordained that " 11000 Acres should be enclosed and " set apart as a Nursery for Timber, that 12868 Acres are in private Estates or Commons, and that the " unenclosed should be commonable to the adjoining Parishes, the Crown having no Right to keep " more than 800 Head of Deer at one Time. Tyringham's Lease of the Mines was renewed for 31 " Years, and it was resolved that the Crown could not grant for a longer Term." The same Year, under the Direction of Henry Marquis of Worcester, Lord Warden, 8487 Acres were inclosed and planted, and the remaining 2,513 soon afterward. The Income to the Crown was then 5390l. a Year.

In 1691, 3 Will. and Mary, a Commission was directed to Henry Duke of Beaufort, Lord Warden, who returned that the Number of inclosed Acres were 9025, and the Value of the Timber, beside Oak, 148,74l. 16s. 8l. About the Year 1705, Edward Wilcox, Surveyor, proposed to the Council, that " if 11000 Acres, planted and inclosed, be divided into sixteen Parts, and one in each, " being 700 Acres, be annually felled, leaving Standards of Oak and Beech, each Cutting would yield " 3,000l. and the other Parts would grow to Perfection." To this Plan Lord Treasurer Godolphin acceded, and a Warrant was issued for the immediate Performance. It is conjectured that the Forest was about this Period in its best State, for though the Forest Courts had not been so regularly held as before the Revolution, yet the greatest Attention was paid by the Servants of the Crown. Different Commissioners were sent by the Treasury to view the Forest, who made the most minute Returns, and as the Cottages were pulled down, it is probable that every Incroachment was reclaimed. But Abuses have since gradually prevailed, and have been suffered to increase, to a Degree that sufficiently accounts for the present unprofitable State of the Forest. Competent Judges have asserted that the Decrease of Timber is more than in a Proportion of four-fifths.

In 1758 a Proposal was made by John Pitt, Esq. Surveyor, for inclosing 2000 Acres more, and ordered accordingly. In the next Year 9200 Feet of Timber were granted by Warrant towards building the Infirmary at Gloucester. An additional Inclosure of 2000 Acres was completed in 1771, at the Expence of 2077l. 16s. 10d.

When the Act for erecting the new Prisons in this County passed, an Order (dated 26 April, 1-80) was issued from the Treasury for the clear Amount of 2000l. to be raised by *Sale of Timber*, and applied to that Purpose.

A Return of Timber felled for the Navy from 1761 to 1786, both inclusive.

Receipts			Loads	Feet		Value	£.	s.	d.
Total felled	Of Oak,	—	16,73	14	—	}	30573	14	4
	Of Beech,	—	871	41	—				
	Cord Wood,	—	2230		—		6955	7	1
	Stakes,	—			—		12	3	10½
	Bark,	—	1510 Tons,		—		2650	1	5
						Total,	41 19 13	7	
						Disbursed,	13610 13		
						Balance,	7,719	6	8½

In the Forest District are 2077 exempted Acres, in *Hudnall's* and *Abbot's* Woods, which are commonable to the Natives of the Hundred and Parish of *St. Briavel's*.†

The Site of the Forest exhibits a great Variety of Ground. It breaks into numberless deep and wooded Valleys, the Acclivities of which are clothed with the impenetrable and matted Foliage of the

* ... this ... Indenture made under the Great Seal between the King and Sir John Wyntour, Knight, dated ... Car. I.
† Report of the Commissioners of Forests and Crown Lands, 1788.

Birch Tree, Hawthorn, and other low Wood, interspersed with venerable Oaks. In most of these are Springs, but not copious, of a very dark ferruginous Colour, and very strongly impregnated with Steel. The high Lands spread into Plains, which are shaded by Forest Trees of almost every Description, and not unusual of singular Size and Beauty. The Timber most natural to this Soil is Oak and Beech, and in the elevated Parts are Apple Trees peculiar to it, called the *Stire*, of which a Kind of Cyder is made of remarkable Strength and Flavour, and of a very perceptible chalybeate Tast.

Most of the useful fossil Productions are found here in great Quantities and Perfection, Iron Ore, Coal &c, Ochre, and Stone.

We collect from very early Records, that the Iron Ore was discovered and made into Bars. The Abbot of *Flaxley* was possessed of a Forge by royal Grant soon after the Foundation of the Abbey in the Reign of HENRY II. and was allowed two Oaks weekly for the Supply of it, a Privilege commuted in 1258, 42 HEN. III. for *Abbot's* Wood of 872 Acres held by the Abbey to the Dissolution.

In the next Reign were many smelting Kilns, which were called "*Forges*" &c. They all paid an annual Rent, or were reserved to the Crown. Large Furnaces now and then were erected in it. It appears from the immense Quantities of Iron Cinders extremely wrought, which are discovered near the Surface, that the Art of smelting the Ore is in much earlier Ages very uncertainly known or practised. The Coal is found at a comparatively slight Depth, and produces a very intense Heat, which renders it the better adapted to the Use of the Forges. The Stone is composed of a deep red Grit, requires Hardness by being exposed to the Air, and is serviceable in Buildings of all Kinds. The Arable Lands are comparatively very few.

The Process used in smelting and preparing the Ore varies at present but little from that described in the MSS of Dr. PARSONS, written about a Century ago, his full Account is thereto subjoined.

MANWOOD

* "... a fossil of a sort, the more common Sort, ... much attributed to the Magnes." "*Terra ferruginea, officinis ... amia ...* of ... the better Quality, called by the Mineralists *Ochre*..." a mixture Variety of forms ... stirred and tempered and tempered ... or the known Dies, very strongly attested by the Magnet. The first Class Collection of small cylindrical Columns, occasioned by the Moulding, like Icicles, an Issue of Fumour from the Midst which the Tipes ...

† The solid part flaming and glossy Appearance, crackles much when drawn, the Fire, has issue hereof and is not left at a time other Sorts.

‡ ... "Rex habuit unum Forum ... tempore actu Operatore, in nemore *Nemus* diffusa in nemore, aped se Forges." ... "Dom. Rex de his ... requiritur in nemore ... Item Dom... ad habit de quibus Fabrica Abbas qua dicitur certus ..."
"... in ob. & commiqua Domini Rex capit de Mine ponitur ad nutum sua Servientis."
MS. Har.... in the Library of *Lincoln Inn*
From these same MSS it appears that in a.... for ... forest two Forges were leased from the Crown, ... forge per Annum a Lit. Dom. R. gis vis fol. & forge operatis p. annum ...

§ "DEAN FORREST

" The Forest of *Dean* comprehendeth that Part of *Gloucestershire* that ... between two Rivers *Wye*, and *Severn*, containing ... at least 20000 Acres, besides the *Lea Bayley*, which is 400 Acres more, and of Coppices and mean Lands thereunto belonging ... appertaining to the Purlieus were mentioned as waste and of little ... 7000 Acres more. So that the whole Dimensions of the Level cometh to at least 27000 Acres, whole Soil is extremely rich in Clay, and in the Winter deep and miry, but in the Summer dry and productive. Vid Phil. Trans. No. ... p 291

* The Springs of the Forest are for the most Part of a Ferruginous Colour, as Col. Coel ... occasioned either by the Veins of Okre of which there is a great plenty, or else through the richly Impregnated of the Materials of the Ore, which superabound in the Forest.
The Ground of the Forest is more inclined to Wood and Coles than Corn, yet they have much of the latter.

* The Inhabitants are some of them a Sort of robust, wild People that are not to be civilized by good Discipline and Government.
The Ore and Cinder wherewith they make their Iron (which is the great Employment of the poorer Sort) is plentiful, as dug in most Parts of the Forest, as one the Level, and some parts in very high Lands.

* For whether by virtue of the Forest Laws or other Custom, the Level or all of the Forest or other Laws doth ... him provided, lives or born in the Hundred of St. *Briavels*, may claim by Men-Courts or whoever, either to dig out Iron-stone or Forest, and dig ore out of Ore and Cinders without any Prohibition.

" There are two Sorts of Ore, the best Ore is your Brush Ore of a bluish Colour, very ponderous, and full of little ... pecks the Grain of Silver, this affordeth the richest Quantity of Iron, but being melted doth produce a ... iron mettle but the Iron ... by this Inconvenience that it will be Cold-shore, which they call being red-share, whereby the Iron may be broken but the Rest of the Ore, after the melting hath been a ... which answers the ... best and the more Quantity ... it the colder Temper of Iron-mettle, for which these are prepared before they are brought to the Forge.

" But this is to be noted, that in former Time, when this Work were few and in Vent small, they used ... of ... the Below ... such as were moved in the Stream of Neat Level Water of their Iron ... mould less ... in them ... the Furnaces are lower go forth hath in them only melted down the purer or Part of the Ore, respecting ... red and ... and not worth their Charge, that they call ... Cinders, and is now found an an excessive Quantity throughout all the Parts of the Country where any Furnaces have been wont to be, which ...

" When they had prepared their Ore, then to Work it reduce to a ... fire to ... it up to the top with Coal and Ore ... full of Proportion in to their ... they leave it ... Coal be called and burn renew the Kilns ... with ... Coals ... without ... in ... Coal ... and ... to ... one the ... the Sides of ... the ... and ... but down ... heat ... within, which are two or other Mettle to ... their Iron ... which be ... said ... about twenty or ... to green the other ... and ... thirty ... their walls and ... such as ... where it is wasted, which is about the Mouth, the Top and Bottom having ... Coppers ... to ... the Lead the ...

MANWOOD (cap I p 6) states that certain Officers are necessary to the Constitution of all Forests to hold the Courts for the due Execution of the Forest Laws These have been in immemorial Usage in the Forest of *Dean*, and peculiar to it is a Court of *Free Miners*, who exercise an independent Jurisdiction

The great Officer is the LORD WARDEN, by Patent, during the King's Pleasure He is the Keeper of the Deer only, and has for himself no Salary, but receives 21*l* a Year from the Treasury, for the [illegible] the Conservators To this Office is annexed the Constableship of the Castle and Hundred of *St Briavels*, from which arises a rent Charge of 40*l* a Year, which is allowed to the Keepers

SIX DEPUTY WARDENS, who preside alternately at the Court of Free Miners

FOUR VERDERERS, whose Duty it is to preserve the Vert* and Venison of the Forest, to prevent Purpresture, Waste, and Assart, and to inflict Penalties where committed Elected by the Freeholders of the County at large They have each an annual Claim of two Fat Deer

CONSERVATOR,

" Egg Behind the Furnace are placed two high Pair of Bellows whose Noses meet at a little Hole near the Bottom [illegible]
" compressed together by certain Buttons placed on the Axis of a very large wheel, which is turned about with [illegible]
" Manner [illegible] Mill As soon as these Buttons are slid off the Bellows are raised again by a Counterpoise of Weights,
" whereby they [illegible] to play alternately, the one giving its Blast while the other is rising
" At first they fill these Furnaces with Ore and Cinder intermixt with Fuel, which in these Works is always [illegible]
" them hollow at the Bottom, that they may the more easily take Fire But after they are once kindled, the Materials run [illegible]
" get [illegible] hard Cake or Lump which is sustained by the Furnace, and through this the Mettal [illegible]
" the Receivers which are placed at the Bottom, where there is a passage open, by which they take away the Scum and [illegible]
" to let out their Mettal as they see Occasion
Before the Mouth of the Furnace lies a great bed of Sand where they make Furrows of the Fashion [illegible]
" their Iron into them when the Receivers are full they let in their Mettal which is made [illegible] by the Violence of
" the Fire, that it not only runs to a considerable Distance, but stands afterwards boiling [illegible] while
" After these Furnaces are once at Work, they keep them constantly employed for many Months together never suffering
" the Fire to slacken Night or Day, but still supplying the waste of Fuel and other Materials with fresh poured in at the
" Top
" Several Attempts have been made to bring in the Use of the Sea Coal in these Works instead of Charcoal, the [illegible]
" [illegible] the latter not [illegible] a great Expence, but hitherto they have proved ineffectual,
" Workmen finding by Experience that a Sea Coal Fire how vehement soever, will not penetrate the most [illegible]
" Ore by which Means they leave much of the Metal behind them unmelted
" From these Furnaces they bring the Sows and Piggs of Iron as they call them to their Forges [illegible]
" though they stand together under the same Roof one they call their Finery and the other Chafery both of them [illegible]
" Hearths upon which they place great Heaps of Sea Coal and behind them Bellows like those of the Furnaces but [illegible]
" near so large
" In their Fineries they first put these Piggs of Iron placing three or four of them together behind the Fire, with [illegible]
" of one End thrust into it where softening by Degrees they [illegible] work them [illegible] till the Mettal [illegible]
" together [illegible] a round Mass or Lump which they call an Half Bloom this they take out, and giving it [illegible]
" their Sledges they [illegible] to a great weighty Hammer raised likewise by the Motion of a Water Wheel [illegible]
" dexterously to the Blows they presently beat it into a thick short square [illegible]
" and [illegible] work it under the same Hammer till it comes to the Shape of a Bar in the middle with [illegible]
" the Ends [illegible] Heatings in the Chafery and more Workings under the Hammer, [illegible]
" [illegible] their Iron into Bars of several Shapes, in which [illegible] they expose them to Sale
All their principal Iron undergoes the aforementioned Preparations, yet for several Uses Purposes [illegible]
" neys Hearths, or Ovens, and the like they have a Sort of cast Iron, which they take out of the Receivers of the Furnaces
" [illegible] melted in great Ladles and pour it into the Moulds of fine Sand in like Manner [illegible]
" and softer Metal, but this Sort of Iron is so very brittle, that being heated, with one blow of a Hammer it breaks all to
" Pieces
Now although this Fault be most found in this Sort of Iron, yet as in the Working the best Sort of Iron they omit any
" [illegible] will be found want some Part of its toughness, which they esteem its Perfection
" Of the Oak in the Forest of *Dean* see EVELYN'S Works, p [illegible]
" MR [illegible] of the same Forest, that in the Reign of Queen ELIZABETH [illegible]
" [illegible] to have (by private Interest) this Wood destroyed but what was not done by those Means, was by [illegible]
" before [illegible] exposed to Sale for Fuel and other Uses

" [illegible] and yellow Ochre the chiefest of which Pits are in *Pecan Cross*, *Little Dean*
" In several Parts of the Forest there are Quarries of [illegible] Grindstones, and Wheel stones [illegible]
" [illegible]

" In the [illegible] King CHARLES I there was a Lord High Constable of the Forest a Lord Chief Justice [illegible]
Officers, [illegible]

1 The [illegible] Centre of the Forest between *Dan' More* and *K[illegible]*
2 [illegible] which [illegible] the upper End of *[illegible] Marsh*, [illegible] the [illegible]
3 *Hat* [illegible]
4 [illegible]
D[illegible] [illegible] upon the *Old [illegible]* near *Lidney*
[illegible] [illegible] from the [illegible]

[illegible]
[illegible]
[illegible]
[illegible] Ball [illegible] Oxon

* [illegible] Woods that are Coverts The *Venison* is every Beast of the Forest and Chase [illegible]
[illegible] MANWOOD, p 6

[illegible]

CONSERVATOR, appointed by the Lords of the Treasury, with a Salary of 64*l* 16*s* a Year His Office is to inspect and preserve the Timber, he employs six Keepers *, who have their distinct Walks or Districts

In the Forest are seven WOODWARDSHIPS, which are held by hereditary Grants Of, 1 *Sarton* and *Bicknor*, 2 *The Bearse*, 3 *Magna Dene* and *Lea Bayley*, 4 *Blakeney*, 5 *Ruar Dene*, 6 *Abbey*, 7 *Blyth's Bayley* The Perquisites of these are the Lop and Top of all felled Timber and all windfall and dotard Trees (*sicca & vento profrata*) within their respective Bailywicks

The CHIEF and eight FORESTERS IN FEE

The CHIEF FORESTER is Bow-bearer to the King He has no Salary, but claims to be entitled to ten Bucks and ten Does in each Season, and to the right Shoulder of every Deer killed in the Forest As Bow-bearer, to attend the King, with a Bow and Arrow, and six stout Bowmen cloathed in green, whenever he hunts within the Forest, and has an unlimited Right of Hunting, Hawking, and Fishing

The GAVELLER †, or Keeper of the King's Gawles, to whom a Fee of 5*s* is due from every free Miner on the opening of new Mines Appointed by the Lords of the Treasury

PRESENT OFFICERS OF THE FOREST OF *Dean*

Lord Warden and Constable of St Briavel's,

Right Hon Frederick Augustus Earl of Berkeley.

Deputy Wardens,

Sir John Guise, Bart
Sir Thomas Crawley Boevey, Bart.
John Colchester, Esq
Edmund Probyn, Esq.
Roynon Jones, Esq
Joseph Pyrke, Esq

Verdurers,

Sir John Guise, Bart.
Edmund Probyn,
Roynon Jones,
Joseph Pyrke, Esqrs.

Conservator,

Roynon Jones, Esq

Woodwards,

William Hall, Lord Viscount Gage,
Charles Edwyn Esq
John Colchester, Esq

George Savage, Esq
Mary and Jane Clarke, Spinsters,
Edmund Probyn, Esq.
John Beale, Gent

Chief Forester in Fee and Bow bearer,

Charles Edwyn, Esq

Foresters in Fee,

Mayor and Burgesses of the City of *Gloucester*,
Mary and Jane Clarke, Spinsters, of the
 Hill Common,
Thomas Foley, Esq
Heirs of Ralph Cohler,
Heirs of Thomas Williams,
Heirs of John Ayres,
Heirs of Sir Robert Gunning, Knight,
Heirs of Henry Yearsley

Gaveller,

George Cæsar Hopkinson, Esq

Steward of the Swannimote,

John Mathews, Attorney at Law

Three Courts are necessarily held for the Government of all Forests, *viz*

1 The Court of *Attachment*, who take Cognizance in all Causes "*de viridi & venatione*," Vert and Venison, enroll the Offenders, in order to present them at the Justice Seat They have a power of Inquiry, but not of Conviction, and are required to meet once in forty Days

2 The Court of *Swannimote* ‡, held likewise before the Verdurers, by the Steward of the Swannimote thrice in the Year Here the Freeholders are summoned to make Inquests and empanel Juries

"*Purpresture*, from the Norman '*pourpris*,' *conseptum*, an Inclosure, but more properly an Incroachment"
 at Ma woor cap X

Affor "Verche when that the pleasant Woods of the Foreste, or thicke bushie Hedges are cut or the lusty feedings of
" wild Beastes, be cutte down, destroyed, or plucked uppe by the Rotes into the same Ground be made Plaine, and turned
" into arable Land This by the Lawes of the Foreste is properly said to be an Affiart or Land affiarted"
 " *Waste* is a Worde chieflie in Use amongst Lawyers, and was brought into this Lande by the Normans, being derived from
" the French Verbe 'gaster' i e wastare to lay waste Ibid cap IX pp 47 49

* These inhabit six Lodges, the King's, York, Worcester, Danby, Herbert, Latimer, with a Salary each of 25*l* a Year
† From "Gavol," in Anglo Saxon, a Tribute, though stated to have been an ancient Office none upon Record prior to 1660
‡ This Term is derived by Lord Coke from the Saxon "Spein," Servant, and "Mote, or Emore," a Court alluding to its being a Court of the Officers of the Forest, and preparatory to the Justice Seat

3 The *Juſtice Seat*, ſummoned by the Chief Juſtice in Eyre South of *Trent*, once only in three Years. Before this Court are heard and determined all Cauſes which reſpect the Franchiſes and Privileges of the Foreſt, and the Treſpaſſes againſt them. Prior to which, the Regarders, or Commiſſioners, muſt inſpect and review the whole Foreſt, in order to make due Preſentments.

All which Courts uſually aſſemble at the King's Lodge, more commonly called the "*Speech Houſe*," ſituate nearly in the Centre of the Foreſt.

Beſide theſe are two others, peculiar to the Foreſt of *Dean*, viz the Court of *Record* for the Hundred of *St Briavel's* (already mentioned in the Account of the Caſtle) and that of the *Free Miners*

The *Mine Law* Court, however ancient, has not been recorded in the Archives of the Foreſt before 1635, 10 CAR I when PHILIP Earl of PEMBROKE, as Conſtable of *St. Briavel's*, claimed to preſide It conſiſts of the Gaveller and a Jury of forty eight Free Miners, who muſt be Natives of the Hundred, and have been employed in a Mine at leaſt for the Space of a Year and a Day Their Privileges are to enact and enforce Bye Laws in remedy of Grievances, or for Accommodation, with the unanimous Conſent of the Jury, and to cut *Wood, but not Timber*, excepting for ſinking the Mines, as well in the Lands of private Perſons, as in the King's Soil, and to ſearch for Ore It has been computed that not leſs than 100 Tons of Wood are conſumed yearly From a late Report of the Gaveller, made to the Commiſſioners for enquiring into the State of the Foreſt, it appears that "there is at preſent no Iron Mine regularly "worked, that 121 Coal Pits produce weekly 1816 Tons, and that the Compoſitions of 662 Free Miners "amount to 215l 8s *per Annum*" This laſt Circumſtance is occaſioned by the frequency of opening new Mines, which is done as ſoon as they are prevented by Water, which commonly happens at a ſhallow Depth As yet, they have not erected Engines of modern Invention, ſo uſeful in other Collieries, and oppoſe every Innovation, as perhaps eventually ſubverſive of their ancient and eſtabliſhed Rights.

XCII. DEERHURST, OR DEORHURST.

AT *Deorhyrste* in the first Periods of the *Saxon* Heptarchy a Cell for Religious was established by DODO, a tributary Prince of the Kingdom of *Mercia*, and much may be collected from the early Chroniclers both of its ecclesiastical and military History.

THE Parish of *Deerhurst* is nearly of a circular Form, the chief of its own Hundred *, and of large Extent. It is distant three Miles South from *Tewkesbury*, and eight from GLOUCESTER on the North. The Soil near the River *Severn* is of a deep Clay, applied more generally to Pasture, and subject to frequent Inundations, but it varies on the higher Grounds †. Upon the Banks of the *Severn* a Tract of Commonable Lands extends for four Miles. A few Years since, the Inhabitants of the adjoining Parish of *Leigh* sunk a Ditch to divide the Commons, but, on being sued, were obliged to relinquish their Plan.

THE Æra of the Foundation ‡ of the Priory of *Deerhurst* is placed about 750, when DODO, already the Founder of *Tewkesbury*, in respect to the Memory of his Brother ALMARICK, who had lived and was interred here, erected over his Grave a stately Chapel, and established a Fraternity of Priests. These were soon dispersed, and the Structure demolished by the Ravages of the *Danes*, but re-built in 980, though it remained in an unflourishing State till it was given by EDWARD the CONFESSOR (1056) to the Abbey of *St Dennis* in *France*, to which it became a Cell of *Benedictine* Monks, and was confirmed to them in 1069 by WILLIAM the CONQUEROR. It possessed eight Lordships, and was accounted worth 300 Marks a Year, when it was sold by the Abbot and Convent of *St Dennis* to RICHARD Earl of CORNWALL in 1250. In 1388, 11 RIC II. some Pretence was found for seizing their Lands, and they were granted to JOHN DE BEAUCHAMP, of *Holte*. It does not appear that they were inherited by that Family, for in 1418, 2 HEN V. when the Alien Priories were dissolved, this was stated to be "Prioratus Indigena," and consequently not subject to that Statute. In the first Year of the next Reign, on the Petition of the Convent and HUGH MACASON the last Prior Alien, the Monastery of *St Dennis* was divested of its Right, and the Nomination of the Prior conferred on the Convent, the Patronage of which was given to the Abbey of *Tewkesbury*. Yet, in the 19th of his Reign, King HENRY VI. endowed his College at *Eaton* with Parcel of their Revenues. The Denization was however revoked by EDWARD the Fourth, who first detached these Lands from *Eaton*, and settled them on the College of *Fotheringhay*, then restored them to *Eaton*, and lastly to *Tewkesbury*. Continued Law-suits were carried on between these Ecclesiastics till the Reign of HENRY the Seventh, when the last mentioned obtained the entire Possession of *Deerhurst*. At the Dissolution in 1543, 34 HEN VIII. it was purchased as Parcel of *Tewkesbury* by WILLIAM THROCKMORTON, and had a yearly Rental, which in the Valuations was included in that of *Tewkesbury*. To JOHN BROMSGROVE, the last Prior, a Pension was assigned of 13*l*. 6*s*. 8*d*. annually. The Site, and an Estate consequently exempt from Tythes, was purchased in the last Century by the noble

* "At the Time of the *Norman* Survey there were more Hundreds than at present, consequently those which now remain do "not always contain the same Places as at that Time, nor do the *Norman* Hundreds always contain 100 Villages. This has "introduced still greater Confusion into Domesday-book." WARTON's *Kiddington*, p. 31. n.

† "The rising Grounds of *Deerhurst* are covered with a red Loam, a remarkable Species of Soil, common to the Hillocks "of the lower *Severn* District, and to the inferior Hills of *Herefordshire*. It is here called "Red Land," and resembles the little "Red Hill of *Nottinghamshire*." MARSHALL's Rur. Econ. of Glouc. vol. I. p. 66.

‡ "DEIRHURSTE IN GLOCESTERSHIR.

"It standith as *Severne* Ryver cummith downe *in læva ripa* a Mile beneth *Theokesbyri*. The Site of the Towne [illegible] "[illegible] Meddow. So that when *Severne* much riseth the Water commith almoste [illegible] the Towne. It is to be sup"posed [illegible] of olde Tyme lesse subjecte to Waters, and that the Bottom of *Severne* then deeper without chokinge of Sandes "[illegible] Houses. It is now but a poore Village, and the Lordship longged a late [illegible] the Abbat of *Tewke*"[illegible] *Persore* had was longging to *Persore* Abbay tyl WILLIAM CONQUEROR gave it away. *Deirhurste* Priory "[illegible] that the House of *Deirhurste* was [illegible] from the Monasterie of *St Dionise* [illegible] "[illegible] Monk of *St Dionise*, was the last Priour there there [illegible] "[illegible] Tyme [illegible] and moste of the Landes of it given *Fotheringay* and *Eton* College [illegible] "[illegible] and the Abbay of *Theokesbyri*, [illegible] "[illegible] the Priorie of [illegible] longgin then newly to *Teokesbyri*, [illegible] with the Landes to *Fotheringay* College "[illegible] mention that yn his Tyme there was a notable Abbay at *Deirhurste* [illegible] "[illegible] as it is said to *Malverne*. The [illegible] Order was [illegible] "[illegible] Bow Shot [illegible] North of the Towne. There [illegible] "[illegible] *Sheperdes* [illegible] and other. But the Buildings of them be gone. There be yet [illegible] "[illegible] Scripture [illegible]" LELAND's Itin. vol. VI. pp. 78, 79.

[illegible]

Family of COVENTRY * GEORGE Earl of COVENTRY was created Viscount DEERHURST, by Patent, bearing Date Apr. 26, 1697, 9 WILL III †

The Church of *Deerhurst* exercises a peculiar Jurisdiction over the following Parishes " *Corse, Forthampton, Hasfield, Leigh, Staverton, Boarngton*, and *Tirley*" These claim archidiaconal Visitation at their Mother Church, and had no Right of Sepulture in their own Cemeteries till confirmed by the Priors The Benefice is unusually small, being only a stipendiary Curacy of 6*l* 13*s* 4*d* a Year, due from the Impropriation, it has been twice augmented by Queen ANNE's Bounty The Family of THROGMORTON continued the Impropriators for several Descents, of whom it was held by the FERMORS Sir JOHN POWELL, Knight, a Justice of the King's Bench in the beginning of the present Century, became the Possessor, and dying in 1713 bequeathed it with other considerable Estates to JOHN SNELL, Esq his Nephew, whose Representative is POWELL SNELL, Esq of *Guiting Grange*

Of the Structure of the Church, dedicated to the *Holy Trinity* and *St Dennis*, the present dilapidated State leaves much room for Conjecture It has a very lofty Nave and Chancel, with two low Aisles, and a Tower at the West End, upon which was a Spire, blown down in 1666

Here was certainly a more ancient Building, with which this is connected Circular *Saxon* Arches are incorporated into the Walls, but the Arches now seen are pointed, the capitals of the Pillars foliated, and the Windows square, a *Style of the later Gothic* Adjoining, and communicating with the Chancel, are Remains of the Priory, now modernized The old Inhabitants of the Village describe a very spacious Hall and other Apartments, which formed the Quadrangle, at this Time almost in Ruins

Prior to the Conquest the Manor was held by the Abbey of *Pershore* in *Worcestershire*, from which it was at that Time forcibly taken and given to the Monks of *Westminster* Their Right was interrupted by ROBERT FITZ HAMAN, but recovered by Law in the Reign of HENRY the Second From that Period till the Dissolution it formed a Part of their Revenues, which were granted to the See of *Westminster* by HENRY the Eighth, and confirmed to the Dean and Chapter by Queen ELIZABETH

In this Parish are four Hamlets, viz

1 *Aperley*, anciently belonging to the Abbey of *Westminster* A considerable Estate, long vested in the Family of LANE, was bequeathed by the last of them to CAPEL PAYNE, Esq in 1755 ‡ A reputed and distinct Manor in *Aperley*, with a capital Messuage, and 400 Acres of Land, were held by EDWARD BRUGES in the Reign of HENRY the Sixth He was succeeded by the Family of THROCKMORTON, from whom it came to POWELL and SNELL

2 *Wightfield* From GILBERT LE DESPENCER this Estate passed to Sir JOHN CASSEY, Knight, Chief Baron of the Exchequer, who died in 1400, 1 HEN IV In 1468 9 EDW IV JOHN CASSEY, Esq was Sheriff of this County This Family retained it till the beginning of the last Century, which is now inherited from Judge POWELL by POWELL SNELL, Esq

3 *Walton* A Manor held likewise under the Church at *Westminster*, which includes, 4 *Hardwick*, of the same Description, which were held by many Descents of the Family of HARRIS, afterward resident in GLOUCESTER

THOMAS DOWDESWELL, of *Pull Court*, as Lessee, holds Courts for *Plaistowe* in this Parish, which have Jurisdiction over all the Manors in the lower Division of the Hundred of *Westminster* In this District all the abovementioned Hamlets are contained, the Convent having procured most of their Possessions in this County to be thus incorporated

The chief Estates in this Parish are vested in the Right Honourable GEORGE Earl of COVENTRY, and the Families of SNELL, PAYNE, and HYETT, of *Painswick*

* See TANNER's Notitia Monastica GLOUCESTERSH No 10 edit NASMITH DUGDALE's Monasticon tom I pp [illegible] 547 tom II p [illegible] [illegible] Historiae de [illegible] Vol Royal de S *Dennis Paris*, Append n cxv In ATKINS's GLOUCESTERSHIRE, pp [illegible] 25, 36, 36[illegible] 3[illegible] 380 4[illegible] 430 460 49[illegible] 537 608 687 788 797 and 847 concerning Manors Impropriations, [illegible] belonging to this Priory, [illegible] GLOUCESTER, [illegible] *St Dennis*, *Compton Parva* [illegible] *Deerhurst*, *Elmstone* [illegible] [illegible] *Hasfield* [illegible] *Leigh* [illegible] *Preston*, *Hawe* [illegible] *Wilford* and *Woolstone*, in this County In NASH's *Worcestershire* vol I p 43 of the Advowson of [illegible] In STEVENS's Supplement vol I p 27, [illegible] EDW II n 17 [illegible] apud *Deerhurst* &c FULLER's [illegible] Hist Book VI p 303 [illegible] *Coventry*

† ATKINS relates, that the following Inscription was placed over the Gate

"Hanc Aulam [illegible] DODO Dux [illegible] Ecclesiam ad Honorem Beatae MARIAE Virginis ob amorem fratris sui ALMARICI"

And in the Year 167[illegible] [illegible] was discovered, which was thus inscribed

"ODDA Dux [illegible] Aulam [illegible] atque dedicari [illegible] S Trinitatis pro Anima Germani sui ELFRICI que [illegible] de hoc loco assumpta est EALDREDUS vero Episcopus qui eandem dedicavit [illegible] Aprilis, XIV [illegible] anno Regni [illegible] WARDI Regis [illegible]

‡ WILLIAM [illegible] LA MARE made a Deed of Gift to the Hospital of *St Bartholomew* in GLOUCESTER of two Circets of Wheat (16 Bushels) to be paid yearly from his Farm at *Apperley*, alias *Happerle*

In

In the Year 1016 a very memorable Treaty was proposed at *Deerhurst*, where the Armies of ED-MUND IRONSIDE and CANUTE the *Dane** were drawn up in order of Battle on either Side the *Severn* The Division of the Kingdom was ratified between them in a small Island called *Oilney*, or *Olney*, but as there is another of the same Name near GLOCESTER, Historians are not agreed, they are however unanimous in asserting that the Truce was completed at *Deerhurst*

BENEFACTIONS

Dr ROBERT HUNTINGTON, Bishop of *Raphoe* in *Ireland*, gave a Rent Charge of 2l. a Year, payable out of Lands, for the apprenticing poor Boys alternately with the Parish of *Leg*

SARAH ROBERTS left Lands, the annual Produce of which now is 2 to be distributed in Bread, on *St Thomas's Day*, amongst such Poor as do not receive weekly pay

CURATES	PATRONS	CURATES	PATRONS
1682 George Styles,	—— Farmer, Esq	1746 Will Palmer, B A	Bishop of GLOCESTER
171 * * *	* * * * *	1750 Charles Bishop, B A	The same
1730 Rich Bashington,	Bishop of GLOCESTER	1773 Will Davies, Clerk,	The same

PRESENT LORD OF THE MANORS,
Of *Deerhurst* and *Plaistow*,
THOMAS DOWDESWELL, Esq

The Persons summoned from this Place and his Hamlets by the Heralds, in 1682 and 1683, were

Edward Harris, Gent of *Walton*   William Lane, Gent of *Apurly*
Edward Smith, Gent   George Banister, Gent
Roger Mortimer, Gent

At the Election in 1776, Thirty-two Freeholders polled from this Parish

The Register begins in 1558, and in 1698 has the following Entry

" The King's Dues upon Marriages, Births, and Burials, were paid until the 20th of October, " 1698, and likewise Batchelors and Widowers," which proves that Tax to be no new Expedient for the Supply of Government

ANNUAL ACCOUNT OF MARRIAGES, BIRTHS, AND BURIALS, IN THIS PARISH

A D	Mar	Bir	Bur	A D	Mar	Bir	Bur	A D	Mar	Bir	Bur	A D	Mar	Bir	Bur
1781	3	23	16	1786	2	18	17	1791				1796			
1782	4	26	16	1787	2	11	11	1792				1797			
1783	1	18	10	1788	5	10	6	1793				1798			
1784	3	13	15	1789				1794				1799			
1785	6	13	31	1790				1795				1800			

INSCRIPTIONS IN THE CHURCH

ON A LARGE GREY MARBLE, THE EFFIGIES OF A MAN IN HIS JUDGE'S ROBES, AT HIS FEET A LION A WOMAN IN THE DRESS OF THE TIMES, AT HER FEET A GREYHOUND OVER THEIR HEADS THE FIGURES OF CHRIST AND St ANNE INSTRUCTING THE VIRGIN FOUR CORNER ESCUTCHEONS, TWO REMAINING †

1 Argent, a Chevron between three Falcons Heads erased Gules, for CASSEY 2 Three Lions passant in Pale

Hic jacet Johes Cassey, Miles, quondam capitalis Baro' Es'cary D'm Regis qui obiit Et XXX die Mau, Anno D'm MCCCC, & Alicia uxor ejus, quor' a'i bus p piciet' Deus. Amen

---

* Ambo reges ad horum qui *Deerhurst* non mutato in unum convenerunt ...

ON A FLAT BLUE STONE INLAID WITH BRASS, THE FIGURE OF A WOMAN IN THE DRESS OF THE TIMES. FOUR CORNER ESCUTCHEONS, ONE ONLY REMAINING

Quarterly, 1 and 4 Argent, a Cross Sable, charged with a Leopard's Face in the Centre Or, BRUGES 2 DE CHANDOS 3 BERKELEY, of *Coberley*

Here lyethe Elyzabethe Rowdon, sumtyme Wyffe to Wyll'm Caffey, of Whyghtfylde, Efquyer, after the Dethe of the fayde Wyll'm was maryed to Walter Rowdon, Efquyer, and was Doughter to Thomas Bruges, of Coberle, Efquyer, which Elizabethe dyed the FFU Day of Januarie, Anno D'ni P̃D.x, for whofe Soule of your Charitie fay a Pater Nofter.

ON FLAT STONES IN THE CHANCEL

Arms, Argent, a Fefs Sable, between three Lions Heads erafed Gules, for FERMOR, —impaling, Argent, three Bars Sable, and in chief three Martletts of the fecond, for CARILL

Hic jacet ELIZABETHA, uxor
Petri Fermor, Armigeri,
te march e hujus Manerii,
Filia JOANNIS CARILL,
de Langley Surria, Armiger,
& ex nobiliffima profapia comitum
Kingtordiæ, oriunda
piiffime obiit ficut
VIXIT II Junii, Anno 1677

Here lyeth the Body of
PETER FERMOR, fecond Son to
HENRY FERMOR, Efq
of Tufmore in Oxfordfhire
He dy Fort the 6th Day of December,
Anno Domini 1641

Arms, Barry of fix Or and Azure, an Inefcutcheon Ermine, on a Chief of the firft, three Palletts between two Gyronnies of the fecond, for MORTIMER, —impaling, Barry of ten Argent and Azure, over all a Lion rampant Gules, for STRATFORD

Here lyeth the Body of
ELIZABETH, the Wife of Roger MORTIMER, Gent.
who departed this Life the 10th Day of January,
Anno Domini 1652.

Here alfo lyeth the Body of
Roger MORTIMER, Gent
who departed this Life the
25th Day of June, Anno Dom 1683

ON A MONUMENT IN THE NORTH AISLE

Arms, Per Pale Azure and Gules three Saltires Or, in the Centre a Mullet of the firft, for LANE

Near the Pew
lie the Remains of WILLIAM LANE, Efq
late of Apperley in this Parifh,
who departed this Life
Auguft, 17, aged 6 Years

ON FLAT STONES

Arms, on three Efcutcheons, 1ft, Parti Per Pale Gules and Azure, three Lions rampant Or, for POWELL 2d, Per Pale Argent and Gules a Lion rampant Sable for ROBERTS 3d, Azure, three Lozenges in Fefs Or, for FREEMAN

MARGARET, the Wife of
JAMES POWELL, Efq Daughter of
JOHN ROBERTS, of Fiddington, Gen
deceafed Sept 5, 1656
M D Q P
KEMMET FREEMAN

THOMAS CLUTTERBOOK,
of Leonard Stanley, Gent
died the 2 d of February, 1656

Here lyeth the Body of
JOHN POWELL, of the City of Gloucefter, Efq
who departed this Life the Day of Nov 1665

Here lieth the Body of
EDWARD GAY, Gent who married
FRANCES, the eldeft Daughter of
JOHN COTHERIDGE, Efq and had by her
fix Sonnes and one Daughter, and was
here buried the fixth Day of
December, Anno 1612

Arms, MORTIMER as before —impaling Ermine, on a Bend Gules, three Eagles difplayed Or, for BACHOT

ELIZABETH, the Wife of
EDMUND MORTIMER, died the 12th Day of
November, Anno Dom 1650

JOSEPH, Son of JOSEPH and ANN WINTLE,
of Hatlow,
died Auguft 8, 1753, aged 12

Alfo ANN, Wife of JOSEPH WINTLE,
died July 20, 1754, aged 48

JOSEPH WINTLE, of Phutlow,
died Oct 30, 1770 aged 51

WILLIAM DUTTER, late of Phutlow,
departed this Life the 25th Day of
January, 1709, aged 47

WILLIAM, Son of
WILLIAM and ANN DUTTER,
died an Infant

Alfo Mrs ANN DUTTER,
Relict of THOMAS WINTLE, of Phutlow,
and late Wife of Mr WILLIAM DUTTER
died Jun 7, 1715, in the 67th Year of her Age

J N

JOHN HERRING
died June 17, 1704, aged 56

PARRY, the Son of JOHN and JOYCE HERRING,
departed this Life the 4th of June, 1689

JOYCE, Wife of RICHARD SCANDRETT,
died August 13, 1694, aged 68

RICHARD, Son of JOHN and JOYCE HERRING,
died an Infant

Hic inhumatur Corpus GEORGII STILES,
hujus Paroch e Clericus
Viginti & novem Annis
Octo trigesimo die Septembris,
Anno Salutis 1711, ætatis 67

ON FLAT STONES IN THE NAVE

Thomas Cox of this Place,
departed this Life the 14th Day of March, 1736,
aged 6.

Mary, the Daughter of
Thomas and Susanna Cox,
departed this Life the 31st of August, 1738,
aged 1.

Susanna, Wife of the aforenamed
Thomas Cox, departed this Life
January the 31st, 1739, aged 61

Mary, Wife of Thomas Cox
died November the 11th, 1750, aged 7

George their Son
died June 23, 1748, an Infant

Thomas Cox, late of Apperley, Gent
died the 24th of May, 17 . . , aged 58

John Ireck, of Apperley
was buried the 7th of ot . . , 1685, aged 6

Susann his Wife
was buried March the 20th, 1703, aged . .
aged . . Years

Also SARAH Ireck her Daughter,
Relict of Arthur Ireck of
Kencheſter in com Hereford, Gent
was buried December 17, 1 . . , aged 6

Also three Grandchildren

MARY, Daughter of John and Mary Cox,
died July 7, 171 , aged .

Here lyeth, by his own express Desire,
the Body of THOMAS Church,
late of the City of Worcester, Baker,
who departed this Life July 26, 176 ,
in the 73d Year of his Age

IN THE CHURCH YARD, ON TOMBS

WILLIAM Peart,
late of the Eye,
died Oct. 29, 1750, aged 45

SAMUEL Healing, of Apperley in this Parish,
died March 10, 175 , aged 72

JOHN Healing, of Whitefield in this Parish,
died Feb 14, 1782, aged 3 ,

ON HEAD STONES

	Died	Aged		Died	Aged
Lawrence Cox, Yeoman	19 Jan 1751	52	Elizabeth, Wife of John Huck, of the Oak	27 May 1697	
Mary his Wife	1 Feb 1 .	72	John Huck, of the Oak Yeoman	12 June, 1 5 6	
Anne, Wife of Thomas Cox	4 Jan 1749	6	Giles Huck of this Parish, Yeoman	Jan 17	
Charles Cox, Gent late of Tewkesbury	16 Jun 1 6	52	Eleanor his Wife	May 74	60
Catharine, the Wife of John Cox Mercer, of Tewkesbury, and Daughter of George Whitmore of Cann Hall in the County of Stafford Esq	26 Jun 1763	3	John his Son	5 Feb 1 .	
			John Huck, of the Oak	20 Mar 1763	
			Susanna his Wife	1 Dec 55	
			William Huck	Apr 162	
Sarah Wife of Thomas Cox of this Parish and late Widow of Giles Surman	3 Mar 1766		Judith his wife	19 May 1743	14
			Edward Huck	2 Oct 1	
Thomas Cox	1 July, 175	73	Joseph Son of John and Susanna Huck of the Oak	2 Nov	3
Giles Surman	7 Apr 1	50	Susannah Nite	9 Feb	
Giles Surman	25 Aug 176	5	William Nite junr	5 May	
William Cox of the Parish Daughter of Thomas and Mary Cox, of Dumbleton	9 Oct 1758		Mary his Wife	2 Mar	
			Thomas Huck	1	
John Cox	11 Apr 175	69	Judith his Wife	1	
Mary his Wife	1 Aug 176	65	John his son	1	
John, Son of John and Ann Cox	3 Dec	5			
Sarah, Wife of William Cox	17 Feb 175				
Edmund Lovett of this Parish	4 Jun 1 3		Thomas Healing	1	
Elizabeth his Wife	8 Jul 175	60	Elizabeth Wife of John Healing	1	
John Lovett	17		John Healing	1	
Edith his Wife	8 Oct 1757	44	Healing	1	
William, Son of John and Edith Lovett	27 Feb 1765	20			
William Huck, of the Oak	9 July 1740	84	Healing	10	

ON HEAD STONES

	Died	Aged
John Haling -	31 July, 170-	77
Judith Daughter of Samuel and Judith Haling	13 Aug 1762	13
Richard Poff Yeoman -	14 Feb 1738	65
Elizabeth his Wife	10 Oct 1733	74
Isabel, Wife of William Eagles	18 Aug 1728	39
William Eagles	2 Jan 1742	52
William Haling	4 May 1782	71
Mary, Wife of William White	5 Mar 1754	50
Mary Wife of Joseph Sheppard	4 Aug 1750	47
John Creswell	29 Jun 1733	70
Mary his Wife -	6 Apr 1736	60
Capel Colchester	1 Apr 1718	54
Anna his Wife	20 Apr 1698	32
William Fewster	20 Sept 1720	86
Mary his Wife -	-7 July, ——	70
Thomas Hampton	7 Mar 1684	50
Elizabeth his Wife	2 Feb 1689	28
Thomas Hampton	17 Oct 1701	76
Margaret his Wife	9 Dec 1682	
Edmund Hampton -	12 Dec 1709	70
Mary his Wife	23 Dec 1704	64
John Hampton, of this Parish	25 Jun 1751	30
William Haynes	28 Oct 1738	65
Dinah, Wife of Stephen Lun	11 Jun 1741	63
Giles Hawker -	29 July, 1685	67
Alice his Wife	22 Mar 1686	
Francis Son of the Rev Francis Lamb -	13 Oct 1755	27
Elizabeth Marshall	— Apr 1743	23
Ann, Wife of Samuel Fox, of Bourton on the Water	16 Oct 1742	72
William Stone -	12 Apr 1761	56
Elizabeth his Wife	3 Mar 1759	
Elizabeth, Wife of Joseph Barnard	2 July 1734	42
William Barnard	14 Oct 1706	70
Sarah, Wife of William Thurston, and late Wife of William Barnard, of Handby Castle	1 Feb 1709	66
Jerrad Pope -	18 Mar 1696	66
Margaret his Wife	21 Jan 1687	59
Mary, Wife of William Allen	25 Mar 1749	32
Benjamin, Son of William and Mary Barnes	5 May 1727	25
Richard Smith Yeoman	6 Feb 1715	65
Joan, Wife of John Wintle	19 Nov 1761	59
Philipp Greenway	9 Dec 1716	93
Richard Beale	8 Nov 1702	67
Joan, Wife of Richard Beale, and late Wife of John Ashley	25 Apr 1711	61
Robert Evans	15 June, 1743	70
Sarah his Wife	3 Nov 1754	61
Thomas Evens - -	16 Oct 1764	75
Mary his Wife	27 Jan 1773	70

	Died	Aged
William Farmer	14 Apr 1782	—
William Farmer	8 Oct 17?7	4
Elizabeth, Wife of Charles Andrews	11 Sept 1760	4
James Gamon	1 Nov 173?	30
Ann Wife of James Gamon	24 June, 1778	83
William Brooks of Deerhurst Walton	3 Feb 1704	48
Joseph Gregory of this Parish	1 Mar 170?	
Elizabeth his Wife	3 Jan 1753	6?
Christopher Shayle, senior	2 Jan 1765	
Thomas his Son	25 July 1763	33
Henry Son of Thomas and Elizabeth Shayle	6 July, 1755	1
Thomas Shayle	10 Apr 1756	8?
William, Son of Henry and Jane Shayle	12 June, 1769	26
Elizabeth, Wife of Christopher Shayle	28 July, 1761	80
Mary, Wife of John Soders	1 Oct 173?	
Thomas Newman	4 Dec 1784	63
Martha, Wife of William Newman, of Apperley	21 Dec 1767	6
William Newman, of Apperley	July, 1781	63
Thomas Butt	6 Nov 1683	
Robert, Son of Thomas and Margaret Butt	9 Oct 1690	8
Edward Munn	6 Dec 1685	
Elizabeth Wife of Edward Munn	8 Jun 1734	40
Edward their Son	8 Jun 1708	
William Windows -	1 Nov 1756	40
Sarah his Wife, and late Wife of Thomas Fluck	26 Oct 1758	71
Elizabeth Lane	30 Dec 1709	8
Sarah Wife of William Clark or	26 Sept 1709	8
William Whithorne	17 May, 174?	
Mary his Wife -	2 July, 175?	54
William Brooks	3 Feb 1764	
Sarah, Wife of William Webb	26 Oct 170?	
Mary, Wife of William Price	12 Aug 1766	63
Philippa, Wife of Thomas Dipper	— Apr 175?	47
William Dipper, senior	30 Sept 1716	57
Hannah, Wife of William Dipper late of Apperley	— Nov 176?	
William Dipper, Yeoman	24 May, 1769	80
Mary, Wife of Robert Witts, first the Wife of Thomas Evens	— Feb 17??	6?
Isaac Pearce	16 Apr 17?5	6?
Thomas Etheridge, senior	13 Apr 17??	6?
Thomas Etheridge, junior	7 May, 1735	
Thomas Dovey	19 June, 1742	5?
Richard Nelmes -	8 Nov 1751	
Esther his Wife	11 Dec 1760	
Richard their Son	21 Dec 1752	
Richard Jones -	11 Jun 1723	
Mary his Wife	2 Nov 1741	62

XCIII. DEINTON, or DEYNTON,

MORE antiently *DONNINGTUNE* though fubfequently to the *Domefday* Survey, in which it does not occur, but as *DIDINTONE*

The Parifh of *Deynton* conftitutes a Part of the united Hundreds of *Langhy* and *Swinefhead*, is nearly three Miles long and two broad, fix Miles from *Sodbury* on the South, four from *Marfhfield* on the Weft, and thirty five in a foutherly Direction from *Gloucefter* The Soil is light and loamy, chiefly Pafturage, with an inconfiderable Proportion of arable Lands At *Bitton* the River *Boyd* interfecting this Parifh runs in Confluence with the *Avon*

The Benefice is rectorial, with an extenfive Glebe, in the Patronage of the Crown, and comprifed within the Deanery of *Hawkefbury*

The Church, dedicated to the *Holy Trinity*, is conftructed with a Nave, North Aifle, and a low em-battled Tower The dividing Arches are maffy and pointed, of early Architecture THOMAS COKER, M A Rector, re-built the Chancel in 1767, and the Nave was lengthened and modernized about two Years fince By the fame Incumbent the Rectory Houfe was erected in a commodious and elegant Style

The Manor was Parcel of the Honour of GLOUCESTER, and held in Fee for many Generations under the DE CLARES by a Family to which it gave Name In 1278, 6 Edw I JOHN DE TRACI purchafed it of THOMAS DE DEYNTON, in whofe Defcendants it remained till the Reign of Queen ELIZABETH, when it was transferred to ARTHUR PLAYER, Efq and others Early in the prefent Century it belonged to the Family of LANGTON The principal Eftate is vefted in WILLIAM GORE LANGTON, Efq which Name he affumed on his Marriage with the Hon

An exempted Manor, called the *Bury*, paffed on the Stiles to the HILLMANS, who now poffefs it *Tracy Park* Lodge was long the Eftate and Refidence of the Family of RIDLEY and by many fubfequent Purchafes is now of ———— BUSH, Efq It pays a Mark only, yearly, in Lieu of Tythes There was anciently a free Chapel adjoining to the Manor Houfe, for the Site of which 5s 4d is ftill due as an Audit to the Crown

The Courfe of the River *Boyd* is through a very deep Channel of Rocks, rifing almoft in a perpendicular Direction, upon either Side of which are very diftinct Vallitions for advanced Tofts, probably communicating with the Military Way from *Aqua Solis* to the *Trajectus*

Lead Ore is found, but not of fufficient Quality to encourage the Eftablifhment of Work Many of the poorer Inhabitants are employed in obtaining the Rock Stone, which produces Lime of remarkable Strength and Whitenefs

---

BENEFACTIONS.

WILLIAM TRACY, Efq by Deed, a certain Land for the Erection of a Poor Houfe

JOHN NEWTON, Efq 100, gave in lock Sums less by certain Lines, the annual Produce is 60

The Rev WILLIAM LANGTON, 1 bequeathed 2 for the Endowment of a School and up-preparing poor Children this Sum he ordered to be laid out in Land the yearly Produce of which they whom Annual Profit of each the reft of which £ to put out poor Children Apprentices

PHILIPPA S for the Relief of the Poor the annual Produce of which is

Mrs S P devifed to apprenticing poor Children, the annual Profit of which

INCUMBENTS	PATRONS	INCUMBENTS.	PATRONS
1278 ——————,	Thomas de Deynton	1678 Joseph Jackson,	King Charles II
—— Arthur Saul,	Queen Elizabeth	* * * * * * *	* * * *
1586 William Dyke,	——————	1720 Rich Furney, M A	King George I
1588 Thomas Cooley,	Sir John Tracey, Knt	1727 James Howe, M A	The fame
1593 Thomas Cozen,		1728 David Duncan, M A	King George II
1613 William Beeley,	King James I	1745 Tho Coker, M A (refigned) The fame
1615 George Beeley,	The fame	1783 Peter Gunning, M A King Geo 3 III.
1640 Robert Wilkes,	King Charles I		

PRESENT PROPRIETORS OF THE MANORS,

Of *Deinton*,
WILLIAM GORE LANGTON, ESQ

Of the *Bury*,
HENRY HILLMAN, ESQ

The Perfons fummoned from this Place by the Heralds in 1682 and 1683, were

Henry Still, Efq
John Parker, Gent
—————— Ridley, Gent.

At the Election in 1776 Twenty three Freeholders polled from this Parish

The oldeft Register bears Date in 1566

ANNUAL ACCOUNT OF MARRIAGES, BIRTHS, AND BURIALS, IN THIS PARISH

A D	Mar	Bir	Bur	A D	Mar	Bir	Bur	A D	Mar	Bir	Bur	A D	Mar	Bir	Bur
1781	1	13	8	1786	3	15	7	1791				1796			
1782	3	7	12	1787	3	7	6	1792				1797			
1783	1	7	6	1788	2	12	8	1793				1798			
1784	4	12	9	1789				1794				1799			
1785	3	7	4	1790				1795				1800			

INSCRIPTIONS IN THE CHURCH

ON A NEAT MONUMENT OF WHITE AND VARIEGATED
MARBLE IN THE NAVE

Arms, Quarterly, Gules and Or, a Bend Argent, for LANGTON,—impaling, Argent, a Crofs Sable, charged in the Centre with a Leopard's Face Or, for BRIDGES

M S
ELIZABETHÆ LANGTON,
Filiæ
EDWARDI BRIDGES, de Cunfham,
in Com Somerfet Arm̄
Uxoris
JOHANNIS LANGTON, de Deinton,
in Com Glouceft Gen
a cujus morte
Vidua vixit annos ultra
quadraginta,
ut Charitate in Pauperes,
Benignitate in fuos,
Pietate in Deum,
Curis foluta
fefe devoveret,
ætat 83, died 33°,
Filæt 24 Mar 1702-3
Sancta Matrona
fuas exuvias juxta
illuftrium Majorum cineres
in Ecclefia de Cunfham

recondi juffit,
fed cum inter multifaria
numerofæ familæ
marmora
in Anguftiis iftius cancellis,
Monumento detur t locus
in hujus Parochia Ecclefiam,
in qua
longam bonis operibus
perigandis
Viduitatem contempfit,
CAROLUS, JAMES & AMY MEREDITH,
Nepotes & Executores,
Marmor hoc gratitudinis ergo
pofuerunt

On a plain Tablet

Underneath lyeth the Body of
MARY, the Wife of EDMUND CHATER,
who departed this Life the 18th Day
of September, Anno Domini 1695,
ætatis fuæ 5—

ON A MONUMENT ON THE NORTH SIDE THE
CHANCEL

JOSIAH JACKSON, M.A.
the faithful Vicar of this Church
41 Years,
died Jan 12, 1719
He was an eminent Pattern
of primitive Piety,
and the perfecting Discipline of the Cross,
found and zealous
in the Faith,
constant and diligent
in his Ministry,
is a true Priest of God
and Disciple of Christ

ELIZABETH his Wife,
an holy and godly Matron,
imitating her Husband's Virtues,
died Feb 1-, 17-1

The Memory of the Just is bless'd.

ON A PLAIN TABLET

Near this Place lieth the Body of
SAMUEL PACKER, of this Parish, Yeoman,
who departed this Life the
6th of September, 17-1, aged 64 Years

The Body of
JOHN PACKER, of this Parish, Yeoman,
lies in this Place, who departed this Life
the 27th of November, 1760,
aged 70 Years

ON ANOTHER TABLET AT THE WEST END

Near this Place was interred the Body of
PHILIP Son of ROBERT PALMER,
by ANN his Wife
He died Sept 26, 1748,
aged 1 Year and 6 Months

Also
PHILIP a second Son of that Name,
died October 13, 1759,
aged 3 Years and 6 Months

Also
BETTY, Daughter of ROBERT and ANN PALMER,
died June 29, 1771, in the 18th Year of her Age

ON TABLE STONES IN THE NAVE

ON A BRASS PLATE

M S

Conjugis sui charissimæ GEORGII WEARE,
de Hæc Parochia, Generosi,
Filii HENRICI WEARE, de Henton,
& P. . . . ILS uxoris ejus
quarum Georgius, placide in
Domino obdormivit 17, & hic sepultus fuit
-1 die Januarii 1656,
ætatis suæ 41

Christianæ filiæ, Mensin . . .
Ann . . .

JOHN ROBINSON
departed this Life May 4, 1670,
aged 38

ELIZABETH his Daughter
died March 8, 1719,
aged 57 Years and 2 Months

SAMUEL PACKER
departed this Life Jan 14, 1712,
aged 62 Years and 6 Months

SARAH, the Wife of
the abovesaid SAMUEL PACKER,
died May 12, 1743, aged 83

SARAH, Daughter of
SAMUEL and SARAH PACKER,
departed this Life Sept 1, 1747, aged 41

WILLIAM their Son
died Sept 3, 1,- aged 41

MARGARET, Daughter of
RICHARD and ANN DAVIS,
died October -3, 1713,
aged 43 Years and 8 Months

ANN, the Wife of RICHARD DAVIS,
Mother of the abovesaid MARGARET,
died August 14, 1735,
in the 97th Year of her Age.

KATHERINE, Wife of THOMAS LEWEN,
died the 8th of June, 1754,
in the 88th Year of her Age

JOHN DAVIS, of the City of Bristol,
departed this Life June 3, 1757,
in the 85th Year of his Age.

MARY, the Wife of THOMAS FARR,
of the City of Bristol, and Daughter of
SAMUEL PACKER, of
the Parish of Westerleigh,
departed this Life February 7, 171-,
in the 5th Year of her Age

ON TABLE STONES IN THE
NORTH AISLE

MARGARET the Daughter of
ARTHUR and DOROTHY PLAYER,
died 22 June, Anno Dom 1596

THOMAS BROWNE
departed this Life April   Anno Dom 1610

JANE RODBOURNE
was buried the 1st Day of July, A.D. 1614

RICHARD RIDLEY,
of Well House in this Parish,
died August -5, 1625

ELIZABETH,

ELIZABETH, the Wife of RICHARD RIDLEY,
deceafed the 1ſt Day of January, Anno Dom 1627.

THOMAS RIDLEY, Gent
was buried Auguſt 12, 1662

RICHARD RIDLEY, Gent
eldeſt Son of the ſaid THOMAS RIDLEY,
died April 17, 1690, aged 62.

HESTER RIDLEY
was buried September the   1671.

ALICE, Wife of THOMAS RIDLEY,
departed this Life the 24th of October, 1678.

JEANY, the Daughter of
RICHARD and SARAH RIDLEY,
departed this Life Auguſt 7, A D 1686,

Here reſteth the Body of
THOMAS and PRISCILLA,
Son and Daughter of JOHN ATWOOD,
who did depart this Life,
THOMAS,
the 12th of Sept Anno Domini 1647,
and PRISCILLA,
the 18th of May, Anno Dom 1650

IN THE CHURCH YARD, ON TOMBS.

The Rev Mr ROBERT WILKES,
Rector of this Pariſh,
was buried November   1677

REBECKAH his Wife
was buried the 9th of December, 1699.

REBECKAH their Daughter
was buried June 1, 1680, aged 14

ANN their Daughter
died January   aged 28

Within this Tomb lies the Body of
the Rev Mr FRANCIS WILKES,
who departed this Life the
21ſt Day of April, 1744, aged 79 Years,
He was many Years the faithful
Miniſter of Rowbarrow and Burnington
in the County of Somerſet,
upwards of fifty-two Years,
and Son of
the Reverend Mr ROBERT WILKES,
formerly Miniſter of this Pariſh

Here alſo lies interred   the well beloved
Wife of the ſaid Mr FRANCIS WILKES,
who died the 20th Day of October, 1738,
aged 78 Years.

RICHARD, Son of
WILLIAM and HANNAH BUTLER,
died May 8, 1763, aged 22

WILLIAM BUTLER, Yeoman,
died June 2, 1763, aged 52

SARAH, Daughter of
WILLIAM and HANNAH BUTLER,
died June 11, 1770, aged 21

HANNAH, Wife of JOHN BRYAN, ſenior,
died Nov 2, 1757, aged 52

JOHN BRYAN, ſenior,
died Sep 25, 1760, aged 84

JOHN BRYAN, junior,
died Feb 23, 1758, aged 53

BETTY his Wife
died May 11, 1735, aged 22

WILLIAM NICHOLLS
died March 18, 1713, aged 40

SAMUEL his Son
died Auguſt 30,

And MARY his Daughter,
May the 10h, 1700

GEORGE, the Son of
WILLIAM and MARY NICHOLLS,
was buried May 30, 1722, aged 26.

JAMES, the Son of
WILLIAM and MARY NICHOLLS,
died March 25, 1740, aged 20

MARY, Wife of WILLIAM NICHOLLS,
died September 15, 1742, aged 71

WILLIAM NICHOLLS
died February 4 1769, in the
68th Year of his Age

ELIZABETH, Wife of WILLIAM NICHOLLS
died April 5, 1775, aged 60

MARY their Daughter died in her Infancy

WILLIAM DAVIS, Yeoman,
died October 7, 1775, aged 67

HANNAH, Wife of EDWARD DAVIS,
died March 26, 1751, aged 62

EDWARD

EDWARD DAVIS
died June 14, 1749, in the 66th Year of his Age

ELIZABETH, Wife of
EDWARD DAVIS, Daughter of
WILLIAM and ELIZABETH SAUNDERS,
died the 20th of March, 1722, aged 39.

ELIZABETH, Wife of JACOB AMOS,
Daughter of EDWARD and ELIZABETH DAVIS,
died October 18, 1748, aged 28

Also two Sons and one Daughter of
EDWARD and ELIZABETH DAVIS, died as follows

SAMUEL died May 3, 1720.

JAMES died Feb 5, 1721

MARY died Jan 17, 1713

ANN, Wife of MOSES TOCHILL,
Daughter of EDWARD and ELIZABETH DAVIS,
died October 19, 1781, aged 71

RICHARD NEALE
died April 11, 1736, aged 77

JANE, Wife of RICHARD NEALE,
died Feb 17, 1704, aged 44

LUCY, Wife of GEORGE TOCHILL,
died Aug 15, 1754, aged 21

JANE, Wife of WILLIAM JONES,
died April 5, 1738, aged 49

WILLIAM JONES
died March 16, 1767, aged about 80

SAMUEL, Son of WILLIAM and JANE JONES,
died Feb 13, 1777, aged 56

SARAH, Wife of GILES BROWNING,
died April 19, 1746, aged 52

GILES BROWNING
died Jan 14, 1772, in the 77th Year of his Age

WILLIAM BROWNE
died May 29, 1783, aged 62

MARY, Wife of RICHARD BENNETT,
and Daughter of TOBIAS LUTON,
died in July 1710, aged 26

THOMAS CREW
died April 24, 1747, aged 52

MARY his Wife
died March 20, 1727, aged 34

SARAH, Wife of MATTHEW SNAILUM,
died April 24, 1775, aged 87

THOMAS their Son
died Oct 21, 1752, aged 32

MATTHEW SNAILUM
died in November 1733, aged 49.

SAMUEL MANNINGS, senior,
died April 18, 1712,
aged 53 Years and 10 Months

SARAH his Wife
died the 6th of May, 1742, aged 82

WILLIAM, Son of
SAMUEL and HANNAH MANNINGS,
died March 19, 1737, aged 17

SAMUEL MANNINGS, Yeoman,
died May 7, 1731, aged 40

HANNAH, Wife of SAMUEL MANNINGS,
died Feb 21, 1761, aged 72

ON HEAD STONES

	Died	Aged
Sarah, Wife of Thomas Gay	5 June, 1711	25
Grace, Wife of Thomas Mannings	8 Nov 1751	51
Isaac Mannings	26 Mar 1751	1
Thomas Godard	17 Apr 1760	6
Ann, Wife of Robert Bolwell	19 Mar 1719	5
Hugh, Son of Robert and Mary Bolwell	5 Jun 1714	12
Mary their Daughter	15 Aug 1745	15
Mary, Wife of Samuel Larcom	May, 1770	50
Sarah their Daughter	1751	15
Esther their Daughter	1731	5
Elizabeth Daughter of Richard and Margaret Strange	19 Jan 1719	25
Ann, Wife of Robert Razey, Daughter of Richard and Margaret Strange, of Wick and Abson	5 Mar 1739	3
June, Daughter of Richard and Mary Strange	Dec 1765	1
Richard Strange, of Wick and Abson	Sept 1761	71
William Elmes	22 May 1769	5
John Simmonds	8 May 1760	
Ann his Wife	9 Aug 1772	
Mary, second Wife of John Pyles	1 Nov 1771	
Mary, Wife of William Nichol	15 Oct 1761	

6 H

ON

ON HEAD STONES

	Died		Age
James, Son of William and Elizabeth Nicholls	29 Jan	1767	27
Elizabeth, Wife of James England	29 May,	1781	50
Thomas Gunning	14 Feb	1780	6
Hannah, Wife of Thomas Gunning,	19 Jun	1770	66
Thomas Pink	2 Feb	1784	60
Hannah, Wife of Thomas Pinker	19 Jun	1737	38
George Davis	15 Dec	1750	44
George, Son of Thomas and Elizabeth Gunning	21 Jan	1764	30
William their Son	8 June,	1765	33
Mary, Wife of Peter Vines, of Dirham	18 May,	1775	43
Charles Thomas	19 Nov	1770	38
John, Son of William and Elizabeth Nicholls	11 May	1777	28
Doctor their Son	4 Feb	1780	
Edward West	2 Oct	1768	58
Ann his Wife	31 Dec	1774	65
John Nicholls	13 Dec	1766	68
Sarah Gunning	14 Oct	1779	47
Elizabeth Stilman, Daughter of John and Mary Gunning	25 Aug	1778	35
Mary, Wife of John Gunning	1 Oct	1774	59
George, Ann, and Sarah, their Children, died young			
Joseph England	29 Aug	1771	80
Sarah, Wife of Joseph England	19 Dec	1756	59
George England	23 Dec	1776	51
Mary, Wife of Tobias Luton	10 Dec	1722	75
Mary Luton, Spinster, Grand daughter of the above	17 May,	1782	66
John Francombe, upwards of 40 Years Clerk of this Parish	9 Mar	1764	76
Edward Fox	3 Jan	1769	49
Jane his Wife	9 Dec	1772	47
Edith their Daughter	2 Dec	1768	72
Margaret, Wife of Joseph England	26 Apr	1723	25
Joseph England, senior	31 Aug	17	79

XCIV. D I D B R O K E

I T S in the Hundred of *Kiftefgate*, three Miles diftant from *Winchcombe* on the North, eight Miles West from *Campden*, and more than eighteen North-eaft from the City of *Gloucefter*. Of the Soil, which is a light Clay, nearly equal Portions are Pafture and Tillage, within a Circuit of ten Miles interfected by the Rivulet *Ifbourn*, which joins the *Avon* near *Lechham*.

The Living, which is a Vicarage in the Deanery of *Campden*, became a Stipendiary of the Abbey of *Hayles* in 1270, with a Penfion of ten Marks a Year, which is now received from the Impropriation. It was at the Diffolution included in the Grant then made to Sir Edward Seymour, and fince transferred to the noble Family of *Tracey*. In 1778, this Vicarage with the Rectory of *Pinnel* and the Chapelry of *Hyde*, were confolidated into one Prefentation by Confent of Dr Martin Benson, the Diocefan, the Patron, and Incumbent.

The Church, dedicated to *St George*, has a Nave only, with a light embattled Tower at the Weft End. It was built at the fole Expence of William Whytchurch, Abbot of *Hayles* between the Years 1470 and 1479. After the fatal Battle of *Tewkefbury* in 1472, it is traditionally faid that fome of the *Lancaftrians*, who had fled to the Church of *Didbroke* for Sanctuary, were there barely put to Death, and that after fuch Pollution it was re-built by an Abbot. Several Portraits in painted Glafs were perfect in the beginning of this Century, which are now mutilated or removed by modern Reparations. In the great Eaft Window were the Figures of two female Saints, and that of the Founder, with thefe Arms and Infcription. " Argent, a Lion rampant Gules within a Bordure bezantée." 2 " Or, a " Spread Eagle Sable," Abbey of *Hayles*. " **Orate pro a ia Wyll't Wytchyrche, qui hoc templum fun-** " **dauit cum Cancello**." And in the Window of the Belfry, the Images of the titular Saint George and Pope Silvester. The Sarcophagus, or railed Tomb in which the Founder is buried, is compofed of blue Marble beneath a Niche on the North Side of the Nave. Upon the Lid was a Crofs florette, on one Side a Chalice, on the other a Mafs Book, but fince defaced.

When the Abbey of *Hayles* was eftablifhed and endowed by Richard the fecond King of the Romans in 1246, this Manor was included in their Rental. At the fuppreffion it was granted to the Progenitor of the prefent Proprietor, and has the principal Eftate annexed.

The Tything of *Cofcombe* contains the firft Grounds on the North-eaft. The ancient Houfe, one of the Refidences of the Abbots of *Hayles*, was rebuilt by Judge Tracey early in this Century. It has fince paffed with a competent Eftate to his Grandfon Robert Tracey, Efq; from whom to Robert Pratt, Efq; whofe Relict has remarried with Stayner Holford, Efq; the prefent Poffeffor. The Chapel mentioned by Atkyns is no longer applied to facred Ufes.

Hamington Grange, Parcel of the Abbey Eftate, was granted to Robert Acton 1541. From this Family of *Jefferies* it is now held by —— Grift, Efq; Other Lands have been long vefted in the Family of *James*. The Intrenchments of fome early Period abound on the Hills.

No Benefactions to the Poor

Incumbents	Patrons.	Incumbents	Patrons.
—— Meredith Evans,		1737 William Winde,	
1556 William Gumpe,	Antony Holokyns	1743 John Holbroke, M.A.	
*	*	1765 John Tracey, D D	
—— Winde,	Lord Tracey	1769 John Tracey, D D	

Present Lord of the Manor,

The Right Honourable Charles Lord Vifcount Tracey, of *Rathcoole* in the Kingdom of *Ireland*.

The Perfons fummoned from this Parifh by the Heralds, in 1682 and 1683, were

Richard Herther, Gent. and Edward Workman, Gent.

At the Election in 1776 Two Freeholders polled from this Parifh

The

The Date of the oldeſt Regiſter cannot be aſcertained.

ANNUAL ACCOUNT OF MARRIAGES, BIRTHS, AND BURIALS, IN THIS PARISH

A D	Mar	Bir	Bur	A D	Mar	Bir	Bur	A D	Mar	Bir	Bur	A D	Mar	Bir	Bur.
1781	3	7	6	1786	5	11	4	1791				1796			
1782	2	11	5	1787	4	9	9	1792				1797			
1783	4	6	4	1788	3	5	5	1793				1798			
1784	1	13	6	1789				1794				1799			
1785	1	7	4	1790				1795				1800			

This Regiſter includes the Inhabitants of *Hayles and Pynnock*

INSCRIPTIONS IN THE CHURCH.

ON A NEAT MONUMENT OF WHITE AND VA-
RIEGATED MARBLE IN THE CHANCEL

Arms, Or, between two Bendlets Gules, an
Eſcallop in the dexter Chief Point Sable, for TRA
CEY,—impaling, Or, a Feſs wavy between ſix Bil
lets Sable, for DOWDESWELL

Near this Place
lies interred the Body
of the Honourable ROBERT TRACY, Eſq
Son of the Right Honourable ROBERT, late
Lord Viſcount TRACY, of Todington
He was Judge twenty ſix Years
in the Courts of Weſtminſter,
but being ſtruck with the Palſy
in the Year 1726, reſigned a Commiſſion
which he had ſo long executed
with the greateſt Knowledge,

Moderation, and Integrity,
to the Honour of his Prince,
and univerſal Satisfaction
of his Fellow Subjects
Obiit 11 Sept Anno 1735,
ætat 80

Benefacere magis quam conſpici

ON A FLAT STONE

In Memory of MARGERY,
Wife of WILLIAM BAYLIS,
of this Town, who died
in September 1742, aged 40.

WILLIAM BAYLIS aforeſaid
died Aug 23, 1757, aged 59.

IN THE CHURCH YARD, ON A TOMB.

JAMES HAYES
died the 23d Day of July, 1718, aged 71

ON HEAD STONES

	Died	Aged		Died	Aged
Thomas Agg	26 June, 1762	63	John Reeve, ſenior	25 Mar 17 6	
Anne his wife	13 Nov 1776	77	Ann, Wife of John Reeve	— May, 1	
... tiam Clare	9 Jan 1 68	52	Richard Baker	6 Feb 1	0
... his Wife	29 Jan 1768	64	Elizabeth, Wife of James Agg	27 Nov 17 53	1
John their Son	1 Sep 1786	29	Ann, Wife of John Buts	11 Nov 58	54
... James the elder	6 Feb 1744	80	Ann, Wife of Thomas Tiff, ſenior	1 Aug 1734	8
Heſter his Wife	10 July, 1764	80	Thomas Tiff, ſenior	7 Nov 1760	9
Margery James	15 Sept 1714	65	Ann, Wife of Thomas Tiff of Southam		
Ann, Wife of Thomas James	2 July, 1744	60	Southam	1 Feb 1 59	1
Thomas James	24 Oct 1751	72	Thomas Tiff of Southam the Pa		
Richard Greening, ſenior	12 June, 1768		riſh of Biſhop Cleeve	Dec 1 2	70
Ann, Wife of Richard Greening	12 Mar 1738	90	Anna Daughter of Thomas and Ann		
John Gibbons	8 Oct 1746	74	Tiff	10 Nov 1	
Anthony Hayns	20 Sept 1726	55			

xcv. DIDMARTON

IS situate in the Hundred of *Grumbald's Ash*, upon the Extremity of the lower *Cotefwold*, bounded by the County of *Wilts*. It is fix Miles distant from *Tetbury* on the South-weft, eight South from *Horton Tinder Edge*, and nearly twenty two in the fame Direction from *Gloucester*. The Circumference of the Parish is from feven to eight Miles, including a light Soil, tilled, with very fmall Exception. The Village lies on the great Road from *Oxford* to *Bath* and *Bristol*.

The Living is a Rectory in the Deanery of *Hawkefbury*, endowed with 52 Acres of Glebe. In 17 , it was united in the fame Prefentation with *Oldbury on the Hill*. The Church, dedicated to St *Lawrence*, is inconfiderable, it has an Aifle projecting from the End of the Nave. Sir R. *Atkyns* affigns the fame Reafon for this Form that induced *Philip* of *Spain* to build the *Efcurial*, with a Reference to the Initial of the Tutelary Saint.

In the oldeft Records we find the manerial Territory extending over the whole Parish, and fucceffively enjoyed by the Families of De *Seward*, *Wroxton*, and *Woughton*. In 1571, Sir *Simon Codrington*, of *Codington*, married *Grisel*, the Co heir of *Richard Secoll*, Efq. and received the Eftate in Dower. Of the lineal Defcendants of this Marriage it was purchafed in 17 by *Charles Noel*, fourth Duke of *Beaufort*. The Manor houfe was built by the *Codringtons* foon after their Succeffion.

Tumuli, or Barrows, the fuppofed Repofitories of Military Antiquities, are fhewn within the Limits of this Parish.

BENEFACTIONS.

Nicholas *Innots* devifed by Will, 1687, Lands, the annual Produce of which is l' for the Relief and Maintenance of the Poor.

Incumbents	Patrons	Incumbents	Patrons
— George Longford,		1735 Thomas Heather, M A	
160 Marmaduke Chipman,	Simon Codrington	175 William Cooke, M A	Charles Noel Duke of Beaufort
167, Thomas Byrton,	Robert Codrington	1780 Edward Steount, Ll D	Henry Duke of Beaufort
1680 ——— Blifs,			
1724 William Skinner, M A			

PRESENT LORD OF THE MANOR,

His Grace HENRY Duke of BEAUFORT.

The Perfons fummoned from this Parish by the Heralds in 1682 and 1683, were

Robert Codrington, Efq. and —— Blifs, Clerk.

It does not appear that any Freeholder polled from this Parish at the Election in 1776.

The Regifter commences in 1675, and is very impeifect.

ANNUAL ACCOUNT OF MARRIAGES, BIRTHS, AND BURIALS, IN THIS PARISH.

A D	Mar	Bir	Bur	A D	Mar	Bir	Bir	A D	Mar	Bir	Bur	A D	Mar	Bir	Bur
1781	—	4	—	1786	—	4	—	1791				1796			
1782	—	2	—	1787	1	2	—	1792				1797			
1783	—	3	—	1788	1	3	2	1793				1798			
1784	—	1	1	1789	2	4	1	1794				1799			
1785	1	3	3	1790				1795				1800			

INSCRIPTIONS

INSCRIPTIONS IN THE CHURCH.

IN THE CHANCEL

ON MONUMENTS.

Arms, Argent a Fef en bit les Sable between three Lions paffun Gules for CODRINGTON ——impaling Lozengy Gules and vaire.

Under the Marble lyeth the Bodies of two Sonns and three Daughters of JOHN and FRANCIS CODRINGTON, that were ftill born

Here lyeth the Bodies of FRANCES the eldeft Daughter, and CHRISTOPHER the fourth Son, of ROBERT CODRINGTON, Efq and AGNES his Wife, who died in the Year of our Lord 1686

ON A FLAT MONUMENT OF VARIEGATED MARBLE

Arms, on three Efcutcheons 1 Quarterly 1ft and 4th Argent three Bugle Horns Sable for FORRESTER 2d and 3d, Azure nine Mulletts Or, for 2 Argent, two Chevron's Azure within a Bordure engrailed Gules, for TYRRELL ——impaling Argent, a Fefs embattled Sable, between three Lions paffant Gules, for CODRINGTON 3 FORRESTER, —impaling, TYRRELL, as before

In Memory of ELIZABETH TYRRELL Widow of CHAS TYRRELL Efq fecond fonn of Sir THOMAS TYRRELL of Thornton in the County of Bucks Baronet and one of the Daughters of ROBERT CODRINGTON, Efq and AGNES his Wife, who died the 30th of July, 1745, aged 70 Years

Alfo of WILLIAM Lord FORRESTER, of Coftorphin in Mid Lothian, who died Oct 16, 1763

Alfo of ELIZABETH FORRESTER, the Widow of JOHN FORRESTER, Efq Captain in his Majefty's Navy, and daughter of the faid CHAS and ELIZABETH TYRRELL, who died Oct 24, 1776

Erected by Order of the faid ELIZABETH FORRESTER, to the Memory of her Mother and Son abovenamed

ON FLAT STONES.

Here lyeth the Body of AGNES CODRINGTON the Wife of SIMON CODRINGTON, who deceafed the 12th of January, Anno Dom 1618

Here alfo lieth the Body of ROBERT CODRINGTON, Efq who departed this Life the 11th Day of June, Anno Dom 1717, ætatis fuæ 66

Here lieth the body of AGNES CODRINGTON, late Wife of ROBERT CODRINGTON, Efq who departed this Life the 25th Day of October Anno Domini 17 7, ætitis fuæ 63

RICHARD CODRINGTON Son of ROBERT CODRINGTON, Efq and AGNES his Wife was interred September 23, AD 1691

R C
Here lieth the Body of RACHEL, the fifth Daughter of ROBERT CODRINGTON, Efq and AGNES his Wife who departed this Life September the 7th in the 16th Year of her Age, A D 1699

F C
Here alfo lieth the Body of FRANCES, the eighth Daughter of ROBERT CODRINGTON Efq and AGNES his Wife Oct Mrs, A D 1712

ON A NEAT MARBLE MONUMENT in the Nave

In Memory of CORNELIUS COFFIN Efteen Parish, Gent who died Feb 1, 1755, aged

And of MARY his Wife who died Sep 24, 1762 aged

Who MARY then Daughter Wife of JOSEPH Efteen Gent She died Apr 12, 18 aged

ON A SQUARE MARBLE TABLET

Near this Place lieth interred the Body of ROBERT CROUCHER, Gent of this Parifh, who departed this Life Dec 19, 1775, in the 82d Year of his Age He was Servant 51 Years to HENRY 3d Duke of BEAUFORT to CHARLES NOEL 4th Duke of BEAUFORT, and to HENRY 5th Duke of BEAUFORT, 43 Years of which Time he ferved the Office of Steward, on their feveral Eftates in the Counties of Gloucefter and Wilts HENRY 5 th Duke of BEAUFORT his caufed this Stone to be erected to his Memory, in Teftimony of his Fidelity, Honefty, and Integrity

ON FLAT STONES IN THE NORTH AISLE

Here lieth the Body of HANNAH REVERELL Daughter of DANIEL REVERELL of Wells, and late wife to ROBERT CODRINGTON who departed this Life the 3d Day of October, 1682, at 2

Here lyeth the Body of THOMAS ODH Gent who departed this Life the 1ft Day of July, aged 70

IN THE CHURCH YARD, ON TOMBS

THOMAS HOLBOROW, of this Parifh, Yeoman, was buried June 1, 1681

ELIZABETH his Wife was buried May 4, 1676

And JOAN their Daughter was buried in 1682

WILLIAM HOLBOROW, 1701

SAMUEL HOLBOROW, Yeoman, departed this Life Oct 6 1732

WILLIAM HAVARD died Sept 26 1779 aged 48

SARAH Wife of JOHN PANE, of Selwood, and Daughter of JOHN AYLER and PHILOPENE his Wife, of the Parifh of Lay, was buried Nov 12, 16 aged 54

MARY LYNES of Afhford in the Parifh of Biddlo buried died Oct, 1608, aged 8

WILLIAM LOING of this Parifh, died Feb 5 1716, aged 4

MARY his fecond Wife died March 25, in the 5th Year of her Age

ANNE his Third Wife died Aug 15, 1710 aged 60

HANNAH, Wife of ALBERT ROPE dier of Veerina died 1738, died 71

CAROLINE ROBBS died Aug 5 1719 aged 45

GEORGE WATTS ended Aug 83 aged 56.

ON FLAT AND HEAD STONES

	Died	Aged		Died	Aged
MARY, Daughter of Robert and Mary Croucher	10 Feb 174	On	with Denny,	2 June 175	
Mrs MARY Hutchin	12 Feb 1755	64	Mary the Daughter, Wife of Joseph Croucher	20 Apr 160	
Robert Croucher, Son of Richard Croucher and Jane Croucher, died Feb 19, 1751 and died Years, 8 Months and 3 Days			Thomas Menty, Mafon	Nov 1	
			Margaret Wife of Thomas Menty	Nov 15	
			Nathaniel Wife		
William Melhuifh fon of John and Hannah Melhuifh	20 Nov 1741	15	Edith Wife of Nathaniel Watt		
			Nathaniel Son of Nathaniel Watt		
Hannah Melhuifh	1 July 1756	79	Ann, Wife of George Watts	July 1744	

IS a Parish in the lower Division of the Hundred of *Grumbald's Ash*, distant from *Sodbury* three Miles on the South east, five from *Marshfield* on the North, and twenty-eight from the City of GLOUCESTER in a Northerly Direction.

The Border is of an oval Form, two Miles in the widest Part and three in length, of a Soil deep in the Vale, but becoming gradually lighter on the Bases of the Hills which furround it on the East and North Sides. Sixty Acres only are tilled in the whole Parish.

The Benefice is a Rectory, in the Deanery of *Hawkesbury*. It appears that certain Tythes were claimed by the Prior of *Stanley St. Leonard* in 1277, and how I find that the Abbey of *Keynsham*, co. Somerset, held what was then ftyled the Rectory.

No Marks of Antiquity remain in the Church, which is dedicated to the *Holy Virgin*, it is of fmall Dimenfions with a low Tower at the Weft End.

WILLIAM the CONQUEROR gave the Manor to the Bishop of *Constance*, and it was held under him for many Centuries by the Defcendants of ROGER DE BERKELEY, of *Dursley*, as Parcel of the Eftate of that Family.* The Heir in 1400 carried it into the Name of DE CANTILUPE by Marriage, and in 1473 it paffed by the fame Circumftance to THOMAS WIKYS. In the Reign of Queen ELIZABETH it was purchafed by GILES CODRINGTON, whofe lineal Defcendant SAMUEL CODRINGTON† re-fold it to the celebrated CHRISTOPHER CODRINGTON‡, Governor of the *Leeward Iflands*, who returned it by his Will, dated 1702, to his relative WILLIAM CODRINGTON, created a Baronet Ap. 21, 1721, the Father of the prefent Poffeffor.

The Demefnes extend over the greater Part of the Parifh, excepting the Little of WATERLANE, Lq.

The ancient Manor houfe owes its Erection to ROBERT WIKYS in 1557. The Front is of part Addition in the beft Style of JAMES the Firft's Reign, and is very fpacious, fituate on an eafy Rife of delightful Lawn, above the Houfe are two very beautiful Sheets of Water formed from the Source of the River *Froom*, and one below it. Much picturefque Scenery is found in the Park, the Ground being broken into many Knowls and Ridges extremely fteep, which are relieved by Trees of great Age and Beauty and Clumps very judicioufly planted. The Refult of the whole is fuch as characterizes the moft admired Refidences of the *Englifh* Gentry. It is very advantageoufly feen through an Avenue near the great Road leading to *Bath*.

Upon the Summits of the furrounding Hills are the Veftiges of a Chain of "*Caftra exploratoria,*" and more advanced on the Plain indubitable Traces of a large Camp.

LELAND relates, that "a Gaftle with Bones in a Sepulchre found by *Dodington* Church on the high "Way. Potts exceeding fadly nelyd and flourifhed in the *Roman's* Tymes, digged out of the Grounds "in the Felds at *Dodington*. Thefe Habitations were afterwards occupied by the *Saxons*, when they repelled the *Danes* Entrance, it Prior to—

Hiftory informs us that King EDWARD the Fourth refted his Army here fome Days, when on his March toward *Tewkefbury*, where he totally defeated the remaining Forces of the *Lancaftrian* Part.

* C. Proceed Introduced to the GALLIENS. Mr. WIKYS of *Dodington* contended by fum Reafon that the Family Seat of "*Dodington* fhould be older than the Limefily, of *Dursley*. But the Name of BERKELEY feems and *Dursley* of whom the Family were called found thereto the contrary. LELANDS Itin. vol. VI. p. 74.

† RICHARD CODRINGTON of KEMBLE Wood, Alderman of Briftol, purchafing of the Priory and Manor of the Counts Hay of *Dodington* and others. Octavo, and wrote, befide many Tranflations, the Life of HENRY Earl of ESSEX, 1646, &c. he died at Iflington in his 90th year.

‡ CHRISTOPHER CODRINGTON was born in the Ifland of *Barbadoes* in 1668, admitted Fellow of *All Soul's College*, then Creating the Directory of a certain Fellowfhip, he entered into the Army, and foon obtained Promotion from King WILLIAM. Conducted himfelf with Bravery at *Klege*, he was appointed Captain General, and Governor in Chief of the *Leeward Iflands*. Some Articles of impeachment were brought againft him before the Courts of *England*, whom however were cleared. Some time previous to his Death he refigned his Government and retired to the enjoyment of a ftudious Life. He died at Barbadoes in 1710. He bequeathed his Eftate to *All Soul's College*, to found and build a Library in which the eminent Man in more Work, Guild, by an Illuftrious Grid and a Buft by Rysbrack. His other Bequefts were equally judicious and munificent. Bee Life vol. III. p. 674 ed. KIPPIS.

§ Itin. vol. VI. p.

No Benefactions to the Poor

INCUMBENTS	PATRONS	INCUMBENTS	PATRONS
1500 ——————,	Abbot of GLOUCESTER	1675 Samuel Hieron,	Samuel Codrington, Efq
1559 Henry Townfhend,	——————	1693 Richard Codrington,	The fame
1578 Thomas Wilfie,		1732 Lingen Unett, Clerk,	——————
1593 John Coyde,	Sir John Poyntz	1738 Thomas Bennet, D D	
1597 Hugh Clunn,	William Herbert, Efq	1750 William Hughes, LL B	Sir W Codrington
1622 Robert Greenhill, or Greenald	——————	1769 Philip Bufs, M A	Sir W Codrington
1661 Thomas Codrington,	——————	1775 Philip Blifs, M. A.	The fame

PRESENT LORD OF THE MANOR,

SIR WILLIAM CODRINGTON, Bart

The only Perfon fummoned from this Place by the Heralds in 1682 and 1683, was
SAMUEL CODRINGTON, Efq

It does not appear that any Perfon polled from this Parifh at the Election in 1776

The earlieft Date in the Regifter occurs in 1575

ANNUAL ACCOUNT OF MARRIAGES, BIRTHS, AND BURIALS, IN THIS PARISH

A.D.	Mar	Bir	Bur	A D	Mar	Bir	Bur	A D	Mar	Bir	Bur	A D	Mar	Bir	Bur
1781	—	5	1	1786	—	2	—	1791				1796			
1782	—	4	1	1787	1	5	—	1792				1797			
1783	1	4	—	1788	—	1	2	1793				1798			
1784	—	—	2	1789	1	3	—	1794				1799			
1785	1	6	0	1790				1795				1800			

INSCRIPTIONS IN THE CHURCH

ON A MONUMENT AGAINST THE SOUTH WALL IN THE CHANCEL

P M
ROBERTI GREENALDI, hujus Ecclefiæ
Paftoris An 38, qui ob t 8
die Jan 1660,
æt 83

ON A MONUMENT ON THE NORTH SIDE

Arms, Per Fefs three Squirrels counterchanged,
for HORLER,—impaling, A gent, a Fefs embatiled
Sable, between three Lions paffant Gules, for CO-
DRINGTON

P M
Quod reliquum eft
JOANNÆ filiæ RICARDI CODRINGTON,
Gen Uxoris Chariffima JEREMIÆ
HORLER, Rectoris de Sodbury
Parva, quæ obiit tertio die Martii,
Anno Dom 1721

Depofitum etiam JEREMIÆ
HORLER prædict qui obiit
primo die Martii, 1723-4

RICARDI CODRINGTON, A. M.
Hujus Ecclefiæ Rectoris
Obiit 1 Feb 1732

ON A FLAT STONE IN THE CHANCEL

Within this Vault under this Stone,
lieth Mr Thomas Codrington,
Lord and Rector of this Place,
who died in the Year of our Lord 1675,
September 13, æt 3ia 14

ON A FLAT STONE IN THE NAVE

Arms, Quarterly, 1ft and 4th CODRINGTON, as
before, 2d and 3d, on a Bend three Rofes — im
paling on a Chevron between three Bears heads
couped, an Eftoile, for CHAPMAN

Here lieth the Body of
Mrs Dorothy Chapman,
Sifter to the Honourable
William Codrington Efq
who departed this Life June 2,
Anno Dom 171.

Alfo the Body of William the Son of
the faid William Codrington
and Elizabeth his Wife
who departed his Life November the 26th,
Anno Dom 1718, aged 12 Days

IN THE CHURCH YARD, ON TOMBS.

ELIZABETH CODRINGTON, the Wife of
SAMUEL CODRINGTON, Esq;
changed Mortality for Immortality,
the 22d Day of February, 1687, aged 82

This Monument was repaired and beautified
by the Executor of SAMUEL CODRINGTON, Esq;
Anno Domini 1717, to preserve the Memory of
the Piety, Charity, and other great Virtues
of the said Mrs CODRINGTON

ARTHUR PARKER
died Dec 16, 1769, aged 66

REBECCA his Wife
died May 31, 1784, aged 78.

MARY, Wife of RICHARD LAEL,
and Daughter of
ARTHUR and REBECCA PARKER,
died Feb 2, 1769, aged 30

JOHN, Son of
ARTHUR and REBECCA PARKER,
died Feb 20, 1784, aged 32

JANE, Wife of
JOHN SARCFAUNT, Daughter of
ARTHUR and REBECCA PARKER,
died Feb 20, 1784, aged 44

ON A FLAT STONE

JOHANNES BATTIN ob 1682

MARIA, uxoris JOHANNIS BATTIN,
quinque liberorum mater, quæ
75 annos nata nunc donata
fuit, anno Dom in 1685

JOHANNIS BATTIN
Obiit anno Dom 69 .
ætatis 87

ON HEAD STONES

					Died	Aged
John Nash	-	-	-	-	15 Sept 1773	52
William Young	-	-	-	-	30 Nov 17	77
Elizabeth, Wife of William Snip	-	-	-	-	29 May 17	55
John, Son of William and Elizabeth Glaskoline	-	-	-	15 Oct 17 3	2
Francis Clark	-	-	-	-	11 Jun, 17	
Sarah his Wife	-	-	-	-	17 Dec 17	10
Samuel Greenald	-	-	-	-	17 Jul 17 1	22
Elizabeth, Daughter of Robert and Elizabeth Holvay	-	-	19 Jan 17	1
Robert Howay	-	-	-	-	13 Nov 173	73
Elizabeth his Wife	-	-	-	-	6 Oct 171	67

IN the Courſe of Topographic Reſearches, many Places neceſſarily occur, which afford no Materials of curious Inveſtigation. Of this Deſcription particularly is *Dorſington*, a very ſmall Pariſh of the Hundred of *Kiſteſgate*, ſix Miles North from *Campden*, ſeven South-weſt from *Stratford upon Avon*, and thirty three computed Miles from GLOUCESTER on the North eaſt. The Terrier of the whole Pariſh does not exceed 1000 Acres, tilled and Paſture in nearly equal Portions, of a very heavy and fertile Soil.

The Rectory is endowed with a conſiderable Glebe, and is in the Deanery of *Campden*.

The Church is deſcribed by Sir R. ATKINS to have been a very inconſiderable Structure, previous to the Conflagration 1754, by which, with a great Part of the Village, it was deſtroyed. It was re-built with Brick on a ſmall modern Plan, and conſiſts of a Nave only.

Of the Manor the ſole Poſſeſſors were the DE NEWBURGHS and BEAUCHAMPS, Earls of WARWICK, for ſeveral Centuries after the Conqueſt. Afterward the Family of DE DRAYTON, from whom, with intermediate Purchaſers of ſhort Continuance, it paſſed to THOMAS RAWLINS, Serjeant at Law, in the Reign of JAMES the Firſt, and with it the Property of the whole Pariſh, which has been tranſmitted to the preſent Poſſeſſor.

No Benefactions to the Poor.

INCUMBENTS	PATRONS.	INCUMBENTS.	PATRONS.
—— Richard Phelps,	—————	1681 Thomas Yeate, M A	The ſame
1571 Thomas Phelps,	—————	1713 William Yeate, M A	—————
—— Thomas Turner, D D	—————	1735 William Bell, M A	—————
1593 John Rutter,	Chriſtopher Turner	1739 Wm Gelſthorpe, B A	—————
1633 Ferryman Rutter,	—————	1777 Edmund Rawlins, M A	Wm Rawlins, Eſq
1668 John Ward, D D	Thomas Rawlins, Eſq		

PRESENT LORD OF THE MANOR,

WILLIAM RAWLINS, Eſq

No Perſon appears to have been ſummoned by the Heralds, in 1682 and 1683.

At the Election in 1776 Three Freeholders polled from this Pariſh.

The oldeſt Regiſter bears Date in 1591.

ANNUAL ACCOUNT OF MARRIAGES, BIRTHS, AND BURIALS, IN THIS PARISH

A D	Mar	Bir	Bur	A D	Mar	Bir	Bur	A D	Mar	Bir	Bur	A D	Mar	Bir	Bur
1781	1	3	4	1786	2	3	2	1791				1796			
1782	—	4	2	1787	1	2	3	1792				1797			
1783	2	2	3	1788	—	3	1	1793				1798			
1784	1	5	5	1789	1	2	4	1794				1799			
1785	—	3	2	1790				1795				1800			

INSCRIPTIONS

INSCRIPTIONS IN THE CHURCH.

ON FLAT STONES

M S
THOMÆ YEATE, M A
hujus Ecclesiæ per xxxii annos Rectoris,
Qui obiit 9 die Novembris,
Anno { Salutis 1713
{ Ætatis 55

Depositum
A YEATE THOMÆ Conjugis,
Quæ obiit Jan 30,
Anno Dom 1742,
æ tis 81

Hic jacet
GULIELMUS YEATE, A M
Vir Literarum amore morum probitate,
Animo hospitali,
Perquam insignis,
In Deum, in patriam, in propinquos pietatis,
In amicos fidei,
Religiosis cultor,
Cunctis ergo bonis flebilis occidit,
utpote cui una cura & studium fuit
Comitate & beneficiis
De cunctis bene mereri
Obiit 4° die Martii, Anno Dom 1734,
ætatis suæ 48

BARBARA, Wife of THOMAS YEATE, Gent
died June 25, 1765, aged 45
She was the eldest Daughter of the
Rev THOMAS WARD,
Rector of Blissworth in the County of
Northampton, and of Bygrave in the
County of Hertford

Depositum
JOHANNIS GELSTHROPE,
Qui obiit decimo die Julii,
Anno { Ætitis 43
{ Sal itis 1718

M S
Fœminæ integerrimæ temper
Colendæ ALICIÆ RAWLINS,
Quæ hac in parœcia nata 1684.

Patre THOMA YEATE, Rectore,
Hic etiam viri sui inter prioris cineres
Exuvias mortales suas pro more
Deponi voluit
Obiit 25 die Aprilis, anno Dom 1770,
æ itis 86

Here lyeth the Body of
THOMAS GELSTHROPE, Gent
who departed this Life
August 31, Anno Dom 1735,
aged 22

In hopes of joyful Resurrection,
here lieth the Body of
WILLIAM GELSTHROPE, A B
38 Years Rector of this Parish
He died August 19, 1777,
in the 63d Year of his Age,
of whom it may truly be said,
that he lived in an uniform and
constant Obedience to those
two great Commandments on which
hang all the Law and the Prophets

IN THE CHURCH YARD.

ON HEAD STONES

						Died	Aged
Richard Dennis	-	-		-	-	12 Ma 1727	7,
Mary, Wife of John Holtham		-	-	-	-	5 Sept 1776	57
Thomas Osborne					-	2 Mar 1704	50
Martha, Wife of John Heming	-		-	-	-	20 May 175,	40
Anne, Daughter of William Durham and Elizabeth his Wife					-	1 May 174,	29
William Holtham					-	6 Nov 1779	72
Mary his Wife	-	-	-	-	-	26 Oct 1780	50
Richard Marriott	-	-	-	-	-	2 Jun 1779	13
Mary Marriott	-	-	-	-	-	28 Feb 1780	72

XCVIII. DOWDESWELL,
OR
DOLSWELLE,

IS one of the Parishes of which the Hundred of *Bradley* is composed, four Miles distant from *Cheltenham* on the East, seven South from *Winchcombe*, and twelve North east from GLOUCESTER

The Boundaries inclose a Tract of a long Form, two Miles in the widest Part, three in Length, and very narrow toward the Extremity Of the Soil the nature varies from deep Clay to Gravel, the greater Portion is applied to Pasture, besides which there are 200 Acres of Woodland

The Living is a Rectory in the Deanery of *Winchcombe*, the Patronage of which has been vested, with temporary Alienations only, in the Family of ROGERS since the Reign of Queen ELIZABETH That the ancient Church has been rebuilt is sufficiently evident from the Style of the present, which consists of a Transept of equal Height and Dimensions The low and massy Spire in the Centre is said to have been completed at the joint Expence of RICHARD HABINGTON and RICHARD ROGERS, as I to s 1577 In the Chancel remains, without Arms or Inscription, the brass Effigy of a Man, in a Robe d r---, with Roses and Fleurs de Lis inserted in the Interstices, but no Mullets, as it has been said Its Head is tonsured, and the ingenious Mr GOUGH asserts it to be the exact Counterpart of that of ROBERT EGLESFIELD, Founder of *Queens College, Oxford*, only smaller, who died in 1349

Bishop TANNER, in his Catalogue of the Abbots of *Hailes*, mentions that ROBERT, an Abbot elected in 380, retired in 1402, and died in 1420 This tradition, this th s to have been a Memorial for one of the Abbots, and the Age, and comparative Circumstances, determine it in some Measure to be the Person abovementioned

In the Church Yard is a Yew Tree of primeval Date, and in a State of very flourishing Vegetation

The Rectory house has great Advantages of Situation, commanding a very beautiful Point of View On either Side a Ridge of Hill, one covered with low Wood, the other breaking into a bare Rock, forming a bold Vista which is terminated by the grotesque Hill of *Churchdown* in the Centre, and the Landscape closed by the Mountains of *Hatterel*, which beautifully blend with the Horizon Of modern Improvements those most eligible have been adopted by the present Incumbent, and with no sparing Hand

The Church of *Worcester*, according to the first Records, possessed the chief Manor, held as of *Whittington* King HENRY the Third by Detachment, gave it to the Knights Templars, at whose Suppression it passed to the College of *Westbury upon Trim* Sir RALPH SADLER afterwards obtained it from whom it was transferred by Purchase to the Ancestor of the present Possessor It then owed Service to the Manor of *Guiting* Upper Dowdeswell belonged in the Reign of HENRY VII to Sir EDMUND TAME, whose nephew sold it to NICHOLAS HABINGTON of a very ancient Family seated at *Hindlip* from whom returned it for several Generations ANTONY HABINGTON, or ABINGTON, was of the Court of Prince HENRY, Son of JAMES I and JOHN his Descendant, was sued to compound with the Committees of Parliament for this Estate, for 64*l* Sir EDWARD RICH succeeded by Purchase, of whose Descendant it was bought by CHARLES VAN NOTEN, Esq who has since obtained the Seignory on P

Sandiwell originally was in the great Lordship of GLOUCESTER, but in the Reign of ELIZABETH this Rectory was purchased by WILLIAM ROGERS, who bequeathed it to JOHN ROGERS, his second Son of his Descendant it was bought by HENRY BRETT, Esq in 1610 who, with the present Mansion house, which was sold by his Son to HENRY Lord CONWAY of the Kingdom of Ireland His Successor for the Earl of HERTFORD resold it to the late THOMAS TRACY, Esq besides the Shire for this

* Sepulchral Monuments p 157
† Although I am much in a Loss how to ascertain the exact what I can View Interspersed chiefly with these Churches A separate Building, how Just the Idea of which as No Rector Abbots present in --- other are explained in Church Yards this Statute must have and probably related to Yews the general of especially being planted there is of much more ancient Date than by Mr in the History of --- ---

County, and it is the prefent Refidence of his Relict, Daughter and fole Heir of Sir WILLIAM Dodwell, Bart of *Sevenhampton* in this County The Houfe is a handfome modern Edifice, inclofed in a Park of lefs than a Hundred Acres in Extent When the Foundations were making, Coffins of Lead were difcovered near the Surface, fuppofed to be of the *Romans*, after the Introduction of Chriftianity

Pegglefworth lies on one of the higheft Summits of *Cotefwold*, the principal Share of it is vefted in JOHN WADE, Efq of *Woodchefter*, and confifts almoft entirely of arable Inclofures

The great Road from GLOUCESTER to *London* has been lately formed, and brought in a new Direction from *Cheltenham*, through this Parifh to *Frogmill*, whereby the Afcent is rendered much more eafy than by the former Courfe up *Crickley Hill*

Near to *Andover's Ford* a very fharp Encounter happened between the Parties during the Civil War [*]

No Benefactions to the Poor

INCUMBENTS	PATRONS	INCUMBENTS	PATRONS
—— Roger Green,	————.	1670 Jofeph Sterne,	
1575 Thomas Childes,	William Rogers, Efq	1701 Charles Neville, Efq	W Rogers, Efq
1597 Robert Temple,	Queen Elizabeth	1717 John Rogers,	The fame
1612 John Crowther,	————.	1768 John Arnold, LL B	
1623 William Driver,		1778 William Baker, LL B	John Read, Efq
————,	W Rogers, Efq		

PRESENT PROPRIETORS OF THE MANORS,

Of *Lower Dowdefwell* and *Rofley*
EDWARD ROGERS, ESQ

Of *Upper Dowdefwell*
CHARLES POLE, ESQ

Of *Pegglefworth*
JOHN WADE, ESQ

The Perfons fummoned from this Place by the Heralds in 1682 and 1683, were

The Heirs of Sir Edward Rich,
William Rogers, Efq

Sir Thomas Earle, Knight,
Paul Dodwell, Gent

At the Election in 1776 Three Freeholders polled from this Parifh

ANNUAL ACCOUNT OF MARRIAGES, BIRTHS, AND BURIALS, IN THIS PARISH

A D	Mar	Bir	Bur	A D	Mar	Bir	Bur	A D	Mar	Bir	Bur	A D	Mar	Bir	Bur
1781	1	11	2	1786	1	5	3	1791				1796			
1782	2	3	2	1787	3	3	2	1792				1797			
1783	1	5	3	1788	3	9	2	1793				1798			
1784	—	6	5	1789				1794				1799			
1785	3	3	4	1790				1795				1800			

INSCRIPTIONS IN THE CHURCH.

ON A TABLET ON THE SOUTH SIDE OF THE CHANCEL

Arms, Argent, a Mullet Sable, and on a Chief Gules, a Hon de lis Or, for ROGERS

Parce te calicole infirmum, hic morte quiefcunt
Funebris hic requies fineri morte erit
Vincula diffolvit Chriftus, Domino tenementur,
Confortes thisfum fe reddere fuis

Upon the Death of WILLIAM ROGERS, Gent
buried June 2, 1649

And of HELEN his Wife
interred February the firft, 1648

ON A MONUMENT AGAINST THE SAME WALL

Arms, ROGERS as before, —impaling, Argent, a Crofs raguly Gules, for LAWRENCE

To the Memory of WILLIAM ROGERS,
of Sandwell in this Parifh of Dowdfwell, Gent
who departed this Life the 11th Day of January
1663, in the 67th Year of his Age

To the Memory of
ELIZABETH ROGERS, Widow,
late Wife of WILLIAM ROGERS,
of Sandwell, Gent
deceafed the 2d of July, 1670

On a handsome Monument supported by
Columns of variegated Marble, with the
Bust of William Rogers, Esq

Arms, Rogers as before

Hic prope jacet
Gulielmus Rogers, Armiger,
Magistrorum Curiæ Cancellariæ nuper primus
Obiit nono die Aprilis, Anno Domini 1734,
ætatis suæ 76
Christianæ Religionis veritatem firmiter credens,
Omnem superstitionem vehementer abhorrens,
Dei unitatem religiose colens,
Christi Redemptionem strenue expectans,
Justum & honestum utili anteferens

ON A BRASS PLATE

Here lyeth the Body of
John Crowther, Master of Arts,
and some time Parson of this Parish,
who departed this Life the 14th day of Sept
in the Year of our Lord 1623

Ætas an virtus (licet ambas sit scio magnas)
Qui novit, dicat quæ tibi major erit,
Anni comperti quatuor bis bisque triginta,
At quis virtutes enumerare potest ?
Tum bene, tu nque diu vita tum morte beatus,
Vixit sic vivam, sic moriarque precor.

ON FLAT STONES
IN THE CHANCEL.

Jane, the Daughter of William Driver,
was buried Feb 23, 1650

Under this Stone lies the Body of
John Rogers, Esq.
who died Dec 2, 1760,
aged 26 Years

The Rev John Arnold, B I
Rector of this Parish and Cobberley,
who died July 17, 1775, aged 46 Years

Underneath lie the Remains of
the late Rev Richard Rogers, LL B
of Chilton Kings
He died March 10, 1780, aged 46 Years

In Memory of John Ailefearth Gent
who died Nov 6, 1755, aged 78

ON FLAT STONES
IN THE NORTH AISLE

In Memory of Gulielmi Rogers, Arm
Obiit August 1, 1678, ætatis suæ 5

In Memory of Anne Poole
Wife of William Rogers, Esq
who died March 15, 1770, aged 3

Anne, Daughter of
William and Anne Rogers,
died February 6 1773,
aged 10 Months and 14 Days

IN THE SOUTH AISLE

ON A NEAT MONUMENT

Arms, Per Pale Sable and Gules, a Cross bot
tonée nichée between four Fleurs de lis Or, for Rich
—impaling, Azure, on a Chevron Argent, three
Roses Gules, for Gilbert

In Memory of
Baily Rich, eldest Son of
Lionel Rich, of Upper Dowdeswell, Esq
He married the only Daughter and Heir of
John Gilbert, of Swindon,
in the County of Wilts, Gent
by whom he had one Son,
born Feb 15 1688,
buried April 18, 1723.

Elizabeth, Daughter of
Edward Gilbert Rich, Esq
and Mary his Wife,
born Aug 10, 1740,
buried April 19, 1741

Here likewise are reposed the Remains of
Mary his Daughter, the beloved Wife of
Robert Lawrence, Esq,
whose Mind was a sweet Assemblage
of every social and benevolent Affection,
eminently displayed by the warm Exertions of
Friendship, the endearing Sympathy of
connubial Love,
and by Meekness and Humility,
and the regular Practice of all those Duties
which are the Result of a truly Christian Faith
Thus lived for a better State,
she calmly resigned her Soul into the
Hands of her blessed Redeemer,
on the 21st Day of January,
in the Year of our Lord 1761, aged 22.

Elizabeth their Daughter died an Infant.

ON ANOTHER NEAT MONUMENT

Arms, Rich as before — impaling Argent on
a Chevron Azure, between three Torteaux Sable,
three Bucks Heads cabossed Or, for

In Memory of Edward Rich,
of Upper Dowdeswell, Esquire
Bencher and Barrister at Law of the
Honourable Society of Lincoln Inne
who deceased the 4th Day of February, A Dom
aged 78 Years

Mary, Wife of Lionel Rich Esq
buried the 7th of February, 1751
aged 69 Years

Lionel Rich Esq
buried April 26, 1750,
aged 71 Years

O N

O N F L A T S T O N E S

Here lieth the Body of
ELIZABETH ABINGTON,
Widow and Relict of ANTHONY ABINGTON,
of Dowdeswell,
who most religiously departed this Life
2, Dec 1640

Here lieth the Body of
MARTHA, the Widow and Relict of
EDWARD RICH, Esq
who died March 30, 1684, aged 73

I N T H E C H U R C H Y A R D.

ON A TABLET AGAINST THE CHURCH

In Memory of
ROBERT ROGERS, Gent.
who departed this Life
Jan 27, 1777, aged 62 Years

SARAH, Wife of
NATHANIEL OKEY,
died March 13, 1717 aged 22

JOHN OKEY, Son of
NATHANIEL and SARAH OKEY,
died January 29, 1769, aged 52

NATHANIEL OKEY
died Feb 12, 1771, aged 84.

O N T O M B S

THOMAS ROGERS,
of the Low House in this Parish, Gent.
died Oct 18, 1731, aged 76.

WILLIAM ROGERS,
of the Lowe House, Gent
died Feb 14, 1777, aged 66

ELIZABETH his Wife
died August 3, 1773, aged 67.

WILLIAM their Son
died July 1, 1754,
in the 14th Year of his Age

WILLIAM MAJOR
died April _, 1729, aged 77.

JANE his Wife
was buried June 2, 1726,
aged 86

REBECKAH, Wife of
THOMAS NEALE, and Daughter of
ANTHONY LAWRENCE, Gent
died the 8th Day of May, 1743,
aged 28

Mrs MARGARET PERRY,
Wife of ROGER PERRY,
died August 27, 1731, aged 52

This Tomb was erected
by Order of her Son
PETER PERRY, Esq
in Memory of the best of
Wives, Mothers, and Women

O N H E A D S T O N E S

					Died		Aged
Edward Land	-			-	21 Ma	1773	51
William Son of James and Parthenia Emes		-	-	5 Oct	1776	10
J Land her Son				19 May	1777	32
John Rogers	-	-	-	-	14 Nov	1765	36
Richard Venfield				29 Mar	1765	76
Ann, Wife of Nathaniel Okey	-	-	26 Jan	1771	84
Francis Ingram				23 Oct	1724	87
James his Wife	-	-	-	-	——	1672	—
John Joynes	-			10 Sept	1727	36
Mary, Wife of Thomas Caudle		-	-	27 Feb	1781	52

4

O N   H E A D   S T O N E S.

	Died		Aged
Elizabeth, Wife of John Cull	9 Aug.	1693	—
John Goodall	31 Aug	1779	59
John, Son of John and Mary Goodall	8 Jan	1771	10
Joseph Bunce	8 Feb	1745	45
Frances, Wife of James Stanley	1 Oct	1759	33
James Stanley	26 Mar	1765	—
John Chappel	29 Aug	1785	79
John Hathaway, senior	26 Feb	1712	72
Eleanor, Wife of James Cooper	9 Nov	1680	94
Joseph Williams	7 Oct.	1764	57
Thomas Mosen	25 Jan	1771	72
Ann Mary his Wife	6 Dec	1768	67
William Mosen	25 Aug	1718	29
Ann Mosen	1 June,	1787	78
James Mosen	10 Feb	1736	76
Sarah his Wife	24 Oct	1740	77
James Batt	30 May,	1786	17

DOWNE AMPNEY.

UNDER the general Denomination, *Omenev* in *Domesday* Book, four Parishes are described, situate on a Rivulet which is not otherwise distinguished than as *Ampn*, *Brook*

Down Ampney, or *Ampney Inferior*, lies on the Eastern Confines of the County adjoining *Wiltshire*, in the Hundred of *Crowthorne* and *Minety*, distant from *Cirencester* six Miles on the South, two from *Cricklade*, *Wilts*, on the South, and twenty three in a similar Direction from the City of GLOUCESTER The Soil, consisting of 2500 Acres, varies from Loam to Gravel, and is equally applied to Pasture and Tillage, the Rivulet intersecting the whole in its course to the *Isis*

The Living is vicarial, the Impropriate Tythes of which were given by King EDWARD I to the Knights Templars, of whom was NICHOLAS DE VILLARS 1268, who probably procured the Donation In 1315, EDW II when the Templars were suppressed, they passed to the Abbey of *Cirencester*, where they remained till 1544, when they were granted to the College of *Christ Church* in *Oxford*, who now present to the Vicarage *

Of the Church, dedicated to *All Hallows*, the Construction is evidently complete and of the same Period, of the latter part of the 13th Century It has a Nave supported by four pointed Arches, with two Aisles, a Transept and a Tower embattled and finished by an ornamented Spire In the Chancel under a plain Arcade, is a Sarcophagus with a Cross Florence, and encircled with a Laurel wreath. In the South Transept under a Niche of Quaterfoils, is a female Figure in Free Stone, supplicating, near it, on a Table of black Marble, a Knight Templar, in reticulated Armour, cross-legged with a Talbot at the Feet and drawing his Sword, the Scabbard of which he holds in his left Hand The Shield is of the Heater-shape, and bears a Cross charged with five Escalops † Adjoining to it is a Slab inscribed with Saxon Characters round the Margin, but totally illegible

The Fraternity of Knights Templars certainly founded the present Church, in which pious Work they were assisted by NICHOLAS DE VILLARS about the year 1260

During the first Century after the Conquest, the Manor was annexed to the Crown In 1250, 46 HEN III EDWARD CROUCHBACK, Earl of *Lancaster*, his second Son, granted it in Fee to NICHOLAS DE VILLERS, whose Family retained it till 1363, 35 EDW III About the beginning of the reign of RICHARD II Sir THOMAS HUNGERFORD ‡ purchased it, and it became the residence of his lineal Descendants to Sir ANTHONY HUNGERFORD, Knt whose Daughter and sole Heir, upon his death in 1645, transferred it to EDMUND DUNCH §, Esq by marriage JAMES CRAGGS ||, Esq Secretary of State to King GEORGE I having bought the manerial Office, bequeathed it to his natural Daughters and Coheirs, ANN, first married to JOHN KNIGHT, Esq of *Gosfield Hall*, Co *Essex* secondly, to ROBERT NUGENT **, Lord Viscount CLARE of the Kingdom of *Ireland*, who assumed the Name of CRAGGS, and died in 1788, and HARRIOT † † the Wife of RICHARD ELIOT, of *Port Eliot*, Co *Cornwall*, whose Son upon the Death of

* "In those times Vicars signified no more than Curates and were removeable at the Will of the Rector But when Churches
" were appropriated to Monasteries and the Religious were obliged to secure a Person of the Globe and Tythes for the mainte-
" nance of a Vicar such a one is called a Perpetual Vicar made perscriptive and institutive." BLOMEFIELD, Norfolk, v I p 13
† NICHOLAS DE VILLERS is recorded in an old Roll of Arms bearing Argent, une Croise Goul's, & cinque Eschalops d'Or
COLLINS'S *Yorke* v IV p 135 says, that NICHOLAS DE VILLERS son of ALEXANDER DE VILLERS et *heresley* Co *Lei*
charged for this, his paternal Coat, Sable three Cinquefoils Argent in 1260 Mr GOUGH (*Sep tm Cent* 13 p 96) notices
this Figure which is very resemblant of those in the *Temple* Church which is empty on his account and sumptuous Work
‡ Sir THOMAS HUNGERFORD, Knight, was elected and constituted the first standing Speaker of the House of Commons in
1370 50 EDWARD III The Duke of LANCASTER sought by right hyant to demand twice when in one Year The Knight was of Parliament, whom the Duke hadde made in hye pleasure did so Despite that the might deliberately mewed hym, for If the other
Knightes in the lower House who had so that shade with the Commonality, he had caused to be mewed except twelve whom
her would not remove Of the greater Part Matter this, the Person was elected to deliver her Answer, who was a Knight
very family with the Duke and in his Steward STOWE'S *Annals*, p 2, 3
§ EDMUND DUNCH Esq of *Little Wittenham* Co *Berks* married this second Daughter and sole Heir of Sir ANTHONY HUN-
" GERFORD Knt of *Black Ampney* which Manor was part of her very fortune £10000 in land a prodigious sum in those
" days By the Protector OLIVER CROMWELL he was created baron Burnell of *East Witenham*, Letters Pate April
† 16 1658 A Vidimus of his Patent is given in the last Edition of Noble's Memoirs of CROMWELL, v II p 161
|| JAMES CRAGGS Esq joint Secretary of State with Earl STANHOPE, died February 16 1720
** COLLINS'S Supplement, P 79
† ALMON'S Peerage of *Ireland*, v II p 18

his Mother and Aunt, became fole Proprietor. He was created a Baron by Patent, January 30, 1784, 24 GEORGE III. by the Title of Lord *Eliot* of *St. German's* in the County of *Cornwall*.

Of the great Manor Houfe, feveral Parts exhibit much higher Antiquity than the Reign of King HENRY VIII. particularly the Porch, the Arch of which is of quarterfoils, and which with the Hall compofes the chief Front. The Arms of HUNGERFORD " Sable two Bars Argent, and in chief three Plates," are very frequently difperfed, particularly on the Bafe of a very fingular Chimney, a Column ornamented with Tracery. A Range of Buildings which connected the great Gateway, and is now deftroyed, completed three fides of the Quadrangle.* The Portal, or grand Entrance, is flanked by two octangular Turrets, embattled, and embellifhed with the Arms of HUNGERFORD, their Cognizance (a Garb between two Sickles,) and the Cypher of the Builder, Sir ANTONY HUNGERFORD. Over the Arch, upon a large Efcocheon, HUNGERFORD,—impaling quarterly, 1 Argent, on a Bend Gules, three Mullets O, for DAUVERS, 2 Gules two Bars, and in Chief two Bucks Heads caboffed Or, for POPHAM, 3 Pert. nebuk. Gules and Or, for DANTESEY, 4th as 1ft. The Hall is very lofty and fpacious, with a Roof of Timber Frame, which is fupported by Cherubs holding Efcocheons charged with Arms, Cognizance and Cypher A H. In the Windows are, Quarterly, 1ft and 4th, HUNGERFORD, 2d and 3d, Per Pale, indented Vert and Gules a Cheveron Or, for DE HEYTESBURY,—impaling, Paly wavy of fix Or and Gules, for MOLEYNS. Upon the Wainfcot, which is of fmall Compartments filled with Mantles, are many grotefque Mouldings and a date, 1537.

We have been the more minute in this Defcription, as there are few fo perfect Specimens of the Architecture of that Age now remaining in this County.

No Benefactions to the Poor

INCUMBENTS	PATRONS	INCUMBENTS	PATRONS
1530	Abbey of Cirencefter	1681 Jofeph Richards, M. A.	———
—15 Bartholemew Ferrars,	———	1687 Michael Bingley, B. A.	———
1585 Simon Preffe,	Anthony Hungerford	1746 Thomas Smith, M. A.	
1590 Henry Bifhop,	John Hungerford	1785 John Morgan, M. A.	
1603 Robert Alford,	R. James	1788 Andrew Price, M. A.	
1679 Henry Green, M. A.	Ch. Ch. College, Oxford		

PRESENT LORD OF THE MANOR,

The Right Honourable EDWARD CRAGGS ELIOT Lord ELIOT.

The Perfons fummoned from this Place by the Heralds in 1682 and 1683 were,

The Heirs of Hungerford Dunch, Efq. and Henry Fletcher, Gent.

At the Election in 1776, Two Freeholders polled from this Parifh.

The oldeft Regifter bears Date 1603, and is written in Latin to 1641.

ANNUAL ACCOUNT OF MARRIAGES, BIRTHS, AND BURIALS, IN THIS PARISH

A D	Mar	Bir	Bur	A D	Mar	Bir	Bur	A D	Mar	Bir	Bur	A.D	Mar	Bir	Bur
1781	4	11	5	1786	2	6	9	1791				1796			
1782	3	7	6	1787	1	10	6	1792				1797			
1783	3	11	4	1788	3	9	7	1793				1798			
1784	4	7	3	1789	2	8	7	1794				1799			
1785	1	4	6	1790				1795				1800			

* Gateways of this kind became a very fafhionable Appendage to the moft magnificent Refidences in the beginning of the Sixteenth Century. They were introduced by HOLBEIN, who defigned that at *Whitehall*. Similar Edifices are at *Dray Hall*, Co. *Wilts*, built by Sir ANDREW BAYNTON, at *Cowbton*, Co. *Warwick*, by Sir ROBERT THROCMORTON and others. Sir ANTONY HUNGERFORD was Knight of the Shire for this County in the firft Parliament of Queen MARY, 1553. He finifhed the building after his marriage with his fecond Wife, ELIZABETH, Daughter of Sir JOHN DANVERS of *Dantefey*, Co. *Wilts* [*Argus B. d.*] (thus I 1ANE, lieu. v. II. p.) hath a little above *Afbney* Town out of a Rok by North, and porth 13 Miles or more to *Down Ampney* where Sir ANTONY HUNGERFORD hath a fayr Houfe of Stone. *fr. so ubi ori. Ampney* goeth in o &c, a Mile between *Down Ampney*, it an Name Eiton in *Wilfhir*.

INSCRIPTIONS IN THE CHURCH.

ON TABLETS IN THE CHANCEL

In Memory of
CÆSAR CHANDLER, Gent
who departed this Life Dec. 6, 1754

In Memory of
ANN the Wife of
CÆSAR CHANDLER, Gent
who departed this Life Oct. 26, 175
aged 65

A MURAL MONUMENT OF ALABASTER, UNDER A DOUBLE ARCADE, TWO FIGURES OF MEN KNEELING IN ARMOUR, A DESK BETWEEN THEM THE ELEMENT FINISHED WITH EMBLEMS AND DEVICE UPON THE ARCHITRAVE, ON SEPARATE ESCUTCHEONS,

1st Gules a Cheveron Ermine between ten Crosses patté Argent for BERKELEY, of Stone, 2 three Eagles displayed, for EARNLEY 3 Gules, a Cheveron vairy between three Crescents Or for GODDARD 4 Gules, three Lucies Haurient, A gent, semée Crosses Croslets Or, for LUCIE In the Centre, HUNGERFORD, Quartering, 1 HUNGERFORD, 2 DE HEYTESBURY, 3 Azure, three Garbs and a Chief Or, for PEVERLL 4 Argent, three Toads erect Sable, for BOTTREAUX, 5 Argent, two Bars Gules, in Chief three Torteaxes, for MOELS, 6 Ermine, within a Bordure Sable, bezantee, a Lion rampant Gules for CORNWALL 8 Or, three Torteauxes, in Chief a Label of three Points charged with three Fleurs de lis each for COURTENAY, 9 Bairy of six Ermine and Gules, for HUSEY, 10 Argent, a Gryphon segreant Gules, for BOTREAUX 11 MOELS 12 Sable, on a Chief Argent, three Lozenges Gules, for MOELS 13 Argent, a Bend Or, and a Label of three Points, for SAINT LOO, 14 Or, a Lion rampant crowned Azure 15 Azure, three Piles direct Or, for MALLETT, 16 HUNGERFORD, as before

In this Chapel lieth the Body of Sir JOHN HUNGERFORD Knight, lineally descended from WALTER Lord HUNGERFORD, Knight of the Noble Order of the Garter, who was beloved both in his Life, service done to his King and Country loyal to his Friend, charitable

to the Poor, and courteous to all.
He first married MARY,
the Daughter of
Sir RICHARD BARKLEY Knight,
by whom he had three Sonnes
and four Daughters
and afterwards ANNA the Daughter of
EDWARD GODDARD, Esq
He died the XVIII Day of March,
in the LXX Year of his Age,
Anno R R CAROLI Decimo,
Annoque Domini 1634

Christus Mihi Via

Sir ANTHONY HUNGERFORD, Knight,
now living (eldest son to this
Sir JOHN HUNGERFORD, Knight),
was first married to ELIZABETH LUCY,
Daughter to Sir THOMAS LUCY, Knight
by whom he had two Daughters,
(one died young, BRIDGET survived,
and was married to
EDMUND DUNCH, Esq),
and afterwards, the said Sir ANTHONY
married JANE EARNLY,
Daughter of MICHAEL EARNLY, Esq
by SUSAN HUNGERFORD
Daughter and one of the Coheirs of
Sir WALTER HUNGERFORD,
of Farley, Knight
He erected this Monument in the
LIII Year of his Age,
for the Honour of his dear Father
and in Remembrance of his own Mortality,
Sept. 30, Anno R R CAROLI XIII
Anno Domini 1637

ON A BRASS PLATE

Christus est refurrectio mortuorum
Hic jacet MARIA Domini HUNGERFORD,
uper uxoris JOHANNIS HUNGERFORD,
de Downe Ampney Militis,
(Jolinque RICHARDI BARKLEY,
Militis) prae Maurício Domino
BARKLEY, per Dominum ISABELLAM
Uxorem ejus, filia RICHARDI
BARKLEY, comitis Cornubiæ,
ut is Romanorum, filii Johannis
Regis Anglia haec dilecter descendebat),
quæ fuit vera pietatis, rarum exemplum,
honorum litterarum valde studiosa,
exquisite pudicitia et in omnibus
morato tua, christi et mortitur dulcis
conjuge et uxoris fua pene
Christi et Bonorum pene
Vixit cum marito fuo conjunctissime

Quadraginta et quatuor annos
Apostema in pectore vitam ejus
finivit decimo octavo die Julij,
vesperi circa horam septimam,
Anno ætatis suæ sexagesimo quinto,
Annoque Domini computatione Angliæ
16-8 { sicut via finis ita.
{ Vivit post funera virtus
Ultimum officii et Amoris mei erga
Landam MARIAM Dominam
HUNGERFORD et verum
Testimonium, WILLIELMUS PLATT

ON A TABLET

Here lieth JOHN, the second Son of
Sir JOHN HUNGERFORD, Knt
who was buried the 5th Day of March,
Anno Dom. 1643

ON FLAT STONES IN THE NAVE

ANTHONY KING
died May 18, 1662

ALICE his Wife,
died Jan 22, 16 8

RICHARD BENNETT
was buried August 30, 1675

MARY, Wife of HENRY FLETCHER,
died August 11, 1707

ANNE, the Wife of
THOMAS HOUSE of this Parish,
departed this Life May 9 1764,
aged 72

IN THE CHURCH YARD.   ON TOMBS

EDMUND HILLIER
died March 15, 1726, aged 70

Also JOHN and ELIZABETH HILLIER,
Father and Mother of the said
EDMUND HILLIER,
and JOHN his elder Brother

THOMAS KING
died July 23, 1767, aged 72

MARY his Wife
died Jan 19, 1771, aged 73

THOMAS CHRISTOPHER, and JANE,
their Children, died young

EDWARD KIMBER
died April 27, 1766, aged 69

ELIZABETH his Wife
died Feb 2, 1742, aged 55

EDWARD their Son
died Nov 14, 1762, aged 45

THOMAS, Son of EDWARD and
ELIZABETH KIMBER,
died March 27, 1779, aged 52

WILLIAM KIMBER, senior,
died August 4, 1782, aged 66

HESTER his Wife
died August 11, 1786, aged 74

LAWRENCE BURGESS
died July 11, 1773, aged 87

ELIZABETH, Wife of CHRISTOPHER
SAUNDERS of CRICKLADE,
Daughter of Mr LAWRENCE BURGESS
ELIZABETH and his Wife,
died Oct 2, 1719,
aged 27 Years 7 Months

HARRY BURGESS, Gent
died April 2, 1723, aged 37

MARY, Wife of JOHN GINGELL,
died April 15, 1725, aged 33

MARY, their Daughter,
died Oct 8, 1754, aged 30

CATHARINE, Wife of
LAWRENCE BURGESS, senior,
died Oct 18, 1777, aged 83

LAWRENCE BURGESS, junior,
Son of LAWRENCE and
CATHARINE BURGESS,
died Jan 18, 1786, aged 58

JOHN GINGELL
died April 9, 1767 aged 54

ON HEAD STONES

	Died	Aged
John Golding, of the Ley	4 Feb. 1776	65
Ann his Wife	19 June, 1776	57
Edward Hayward	9 Apr 1752	69
Anne his Wife	27 June, 1767	70
John Howse, senior	30 July 1745	95
Mary his Wife	17 Nov 1732	80
John Howse	31 May, 1786	73
John, Son of Thomas and Sarah Golding	12 June, 1787	17
Sarah, Wife of Thomas Golding	19 Nov 1782	44
Robert Archer	23 June, 1740	75
Ann his Wife	29 ——— 1751	60
John Son of John and Mary Hewer	30 May 1730	17
Mary his Mother	2 Jan 1766	91
Henry Hewer	9 Feb 1749	74
Mary, Wife of Richard Hewer	15 June, 1742	26
Betty Wife of Giles Hewer	22 Dec 1777	48
John Hodges	26 Sept 1750	82
Amy Wife of David Archer	24 Nov 1769	31
Margaret, Wife of John Archer	2 Sept 1747	77
John Archer	7 Mar 1730	61
John, Son of John and Margaret Archer	22 July, 1761	62
John Archer	4 Feb 1716	66
Robert their Son	16 Dec 1760	77
John Archer	3 June 1687	35
David Son of John and Jane Archer	11 June, 1749	63
Mary Wife of Richard Archer	6 Aug 1708	19
Richard Archer	14 Mar 1737	63
William Mealing	14 Feb 1698	35
Ann, Wife of William Mealing	17 Oct 1727	59
Ann, Daughter of John and Elizabeth Archer	13 Feb 1752	57
John Creed	16 Jan 1732	73
Elizabeth Creed	21 Nov 1754	60
Anthony Creed	6 Dec 1691	59
Elizabeth his Wife	5 Oct 1704	62
Thomas, Son of Thomas and Elizabeth Adams	18 Feb 1752	45

	Died	Aged
William Kimber	23 Dec 1760	69
Mary his Wife	13 Aug 1762	54
Mary, Wife of Anthony King	21 Apr 1771	64
Jane their Daughter	25 Mar 1756	33
Anthony King	30 May, 1755	44
Elizabeth his Wife	9 July, 1745	34
Alice, Daughter of Christopher and Elizabeth King	11 Nov 1785	19
Christopher King	13 June, 1740	37
Francis, Wife of Thomas King	15 June, 1729	81
Thomas King senior	1 Jan 1733	85
Sarah, Wife of Henry Hathaway	2 Feb 1780	53
John, Son of Henry and Mary Smith	1 July, 1781	56
Sarah, Wife of John Smith,	9 Oct 1782	49
John Kimber	30 Dec 1744	50
Robert, Son of William and Ann Mealing	18 Aug 1753	49
Alice Daughter of William and Ann Mealing	12 Oct 1766	77
Thomas Trinder	6 Nov 1759	72
Margaret his Wife	4 Oct 1758	66
Edmund, Son of Edmund and Priscilla Trinder	29 Nov 1780	24
Priscilla Wife of Richard Harrison Daughter of Edmund and Priscilla Trinder	1 July, 1785	21
Edmund Betterton	14 June, 1767	63
Mary, Wife of Walter Betterton	5 ——— 1754	71
John, Son of Lawrence and Catharine Burgess	18 Mar 1663	51
Harry their Son	18 May 1763	51
Deborah, Wife of Philip Ludlard	11 June, 1765	64
Edward, Son of Thomas and Edith Pitts	8 Dec 1726	56
Margaret Pitts	24 Aug 1746	57
Thomas, Son of Lawrence and Catharine Burgess	31 Jan 1765	
Thomas Matthews	19 Apr 1737	69
Ann his Wife	19 Feb 1759	65

C. DOWNE-HATHERLEY

IS a Parish of small extent, in the Hundred of Dudstone and King's Barton, situate in the great Vale of Gloucester, from which City it is distant four Miles on the North-east, six from Tewksbury in the opposite Direction, and at equal Distance from Cheltenham on the West. Of the Soil an exact Description is subjoined — it is chiefly in Tillage. The Terrier contains nearly 700 Acres, including a common Meadow of more than Sixty.

The Benefice is a Vicarage in the Deanery of Hembe, and the Church dedicated to St Mary, and Corpus Christi, a small unornamented Building, with no interesting Vestige of Antiquity.

Domesday Book records this Manor, under the Title of "Terra Regis," it was, on the Creation of the Barony of Gifford of Brimpsfield annexed to it, and held by Knights Service in 1311, 4 Edw II by Sir John de Antioch St Thomas Berkeley Sq, 17 Rich II having married the Heir of his Descendant, several Time. With the large Estates of that Family reputed by Inheritance to the gallant and ... Sir Fulk Greville, created Baron Brooke of Beauchamp Court in 1620, of which whom in 17.., the Eliz Nicholas Norwood, Esq (of the Family, settled at Champton, Spinster Cd the several Title, from which last it was transferred to that of Gwinnett, of Badgecombe ... prete the Representative of which Family is William Catchmay, Esq who assumed the arms and Arms of Gwinnett by royal Sign manual. But the Property of the largest Rate was ... in 1768, 41 Edw III in John At Yate, from whom it passed to the Berkeleys, of B.. e ... in the last Century the Family of Britt was established at Hatherly they were ... of th of Gibbes, about the Year 1720 and by William Gibbes, Esq who died ... the property that was bequeathed to Richard Sutton, of Norton Park, co Notts, who was created a Baronet, by Patent, dated 25 Sept 1772, 12 Geo III.

The Parish does not afford any other Subject of Remark

BENEFACTIONS

William Drinkwater, by Will, 1613, left 10s. a Year, to be given to the Poor at Christmas, payable out of an Estate.

—— Cox, 1654, gave 20s. a Year, payable out of an Estate at Upton St Leonards, to be distributed among such Poor as do not receive Alms at Christmas.

Henry Britt, Esq 1711, gave a Cottage, and three Acres of Arable Land, the Annual Produce of which now is 12 s.

Incumbents	Patrons	Incumbents	Patrons
1305 ——	Priory of St Oswald in Gloucester	—— Anthony Robertson,	——
	Priory of Usk	1660 John Fox,	Charles Norwood, Esq
1500 ——	Abbey of St Peter in Gloucester	—— Humphry Randal,	K Charles II
		1671 Samuel Broad, M A	
—— James Welham		1707 Thomas Pugh,	Q Anne
1563 Henry Argull, M A	Q Eliz	1727 Samuel Gwinnett, M A	K George I
16.. John At Argull, D D	King James I	775 Martin Bury, L.. B	K George III

* "On examining the Soil of a Ground which is deservedly esteemed the best Piece of Land in the Parish of Downe-Hatherley ... and observations to Committees ... of the Hay, I found as follow — the first in Inches a thin open Loam (a Mixture of Clay and Sand) free-... Matter, from 6 to 9 Inches a dark brown Clay ... adds ... more colour ... from 15 to 18 Inches a stronger Earth Clay still more ... the six Inches ... mixed with Fibres which ... th Depth ... of ... In these Soils ... full of them. Hence appears the Value of such Soils to to Corn Land ... I observed It ... the product acquired Phos ... was ... to continue in full Vigour for ... twelve Grass ... that the soil under ... does not ... in a ... for ... in Moisture ... Clover is unco ... rapid." Marshall's Rural Econ of Gloucestersh Vol I p 10..

PRESENT LORD OF THE MANOR,

WILLIAM CATCHMAY GWINNETT, Esq

The Perfons fummoned from this Place by the Heralds in 1682 and 1683, were
Samuel Broad, Vicar, and Richard Bifley, Gent

At the Election in 1776 Ten Freeholders polled from this Parifh

The Register has its firft Date in 1563, and is chiefly written in Latin.

ANNUAL ACCOUNT OF MARRIAGES, BIRTHS, AND BURIALS, IN THIS PARISH

A D	Mar	Bir	Bur	A D	Mar	Bu	Bur	A D	Mar	Bir	Bur	A D	Mar	Bir	Bur
1781	2	6	2	1786	—	3	3	1791				1796			
1782	2	5	5	1787	—	1	4	1792				1797			
1783	1	5		1788			3	1793				1798			
1784	3	—	—	1789	4	2	5	1794				1799			
1785	—	4	11	1790				1795				1800			

INSCRIPTIONS IN THE CHURCH.

ON A COARSE STONE AGAINST THE WALL IN THE
CHANCEL

Arms, Cheequy, Argent and Sable, on a Bend
Gules, three Efcallops Or

Vita fumo fugacior.

Here lyeth buried the Body of
WILLYAM PARTFREDGE, Efquier,
who departed this Life the
15th of Aprill, 1609

Memento quam fis brevis ævi

ON A MONUMENT ON THE SOUTH SIDE

Arms, on three Efcutcheons, 1 Gules, a Fefs
dauncette Argent, between 11 Billets Or, for BRETT
2 Brett, —impaling, Or, on a Fefs Sable three
Bezans, and in chief a Greyhound current of the
fecond, for LYANS 3 Or, a Saltire engrailed,
between four crofs Crofslets Sable

To the pious Memory of
HESTER, the beautiful Daughter of
RICHARD and MARGARET LYANS, of
Inftone in Oxfordfhire, Gent
The virtuous Wife of HENRY BRETT,
of Hatherley, Efq who died June 7,
Anno ætt 38 Sal 1696

Alfo
to the pious Memory of GEORGE BRETT, Efq
and JOYCE his Wife,
Father and Mother of HENRY,
who were here buried,

GEORGE, Anno ætt 4 Sal 1667

JOYCE, Anno ætt Sal 1662

ON FLAT STONES
IN THE CHANCEL.

ANNE BRETT, the Daughter of
GEORGE BRETT, Efq and of JOYCE his Wife,
was buried the 10th Day of July, A D 1662

ROBERT, Son of HENRY BRETT, Efq
and HESTER his Wife,
deceafed June Anno 16 aged 6 Mont's

HESTER, Wife of HENRY BRETT, Efq
departed this Life the 7th Day of June,
in the Year of our Lord 1696, aged 38

ARTHUR BRETT, Son of
GEORGE BRETT, Efq and JOYCE his Wife,
was buried March 20, 1661

HENRY BRETT Son of
GEORGE BRETT, Efq and JOYCE his Wife
was buried July 2, 1663

HESTER, Relict of JOSHUA BRETT,
Doctor in Divinity
died May 27, 1690, aged 51

The Rev. Thomas Piggott,
Vicar of this Church many Years,
died August 13, 1727, aged 57

Sarah Williams, his Sister
in Law, lies near this Place, 1726

In Memory of Susannah,
the Wife of Martin Barry, Vicar of this Parish,
Daughter of Gabriel Harris,
Alderman of Gloucester,
who departed this Life Nov. 2, 17--, aged 3

Also of Susannah his Wife
Daughter of Daniel Ellis of Mistleworth,
who died Jan. 9, 1754, aged 34

Also of Barbara his Wife
Daughter of James Rook, Esq.
of Bigsware, in the Parish of St. Briavels,
who died May 12, 1785, aged

On a large Monument, white & variegated
Marble, in the Nave

Arms, Argent, three Battle-axes sable, for Gibbes

To the Memory of
Wintchion Gibbes, Esquire, and
Elizabeth-Bathurst Gibbes,
This Monument was erected, agreeable
to the Direction of the last Will of the late
William Gibbes, Esq. of this Place,
as a testimony of his Regard and Esteem,
A.D. 1785

Wintchion Gibbes,
ob. 9 May, 1778, æt. 32

Elizabeth-Bathurst Gibbes,
ob. Mar. 15, 1763, æt. 71

IN THE CHURCH YARD, ON TOMBS.

Arms, on three Escutcheons, 1 Chequy, for
Aiscull 2 on a Fess three Crosses patée fitchy,
and on a Canton a Fleur de Lis. 3 On a Cross
five Cinquefoils, for Villiers

Hic jacet sepultus venerabilis
Vir Henricus Aiscull, Ecclesiæ
Cathedralis Menevensis Cancellarius,
Gloucestrensis Præbendarius, necnon
hujus Parochiæ Vicarius,
qui obiit in Domino Junii 18,
Anno Dom. 1620

William Drinkwater
was buried the 29th of January 1615,
who (in Zeal to the Worde)
give Forty Shillings yearly for ever, towarde
the Maintenance of a Preacher in Gloucester,
and Ten Shillings in Church, Ten Shillings
yearly to the Poor of Hatherly for ever

On a raised circular Tomb

Arms, on two Escutcheons 1 a Chevron between
three Sucars Heads, for Gwinnett 2 On a Fess
a Lion passant

Hæc urna colligit cineres
& impletur
quod est mortale Anne Gwinnett,
cujus formam mentemque honestam
... venerabor
& infamiæ vere potuit & duravit

Socratica virtus καλον ει αγια;
suis moribus & elegantiis ornata
suis, amicis, notis,
vivit etiam,
& omnibus vitæ partibus bene peractis
decessit plorat
Anno { Ætatis 74
{ Salutis 1768

Hos cineres
nec mitrata violet insolentia,
nec mitrata lædat aut malitia,
heu! sordidæ remittque mentis vitium,
& iterum ing. mœque prorsus aliena!
Nec polluant intus infirmum pavet,
quippe his tuberis olim ingurgitarunt
mores & intueri
Sit Samuelis Gwinnett, pastoris fidi,
nec verborum adulterantes, nec pietis apponitis,
ut in hujus Ecclesiæ munus obeundis
largus, simplicis, amœni, institutis,
sub cervis horis dedit residentia,
at inter hasce exeriones disciplinas
nec turbamus, nec iniecuris,
denique per vitam honestam & decoram
homo vere philosophicus fludiit,
civilis excoluit
Anno { Vicariæ 45
{ Ætatis 71
{ Salutis 1776

On the Base

Talais hunc lapide... parentibus
potui...
& lachrymis fudique averfi
... extrema rite persolvit

ON

ON HEAD STONES

	Died	Age
George Piffe, fenior,	2, June, 173_	5.
Betty, Wife of George Pifle	3 Feb 1760	_6
John Betty	24 June, 173_	
Anne his Wife	1. Apr 174.	4
Thomas Butt, fenior	28 May, 17..	6o
Mary his Wife	16 Feb 173.	(4
Thomas Butt, junior	24 Aug 17.7	51
Sarah, Wife of Thomas Holder, of Churchdown	2 Dec 1714	6o
Thomas their Son	11 Feb 171.	2.
Adam Jackfon, of Longford in the Parifh of St Mary de Load	14 Feb 1,06	101
Efther his Wife	6 Sept 1759	73
John Martin	_o Nov 1693	34
Anne his Wife	13 Sept 1708	—
David their Son	11 Apr 1712	_1
Thomas Thayer, of the Hamlet of Twigworth	11 Sept 1720	8o
William Thayer	2 Dec 1714	
John Lett	11 Nov 1762	80
Mary his Wife	2 Apr 17.4	60
Mary Wife of Francis Lett	31 Oct 1761	21
John, Son of Edward and Jane Prefton, of the Hamlet of Twigworth	15 Oct 1776	24
Jane their Daughter	5 May, 1786	24
Elizabeth, Wife of William Prefton	16 May, 1786	21
Edward Roane	25 Feb 167.	52
Joan his Wife	16 Apr. 1695	60
James their Son	3 Jan 1689	24
Giles Edwards, of Twigworth	12 Mar 1701	,7
John Edwards, of Twigworth	25 Jan 1684	69
Emmanuel Lane, Gent	29 July, 1698	—
Ann, Relict of William Randall, Gent	18 May, 1699	—
Jane, Wife of Emmanuel Lane, Gent	2 Nov 1694	5.
Sarah, Wife of John Vernon	22 Aug 1714	54

ci. DRIFFIELD, OR DRYFFELDE.

THIS Parish is included in the Hundred of Crowthorne and Minty, four Miles distant from Cirencester South-eastward, three in the opposite Direction from Crica de in Hampshire, and twenty-one from Gloucester. Within the Boundaries about a thousand Acres are included, the Grass Lands are cold and unproductive, here tilled are of a light Soil, yet not uncertain. The Common Fields are hitherto unenclosed.

All the impropriate Tythes have been allotted to the Vicarage since the Suppression of the Abbey of Cirencester, who held them with the Advowson, and forty-one Acres of Glebe were then added. It belongs to the Deanery of Cirencester.

The Church, dedicated to St. Mary, was rebuilt about thirty Years since, at the sole Expence of GABRIEL HANGER, Lord COLERAINE. It is a Edifice in the modern Style, of great simplicity and Neatness especially in the internal Decorations. SIR R. ATKYNS remarks of the old Church, that "it "was a strong Building with a Tower at the West End, and that there was an Inscription in the Chancel "cell for Sir JOHN PRETTYMAN Knight, Lord of the Manor, who died in 1638." Now destroyed.

Amongst the Possessions of REMB the Priest, the Manor of "Dryffelde" was enrolled, and given to the Abbey of Augustine Canons at Cirencester by King HENRY I. By the Charter or Confirmation granted by EDWARD III. they possessed here eight Hides of Land. In 1546 these Lands were given in Exchange for others at Halstan, co. Essex, to HUMFREY and GEORGE BROWNE by MARY the elder Cohen of Sir HUMFREY BROWNE, Knight, of Ridley Hall, co. Essex, and one of the Justices of the Common Pleas, they passed in Marriage Settlement to THOMAS WILFORD, Esq. prior to 1608, to whom succeeded Sir JOHN PRETTYMAN. JOHN D'AENOUR, of HANGER, a Merchant in London in the Reign of CHARLES I. purchased the manorial Estate extending over the whole Parish. His Descendant GABRIEL HANGER was created Baron COLERAINE, of Coleraine, in the County of Londonderry, in Ireland, Dec. 1, 1762, 2 GEO. III.

Upon the Site of the Manor house, modernized and improved by its later Possessors, was a country Residence of the Abbots of Cirencester. To this Place, at the Dispersion of their other Property, JOHN BLAKE, the last Abbot, was permitted to retire with a Pension of 220l. a Year, and sent several Years in Acts of religious Retirement. He was buried in the Chancel under an uninscribed Stone, nor can the Date of his Death be ascertained by any authentic Document. Parts of the present House are of the Style of the Commencement of the last Century, others more modern.

BENEFACTIONS

Five Pounds a Year are given by the Society for the Incouragement of Sunday Schools, to teach forty poor Children to read.

Incumbents	Patrons	Incumbents	Patrons
10 1539	Abbey of Cirencester	1654 Ric Parsons, LL B	Bishop of Gloucester
—— John Adams,	William Adams	17.. Thomas Ward	Robert Vele Gent
1583 Hen. v Hill,		17.. Richard Arthur, B A	Thomas Humphrys
—— Samuel Michel,	Sir John Prettyman	17.. Thos Humphrys, Clerk	—— ——
166. Sam Rich D D	indif { Wm Prettyman	1745 Thomas Jay B D	Cob Hinder, Esq
1668 Sam Rich D D	{ part { Bp of Gloucester	1777 Richard Denison Cum	
16.. Thomas Mole,	—— Gulim, Gent	Ireland, LL B	Thomas Smith, Esq

* Richard Parsons was born in 1643, Fellow of A College Oxon, LL B they appointed Chancellor of the Diocese of Gloucester 1672, LL D of the Middle in 1676.
* Dr Francis Parsons, while Chancellor of the Diocese of Gloucester, took an Opportunity to the back Archives deposited with the Cathedral and Deeds in the Registry of the Records to his publication of the New "History of the Antiquities of Gloucestershire and Diocese. A Design which he hoped to have completed... Method of arranging all the matters collected from History... he has ventured a Mention and Catalogue of all the present Cathedrals, Churches... to the Approved Valuation with Decline. The last of his New... and one time published the Parochial Diocese 1693 What he intended then, to print the proposed..." the Parish had preserved the detailing of Gloucestershire Topographia.

PRESENT LORD OF THE MANOR,

The Right Honourable JOHN HANGER Lord COLERAINE

The only Perſon ſummoned from this Place by the Heralds in 1682 and 168;, was
George Hanger, Eſq

At the Election in 1776, only One Freeholder polled from this Pariſh

The Regiſter commences with the Year 1560

ANNUAL ACCOUNT OF MARRIAGES, BIRTHS, AND BURIALS, IN THIS PARISH

AD	Mar	Bir	Bur	AD	Mar	Bir	Bur	AD	Mar	Bir	Bur	AD	Mar	Bir	Bur
1781	2	3	2	1786	1	6	2	1791				1796			
1782	—	3	1	1787	2	3	1	1792				1797			
1783	1	4	2	1788	1	2	—	1793				1798			
1784	—	3	6	1789	1	1	4	1794				1799			
1785	1	2	1	1790				1795				1800			

INSCRIPTIONS IN THE CHURCH

ON A TABLET IN THE CHANCEL

Arms, a Griffin ſalient per Feſs for HANGER

Near this Place lies interred the Body of
GEORGE HANGER, Eſq
who departed this Life, the 30th of May,
Anno Dom 1688, in the 74th Year of his Age

Arms, on a Lozenge a Lion rampant regardant

Near this Place lies interred the Body of
Mrs ANNE HANGER, late Wife of
GEORGE HANGER, Eſq deceaſed,
who departed this Life the 2nd Day of July,
Anno Dom 1678, in the 70th Year of her Age

ON A NEAT MARBLE MONUMENT

Arms, HANGER as before

Near this Place
lies the Body of Sir GEORGE HANGER, Knight,
who departed this Life the 24th Day of Nov 1731,
aged 80 Years

Near this Place
lieth the Body of Dame ANN HANGER,
Relict of Sir GEORGE HANGER, Knight.
She was Daughter and Coheireſs of
Sir JOHN BEALE, of Faringham
in the County of Kent, But
and departed this Life the 19th Day of November,
17—, aged 73

ON A SMALL NEAT MARBLE TABLET

Near this Place
lieth the Body of Mrs JANE HANGER,
Daughter of Sir GEORGE HANGER
who departed this Life the 7th Day of January,
Anno Dom 1764 aged 20
Relations and Friends erected this Memory,
for Proof of their Love and
the aſſurance of their Religion,
and in full hope of a bleſſed Reſurrection

ON ANOTHER TABLET NEAR THE FORMER

Here reſteth the Body of
Mrs MARY HANGER,
Daughter of Sir GEORGE HANGER, Knight,
who departed this Life the 17th Day of June,
Anno Dom 1722
She was pious, virtuous, and charitable,
and endued with
all thoſe amiable Qualifications
that could render her Truly deſirable,
and her Change happy

ON AN ELEGANT MARBLE MONUMENT

Arms, Quarterly, 1ſt and 4th, HANGER as before, 2d and 3d Sable, on a Chevron Or, between three Griffin Heads eraſed Argent, three Flores Gules for BEALE On an Eſcutcheon of Pretence, quarterly, 1ſt and 4th, Argent a Chevron Or, between three Demi Lions rampant Gules for BEALE 2d and 3d, Sable, a Chevron between three Boars Heads couped at the Shoulders Argent, for VAUGHAN Motto, as it went

Here lieth
in Expectation of the laſt Day,
GABRIEL HANGER, Lord COLERAINE
whoſe manner of Mind he was
that Day will diſcover
He died June 24, 17—, aged 75

Here also,
in hope of a joyful Reſurrection,
lieth buried with her Lord,
ELIZABETH lady COLERAINE,
Daughter and Heireſs of
RICHARD BOND, Eſq of Combury
in the County of Hereford
She died Dec 10, 17—
16,

O N   F L A T   S T O N E S

Under this Stone lieth the Body of
GABRIEL HANGER, Son of
GABRIEL HANGER, Esq of Dryffield,
who died the 28th Day of July,
Anno Dom 1747, aged 9 Years

Here lieth interred the Body of
JOHN HANGER, of London Merchant,
deceased the 10th Day of May, 1654.
Also of Mrs. MARTHA TROTT,
the Daughter of the said JOHN HANGER,
who deceased October the 10th, 1688

I N   T H E   C H U R C H   Y A R D ,   O N   T O M B S

FRANCIS RADWAY
died April 22, 1761, aged 76

ANN his Wife
died Dec 10, 1748   aged 76

ANNE their Daughter
died August 9, 1715, aged 6

RICHARD HOWSE, senior,
died May 5, 1730, aged 68.

ANNE his Wife
died Feb 5, 1757 aged 99.

ELIZABETH SUDELL, of this Parish,
Wife of JOHN JONES, RICHARD CRAFTS, and
OBADIAH BLACKWELL,
all Citizens and Stationers of London,
departed this Life the 22d Day of Oct 1709,
aged 83 Years

ELIZABETH, Wife of JOHN FORSHEW,
died March 23, 1739, aged 72

ANN FORSHEW
died the 7 May, 1719, aged 31

THOMAS HAYWARD,
Clerk of this Parish,
died July 1, 1731, aged 74.

ELIZABETH his Wife
died Oct 18, 1691, aged 44.

JANE his second Wife
died Oct 5, 1720, aged 61

ANN, Daughter of
THOMAS and ELIZABETH HAYWARD,
died Dec 25, 1756, aged 72

JOHN HAYWARD
died Dec 10, 1739, aged 45

O N   H E A D   S T O N E S

	Died		Age
Henry Adams	6 Apr	1746	77
Mary his Wife	30 Mar	1753	77
Michael Dubber	18 Jan	1735	—
Sarah his Wife	18 Sep	1743	66
John Adams	27 Apr	1729	65
Rebecca his Wife	30 Jan	1739	63
Thomas Kilby	4 Oct	1755	90
Margaret, Wife of Thomas Kilby	1 Apr	1739	67
John Kilby	9 Jan	1749	50
John Lane	3 Nov	1744	71
Jane, Wife of John Ficketts	13 Feb	1749	43
Peter Wakefield	28 Apr	1754	86
William Eldridge, senior	31 Dec	1750	51
Mary his Wife	22 Sep	1711	75
Elizabeth, Wife of John Weekes	2 Dec	1755	64
Jane, Wife of William Brush	2 Dec	1758	40
Michael True	19 Mar	1750	51
Sarah Wakefield	2 Apr	1751	77
Katharine, Wife of William Goodrick	4 Dec	1779	94
William, Son of John Lane	25 May, 1774		65
Joan, Wife of John Kilby	28 Mar, 1774		76
William Ayliffe	20 July, 1748		52

CII. DUMBLETON.

THE Distance of this Parish, which lies in the Hundred of *Kiftefgate*, from *Teesban*, in *Worcefter*, is six Miles on the South, four North from *Winchcombe*, and eighteen North-eastward to the City of *Glocester*. Two thousand five Hundred Acres are described in its Terrier, one fourth only of which is in Tillage, of a strong Clay Soil, and singularly fertile, near the Rivulet *Ifbourne*.

The Benefice is rectorial, in the Deanery of *Campden*, charged with 10s. a Year to *Trinity College, Oxford*, which is invested with certain impropriate Tythes, of the yearly Value of 10l., and with the Remainder and Glebe of eighty Acres, the Vicarage is endowed.◊

There are good Reasons for Conjecture that the Church, dedicated to *St. Peter*, was erected at the Charge of the Abbey of *Abingdon*, co. *Berks*, in the 13th Century, who bound themselves to the Repairs of it, an Expence from which the Parishioners are still exempted. It consists of a Nave, a low South Aisle, and a sepulchral Chapel, projecting as a Semi transept from the North Side, with a massive embattled Tower. This Dormitory may have been coeval with the other Building, it was erected by Robert Dastyn, or Daston. Around the Margins of Slabs are these mutilated Inscriptions, in the Norman Language, and partly *Saxon* Character. "ROBERT DASTYN JANDER D." "DEV DEL AIME EYT MERLI" Upon the other, "MARKERIC DASTIN GIST ICI." "DEV DEL AIME" Such Memorials were not unfrequent as late as the Reigns of the three Edwards.† *Jesus College, Oxford*, as holding the former Property of this Family, is liable to Repairs of this Part only.

King ATHELSTAN ‡, in 931, included this Manor, taxed at seven Hides and a Half (750 Acres) in his Charter of Foundation of the Abbey of *Abingdon*, and in 15 EDW. I. 1287, the Abbot proved his Right of free Warren, &c. When that House was dissolved in 1543, the Manor and Advowson were granted to THOMAS Loucher Lord AUDLEY, and Sir THOMAS POPE, Knight, in Exchange for *Iver Marney*, co. *Essex*, but confirmed to the latter two Years afterward. He bequeathed this manorial Estate to EDMUND HUTCHINS ◊, by his Will, dated 1556, the Son of his second Sister ELIZABETH, who had married RICHARD HUTCHINS, of *Chipping Norton*, co. *Oxford*. Dying without Issue he gave it to his Wife DOROTHY, Daughter of THOMAS COCKS, of *Cleeve* who settled it on her Brother CHARLES COCKS and his Heirs in 1646, the Progenitor of the present Proprietor. Upon the Demise of Sir ROBERT COCKS in 1705, the fourth in Descent from RICHARD COCKS, created a Baronet in 1666, it lapsed to the Hon. General CHARLES COCKS, of *Castle Ditch*, co. *Hereford*, who was created a Baronet Sept. 1, 177 , and a Baron May 7, 1784, 24 GEO. III. by the Title of Lord SOMERS, Baron of LVESHAM.

The Manor-house is now partly taken down and rented as a Farm: it was large and commodious, and the constant Residence of the Family.

A Portion of Division of the rectorial Tythes of this extensive Parish (together with a Pension of 10s. charged on the Vicar-age) formerly belonging to the Abbey of *Abingdon* was given to *Trinity College, Oxford* by the Tenure of Sir THOMAS POPE about 157 . This Estate evidently is the Beginning of the Rental JAMES I. paid annually to the College 4 l. 9 s. in Money, together in Content the Quarters of Wheat, one ton of Malt with the same Proportion in three Periods. Under CROMWELL it is no better: Dr. KEN HARRIS, the interposing President of the College, with his Fellows to retain the uncertain Value and Establishment took an exorbitant Fine for this Lease. At the Restoration, the reinstated President and Fellows applying to the Lessee to Renew, the Case was referred to the Lord Chancellor who was of Opinion that the College, by her Tenure of the Fine, would sell out almost the whole preferment to reversionary Benefit in this Property, and therefore heard the original, which he conceived to a demand Improvement to the College. The President is remaining to let the Chancel of this Parish with that (of Longney) interposed by the Foundation of Jesus College, Oxford, as demonstrated in Note (p.). The Founder commands only the Nave of this Manor with Sexton, presupposes them to repair, in public Obligations preceded in the estate. The President is therefore exhibited in repairing any part of the private. The particular Privilege. We are ever willing to avail ourselves to the obdurate ability to prosecute such demands, but especially if what has been alleged comparably ceases Prejudice in any Quarter.
                                        Sir Green, Hill, day Of 5

‡ Given Sep. Men. Third p. 1551
* JAMES Notes Life Note. DAVIS's Supplement I p. 50 . Preface 5 Hist. I. Qu. Warren del. Ibot.
D. Sai.
§ DOMESDAY Hutchins was one of the Scholars of *Trinity College, Oxford*, support I. by the Founder, and inherited when bequeath for 1553. By his Will declared Life 16. for the estate by the Abbot first the Estate will that work of COST. Now partly by applied to Lands, the which further than Parish estate, so that his chosen by formula, the found who was made a Dean and buried 1563. Upon that portion College the whole remained in not part of Lands the Son. *Jesus College, Oxford*, Warden . . . his continued Hutchins. Warden. Liberal and Dean, Jesu.

Another confiderable Eftate is attributed in *Domefday* Book to WILLIAM GOIZ NBOLD, which, in th early fucceeding Centuries was transferred to the Family of DASTON. Parcel of th's Eftate was purchafed in 1629 by the Executors of Sir Thomas WYNNE, Knight, and the Principal and Fellows of *Jefus College*, Oxford, were enfeoffed of it, for the Main chance of one Scholar on their Foundation, and other Purpofes *

Such is the Hiftory of the Property of this Parifh, which furnifhes no botanical Rarity, nor would enrich with its Productions the Claffes of the Foffilift

BENEFACTIONS

JOHN COCKS, Efq 1723, bequeathed Land, the Yearly Rent of which, now is £ 4s five of which, to place out fome Boy or Girl Yearly, or at two or three Years, as his Executors fhall think fit, the remaining Part to be diftributed amongft fuch Poor as do not receive Alms

INCUMBENTS	PATRONS	INCUMBENTS	PATRONS
To 1543,	Abbey of Abingdon	1733 William Cockes, B A	— — — —
1581 Oliver Dafton,	Edmund Hutchins, Efq	1754 Kynard Baghett, B A	Will Baghett, Efq
1615 Michael Willington,	William Dobyns	17., Thomas Paghett, M A	The fame
1640 Tho Wafhbourne B D	— — —	1762 John Baghot De la bere,	William Baghott De la Bere
1687 Charles Cockes, M A	Sir Ric Cockes, Bart		

PRESENT LORD OF THE MANOR,

The Right Honourable CHARLES Lord SOMERS, Baron of EVESHAM

The only Perfon fummoned from this Parifh by the Heralds in 1682 and 1683, was Sir Richard Cockes, Bart

At the Election in 1776 Two Freeholders polled from this Parifh.

ANNUAL ACCOUNT OF MARRIAGES, BIRTHS, AND BURIALS, IN THIS PARISH

A D	Mar	Bir	Bur	A D	Mar	Bir	Bur	A D	Mar	Bir	Bur	A D	Mar	Bir	Bur
1781	2	8	4	1786	1	6	4	1791				1796			
1782	2	11	6	1787	3	6	4	1792				1797			
1783	4	11	4	1788	5	6	4	1793				1798			
1784	—	12	12	1789				1794				1799			
1785	1	7	10	1790				1795				1800			

INSCRIPTIONS IN THE CHURCH

UNDER AN ARCADE, TWO FIGURES KNEELING, IN THE DRESS AND STATE OF THE TIMES

Arms, On Efcutcheons, quarterly, Or, a Lion rampant Azure, for PERCY, 2d and 3d, Gules, three Lucies hauriant proper, for Lucy, impaling, Sable, a Chevron between three Stags Attires, Argent for COCKES

Here lye the Bodies of Sir CHARLES PERCY, Knt 3d Son of the Earle of Northumberland, and of Dame DOROTHY his Wife, the Daughter of THOMAS COCKES, of Cleeve, Efq and of ANNE their Daughter. Sir CHARLES was buried the 6th D of July, Anno Domini 1628 Dame DOROTHY, the 28th of June, Anno Domini 1640

ON A HANDSOME MARBLE TABLET

ARMS COCKES IMPALING

Memoriæ Sacrum
CAROLI COCKS Armigeri, Filii natu
THOMÆ COCKS, de Cleeve, in Agro Gloucestriæ,
Armigeri, qui obiit decimo quinto die Augusti,
Anno ætatis fuæ octogefimo tertio,
Anno que Domini MDCLIV

RICHARDUS COCKS, Baronett, nepos ejufdem
CAROLI & curatrum Heres hoc parental love
CAROLO hoc Monumentum Amoris
& Gratitudinis ergo
extruxit

Upon a large Monument

Arms, Cockes,—impaling, P ly of fix Or and Gules, on a Bend Sable three Mullets of the Field, for Elton

In Memory of

Sir Richard Cocks, Baronet, and of Dame Susanna his Wife He was the fecond Son of Richard Cocks, of Castle Ditch in the County of Hereford, Efq and of Judith his Wife, Daughter and Coheir of John Elliott, Efq She was the th Daughter of Ambrose Elton, of the Hasle in the County of Hereford, Efq and of Anne his Wife, Daughter of Sir Edward Aston, of Tixill in the County of Stafford He, in his younger Days, accompanied his Uncle Christopher Cocks, who was honoured by King James the Firft, with a public Character into Mufcovy, and after his Return he retired into the Country, and was concerned with no publick Matters, more than the Offices of Justice of the Peace and High Sheriff She was a Lady distinguished by very great Ornaments of Mind and Body the visible Remains of which continued with her to her last Hour They kept good Hospitality, loved their Tenants and Neighbours, and on all Occasions did them all the Service they could He lived peaceably with them, and kept them in Peace one with another He was a great Sufferer for his Love to the Royal Family, and for his Zeale for the Laws and Eftablished Religion of his Country. They were indulgent Parents, good to their Servants, and charitable to the Poor They gave their Children good Fortunes, and liberal Education They had three Sons, Richard, Charles, and John, and two Daughters, Judith and Elizabeth But John the younger, and Elizabeth, the Relict of Sir John Fust, of Hill in this County, Baronet, only furvived them, fhe, out of a juft Remembrance, and Gratitude to fo good Parents, and believing the Memory of them would be grateful to their Neighbours, ordered her Brother John Cocks to erect this Monument for them. He died September 16, A D 1684, aged 82. She died March 10, A D 1689, aged 84

Against the South Wall in the Chancel, on a fquare Marble Tablet

To the happy Memory of Mrs Dorothy Cocks She died the 29th Day of October, 1714, in the 58th Year of her Age, and lies interred in the Chancel near the Communion Table She was eldeft Child of Richard Cocks, Efq and of Mary his Wife, the youngeft Daughter of Sir Robert Cooke, of Hynron, by his firft Wife, her Father and her Mother both died when fhe was about 14 Years old She was of a middle Stature, covered with great Ornaments of Body and with all the care of the Mind She was a Woman of a very good and compaffionate Nature, of a great Underftanding, and made a very good Ufe of it, fhe endeared to her Mother to her younger Sifters, than to be engaged in another Family, and by her good Inftructions, fhe helped to bread them up in Piety and Religion,

and other neceffary Knowledge. Envy itfelf cannot charge her with an unbecoming Action, or Expreffion, in her whole Life She was a Woman of great Piety, Patience, and Humanity, fhe fpent great Part of her Life in her Devotions and Prayers, for herfelf, her Friends, and her Country, fhe bore a tedious Sickness, and other Misfortunes that attended her infirm Body with all Cheerfulnefs and Refignation, fhe made Ufe of her Time and Fortune, not only to ferve Friends and Relations, but even Strangers that were diftreffed Therefore Sir Richard Cocks, her eldeft Brother, out of a grateful Remembrance of thefe Virtues, has chofe rather to fet up this true and juft Epitaph, than a magnificent Monument, with an Intention to make her Family blufh, when they deviate from fuch a Precedent, and that they and others may imitate her Example in this World, *and be happy with her in the next.*

IN THE NAVE.

On a large Marble Monument

Arms, Cocks as before,—impaling, Gules, a Saltire Argent, charged in the Centre with a Rofe of the firft, for Neville.

To the facred Memory of Frances Lady Cocks, dearly and defervedly beloved Wife of Sir Richard Cocks, of Dumbleton in the County of Gloucefter, Bart She was the fifth, and youngeft Daughter of Colonel Richard Nevill, of Billingfbeat in the County of Berks, who was defcended from a younger Son of Lord Abergavenny and of Anne his Wife, one of the Daughters of Sir Christopher Heydon, of Bocanfthrop in the County of Norfolk She was a Lady endowed with all the Accomplifh-ments Nature or Education would beftow upon or form in her, fhe was eminently pious and zealous for the eftablifhed Government and Religion, which was demonftrated by the many Hours fhe daily fpent in her private Devotions, and her conftant Attendance, even to the Hazard of her Health, upon the Service of the Church She was an Ornament to the Honourable Family from which fhe defcended, and was efteemed an Honour and a Bleffing to the Family fhe came into She was an obliging good Neighbour to the Rich, charitable to the Poor, the kindeft Miftrefs, and the beft of Wives She lived more than 3 Years in Peace, Harmony, and Tranquillity with her Husband, as far is human Imbecilities common to the beft of Mortals would permit, fhe continued, in delight of, and the Infirmities incident to, Mortality, cheerful and comely to the laft Minute of her Life She died, after a fhort Indifpofition, of a Fever, and upon a Cold, the 1ft of Feb Anno Dom 17 in the fixtieth Year of her Age Her Husband therefore expreffeth his Gratitude to Heaven for his folong enjoying fo great a Bleffing and Comfort, and to all the Remembrance of her fhould, with with the Memory of the Generation to perpetuate, and for is in him lies, the Virtues of fo excellent a Perfon, his ordered this Monument to be erected

ON A NEAT TABLET OF WHITE MARBLE

In Memory of Sir Robert Cocks, Bart
who, after suftaining with Christian Fortitude
and Refignation the most affecting Loss of
an amiable Wife and three Children
in the course of a few Days by a cruel
Diftemper which attacked his Family,
had the Misfortune to lose his own
Life, by a Fall from his Horse in April 1765,
and lies buried near this Place

IN THE SOUTH AISLE

ON A MARBLE MONUMENT, WITH ELEGANT
SCULPTURE AND DEVICES

ELIZABETH,
Wife of Sir Robert Cocks, Bart
and Daughter of James Cholmeley, Esq
of Eaiton in the County of Lincoln,
with three of her Children,
CHARLES, ANN, and CATHERINE,
were carried fuccessively, by the fame fatal Sicknefs,
a Fever and a fore Throat,
to the Grave
in a few Days
A most excellent and amiable Mother,
the two youngest in the brighteft Dawn of Hope,
the eldest in the fweeteft Bloom of Virtue,
growing up like the fineft Flowers,
like the fureft Flowers
were cut down
This Place where they fleep
is marked out by the unfeigned Grief of a Husband,
mixed with the Tears and unflattering
Praife of furviving Friends,
unhappy in being Survivors,
unlefs they tread in the fame blamelefs Steps,
happy could they, by keeping her in Remembrance,
each the fame fhining Heights
of Lovelinefs, Virtue, and Religion

CHARLES,	died Jan 21, aged	3 Years,	
ANNE,	Jan 26,	8,	
ELIZABETH,	Jan 30,	9,	
CATHERINE,	Feb 7,	10,	
	A D 1749		

Alfo three other Children,

CHARLES,	died April 3, 1733, aged 1 Year 8 Mo	
ELIZABETH,	July 2, 1738,	9 Months
ROBERT,	Sept 27, 1740,	10 Years

ON ANOTHER ELEGANT MARBLE MONUMENT

Arms, Cocks as before

To the Memory of
Miss DOROTHY COCKS,
the youngeft and only furviving Child
of Sir Robert Cocks, of Dumbleton, Bart
who died, April 24, 1767, aged 18 Years,
much lamented by all who knew her,
A fair Flower
cut off in the Bloffom of Life,
amiable in her Perfon,
fenfible and prudent in all her Actions,
untainted with the Follies
and Difsipation of the Age
in which fhe lived
This little Monument, in Teftimony
of her great Love and Affection,
is erected by her Aunt
Miss SARAH COCKS

ON FLAT STONES IN THE NAVE.

Here lieth the Body of
ANTHONY, the Son of Anthony Best, Gent
He lived in the Parifh of St Clement, London,
and laid here to reft, in Hope of a joyful
Refurrection
A Man faithful to his Friend,
and loving to the Poor
He gave to this Parifh twenty Pounds at his Death.
He was buried the 14th of Sept 1687,
æt æis fuæ 21

Mr ANTHONY BEST the elder
departed this Life the laft Day of Auguft,
in the Year 1685, ætat fuæ 75.

Alfo ANNE his Wife
died Jan 15, 1699

In Memory of Mrs ELIZABETH KEEN,
who was twenty Years Houfekeeper to
Sir Robert Cocks, Baronet
She departed this Life June 11, 1753,
aged 51 Years

IN THE NORTH AISLE

ON A FLAT STONE WERE THE FIGURES OF A MAN
AND WOMAN IN BRASS AND AT THEIR FEET THIS
INSCRIPTION, ALL OF WHICH ARE NOW ENTIRELY
DEMOLISHED

Orate p a'ibus Willi Dafton, filii Joh'is Dafton
et Annæ uxoris ejus, qui quidem Willi us, obiit
Anno Domini M'illmo CCCC XXX°. quor
a't'ab' p picietur Deus

IN THE CHURCH YARD, ON TOMBS

JOHN INGLIS
died   1647

JOHN STATE, Yeoman,
died Aug 1, 1728, aged 59

ANN his Wife
died Jan 6, 1721 2, aged 44.

JOHN AGGE
died April 8, 17?5, aged 62

JOHN his Son, by SARAH his Wife,
was buried Dec 11, 1677, aged 8 Months

SARAH Wife of JOHN AGGE,
died May 7, 1729, aged 77

HANNAH, Wife of JOB STOCK,
died May 17, 17?2, aged 5?

ON HEAD STONES

	Died	Aged
Mary, Wife of John Timbrell	20 Sept 17?6	89
John Timbrell	1? Dec 178?	8?
Mary, Daughter of John and Mary Cowles	20 Feb 17?7	4?
Mary, Wife of John Field	14 Feb 1773	??
Richard James	3 Aug 177?	6?
Mary, Wife of Robert State	5 Sept 17?9	?6
Thomas Pilman	6 Nov 1720	?5
Elizabeth his Wife	30 Aug 1771	?9
Richard Dobbins	18 May, 1754	?3
John Harris	18 Sept 1752	?5
Mary, Wife of James Dunn	6 Sep 176?	49
Joseph Wheeler	2 Dec 7?2	5?
Mary his Wife	6 —— 1747	77
Richard Baker	9 Mar 1742	6?
John Andrews	5 July, 1744	8
Elizabeth his Wife	25 Mar 1729	54
David Phillips	22 Dec 1?66	3?
Francis Dunn	15 Feb 1770	8?
James Dunn	15 Feb 178?	6?
Elizabeth, Wife of Richard James	16 Oct 1745	31
Richard James	3 Aug 177?	6?
John his Son	2 July, 1774	?9
Edward Foot	10 Jun, 17?0	?7
Elizabeth, Wife of Edward Clayton	4 Sept 1729	30
Henry Clayton	27 Jun 174?	??
Ann his Wife	1 Dec 17?3	6?
Sarah, Wife of John Cullabine	3 Mar 17??	??
John Cullabine	6 June, 1782	6?
Mary, Wife of John Baylis	15 Feb 1781	??

CIII. DUNTESBORNE ABBATIS,

OR

UPPER DUNTESBORNE,

A PARISH situate on the South-west side of the *Irmin-street*, or *Foss* Road, from *Cirencester* to *Gloucester*, from which it is distant twelve Miles South-eastward, and from the former Place five, in the precisely opposite Direction. The Soil is chiefly high, and in Tillage, by a proportion of three fourths, of considerable Extent, and divided between the Hundreds of *Crowthorne* and *Minety*, and *Rapsgate.*

Of the Benefice, a Rectory in the Deanery of *Cirencester*, the Advowson originally annexed to the Manor, is said to have been obtained from the Crown by Esmé Stuart, Duke of *Richmond*, in 1611, 8 James I, but it does not appear, that he presented. From the Family of Estcourt and others, who have been Patrons since 1583, it was transferred to the last, and is now vested in the Family of the present Incumbent.*

The Church, dedicated to *St. Peter* (the Tutelar of its Patron Monastery at *Gloucester*), is an inconsiderable Structure, with a low-roofed Tower at the West end. It is a Member of the Deanery of *Cirencester.*

When *Domesday* was compiled, a noble House of the *Normans* held the greater Division of *Duntesborne*, but none is Property specified, and in divers Portions. The Vill and Manorial Rights, consisting of 5 Hides (nearly 600 cultivated Acres), were granted to the Abbey of *St. Peter* in *Gloucester*, by ... , Relict of Walter de Lacy, upon his sudden Death in 1085, and, in 1100, Gilbert de Esketot ... and other Lands. These Estates were purchased out of the Court of Augmentations in 1548, 1 Eliz. by William Morgan and James Doile, in the Descendants of which last they remained, to Oliver Doile in 1669, though with considerable diminutions. The Family of Pleydell, of Coleshill, co *Berks*, long after their Possession of other Estates in this Parish, purchased the Manor. Sir Mark Stuart Pleydell, Baronet, about thirty Years since built a House, on a singular Plan, on an Eminence in this Parish, which he erected for the very beautiful rural Scenery which it presents, and to which he frequently retired. Upon his Death, in 1770, he devised this Manor and Estate to the present Earl of Radnor, Son of William Bouverie, Viscount *Folkstone* (created Earl of *Radnor*, Oct. 3, 1765, 5 Geo. III.) by Harriot his Wife, sole Daughter and Heir, then deceased. One Hide, given by Richard Murdac, in 1149, to the Prior of *Llanthony*, in the Year 1544, to Richard Andrews and Richard Leonard.†

The only Hamlet *Duntesborne Lear*, or *de Lear*, which is part of the Hundred of *Rapsgate*, held at the Conquest by the Abbey of *Lire*, in *Normandy*, and transferred at the Suppression of Alien Priories to the *Augustines* of *Cirencester* in 1416, 3 Hen. V. In 15 ... , 4 Eliz. it was bought by John Pleydell, of *Berks*, co *Berks*, and incorporated with the Manorial Estate. It is anciently recorded as a separate Manor, and included *Sumner Farm.*

Other Property, exclusive of the principal, is vested in the Families of Chapman, Field, and Hard.

BENEFACTIONS

Thomas Meceleton, 1652, gave by Will a Freehold Pasture Ground in this Parish, now let at ... per Annum, to be given to the Poor of the Parishes of *Duntesborne Abbatis*, *Winstone*, and ... in the following Proportions, ... to this Parish, and the produce of a Coppice Wood growing thereon (cut every 12 Years) directed to be yearly divided between the Poor, ... deducting 1s. for his Use, ... of *Duntesborne Abbatis* for their Trouble.

William Harding, 1833, by Will gave Twenty Pounds ... thereof for instructing poor Parish Children in the Officer's Handicraft.

A School has also been built by the Parishioners.

Incumbents	Patrons	Incumbents	Patro s
1541 ———,	Abbey of Gloucester.	1620 William Poole,	The same
1573 James Ballard,	Bishop of Gioucester	1661 Thomas Phipps,	Wm Morse and J Loud
1575 Hugh Humphrys,	Anthony Herbert	1714 William Phipps,	Joseph Jones, Gent
1583 Thomas Knight,	Thomas Eftcourt, Efq	1733 Tho Davies, B A	Edmund Davies, Gent
1594 Giles Dymoke,	The fame	1772 Jol Chapman, B A	James Clutterbuck Es
1613 Thomas Cole,	Sir Thonas Eftcourt.		

Present Lord of the Manor of *Duntefborne Abbatis* and *De Lyra*

The Right Honourable Jacob Pleydell Bouverie Earl of Radnor

The Perfons fummoned from this Place by the Heralds in 1682 and 1683 were,

William Phipps, Rector, and Oliver Dolle, Gent

At the Election in 1776, Fourteen Freeholders polled from this Parifh, and the Hamlet of *Duntefborne L*

The oldeft Regifter bears Date 1683

Annual Account of Marriages, Births, and Burials, in this Parish

A D	Mar	Bir	Bur	A D	Mar	Bir	Bur	A D	Mar	Bir	Bur	A D	Ma	Bir	Bur
1781	2	7	2	1786	2	8		1791				1796			
1782	2	17	2	1787	1	9	8	1792				1797			
1783	2	8	4	1788	—	12	7	1793				1798			
1784	1	13	5	1789				1794				1799			
1785	3	9	14	1790				1795				1800			

INSCRIPTIONS IN THE CHURCH

ON FLAT STONES IN THE CHANCEL

In Memorium
Maria uxoris Thomas Phipps,
Rectoris hujus Ecclefie, quæ
fepulta fuit decimo die Januarii,
Anno Salutis 1694

Mr William Phipps,
Rector of this Church,
was buried Dec 17, 173-, aged 71

A n, the Daughter of
John Partridge,
and Wife of
Thomas Phipps,
Rector of this Chuch,
was here buried

Here refteth the Body of
Oliver Dolle, Gentleman,
who departed this Life
the 2d Day of September,
An o Dom 160

Here lieth the Body of
Anne, the Wife of Thomas Limerick
She d'ed the 1th Day of April,
aged 5

IN THE CHURCH YARD

Against the Porch

Beneath this Place lieth Anthony Sly,
of this Parifh
He died the 9th Day of July, 736,
aged 9 Years

On a Tomb

William Freeman, of this Parifh,
died March 13, 17 9, aged 9

Mary his Wife
died Oct 9 176, aged 6

ON FLAT AND HEAD STONES

	Died	Aged		Died	Aged
Jofeph Saver, fervant of Dunfborn			William ?eams		
Loufe	1 June, 7 9		Phineas son of John and Mary Lwle	3 July	
Jofeph ryer junior,	14 July, 25 9	15	or Wite of James Hobbs	21 Ma 1,	
Joan Vite of Jofeph Saver	6 Ma 17 0	—	John on of Thomas and May		
Richard on of William and May			Huim	6 July 1 t	
Freman	6 Dec 1,18	7	Thomas Huding	10 Jan 1753	
Thomas Frid,	Aug 1, 9	36	Mary his wife	4 Ma 1 4	
Joh n	Oct 1751	57	William Huding,	30 June, 1785	
William ell	June, 175	65	Here, the first on o Thomas		
r ohl d	Aug 1 5	55	and Mary Huding	18 Ma 17,	
Thomas e 1	7 July, 1,44	47	Mary der of Anthony Sly	3 Jan 1	
Here iche Ruth onto sh no			Mary, Wife 1 j La Eid	22 Ju 17 5	
and Anthon y	15 De 1, 4		Eli beth Wife of William Ruth	3 June, 1713	
Mary Wife of Thoma Clark, and			Sarah vfe William Huding	6 Feb 1 9	
Daughter of Edward and			Thomas Truftman	July 1 9	
IKl	1 Jan 1737	98	Here n Wife of Thomas Truftman	10 Oct 1,	
Mary Wife of John Pice	June 9	7	Jerem ah Griffith	— 1 9	

CIV. DUNTESBORNE MILITIS RUFI,
OR
LE ROUS.

IT was cuftomary, with the *Norman* Followers of the Conqueror, to apply their Surnames from any Perfonal Singularity, and amongft many other inftances, RUFUS, BLONDUS, and NIGELLUS were the Progenitors of the modern Families of ROUS, BLOUNT, and NEALE. The former were the early Poffeffors of this Parifh, called like the *Lower Duntefborn*, with a Reference to its Situation on the Bourn or Rivulet, and its Vicinity to *Cirencefter* about four Miles on the North eaft. It lies in the Hundred of *Crowthorne* and *Minety*, of a ligh Soil richly tilled, forming a Terrier of 1800 Acres, one Hundred of which are Woodland.

The Living, which is a Rectory in the Deanry of *Cirencefter* is charged with the annual Payment of a Mark to the Crown, formerly due to the Knights Hofpitallers of St *John* of *Jerufalem*, who were Patrons. It is evident that the Advowfon was detached from the Manor, as we find it purchafed by Dr ROBERT MORWENT, the fecond Prefident of *Corpus Chrifti College Oxford*, who, on his Demife in 1557, bequeathed it to that Society.

In the Church, dedicated to St *Michael*, nothing occurs worthy notice. The dimenfions are very fmall. Under the Chancel is an Arched Vault communicating with the Church, probably not fepulchral, but ufed in certain Ceremonies of the Romifh Worfhip.

King WILLIAM, foon after the Conqueft, gave this Manor to his Coufin WILLIAM DE OVE, afterward to JOHN RUFUS MILES, or LE ROUS, the laft of whofe race was attainted for Rebellion with JOHN GIFFARD, Baron of *Brimpffield*, in 1322, and his Lands confifcated. By the Family of MULL, or MILLES, it was likewife forfeited for their Attachment to the *Lancaftrian* Caufe, and granted by EDWARD IV in 1465, to THOMAS HERBERT, and, in 1474 to Sir RICHARD BEAUCHAMP. Dr RICHARD FOX, Bifhop of *Winton*, obtaining this Manor, fettled it upon *Corpus Chrifti College Oxford*, by his Charter of Foundation in 1517, who have been the fubfequent Proprietors.

The Ancient Manor and Park of *Pinbury*, chiefly in this Parifh, was given by the Conqueror to the Nuns of *Caen*, in *Normandy*, and then taxed at five Hides. In 1416, 2 HEN V it was given with *Minchin Hampton*, and *Avening*, parcel of the fame Eftate, to the Nunnery of *Syon*, in who had a Cell here, and upon the general Suppreffion, granted in 1543 to ANDREW Lord W in exchange for *Stanwell*, co *Middlefex*. It next paffed by Purchafe to Sir HENRY POOLE, in 1600, from that Family to Sir ROBERT ATKYNS, fen (1660) whofe Son Sir ROBERT built the prefent dilapidated Manfion Houfe, and made it his refidence till the Death of his Father in 1710. EDWARD ATKYNS, Efq of *Laft Sheen*, co *Surrey*, the Heir general, fold this Manor in 1730 to the Right Honourable HENRY BATHURST, Lord APSLEY. The Site confifts of deep Dells, through which is the winding Courfe of the Rivulet *Froome*, pleafingly diverfified with Beech Woods.

Part of Earl BATHURST's Eftate at *Oakley* is within the Boundary of this Parifh.

No Benefactions to the Poor

Incumbents	Patrons	Incumbents	Patrons
1557 Robert Morwent, B D †	———————	1679 James Seffions, B D	Corpus Chr Col Oxford
1558 Richard Woodward, B D	Corpus Chr Col Oxford		
		1695 James Dockwra, B D	The fame
1561 William Bocher, B D ‡	The fame	1738 William Marfhall, M A	The fame
‡ ‡	‡ ‡	1745 Edward Ford, B D	The fame
1603 John Hampton, B D	The fame	1762 Thomas Pettener M A	The fame
1634 William Symes, B D	The fame	1771 William Linden, B D	The fame

* *Caen* is the Capital of Lower *Normandy*, in the Diocefe of *Bayeux*, in which City are two Abbies, one for Monks, and the other for Nuns. The Nunnery of the Holy Trinity was founded about the Year, 1064, by MATILDA, Wife of WILLIAM the Conqueror, whofe Monument remains at this Day.

KEEBLE's *Duntifbourne* p 57. TANNER's Not Mon 777. 67. Nº. VII. LELAND's Munerium vol II p 776.
† Wood's Fafti Oxon Vol I p 661. Antiq Univ Oxon edit Gutch p 76.
‡ WILLIAM Bocher, B D Prefident of Corpus Chrifti Coll, in 1600, when he honourably quitted that Station to the heir, and, retiring to his Rectory of *Duntefborne Rous* co *Gloucefter* till his Death, there beftowed on that At length giving way to his years, buried in the Church there, Nov 1 1633. Vide Fafti Vol I p 161, and Antiq Univ Oxon p 376. Edit Gutch.

PRESENT PROPRIETORS OF THE MANORS,

Of *Duntesborne*,

The Prefident, Fellows, and Scholars of *Corpus Chrifti College, Oxford*

Of *Pinbury*,

The Right Honourable HENRY Lord APSLEY

The only Perfon fummoned by the Heralds, in 1682 and 1683, was
Thomas King, Gen

It does not appear that any Perfon polled from this Parifh at the Election in 1776

The earlieft Date in the Regifter occurs in 1545

ANNUAL ACCOUNT OF MARRIAGES, BIRTHS, AND BURIALS, IN THIS PARISH

A.D	Mar	Bir	Bur	A.D	Mar	Bir	Bur	A.D	Mar	Bir	Bur	A.D	Mar	Bir	Bur
1781	—	3	2	1786	—	1	2	1791				1796			
1782	—	1	2	1787	2	—	1	1792				1797			
1783	—	1	2	1788	1	5	3	1793				1798			
1784	—	1	3	1789				1794				1799			
1785	2	5	3	1790				1795				1800			

INSCRIPTIONS IN THE CHURCH.

ON FLAT STONES IN THE CHANCEL

JACOBUS SESSIONS,
Hujus Ecclefiæ Rector,
infra jacet fepultus
Obiit Augufti XXVI
Anno Domini 1695
A cœnn Domini
ad cœnn Agni

Trin... minor
JACOBI & ELIZ SESSIONS,
Nti us fui tertio,
Denatus 10 Sept 1687

Gloria Deo opt max
qui repetit
Animam Jofiæ Filii natu max
JOSEP DOCKWRAY,
VII Id No
Anno { Lætitis tuæ 12
{ Salutis 1709

Prope jacent offa REBECCÆ MITRIS,
co juventis
Depofita VI Julii, 1700

ON A BRASS PLATE AGAINST TH SOUTH WALL IN THE CHANCEL

Underneath are the
Remains of the
Rev THOMAS PETTENER,
formerly Fellow of
Chrift College Oxon,
and late Rector of this Parifh,
who departed this Life
the 24th Day of April, 1771,
in the 37th Year of his Age

IN THE CHURCH YARD, ON TOMBS

JOHN JEFFERIS, of Dunfburne
deceafed the 12th Day of Sept 1611
(this JOHN JEFFERIS, deceafed was the
youngeft Son of his Father,
RICHARD JEFFERIS, of Dunfburne)

By ELIZABETH his Wife he had eight
Children four Sons and four Daughters

JOHN,	ELIZABETH,
GEORGE,	ANNE,
THOMAS,	SUSANNA,
JOHN,	ELIZABETH

THOMAS, youngeft Son of
THOMAS JEFFERIS Gent
died February 10 Anno Domini 1696.

MARGARET firft Wife of
THOMAS JEFFERIS Gent
fecondly the Wife of
WILLIAM MARSHALL, Gent
died Jun... aged 75

CATHARINE JEFFERIS,
Daughter of RICHARD JEFFERIS
departed this Life the Day of
Dec 1680

ANN, Widow of PAUL JEFFERIS,
was buried May 16, 168

RICHARD HOWES
died June 29, 1695

ANN his Wife
died May 1, 1696

MARY Wife of JOHN HAYNES,
of this Parifh Yeoman,
died the 11th Day of Oct 17 , aged 27

RICHARD Son of
JOHN HAYNES, Yeoman
was buried Dec 11, 1 , aged , Month

ELIZABETH fecond Wife of
JOHN HAYNES of th Parifh Yeoman,
deceafed the 8th Day of Auguft, 17 ,
aged 6 Years

M S
EDWARD BORN, S T P
C C C apud Oxonienfes nuper f...
hunc fordem Ecclefia prefedit
I vocat
Quibus erit,
In excol ndis Tyron in... ...iis
Pul... ... Argumentis tobi
I ... fitis,
nec hus fuæ
In aliis his Domini ... ...tuendis
ipfe enim e principue Academic
V y ... ...um
I am fe ... ...tiffimo mani ... ...
...olun h ... ...
... ...
Obiit , Octob... die,
et it 4

I ... ... his V ...
was l buried near hi
D 1 , 1 ,

ON FLAT AND HEAD STONES

	Died	Aged			Died	
Richard Howes	2 Dec 1724	7	Stephen Pitt		July	
Richard Smart	20 Feb 176		Catherine his Wife		May	
John Cox	29 Jun 146		Thomas Ho... yeoman		Apr	
Thomas Tombs	11 May 134	5	Anne, Wife of Thomas Ho...			
Thomas Tombs	1 June 180		...		Dec	
Giles Tombs, junior	Jun 1 ,		Giles Ho...		Sep	
Mary Wife of William Tombs	2 Dec 1740	3	Mary his Wife		May	

4

DURSLEY

CONCERNING which, the following very minute and authentic Account is given in the Collections of JOHN SMYTH, Esq preserved amongst the Archives in *Berkeley Castle*.

" *Durseley*, in *Domesday* Book written *Dersilege*, and soone after *Dueslega*, wherein WILLIAM the
" CONQUEROR had three Hides of Land in Demesne, as that Booke shewethe, which with one other Hide
" of Land, the old Inheritance of the *Berkeleis*, were late the Inheritance of Sir THOMAS ESTCOURTE,
" Knight, who dyed without Issue in 22 *Jac Regis*, and nowe of THOMAS ESTCOURTE, Esquior, Son
" of EDMOND, Brother of the said Sir THOMAS, all holden of the Kinge, by Tenure of Knightes Ser-
" vice in *Capite*   The Name of this ancient Towne, I conceive to come from the British Word *Dwr*,
" which signifieth Water, which plentifully ariseth by, and runneth through the same, and the *Saxon*
" Word LEIA, LELE, or LEY, which, being all one, doe sometimes signifie Water, and sometimes
" Place, the Water running through this Towne, is at this Day *Twenni*   The Towne gives Name to
" one of the Deaneries of this County, wherein are the Churches of *Berkeley*, of *Slymbridge*, of *Cowley*,
" of *Camme*, of *Frampton*, of *Durseley*, of *Owley*, of *Newenton*, of *Beverston*, and of *Wotton*, as by
" the ancient Roll of Taxation, in 20 *Edw* I in the Tower of *London* appareth   The Rectory of
" *Durseley* is accompted the Corps or Body of the Arch Deaconry of this County of GLOUCESTER   and
" is of Custom and Right the Incumbency of him, that is, for the Time " Oculus Episcopi,' the Arch-
" Deacon, which is at this time HUGH ROBINSON, Doctor in Divinitie

" The foresaid Hide of Lande was the old Habitation of the ancient Familie of the BERKELEIS
" called of DURSELEY *, in a Castle by them built, before the Conquest (the ruins where of now hime
" full, with Bailey and Worke there growinge), and they afterward alsoe held from EDWARD CONFESSOR,
" and from WILLIAM the CONQUEROR, and from his two Sons WILLIAM RUFUS and HENRIE I, and
" alsoe halfe the Raigne of K STEPHEN   the first mentioned three hides in *Domesdie* Booke, with the
" whole Manor of *Berkeleis* (in effect) and all *Berkeley Hernesse*, whereof *Dursley* was an Hamlet or
" Parcell (of those Kings) in Fee Fame, at the Yearlie Rent of 500*l* 17*s* 2*d* as the great Roll of the
" Pipe in the first Yeere of the Raigne of K HENRY II doth shew   The first of which Familie,
" whose Name I can certainlie fasten upon, is ROGER BERKELEI, mentioned in the said Book of *Do-*
" *mesdie*, who also lived in the Reign of EDWARD CONFESSOR, and was Father of WILLIAM BERKELEI,
" who, in the Rign of K HENRY I founded the Abbey of *Kingswood*, by *Wotton Under Edge*, in that
" one, and after, called the Manor of *Achoue*, as, amongst many other Prooves, the continuation of K
" HENRY the second made in the eleventh Yea of his Raigne to the Abbott of that Monastery, for ten
" Markes Fine, speaketh, specified in the great Pipe Roll in the Exchequer for that Yeare   Which
" WILLIAM BERKELEY was father of ROGER BERKELEY, who lived in the time of K STEPHEN, who,
" by HAVISIA his Wife, was Father of ROBERT, who, by HELENA his Wife, Daughter of the Lord
" ROBERT Sonne of HARDING, first Lord of BERKELEY, had from her Father Gift the Manor of
" *Dursley*, in Fee Simple, for her Marriage Portion   Between whom was Issue ROGER, who, by
" HAVISIA his first Wife, had Issue, HENRY, which HENRY, by AGNES his Wife, had Issue, JOHN,
" which JOHN, by SIBILL his Wife, had Issue HENRY, which HENRY, by JOANE his Wife, had Issue
" WILLIAM, JOHN, and HENRY, which WILLIAM and JOHN, dying without Issue, left the Manor to
" descend upon the said HENRY then Brother, which HENRY had Issue JOHN, who, by his first his
" Wife, left Issue, NICHOLAS and MAUD   Which NICHOLAS married CICELY, Sister and Heire of
" Sir JOHN DE LA MORE of *Britton*, but died without Issue, 6 RICH II 1382, whereby this Manor d
" scended to the said MAUD his Sister, who was married to ROBERT DE CANTELUPO, and died in the 4th
" HENRY IV   by whom she left Issue ROBERT, who died in 14 , having Issue ELIZABETH, his
" only Daughter and Heire, married to RICHARD CHEDDER, which RICHARD and ELIZABETH his Wife
" were they who, in 13 HENRY IV sold by Fine then levyed, the Advowson of the said Abbey of

* *Deseender dise Persons* It is certaine in the Tower (of *Kingswood*) a Quire of Toph there by *Dessalage*, where of much
of the Castell was builded   Part of *Dowle's* Castell brought, a stroke in the Houses at *Dedington* PERAMBUL Ita V f 175
Dwr   is a prity letting Towne finding or place of the elysy, as a Hed privileged at 9 Yeare fine with 1 Market
taxe with To be set free, a die, Spurge   and as is the principal Head of the Brooke, bringge the Ensign, Mills, as at the
Towne   The Water of which into *Severne* that is about four Myles of certain, by the weary turne other abbies   That it was
hold of old in ancient fine or or longevng to the BERKELEYS first to the WEST Inefell to Decay, and such rent of old as yet
hold of old and Dites about yet and wa in the most Parte made of   Stone full of Pore and Hole lyke a Fume
Deser er Ouire of the stone that in *Dursei*, and it will fill very longe   PERAMBUL Ita V 7 f   178
The Spacous of ere is called *Tophus* by Lathius and for is of the hightness and extreme durability very compactly
closes a viding, Crustings, felt between the Ribs of the springe, Arches   The Higher Court of the Cathedral a Church
the Spacous   Upon application in the Hen the High Arcenes for the in the Houses and the lower parte of the
In *Davie* and the serpent Parishes there hold up the the other over   South summer the Cold and reductive
* To the sides of these Mollie, the Prime Minister, Efful Abbas Columna founded an other Edwin ruins in these smaller
taxe   Well persnied Wood, the Inspections These are particularly in the filth fore

" *Kingswood* to THOMAS, then Lord BERKELEY, the fourth of that Name whereof WILLIAM BERKE-
" LEY, in the time of K. HENRY I was Founder. After the Death of which RICHARD CHEDDER and
" ELIZABETH, in the time of Kinge HENRY VI the Manor of *Dursley* came to THOMAS WILLIAM this
" WYKYS, in 1464, leaving Issue JOHN WYKYS, who died in the time HEN. VII and was Father of
" LOMOND WYKYS, who died in the 6th of Henry VIII Father of NICHOLAS WYKYS, who died with
" PHIL and MARY whose Sonne JOHN WYKYS died in the Life time of his Father, leaving Issue
" POLLET WYKYS, who, in the 9th of ELIZ sold the Manor of *Dursley*, to RICHARD
" BIRD, and his Heires, and he shortlie after to LEMOND WOOLWORTH alias WIBBE, who died
" leaving Issue, WILLIAM, who, in 9 ELIZ sold the same to THOMAS ESCOURT, Esq who died in
" — ELIZ leaving Issue, Sir THOMAS ESCOURIE, Knt who, dying in 22 JAMES I left the same to
" THOMAS ESCOURT his Brother EDMOND's Sonne, as is aforesaid. Howbeit, RICHARD WIBBE alias
" WOOLWORTH, Son and Heir of the said WILLIAM, to this Day receiveth 20*l.* per Annum of the
" Manor for his Life, now the Heir of the said RICHARD BIRD.

" It can not be unpleasinge to *you*, delighting in such reverend Antiquities, to reade out of that vene-
" rable Booke, called the red Booke, in the Office of Kinge's Remembrancer in the Exchequer, the
" Certificate of the said ROGER BERKELEY, made to K. HENRY II in the 13th Yeere of his Raigne,
" the original wordes thus, " *Cuta ROCFRIDE BERKELAY.* Sciat Dñs Rex quod habeo duos Milites
" & Dimid feotros de veteri Feofamento, unde HUGO DE PLANCA tenet dimidiam Hid. in L. de his
" integrum militem habetis ad dimid faciend. Tenent viz RADULPHUS DE YWELLE dimid In hac,
" Lauina RADULPHI CANTELENI dimid hidam ROGERUS DE ALBA MARIA unam Virgatam Sin...
" DE COLLECT unam Virgatam, e he habetis dimid militem. Ad alterum Militem faciend WALTE-
" RUS DE HOLCOMBE tenet tres hidas & dimid REGINALDUS DE ALBA MARA tres hidas. Et ita tenent
" isti tres decem Hidas, unde nolunt mihi facere Servicium, nisi de tribus virgatis seu unuiquisque de
" una virgata. Et ita habet duos Milites & dimid feodatos, & nullum habeo feofatum de novo, in
" meo tempore. Si vobis in antea de Domo meo placet audire. In manerio meo de *Coverley*, habeo
" Feodum duorum Militum, apud *Stanley* Feodum unus Militis cum una hida de *Chedrington*. In *Nea-
" aton* habeo Feodum unius Militis. In *Durflege* unam hidam, *Osterword* dimid hidam. In *Dursley*
" tres hidas & dimid. In *Sumbrugge* tres hidas, quas Ego istensu vestro, dedi MAURICIO filio ROBERTI,
" unde nullum habeo Servicium. *Kingswodum* tenet *Abbas Moraehi* ex dono WILLIAM DE BELL FAI,
" unde vobis integrum Militem facio, quare ipsi mihi nullum servicium reddere volunt. " Thus that
" Certificate. Aere upon his Hide of Land in *Dursley*, doubtless was his dwelling Place or his Castell,
" ancientlie built thereon, which was an olde Freehold of itselfe, and not Parcell of the Manor, either
" of *Berkeley*, or *Dursley.*

" An ancient Booke of Knightes Fees in the time of EDW. I in the Exchequer, with the Reference
" or to the Lord Treasurer, this " HENRICUS DE BIRKELAY tenet *Dursley* & *Newnton* Comitatum
" *Capite*, per Servicium duorum Militum." An Inquisition in the Tower, in the EDW. No. 18, saith
" that HENRY BERKELEY dyed, seized (inter alia) of the Manor of *Stanley St Leonard*, quod pertinet
" ad Baronium de *De silege*, and that WILLIAM was his Son and Heire, 13 Yeeres old. Hac Rot
" Membris 2 and 6, 38 HENRY III shews that the King granted Liberty to WILLIAM BERK of
" *Durs*, for terme of Life to hunt the Fox, Wolfe, Hare, Wildcat, Badger &c. and that he and...
" not be returned upon any Jury, nor be made Sheriffe, Coroner, &c. again this WILLIAM. And with
" *Pat Rot*, 39 HENR III Pag 2, this W. DE BIRKLAY was Valettus regis, one that serve in
" the King in his Bedchamber, and, by *Pat Rot* 53 HEN III This W de B was pardoned by
" the King his partakinge with ROGER DE CLIFFORD, his Rebellion and Stirres against the King,
" because he would not keep the Statutes and Provision of the Parliament made at *Oxford*. This HENRY
" de BERKELEY Lord of *Dursley* had, in the 9th EDW I a travall with THOMAS Lord BERKELEY, the
" second of that Name, for the Liberties thereof. And in the said 9th and 13th of the same, it ere
" seems, put forward two Writs of *Quo Warranto* against the said THOMAS Lord BERKELEY, which,
" coming to a trivall at GLOUCESTER, the Jury found that the Ancestors of the said THOMAS in the
" Reigns of HENRY II and King JOHN, used, that if any Thieves, either in the Courte or in the Leets
" of *Dursley*, to bring them the same Day to the Castell at *Berkeley*, if the Day allowed, where they were
" accustomed to receive their Judgment, and to have Justice executed upon them. The booke in the
" Exchequer called the " *Nomina Villarum*," compiled in 9 EDW II sayth, that in the Hundred of
" *Berkeley*, are two Burrowes Townes, viz *Berkeley*, whereof THOMAS Lord BERKELEY is Lord, and
" *Dursley* whereof JOHN Son of WILLIAM BERKELEY is Lord. The said John Son of William
" BERKELEY, takinge Advantage in the 1st EDW III, while THOMAS Lord BERKELEY, Grandfather
" Heire to the last mentioned, was in trivall by Parliament about his Life and Fortune...
" of K. EDW II and *Isabel his Queen*, exhibits his Petition in that Parliament, alleging that he
" himselfe holds the Manors of *Newnton* and *Dursley* of the King, by and immediately in Capite.
" And that the said THOMAS Lord BERKELEY being one of the Greatest...
" by his Servicy to his uses, often wrongfully distrained him by his Ploughs Cattle, and the rather
" would he make him... by the Sheriff, nor by his Bayl, nor other Minister...
" his Freeman and some of his household Servants, and for, by his Serjeants and Bailiffs
" colour of this... he hath made, in... the Aid of... his
" King's Comminders, to his Returne of Writs and all other royal Franchises...

" ... Parties... lately specified, and with some Variation in the Elder Notes...
" ...

"Berkeley, which before was guildable, would encroach to him the Attendance and Seignory of him the said John, to his Diſinheriſon, and the Damage of the Kinge, whereof hee now prayes Remedy in this High Court of Parliament, whereto the Anſwer was, that the Rolles of the Chancery, ſhould be viewed, and more, I thinke, followed not hereupon

"In this Towne is a Markett each Thurſday, and two Fayre Days, the one on the 25th of April, called St Mark's Day, the other on the 25th of November, called St Clement's Day, but when, or by what Kinge granted to the Lord hereof, I have not obſerved The Governmente of this Towne is by a Magiſtrate called a Bayliſte, yeerelie choſen by the Lord's Steward, and the Jury at the Leete, or Law Day holden within a Month after Michaelmas.

"In this Towne is a Rock of ſtrange Stone, called a Puſf ſtone, or, as ſome pronounce, a Touſe-ſtone, wherin is no Chink, Cricke, Chop, or Cure, at all, like a Sponge, of an incredible Durance, as the Walls of Berkeley Caſtell, made of Rumes of the Nunnerie there, demoliſhed neere 700 Yeeres agoe, may witneſs, very eaſy to be cut, and ſoft Through which Rocke, divers Vautes, Hauſes, Cellars Milles, and Water courſes, in the Towne are cutt and runne the like is ſaid not to be eli where to una and by it, and through Part of it runneth the Streame from the firſte Fountain, called Excelme, anciently in the Time of Henry III, and afore written Heaelme in divers Deeds

"To have viſited an ancient Hermitage, ſeated in the Midſt of the Deſart Woodes, hanging over this Towne may ſeeme in Daies of ſuch Belieſ to have been an Expiatorie or meritorious Worke, through the pains takinge in the uneaſy and dangerous Clyming and Acceſs to the Hermites Celle, up and downe the craggy Hills leading therto The laſt Time I finde Mention of Hermite, or Hermitage, is in the Court-roll of the Manor of Hamme, in 8 Henry VIII, when hee was awarded at that Courte (bona manu), with two Handes, to prove that the Horſe, which had hither ſtrayed, and there taken up, was not thence ſtolen by him, but his owne proper Goodes, but though hee had Reſtitution, yet doubtleſs moſt of them were hipocriticall Knaves."

The Town of Dursley is ſituate at the Baſe of a ſteep Hill, covered with hanging Beech Woods, four Miles on the North from Wotton Under Edge, and fifteen ſouthward from Gloucester The Streets are planned irregularly, and of no great Extent, with many reſpectable Buildings unfavourably placed +. In Dr Parsons's MSS it is ſaid that the firſt Charter for the Market and Fairs was obtained in 1471, 11 Edw IV by William Lord Berkeley, and renewed, in 1612, on the Petition of Sir Thomas Estcourt, Knight The old Croſs, which was in open Arcade, falling to decay, the preſent very commodious Market-houſe was erected in 1738 at the ſole Expence of the Lord of the Manor The Office of Bailiff is certainly of very ancient Eſtabliſhment, though no Evidences ſupplying a Catalogue of them prior to 1567 have reached us Their preſent Office is to ſuperintend the Police of the Town, and adjuſt annually the Weights and Meaſures, in early Times, it is probable, they exerciſed more extenſive Juriſdiction

PRÆPOSITI, OR BAILIFFS

A D		A D	
1567	James Smallwood	1589	John Plomer
1568	Roge Pitt	1590	Thomas Auſten
1569	Chriſtoph Webbe, alias Woolworth	1591	Richard Martin
1570	William Berry	1592	Richard Browninge
1571	Richard Berry.	1593	.
1572	William Webbe, alias Woolworth	1594	
1573		1595	. .
1574		1596	.
1575		1597	.
1576		1598	.
1577	. .	1599	.
1578		1600	
1579	Richard Mixtone	1601	
1580	William Trotman	1602	.
1581		1603	John Plomer.
1582	Alexander Burton	1604	
1583	Thomas Trotman	1605	
1584	Thomas Purker	1606	
1585	John Tyler	1607	
1586	Richard Mixtone	1608	
1587	William Purnell	1609	
1588	Thomas Trotman	1610	
		1611	Maurice Tyler

* In the Iteration of Style, theſe are now held on the 6th of May, and the 6th of December
+ There are ſeveral very old Dwelling houſes in this Town, one of which bore a external Date 1520 within Theſe of Oak Wainſcot and arched Roof of Timber Frame, the Beams highly carved and ornamented with a Cypher, Theſe would have belonged to the Webbes, alias Woolworth, of the Webbes

A. D.		A. D.	
1612	Arthur Vizar.	1681	William Tippetts.
1613	Richard Tippetts.	1682	Samuel King
1614	John Martin.	1683	Richard Tippetts.
1615	.	1684	Walter Maye
1616	William Harding.	1685	Jacob Wallington.
1617	Isaac Smith.	1686	John Williams
1618	.	1687	Isaac Smyth.
1619	. . .	1688	William Lytton.
1620	Richard Tippetts	1689	Thomas Purnell.
1621	Henry Trotman	1690	John Partridge
1622	. . . .	1691	John Purnell
1623	. . . .	1692	Benjamin Symonds
1624	William Harding	1693	Samuel Clarke.
1625	Thomas Hyett	1694	John Webb.
1626	Thomas Smyth.	1695	Robert Whateley.
1627	Richard Merick.	1696	Richard Merrick
1628	Philip Biggs	1697	Thomas King.
1629	Richard Browninge.	1698	Joseph Pulley
1630	Isaac Smith	1699	Maurice Philips
1631	Richard Oliver	1700	Samuel King
1632	John Tyler	1701	Richard Tippetts.
1633		1702	James Bayley
1634	Nicholas Dangerfield.	1703	William Purnell
1635	George Grace.	1704	Jacob Wellington.
1636	Thomas Watkyns.	1705	Isaac Smyth.
1637	John Browninge.	1706	Isaac Smyth
1638	Samuel Harding.	1707	John Philips.
1939	William Hill	1708	Maurice Smith
1640	Henry Smith.	1709	. .
1641	John Tucker	1710	. . .
1642	Nicholas Dangerfield.	1711	
1643	William Pitt	1712	Roger Whateley.
1644	. . . .	1713	William Symondes
1645	John Hodges	1714	Josiah Arundell.
1646		1715	.
1647	John Philips.	1716	.
1648	Augustin Philips.	1717	. .
3649	George Martin.	1718	.
1650	William Tippetts.	1719	.
1651	Henry Adey	1720	. .
1652	John Arundel	1721	. .
1653	Isaac Smith	1722	.
1654	John Purnell	1723	. .
1655	Obadiah Webb	1724	
1656	William Purnell	1725	
1657	John Watkins.	1726	
1658	John Arundell	1727	. .
1659	John Oliver.	1728	
1660	John Till Adams.	1729	
1661	William Partridge	1730	Selwyn James
1662	Edmond Perrott.	1731	Giles Hodges
1663	John Tucker.	1732	John Purnell
1664	William Tippetts	1733	Richard Oliver
1665	Thomas Everett	1737	James Nicholas
1666	Henry Smith	1735	Samuel Wallington.
1667	Samuel Symonds	1736	Thomas Morse
1668	John Arundell	1737	Timothy Wallington
1669	William Smith	1738	Samuel Clarke
1670	William Lytton	1739	Richard Cooper
1671	John Purnell	1740	Jacob Stiff
1672	Arthur Crew	1741	Thomas Purnell
1673	William Powell.	1742	Josias Clarke
1674	John Oliver.	1746	Thomas Willington
1675	William Merrick	1744	William Browning
1676	. .	1745	John Moodey
1677	William Partridge	1746	John Gethen
1678	Daniel Knight.	1747	George Linthorne.
1679	Thomas King	1748	Nathaniel Lawson
1680	Thomas King	1749	Joseph Till Adams

A. D	1750	Richard Tippetts	A D	1770	Benjamin Millard
	1751	Maurice Smith		1771	Richard Williams
	1752	John Plomer		1772	Isaac Danford
	1753	Lewis Hoskins		1773	Isaac Jones
	1754	William Long		1774	John Bull
	1755	Joseph Fairthorne		1775	William Roach
	1756	William Heaven.		1776	William Drew
	1757	John King		1777	Samuel Griffin.
	1758	William Plomer		1778	William King
	1759	William Blake		1779	Thomas Lewton.
	1760	Samuel Lewton		1780	Benjamin Millard, junior.
	1761	Thomas Cam.		1781	Daniel Dimorey.
	1762	Josiah Tippetts		1782	William Jackson.
	1763	Samuel Phillimore		1783	John Willington.
	1764	Morgan Pulley		1784	James Wheeler
	1765	Hugh Everett, senior		1785	Nathaniel Blackwell
	1766	Thomas Morse, junior.		1786	Richard Williams, junior
	1767	Thomas Tippetts		1787	Jonathan Hitchins
	1768	Benjamin Smith		1788	Thomas Moore.
	1769	Samuel Wallington		1789	John Long

The Boundaries of the Parish are found by the last Perambulation to exceed eight Miles, of a Soil light and gravelly, mostly in Pasture, with 2000 Acres of Woodland. Exclusive of the manorial Estate, the chief Property is held by the Families of PHILPS, the two distinct Families of PURNELL, the Mayor, Aldermen, and Burgesses of the City of *Bristol*, and the Families of TIPPETS, VIZARD, ADEY, WALLINGTON, and BLACKWELL.

Of the Manor so accurate an Account has been given, as to preclude the Necessity of adding more than that it still is vested in the last mentioned Name and Family.

As early as HENRY the VIIIth's Reign, the Castle was become a mere Ruin, it was a Baronial Residence only, for the Site is so commanded by surrounding Hills as to render it ineffectual to any military Purpose, even upon the ancient System of War. It has been stiled the Barony of *Dursley*, although none of this House of BERKELEY have ever received Summons to Parliament, but in 1679, 31 Car. II GEORGE Baron BERKELEY was created Viscount DURSLEY by Patent *

The Manufacture of Cloth was established in this Town and Parish soon after its more general Introduction from *Flanders*, and has enriched many Families. It still employs the poorer Inhabitants, and is conducted with Reputation and Success.

The Benefice is a Rectory, anciently charged with a Payment of 1l. 6s. 8d. to the Priory of *Stanley St. Leonard*, and in the Patronage of the Abbot of GLOUCESTER, who in 1475, at the Instance of JOHN CARPENTER Bishop of *Hereford*, annexed this Rectory to the House of the Archdeacon of GLOUCESTER, to which Dignity it was then appropriated, and has since continued to be annexed.

It is the Chief of its own Deanery.

The Church, dedicated to St. *James*, consists of a spacious Nave, two Aisles, a Tower of noble Gothic, and a very handsome Portal. The dividing Arches are light, carried on the Lamb, heightened with the Arms of BERKELEY † and FITZHARDING, and the Device of THOMAS TANNER ‡, who, in the Reign of HENRY the VIth, erected a Chapel at the End of the South Aisle, for the Reception of a Chantry, in which is the Figure of a Skeleton beneath a Canopy, intended for a Memorial of him. It is probable that he contributed to the external Embellishment of the Chancel or South Side of the Church, which is in the best Style of that Age. The old Spire fell in 1699, whilst the Bells were rung, in which Accident several Lives were lost. It was rebuilt and finished in 1708, at the Expence of the Parish. The Chancel was likewise re-erected in 1750, and neatly fitted up.

* Collins Peerage, vol. III. Title PURNELL
† Notes of BERKELEY, whose Arms also be seen in three Ancient Glass in the Church Glaze pane, about at the Nave of Gentry retrieved by the examination in 1475 ...
‡ Priest THOMAS TANNER a Dean, a great Worthy ...

A small Turret, which contained the Saints Bell *, still remains, and a Shrine at the end of the North Aisle, where was the other Chantry, of which RICHARD BREIC was the last Incumbent

With *Woodmancote*, the only Hamlet in this Parish, Mr SMYTH proceeds with his usual Accuracy and Minuteness

"*Woodmancote*, anciently written *Wodemancote*, is an ancient Manor, with the Parish of *Dursley*, "holden of GEORGE Lord BERKELEY of his Manor of *Berkeley*, by half a Knighte's Fee, and Sute to "his Hundred Courte, and before the charteringe thereof, by several Sales   The Scituation of the ca- "pitall Mailage, and Manor house of this Village or Township of *Woodmancote* assureth us from "whence the Name is derived, as that it was the Cote or Dwelling-house of the Woodman or Wood- "ward, wholly inclosed almost with the Woods of that Manor, and of the Manor of *Dursley*, lying "together, as alsoe did spacious Woods of other Manors therto adjoininge   For the ancient Owners "of this *Woolmancott* from the Time of WILLIAM the CONQUEROR, or before, untill the Tyme of "HENRY IIId, I referre you to what I have formerlie written of *Nybley*   And in that Kinge's Reign "it was the Land of OTTO, alias OTHO, the Sonne of WILLIAM, and of WILLIAM, the Sonne of "OTHO, I suppose that two of that Name succeeded the one the other, and after of THOMAS, Sonne of "OTTO, who dyeing, 2 EDW I lefte it to OTTO his Sonne, then but 9 Years olde, as an Inquisition "shewith   From whom it came to ROBERT DE SWYNEFORNE, who dying in 19 EDW II left the "same to his Son THOMAS DE SWYNEBORNE, and after it came to MARGERY DE SWINEBORN, upon whose "Death, in 16 EDW III controversie arose about this Manor, and WARREN FITZWARREN (who "dwelte where I now doe) cept into the Possession therof, who after, with THOMAS his Brother, and "CATHERINE then Sister, in 25 EDW III released all their Interest to another ROBERT DE SWYNE "BOURNE and his Heires, from whom, by his Deede inrolled in the Court of Common Pleas (the said "25 EDW III Rot 2), it came to WILLIAM DE CHELTENHAM and WILLIAM DE WESTAL and "their Heires, who beinge Servants in the House of THOMAS Lord BERKELEY, the third of that "Name, according to the Trust in them reposed, conveyed the same to the Lady KATHERINE, "the second Wife of him the said Lord BERKELEY, and to MAURICE their Sonne (then very "younge), and to the Heires Males of his Body, with divers other Remainders over, as by the "Deede in *Berkeley* Castle appears, by which Purchace and Entayle this Manor came unto, to, and "settled in, Sir JOHN BERKELEY, Brother and Heire Male of the said MAURICE, for that the said "MAURICE in his Minority dyed without Issue   Which Sir JOHN BERKELEY, after the Death of the "said Lady CATHERINE, who died 9 RICHARD IId held this Manor, and died seised thereof, to him "and the Heirs Males of his Bodie in 6 HEN VI leaving Issue MAURICE BERKELEY, Father of "MAURICE and EDWARD, which MAURICE had Issue WILLIAM, which WILLIAM died without Issue "Male, and the said EDWARD was his Unkle and Heire Male, by Force of the said Entayle, which "EDWARD had Issue THOMAS and WILLIAM, the said THOMAS had Issue JOHN, who died without Issue "Male of his Body, and the said WILLIAM was his Unkle and Heire, which WILLIAM died, 5 EDW VI. "having Issue JOHN BERKELEY, who in Easter Term, 9 ELIZ sold this Manor of *Woodmancott* to "RICHARD LAMBERT, a Merchant in *London*, by whose Death, in 30 ELIZ it descended to WINIFRID "his Daughter and Heire, whose Mother was re married to Sir HENRY WINSTON, Knight, and the "said WINEFRID was in Ward for this Manor to HENRY Lord BERKELEY, who dying in her Minority "without Issue, the same descended to her Unkle EDMOND LAMBERT (afterward written EDWARD), "Brother of the said RICHARD the Purchaser, which EDWARD, after in his Life Time, in the Tyme "of King JAMES, and his Feoffees in Trust after his Death, in 7 JAC I for raising of Portions for his "Daughters, for scattered all not all the Lands of the Manor by their several Sales, in scrip JAC I "to particular Men, that it is now in 1639, is Cantoned the Inheritance of 38 Freeholders

"Pui..th this Manor is not named in the Booke of *Domesday*, either is a Member of the Manor "and Priory of *Berkeley*, or is a Parcell of the ancient Possessions of the BERKELEYS, of *Dursley*, "was... but in this Countie not set downe, nor in the Certificate of ROGER BERKELEY, made to "KING HEN IId, of all the Lands that hee or his Ancestors held, I cannot resolve otherwise but "that it was Freehold in the Hand of one ancient Saxon or other, holden of the Lady Abbatise and "Nunns of *Lacock*, unless I should say, it is in *Domesday* Boke comprehended under the Manor of "Cam, where of some Inquisitions finde it to be holden of the Manor and an Humble thereof, where in so "I doe not... Though the Inhabitants of this Manor claim to have a Leet or Lawe Day amongst "themselves, yet the Intanglement creof, with some of this Manor on Tything of *Woodmancote*, apper "...ce in the Yeare that Leete holden at *Berkeley*, for the Hundred of *Berkeley*, and so far as to the "Courtship there   In the Time of HENRY VI arose a Question between the Inhabitants of *Wood* "mancote, and each of the Inhabitants of *Nybley* is called *Warrens* Tenants about paying the "to the Kings Silver   Here are divers Lands and Tenements called *Cliffords* Landes to ance "the Lands of *Cam* in some Recordes and Evidences called a Manor, holden of this Manor of *Wood* "mancote, now the Inheritance of certaine Feoffees to the Use of the Citie of *Bristol* who by their "Attorney doe Suite at the Court of the Hundred of *Berkeley*, and pay the yearlie Rent of 4s to the

" Lord BERKELEY's Manor of *Came* Touchinge which Land are feveral Inquifitions, after the Death
' of ALEX ADER FRADWAY, in 19 HEN VII and another after the Death of JAMES CLIFFORD, 37
" HEN VIII and another after the Death of HENRY CLIFFORD in 1 ELIZ who left Iffue JAMES, who in
" ELIZ alienated the fame, and mentioned therin to be 8 Meffuages, and 192 Acres of Land, holden
" of the Manor of *Durfley* by 17s Rente "

From other equally authentic Evidences, with which we have been favoured, it appears, that in 1670,
22 CHARLES II it was transferred by Purchafe from WILLIAM LUDEN and ELIZABETH his Wife, Sifter
of ARTHUR BROMWICH, Efq to JOHN ARUNDELL In 1762 it was fold by the Coheirs of JOHN ARUN-
DELL, Gent to JOHN DE LA FIELD PHELIS, Efq the Father of the prefent Poffeffor The Homage
paid twice a Year to the Court at *Berkeley*, is a Thong of blue Leather, tagged with Tin at each End

The Village of Woodmancot contains many Houfes, and adjoins the Town of *Durfley*.

EDWARD FOX *, Bifhop of *Hereford*, a very ftrenuous Promoter of the Reformation, was a Native of
this Place.

B E N E F A C T I O N S

A Tenement, now called the Church Houfe, and a Piece of Land called the Torch Acre, to Feoffees
for ever, for repairing the Church +

The Houfes, now called the Alms houfes, to Feoffees for ever, for the Benefit of the Poor

Mr SHILMAN, by Deed gave to Truftees, an Eftate for ever, in the Parifh of *Standifh*, of the yearly
Value of 4*l* for the Ufe of the Poor

Mr HENRY STUBBS gave 10s yearly, to buy Books for poor Children

Mr HUGH SMITH, of *Durfley*, by Will, Jan 1, 1637, gave two Tenements at the Broad Well, for
repairing the Church

Sir THOMAS ESTCOURT, by Will, Aug 10, 1642, gave a Moiety of the clear yearly Rents of his
Tenements in *Tetbury*, after deducting 40s a Year for the Relief of the Poor, now fettled at 10*l* a Year.

Mr THROCKMORTON TROTMAN, of *London*, by Will, Oct 30, 1663, gave 15*l* a Year for ever, for a
Lecture to be preached every Thurfday

Mr JOHN ARUNDELL, of *Durfley*, by Will, May 19, 1703, gave an Acre of Ground, in the Parifh
of *Cam*, to Truftees, for ever, for buying Books, and teaching poor Children to read

JOSIAH SHEPHARD, by Will, in 1726, bequeathed 100*l.* for the Support of a School, 265*l* more were
added by Subfcription, the Income of which is 24*l*

Mrs ANN PURNELL, of *Durfley*, Widow, by Will, Dec 21, 1759, gave to Truftees 100*l* for purchafing Lands, the Income of which to be applied as followeth 10s to the officiating Minifter to preach
every Good Friday in the Afternoon the Remainder for teaching poor Children to read and alfo 6*l*
to be laid out as followeth 10*l* to the officiating Minifter for preaching a Sermon on New Year's Day
in the Morning for ever, and the Remainder to be equally divided amongft Forty poor Widows of the Parifh

NATHANIEL LAWSON, Gent in 1766, left 2*l* 5s 7d to be diftributed in Bread yearly, amongft the Poor

JACE SELFE, Gent bequeathed, in 1769, 1*l* 10s to be annually applied to the fame Purpofe

INCUMBENTS	PATRONS	INCUMBENTS	PATRONS
1541 Nich Wootton, LL D	Bp of Gloucefter	1662 Edward Pope, M A	Bp of Gloucefter
1543 John Williams, LL D	The fame	1671 John Greenow, M A	The fame
1559 Guy Eaton, B D	The fame	1678 Thomas Hyde, M A	The fame
1574 George Steele, LL D	The fame	1701 Robert Prior, M A	The fame
1602 Robert Hill, B D	The fame	1714 Nathaniel Hyde, D D	The fame
1606 Samuel Eaton, M A	The fame	1731 William Geeke, D D	The fame
16.. Hugh Robinfon, D D	The fame	1767 Richard Hurd, D D	The fame
——————,	The fame	1774 James Webfter, LL B	The fame
1660 John Middleton,	The fame		

PRESENT PROPRIETORS OF THE MANORS,

Of *Dursley*,   Of *Woodmancote*,
THOMAS ESTCOURT, ESQ.   JOHN DE LA FIELD PHELPS, ESQ.

The Persons summoned from this Place by the Heralds in 1682 and 1683 were

William Purnell, Esq.   Francis Whitney, Gent
John Arundell, Esq.   Thomas Bailey, Gent
William Smyth, Gent

At the Election in 1776, Thirty-nine Freeholders polled from this Parish

The Register commences in 1640, one prior to it has been destroyed, bearing Date 1535

ANNUAL ACCOUNT OF MARRIAGES, BIRTHS, AND BURIALS, IN THIS PARISH.

A D	Mar	Bir	Bur	A D	Mar	Bir	Bur	A.D	Mar	Bir	Bur	A.D	Mar	Bir	Bir
1781	13	43	27	1786	11	59	45	1791				1796			
1782	16	54	21	1787	18	62	52	1792				1797			
1783	28	46	25	1788	15	61	37	1793				1798			
1784	14	66	39	1789				1794				1799			
1785	18	51	44	1790				1795				1800			

INSCRIPTIONS IN THE CHURCH

ON MONUMENTS IN THE CHANCEL

Arms, Vert, a Chevron between three Lions Heads erased Or, for PLOMER

To the Memory of
WILLIAM PLOMER, of the City of
Bristol, and also of
HANNAH his Wife,
Daughter of SAMUEL CLARK,
of this Town, Mercer, who died, viz
he April 2, 1735, aged 35
and she July 1, 1734, aged 41

Near this Place lies the Body of
JOHN PLOMER of this Town Mercer,
Son of the said WILLIAM and HANNAH,
who died November 23, 1757, aged 30

Arms, Per Pale a Wolf falient, between six Crosses Crosslets, for PHELPS
—impaling, quarterly, Azure and Or
in the first Quarter, a Hawk's Lure of
the second, for FOWLER

To the Memory of JOHN PHELPS, Esq
who died June 16, 1735
in the 44th Year of his Age
This Monument was erected by
his eldest son
JOHN DE LA FIELD PHELPS

Near this Place lies interred
JOHN DE LA FIELD PHELPS, Esq
who died April 21, 1771,
in the 37th Year of his Age
He was many Years in the
Commission of the Peace, and served
High Sheriff in the Year 1761

Also ESTHER his Daughter,
who died April 6, 1767,
in the 5th Year of her Age

In the Chancel (with the Family)
lieth Mr WILL PURNELL Merchant,
Son of JOHN PURNELL, Gent
Obiit 18 June, 1715, et 59

Arms, on a Fess between three Lozenges three Cinquefoils for PURNELL
—impaling, on a Bend three Roses, in the sinister chief Point a Chessrook, for SMALL

H S E
THOMAS PURNELL, de Kingshill, Arm.
Vir ingenio admodum humanis,
moribus gravis, a te integerrima,
qui cum patria, dum it civisfit
amicis præter actuallicitus ea us,
annis audem & honore gratis
animam Deo reddidit die Octob XXIX
A D MDCCXXIX ætatis suæ LXII
Non procul ab hoc marmore jacet
filius natu minimus NATHANAEL,
optimæ spei adolescentulus
Obiit X Octob MDCCXVIII
Anno ætatis XVII

Et ANNA, uxor THOMÆ PURNELL, Arm
quæ hanc vitam discessit vicesimo
die Februarii MDCCXXXV
ætatis suo octogesimo uno

Et GULIELMUS PURNELL, Generofus,
filius prædicti THOMÆ secundus
qui postquam inter Rutinos a netto
Mercatoris officio, interris patriæ suæ,
diu interfuiset com modo in prope re
reversus in placido apud Tiltown,
receffu vitam continuavit
XXIV die Octobris
A D MDCCLII ætat LVII

Near this Place lieth the Body of
WILLIAM LITTON, Clothier
who departed this Life the
3d Day of June in the Year of our Lord
1703, aged 61 Year

Also the Body of
ANNA, Daughter of
ROBERT CLARKE Gent
first Wife of the above named
WILLIAM LITTON and, after Wife of
JOHN HYETT Esq received
late Mayor and one of the Aldermen
of the City of Glouchester,
who departed this Life in the Year 1735
aged 71 Years

Arms, on a Bend between two Roundlets, three Swans, for CLARKE

Near this Place was interred
SAMUEL CLARKE
of this Town, Mercer
and also HANNAH his Wife
He died Dec 18, 1737 in the
73d Year of his Age
and she Sept 8, 1729, aged 65

Also near this Place resteth the Body of
SAMUEL CLARKE, Mercer,
Son of the aforesaid
SAMUEL and HANNAH CLARK
who departed this Life Dec 21, 1747,
in the 56th Year of his Age

Likewise near this Place resteth
the Body of WILLIAM Son of the
aforesaid SAMUEL and
HANNAH CLARKE
who departed this Life April 28, 1749
in the 56th Year of his Age

Also near this Place resteth the
Body of JOSIAH CLARKE, Mercer
Son of the said SAMUEL and his
Wife who died May 1, 1734
in the 54th Year of his Age

ON A PAVEMENT

Within the Rails of the
Lozenges on a Brass Plate is the
Inscription on it

To the Memory of
Mr FRANCIS WALKER
Sister of WILLIAM WALKER to
a Sheep of Clear sense
a Woman of these her conduct dark
with all moral prudence, to her
Honour
She was born Nov 28th 1715
Nov
died at the Presence on this Life
April 8, 1781
his loved friend
reits this Life

On the second

To the Memory of
ELIZABETH WEBSTER, eldest
Daughter of JAMES WEBSTER, LL B
Archdeacon of Gloucester,
and of SARAH his Wife
Her Days were few, innocent, and
without reproach
She was born at Brant Broughton,
Lincolnshire
Jan 15, 1762,
died at the Parsonage in this Town
June 2, 1780,
and was interred
near this Place

On the third

To the Memory of
FRANCES WEBSTER, the third
Daughter of JAMES WEBSTER, LL B
Archdeacon of Gloucester,
and of SARAH his Wife
Her Person was amiable, and her Life
blameless
She was born at Brant Broughton,
Lincolnshire,
June 16, 1764,
died at Taunton, Somersetshire,
Dec 9 1785,
and was buried
near this Place

Here lyeth the Body of
ELIZABETH, Wife of
HENRY ARUNDELL, Clothier,
who departed this Life the
26th Day of   16   aged

Here resteth the Body of
JOSIAH ARUNDELL,
of this Parish, Gent,
who died April 21, 1736,
aged 72 Years.

Here resteth the Body of
ANNE, Daughter of JOHN ARUNDELL

In Memory of
NATHANIEL WEBB, of this Town,
who departed this Life April 2, 1739,
aged 76

Also of MARGARET his Relict,
and Daughter of
EDMUND SEME, of Howlshill,
in the Parish of Walford,
in the County of Hereford, Gent
who departed this Life
the 29th Day of November, 1741,
aged 66

Here resteth the Body of
ANNE, Wife of THOMAS NICHOLAS,
of Wantwell, in the Parish of Berkeley,
who departed this Life June 21, 1746,
aged 78

Also the Body of
Mr JOHN NICHOLAS,
of this Town, Clothier
who departed this Life Feb 7, 1754,
aged 41 Years

Also the Body of
ANN, the Wife of JAMES NICHOLAS,
Clothier,
who departed this Life July 9, 1755,
aged 21

Here lyeth the Body of
WILLIAM PURNELL, Clothier,
who departed this Life October 29, 1633,
aetatis sue 54

In Memory of
THOMAS PURNELL, of Kingshill, Esq
Son of WILLIAM PURNELL,
of this Town,
who died October 29, 1729,
aged

Also ANNE, Wife of
THOMAS PURNELL, Esq
departed this Life in February 1745,
in the 80th Year of her Age

And also WILLIAM PURNELL,
of Filldown, Gent
Son of the said THOMAS and ANNE,
who died the 2   aged

Here lyeth the Body of
JOHN, the Son of JOHN PURNELL,
Clothier
who died June 30 1712
aged 2 Year

Here lyeth the Body of
ANNE, the Wife of JOHN PURNELL,
who departed this Life the 8th Day of
September, 1695, aged 71

Also the Body of
JOHN PURNELL, Clothier,
who departed this Life the 15th Day of
June, 1714, aged 51 Years

In Memory of
ANN PURNELL, eldest Daughter of
JOHN PURNELL, of this Town, Gent
who died August 28, 1729, aged 79

JOHN PURNELL, senior, Clothier,
was here buried the 23d Day of
February, 1666

Here lyeth the Body of
ANN, the Daughter of
JOHN PURNELL, Clothier,
who departed this Life the 25th Day of
September, 1710, aged 17 Years

Here lyeth the Body of
ANNE HUNT, eldest Daughter of
THOMAS PURNELL, Esq
who died April 15, 1702, aged 74

RICHARD, the Son of
RICHARD MORGAN, Gent
died the 28th Day of Dec 1742,
aged 2 Months

On a marble Tablet

In Memory of THOMAS PURNELL, Esq
and   AN his Wife,
who departed this Life
the April 1743, aged 51
and the May 23, 1765, aged 71

Also JOHN their Son
departed this Life May 6 1752,
aged

And also WILLIAM JONES, Gent
was buried here Nov 26, 1755, aged 39

In Memory of
MARTHA, Wife of THOMAS BAVIN,
and Daughter of JOHN PURNELL, senior,
of this Town, Gent
who departed this Life the 14th Day of
May, 1734, in the 71st Year of her Age

Here lyeth the Body of
ESTHER, the Widow of
THOMAS FAXER, of this Parish,
Clothier
She was the Daughter of
THOMAS TYNDAL, of Stinchcomb,
Gent, and was first married to
JOHN ELLIOTT, Clerk
some time Curate of this Parish and
afterwards Rector of Edgworth,
in this County
She died April the 30th, 1743,
in the 82nd Year of her Age

Also HANNAH Daughter of
the said JOHN and ESTHER ELLIOTT,
who died Sept 16, 1698,
in the 4th Year of her Age

Also ELIZABETH their Daughter,
and Widow of SAMUEL YATES,
of the Parish of Minchinghampton Dyer
She died July the 26th 1756,
in the 64th Year of her Age

Also of ONESIPHORUS ELLIOTT Clothier,
youngest Son of the said
JOHN and ESTHER,
who died April 9 1766,
in the 65th Year of his Age

Here lyeth the Body of
MARY, Wife of
GEORGE LAITHORN, Clothier,
who died Sep 18, 1748,
aged 23 Years

Also the said GEORGE FAITHORN,
died Sept 29, 1755, aged 29 Years

Here resteth the Body of
JOHN PURNELL, senior,
Clothier, in Dursley,
who departed this Life the 12th of May,
1692

Also the Body of
MARGARET, the Wife of
JOHN PURNELL, senior Clothier,
who died the 10th Day of January, 1712,
aged 73

And JOSEPH their Son
departed this Life January 14, 1732,
in the 63d Year of his Age

And MARY his Wife,
aged 56, 1743

In the Nave

On a marble Monument fixed
against a Pillar

Near this Place lieth the Body of
FRANCES Wife of JOHN A WOOD,
Gent and Relict of JOHN PHILLIPS,
She died Jan 27, A D 1728,
aged five 7

Also of JOHN PHILLIPS,
Son of the said FRANCES,
by her former Husband
He died Jan 19, Anno Dom 1709,
aged 28

Also two Sons and one Daughter of
WILLIAM PURNELL and ANN his Wife,
Daughter of the said FRANCES,
they died in their Childhood

ON MONUMENTS IN THE NORTH AISLE

Arms on a Chevron between three Depui, i, three Griffes or, a for Id...

In Memory of WILLIAM LLEWIS,
of this Town Clothier
and HANNAH his Wife
He dec'd March 3, 1735, aged 51
She Decemeber 15 ... aged 51 ...

Also SARAH Wife of
THOMAS Lee ... the ...
who d'd November ... 1755, aged 31

Likewi.e ANN CORNWALL,
Daughter of the above
WILLIAM and HANNAH
died Feb 28 ... aged 5...

Also the ... THOMAS TIPPETTS,
... Ma ... 1 ... 9 at 60

Arm ... on a le ... ds ... e three Leopards
... es of the he ... o ... Ann ...

M.S.
HENNY ... s ... Cl ... an
died Jan 7, 1735 ... in ... 44 Year

Cr ... IAN his Wife
died Jul 30 1754, aged 15 Years

Their Chi ... en
WILLIA ...
dec'd Feb 19, 1 ... aged 9 M ... ths

A ... s
died Dec ... 9 ... 1 ... aged ... Years

MARTHA
died May 1,, 1 ... aged 29 Year

HENRY
d'd Aug 19 ... 7 ... aged 75 Years

Also JEMIMA, Wife of
HENRY ANSS, jun
died July 10 1755, aged 30 Year

Anne, P ... s ... nupt ... g, HANNAH ...

Jenner o Mort
In this life
are deposited the Remains of
JOHN PURNELL ... n and MARY his
Wife
He departed this life July 27 1, ...
aged ... Years
She was interr'd Feb ... 174 ... aged 4

H ... ha ... N
... beloved Daughter of the ...
Jo ... n and MARY ...
... kdied N ... ber ... 1755
... ed 35 Years

... ted in me ... ory of
J ... s ... S ... this Town,
who d'parted this Life ... 1 ... 1 ... 1,
... an 6 ...

A ... As ... In D ... a ...
A ... ll ... o ... R ... n
deparnu ... is ... f ... i ... 1 ... is ...
... ed ...
A ... the H ... t ... t ... J ... a ...
S ... n the above L ... s his ...
who d'parted this li ... 1 ... 0 1, ...
... the 3 ... Year of his A ...

Al ... hes ... here the ... dy of
A ... of ... s ... of ... wife ...
... In this Town ...
who de ... 1 ... 1 ... 1, aged ...

In ... ... Ann ... of W ... ...
... John ... ... the ... ...
Item ... C ... D ... W ... of ...
... li ... ed ... between two per ...

SARAH D ... ch ... et
G ... and SARAH ...
was buried ... p ... l ... 1735
... ed Y ...

ANN the Daughter of
RICHARD H ... y ... Clothi ... D ... sley,
d'd Jan ... 1 ... 1

Her ... with the lady of
RICHARD H ... e
who departed this Life the ... D ... ...
August Anco 1711, age 49 Years

ANN the Wife of RICHARD H ... y,
her ... ed Dwe ... of M ... 1 4
... 6 ... Yea ...

Here reacheth the body of
A ... N ... of C ... l ... RNELL,
Clari of North Nly ...
who d'ed M ... 12 ... 1 ... 0 ... 75

Here ... th the ... y of
MARY A ... of ABRAHAM DAVID
who departed this Li ...
April ... 47 aged 70 Ye ...

A ... n ... D ... P ... re ... don ...
d'd A ... o D ... m ... 9

Also ... of PHILLIP ... m ...
died Ann Domini 1 ...

Likewi.e SAMUEL C ... N ... LAIN
old dep ... 1 ... 1 ... Yea ...

In M ... o ... f
NICHOLAS N ... A ... Clo ...
who died Dec ... 17 ... d 65

ANNE of R ... e ... his Wife
who died Oct 21 1 ... d 5

A ... of
... of th ... on, ... bo d ... l ... b ...

Here re ... th the Bod ... of
... o ... h ... s ... his ... nna Cloth ...
who ... part ... he Li ... 26th Day of
July 1716, ... d 5 ... ear ...

Also S ... an W ...
I ... s C ... n ... da ...
d ... the 6th Dec ... M ... 7

SAMUEL ... b ... h ... s ... n Clothi ...
d'd Jun ... 1 ...

In the ... nth ... l ... t
J ... n Pe ... p ... n
who dep ... e ... th
the 8th D ... of ... 196

ELIZA ... Wife of D ... x ... IGGS,
died Au ... 9, 1

Also J ... e ... nd
M ... en ... d J ... s K ... th,
who ... d, 1 ... infan ...

Here re ... eth the Bod ... of
R ... R ... n ... Clo ...
A ... ed July 1 ... 7 ... 9 d 55 Ye ...

MARY HA ...
Daughter of C ... n A ... y
and De ... y ... s ... lo ... e ...

In the Me ... y of the
Fa ... t S ... y
are contained in th ... S ... n ... ent

In M ... y H ... A ... ts 1735,
who died L ... 17 ... 747,
... ed ... Years

Also SAR ... Wife of
J ... ss ... n ... t
... d N ... v ... ... d ... Years

Here re ... th the b ... y of
R ... r ... l ... s ...
... th ... Town C ... ier
who d'd Feb 1 ... 10,
aged 4 ... Yea ...

In Me ... ry of ... s WAT ...
who died M ... 1 ...
... ed ... Years

... 1 ... ... of ... s 1755,
the A ... of J ... M ... 1735 ...
... the Tow ...
who s ... Oct ... 1 ...
... d ... Year

In Memo ... f JAM ... C ... AS
d ... d L ... s ...
who died ... an ... 7 ...
aged ... Y ...

... o ... o ...
who ... d ... 1 ...
... 18 Yea ...

A ... dif ... h ... ...
of the T ... n C ... h ...
who d'd M ... 1 ... 1755
... ed Yea ...

A ... t o ... s ...
JOHN and MARY ...,
wh ... d d ...

W ... t ...
Sept ... 17 ... 1 ... Ye ...

I ... ard ...
March ... 1 ... 1 ... ed ... Ye ...

ON MONUMENTS IN THE SOUTH AISLE

Arms, Per Ch ... on and ... lez, in
Chie ... d th ... in bal ... two per ...
in ... re — ... for ... re ...

In Me ... y of
L ... N ... in the Ne ... Ha ... in 1 ...,
he dep ... e ... ie L ... 1 ...
in the 57th year of ... s A ...

Also M ... J ... n ... 1 ...,
who d ... 1 ... 1 ... d ... Ye ...

Near th ... ly ... the rem ... d
th ... H ... J ... n WOOD,
... f ... s ... Cler ...
who s ... 6 ... 1 ... 1735,
... ed ... Year ...

To the Memory of
ANN BARNES, Relict of JOHN BARNES,
Surgeon, and only Sister of
NATHANIEL HICKES, of Weſtend,
in this County, Eſq
She died the 9th of April, 1768,
ætat 57

ON FLAT STONES

Under this Stone is depoſited
the Body of JOHN BARNES, Gent.
eldeſt Son of JOHN BARNES,
of Gannerew, near Monmouth
in the County of Hereford, Gent
who departed this Life the firſt Day of
July, in the Year of our Lord 1761,
in the 55th Year of his Age

BRETT RANDOLPH Eſq
late of Warwick on James River,
Virginia,
born Sept 4, 1732,
died Sep 4 1759

Alſo MARY, Relict of
the ſaid BRETT RANDOLPH,
died Nov 24, 1779, aged 49 Years

Memoria GULIELMI SMITH Gene. oſi,
qui mortem obiit vicesimo tertio die
Junii, A D 1733, ætatis 34

In Memory of DANIEL WHITE,
who died Jan 31, 1744, aged 53

ELIZABETH, Wife of
JOHN LAWSON,
died March 29, 1756

Alſo ANN their Daughter
died .

ON MONUMENTS AGAINST THE BELFRY

NORTH SIDE

Arms, Chequuy Or and Azure, on a
Feſs Gules three Lozenges Argent, for
CAPEL Creſt, three Oſtrich Feathers
Argent

Near this Place lyeth the Body of
DANIEL CAPEL,
Vicar of Cam and Curate of Durſley,
who departed this Life May ,
A D 1737 aged 68 Years

SOUTH SIDE

Arms, Argent, on a Feſs Sable, between three Lozenges Gules, three
Cinquefoils of the Field, for PURNELL
—impaling, Argent, a Chevron Azure,
between three Falcons riſing proper, for
PHILIPPS

In Memory of
WILLIAM PURNELL, Gent
who departed this Life Jan 4, 1743,
aged 69

And of ANN his Wife,
who died May 11, 1760, aged 76.

And of their Son
JOHN PURNELL, of Newhouse, Eſq
who, adorned with every ſocial
and Chriſtian Virtue,
as a Son, a Husband, a Father, and
a Friend,
drew his laſt Breath without a Groan,
and crowned a Life of Piety
by a Death of Peace.
He married ANNA, Daughter of
JOHN PHELIS Eſq
by MARY, Daughter of
JOHN ARUNDELL Eſq
whoſe congenial Benevolence, and
amiable Conduct in the
female Duties of domeſtic Life
rendered her Death ſeverely felt,
and ſincerely lamented
She died March 18 1762, aged 38
He died October 31, 1762 aged 6

IN THE CHURCH YARD, ON TOMBS

WILLIAM MAY
was buried June 27, 1685.

Two Daughters of
JOHN and MARY KING

ANN died 18 December, 1685

ELIZABETH died 6 January 1686

THOMAS KING, of this Town,
who died the 8th of January, 1689,
aged 74

THOMAS KING,
of this Town Junior Baker
died March 30, 172 aged 85 Years

MARY his Wife
died April 24 1717, aged 84 Years

HENRY their Son
died April 15, 1733, aged 60 Years

THOMAS their Son
died Oct 23, 1746 aged 49

ANN their Daughter
died Dec 20, 1759 aged 30 Years

MARY, Wife of
RICHARD ROE, of this Town, ſenior,
died Jan , 1760, aged 75

Alſo EDWARD and WILLIAM their Sons
were buried here

Alſo the ſaid RICHARD ROE
died April 17, 1770, aged 85 Years

ELIZABETH and ANN,
Daughters of RICHARD ROE,
were buried here

JUDITH, Wife of THOMAS KING,
died Feb 14, 1737, aged 35 Years

ELIZABETH her Daughter
died Dec 11, 1734, aged 3

THOMAS TAYLOR,
of this Town, Baker,
died Aug 13, 1752, aged 33.

Two of his Children by MARY his Wife
are buried here

THOMAS, Son of
WILLIAM and MARY TAYLOR,
died Nov 3, 1710, aged 9 Months

MARY JENKINS, Daughter of
WILLIAM and MARY TAYLOR,
died June 14, 1780 aged 71

HANNAH her Daughter
died Oct 4 1799, aged 37

SARAH, Wife of WILLIAM TAYLOR,
died May 9 1751, aged 69

Alſo five of her Children
four died in their Infancy

HANNAH died in the 15th Year of her
Age

SARAH Daughter of
JOHN and LILL EVERETT
died Sept 12, 1747, aged 22

ELIZABETH Wife of
JOHN EVERETT,
died Aug 6, 1767, aged 68

MARY, Wife of
THOMAS COLLIER, ſen
died Oct 8 1780, aged 66 Years

HESTER their Daughter
died March 13, 1748, aged 4 Years

THOMAS COLLIER jun
died Jan 8, 1785 aged 36

Here reſteth the Body of
JOHN HALLOWS the Clerk of this
Pariſh,
who died Jan 7, 1743,
in the 61ſt Year of his Age

Alſo JOAN, Wife of
the ſaid JOHN HALLOWS

JOSEPH HALL
died May 3, 1767, aged 41

JANE, Wife of JAMES GETHEN of this
Town Baker

Alſo four of their Children

Under this Tomb lie the Bodies of
THO ASCOTH, and MARY his Wife

THOMAS their Son
died Dec 6, 1757, aged 67

ANN Wife of JOHN GETHEN and
Daughter of ROBERT BENNETT of
Wotton Under Edge, Writing Maſter
died March 3, 1749 aged 48 Years

JOHN GETHEN died Dec 7, 1761
aged 69 Years

Thomas and William,
Son of John and Mary,
were buried here Infants

Peter Dixon, one of Thomas and
Mary Bayley, died Sep 14, 1746,
aged 12 Years

Mary, wife of James Bayley John 1,
died Nov 5, 1741, ...

Sarah Second Wife
died June 11, 1784, aged 78

Susanna Daughter of
Francis Whitney
died Nov 1, 1773, aged 9

Francis Whitney, of this Town,
Clothier, died April 4, 1727, aged 60

Mary, wife of James Nicholas,
of Nov 5 1733, died ...

James, their Son died Jan 10, 1774,
aged 4 Years

Mary, their Daughter died April 14,
1774, aged 1 Year

Mary, Wife of Francis Whitney,
died Jan 26, 1757, aged 30

Four Children died in their Infancy

Francis Whitney
died Oct 18, 1702, aged 7 Years

Mary, Wife of Francis Whitney,
died Aug 6 1690

Also here lyeth Robert Whitney,
their Son

Charles Whitney, Clothier,
died Jan 6, 1733, aged 59

Mary, their Daughter, was buried
Dec 2, 1734, aged 30

Mary, Wife of Thomas Hill, jun
died Nov 9 1763, aged 35 Years

Thomas Hill, jun
died May 20, 1777, aged 61

Edward Hill ...
died April 28, 1744, aged 49

Elizabeth, his Wife, Daughter of
Thomas Hill
died Jan 20, 1676, aged 43

Edward their Son, Aug 23, 1733,
aged ... Years

Thomas Hill
died June ...

Hannah, Wife of Thomas Hill,
died Jan 19, 1766, aged 77

William ...
died Sep ..., aged 5

... Children, viz
Mary ...
died ...

Thomas Tittadam, Cardmaker
Dec 18 1744 ... aged 58

Joseph, Son of Thomas Tittadam,
died Oct 8 1769, aged 53 Year

Elizabeth his Daughter
died June 6, 1779, aged 19 Years

Thomas Tittadam
died July 31, 1700, aged 48 Years

Deborah Wife of
Thomas Tittadam, Cardmaker
died April 2, 1751, aged 59

Also Six Children

Mary, Wife of
Thomas Tittadam, jun
died Oct 9, 1748, aged 5

John their Son April 5, 1744,
aged 6 after his

Sarah, Wife of
Joseph Tittadam
died May 15 1767, aged 39 Years

Hic jacet Reliquiæ
Samuelis Rogers

Hic jacet Corpus Jacobi Bayley,
de London Gent
Obiit die Novembris 1731

Obadiah Webb Mercer,
once Bayliff of this Town,
buried Oct 9 1665, aged 49

Elizabeth his Wife
Oct 1, 1692, aged 7

Robert their Son
died Jul 21 1666, aged 19

Samuel their Son
died July 20, 1697, aged 27

Mary, Feb 1670, aged 10

Mary Hicks was buried
Sep 6, 1742, aged 40

John Webb Mercer
died June 30, 1745, aged 64

Elizabeth his Daughter
died ...

Sarah his Wife
died Jan 31, 1733, aged 58

... son of ... John Cam
of June, 1666, aged ...

... of the John Cam ...

He, April 24, ... aged ...
the ... July 1753, aged 67

... his Daughter Mary ...
William Knight
died Sep ... aged 55

Mary, Wife of ...
and Daughter of John and
Hannah ...
died July ..., aged ...

Martha Knight,
... died in her ...

Hannah Knight
on May 6 ...

Muriel Butler, Wife of Cam,
died June 21, 1777, aged 70

Sarah his Wife Daughter of
Robert and Sarah Webb
died Oct 4, 1710, aged 29

Robert Webb
died June 9, 1748, aged 53 Year

Sarah his Wife
died May 2, 1741, aged 63

Peter, their Son was buried here

Maurice Forshew,
of this Town, Cardmaker,
died April 2, 1773, aged 59 Years

Ann Smith, Relict of
Samuel Smith and Daughter of
John and Alice Lamb,
died Nov 25, 1773, aged 74

Charles Cooper
died July 10, 1777, aged 64, ...

Hester his Wife
died June 22, 1767, aged 73 Years

John, Charles and William,
their Sons died Young

Daniel their brother
died Dec 10, 1751, aged 49

Mary, Wife of William Drew,
died Oct 29, 1777, aged 49 Year

Elizabeth Workman,
died March 10, 1779, aged 73

Here lyeth the Body of
Henry Avery,
who departed this Life
August 9 1664

Martha the Wife of Henry Avery,
was buried Oct 26, 1715, aged 68

Here lyeth the Body of John Fisher,
who died May 14, 1667, aged 85

Here resteth the Body of
Henry Avery of Dursley Clothier,
who departed this Life the 16th day of
May Anno Dom 1701 aged ...

Here resteth the Body of
John Avery
who died ...

Thomas ... Son of ...
John Avery Clothier,
died ...

John ...
John Avery ...
died ...

John Avery ... Daughter ...
died July ...

Henry, Daughter of John Avery,
died ...

John ...
died ...

John Hill ...
died ...

JOYCE, he Daughter of
JOHN and JOANNA HEALSTONE,
died April 21, 177, aged 30

ELIZABETH the Wife of
SAMUEL TROTMAN Daughter of
RICHARD and SARA MERRICK,
died March 16, 171, aged 63

RICHARD MERRICK fon Mercer,
died May 10, 1714, aged 4

WILLIAM MERRICK, Mercer,
was buried Aug 20,

D t, Son of WILLIAM MERRICK,
died　　　　day of January

ISAAC SMITH,
of the Parifh, Clother,
died May 17, 1726, aged 71

H I E
AN , Filix plurimum dr th
JOHANNIS BERRIMAN, hujus Parochiæ,
In fum cons t, quæ decefsit
16 die A t Ann 17 5
Æt t , te deam require

ELIZ Filiæ JOHANNI &
JOHANNÆ BARNES, vivit migravit
A t 174 , & An t hæ tuæ

JOHANNA, Uxor JOHANNI BARNES,
obiit 25 Auguft Vinoque Dom 4
L at fut 49

Here lieth the Body of
WOOLVIN BA N
who died Aug 11, 160,
Ætatis fuæ

JOHN GRIFFITS, fon
of the New Mills, Clother,
departed this Life, May 31, 1706,
aged 5

MARY his Wife
died Nov 4, 1727, aged 67

MARY and REBECCA
Daughters of the id JOHN and MARY,
interred here

JOHN GRIFFITS,
of the New Mills, in his Lifetim Clother,
died July 17 1736, aged 4

JOHN the Son of
JOHN and ANN GRIFFITS
died Ju 17, 1736, aged 6 Years

ANN Relict of
JOHN GRIFFITS Clother
died Sept 6, 1738, aged 57

MARY, Wife of JOSEPH PEACOCK,
Daughter of JOHN and ELIZ GRIFFITS,
died April 8, 179, aged 47

Th Brice
JOHN NISBERRIMAN,
hujus opp li
The a ter oh concer mis
qui bui e tuo quæ du
Mortis Sub vano Dom a 178
Late brie e
J t te Ann blandus
C n i e en ten
en nt e tu i
n tit all ber e
ll e i ite

M t F e ing He an,
e i t l t
ele e tte un t he t e i
t t Jam e

WILLIAM PARTRIDGE, Mercer,
died Feb 2, 1682, aged 54

ELIZ Wife of
WILLIAM PARTRIDGE, Mercer,
died Oct 12, 172 aged 75

WILLIAM, Son of
WILLIAM PARTRIDGE
died Nov 1, 1663, aged 2 Years,

ANN DAVIS
died April 15 1754 aged 75
SAMUEL Son of BENJAMIN and
ELIZABETH HILL,
died Feb 28, 1759, aged 7 Years

WILLIAM PARTRIDGE,
of Durfley Clothier,
died the laft day of Feb 1690,
aged 20 Years,

JOHN, Son of GILES and
ANN WORKMAN,
died Sep 23, 1748 aged 8

ELIZ Relict of JOHN WORKMAN,
and Wife of SAMUEL GARDNER,
died April 19, 1744 aged 2

MAURICE SMITH
died Dec 4, 1736, aged 60

ELIZABETH, Wife of
MAURICE SMITH
died Nov 29, 1738, aged 54 Years

Three Children of
MAURICE and ELIZABETH SMITH
died young

ANN WATKINS,
Wife of JOHN WATKINS, Mercer,
who deceafed Feb 15, 1660,
being aged 50 Years

JOHN WATKINS, of Durfley, Mercer,
died Oct 6, 1691

ELIZAB TH Wife of
SAMUEL KING, Daughter of
JOHN WATKINS
buried here Dec 5, 1704

NATHANIEL, Son of SAMUEL KING,
died Oct 22 1704

ELIZABETH, Wife of
MAURICE SMITH Daughter of
SAMUEL KING
died Dec 2, 1704

Alfo SAMUEL KING, Mercer,
died Oct 2, 1708

MAURICE PHILLIS
of this Town, Clother,
died March 5 1720, aged 86,

ELIZABETH, Wife of
MAURICE PHILLIS,
died Oct 1, 1730, aged 95

They lived in Wedlock 65 Years

SAMUEL and ELIZABETH PHILLIS
He died Feb 6, 1746
aged 84 Years
She died Dec 14, 1

JOHN their Son
died Nov 12 1743, aged 2

WILLIAM
died 1 3, aged 30

ELIZ Daughter of
t t F nd Wife
d Nov t 2 aged 26 Year

HENRY WILLIAMS
died Dec 16 1694

EDMUND, Son of
EDMUND and JANE HORT,
died May 20, 173, aged 2

THOMAS their Son
died Jan 29, 1738, aged 2, Years

Four more of their Children buried here

NATHANIEL
died May 29, 1723, aged 5 Years

JANE
died Sept 12, 1728, aged 2 Years

JOHN
died May 30, 1733, aged 3 Years

ALICE
died Jan 12, 1773, aged

EDMUND HORT, of Durfley,
died Aug 4, 1738, aged 57

JANE his Wife
died Jan 13, 17

SARAH Wife of RICHARD COOPER,
died April 5, 1744, aged 59

MARTHA their Daughter
died Aug 20, 1736, aged 13 Years

RICHARD COOPER
died Jan 19, 1749, aged 64 Years

MAURICE ANDREWS
died Sept 22, 1749, aged 9

MAURICE, Son of JOHN ANDREWS,
died May 12, 1712, aged 54

JOHN, Son of the faid
MAURICE ANDREWS

ELIZ Wife of MAURICE ANDREWS,
died Sept 14, 1759, aged 80

JOHN ANDREWS
died March 26 1752, aged 2

NATHANIEL WENT
died March 29, 1759 aged 54

HANNAH WENT
died Aug 15, 1744 aged 42

JOHN WENT
died Oct 9, 1772 aged 62

HANNAH BLACKWELL,
died Aug 16, 1744, aged 4

ANN GEORGE
died Jan 15, 182, aged 81

JACOB WALLINGTON, Efq
was buried March 24 174
aged 8 Years

NICHOLAS NEALE, Clother,
was buried Oct 26, 170 , aged 6

ALICE his Wife
died Jan 14, 1734, aged 60

THOMAS NEALE,
of this Town, Clother
died March 8, 1754, aged 7

ESTHER Daughter of JOHN NEALE
of this Town
died May 5 1751 aged 6

MARY Daughter of THOMAS NEALE
died Feb 27, 17 , aged 36 Year

WILLIAM SANIGEAR,
of this Town,
died Feb 4, 1771, aged 70

MARTHA his Wife
died March 9, 1753, aged 55

MARY, Daughter of
WILLIAM SANIGAR, jun
died Feb 24, 1739, aged 2 Years.

SARAH, Wife of ABRAHAM SANIGEAR,
Daughter of
THOMAS and ANN LEWTON,
died June 14, 1770, aged 34 Years

WILLIAM their Son
died July 14, 1760, aged 7 Years

JOSEPH JONES,
died May 2, 1755, aged 42
LUCAS his Son
died June 15, 1763, aged 35
JOSEPH Son of JOSEPH JONES,
died July 23, 1769, aged 39 Years
ELIZABETH, Wife of
JOSEPH JONES, junior
died May 3 1770, aged 39 Years

JACOB STILE
died Nov 18, 1733, aged 56 Years
ANN, Daughter of
JACOB and his Wife
died Nov 24, 1735, aged 7
Three more of their Children were
buried here

MARY, Wife of JOSEPH CARTER
died April 18, 17 , aged

Three Children died young

JOSEPH CARTER
died June 20, 1780, aged 40

Four Children of
THOMAS and MARY SMITH

THOMAS SMITH
died April 19, 1768, aged 58 Years.

ON FLAT AND HEAD STONES

	Died	Aged		Died	Aged
James Griffin, Baker	22 Apr 1764	28	Mary, Wife of Thomas Green	6 Feb 1757	54
John Griffin Baker	18 July, 1755	53	Thomas Green	25 Feb 1738	54
John his Son	10 Aug 1746	11	William Wood	8 Sept 1760	29
Christopher Pincott	23 Oct 1782	68	Judith his Wife	13 Mar 17 7	81
Elizabeth his Daughter	25 June, 1733	12	Elizabeth, Wife of Jacob Clark	8 Mar 1755	73
James Pinco	15 Sept 1748	20	Mary his second Wife	17 Nov 1770	52
Daniel Pincot	7 Mar 1772	72	John Higgins	20 Sept 1776	81
Mary his Wife	14 Jun 1757	60	Mary his Wife	— Nov 1770	70
Ann, Wife of Thomas Williams	4 May, 1770	37	Joseph Suntum	2 Dec 1763	57
Two Children of Robert and Christian Thurston	in Infancy		Arthur Vizard	26 Sept 1784	17
Richard, Son of John Pingrey, of Acton, in Worcestershire	19 June, 1753	56	Mary, Wife of Jacob Walley, Basketmaker	30 July, 1765	71
Joseph Vetvet	21 Jan 1750	45	Arthur Perry	1 Dec 1747	—
Three Children of Joseph and Sarah Stephens	—— 1717	—	Mary his Wife	— July, 1743	—
			Thomas Gibbs	10 May, 1745	37
Henry, Son of Daniel and Ann Budding	9 Jun 1715	—	Sarah his Wife		
			Nicholas Neale, of this Town jun	4 Nov 1770	52
Robert How	30 Oct 1723	60	Ann his Wife	2 Sept 1781	65
Nathaniel Newth	5 July, 1763	61	John Morgan		
Ann his Wife	20 Oct 1748	49	Sarah Wife of James Morgan	2 May 1767	—
John, Wife of John Vizard, sen	—— 1718	—	Joseph Oliver Clothdresser	— Nov —	45
William Hallowes and he	21 July, 1718	—	Abraham, Son of Thomas and Esther Stiff	10 Sept 1738	—
Ann his Wife	20 Oct 1723	—	Elizabeth, Wife of Thomas Oldland	20 May, 1752	39
Samuel, Son of the said William and Ann	4 July, 1714	21	Elizabeth Harold	16 Feb 1784	82
Sarah Hallowes Widow	23 Mar 1723	87	Elizabeth her Daughter	21 Apr 1762	0
James Barnfield	24 Jun 1721	17	John Lance	13 Mar 1784	45
Robert Belcher	15 May, 1727	23	Frances Elder	1 June, 1762	—
Ann, Daughter of John and Elizabeth Belcher	15 July, 1718	—	Martha, Daughter of John and Susanna Dando	12 May 1759	2
Samuel Belcher, Joiner	2 Sept 1761	52	Stephen, Son of the said John and Susanna	4 May, 1759	—
Mary Wife of Thomas Everatt	19 Aug 1762	83	Thomas Brown Wheelwright	9 Sept 1755	—
Thomas Everatt	11 Sept 1764	76	William Son of John Collins		
Martha Wife of John Hickes Surgeon	17 Apr 1709	58	Timothy Linton, Baker	Sep 1718	60
			Mary his Wife	Oct 1713	61
Thomas Hickes, Surgeon, Son of John and Martha	7 May, 1732	42	Christian, Daughter of Robert and Ann Smith	5 Apr 1779	
Sarah, Daughter of Joseph and Sarah Weaver	18 May, 1723	1	Richard Comock	7 Nov 1761	77
			Mary, Wife of Thomas Smith, jun	Jun 1772	2
John Hurt	23 Feb 1774	37	Ann, Daughter of John Cock	9 May 1767	11
Joan his Wife	18 Feb 1721	22	Sarah Wife of Thomas Hughes	4 Jul 1734	38
Mary, Wife of Joseph Williams	2 Feb 1715	68	Elizabeth, Wife of Benjamin Millard, senior	6 Oct 1755	4
Three of his Wives and two Children	——	—	Three of their Children		
Benjamin Hallows	7 May, 1744	68	Sarah Wife of John Wilkes	1 Feb 1770	55
Sarah his Wife	7 Apr 1720	52	Ann her Daughter	2 Sept 1770	2
William Stevens, Mason	6 Aug 1759	60	William, Son of William and Hannah Wood	6 May 1759	3
Mary Wife of Thomas Curtis	22 Mar 1747	50	John Wood	Apr 1762	71
Thomas Son of Thomas and Sarah Nichols	18 May, 1769	13	Sarah his Wife	25 Apr 1762	74
Thomas Nichols	11 Dec 1771	7	Samuel Smith Butcher	1 Sept 1757	0
Richard Son of James Tull	— Jun 17	5	Samuel his Son	10 Jul 1766	31
Ann Tullin	5 May 1735	—	John Ireland, senior	1 Apr 1691	56
John Puller	12 June 1735	4	Rebecca his Wife	27 Feb 1712	78
Mary Wife of Jonathan Tomb	6 June, 1741	59	William his son	21 Jan 1696	15
Margaret his Daughter	29 Jan 1738	7	Francis Curtis	2 Apr 1716	77
Hugh Everatt	1 Oct 1781	52	Katharine his Wife	2 Feb 1	78
Joseph his Son	11 Oct 1770	6			

ON FLAT AND HEAD STONES

	Died	Aged		Died	Aged
Francis Curtis, Clothier -	8 Mar 1759	66	Two Sons and two Daughters of Joseph and Hannah Williams		
Elizabeth his Daughter			John Weight		
Thomas Curtis Carpenter -	9 Sept 1756	65	John Millard	6 Jan 1,3	
Mary, Wife of Thomas Grace	1 Jan 1767	38	John his son		
Edmund Lewis, of the City of Bristol Blacksmith	4 Aug 1752	—	Elizabeth his Wife	17 Jan 1,3,	81
			Esther, Wife of John Phelp	2 Jan 1,31	
Judith, Wife of John Smith, Cardmaker	30 Apr 1737	60	Richard Wyman Fuller	1 De 17,3	
The said John Smith -	1 May 1760	84	Mary his Daughter	15 Apr 1730	
Mary Wife of Thomas Wyman	6 Apr 1770	50	Two Children of Thomas and Elizabeth Harman		
Elizabeth their Daughter	17 Aug 1764	18			
William, Son of William and Sarah Blake	8 Feb 1784	—	Ann, Wife of Samuel Stockwell	7 May 1746	
			William Browning -	25 Dec 1745	6
William Blake, senior -	2 Apr 1766	59	Elizabeth his Wife	11 Apr 1725	51
Daniel Cull	4 Mar 1785	63	Daniel their Son	2 Dec 1,1,	
Mary Daughter of John and Mary Cull -	17 June 1786	23	Martha, Wife of Thomas Heath	18 Apr 1,3	63
Edward Wells -	17 May 1734	72	Sarah their Daughter	21 Sept 1734	65
Sarah his Wife	12 Dec 1747	80	Elizabeth, Daughter of Thomas and Elizabeth Dawes, of North Nibley	8 Apr 1759	
John Harding, Cardmaker	23 Dec 1701	60	Thomas Daw	25 May 1771	
Elizabeth his Wife	29 Aug 1767	64	Thomas Cook, Glover -	12 Sep 1736	
Elizabeth, Wife of Thomas Brothers	9 May 1722	48	Samuel Morgan -	11 Dec 177	
Thomas Brothers	11 June 1728	62	Mary his Wife	23 July 1760	
Joseph Ketching Cordwainer	9 Dec 1736	73	Three of their Children died young		
Elizabeth his Wife	—	67	Jacob Clark, senior	4 Apr 16,	
Joseph their Son	3 Dec 1759	61	Esther his Wife	1 Apr 170	
Daniel, Son of Daniel and Sarah Workman -	14 Sept 1758	3	William their Son -	11 Fel 1757	9
Robert Workman	— Dec 1758	65	James Gething, Cardmaker	20 May 1756	85
Sarah his Wife	11 Aug 1755	42	Lois his Wife	5 Oct 1735	69
Elizabeth, Wife of Samuel Hill	6 Mar 1737	54	Betty, Wife of Nathaniel Young	19 Dec 175	5
William Holder	23 Sept 1767	66	Daniel Young	Jul 1743	
Hester his Wife -	6 Dec 1746	57	Sampson Browning -	10 Aug 1740	4
William their Son -	31 Apr 1732	27	Elizabeth, Wife of Sampson Browning senior	— July 127	
Elizabeth their Daughter -	8 Oct 1766	32	Mary, Wife of Thomas Wyman	4 Jul 17,	
Robert Clark -	8 May 1721	76	Thomas Wyman junior	1 Dec 1722	
Robert Cobley	2 Aug 1704	65	Daniel Ricketts	— Sept	
Martha his Wife -	2 Feb 1747	47	William Trotman	9 July 1730	
Nathaniel their Son	14 Oct 142	16	Edward and Mary, Son and Daughter of —— Southern		
Thomas their Son	20 June 1704	—	John Grace		
Nathaniel Pitt -	12 Aug 1733	72	John Danzel	May 1736	51
Mary his Wife -	23 Dec 1741	73	Mary his	Oct 175	
Daniel Igby -	13 Feb 1737	65	John ... Daniel ...	13 A	
Sarah his Wife	17 Jan 1750	84	James Mann	15 O	
Daniel their Son -	18 Dec 1778	62	Thomas his Son	11	
Sarah his Wife, Daughter of William and Sarah ...	14 Oct 170	64	Elizabeth Wife of Thomas ...	1 Feb	
			Sarah Wife of Thomas J...	1	—
William Ketch	3 July 123	7	Richard ...	1	
Hannah his Wife	— May 1 6,		Mary Jones	1	
Judith Ketch their Son	5 Oct 1753	7	M ...		
Ann Wife of Benjamin Ketch	— May 17		Hester	O	
John Lamb	— Aug 1 31				
... Roberts	7 Oct 1,10	—			

IS a very large Parish, in the Hundred of *Botloe*, contiguous to the County of *Hereford*, three Miles and a half distant from *Newent*, eleven Miles North from *Michel Dean*, and seventeen North-west from the City of GLOUCESTER Its Extent is nearly six Miles each Way, being of a circular Form, the Soil, one Part in seven, light and sandy, and the Remainder Clay, peculiarly favourable to the Growth of Oak Timber, and very numerous Orchards, as the Fruit Trees are frequently planted in the arable Fields *

The Living is a Vicarage, endowed with Tythes, though of late Years stipendiary only from the Impropriation † It was confirmed in 1242 by the Bull of Pope ALEXANDER III to the *Benedictine* Abbey of *Cormeilles*, in *Normandy*, " Ecclesiam de *Dimoc*, cum omnibus pertinentiis suis, & decimis apud Di-" moc 40 Solid decimam de toto Domino, & unam virgatam terræ in eâdem villâ ‡," which was transferred to the Master and Fellows of the College of *Fotheringhey*, co *Northampton*, when founded by King HENRY IV § At the final Suppression of Monasteries, the said Master and Fellows surrendered the Impropriation, by Deed of Exchange, to King HENRY VIII in the 38th of his Reign, 1547, and in the 1st of EDW VI Sir RICHARD LEE, Knight, procured a Grant of it in Fee, at the yearly Rent of 40*s* The Family of WYNTER, eminent for their Attachment to the STUARTS, afterwards held the Rectory, with the Advowson, which in 1652 (the Estates of Sir JOHN WYNTER being confiscated by the Parliament) was sold to DANIEL WYCHERLEY and THOMAS MILWARD, Esqrs Of Sir ORLANDO HUMPHREYS it was purchased by GEORGE PRITCHARD, Esq whose Daughter and sole Heir, deceased, was the Wife of HENRY LAMBERT, Esq by whom she left one Daughter, SUSAN LAMBERT PRITCHARD, whose Property it now is

The Church is dedicated to *St Mary*, and is included in the *Forest* Deanery The Nave is long and spacious, with a Transept of unequal Height, and not opposite. In the North is a Gothic Arcade, which contained the Image of the *Virgin*, the last Chaplain of the Chantry dedicated to her was JOHN WOOD Against the Tower, which is massy, with a very obtuse Spire, are, two Escocheons, bearing, 1 Three Pheons, for FORSTER; 2 Two Bendlets, charged with Barrs dancettè In the Vestry is an old mural Monument, intended for the Family of BRYDGES, to which Brasses were once affixed The original Form of the Building is much altered by frequent and modern Repairs

It appears, that the Village of *Dymock* was in early Times privileged with a Market and Fairs, that it was of greater Extent and more populous, and that the Inhabitants were exempted from certain County Rates, by King HENRY the Third To the Collectors of the King's Tenths and Fifteenths it then paid 6*l* 16*s*. 6*d* from which 2*l* 16*s* 6*d* were deducted

What Accounts of the Descent of the Manor have been transmitted to us are vague and uncertain, for it has been divided, and the Portions inaccurately specified By the Crown it was given and annexed to the Earldom of *Hereford*, it is afterward said to have belonged to the Families of CLIFFORD and GRANDISON In 32 HEN VI Sir WALTER DEVEREUX and ELIZABETH his Wife, claimed four Parts of the Manor, which were vested in 1565, 7 ELIZ in WALTER Viscount HEREFORD, by whom they were settled in Jointure on LETICE his Wife (re married to ROBERT DUDLEY, Earl of *Leicester*),

---

* " In the deep soiled District about *Dymock* where the whole Country may be said to be a Forest of Fruit Trees the Occupiers
" of Fruit Grounds, experiencing the Evil of Trees in arable Lands, are planting in their Grass Grounds This however, appears
" to be a wrong Principle Let them lay their old Orchards to Grass, and if they plant break up their young Orchards to
" Arable, this will be changing the Course of Husbandry, and be it once beneficial to the Land and the Trees "

MARSHALL's Rur Œc vol II p 187

† " Vicar,,, Decim ibidem Alb *annexly*, olim Imp 9*l* 13*s* 4*d*. BACON's Lib Reg p 333

‡ DECEM Mon vol II pp 66 , 967 " Valor annuus Ecclesiarum De *Newent Beckford & Dymoc*, quæ sunt Possessiones
" Spiritures et Priomdum de *Newent* spectantes pro quibus JOHANNES CHEYNE, Chivaler, & THOMAS HORSTON, Cler nuper
" Firmarii eatum farum 15 Marcas annuatim nobis per literas presentes reddere tenebuntur "

§ 67*l* 6*s* 8*d* quondam annuam firmam quam JOHANNES CHEYNE, Chivaler, reddere tenetur annuatim pro custodia Mane riorum temp ordin de *Newent* &c Ibid vol I p 159

The Vicar for many Years past has received in annual Stipend from the Impropriation of 40*l* and lately of 60*l* But it appears by the Return made by the Commission to ascertain the first Fruits due to the Crown, under the Statute of 26 HEN VIII that the Vicar was then entitled to vicarial Tythes, and by the Charters of *Fotheringhey*, temp HEN IV and RICH III. that such were of the said Tenth exempted those of Corn and Grain

6 X

and

and whose Right was proved in 1581   Giles Forster, Esq was the Proprietor in 1608, and soon after

* The Customs of *Dymock* were investigated by the Committee of the House of Commons for scrutinizing the Votes at the contested Election in 1776, when the Tenants of the Manor were declared to have given legal Suffrages

A Schedule indented, of the old and ancient Custom of the Manor of *Dymock* in the County of Gloucester, made and enrolled the fifth Day of April, in the Seventh Year of the Reign of Queen Elizabeth used within the said Manor, by the Custom and ancient Demeyne Tenants of the said Manor Time out of Mind, or the Remembrance of any Man, between the Right Hon Walter Vicount Hereford, Lord Ferrers of Chartley, and Lord of the said Manor of *Dymock*, of the one Part, and the ancient Demeyne Tenants of the Manor aforesaid of the other Part as herafter be expressed

1 Imprimis, The Custom of the said Manor of *Dymock* is, and always has been for the Time aforesaid, that the customary and ancient Demeyne Tenants of the said Manor as aforesaid do hold their Lands to them and to the Heirs of their Bodys lawfully begotten the Reversion and Remainder thereof, in Fee, to the Lord of the said Manor as aforesaid

Item 2d That they have used always, all the Time aforesaid when they be disposed to will, sell, give, grant, or alienate their Lands or Tenements to any Person or Persons whatsoever, to make Estate thereof by free Deed indented or poll Deed, to such Persons whatsoever, to have and to hold to them and to the Heirs of their Bodys lawfully begotten the Rent and Remainder thereof to the Lord of the said Manor and his Heirs for ever, with Lycence of the Lord of the Manor in that Behalf obtained

Item 3d, The Custom is that the Lord of the Manor, for the Time being, have always used for the Time aforesaid, to give and grant in the Court or Court Baron there, within the said Manor upon Request of any Tenant or Tenants disposed to make Alienation, as is aforesaid, such Lycence to do the same, and the Lycence to be enrolled in the Court Roll, of the said Manor by the Steward for the Lord for the Time being

Item 4th, That the Tenants aforesaid, for such Lycences and Alienation as is aforesaid have used to pay to the Lord of the Manor one Year's Rent, by the Name of Relief, and to the Steward for the Copy of the said Lycence Two Shillings

Item 5th, The Custom is, that the Lord of the Manor shall keep yearly, Two Times in the Year keep his Law Days and Court Barons in Manor and Form following that is to say, one within a Month next after the Feast of Saint Michael the Archangell, and the other within a Month next Hock Tuesday

Item 6th The Custom is, that all and every such Alienation made of Lands or Tenements, with Lycence as aforesaid, shall be Barrs for ever, by Custom of the said Manor, to the Heir or Heirs of such Tenant or Tenants, and also to the Lord of the said Manor and his Heirs, to demand or claim any of the Lands and Tenements so alienated, as is aforesaid and in default of Issue of the Body of the Tenant that alienateth and that no Writts of Forme, donne or descendr for the Heir, nor Remainder for the Lord hath been used to be commenced or brought within the said Manor, or at Common Law, by any Heir or Heirs of the Tenant aforesaid, or by the Lord or his Heirs, for the Lands alienated, with Lycence as is aforesaid, for that every such Tenant, may alienate, as is aforesaid, by the Custom of the said Manor

Item 7th, The Custom is that every Tenant that said pay to the Lord and his Heirs at their Deaths his best Beast that in Value shall be the best, for Herriotts and Relief, which is one Year's Rent for every Mense whereof every such Tenant shall dye seized not otherwise, except it be specially reserved upon their Grants heretofore made, if the Tenant that deceased having no Cattle of his own, then to pay his best Implement of Household Stuff for the Herriot, and for his Relief a Year's Rent

Item 8th, The Custom is, to have a Three week's Court, if there be any Plaints of Debts, Trespass, or otherwise, according to the Custom of the said Manor, affirmed by any Person within the same Manor, till the same be ended and tryed and that all the Custom, Lands, and Tenements, within the said Manor, be pleadable within the said Manor, by Writt of Right or Close, and not at Common Law

Item 9th, The Custom of the said Manor is that if any do demand any Customary Lands within the said Manor, by Writt of Right or Close against any Tenant within the Manor aforesaid that is to be brought according to the said Custom of the said Manor, that upon sufficient Warning to be given unto the Lord or his Steward of the said Manor, they are always to have a Three weeks Court, untill the Matter in controversie be tryed

Item 10th, The Custom is, that if a Writt of Right or Close according to the Custom of the said Manor, by one that has Cause to demand customary Lands, the one, that he that purchase or bring such Writt shall at the Law Day or Court Baron, deliver the same Writt unto the Steward in the Presence of the Court, and the Steward to break the same Writt in the Face of the Court and to read the same, and to have Six Shillings and Eight Pence for breaking the Writt and the Bailiff Three shillings and Four Pence

And then always after the Steward or his sufficient Deputy every Three Weeks to keep the Lord's Court within the said Manor till the Matter be tryed, according to the Custom of the said Manor or otherwise made a End off, by any Ways whatsoever, to that he that brings the Writt shall bear the Steward Charges

Item 11th, The Custom is, that the Lord to have a Steward certain of the said Manor who shall always keep his Courts with sufficient Warrant from the Lord of the said Manor, under his Hand and Seal of Arms, and the Warrant of the said Steward always at every Court, upon Demand to be read in open Court for the true knowledge of the Tenants, the same out of the said Court, if it be required and the same Warrant to be immediately after delivered unto the Tenants aforesaid according the Custom of the said Manor to be read unto for the said Steward &c

Item 12th The Custom of the said Manor, for the Time aforesaid have been that all the Tenants of the said Manor that do any Service in the Household charged or any other, being in any Office, that Day of the said Two Courts all Courts to be twice holden by the Year is bound to have her Dinner at the Lord's Expence

Item 13th That the Custom is that the Lord, or his Steward for the Time being, at every his said Two Courts as is aforesaid, shall chose one of his Free Berchers or Free Suiters of the Court, and the Tenants to chose another and that they do that same elect and chose the Twelve Men every their Court Days for the Lord's Homage, if they cannot agree, then the Steward of the Lord shall chose indifferent the Twelve Men indifferently between the Lord and Tenants aforesaid

Item 14th The Custom is, that if any of the Lord's Tenants do commit any Felony, and thereof be attainted by Law, or any Means whatsoever that then the said Lord of the said Manor shall not have his Lands holden by Tenant for the said Moiety the Day, Year, and Waste, but he next Heir immediately must have the same, for that the Father ought to go to the Bough, and the Son to the Plow

Item 15th, The Custom is that no Tenant may alienate, give nor grant his Lands or Tenements, or Parcell thereof otherwise than is aforesaid, without the Lycence of the Lord upon Pain of Forfeiture of his Lands and Tenements, and only for Twenty one Years in Possession or under by Lease upon reasonable Sum and required

Item 16th, The Custom is, that every Court that is to be holden within the said Manor there must be a Free Bench for its Free Suiters to the Court of the Lord, or else no Court to be holden within the said Manor, and the Bench is to be only by the Steward's Direction

Item 17th, The Custom of the said Manor is, that the Lord's tenant may show any of the said Two Days deny in the Roll of such Defence any Tenant within the said Manor holdeth his Lands by and if that any of them refuse it from the same to be Stewed at the next Law Day, to the Lord it may be enrolled and no Inheritance Court by Tenants of the said Land alienate, or such like, why the same cannot be shewed, then the Lord shall seize the Lands till the Evidence be shewed

Item 18th The Custom is that if any Tenant he after have any Deed of Intail made to him by Lycence and relief shall within one Year next after a Copy out of the said Deed of Intail, bring the same to be Stewed to be enrolled upon Pain of Forfeiture which is to be paid for his Lycence

Item 19th, The Custom is that every Tenant which shall have Lycence granted to alienate shall cause to have within a Month and one Day next out the Date, else the Lycence to be void

Itu 1

after Sir John Winter, of *Lydney*, and having been fold by Parliament, as the Impropriation had been, it paffed in 1657 to Evan Seys, Serjeant at Law, who re-fold it to Edward Pye, Merchant. Edward Pye Chamberlayne, Efq received it from the laft mentioned by Will in 1712, and his Son transferred the Manfion-houfe called the *Boyce*, with the manerial Eftate, to Ann Cam, Spinfter, by Purchafe, upon her Death, in 1790, fhe was fucceeded by John Mogeridge, Efq of *Bradford*, co *Huts*, in the Eftate, and by John Thackwell, Efq. of *Berrow*, co *Worcefter*, in the Manor.

In this Parifh are five Tythings, thus divided. In *Wood End* Divifion, the Tythings of *Flaxley* and *Gamage Hall*. Thefe, by long Ufage, are now called the Manor of *Little Dymock*. The Abbey of *Flaxley*, by Charter of Henry Duke of Normandy, poffeffed " all the Demefnes in *Dymock*, and half " the Wood there," and by a fubfequent Charter after his Succeffion as K. Henry II " All the Demefnes " at *Dymoc*, and five Yard Lands and a Half, befide the Demefnes, and half the Wood *." Sir Anthony Kingstone procured a Grant of this laft to the Suppreffion, which is confequently exempt from Tythes. In 1582 Thomas Wenman purchafed it, and from the Wenmans it defcended to Winman Wynniatt, Efq and it is now vefted in the Rev. Reginald Wynniatt, M A of *Staunton*. *Gamage Hall*, is the Manor houfe detached by Sale from the Eftate about 60 Years fince, when the Privilege of holding Courts there was referved, it is now the Property of Richard Sergeant, Gent. In former Centuries, it was held by the Families of De Gamage, Pembruge, and Monnion, and exercifes the fame Jurifdiction within itfelf as the greater Minor. By the Family of Hill, feveral good Eftates in this Tything have been poffeffed for many Generations.

Ryeland Divifion contains the Tythings of *Ryton* and *Ockington*. An Eftate called *Cowfield* was purchafed by Matthew Paul, Gent of a Branch of the Family of Hill, and another called *Pit Leafow* is now held by George Hayward, M A of *Proceſter*.

The *Ketford* Eftate in 1456, 36 Hen VI was vefted in the Family of Handborough. Thomas Brydges (of the Chandos Family) received it in Dower with Maud his Wife, Daughter of Thomas Handborough. Sir John Brydges, Lord Mayor of *London* in 1521, 12 Hen VIII was her Son, and a Native of *Dymock*. It includes two large Farms, *Great Ketford*, bought in 1670 of William Grove, Gent by Thomas Wall, Efq in Truft for his Son in law Rich Yate, of *Bromeſberro* the other called *Hill Place*, purchafed in 1732, by Colonel Walter Yate, of the Relict of Chriftopher Woodward, Gent of *Newent*, in whofe Family it had been vefted fince 1598, 40 Eliz then transferred by Sale from Humphry Forster, Efq of the *Boyce*.

The capital Meffuage called the *Callow*, was purchafed in 1687 by Rich Yate, Efq of the Family of Sheale, and another Eftate called *Cutt Mill*, was bequeathed in 1664 to Catherine his Wife, by her Father Thomas Wall, Efq of *Lintridge*, all which Property is now inherited by Walter Hollywood Yate, a Minor, eldeft Son of the late Robert Gorges Dobyns Yate, Efq deceafed. *Great Lintridge* was long the Refidence of the Walls, an ancient and opulent Houfe, from them it paffed to George Pritchard, Efq from whom, with the Impropriation, to Henry Lambert, Efq. *Ockington* was the Eftate of the Family of Weall, now of Bayliss, by Purchafe.

In *Tedington* Divifion, the Tything of *Leadington*, fituate near the Rivulet *Leedon*, a competent Eftate, now belonging to Thomas Hankins, Gent has been the Refidence of his Progenitors for many Centuries. John Cam, M D of *Hereford*, has other Property in this Tything.

During the Civil War a Garifon was fupported at *Dymock* for the King, by his ftrenuous Partizan Sir John Winter †.

Roger Dimoc, a learned *Dominican*, who died in 1390, is faid to have been born here, and Robert Burhill, D D in the laft Century ‡.

---

* Atkyns's *Gloucestershire*, p. 438 Dugdale's *Monaft* vol I p 884
† Corbet's Military Government of *Gloucester*, p 64
‡ Of whom fee Wood Athenæ, vol II p 4

BENEFACTIONS

BENEFACTIONS.

1650 WILLIAM SKINNER, LL. D gave Land for the Benefit of the Poor, which now produces 4*s* a Year

WILLIAM WALL, Efq gave Land, Seventy-two Yards in Length, and Eleven in Breadth, to poor Cottagers

1717 ROBERT WYNTER, Gent bequeathed Lands, the annual Produce of which is 30*l*. to cloath Twenty poor People

1719 WILLIAM WEALE, Citizen of *London*, gave 100*l* the Interest of which to be laid out in Bread, yearly, at Christmas

1734 WILLIAM HOOPER, Gent left a Rent Charge of 3*l* a Year for instructing poor Children

THOMAS MURREL gave 10*s*. yearly, to be given to Ten poor Widows, and 10*s* to the Minister of the Parish for a Sermon recommending Charity, upon Candlemas Day

In the Year 1785 certain Premises were purchased and fitted for the Reception of a School, by a Sub-scription of 140*l* raised by the Parishioners, for educating the Children of the industrious Poor on Sundays, agreeably to the late Institution

INCUMBENTS	PATRONS.	INCUMBENTS.	PATRONS.
1577 Walter Coulfey,	Bp of Gloucester	1667 Grindal Wilson,	John Sheyle, Gent
1588 James Thomas,	Queen Elizabeth	1720 Samuel Savage,	Sir W. Humphreys
162. William Morgan,	Wm Wynter, Efq	1761 Wm. Hayward, M.A.	Geo. Pritchard, Gent
1664 Thomas Eaton,	Wm Wynter, Efq.	1787 Jof Symondes,	Henry Lambert, Efq

PRESENT PROPRIETORS OF THE MANORS,

Of *Great Dymock*,
JOHN THACKWELL, Esq

Of *Little Dymock*,
REGINALD WYNNIATT, M. A.

The Persons summoned by the Heralds, in 1682 and 1683, were

William Wynter, Efq
Edward Pye, Efq
Grindal Wilson, Vicar,

William Wall, Efq.
John Camm, Gent
John Holmes, Gent

At the Election in 1776, Thirty-four Freeholders polled from this Parish and its Hamlets.

The earliest Date in the Register occurs in 1538.

ANNUAL ACCOUNT OF MARRIAGES, BIRTHS, AND BURIALS, IN THIS PARISH

A D	Mar	Bir	Bur	A D	Mar	Bir	Bur	A D	Mar	Bir	Bur	A D	Mar	Bir	Bur
1781	6	39	23	1786	—	38	10	1791				1796			
1782	5	33	16	1787	7	37	19	1792				1797			
1783	7	28	29	1788	4	34	16	1793				1798			
1784	7	39	14	1789	6	41	9	1794				1799			
1785	2	35	37	1790				1795				1800			

INSCRIPTIONS IN THE CHURCH.

ON MARBLE MONUMENTS IN THE CHANCEL

..., Quarterly, 1st and 4th, a Cross, in WALL; d and 3d, Checquy Or and Azure, on a Fefs Gules, three Lozenges Argent, for CAPEL, —impaling, Gules an Inefcutcheon Argent, within an Orle of Mullets Or, for CHAMBER-LAYNE

In the pious Memory of THOMAS WALL, Efq a Graduate at the University of Oxford, who departed this Life the 15th of March, A D 166., aged 64

And also of DOROTHY his Wife, descended from the Family of the BERKELEYS, in the Countie of Worcester who departed this Life the 4th of May, A D 1672, aged 66

And to the pious Memory of WILLIAM WALL, Efq only Son of the said THOMAS and DOROTHY, Vic Com Glouc, A D 1682

And also of DOROTHY his Wife, descended from the Family of CAPEL, in the County of Hereford

And likewise to the pious Memory of THOMAS WALL, Efq Son and Heir of the said WILLIAM, descended from the Family of CHAMBERLAIN, in the County of Warwick, He died Nov 9, 1694

Arms

Arms Sable, a Fefs Ermine, a
Mullet for Difference WYNTER

Here lies interred the
Body of ROBERT WINTOUR,
of the Inner Temple, London Gent
Son of WILLIAM WINTOUR,
of Dymock, Efq
the laft of the Heirs Male
defcended from that ancient and
honourable Family,
who departed this Life
the 21ft Day of February, 1718,
aged 61 Years,
and was a good Benefactor
to the Poor of this Parifh

ON FLAT STONES

Arms WYNTER —impaling, a Fefs
between three Lions Heads erafed, for
FARMER

Here lyeth the Body of
Captain WILLIAM WINTOUR, Gent
who departed this Life Jan 20,
A D 1666

Here lyeth the Body of
MARGARET WINTOUR,
late Wife of
Captain WILLIAM WINTOUR, Gent.
who departed this Life
the 8th Day of January, A D 1674

Underneath this Stone lies the Body of
ROBERT WINTOUR,
of the Inner Temple, London, Gent

Here lyeth HESTER,
the Daughter of WILL WINTOUR, Efq
and of HESTER his Wife,
who died the 1ft Day of September,

IN THE NAVE

ON A MARBLE MONUMENT

Arms; Ermine, a Bend lozengy Gules
for PYE Crest, a Crofs fitchy, between
two Wings

In Memory of
EDWARD PYE CHAMBERLAIN, Efq
of the Boyce, in this Parifh,
who died April 20 1729,
aged 38 Years

Likewife of
ELIZABETH his Wife,
who died Nov 19, 1775,
aged 76

And alfo of four of their Children
who died Infants

This Monument was erected by
EDWARD PYE CHAMBERLAYNE, Efq
in Duty to his worthy and deceafed
Parents

AGAINST THE NORTH WALL UPON A
HANDSOME MARBLE MONUMENT

Arms, a Crofs engrailed, for CAM

Near this Place lies interred
JOSEPH CAM, Son of JOSEPH CAM,
Citizen of London
Died Oct 20, 1719, aged 12.

MARY PARSONS,
Mother of MARY CAM
Wife of JOSEPH CAM, fenior,
died May 24, 1714 aged 60

JOSEPH CAM Citizen of London,
died Aug 5, 1720 aged 63

ANN CAM, Daughter of
the faid JOSEPH,
died Sept 22, 1734, aged 21

MARY CAM Wife of
the faid JOSEPH
died Oct 8, 1752, aged 71

JOSEPH CAM, Son of
WILLIAM and MARY CAM,
Citizen of London,
died Oct 3, 1753, aged 26

MARY CAM, Wife of
WILLIAM CAM,
died June 3, 1774, aged 72.

Alfo two Infants,
the Children of the faid
WILLIAM and MARY CAM

ON FLAT STONES

In Memory of
THOMAS WALL, Efq
who died Nov 9 1694, aged 33 Years.

Near this Place lyeth
PENELOPE the Daughter of
WILLIAM WALL of the Park,
in the County of Hereford Efq
by KATHARINE his Wife
She departed this Life January 5 1719,
aged 1 Year and 6 Months

Here lyeth the Body of
MARY CHAMBERLAIN, Widow,
and Relict of THOMAS WALL
of Lintridge, in this Parifh Efq
of the Family of EDWARD PYE, Efq
Lord of the Mannour of Great Dymock,
and had by her faid Hufband
one Son and two Daughters
DOROTHY, WILLIAM and
ELIZABETH PYE
She departed this Life May 1707,
in Hopes of a bleffed Refurrection to
eternal Life

Here lyeth the Body of
EDWARD PYE, of Boyce Efq
who departed this Life
in Hopes of a better,
the 31ft of Auguft 1692,
in the eightieth Year of his Age

IN THE NORTH TRANSEPT

Arms on a Fefs between three Anchors
a Griffin paffant, for WYNNIATT

Jufta hoc marmor
JOHANNES WYNNIATT, Cener
Vir pius & probus, liberalis in omnes,
Pauperibus larga manu beneficus
eauvias depofuit 13 Octob 1670

RICHARDUS WYNNIATT, Filius,
Pietatis ergo pofuit

Arms, two Bars in chief a Lion
paffant

In Memory of
RICHARD HILL of this Place,
who departed this Life
June 3 1771, aged 50

Alfo MARY his Relict
who departed this Life
April 1776 aged 70

Alfo THOMAS ROOKE MOORE,
Son of the above
RICHARD and MARY HILL,
who departed this Life
July 16 1746 aged near 6 Months

Arms Barry, wavy of fix a Bar a
Lion paffant, in Fefs, and in Chief, three
Roundlets

Near this Place is interred
the Body of WILLIAM HANKINS Efq
late of the Greenhoufe, in this Parifh,
who departed this Life
Nov 9, 1771, aged 54

Alfo JOHN, Son of
WILLIAM HANKINS Efq
by MARY his Wife,
who departed this Life
Feb 15, 1775, aged 56

ON FLAT STONES

Here lyeth the Body of
ELIZABETH the former Wife of
JOHN HANKINS

Alfo URSULA the Wife of
WILLIAM SWAYNE of the
Parifh of Newnham, Daughter of
JOHN HANKINS, fen
of the Greenhoufe
She died Oct 7, 1742, aged 50

Here lyeth the Body of
JOHN HANKINS, jun
of the Greenhoufe
who departed this Life
Sept 10 1738 aged 39
He was a loving Hufband,
a tender Father, and a faithful Friend

Alfo in Memory of
ANN, the Wife of
THOMAS BAILEY of Woodfields,
and Daughter of
JOHN HANKINS above-mentioned
by ANN his Wife
She died Oct 21, 1780, aged 63
She was a loving Wife
a good Chriftian, and a fincere Friend

In Memory of
ANN HANKINS, Wife of
JOHN HANKINS,
of the Greenhouse, senior
She died the 14th Day of December,
1776 aged 86 Years.
She was a good Wife
a tender Mother and Grandmother.

ON A TOMB IN THE VESTRY

Arms, Quarterly, 1st and 4th, Gules,
a Chevron vairy, between three Pelicans
Heads erased Sable for MACHEN, 2d
and 3d, three Holly Leaves

Here lyeth the Body of
Mr JAMES MACHEN, senior,
who died March 10, 1760, aged 58

Here also lyeth the Body of
Mrs SARAH, the Wife of
the above Mr JAMES MACHEN
She departed this Life
July 23, 1763, aged 67

ON A MONUMENT AGAINST THE
CHURCH

Near
this Stone are the Remains
of HANNAH,
late Wife of JAMES AMOTT
(Officer of Excise)
She was born at Uttoxeter,
in Staffordshire,
and died March 21, 1770,
aged 24 Years

IN THE CHURCH YARD, ON TOMBS.

THOMAS COMMINS
died May 20, 1780, aged 78
ANN his Wife
died July 21, 1761, aged 62
WILLIAM SMITH
died Dec 13, 1716, aged 74
JONE his Wife
died Aug 1, 1723, aged
Father and Mother to the above
ANN COMMINS

JOHN CAM
died Jan 10, 1679, aged 60
ANN his Wife
died Sept. 11, 1701, aged 75
JOHN their Son
died June 10, 1707, aged 56
ANN his Wife
died April 12, 1742, aged 88
JOHN, Son of
the latter JOHN,
died Sept 11, 1739, aged 60
WILLIAM CAM, Esq
died April 22, 1767, aged 85
JOHN CAM, Esq his Son,
died June 11, 1767, aged 52

JOHN CAM
died Nov 5, 1753, aged 75
ANN his Wife
died Sept 24, 1754, aged 80
ROBERT CAM
died Nov 30, 1683, aged 32
DORCAS his Wife
died Sept 15, 1712, aged 60

THOMAS GREENE
died Feb 22, 1707, aged 86.

WILLIAM LOVERIDG
died   17, 1709, aged 66
MARY his Daughter
died May   1677,

RICHARD SKIPP
died Aug 1, 1785, aged 40.
ROBERT his Son
died March 12, 1781, aged 6 Weeks
ROBERT, another of his Sons,
died Dec 28, 1783, aged 1 Year

RICHARD HILL
was interred May 27, 1756, aged 43
RICHARD HILL, jun
died June 16, 1763, aged 28

HESTER, Relict of
WILLIAM MANN,
died Oct. 3, 1720, aged 60
RICHARD HILL
died Sept 13, 1729 aged 66.
SUSANNAH his Wife
died July 14, 1730, aged 52
RICHARD HILL
died March 5, 1711 aged 79
JANE his Wife
died June 1, 1715, aged 72

SARAH, the Wife of
RICHARD HALL,
died Nov 17, 1760, aged 42
RICHARD HALL
died Feb 26, 1780, aged 69.
ROBERT HALL
died March 17, 1715, aged 45
ROBERT his Son
died Aug 27, 1711, aged 3

PROFET NASH
died Nov 12, 1785

WILLIAM WEALE, Gent
died Jan 1, 1721, aged 74.
WILLIAM his Son
died in his Infancy
MARGERY his Wife
died Dec 31, 1731, aged 83
WILLIAM his Son
died Jan 6, 1735, aged 45.
JOHN WEALE
died Sept 12, 1739, aged 83

JOSEPH WEALE
died April 29, 1757, aged
HESTER his Wife
died Dec 3, 1735, aged 43
ANN their Daughter
died May 20, 1740, aged 2

ON FLAT AND HEAD STONES.

	Died	Aged
Ann, the Wife of Edward Smith	18 Jan 1758	22
William Hodges	22 Sept 1733	52
Judith his Wife	15 Sept 1729	51
Richard the Son of William and Hannah Hodges	11 June, 1758	4
Richard another of their Sons	23 Mar 1766	6
Thomas their Son	26 Oct 1775	30
John their Son	3 Jan 1777	29
John the Son of Jonas Powell	26 Dec 1764	47
Jonas Powell buried	20 Dec 1755	57
Younger Son of William and Sarah Hooper	12 Dec 1775	44
Sarah Hooper	15 Apr 1751	31
Mary, Wife of Richard Jenkins	6 May, 1733	76
Mary Daughter of Benjamin Binks, buried in the 22d Year of her Age		
Mary, Wife of Richard Williams	17 Aug, 1735	63
Richard Williams	4 June, 1734	62
Joseph Tyler	14 Aug 1738	29
William, Son of Joseph Dobbs	14 Aug 1785	25
Sarah, Wife of William Stone	16 Mar 1700	50
Samuel Son of William Stone	12 Feb 1712	19
William Stone	11 June 1733	78
Margaret the Wife of Philip Mail	22 Aug 1766	63
Ann Roberson Widow	2 May, 1729	71
Henry Roberson	13 Mar	—
William Powell	14 Aug 1712	80
Benjamin Philips	13 Sept 1734	24
Richard Wintour	11 July, 1732	—
Joseph Webb	26 Dec 1783	49
Daniel his Son	31 Dec 1779	5
Joseph Robinson and } both buried	8 Apr 1726	36
Mary his Wife }		48
Jonathan Drew	9 Mar 1737	
Thomas Drew	15 Mar 1760	37
Edward Tyler	19 Jan 1789	82
Mary, Wife of John Hodges	9 Dec 1745	26
John Pimbley	19 Mar 1782	44
Nancy, the Daughter of Daniel and Mary Woore	26 Oct 1769	7
Elizabeth, Wife of John Burgom	27 Apr 1729	56
John Burgom	25 Mar 1733	52
George Hankins	11 June, 1774	62
Ann his Daughter	14 May, 1785	27
Elizabeth, Wife of John Puckmore	27 May, 1731	29
John Puckmore	15 Oct 1747	62
John his Son died young		
Mary, Wife of William Puckmore	9 June, 1762	56
Elizabeth, Wife of Robert Millard	— Sept —	64
Jane, Daughter of Thomas Gutcher	20 Mar 1768	51
Elizabeth, Wife of John Boswood	15 May, 1771	67
John Wigmore	17 Sep 1782	52
William his Son	6 July, 1760	
Elizabeth, Wife of John Hill	14 July, 1752	
Sarah, Wife of John Hill		—
Hannah, Wife of Thomas Hill	30 Dec 1751	60
Thomas Hill	27 Sept 1756	69
Sarah his Daughter		
Ann, Daughter of John Hill	14 June, 1785	3
John Hill	23 Dec 1760	27
Ann Hill buried	5 Mar 1720	66
John Hill buried	11 Sept 1744	71
Richard, Son of William Thurston	8 Sept 1779	
William, Son of James Wingod buried	16 Jan 1741	34
Jane, Wife of Thomas Stephens	29 Apr 1761	67
Thomas Stephens	15 Feb 1767	76
Hannah, Wife of Thomas Stallard	18 Dec 1733	35
Elizabeth, Wife of Jonathan Landon	31 Aug 1729	74
Mary Daughter of James Barnes	30 Mar 1770	12
James Barnes	26 Jan 1782	59
Richard Son of John Williams	23 Dec 1745	19
William Morton	3 July, 1753	54
Anna his Wife	24 June, 1776	74
George Sier Mason	14 Oct 1778	38
Susannah, Wife of William Davis	4 Feb 1758	58
John Davis buried	6 Apr 1727	70
Ann, Wife of Benjamin Parsons	10 May, 1733	40
William Jones	25 Aug 1760	58
Mary his Wife	8 June, 1787	74
Edward their Son	21 Jan 1766	12
Betty their Daughter	11 Nov 1780	39
Mary their Daughter	20 May, 1777	31
John Jones	2 July, 1760	29
Three of his Children died young		
William Handen and	7 Dec 1773	51
George Price	3 Oct 1720	47
Abigail his Wife	21 Dec 1724	37
Mary Wife of William Botworth	21 Oct 1762	77
Thomas, Son of William Smith	5 June, 1726	25
Margaret, Wife of William Williams	30 Mar 1733	36
Margaret Powell	6 Nov 1748	62
Betty Wife of John Pewtriss	10 Mar 1738	39
Daniel Packer	2 Nov 1743	52
John Selwin	23 July, 1693	—
William Selwyn	8 Oct 1781	77
John, the Son of Thomas Gunter	4 Aug 1733	33
John Walker	10 Jan 1738	31
Hannah his Wife	11 Aug 1737	32
Thomas Gunter	8 Sept 1722	60
William Hope	1 Nov 1770	65
Mary his Wife	7 Mar 1782	83
Jonathan Williams	2 May, 1770	61
Sarah his Wife	21 Nov 1758	49
Sarah, Wife of William Davis	29 Mar 1729	47
Comfort, another Wife to the above	14 June, 1773	78
Comfort their Daughter	9 Feb 1763	24
Two more of their Children died young		
Lydia Wife of Edward Grundy	22 Nov 1779	54
Ann their Daughter	26 Mar 1766	10
Ann, the Wife of Edward Grundy	15 Mar 1754	60
James Cooper, senior	13 June 1746	74
Sibil his Wife	8 Jan 1758	84
Elizabeth their Daughter	14 July, 1747	4
Jane, Daughter of James Cooper, junior	14 Mar 1765	2
James his Son	9 Mar 1765	—
James Cooper	6 Mar 1777	6
Elizabeth, Wife of John Evans	3 Feb 1763	7
Thomas Adams	1 Apr 1758	70
Walter Chambers senior	1 Mar 88	66
Walter Chambers junior	16 May, 1788	32
Richard Phelpotts	30 Aug 1709	
Jane, Wife of Charles Rook	1 Dec 1784	84
Mary Seaton	8 Dec 1785	27
Elizabeth Murrell buried	23 May, 1733	62
John Moyle	17 Apr 1766	69
Richard Turner	22 Feb 1761	60
Elizabeth his Wife	7 Apr 1757	55
Thomas Attwood died in his infancy		
John Moyle	6 Aug 1732	44
Elizabeth, Wife of Joseph Cummins	2 Feb 1758	8
Lucy, Relict of Thomas Hames	14 Dec 1741	65

CVII. DYRHAM, or DEREHAM.

THIS Parish lies in the Hundred of *Grumbald's Afh*, Four Miles Weſt of *Marſhfield*, Five South from *Chipping Sodbury*, Eight Northward from *Bath*, and Thirty-one Southward from the City of GLOUCESTER It is nearly Eight Miles in Extent, of a rich Soil, chiefly applied to Paſture In the Two common Fields are Seven Hundred Acres, excluſive of the incloſed Arable Land The Village is ſituate on the Baſe of a very narrow Amphitheatre formed by ſteep Acclivities, from which flue many ſmall Springs, the Source of the River *Boyd*

Of the Benefice, which is a Rectory in the Deanery of *Hawkeſbury*, the Advowſon has never been alienated from the Manor The Glebe exceeds Eighty Acres

It is traditionally aſſerted, that the Church, dedicated to *St Peter*, was built by Sir MAURICE RUSSELL, Knight, before the Year 1401 The Style of Architecture is evidently of that Age, a Nave, Two Aiſles, and embattled Tower, of regular Gothic In 1520, Sir WILLIAM DENYS and ANNE his Wife founded a Chantry Gild, and erected, or prepared, the South Aiſle for the Reception of its Service

The

---

* Sir WILLIAM DENNIS and others founded a Gild in this Church, 1520 The Method of its Foundation, and its Statutes, are ſtill preſerved, and are here inſerted which may ſhew the Nature of Gilds in general

Memorandum, In the Year of our Lord 1520, October the firſt, in the twelfth Year of King HENRY the Eighth, Sir WILLIAM DENNIS, Knight Dame ANNE his Wife, ROBERT LEEN Parſon of the Church of *Dyrham*, THOMAS ILES, and WILLIAM WERE, who were Servants to the ſaid Sir WILLIAM and Dame ANNE, founded firſt a Prieſt to ſing Maſs every within the Pariſh Church of *Dyrham* within the Chapel of *St Denys*, to pray for the Founders of the ſaid Maſs, and for all thoſe that will become Brothers and Siſters, or any thing helping for the Maintenance of the ſaid Fraternity or Gild

Item, The ſaid Prieſt ſhall, or may ſignify before he begin his Maſs, pray in general for the good State of the Founders, and Brothers, and Siſters, and for all Benefactors to the ſaid Gild

Item, The ſaid Prieſt, at his coming to the Savetory, ſhall ſay for the Souls of the ſaid Founders, Brethren, and Siſters, which be Dead *De Profundis*

Item, The Proctor of the ſaid Gild, for the Time being, ſhall cauſe four ſolemn Dirges and Maſſes, according to Note, to be ſung at four Times within the Year, which Times ſhall appear following theſe words "Let us Pray"

Item, The Dirge and Maſs to be kept upon *St Denys* Eve, and the Maſs upon the Day, which ſhall be he ninth Day of October

Item, The ſecond Dirge and Maſs to be kept the eighth and ninth Day of January

Item, The third Dirge and Maſs to be kept the twenty ninth and thirtieth Day of March

Item, The fourth Dirge and Maſs to be kept the twenty ſeventh and twenty eighth Day of June

Item, The ſaid Prieſt before he goeth to the Quarter Maſs ſhall pray for the State of the Founders, Brothers, and Siſters, and for the Souls of them that be dead generally, or eſpecially, is he hath Time

Item The Proctor of the ſaid Gild ſhall retain, at every Quarter of the Year, to be at that ſolemn Maſs, the Parſon of the Church, or his Prieſt in his Abſence, with four other honeſt Prieſts to help to ſing the Dirge, and to ſing Maſs on the Morrow

Item The Proctor of the ſaid Gild ſhall, of the Stock of the ſaid Gild, pay every Prieſt for his coming, and for his devout Doing, 6d and to the Ringer 4d

Item, Such Perſons as ſhall be named and choſen to be Proctors of the ſaid Gild, ſhall be every Year named and cauſed the firſt Day of February

Item, The ſaid Proctors ſhall make their Account every Year upon the firſt Day of February

Item, The ſaid Proctors ſhall make their Account upon the ſaid Day within the Church of *Dyrham*, within the ſaid Chapel, and to lay down the Money of their Collections upon the Altar there

Item, The Account ſhall be made before the Lord of the Lordſhip, or the Lord's Bayliff in his Abſence, the Parſon of the Church, or his Prieſt in his Abſence, and two of the eldeſt Brethren within the Pariſh, and all the Brethren within the ſaid Pariſh, if they will be at it

Item At the Account the old Proctors before they be diſcharged ſhall name to the ſaid Lord or to his Bayliff, the Parſon or his Prieſt ſuch as ſhall take the Account, ſix Perſons, of the which ſix, the ſaid Lord, or his Bayliff, the Parſon or his Prieſt, that taketh the Accounts, ſhall name two to be Collectors and there, openly, the ſaid Lord, or Bayliff, Parſon or Prieſt, which taketh the Account ſhall deliver the ſaid Money to the new Proctors

Memorandum That WILLIAM WERE hath given to *St Denys* Chapel a Challice of Silver

Memorandum, That where Sir WILLIAM DENNIS and Dame ANNE his Wife, and ROBERT LEEN, Parſon of the Church of *Dyrham* THOMAS ILES, and WILLIAM WERE, having conſtituted and ordained a Prieſt to ſing daily in *St Denys* Chapel within the Church of *Dyrham* for the Maintenance of the ſaid Prieſt Sir WILLIAM DENNIS hath promiſed to give to the Proctors and their Succeſſors of the Gild of *St Denys*, for the foreſaid Maintenance of the ſaid Prieſt 16 Kine

Item, He and Dame ANNE by the Licence of the ſaid Sir WILLIAM her Huſband have promiſed to give a Kine

Item, ROBERT LEEN, Parſon of the foreſaid Church, hath promiſed to give 100 Sheep

Item, THOMAS ILES 50 Sheep

Item, WILLIAM WERE in Oxen and Kine of

Item, There is let to JOHN PAKER of *Hincle Farm* 8 Kine of *St Nicholas* ſtock, paying yearly he Year, for every Cow

Item In like Manner to the ninery Life, of *St Nicholas* ſtock, 4 Kine

Item To JOHN WARE of *St Nicholas* ſtock, 4 Kine

Item, The Proctors of *St Denys* Gild ſhall pay, quarterly, to the Prieſt that ſingeth in the ſaid Chapel, for his ſalary, to

The Manor was once a Barony   Soon after the Conquest it paſſed to the Family of NEWMARCH (DE NOVO MERCATU), and JAMES, ſtyled Baron of *Newmarch* and *Dereham*, dying in 1199, 17 JOHN, bequeathed this Eſtate to ISABEL his Coheir, the Wife of RALPH DE RUSSEL   In this knightly Family (the Anceſtors of the Duke of BEDFORD, and GORGES, of *Somerſetſhire* and *Herfordſhire*) it deſcended to Sir MAURICE RUSSEL, who died in 1501, then Sheriff of this County, which Office he had before borne in the Year 1396   He left this Manor in Moiety, between his Coheirs MARGARET, the Wife of Sir GILBERT DENNIS, and ISABEL, married to Sir JOHN DRAYTON, who were jointly ſeiſed of it in 1415, 3 HEN V   In 1422 the former died poſſeſſed of the whole Title, the Moiety of which he had purchaſed + Sir WALTER DENNIS was the laſt Poſſeſſor of that Name for, joining with RICHARD DENNIS, Eſq his Son, he transferred it to GEORGE WYNTER, Eſq Brother of Sir WILLIAM WYNTER, of *Iſdney*, by Deed, bearing Date 1571, 13 ELIZ   Here they reſided in Splendour till the Death of JOHN WYNTER, Eſq in 1668, whoſe only Daughter and Heir had married WILLIAM BLATHWAYTE ‡, Eſq of a Family ſettled in *Cumberland* and whoſe lineal Deſcendant is the preſent Proprietor of the manerial Eſtate, which includes the greater Part of the Pariſh

LELAND ſpeaks very copiouſly of *Dyrham*, " wher Maſtar DIONISE dwellith, havinge a faire Howſe " of achelie Stones, and a Parke   *Dereham* Village is a 2 Miles from *Tormerton*   Ther is a fair Maner-" place longinge to Maſta DIONISE   The Lordſhippe of auncient Time Is ſaid to the RUSSELS   One " JOHN RUSSEL and ELIZABETH his Wife lyethe buried in the Paroche Churche, but they had but " a meane Houſe there   From them it cam by Heire generall onto the DIONISIES, of whom one " GILBERT DENNIS was accountid, as one of the firſt that they poſſeſſyd   Then cam MAURICE, and " hee ther buildid a new Courte   And Ser GULIAM DIONISE buildid another Courte of late Yeres " The DIONISIS hathe here a fayr Parke, and alſo a fair Lordſhippe §"

Upon the ſame Spot, the preſent very ſumptuous Manſion was erected by WILLIAM BLATHWAYTE, Eſq Secretary at War and of State in the Reign of King WILLIAM III   It has an Air of great Magnificence on its firſt breaking on the Sight, but the Elevation is neceſſarily unfavourable, from the Confinement of the Hills, which, excepting on the South-weſt, riſe almoſt perpendicularly above it   The Building was compleated in 1698 from a Deſign of WILLIAM TALMAN ||, who conducted the whole ſe in immenſe Coſt   An Elevation of it is publiſhed in CAMPBELL's " Vitruvius Britannicus," vol II p 94 and another in Sir R ATKINS's Hiſtory, by Kip, with more than his uſual Fidelity   His Delineation is the more valuable, as exhibiting a Bird's Eye View of the Pleaſure Grounds now reconciled to modern Taſte, which were deſigned by LE NOTRE, and were the firſt Specimen in that Day, of Caſcades and Jets d'Eau carried to the very Summit of the Hill   Every Caprice of the *Dutch* Style, which could be effected by Art, abounded at *Dyrham*, where ſuch Ornaments were ſo numerous and ſumptuous as to defy both Expence and Imitation   The Houſe conſiſts of Two Fronts, the principal of which extends 130 Feet   There are beſide, Two Wings and a Quadrangle of Offices   The Baſe is of ruſtic, and the firſt Floor contains a Suite of many excellent Apartments   The Windows are decorated with alternate Pediments, and the Cornice finiſhed with Trophies, Urns, and a Profuſion of Ornament   The Park is extenſive and well planted firſt incloſed by Sir WILLIAM DENNIS, one of the Eſquires of the Body to King HENRY the Eighth, from whom in 1512 he obtained Licence " to impark 500 Acres within his " Manor of *Dereham* ** '

Item, The Proctors ſhall receive the Money for the Payment of the ſaid Prieſt, as followeth

	£	s	d
Of Sir WILLIAM DENNIS, quarterly, till the ſaid 16 Kine be delivered to the Proctors of the ſaid Gild, for the Time being,		6	8
Of Dame ANNE DENNIS		3	4
Of Mr ROBERT EEN, Paſtor of the ſaid Church		6	8
Of THOMAS EEN,		3	4
Of WILLIAM WEE,		6	8
Of JOHN LOLD		3	4
Of HUMFREY EEN,		1	8
Of JOHN WARD,		1	8
	13	1	

Memorandum The ſaid Prieſt ſhall find himſelf fit or to ſing at the ſaid Altar, Bread, Wine, and Wax

Many were the brethren and ſiſters of this Guild, who were provided up to to contribute towards its Maintenance which Perſons lived in ſo ſeveral Pariſhes it ſeith, in I Bol Bath *Somerſetſhire*, and *Glouceſterſhire*, and might amount in Number to 300 Perſons   The uſual payment each Perſon was to or ſed quarterly

* COLLINS his Baronage vol I p 244

+ It is probable that he followng anncient Inſigina, (mentioned in MS of JOHN SMYTH, Eſq of North Nibley in 1607, and now in the College of Arms Louvan') were formerly unemblazoned in the Windows of the Church   Gules, a fred on chief Azure, between three Leopards Faces gulant Or   DENNIS quartering Azure, 2 Chevrons Gules, between three Azure   BASKERVILLE quarterly   DENNIS   Argent on a Chief Gules three Bezants Azure a Lozenge Or and Azure, a Chevron Gules Corbet   4 Azure a Croſs molme Or, MORE Or 3 Quarterly Gules ſaltie, DENNIS Gules and Azure —impaling BERKELEY, MONTRAVERS, BROTHERTON, and WAKE, quarterly   Argent three Lozenges conjoined in feſs Gules MONTACUTE   Or three flotteauxes and a Label Azure COURTNAY   of Vair Or and Gules FERRARS 7 Azure two Chevrons Gules, and a Label Azure ST MAURE or   Or, a fron impaling   Or, a fron impaling Argent 3 Martlets Azure a Griffin ſejeant Gules   BOTREAUX   5 Gules, four Lozenges Argent each charged with a Mullet Azure Guis 10 MORTIMER or MOREYNS 11 Gules 12 Lozenges, Gules and Ermine BOTREAUX 13 DENNIS 14 RUSSEL quartering, Gules 2 15 Azure, two Bars dancette Or, DE LA RIVERE —impaling Reſit and Gules quarterly Gules 8   16 COURTENAY 17 HYTISLEURY quartering HUNGERFORD, in it DUTONE Empires

‡ WOOD vol II p 632 ATKINS Glouc p 414

§ Itin vol VII pp 72 7

|| WALPOLE's Anecdotes of Painting vol III p 263

** " GUILIELMUS DENNIS, unus Armig pro corpore Regis 5 Junii, 4 HEN VIII habet licentiam imparcandi 500 acras " terræ apud *Kellworthy*, infra mainerium ſuum de *Dereham*, cum Grava cum libera warenna ' Pell firma 4, HEN VIII

Hinton, or *Henton*, is the only Hamlet, originally a diſtinct Manor held by the Family of DE LA RIVERE, or DE RIVARIIS, of whom, having been purchaſed by the Ruſſels, it was conſolidated with the Demeſnes. The Coheirs of Sir MAURICE RUSSEL detached the chief Eſtate by Sale to THOMAS WHITE, Eſq who was Mayor of *Briſtol* in 1530, 21 HEN VIII and which, then producing 25l 12s per Annum, he gave by Deed, Jan 14, 1541, to exempt the *Severn* Veſſels from the Cuſtoms of the Port of *Briſtol*, and other charitable Purpoſes *

In the very remote Æra of the *Britiſh* and *Saxon* Wars, *Dyrham* was the Scene of many military Tranſactions. In an ancient Map of the *Saxon* Heptarchy "Deopham" is deſcribed as a Place of Conſequence † FLAND, enumerating the Encampments which are to be traced on this Chain of Hills, ſpeaks of three " by *Derham* Military Dioniſes Houſe, and all towchinge on one Hilly Creaſte "

The Camp on *Hinton Hill* incloſes at leaſt Twenty Acres of Ground, and is ſuppoſed to have been occupied by the *Saxons* in 599, when they gained a ſignal Victory over the *Britons*, ſlew three of their Princes, and took the Cities of *Cirenceſter*, *Glouceſter*, and *Bath* ‡

BENEFACTIONS

Mr WILLIAM LANGTON, formerly Rector of this Pariſh, left by Will, dated July 20, 1668, 600l for the Uſe of the Poor of the Pariſhes of *Dyrham* and *Deynton*, in the County of *Glouceſter*, which Sum he bequeathed to twelve Perſons therein named, in Truſt, for the Intent and Purpoſe of purchaſing Land in Fee Simple, the Profits, or Rents thereof to be laid out thus 10s a Year to be paid to the Miniſter of this Pariſh, or his Repreſentative, for ever, to preach a Sermon every Year on Eaſter Monday, the Reſidue of the Rent to be divided into three Parts, two thirds to be paid to the Churchwardens, or Overſeers of the Poor of this Pariſh for ever, to be employed by them with the Diſcretion and Conſent of the Miniſter, and ſome of the Truſtees, or chiefeſt of the Pariſhioners, for the educating or teaching any poor Children whatſoever, and for binding Apprentices of ſuch poor Men's Children as receive no Alms of the Pariſh, the other third Part of the Rent to be paid to the Churchwardens, or Overſeers of the Pariſh of *Deynton* for ever, to be employed by them in the Manner preſcribed to the Churchwardens and Overſeers of this Pariſh, when ſix of the Truſtees are dead, the ſurviving Truſtees are directed to convey the Land to twelve other Perſons, to be ſucceſſively choſen by the Miniſters of the Pariſhes of *Dyrham* and *Deynton*, together with the Churchwardens and Overſeers of the Poor, and moſt ſubſtantial Inhabitants of theſe Pariſhes for the Time being, the annual Produce of theſe Lands now are 35l

On the firſt of February, 1774, Mr PETER GRAND, the preſent Rector of *Dyrham*, did purchaſe in the public Funds, out of ſeveral Years' Savings, proceeding chiefly from a Coal Mine, 100l Stock in the Conſolidated 3 per Cent Annuities, in his Name, and for the ſole Uſe of, and Benefit of that Part of Mr LANGTON's Charity, which is now, or may hereafter be due to this Pariſh

A School Houſe was alſo built by Mr GRAND, at his own Expence, 1770

INCUMBENTS	PATRONS	INCUMBENTS	PATRONS
1520 Robert Iken,	Sir William Dennys	1638 Wm Langton, M A	Sir George Wynter.
		1668 Henry Hoſkins,	John Wynter, Eſq
1570 Walter Dennys,	Edward Dennys, Eſq	1680 Sam Trewman, B D	The ſame
1577 John Hall,	George Wynter, Eſq	1699 Mervin Perry,	Wm Blathwayte, Eſq.
1587 John Hawling,	Queen Elizabeth	1753 Peter Grand, M A	Wm Blathwayte, Eſq

PRESENT LORD OF THE MANOR,

WILLIAM BLATHWAYTE, ESQ

The Perſons ſummoned from this Place by the Heralds in 1682 and 1683 were

John Wynter, Eſq and Thomas Weare, Gent

At the Election in 1776, Two Freeholders polled from this Pariſh

The Regiſter has its firſt Date in 1567

ANNUAL ACCOUNT OF MARRIAGES, BIRTHS, AND BURIALS IN THIS PARISH

A D	Mar	Bir	Bur	A D	Mar	Bir	Bur	A D	Mar	Bir	Bur	A D	Mar	Bir	Bur
1781		11	6	1786		11	6	1791				1796			
1782	3	7	5	1787	5	12	10	1792				1797			
1783		14	5	1788	3	11	5	1793				1798			
1784	1	9	7	1789				1794				1799			
1785		9	8	1790				1795				1800			

* Barret's Hiſtory of *Briſtol*, pp 13, 613
† Saxon Chronicle, vol II Append II to XX p 27 CAMDEN's Britannia
‡ Anno 580 XOVII Sax CLAUDEN, & filius ejus CUTHWINE in loco qui vocat Deorham, cum Britannis dimicant in loco qui vocat Deorham, cum Britannis dimicant, tam cum Regibus MAIL, CONIDAN & FARNMAIL, cum multis aliis, trucidaverunt, utilique treo civitates abſtulerunt, Glouceſtre & Bathmetiſe, addiderunt
FLAND, Colleet vol II pp 279 9, CAMDEN's Britannia, vol I p 285 HOLINSHED p 147

INSCRIPTION

INSCRIPTIONS IN THE CHURCH

Upon a Marble Slab, inlaid with the Figure of a Knight and his Lady for Sir Maurice Russel and Dame Isabel his Wife these Verses in the Gothic Character

Intus probatio vita jacet hic tumulatus
Sub petra stratus Mauricus Russel
vocatus
Habet sponsa suæ hujus militis illa
Quæ jacet abscons sub marmore
modo alto
Cœli columen Trinitas eis conferat,
Amen
Qui fuit, est et erit, concita morte
perit

On a large Freestone Monument in the Chancel

Arms, Quarterly, Gules and Or, a Bend Argent, for LANG on

M S
GULIELMI LANGTON, A M
hujus Ecclesiæ
Pastoris super vigilantissimi,
de grege suo multis aliis
optime merentis
Qui quum id ratus sit pietatis
tum charitatis
800 l non à minus
dedisset,
Post laudabilis vitæ
(Annorum fer 59) Exidium
Ad Patrium cœlestem eventus,
Quod mortale in eo fuit
hoc pulvere
Deponendum
curavit

Obiit
Sepultus } Aug { 7 } 1668
          { 17 }

Amoris gratitudinis ergo,
posuit JOHANNES MEREDITH   Armiger

On a painted Board against the South Wall of the Chancel,

Near this Place lieth the Body of
The Rev Mr MERVIN PLEURY,
who, after being Rector of this Parish
53 Years, died much lamented
by all his Parishioners
Dec 17, 1753, æt. suæ 88

Also of ELIZABETH his Wife,
who died March 6, 1752 æt su 70

ON INSCRIPTIONS IN THE CHANCEL

In spem
Gloriosæ Resurrectionis
Exuviæ his reponuntur
GULIELMI LANGTON,
Fidelissimi hujus Ecclesiæ
Pastoris
Qui post annorum ferme 30,
labores et less ibidem
Exantlatos
Mortalia hic exceutus
in Christo placidissime
requievit
Anno Christi æratis 1668,
Ætatis suæ 59

Here lieth the Body of ANNE,
the Wife of SAMUEL TILLYMAN,
Rector of this Parish and
Daughter of THOMAS SYMES,
late of Winterborn, Esq
who departed this Life
Oct 27, 1673, aged 26 Years

SAMUEL TILLYMAN S T B
hujus Ecclesiæ Rector
obiit XXX Die Martii Domini
MDCLXXXVIII

IN THE SOUTH AISLE

Under a Canopy, supported by Pillars of the Corinthian Order, the Cumbent Figures of a Man in Armour and his Wife, suitebly cut in

Arms, Sable a Fess Ermine, for WYNTER, — impaling quarterly first and fourth, Sable, on a Fess, between three Bugles, Argent, a Hemp brake, Gules, for BRAIN, — a Cross ingrailed 3 Piles, ten Plates, on a Chief of the 2d, a Lion passant of the first, BRIDGEMAN

GEORGIO WYNTER,
Armigero (qui animam efflavit XXIX die Novembris, anno Domini 1581) ANNA WYNTER uxor pietatis conjugi hoc Monumentum posuit, statuens cum et ipsi Dei justæ vitæ injusti rationem peregerit, hic juxta mariti funus suum quo que reponi ut quibus viva unus erat animus, eidem et mortuis unus esset corporum quiescendi locus, sub spe futuræ Resurrectionis

Mole sub hac placidem capiunt en Membra GEORGII WYNTERI Requiem, duos peritape labores qui solicit in terram fluctuantibus undis et pace in noctua simul, et pugnacibus unis fustinunt Patriæ dum publica munia cessit

Anna tu quondam marito fidissima conjux,
Undenas, thalamo, sobole tulit isti viriles
Quatuor, et septem generose Feminate
niteis

On another stately Monument of variegated Marble

Arms Two Bendlets engrailed, BRATHWAYTE quartering WYNTER defto, BRATHWAYTE — impaling Argent, on a Bend engrailed Gules, a Bezant between two Swans Argent

D O M
Immortali
In piam Memoriam
JOHANNIS et FRANCISCÆ WYNTER,
Necnon MARIÆ consequentissimæ
ipsorum Filiæ et Heredis,
Hic Antecessorum relicta Posteris
Tabulam hanc cum editio
qui prius dehinc to,
nunc perstat
GULIELMO BRATHWAYTE,
MARITI
Christianis et amantibus
Corpus
D D D CC
Anno salutis
MDCCXI

FRANCES, Wife of
JOHN WYNTER Esq
departed this Life, Nov 20, 1691

ANN the Daughter of JOHN WYNTER,
of Durham in the County of
Glocester, Esq
departed this Life, Jun 30, 1684

JOSEPH BRATHWAYT, Son of
WILLIAM BRATHWAYT, Esq
and THOMASINE his Wife,
died Jun 28, 1741 aged 15
WILLIAM BRATHWAYT Esq
died March 24, 7   aged 50
Also Mrs THOMASINE BRATHWAYT,
died Feb 4, 1774   aged 77

INFANTIE Relict of JAMES BRATON,
of the City of bath, Mercer,
died Feb 8, 1725 aged 82

ON MONUMENTS IN THE NORTH AISLE

Near this Place, lieth the Body of
ISAAC TYLER,
who departed this Life, Dec 11 1693,
Aged 65 Years

Likewise EDITH, the Wife
of the said ISAAC TYLER,
who died July 2 1715

Near this Place lyeth the Body of
ANN, the Wife of ISAAC TYLER,
who departed this Life Jan 29, 1682,
Aged 40 Years

Arms three Lozenges, for FREEMAN —impaling on a Fess, between two Leopards, Passant Or dant, three Crescents for TYLER

In Memory of FRANCES FREEMAN,
of Norton maiereand in the
County of Somerset Esq
He died Oct 18, 175, aged 70,
and he interred in a Vault about nigh Place

Also of MARY his beloved Wife
Daughter and Heiress of ISAAC TYLER,
formerly of this Parish Gent
she died Dec 28 17   aged 67,
and les interred in the same Vault

ON INSCRIPTIONS

MARY late Wife of HENRY WYATT,
died Apr 12, 1633 aged d
THOMAS WYATT, of this Parish Gent
died Oct 26, 16   in the 6th Year
of his Age

PRUDENCE, late the Wife of
HENRY WYATT
died Aug 14, 1693, Aged 65

WILLIAM WYATT of this Parish Gent
died June 9 1697 in the 58th Year
of his Age

WILLIAM NEAT
departed this Life the 19th Day of
January Anno Domini 17 4
MARY NEAT,
died Jun   169

JOHN NEALE, junior,
died Oct 27, Anno Dom 1671

JANE, the Wife of THOMAS HURNALL,
departed this Life Sept 25, 1702,
Ætatis suæ 32

Also ELIZABETH their Daughter

ELIZABETH, Wife of
JOHN HURNALL, Yeoman
departed this Life, Aug 10, 1674.

Here resteth the Bodie
of RICHARD CODRINGTON,
of blq
who departed this Life, May 20, 1635

Here lies interred the remains of
WALTER TYLER of this Parish Gent
who died Jan 19 1715, aged 8

Also ELIZABETH his Wife,
died Feb 15, 1766, aged 73

Also of WILLIAM and JOHN, their Son

IN THE CHURCH YARD, ON TOMBS

RICHARD BOLWELL of the Parish of
Walcot, near Bath Son of
HUGH and GRACE BOLWELL,
of the Parish of Coldashton,
died Dec 19, 1750, aged 53

MOSES BUTLER, Yeoman,
died June 18, 1761, aged 60

JOHN TYLER, Yeoman,
died Dec 2, 1705

FRANCES his Wife,
died Aug 17, 1699, aged 68

JOHN their Son,
died Feb. 1725, aged 49

WILLIAM Son of WILLIAM TYLER,
died Dec 18, 1716.

MARY Wife of PHILIP WEST,
died Aug 22, 1745, aged 26

JOHN Son of PHILIP and
ELIZABETH WEST
died March 7, 1726 aged
JANE their Daughter,
died July 14, 1730, aged 22

PHILIP WEST, the Elder,
died May 11, 1738, aged 69
ELIZABETH his Wife,
died April 10, 1744, aged 71

ROGER HAWKINS
late Servant to
WILLIAM BRAITHWAYT, Esq.
died Nov 15, 1761, aged 52

EDWARD TOGHILL, sen
died Sept 24 1747

MARTHA Wife of STEPHEN TOGHILL,
died Jan 23, 1784 Aged 42

MARY CREW
died May 5, 1776, aged 72

THOMAS CREW her Husband aged 32,
was buried at Doynton

JOHN the Son of
JEREMIAH and MARY NORTH,
died Nov 5, 1727, aged 2
JEREMIAH their Son
died Feb 28, 1722, aged 9

JEREMIAH NORTH
died Sept 23, 1731, aged 53
MARY, Wife of JEREMIAH NORTH,
died Dec 21, 1776 aged 88

SAMUEL NORTH,
died Nov 27 1787, aged 63

ON HEAD STONES

	Died	Aged		Died	A d
William Bryan	3 Apr 1767	65	Ann, Wife of John Brimble	28 June, 1749	23
Mary his Wife	2 Apr 1745	45	Benjamin Smith	4 Nov 1779	83
Hannah their Daughter	25 Nov 1745	4	Ann his Wife	22 May 1770	70
Edward, Son of Guy and Mary Bryan	28 Oct 1745	4	Edward Maud	27 Oct 1773	71
Betty their Daughter	1 Jan 1766	30	Ann his Wife	12 Feb 1780	84
Francis Hathaway	29 June, 1766	90	William, Son of William and Mary Looker	28 Aug 1766	20
Elizabeth Wife of Francis Hathaway, of Pucklechurch	2 May, 1747	57	James Adams	25 Feb 1757	36
Edmund Matthews	5 Mar 1757	49	Philip Harding	22 Sept 1758	41
Jane his Wife	14 Aug 1749	46	Hannah, Relict of the above, and late Wife of William May	25 July, 1775	61
George, Son of George and Sarah Butler	30 Apr 1763	24	James Hill	7 June 1740	60
William their Son	6 Jan 1755	3	Nathaniel Hill of Margotsfield	6 Sp 1759	78
Richard their Son	5 Sept 1751	7	Edward Osborne	15 Sep 1743	50
David West	— Dec 1742	26	Ann Summers Widow	25 Dec 1741	66
Jane, Daughter of George and Martha Anstee	11 Dec 1771	24	Robert May	1 Aug 1758	69
John their Son	21 Nov 1771	33	Sarah his Wife	20 Sep 1708	87
George their Son	16 May, 1770	29	Edward Comey	15 Oct 1770	64
Robert their Son	16 July, 1762	13	Prudence his Wife	6 Mar 1717	67
Anne, Wife of Robert Anstee	5 Oct 1761	82	Ann Comey	22 June, 1749	53
Robert Anstee	5 Apr 1762	79	John Limb of the City of Bristol	13 Jan 1765	44
Mary, Wife of Robert Anstee	25 June, 1723	34	Elizabeth, Wife of Francis Pipp of the City of Bristol	19 July 1770	53
John their Son, died Young			Richard Somner	1 Dec 1753	38
Robert Anstee	10 Dec 1775	85	Mary Wife of Richard Somner	10 Aug 1753	54
Selah, Daughter of Richard and Diana Collins	5 Nov 1752	11	William Son of City and Mary Bryan	24 June 1755	7
Richard Collins	6 Feb 1748	42	Edward their Son	25 Oct 1755	1
Richard Son of Richard and Diana Collins	5 Aug 1780	35	Ruth their Daughter	5 Mar 1756	1
Hannah their Daughter	22 May, 1781	34	Melior Wife of Thomas Sloper, Daughter of Charles and Ann Snell of this Parish	29 May 1777	7
Abraham, Son of William and Rebecca Collins	21 Jan 1779	10	Thomas Sloper Son of Thomas Sloper of Aston Turville, in this County and late of this Parish by Sarah his Wife Daughter of John Nettle, of this Parish	11 Jan 1771	6
Mary, Wife of William Newman	6 Mar 1787	51			
Joanna, Wife of Robert Brimble	1 Dec 1773	42			

EASTINGTON

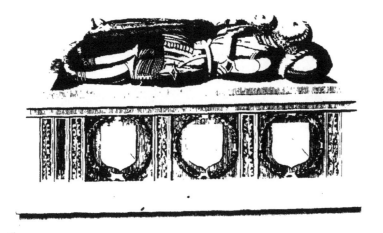

Tomb of EDWARD STEPHENS Esquire
and JOAN his Wife 1587

CVIII. EASTINGTON.

OF this Parish no separate Account is given in *Domesday* Book, and it is conjectured to have been then included in the adjoining Lordship of *Frampton*.

The Village of *Eastington* is situate in the lower Part of the Vale of *Stroud water*, in the Hundred of *Whitstone*, upon the River *Froom*, by different Branches of which the Parish is intersected. It is distant from *Stroud* six Miles westward, six North from *Dursley*, and from *Gloucester* ten on the South. About 2000 Acres are described in the Terrier, of a Soil varying from Gravel to Clay, chiefly Meadow and Pasture, in a Proportion of three fourths. The Inhabitants occupying Lands have a Privilege of Common in a Meadow of 70 Acres, restricted to certain Seasons of the Year.

The Benefice, which is Rectorial *, is a Member of the Deanery of *Stonehouse*, and is endowed with an extensive Glebe. Sir R. ATKINS, in asserting that the Advowson belonged to the Benedictine Nuns of *Clerkenwell*, in the County of *Middlesex*, has mistaken this Parish for that of *Eastington* or *Ampney St. Peter*, in this County, for it certainly was never detached from the Manor. In the Church, dedicated to *St. Michael*, there is ample Room for Investigation. It has a Nave and North Aisle, with a plain embattled Tower at the West End. Whatever be the Date of the first Structure, indubitable Proofs remain of its having been internally decorated, and the Aisle probably built, by the munificent and unfortunate EDWARD STAFFORD, the last Duke of *Buckingham* of that Family. The whole Roof is of Oak, very richly framed and jointed with Rosettes. Upon the Architrave of the South Door, intermixed with Foliage, are the Gothic Letters **S. B** (STAFFORD and BUCKINGHAM) and between them a ducal Coronet, charged with the Roman Letter W. These appear likewise in painted Glass in the Nave, with the Addition of a Gothic **D** inclosing a **b** for *Dux Buckinghamensis*, the usual Cypher and Cognizance of that Nobleman +. Upon other Panes were the Arms of CLARE and DE AUDLEY, Earls of GLOUCESTER. The Font is very ancient, a single Column with Sculpture in a peculiar Style.

Preserved in a Window of the Rectory House (of several Centuries standing) is a Series of Compartments of stained Glass, exhibiting the Arms of Queen ELIZABETH, and nine others of Soldiers performing different military Exercises, they are ?, some Half Head, and very delicately and correctly finished.

The History of the Descent of the Manor may be accurately stated, although the Name does not appear in the *Domesday* Survey. We collect that WINEBALD DE BALUN or PAGANUS, a *Norman Knight*, received it from the Conqueror. In 1319, 12 Edw. II there DE AUDLEY married LORD DE PARCE, the sole Heir of that Family; and in the next Reign it passed in Dower to Katherine Baron Stafford with MARGARET AUDLEY. Being annexed to the ancient Estates of the STAFFORDS, it remained with them 'till the Attainder and Death of EDWARD Duke of BUCKINGHAM in 1521, 13 Hen. VIII. then a Life Interest was granted to THOMAS HENEAGE, Esq. and CATHERINE his Wife. By their Decease in 1632 the Manor reverted to HENRY Lord STAFFORD, whose Son EDWARD sold it to EDWARD STEPHENS, Esq. in 1573, 15 Eliz. in whose lineal Descendant it is now vested. He was the Ancestor of the four very opulent and respectable Families of STEPHENS, settled at *Eastington* and *Chavenage*, *Lypiate*, *Little Sodbury*, and *Cherington*, all at one Time resident in this County, which they have frequently represented in Parliament. NATHANIEL STEPHENS, Esq. who died in 1660, very zealously promoted the republican Interest, and exerted his local Influence to that Effect with great Success. He was an active Commissioner in all the Transactions of that Part. ‡

The Manor House, which was during those Commotions used as a Garrison, was built by EDWARD STEPHENS, Esq. in 1578. It was remarkably spacious, and in the best Stile of that Day, with a Front of very curious and expensive Masonry. It was levelled with the Ground in 1775, and the Materials dispersed and sold.

---

* "A Portion of Tythes in *Eastington*, was granted to the Monks of *Bermondsy* in 1100, 1 W ...."
† R. Atk.

" Pens ..... Vicario de *Frocester*." BACON's Lib. Reg. p. 243.
Advowson of *Eastington* (or *Ampney St. Peter*) granted to the Nuns of *Clerkenwell*, DECANAT. Men. Vol. I. p. 4 ... Newcourt Dic. Lond. Vol. I. p. 157. TANNER, No. Mon. N. V. *Middlesex*.

† "Arms Argent a file of five Lambeaux azure anciently set up in the Church of *Eastington*, ... Gloucester ..... Earls of *Huntington*." GUILLIM's Heraldry, ed. I. p. 2 ..... Edit. 1679.

‡ WOOD's Athen. Vol. II. p. 471. CORBET, &c.

Here are several considerable Estates, called corruptly *Mill End*, *Nup End*, *Nast-End*, the two latter mean the Upper and Last End of the Parish. These, though once perhaps annexed to the Manor, were in the Tenure of *Walter Clutterbuck*, Gent. soon after the Year 1557, 2d Mary. His Sons, Richard, Peter, and Fabian, were Progenitors of three distinct Families of good Repute, each settled on their own Estate.

Millend House, built by his eldest Son, is the ancient Residence, and now belongs to WILLIAM FRYER Esq. in Right of his Wife, the Relict of RICHARD CLUTTERBUCK, Esq. the last Heir Male of that Branch.

Another principal Estate was held by NATHANIEL CLUTTERBUCK, Gent. who married MARY the eldest Coheir of JOHN CLIFFORD, Esq. of *Frampton* upon *Severn*, and is now inherited by ELIZABETH PHILIPS, Relict of EDMUND PHILIPS, Gent. of the City of GLOUCESTER.

Nup-End, now vested in the Family of PURNELL, was purchased of the CLUTTERBUCKS by JOSEPH LILE, Esq. by whom it was resold in 1760.

Framilode Mills, within the Limits of this Parish, were once the Property of Ecclesiasticks. In the Charter of Foundation of the Abbey of *St. Peter* in GLOUCESTER is recited " Molendinum de Framiloda " quod *Winebaldus de Baladona* reddidit Ecclia ✝," and in a Terrier of their Possessions dated 1575, two Mills at *Framelode* are specified. The Abbey of *Winchcombe* were Proprietors " de Medietate Gur-" gitis de *Framelode* in aqua *Sabrina.* "

The only Hamlet, or Tything, is *Alkerton*, or *Alcrinton*, which, though a distinct Manor, has been jointly held for many Ages.

Neale's Place, the chief Estate in this Division, was purchased early in the present Century by JOHN KING, Gent. (who was of an ancient Family, settled at *Blackhall* in the Parish of *King's Peon* in *Herefordshire*), and is inherited by his Grandson, RICHARD KING, Esq.

Near the Mansion House, a Spring of Medicinal Water was discovered by sinking a Well about thirty Years since, which has very strong cathartic Qualities ‡

Other Lands formerly the Property of HORTON, of *Wootton*, are now severally vested in the Families of FORD, BICLAND, TALBOYS, and KNOWLES, and the Estate, called *Puddle Wharf*, is held by the Relict of SAMUEL SHEPPARD, Esq. of *Minchin-Hampton*.

The Prior of *Stanley St. Leonard*, presented to the Chantry of *Alkerton*, in the Church of *Eastington*, and in 1339, procured an Inhibition that the Inhabitants should attend divine Service in no other Church.

The Navigable Canal from *Walbridge* to *Framilode*, which was completed in 1779, extends two Miles through this Parish.

B E N E F A C T I O N S

RICHARD CLUTTERBUCK, of *Nup End*, Gent. by Will, 1735, gave 15s. to the Minister, and 5s. to the Clerk of this Parish, to be paid every Year, for a Sermon preached yearly on Ascension Day.

He also gave another Sum of 2l. to be paid Yearly on Christmas Day to poor Housekeepers, and charged his Estate in the said Parish with the Payment of the aforementioned Sums to the Minister, Clerk, and poor Housekeepers, for ever.

Dec. 20, 1764, the Sum of 537l. 5s. 11d. was subscribed by RICHARD STEPHENS, Esq. ROBERT STEPHENS, M.A. Clerk, PHILIP SHEPPARD, M.A. Clerk, SAMUEL GRASSI, M.A. Clerk, WILLIAM KNIGHT, JOSEPH ELLIS, RICHARD CLUTTERBUCK, and ONESIPHORUS ELLIOT, Gent. vested in Truste, the annual Produce of which is 6l. 2s. 4d. for teaching poor Children to read.

1712 JOHN BRANCH, Gent. left by Will 100l. which, being laid out in the South Sea Stock, produces 5l. 3s. 8d. which is divided between ten poor Housekeepers on Michaelmas Day.

INCUMBENTS	PATRONS	INCUMBENTS	PATRONS
1319 ——	Hugh and Ifolda de Audley	1635 William Mew,	Nathan Stephens, Esq
1343 ——	Hugh Baron Stafford	1665 Samuel Mew, B D	Richard Stephens Esq
* * * *	* * *	1707 Wm Dighton, M A	Nathan Stephens, Esq
1571 Richard Syrrel,	G Fettiplace, and others	1760 Rob Stephens, M A	——
1581 Robert Ball,		1776 Wm Davies, M A	R Stephens, M A
1613 R Capel*, M A	Nathan. Stephens, Esq		

PRESENT LORD OF THE MANOR,

HENRY STEPHENS, Esq who holds Court Baron for the Hundred of *Whitstone*

The Persons summoned from this Place by the Heralds in 1682 and 1683 were,

Nathaniel Stephens, Esq.
Richard Stephens, Esq

Nathaniel Clutterbuck, Gent
William Clutterbuck, Gent of *Alkerton.*
Samuel Mew, Rector

At the Election in 1776, Nineteen Freeholders polled from this Parish

The first Date of the Register is in 1558

ANNUAL ACCOUNT OF MARRIAGES, BIRTHS, AND BURIALS, IN THIS PARISH

A D	Mar	Bir	Bur	A D	Mar	Bir	Bur	A D	Mar	Bir	Bur	A D	Mar	Bir	Bur
1781	5	19	16	1786	8	20	18	1791				1796			
1782	8	24	15	1787	3	43	12	1792				1797			
1783	2	16	22	1788	6	23	17	1793				1798			
1784	5	14	14	1789				1794				1799			
1785	9	24	18	1790				1795				1800			

INSCRIPTIONS IN THE CHURCH.

IN THE CHANCEL

Upon a raised Altar Tomb of Free ſtone the cumbent Figure of a Man and Woman in the Dreſs of the Times Repreſented on different Compartments, Parti per Chevron Azure and A gent in Chief two Falcons rifing Or, for STEPHENS On an Eſcocheon fixed to the Wall STEPHENS —impaling quarterly, 1ſt and 4th a Conquefoil and in Chief a Lion paſſant, for FOWLER, 2d and 3d, on a Bend three Croſs Croſslets

On a blue Marble Slab, the Effigy in Brafs of a Woman in a Mantle bearing the following Arms Quarterly 1 Argent, a Bend Sable, within a Border encircled Azure, KNEVIT 2 Argent a Bend Azure, and Chief Gules CROMWELL 3 Chequy Or and Gules, a Chief Ermine, TAISHALL, 4 Chequy Or and Gules a Bend Ermine, DE CAILLI, or CLIFTON, Paly of ſix within a Border bezantè 6 Bends of ſix a Canton ... four ... Eſcocheon ... before 2 or 1 Dozengel Quarterly, 1 KNIVET, 2 CROMWELL, 3 TAISHAL 4 CAILLI, 5 De

Woolſtock, 6 Paly of ſix within a Bordure bezantè, 7 Bench of ſix a Canton 8 Or 1 Chevron Gules STAFFORD, 9 Azure a Bend cottiſed, between ſix Lioncels rampant, Or, DE BOHUN The others effacée

Inſcrip on round the Verge

Here lyeth Elizabeth Kneuet ¦ Daughter of Sir Will Kneuet Knight whiche Elizabethe deceaſed the firſt Daie of Novembre in the Yere of our Lord God MD and LVIII On whoſe Soule Jeſu have Mercy Amen

---

* "RICHARD CAPEL was born of good Parentage, within the City of Glouceſter, educated in Grammar Learning there became a Commoner of St Alban Hall in 1601, et ... Demy of Magdalen College ſoon after, and in 1609 made Fellow of that Houſe being then M A which was the higheſt Degree he took in this Univerſity While he continued the ... Eminency ... was reſorted to by noted Men eſpecially of the Calvinian Party, and many Pupils put to his Charge, of whom divers afterward became noted for their Learning, as Accepted Frewen, Archbiſhop of York Apoſtle and others Afterward leaving the College upon obtaining the Rectory of Eaſtington in his own County, became eminent there among the Puritan Party for his painful and practical Way of preaching, his exemplary Life and Converſation and in doing many good Offices for thoſe of that Function When the Book concerning Sport on the Lord's Day was commanded to be read in Churches in 1633 he refuſed to do it, and thereupon within ... relinquiſhing his Rectory obtained Licence to practiſe Phyſick from the Biſhop of Glouceſter ſo that ſetting it Practical near to Stroud in the ſaid County (where as ... a remoned Eſtate) was reſorted to eſpecially by thoſe of his Opinion for he ... in the Faculty In the Beginning of the grand Rebellion he cloſed with the Presbyterians was one of the Aſſembly of Divines, but refuſed to ſit many of them, and was, I conceive reſtored to his Benefice, or elſe had a better content of up ... He paid his laſt Debt to Nature at Pitchcome, Sep 21 1656 and was buried within the Precincts of the Church there His Father Nine was Chriſtopher Capel a ſtout Alderman of Glouceſter, and a good Friend to ſuch Miniſter as had ſuffered for Nonconformity Wood's Athen vol II p 18

Of all which, which remain ... Teſtimonies are the now exceedingly ...

WILLIAM PRINNE born in A ... went to Magdalen College, in this ... part uſed force ... but under R CAPEL became noted for a famous Preacher ... with a ... and on ... to the ... much beloved. At which Accompliſhment were knit together in a Body of about 4 Years of Age which he failed to ſtudious would have a Body of Learning At the ... ſooner the Book as ... was ... 47 ... he left a Library ... Perſon in the Year 16 ... and was buried in th Yard under the great New ... within ... in a deep Church

Wood's Athen vol II p 165

... ſhew the Deſcent of WILLIAM KNIVET Knt of Berg and Cailli, in the County of Norfolk ... Wife, one of Lewes ... Duke of BUCKINGHAM, commonly ſtyle Henry Bohun ... Edward ... vol I pag ...

ON A HANDSOME MARBLE
MONUMENT

Arms, Per Chevron Azure and
Argent, in Chief two Falcons rising
Or, for STEPHENS —impaling, two
Helmets in Chief, and a Garb in Base,
for CHOLMLEY

To the Memory of
RICHARD STEPHENS, Grandson of
RICHARD, and Son of
NATHANIEL STEPHENS, Esqrs
Lords of this Manor,
Persons of great Worth and useful
in their Times

NATHANIEL dyed May 22 1660,
aged 71 Years

His Son RICHARD dyed March 7, 1748,
aged 38 Years
Hee married ANN daughter of
Sir HUGH CHOLMLEY,
of Whitby, in Yorkshire,
Kt and Barronet
and had by her five Sons and three
Daughters all living at the time of
his Death who in his Life gave
signall Proofs of his Piety,
Wisdome, and Patience
of a generous Spirit
joyned with an humble Minde

Arms, STEPHENS, as above

To the Memory of
ROBERT STEPHENS, of the
Middle Temple,
Serjeant at Law, Son of
NATHANIEL STEPHENS,
Brother of RICHARD STEPHENS,
of this Place, Esqr
Lord of this Manner
borne July 23, 1622 died Nov 4, 1675,
aged 53
He was exquisitely knowing in the
Lawes of this Kingdome, and in
all other reall and solid Learning
a publique Loss to his Country and
Age in which he lived

ON A MONUMENT AGAINST ONE
OF THE PILLARS

Arms Sable, a Chevron between
three Griffins Heads erazed Or charged
with three Mullets of the Field, for
BEALE, —impaling, Chequy, Or and
Sable, for a Base

Memoriæ Sacrum
Dominæ EDITHÆ BEALE,
Uxoris et Viduæ ROBERTI BEALE,
de Prioris Manston in com Warwick,
Arm. reliquæ ELIZABETHÆ
Consilio Regio et Epistolis,
& in Boreali horis Angliæ partibus
Secretarii (qui diem clausit extremum
27 Maii, An D 160 †
& Filiæ HENRICI SAINTBARB
ex antiquissima SAINTBARBORUM,
de Ashington, in com Somerset, Arm
Familia, & ELEONORÆ JENINGS,
de Tinten, in com Sussex
quam pulcherrima prole ditavit
filios habuit duos FRANCISCUM &
ROBERTUM, et filias FRANCISCAM
UR...AM...BETH...RIAM MARGARETTAM
(nuptam HENRICO YELVERTON, Mil)
...

MA...STEPHENS, CATHERINA,
(Neptum NAT...S...NS)
de Eddington in Com Gloucer
Arm ANNAM, et A...IAM
Foemina pudica, prudentissima,
pudicissime et religiosiss...
mur...centissima ejus beata Anima
...terrestri carcere emerita...
12 Julii, A D 1628 ...Ætat...
et corpus in hoc Sepulchro...
de Lathington sepulchris recondite
reconditum in certissima...gloriosæ
Resurrectionis spem

ON A BRASS PLATE IN THE OLD TEXT

Arms, STEPHENS, Crest a Demi
Eagle

Here underneath lye buried the Bodies
of Edward Stephens Gentleman and
Joan his Wife which both feared God
hated Evil were helpfull to the Poore, of
good Report and toward their later Dayes
having heere settled he was Patron of this
Church the Ministery of the Word they
were diligent Hearers and Embracers of the
Truthe. He dyed ... of October 15.. 2
Regine Elizabethe beinge about 61
Yeares of Age and she the 5 of August in the
same Yeare aged about 62 Yeares leaving
behind them ... Sonnes and Daughters
living.

ON ...LATIONIS

Here resteth the Body of
JAMES STEPHENS, Clother,
the Sonne of
EDWARD STEPHENS, Gentleman
Wayting for the ... rection to Come,
he deceased on the 10th Day of
February 159...

Here lyeth the Body of ...A
the Daughter of JAMES STEPHENS
she died 27 June aged six Yeres
and seven Months, 1636

Here lyes the Body of RICHARD,
son of WILLIAM CLUTTERBUCK,
of this Parish, Clother,
who died June 26 1714,
in the 64th Year of his A...
Here also lyeth the body of
HANNAH, the Wife of
RICHARD CLUTTERBUCK
and Daughter of GILES NASH
of Stonehouse who died July 6 1746,
in the 67th Year of her Age

Here lyeth the Body of
REBEKAH, the Wife of
WILLIAM CLUTTERBUCK,
Daughter of THO PIERCE,
of Wotton under Edge, Gent
who died 4 April, 1706

Here lyeth the Body of
WILLIAM, Son of
RICHARD CLUTTERBUCK, Clother,
who died the 10th of July, 17..
in the 84th Year of his Age

Also
Here resteth the Body of
GILES CLUTTERBUCK, Gent
Son of RICHARD and HANNAH
CLUTTERBUCK
He was born May 7, 169...
died January 25, 16...

Here lyeth the Body of
MRS ANN CLUTTERBUCK
Relict of Mr GILES CLUTTERBUCK,
who departed this Life
Nov 10, 17.., aged 67 Years

Here lyeth the Body of
the late ... of
WILLIAM MEW, M A
Rector of this Church
formerly the Widow of
WM CLUTTERBUCK, of this Parish,
Clother, who departed
this Life ... April ...
of her Age 70

Here resteth the Body of
RICHARD CLUTTERBUCK,
the Sonne of
WILLIAM CLUTTERBUCK, Clother,
Wayting for a full Resurrection to Glory
He fell on sleep the ... Day of June
Anno 16..

Here lyeth A...D... of...
Da...er Tewksbury of Stonehouse,
Gent and ...t
RICHARD CLUTTERBUCK
of this Parish, Clother,
buried Oct 4, 16..

Here lyeth the Body of
RICHARD CLUTTERBUCK,
late of this Parish ...
who died ...
...he was loving ...
World ...
which he came ...
...during the whole Course of his
May the Lord ...
of this even in Death ...
which removed him ...
make our Hearts to meditate ...

...THO WELL he died ... M...
He died September 27, 17..,
aged 53

ANNE STEPHENS —impaling, A...
...and a Fess Sable three ...
On a Field Azure, for ...

MARGARET, the Widow of
RICHARD STEPHENS ... Esq,
Daughter of THO PIERCE,
EDWARD SAINTBARB Esq...
and Matron of ... Wife
here interr'd, ... Buck
As brief as was her life and ...
to her End well fill'd ...
He that ... keep Minister ...
living her entire and ...
Daughters

How long, O Lord! How endureth...

H.c jacet quod mor ale tuit
HANNÆ ux GUALT MARSHALL,
filiæ GULIELMI CLUTTERBUCK
quæ obiit 12 die Septembris,
anno Domini 1683, ætat suæ 27°
Etiam GUALT MARSHALL, Gen
qui obiit Apr 6°,
A D 1732, ætat suæ 78
Etiam MARGARETTÆ
GUALT MARSHALL, Gen Uxoris
JOSEPH AYLOFFE,
è Gray's-Inn, Armigr filiæ,
quæ obiit die Julii 15°,
Anno Dom 1758, ætatis suæ 68
Ac etiam ANNÆ, filiæ
NATH is POOLE, quæ obiit,
18 die Octob anno Dom 1717

Arms, STEPHENS impaling BEALE

Here resteth the Body of
CATHARINE the Wife of
NATHANIEL STEPHENS, Esq
the Daughter of
ROBERT BEALE, Esq
Clerk of the Councell to Queen Eliz
who lived in Honour, and dyed in the
Faith of our Lord Jesus,
Feb 22, an 1632,
She left behind her in this Vale of
Teares 3 Sons, HENRY, RICHARD,
and ROBERT, and 5 Daughters,
MARGARET, CATHARINE, SARAH,
HANNA and ABI GAIL
expecting a joyful Resurrection, and
an immortal Crown of Glory at the
last Day

Here lieth the Body of
EDITH STEPHENS
second Daughter of
NATHANIEL STEPHENS,
of Ladington, Esq nei,
who died the 6th Day of
September in D 1632
being 14 Years old

Here lyeth the Body of
FRANCIS, Son of
NATHANIEL STEPHENS, Esq
who died the 31 Day of March, 1701,
aged near ten Months

Also FRANCES his Daughter,
who died the 10th Day of March,
aged 1 Year and   Months

IN THE NORTH AISLE

F AT STONES, ON BRASS PLATES

Here lyeth the Body of
KATHARINE the Wife of
EDWARD STEPHENS,
of this Parish, Gent Daughter of
SAMUEL FREWMAN,
Rector of Parkham in this County,
who departed this Life the
23d Day of April An Dom 1705,
Ætatis suæ 57

Here lyeth the Body of
EDWARD STEPHENS Gent
of this Parish of Listing on,
who departed this Life
the 9th Day September, 17..
in the 6 d Year of his Age

IN THE SOUTH AISLE

To the Pious Memory of
SARAH, the Daughter of
JOHN KING Gent and Wife of
NATHANIEL STEPHENS Gent
who died the 13th of December,
1736, aged 54 Years

Near this Place lie the Bodies of
RICHARD and CATHARINE,
Son and Daughter of
NATH STEPHENS RICHARD died the
1st of June, 1742, in the
29th Year of his Age
CATHARINE died March 29, 1741,
aged 26 Years

Also of NATHANIEL STEPHENS, Gent
who died Aug 8 1744
aged 67 Years

ANNE Wife of ELLIS JAMES,
of this Parish, Gent
and Daughter of
EDWARD STEPHENS, Gent
and CATHARINE his Wife,
died 15 Dec 1766, aged 52

ELLIS JAMES their Son,
died 2nd Dec 1774, aged 27

MARY their Daughter
died 26 Oct 1782 aged 39

The above mentioned Mr ELLIS JAMES
died 17 March, 1790, aged 85

IN THE CHURCH YARD

WILLIAM PEMBLE, Master of Arts,
and Preacher, which was here buried
September 23d 1623

ON MONUMENTS AGAINST
THE EAST END OF THE
CHURCH

Arms Azure a Lion rampant, and
in Chief three Scallop, Argent for
CLUTTERBUCK on an Escutcheon of
Pretence Cheqy, Or and Azure on a
Bend Gules three Lions passant of the
last for CLIFFORD

In Memoriam
NATH is CLUTTERBUCK Gen
qui obiit 13 die Oct 1us, 1680
Pronepotis GULIELMI Jun
Nepotis RICHARDI, J CLUTTER
Filii GULIELMI jun } BUCK
Qui onno con habitaverunt
Nutterum in hac Parochia
Et MARIÆ uxor cius 2da filia natu
maxima et unica Cohæredem
JOHN is CLIFFORD Gen de Frampton,
sup Sabrina qui obiit
7 die Oct 1b 1680,
CUTHBERTUS Filius, natu maximus
aplor NATH is & MARIÆ, ex prece
eigil nenies mæ relique suis,
hoc ponit

In Memory of
JUDITH HICKS, Widow,
who died the 16th of Feb 1760,
aged 80 Years

Near this Place lieth the Body of
WILLIAM Son of
GILES CLUTTERBUCK, Gent
by ANN his Wife, born Nov 23, 1724,
died May 19, 17..

Also of CATHARINE their Daughter
She was born Dec 11 1727,
died Aug 14 1738

ON A FLAT RAISED TOMB

Arms STEPHENS impaling CHOLM
LEY as before

ROBERT STEPHENS *, Esq
fourth Son of
RICHARD STEPHENS, Esq
Lord of this Manor,
died 12 Nov 1732 aged 67
He was Bencher at Law of the
Middle Temple
and Somerset of the Customs other
late Majesties Queen ANNE and
King GEORGE the First
In this voluntary Resignation of which,
he was for a Testimony of his Fidelity
made Histories upteer
A Gentleman for his Skill in the Law,
Antiquity, and Police Learning,

and for his Justice and Integrity
in all his Actions,
worthy to be remembered
He married MARY Daughter of
Sir HUGH CHOLMLEY Bart
of Whitby in the County of York,
and Relict of NATH CHOMBEY,
of Leicestershire Esq
who, surviving, erected this Monument

HANNAH Wife of
WILLIAM DIGHTON,
Minister of this Parish,
and Daughter of THOMAS TYNDALL,
of Stinchcomb, Gent
died Dec 1, 1716
in the 73d Year of her Age

Also WILLIAM DIGHTON,
who was Minister of
this Parish 53 Years,
died Feb 1, 17..,
in the 93d Year of his Age

ROBERT BALL who was Pastor
of this Church, Years,
died July 1, anno 1613, ætatis suæ 63

D ROT.. Wife of
RIC A .CA.. .. ..her,
.. D ...
..AH PLLM.. D of Plinhead,
.. Norfolk ...
.. Sept 14, .. , ... 8

RICHARD CLUTTERBUCK Gent
died Nov .., 173., aged 85 Years

CRAC.. .s wife (and Daughter of
Mau .. .. Grace Dyer .. of
Redwick in the Parish of Henbury)
died June 9 1720,
in the 6.th Year of her Age

CHA.. CLUTTERBUCK Gent
died the 28th Day of M.., 1741
aged 49 Years

SARAH, Wife of EDWARD COX,
and Sister of
CHARLES CLUTTERBUCK, Gent
died Sept 18 1758, aged 36

In Memory of
JOSIAH CLUTTERBUCK of this Parish,
who died Feb 26, A D 1741,
in the 81st Year of his Age

Also A.. his Wife,
who died Feb 14 A D 1730,
in the 69th Year of her Age

MARY Relict of DANIEL P...,
and Wife of JOHN PEER, of Stonehouse,
died March 13, 1777, aged 63

Hic.. contigue reconduntur cineres
NATHAN CLUTTERBUCK Gen
qui obijt 13 die Octob 1650,
MARGAR.. uxcr.. cjus prima,
qu.. .. 8 Mar 1657
...
JOHANNIS CLUTTERBUCK ...
Nepus EATTANT CLUTTERBUCK,
& Nup n.. Prompt s
WILLIELMI CLUTTERBUCK,
ac N.ttest
It NATHAN his ...,
qui obiit 18 Juni 1656,
ac etiam MARIAM un.. ejus secunda,
.. 7 Octris, 1650
MARI.. qu.. 7 Ju.. 1650
...
ip.o .. NATHAN.. & MARIA
N...
MAR.. ...
CUIT CLUTTERBUCK
Gen.. N.. 18 NATH.. & MARIA
..12 Sept 1684

WILLIAM CLUTTERBUCK,
of Nupend Gent
died June 11, 1700
in the 7.th Year of his Age

Also three of his Children, viz

JOHN, died Nov 5 1696, aged ..

HENRY, died Jan 6 1689 aged 28

MARTH.., died June 24, 1688 aged 24

MARTHA his Wife and Daughter of
RICHARD CLUTTERBUCK of Mill End,
Clothier,
died April .., 172., aged .. Years

Also WILLIAM and Son and
Daughter of WILLIAM CLUTTERBUCK
WILLIAM died March 1, 1707,
aged 59,

died Sept 6, 1713 aged 60.
She was the Wife of JO.. POPE of Cam,
Clothier

Also JOHN CLUTTERBUCK, sen
died Oct .1, 1694

Also ANN his Wife
Daughter of HENRY FOWLER, Gent
who was buried Oct .., 16..

JAMES BUDDING of this Parish,
died Sept 13 17., aged 72 Years

Also GEORGE BUDDING,
August 16, 1713

Also GEORGE BUDDING,
Feb 18, 1694, aged 73

WILLIAM BUDDING of Nupend,
died Feb 26, 17.5, aged 54 Years

Also MARY his Wife
died Dec 1, 1741, aged .. Years

ELIZABETH Daughter of
WILLIAM BLANCH,
died April 26, 1656

ELIZABETH, Wife of THOMAS BLANCH,
Nov 10 1701, aged 4.

THOMAS BLANCH,
Feb 24 1700 in the
61st Year of his Age

MARY his first Wife
died March 0 1693

Ad Memoriam Echrem MARIÆ,
uxoris Christinæ
JOHANNIS BLANCH Filii
RIDIAL.. CABRID..
quæ obiit 11 Juni, anno 1686,
ætatis 25

RICHARD BLANCH
December 19, 1736

CATHARINE Daughter of
THOMAS BLANCH,
June .., 17.., aged 44

HANNAH Wife of
THOMAS SOUTHERLAND of London,
June 4 17.0
in the 73rd Year of her Age

ELIZABETH, Wife of
WILLIAM BLANCH, May .., 164.

MARY Wife of THOMAS CREST
and Daughter of THOMAS BLANCH,
died May 25 17..
Aged in ..8

R... their Daughter
June 22, 1700, aged 2 Days

SUSANNAH BISHOP,
July 3., 1722, aged 62

JOHN KING buried Sept 2, 72..,
aged 66 Years

Also CATHARINE his Wife
buried Oct 16, 1704, aged 43 Years

Also five of his Children viz
JOHN buried Oct 6, 1704,
aged 20 Years

ELIZABETH, buried April 2, 16..,
aged 30 Years

RICHARD, buried Sep 26, 1694,
aged 5 Years

CATHARINE, buried Oct 9, 1694,
aged 3 Years

ESTHER, buried Sept 1, 1701,
aged 3 Months

RICHARD, Son of JOHN KING,
January 28 1747, aged 31

ELIZABETH his Daughter,
May 7, 1745 an infant

ELIZABETH, Wife of the above
RICHARD, April 18, 178.,
aged near ..

Also CATHARINE Daughter of
RICHARD and ELIZABETH,
Dec 2, 1773, aged 36

SAMUEL KNIGHT,
Dec 1.. 118., aged 86

JOSEPH his Son March .. 17..,
in the 80th Year of his Age
MARY, Relict of Mr EDWARD SMITH,
Vicar of Frocetfe,
formerly Relict of Mr JOSEPH KNIGHT,
buried March 27 17..,
aged 68 Years

NATHANIEL IVY
Son of NATHANIEL BROOKET Esther,
July 3., 17.. aged .. Years

JONATHAN BISHOP Son of
WALTER BISHOP, Clerk
March 19 17.7 aged 1 Years

JOHN HIGHWAY died J.. 22, 17.5,
aged 45 Years

SARAH wife of JOHN HIGHWAY,
and Wid.. of WILLIAM HIGHWAY,
died Feb .. 1754, aged .. Years

J.KIAH his Son, Nov 5, 1.4.,
aged 9 Years

MARTHA his Daughter
April 20, 173., aged 5 Years

ON A PLATE

JOHN WARNER Jan 3., 1762,
aged 5 Years

Four of his Children, viz
WILLIAM, died Feb 11, 1767,
aged 13 Weeks

MARY, died April 18 17..,
aged 2 Years

CHRISTIAN June 26, 17..,
aged 6 Years

AN.., Oct .. 17.., aged 14 Years

ON FLAT AND HEAD STONES

	Died	Aged		Died	Aged
Dorothy, Wife of William Stone	2 Mar 17-7	50	Thomas Browning	8 Mar 1771	8
John Wilkins, Clerk of this Parish, Years	13 Sep 1756	79	Sisal his Daughter	19 Apr 1754	9
Abigail his Wife	9 Oct 145	49	John Son of Richard and Elizabeth Kesley	31 May 1779	2
Elizabeth his second Wife	12 May 7 1	75	Sus Bira	10 1 1	1
John, Son of John and Abigail Wilkins	15 May 1756	6	benjamin Jaboys	1 Oct 1700	13
Sarah their Daughter	7 Apr 1751	6	Mary his Wife	3 Dec 1 3	
John Peglar	Nov 70	70	William Burcy	9 Oct 69	52
Elizabeth his Wife	21 Apr 1755	60	Mary, Wife of Richard Wicet	Apr 1 43	28
John their Son	11 Apr 1770		Rachel Wife of Joseph Oyles	1 June 1704	—
Hannah Wife of Nath Perkins	13 Sep 1750		Sarah, Daughter of Samuel and Elizabeth ashton	2 July 1742	6
Nathaniel their Son			Samuel Bell p	Jan 176-	71
Ann, Daughter of Joseph Peglar	28 Aug 1 1	1	Elizabeth Wife of John ashton, ter	5 Feb 1767	71
Nath Pitt	1 May 165		John Linton, ter	4 June 1 3	82
Thomas, Son of Thomas Bird	17 Dec 1702	17	Le	9 Feb 1 3	28
Richard Smith	15 Apr 17 7	77	Hannah Linton	25 May 1 44	46
Joshua Palmer	Nov 172	72	Sus others	Aug 1 1	50
Sarah his Wife	10 Nov 1704	65	Hannah his Wife	14 Oct 1756	6
Ruth, Wife of William Leeman	14 Jun 1710		Elizabeth Wife of Joseph Evans	Oct 71	
Sarah Wife of Abraham Freeland	Apr 1 51		Nathaniel Evans	8 Nov 1756	74
Mary Wife of Samuel Bird			Sarah, Wife of Joseph Pitt	9 May 1728	3
William Godwin	17 June 17	77	Jane his Daughter	14 Oct 1713	11
Angel his Wife	15 Nov 170	70	Edward Verry	15 June 1 65	51
Jane, Wife of Richard Smith	7 Feb 168	52	Joan Wife of John Verry	2 Jun 1709	
Nathaniel Miles Junior	13 Feb 1 3		Ruth Wife of John Ford	7	53
Elizabeth his Wife			Rebecca Daughter of Samuel Hogg and Wife of William Hoots	10 Oct 1715	28
Joan Miles	5 Nov 1 0	60	John Son of George Knowles	6 Apr 17 7	1
Hannah his Wife	13 Aug 1756	7	Ann, Wife of Richard Wilton	Nov 1692	
Hannah Wife of William Mower	May 17 3	53	Richard Knowles	20 Dec 1691	57
Jane Daughter of Will King	May 1751		Richard Hytt	Dec 1 0	
Mary Wife of Nathaniel King	May 1 6		William Hopkin	17 Dec 1655	
Richard Pughs	4 Apr 1 8		Hannah Wife of Joan Davis	25 Oct 1701	1
Mary his Wife	Mar 6	5	Daniel Cra	28 May 1750	68
Hester Browne	7 Oct 172	13	Elizabeth his Wife	2 May 1740	60
Thomas Browning, an Infant	9 Mar 17		Samuel Evans of Stroud	7 Jul 1773	30
Richard his Father	1 Nov 1729	0	Edward Evans of Hardwick	7 Apr 1771	60
Thomas Evans	6 July 1 3	66	John Evans, ter	15 June 1 68	57
Sarah his Wife	6 Jul 1733	40	Elizabeth his Wife	Feb 1 5	3
Sarah Wife of William Evans	7 Sept 1756	3	Jane their Son young	Feb 1 1	
John and Sarah their Children			Edward Evans	1 Nov 1770	1
Catharine his Wife	23 Oct 1740		Jane Evans	2 Nov 17 1	
William Evans	13 Mar 1749	7	Jane Wife of Robert Morgan	Oct 17 3	62
Mary his Wife	13 Apr 1715	4	W ts, Son of Robert and Jane	Nov 1	
Edward Evans buried	13 Dec 1 30	54			
John, Son of William Evans	24 Mar 1 6	58	Dorothea their Parents		
Sarah, Daughter of John Evans	5 Jun 1 5	4	Joseph Elliott		
Ann, Daughter of James and Margaret Hyatt	21 Aug 1 5		Sarah daughter of Joseph and Elizabeth Elliott	3 1	
James Wermore	9 Jan 1772	85	Joseph Elliott son to the said Sarah	2 Nov 1650	
Sus his Wife	11 Jun 1751	6	William and Sarah Lucy		
Sarah, Mary, and Elizabeth their Children			Isaac Lucy		
James Hyatt	6 Apr 177	62	Richard his Wife	8 Feb 1 65	1
William Hyatt	1 Nov 1 1		Elizabeth Wife of Daniel Clarke	9 Jan 17 0	6
Elizabeth, Wife of Samuel Lom	17 Mar 1 1	21	Ann L ce	7 Jun 1700	6
Joseph Willard	1751		Richard Lucy	Feb 1 5	4
Ann Jones	1		John Son of Joseph n	June 1751	45
Samuel Jones	1		Father Son of John n	15 Oct 1 5	15
George Howard	1 Jan 1	68	Jane Lucy	15 Mar 1 55	
Elizabeth his Wife	19 Jan 1 67	81	Mary Wife of Richard tock, of Hurst, Esquire	3 Mar 73	5
Thomas Clutterbuck	16 Dec 1		Ann their son of Edmund and Sarah	Nov 1 11	18
Sarah his Wife	21 Jun 1 3		Mary their Daughter	Nov 1	
Nathaniel Clutterbuck	5 Apr 1	15	Richard and	1 Mar 1704	71
Sarah his Wife	25 Jun 1 0	7	Mary his Wife, Daughter of Richard Evans	6 Jul 1	57
Nathaniel Hayward	1 Nov 1 4	7	Samuel Son of Samuel Lucy	11 June 1 1	
Ann his Wife	6 May 1 14	19	Samuel Lucy	Dec 1707	52
Daniel their Son	Apr 1 5		Ann his Wife		
Hester, Wife of John Hayward	26 Jun 1682	51	Thomas Son of William Lucy	14 Dec 1 53	10
William Hyatt	24 Apr 1715	71	Sarah his Wife	6 Jun 81	69
Sarah his Wife	Jan 1 4	71	Elizabeth, Daughter of William Lucy	8 Jun 1 20	40
Elizabeth Wife of William Gibbs	15 Feb 1 41		Nehemiah, Son of Thomas and Sarah Lucy	1 Oct 1757	—
Mary, Wife of Thomas Underwood	1 June 1 5	50			
John Clutterbuck	11 Apr 1 65	60			
Elizabeth Wife of Thomas Underwood	15 Apr 1714	43			
Richard his Son buried	3 Apr 1759				

ON FLAT AND HEAD STONES

	Died	Aged		Died	Aged
Elizabeth their Daughter	6 Sept 1778	3	Ann his Wife	31 Jan 1768	61
Mary their Daughter	8 May, 1761	1	William their Son	15 May, 176	19
John their Son	10 Apr 1789	2	Hannah, Wife of William Stone	11 Nov 1760	52
William Wetmore	9 Jan 1733	79	Abraham Watkins	14 Sept 1727	58
Sarah his Wife	15 Nov 1731	83	Elizabeth his Relict, and Wife of		
Thomas, Son of James Wetmore	27 Oct 1777	48	Nathaniel Simmons	12 Feb. 1732	—
Sarah, Daughter of William and			William Peglar	16 June, 1729	—
Sarah Wetmore	21 July, 1735	12	Abigail his Wife	24 May, 1748	85
William Wetmore buried	14 Sept 1765	75	Nathaniel King, sen buried	28 Feb 1733	6
Richard Fennell	10 Nov 1719	33	Nathaniel King, jun	24 Jan 1759	69
Sarah his Wife	18 Oct 1761	81	Abigail his Wife	27 Aug 1729	73
Leonard Knowles	11 July, 1764	69	John Miles of Stonehouse	13 May 1744	79
Betty his Daughter	20 June, 1754	4	Hester his Wife	3 Dec 1784	90
Richard Cooper, Gent	29 Aug 1719	77	Thomas Miles	28 Nov 1695	54
John Marshall, Gent.	12 Aug 1743	80	Elizabeth his Wife	2 Aug 1728	72
Thomas Davis	16 Apr 1756	6	Nathaniel Miles, sen	23 Oct 1736	60
Mary his Wife	15 Mar 1762	56	Ann his Wife		
Nathaniel Perkins	30 Oct 1768	74	Elizabeth, Wife of Nathaniel Miles	10 Feb 1700	26
Elizabeth his Wife	16 Apr 1754	70	Randford Brain	16 June, 1735	61
George Perkins	10 Sept 1767	66	Ann his Wife	19 Dec 1731	60

East Leach St Marten and East Leach Turville

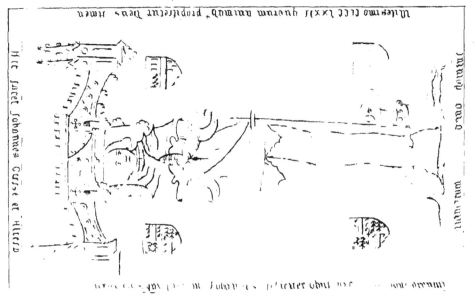

EAST LECHE ST. MARTIN,
OR
BURTHORPE.

THE Name *Leche* in *Domesday*, and other early Evidences, was applied indistinctly to four several Parishes, from the Rivulet on the Banks of which they are situate.*

This Village is in the Hundred of *Brightwell's Barrow* eight Miles from *Northleche* on the South-east, three Northward from *Lechlade*, and twenty-seven due East from the City of GLOUCESTER The Parish is of an oval Shape, about two Miles across in the widest Part, containing 1500 Acres, of a light stony Soil, three fourths of which are tilled

DROGO FITZ PONS (the Ancestor of the Families of POINTZ and CLIFFORD) obtained the Lordship of *Leche* from the CONQUEROR, which was granted by RICHARD FITZ PONS, in the Reign of HENRY the First, to the *Benedictine* Priory of *Great Malverne*, com *Vigorn* † His Descendant WALTER DE CLIFFORD reclaiming it, gave it to the Abbey of *St Peter*, in GLOUCESTER ‡ ALDRED Bishop of WORCESTER, upon the Pretence of encreasing Hospitality, appropriated thus and other Manors to his See, and upon his farther Promotion to *York* annexed them to that Archbishoprick These were afterward restored to the Abbey by his Successor THOMAS DE BAION in 1095, with great Contrition § In 1114, and the 9th of his Reign, King STEPHEN granted a Charter of Confirmation to the Monks of GLOUCESTER, in whose Hands this Manor remained, till their Suppression, when it was added to the Revenues of the Dean and Chapter, then about to be established

The larger Estate, including the Hamlet of *Fifield*, was long held by the Family of TRINDER In the Beginning of this Century JOSEPH SMALL, Gent became Lessee, who built the Manor House After the Decease of his Son VINER SMALL, M.D. it was transferred to —— JERVIS, who was succeeded by SLADE NASH, Esq

Burthorpe Farm, held likewise under the Church, was first in Lease to a Branch of the Family of BLOMER, of *Hatherop*, and for many Years to the DOWDESWELLS, of *Pull Court*, com *Vigorn* Upon the Death of the Right Honourable WILLIAM DOWDESWELL, Esq in 1775, this Estate was purchased by TIMOTHY KIMBER, Gent Two Freehold Estates, of nearly 120 Acres each, belong to the Reverend BENJAMIN BOYES, Clerk, and the Family of BUTLER, of *London*

The Living is a Rectory, in the Deanery of *Fairford*, and in the Patronage of the Crown.

Of this Church, dedicated to *St Martin*, and that of *East Leche Turville*, the Style of Building are exactly correspondent, both of high Antiquity, with a Nave, semi Transept, and slated Tower They are situate at about 120 Yards Distance on either Side the River *Leche*, which is the common Boundary of both Parishes

The Rectory House, which is very commodious, was re-built by HENRY SMITH, D.D. a former Incumbent

BENEFACTIONS

Dr HENRY SMITH, by Will, 1702, bequeathed 50l the Interest of which to be given five Poor Persons, on St Thomas' Day, according to the Direction of the Rector

* " Clere Coln and lovely *Leche* to down from *Coteswold's* Plaine
" At *Leche* looking hands come likewise to support
" The Mother of good *Coln* DRAYTON's Polyolbion, book IV p 233
† DUGDALE's Mon vol I p 365 TANNER's Notitia *Worcestershire*, Nᵒ 15 Pat Rol 20 Edw III m 18 Pro Ecclesia de *Leche* &c appropriandis
‡ " Totum Territorium de Manerio *Estleche* quam pro Manerio *Glastlerie* de WALTERIO CLIFFORD exceimerunt ' DUGDALE Addit in vol I p 9
§ " MEREDUS WIGORN Epi opus hospitii fui ea usa abstulit a con nomen *Leche*, *Odynton*, & *Staywich* cum *Barona* retinens in " annum fui Eundem in Archiepiscopum *Ebor* consecratur qui ipsi manerii Ecclesia *Ebor* appropriavit Anno 1095. " Idem sua Archiepiscopi opis *Ebor* villa *Leche* &c reddidit Gloucerensi Ecclesia, semetipsum graviter inculpando, pestes rudendo, " genu flectendo, quin injurias eis tandem remiserat DUGDALE, vol I p 110

INCUMBENTS

INCUMBENTS	PATRONS	INCUMBENTS	PATRONS
1578 Lewis Padwyn,	Queen Elizabeth	1688 Henry Smith, D D	King James II
1583 Simon Perrett,	The same	1702 Thomas Burton, D D	Queen Anne
1600 Rowland Stutchfield,	The same	1720 William Asplin, M A	King George I
1622 John Wall,	King James I	1758 James Parsons, M A	King George II
. . . .	. . . . . .	1785 Hon Fran Knollys, M A	King George III
—— Edward Be,			

PRESENT LESSEE OF THE MANOR,
SLADE NASH, ESQ

There does not appear to have been any Person summoned from this Place by the Heralds in 1682 and 1683

At the Election in 1776 only One Freeholder polled from this Parish

The Register is curiously preserved, commencing in 1538, and is continued in one Volume to the present Time

ANNUAL ACCOUNT OF MARRIAGES, BIRTHS, AND BURIALS, IN THIS PARISH

A D	Mar	Bir	Bur	A D	Mar	Bir	Bur	A D	Mar	Bir	Bur	A D	Mar	Bir	Bur
1781	1	8	3	1786	3	4	4	1791				1796			
1782	2	4	1	1787	1	6	7	1792				1797			
1783	2	2	6	1788	2	3	5	1793				1798			
1784	1	5	7	1789				1794				1799			
1785	—	2	5	1790				1795				1800			

INSCRIPTIONS IN THE CHURCH.

IN THE CHANCEL

ON A MONUMENT FIXED IN ONE OF THE WINDOWS IN THE SOUTH WALL

M. S

Mariæ, filiæ Johannis
. . . . de Hornton,
in . . . Oxon, generosi,
Conjugis vero conju,
Willielmi Asplin, Clerici hujus
Ecclesiæ . . . qui omnibus
. . . .
. . . . redidit
A D MDCCXXVI at sua I
. . . . hic deposuit
Matri hic etiam eodem sub lapide,
A I 1730 æt suæ 71,
Sepultus est, prædictus
WILLIELMUS ASPLIN, A M
Alkibit I Author, vere & æqui custos,
pacis amator nemi invidens,
Hic tamen (inimicorum utpote
infimum) summum sibi
. . . . dixit quod nulli ulque invisus
fuerit
. . . . am
. . . Pri xl 5

ON FLAT STONES.

Here lieth the Body of
ELIZABETH, the Wife of
RICHARD BLOMER, Gen
deceased the 1st Day of Nov
Anno Domini 1611

Arms . . . le, 3 Leopards Face
in Centre Or, between three Crosses
patte . . . Argent, for . . . RONS

Beneath this Stone are deposited the
Remains of the
Rev JAMES PARSONS, M A
for many Years Rector of this Parish
With a manly Zeal for the Cause of
Religion and Virtue, he possessed that
amiable Simplicity of Manners
which endeared him . . . universal
Esteem and Veneration
He died Aug 5, 1785,
in the 67th Year of his Age

In a Grave adjoining were interred
JANE, the Wife of the
Rev JAMES PARSONS,
who died Oct 14, 1780,
aged 53 Years,
and CATHARINE COTT, her Aunt,
who died Aug 16, 1765.

Here lyeth the Body of
RICHARD BLOMER, Gentleman,
who deceased the ninth Day of July,
Anno Domini 16 1

Here . . . the body of
EDWARD BELL, Rector of this Church,
who died the . . th Day of October,
Anno Domini 1685, aged 78 Years

IN THE CHURCH YARD

ON A TOMB

GEORGE BUTLER, &c
who . . . . 1 May 23, 1777,
aged 77 Years

Also of ELIZABETH, Wife of
GEORGE BAXTER
who died Feb 2 , 17 . t
aged 4 Years

ON FLAT AND HEAD STONES

	Died	Aged		Died	Aged
. . . . Wife of Richard Baxter	25 Oct 1698	61	John Curtis —	17 Feb 1 5	5
Charles Baxter	5 Feb 1700	—	Richard his son	30 June 176	14
Richard, son of Richard and Sarah			Mary Wife of George Curtis	Sept 176	4
Baxter of Bury Vere Perihut	19 Sept 1711	84	Eleanor heir Da . ter	20 Jun 1 5	
and Daughter of . . . and Eli			Curtis an Daughter (an Infant)		
zabeth Perit	5 Feb 171	—	Robert Green	6 Feb 1784	
Charles th . . son	5 Feb 1 , 20	20	Jacob Stephens	20 Apr 17	
. . . .	27 Nov 17 0	5	D . . ns his Wife	6 Feb 17	
. . . . Wife of . . d Baxter	5 Nov 1 16	63	Mary Wife of John Kibble of L. . .		
Mary Baxter	15 Feb 1691	—	field	18 Oct 1784	70
. . . Hugh	5 Apr 1713	52	Mary Wife of Job Bishop their		
. . . .	23 Jul 1 1	77	Daughter	8 Mar . t	
. . . . Newman	14 Dec 1 01	6	William, son of George and Mary		
. . . .	16 Sep 1685	—	Longford	29 Nov 1781	4
. . . . dall	5 Nov 1708	—	John Frechbury	9 Fe . t	
. . . .	18 July 1716	37	Martha, Wife of Thomas Frechbury	6 Apr 178	5
. . . h Wife	1 Nov 1748	62	William son of John and Catha		
. . . . . . Phill	6 Aug 1742	55	rine Green	6 Mar 1	—
Mary Wife of Thomas Hareson	2 Nov 1741	41	Mary, Wife of Daniel Thomas	20 Sept .	
. . . .	5 June 1741	31	Ann, Wife of John Wheeler	11 Feb t	
. . . . . Wife of Jonathan Call	4 Feb 1750	4	John their son	15 June t	
. . . his son and Wife	10 Dec 1756	40			

Consecrated July p . t Aug 1611, but held this Rectory in Commendam
. . . Josephus Osbrton, see Gent Mag vol XLVIII p 2 1

CX I A S I

THL Account of the preceding Parish applies likewise to this ... District, Distance, and soil excepting in the Extent of the Terrier, which exceeds it by ... by a thousand ... Although the addition ... Name be taken from the Family of I... , or Tur...le, no Proof ... of their having possessed any Lands in this Parish A general Inclosure has ... made of the Lands, upon which large Flocks were formerly fed

The Living is a stipendiary Curacy in the Deanery of I...ford, ... Impropriation was given to the Benedictine Abbey of Te..ksb..y, by their Founder Robert ... Hives, ... Earle It passed in 20 Edw. III 1347, to the Abbey of Gloucester, and is now held in Lease under the Dean and Chapter, charged with 30l a Year to the Curate

From the Church, dedicated to S... Andrew, a cumbent Frame, under an Arch, and the Portrait of John di Leche, a Priest in painted Glass, are now removed The Door ... has some curious Saxon carvings Very considerable repairs have been lately made

Rogir di Laci received the Manor from the Conqueror, and it descended to the Di Ciiaes, a line of Gloucester ... to whom, through the Audleys, it was inherited by Edward Stafford, Duke of Buckingham, and upon his attainder was confiscated to the Crown Sir Edward Lest, Knight, purchased it of K Henry VIII and from one of his Co-heirs, passed to Sir Thomas Vachel, Knight, of Compton Mordac, to Harctt By his Descendant it was transferred to William Brewer, Esq before 1608, from whom, by Heirship, it now belongs to Sir John Wine, Bart of Engold, com. Dorset, and Hatherop in this County

But it appears that this principal mineral Title was held by ... in fine Lands, for near two Centuries, by the Family of I...es... ... this ... of ... A ... reputed Manor with a competent Estate, was given by William C... to the College in Priory of Pri... in Oxfordshire, which after their Suppression was granted to John Doctor Cox and Jo Jackson in 1559 Richard Keble (a Descendant of Sir H... ... Keble, ... and Mayor of London in 1510 ...) purchased it of them, and it was transmitted from him to ... for several times of the same Name, by the last of whom it was sold to Sir John Wine, Bart and is now ... the whole Property of the Parish

Several Springs here are very strongly impregnated with different minerals, chiefly of ... an Ochre

---

BENEFACTIONS

Thomas Howis, by Will, dated April 27, 1760, gave 25l the Interest thereof to be distributed in Bread to the Poor on Easter-Day

The present perpetual Curate is John Chaundler, M A The following ... communicated ... the Book of the Register of this Parish with my ... direction

Present Lord of the Manor,
Sir John Wine, Bart

The only Person summoned from the Parish by the Heralds Office in 1683, ...
Richard Keble, Esq

It does not appear that any Freeholder polled from this Parish to the Heralds in 1776
The present Register commences in 16...

An Account of Marriages, Births and Burials from the Parish

A D	Mar	Bur	Bur	A D	Mar	Br	Bur	A D	Mar	Br	Bur	A D	Mar	Br	Bur
1781	1	1	9	1786	3	14	2	1791					1		
1782	7	1	6	1787	1	10	5	1792					1		
1783	1	1	2	1788	—	9	6	1793					1		
1784	—	1	5	1789	1	14	3	1794					1		
1785	2	9	1					1795					1		

* Du ...
† Co... William Ca...
‡ ... Curate Johnson, Do...
... Dugdale's Warwickshire, p 41...

INSCRIPTIONS

INSCRIPTIONS IN THE CHURCH

ON FLAT STONES IN THE CHANCEL.

Arms, Per Cheveron Argen, and Sable, three Elephants Heads erased counterchanged

In Memory of ANTHONY SAUNDERS, Rector of East Leach Turvill, who died the 25th Day of March, Anno Domini, 1731, Ætat 72

Here lies interred the Body of ELIZABETH, Wife of ANTHONY SAUNDERS, Gent who departed this Life, May the 9 h, 1743, aged 63 Years

Also in Memory of JOAN, Wife of WILLIAM MEATING and Sister to the abovemention'ed ELIZABETH SAUNDERS, who departed this Life May 11, 1743, aged 63 Years

He e lye h the Body of FRANCES SAUNDERS Wife and Relict of THOMAS SAUNDERS, Gent deceased the 18th of January 1703, aged 73

In Memory of JOHN SAUNDERS, Gent who died the 27th Day of June Anno Domini 1710, Ætat 48

RICHARDUS KELLE Gen N tus XXXI Octobris MD Obiit XXV July MDCC

Here lyeth the Body of WALTER ADDERTON, Clark, who deceased the Day of July

MARY, the Widow of RICHARD KEBLE, Gent died January the XX A D MDCCXII Æt LXX

Here lyeth interred the Body of JOHN PORTER who departed this Life the 29th Day of March 1721, aged 47 Years

Also here lyeth interred the Body of ELIZABETH, Wife of the above mentioned JOHN PORTER who died July the 1st 1738, aged 89 Years

IN THE NAVE

ON A HANDSOME MARBLE MONUMENT

1770
SARAH ANNE, Daughter of BENJAMIN and MARY BOYES, departed this Life July 6, aged 1 Year

Near this are reposited the Bodies of RICHARD and DINAH BOYES She departed this Life the 11th Nov 1771, in the 71st Year of her Age He the 23d of Dec following aged 83, BENJAMIN Son of R and MARY BOYES, departed this Life Oct 13, 1788

ON FLAT STONES IN THE NORTH AISLE

Here lies the Body of MARY, Daughter of JOSEPH TRINDER, and KATHARINE his Wife who departed this Life, March 18, 17

Here lies the of DOROTHY, Daughter of JOSEPH TRINDER, and KATHARINE his Wife, who departed this Life, August the 25th, 1696

Here lyeth the Body of KATHARINE, Wife of JOSEPH TRINDER who departed this Life the 5th of November 1706

Here lyeth the Body of CECILY, the Wife of ROBERT JONES Yeoman, who departed this Life, August the 12th, Anno Domini 1656

Here lyeth the Body of WILLIAM SWELL, who was buried October the 13th 1687

IN THE CHURCHYARD, ON A TOMB

THOMAS HOWES died 27 April 1762, aged 76 Years

ON FLAT AND HEAD STONES

	Died	Aged		Died	Aged
Mary, Wife of Joseph Porter, and Daughter of John and Eleanor Newport	11 June, 1759	31	Sibilla, Wife of William Clark	18 Mar 1734	71
Richard, Son of Thomas and Frances Tuckwell	30 Nov 1709	14	Isley Bridshaw	4 May 1738	70
Sarah, Wife of Jacob Porter	28 Dec 1,67	44	Mary, Wife of Richard Browne	30 July, 17-0	71
Susannah his Wife, and only Daughter of John and Mary Wakeheld	23 Nov 1728	2	Elizabeth, Daughter of John and Elizabeth Por er	26 Dec 17 6	13
Richard Tuckwell	29 Jan 1,55	74	Peter Herbert	5 Au 1,65	5
John Collier	23 Jul, 1726	71	Richard the Son		
John Jones	16 Dec 1762	65	Mary Wife of John Clarke	26 June 1760	5
Elizabeth his Wife	21 Aug 1727	25	William Clark	12 Sept 1766	71
Mary his second Wife	— 1770	55	Frances, Wife of Adam Clarke and Daughter of Richard and Susannah Tuckwell	6 Feb 1736	53
John Howes	29 May 1722	74			
Elizabeth his Wife	23 Aug 1729	72	Jasper, Son of Adam and Frances Clarke	15 Apr 1736	1
Ann then Daughter, and Wife of Richard A ton	5 Dec 1750	71	Adam Clarke	6 Nov 1763	76
John Howes	6 Mar 1785	71	Ann his Wife, and Relict of John Lapworth	17 Oct 1775	8
Thomas, Son of John and Elizabeth Porter	4 June, 1729	21	Henry Lackley	21 July 1744	
Samuel, Son of John and Anna Porter	11 May, 1710	24	Grace Lifeley	4 Nov 1751	61
Henry Newport buried	27 May 1731	69	Mary Wife of John Wakefield	5 Sept 17	83
Mary his Wife	7 July, 1726	63	John Wakefield	4 Jan 17 1	93
Dorothy, Wife of Richard Lapworth	21 Jan 1739	70	John Wakefield, jun	29 Dec 17 1	68
Henry Lapworth	19 Jan 1741	71	Thomas Tuckwell	6 Jan 1745	6
William Smith	9 Sept 1770	39	Robert Richins	21 Jan, 17 0	
William Jones	18 Nov 1763	81	Catharine Richins	26 Jan 1703	
Daniel Jones	21 Feb 1741	73	Justinian Lovely	11 Dec 1755	7
Jane his Wife	17 Apr 1752	84	Robert Sermon, Gent	3 Jan 1,	83
William Dunn	20 Sept 1763	66	Thomas, Son of Thomas and Elizabeth Brown	3 Jan 1765	22
Anne his Wife	6 July, 1776	73	Sarah then Daughter	16 Apr 1765	26
Anne, Wife of William Iles	29 Oct 1766	39	John Lapworth	11 Apr 17 1	71
William their Son	—	—	Elizabeth Trinder	7 May 1708	15
			Robert Trinder	29 Jan 1 36	
			Hester Woodward	5 Aug 1, 2	

CXI. EBRINGTON, OR EBBURTON,

LIES in the Hundred of *Kiftsgate*, two Miles diftant North-eaft from *Campden*, and twenty three in the fame Direction from the City of GLOUCESTER.

The Boundaries of this Parifh are of an oval Shape, two Miles long, one broad, and fix in Circumference, of a Soil light and gravelly, and chiefly applied to Tillage.

The Living is a very fmall Vicarage, in the Deanery of *Campden*, the Emoluments of which arife principally from Stipends, 8*l* per Ann paid by the Earl of GAINSBOROUGH, in Lieu of Tythes in the Hamlet of *Charingworth*, and 10*l* the Benefaction of Sir WILLIAM KEYTE, Bart. It is not in Charge. In 1377, WILLIAM LE ZOUCH, of *Charingworth*, gave lands to the Ciftertian Abbey of *Biltlefden*, com *Bucks*, annexing to it the Impropriation, which were granted in 1607 to ANTHONY and GEORGE BONNER *. The Tythes of *Charingworth* abovementioned were once held by the Abbey of *Winchcombe*.

The Church is dedicated to St *Eadburgh*, and is fpacious and neat. It has a Nave, a femi tranfept and low Tower. In the Chancel, which is more modern, are Hiftorical Paintings in the Eaft window, from the Story of JOSEPH and his Brethren, with the Arms of the Donor Sir WILLIAM KEYTE, very well executed.

In *Domefday*, *Ebrington* is not mentioned. Some have conjectured that it is there defcribed as "*Brifentune*," the Property of WILLIAM GOIZENBODED. In the 55th of HENRY III it was claimed by ROGER DE QUINCY, Earl of *Winchefter*. The Family of DE BOSCO, or BOIS, were the Poffeffors for feveral Generations, who, in 1331, 3 EDW III were fucceeded by Sir ROGER CORBET.

Of Sir ROBERT CORBET it was afterwards purchafed by that great Luminary of the Law, Sir JOHN FORTESCUE †, Lord Chancellor of *England* in the Reign of HENRY Sixth. Being a zealous Lancaftrian, after the decifive Battle of *Tewkefbury*, he was attainted, and his Eftates confifcated, yet he was permitted to retire to his Manor of *Ebrington*, where he died and was interred. Upon the Death of Sir JOHN BRUGGE in 14 1, who had obtained this Eftate, it was reftored to the FORTESCUES, in which noble Family it has been without Interruption, and is ftill vefted.

The manerial Houfe is large, in the Style of the laft Century.

This Parifh comprifes three Hamlets, 1 *Ebrington*, 2 *Charingworth*, which is diftinctly fpecified in *Domefday*, belonging to RALPH DE TODENI, and containing ten Hides of cultivated Land. It is a Liberty which owes Suit and Service to the King's Court, held at *Afton Subedge* ‡.

From the FURSTANES the chief Eftate paffed to the GREVILLES, who retained it for feveral Centuries. It has been fubfequently the Property of the Earls of GAINSBOROUGH, and the Family of BARNSLEY.

3 *Hidcote Bois*, or *Cote*, given in *Saxon* Times to the Benedictine Abbey of *Evefham*, com *Vigorn*. For many Centuries the greater Part of this Tything belonged to the KEYTES. Sir JOHN KEYTE was created a Baronet in 1660, in Reward of his Services to the Royal Caufe during the Rebellion. His Grandfon, Sir WILLIAM KEYTE, rebuilt their Refidence called "*Norton*," at a very confiderable Expence. In 1741 this Edifice was confumed by Fire, and its Poffeffor perifhed in the Flames §. Soon after that Event, the Eftate was fold by the Executors of Sir DUDLEY RYDER, whofe Son the Right Hon NATHANIEL Lord HARROWBY has fince fucceeded.

The higher Grounds in this Parifh afford many extenfive Profpects over the Vale of *Evefham*, but of Antiquities or Natural Curiofities few Specimens have been difcovered.

---

* "Wm Zouch de *Charingworth* dedit feptem Acras terra Abb & Conv de *Laddefden*, com *Bucks*, et appropriavit Ecclefiam om 1377." Pat. Hen VI in S PAROCH.

† Sir John Fortefcue was the fecond Son of Sir HENRY FORTESCUE Lord Chief Juftice of the Common Pleas in *Ireland*. He was created to the Degree of Serjeant at Law in 1430. In 1442, he was made Lord Chief Juftice of *England* and laftly, Lord High Chancellor. Sir HENRY Sixth. After King EDWARD the IV was feated on the Throne, he followed the Fortunes of the unfortunate Houfe of LANCASTER, and was many Years in exile with Queen MARGARET and Prince EDWARD her Son, previous to the Battle of *Tewkefbury*. His celebrated Book "De Laudibus Legum Anglie" was then written, and dedicated to that Prince. It has fince been publifhed in Latin and Englifh, to one of which Mr SELDEN wrote Notes. His other Work, "On the Difference between an Abfolute and a Limited Monarchy," was publifhed by JOHN FORTESCUE ALAND, fince Lord FORTESCUE. See 1714. Ch at 90.

‡ See Dugdale's Bar. COLLINS, vol VII p 351. GRANGE's Biography, vol I p 57 &c

§ Of this Cataftrophe a very minute Account is given in the Gentleman's Magazine for Apr 1741.

BENEFACTIONS

B E N E F A C T I O N S

WILLIAM KEYTE, Efq in 1635, gave by Will, the Milk of ten fufficient new Milch Kine, from the tenth of May, untill the Feaft of All Saints every Year, to be difpofed of to fuch Poor Perfons as fhould be thought fit by his Executors and Heirs and the Church-wardens for the Time being

INCUMBENTS	PATRONS.	INCUMBENTS	PATRONS
	From 1377 to 1541 Abbey of Bittlefden.	1616 Francis Hains	The fame
1575 Thomas Sweetnam,	Queen Elizabeth	1622 ————	————
——— Thomas Gyles,	The fame	1638 ————	————
1577 Roger Williams,	Bifhop of Gloucefter	1704 Baptift Hickes,	————
1610 Thomas Hawling,	King James, or Bifhop of Briftol *	1715 Thomas Andrews,	Queen Anne
		1759 Jacob Mould, Clerk.	King George II.

PRESENT LORD OF THE MANOR,

The Right Hon MATTHEW Earl FORTESCUE †.

The Perfons fummoned from this Place by the Heralds in 1682 and 1683 were

Sir William Keyte, Bart   Francis Keyte, Efq

At the Election in 1776, Four Freeholders polled from this Parish

The Regifter has its firft Date in 1680

ANNUAL ACCOUNT OF MARRIAGES, BIRTHS, AND BURIALS, IN THIS PARISH

AD	Mar	Bir	Bur	AD	Mar	Bir	Bur	AD	Mar	Bir	Bur	AD	Mar	Bir	Bur
1781	—	22	7	1786	6	16	10	1791				1796			
1782	2	13	4	1787	4	18	4	1792				1797			
1783	2	13	6	1788	7	17	13	1793				1798			
1784	1	12	5	1789	3	13	13	1794				1799			
1785	1	15	11	1790				1795				1800			

INSCRIPTIONS IN THE CHURCH

IN THE CHANCEL.

ON MONUMENTS

Arms; Azure, a Chevron between three Kites heads erafed, Or, for KEYT, a KEYT impaling Or a Cheveron Sable between three Croffes patee fitche Gules, for RILEY, KEYT impaling, quarterly firft and fourth, Sable three Sammons hau rient Argent, for SALMON 2d and 3d Argent, a Bend Azure, between a Mullet and Annulet Gules, for

DOM

In Memoria æterna erit juftus

D pofitum GULIELMI KEYT,

At mirch hic tub r it nunc præ ftolitur, Jefus dorent fius tube c impore exurgere & c reipici nem incorruptionem induere vollent Conftatus W gouin ah vicecom as othero fundus cil

Familia ho int's antiqua, ii quir per trie ateo plus n in fe m in ville hujus primat n hin in Duxit in Uxorem TEL WTINAM RILEY a quo duos filios, JOHANNEM & GULIELMUM, totidemque fufcepit filias ANNAM nempe et ELIZABETHAM

E h nefter erat i us habuitque erga pauperes (viri prefertim hnio)
ΣΤΗΛΗΓΝΑ ΟΙΚΤΗ ΜΕΙΝ utpote qui decem vi tarum uberibus

diftentis lac, a decimo die Maii ufque ad primum Novembris in perpetuum ip orum alimentum mifericors legavit Amicis jucundiffimus, cunct s gratiffimus, optimus fenex lenio confectus, (fummo Bonorum omnium luctu ac defiderio) mortalitatem cum perennitate Placide commutavit, idibus O tobris, Anno Verbi Incarnati 1632, Ætatis fuæ 78 Jo KEYT filius mœftiffimus, entiffimo parenti Hoc pietatis ergo pofuit ΜΝΗΜΟΣΥΝΟΝ

UPON A TABLE T MB, THE EFFIGY OF A MAN RECUMBENT IN A JUDGE'S ROBES

Arms azure, a Bird engrailed, Argen between two Cottile Or FORTESCUE — impaling, Giles Clarions Or GLANVILLE Argent three cros Croflets in Bend able, as before a or i cut a O RWen proper Cubret, Gule n Mul t in Chief, in la Crefcent in Bile Argen 4 on a Bend three Crob is Gules between 6 cros Croflets 6 FORTESCUE

In falutem et in mortu m Memoriam viri Domini JOHANNIS FORTESCUTI, militis grandevi Angliæ Judicis primarii, et precellu tempor fub HENRICO VIto Rege et EDVARDO

principe fummi Cancellarii, Confiliarii Regis prudentiffimi, Legum Angliæ peritiffimi nec non earundem hyperafpiftis fortiffimi qui corporis exuvias latam refurrectione expectantes hic depofuit, Marm oreum hoc Monumentum poh um eft
Anno Domini MDCLXXVII
Voto et expenfis ROBERTI FORTEscuti, Arm i, e uidem I ummæ hæredis nuper defuncti Angligenas intra cancellos jur in et æqu, Cui tenuit cineres jam tenet in via Lex viva ille fuit, patriæ lux fplendida Legis, Forte bonis fcutum fontibus at cutica Clarus erit titulis, clatus myurris arte Clarus virtute aft clarior emicuit Jam n cat in tenebris feluti e ibun cula in orbi N um Virtus rid os non dare tanta ne quit Vivit idhuc FORTESCUTUS laudatus in æva Vivit in Legum Laudibus ille fu

To perpetuate the Memory of that learned and excellent Men Chancellor FORTESCUE this Monume it was repaired by his Defcendant, MATTHEW Lord FORTESCUE, in the Year 176,

* Created Barun FORTESCUE of Cafile Hill, July 5, 1746, 20 Geo II Lord FORTESCUE, and Vifcount EBRINGTON, Auguft 18 1789, 29 Geo III
† See BARRET's Briftol, p 517

On an elegant Marble Monu
ment with two Busts

Arms, 1 Keyt, 2 Sable, three
Bens Argent, a Canton Ermine Porter,
3 Salmon 4 Argent, 1 Bend Azure,
between a Mullet and Annulet Gules
Gules, a Fess between fix Billets Ar
gent, Staveley 6 Keyt,—impal
ing, Ermine, on a Chief indented Gules,
three Escallops O Taylor

Dominus Johannes Keyt,
Jo Fil Guil Nep Baronetti,
(Qui nuperis motibus ex parte Regis
Propriis sumptibus Hippirch is fuit)
Ex Margareta, Guil Tayler
Armig Hærede
sobolem suscepit
D Guil Keyt Baronettum
Joannem Thomam, et Francicum,
Filios,

Elizabetham, Uxorem
Jo. Talbot de Lacock, eq aur

Margaretam Uxorem
Jo Packington, Fil et Hæredis
Jo Packington, Baronetti

Diem obiit ille 26 die Aug
A. D. MDCLXII

Diem obiit illa 28 die Jun
A. D. MDCLXIX

On a large Marble Flat Stone,
with the Inscription round
part of the Verge

Arms 1 Keyt,—impaling Gules,
a Lion Rampant within a Bordure en
grailed Or, Talbot, 3 Taylor, on a
large Escocheon, Talbot, with twenty
four Quarterings

Hic requiescit in Domino
Elizabetha, Johannis Talbott
Conjux, Johannis Keyt
Armigeri primogeniti corporis
formæ extima animi autem dotibus
major, quæ cum peperisset
unicum filium sibi superstitem
religiosissimo exitu vitam clausit,
cujus anima in cœlestem
patriam evocata, placide prope
emigravit, et deposuit quod mortale
fuit, certa spe resurgendi indutum
gloria, obiit primo Aprilis,
Anno Domini 1656, ætatis 21

ON FLAT STONES

Arms Keyt,—impaling on a
Fess three Eaglets displayed, Harri
son

Margaretta
Filia Guilielmi Harrison,
de Caddicroft in com Wigorn, Gen
Uxor secunda Johannis Keyt,
de Ebbrington, in com Glouc
Ar juxta quem hic fita est
Diem obiit Februarii 8, A D 1667,
Ætatis suæ 78

Arms, Keyt, quartering Taylor
Sable, a Fess Ermine, between thre
Crescents O, for Coventry

H S E
De Thomas Keyt
Dni Guilielmi Keyt Baronetti
Et Dnæ Elizabethæ uxoris ejus,
Hon'biles Dno Francisci Coventrye,
Armiger filia natu maxima,
Filius filii in nomine
Summa in Pirentes obfervantia
nulli fecundus
Cœlibum pudicitiam colentium
facile primus, moribus ideo cassus,
e pudore integer,

Secto licet corruptissimo
Cras constituentiæ suspicione obesset,
Natus XIV Cal Sept MDCLXXII
Denatus IV Cal Ju. MDCCII
Qui rem familiarem
Dilectissimo Fratruo Francisco Keyt
Tabellis Testamentariis legavit

Arms, Keyt,—impaling, Porter,
as before

Memoriæ Sacrum
Johannis Keyt Armiger,
Gulielmi filii primogeniti,
Qui reclinavit annos in hoc
pulvere depositum Consortem tori
fidelissimam prudentem providam,
et puerperam Thomæ Porter
Generosi, filiam duxit Janam, quæ
charissima reliquit conjugi pignora
Septem filios, et quinque filias,
Prius a Wigornia postea Glocestria,
V dit Vi comitens, Pacique præpositum
Regis, Reipublicæ, Religionis ergo Dux,
Vicecomes, Tetarches bellum fortiter,
pacem civiliter, gessit coluitque
Nobilis ingenui, vitæ intemeratæ,
Pietatis } in { Deum Principem,
Fide itatis Principem,
Charitatis } { Proximum
Exemplar æmulandum Communi
procerum populique jactura
Ho occubuit Aprilis 23,
Anno Salvatoris 1662, ætatis 76
Johannes Keyt, Baronettus, filius
natus posuit

Arms Quarterly, Keyt, Porter,
Salmon, and Taylor On an Esco
cheon of Pretence, Coventry, as be
fore

H S E
Hic U Gulielmus Keyt, Baronettus,
Qui uxorem duxit Elizabetham,
Honorabilis Francisci Coventrye,
Filiam e Honoratissima
Thomæ Baronis Coventrye,
Magni Sigilli Custodis Nep'tem
Ex qua suscepit quatuor filios,
Johannem, Anconimum,
Gulielmum Thomam,
(Quibus omnibus superstes fuit)
Filiasque duas Margaritam et
Dorotheam Pauperibus et operariis
indies benevolum Regibus etiam
exultantibus, semper fidelem
Hujus Ecclesiæ Pastoribus
(quibus annuatim solvendi decem
legavit libras)
In perpetuum se præbuit munificum
Mortiferum (quo laboravit)
morbum anno vere Christiano
perpessus, tandem placide obdormivit
S Andreæ Festo
Anno Christi incarnati MXCIIIo
Ætatis suæ supra LXm VIo

Arms, Quarterly of 6, Keyt, as
before a Label for Difference

Fratrum utero haud ita pridem de
functo, Familiæ ejusdem et luctum
renovavit Mœss præmatura ademus via
Wilhelmi Keyt, Armigeri
Dni Wilhelmi Keyt Baronetti,
Filii natu tertii, et, fi Deus minuisset,
Hæredis futuri
Qui ex Generis Thalamique
Consorte fidelissima,
Meritoque dilectissima, Agnete
D mi Johannis Croston de Clopton
Equitis Aurati filia primogenita,
Postquam septem procreasset Filios,
Wilhelmum, Coventrium,
Thomam Gilbertum
Johannem, Franciscum,
et Hastingum et tres Filias,
Elizabetham Barbaram et
Margaretam, ab omnibus

deploratus hinc emigravit
Festi Omnium Sanctorum Vigilia
Ad participandam Sanctorum in hac
sortem Anno post Christum natum
MDCCIIo, Ætatis suæ XXXIX

Arms, Keyt,—impaling Argent,
on three Bars Sable fix Cinquefoils of
the Field for Dayrell

Memoriæ Sacrum
Thomæ Keyt de Wolford Armiger,
Johannis filii natu minoris,
Cognatis et necessariis amicissimi,
Ægrotis et egenis munificentissimi,
Omnibus humanissimi, fato perfunsti
V Idus Januar Anno Salutis MDCCI
Ætatis suæ LXXX
Wilhelmus Keyt, Armiger,
Quem Hæredem ex asse natum
Lapidem hunc sepulchralem posuit

Arms Keyt, impaling Dayrell

Mors sexuvias in hunc Tumulum
recondidat certa spe resurgendi ad
vitam immortalem
Matron pientissima
Maria Gualteri Dayrell
de Abendon in agro B rcheria
Armigeri, Filii qui taxit et functer
bis nupta sui primum, Reverendo
Johanni Morris, S I D
Ædis Christi apud Oxonienses
Canonico, et Linguæ Ebrææ Profeffori
Regio D uade rei militaris peritissimo
Duci, Thomæ Keyt,
de Wolford Magna,
In comitatu War vici Armigero
Nullam post se reliquit sobolem,
Non en vero nælius et multo perennius,
quam quod habere poterat a filius
et filiabu Postquam annos plus
minus septuaginta pud c,
sancte, p e peregisset,
Terreni m deposuit tabernaculum,
Ut æ ernum in Cœlis habere
domicilium, nono Kalendas Novembris,
Anno Æræ Christianæ MDCLXXXI

Here lyeth the Body of
William Keyt second Son to
William Keyt, Esq
who departed this Life March 28
Anno Domini 16 , ætatis suæ 57

Arms, On a Lozenge, Keyt

Here lyeth the Body of
Miss Jane Keyt Daughter of
Mr Francis Keyt,
and Anne his Wife of Hitchcoate,
who departed this Life
the 30th Day of June An Dom 164
Ætatis suæ 2d

Arms, Keyt,—impaling, quar
terly, Argent and Gules in the 2d and
3d a Fret Or over all, on a Bend
ble, three Leopards of the fir for
Spencer

Here lies the Body of
Anne Keyt Daughter of
Sir William Spencer,
of Yardington in the County of
Oxford, Baronet and of
Constance his Wife the Daughter of
Sir Thomas Lucy of Chilecott
in the County of Warwick which said
Anne was the late Wife of
Francis Keyt of Ebbrington, Esq
and deceased the 29th of May,
in the Year 1687
A Lady dignified not only by her Birth,
but besides her other Virtues, for her
Love and Fidelity to her Husband

O 4

ON FLAT STONES IN THE NAVE.

Here lieth the Body of
the Rev Mr WILLIAM STANTON,
Minister of this Parish
who departed this Life,
April 7, 170. aged 33
declared as ch xli v 13

Here lyeth the Body of
FRANCES, the Wife of the
Rev Mr THOMAS ANDREWS,
Vicar of this Church,
and Daughter of MILDMAY,
Son of the Hon W FANE D D
Sixth Son of the Right Hon
Sir FRANCIS FANE, Earl of
WESTMORELAND She died
March 1, 1720, aged 32

To the Memory of the
Rev Mr THOMAS ANDREWS,
Vicar of this Church,
who departed this Life July 21, 1738,
aged 68

To the Memory of DOROTHEA,
the second Wife of the
Rev Mr THOMAS ANDREWS,
Vicar of this Church,
and Daughter of
Mr WILLIAM KEYT, of this Town,
who departed this Life
the 26th of Jan 173½, aged 34

Here lyeth the Body of
WILLIAM DANIEL, Son to
ROBERT DANIEL He married
MARGARET, the Daughter of
WILLIAM MILWARD of Stourton,
i com Warwick deceased the
5th March A D 1647 æt suæ 89

Here lyeth the Body of
THOMAS BARNSLEY,
of Charringworth Gent
who departed this Life, Sept 13, 1711.

IN THE SOUTH TRANSEPT

ON A NEAT MARBLE MONUMENT

Underneath lieth the Body of
JOHN JONES Esq He died the
5th of Sept 1786, aged 41
From his benevolent Disposition,
gentle Manners, and amiable Character;
he will always be remembered by
those who knew him with a tender
Concern From his affectionate
Temper, steady Friendship, and
honorable Principles,
his Loss will he ever felt by a Brother
(who caused this Stone to be placed
here in testimony of his Virtues)
until he himself mingles with the Dust

Here lyeth the Body of
Mr JOHN BARNSLEY,
the Son of Mr THOMAS BARNSLEY,
of Charringworth Gent
who departed his Life 20 April, 1767,
aged 76 Years

Here lyeth the Body of
JOHN BARNSLEY Gent
of Charringworth
who departed this Life,
Dec 6, 1778, aged 6,

Here also lieth the Body of
MARY, the Daughter of
THOMAS BARNSLEY, Gent
of Charringworth, who departed this
Life Nov 23, 1708

In Memory of SUSANNAH,
the Wife of Lieut SAMUEL BARNSLEY
of Hurst near Reading,
in the County of Berks,
who departed this life the 8th Day of
Sept 1776, aged years

On a very old Tomb are the Arms of
KEYT, impaling RILEY

ON A FREE STONE MONUMENT AGAINST THE WEST END OF THE CHURCH

To the Memory of
MICHAEL WESTON and ELIZABETH
his Wife He died March 20, 1756,
aged 55 Years, she died Aug 29, 1769,
aged 65 Years

In Memory of
MARY, Wife of JOHN MOULD
(Nephew to the Rev Mr Mould)
who in a Journey from Town to see her
Friends was arrested by Death
The Soul took its flight into the
invisible World and her Remains are
consigned to rest here till the Resurrection,
she died Sep 5, 1775,
in the 29th Year of her Age

In Memory of ELIZABETH,
Daughter of the Rev Mr TYRER,
and MARY his Wife,
who died July 7, 1761,
in the 13th Year of her Age

Also in Memory of THOMAS,
Son of the Rev Mr MOULD,
and SARAH his Wife
who died Sept 25, 1761,
aged four Months

ON FLAT AND HEAD STONES.

	Died	Aged		Died	Aged
Mary, Wife of John Leeke, and Daughter of Sam and Eliz Keyte	19 Sept 1704	28	Richard Fletcher	7 June 1779	67
William Keyte	29 Sept 1769	30	Susannah his Daughter	27 July 1783	23
Mary, Wife of William Whitehead	7 Jun 1727	60	Samuel Southam	11 Mar 1771	66
William Whitehead	Mar 1730	94	Sarah his Wife	1770	
Mary, Wife of John Purser	22 Apr 1756	67	Elizabeth Daughter of Thomas and Hannah Southam	2 Sept 1743	0
Richard Keyte	19 Sept 1784	70	Thomas their Son	16 Apr 1741	3
Judith, Wife of William Whitehead	18 Mar 1780	62	Mary and Hester their Daughters	1 Nov 1742	13
John Purser	11 May, 1770	80		2 July, 1752	12
Robert Purser	30 July, 1707	60	Hannah Southam	16 Jun 1747	60
Hannah Wife of John Purser	11 Oct 1731	75	James Righton	14 Dec 1755	72
Elizabeth their Daughter	4 Mar 1738	38	Ann his Wife	13 Nov 1757	21
John father of Hidcott son	3 Mar 1722	55	Samuel Righton of Hidcott	14 Feb 1773	6
Joseph Purser	2 Jun 1776	60	Thomas, son of Thomas and Sarah Jones	6 Dec 1760	—
Mary, Wife of Thomas Lawney	22 June, 1729	23			
William Fletcher	29 Feb 1752	87	Elizabeth, Wife of Richard Smith	Nov 1783	52
Valentine his Wife	2 Mar 1732	69	John Huson	11 Apr 1764	55
Thomas Fletcher	11 June, 1770	71	Thomas Procter	1 Dec 1776	61
Elizabeth, Daughter of Robert and Ann Shorte	1 Dec 1749	1	Agathe his Wife	24 Sept 1770	51
			Thomas Booker	16 Mar 1771	6
William Hobbins	13 June, 1776	67	Elizabeth his Wife	Aug 1761	65
Ann his Wife	11 May, 1780	71	John Gibbs	14 Apr 1780	30
Dinah Unit, Son of Nathaniel and Mary Unit	22 Mar 1777	28	Jane Daughter of William and Alice Purser	6 Feb 1757	
Mary their Daughter	1 Feb 1764	23	Alice Wife of William Purser	10 Nov 1760	85
Nathaniel Unit	23 Jun 1789	80	William Purser	9 Feb 1776	66
Mary his Wife	5 Feb 1769	61	Mary Purser	1 Jun 1774	42
John Keyte	20 Dec 1776	56	Thomas Smith	3 Aug 1784	17
Mary Beard	24 Aug 1763	21	Ann, Wife of Thomas Roberts	6 Apr 1765	38
Susannah, Wife of Richard Fletcher	2 Sept 1751	77	Thomas Roberts	2 Oct 1765	28
Richard Fletcher	13 Nov 1766	84	Sarah his Wife	23 Sept 1773	60
Ann, Daughter of Richard and Sarah Fletcher	20 Mar 1762	9	William Carter	11 Jun 1774	81
Agathe their Daughter	21 Mar 1773	3	Mary, Wife of Charles Ueal	16 Mar 1744	41
Joshua their Son	20 June, 1776	—	Samuel, Son of William and Elizabeth Keyt	6 May, 1710	20
			Elizabeth, Wife of Samuel Keyt	16 July, 1708	20

CXII. EDGEWORTH.

A NAME defcriptive of the Situation of this Village upon feveral eafy Acclivities. It is a Parifh of no great Extent in the Hundred of *Bifs*, fix Miles Northweft from *Cirencefter*, in twelve in the precifely oppofite Direction from the City of Gloucefter. The Parifh contains 2021, or Acres, including the common Fields and Woodlands, of a light Soil and chiefly in Tillage; in the Valley are fertile Meadows on the Banks of the Rivulet *Froome*.

The Benefice, which is rectorial, is a Member of the Deanery of *Stonehoufe*, and the Church has *St. Mary* for its Patron Saint. It is conftructed with a Nave or Pace only, with a great embattled Tower, at the Weft End, of early Norman Architecture. The few Veftiges of Antiquity it exhibits, are the Portrait of a Prieft epifcopally habited, a Lavatory and curious Subfellium of Stone Bench, on the left Side of the Altar, with the Steps of the ancient Rood Loft. *Domefday* Books records *Ricardus* in Fact as the Proprietor of "Egefwrde," which Manor was originally connected with *Painfwick*, having been jointly inherited by AUDOMIR DE VALENCE, Earl of *Pembroke*, in 1324, 17 Edw. II. In the fucceeding Reign it paffed in Dower to the noble Family of TALBOT, of *Goarton Caftle* in *Herefordfhire*. In 1397, 20th RICH. II. it was leafed by RICHARD Lord TALBOT, by fervice of half a Knights Fee to THOMAS RALEGH, Efq of *Farnborough* in the County of *Warwick*, whofe Defcendants held by Soccage as of the Manor of *Painfwick*, during a Courfe of more than 20 Years; Sir GEORGE RALEGH, Knt joining with EDWARD his Son, in 1602, 44 Eliz. conveyed it by Deed of Sale to Sir HENRY POOLE, Knt of *Saperton*. About 1670, when the Property of that Family in this County was difperfed, *Edgeworth* was purchafed by NATHANIEL RIDLER, Efq. who built the prefent Manerial Houfe foon afterwards, and made it his Refidence. Upon the Death of THOMAS RIDLER, Efq. a Partition of the Eftate was made between his three Co-heirs ELIZABETH, the Wife of WILLIAM KINGS, of *Charlton Kings*, whofe Share is inherited by DODINGTON HUNT, Efq. and MARY, who died unmarried in 1774, and bequeathed her Share with the Manor to her Nephew, THOMAS BRERETON, Efq. after the Deceafe of her younger Sifter BARBARA, late the Wife of the Rev. RICHARD BRERETON, M. A. Rector, who now holds the third Portion in her Right. There is a fmall Freehold only in this Parifh, excepting a Part of *Pinbury* defcribed under *Duntifborne Militis*. A Mill and Meadow, originally given to the Abbey of *St. Peter* in GLOUCESTER, now belongs to the Manor. The Face of the County in this lone *Cotefwold* is well cultivated, and derives much picturefque Beauty from the numerous Woodlands and Groves of Beech, which grow fpontaneoufly, the natural Produce of the Soil.

BENEFACTIONS

JOAN RIDLER, by Will, dated Aug. 27, 1714, and MARY RIDLER, May 9, 1715, devifed 100l. the Intereft to be applied to teach poor Children to read.

THOMAS RIDLER, Rector in 1701, bequeathed the Intereft of 5l. to the Poor for eve.

JOHN RIDLER in 1724 left the Intereft of 50l. for the fame Purpofe.

ANNE RIDLER, Widow, gave by Will, April 1, 1717, 100l. the Intereft to be diftributed annually, according to the Difcretion of the Truftees.

—— WARD, Relict of THOMAS WARD, Rector, gave 5l. the Intereft to be applied as the other Charities. The Date of this Donation is not known.

INCUMBENTS	PATRONS		INCUMBENTS	PATRONS
16— Henry Hayward,	————		1703 Will. Dighton, M. A.	The fame
—— Thomas Ward			1707 Edw. Jogger Griffin,	The fame
—— Nathaniel Capel	Sir Henry Poole		1729 Samuel Ridler, H. B.	Thomas Ridler, Efq
1684 Thomas Ridler	Nathaniel Ridler, Efq		1765 Rich. Brereton, M. A.	Upon his own Prefentation
1701 John Ellis,	The fame			

PRESENT LORD OF THE MANOR.

THOMAS BRERETON, Efq.

* See the Pedigree of DE VATTE *Warwickfhire* p. 380.
† It appears that this Vill was not included in the Tenure of the Manor of *Painfwick* while *Edwarde* was feifed at the Conqueft by Jun, as held in 1356 by JOHN, after which Each of *Cirewarden* and where now in the *fame* and *Weston*.

The

The Persons summoned from this Place by the Heralds in 1682 and 1683 were,
Nathaniel Ridler, Esq and Henry Wyndowe, Esq

At the Election in 1776, Two Freeholders polled from this Parish

The first Date of the Register is in 1556

ANNUAL ACCOUNT OF MARRIAGES, BIRTHS, AND BURIALS, IN THIS PARISH

A D	Mar	Bir	Bur	A D	Mar	Bir	Bur	A D	Mar	Bir	Bur	A D	Mar	Bir	Bur
1781	—	3	3	1786	1	2	3	1791				1796			
1782	—	2	3	1787	1	4	4	1792				1797			
1783	—	3	5	1788	—	2	1	1793				1798			
1784	3	5	1	1789	—	2	1	1794				1799			
1785	1	2	3	1790				1795				1800			

INSCRIPTIONS IN THE CHURCH.

IN THE CHANCEL

ON A MARBLE MONUMENT

In the Church-yard adjoining
lie the Remains of
Mrs BARBARA BRERETON,
one of the co heiresses of
THOMAS RIDLER, Esq
and Wife of the
Rev RICHARD BRERETON,
Rector of this Parish
To her Family and near Connections
she was an invaluable Friend,
to the Poor a liberal Benefactress,
to all an Example of Sincerity,
Generosity, and unaffected Piety.
She died suddenly but not unprepared,
Aug 23, 1767, at 64

ON A FLAT STONE

In Deum pius, in uxorem et liberos
amans, in conjunctos benignus,
in omnes dum vixit isti issue
sub hoc lapide, gloriosam expectans
resurrectionem in Domino, mortuus
et sepultus est, IRA CIRCIS MARSHE,
Generosus Junii, A D 1630

ON FLAT STONES IN
THE NAVE

Here lyeth the Body of
ANTHONY SADLIER, Gent
who was charitable to the poor of
this Parish and lived above
One Hundred Years, who died and
was buried the 2d day of February,
Anno Domini, 16

On the left side of this Stone
is interred waiting to be raised to
eternal Glory, the Body of
Mrs ANN GODDARD Relict of
Mr RICHARD GODDARD and the
Daughter of Mr ANTHONY SADLER,
who lived to a good old Age,
the first day of November, 16

Here lyeth the Body of
JEROME JEFFEREYS, of West Hood,
who died the 7th of June,
Anno Dom 1606

In Memory of
RICHARD GODDARD, Gen who
was buried the 26th day of June 170

IN THE CHURCH YARD, ON TOMBS

HENRY WITTS,
buried Oct 15, 1730, aged 83

ANN, his Wife,
died Jan 0, 1739 40, aged 86

HENRY WITTS, Jun
died Sept 6, 1732, aged 7

GEORGE WITTS,
died Dec 6, 1761, aged 7

JOHN BROWN
died March 3, 1726,
aged 63

MARY RIDLER, 2nd Daughter of
THOMAS RIDLER Esq
died Nov 19, 1774 aged 5
ANN, Relict of THOMAS RIDLER, Esq
April 25, 1760, aged 7

ON FLAT AND HEAD STONES

	Died	Aged		Died	Aged
Charles Billinger, sen	10 Aug 1730	64	William their Son	20 Oct 17	—
Hester smith	2 Sept 1754	14	Elizabeth their Daughter	16 June, 17 3	
Mary Smith	6 Mar 1680	—	Ann Wife of Benjamin Dodge	1 Oct 1740	38
John smith	12 Apr 1735	58	Mary Wife of James their Son	29 July 1767	25
June, Wife of Henry Coal	21 June 1771	55	John Parsons of Dunsbourne Rous	22 Mar 1771	86
George Blackwell	28 Nov 1771	73	Elizabeth his Wife	20 July, 1702	6
Mary his Wife	, July, 1762	1	June Wife of John Brown	28 Jan 1745	
Mary their Daughter	19 Feb 171	11	Mary Hilles buried	18 Mar 1742	11

CXIII. ELBERTON.

IS fituate in the lower Divifion of the Hundred of *Berkeley*, eleven Miles North from *Briftol*, and twenty eight from *Gloucefter* on the South-weft   The Village lies in the Vale   on the Laft fide of the River *Severn*, the Soil is a ftrong red Clay, and produces excellent Herbage, a very fmall Portion of the Lands are in Tillage

In Mr SMYTH's MSS are the fubjoined Notices

" *Elberton*, or *Alberton*, *Ethrigeton*, or *Eldberton* quifi, the old Barton, or Farme Place   In D nefile
" Booke it is written *Eldberton*, where WILLIAM the Conquerour had five Hides of Land in Demefne
" The Manor is now the Inheritance of HUMFRY HOOK, a Merchant of *Briftol*, who purchafed the
" fame of Sir ARTHUR SMYTHES, Sonn of GEORGE SMYTHES, a Goldfmith in *London*   who purchafed
" the fame of WALTER WALSH of *Sodbury*, Efq to whom HENRY WALSH his Cofen (afterwards flaine
" in fingle Combat, by Sir EDWARD WINTOUR) conveyed his and other Manors, which HENRY was
" the Sonne of NICHOLAS WALSH, Sonne of MAURICE WALSH (who dy'd in 4th MARIA) fon of Sir
" JOHN WALSH, Sonne of Sir JOHN WALSH of Or *ton*, and ELIZABETH his Wife, Daughter of
" RICHARD FORSTER, als FORSTER of *Sodbury*   It is holden by Knight's Service in Capite of the
" Crowne   This Manor was Parcell of the Hernefe viz Nookes or Corners of the great Manor of *Bereche*,
" and by Kinge HENRY Second in the firft Yeare of his Raigne, granted (inter alia) to ROBERT, Son
" of HARDING and his Heirs, who afterwardes about the 12th of the faid King gave the fame to
" ROBERT his thirde Sonne and his Heires, and dyed 5 Yeares after, and by the Death of the faid
" ROBERT, Sonne of ROBERT in the Time of King JOHN, it defcended to MAURICE DE CANT his Son
" and Heire, by whofe Death without Iffue in 14th of HENRY III the Manor came to ROBERT DE
" GOURNAY, Son and Heire of EVA, Sifter and Heire of the faid MAURICE, which ROBERT, dying in
" 53d HEN III left it by Defcent to ANSELM DE GOURNAY his Sonne, and by his Death in 1 EDW I
" it defcended to JOHN DE GOURNAY his Son, who dying without Iffue, five Yeares after his Father left
" the fame to ELIZABETH his Sifter and Heire, who was married to Sir JOHN AT ADAM, who di d
" in 5th EDW II leaving Iffue, by his faid Wife, THOMAS AT ADAM, who by Fine and other
" Affurances in 4th EDW III fold this Manor with *Kingfweston* to MAURICE BERKELEY, Knt and his
" Heires, fecond Son of MAURICE, Lord BERKELEY, the thirde of that Name, who had Iffue, Sir
" THOMAS BERKELEY, called of *Ewelme*, and died 21 EDW III leaving Iffue MAURICE BERKELEY,
" who died 2 HEN IV leaving Iffue, Sir MAURICE BERKELEY, borne after the Death of his Father,
" who dyed the 4th EDW IV leaving Iffue Sir MAURICE BERKELEY, Knt to whom this Manor
" defcended, as the Inquifition, found inut Heire after his Death, theweth   The faid Sir WILLIAM,
" then 28 Yeares old, died in 17 HEN VII leaving Iffue Sir ROBERT BERKELEY   But, forafmuch as
" the faid Sir WILLIAM BERKELEY was in the 1ft HEN VII attainted of High Treafon by Parliament,
" for partaking with Kinge RICHARD III and this Manor granted by King HENRY VII to JASPAR,
" Earle of *Pembroke* in Taile, though the faid Sir WILLIAM was reftored to moft of his Lands after
" Compofition made with the faid Earle and his Sonne, Sir RICHARD, his Father's Death, yet
" with neither of them are found to dye feized of the Manor, nor to fue Livery thereof nor any of their
" Pofteritie after them, I cannot but conceive, but that one of them fold away the fame, but when or
" to whom I have not obferved

" In this Parifh of *Alberton* is one ancient Freehold, created by the Ifoe of he ANSELM DE GOURNAY,
" by a Grant thereof made to THOMAS NORRY and his Heires, who after fold the fame to THOMAS
" TROYN and his Heires, and he to JOHN CHAMBERS and his Heires, all which feveral Altera-
" tions are laid downe in a Prebon, dated July 18, 10 EDW III being made without Lycence   Yet,
" that Recorde faith that thefe Landes were holden of JOHN INDIAN in Capite and are now (Anno 1639)
" the Inheritance of THOMAS HORTONS in Right of JAMES SEGAR, worth 10s per ann', which had in the
" Name and Pofteritie of CHAMBERS continued in lineal Defcent till EDMOND CHAMBERS (that yet is),
" and his Father fold the fame of late Yeares

" The Church of *Elberton* is in the Deanery of *Briftol*, and in fome Deeds faid it alfo *Elton* to
" belong to the Mother Church of *Almondfbury*, as Chapels the col

Notes relative to *Elberton* are found in the following Record
   Inquif 5 HEN III poft Mortem ROBERTI DE GOURNAY
   ——— 1 EDW I poft Mort ANSELMI DE GOURNAY
   ——— 21 EDW III poft Mort MAURICII DE M DEL BERKELEY
   ——— 29 EDW III poft Mort THOMAS BERKELEY DE UI Y Canah
And of the detached Freehold
   Inquif 11 EDW I poft Mort JOHANNIS TROYNS
   ——— 13 EDW III Writ " Ad quod damnum   SMYTH MSS "

1   1o

To this accurate Account of the Property of this Parish it remains only to be added, that the manerial Estate paffed in Dower about the Middle of the laft Century with CECILY, Daughter of the abovementioned HUMPHRY HOOKE to Sir ROBERT CANN, Bart and continued in that Family till the Death of the laft Baronet in 1765 leaving no Iffue, he was fucceeded by his Nephew ROBERT CANN JEFFERIES, Efq who died in 1773 unmarried His Sifter, who is the Relict of the late Sir HENRY LIPPINCOTT, Bart inherited from him The Freehold, above deferibed, is now divided amongft feveral Proprietors, the larger Part of it has been transferred from the Families of BROWNE and VAUGHAN to the GOLDNEYS of Clifton Lands in Ailberton once belonged to the Monaftery of St Auguftine near Briftol " Ex dono WILLIELMI filii GREGORII, 40 folidatas Terrra in Ailberto e ficut comes WILLIELMUS " eas confirmavit *

The Living is a Vicarage, or Chapelry, in the Diocefe of Briftol, but in the Archdeaconry of GLOUCESTER, of the certified Value of 46l per ann confolidated with Olvefton in 1767 By the Act of Union the Dean and Chapter of Briftol prefent twice, and the Bifhop once, the latter has the intermediate Turn † The Impropriation valued, at the Diffolution of St Auguftine's, at 6l has been fince given in Augmentation of the perpetual Curacy of Horfield

There are grounds for Conjecture, that the Church, dedicated to St Mary, was built by the Convent, in the 13th Century It has a Nave, two Ailes, with a Tower and Spire in the Middle The whole is now under complete Repair, having been much dilapidated from Age No veftiges of Antiquity remain, excepting a large ftone Sarcophagus, without Arms, Ornament, or Infcription Upon the rifing Grounds, above the Church, a Camp or Outpoft, probably Roman, and commanding a fine View of the River, is ftill eafily to be traced

---

BENEFACTIONS

JOHN HICKS by Will bequeathed 40l the Intereft of which to be diftributed on the 27th of December yearly in Bread and Meat

The prefent Incumbent is JOHN CAMPLIN, D D prefented by the Dean and Chapter of Briftol in 767

PRESENT LADY OF THE MANOR,

Dame CATHERINE LIPPINCOTT

It does not appear that any Perfon was fummoned from this Parifh by the Heralds in 1682 and 1683

At the Election in 1776, Two Freeholders polled from this Parifh

The earlieft Date in the Regifter occurs in 1653

ANNUAL ACCOUNT OF MARRIAGES, BIRTHS, AND BURIALS, IN THIS PARISH

A.D	Mar	Bir	Bur	A D	Mar	Bir	Bur	A D	Mar	Bir	Bur	A D	Mar	Bir	Bur
1781	—	4	3	1786	—	—	1	1791			1	1796			
1782	3	1	5	1787	—	1	2	1792				1797			
1783	—	1	5	1788	—	3	3	1793				1798			
1784	1	—	5	1789		2	2	1794				1799			
1785	3	2	1	1790				1795				1800			

INSCRIPTIONS IN THE CHURCH.

IN THE NAVE
ON FLAT STONES

ON A BRASS PLATE

Her lyeth the Body of
Jofeph Fricker Jun fon of
Jofeph Fricker, M D of Locking on,
Qui obiit Aug 2/, 1707

In Memory of Eufeta, the Son of
Thomas Edmonds, who died
17th July, 1781, aged 7 Years

Here lyeth the Body of
Thomas Winfield Yeoman,
buried 9th May A D 1671

Here lyeth the Body of
JOSEPH FRICKER, late of Olvefton,
Gent and SARAH his Wife,
who were buried,
SARAH the 29th of June, 1711,
JOSEPH the 13th of Feb 1710

CHRISTIAN the Wife of
THOMAS EDMONDS of this Parifh,
and Daughter of the aforefaid
JOSEPH FRICKER, departed this Life
the 21ft Day of July, 1731
in the 30th Year of her Age

Here lyeth the Body of
JOHN WALL of this Parifh, Yeoman,
who departed this Life 4th of July,
1741, aged 74 Years

Here lyeth the Body of
BRIDGET SMITH, Widow,
who was buried May 8, 1671,
Ætatis fuæ 82

ROUND THE VERGE

Here lie buried the Body of
HENRY SMITH, who deceafed
October 11, 1651

ADJOINING

Alfo the Body of MARIAN SMITH
Widow She died June 1671
Ætatis fuæ 75

---

* DUGDALE'S Mon vol II p 213
Thefe LANDS were granted to PAUL Bufh and his Succeffors, Bifhops of Briftol, June 10, 1541, 34 Hen VIII
BARRET Briftol p 13

† BACON'S Liber Regis, p 118

IN THE CHURCH YARD, ON TOMBS.

ANN, Wife of JOHN HICKS, jun
buried June 8, 1724 aged 53

JOHN HICKS fen.
died Oct 16, 17 7,
in the 69 h Year of his age

JONE his Wife buried Nov 11, 1688,
aged about 50

JOHN HICKS died Sept 10, 1733,
aged 54

JOSEPH STEPHENS died Dec 8, 1745,
aged 55 Years

ELIZABETH his Wife
died July 14, 1723,
aged 40 Years
SARAH their Daughter,
died Oct 19, 1743, aged 26 Years

JOSEPH and RACHAEL, their Children,
died young.

THOMAS JOHNSON fen
died July 1, 1766, aged 82 Years

ELIZABETH his Wife
died April 15, 17 3,
in the 88th Year of her Age

JOHN HIGNELL, Son of
ANTHONY and ELIZABETH HIGNELL,
died Feb 18, 1782, aged 70

ESTHER his Wife
died Dec. 15, 1,86 aged 57

JACOB MILLETT,
died Feb 14, 1776, aged 73

BENJAMIN his Son
died Dec 12 1761, aged 24.
JOSEPH his Son
died Feb 22, 1766, aged 32

ELEANOR and ANN his Daughters
died Young

MARY PARTRIDGE
died March 20, 1766, aged 88.

ON HEAD AND FLAT STONES

	Died	Aged		Died	Aged
Henry Hicks	4 Mar 1766	80	Mary their Daughter	2 Nov 1725	16
Martha his Wife	15 Feb 17,7	52	Betty Wife of Moses Hignell of Ol veston	23 Mar 1745	60
Several of their Children died Young			William Smith	29 Apr 1713	66
Elizabeth, Wife of John Johnson,	27 Feb 1762	45	Abigail his Wife	13 Jun 1729	84
Hannal their Daughter died an Infant			Thomas their Son	1, Feb 1713	27
William Johnson	12 July, 1751	51	Thomas Davies	12 Aug 1737	70
Susannah his Wife	19 Dec 1785	82	Thomas Smith Davies	14 June, 1741	27
Ann, their Daughter, and Wife of John Cox	15 Dec 1756	23	Mary Wife of Thomas Davies	18 Apr 1744	65
Mary, Wife of John Johnson	4 Mav 17 9	33	Elizabeth Wife of Zachariah Jones	31 Nov 1767	61
John Johnson	11 Apr 1758	47	Mary, Wife of James Kennion, and Daughter of Thomas and Mary Davies	23 Feb 1750	55
William Bradley	7 July, 1729	65			
Mary his Widow	29 Apr 1738	—	James Kennion, fen	10 June, 1777	60
William Gunter	10 Oct 17,7	64	Mary and Elizabeth Daughe of Richard and Mary West of West bury, died Infants		
Mary his Wife	27 Dec 1741	66			
William their Son	15 Mar 1759	40	Mary, Daughter of Benjamin and Eleanor Hignell	15 Sept 1740	—
Samuel Bayley	11 May, 1753	59	Mordecai their Son	15 Feb. 1742	—
Joseph Bayley	16 Jan 1724	70	Elizabeth Smith, Spinster,	4 Aug 1710	60
Mary his Wife	6 July, 17,6	81	John Pearce	4 Oct 1721	82
Anthony Hignell	14 Sept 1720	52	Mary, Wife of John Johnson	4 May, 1719	33
Elizabeth his late Wife	25 July, 1748	69	John Johnson	11 Apr 1758	47
Thomas, } their Sons {	2, Jan 1729	31	Susannah, Wife of Thomas Hignell	0 June, 1779	35
Mordecai,	23 Aug 1748	19			
Sarah their Daughter	1 Mar 1759	42			
Stephen Hignell of Cote	10 Sept 1742	72			
Dinah his Wife	11 Nov 1737	66			

CXIV. ELKESTONE,

OR ALFDESTANE as denominated by the *Saxons*, is a Parish of the middle Dimensions, situate in the Hundred of *Rapsgate* near the great Foss Road to *Cirencester*, from whence it is distant eight Miles on the North-west, seven South from *Cheltenham*, and ten Eastward from GLOUCESTER.

Fifteen Hundred Acres, by Computation, are included in the Terrier, of a dry and stony Soil, principally tilled, the Harvest, though unusually late, is very productive. The Plan of large Inclosures has been lately very generally adopted in this District.

The Living is a Rectory in the Deanery of *Stonehouse*, endowed with a Glebe of 100 Acres, and all Tythes.

Of the Church, dedicated to *St. John th Evangelist*, the original Construction is evidently as early as the *Saxon* Æra. It has a Nave only, with a Tower at the West end, sixty-six Feet high, and of plain Gothic Proportions. To the Walls are affixed four Escocheons 1 Quarterly, over all a Bend FITZ NICHOL 2 Quarterly, per Fess indented ACTON 3 Barry of eight,—POYNTZ 4 Effaced. By these its Date is ascertained during the Reign of RICHARD II and the probable Founder to have been Sir JOHN POYNTZ, Knt to whom the Manor and Advowson had descended by Heirship. The Tower is connected with the Nave, by a very lofty and elegant Gothic Arch. On the outside of the whole Building, under the Roofing on either Side, is a Series of Heads and Beasts placed horizontally. They exhibit the Sculpture of a very remote Age. The Door case is finished by a Saxon Bas relief, representing CHRIST sitting on a Throne and holding a Book, with his Symbols, a Lamb and a Dove. But the most perfect Specimen of that Style is the Inside of the Chancel, which, externally more lofty than the Nave, is not above 12 Feet in height, with a vaulted Roof of circular Arches, enriched with Scrolls of various and elaborate Sculpture *.

In the most ancient Records of the Manor, the Families of DE ACTON and POYNTZ are recited. JOHN DE ACTON held it in 1315, 8 EDW II. In 1377, 1 RICH II. Sir JOHN POYNTZ of *Iron Acton* inherited this with the other Estates of that Family, in right of his Mother, and it continued in his Descendants for many Generations. It passed from them about the Commencement of the last Century, when, JAMES HUNTLEY, Esq second Son of GEORGE HUNTLEY, Knt of *Frocester Court*, occurs as Proprietor, and about 1630, it was sold by him or his Heirs to WILLIAM, afterwards Earl CRAVEN. From that Nobleman it has been transmitted to the present Possessor, whose Patent of Creation bears Date, Dec 11, 1665, 17th CHARLES II †

HAMLETS *Cockleford* situate on the Banks of the Rivulet *Churn*. 2 *Combend* lies upon an Acclivity, about a Mile eastward from the Church. It includes a very considerable Estate, which claims the Privilege of a Manor, and became the Property of the Family of ISTCOURT, prior to 1599, 41 ELIZ, when, THOMAS ISTCOURT, Esq dying bequeathed it to his Son. About 1614, it was transferred by Sale to Sir JOHN HORTON, Knt of *Broughton*, com *Wilts*, who built or enlarged the Mansion house, now taken down, which his Descendants made their Residence. THOMAS HORTON, Esq died in 1727 and was succeeded in this Estate by WILLIAM BLANCH, Esq one of his Heirs at Law. Upon his Death in 1766, he gave a Life Interest in it to his Relict, afterwards the Wife of SAMUEL WAIBANK, Gent who, joining with the Family of ROGERS of GLOUCESTER the other Claimants, conveyed it by Deed of Sale, in 1778, to SAMUEL BOWYER, Esq the present Proprietor.

The *Roman* Antiquities discovered on this Estate were in that Part of it which extends into the Parish of *Colsbourn* ‡.

No Benefactions to the Poor.

INCUMBENTS	PATRONS	INCUMBENTS	PATRONS
—— James Huntley,		1624 William Poole,	
1570 John Brooke,	Sir George Huntley	1665 Samuel Rich, D D	William, Earl Crave
1582 William Broad,	Q Elizabeth	1682 William Prior,	The same
1594 Edward Print,		1727 Humphry Lloyd, B D	William Lord Craven
1611 Timothy Crue, M A	James and Walter	1779 Charles Bishop, M A	William Lord Craven
	Huntley, Esqrs	1788 Fulwar Craven Fowle, M A	The same

* " All ancient Stone Churches built in consequence of the Conversions made by the Roman Missionaries were built with " semicircular Arches * more & open to Rome. This Species of building, the same in *Cutland* as in *England*, prevailed " down to the 10th, 11th, and 12th Centuries, has been generally referred to as *Saxon*, and commonly so called."
Archæologia, vol IX p

† COLLINS & PORTER, The CRAVEN, vol VII p 93
‡ A circum Description and a Description of these Discoveries were communicated to the Society of Antiquaries by S L
Esq F A S and published in the Archæologia, vol IX p 319

PRESENT PROPRIETORS OF MANORS,

Of Elkeftone,   *Of Combend*

The Right Honourable WILLIAM Lord Craven   SAMUEL BOWYER, Efq

The Perfon fummoned from this Place by the Heralds in 1682 and 1683, was
Thomas Horton, Efq.

At the Election in 1776, Six Freeholders polled from this Parifh

The earlieft Date in the Regifter occurs in 1592

ANNUAL ACCOUNT OF MARRIAGES, BIRTHS, AND BURIALS, IN THIS PARISH.

A D	Mar	Bir	Bur	A D	Mar.	Bir	Bur.	A D	Mar	Bir	Bur	A D	Mar	Bir	Bur
1781	3	5	3	1786	—	8	8	1791				1796			
1782	4	10	4	1787	2	6	2	1792				1797			
1783	—	9	5	1788	—	7	3	1793				1798			
1784	1	5	2	1789				1794				1799			
1785	2	15	5	1790				1795				1800			

I N S C R I P T I O N S   I N   T H E   C H U R C H

IN THE CHANCEL

ON A TOMB

Here lyeth the Body of
WILLIAM POOLE, Minifter
of this Parifh of Elftone
above forty Yeares, who died
the 26th Day of February
Anno Domini 1664.

ON A MARBLE MONUMENT AGAINST THE WALL, SOUTH SIDE THE NAVE

Arms, Sable, a Buck's Head ca
bofled Argent, attired Or, in Chief a
Crefcent for the fecond for HORTON

Over againft this Place lies interred
THOMAS, the Son of
THOMAS HORTON, Efq
who whilft living was an
example of piety and fobernefs
to the Gentleman Comoners of
Lincoln Colledge in Oxford,
And afterwards to thofe of
the Middle Temple
in London,
where he died on the 21ft of May
in the Year of our Lord 1687,
in the 25th Year of his Age

ON A FLAT STONE

THOMAS HORTON, Efq.
who died Oct 24, 174?,
aged 51 Years

Here lyeth the Body of
JOHN, the Son of
THOMAS HORTON
of Combend, Efq
who departed this Life,
April 6, 1707,
aged eleven Weeks

Alfo MARY his Daughter,
who departed this Life,
Feb 23 1708,
aged feven Weeks

I N   T H E   C H U R C H Y A R D   O N   T O M B S

WILLIAM KENDALL,
died April 5, 1753

REBEKAH his Wife,
Oct 6, 1773, aged 72

NATHANIEL POOLE,
July 16, 1692, aged 65

MARGARET his Wife,
May 27, 170?, aged near 70
JOSEPH their Son,
Feb 14 1697, aged 19

LYDIA their Daughter,
1697, aged 17

RICHARD WALKER,
Sept 11, 1697

JOHN FLETCHER,
May 25, 1771,
in the 55th Year of his Age.

O N   H E A D   A N D   F L A T   S T O N E S.

	Died	Aged		Died	Aged
Richard and Ann, Children of John Fletcher Infants			Anthony Sadler	31 May, 1771	76
			Henry Bubb, fen	9 July, 1758	55
Ann, Wife of Anthony Sadler	22 Nov 1744	60	Henry Bubb, jun	21 Dec 176?	39

NO mention of this Place occurs in *Domefday* Book, neither is it known to which of the adjoining Parifhes it was annexed, nor at what Period it gained parochial Rights. It lies in the Hundred of *Dudftone* and *King's Barton*, five Miles North-eaftward from *Newnham*, and four in the oppofite Direction from the City of GLOUCESTER. Within the Boundary are comprifed about 2000 Acres, much of which is uninclofed, in fpacious Meadows on the Banks of the River *Severn*, and fubject to Inundations. The Soil is a deep Clay, of which not above one eighth Part is in Tillage, it is peculiarly favourable to the Growth of Oak and Elm Timber, chiefly in the Hedgerows * There are, befide, more than fixty Acres of Woodland By the *Severn* the North weft Termination of the Parifh is formed, excepting at "*Elmore's* " *Back* ‡," where a Part of *Minfterworth* extends on this fide of the River.

The impropriate Tythes were given in 1137 by MILO, Conftable of GLOUCESTER, to the Priory of *Llanthony*, and the vicarial to the Church of *St Owen* in that City to which they were confirmed by WALTER DE CANTILUPO, Bifhop of *Hereford*, in 1236 ¼, both paffed at the Diffolution to the knightly Family of GUISE. The perpetual Curacy was augmented by Lot in 1746, and the privy Tythes have been added by the Impropriator

In the Church, confifting of a Nave and North Aifle long and fpacious, with a low embattled Tower, no ftriking veftiges of Antiquity remain, owing probably to the Repair lately made It is in the Deanery of GLOUCESTER, and dedicated to *St John the Baptift*

Of the Manor the earlieft Poffeffor upon Record was HUBERT DE BURGO, Earl of *Kent*, and chief Juftice of *England* in the Reign of HEN III who granted to the Monks of *Llanthony* the Tythe of Lampreys and all Fifh taken in his Gurges or Fifheries at *Elmore* § JOHN DE BURGH, his Son, held it with Privilege of Free Warren in 1260 44 HEN III and foon after gave it in Dower with one of his Kindred to NICHOLAS, Son of ROBERT GYSE, of *Afpley Gowiz*, com *Beuford*, where they had been fettled fince the Conqueft Sir ANSELME GYSE was confirmed in the Property of this Parifh by a farther Grant, dated 1274, 2 EDW I at the yearly Rent of a Clove gilliflower, in ackrowledgment of the Gift, with the Conceffion of his own Coat armour ‖ It appears, however, that the Family of GYSE were Mefne Lords only, under the Priory of *Llanthony*, for Sir JOHN DE GYSE invefted them with the Lordfhip, referving a Fee farm Rent, in the Reign of EDW III **

It was likewife acknowledged to be Parcel of the Honour of *Hereford* in 1359 and 1373, the 23d and 46th of EDW III, and in 1558, 5th of Q MARY Sir WILLIAM GYSE, Bart fifth in Defcent from Sir CHRISTOTOPHER GUISE, whofe Patent of Creation bears Date July 10, 1661, 13th CHARLES II died unmarried in 1783, and bequeathed this with other Eftates to his Sifter and Heir JANE, the Wife of the Hon and Right Rev SHUTE BARRINGTON, Lord Bifhop of *Sarum*, after whofe Deceafe they are devifed to Sir JOHN GUISE, Bart of *Highnam Court*

Elmore Court, the manerial Manfion, is of very high Antiquity It was rebuilt in the Reign of Q Eliz by JOHN GUISE, Efq with Stone brought from the Caftle of the DE BOHUNS, Earls of *Hereford* at *Harf-combe* Over the Gateway of the Offices then erected, which include a private Chapel, are Arms, Quarterly 1 and 4 Gules 7 Lozenges conjoined vaire, on a Canton, or a Mullet pierced Sable—GUISE 2 and 3 Sable a Fefs between fix Mullets, Argent—WYSHAM ‡‡ Many Alterations and Additions have

---

* "Mr GYSE hath, at his Manor of *Elmore* in GLOCESTERSHIRE, Okes the Rootes within the Ground, whom he converted into very hard Stone And they fum fay, that there is Ground, that if a Man cut a Piece of Wood there and ftrike it in, it will grow " LELAND Itin vol III p 105

† "*Bick* or *Bee*, is an ancient Word fignifying a Ferry "

‡ Carta *Milonis Conft* Creatae ' Capelli de *Elmore* cum tota Decima Dominii in omnibus & omnibus Decimis vicinariis cum tertia quadam id colligendum Pecuniam ' DUGDALE, Mon Angl vol II p 71

§ Regift Prioratus de *Llanthony*, t 48 Tefte RICARDO CICESTRENSI Epifcopo.

‖ HUBERT DE BURGO, Earl of *Kent*, printed Lands to ANSELME DE GEE in the Counties of GLOUCESTER and Ludlow whereupon the faid ANSELME bare the fame Coat with a Canton Or, charged with a Mullet of fix Points pierced Sable CAMDEN's Remains, p 216, &c

* Priorat de *Llanthony* pro Minerio de *Elmore* Pat Rot 32 EDW III p 1 m 26 TANNER's Not Mon The Manor valued at 12l per ann was vefted in WILLIAM HAYBARARD, ROBERT DE LITTLE, and RICHARI SROUT, Clerks in Truft for the Priory But the Redeofforment was made by WILLIAM the Prior, and the Convent, dated April 5, 1359, granting to Sir JOHN GYSE, Knt an Annuity of 20l for his Life, and 12 Yards of the Suit of the principal Clerks, and one Robe for his Efquire, and another for his Chamberlain And they engage to celebrate Maffes and Requiems for the Souls of his Anceftors daily, and one folemn Anniverfary yearly for ever

‡‡ Several curious carved Chimney pieces are preferved, upon which are the following Arms,—1 GUISE quartering WYSHAM and CUES, a Fefs between fix Billets Or BEAUCHAMP of *Holt* 2 GUISE impaling Gules three Lioncel, rampant, Or PAUNCEFOOT 3 GUISE impaling Gules, a Bend engrailed Azure, between three Leopards heads jeffant de Lis, Or DENNYS

Sir JOHN GUISE was created Knight of the Bath at the Inftallation of ARTHUR Prince of WALES LELAND's Collect vol IV p 252 He is likewife mentioned in HOLLINSHED's Chronicle, p 1450, as a Knight of this County

3

tttt

been subsequently made, upon a Plan which has never been completed, chiefly by Sir John Guise, about the Commencement of this Century. For many Years past it has ceased to be the Residence of the Family. The Situation is advantageous, upon an easy Acclivity, commanding a widely extended Prospect of the Vale, surrounded with the *Cotefwold* Hills, and on the opposite Side, of the Forest of *Dean*.

The Property independent on the Manor is inconfiderable, though there are feveral Copyhold Tenures of different Value.

Of natural Curiofities the principal is a Ridge of Rocks crofling the *Severn*, at a Place called " *Stone* " *Bench*," about 100 Yards over, in an oblique Direction, to near the furface at low Water is to impede Navigation. The Tide, from the fudden Contraction of the Banks of the River, gains fuch Force as to rife many Feet above the Surface, producing a very fingular and beautiful Effect.

B E N E F A C T I O N S

3*l* 10*s* a Year, vefted in Truftees, were given by Deed, the Deed and Time unknown, to repair the Severn Walls, or to repair the Church, Bridges, Highways, or to furnifh Horfe and Harnefs, &c. and for the King's Service, the Refidue for the Succour and relief of the Poor, if any remain.

Oct 6, 1620, Giles Cove, bequeathed by Will 1*l* 2*s* yearly, for the Relief of the poorer Houfe-keepers, who do not receive pay from the Parifh.

Incumbents	Patrons	Incumbents	Patrons
1620 John Blanch	——	1716 Wilhur James,	Sir John Guife
1625 Valentine Marfhall,	——	1744 John Will, B A	Sir John Guife
166— —— Lytelton, Clerk,	Sir Chriftopher Guife	1764 John Lewis,	Sir William Guife
—— Ben. Saunders, Clerk,	——	1774 Jofeph Chefter, M A	The fame
1701 ——			

PRESENT LORD OF THE MANOR,

The Hon and Rt Rev SHUTE, Lord Bifhop of SALISBURY

The Perfon fummoned from this Place by the Heralds in 1682 and 1683, was

SIR JOHN GUISE, Bart

At the Election in 1776 Ten Freeholders polled from this Parifh

The Regifter has its firft Date in 1560, but at the Conclufion of the firft Volume is a Part thus entituled " Of Baptifme, Weddings, and Burialls, happening at *Elmore*, out of the Worfhipfull Houfe of GUYSE, fythens the 6th Day of December 1556."

ANNUAL ACCOUNT OF MARRIAGES, BIRTHS, AND BURIALS, IN THIS PARISH

A D	Mar	Bir	Bur	A D	Mar	Bir	Bur	A D	Mar	Bur	Bur	A D	Mar	Bir	Bur
1781	2	9	7	1786	3	17	15	1791				1796			
1782	1	16	4	1787	2	10	5	1792				1797			
1783	—	5	8	1788	7	9	4	1793				1798			
1784	1	4	5	1789	—	16	4	1794				1799			
1785	2	10	5	1790				1795				1800			

INSCRIPTIONS IN THE CHURCH

IN THE CHANCEL

Upon a Raifed Tomb

The figure of a Man in Armour carved in a Slab of white Marble with blue Lines. Four Corner Letters. Guife quarterly fecond Wyfham 2 Guife quarterly Wyfham Giles, a Lefs between fix Billets, Or, Beauchamp of Holte.

Inteription on Ground near

Hic jacet Johannes Guife et Alicia uxor ejus qui quidem Johannes feliciter obiit in communione omnium animarum anno Domini Milefimo &c &c &c CCCCLLLIII Quorum animabus propicietur Deus Amen.

On a Monument of Freestone

Arms Quarterly a Bend 1 3th Guife 2 Beauchamp 3 Wyfham This for the Worthy Memory of Sir William Guife who deceafed Sept 19 1642

And of William his eldeft Son by his firft Wife Agnes, &c. Dorothea — Curt —— fon Efq who married Chriftian Daughter of John Dean of Truckenham Efq by whom he had four fons and three Daughters He deceafed Auguft — 1655.

On a Marble Monument

Arms Guife impaling quarterly Cole and Auriol a Crefs Moline for creft

In Memory of William Guife Efq eldeft Son of the Guife of Elmore He was eldeft Son of Major Henry Guife and Margaret his wife in the county of Gloucefter William Guife Efq of the Temple —— ——

Lyeth here interred with WILLIAM his 4th son. Also DOROTHEA his Wife, departed this Life June the 12th, 1728, aged 76.

A Lady remarkable for her strict Piety, diffusive Charity, and engaging Courteousness of behaviour flowing from the truest ornaments of Religion Goodness and Humility

She was the only Daughter of JOHN SNELL* Esq Lord of the Manor of Ufleton, in the County of Warwick, which Manour with Lands to the Value of near a Thousand Pounds a Year, he gave by Will to support the Interest of Episcopacy in Scotland but this Application of his intended Benefaction being defeated by the Union, a Decree was obtained in the High Court of Chancery for settling the Estate on Baliol College, in Oxford, for ever to maintain, support and educate certain Scholars to be sent thither by the University of Glasgow, allowing to each Fifty Pounds a Year, for Ten Years, only eight partake at present of these Exhibitions, though he there may be deemed capable of supporting a greater Number

She had Issue three Sons and one Daughter

JOHN the eldest died aged 21 Years He was a Gentleman of a very extraordinary Genius, and eminently studious, having in that early time of Life acquired a perfect knowledge of all the polite Languages, Ancient and Modern

WILLIAM the Second Son died aged 12 Years

HENRY the third Son is still living, under care of this Inscription

And Than on is the Daughter was married to DENNIS COOKE, of Highnam Esq and has interred in Highnam Chapel

ON FLAT STONES

Arms, GUISE impaling SNELL, Crest, a Swan proper issuant from a ducal Coronet

WILLIAM GUISE, Gent of Gloucester, DOROTHEA GUISE, WILLIAM GUISE Deposited in this Grave, with their Ancestors, are two Sons of HENRY GUISE, Esq of Gloucester, or of Upton St Leonards, by MARY his Wife, Daughter of EDWARD COOKE, of Highnam, Esq EDWARD and WILLIAM both died Infants, one anno 1736, the other anno 1737

Arms quarterly GUISE and SNELL, on an Escotheon of Pretence, Or, a Chiveron chequy Gules and Azure, between three cinquefoils of the second for Cook.

Here lyeth the Body of HENRY GUISE, Esq of the City of Gloucester, youngest Son of WILLIAM GUISE, Esq who lies interred in this Chancel a Gentleman in his private Conversation, well known for his engaging affability, in publick, for his strict Administration of Justice. He died much lamented the 23d of Oct, 1749, aged 51

IN THE NORTH AISLE

ON A FLAT STONE

J B BISHOP, departed this Life Feb 10, 1784, aged 30 Years

IN THE NAVE

ON A NEAT MARBLE MONUMENT

Arms, Azure on a Fess Argent, a Lion passant Gules, between three Boars heads couped of the 2d for GOUGH

In Memory of the Rev Mr WILLIAM JAMES, late Minister of this Church, who died October 11, 1744, aged 59

Also MARY his Wife, Daughter of JOHN GOUGH, late of Stonehouse in this County She died June 5, 1747 aged 54

Also ANNA, their Daughter who, in regard to the Memory of her dear Parents caused this Monument to be erected She died Oct 7, 1755, aged 22 Years

ON FREESTONE MONUMENTS

In Memory of RICHARD LEIGHTON, and SUSANNAH his Wife She died May 20, 1683, æt 38, and he Sept 13, 1718, at 87

Also of WILLIAM CRUMP, of the Parish of Minsterworth, who died May 30, 1743 Aged near 70 Years

In Memory of SUSANNAH, Daughter of DANIEL and SUSANNAH ELLIS, who departed this Life March 21, 1739, Also of ELIZABETH their Daughter, who died Feb 19 1742, both in their infancy

ON A FLAT STONE

Here resteth the Body of the Rev BENJAMIN SAUNDERS, late Minister of this Parish who departed this Life the 17th Day of January, anno Domini 1701

IN THE CHURCH YARD,

On the side of four Arches finished with a Pyramid of Freestone, erected over the Vault of the Family of GUISE.

ON TOMBS

Here resteth the Body of the Pious and sincerely eminently Pious and pundus Divine, Mr VALENTINE MARSHALL, of this Place preacher 30 Years, and died in the 63d Year of his Age, and was buried Oct 3, 1661

WILLIAM BRADLEY late of Hardwick, died July 7, 1779, aged 60

JOHN BRADLEY died Oct 18, 1751, in the 63d Year of his Age

JANE Wife of JOHN BRADLEY, died Feb 15, 1769, aged 60

HENRY Son of JOHN BRADLEY, died Dec 6, 1763, aged 35

ELIZABETH, Wife of ARTHUR KNOWLES, buried March 1, 1767, aged 46

ARTHUR KNOWLES Gent died April 6, 1711, aged 65 Years

ARTHUR their Son, died Nov 19, 1705, aged 1

ELEANOR, Daughter of the Rev Mr NATHANIEL HAWKINS, late Minister of Coln Rogers in this County, died 18th of April 1719, aged 9 Years.

HANNAH, Wife of the said Rev Mr HAWKINS, died 23d of Oct 1720, aged 60 Years

JOSEPH LEES, died Nov 9, 1740, aged 57

ELIZABETH his Wife died Sep 26, 1736, aged 50

ELIZABETH their Daughter died Oct 16, 1744, aged 17

JOHN HOPKINS, Son Mariner, died May 7, 1696

GRACE CUTTING died Nov 1, 1731 aged 72 Years

EDWARD CUTTING, Steward to Sir JOHN GUISE, Baronet died one in the 53th year of his Age

ELIZABETH his Wife died 1762, in the 53d year of her Age

WILLIAM ASTMAN of the Parish of Hardwick, died May 22, 1737, at 71

SARAH his Wife died March 11, 1693, at 51

JOHN BREBTHER of Hardwick, died March 16, 1691, aged 65

WILLIAM ASTMAN of Hardwick, died Jan 31, 1763, aged 65

MARY Wife of WILLIAM ASTMAN, and Daughter of HENRY BRADLEY, buried May 17, 1731, aged 51

ANSELM HARMAN died Nov 6, 1730, aged 55

JOHN HARMAN, of Bio the Mill died July 12, 1751, aged 52

WILLIAM JAMES died April 15, 1713, aged 60

RICHARD KNOWLES, Gent died April 12, 1720, aged 73

A 1

ANN, Wife of RICHARD KNOWLES, died Feb 20 1692 aged 62

HENRY BRADLEY, sen died May 3, 1675, aged 56

MARY his Wife, died Jan 7 171, aged 91

MARY that Daughter, died Jan 11, 16, aged 18

ALICE FREEME, Daughter of JOHN SAPTON, late Wife to RICHARD BULLOCK, died Septemb 15, 1688

HESTER Wife of JAMES BREWER, died Feb 18, 1781, æt 49 Years

MARY, Wife of JOHN WALL of Hardwick, died Sept 14, 1758 aged 71

JOHN WALL died July 25, 1778, aged 7,

JOHN, Son of JOHN and JANE BRADLEY, died May 14, 1760, aged 41 Years

---

ELIZABETH his Daughter died Nov 22, 1757, aged 4 Years

SILVANUS VICK died June 18, 1773, aged 56 Years

SARAH his Wife died July 17, 1765, aged 51 Years

GRACE, their Daughter, died June 2, 1765, aged 16 Years

ANN, their Daughter died March 2, 1773, aged 14 Years

MARGARET, Daughter of RICHARD TOWNSEND, died Dec 15, 1681, et suæ 8

WILLIAM RANDALL of Hareshcid, Gent died Feb 19, 178-, aged 56 Years

---

JOYCE Daughter of HENRY BRADLEY, died May 18, 1757, aged 6

HENRY Son of HENRY BRADLEY buried April 18 1730, in the 4th Year of his Age

---

HANNAH Wife of HENRY BRADLEY, died April 19, 1778, aged 70

WILLIAM Son of JOHN BRADLEY, died March 7, 1743, aged 41 Years

---

ON FLAT AND HEAD STONES

	Died	Aged
William Jones	14 Sept 1754	41
Hester his Wife	22 Sept 1770	61
John Harber	19 Oct 1757	33
Daniel Lane	26 July, 1746	61
Abigail his Wife	4 Jan 1755	78
Susannah and Esther their Daughters,	16 Mar 1729	20
	12 Sept 32	17
Daniel their Son	4 Jan 1773	54
Henry Ockell	— Aug 1767	79
Harry Ockell	10 Mar 1781	57
Elizabeth his Wife	11 Oct 1770	42
Robert James,	1 Dec 1755	56
Thomas James,	22 July, 1759	67
Elizabeth his Wife	6 Mar 1778	80
Ann, Daughter of Silvanus and Sarah Vick	17 June, 1730	2
Sarah, Daughter of William Rowles	6 Mar 1759	11
Betty Rowles	15 Nov 1762	20
Sarah, Daughter of Silvanus and Sarah Vick	20 June, 1764	8
Sarah, Wife of Ephraim Smith of Saul	25 Sept 175	77
Silvester Daughter of Matthew Lane	7 May, 1734	30
Joseph Leighton	1 Aug 1729	42
Margaret Daughter of Phillip Townsend	1, Dec 1781	8
Richard Ellis	Jan 1676	—
William Ellis	20 Apr 1683	—
Ann, Wife of Richard Leighton	24 Nov 1764	63
Margaret Daughter of William Ellis	20 Mar 1668	—
William his Son	7 Feb 1676	—
Elizabeth his Wife	12 Mar 1711	76
Margaret Wife of William Vick	23 July, 1755	80
William Vick	11 May, 1761	7,
Dinah Wife of Richard Ellis,	6 Apr 1775	45
Elizabeth Ellis	29 Nov 17,5	46
Joseph Ellis	15 Apr 1715	—
Smith his Wife	15 Apr 1758	70
Daniel Ellis son	6 Aug 1784	—
Elizabeth his Wife	21 May, 1586	—
Daniel their Son	15 Dec 16 2	—
Joseph Ellis	5 Sept 1700	54
Richard Scilly	15 Jun 1777	7,
Mary his Wife	— May, 1772	60
Susannah, second Wife of Nathaniel Hawkins	23 Dec 1738	39
William Layton	18 Nov 1603	48
Sarah Daughter of Phillip Wall	20 Apr 1721	1,
Thomas his Son	18 Apr 172	24
Mary Wall buried	17 Dec 1729	5
Joseph her Son ditto	15 Nov 1729	14
Daniel Hawkins	21 Nov 1750	51
Phillip Wall	11 Dec 1762	67
Thomas his Son	7 June, 175	7
Mary his Daughter	30 Jan 1749	17
David Richards	15 Sept 1726	71
Ann his Wife	6 Feb 1733	0
Phillip Wall	1,12	53
William his Son	10 May 1765	59
Elizabeth, Wife of Robert Hamlett	15 Feb 1780	6,
Robert Hamlett	19 Jan 1756	77
Ann his Daughter, and Wife of John Griffiths	6 Aug 1780	7
George Gulding	2 Nov 1731	71
Mary his Daughter	10 Apr 1732	5
John Smith	20 July, 1726	5
Sarah his Wife	7 Dec 1731	61
Daniel, Son of Daniel and Mary Gulding,	16 July, 178	1,
John Hill	12 June, 1737	60
Hannah, Wife of Joseph James, and Daughter of James and Elizabeth Prosser	16 Nov 1769	26
Joseph James	15 May, 1775	59
James Prosser	1 Oct 1766	60
Elizabeth his Wife	10 June, 1750	65
William Cam	7 Oct 1765	1,
Joseph Prosser	13 Sept 1755	51
Ann his Wife	11 Sept 1755	59
Mary, Wife of Giles Hooper	16 Feb 1752	5,
Mary his Daughter	2 Feb 1759	43
Mary Wife of George Ferebury	2 Aug 1733	62
George Ferebury	18 Jun 1766	66
John their Son	26 May, 1742	6
Charles, son of William and Sarah Dowel of Mutherworth	Mar 1760	6

CXVI. ELMSTONE,

MORE anciently "AILMUNDISTAN," is a Parish of the middle Size, in the Vale of Gloucester, from whence it is distant eight Miles on the North, five South-east from Tewkesbury, and from Cheltenham four on the North west. It is divided between the Hundreds of Westminster and Deerhurst, containing by Computation about 1600 Acres, of a Soil varying from Clay to deep Sand, three fourths of which are in Tillage, the whole is intersected by the Rivulet Swillyate in its Course to the Severn.

The Living is a Vicarage, not in Charge, in the Deanery of Winchcombe, of which the Impropriation and Appointment formerly belonged to the Abbey of Tewkesbury. In 1612, 10 James I the impropriate Tythes were purchased of the Crown, who retained the Advowson, by Antony Cole, which in 1630 were resold to the Principal and Fellows of Jesus College, Oxford, under which Society the Family of Gwinnett of Bengeworth, long held them, and the Lease descended by Heirship to William Cachmay Gwinnett, Esq in 1782.

Nothing worthy Remark occurs in the Church, which is dedicated to St Mary, it has a Nave and South Aisle, with a strong embattled Tower on the West end.

Originally the Manor was included and described as Parcel of the Manor of Deerhurst, and was un-... taken from the Monks of Westminster by Robert Fitz Haman, but restored to them by a Suit at Law in the Reign of Hen II † At the Suppression of the Monastery it was confirmed to the Dean and Chapter of that Church, who are the present Proprietors. The Family of Buckle have continued Lessees since the Reign of K James I ‡

HAMLETS

Hardwick, or Elmstone Hardwick, lies in the lower Part of the Hundred of Westminster, and is a distinct Manor. In Domesday it is stated to contain five Hides of Land, and to be a Member of Deerhurst Maurice Lord Berkeley died possessed of it in 1524, 15 Hen VIII From that noble Family it passed to Richard Lygon, Esq of Ash court in 1567, 9 Q Eliz At the Commencement of this Century Richard Dowdeswell, Esq of Pull court, com Vigorn, was Lord of this Manor, which is now held in Jointure by Bridget, Relict of the Rt Hon William Dowdeswell, late Chancellor of the Exchequer, who died in 1775.

Uckington, is a Tything and Manor in the lower Division of the Hundred of Deerhurst, the Jurisdiction of which extend over the adjoining Parish of Staverton. It has its own Constable. In a Deed dated in 12.., 50th of Hen III of the Lands transferred from the Priory of St Denis to that of Deerhurst, are the following Particulars, ' Prior de Deorhyrste habet xii bovis terre apud Okintune, et reddunt per " Ann xx Sol Item, habet iv ... ... de reddit issus cum auxilio rusticorum In Villenagio " iv ... ... Item, Meatuum illud nullum potest sufficere Instrumentum, quia nullum habet " Pratum, nisi tantum de quo potest recipere unam Karittam Feni, et reddit is Dni Robert Meseros " de mid Mirea Summa redditum cum liberorum quam rusticorum cum xxii precariis Lovatis " xl ... iis and § After the Death of Edward Earl of Oxford in 1741, it was sold by his Executor to the Family of Rogers of Dowdeswell, and is now the Property of Joseph Berwick, Esq of Hallow in Right of his Wife, Ann, Daughter and sole Heir of John Rogers, Esq A competent Estate in this Tything belongs to John Buckle, Gent which has for several Generations been vested in that Family.

A very valuable landed Property in this Parish is now held by ——— Hancock, Esq of Oxfordshire.

In the Record of the Abbey of Cirencester, preserved by Dugdale, one Hide of Land in Elmondstan is specified ||

---

* Several Benefactions, amounting to 1350l were laid out in 1630, by Sir Baptist Hicks, Knt Principal to the different Improprietors and Rent Charge in Cirencester registers. Willis Hist Cur Compl p 523 cht Cirencester ... And sv Esq p Cr.

† By Deed dated 14th Sept 10 James John Lygon, Esq of ... conveyed the Manor of Uckington to Matthew Lord ... Coventry. Atkins Smith.

§ Dugdale Mon Angl vol I p 548

|| Ibid vol II p ...

3

No Benefactions to the Poor.

INCUMBENTS	PATRONS.	INCUMBENTS.	PATRONS.
—— Richard Mudwell,	Abbey of Tewkesbury.	1738 William Williams, B.A.	The same.
1594 Edward Prince,	Q. Elizabeth	1747 ——	
* * * * * * *		1763 Anthony Freeman, M A	Geo III
1694 George Styles, B A	William and Mary.	1789 Vacant	
1733 Cornelius Bond,	Geo II		

PRESENT PROPRIETORS OF THE MANORS,

Of Elmstone,   Of Uckington.   Of Elmston Harawick

JOHN BUCKLE, Gent   JOSEPH BERWICK, Esq   BRIDGIT DOWDESWELL,

The only Person summoned from this Parish by the Heralds in 1682 and 1683, was
THOMAS WELLES, Gent of Uckington

At the Election in 1776 Six Freeholders polled from this Parish and its Hamlets.

The present Register commences in 1564.

ANNUAL ACCOUNT OF MARRIAGES, BIRTHS, AND BURIALS, IN THIS PARISH.

A D	Mar	Bir	Bur	A D	Mar	Bir	Bur	A D	Mar	Bir	Bur	A D	Mar	Br	Bur
1781	2	5	3	1786	3	14	7	1791				1796			
1782	5	9	6	1787	5	4	1	1792				1797			
1783	3	7	2	1788	2	7	6	1793				1798			
1784	1	8	3	1789	—	10	3	1794				1799			
1785	1	9	6	1790				1795				1800			

INSCRIPTIONS IN THE CHURCH.

ON A FLAT STONE

Here lieth the Body of the
Rev Mr WILLIAM WILLIAMS,
Vicar of Elmstone and Athchurch,
who died April 2, 1747,
aged 61 Years

Also the Body of FRANCES, the Wife
of the Rev Mr WILLIAM WILLIAMS,
who died July 6, 1762, aged 69 Years

ON A MONUMENT IN THE
SOUTH AISLE

In Memory of HENRY PACEY,
late of Norton Poll
in the Parish of this in this County,
who departed this Life Oct 7, 1733,
aged 33 Years

ON FLAT STONES

Here lieth the Body of
WALTER BUCKLE who is buried
the 5th of Oct A D 1641

Here lieth the Body of
THOMAS BUCKLE who departed
this Life Sept 22 1661

Here lieth the Body of
ELIZABETH BUCKLE,
the Daughter of THOMAS BUCKLE,
who departed this Life the 8t of Sept
Anno Dom 1664

Here lieth the body of
ELIZABETH, the late Wife of
THOMAS BUCKLE deceased,
who departed this Life
the 8t of March 1668

Here lieth the Body of
ELIZABETH, Wife of
THOMAS BUCKLE and Daughter of
JOHN STERMS of Swindon Gent
who departed this Life the
20th day of June, Anno Dom 1709,
Anno aetatis 36

In Memory of JOHN BUCKLE, son of
THOMAS BUCKLE, who died the
11th of March, Anno Dom 1716

Near this place are also buried
ELIZABETH and WILLIAM, children of
the said Thomas Buckle
Elizabeth was buried June 4,
Anno Dom 1023 and
William was buried March, 1708

In Memory of THOMAS BUCKLE,
late of this Parish Gent who
departed his Life Dec 13 A D 1709,
Aetatis suae 73

Here lieth the Body of MARY,
Wife of the Rev Mr THOMAS BUCKLE,
Vicar of this parish who departed this
Life the 5th day of Feb 1751,
aetatis suae 55

Also here lieth the Body of the
Rev Mr THOMAS BUCKLE
who departed this Life April 30, 1758
aetatis suae 61

In Memory of THOMAS the son of
WILLIAM and SARAH BUCKLE,
who died Dec 21 A D 1752,
aged Year

In Memory of MARY BRISTOW,
Wife and Daughter of
Mr THOMAS BUCKLE
buried Dec 11, 1714, aged 6
ELIZABETH BURGESS, Daughter of the
Rev Mr BUCKLE
obiit Oct 18 aged 45

Here lieth the body of
LUCY, the Daughter of
THOMAS and SARAH BUCKLE,
who departed this Life April 16, 1756,
aged 1 Year

IN THE CHURCH YARD, ON TOMBS

JOHN GRAVES, died June 11, 1628.
MARGARET his Wife,

GEORGE LONG, sen of Badgworth, died Sept. 17, 1726, aged 78 Years.
ELIZABETH his Wife, died July 22, 1731, aged 69.
GEORGE LONG, jun. obiit Feb. 14, 1754, æt 72

ANN, Daughter of GEORGE and ISABELLA LONG, obiit April 18, 1745, æt 16 Years

ON FLAT AND HEAD STONES

	Died	Aged		Died	Aged
John Little of Boddington -	6 Feb 1728	49	Sarah, Wife of Giles Roan of Maisemore	25 Apr 1735	51
Mary his Wife, Daughter of Richard and Ann Buckle	1 Mar 1728	35	William Sowle -	7 May, 1711	36
Thomas Little buried	7 Dec 1711	36	Mary his Wife -	2 Jan 1749	56
Mary his Wife buried	7 Nov 1711	22	Ann their Daughter -	18 May, 1744	19
Elizabeth, Daughter of Phillip Dance	31 July, 1729	17	John, Son of Fereby and Ann Stait	22 May, 1734	4
Susannah Little, buried	9 Mar 1695	61	Fereby Stait	12 Mar 1708	58
Alice Little, widow -	9 Jan 1707	99	William Fisher buried	30 June, 1688	38
Adam Little -	20 Apr 1713	61	Mary his Wife buried	28 May 169	4
Elizabeth his Wife	22 Mar 1687	31	Elizabeth, Wife of William Freeman	14 Aug 1733	40
Seven of their Children, five Sons and two Daughters			Sarah Wife of George Marshall	11 July, 1735	90
John, Son of Phillip and Hannah Dance	7 June, 1743	23	William their Son	10 Feb. 1738	15
Phillip Dance -	8 Aug. 1724	48	Elizabeth Kare -	8 Feb. 1764	61
Adam Dance -	12 Jan 1767	49	William Collins -	3 May, 1745	53
Betty, Daughter of John and Elizabeth Piff	13 June, 1738	3	Elizabeth, Daughter of Thomas and Elizabeth Piff	4 June, 1779	1
Mary, Wife of William Cook, and Daughter of John Roan of Maisemore	28 Apr 1743	12	John their Son -	10 Jan 1771	6
John and Mary their Children			Richard their Son -		
Jonathan Marshall -	21 Jan 1721	60	John, Son of Thomas and Joyce Piff	25 July, 1766	31
John Cook -	13 Apr 1780	43	Thomas Piff -	10 Apr 1750	47
Elizabeth his Wife	4 Dec. 1761	55	William his Son	14 May, 1740	
George, Son of Daniel Cook	31 May, 1739	28	Ann his Daughter -	14 Mar 1761	18
John Little, jun	25 Dec 1717	20	Francis Tombs -	20 Mar 1782	12
John Butt	21 Aug 1711	48	Alice his Wife -	25 Sept 1771	66
Thomas Butt -	1 June, 1722	24	Elizabeth, Wife of Samuel Pye, jun	1 Feb 1738	17
Jane, Wife of John Cook	18 Jan 1739	56	Elizabeth, Daughter of William and Margaret Pyff	4 May, 1770	14
John Cook -	25 Feb. 1728	26	Ann their Daughter -	10 Mar 1761	2
Daniel Cook -	48 Dec. 1762	77	Thomas Son of Thomas and Elizabeth Chadbourne	23 May, 1762	3
Richard Jacksons -	5 Nov 1743	45	John Piff -	6 May, 1754	37
Ann his Wife -	10 July, 1745	35	John, Son of John and Mary Piff	18 Apr 1734	31
			Hannah their Daughter buried	6 May, 1746	32

FAIRFORD

CXVII. FAIRFORD.

IT is acknowledged, that few Districts in this County enjoy greater natural Advantages of Situation than this Parish, which is a Part of the Hundred of *Brightwell's Barrow*, four Miles distant on the West from *Techrid*, and eight easterly from *Cirencester* on the great *London* Road. From GLOUCESTER it is more than 25 Miles, inclining to the South. By Computation about 3,000 Acres lie within the Boundaries, which are four Miles in Extent, and two across, of a Soil light, and intermixed with Gravel and Limestone, mostly in Tillage, and productive of several Grasses in great Perfection. Near the River *Colne*, which intersects the Parish, are many Meadows. The Woodlands do not exceed 100 Acres. In 1754 the first Inclosure and Allotment of the Commonable Lands were made, and completed in 1769.

This pleasant and spacious Village has been considered by Topographers as a Town, since 1668 when ANDREW BARKER Esq procured a Charter for a weekly Market on Thursday, and two annual Fairs for Cattle, now held upon the 14th of May, and the 12th of November [

The Plan of the Town is regular, consisting of two Streets neatly built, most of the Houses are held by Lease under the Manor.

The Benefice is vicarial, and the Chief of its own Deanery, originally in the Appointment of the *Benedictine* Abbey of *Tewkesbury*, and, since the Restoration, of the Dean and Chapter of GLOUCESTER. In 1313, 8 EDW II the impropriate Tythes of Corn were confirmed to that Monastery by Patent, having been Parcel of the Grant of their Founder ROBERT FITZ HAMON. When the Dean and Chapter of GLOUCESTER were established in 1544, they were given to them, and leased soon after to NICHOLAS OLDISWORTH, Esq whose lineal Descendants have held down to the present Lessee the Rev. JOHN OLDISWORTH §, Clerk.

The Church retains many Attractions for the Virtuoso and Antiquary. It is indeed a very finished Specimen of the purest Gothic Architecture that prevailed about the Close of the Fifteenth Century. This Structure consists of a lofty Nave, two Aisles, and a Tower in the Middle 120 Feet in Length, and 54 broad. The whole is embattled, a Series of grotesque Figures surround the Architrave of the Tower, which is so low in Proportion that it has been thought a Spire was originally intended, the Form has some Peculiarities for the Buttresses are flattened, and gradually diminished to the Top, and upon the Bases are Figures as large as Life, of rude Sculpture, so that it appears to be almost of a small Distance. The Parapet is ornamented with five Escocheons on each Side, the four larger of which bear the Arms of DE CLARE, DE SPENCER, NEWBURGH, and LAMB. Others are charged with the ragged Staff and Fetterlock, the Cognizances of the House of BEAUCHAMP. There are many Niches, which when filled with the highly finished Images, now removed, must have added much to the original Beauty of this Face. Of its internal Form and Imbellishments the most minute Description we can offer, can scarcely be deemed superfluous. The Aisles are divided from the Nave by four Arches, the Pillars light and few enough to admit a Range of Windows above them. The Tower then interposes. The Aisles are continued parallel with the Chancel, with which is a Communication by two Arches of equal Height. A Screen surrounding the Chancel is of very beautiful Gothic Carving in Oak, with Stalls in the same Taste. On the left Hand of the Altar are three Niches, or Tabernacles, formerly of delicate Ornamental Work. The upper Division of either Aisle closes in a Chancel to the Vicar, and Lord of the Manor. The near Pavement, into the very suitable Ornament, have been over several Times given by the Lords of BATHER, and their Connections. The Church owes its Re-erection to JOHN LAMB, a Merchant

* The Right Honourable WARE HILL, Earl of *H borough*, was created Viscount *La ford, by* Patent dated Aug 8, 17. He was summoned May 14 19

† M S Lansdown & the ANT A WOOD, Mss. Ashmol Oxon

‡ From *Leon to Fairford* there are Miles, it by the Ground in a Manor in a Level, most apt for Grass. Those by here from the Woods. It is a pretty uplish Towne, and much resorted, both the Lords by the fashion, the Oldisworth Abbey Fair...

... confirmed there the communion of the *Dean* ... Lamb... between...

From *Techrid* to *Fairford*, which was a TRANSLATION of a right full... Times, wholed in the charge of *John* Lamb (temp Hen IV) here he settled ... here of Manor in the Vicarage ... Hine at never discontinued but by her Endeavours, and his Son Edward, the continuation linked the 6th...

M Lee A Wood ut sup

§ I cannot find several particulars concerning the present Deanery...
Prebendal de *Hookes & Corp* appropriate and ... Rectory Nicholas...
The appropriation was confirmed to the Monastery of *Tewkesbury* by the Dean of OXFORD ... 1533, it is subjoined to ... Chapter XII. The valuation Edw VI... p 170

§ Upon the general Inclosure in 1760... to Join the Commutation Tabula Acts ... Orchard Lane
... the Houses ... opposite the Vicarage, and given in Presentation of the Ground, and part appropriate...
... and ... Vicarage

chant, of a Family fettled in *London*, where feveral of them had ferved the Office of Sheriff * About the Year 1492, foon after the Siege of *Bo'ogne*, a Veffel bound to the Port of *Rome*, from the *Low Countries*, and laden with painted Glafs, is faid to have been taken by him, who inftantly determined on preparing a Church here for its Reception The Dedication of it to the *Virgin Mary* was celebrated in 1493, the probable Date of its Foundation, for the whole was not completed by JOHN TAME, who died in 1500, but remained to be finifhed by his Son Sir EDMOND TAME, Knight †. A Series of Scripture Hiftories, fo numerous and exquifitely penciled, even before the barbarous Demolition of monaftic Splendour, the whole Kingdom had not to fhow. During the Commotions in 1642, when the Republican Army were on their March towards *Cirencefter*, WILLIAM OLDYSWORTH, Efq the Impropriator, fearing its Deftruction, caufed the whole to be taken down and concealed, and to him the Lovers of ancient Art are indebted for its prefent Exiftence, which, although mutilated in many Parts, is ftill unrivalled ‡

In

* STOWE's *London*, p 504
† ' JOHN TAME began the fair new Churche of *Fayrford*, and EDMOND TAME finifhed it " LELAND, vol II p. 22.

‡ Of thefe " ftoried Windows richly dight,
Cafting a dim religious Light,"

(for furely none can more completely anfwer the Idea of the Poet) it appears that a Defcription was engroffed on Vellum by order of Sir EDMUND TAME, and preferved in the Church Cheft It is now loft, but a Paper Roll copied from it, falling into the Hands of Mr MURRAY, was publifhed by HEARNE, in his Edition of ROPER's Life of Sir T MORE, p. 273, 8vo In 176?, another Account collected chiefly from the Former, and popular Tradition, was printed at *Cirencefter*, of which fome Part are rather inaccurate There are twenty eight Windows with four, or more, Compartments in each, all of which deferve a minute and feparate Inveftigation, both of the Subjects, and the prefent State If we follow the Series of Scripture Hiftories exhibited in thefe Delineations, the Account muft commence with the fifth Window, in the North Aifle, in which it may be obferved, they are in much the beft State of Preservation

1 Mifcellaneous and rather imperfect The Serpent tempting EVE JOSHUA in Armour, kneeling MOSES, and his Divine Legation, from the burning Bufh The Queen of *Sheba* offering Gifts to King SOLOMON The third and fourth Subjects are exquifitely coloured

2 Very imperfect The Hiftory of the Miffion of our SAVIOUR, beginning with the Marriage of ZACHARIAS and ELIZABETH, the Birth of JOHN BAPTIST, the Interview between MARY and ELIZABETH, and the Betrothing of JOSEPH and MARY

3 Very perfect and excellent The Salutation of the VIRGIN Legend on a Scroll, " **Abe Maria Gra' plena Dns tecum** " the Birth of CHRIST, the Offerings of the Wife Men the Purification of the bleffed VIRGIN, and the Circumcifion of our LORD In this Window it would be difficult to point out which has the greater Merit, the Air and Character of the Figures, or the perfpective View of the Infide of the Temple

4 Perfect The Flight into *Egypt* the Affumption of the bleffed VIRGIN, JOSEPH and MARY feeking CHRIST after the Feaft, whom they find difputing with the Doctors in the Temple

5 The great Eaft Window in the moft perfect State The triumphant Entry of JESUS into *Jerufalem*, ZACHEUS and Figures with a Label " **Gloria, Laus, et Honor tibi fit**," his Agony in the Garden JUDAS betraying him PILATE fitting in Judgement againft him, the Jews fcourging him, and compelling him to bear his Crofs In the upper Compartments the Crucifixion MARY, and the other Women, Roman Soldiers, &c The moft ftriking Parts of this Window are, a Book covered with crimfon Velvet and gilt, the Countenances of PILATE, and of MARY with the fuperb Caparifons upon the Horfes of the Soldiers

6 Rather perfect The taking down from the Crofs JOSEPH of *Arimathea* and NICODEMU receiving the Body, and laying it in the Sepulchre St MICHAEL contending with BEELZEBUB, who is overcome, and confined within a fiery Grate The dead Body is admirably characterized

7 Perfect, and well defigned The Imbalming of our LORD, the Angel in the Garden having rolled away the Stone the Transfiguration with MOSES and ELIAS attendant Difciples, Saints PETER, JAMES, and JOHN, JESUS appearing to his Mother, with this Salutation, " **Salve fancte Parens** " This Piece excels in perfpective particularly a View of *Jerufalem* from the Garden, and a *Flemifh* Caftle of three Towers to fignify the three Tabernacles

8 CHRIST appearing to two Difciples going to *Emmaus*, manifefting himfelf to the Twelve, Unbelief of THOMAS

9 Rather perfect The miraculous Draught of Fifhes the Afcenfion, and the Day of Pentecoft
The three Succeffive Windows contain Portraits of the twelve Apoftles, over the Heads of whom, on Scrolls, are difpofed certain Sentences of the Creed All of them in good Prefervation

10 St PETER ' **Credo in Deum omnipotentem Creatorem Celi et Terre** '
St ANDREW " **Et in Jefum Chriftum filium ejus unicum D'num noftrum** '
St JAMES **Qui conceptus eft de Spiritu S'cto, natus ex Virgine Maria** '
St JOHN " **Paffus eft fub Pontio Pilato crucifixus mortuus et fepultus**,"

11. St THOMAS ' **Defcendit ad Inferna tertia die refurrexit a Mortuis** '
St JAMI MINOR ' **Afcendit ad Celos fedit ad dextera Dei Patris omnipotentis** "
St PHILIP **Inde venturus judicare vivos et mortuos** '
St BARTHOLOMEW **Credo in Spiritum Sctum** '

12 St MATHIAS ' **Sanctam Ecclefiam Catholicam** '
St SIMON " **Peccatorum remiffionem** "
St JUDE ' **Carnis refurrectionem** '
St MATTHEW ' **Et vitam eternam. Amen** '

13 Imperfect Four primitive Fathers of the Church St GREGORY, habited as Pope, St JEROME, as Cardinal St AMBROSE and St AUGUSTINE, as Bifhops

14 Very imperfect DAVID fitting in Judgement againft the *Amalekite*, for cutting off the Head of SAUL

15 The great Weft Window, perfect, and exhibiting a View of the Laft Day, our SAVIOUR coming to Judgement a Sword in his left Hand, " **Juftitia** " a Lilly Branch in his right **Mifericordia** In the lower Compartment, St MICHAEL in Armour, weighing Souls The general Refurrection an Angel conducting a Saint to Heaven over a Scroll of the **Emanio fpecies Ifaida Deum** St PETER, with the Symbol admitting the bleffed Spirits ' **Gratias ago D'ne Deo pro** ' to who have pulled the Service are clothed in white Robes, and reprefent a Pope, a King, a Bifhop, and a Monk, **Benedictus fit** ' **Deus in Donis fuis** On the other Side are the Infernal Regions Devils tormenting the condemned Souls **Ite in Damnationem paratam vobis** Gothic Fancy was never more happily difplayed than in thefe Defigns, it once humble tradition of The Brilliancy of the ftrong Tints, and the Delicacy of the Drapery of the fmaller Figures form a fingularly excellent Specimen of ancient Art

16 Imperfect The Judgement of SOLOMON SAMSON flaying the *Philiftines* DAVID after cutting off his Hair, two Rabbies Doctors difputing on Point of the Law Thefe are exquifitely finifhed, the Characters of the Head very bold, the Drapery and fword the Embellifhments innumerable

17 Imperfect The four Evangelifts, the Head of St MARK, very excellent

19 laft

In 1725, to prevent farther Injury, the Honourable ELIZABETH FERMOR, Daughter of WILLIAM Lord LEMPSTER, by JANE his first Wife, Daughter of ANDREW BARKER, at the Expence of 200*l.* secured each Window with a Lattice of Wire

When *Domesday* was compiled, the Manor of *Fairford* was stated to contain twenty one Hides of Land, with thirty Plow Tillages, and was reserved by the King, under the Title of "Terra Regis In 1263, 47 HEN. III RICHARD DE CLARE, Earl of *Gloucester* and *Hertford*, obtained this Lordship, with Privilege of a Market and Fairs, which in the succeeding Reign was confirmed to GILBERT his Son, whose Sister and Coheir ELIANOR, conveyed it by Marriage to HUGH LE DESPENCER the younger, in 1314 From this last Family it descended to the BEAUCHAMPS and NEVILLES, Earls of *Warwick*, and was one of the hundred and fourteen Manors which were fraudulently obtained from ANNE Countess of WARWICK * by King HENRY VII by a Deed, dated Dec 13, 1488 JOHN TAME aforementioned purchased this Manor of the Crown in 1498, several Years prior to which he had been settled here † He was succeeded by his Son and Grandson, both Knights, and of the same Name The last Sir EDMUND left three Sisters and Coheirs, but *Fairford* was held in Jointure by CATHARINE his Relict, twice married after his Decease to Sir WALTER BUCKLER, Knight, who procured from Queen ELIZABETH a farther Confirmation of the Demesnes ‡, and, lastly, to ROGER LYGON Esq Sir THOMAS VERNEY, Knight, of *Compton Murdac*, co *Warwick*, having married ALICE, the second Coheir, purchased the Shares of the other two, MARGARET, the Wife of Sir HUMPHRY STAFFORD, Knight, and ISABEL, the Wife of LEWIS WATKYN, Esq subject to the said Jointure, by Deed of Sale, dated Feb 26, 1547 About the Commencement of the last Century, Sir RICHARD VERNEY, Knight, transferred this Estate to Sir HENRY UNTON, and JOHN CROKE, Esq who soon after re sold it to the Family of TRACEY, for in 1608 Sir JOHN TRACEY, Knight, occurs as Lord of the Manor

18 Perfect and contains with two others, Portraits of twelve Prophets, with Labels over the Head of each
HOSEA   O mors ero tua '
AMOS   ' Qui ædificat in Cælum ascensionem "
MALACHI   Ad vos judicio et ero testis velox,'
JOEL   ' In valle Josephat judicabit omnes Gentes "
19 Perfc   SOPANIAH   " Invocabuntur omnes eum et servient ei "
MICAH   Cum omnium haberis dimissi '
EZEKIEL   Aperiam vos de Sepulchris vestris Populus meus"
OBADIAH   Et erit regnum Dei
20 Perfect   JEREMIA I   ' Patrem invocabitis qui fecit et invisit Cælos "
DAVID   Deus dixit en Filius meus es tu ego hodie genui te,'
ZACARIAH   Suscitabo filios tuos "
21   The Persecution of the Church DOMITIAN, TRAJAN, ADRIAN.
22   ANTONINUS NERO MARCUS AURELIUS
23   HEROD SEVERUS, MAXIMINUS.
24   DECIUS ANANIAS and CALEB who bought our SAVIOUR of JUDAS
25, 26, 27, 28   Twelve Roman Emperors Persecutors of the Church In the Reign of CHARLES the First, before their Removal, these Windows were inspected by Sir ANTONY VANDYKE, who says HEARNE " often affirmed both to the King " and others, that many of the Figures were so exquisitely well done, that they could not be exceeded by the best Pencil The Drawings are attributed to ALBERT DURER but it is improbable that at the Age of 20 Years he could have attained such Experience for he was born in 1471 and the Glass was taken in 1492 Who was the real Artist is a Circumstance involved in some Obscurity Neither LUCA VAN LEYDEN nor GOLTZIUS could have been employed as they both flourished after the Church was finished but for this, the extreme Resemblance of the Style or the well known Etchings of these Masters would induce us to attribute this beautiful Work to them May we be allowed a Conjecture that the Designer was FRANCESCO FRANCIA who was born at *Bologna* in 1450 where he lived till 1518, peculiarly eminent in the Art of encaustic Painting.
In a Dissertation on these inward Ornaments of our Churches were held by our pious Reformers may be seen in HARRISON's Description of *England* Book II chap 1 p 138 col 30, printed in 1580, and prefixed to HOLINSHED's Chronicles, where he speaks " that white Glass may be provided, and set up in their Rooms"
STOW in his Annals p 865 says, that Queen ELIZABETH issued out her Proclamation, prohibiting any Persons, under severe Penalties from defacing Monuments, and from breaking any Image in Glass Windows

* DUGDALE's *Warwickshire* p 300
† " Sir EDMUND TAME, of *Fayrford* up by *Crekelade*, came out of the House of TAME, of *Stowel* TAME that nowe is at *Fairford* hath be maried a xii Yere and hath no Childe Wherefore be likelihode Sir HUMFRE STAFFORD, Son to old " STAFFORD, of *Northamptonshire* is like to have the Landes of TAME of *Fairford* for he maried his Sister, and so the " Name of the TAME is like soe to Decay ' LELAND Itin vol VI p 18
" Of this Family were the Sheriffs of this County in the Years 1506, 1519, 1523 1526 '
FULLER's Worthies, *Gloucestershire*, p 367
Sir EDMUND TAME after finishing the Church at *Fairford*, erected that at *Rendcombe* and *Barnsley* and built several large Inns
' Some thinke that the *George Inn* in *Fairford* was a Chauntrie House for Priests to celebrate for the Soules of the TAMES " in the Parish Church There is the same Likeness of a Man cut in stone over the Door as is on the Tower of the " said Church perhaps of one of the TAMES
' Note, That in the olde House at the West End of the Church at *Cirencester* are in every Window therein old Cotes of " Arms viz of the TAMES of *Fairford* with the Impalements of that Family It is an olde House built with great store " of Timber, known nowe by the Name of the *Ram*, in temp HEN VIII by Sir E TAME, who built *Fairford* Church '
A Wood's Itin MS ut supra
‡ WALTER BUCKLER, originally Fellow of *Merton* College, afterwards Canon of *Cardinal* College, was admitted B D June " 25 1534 though not in priestly Orders This Person was the second Son of JOHN BUCKLER of *Causey* in *Dorsetshire*, and " had been lately a Student in the University of *Paris* was afterward promoted by the King, to be Steward of his College at " *Oxford*, founded on part of the Cardinal's and about the same Time was sent on State Affaires to *Paris* where he performed " with good liking, to the said King In the of EDWARD VI he received the Honour of Knighthood and when Queen " ELIZABETH came to the Crown he was made one of her Privy Council He died at *Fairford* in *Gloucestershire*, having married the Widow of Sir EDMUND TAME, Knight, Lord of that Manor, and was buried in the Church there Over whose " Grave, though there be no Inscription yet his Contemporary in *Merton* College, named JOHN PARKHURST, hath perpetuated " his Memory by certain Epigrams WOOD's Fasti, vol I p 66

2   ANDREW

ANDREW BARKER, Esq of the very ancient Family of BARKER, alias COVERALL, of Coverall and *Hopton* Castles, in the County of *Salop*, became possessed of this manerial Property about the Time of the Restoration of CHARLES II and left one Son, SAMUEL BARKER, Esq Upon his Death in 1708, he was succeeded by his only surviving Daughter and Heir ESTHER, married to JAMES LAMBE, Esq of *Hackney*, co *Middlesex*, who died without Issue in 1761 His Relict dying in 178 , bequeathed *Fairford*, and other Estates, to JOHN RAYMOND, Esq who has since assumed the Name and Arms of BARKER, by royal Sign manual, duly registered in the College of Arms

There was very anciently a manerial Residence near the Church, erected by the Earls of *Warwick*, and called *Beauchamp* and *Warwick Court* It appears that it was re built by one TAMES, for LELAND observes, " there is a fayr Mansion Place of the TAMES hard by the Churche yerd, builded thorow ly " by JOHN TAME and EDMUNDE TAME, the Backhde therof goithe to the very Bridg of *Tanfe d* " This House was taken down by ANDREW BARKER, Esq who, with the Materials of it, built the pre sent Mansion, some Furlongs distant in linking the Foundations of which, Urns and Roman Coins are said by Dr PARSONS to have been discovered It is a large and commodious Edifice, and has been considerably improved by the present Proprietor

Within the Park Pale, about 200 Acres are inclosed, well planted, with an Avenue of a Mile in Length The Pleasure Grounds were long and deservedly admired, when in that Style of Embellish ment, which distinguished the Close of the last Century From the modern Art of Gardening, very judiciously employed, they have gained additional Beauty The River, widened for a great Distance, with its Extremities artificially concealed, gives an Air to the Landscape which a Situation of fewer natural Advantages could scarcely command The Plantations and Walks are so disposed as to produce, that just Combination of Nature and Art by which alone Scenes of real Taste are made complete

In the Reign of HENRY the Eighth, JOHN MORGAN, Esq of the Family of *Tredegar* com *Monmouth*, who had been a Colonel in the Army in the preceeding Reign, being connected with the Family of TAME and OLDYSWORTH, settled in this Parish His House has been inherited by his Descendants till 1773, when it was sold by ROBERT MORGAN, Esq to the present Lord of the Manor CHARLES TYRRIT MORGAN, M A Barrister at Law, now resides in the House inhabited by his Ancestors, to which he has lately added many Improvements

In this Parish are three Tythings 1 The *Borough*, which has its own Constable, 2 and 3 *East End*, and *Milltown End*, to each of which a Tything Man is distinctly assigned. The Church of GLOUCES TER held two Hides of Land here in Saxon Times § Every Estate in the Parish is dependent on the Jurisdiction of the Court La

Fairford, as indeed all the upper District of *Cotswold*, is very productive of extraneous Fossils

---

B E N E F A C T I O N S.

Nov , 1632 THOMAS MORGAN, Gent bequeathed by Will 100l now vested in the Minister Church Wardens, and Overseers of the Poor, the Interest of which to be distributed annually on Good Friday amongst the Poor

Dame JOAN MICO, Relict of Sir SAMUEL MICO, bequeathed by Will a Rent Charge on Land the annual Produce thereof is 5l 4s to be laid out in the purchase of Bread, to be distributed among the Poor on every Sunday in the Year

She also bequeathed by Will 400l which are laid out in Lands in the Parish of *Leachlade*, and vested in Feoffees, for the apprenticing of poor Boys

MORGAN EMMOTS gave 5l which are laid out in Lands in the Parish of *Leachlade*, and vested in Feoffees

Mr SMITH, of *London*, bequeathed by Will a Rent Charge on an Estate now belonging to J RAY MOND, Esq , the annual Produce 1l 1s for teaching poor Children to read

Hon ELIZ FERMOR, and MARY BARKER, Spinster, bequeathed by Will 60l yearly laid out in Lands and vested in Feoffees for the Establishment of a Free School for teaching poor Boys

June 17, 1715, WILLIAM BUTCHLE bequeathed by Will 50l now vested in the Minister and Church Wardens, the annual Produce is 2l to be laid out in Bread, and distributed among the Poor in the Church every Year

---

* CAMDENS Britannia ed GIBSON, vol II p 216
† LELAND Itin vol II p 2
‡ THOMAS OLDYSWORTH Esq the seventh in lineal Descent from Sir LANCELOT OLDYSWORTH Knight, died 33, 33 HEN VIII He married D daughter of JOHN MORGAN, Esq of Wells Court, in the County of Pembroke
M Ledger
§ " Burgum hus Rex Britannia reddit Abbas habuit tempore Gloucestra & nonnulli habeus hoc distribui a terra quod Abbas " tempore Regis Abbatis Dec Ann Mon Angl vol I p 115

Sir Edmund Tame & Katherine his Wife

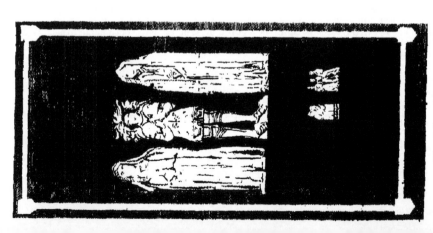

April 28, 1738 Rev FRAMPTON HUNTINGTON bequeathed by Will 10ˡ now vested in the M---ᵉ and Church Wardens, the annual Produce, 10s to be laid out in Bread, and distributed on the 2nd of August in each Year, among 20 such poor Families as should constantly attend the Church, and do not receive Alms

1770 Mr ROBERT JEANES bequeathed by Will 10ˡ now vested in the Minister and Church Wardens, the annual Produce, 10s to be distributed annually among five poor Widows

1773 ALEXANDER COLSTON, Esq bequeathed by Will 1---, now vested in the Minister and Church Wardens, the annual Produce, 5ˡ 5s to be distributed on Old Candlemas Day in each Year among poor Widows

INCUMBENTS	PATRONS.		INCUMBENTS	PATRONS
1273 Ralph Hengeham,	From 1315 to 1541 Abbey of Tewkesbury		1686 Edw Shipman, M A	Dean and Chapter of GLOUCESTER
—— William Salway,			1712 Frampton Huntington, M A	The same
1585 Henry Dun,	John Jones		1738 Joseph Atwell, D D	The same
1585 Edmond Janes,	George Lygon, Esq		1768 Daniel Ivins, Clerk,	The same
1617 Christoph Nicholson,	Rob Oldysworth, Esq		1778 Edward Sparkes, M A	The same
* * * *	* * * *		1785 James Edwards, B D	The same
1657 John Shipman,	——————			

PRESENT LORD OF THE MANOR,

JOHN RAYMOND BARKER, Esq

The Persons summoned from this Place by the Heralds in 1682 and 1683 were

Andrew Barker, Esq   Robert Morgan, Esq
William Oldysworth, Esq   John Shipman, Vicar

At the Election in 1776, Eight Freeholders polled from this Parish

The earliest Date in the Register occurs in 1617

ANNUAL ACCOUNT OF MARRIAGES, BIRTHS, AND BURIALS IN THIS PARISH

A D	Mar	Bir	Bur	A D	Mar	Bir	Bur	A D	Mar	Bir	Bur	A D	Mar	Bir	Bur.
1781	6	18	10	1786	9	35	22	1791				1796			
1782	15	30	14	1787	11	35	26	1792				1797			
1783	12	22	14	1788	6	41	20	1793				1798			
1784	4	34	21	1789	8	40	11	1794				1799			
1785	17	38	14	1790				1795				1800			

ANCIENT MONUMENTS IN THE NORTH AISLE

A Table Tomb of Italian Marble* Upon the Slab the Images of a Man in Armour, and a Woman in the Dress of the Times Four Corner Escutcheons, 1 Argent, a Lion Azure combatant, with a Griffin Vert, Tame 2 Argent, a chevron Gules, between three Poppinjays proper, TWYNHOW. At their Feet TAME impaling TWYNHOW

Legend   " For Jesus Love pray for me,
          " I may not pray nowe—pray ye
          " With a Pater Noster and Ave,
          " That our Paynys relesid may be "

Around the Verge " Orate pro animabus Johis Tame armigeri et Alicie uroris ejus, qui quidem " Joh'es obiit octavo die mensis Maii, Anno D'ni Millesimo quingentesimo, et anno regni Regis Henrici " Sept'i serto decimo Et predicta Alicia obiit vicesimo die mensis Decembris, Anno D'ni Millesimo " CCCC septuagesimo primo quorum a abus propicietur Deus "

A blue marble Slab, inlaid with the Effigies of a Man in Armour, upon his Surcoat the Arms of TAME, between two Women upon the Mantle of the first, Sable, on a Cross, within a Bordure, both ingrailed Or, five Pellets for GREVILLE, on the other, Or a Saltire Sable, for TWINIHAM The same Arms repeated upon four corner Escutcheons Inscription round the Verge " Of your Charitie pray for the Soule of Edmond Tame Knyght, heere under buried which deceessd in the Yere of our Lord God a Thousand CCCCLXIII, and for the Soule of Agnes his first Wife, which deceessd the FFCII Day of July, Anno D'ni Millesimo CCCCCIII, and on all their Soules J'hu have Mercy Amen."

* See in Engraving annexed
7 K

Upon

Upon a Slab affixed to the Wall The Effigies of the same Persons kneeling before Desks, upon which are Books opened Scrolls and Inscriptions changed as before Upon three separate Labels, "**Jesu Lorde that made us**" "**And with thy Blood us bought**" "**Forgive our Trespass**" Inscription at the Feet, "**Hic jacent Edmondus Dame Giles et Agnes et Elizabet uxores ejus, qui quidem Edmondus Obiit primo die Octobris Anno D'ni M. D LIIJII at Anno Regni Regis Henrici Octavi vicessimo sexto quorum A'iarum propicietur Deus, Amen**"

* Upon a Table Tomb, the Effigies in Freestone of a Man in Armour recumbent, and a Woman in the Dress of the Times Upon Escocheons repeated Arms, Argent, two Lions passant Gules Tracy impaling quarterly 1 Gules a Bend engrailed Azure, between three Leopards faces jessant de Lis, Dennys 2 Or a Raven proper within a Bordure Gules, charged with Bezants, Corbet 3 Argent on a Chief Gules three Bezants, Russell 4 Lozengy, Or, and Azure, a Cheveron Gules Di Gorges

ON MONUMENTS

Arm Topiz an Escallop Diamond between two Bendlets it by for Tracy impaling Argent, a Cheveron between three Leatherps Sable for Lygon

Near this Place lieth the Body of the Lady Bridget Tracy, Wife to the Right Hon the Lord Tracy She was buried the fifth of Nov 612 She was Lady of excellent natural parts she understood the Latin Tongue and other useful Parts of Learning, but, that which excels all she was truly pious and charitable Here allo lieth buried her eldest Daughter Mary, who was married to Sr William Poole of Saperton Her youngest Daughter was married to William Somervil, Esq whose youngest Son, Mr Penrudd, was a very beautiful Person and an excellent Scholar for which he was most entirely beloved of his Mother She bred him up at Eton School, and from thence removed him to Oxford, where he died in the nineteenth Year of his Age and was buried here by his Grandmother Tracey, December 3, 1680 This Monument was erected by the Hon Mrs S Somervill the worthy Memory of her most dear Mother Sister and Son

Arms Cules on a Fess Argent three Lions passant purpure for Oldisworth

Gulielmi Oldisworti, hujus Ecclesiae rectoris Jacobi Oldisworth Rectoris de Kencott, in comitatu Oxon Obiit Decem 22 An Salutis 714, Aetatis 54 Vixit purus Religionis Omni, casique Virum ib ipsis incunabulis, meri reverentia cultu Matibus, Pauci indoris & Veritatis, Cujus spite tu quod aliena bene retulis, apud omnes amicis benemus Oris laboris Moderne benedict, Fatis facris horus Celebs

Arms, Oldisworth as before

Underneath lie the Remains of Mrs Muriel Loggan (Daughter of James Oldisworth, Rector of Kencott in Oxfordshire), who died April 18, 1734 aged 74 Years A Woman of superior Strength of Understanding without Affectation, whose extensive Benevolence of Heart to the Poor and warmest Affection to her Relation, whose truly zealous and uniform Devotion and most earnest Desire of doing Good to all, made her greatly respected when living, and sincerely lamented when dead To whose Memory this Monument was erected by her very Affectionate and grateful Relation Mrs Mary Mann of Tewkesbury

Arms, Oldisworth, Crest, a Lion rampant, Gules, holding a Scroll, Or

Sacrum Reliquiis Venerabilis Viri, Jacobi Oldisworth, Cujus, In Deo colendo Pietatem, In curandis animis Diligentiam, In Pauperibus Regimine Authoritatem, In Tentationibus fugiendis Fidem, In Oeconomia ordinanda Prudentiam, In Hospitis celebrandis Affabilitatem, In Egenis ornandis Munificentiam, In omni demum vitae studio, & colore Integ a Virtutes, morefque castos & vere Christianos, In Throe Virinia Et omnium quibus innotuit, Plurim laciment laudibusque celebrant, Duris in Potertis efferunt (Quod Historiam potius quam Epitaphium videtur) Rerum & memorabile Exemplar Obiit certo die Septembris MDCXXIIo, Aetatis LXXXIIo

Arms, Oldisworth impaling Argent on a Fess between two Cheverons Sable three Croterons, Or, for Austin

M Gulielmi Oldisworth, Armigeri Deum observan er cor this, Matris peramantis, Patris prudenter indulgentis, Amici fidelis, Pauperibus A voc i,

Medici & Dispersatoris Uxorem duxit Mariam, Gulielmi Austin, in Comitatu Suthriensi Armigeri Filiae, per quam multiplicem habuit prolem Obiit 3o Die Octobr 1680, Anno Aetatis suae 71o

ON FLAT STONES

WITHIN THE RAILS

Depositum Austini Oldisworth, Praecipua vero utroque Nomine, oriundi viri, Inter Ecclesiae Anglicanae Favores Inter Rei Antiquariae Studiosos, Inter Affines Cives, Amicos, Et Familiares suos, diu multumque desideratu Obiit 27 Die Augusti, Anno Salutis 1717, Aetatis Climacterico

Here lyeth the Body of **William Oldisworth**, the eldest Son of James Oldisworth, who departed this Life the 22d of December 1714, aged 42

Here lieth **William Oldisworth**, Esq who was buried in 1680.

M Kille 1744

A Kibli 15

ON A FLAT STONE WITHOUT THE RAILS

Here lieth interred the Body of William de Tenier, Saddler who gave Forty Pounds for to be to be given Weekly in Bread to the Poor of this Parish for ever, and here departed this Life the 17th Day of June in the Year of our Lord God 1715, and the 66th Year of his Ye

* This Monument was put up or was erected to the Memory of Roger Lygon Esq and Katherine his Wife [...] She was the Daughter of William Denny, Esq of Pucklechurch, and Relict of Sir Thomas Lamb at Sir Walter Overbury, Knight

ON ATCHIEVMENTS IN THE NORTH AISLE

N° 1 Azure, five Fcallops in Crofs Or, for BARKER on an Efcocheon of Pretence Ermine on a Bend Sable three Crefcen s Argent, for

N° 2 Quarterly 1ft and 4th BARKER 2 Gules, a Fefs between three Saltires Argent charged with three annulets Sable, for GOLDSTONE 3 Argent on a Fefs between fix Crofcroflets Sable, three Efcallops, Or for LAVETELY

N° 3 Quarterly 1ft and 4th Sable on a Fefs Or, between three Cinquefoils Ermine a Lion paffant Gules between two Mullets fable for LAMB, 3 and 4d Argent, a Bull paffant fable, armed Or within a Bordure of the fecond bezantee COTE

BANNEROIS

1 BARKER impaling Argent, a Pomegranate proper for

2 BARKER impaling Argent a Chevron Gules fretté Or, between three Billets fable

---

ON MONUMENTS IN THE SOUTH AISLE

Arms; Argent a fefs Sable on a Chief Gules three Mullets, Or, for HUNTINGTON

Ifria Sepultum at Corpus
IRAMPTON HUNTINGTON A M
Qui in hoc mortali Ivo
Vixit Annos 5 et fuit hujus Ecclefiæ
Vicarius 27, unde
Ex hac ærumnofa Vita
Ad Dominum migravit 8vo Die Aug
Annoq Domini 1738

Arms, Argent three Crofcroflets fable, on a Chief Gules a Lion paffant Or, for READS

Near this place lieth the Body of SARAH who was the Wife of THOMAS TOWNSEND of Sadeley in this County Gentleman And after of ALEXANDER READY, of this Place, Gentleman. She was an excellent Wife to both and had deservedly the Character of a very good Woman She died Oct 5, 1731, ætat 39

Arms, Azure an Anchor erect Or between two Dolphins Argent collared and chained of the fecond for COTSTON

Sacred to the Memory of
ALEXANDER COTSTON,
late of Filkins in the
County of Oxford, Efq
and one of his Majefty's Juftices
of the Peace for this County
He died December 1, 1775
in the 84th Year of his Age
He was always refpected for the
Solidity of his Underftanding
and Judgment efteemed for his
amiable difpofition, and beloved
for the Virtues of his Heart

ON A FLAT STONE

Here lyeth the Body of ANN, the Wife of Mr WILLIAM HAYNES, who died March 21, 1723,

Alfo the Body of MARY HAYNES, who died the 27 of March 1754

Alfo the Body of WILLIAM HAYNES, who died the 5th of August, 1758

ON MONUMENTS AGAINST THE EAST END OF THE CHURCH.

Arms. Or a Cryphon fegreant Sable, for MORGAN impaling Gules three Chevrons Argent within a Bordure of the fecond, for AVERY

To the pious Memory of MARY,
the Dearly beloved Wife of
EDMUND MORGAN, Gent
of Fairford in Gloucefterfhire,
and Daughter of
AVERY TIRREL Gent
and MARY his Wife,
of Weft Hagbourn in Berkfhire
She was an ingenious and virtuous
Woman, a moft excellent Wife,
a kind Mother,
a good Neighbour
and charitable to the Poor
She died on 18th March 1713,
in the 33d Year of her Age
in the 2nd of Wedlock,
leaving little one Son
This Monument was erected
by her ftill loving
and forrowful Hufband

Near this Place lieth the
Body of ... the ...
JOHN EDELMAN HATCHARY
of ... in ...
who departed this life
the 25th day of January,
in the 53d Year of his Age

Arms, Or a Cryphon fegreant Sable, for MORGAN 2 and Gules, a Fefs vairé between three Unicorns Heads couped Or, for SAVERY

In Memory of
CHARLES MORGAN, Gent
of this Parifh,
who departed this life
the 18 day of Auguft 1754,
in the Fortieth Year of his Age
He was the only furviving Defcendant
of a very antient Family,
whofe Virtues together with their
Poffeffions he inherited
by the uniform and unaffected
Practice of the one as well as by a
liberal ufe of the other,
he truly merited and univerfally
obtained the diftinguifhing Character
of a faithful Friend,
a good Neighbour,
and a very honeft Man

Alfo to ELIZABETH his Wife,
who exchanged this Life for a better
the 12th day of October 1772,
aged 55 Years
She fucceeded her Confort
in the Care and Education
of a numerous Family of Children,
a Charge which fhe not only
affectionately undertook
and happily lived to accomplifh,
and at her departure the left them,
as the beft Rule of their future
Conduct the imitable pattern of
her own Life and Manners
In grateful Teftimony of fo
much maternal excellence
they wrote their
Common Tribute of
filial Regard and Veneration
to the beft of Mothers

THOMAS MORGAN,
was buried Nov 28, 1632 aged 30

ELIZABETH Wife of
ROBERT MORGAN, Gent
buried 11th of June 1688
She was Daughter and Heirefs
of RICHARD HERFORD Gent
She had Iffue one Daughter
named ELIZABETH, and two Sons viz
RICHARD, ROBERT, EDWARD and
HENRY, which RICHARD
was buried 15th of Sep 1705,
aged 17 Years

WALTER MORGAN
died 28th of September 1705,
aged 57 Years

Mr ROBERT MORGAN,
son of EDMUND and
MARY MORGAN,
died on the 6th of June 17 H
in the 7th Year of his A..

MARY Wife of
CHARLES MORGAN, who
died the 8th of June 1751
in the 63th Year of her Age

Mr THOMAS MORGAN, Widower
of ... and
... MORGAN
died the ... died
the 2th of March 1751
in the 59th Year of his Age

CHAPEL

CHARLES MORGAN, sen Gent
died June 30, 1738,
in the 83d Year of his Age

RICHARD COMLEY,
Son of Lawrence and Sabina Comley,
departed this Life Nov 7 1752,
in the 57th Year of his Age

VALENTINE STRONG (Freemason)
departed this Life Dec 26, A D 166

MARY, Daughter of Den is Por—,
died 14, 171?,

JACOB TELLING,
Son of William and Mary Telling,
died July 10, 1784, aged 29 Years

WILLIAM TELLING
died Sept 3, 1778, aged 50 Years

MARY his Wife
died Feb 3, 1784 aged 62 Years

ISAAC TELLING their Son
died Jan 2, 1776, aged 12 Years

WILLIAM COOPPER jun
Son of William and Ann Coopper,
died June 10, 1754, aged 25 Years

ANN his Grandmother
died May 25, 1729, aged 61 Years

CHARLES WEEKS, Gent
died June 26, 1740
in the thirty third Year of his Age.

ANN his Daughter
died Oct 1, 1739

Arms Per Saltire Ermine and lo
zengy Or and Gules, for BEDWELL

ELIZABETH Wife of
THOMAS BEDWELL,
of Furzy Hill,
died Aug 18, 1740, aged 29 Years

Also ELIZABETH their Daughter

SARAH PRIOR, Daughter of
THOMAS and JANE HITCHMAN,
of Blunsdon in the County of Wilts,
and Wife of JOHN PRIOR,
Master of the adjacent Free School,
died March 22 1787,
in the 48th Year of her Age

Six of their Children died in their
Infancy

WILLIAM WILLIAMS senior,
died June 21, 1762, aged 54 Years

ANN his Wife
died Oct 11, 1766, aged 68 Years

JOHN their Son
died April 21, 1777 aged 49 Years

JOSEPH LEWIS,
Son of Henry and Mary Lewis,
of his Town,
died Jan 11, 1780, aged 5 Years

JOSEPH WHITFORD
died Aug 10, 1722, aged 5?

WILLIAM LAKE
died July 10, 1751, aged 85 Years

ELIZABETH WHITFORD,
aged 76

ON A MONUMENT AGAINST THE FREE SCHOOL

Near this Place
lie interred the Remains
of Mr RICHARD GREEN
late Master of this Free School
who departed this Life the 9th Day of
November, 1707, in the fifty fourth
Year of his Age
The Integrity of his Life and Manners
had gained him the sincere Respect
of his Neighbours, and the
uncommon Assiduity and Abilities
with which he discharg'd the
Duties of his Profession for more than
fourteen Years in this School,
have made his Death a publick Loss,
and he will be long lamented by
all those that knew the Value
of so useful a Character

ON FLAT AND HEAD STONES

	Died	Aged		Died	Aged
George Messeter	27 Aug 1755	33	Martha his Wife	10 Mar 1751	81
John and Ann Peachy			Elizabeth Daughter of Charles and Sarah Herbert	23 Nov 1763	36
Ann, Wife of Edward Trinder	15 Nov 1759	63	Sarah Wife of Charles Herbert	1 Jan 1768	—
William Smith	17 Jan 1763	48	Esther his former Wife	17 Oct 1732	—
Hannah, Wife of Solomon Clinch	24 Aug 1786	56	Sarah, Daughter of James and Sarah Carter	21 Jan 1766	24
Sarah their Daughter	1 Jan 1771	17	Sarah, Wife of James Carter	24 Oct 1769	74
William their Son	10 June 177?		James Carter, senior	10 Dec 1752	59
Charles Price	9 Jan 1755	27	John Carter	15 Oct 1784	60
Thomas Longden	4 Jan 1762	54	Elizabeth his Wife	1 Aug 1765	40
Edward Hicks	15 June 1776	66	Daniel, Son of James and Sarah Carter	15 Apr 1734	3
William Howes	16 Apr 1764	64	Daniel, Son of James and Sarah Carter	28 Mar 1754	19
Catherine Howes	8 Aug 1728	58	Sarah Daughter of John and Elizabeth Wheeler	23 Dec 1749	19
William Howes senior	8 Oct 17?5	72	Elizabeth, Wife of John Wheeler buried	19 Feb 1733	40
Richard, Son of Thomas and Mary Howes	6 July 1727		Charles Wheeler	10 Oct 1743	27
Thomas Price	6 Apr 1747	6	Sarah his Wife	23 June 1752	3?
Mary, Wife of John Bailey, junior	16 June	—	Ann, Wife of Charles Betterton	7 Feb 1742	50
Thomas White	1 Ap 1748	71	John Betterton	6 Mar 1761	60
Mary his Wife	29 Aug 1779	96	Robert his Son	4 June 17?	0
William their son	30 July 1773	38	Robert Coddall	2 Aug 1769	61
Sarah Wife of Thomas White	27 Oct 1731	29	John, Son of John and Jane Barrow	6 Mar 1713	6
John, Son of John and Sarah White	16 Mar 179	8	George, Son of John and Jane Barrow	2 June 73	—
George White senior	24 June 1759	81	George Barrow, senior	25 Sept 1731	7
Mary his Wife	22 Apr 1753	73	Richard Coe	Dec 1??	
George and their Sons, buried	2 July 1750	2	Mary, Daughter of Henry and Alice Simpson	1 Nov 1??	1?
Edward	30 May 1734	2	Henry Simpson, senior	25 Mar 1??	54
Mary, Wife of Robert Hurt	17 Feb 1747	93	Alice his Wife	2 Jan 1760	
Jane, Daughter of George and Mary Price	2 Nov 1754	4?	Sarah, Wife of Allen Simpson	25 Apr 1753	
Ann Higgins	18 Sept 1773	32			
... Wife of ... Clinch	? Mar 17?4	5?	John Telling	5 July 17?	
... Clinch junior	2 Jan 17?4	83	John Telling	14 Jan 17?8	
... Horn	13 Jan 1753	82	Elizabeth, Wife of William Henry	1 Oct 17?	
...	4 Nov 175?	80	...	1? July 1??	
... Thomas Price	11 Jan 1750	64	... Daughter	1 Apr 1??	
... and Mary Hill			...	25 May 1??	6
...	28 Mar 1777	16	...		
...	12 Nov 1734				
...	4 Oct 17??	31			
...					
...	? Nov 17??	36			
...	1 June 17?2	7?	Elizabeth, Wife of John Long	2 May 17?1	

ON FLAT AND HEAD STONES

	Died	Aged
William Firly		
Mary Fury	5 Nov 1755	57
William, Son of Richard and Mary Collett	12 Dec 1752	57
William Early Collett	28 Dec 1761	—
Mary wife of Thomas Fycott	20 Apr 1772	—
Rebecka, wife of William Early	13 Sept 1733	95
Thomas Cooper	30 Jan 1769	73
Elizabeth his Daughter	25 Oct 1756	48
Jane, Wife of Henry Delawell	1 Aug 1752	—
Mary Wife of Richard Blowing	27 Aug 17—	—
Hannah Wife of Charles Heo	24 Sept 1755	51
Deborah Wife of Thomas Lind	5 Apr 1757	48
Elizabeth Wife of John Price	13 Dec 1702	4
Mary her Daughter	13 Mar 1777	71
Ann her Daughter	29 Sept 1761	2
Three more of their Children died in their Infancy	—	—
John Turner, junior	1 Mar 175-	39
Miss Turner	1 June, 1730	65
William, Robert Thomas and Anne, Children of William and Anne Williams, all died in their Infancy		
William Son of William and Elizabeth Green	23 Dec 1745	3
John Loves	19 Jan 1766	45
Ann his Wife	9 Jan 1760	46
Richard Tovey	10 July 1780	24
John Son of John and Ann Tovey	16 May 1716	19
Sarah, Wife of William Gillett	20 June 1765	50
Edward Lanting	2 June 1751	40
William, Son of William and Sarah Ody		
Sarah, Wife of Richard Brewer	2 Aug 1753	72
Harry Turner, senior	21 Jan 1724	21
Alexander his Son	26 Nov 1731	72
Deborah, Wife of Giles Newman	21 Jan 1729	9
Alice Wife of Hugh Hufeter	— Feb 1744	33
Hugh Hufeter	1 Jan 1742	66
William Son of Robert and Betty Bartlet	23 Dec 1738	72
Ann, Daughter of Henry and Esther Tovey	26 Apr 1761	4
Henry Tovey	4 July 1724	2
Esther his Wife	2 Sept 1740	40
Richard their Son	4 June 1766	6
William Ellsworth Lewis, Son of John and Ann Lewis	1 Aug 1770	26
Ann, Wife of John Lewis, and Daughter of Richard and Ann Ellsworth	2 Mar 1716	23
Mary, Wife of Henry Lewis, senior	14 Jan 1753	30
Henry Lewis, senior	13 Jan 17--	72
John Lewis	5 Sept 1748	63
Ann, Daughter of Henry and Mary Lewis	13 Mar 1763	4
	11 Dec 1767	60

	Died	Aged
Henry Lewis, junior	17 Oct 1766	55
Sarah, Wife of William Scotford	1 Oct 1761	77
William Cowle	7 June 1660	54
Elizabeth his wife		
Richard Cowley		
Mary Wife of Ambrose Tucker, of Oxford and Daughter of John and Mary Cowley	1 July, 1748	86
Mary Wife of John Cowley	2 Mar 1788	54
Ann Boy their Daughter	6 Apr 1776	72
William Cowley	13 Sept 1760	2-
Alice his Wife	18 Sept 1736	64
William Reeves junior	23 Jan 1731	62
Thomas Reeves	27 Mar 1733	20
Mary his Wife	5 May 1775	46
Thomas Reeves, senior	5 May 1756	2
Samuel Callie	29 Jan 1763	72
Anne his Wife	— Jan 1749	55
Hannah Palmer buried	5 Feb 1767	85
Sabina, Daughter of John and Mary Palmer buried	11 Dec 1764	82
John Herbert	22 Aug 1760	—
John Lackley	Apr 1706	0
John, Son of William and Elizabeth Neal	Oct 1721	7
Elizabeth Wife of William Neal	8 Sept 1742	24
Samuel Neal	16 Apr 1713	0
Charles Herbert	14 July, 1716	59
Thomas, Son of George and Mary Phillips	5 Nov 1776	49
James mother of their Sons	1 Nov 1769	0
George Phillips	9 Feb 1783	2
John Peachy	21 Sept 1760	4
Arabella his Wife	25 Apr 1740	
Sarah Wife of Harry Herbert	2 Mar 1727	70
Harry their Son	6 Apr 1716	76
John Adams	1 May 1748	
John, Son of Thomas and Hannah Ruffel	7 June, 1762	60
Thomas, Son of Robert and Able King	9 May 1729	55
John Luckman	13 Sept 1753	25
Richard Luckman, senior	14 Nov 1758	60
Elizabeth his Wife	16 Mar 1734	60
Richard Luckman junior	11 May, 1744	45
Mary, Wife of Richard Winklet	8 July, 1755	
Robert Canbry	12 Sep 1712	69
Robert Bishop	— June 1760	63
Robert Humphris	4 Dec 1769	30
Richard, Son of Richard and Mary Humphris	16 Jan 1731	62
Richard Humphris	1 Jan 1760	56
Mary his Wife	25 Aug 1769	68
Charles Petterson	19 Apr 1753	60
Sarah his Wife	14 Nov 1741	65
	6 Sept 1764	56

CXVIII. FARMINGTON,

AND in the moſt ancien Records *Tormentone*, or *Tormertane* Names, which from their Reſemblance of *Tormart .*, another Pariſh in this County, have occaſioned no inconfiderable Confuſion in the Hiſtory of Property

This Pariſh is ſituate in the open *Coteſwold*, in the Hundred of *Bradley*, two Miles Northward from *Northleche*, eight Weſtward from *Burf rd*, in *Oxfordſhire*, and from GLOUCESTER twenty-one on the Eaſt. In Boundaries form an oval of about nine Miles in Circumference The Soil is light, inclining to Gravel, moſtly incloſed, and in Tillage, with 60 Acres of Woodland This Diſtrict is deſervedly famed for every ſuperior Breed of Sheep

The Benefice is rectorial, in the Deanery of *Cirenceſter*, and appears to have been originally connected with *Nor blech*, where the Inhabitants had a Right of Sepulture, and a Penſion of 6s 8d is claimed annually by the Vicar

In the Church, dedicated to *St Peter*, are no ſtriking Remains of Antiquity. It is a plain Building, with a low embattled Tower

Tormentune was originally Parcel of the great Manor of *Leche* In 1298, 26 Edw I it was granted by the Service of one Knight's Fee to HENRY DE ST PHILIBERT, a Pictovin His Grandſon, Sir John DE ST PHILEBERT, in 1352, 25 Edw III transferred this Manor, with the Advowſon of the Chapel by Deed of Sale for the Sum of 200 Marks, to WILLIAM DE EDINGTON, Biſhop of *Winton*, with which he endowed the College he had founded at *Edington*, co *Wilts*, for a Dean and twelve Prebendaries, afterwards a Priory of the Order of *Bonhommes*, of *St Auguſtine* * A Confirmation of which Grant to them, and their Succeſſors, paſſed the great Seal in 1362, 35th of the ſame Reign †

At the Diſſolution this Manor was purchaſed from the Court of Augmentations by MICHAEL AYS-HIELD, or ASHFIELD, whoſe Deſcendant ROBERT ASHFIELD, Eſquire, re-ſold it to Sir RICE JONES, Knight, about the Year 1610 Sir HENRY JONES diſtinguiſhed himſelf in ſeveral Victories obtained in *Flanders*, in one of which he was ſlain Upon his Death, this Eſtate paſſed to the Right Honourable RICHARD LUMLEY, the firſt Earl of *Scarborough*, who had married FRANCES his only Daughter and Heir July in the preſent Century it was transferred by Purchaſe to EDMUND WALLER, Eſq of *Beaconsfield*, co *Bucks*, the Father of the preſent Proprietor About the ſame Time the Manor houſe was built in a modern Style, and is handſome and commodious

The great Road from *Gloucefter* to *Oxford* leads nearly two Miles through this Pariſh.

No Benefactions to the Poor.

INCUMBENTS	PATRONS	INCUMBENTS	PATRONS
1 ., ———,	Henry de St Philebert	1690 Jacob Finnimore,	———
1 ., ———,	Priory of Edington	169 Chriſtopher Baynes,	Earl of Scarborough
10 7 W lliam Aſhfield,	Robert Aſhfield	1718 John Eykyn, LL B	Hon Thomas Lumley
16 1 Thomas Pughe,	King James	173+ Charles Spendelowe,	Edm Waller, Eſq
.. Humphry Smith, M A	Richard Jones, Eſq	173 Thomas Beynon,	The ſame
16 9 Michael Gold s,	Sir Henry Jones	1785 Harry Waller, M A	Edm Waller, Eſq

* WILLIAM DE EDINGTON, Biſhop of *Winton* founded at his native Place a like Chauntry or College, dedicated to *St Mary St Katharine*, and *St John* about the Year 1347 Theſe were afterward at the Requeſt of Edward the Black Prince, on his return redeemed out of Hand of the Order of *St Auguſtine*, called *Bonhommes* who were ſettled there under a Governor or Rector, 1358 It yearly Revenues amounted to 442l 9s 7d Ducdale 521l 12s 3d Speed
TANNER'S Not Mon

† That Chauntry or Oſfice, called the Manor of *Tormentune*, in com *Glouceft enſ*
‡ COLLINS, Vol IV p Title Scarborough

4

PR NT

PRESENT LORD OF THE MANOR,
EDMUND WALTER, Esq

The only Person summoned from this Parish by the Heralds in 1682 and 1683 was
Humphry Smith, Rector

At the Election in 1776, Three Freeholders polled from this Parish

(The Register cannot be precisely ascertained, as to its earliest Date

ANNUAL ACCOUNT OF MARRIAGES, BIRTHS, AND BURIALS, IN THIS PARISH

AD	Mar	Bir	Bur	AD	Mar	Bir	Bur	AD	Mar	Bir	Bur	AD	Mar	Bir	Bur
1781	2	6	3	1786	6	7	5	1791				1796			
1782	2	8	4	1787	—	3	—	1792				1797			
1783	1	8	5	1788	2	8	6	1793				1798			
1784	2	9	2	1789	2	8	4	1794				1799			
1785	1	7	4	1790				1795				1800			

INSCRIPTIONS IN THE CHURCH

IN THE CHANCEL

ON AN ATCHIEVEMENT AGAINST THE SOUTH WALL

Sable, a Cheveron Or between three
Snaffles Argent for MILLS —impaling,
Ermine, a Lion rampant gardant Gules
on a Canton Argent, a Spread Eagle of
the third, for

ON FLAT STONES

Arms, Sable, an Eagle displayed
Ermine, for SMITH

Hic jacet, vir doctrina,
moribus, & pietate insignis
HUMFREDUS SMITH, A M
et hujus ecclesiæ tantis
plusquam quadraginta rector,
qui obiit Feb 26, 1687 8,
anno ætatis suæ 7,

MARIAM juxta Uxorem
JOHANNES EVKYN, LL B
hujus ecclesiæ rector,
diem hic expectat
supremum
Tu vero lector vigil!
Ne dies tremendus ille
tibi superveniat
in pœnam

I F	obiit	July 1, 1734	æt	63
M E		Nov 24 1749		66

C B *
hujus ecclesiæ Rector,
obiit
die Septembris,
Anno Dom
MDCCXVIII
ætatis suæ LIII

Here lie the Remains of
ELIZABETH,
the Infant Daughter of
ROBERT and BARBARA DENLEY
She departed this Life
the 3d of September, 1789,
aged 4 Months

ON BRASS PLATES

Here lieth the Body of
WILLIAM SMITH,
late Wife of
HUMBERLY SMITH Clerk,
who departed this Life
Feb 20, 1632

Here lieth the Body of
DOROTHY SMITH,
the Wife of
WILLIAM ....
of Alvescot, in the County of Ox,
Clerk
who died April 16

Here lieth the Body of
B .... ,
th Son of
HUMFREY SMITH
who departed this Life
July 23 16
aged 12 Years and 6 months the

Here lieth the Body of
THOMAS COX
of .... his son ....
who departed this month of late
May 18, 1656

ON AN ATCHIEVEMENT
AGAINST THE NORTH WALL
IN THE NAVE

.... the Valiant Lion's Other
.... two Bendlets ....
.... —impaling ....
.... for THOMAS COX ....
.... an Oak Tree ....
....

IN THE CHURCH YARD, ON A TOMB

CHARLES MILLER, Gent
died October 7, 17

* CHRISTOPHER PAY

ON HEAD AND FLAT STONES

	Died	Aged		Died	Aged
Elizabeth, Wife of William Joynes	27 July, 1767	33	Hannah, Wife of Edmund Addams	8 Aug 1752	22
Sarah their Daughter -	6 Apr 1776	12	Edmund, Son of Gabriel and Susannah Adams -	15 July, 1753	26
John Joynes -	2 Mar 1748	72			
William Joynes buried	17 Aug 1762	83	Elizabeth, Wife of Gabriel Addams	28 Jan 1786	57
Anna Maria his Wife buried	4 Aug 1741	45	Ann, Wife of Thomas Joynes	6 July, 1788	34
Anna Maria Daughter of William and Elizabeth Joynes	18 Sept 1763	1	Thomas Joynes -	5 July, 1780	54
			James, Son of Charles and Mary Gillett	28 Sept 1779	
Elizabeth, Wife of Thomas Joynes	3 Nov 1763	41	Rebekah their Daughter	27 Mar 1781	
James and Joseph their Children died Infants			John Townsend	14 July 1740	60
Thomas Simmons -	3 Nov 1736	65	Mary their Daughter -	25 May, 1731	38
Anne his Wife -	1 Feb 1765	78	Mary his Wife - -	—— —— 1720	—
John Joynes Son of Thomas and Elizabeth Humphris	21 Dec 1772		William their Son -	—— —— 1728	—
			Jos Hall -	23 Nov 1781	57
Susannah, Wife of Gabriel Addams	3 Nov 1752	50	Betty Hall, Daughter of Caleb and Betty Hall	12 Feb 1786	28
Gabriel Addams -	4 Dec 1774	90	Caleb their Son -	27 May, 1770	11
Betty, Wife of Charles Gillett	23 Mar 1772	36	John their Son -	14 June, 1760	12
John their Son -	19 June, 1770		Petty Hall -	30 Oct 1782	54
John Pearce - -	29 Dec 1757	90	Ann, Wife of Thomas Rose	20 Oct 1779	19
Mary, Wife of John Curtis	2 Feb 1788	65	John, Son of Tho and Eliz Wheeler	9 Sept 1779	29
Elizabeth, Wife of John Joynes, of Hazleton -	25 July, 1789	72	John their Son -	7 Sept 1744	
			Alice their Daughter -	11 Sept 1758	1
Thomas, Son of Thomas and Elizabeth Humphris, of Windrush	12 Jan 1783		Alice their Daughter -	27 Sept 1758	
			Ann their Daughter -	17 June, 1759	11
Richard, Son of Richard and Martha Duffell -	6 May, 1742	24	William Jones - -	26 May, 1717	—

T S a Parish of small Extent, in the lower Division of the Hundred of *Berkeley*, situate on the gr
Road from GLOCESTER to BRISTOL, from the former of which it is distant thirty, and from the
other four Miles. The Boundaries are nearly two Miles each Way, forming a Square, and the Soil,
which is of a stiff Clay, is with small Exception applied to Pasture. From a Survey made in 1791, it
appears that in this Parish are 17 Houses and 113 Inhabitants.

The following account is transcribed from Mr SMYTH's Collections

" *Filton*, alias *Filton* and *Hay*, written also *Filton*, a Township not mentioned in the Booke of *Domef-*
" *dei*, but went under the Name of *Horfield*. In this Village are six Messuages, Parcell at this Day of
" the Possessions of the Bishopricke of *Bristol*, erected in , Hen VIII and were Parcell of the Lands
" of the Monasterie of St *Augustine*, founded by ROBERT Son of HARDINGE, in the Time of Kinge
" STEPHEN. But in what Parish these six Messuages doe lie, Question hath of late been moved by the
" Inhabitants, which I determine not. The Bishop, being Lord also of *Horfield* adjoininge, draweth
" these six Households to his Leet at *Horfield*, who are reputed a little Minor of themselves. The other
" Part of this Village is, at this Day, the Inheritance of WILLIAM BALDWYNE, of *London*, Diaper, whose
" Father WILLIAM BALDWYN, was by Inquis 19 Jac I found to dye seized of the Manor of *Filton*, holden
" of the Kinge by Knight's Service, but not *in Capite*. This little Minor consisteth of eight Households
" who are all within the great Leet of the Hundred of *Berkeley*, whereat they appear twice in each Yeere, and
" whereto the Waste Grounds doe belong. And this eight rule and order the other 6 Households, who
" are bound by what these doe (as all the 45 Yeeres or my being Steward hath byn accustomed), and ap-
" pear thereat, by the Name of the Tything of *Filton* and *Hay*. As for that Part, called *Hay*, only
" one House is nowe standinge thereon, the Inheritance of JOHN MALLET, Esquier. The said WILLIAM
" BALDWYN, Father of WILLIAM, purchased the Manor of JOHN YOUNGE, and hee of RICHARD NE-
" VILLE "

" The doe rest that concerneth this Village, as I observed in the Recordes mentioninge it

" By Patent Roll, in the Tower of *London*, 27 Edw I ELIAS DE FILTON arraigned in Assize against
" the Abbot of St *Augustine*, for common of Pasture there. By Inquis in 4 Rich II after the Death
" of EDMOND BRENT, it is found, that he held joyntlie with his Wife MARGARET, who survived, the
" Moietie of the Manor of *Filton* by Gift of THOMAS FITZ NICHOL and MARGERY his Wife, holden of
" REGINALD DE COBHAM in Right of ALIENOUR his Wife, by Knight's Service, and that WILLIAM
" BRENT is his Son and Heire

" By Rot Claus 7 Ric II mem 22 upon a "non intromittendo" to the King's Eschaetor, it is re-
" cited that where is EDMOND BRENT, deceased held joyntlie the Minor of *Filton*, not holden of the King,
" that the said Moietie should be delyvered to MARGARET his Wife

" By Inquis 7 Ric II upon a Writ of "Ad quod Damnum" it was found, that beside other Mi
" nors entayled by the said Sir THOMAS FITZ NICHOL, there remained to him the Moietie of the Mi
" nors of *Filton* and *Harridocke*, holden of RICHARD COBHAM, by Knight's Service, in Right of Li-
" NOR his Wife. In *Berkeley* Castell is a Court Roll, 11 Hen IV which shews, that ELIAS DE FILTON,
" Son of RALPH DE FILTON, was then Lord thereof

" Inquis 6 Hen V after the Death of Sir THOMAS FITZ NICHOL, shews that he held the Minors of
" *Filton* and *Cobham*, of the Lord of BERKELEY, but by what Service the Jurie find no, and that
" KATHERINE, the Wife of Jo TOUNEY, and John Son of JOHN POYNTZ and ELEANOUR his Wife,
" are as well Heires of the said Sir THOMAS, the said KATHERINE and MARIE being both his Daugh-
" ters and Coheires

" Inquis 8 Hen V after the Death of JOHN, Son and Heire of JOHN BROWNING, findes that hee
" dyed seised of the Minor of *Filton* and *Harridoke*, holden of the Lord BERKELEY, and that WILLIAM
" his Brother and Heire is then 23 Yeers olde

" Inquis 3 Hen VI finds that WILLIAM, sometime the Wife of John BRENT, held for her
" Life the Minor of *Filton* of the Heire of ELEANOUR SEYNT, deceased; and the PERSON BRENT
" was her Sonne and Heire. See also the Record of Michaelmas Term, 20 Hen VI in Scaccario
" item Thesaur "

M Filton

From the Family of MALLET, the Manor paſſed to JOHN POPE, Eſq of *Briſtol*, about the Beginning of this Century, and now belongs to the Right Honourable FREDERIC AUGUSTUS Earl of BERKELEY The chief Eſtate was transferred to JOHN BRICKDALE, Eſq and with another, the Property of the Family of GAYNER, is held under the Manor

The Church, dedicated to *St Peter*, is a ſmall and low Fabric, conſiſting of a Nave and Semi tranſept, projecting on the South Side

The Benefice is a Rectory in the Diocese and Deanery of *Briſtol*, originally appropriated to the Abbey of *St Auguſtine*, charged in the King's Books at the clear yearly Value of 36*l* 11*s* 8*d* * The Advowſon was formerly attached to the Manor

In the Sale made of Episcopal Eſtates, Jan 30, 1649, the Manors and Impropriations of *Horfield* and *Filton* were purchaſed by THOMAS ANDREWS for 1256*l* 14*s*, but it appears, that the ſix Meſſuages before mentioned were the whole Property of the Biſhop in this Pariſh †

BENEFACTION

JOHN SILCOCKS, Gent by Will, dated July 22, 1741, bequeathed the Sum of 200*l* to CHRISTOPHER GRYFFITH the elder, and CHRISTOPHER his Son, and their Aſſigns, and the Miniſter and Churchwardens of the ſeveral Pariſhes of *Filton, Stoke Giffard, Winterbourne,* and *Almondſbury*, in Truſt, to apply the Intereſt to teach poor Children to read, whoſe Parents do not receive Alms, in an equal Number for each Pariſh The annual Proportion of Intereſt to *Filton* is 2*l* 10*s*

INCUMBENTS	PATRONS		INCUMBENTS	PATRONS
—— Richard Knevett,	————,	1683	Scudamore Godwyn, B A	————
1663 Richard Johnſon,	————	1702	Samuel Godwyn,	
1597 William King,	————	1705	James Pidding §,	Eliza Pope
1645 Will Blackwell ‡, B A	John Mallet, Eſq	1730	Francis Baker,	Charles Hawkins
1662 Thomas Stephens,	————	1735	John Bound, M A	The ſame
1668 Thomas Godwyn,	————	1766	John Davie, M A	Matt Brickdale, Eſq
1675 Thomas Godwyn,	————	1779	Edw Blakeway, M A	The ſame

PRESENT LORD OF THE MANOR,

The Right Honourable FREDERIC AUGUSTUS Earl of BERKELEY

No Perſon was ſummoned from this Place by the Heralds in 1682 and 1683

At the Election in 1776 One Freeholder polled from this Pariſh

The Regiſter has its firſt Date in 1654

ANNUAL ACCOUNT OF MARRIAGES, BIRTHS, AND BURIALS, IN THIS PARISH

A D	Mar	Bir	Bur	A D	Mar	Bir	Bur	A D	Mar	Bir	Bur	A D	Mar	Bir	Bur
1781	—	1	6	1786	1	6	—	1791				1796			
1782	—	5	1	1787	1	5	3	1792				1797			
1783	—	2	1	1788	—	4	7	1793				1798			
1784	1	4	3	1789	2	3	3	1794				1799			
1785	1	2	1	1790	—	3	1	1795				1800			

INSCRIPTIONS IN THE CHURCH.

ON FLAT STONES IN THE CHANCEL

Here lyeth the Body of JANE, Daughter of JAMES PIDDING, Rector of this Pariſh, who departed this Life Dec 1714, aged 13 Years and Months

Alſo her lieth THOMAS, Son of the ſaid JAMES PIDDING, who departed this Life April 9, 1721, aged 3 Years

Here lieth the Body of JANE, Wife of JAMES PIDDING, Rector of this Pariſh, who departed this Life Sept 1, 1723, ætatis ſuæ 52

---

* BACON's Liber Regis, p 18

† EDWARD COLSTON, Eſq who died in 1721, gave 6,000*l* to augment ſixty ſmall Livings, of which Benefaction *Filton* partook in 1727

‡ BARRET's Briſtol, p 516 Ecton's Thesaurus, ed WILLIS.

‡ Ejected for Nonconformity in 1662

§ At his own Coſt he built the Eaſt End of the Parſonage Houſe in 1716, and in 1714 paved the Chancel with Brick

He -

Here lieth Abigail Hull,
who lived 13 Months,
and died Feb 17 1637

Also here lieth the Body of
Elinor Wade the Wife of
the above said John Wade,
who departed this Life April 19, 1741,
aged 80 Years

Here lyeth the Body of
Grace Blake
the Wife of John Blake,
of this Parish, Yeoman,
who departed this Life the d of April,
1690, aged 70

IN THE SOUTH TRANSEPT

Here lieth the Body of
John Wade, of this Parish, Gent
who departed this Life May 7, 1716,
aged 49 Years

Here lyeth the Body of
John Blake
who died Dec 1692 aged

IN THE CHURCH YARD, ON TOMBS

William Bysse,
died Nov 1, 1656 ætatis 44

Anne his Wife
died April 5 1689 ætatis suæ 80

George Fretwell
and
Mary his Wife

Here lyeth the Body of
Thomas Austin Ship Carpenter,
who departed this Life
the 6th Day of May, 1672, aged 55

ON HEAD STONES

	Died	Aged		Died	Aged
William Millett, Yeoman	10 May 1750	48	John Wade, Yeoman	14 Oct 1760	64
Elizabeth his Daughter	21 Nov 1745	17	Mary his Wife	11 Oct 1737	4
Thomas his Son	17 Nov 1745	—	Ann his Wife	7 Jan 1734	68
Mary his Daughter	2 Nov 1745	19	Joseph son of Jacob and Mary M	1716	
William his Son	21 Nov 1745	6	lett		
Thomas Harding, of Bristol, Carpenter	19 Dec 1765	47	Joseph, Son of Jacob and Mary Mil lett	1732	—
Richard Hancock, of Pen Park, in the Parish of Westbury on Trim	6 Dec 1766	47	Hannah Daughter of Jacob and Mary Millett	1723	—
Sarah Lewis, of Horfield	7 May, 1760	61	Mary Daughter of Jacob and Mary Millett	1730	—
Stephen Humphrys, Blacksmith	7 Feb 1741	30	Hester, Daughter of Jacob and Mary Millett	1716	—
Martha his Relict, and Wife of John Spear, of Baptist Mills, in the Parish of St Philip and Jacob	28 June 1768	—	William Owen	7 Feb 1725	49
John West	5 Nov 1748	—	Hannah his Wife	5 Oct 1711	30
William Fake, of Bristol,	7 Oct 1758	55	Ann their Daughter	5 July, 1743	40
Thomas Wade	11 J 1744	65	William Mary, and William their Children died in their Infancy		
John Wade, Gent	13 Apr 1705	83			

CXX. FLAXLEY.

THIS Parish is a Part of the Hundred of *St Briavel*, in the Purlieus of the Forest of *Dean*, eleven Miles distant from GLOUCESTER on the North-east, and three from *Newnham* The Bounds include about 1400 Acres, of a Soil varying from red Marl to Lime Stone, and chiefly in Pasture and Woodland In the earliest Records Iron Forges are said to have been established here, and the Iron of this Manufactory has long been esteemed of an excellent Quality

The Abbey of *Flexely* or *Dene* was founded for *Cistertian* Monks, in the Reign of King STEPHEN, about the Year 114-, by ROGER FITZ-MILO, the second Earl of *Hereford*, after the Conquest, in a Valley called *Castiard*, which was, from its retired and beautiful Situation, peculiarly adapted to that order of conventual Hermits Their Endowment, originally simple, was confirmed and extended by various Charters (which are subjoined), during the reigns prior to the Dissolution†. It does not, however, appear that their Number was ever great, and, as the Abbots had no pontifical Privilege, no Documents have reached us, by which their Succession might have been more regularly ascertained, than by the Register of the Diocese of *Hereford*

ABBOTS.

1288	Nicholas	1509	John
1314	William de Rya.	1528	William Beawdley ‡
1372	Richard Peyto	1532	Thomas Ware §

By which last, the Abbey was surrendered to the Commissioners in 1541, at which Time there were Nine Monks, whose Revenues were valued at £112 13s 1d according to DUGDALE A Grant and Confirmation of these were made to Sir WILLIAM KINGSTONE ‖, Knight, by King HENRY VIII in 1545, from which we collect that the conventual Church, Tower, Chapter-house, &c were then undemolished He made it his Residence, and was succeeded by his Son Sir ANTHONY ** and his Descendants

* *Cistertian* Monks were a Branch of the *Benedictines*, so called from *Cistertium* or *Cisteaux*, in the Bishoprick of *Chalons* in *Burgundy* This Order, called likewise *Bernardines* was established in 1098 Their Monasteries, which became very numerous (for STEVENS, vol II p. 31 says that they had in all 6000 Houses), were generally founded in solitary and romantic Places and all dedicated to the Blessed Virgin DUGDALE's Mon vol I p 891 STEVENS Mon vol II pr 37 39

† See in DUGDALE's Mon An, vol I p 884, the Charter of HENRY Duke of NORMANDY and mother, when King HENRY II confirms the Donation of Earl ROGER, Pat 22 RICHARD II p , 11 16 grants them in the County the Mill and in-propriate Church of *Flaxley* the Manors of *Blaisdon*, *Newnham*, and *Ruerdeane*, distinct Manors in the Parishes of *Dio Parva Dymock* and *Alingham* a House in *Abbenhall*; and an Iron Forge in the Forest of *Dean* and for the supply of it two Oaks Weekly, which being found prejudicial a Wood called *Abbots Wood* was given by Patent 42 HENRY III, in Lieu of it ten The Foundation Charter gave them the Tythe of all the Chesnuts growing within the Forest (*Decimam omnium Castanearum*) then producing a considerable Income Certain Tenants within the Purlieus of the Royal Forests, had the right of Pannage or Pannage i e of turning in a certain Number of Hogs to feed on the Acorns and Masts from the Feast of St Michael that of St MARTIN The frequent instances of the Roofs of ancient buildings having been constructed with Chesnut proves that it was generally cultivated in England as a Timber Tree, and the Fruit emigrated by the lower rank of People is considered as of greater Value than Acorns, and consequently subject to Decimation It be admitted that the Timber was valuable the Revenue must have been very considerable By the same Grant they had Fishers, and *Adciam que dicitur Nase* and a Moiety of the Fishery in the *Severn* called *Bunware* Rot in Turr *Lond* N N 39 Pat 54 HEN III n 58 And a Charter dated 2 EDWARD III 13,2 an annual Rent Charge of 36l 19s 1d from the King's Tenants in the Forest of *Dean* In 2 RICHARD II 1387, certain Tenements in *Leye*, *hostelry*, and *Kidney* Pat p 2 m 2b For further Particulars consult TANNER's Not Mon ed NASMITH GLOUCESTERSHIRE, N° XI

LELAND in his Itinerary, Vol IV p 83, says, '*Flaxle* Abbey of White Monks stode in *Dene* Forest a mile 6 Miles from *Gloustre*,' and vol VIII p 36, "ROGERUS Earl of HEREFORD Founder of *Flaxley* in the Forest of *Dene* That was a Brother of ROGERUS Earl of HEREFORD that was kylled with an Arowe in Huntinge in the very Place where the Abbay is was made There was a Tabull of the Matter hanggid up in the Abbay Church of *Flaxley* There was a Bishop of H a FORD that holpe moche to the buildinge of *Flaxley*"

"ROGER Earl of HEREFORD having, in the decline of Life taken the Habit of a Benedictine, died St in the Abbey of St Pet in *Gloucester* in the Year 1143, 12 HENRY II DUGDALE's Baronage, vol I p 538

‡ "1528, June 18 Father WILLIAM BRAWNLEY, Abbat of *Flaxley* of the Cistertian Order, opponent in Divinity Woods Fasti, vol I p 1 c

§ THOMAS WARE, a Monk of the Cistertian Order, and some time a Student in St Bernard College in Oxon He afterwards became the last Abbot of *Flexe*, in *Gloucestershire* (in the Place of W BEAWLEY) and living to see his Houses suppressed himself and his Brethren turned out thence he retired to *Astbroke* convent in *Oxon* where, spending the remaining Part of his Life in Devotion and Retiredness he in a great way it might be Fothergild old Age Anno 1558 when aged He was buried in the Yard belonging to the Church there Wood's Fasti vol I p 62, WILLIAM's Athena Oxon, vol II p 82

‖ Of Sir WILLIAM KINGSTONE I revive thus see (Worthies, p 363) that "he was one of the best Courtiers and Soldiers, one of the best Captains at Sea, and one of the most valiant and skilful Commanders by Land He was knighted for his Service in *Tournay* and made Marshal of the field at *Flodden* Field Afterwards Captain of the Guard to King HENRY VIII and Constable of the Tower and conducted Cardinal Wolsey upon his Attendance upon the Disposition so that he frequently showed very largely having received from time to time several Manors in the County belonging to the Duchy Harl es of *Lancaster* and *Berkeley* Fuller's Worthies p 38

** "HENRY VIII, by his Letters Patent 1545 regranted to Sir ANTHONY KINGSTONE the Site of the late Abbey of *Flaxley* and all the Church Bell Lead and Church Yard of the same and all the House, Garden & of *Flaxley* within the said ground and all other the Manors and tenements of *Flaxley*, He also granted and confirmed to him the Bailiwick *Forgeam*, le *Knolle*, *Knowles*, *Nether*, *Dene Parva Newnham Walton*, and *Dymock* with their Right, & in the County of *Gloucester* and the Hundred and Manor of *Rochford*, with certain Services belonging to the same and all Acres of it is their own use & of the said Monastery the appurtenances thereof the said Monastery, the yearly payment to be 24 at the Crown

Early in the present Century, that Part of this venerable Pile which had been inhabited by the Abbot and Monks, remained nearly perfect * It was a low Structure of great Length, containing in Front the Refectory, sixty Feet long, twenty-five wide, but fourteen only in height, the whole arched with Stone, with plain and massy Ribs, intersecting the Vault The first Floor consisted of a very long Gallery, with which the Dormitories or Cells were connected and at the South End a very spacious Apartment, which is conjectured to have been the Abbot's chief Room or used for the assembling of the Convent These are certainly Parts of the original Structure, much of which was destroyed by Fire in 1777, which has been since restored, and many Additions made by the present Possessor In several of the Apartments are some fine old Portraits of the Families of CLARKE and BOEVEY In 1788, the Site and Floor of the Chapter house were discovered at a small Depth in the Garden, extending about forty five Feet, and twenty-four wide, at the upper End a circular Stone Bench, and in the Centre the carved Base of a Pillar Seven Coffin Lids of Stone were then found to be buried, with an carved Crosses, but upon one a right Hand and Arm holding a Crosier, which Circumstance imports it to have been the Memorial of one of the Abbots, as their Office had not the Privilege, as that of Bishops, of conferring Benediction

In the Park, on the North east, is a natural Terrace of considerable Extent commanding a most interesting View of the cultivated Vale of Severn and the City of Gloucester, flanked by the whole Chain of the Cotswold Mountains from Bredon to Sodbury Hill, a Line of more than fifty Miles The frequent Windings of the River in the Fore-ground appear like so many Lakes in Succession, and give a highly picturesque Effect to this singularly pleasing Landscape The Benefice is a Donative, which receives 8l per Annum from the Impropriation, and is further endowed with the Profits of an Estate purchased with 1200l bequeathed by CATHERINE BOEVEY, Relict of WILLIAM BOEVEY Esq for this Purpose In Pursuance of her Request, the Church was re-built by her Executrix Mary Pope about the Year 1730, which is small, with a low Spire, but on the Inside peculiarly neat The Archdeacon of Hereford visits it, as a Member of his Archdeaconry in the Diocese of GLOUCESTER

Before the year 1650, ABRAHAM CLARKE, Esq purchased the manor and Estate, including the greater Part of the Parish, of ANTHONY KINGSTONE, Esq the fifth in Descent from the first Proprietor and who left no Issue He was succeeded by his Son ABRAHAM after whose Death WILLIAM BOEVEY, Esq enjoyed it By his Will, dated 1697, it passed, subject to Joint ce, to THOMAS CRAWLEY Esq of GLOUCESTER, who assumed the Surname of BOEVEY, from whom it has descended to his Grandson, who, in 1789, succeeded to the Dignity of Baronet, in virtue of a Limitation in the Patent of Creation of Sir CHARLES BARROW, Baronet, of Highgrove, bearing Date Jun 22, 24 Geo III 1 84 An Estate, called the Grange, now vested in the Family of SKIP, is held by Lease under the Manor

B E N E F A C T I O N S

1620, May 8   GEORGE CULLIMANS, Gent gave, by Will, Moneys, now producing 1l a Year, to be given to the Poor

1692, 1 Aug   WILLIAM BOEVEY, Esq by Will so dated, bequeathed 400l which Legacy was confirmed by his Relict CATHERINE BOEVEY, by Will, dated March 3, 1726, to be applied to the apprenticing poor Children of the Parish of Flaxley, the annual Produce of which is 1l

PERPETUAL CURATES	PATRONS	PERPETUAL CURATES	PATRONS
1727 Thos Tyler, M A	Thos Crawley Boevey, Esq	1742 Wm Crawley M A	J Crawley Boevey, Esq
—— William Lloyd, M A		1780 John Longden, M A	J Crawley Boevey, Esq

PRESENT LORD OF THE MANOR,
SIR THOMAS CRAWLEY BOEVEY, Baronet

The only Person summoned by the Heralds, in 1652 and 1683, was
Abraham Clarke, Esq

At the Election in 1776 Two Freeholders polled from this Parish.

INSCRIPTIONS IN THE CHURCH
ON MONUMENTS IN THE CHANCEL

Arms Ermine, a Bend, Party per Bend Gules and Sable, charged with two Cuttes d'Or, between three Cornish Choughs of the third, for BOEVEY — impaling, Argent, three Annulets Azure, for RICH

M S
GULIELMI BOEVEY, Armig
Qui fide et fumma ornatior in,
non sui pa cis si it appetens them,
ne sui notos ex i juria
I benef ent a munere is
Maximum vitae partem felici er transegit
tandem vero
Cum mole corporis ob fillim anima
oppress i spiraret gravter et gemere

ut illens in sui optim bibert,
Deo indicite
id super singu a facultad
Aet XXVI A D MDCXVII
it i XXXV

H M
Catharina
conjux fidissima
M P

Arms BOEVEY as before

Hic deniqit
ABRAHAMUS CLARE, Armiger
fertam schutectitenotu esp Liti

monim vita m fili in Comiti
jillitii opti. ti cultoris rebus,
fui inti moni et it tide,
ver et Deum
I memoria er p patroni,
erphic i rum patet
iberalitatem cresce in ordinat
qui in ordine tue ha ec antificanti,
redi perant Deum
tere limitet
et i i ti amenti et varti in
eventu et i i i ti et a i i um
erti es to Old in si
4 anno Domini i i i
i iti noti i

* See Kip's View of Flaxley Abbey, Atkyns's Antiquities of Gloucestershire
7 N

Arms, Ermine, a Saltire Gules, for
LLOYD

Hoc juxta marmor
depositi conduntur cineres
GUILELMI LLOYD, A. M.
de Stow cum novent eculis
in agro Northonienti
Per annos XXXIV rectoris
Viri
eximiâ probitate fide & eruditione
inftruétissimi,
& cuilibet vel in ecclesia vel in orbe
literito muneri,
five sufinendo, five ornando,
nifi sua obtinisset modesti a
non imparis
In hac capella concionatoris munere
per anno. con plures
feliciter perfunétus est
Londini natus,
in Oxoniensi academia enutritus,
bene lituit & bene vixit,
donec id vitam beatiorem hinc
translatus est
Julii XI die,

anno ætatis suæ LXIX,
& æræ Christianæ
MDCCLIV

Arms Or, on a Chevron Sable three
Elfoiles Argent, for CLARKE

Here lyeth entombed the Body of
JOANNA CLARKE, Lady of Flaxley
who deceased this Life, in the Feare of
GOD, upon Palm Sunday
the 3d of April in the 59th Year of
her Age, and in the Yeir of
our Lord GOD 1664

ON FLAT STONES

JAMES the Son of
ABRAHAM CLARKE, Efq
died Feb 11 1669 aged 6 Days

JANE his Daughter,
born March 6, 1670,
and died Sept 9, 1677

ELIZABETH his Daughter,
born April 22, 1672
and buried in this Chapel
Dec 6, 1677

ANNE RICHES,
Daughter of JOHN RICHES, Efq
and onely Sister to Mrs BOVEY
of Flaxley, departed this Life
Oét 5 1689
which she had passed
in a religious Obfervance of her Duty
towards God and her Parents,
in tender Affeétion to her Relations,
in Charity and Kindnefs to all
ended with his early Habit of Vertue,
Death, however suddain,
did not furprife her
unprepared

ON A LARGE PLAIN TABLET OF WHITE MARBLE

In the Vault near this Chapel is repofited the Body of
Mrs CATHARINA BOVEY Daughter of JOHN RICHES Efq of London, Merchant
She was married to WILLIAM BOVEY, Efq Lord of this Mannot of Flaxley, at the Age of 15,
was left a Widow, without Children, at the Age of 22 and continued fo all the reft of her Life
She entertained her Friends and Neighbours with a moft agreeable Hofpitality but always took Care to
have a large Referve for Charity, which she beftowed, not only on fuch Occafions as offered,
but ftudied how to employ it fo as to make it ufeful and advantageous
Her Difpofition to do good was fo well known in the Diftrict about her, that she eafily became acquainted with
the Circumftances of thofe that wanted; and as she preferved many Families from Ruin by feafonable Loans or Gifts,
fo she conveyed her Affiftance to fome of better Rank, in fuch a Manner as made it doubly acceptable
How far her Bounty extended was known to herfelf alone but much of it appeared, to her Honour and God's Glory,
in frequent Diftributions to the Poor, and efpecially to the Charity Schools round about the Country
in relieving thofe in Prifon, and delivering many out of it in contributing to Churches of the Englifh Eftablifhment
abroad, as well as aiding feveral at home, in cloathing and feeding her indigent Neighbours,
and teaching their Children fome of whom every Sunday by Turns she entertained at her Houfe
and condefcended to examine them herfelf befides this continual it might be faid this duty, Courfe of Liberality
during her Life She bequeathed at her Death toward founding a College in the Ifland of Bermuds 500 l,
to the Grey Coat Hofpital, in St Margaret's, Weftminfter, 500 l,
to the Blue Coat Hofpital in Weftminfter 500 l
to the Charity School of Chrift Church Parifh of Southwark, 400 l
to augment the Living of this Place, 1200 l,
to put out poor Children Apprentices the Intereft of 400 l for ever of which Summe 160 l had been
left by Mr CLARKE and Mr BOVEY
to be diftributed, as her Executrix fhould think fit, among thofe whom she had put out Apprentices in her Life time 400 l,
laftly, she defigned the re building of this Chapel, which pious Defign of hers
was fpeedily executed by Mrs MARY POPE

A MONUMENT IS ERECTED TO HER MEMORY IN WESTMINSTER ABBEY, WITH THE FOLLOWING INSCRIPTION

To the Memory of Mrs CATHARINA BOVEY
whofe Perfon and Underftanding would have become the higheft Rank in Female Life, and
whofe Vivacity would have recommended her in the left Converfation but by Judgment,
as well as Inclination she chofe fuch a retirement as give her great Opportunities in Reading and Reflection,
which she made Ufe of to the wifeft Purpofes of Improvement in Knowledge and Religion
Upon other Subjeéts she ventured far out of the common Way of thinking but in Religious Matters
she made the Holy Scriptures, in which she was well skill'd, the Rule and Guide of her Faith and Aétions,
efteeming it more fafe to rely upon the plain Word of God than to run into any Freedoms of Thought
upon revealed Truth the great Share of Time allowed to the Clofet was not perceived in her Œconomy
for she had always a well ordered and well inftructed Family, from the happy Influence,
as well of her Temper and Conduét, as of her uniform and exemplary Chriftian Life
It pleafed God to blefs her with a confiderable Eftate, which, with a liberal Hand
guided by Wifdom and Piety, she employed to his Glory and the Good of her Neighbours,
Her domeftick Expences were managed with a Decency and Dignity fuitable to her Fortune,
but with a Frugality that made her Income abundant to all proper Object of Charity,
to the Relief the Neceffitous, and I mean igreat relief of the Inftitution and the Inftruction of the Ignorant
She deferved not only with Cheerfulnefs, but with Joy which upon fome Occafions of railing and
refrefhing the fpirit of th Afflicted, she could not refrain from breaking forth into Tears,
flowing from a Heart thoroughly affeéted with Companion and benevolence
Thus did many of her good Works, while she lived go up as a Memorial before God
and fome she left to follow her

She died Jan 21 1726, in the 57th Year of her Age
at Flaxley her feat in Gloucefterfhire
and was buried there where her Name will be
long remembered, and where feveral of her Benefaétions
to that Place, as well as to her, are particularly recorded

This Monument was erected with the utmoft Refpeét
to her Memory and Juftice to her Chiraéter by her
Executrix Mrs MARY POPE, who lived with her near
40 Years in perfeét Friendfhip, never once interrupted
till her much lived ed Death

To the Memory of MARY POPE,
Daughter of JOHN POPE of Briftol Merchant,
the Friend of Mrs BOVEY, and Partner of her Virtues who after a Life fpent in
exemplary Piety, and full of good Works died March 24,
in the Year of our Lord 1746, aged 81 Years

IN THE CHURCH YARD

ON A TABLET AGAINST THE CHURCH
In Memory of the
excellent Mrs. ELIZABETH COWLING,
Daughter of JOHN COWLING Esq.
who left this Life for a blessed Eternity,
Sept. 16, 1759, aged 42 Years

ON TOMBS
WILLIAM HEYLEY,
died July 20, 1784, aged 76
ELIZABETH his Wife
died July 25, 1785 aged 83

EDWARD WILLIAMS
died June 5, 1755, aged 31
CECIL his Mother
died Jan 25, 1773, aged 84

THOMAS HULL
died Oct. 27, 1764 aged 83
ELIZABETH his Wife
died March 26, 1722, aged 39,
MARY his second Wife
died Sept. 28, 1723

EDMUND GREEN
died Sept 8, 1721, aged 73
LIBRAIN his Son
died Sept 5, 1705, aged 12
MARGARET GREEN
died Dec. 30 1732, aged 72

EDMUND GREEN,
died April 23 1748, aged 52
BLANCH the Wife of
JOHN SMITH, of the Grove,
in the Parish of Westbury,
died Jan 13, 1783, aged 74

ON HEAD AND FLAT STONES

	Died		Aged		Died		Aged
Elizabeth Wife of Charles Rose, of the Parish of Chapel Hill, in the County of Monmouth	2 Apr	1775	42	Mary, Wife of Thomas Lodge	28 Nov	1708	—
				Thomas Lodge	7 Apr	1722	55
Elizabeth Wife of Charles Rose	31 Mar	1780	47	Richard Constable	3 June	1753	35
Mary Trefford	7 Mar	1778	63	Ann, Wife of Roger Blewett	8 Mar	1721	79
Arnel Wallington	1 Jan	1765	64	Robert Hillier	12 Feb	1779	67
John Evens	21 Nov	1733	45	Mary, Wife of Edmund Green, late Wife of Thomas Hill	7 Oct	1763	62
Sarah his Daughter	—	1733	6	James Mann	1 Nov	97	59
Thomas Burgum	25 Nov.	1740	69	Mary his Wife	8 Dec	1676	
William Nourse	11 Aug	177	68	Richard Hazell	6 May	1701	52
Mary his Wife	12 Oct	1740	45	Richard Hazell	12 May,	1722	—

FORTHELMINTON, or commonly _Forthington_, is a Parish of about five Miles in Extent, in the lower Division of the Hundred of _Tewkesbury_, from whence it is three Miles distant West, and and eight North from the City of GLOUCESTER The Boundaries are closed on the North by a part of _Worcestershire_, and the River _Severn_ forms them on the East The Soil is chiefly of a deep Clay, and applied to Pasturage it is likewise very productive of Oak and Elm Timber

The Benefice is a Cure, stipendiary from the Impropriation, and in the Appointment of the Impropriator, who is charged with a yearly Payment of 13l 6s 8d is settled upon the Suppression of the Abbey of _Tewkesbury_ It is a Peculiar of _Deerhurst_

In the Year 1789, such Repairs were made to the Church that no discriminating marks of Antiquity remain It is a spacious Building, dedicated to St _Mary_, with a strong embattled Tower The Pews were made at the Expence of the Lord of the Manor

As a Member of the great Lordship of _Tewkesbury_, this Manor was retained by the Crown, at the Compilation of Domesday King HENRY II granted it the _Benedictines of Tewkesbury_, by Royal Charter, in whom it was vested till the Dissolution The Abbot had here a Country Residence and private Chapel, the Site and Parts of which are the present Mansion JOHN WAKEMAN, the last Abbot, after his Resignation and Consecration as first Bishop of GLOUCESTER, frequently retired here, and died in 1549 But he must be considered as a Tenant only, for the Demesne was granted to GILES HARPER in 1542, 23 HEN VIII

The Manor reverting to the Crown, was given by K JAMES, in 1607, the 5th of his Reign, to ROBERT CECIL, Earl of _Salisbury_, and was afterward transferred to ARTHUR CAPEL, Earl of _Essex_, in the Reign of CHARLES II His Son sold it to CHARLES DOWDESWELL, Esq Son of RICHARD DOWDESWELL, Esq of _Pull Court_, who was succeeded by his Sons CHARLES and RICHARD CHARLES DOWDESWELL, Son of the last mentioned RICHARD, conveyed it, by Deed of Sale, to SAMUEL CLARKE, Esq from whom it passed, in the same Manner, to Dr ISAAC MADOX, Bishop of _Worcester_, about 1750, whose Daughter and sole Heir is the Wife of the Hon Dr JAMES YORKE, successively Bishop of St _David's_, _Gloucester_, and _Ely_, who, in her right, is the present Proprietor

The Family of HAYWARD, otherwise COX, in the beginning of the last Century, became possessed of considerable Property in this Parish, a great Part of which was lately purchased by the present Lord of the Manor HOPEWELL HAYWARD, Gent has the only exclusive Estate of consequence

HAMLETS —_Swailley_ and _Down End_, of which is nothing worthy remark

BENEFACTIONS

1617 JOHN RESTELL gave, by Deed, Land for the Use of the Poor now producing yearly 13s
1738 Dec 20, ELIZABETH HAYWARD bequeathed 5l for Bread to be given to the Poor
1784 Dec 3 ELIZABETH NEWMAN left Money, the Annual Produce of which is 5l, to be given to the Poor, at the Discretion of her Executor

* " Ego autem ipse Rex HENRICUS dedi eidem Ecclesiæ unam villam quæ fuit de honore ROBERTI, filii HAIMONIS, post " mortem quidem ROBERTI dedi eum et pro anima ipsius Villa ipsa voc to _Forto acror_ " DUGDALE Mon vol I p 161, Pit 36 Hov III m 13 " Protenementis in _Forthampton_ "
† " Maner Place longing to the Abbate of _Tewkesbury_ for description of this Place upon Severn in dextra ripa, a Mile beneath _Tewkesbury_ " LELANDS Itin vol VI p 9.
‡ JOHN WAKEMAN, alias WICH, or is WOOD (LELAND, vol I p 49) calls him, ROBERT WAKEMAN, was the last Abbot of _Tewkesbury_ He continued till the Dissolution 1539, when he surrendered the Abbey with thirty five of the Monks, and his Pension assigned to him of 266l 13s 4d per annum is may be seen in BURNET's History of the Reformation In September 1541 being then B D he was consecrated the first Bishop of GLOUCESTER He died about the Beginning of the year 1549 In his Life time he erected a Tomb for his Place of Burial in the Abbey Church at _Tewkesbury_, in the North Side of which Chapel standing So that from the high Altar Bishop GODWYN (_de Præsulibus Angliæ_), thus I was buried at Home at his own dently meaning, _Forthington_) in the County of GLOUCESTER, where he had House and Chapel WRITES Mr ATKYNS
It is said in HEARNE's Preface to ROBERT of GLOUCESTER, p xxi that in 1540 at a Convocation several Bishops were appointed to peruse the Translation of the Bible and that the Revelations of St John were assigned to JOHN WAKEMAN Bishop of GLOUCESTER, and JOHN CHAMBERS, Bishop of _Peterborough_

1

Perpetual Curates	Patrons
1781 William Parsons, LL B	Dr James Yorke, Bishop of Gloucester
1789 Charles Platt, M A	Dr James Yorke, Bishop of Ely

Present Lord of the Manor,

The Honourable and Right Reverend James Lord Bishop of Ely

The Person summoned from this Place by the Heralds in 1682 and 1683, was Charles Dowdeswell, Esq

At the Election in 1776, Four Freeholders polled from this Parish

The earliest Date in the Register occurs in 1678

Annual Account of Marriages, Births, and Burials, in this Parish

A D	Mar	Bir	Bur	A D	Mar	Bir	Bur	A D	Mar	Bir	Bur	A D	Mar	Bir	Bur
1781	4	10	4	1786	5	10	10	1791				1796			
1782	1	14	9	1787	3	17	3	1792				1797			
1783	4	11	6	1788	5	11	11	1793				1798			
1784	4	16	9	1789	6	13	8	1794				1799			
1785	1	16	11	1790	1	18	6	1795				1800			

INSCRIPTIONS IN THE CHURCH

IN THE CHANCEL

On a Marble Monument

Arms Or, a rel [illegible] wy, between six Billets Sable, for Dowdeswell, impaling Gules, a Chevron Argent pellettee, charged with two B[illegible] Gemelles of the Field, between three Lions Heads, erased Or, for Colles

Hic infra Recon[illegible]tur
Cineres N[illegible] viri Caroli
Dowdeswell [illegible] ex hac Parochia
Armigeri
Filius erat Richardi Dowdeswell,
nuper de Pool-Court,
in Comitatu Wigorn
Arm[illegible]
vir Probitate [illegible] Industria insigni
quippe qui [illegible] ope [illegible]
modo [illegible]
Duos filios, Carolum [illegible]
et Richardum [illegible] filias,
M[illegible]
Georgii Smyth
Armigeri, de North Nibley,
in hoc comitatu nuptam
Elizabetham [illegible]
Yate de Bromsberrow
[illegible]
et Annam adhuc Virginem,
superstites [illegible],
ex Elizabetha [illegible] Cecil,
de [illegible] in comitatu Hertford
Armigeri [illegible] Annos vixit
[illegible]
[illegible]
[illegible]
obiit [illegible] die Octobris,
Anno Christi 1706

On a small Tablet

To Memory of my much honoured
Husband John Colles,
who died in the Year 1631
Elizabeth [illegible]
[illegible], did this

ON FLAT STONES

Here lieth the Body of
Thomas Cockes alias Hayward,
who died the 15th of May, 1[illegible]0

Here lieth the body of
Thomas Hayward
of the Lower House,
who died Dec 18, Anno 16[illegible]4

Here lieth the body of
William Underhill the Sonne of
John Underhill [illegible] Forthampton,
in the County of Gloucester,
who departed this Li[fe]
the [illegible] Day of April
Anno Dom [illegible]647

On a Marble Stone

Arms Dowdeswell as before, impaling [illegible] between [illegible] Gules, [illegible]

This Marble Stone was laid
by the Widow, 17[illegible]
in Memory of her much honoured
Husband Charles Dowdeswell, Esq
late of Forthampton Court
He married Anne eldest Daughter
of the Hon Mr Justice Tracy
[illegible] whom he had two Children
His Son Charles is interred with him
His Daughter Ann survived him,
He died very much lamented,
the [illegible] of May 17[illegible],
in the [illegible] Year of his Age

Here lyeth the Body of
Margaret, the Wife of
[illegible] who departed this life the
18th of Oct [illegible], Year

ON FLAT STONES IN THE NAVE

Arms On a Bend cottised three [illegible] [illegible] impaling Colles as before

Here lieth the Body of
Alice [illegible], Widdow
Wife of Richard [illegible], Gent
and Daughter of John Colles, Esq
who died July [illegible] 169[illegible]

Arms Argent, on a Fess [illegible] three Fleurs de Lis, Or [illegible] Chief [illegible] second a Lion Passant, [illegible] third, for Hayward, impaling a Cross patonce for Ward

Motto, [illegible]
H S E
Hor[illegible] Hayward Gen
pro[illegible] et industria insignis
Obiit 20 Die Jan Anno Dom 1[illegible]22,
Ætatis [illegible]6
Hic quoque jacet
Elizabetha Hayward
ejus Uxor Septem Liberorum [illegible]
[illegible]
[illegible]
[illegible] Ob [illegible]6
Feb [illegible]

H S E
24° Decembris 175[illegible],
Maria Christiana Uxor
Horatii Hayward Gen
filia Gulielmi [illegible] de [illegible]ington
in Com [illegible] Armigeri,
[illegible]
Mater [illegible] filii
Horatii [illegible]
[illegible] et Mariæ [illegible]
et una filia Elizabeth[illegible]
[illegible]
[illegible] Hayward
et Eliz[illegible] Hayward
[illegible]
[illegible] Hayward
[illegible]
[illegible]
[illegible] Oct [illegible],
[illegible]

IN THE CHURCH YARD, ON TOMBS.

PHILLIP HAYWARD, Gent
died June 3, 1714, aged 62 Years

PHILIPPA and ELIZABETH
twin Daughters of the said
PHILIP HAYWARD
died the 25th May 1715,
ELIZABETH died the 9th Oct. 1718.

———

THOMAS HAYWARD, Gent
died July 31, 1742 aged 66

MARY his Wife,
died April 18, 1759,
in the 9[?] Year of her Age.

———

Job C 17 and 14
MARY, Wife of
PHILLIP HAYWARD, Gent
and Daughter of JOHN STURMY,
of Swindon in this County, Gent
died August 22, 1683, aged 34

Also Mrs ELLANOR STURMY,
only Sister to Mrs MARY HAYWARD,
died Sept 5, 1693, aged 54

———

SUSANNAH Wife of RICHARD HILL,
of Dymock, Gent
died July 14, 1750, aged 52 Years

———

JOHN IRELAND, sen
died April 12 1785, aged 77 Years

MARY his Wife,
died Ap l 30, 1729, aged 77 Years

MARY Daughter of
EDWARD and SARAH IRELAND,
died Jan 10 1784, aged 2 Years

EDWARD their Son
died Dec 9 1785, an Infant

PRISCILLA their Daughter,
died Oct 18, 1787, aged 11 Months,

SARAH his Wife,
died Jan 6, 1789, aged 7 Years

ON FLAT AND HEAD STONES

	Died	Aged		Died	Aged
John Neast -	16 Apr 1755	62	Elizabeth his Wife, Daughter of the Rev Mr Thompson, Vicar of Eldersfield,	14 Apr 17 8	63
George Rider -	13 June, 1761	58			
Samuel his Son by Ann his Wife	13 Nov 1769	26			
Richard Newman -	23 Dec 1732	60	Hannah their Daughter	8 June, 1717	19
Benjamin his Son -	1 Feb 1, 29	19	John Willis	17 Jan. 1725	57
Richard his Son -	24 Oct 1766	56	Richard Foaks -	2 June, 1731	67
William Penfon -	10 Nov 1766	66	Thomas Smith	13 July, 1741	23
Sarah his Wife -	4 May 1744	35	Mary Wife of John George -	30 Apl 1746	46
Mary Wife of John Brookes -	2 Sept 1691	60	Mary Daughter of Thomas and Mary Penfam	29 May, 1770	
Ann Wife of Jonathan Stephens	2 May 1707	—			
Richard White -	17 Mar 1721	70	Margaret Tomb -	2 Feb 1746	40
Margaret his Wife	15 July, 1750	76	Elizabeth Hartland -	22 Oct 1749	37
Nicholas Hatton, Sen Gent -	17 May 1681	74	Samuel Jefferies sen	15 Aug 1761	64
John Hatton	4 Aug 669	—	Samuel Jefferies, jun	29 Oct 1757	24
Elizabeth his Wife -	1 Dec 1692	—	Sarah Wife of John Jefferies -	10 Dec 1701	—
Cannan Wife of John Hatton	6 June, 1700	53	John Son of Peter and M Whithorne	25 Aug 1759	23
John Parish -	21 Sept 1785	51	Mary his Mother	13 Feb 1777	68
William Perkins -	13 Sept 1734	42	Thomas Howbrook -	21 Dec 1754	39
Sarah his Wife -	9 Feb 1774	76	John his Son	14 Dec 1784	15
John their Son -	9 May 1767	56	Thomas Weston -	23 Apr 1789	61
Two of his Children died Infants			Elizabeth his Wife -	10 Aug 1788	58
William Mayhe of Longdon	23 Feb 176	56	James Evans -	11 Sept 1734	62
John Man -	4 May, 1687	—	Elizabeth his Wife	18 Mar 1790	50
Mary his Wife -	22 Apr 1705	—	Two of their Children died Infants		
John Man, Sen -	12 Aug 1714	58	John Stubbes	2 Jan 1753	52
Margaret his Wife -	6 Feb 171	55	William Son of John and Hannah Bennett	5 Jan 1763	7
Mary Wife of William Man -	24 Nov 1766	78			
Mary Wife of Charles Maton -	27 Feb 1730	—	William their fixth Son	26 Dec 768	
Robert Newman -	5 Aug 1743	40	John Crees	24 Dec 1783	41
Margaret Wife of John Willis -	17 Mar 1726	53	Susannah his Daughter died an Infant		

CXXII. FRAMPTON COTTEREL,

OR *COTEL* the Name of its ancient Proprietors, is a Parish in the Hundred of *Langley* and *Swineshead*, five Miles distant from *Sodbury* on the South-west, seven South from *Thornbury*, and ... in the same Direction from the City of Gloucester. The Soil is a red Grit, mixed with ferruginous Particles, and the greate Portion in Pasture, including more than 2000 Acres.

The Benefice is a Rectory, in the Deanery of *Hawkesbury*, endowed with an extensive Glebe, the Advowson of which was formerly annexed to the Manor. In 1744 William Southwell Esq who had purchased the Estate of the Family of Symes in this Parish, presented on his Claim, but in the Year ..., it appearing that the Right had descended in certain Parts to the Coheirs of Henry Symes Esq. and their Representatives, the following Arrangement of Presentation was confirmed. 1 His Grace Henry Duke of Beaufort, by Descent from Elizabeth the eldest Daughter of the said Henry Symes, the Wife of Richard Berkeley, Esq. of Stoke Gifford. 2 and . William Southwell, Esq. by Purchase from Edward Bisse Hale, Esq. whose Grandmother was Jane, the second Daughter and Wife of Edward Bisse, Esq. of Bigleicombe, co Somerset. 4 Robert Buxton, Esq. Nephew of the late John Jacob, Esq. of Norton, co Wilts whose Mother was Susannah, the youngest Daughter and Coheir, Duke of Beaufort. 6 and 7 W Southwell, Esq. 8 Robert Buxton Esq. 9 W Southwell, Esq.

The Church, dedicated to *St Peter*, is a Building in the neat Gothic Style of the middle Century, with a South Aisle, and a Tower embattled and pinnacled, with Niches, in which are Images of Saints. The High Altar was dedicated in July 1315, by Walter de Maidenstone, Bishop of Hereford. A MS of Mr Smith, dated 1607, mentions the following Arms as then remaining in the Windows. 1 Ermine, a Fess cheque, Or, and Azure, Arden impaling Quarterly per Fess, indented Argent and Azure Acton. 2 Acton impaling Argent, a Cheveron between three Falcons rising, Gules. 3 Gules, three Lozenges Fess Ermine, D'Aleny impaling Sable six Swallows in Pile, Argent, Arundel. 2 Azure a Bend and I Fess of three Points Or, Carminow. 3 Gules an Orle, within an Inescutcheon, Argent, Crmock, 4th as first. 4 Barry of 8, Or, and Sable, Poyntz. In 1315, 7 Edw II the Family of Acton were seised of a Mill and eighty Acres in this Parish, and were probably Contributors to this Edifice.

In *Domesday*, the Manor taxed at five Hides was given by the Conqueror to Walter, *Balistarius* ... or the Crossbow man of the King's Person. The Descendants took the Surname of Cotel which may become extinct in 1259, 9 Hen III. To them succeeded Robert Waleran, who in 1289, 15 Edw I proved upon a *quo warranto* his Right to Markets and Fairs. In the next Reign 31, John de Willington held it of the Honour of Walleran ford whose Descendants possessed it until it passed by Marriage of John Willington to John Watte of Wotton ... in 1397, 20 Rich II. John their Son dying S P in 1412, this Manor was divided between his two Sisters, Elizabeth the Wife of Sir William Pulton, and Isabel the Wife of William Beaumont, who inherit their Sisters Moiety. Sir Thomas Beaumont Kt Hen III in 1431, 9 Hen VI, and in 1459, 20th Henry VI th Manor was conveyed to the Crown. Henry, Giles Baron Daubeney, was appointed Constable of the Castle of Bristol, and had this Manor in Fee, in both of which in the next Reign he was succeeded by Edward Seymour Duke of Somerset. After his Attainder, the Manor was demised from the Crown in 1567 to the Family of Bisse Anno 1590 it was granted to William Playne, Esq. of Manor held until later by, whose Descendant left it to Charles Bragg, Esq. in 1675. In 1728 Robert Jefferis Gent became possessed of it by Purchase from Edward Hoskins, Esq. For the Church Estate, upon which is a very large ancient Mansion, was detached from the Manor by K Henry VII and given to Sir John Seymour, the Father Edward Duke of Somerset, and Sir Henry Seymour, to the latter of whom he bequeathed it. His Son and Successor was Sir John Seymour of Berton and Frampton Cotel, Knight of the Shire for this County. Anne his eldest Coheir was the Wife of Henry Symes, Esq. who purchased the remaining Interest of their Heir. Edward Bisse, Esq. received it in Dower with Jane second Daughter and Coheir of ... Elizabeth his Son. Amy Daughter of Edward Bisse, married Garret Hale of Alderly, Grandson of Chief Justice Hale, and was

* King William the Conqueror constituted an Officer called *Arcubalistarius Reg...* who was retained by his ancestor. His Lands were held in Capite of the King by the Service of preferring annually a Crossbow and of kindred ... down according to whatever was offered. The King paid that through ... certain Lands ... *Domesday*, p 157. In later Records ... Jeane ... pp 57 ... &c. In the *Great Antiquity* ...
† *Blount's Tenures*, p 6

Preceded by Lowa s Biss, Hal, Esq who died in 17.., and to whose was soon after soll to William Southwell, Esq who is the present Proprietor

Wickwer is the oti ...ing and is confidered as a feparate Manor ... ...ongrily a Part of the Eftate of the Seymours in this Parifh In the Reign of Q Eliz it paffed to Roger Kemys, Efq and continued in his Defcendants till it was conveyed by ... ... to Robert Brown Gent with Ann the elder Co-heir of William Kemys, by who the ... Daughter Mary afterward Wife of Clayton Milborne, who died in 1712

Francis Brown, Efq was the fubfequent Poffeffor, whofe eldeft Daughter married John Da. Efq of Biya, who inherits in her Right

No Benefactions to the Poor

INCUMBENTS	PATRONS	INCUMBENTS	PATRONS
15.3 Thomas Dylke,	Q Mary	1667 Miles Muggleworth, M A	The fame
Davil Jones,		167. Samuel Alwiy,	Henry Walborot
15.. John Albert,	John Seymour, Efq		John Clements, proc
15.3 Daniel Lane,	Arthur Baffet, Efq	1704 George Prance,	John Berkeley, Efq
1574 Robert Colmore*,	Arthur Baffet, Efq	1745 Thomas Moore, D D	Will Southwell, Efq
1622 Henry Bynnam,	John Gilbert	1765 John A kes,	The fame
16.9 Thomas Day s, A B	Ann Brynham	1.70 Phillip L. s, M A	John Jacob, Efq
1667 Edward Batten, M A	Humph Hooke, Efq		

PRESENT PROPRIETORS OF THE MANORS,

Of Frampton Cotterel   *Of Wickwer*

ROBERT TUCKER, Gent   JOHN DAUBENY, Efq.

The only Perfons fummoned from this Parifh by the Heralds in 1682 and 1683, were

Henry Symes, Efq and Clayton Milbourne, Efq

At the Election in 1776 Twenty eight Freeholders polled from this Parifh and its Hamlets

The prefent Regifter commences in 1.61 and is perfect to 1639 from which Period to 1653 no Entries were made, from 1653 to the prefent Time it is accurate and entire

ANNUAL ACCOUNT OF MARRIAGES, BIRTHS, AND BURIALS, IN THIS PARISH

A D	Mar	Bir	Bun	A D	Mar	Bir	Bun	A D	Mar	Bur	Bun	A D	Mar	Bur	Bur
1781	4	30	12	1786	3	28	14	1791				1796			
1782	3	30	19	1787	13	42	18	1792				1797			
1783	5	28	14	1788	7	30	1..	1793				1798			
1784	5	17	2.	1789	5	41	20	1794				1799			
1785	11	35	24	1790				1795				800			

INSCRIPTIONS IN THE CHURCH

IN MILBORNS AISLE

ON ATCHIEVEMENTS

.. Sable, a Cheveron between three Mules Argent for Brown, impaling, Vert on a Cheveron Argent three Fleurs Sable for Kemys.

2 Brown, quartering Kemy

3 Argent, a Crofs moline Sable on the dexter Chief Point a Mulet Gules, for Milborne, on an Efcutcheon, Browne, quartering Kemys

ON FLAT STONES

Here lyeth the Body of Mary the Wife of Clayton Milborne, Gent only Daughter and Heir of Robert Brown Gent by his Wife Ann Daughter and Co-heir of William Symes of Wickwick, Efq who died January 1, 1707

Alfo here lyeth the body of the faid Clayton Milborne, Efq who died January the 5th 17.., aged 6. Years

Alfo Here lieth the Body H. Milborne Gen onely Son ... th ...

Clayton Milborne bur ...at Mary his Wife who died the 19th March 1715, aged 45 Yea..

Here lyeth the Body of Ann Milborne Daughter Clayton Milborne Efq by Mary his Wife who departed this Life the 4th Day of January 1715

" It appears from the Books of the Regifter of this ... th this Prefentation was difputed by John Seymour Efq " who nominated Walter Roch, Clerk A Writ " De jure Patronatus" to enquire into the Right of Election, was iffued " from the Chancellor's Court, Dec 4. 5 4, and .de.r 3, 1574 5, when Lafcel Colmore Lord of the Manor was " confirmed, and Robert Colmore received Inftitution "

5   He

Here lyeth the Body of
ROBERT BROWN, Gent
who died in September 16,9

Here lieth the Body of
ANN, Daughter and
Coheir of WILLIAM KEMYS,
of Wickwick, in this Parish, Esq
and Wife of ROBERT BROWN, Gent
who died in September 1692

Within this Ile are likewise
interred the Bodyes of ne
said WILLIAM KEMYS
her Father, ARTHUR KEMYS her
Grandfather, and ROGER KEMYS her
Great grandfather, Esquires

Arms on a Lozenge, a Fess cotised, and in Chief two Mullets for
PLAYER

Here lyeth the Body of
MRS ISABELLA PLAYER,
Daughter of WILLIAM, and Sister of
THOMAS PLAYER, Esq
the present Lord of this Manor,
who departed this Life
the 16th Day of June, 1736

Here lyeth the Body of
JOHN SYMES, of Poundsford,
in the Parish of Pitminster
in the County of Somerset, Esq
He was born on the 4th Day of March,
1572
He lived soberly, righteously, and godly,
and dyed on the 21 Day of
October, 661

Arms Azure, three Scallops in
Pale Or, for SYMES

Here lyeth the Body of
HARRY SYMES, Esq
Son of JOHN SYMES, Esq
under the adjacent Marble,
who married the Daughter of
Sir JOHN SEYMOUR, Knight,
formerly of this Parish
He departed this Life
the 1st Day of November,
Anno Domini 1682. ætatis suæ 73
He was a loving Husband, a good
Father, and ever a constant Friend,
where he professed Friendship

Here lyeth the Body of
ANN SYMES, Widow
and Relict of HARRY SYMES, Esq
who departed this Life
on the 25th Day of May A D 1686.
She was the Daughter of

Sir JOHN SEYMOUR, Knight,
formerly of this Parish,
by Dame ANN his first Wife,
the Daughter of WILLIAM POULETT,
of Cottles, in the County of Wilts, Esq
Son of my Lord GILES POULETT,
fourth Son of WILLIAM POULETT,
Marquis of Winchester, and
Lord High Treasurer of England
Catw t her Birth greater her Virtues,
the best of Wives, the best of Mothers,
the best of Women

Reader! thou standest on the sacred
Dust of a virtuous handsome Maid,
AMY, the Daughter of
HARRY SYMES and ANN his Wife,
Daughter of Sir JOHN SEYMOUR
She was in her Deportment to her
Parents continous resplendid, dutiful,
obedient to the Proverb
She have give them cause to
ask her, why do you this?
She was snatched from them by a
violent Sickness, which makes them
daily wash their eyes without Water
She is here in a still and quiet Sleep,
not to awake but by a loud Trump
and then to rise in white, to sing
Hallelujahs to the Great God and Lamb
for ever Amen.
She deceased Jan 9,
was buried Jan 13, 1678.

ON A BRASS PLATE

Arms, Azure, three Escallops in Pale, Or, for SYMES,—impaling, Sable, two Hounds passant Argent, for HORNER

Reader, thou treadest on the sacred Ashes of JOHN SYMES, Esquire, who, in the late unhappy Times of Rebellion was forced (for his faithful Loyalty to his Prince) to leave his former Habitation at Poundsford in the Parish of Pitminster, in the County of Somerset and
to seek a help here for his old Age in this Parish He was a Man greatly renowned for
Wisdom, Justice, Integrity and Sobriety which Talents he did not hide in a Napkin but
religiously exercised in the whole Conduct of his Life especially in the Government of
that County wherein he bore all the honourable Offices incident to a Country Gentleman as
Knight of the Shire (elected, nemine contradicente) for the Parliament held at Westminster, in the 21st Year of King JAMES, High Sheriff, Deputy Lieutenant for many Years,
and Justice of the Peace for 40 Years and upwards And as he was careful and solicitous
to discharge his Duty to God his Soveraigne and his Country, so God was pleased to
bestow on him severall Badges (also) of his speciall Favour as Length of Days, accompanied with a most Healthy Constitution of Body for above 80 Years and of his Mind
to the last as also numerous Posterity, even of Children and Childrens Children, to the
Number of 100 and upwards, descended of his Loynes (by his only Wife AMY, the
Daughter of Thomas Horner of Cloved, in the County of Somerset, Esq)
And when he was full of Days and Honour, having lived 88 Years 7 Months, and 17 Days, and
after the safe Return of his Prince to his Crown and Kingdoms, after a long and horrible
e il, and thereby the flourishing Condition both of Church and State, having finished
his Work on Earth he cheerfully resigned his Soul to God that year the 21st Day of
October, Anno Domini 1661, in full Assurance of a joyfull Resurrection

ON FLAT STONES IN THE CHANCEL

Here lyeth the Body
of JONATHAN DAVIS,
who deceased this
Life October the 6th
aged 39 Year
Anno Domini 169

M S
FRANCIS AND ELIZABETH
...

M S
HERE LYETH MAURICE SMYTH,
Rector of Henton Bluet
in this County sometime
...
Here lyeth Jacob
ELIZABETH the Wife of
HENRY DAVIS,
of this Parish,
who departed this Life
the 14th Day of February,
A D 17 9 aged 52 Years

HENRICI DAVIS,
hujus parochiæ, generosi
Obiit July 1d, A D 1754, at 74

Also here lyeth the Body of
ELIZABETH, the Daughter of
HENRY and SUSANNA DAVIS,
who departed this Life
the 1st Day of January,
A D 1732 aged 9 Weeks

Here
lyeth the Body of
JANE, the Daughter of
SAMUEL HALL, Esq
and Mary his Wife
who departed this Life
November
...

Arms ; Sable, three Efcallops in Pale
Argent for Biss —impaling, Azure,
three Efcallops in Pale Or, for SYMES

Here lyeth the Body of
JANE, the Wife of
EDWARD BISS Efq
and Daughter of
HENRY SYMES, Efq
both of this Parifh,
who died the 6th Day of Auguft, 1704

Here lyeth the Body of
EDWARD BISS, Efq
who departed this Life
the 20th Day April, 1696,
ætatis fuæ 48

Here lyeth two Beauties,
two Vertues,
Daughters of HARRY SYMES, Efq
and ANNE his Wife,
the Daughter of
Sir JOHN SEYMOUR, of this Parifh
ELIANOR,　　　FRANCES,
deceafed
Sept 26, 1672,　　Dec 17, 1671
buryed
Oct. 1, 1672,　　Dec 21, 1671

IN THE CHURCH YARD　ON TOMBS

Here lyeth the Body of
DANIEL HOLDER,
of this Parifh, Yeoman,
who departed this Life
the 27th Day of March, 1776,
in the 70th Year of his Age

Alfo
SAMUEL, Son of
DANIEL and MARY HOLDER,
who died Sept 18, 1773,
aged near 40 Years.

Alfo
JAMES their Son
departed this Life Jan 29, 1776,
aged 28 Years

Underneath this Tomb
refteth the Body of
JOSEPH MILLETT,
of this Parifh, Yeoman,
who departed this Life
the 20th Day of Auguft,
Anno Domini 1690,
aged 57 Years

Alfo
underneath refteth the Body of
FRANCES, the Wife of
JOSEPH MILLETT,
who departed this Life
the 17th Day of December,
Anno Domini 1702,
aged 65 Years

In Memory of
JOSEPH MILLETT,
late of Stoke Gifford,
in this County,
who departed this Life
the 6th Day of January, 1768,
aged 85 Years

In Memory of
JOHN, Son of
JOHN and HESTER HORWOOD,
alias HARWOOD
of Grovenend in the
Parifh of Alvefton
who departed this Life
the 23d Day of January, 1748 9,
aged 22 Years

Here lyeth the Body of
ANN WHITE,
of this Parifh, Widow,
who departed this Life
the 14th Day of December, 1784,
ætatis fuæ 92

Here lyeth the Body of
WILLIAM SLOND,
of this Parifh,
who died April 3, 1716,
aged 30 Years.

Here lyeth the Body of
GEORGE, the fecond Son of
GEORGE RODMAN and
HANNAH his Wife,
of this Parifh
who departed this Life
the 2d Day of December,
Anno Domini 1708,
aged 16 Years and 10 Months

Alfo
here lieth the Body of
WILLIAM GINGELL,
of this Parifh,
who departed this Life
the 10th Day of February, 1750,
aged 44 Years

Here alfo lyeth the Body of
ELIZABETH his Wife
who died January 16, 1780,
aged 78 Years

In Memory of
ANN, the Wife of
EDWARD FREEMAN
of the City of Briftol,
and Daughter of
JOHN MILLETT and MARY his Wife,
of this Parifh,
who died Auguft the 10th 1733,
in the 48th Year of her Age

Alfo in Memory of
the aforefaid
EDWARD FREEMAN,
of the City of Briftol,
Haberdafher
Son of FRANCIS FREEMAN,
of Bifhops Froom in the
County of Hereford Gent
who departed this Life
the 7th Day of May 1739,
aged 41 Years

Here lyeth the Body of
JANE, Wife of WILLIAM MILLETT,
of this Parifh Curt
and Daughter of DANIEL CURTIS,
of the Ifland of Jamaica, Efq
who died May 6. 1705,
aged 51 Years

Alfo
here lyeth the Body of the
aforefaid WILLIAM MILLETT, Gent
who departed this Life
December 22, 1769,
aged 53 Years

Here lyeth the Body of
JOHN WATKINS,
who departed this Life
January 6, 1702, ætatis fuæ 60

Here lyeth the Body of
SARAH the Wife of
JOHN WATKINS,
who departed this Life
June the 11th 1712,
ætatis fuæ 72

Underneath
lie the Remains of
the Rev JAMES BULLER, M A
Vicar of Kilton,
in the County of Somerfet,
who departed this Life
April 11, 1772, aged 72

H H T
GEORGIUS BRYAN,
H I R
Obiit Martii 70,
A D 1744,
æ 71

In Memory of
MARY the Wife of
ABRAHAM DAVIS
of this Parifh, Yeoman
who departed this Life
June the 25th 1702,
aged 39 Years

Alfo
MARY their Daughter,
who departed this Life
November 15 1712,
in the 7th Year of her Age

Alfo
in Memory of
the aforefaid ABRAHAM DAVIS,
who was buried
the 25th Day of December, 1744,
in the 62d Year of his Age

ON HEAD STONES

	Died	Aged		Died	Aged
Mary, Hannah, and Elizabeth, Daughters of Thomas and Betty Pullin, feverally died as follows			Luke Webb	8 June, 1753	50
Mary, June 2, A D 1770, aged 11 Years			Mary Webb, Spinfter	26 July, 1775	50
Hannah, June 6, A D 1770, aged 8 Years			Mary, Wife of Ifaac Jarrett	20 Jan 1737	72
Elizabeth, July 26, A D 1770, aged 14 Years			Ann, Daughter of Ifaac and Mary Jarrett	22 July, 1737	14
Likewife Sarah their Daughter, who died Dec 29, 1772, aged near 6 Months			Sufanna Wife of Stephen Stout	8 Dec 1737	67
Henry Hibbs	25 Aug 1763	53	Stephen Stout	10 Sept 1760	61
Joanna, Wife of Daniel Halder	10 Oct 1765	40	Elizabeth Wife of Stephen Stout	9 Feb 1742	8
Martha, Wife of Francis King	2 Nov 1730	31	Simeon Turner	14 Sept 1768	36
William Harris	28 Apr 1755	65	Simeon his Son	20 Jan 1767	6
John Embly	17 Nov 1770	50	Elizabeth their Daughter	5 June 1770	1
Elizabeth Wife of John Bennett	4 Oct 1725	53	Thomas Blanchard	7 June 1778	84
James Gifford	1 Apr 1737	50	Ann Wife of John Webb	8 June, 1786	47
Ann, Wife of James Gifford	13 Nov 1779	75	Elizabeth, Daughter of Thomas and Betty Hawkins	14 May, 1770	4
George Bryant	23 Jan 1778	86	Joseph Rodman	8 Jan 1740	44
Elizabeth Wife of George Bryant	14 Dec 1753	74	John, Son of William Millett, fenior	13 Ap 1726	46
Sarah, Joseph and Jane Son and Daughter of John and Martha Cook Sarah died in 1743, aged 7 Weeks; Joseph, in 1751, aged 15 Years, and Jane, in 1753, aged 9 Years			George, Son of William and Jane Millett	14 Aug 1737	58
			William Millett, fenior	26 May 1726	84
Ralph Wickham	8 May 1755	70	George Bank	15 Dec 1745	72
Charles Parker	20 July 1713	55	Mary his Wife	10 Jan 1726	47
Sarah Wife of Charles Parker	— Nov 1713		Rachel and Martha, two of their Daughters Rachel	13 Aug 1712	12
Abraham Huggins	1 Apr 1729	7	Martha	6 Jan 1715	10
Sufanna Wife of Abraham Huggins	16 Mar 1766	57	Hannah Daughter of Thomas and Hefter Smith	16 June, 1719	8
Abraham Son of Abraham and Sufanna Huggins	3 May 1756	13	Steven Turner	4 Sept 1711	49
Ann Hale their Son	6 Jan 1774	51	Harry Chefter	22 Sept 1731	16
Jacob Huggins, a Father of the fame	1 Apr 1709	4	Thomas Chefter	20 Sep 1733	38
Joseph Gingell fenior	9 Jan 1707	51	Hannah Relict of Thomas Chefter	— Jun 1745	55
Joseph Gidgell, junior	3 Mar 1705	45	Behrah Turner	23 Oct 1753	43
Ann Wife of Joseph Cowell fenior	11 Jan 1726	52	Richard Price	24 Feb 1757	26
Ann Widow of Joseph Cowell, fen	6 Nov 1762	13	Ann Wife of Mofes Pocock	1 Feb 1779	51
Ann, Wife of Edward Webb	13 Aug 1750	13	John the Son of Mofes and Ann Pocock	14 Jan 1766	1
John Webb fenior	21 Apr 1714	66	Jane Cfter	11 Jan 1775	17
Joseph, Son of John Webb	1 Jan 1717	11	William Ofter	8 Sept 1761	
			Martha his Wife	6 May, 1784	4
			William Flower	6 Apr 1784	55
			Dinah, Wife of John Davis	1 Jan 1715	12
			Betty Wife of Thomas Davis	6 Jan 1711	74
			John Son of Thomas Davis and Betty his Wife	1 Aug 1717	

FRAMPTON UPON SEVERN

CXXIII. FRAMPTON UPON SEVERN.

IN Diſtinction, with reſpect to the preceding Pariſh, is ſituate in the Hundred of *Whitſtore*, which exerciſes mineral Rights as paramount over all Pariſhes within its Diſtrict. It is diſtant from *Stroud* eight Miles weſtward, ſeven North from *Durſley*, five South from *Newenham*, croſſing the River, and from GLOUCESTER ten on the South-weſt. The whole Pariſh is about two Miles ſquare, of a Soil chiefly of fine Gravel, nearly equal Portions in Paſture and Tillage, including common arable Fields of 300 Acres. The Inhabitants have a Right of Commonage in *Slimbridge Warth*. The *Severn* forms the South-weſt Boundary, and is more than a Mile acroſs, from the Shifting of the Sands, the current of the River is diverted from one Shore to the other, and it is remarkable, that of late Years, all Endeavours to prevent its Encroachments, have been inſufficient.

The Living is vicarial, in the Deanery of *Durſley*. It is endowed with one third of the Profits of the Impropriation, and the Privy Tythes. It is ſaid, that the Impropriation belonged to the Abbey of *Cirenceſter* but is ſo ſpecified neither by DUGDALE or TANNER.* The Advowſon is annexed to it, and both were obtained by the Family of CLIFFORD, from whom they were transferred about the Beginning of the preſent Century, and are now veſted in ELIZABETH WICKS, Widow.

The Church was conſecrated, and dedicated to *St. Mary*, in July 1315, by WALTER DE MAYDENSTONE, Biſhop of *Hereford*.† It is conſtructed with a Nave, two Aiſles, and a Chapel on either Side the Chancel. The Tower is of neat Gothic Architecture, having a deep and open embattled Parapet, with Pinnacles. In the North Aiſle and Chapel, under Arcades, are two recumbent Effigies in Free ſtone, of a Crofalder in a Lady, certainly of the CLIFFORDS, and a Conjecture is allowable, from the Date of the Dedication of the Church, and other Circumſtances, that they were intended for WILLIAM CLIFFORD, who died in 1321, and CATHERINE DE MALTON his Wife. In the Eaſt Window are Arms and Portraits of Saints 1 Chequy Or and Azure, on a Bend Gules, three Lions paſſant Or, CLIFFORD

* Dr. PARSONS ſays, that the Advowſon belonged to the Abbey of GLOUCESTER, and it ſeems to have been originally dotted from the Impropriation. There is more room to ſuppoſe, that the Great Tythes were veſted in the Family of CLIFFORD at the Diſſolution, and the continued, than that they were forfeited by Attainder, ſince that Period, as Sir R. ATKINS aſſerts. For the MUND CLIFFORD preſented ſo lately as 1691, in Right of the elder branch of the Family after the Diſperſion of their other Property. Mr Frith, purchaſed with Queen Anne's Bounty, in the Pariſh of *Slimbridge*, producing a ... annual Income of ...

† The Survey of the Cathedral of *Gloucester*, p. 162.

2 Argent, a Crofs voided Gules, DE MALTON 3 Gules, on a Bend Argent, a Martlet Sable, HOARE anciently 4 Sable, an Eagle with two Heads difplayed Argent, within a Bordure engrailed of the fecond, HOARE modern In another Window, BERKELEY *

The CONQUEROR gave this Manor, taxed at nine Carucates or Plough tillages, with other extenfive Grants in the Counties of *Hereford* and *Worcefter*, to his Follower DROGO FILIUS PUNTII, or FITZ-PONS, who died without Iffue in 1089 He was fucceeded by his Brother RICHARD +, who fettled it on his fecond Son WALTER, Lord of *Clifford Caftle*, co *Hereford*, the Father of "*Fair Rofamond*" RICHARD CLIFFORD ‡, a younger Son of the preceding, obtained it, and to Sir HUGH CLIFFORD his Heir, a Grant of Markets and Fairs was made in 1254, 38 HEN III which was confirmed in 1311, 4 EDW II In that Reign, it paffed to Sir JOHN CHIDIOCKE, who had married ISABEL, fole Daughter and Heir of ROBERT CLIFFORD CATHERINE CHIDIOCKE was the Wife of Sir JOHN ARUNDEL, of *Lanherne*, in *Cornwall*, who died feized of the Manor in 1479, 19 EDW IV and bequeathed it to his Son Sir JOHN ARUNDEL, JOHN ARUNDEL, Efq occurs in 1608, who, about 1630, fold it to HUMPHRY HOOKE, Alderman of *Briftol* Sir HUMPHRY HOOKE died about the Clofe of the laft Century, leaving three Coheirs, from one of whom, the Family of GROVE, of *Ferns*, co *Wilts*, derive their Right

Concerning other Property, it appears, that HENRY, Brother of Sir HUGH CLIFFORD, purchafed Lands in *Frampton* of confiderable Value in 1284, 12 EDW I which paffed by regular Defcent to JOHN CLIFFORD, Efq who died in 1684 MARY, the eldeft of his three Coheirs, married NATHANIEL CLUTTERBUCK, of *Eaftington*, whofe Grandfon RICHARD CLUTTERBUCK, Efq dying in 1775 left a Life Intereft in this Eftate to EDMUND PHILLIPS, Gent and ELIZABETH his Wife, Daughter of WILLIAM BELL, Efq of *Saintburft* and *Gloucefter*, by CATHERINE his only furviving Sifter, and after their Demife to NATHANIEL WINCHCOMBE, Efq of *Stratford Houfe*, in the Parifh of *Stroud*, and his Heirs, he being the only Son of ANNE, fecond Daughter of the faid WILLIAM BELL, a lineal Defcendant from Sir THOMAS BELL, Knight, the munificent Mayor of *Gloucefter* in the Reign of King HENRY the Eighth §.

Upon the ancient Site, in 1731, R CLUTTERBUCK, Efq began the prefent Manfion, which is a large and handfome Edifice. The Houfe occupies the Centre with fpacious Wings as Offices, it is ornamented with Ionic Pilafters, and upon the Pediment, in bas relief, is an Efcutcheon, bearing, Quarterly, 1ft and 4th, Azure, a Lion rampant, and in Chief three Efcallops Argent, for CLUTTERBUCK, 2d and 3d, CLIFFORD The extenfive Pleafure Grounds are very regular and neat, in the old Style of Gardening

An Area, called *Rofamond's Green* **, of 750 Yards in length and 150 broad, forms the Entrance to this pleafant and populous Village on the North-eaft from the Church, and gives it an Air of fuperior Neatnefs and Cultivation Thefe Improvements were made when the Manfion Houfe was re-built, and at the Expence of the fame Perfon

Of another confiderable Eftate the earlieft Proprietors we can trace are as follows from HENRY CLIFFORD it paffed in Dower with ALICE his Daughter, and Heir to WILLIAM FUST, about 1470, who was

---

* " In 1491, upon the Difinherifon of MAURICE LORD BERKELEY by the Will of WILLIAM Marquis of BERKELEY he regained a yearly Rent of twenty-two Marks in *Frampton*, which could not pafs in the Settlement " DUGDALE, Baron Vol I p 366

+ WALTER FITZ PONS having the Caftle of *Clifford*, Co *Hereford*, in Dower with MARGARET Daughter and Heir of RALPH BARON DE TONEI affumed that Name WALTER his eldeft Son, was the Progenitor of the noble Branch of this Family created Barons of CLIFFORD with the inherited Baronies of DE VIPONT, WESTMORELAND, and VESCI in 1356, Earls of CUMBERLAND in 1525 Barons CLIFFORD of *Chudleigh*, Co *Devon* in 167 RICHARD, the younger Brother, was the immediate Anceftor of the CLIFFORDS of *Frampton*

‡ In 1303 2 JOHN, a Fine was levied between RICHARD DE CLIFFORD Petent and WALTER CLIFFORD the elder Brother, Tenant of the Manors of *Lafham Cuy Culmerton* and the Hay of *Trnefcar*, Co *Salop*, who were releafed to WALTER, who granted to RICHARD and his Heirs, by LETITIA DE BERKELEY his Wife, the Manor of *Frampton* to be held of WALTER by the fervice of one Knight's Fee to the Caftle Guard of *Cliffod*, Co *Hereford* for 40 Days, and paying to RICHARD for his Life, an Annuity of ten Pounds by the hands of HUGH DE DENE and JOHN DE SOLERS Fine levat in Com Sa p 2 R Joh in Cur Recept Scaccar Of this Family the following have been Sheriffs of this County In 1377 JOHN DE CLIFFORD 1446, HENRY CLIFFORD, 1450, JAMES CLIFFORD, and in 1538, JAMES CLIFFORD, Efq was fummoned as one of the Confervators of the Peace FULLERS Worthies, p 363

§ Monf Ledbree

** In the Manfion houfe is preferved a Portrait of ROSAMOND which is fomewhat different from one defcribed by HEARNE " An Ancient and fine Picture of the beautiful Rofamond is now in the Poffeffion of SAMUEL GALE Efq who purchafed it " accidentally, and it was from him that I received the following Account of it It is painted on a Pannel of Wainfcot and " reprefents her in a three quarter Proportion, dreffed in the habit of the Times—a habit of a Gown of ch neat coloured Velvet, " with large fquare Sleeves of black flowered damafk facings, turned up above the Bend of her Arms and clofe Sleeves of a " Pearl coloured Sattin, puffed out, but buttoned at the Wrift, appearing from under the large ones She has feveral Rings fet " with precious Stones on her Fingers Her Front covered with a fine flowered Linen gathered clofe at the Neck like a Ruff " Her Face is charmingly fair, with a fine blufh on her Cheeks Her Hair of a dark Brown, parted with a feam from the " Middle of her forehead upwards, under her Coiffure, which is very plain but could I fee it appears above it and that co " vered with a fmall Cap of Silk She is looking very intently on the fatal Cup which fhe is trying to drink fhe holds it in " one hand and the Cover in the other Before her is a Table of black Damafk on which is the fame Prayer book open written " in the Black Character " Mr GALE fuppofes this Piece to have been done about HALE the feventh's Time " LANGTOFTS Chron p 561 8vo

Although every Portrait of ROSAMOND muft be imaginary it is thought that the genuine Account would not be unentertaining to fome of our Readers There is an Anachronifm with refpect to the Dref, which is that of the Court in the Reign of EDWARD IV and HENRY VII with little Variation but as no authentic Hiftory of her birth contradicts any Account in the Englifh Hiftory contradict that Tradition

fucceeded

succeeded by Lawrence Test, whose Son Giles was an Ecclesiastic, and at his Death in 1545 bequeathed it to Mary his Sister, the Wife of Ambrose Codrington He was succeeded by Francis Codrington, Sheriff of *Bristol*, who died seised of it in 1558 From this Family it was transferred by Deed of Marriage Settlement of Margaret, Daughter of Francis Codrington, to Edward Bromwich, Esq of *Bromesberrow*, about 1650 In 1670, it was sold to Colonel Rice Yate, and several Purchases were subsequently made by Walter Yate, Esq his Son Robert Gorges Dobyns Yate, Esq in 1779, sold it to Samuel Peach, Esq of *Bristol*, by whose Will it passed to Samuel Peach Crueir his Grandson, who assumed the Name of Peach by royal Sign Manual in 1787 The ancient House of Timber Frame is now occupied as a Farm, in the Windows of which, these Arms are emblazoned 1st, Argent, a Fess counter-embattled Sable, between three Lions passant Gules, Codrington 2 Codrington, impaling, Sable, on a Chevron Or, between three Falcons rising Argent is many Roundlets 3 Clifford A Cypher F C (*Francis Codrington*) is very curiously flourished *

There were other competent Estates, now dispersed, held by the Families of Selwyn and Haines, but excepting those already specified, the principal Landholders are Nathaniel Winchcombe, Esq and Richard King, Esq of *Alkerton*

Richard Fitz Pons gave two Yard Lands in *Frampton*, of the yearly Value of 20 Shillings to the Knights Templars †, which Rent is now paid to *Corpus Christi College, Oxford*

Iron Armour, consisting chiefly of Weapons of a rude Form, has been ploughed up in a Field there, where was traditionally a Skirmish between the *Saxons* and *Danes*

No Benefactions to the Poor.

Incumbents.	Patrons	Incumbents	Patrons.
—— Richard Sheppard,	————.	1648 John Barnsdale,	The Parliament.
1554 Thomas Mason,	Henry Clyfford, Esq	1662 Jonathan Heskyns,	Christian Clifford
1558 John Robyns,	The fame	1667 Nich Paul, M A	S Leet & Christian his Wife
—— Peter Ovett,		1691 William Done,	Edmund Clifford
1573 John Savacre,	James Clyfford, Esq	1698 William Smith,	
—— Walter Wint,		1721 Charles Wallington,	
1578 ———— Clutterbucke,	————.	1765 John Wicks, M A	John Wicks
* * * * *	* * * * *	1770 William James, B A	Elizabeth Wicks
1621 Thomas Pill,	John and Mary Cage	1773 William Ellis, M A	The fame
1622 Alan Bishop,		1777 Thomas Rudge, B D	The fame
1624 Thomas Pill,	John Cage, Esq.	1784 William Jenkin, LL B	The fame.

PRESENT LORD OF THE MANOR,

Thomas Grove, Esq

The Persons summoned from this Parish by the Heralds in 1682 and 1683 were

John Clifford, Esq. and George Lloyde, Gent.

At the Election in 1776, Twenty-nine Freeholders polled from this Parish

The Register commences with a Date 1624 ‡

Annual Account of Marriages, Births, and Burials, in this Parish

A D	Mar	Bir	Bur	A D	Mar	Bir	Bur	A D	Mar	Bir	Bur	A D	Mar	Bir	Bur
1781	12	21	13	1786	4	20	17	1791				1796			
1782	3	30	28	1787	5	27	9	1792				1797			
1783	5	50	20	1788	12	31	13	1793				1798			
1784	7	1	21	1789	6	22	17	1794				1799			
1785	5	17	25	1790				1795				1800			

* For several Years past the River has taken its Course near the Banks which are in this Parish These have been lately broken down and every endeavour to keep the Flood within its bounds has failed so that the high Spring tides overflow the Grounds adjacent to the Church undermine the Banks and encroach on the Land whereby many Acres are lost and are still losing from this Estate occupied by Mr Wate which sink into the bed of the River

† Apud *Framptonum* ex dono Ricardi Filii Ponzii duas virgatas, quas tenet Rogerus de Caldeio pro xs £1' *Ducat Mon* Vol II p 50 These Rents were originally paid to the Preceptory at *Quenington*, and were, soon after the Dissolution, purchased by *Corpus Christi College Oxford*

‡ In the Register is a long detail of Damage done by a Storm on the 18th of Feb 1662, which, in the space of four Hours, destroyed twelve Houses, one dwelling house, and rooted up 357 Trees, chiefly in Orchards The Account is subscribed "John Barnsdale, Vicar"

INSCRIPTIONS IN THE CHURCH

ON FLAT STONES IN THE CHANCEL

Here lieth the Body of
CLUTTERBUCK, and Vi
care of this Church deceased
the 30 Day of September, A no
Domini 1579 annoque Regni
Reginæ ELIZABETH vicesimo

Here lieth the Body of
WALTER WIAT,
Preacher and Vi
care of this Ch
he deceased the 30
Day of September,
Anno Domini 15
78 Annoque regni
Reginæ ELIZABETH
vicesimo

MARY the Wife
of THOMAS BOWSER,
departed this Life the 2d of Sept 1612

THOMAS BOWSER, Gent
departed this Life July, 1651

Here lieth the Body of
ELEANOR, the W of THO BOWSER,
who died Sept 20 1669

Here lieth the Body of
ALICE, the Wife of
JOHN BOWSER, Gen
who died the 19th Day of
October 1669

ON FLAT STONES IN THE NAVE

BRASS PLATES INSCRIBED
To the sacred Memory of
JOSEPH MORGAN
of this Parish Gardener,
and MARY his Wife
He was buried Sept 15, 1766, æt 69
She Jan 12, 1763, æt 63

Underneath are interred the
Remains of RICHARD CORK,
of this Parish, Surgeon,
who was buried the
5th Day of October, 1769, aged 62
Also of MARY his Wife
and Daughter of MILES OATRIDGE,
of the Parish of Conley Gent
who was buried the
15th of October, 1759, aged 59 Years
Also of MARY their Daughter,
who was buried the
4th of September 1785 at 42

ON MONUMENTS IN THE NORTH AISLE

Arms, Checquy Or and Azure on a
Bend Gules, three Lioncels passant of
the first, for CLIFFORD

In Memoriam
JOHN CLIFFORD, Gen
Masculorum antiquissimi
Nominis CLIFFORDIORUM,
Infra hanc Parochiam,
Qui obiit XXVII die
October Anno Domini 1754,
Hoc erigitur

Arms Azure on a Saltire between
four Fleurs de Lis Or five Escallops Sa
ble, for WADE;—impaling, Sable, a
Chevron Or, between three Towers triple
towered Argent, for DUNCH

ANNA WADE,
filia natu tertia JOHANNIS DUNCH
de Pusey, in Comitatu Berks, Armigeri,

Annæque uxoris ex majorum
apud Hamptonien. s Domo Familiis
Ambabus Religione parit ac
genus splendore conspicuum origina
Propago, conjux inter se Christiani
THOMÆ WADE, Armigeri
hujus oppiduloque Generosi cui
quatuor peperit Liberos
(uno eode nquæsuavi dno almoq. sita)
Rei domesticæ studiosæ p
nec minus in rebus Dei assiduæ Servit
Ux. Mater, Domina Verna
Amica, Pœnitarum Lætissimus
annuetim inde s peperit exti
Arcer is eum corripit
Ardentior adhuc amor in
Pater in charum Redemptoris
Brachia subitam expiravit annum
mensis Julii DCXVII,
Anno Æræ Christianæ MDCLXXXVII,
et ætatis XX.
Charissimæ Uxoris M S
M P THOMAS WADE

Arms Quarterly, 1st and 4th Azure
a Lion rampant, Or in Chief three Es
callops Argent for CLUTTERBUCK;
2d and 3d CLIFFORD, as before

M S
GULIELMI CLUTTERBUCK,
hujus Parochiæ Generosi,
qui 15 Kal Anno Æræ Christianæ
MDCCXXVII,
ex hac vita decessit Annos 67 natus
Alias CLUTTERBUCK, de Nailsend,
in Parochia Lassington,
in ipso Agro natus est,
Unius ex MARIA,
Uxore JOANNIS CLIFFORD,
hujus Parochiæ Generosi
maxi menda filii charam cum aliis
Hæredem Inter eliquerit

ON A STALE FREESTONE TABLET
Arms CLIFFORD, as before

In Memoriam ANTHONII CLIFFORD,
Defuncti RICHARD CLIFFORD,
posuit

ON A NEAT MARBLE TABLET
Arms Quarterly, 1st and 4th Azure,
on a Cheve on c.d ted between three
Lapwings Or as many Cinquefoil of the
Field, on a Chief of the second a Fleur
de Lis between two Spears Heads of the
first, for WINCHE MARE d and 4th
Sable a Chevron Ermine between three
Griffins Heads er died Or forGAY DINER
Upon an Escutcheon of Pretence quar
terly of 12, 1 Argent a Chevron be
tween three Bells Gules charged with
two Bars gemelle of the Field, in Chief
of the second a Hawk's Lure between
two Hawks of the Field, PITT 2 azure,
a Lion rampant and in Chief three Escal
lops Argent, for CROMER DUCK 3
CROMER 4 HOARE anciently
HOSTILINTON 6 HEART modern 7
Ermine three Bars Gules HUSSEY 8
Argent on a Fess nebulé Sable three
Hares Heads coupled Or HAREWELL
9 Argent a Chevron Gules in chief
two Castle pieces, in base a Saltire of
the second BLATENY 10 Argent,
three Moor Cocks proper PONANORT
11 Argent a Chevron between three
Eagles displayed Azure CROFTES 12
Vert, a Chevron between three Wolves
Head erased Argent MIDDELTO

NATH WINCHCOMBE, Gent
died October 2, 176

ANN his Wife Daughter and Coheir
of WILLIAM PITT, Esq
of Gloucester, and was there in this

Cou ty, by CATHARINE Es his Wife
Daughter of WILLIAM CLIFT KEN
Gent of this Parish died Xbr 7, 1679

ON A FLAT STON
On a large blue stone, with a bra
Fillet SEAL with ALABAST

Hic jacet humatum corpus Elisab the
Clifford, quæ obiit tricessimo quarto die Mensis
Septembris anno Dni Gulielmo
MDCCLII Sub eodem vero lapide ja
cet corpus Johannis Isiford qui obiit
Maii in Dni Gulielmo MDCCLIIII,
quorum animabus propitietur Deus Amen

Arms, CLIFFORD, as before

ANTHONIUS CLIFFORD
Ford Omit hic posuit
the Jul. AD 1750

Arms CLIFFORD as before
JOHN CLIFFORD Cur
1st October 1684

Hic jacet
JOANA Uxor JOHANNIS
CLIFFORD, Curie
obiit bi ar ie

Arms Quarterly 1st and 4th, Cut
TER TUKE 2d and 3d, CLIFFORD,
imp hac WADE as before

Quod mortale fuit SA x
nuper Ux WILL CLUTTERBUCK,
Gen & nunc JOHIS WADE, Ar
sub hac Petra apolit in cet
quæ obiit 25 di Junii
Anno { ætatis suæ 8
{ Salutis 1685

Hic reconduntur Cineres
CLIFFORD CLUTTERBUCK,
Filii trium
WILL CLUTTERBUCK Gen
Qui obiit Nov 1769

Arms, WADE impaling DUNCH,
as before

ANNA WADE Uxor THOMÆ WADE,
Generosi, dum ibus puerperium prius
feverit tandem Secunda provimus febri
Accerbum monumentum non itaque
die quis hic juxta uti tuturi
exhibet in majorum urn in Hujus
ut eam inutantibus in matre verae
conclusus est tumulus In XIV
a quo ex inter omnium ex Jesus
huius

Hic lieth the Body of
RICHARD CLUTTERBUCK
one of the
NATHANIEL CLUTTERBUCK Gent
who died Oct 12 1750
aged three Years

THOMAS CLUTTERBUCK,
eldest Son of the said
NATHANIEL, who died Feb 1, 1651,
aged three Years

Here lieth Ann
1st on Wife of Mr CLUTTERBUCK,
of this Parish Gent
Daughter of Wm CLUTTERBUCK of
Nailsend in this Parish in this Coun
who died Aug 15 1707

All the rest lieth th deceased son
WILLIAM CLUTTERBUCK,
his son Luttin,
who died Feb 15

SARAH, Daughter of
WILLIAM CLUTTERBUCK, Gent
died October 27, 1709

MARY CLUTTERBUCK
Daughter of Wm CLUTTERBUCK, Gent
died Jan. 17 1711

Hic situs NICHOLAUS PAUL, A M
hujus ecclenæ vicarius, vii integer
vitæ, regis subditus fidelis ecclesiæ
Sancti Catholicæ filius verus,
qui cum sep em ot octaginta annos
Dom ino t regit die Passionis
Dom ni de e sit MDCLXXX
Juxta m eum depo tui SAMUEL PAUL,
filius ejus i tu minimus,
vigin t annos natus, natura
exit Jai uar 17, 1670

Underneath is interred
the Body of ANN, the Daughter of
JOHN and ELIZABETH PLANELI,
who died Dec 11 1763, aged 25 Days

JOSIAH TIPPETTS
died April 24, 1783, aged 65

MARY CLUTTERBUCK,
Daughter of W CLUTTERBUCK, Gent
died Jan 11, 1711.

IN THE SOUTH AISLE

ON A TOMB

HERE LIETH THE BODI
OF THE RIGHT WORSHIP-
FUL HENRY CLIFFORD, ESQUIER,
WHO DECEASED THE 4
DAY OF JUNE, 1558, AND
THE BODY OF MABEL HIS
WIFE, ONE OF THE DAUGH-
TERS OF SER JHON WE
LCHE, KNIGHT, WHO DE
CEASED IN SEPTEMBER
1592, AND THE BODI
OF ANNE WATSON, DAUGH-
TER OF THE SAIDE
HENRY AND MABELL,
AT THE PROPER CHARG
OF WILLIAM WATSONE,
GENTLEMANE, 1595

ON FLAT STONES.

Here lieth the Bo-
di of JOHN SIDENHAM,
decesed the 16 Day
of March, anno
Domini 1585

Here lieth the Bo-
di of MARI SIDENHAM,
deceesed the Day
of Jan Anno
Domini 15

Here lieth the Bo
dis of NICHOLAS SID-
ENHAM, deceesed the
11 Day of December,
Anno Domini 1584

Here lieth the Body of
RICHARD BROMWICH, the Son of
EDWARD BROMWICH, Esq
who died the 1st Day of   1626.

ON A MARBLE STONE

Inter CLIFFORDORUM cineres hic
jacet EDRUS HAYNES, un Attornat
Cur de Com Banco, in cujus memor
ROSAMUNDA, filia JOHS CLIFFORD,
necessissima si a relicta, hoc posuit,
ob. 11 Junii, 1668

Here lieth the Body of
CHARLES, the Son of
ZECHARIAH WINTLE,
who died May 10, 1682, aged 12 Days

Also ROSAMUND his Daughter,
who died March 6, A. D. 1685,
aged almost 2 Years

Here lieth the Body of
ROSAMUND, the Wife of
ZACHARIAH WINTLE,
and Daughter of JOHN CLIFFORD, Gent
who died the 23d of November,
A D 1686

In Memo v of MARY,
Wife of THOMAS PEARSON, and
Daughter of EDWARD HAYNES, Gent
who died April 7, 1741, ætitis sua 15

Also of MARY the Daughter of
THOMAS and MARY PEARSON
who died June 8, 1757, aged 65

In Memoriæ THOMÆ PEARSON,
qui obiit 27 Junii, A. D 1777,
æt. tuæ 51

In Memory of MARY,
Daughter of Wm CLUTTERBUCK,
of Mill End, in the Parish of Eastington,
in this County, Gen
who died Feb 17, A. D. 1720 1

Also of SARAH, Daughter of
Wm CLUTTERBUCK aforesaid,
who died Jan 17, A. D. 1723

In Memory of
JOHN WICKS, of this Parish, Gent
who died Oct. 29, 1746, aged 60 Years.

Also MARY his Wife
died Dec 25, 1745, aged 60 Years

Sacred to the Memory of
JOHN WICKS Son of
JOHN and MARY WICKS,
of this Parish, Clerk,
Rector of Frampton Cotterel,
in this County, and Impropriator of he
Great Tythes of this Parish,
who departed this Life the 21st of May,
1770, aged 50 Years

Here lie the Remains of
JOSEPH WICKS, Gent
Son of JOHN and MARY WICKS,
of this Parish,
who resigned this Life the 3d Day of
November, 1771, aged 45 Years

In Memory of
the Rev STEPHEN MIDWINTER,
Curate of this Parish,
who died the 11th of October, 1737,
aged 42 Years

Also of HESTER his Wife,
who died March 31, 1776, aged 82

Inscribed
to the sacred Memory of
ROBERT VERREY, of this
Parish, Yeoman and
ELIZABETH his Wife.
She died May 25, 1778, aged 59.

IN THE CHURCH YARD.

ON A FREESTONE MONUMENT AGAINST
THE SOUTH CHANCEL

In Memory of
JOHN BOND, of this Parish, Yeoman
he died Jun 29, 1733, ætat 75

SARAH the Wife of JOHN BOND,
died March 10, 1789 aged 38

JOHN, the Son of JOHN BOND,
died May 18 1724

Also of MARY his Daughter
died May 8, 1724

ON TOMBS

HENRY WINCHCOMB
died Dec 0, A D 1723,
aged 74 Years

Alice his Wife
died June 9, A D 1715,
aged 60 Years

ANNE their Daughter
died September 17, 1710,
in the 16th Year of her Age

Alice their Daughter
died April 1723 aged 27 Years

JOHN, Son of HENRY WINCHCOMBE,
died July 22 1734, in his 4th Year

ELIZABETH his Wife
died Dec 8, 1728, aged 39 Years

THOMAS their Son
died Aug 26, 1719 aged 11 Months

JOHN their Son
died March 27, 1747, aged 1 Years.

ANNE their Daughter
died June 4, 1735, aged 13

Alice their Daughter
died Jun 18, 1723, an Infant

MARY.

MARY, Daughter of
JOHN and ELIZABETH WINCHCOMBE,
died Jan 10 1755, aged 36 Years

ELIZABETH their Daughter
died April 23, 1770

THOMAS ROGERS
died June 19, 1703 in the
god Year of his Age

ABIGAIL his Wife
died June 8, 741 aged 74 Years

ELIZABETH their Daughter
died in 1693

ABIGAIL their Daughter
died in 1699

THOMAS ROGERS Cler A M
Cujus ne pl res quae lector, titulos
quos si men tuletur, narratffe conftat
(nec qui tulit magnus, fed qui meruit)
fama ille amen in comvid ho ores
quæfitos in cntis quos incorrup a fides
implicitas pudor nudique veritas
morumque integritas, quam edocto
ingenio quo felicius alios docect,
adjunxit al unde et tribuerunt
Vita his artibus culta atque honeftata
vacua fuc pigri crucia u norbi
(ipfa profecto morte gravioris)
Telo lethinæ improvifo in via
effe illius equo difceffit
Difce hoc exemplo, mortem viro bono
quæ fuk it vim venire optimam
Ob die 17° Martii, A D 1736, æt 38

RICHARD DAVIS
died March 30, 1725, aged near 37

ELIZABETH KING,
Relict of RICHARD DAVIS,
died Oct 3, 175*, aged 59

THOMAS their Son
died Jan 5 1761 aged 40

HESTER his Wife
Daughter of WM MAYO, of Slimbridge,
died Sept 16, 1763, aged 43

They left four Children

THOMAS BRADFORD
was buried June 11 1748,
aged 80 Years

ESTHER his Wife
died April 11, 1731, aged 57 Years

ELIZABETH their Daughter
died April 23 1712, aged 5 Years

MARGARET the firft, and
MARGARET the fecond,
their Daughters died Infants

CORNELIUS BRADFORD,
buried April 9 1757,
aged near 37 Year

MARY, Wife of
THOMAS EVANS and Daughter of
THOMAS and ESTHER BRADFORD
buried Dec 26 1739,
aged near 41 Years

JOHN BRADFORD
died Sept 15, 1784 aged 76 Year

MARY his Wife
buried June , 17 7, aged 64 Years

THOMAS WARNER
died Feb 1, Anno Dom 1614

WILLIAM HINTON
died Nov 7 Anno Dom 1684

WILLIAM his Son
died Feb 1, 1682

LYDIA HINTON
died July 23, 17-1 aged 77

LYDIA their Daughter
Wife of the Rev Mr BROADHURST
buried July 14, 1722, aged 51,
leaving two Daughters,
LYDIA and ELIZABETH

ANN, Daughter of WILLIAM HINTON,
died May 25, 168_

RICHARD LONGSTREETH
was buried Jan 23, 1737

JOHN his Son
buried April 23, 1755, aged 55

RICHARD, Son of
JOHN LONGSTREETH,
buried Jan 1, 1756 aged 20

ELIZABETH his Daughter,
buried April 14, 1753, aged 21

ANN eldeft Daughter of
RICHARD LONGSTREETH, Wife of
BRICE SLEDE of Bristol
died Oct 14 1766 aged 60

JUDITH his youngeft Daughter,
Wife of THOMAS DAVIS,
Millwright, of Stroud,
buried Nov 1, 1771, at 55,
leaving one Son

JOHN GARDINER,
buried May 19 1691

EDWARD his Son
died Sept 19, aged 42 Years

EDWARD GARDINER
buried May 6, 1761, aged 70 Years

EDWARD his Son
died June 24, 1715, aged one Month

JOHN his Son
died in 1744, aged 23

ROSAMUND his Daughter
was buried Oct 19, 1742,
aged 2, Years

THOMAS ADY, of Freethorn,
buried June 23, 1756, aged 80 Years

ELIZABETH his Wife,
buried May 19 1746, aged 64,
with feveral of their Children

THOMAS their Son,
buried June 23, 176 aged 45 Years

MARY his Wife
died May 9, 1789 aged 5 Years

JOHN HAWKINS
died April 24, 1731 aged 45 Years

MARY his Wife
died April 10, 1722 aged 53 Years

JEREMIAH their Son
died March 21, 1714 aged 18

JOHN their Son
died Aug 11, 17 , aged 1

DEBORAH their Daughter
died June 10, 1 ,

SARAH their Daughter
died Jan 13, 1 , aged 5 Weeks

ELIZABETH their Daughter
died July 24, 17-0, aged 14

ELEANOR their Daughter
died Feb 2, 176 aged 20

SAMUEL HAWKINS,
buried July , 1756 aged 59 Years

THOMAS WINTLE, Clothier,
died Aug 26, 1728, aged 37 Years

ANNA his Wife
died March 25 1725, aged 3 Years

ANN Wife of
CHARLES KNAPP, Daughter of
RICHARD and ELIZ BOND, of Pitchcomb,
died Feb 5, 1769, aged 51 Years

JOHN WILLIAMS Gent
late of Goodrick, Herefordfhire,
who died by a Fall from his Horfe
June 8 1774 aged 73 Years

SEYMOUR BUCKINGHAM,
died Aug 9, 1704, aged 56 Years

HANNAH his Wife
died Dec 17, 1728, aged 6, Years

THOMAS their Son
died Sept 26, 1761, aged 57 Years

MARY his Wife
died July 13, 1737, aged 49 Years

SEYMOUR his Son
by SARAH his Wife
died an Infant

GILES HIERON
died June 11 1727

MARY his Wife
died Auguft 5, 1744

ELIZABETH, Wife of
JOHN HIERON, jun
his Grandfon, Daughter of
ROBERT and ELIZABETH HALL,
of Slimbridge
died July 31, 1787, aged 26 Years

SARAH Wife of SAMUEL COTTIN,
died Aug 5 1782, aged 5, Years

THOMAS, Son of
Jno HIERON and SARAH his Wife
(their Daughter)
buried Feb 10, 177

All two more Children died Infants

THOMAS BARNARD
died June 17, 17 9 aged 5 Years

ELEANOR his Wife
died Mar 6, 1704 aged 65

ELIZABETH, Daughter of
WM and ELIZ BARNARD
died Nov 3, 17 , d 1 Years

JOHN BARNARD
died April 21, 17 , aged 18

In Memoriam
JOHANNIS SEYMORE,
qui obiit 27 die Junii, A D 1673

THOMAS SAUNDERS
died May 31, 1719, aged 50 Years.

MARY his Wife
died June 6, 1733,
in the 63d Year of her Age.

SARAH their Daughter,
buried June 9, 1751, aged 51 Years

MARY, another of their Daughters,
Wife of THOMAS FOWLER,
of Ouldings, in the Parish of Stonehouse,
buried April 20, 1770, aged 60 Years

MARY, Wife of
PHILLIP GUY,
died Jan. 29, 1767, aged 27

ON HEAD AND FLAT STONES.

	Died	Aged		Died	Aged
Richard Blanch	11 Mar 1745	58	John Johnson, of Fframbridge	8 Apr 1778	45
Elizabeth his Wife	8 Feb 1744	51	Ann his Wife	24 Aug 1781	47
Joannah Pearson	20 Jan 1729	70	Thomas, Son of James and Eliza-beth Barnard	17 Dec. ——	—
Joseph Packer, Butcher	2 Jan 1788	67	Sarah, Daughter of James Barnard	5 Feb 1720	8
Esther Wife of John Verney	14 Apr 1742	52	Samuel his Son buried	11 Dec 1743	4
John Verney	28 Oct 1746	51	James Barnard, Butcher	8 Dec 1757	63
Elizabeth, Wife of Joseph Merrett	6 Jan 1730	44	Elizabeth his Wife buried	3 Oct 1741	41
Joseph Ayland	—— 1725	—	John their Son	9 Oct 1741	9
Judith, Daughter of William and Elizabeth Fryer	17 Oct 1761	63	Sarah their Daughter	20 May, 1765	—
Thomas Ayland buried	26 Dec. 1757	62	Abraham Lane	18 Feb 1752	4
Mary his Wife	16 Oct 1760	68	Anna, Wife of John Frape	29 Mar 1756	36
Thomas his Son	— Jan 1721	2	Sarah their Daughter	26 Sep 1740	14
George Day	— 1711	—	Ann, Wife of Ephraim Smith	11 Jan 1693	31
Daniel Hewlett	2 June, 1765	47	Margaret, Wife of Charles Ricketts	15 May, 1761	28
Mary, Wife of John Hyett	11 Nov 1747	74	Sarah their Daughter	7 Sept 1761	2
John Hyett	14 Nov 1747	67	Lydia, Wife of William Browning	19 Mar 1736	50
Elizabeth their Daughter	21 June 1744	33	Samuel their Son	7 Oct 1747	18
Thomas George	24 Mar 1748	60	William Browning and Mary his Wife		
William Burley, buried	26 June, 1744	48	Mary, Daughter of Thomas Evans, and Wife of William James	19 May, 1734	24
Ann his Wife buried	29 Aug 1747	51	William their Son	19 Nov 1732	—
Ruth, Wife of William Burley	9 Jan 1715	61	Mary Evans	18 Apr. 1721	50
William Burley, junior	13 Jan 1729	—	William, Son of Thomas Evans	19 Jan 1743	49
Daniel Burley	16 July, 1739	41	Elizabeth, Daughter of Thomas and Mary Evans	20 Jan 1734	29
Sarah his Wife buried	12 Nov 1771	72	John, Son of Thomas Evans	21 Oct 1788	1
Edward Evans	24 Dec 1758	39	Samuel, Son of Thomas Evans	— June, 1764	—
John, Son of Edward and Mary Evans	24 Apr 1751	45	Mary, Wife of John Wakefield, of Newnham, Mariner	5 May, 1761	25
William their Son	26 Aug 1783	29	Edward Evans	18 May, 1746	43
James Evans	12 Mar 1777	53	William his Son	5 Dec 1744	13
Sarah his Wife	7 Feb 1784	65	Thomas his Son	25 Oct 1748	27
Thomas their Son	22 Dec 1762	3	Martha his Wife	9 Mar 1750	48
Sarah their Daughter	26 July, 1763	—	John, Son of Richard and Katharine Rowles	22 Sept 1734	3
John Vaughan	17 Sept —	20	Daniel King	23 Mar 1775	57
John his Son	26 Oct 1762	32	Mary his Wife	15 July, 1770	60
John Spencer	5 Nov 1747	40	Susannah, Daughter of John and Hannah King	27 Oct 1778	—
John his Son	26 Oct 1747	10	Susannah the second, their Daugh-ter	14 July, 1785	2
Mary, Daughter of Richard Avad	18 Feb 1718	2	William Gundon	25 Feb 1762	39
Richard Avad	12 Jan 1729	52	Elizabeth his Wife	19 June, 1785	76
Susannah his Wife	3 Nov 1728	—	Mary their Daughter	6 Aug 1752	15
Samuel Guy	6 June, 1779	41	Sarah Ricketts, their Daughter	12 Nov 1746	27
Thomas Guy	12 Nov 1742	83	Richard Sanigear	15 Dec 1765	57
Ann, Wife of William Guy	6 Nov 1762	59	Dinah, Daughter of Richard Blaynch	3 Feb 1701	—
John Parslow	25 Mar 1744	49	Thomas Haynes	7 Apr 1734	—
Mary his Wife	3 June, 1734	28	Joseph Haynes, Gent.	6 Nov 1712	—
Deborah their Daughter	11 Mar 1739	11	Susannah, Daughter of Thomas and Elizabeth Holder	24 May, 1727	1
Samuel Parslow	— 1750	4	Elizabeth, Wife of Joseph Canter	19 Dec 1766	63
John his Son	—— 1740	-1	Elizabeth their Daughter	3 Aug, 1765	5
Margaret Bridford	24 May, 1738	63	Samuel, Son of Samuel and Sarah Dew	31 May, 1772	1
William Waring	9 June, 1740	40	Hester their Daughter, buried at King Stanley	— June, 1770	24
Richard Roe buried	25 May, 1766	52	Thomas Bevan, Butcher buried	— May, 1749	—
Anne his Wife	—— ——	—	Sarah his Wife buried	6 Feb 1725	—
Richard their Son	17 June, 1744	2	William Rogers	20 Mar, 1695	60
Betty and Ann their Daughters, bu-ried at Dursley			Timothy his Wife	21 Oct 1743	91
David Fletcher	8 May 1770	52	Mary their Daughter, Wife of John Hill	15 May 1748	74
William Fletcher	9 Aug 1743	28	William Knight	4 Jan 1765	6
Elizabeth his Wife	5 Dec 1736	49	Susannah his Wife	15 Aug 1760	55
John Fletcher	2 Dec 1754	52	John, William, and Joseph, their Sons		
Betty his Wife	17 Mar 1741	46	James Knight buried	13 Dec 1719	67
John their Son	31 May, 1743	7			
Paul Edwards	20 May, 1729	81			
John his Son	15 Sept 1723	31			
Esther, Wife of Paul Edwards	1 Aug 1744	63			
Joseph Guy, of Troombridge	4 Nov 1766	83			
Sarah his Wife	1 Dec 1767	68			
William Webley Coley, Son of William and Elizabeth Frome Coley	21 Dec 1783	—			
George Coley	10 June, 1771	37			

ON

ON HEAD AND FLAT STONES

	Died	Aged			Died	Aged
James his Son - -	27 May, 1751	12	John their Son, Surgeon -		8 June, 1727	41
John his Son - -	3 Apr. 1730	36	John Mills Bricklayer	buried	15 Mar 1761	52
John Carefield -	18 May, 1738	43	Mary his Wife		20 Dec 1780	63
Mary his Wife -	2 Mar 1765	63	John Mills - -	buried	4 Mar 1721	55
Elizabeth their Daughter	7 July, 1732	—	Rosamund his Wife	buried	23 May, 1712	41
John Carefield, son	3 Feb. 1732	65	William Fords		11 Sept 1741	61
Anne his Daughter	13 May, 1733	6	Ann his Wife		11 Jan 1730	54
Jane, Wife of John Carefield	13 July, 1761	68	William Iskell -	buried	6 May, 1718	80
William Carefield	8 Feb 1774	38	Judith his Wife -	buried	12 Aug 1728	45
Mary, Wife of John Carefield	—— —— 1727	—	John their Son -	buried	11 July, 1729	25
Nathaniel, Son of John and Sarah			Joseph their Son -	buried	6 Jan 1743	25
Haynes, Clerk of this Parish	23 Apr 1749	39	Sarah their Daughter, Wife of John			
Sarah his Wife -	3 Oct 1755	—	Spencer	buried	1 Dec 1732	27
Thomas and Edith their Children			Susannah another Daughter	buried	28 Nov 1781	72
Joseph, Son of Joseph and Hester			James Keylock		1 Apr 1751	29
Brother - -	2 Apr 1730	—	John Keylock -		29 May, 1760	56
Elizabeth, Wife of William Wintle	7 Aug 1666	—	Thomas Keylock - -		14 Oct 1781	67
Elizabeth, Wife of Zechariah Wintle	4 Mar 1710	—	Richard Davis -		30 Mar 1725	36
William Wintle -	5 Oct 1690	—	Elizabeth King, Relict of the said			
William his Son -	10 Dec 1692	—	Richard Davis -		23 Oct 1752	53
Zechariah Wintle -	11 Sept 1659	—	Thomas their Son -		9 Jan 1761	40
Ann, Wife of Jacob Osborn, of			Helen his Wife, Daughter of Wil-			
Gloster and Daughter of Thomas			liam Mayo, of Slimbridge		16 Sept 1763	45
and Mary Haynes	21 Dec 1776	60	Johanna, Daughter of Robert Tip-			
Edward Cage - -	13 June, 1695	—	petts, by Sarah his Wife, Daugh-			
Judith his Wife - -	26 Feb 1740	—	ter of John and Mary Hawkins		9 Aug. 1774	43

In Memory of JOHN GRIFFIN, his six Wives, and four Children
He was Lay Clerk of this Parish upwards of 50 Years,
and died Feb 15, 1788, aged 84

CXXIV. FRETHERNE.

THIS small Parish lies in the Hundred of *Whitstone*, three Miles South eastward from *Newnham*, eight Northward from *Dursley*, and nine from GLOUCESTER on the South-west. The Western Boundary is made by the *Severn*, the whole not exceeding six Miles in Circumference. The Soil is universally a very stiff, moist, Clay, nearly in equal Portions, Pasture and Tilled. In parochial Payments it is jointly rated with *Saul*, and *Putloe*, a Hamlet of *Standish*, with the former of which it is intermixed.

The Living is a Rectory, in the Deanery of GLOUCESTER, anciently endowed with forty four Ridges of Land, the Advowson is vested in the Family of YATE, of *Bromesberrow* *. The Church, dedicated to St *Mary*, is plain and small †

Domesday states this Manor to have been valued at three Hides only. In 1316, 9 EDW II it was the Property of NICHOLAS LE VILE, and a Family styled DE FRETHERNE held it for several successive Centuries. HENRY CLIFFORD obtained it by Deed, dated Oct 25, 1425, 3 HEN VI, from JOHN and LAWRENCE PRIDE, and LAWRENCE BAKER. JAMES CLIFFORD, Esq is recorded in 1608. He was an Officer of the Houshold to Queen ELIZABETH, and is said to have built a very sumptuous House in the Style of that Day for her Reception in her Progress to *Bristol* in 1574. It had an eligible Situation, above the Church, commanding a very advantageous View of the *Severn* ‡

After remaining long in a State of Dilapidation, it was entirely taken down about 1750, and several of the architectural Ornaments were removed to *Arlingham Court*.

About the Year 1623, the Manor passed to the Family of CAGE, or GAGE, Citizens of *London*, but whether by Connection or Purchase is not known. JOHN CAGE married MARY, only Daughter and Heir of JAMES CLIFFORD, who sold it to WILLIAM BAYLY, Barrister at Law, soon afterward, and it continued with the Descendants of the last mentioned for several Generations. In 1744 and 1745 the Manor was bought by the Trustees of Colonel WALTER YATE, in pursuance of his Will, one undivided fourth Part of JOHN PRITCHARD, and three fourths of WILLIAM HAYWARD, Serjeant at Law. In 1777 ROBERT GORGES DOBYNS YATE, Esq re sold it to RICHARD STEPHENS, Esq of *Eastington*. Other Estates belong to JOHN SKINNER STOCK, Esq Barrister at Law, THOMAS MORSE, Esq of *Dursley*, and the Family of SAUNDERS. The Parishioners anciently claimed an Exemption from all Tolls of Fairs, and a free Passage over the *Severn*, but by what Authority is not now to be collected.

Fretherne Cliff is a Hill rising gradually to the Height of sixty Feet above the Surface of the River. The Soil, of blue Clay, is hard and unfertile, in which these several Sorts of Fossils are found, beautiful Masses of Mundic and Ammonites mundicifed, Gryphites, Asteriae, Ostracites, and huge Bivalves. In some Places Layers of Coal, very thin, but of a fine Quality, are inserted in the Beds of soil, likewise some Fragments of the pearly shelled Nautili, of the Tugell Species.

In the Road leading to this Place is a House, which according to the most ancient and generally received Tradition, was the Site of the Residence of WALTER Lord CLIFFORD, where his Daughter " Fair ROSAMOND, was born.

* DOROTHY BAYLY, Spinster, who died in 1720, left her Estate called *Yelmsdon* in the Parish of *Tewksbury* to the Bishop and Dean of GLOUCESTER in Trust, who shall appoint a Curate. He being bound to take care of and find the other Moiety to the Rector of *Fretherne* for the Time being
† Deed recited 13, THOMAS's Survey of *Worcester* Cath p 216
‡ *Fretherne* Lodge, which is a stately House, with a most noble Staircase and Turrets to *Fretherne* belonged to the Cliffords who had here a Park. It was built by JAMES CLIFFORD, who by Deed of covenant in Queen Elizabeth's Time...

No Benefactions to the Poor.

INCUMBENTS	PATRONS	INCUMBENTS.	PATRONS
—— William Luffingham,	John Rolles, by Grant from James Cliflord and Dorothy his Wife	1690 Henry Higford,	William Bayly, Efq
		1695 John Talbot,	The fame
		1705 William Smith,	The fame
		1720 Vincent Rice,	The fame
1582 James Luffingham,	The fame	17—— William Deane,	The fame
—— Richard Luffingham,	The fame	1754 Yate Bromwich M A	The fame
1663 Thos Wootton, B A	William Bayly, Efq	1786 Henry Gorges Dobyns }	} R G. D Yate, Efq.
1673 George Perkins, M. A	The fame	Yate, LL B }	

PRESENT LORD OF THE MANOR,

HENRY STEPHENS, Efq

The only Perfon fummoned by the Heralds, in 1682 and 1683, was

William Bayly, Efq

At the Election in 1776 Eleven Freeholders polled from this Parish.

The first Date of the Register is in 1631

ANNUAL ACCOUNT OF MARRIAGES, BIRTHS, AND BURIALS, IN THIS PARISH

A D	Mar	Bir	Bur	A D	Mar	Bir	Bur	A D	Mar	Bir	Bur	A D	Mar	Bir	Bur
1781	2	7	3	1786	—	6	5	1791				1796			
1782	1	6	—	1787	5	5	8	1792				1797			
1783	—	2	2	1788	2	7	4	1793				1798			
1784	1	7	3	1789	2	9	1	1794				1799			
1785	5	4	8	1790	3	6	3	1795				1800			

INSCRIPTIONS IN THE CHURCH

IN THE CHANCEL, ON FLAT STONES

HIC THOMAS

WOTTON TROLLES

TU TUTO JACET ANA

DUM VENIET CHRIST

SUFFICIT ISTA DOMUS

VO ID EBR

1664

HEARE RESTETH
THE BODY OF ANN
BAYLY, DAITER OF
WILLIAM BAYLY, ESQ
VILR, WHO DEPARTED
THIS LIFE THE 27 OF
AVGVST, IN THE
YEAR O OUR LORD
GOD
1666

ON A TOMB

Arms In a Lozenge, an Efco
cheon of Pretence. Party per Pale
for BAYLY —impaling, Gules, three
Stirrups leathered and buckled Or, for
SCUDAMORE

Her lies the Body of
RADIGUNT, eldeft Daughter of
JOHN SCUDAMORE,
of Kentchurch in the
County of Hereford, Efq
and Relict of WILLIAM BAYLY,
of Fretherne, in the
County of Gloucefter, Efq
who finifhed virtuous Life June 15,
in the Year of her Age LXXX,
and of her Redemption 1702

In Memory of
Mrs DOROTHY BAYLY
fecond Daughter of WM BAYLY
of Fretherne Efq
She departed this Life
the 25th Day of June,
Anno Domini 17—
and lies here buried
in the 76th Yeare
of her Age

Her resteth
the Body of JOYCE
BAYLY, de
cefted the 9 Day
of December,
1623

IN THE CHURCH YARD, ON TOMBS

Near this Place lieth the Body of
Mrs JANE DEANE,
Relict of the Rev Mr DEANE,
Rector of Colmboe, in the
County of Nottingham,
the Gift of his Grace the
Duke of KINGSTONE
She was the excellent Mother of
twelve children and worthy of all
Honour,
Grandmother to the Rev Mr W DEANE,
late Rector of this Parish,
Minor Canon and Sacrist of the
Cathedral Church of Gloucester
He departed this life the
9th of November, 1753 aged 42,
and lies buried on the Right Hand
of that Choir

Mrs DEANE died June 11, 1738,
and this Stone was directed to be

placed here by her Daughter
Mrs ELIZABETH BAYLY,
third Wife of WM BAYLY, Esq
the last of that Name that possessed
Frethorn Lodge,
in his time a good old Seat,
remarkable for a fine Staircase,
built by the noble Family of the
CLIFFORDS

WILLIAM BAILY, Esq
died at Worcester Aug 20 1726,
and was buried in the Chancel of
St. Swithin in that City

WILLIAM ROWLES, Yeoman
died Feb. 28, 1720, aged 38 Years.

ELIZABETH his Daughter
died Nov 20, 1719, aged 2 Years.

ELIZABETH, Wife of
JOSEPH SINDERLY,
died April 19, 1754,
aged near 67 Years

TOBIAS COULES,
1630

MARGARET, Wife of
THOMAS KING,
died Jan 2, 1731
in the 64th Year of her Age.

RICHARD their Son
died Dec 1, 1738, aged near 30 Years.

THOMAS KING
died Sept 15, 1746, aged near 79 Years

JANE, Wife of
WILLIAM MIDDLETON
of the City of Gloucester, Gent
died Jan 8, 1777, aged 52 Years.

ON HEAD AND FLAT STONES.

		Died	Aged			Died	Aged
Pearce Smith	- -	8 — 1655	—	Ann, Wife of William Evans		12 Nov 1746	27
Joseph his Son	-	5 Mar 1676	16	Ann their Daughter	-	in Infancy	
—— Wife of P Smith	-	— Oct 1668	—	John Cowmeadow	-	4 July, 1745	54
Edward Bendal	buried	— 1684	—	Elizabeth his Wife		11 Jan. 1743	59
Thomas Evans	-	12 Mar 1773	38	Elianor Warren	both drowned	17 June, 1757	6
Mary his Wife	-	3 Jan 1770	35	William Warren		17 June, 1757	27
Mary Betty, John, Mary, and				John Warren		19 June, 1778	63
Thomas, their Children, died				Elizabeth, Wife of William Vaile		7 Jan 1786	58
Infants.				Hester, Wife of Joseph Hale		7 Aug 1787	65

FROCESTER

CHAPEL FROCESTER

CXXV. FROCESTER

LIES in the Hundred of *Whitstone*, four Miles North-east from *Dursley*, five West from *Stroud*, and eleven South-west from *Gloucester*. The Soil is very fertile, chiefly Pasture, in some Parts a fine binding Gravel or rich Brash, and in a small Proportion Clay. The common Arable Land is divided into six Fields, containing collectively 270 Acres. Upon a late Survey, the Terrier was found to include 1174 Acres belonging to the Right Honourable ~~George Earl of Warwick~~, and 600 of Pasture to the Right Honourable FRANCIS Lord DUCIE, beside Woodland, called the *Buckholt* *, of uncertified Extent. In this Wood arise several Springs which form a Rivulet intersecting the Parish in its Course to the *Severn*, about two Miles below.

The ancient Village is said to have been contiguous to the Church, but having been destroyed by Fire, was re-established at the Distance of a Mile from it, upon the great Road from *Gloucester* to *Bath*, from the former of which this Place is the first commodious Stage.

The Living is a Vicarage in the Deanery of *Stonehouse*, and not in Charge in the King's Books, originally, with the Manor, belonging to the *Benedictine* Abbey of *St. Peter* in *Gloucester*, to whom the Church is dedicated. It has a Nave and South Aisle of equal Length with the Chancel, and a low obtuse Spire. The only Reliques of Antiquity are several Stone Coffins, having Lids inlaid with the Crosses of Alabaster. In the last Century it was thought expedient to build the Chancel now required, for which purpose the Site was given by ANNE Baroness Dowager BROOKE, where all parochial Offices are now performed, excepting Sepulture.

Ecclesiastics are said to have been settled at *Frocester* † in the very remote *Saxon* Æra, which were made dependant upon the Abbey of *Gloucester* by CLINE of RAVENSWART, Brother of BEORNULF King of *Mercia*, in 822 ‡.

The Manor, stated in Dome'day to contain five Hides of Land, having been alienated, and annexed to the See of *York* by WOLSTAN the Archbishop, was regained by Abbot SERLO in 1072, from which time to the Reformation, it continued their Property §. In 1547, 1 EDW. VI. it was given to the Protector EDWARD Duke of SOMERSET, upon whose Attainder it was confirmed, in lieu of Dower, to ANNE his Relict. It lapsed to the Crown on her Decease, and in 1575, 17 ELIZ. was regranted to Sir CHRISTOPHER HATTON, Knight. Sir WILLIAM DODINGTON, Knight, of *Bremer* co. *Hants*, is recited in 1608 as Possessor of the Manor, whose Son JOHN DODINGTON, bequeathed it to his Daughter, and, at length, for her, ANNE the Wife of ROBERT GREVILL, the fourth Baron BROOKE, in which noble Family it is now vested.

When the Lands of the Abbey at *Frocester* was disposed of, the ancient Grange, Mill, &c. with the Demesne Lands (now consequently exempted from Tithes) and the Impropriation, were purchased from the Court of Augmentations by JOHN HUNTLEY in 1551, which were held by Sir GEORGE HUNTLEY, Knight, and his descendants, who sold them to Sir ROBERT DUCIE, Bart. about 1612. The Right ~~Honourable~~ FRANCIS Lord DUCIE derives his Right to them from the last mentioned Family.

The Court House appears to have been built by the HUNTLEYS in the Reign of Q. ELIZABETH, and ~~was appropriated for her Reception here~~ It formerly made three Sides of a spacious Quadrangle, with large Windows and other Ornaments in the Style of that Day. But a greater Curiosity

---

is the old Conventual Barn, which is 70 Yards in Length, and full entire No Date of its building, which is usual in others in this County, has ever been discovered

Southward from the Village is a very lofty Hill, the Summit of which seems evidently to have been one of the Fastnesses formerly occupied by the *Danes*, a Conjecture formed from the Appearance of Intrenchments and the Discovery of Skeletons The Road leads down a winding Terrace, the Acclivities of which are made very picturesque by beautiful Beech Woods Following this singularly magnificent Prospect, as it presents itself, flanked on the left Side by *Cam* Down, of a volcanic Shape, and the bold Promontory of *Stinchcombe*, two wide Reaches of the *Severn* are seen in the Foreground—an expansive and cultivated Vale, interspersed with Village Churches, which pleasingly mark the Distances Beyond, are the Forest Hills, and, as we descend, the Landscape is closed by the blue Mountains of *Malvern* and the Turrets of *Gloucester* *.

Considerable Property is held by renewable Life Leases under the Manor, the chief of which are the Estates of the Rev. GEORGE HAYWARD, M A Vicar, RICHARD BIGLAND, Esq and the Families of MILES, WITMORE, BROOKE, WEBB, HEAVEN, SMITH, DRIVER, BARNES, GARLICK, and SANDFORD

B E N E F A C T I O N S.

RALPH BIGLAND, Esq Garter Principal King of Arms, by Will, dated 1784, gave 100*l* to purchase Land, vested in Trustees, the Produce, Interest, or Rent, arising from the said Donation, to be disposed of as follows 20*s* for a Dinner, annually, 2*s* 6*d*. to the Parish Clerk, and the Remainder to the worthy Poor of the Parish of *Frocester* for ever A Ground, called *Wet Mead*, in the Parish of *Coaly*, formerly belonging to ―――― BROWNING, Esq containing 2 Acres, 1 Rood, and 16 Perches, is appropriated for the Purpose directed by the said Will

A Tenement and Three Acres of Land, lying in the Parish of *Coaley*, were given for the Repairs of the Church, the Donor, and the Time of Donation, unknown

INCUMBENTS	PATRONS.	INCUMBENTS	PATRONS
—— Kenelm Dene,	Abbey of Gloucester	* * * * * * *	* * * * *
1552 John Dyston,	Edw Walsh, by Grant from the Abbey of Gloucester	1663 Philip Lawrance	Sir William Ducie
		1664 Eliezer Marshall, M A	The fame.
1554 Edward Rutter,	George Huntley	1668 John Marshall	The fame
1567 William Johns,	The fame	1686 Thomas Burton,	Frances Visc Downe
1570 William Tully,	George Huntley, Esq	1692 Edw Smith, M A	The fame, and Philip Sheppard, Esq
1609 Nath Baxter, B D	Sir George Huntley	1729 John Hayward, M A	Matt Lord Ducie
1610 Richard Hathaway,	The fame	1776 Geo Hayward, M A	Thos Lord Ducie

PRESENT LORD OF THE MANOR,

The Right Honourable GEORGE Earl of BROOK and WARWICK

The only Person summoned from this Place by the Heralds in 1682 and 1683 was
John Marshall, Vicar

At the Election in 1776 Six Freeholders polled from this Parish

The Register has its first Date in 1559

ANNUAL ACCOUNT OF MARRIAGES, BIRTHS, AND BURIALS, IN THIS PARISH

A D	Mar	Bir	Bur	A D	Mar	Bir	Bur	A D	Mar	Bir	Bur	A D	Mar	Bir	Bur
1781	3	6	7	1786	4	7	7	1791				1796			
1782	2	9	9	1787	6	15	9	1792				1797			
1783	2	2	4	1788	2	10	6	1793				1798			
1784	2	11	4	1789	5	14	10	1794				1799			
1785	6	9	20	1790	3	17	8	1795				1800			

* The Road descending from the Hill, which was formerly very narrow and steep, has been diverted and brought by an easy regular and easy Course from *Nympsfield* across *Coaley Pike* This Improvement was suggested by the present Vicar of *Frocester* and completed in 1783, under his Inspection, to the great Accommodation of the Public

INSCRIPTIONS IN THE CHURCH.

ON A FLAT STONE IN THE CHANCEL

ANNO DOMINI 1570,
THE 14 OF AUGUST,
WAS BURIED THE BO-
DY OF JHON HVNTLEY,
THE SONNE AND HEYRE
OF GEORGE HVNTLEY,
ESQVIER, AND IN
THE 12 YEARE OF
THE RAIGNE OF OVR
SOVERAGNE LADY
ELIZABETH QUEENE

ON FLAT STONES IN THE NAVE

Under this Stone are deposited
the Remains of ELIZABETH,
the Wife of EDW SMITH,
Vicar of this Parish,
who was buried Feb 8, 1712 13

In Memory of the
Rev Mr EDW SMITH, M A.
late Vicar of this Parish,
who died March 25, 1729,
aged 70 Years

In Memory of
MARY, Relict of the
Rev Mr EDWARD TURNER,
late Vicar of Cam,
who deceased May 3,
Anno Domini 1738

ON A BRASS PLATE

In Memory of
SAMUEL HALLIDAY and of
ELEANOR his Wife.
He died the 24th Day of August, 1684,
aged 50 Years
She died the 24th Day of June,
in the 80th Year of her Age, 1720

IN THE NORTH CHANCEL, ON AN ALTAR TOMB

Hic jacet sub hoc tumulo
Corpus JOHANNIS HUNTLEY, Armigeri,
qui hanc vitam discessit
decimo quarto die Augusti,
Anno Dom 1570,
et etiam Corpus
GEORGII HUNTLEY, Militis,
& eidem JOHANNI
prædicto Hæredis, qui
hanc vitam discessit
decimo tertio die Septembris,
Anno Domini 1622

ON FLAT STONES, WITH A WALL BEFORE THEM.

Here lyeth the Body of
ELIZABETH, Daughter of
the Rev JOHN HAYWARD
She died Jan 2, 1768, aged 34.

Here lyeth the Body of
MARY the Wife of
the Rev JOHN HAYWARD,
Vicar of this Parish,
She died May the 12th, 1768,
aged 58

Here lyeth the Body of
the Rev JOHN HAYWARD, M A
Vicar of this Parish 47 Years
and 18 Years Rector of Nymphsfield.
He died July 1776, aged 71

Here lieth the Body of
MARY Wife of
WILLIAM HOPTON,
and Daughter of
the Rev JOHN HAYWARD
She died June 21, 1769, aged 38

IN THE CHURCH YARD

ON TOMBS

Arms, Erminois, on a Bend Azure,
cottised Sable three Martlets Argent,
a Canton Or, charged with a Rose Gules,
for WILKINS, on an Escocheon of Pretence, Argent, on a Cheveron engrailed
Sable, between three Fleurs de lis Gules,
as many Bezants, for WOOD

In Memory of
JOHN WILKINS, of this Parish,
who died the 29th of April, 1736,
aged 69 Years

Also of
ANNE, the Wife of the said
JOHN WILKINS,
who died the 20th of July, 1730,
aged near 58 Years

In Memory of
ELIZABETH, the Daughter of
JOHN WILKINS
and ANNE his Wife,
who died June the 17 1729,
in the 28th Year of her Age.

Also of
JUDITH, the Daughter of
JOHN WILKINS,
by ANNE his Wife,
who died the 14th of May, 1730,
in the 23d Year of her Age

Near this Place lie the Bodies of
JOHN WILKINS,
late of this Parish,
and ELIZABETH his Wife,
the Daughter of CHARLES WOOD,

of Stanley St Leonard, in this County.
He departed this Life the
9th Day of March 1758, aged 64 Years,
and she on the 8th Day of August 1739,
aged 49 Years

SARAH
their only surviving Daughter
(Wife of MILES OATRIDGE, jun
of Coaley, in this County)
as a Pledge of her filial Affection,
caused this Monument to be erected
to their Memories, anno 1760

Also to the Memories of
JOHN (eldest Son of the said
JOHN and ELIZABETH WILKINS),
who died March 7, 1747,
aged 29 Years, and was buried here;

CHARLES, second Son,
who died in London
Sept 18 1740 aged 19 Years
was buried at Stepney in Middlesex

ANNE, eldest Daughter,
Wife of RALPH BIGLAND,
Citizen of London
(now Somerset Herald),
who died there Dec 1, 1738,
aged 25 Years,
and was buried at Stepney,
in the County aforesaid

ELIZABETH, second Daughter,
Wife of ARTHUR JEFFSON,
Citizen of Bristol
who died there Sept 12 1731,
aged 31 Years,
and was buried in St Werburgh
Church

MARY, Daughter of
RICHARD and MARY BIGLAND,
died Nov 5 1766,
aged 16 Months

JOHN WEBB
died Aug 1, 1686, aged 70.

JOHN his Son
died Jan 22, 1676
aged 1 Year and 9 Months

EDWARD BROWNING,
Son of EDWARD BROWNING
died the 2d Day of April, 1687

THOMAS BROWNING,
died in October, 1737, aged 76

JUDITH his Daughter
Wife of SAMUEL FLETCHER,
died April 8, 1775, aged 74

SAMUEL FLETCHER
died March 5, 17 aged 0

THOMAS IVAN
died July 30, 1779 aged 27

ELIZABETH, Wife of
NICHOLA BARON
was here buried April 25,
A no { Domini 1743,
{ ætatis 80,

THOMAS BARON
died Sept 11 1766 aged 64

MARY his Wife
died Nov 4 1784, aged

THOMAS

THOMAS WETMORE, Yeoman,
died August 24, 1759, aged 71.

ELIZABETH his Wife
died April 25, 1748, aged 30

MARY his second Wife
died March 6, 1779 aged 60

ELIZABETH Daughter of
WILLIAM and SARAH WETMORE,
died May 31, 1767, aged 6 Years

ELIZABETH Wife of
WILLIAM IRONMAN,
died Sept 20, 1771, aged 0

Three of their Children died Infants

ON A BRASS PLATE
JOHN HEAVEN,
late Servant to the
Rev PHILIP SHEPPARD 23 Years
He departed this Life Oct 7, 1779,
aged 66 Years

ON A FLAT STONE
In Memory of
SAMUEL, the Son of
NATHANIEL WILKINS,
of this Parish,
and of ELIZABETH his Wife,
the Daughter of JOHN PICKER,
of Nymphsfield,
who died at Leghorn anno 1738,
aged near 40 Years

Also of
NATHANIEL WILKINS aforesaid,
who died February 1764,
aged 6 Years

ELIZABETH his Wife died in 1784,
aged 84

ELIZA their Daughter
Wife of JAMES BAILIS
died March 3, 1753, aged 37 Years
JOHN 4th Son of the said NATHANIEL
and ELIZABETH, died in London,
Jan 15, 1766, aged 22
NATHANIEL, 2d Son
died in London, 1782, aged 60
WILLIAM, 3d Son, died 1782, aged 49

ON FLAT AND HEAD STONES

	Died	Aged		Died	Aged
William Chapman -	16 Nov 1692	61	George, Son of John Smith	14 Sept 1720	—
Mary his Wife	21 Nov. 1726	84	Margaret, Wife of John Smith	27 Aug 1721	—
Rebekah, Wife of Joseph Wilkins	25 Dec 1675	—	William Smith -	28 Dec 1728	—
William Wilkins	4 Sept 1711	35	William Smith -	16 Apr 17 9	30
George Chapman Wilkins, Son of John and Ann Wilkins buried	27 Dec. 1712	—	Margaret Smith - buried	15 Jun 1768	10
Joseph, Son of John Wilkins	3 Mar 1717	—	Thomas Son of William and Margaret Smith buried	4 Apr 1781	53
Mary, Daughter of Nathaniel Wilkins	4 Sept 1714	3	Sarah his Wife buried	29 Dec 1779	50
Hannah, Daughter of Miles and Mary Oatridge	28 July 1714	1	William Wood	11 Apr 1729	73
John, Son of John Heaven	12 July, 1707	8	Elizabeth his Wife	14 Oct 17 4	—
Edith, Relict of William Heaven, senior	30 Jun 1708	79	James their Son	14 May, 1704	—
Ann, Daughter of William Heaven	4 Mar. 1728	1	Sarah their Daughter -	6 Jun. 1724	—
Ursula, Daughter of William Heaven	4 May, 1736	19	John their Son	10 Mar 1709	7
Edward Son of William Heaven	11 June, 1743	37	Elizabeth his Wife	29 Mar 1748	46
Elizabeth, Relict of William Heaven, junior	19 Feb 1744	75	William, Son of John and Margaret Wood	31 July, 1789	36
John Heaven	8 Feb 1739	33	Mary Daughter of John and Margaret Wood	11 May 1792	41
Martha his Daughter -	31 May, 1745	8	Margaret, Wife of George Baron	3 Oct 1665	—
Thomas Heaven	20 Oct 1754	44	Nicholas Baron -	— May 1 65	—
Alice Wife of Richard Ronalds, and Relict of Thomas Heaven	30 Oct 1770	64	Charles his Son -	— 1 53	33
Sarah Wife of John Wettmore	6 July, 1711	—	Mary, Wife of George Baron	6 Aug 1726	26
Thomas Wettmore, senior	5 Apr 1727	82	George Baron buried	8 Nov 83	42
Henry Wetmore	14 Apr 1729	97	Sarah their Daughter died in Infancy		
Mary, Wife of John Wettmore	27 Aug 1742	46	Richard Barnes	13 Nov 1748	50
John Wettmore	14 Sept 1745	62	Hannah his Wife	29 Sept 1756	39
Thomas their Son	2 Nov 1753	26	Hannah Wife of Samuel Barnes	1 July, 1758	66
William Daw	6 June 1723	63	Daniel Bennett	26 Nov 1728	66
William Son of William Daw, jun	26 Apr 1727	—	Hannah his Wife	15 Sept 1735	66
James, Son of William Daw, jun	12 Oct 1734	—	Daniel Bennett	4 Feb 1768	48
James, Son of Wm Daw	21 Nov 1727	—	Sarah his Wife	5 Feb 17 3	75
Hannah, Relict of William Daw	19 July, 1733	—	Richard Ronalds -	18 Oct 1731	42
Margaret, Daughter of Will Daw	4 Jun 1744	9	Richard Ronalds	11 May, 1771	54
William, Son of George Smith, of Chester	21 May, 1758	4	Mary Ronalds -	23 Ju 1	5
William Daw -	23 July 1760	57	William Andrews -	11 Jun, 1777	69
Sarah his Wife	28 Oct 1777	71	Richard, Son of Giles Heaven	18 June 1757	13
George, Son of William and Sarah Daw	20 Jun 1788	58	Richard Heaven	24 Aug 175	30
William and William, Sons of George and Sarah Daw died Infants			Anne, Wife of Samuel Heaven	6 Apr 1746	36
John Phelps	22 Dec 1756	51	Anne their Daughter	15 Dec 1758	1
Margaret Phelps -	2 Dec 1757	67	Samuel Heaven	25 Apr 1767	46
Ann Daughter of John Phelps	3 May 17—	12	Richard Heaven	4 Mar 1759	62
George Pegler	16 Dec 1679	63	Mary his Wife	25 Apr 1748	85
Thomas Pegler	26 Feb 1692	—	Mary, Daughter of William and Sarah Heaven	24 Jun 1	18
Sarah, Wife of George Pegler	27 Oct 1719	36	James Wilkins	18 Mar 17 2	51
George Pegler	22 Aug 1722	65	Sarah his Wife		
John, Son of George Pegler	3 May, 1721	—	Ann, Wife of William Wilkins	1 Mar 1 50	—
James, Son of George Pegler	3 Mar 1727	11	Susannah, Wife of John Wilkins	24 Nov 17 2	23
George Pegler	16 Oct 1738	27	Abigail, Wife of William Varney	25 Apr 1 45	—
Thomas Pegler -	26 Feb 1764	48	Mary, Wife of Samuel Wilkins	2 Nov 1 7 2	5
Mary, Wife of Thomas Pegler -	9 May, 1776	63	Samuel Wilkins	17 July 1 7	—
John Smith			Thomas Wilkins -	— Mar 1 81	65
Sarah Wife of John Smith, senior			Sarah, Daughter of Samuel and Mary Wilkins		
Richard Smith -	20 Nov 1686	—	Mary Wife of Samuel Wilkins	16 May, 1794	45
John Smith - -	5 Oct 1701	—	Samuel Wilkins	4 Dec 1786	65
Michael Smith	30 July, 1702	—	William, Son of Thomas Wilkins	1 June, 1776	—
			Thomas Wilkins	19 Dec 17 0	—
			Sarah his Wife	24 Mar 1 57	—
			Thomas Wilkins such smaller	21 Nov 1 57	—
			John Wilkins	8 Jun 1 3	5

ON FLAT AND HEAD STONES

	Died	Aged
William, Son of William Nurse	27 June, 1662	—
Samuel Nurse	11 Dec 1711	36
Sarah Wife of George Nurse	8 Dec 1755	—
Mary, Daughter of George Nurse	— Sept 1768	4
John Webb, senior		
John Webb	17 Oct 1742	53
Charles, Son of William and Ann Webb	19 Feb 1787	—
Ann, Wife of Simon Neall, of Cowley	26 Jan 1740	—
Sarah, Daughter of Daniel Neall, senior	16 Mar 1744	—
Sarah, Daughter of Daniel Neall, junior	28 Nov 1752	3
Mary Wife of Richard Horstone		
Lucy Llan	14 Sept 1747	—
John Davis	12 Jan 1731	26
Edith his Wife	5 May, 1736	29
Thomas Davis, Butcher	20 May, 1787	81
William King, a Native of North Britain	28 Oct 1748	34
Elizabeth, Wife of Nathaniel Stephens	21 June, 1735	65
Mary their Daughter	11 Aug 1762	60
Samuel Wilkins	— 1784	—
Judith, Wife of John Parslow		
Elizabeth, Wife of Roger Parslow	31 Dec 1732	64
Robert their Son	28 Dec 1732	44
Bartholemew Wicks	30 Apr 1684	—
N Adams	1 Oct 1728	68
Judith his Wife	1 Oct 1725	63
Andrew Fletcher	1 Jan 1734	41
James, Son of John Fletcher	28 May, 1738	32
Robert Collins	— 1742	—
Betty his Wife	— 1748	—

	Died	Aged
Betty, ⎫ Daughters of W Collins	— 1760	—
Sarah, ⎭	— 1759	—
Stephen Hoskins	24 June, 1733	70
William Cowley Clerk of this Parish	30 Mar 1753	77
Hannah his Wife	30 July, 1731	43
Samuel his Son	28 May 1731	—
Samuel Woodman	28 Aug 1753	64
Also five of his Children		
Mary, Wife of Thomas Woodman	19 Apr 1755	33
Sarah, Wife of John French	29 Oct 1789	69
Mary, Wife of John Turner, and Daughter of John and Sarah French	21 Aug 1786	42
Joseph Churches	9 May, 1767	76
Martha his Wife	28 Apr 1743	63
Arthur Watts, Son of Arthur Watts	17 Feb 1721	43
William Clark	— May, 1753	—
Sarah his Wife	28 Apr 1778	69
Hannah Clark	28 June, 1754	23
William Clutterbuck	17 Dec 1785	36
Sarah his Daughter	26 Feb 1780	1
Thomas Son of Thomas and Sarah Buckingham	16 Mar 1769	5
Thomas, George, Thomas, James, and Joseph, their Sons, died Infants		
Anthony Rowles	4 Feb 1789	77
John Crols	19 Apr 1731	50
Mary his Wife	1 Apr 1752	53
John Trotman	7 May, 1747	52
Samuel Browning	17 Oct 1731	39
George Perkems buried	22 Apr 1712	—
Also three of his Children		
Sarah, Wife of John Bond, of Stroud	4 Sept 1783	58

MORE commonly called *NETHER GUITING*, is a Parish of considerable Extent, in the lower Division of the Hundred of *Kiftesgate*, six Miles distant Westward from *Stowe*, six Eastward from *Winchcomb*, and nineteen North east from the City of GLOUCESTER The Soil is of light stone Brash, including about 4000 Acres; arable in a far greater Proportion, with spacious Downs and Woodlands The Downs are commonable, and are remarkable for the natural Produce of a great Number of Hawthorns

The Living is a Vicarage, the Impropriation of which was given to the *Cistertian* Abbey of *Bruerne*, in *Oxfordshire*, soon after its Foundation in the Reign of King JOHN. The greater Part of the impropriate Tythes now belong to *Christ Church* College, *Oxford*, and the Remainder to the Trustees of certain Charities, bequeathed by GEORGE TOWNSEND, of *Rotwell*, in this County, Esq anno 1683

The Church, dedicated to *St. Michael*, retains the Architecture of the early *Norman* Centuries The two opposite Door cases consist of indented Mouldings, and what is remarkable, the Arch dividing the Nave from the Chancel, which is very pointed, has the same Ornament There is an embattled Tower at the West End.

The Manor was given by the CONQUEROR to WILLIAM GOIZENBODED, from whom it descended to the DE QUINCEYS, Earls of *Winton*, under whom it appears to have been held by Lease by the Master of the Knights Templars. ROGER DE WATTEVILLE had previously granted to them wo Yard Lands, and certain Immunities, in this Parish In 1314, 14 EDW II it was found by an Inquisition, *post mortem*, that ROGER CORBET had died seized of this Manor, with those of *Ebrington*, *Cuttesluat*, and *Barnecott*, from which Circumstance it seems that it was about that Time included in the Manor of *Ebrington*, which still exercises manerial Jurisdiction as Paramount ADAM DE HERMINGTON, and Sir JOHN BOTELER, of *Sudley*, are next mentioned as Proprietors In the Reign of HENRY the Eighth it was transferred from the Crown, where it had lapsed by Attainder of the BOTELERS, to WILLIAM WHORWOOD, Esq Attorney General, who left two Daughters and Coheirs, ANNE the Wife of AMBROSE DUDLEY, Earl of *Warwick*, and MARGARET, of THOMAS THROCKMORTON, of *Coughton*, co *Warwick*, Ancestor of the present Sir ROBERT THROCKMORTON, Baronet, the former of whom dying without Issue, one Moiety was inherited by her Nephew THOMAS WHORWOOD in 1573, 15 ELIZ

The ancient Family of STRATFORD, already possessing large Property in the Parish purchased the Manor about 1600, and retained it till 1715, when it was transferred to Sir JAMES HOWE, Bart of *Berwick St Leonard's*, co *Wilt*, by Marriage with ELIZABETH Daughter and Heir of HENRY STRATFORD, Esq In 1720 DAVID HUGHES, Esq held the Manor of *Guiting Poher* and was succeeded by his Son, who, dying without Issue in 1757, it passed in equal Parts to his three Sisters and Coheirs the eldest of whom was the Wife of JOHN VERNON, Esq Barrister at Law, the second of WILLIAM SMART, Gent. and the youngest of THOMAS HOLLAND, Gent of *Mickleton*

HAMLETS

Fermecotte, or *Farmcote*, distant from the Church about three Miles, is a distinct Manor, and is said to have had anciently parochial Rights It is a Chapelry annexed to *Guiting Poher*, to which it pays, in Lieu of Tythes, 6l 8s 4d by an old Composition It is recited in *Domesday*, and in the following Centuries passed to the Families of CORBET and GREVILLE JOHN STRATFORD a Witness summoned to Parliament 12 EDW II 1320, then held this Manor JOHN STRATFORD, the eighth in descent from the abovementioned, was the Progenitor of three opulent Families settled at *Farmcote*, *Great Gritting*, and *Halling* For this Estate WILLIAM STRATFORD, Esq paid to the Parliament 763l 15s on account of his Loyalty About the beginning of the present Century it became by Purchase the Property of ROBERT TRACY, Esq of *Corscombe*, who, dying without Issue, left it to ROBERT PRATT, Esq whose Relict, remarried to STEVENOR HOLFORD, Esq (since deceased) is the present Possessor

In the Chapel, which is apparently ancient, is a Tomb for HENRY STRATFORD, Esq in the Style of Queen ELIZABETH's Time, without Inscription The Preceptory at *Quenington* and the Abbey of *Hayles*, both held Lands in this Hamlet

Farmcote Wood, of 200 Acres, as appendant on the Loidship of *Sudley*, belongs to the Right Honourable GEORGE LORD RIVERS.

2 *Guiting Grange* included the manerial Lands originally granted to the Abbey of *Bruerne*, and was the Grange in which their Corn rents were received * Upon the Diffolution, thefe Lands were fold, fubject to a referved Rent to the Crown, to ANTHONY STRINGER and JOHN WILLIAMS in 1545 They were bought in 1620 by WILLIAM GARDYNER, Efq of *Bermondfey* in the County of *Surrey*, and by his Grandfon re fold, about 1720, to JOHN SNELL, Efq of *Gloucefter* The Manfion houfe is compact and elegant, fituate in a fmall Park, which abounds in very beautiful Scenery The *Cotefwold* Vallies, fuch as thefe are, fhew a fuperior Cultivation

3 *Catteflade*, or *Caftellet*, for it is faid, that a Caftle built here was held by EDMUND Earl of STAFFORD, in the Reign of HENRY the Fourth † This Hamlet is likewife mentioned in *Domefday* It became the Property of DAVID HUGHES, Efq by Marriage with the Heir of the Family of COLLES, and is now that of the Reprefentatives of his Coheirs, THOMAS VERNON and THOMAS HOLLAND, Gents

A Stream which is the Source of the River *Windrufh* has its firft Rife in this Parifh

BENEFACTIONS

1615 THOMAS COMPEER, Gent bequeathed 100*l* the Intereft of which to be expended in buying Materials for fetting the Poor to work, or to be given them in Bread
1635 THOMAS DEAN gave 30*l* to the Poor
1682 GEORGE TOWNESEND, Efq of *Rowell*, left Lands, the Income of which is 2*l* 12*s* to be laid out in Bread, and other Lands, which produce 5*l* a Year, for apprenticing a poor Boy, either from this Parifh, or *Blockley* in *Worcefterfhire*

INCUMBENTS	PATRONS.	INCUMBENTS	PATRONS
1560 Baldwin Johnfon,	———	1737 John Parfons, M A	Coheirs of D Hughes, Efq
——— Thomas Wood,			
1588 Henry Scriven,	Henry Stratford, Efq	1760 Thomas Darke,	Thos Vernon, Efq and David Hughes Holland, Gent.
1621 William Gorton ‡,	Henry Stratford, Efq		
1658 Miles Huatfon,	Wm Stratford, Efq		
* * * * * *	* * * * *	1769 Erafmus King,	The fame
1712 Thomas Humphreys,	David Hughes, Efq	1777 Charles Bifhop, M A	Elinor Vernon and John Holland
1727 Henry Savage, B A.	The fame		
		1780 Thomas Symondes,	The fame.

PRESENT PROPRIETORS OF THE MANORS,

Lord Paramount of *Guiting*, *Catteflade*, and *Farmcote*.
The Right Honourable HUGH Earl FORTESCUE

CLAIMANTS,

Of *Guiting* and *Catteflade*,   Of *Farmcote*,
ELEANOR VERNON, Widow,   MARY HOLFORD, Widow.

Lord of the Manor of *Guiting Grange*,
POWEL SNELL, Efq

The only Perfons fummoned from this Parifh by the Heralds in 1682 and 1683, were William Gardyner, Efq and John Colles, Gent of *Catteflade*

At the Election in 1776 Twelve Freeholders polled from this Parifh

The firft Date of the Regifter is in 1560

ANNUAL ACCOUNT OF MARRIAGES, BIRTHS, AND BURIALS, IN THIS PARISH

A D	Mar	Bir	Bur	A D	Mar	Bir	Bur	A D	Mar	Bir	Bur	A D	Mar	Bir	Bur
1781	4	16	10	1786	3	21	7	1791				1796			
1782	2	15	10	1787	6	11	15	1792				1797			
1783	1	12	12	1788	5	14	7	1793				1798			
1784	3	13	20	1789	3	12	7	1794				1799			
1785	7	11	12	1790	1	14	7	1795				1800			

* DUGDALE's Mon vol I p 63, Chart 3) Tow III m' pro b' ca w itenna in *Cuyting Poer*, &c '
† M. N II
‡ WILLIAM GORTON B D of the Univerfity of *St Andrew* was incorporated July 9, 1619 He was then Vicar of *Bourton* Gare on Grace Woods Fafti Oxon vol I p 858

/ U   INSCRIPTIONS

INSCRIPTIONS IN THE CHURCH

ON FLAT STONES IN THE CHANCEL.

Arms Gules, a Cheveron vaire between three Crescents Gules. Crest a Buck's Head affronte Gules attired Or

HIC JACET CORPUS
EDMONDI GODDARD, DE SWINDON
IN COMITATU WILTONIENSI,
GENEROSI.
OBIIT 18 OCTOBRIS,
ANAQUI. DOM 1676,
ÆTATIS SUÆ 61

Here lieth the Body of
WILLIAM COLES, Gent.
who departed this Life

December the 5 1699,
and in the 76 Year of
his Age

ON A BRASS PLATE AGAINST THE NORTH PILLAR BETWEEN THE NAVE AND CHANCEL.

Memoriæ Sacrum
Prope hunc locum in his cancellis
jacet Corpus MILETII HUATSONII,
Clerici,
PETRI HUATSONII Filii
de Docker, Baronetæ,
Candaliensi comitatu Westmorlandiæ,
hujus Ecclesiæ plurimis annis pastoris
Obiit die mensis Julii 3,
anno æt 79, & anno Salutis 1712
Qui requiescit in Domino

IN THE NAVE

ON A FLAT STONE

In Memory of THOMAS CHARLES,
Mercer,
And of MARY his Wife.

THOMAS died Nov 2, 1727, aged 42
MARY died Aug 10 1731, aged 41

Their Son RICHARD SMITH CHARLES
died greatly lamented, and was buried
here March 23 1755,
aged 38 Years

IN THE CHURCH YARD, ON TOMBS.

WELTHIN, Wife of
HENRY HUMPHRIS
died Jan 27, 1758, aged 74.

HENRY HUMPHRIS
died Dec 9 1781, aged 87

HENRY FREEMAN
died July 8, 10 7.

JOHN FREEMAN
Sept 3, 1731 aged 48

WILLIAM FREEMAN, Free Mason,
died Jan 31, 1730, aged 46

THOMAS FREEMAN
died Feb 26 1775, aged 86.

Here lieth
a truly honest Man,
JOHN HOWER,
Dyer, who
departed this Life the 26th Day of May,
1787, aged 77 Years,
by whose unremitting Industry
the Poor of this and the adjacent Parishes
were many Years greatly relieved, by
the Employment of them
in the various Parts
of his Trade
By an uniform Respect for his Superiors,
he gained their good Will,
by a Generosity and Hospitality to his
Equals
he was blessed with their Friendship;
and,
by a Hand ever open to the distressed,

he procured their unfeigned
Benedictions
This small Tribute to his Memory
is placed by a near Neighbour

Ye, to whom once this mortal Clay was
known,
Whose social Tongue oft chear'd the
Winter's Day,
Drop one soft Tear of Pity on this Stone,
Then move in sacred Thoughtfulness
away;
'Twas mine 'tis yours (perchance with
Grief) to see
The Trifles of more fleeting Years re
turn
Then let I redeem what's lost with
Piety,
Lest ye too late your Negligence
should mourn

ON HEAD AND FLAT STONES

	Died	Aged		Died	Aged
Charles Black ell	16 Mar 1716	—	Elizabeth, Wife of John Williams	28 Apr 1742	64
William Hanks	5 Aug 1757	36	Joseph Thorndell	1 Nov 1785	65
Mary, Wife of Thomas Hyett buried	19 June, 1747	—	Sarah his Daughter, Wife of John		
Mary Wife of Edward Wood	24 Aug 1762	58	Harris	28 Sept 1776	9
Esther, Wife of William Hayward	15 Aug 1762	56	Sarah, Wife of Joseph Thorndell	5 Apr 1784	60
Thomas Jones	9 Aug 1715	15	William Thorndell	27 July 1782	6,
Margaret his Wife	10 Oct 1754	73	James Taylor	22 Nov 1755	53
Deborah, Daughter of William and			Hannah, Wife of Adam Millin	10 Nov 1789	28
Deborah Norton of Hannai			Harry Hayward	25 Dec 1776	42
and Wife of J. Hayward	11 Aug 1776	56	Thomas Freeman	10 Mar 1729	—
Ann Daughter of John and Debo			John Freeman	4 Feb 1761	45
rah Hayward	18 Aug 1778	2	Elizabeth Rick	8 June, 689	65
William Thipps late Bayliff to			Elizabeth Wife of William Hunt	12 Apr 1767	5
Powell Snell, Esq	8 Aug 1743	60	John Son of Thomas and Mary		
John Lucett	23 Oct 1780	66	Buttler	21 Feb 1736	1
Ann Wife of William Arkell of			John Wood	5 Oct 1749	71
Calcutt	12 Feb 1771	31	Mary his Wife	10 Nov 1761	6,
Sarah, Wife of William Luckett			John Wood of Barton	28 Dec 1751	35
late of his dwell	3 Oct 1782	78	Edward Wood	— 1673	—
Elizabeth Wife of Robert Beddon	11 Apr 1784	19	Hannah Daughter of John and		
Ann Wife of Nathaniel Milton	10 Aug 1784	50	Mary Wood, and Wife of Edward		
Elizabeth Wife of William Hunt	2 Apr 1767	1,	Mathews	15 Aug 1743	25
Jane Wife of Benjamin	6 Dec 1788	71	Hannah Wife of John Wood, of		
Ann, Wife of James Taylor	15 Jan 1783	6.	Barton	— 1715	—

ON

ON HEAD AND FLAT STONES

	Died	Aged		Died	Aged
Augustine, Son of Augustine and Mary Greening	9 Apr 1745	4	Thomas Wood	18 Jan 1769	41
Thomas, Son of Augustine and Mary Greening	17 Jan 1745	1	Sarah his Wife	24 Aug 1731	45
Augustine Greening	23 Dec 1782	70	John their Son	27 May 1763	70
Mary King	20 May 1745	—	Mary, Daughter of Richard and Mary Belcher	18 Apr 1762	16
Benjamin Charlwood	3 Aug 1747	40	Eleanor, Wife of Justinian Hatheway	23 Sept 1744	69
Mary his Daughter	15 Apr 1745	4	Sarah, Wife of Joseph Mutco buried	21 Dec 1760	53
Elizabeth, Wife of Edward Smith, junior	24 May 1757	76	Anne, Wife of Thomas Hatheway	15 Dec 1751	68
Hannah, Wife of John Turner	20 Apr 1762	61	Anathan Hatheway	—	—
John Turner	28 Nov 1778	78	Anne, Daughter of Joseph	— Nov 1729	—
Thomas Greening	21 May 1730	—	Robert Etheridge	6 Aug 1746	17
Grace his Wife	15 Mar 1726	66	John Etheridge	17 Jan 1748	48
William, Son of William Preston, of Yanworth	9 June 1722	26	John, Son of John and Elizabeth Etheridge	30 Nov 1749	24
Elner, Daughter of John Skinner	25 Sept 1701	24	Elizabeth, Wife of John Etheridge	13 Aug 1773	81
John Stephens, senior	12 Oct 1729	75	Elizabeth Wife of John Humphris	4 Nov 1739	78
John Stephens, junior	19 Mar 1770	67	John Humphris	6 Mar 1680	—
Hannah, Wife of John Stephens	6 Mar 1747	45	John Humphris	7 May 1740	57
Hester Wife of James Humphris, of Kyneton	11 June 1725	49	Ann, Wife of Rich Williams, senior	14 Nov 1724	67
Alice, Wife of John Humphris	10 Mar 1782	59	John Williams	7 July 1776	85
Henry Humphris, of Kyneton	16 Nov 1765	35	Mary his Wife	20 Oct 1747	46
Elizabeth, Wife of John Turner	12 Dec 1770	71	Michael their Son	12 Nov 1732	29
			Mary, Wife of Timothy Sadler	2 May 1781	63
			Ann, Daughter of Anthony and Ann Sadler	24 June 1752	26
			John Blackwell	8 Dec 1714	

IN THE CHAPEL AT FARMCOTE

On a Tomb on the North Side of the Chancel are the Effigies of a Man in Armour, with a Woman, in the Dress of the Times supplicating and the following Arms, but no Inscription —Barry of 10 over 111 a Lion rampant, for STRATFORD —impaling a Bend engrailed, a Crescent for difference

ON FLAT STONES IN THE NAVE

Here lieth the Body of
ARABELLA, the Daughter of

Thomas and Betty Baker,
who departed this Life the
2d Day of June, in the Year 1765,
aged 17 Weeks

Also here lieth the Body of
BETTY, the Daughter of
THOMAS and BETTY,
who departed this Life
the 11th Day of November,
in the Year 1767, aged 16 Years

Heare
resteth, in hopes of a joyfull
Resurrection, the Body of
THOMAS BAKER,
who departed this Life
the 30th Day of September 1785,
aged 64 Years

ON HEAD STONES IN THE CHAPEL YARD.

	Died	Aged		Died	Aged
Hannah, Wife of Robert Baylis	26 June, 1750	53	William, Son of Richard Baker, of Didbrooke	30 Aug 1761	26
Three of their Children died in their Infancy, buried within the Entrance of the Chapel			Anne Wife of Thomas Wilson, of Camden, and Daughter of Robert and Hannah Baylis	24 Dec 1774	49
Robert Baylis	21 Apr 1767	64	Jane Daughter of John and Ann Chadbourn	19 Nov 1748	73
Moses Son of Robert and Ann Baylis	15 June, 1766	26			
Caleb, Son of Robert and Hannah Baylis	22 Oct 1773	42			

CXXVII. GUITING MILITUM TEMPLI,
OR
TEMPLE GUITING.

ADJOINS the preceding Parish, and is situate in the lower Division of the Hundred of *Kiftef gate*, feven Miles North weftward from *Stow*, five Eaftward from *Winchcombe*, and twenty from GLOUCESTER on the North eaft. More than 4000 Acres are included within the Boundaries, of a light ftony Soil tiled, with 400 Acres in Woodland, and very extenfive commonable Downs, upon which large Flocks are fed

The Living is a ftipendiary Curacy, of the certified Value of 20*l* 5*s* paid from the Impropriation, which, upon the Diffolution of the Knights Hofpitallers of *St John* of *Jerufalem*, was granted to *Chrift Church* College, *Oxford*

The Church, dedicated to *St Mary*, is conftructed with a Nave and a ftrong embattled Tower at the Weft End, but the Chancel is evidently more ancient, fo that it appears, that the original Edifice was re-built, and moft probably by the Knights Hofpitallers. Dr TALBOT, the late Incumbent, in 1745, it the Expence of 1,000*l* entirely re modelled the Infide in a high Style of modern Decoration, with a flat Roof, and furrounding Cornices

Amongft the hundred and fixteen Manors given by the CONQUEROR to ROGER DE LACI (fixteen of which were in this County) was "*Getinge*" His Defcendant GILBERT DE LACI gave in 1120 twelve Hides and one Virgate of Land, with the Demefnes in *Guiting* to the Knights Templars, and afterward profeffed himfelf of that Order But the Manor was referved to his Heirs, and held by Leafe in 1324, 17 EDW II from ALICE Countefs of LINCOLN by the Templars, who were about that Time fucceeded by the Knights Hofpitallers * It was inherited by the Family of CLINTON DE SAY, and in the Reign of HENRY VIII was purchafed of Sir JOHN HUDDLESTONE, Knight, by Dr RICHARD FOX, Bifhop of *Winchefter*, who fettled it on the Prefident and Fellows of *Corpus Chrifti* College, *Oxford*, by Charter of Foundation in 1517

The only Freehold Eftate in *Temple Cuting* became in 1590 the Property of THOMAS BEALE, Gent JOHN BEALE, Gent dying in 1774, bequeathed it to his Daughter and fole Heir MARY, the Wife of JOHN BROWNE, Gent of *Cold Salperton*, whofe fecond Son THOMAS BEALE BROWNE, a Minor, is the prefent Poffeffor The principal Leffee under *Corpus Chrifti* College is GEORGE TALBOT, Efq of an Eftate, long held by the Family of ALLEN For more than a Century, the impropriate Tythes have been leafed by *Chrift Church* College to the Family of HAYWARD

HAMLETS

1 *Ford* is a Conftablewick annexed to *Pynock*, and had formerly a Chapel, now applied to fecular Ufes It claims diftinct manorial Rights, and forms a Part of the Eftate of the Right Honourable THOMAS CHARLES FITCH, Lord Vifcount TRACY. The Abbey of *St Peter* in *Gloucefter* held a Mill here, the Donation of ROBERT CONSEL in 1120, during the Abbacy of WILLIAM GODEMON

2 *Barton* was Parcel of the Templar's Eftate in *Guiting*, where they had two Mills, one of them a Fulling Mill, erected by the Hofpitallers, probably in the Reign of EDW III and amongft the firft in this County † The chief Leffees under *Corpus Chrifti* College are WILLIAM RAIKES, Efq of *London*, and

---

* At *Quenington*, in this County, was a Preceptory of Knights Templars appendant on their chief Houfe in *London* A few of them refided there, for the Purpofe of receiving the Rents of Lands contiguous, and belonging to them Upon their Diffolution in 1340 the fame Eftablifhment were kept up and called Commanderies by the Knights Hofpitallers
† Summa redditus pertinentium ad *Guiting* xij *s* vid ob' DUGDALE Mon vol II p 529
† Ibi etiam fecerunt unum Molendinum fullereticapud *Bertone*, quod tenet *Wretone* pro xxxti Item ipfi fecerunt aliud Molendinum apud *Bertone* quod tenet eum *Wretone* pro xiij DecTali ut fupra This, it is prefumed, is the firft Notice of any fulling Mill erected in this County, and it is certain that the Manufacture was eftablifhed in the Town of *Campden* Norton Burford Cirencefter and the adjacent Villages, before it was extended to the Diftrict called Stroud water For the greater Encouragement of it an Act of Parliament was made in 1376, that no woollen Cloth fhall be carried out of the Realm to be fulled which were continued by fubfequent Statutes in RIC II ch 7 HEN IV ch 3 HEN VII ch EDW VII ch 14 to this Period the Wool was on the contrary exported to *Flanders*, from whence this Kingdom was fupplied with Woollen Cloth

JOHN

John Inglett Fortescue, Esq of *Dralish*, co *Devon* Maurice Rodney held this Manor by Grant from Queen Elizabeth in the first Year of her Reign

3 *Kyngton* in 1350 belonged to the Families of Cook and Coletti, but is now divided into several small Freeholds One of the large Common Fields is appropriated to this Hamlet

In a Survey made in 1770, the whole Parish was found to contain 75 Houses, and 426 Inhabitants

INCUMBENTS	PATRONS	INCUMBENTS	PATRONS
1711 William Winde,	Christ Church Coll Oxf	1777 Charles Bishop,	Christ Church Coll Oxf
—— Parsons,	The same	1786 Thomas Symonds,	The same
1769 Erasmus King,	The same		

PRESENT PROPRIETORS OF THE MANOR,

The President, Fellows, and Scholars of *Corpus Christi* College, Oxford

The Persons summoned from this Place by the Heralds in 1682 and 1683, were

William Stratford, Esq and John Beale, Gent

At the Election in 1776, Three Freeholders polled from this Parish

The earliest Date in the Register occurs in 1679

ANNUAL ACCOUNT OF MARRIAGES, BIRTHS, AND BURIALS, IN THIS PARISH

A D	Mar	Bir	Bur	A D	Mar	Bir	Bur	A D	Mar	Bir	Bur	A D	Mar	Bir	Bur
1781	7	9	11	1786	3	10	14	1791				1796			
1782	4	7	6	1787	2	9	11	1792				1797			
1783	2	10	6	1788	5	12	12	1793				1798			
1784	5	9	11	1789	2	14	4	1794				1799			
1785	4	11	15	1790	3	9	8	1795				1800			

INSCRIPTIONS IN THE CHURCH

ON FLAT STONES IN THE CHANCEL.

To the Memory of
RICHARD HAYWARD, Gen
Impropriator of this Parish,
& ANN his Wife,

He died the 21st of January, 1703,
aged 60

She died the 24th of June, 1714
aged 80

ROGER and SUSANNAH
two of their Children, died Infants

Here lieth the Body of
AGNES HAYWARD,
Daughter of the
Richard and Ann Hayward
She died April 8, 1765 in her 31st Year

To the Memory of
CHARLES HAYWARD, Gent
Impropriator of this Parish
who departed this Life
the 25th Day of January,
in the Year of our Lord 1765,
aged 63 Year

To the Memory of
CHARLES HAYWARD, Gent
Impropriator of this Parish
who died July 25, 1764, aged 76

Also of ANNE HAYWARD,
Wife of THOMAS HAYWARD, Gen
who died the 8th Day of October, 1714,
aged 70 Year

To the Memory of
THOMAS HAYWARD, Gent
who departed this Life
the 16th Day of August,
1733, aged 57 Years

Here lieth the Body of
JOHN ALLEN
Citizen and Apothecary of London,
who died 1744, by Reason
he married a Town Wife,
three sons John, Richard and Samuel,
and two daughters,
Elizabeth and Margaret

He died June 10, 1752,
aged 71 Year
I whose Virtues he receiveth
Comfort

ON FLAT STONES IN THE NAVE

Here lieth the Body of
MARY, the Wife of THOMAS DEANE,
of the Woodhouse, Gen
who departed this Life
he 3d Day of October in Anno Dom 1708,
aged 5 Years

In Memory of
MARGARET the Wife of
LEWIS ADAMS of the Woodhouse,
Gen
the only Daughter of JAMES ROSE,
of the City of London Gent
who succeeded in such matters of Family
of the Woodhouse Killick and
Parsons Cottage into older of his,
in the Northern part of
He the first went Secretary to his Uncle
Richard Rose,
late Archbishop of Canterbury in the
Reverend King, late the Lyth and
he first led his Lyth and
Then ADAMS she bore him four
Daughters she died in this Life
June 1, 1744, aged 42 Years

Here lieth the Body of Mrs KATHERINE BRAYNE, of Barton, Relict of Mr WILLIAM BRAYNE,
of Little Dean, in this County   She died Nov 22, 1727, aged 82 Years

Also the Remains of ELIZABETH CURTIS, of Stow, in the County of Gloucester,
who died the 22d Day of Feb 1758, aged 72 Years.

ON MARBLE MONUMENTS IN THE NORTH WING

Arms, on a Chevron, between three Griffin's Heads crazed, as many Mullets

In a Vault near this Marble
lie the Remains
of JOHN BEALE, Gent
descended from an ancient Family of this Place
He died the IX Day of August, MDCCLXXIV, aged LXXIV Years

Also
in the same Vault are deposited the Remains of
JOHN BEALE, of the City of London Merchant,
a Gentleman justly esteemed for his Integrity and Friendship
He died the XXVII Day of October, MDCCLXXIV, aged XXVIII Years,
justly lamented by all who knew him
He was only Son and Heir of the first named
JOHN BEALE and MARY his Wife
Daughter, and sole surviving Heir
of THOMAS ROBBINS, of Maugersbury, in this County

Arms, Gules, a Lion rampant within a Border engrailed Or, a Mullet for difference for TALBOT —impaling, Per Fess Or
and Argent, an Eagle displayed, with two Heads Sable on the Breast an Escocheon Gules, charged with a Bend Vaire, for
BOUVERIE

Sacred to the Memory
of that truly great and pious Divine the Honorable and Reverend GEORGE TALBOT, D.D
(youngest Son of CHARLES Lord TALBOT, Lord High Chancellor of Great Britain)
who finished his glorious Course of Life on the 19th of November, 1765 in the 71st Year of his Age
Stedfast from his Infancy in the Profession of the true Faith, and constant in the Practice of every Virtue,
he became in early Life and continued to his last Hour,
a shining Pattern of Christian Excellence and an Ornament to Human Nature
Though blest with every Endowment to discharge with Dignity and Lustre the Duties of the highest Office,
his Humility confined him to the lowest in the Ministry
Conscious of the Good he did in this Curacy and dreading the Responsibility of a more extensive Trust,
he refused a Bishoprick
and for near thirty Years, until disabled by Infirmities taught in this Church,
with the purest Zeal and most persuasive Eloquence
the saving Truths of the Gospel and converted men to Righteousness
His Charities were diffusive, but directed by Wisdom his Benevolence was unbounded
and his Labours to promote Peace, and the Temporal, as well as the Spiritual Interest of all his Fellow Creatures,
ceased only with his last Breath
He passed through Life without an Enemy and with the Affection and Veneration of all who knew him
This Fabrick, substantially repaired and beautified at his sole Expence
and the Hospital of this County which his Liberality and Exertion greatly contributed to found and establish,
will be lasting Monuments of his Piety and Humanity
but his good Name will survive both

This was erected by the Honourable CHARLOTTE BOUVERIE at her express Desire

---

IN THE CHURCH YARD, ON TOMBS

MARY WINDE, Relict of
JOHN WINDE of Bruckthrop,
and Daughter of WILLIAM RANDAL,
of Cowley who was buried
Feb 28, 1684.

JOHN WILLIAMS,
Sept 26, 1680

JOHN WILLIAMS,
1696

JOHN WILLIAMS,
Sept 2, 1745

THOMAS WILLIAMS of Kyneton,
May 26 1755, aged 70

RICHARD TOWNSEND Gent
departed this Life MDCCLXXXIV

SARAH KICK, Daughter of
ANTHONY and MARY KICK,
of Swindon in this County,
died June 5, 1753 aged 12 Years

ELIZABETH, Daughter of
JOHN and JOAN CLARK
died May 21, 1760, aged 22 Years

JOAN, Wife of JOHN CLARK,
died Jan 27, 1783, aged 84 Years

RICHARD their Son
died in his Infancy

ERASMUS KING Clerk
a few Years Vicar of
Upper and Lower Guiting
died March 1, 1777, aged Years

Clear was his Voice, and was his Kneeling
strong,
With pious Care his well taught Flock he
led,
He shewed of Holy Writ the choicest
Store
Well skilled he was in Theology and Love
On his persuasive Lips Attention hung,
For Truths divine flowed free from
his Tongue

Rev CHARLES BISHOP M.A
Minister of this Parish,
Vicar of Lower Guiting
and of Sedgeworth in this County
died May 14, 1780, aged 28 Years

It was by some Son (sure Ally of Death)
Prey on him that Limbs and Lungs
faith

Reader! he taught without Complaint
his Text,
He bore with patient Chearfulness to
bear
And when the long impending Stroke is
ever
Calmly resign, saw him, this World for
Heaven

ON FLAT AND HEAD STONES

	Died	Aged
Betty Crips	13 Sept 1778	60
Richard Crips	9 Apr 1769	48
Betty their Daughter -	25 June 1772	9
Giles Crip	28 May 1737	30
Elizabeth his Wife	31 Mar 1734	44
Mary their Daughter -	1 Aug 1745	10
William Crips	1747	
Elizabeth Daughter of Richard and Elizabeth Crips	21 June, 1757	—
John Crips	14 Feb 1756	83
Thomas Son of John and Mary Crips	17 July, 1788	72
Mary Daughter of Richard and Elizabeth Smith of Clberry, and Wife of Thomas Tutter	16 Aug, 1777	33
Joseph Keck	5 Dec 1729	75
Sarah Keck Relict of Joseph Keck	12 Aug 1762	100
Hester Wife of Robert Keck	11 Feb 1754	33
Robert Keck	4 July, 1757	76
Mary Keck, Wife of Anthony Keck	2 Nov 1759	56
William, Son of Joseph and Sarah Keck	23 Jan 1757	70
Elizabeth Daughter of Joseph and Ann Keck	31 May, 1767	39
John Jones, Son of George Gibert and Margaret Jones, of Ford	18 Apr 1771	21
Ann her Daughter	11 Apr 1773	21
Margaret, Wife of George Gibert Jones	7 Oct 1773	54
George Gibert Jones	15 July, 1778	59
George Gibert Jones	12 Dec 1777	32
Mary Wife of William Freebury, of Ford Junior	27 May 1777	29
Thomas Vere	24 May, 1736	65
Mary Daughter of William and Frances Dowty	— Mar 1736	
Mary Wife of Richard Collett	21 Apr 1753	65
William Collett	30 May, 1722	
Sarah Wife of Thomas Dunce of Corndeot	15 Oct 1746	27
John Wigget	2 Feb 1753	—
Alice, Wife of John Snow, of Ford	19 Oct 1780	31
William their Son died in his Infancy		
Thomas Morris	3 Jan 1766	82
Anne his Wife	11 Aug 1721	51
Anne their Wife	13 May 1714	42
Anne Wife of James Parden of Ford	9 Oct 1758	53
Anne their Daughter	3 Jan 1756	21
Anne, Daughter of James and Anne Parden, of Ford	21 Aug 1734	
Benjamin Crips, Son of John and Mary Crips	— Oct 1728	9
John their Son	24 Aug, 1728	16
Mary Wife of John Crips, senior	25 Feb 1771	84
June, Wife of William Bayly, Daughter of William and Mary Ansel	1768	35
Robert Son of William and Mary Church, died in his Infancy		
Betty their Daughter	15 Sept 1768	73
James Wife Mary Ann Harriett	12 Feb 1770	80
Joseph Chandler	8 Mar 1771	—
Giles Wilcox	6 Aug 1764	56
Ann Wife of Joseph Chandler		
Robert Chandler of Kynton	11 Feb 1734	52
Martha Wife	14 Aug 1745	6
Elizabeth Wife of Richard Smith and Daughter of Robert and Sarah Hughes, of Ford	28 Jan 1761	39

	Died	Aged
Robert, Son of Richard and Elizabeth Smith	22 Mar 1761	—
William their Son -	7 Apr 1764	11
Robert Baylis of Sudeley	4 Mar 1723	59
Jonannah his Wife buried	10 Jan 1733	5
Ann, Wife of John Lyes buried	22 June, 1776	—
Elizabeth, Daughter of William and Elizabeth Baylis	4 May, 1728	22
Ann Daughter of William and Elizabeth Baylis	— June 1713	—
William Baylis senior	May, 1724	63
Elizabeth his Wife	14 Mar 1756	77
John Smith, of Ford	29 Sept 1769	69
Elizabeth his Wife	4 Apr 1713	50
Richard Smith	1 May, 1762	66
Mary his Wife	25 Feb 1745	58
Mary their Daughter -	5 July, 1747	
Mary, Wife of Richard Perrett, senior	30 May 1754	70
John, Son of Richard and Mary Perrett	16 Mar 1784	68
Sarah, Wife of Richard Perrett, junior	5 Apr 1776	63
Mary, Wife of William Dowdeswell	8 Feb 1787	35
Mary their Daughter died in her Infancy		
John Periat	28 June, 1688	41
Richard Surman	10 Dec 1710	
Lucy, Wife of James Griffin	25 Feb 1766	76
James Griffin	25 July 1764	80
John Dowdeswell	17 May 1764	65
Elizabeth his Wife	6 Jan 1761	59
Elizabeth, Wife of Thomas Dowdeswell	18 Feb 1745	61
John, Son of John and Elizabeth Dowdeswell	10 Mar 1774	27
Elizabeth their Daughter died in her Infancy		
Mary Daughter of John and Elizabeth Smith	30 Jan 1773	19
Mary, Daughter of Richard and Sarah Smith	25 Sept 1715	24
John Clark -	14 Sept 1767	66
Samuel Dowdeswell -	3 Apr 1726	71
Anthony Dobbins -	23 June, 1708	70
Anthony Dobbins -	24 Sept 1779	77
Eleanor, Wife of William Winchester	14 Feb 1712	30
Adam their Son	7 Feb 1782	—
William Timmins -	2 Mar 1720	60
Sarah his Wife	3 July, 1714	86
Sarah Timmins	21 July 1765	61
Jane Timmins	16 Mar 1766	55
Mary Wife of William Procter	4 Feb 1783	69
Katharine Luker	5 Mar 1735	77
Adam Winchester	30 Sept 1754	55
Elizabeth, Wife of Richard Tomkins	25 Oct 1738	60
Thomas Yurlington of Sudeley, in the Parish of Winchcomb	6 Mar 1761	82
Edward Humphris	24 July, 1766	53
Sarah Wife of William Collett	7 Jan 1784	29
Neart Wife of John White and Daughter of Thomas Dunce, Gent	14 Apr 1742	79
Anne Williams	3 Jan 1767	—
Anne, Wife of William Williams	1 Feb 1781	70
William Williams	3 June 1717	50
John Williams	17 Mar 1760	—
Anne his Wife	17 Aug 1762	18
Thomas Comper	6 Mar 1789	
William Baylis -	14 Feb 1756	54

ON   FLAT   AND   HEAD   STONES

	Died	Aged		Died	Aged
Charles, Son of Charles and Lucy Williams	29 Feb 1772	7	Ann Deane - -	25 Dec 1730	—
Thomas Williams -	6 Mar 1758	61	William Hatfield -	14 Dec 1787	41
Charles Williams	12 Mar 1766	55	Ann, Daughter of William and Sarah Hatfield died in her Infancy		
Ann, Wife of Thomas Williams	20 Dec 1775	77	Sarah, Daughter of William and Sarah Hatfield -	19 Feb 1787	5
William Compere -	16 June, 1690	81	William Johnson - -	— May, 1721	22
Dorothy his Wife -	3 Sept ——	—			
Thomas Smith - -	25 May, 1745	61			

The Honourable and Reverend
GEORGE TALBOTT,
D D
died November 19, 1785,
aged 70

AN INDEX

OF

HAMLETS, TYTHINGS, AND PLACES, SITUATE IN THE DIFFERENT PARISHES.

A N

A N

I N D E X

O F

ARMS in CHURCHES, and AFFIXED to MONUMENTAL INSCRIPTIONS.

672

A N

I N D E X

O F

NAMES, AS THEY OCCUR IN THE MONUMENTAL INSCRIPTIONS.

₊ *The Figures refer to the Number of each Parish.*

DIRECTIONS FOR PLACING THE DETACHED PLATES IN VOLUME I.

END OF THE FIRST VOLUME.

CAMPDEN · CERNEY (South) · CERNEY (South) · CHARFIELD · CHARLTON =

Smith · Hickes · Noel · Rich · Bigh · Hickes · Brereton · Ive

= KINGS · CHELTENHAM

Lygon · Rich · Lygon · Dormer · Packer · Roberts · Wood · Delabere

CHURCHDOWN · CHURCHAM · CIRENCESTER

Austen · Windowe · Oldisworth · Arnold · the Abbes · Routhale · D.Anvers · Nottingham

CIRENCESTER

Dirton · Bathurst · Master · Selfe · Menew · Cornell · Athens · Perry

CIRENCESTER · COBVRN · CLIFFORD CHAMBERS

Gregoy · Huddlestone · Delaber · Bedingafeld · Cocks · Norwood · Dighton · Ravnesford

COALLY · COBERLEY · COLSBORN

Brereton · Harding · Berkeley · Bruges · Butler · Castleman · Hung. · Shappard

COLNE S. Aldwyns · COLNE (Denis) · COMPTON (Parva) CONDICOTE · CORSE · CROMHALL

Kirtplace · Poole · Kemp · Turton · Hide · Grail · Hickes · Codrington

CROMHALL · DEAN (Magh) · DEAN (Parva) · DERHERST

Welsh · Baventham · Holmes · Samavine · Dutchman · Cryer · Lovier · Mortimer

DEERHURST — DEYNTON — DIDBROKE — DIDMARTON — DODINGTON — DOWDESWELL

Lane — *Cassell* — *Langton* — *Tracey* — *Codrington* — *Codrington* — *Rogers* — *Fitch*

DOWNE AMPNEY — DOWNE HATHERLEY — DUMBLEDON — PURSLEY

Villars — *Hungerford* — *Partridge* — *Jacks* — *Brett* — *Percie* — *Cookes* — *Huttington*

DURSLEY — DYMOCK — DYRHAM

Pratts — *Purnell Von Rouse* — *Capel* — *Wynter* — *Pye* — *De la Riviere* — *Rossell* — *Dennie*

DYRHAM — EASTINGTON — EAST LECHE I Martin — EAST LECHE Burrell

Wynts — *Bathurst* — *Stephens* — *Stafford* — *Inwood* — *Clutterbuck* — *Irefons* — *Saunders*

EBRINGION — ELKSTONE — ELMORE — FAIRFORD

Kayle — *Fortgue* — *Huston* — *Brown* — *Guise* — *Lane* — *Tippin* — *Inrea*

FAIRFORD — FLAXLEY

Oldsworth — *Hamington* — *Unpin* — *Lawks* — *Allin* — *Raaly* — *Brena* — *Hope*

FLAXLEY — FORTHAMPTON — FRAMPTON Clutt

Pask — *Dardswell* — *Chamorel* — *Inman* — *Inman* — *Lapp* — *Veln* — *Senn*

FRAMPTON upon Severn — PROCTER — CUTSING Lane — CUTSING Empl

Lightning Source UK Ltd.
Milton Keynes UK
UKHW050815220822
407644UK00006B/691